TRADEMARK LAW
An Open-Access Casebook

Version 10 (2023)

www.tmcasebook.org

Volume I

Barton Beebe

John M. Desmarais Professor of Intellectual Property Law

New York University School of Law

This work is licensed under a Creative Commons Attribution-NonCommercial-ShareAlike 4.0 International License.

Volume I

i

V10.0/2023-07-22

Volume II

V10.0/2023-07-22

Preface

Thank you for your interest in *Trademark Law: An Open-Access Casebook*! I hope that you find it useful.

I should say a word or two about the court opinions included in this casebook. As with any casebook, students should ask themselves as they come upon each particular opinion: Why is this opinion being presented to me? What is it doing here? This casebook includes some opinions because they are leading opinions that continue to have a significant influence on the course of American trademark doctrine. Other opinions are included because they are simple, straightforward examples of the doctrine being applied. Still other opinions are included because they are problematic and almost certainly wrong. Finally, some opinions are included because they are all of the above. Though the casebook does sometimes point out which opinions have proven to be highly influential, you are nevertheless invited, as you proceed through the casebook, to decide for yourself how each opinion should otherwise be characterized.

The opinions are sometimes lightly edited and may retain many of the citations included in the original opinion. They may also retain paragraphs that review doctrine previously covered. This may be frustrating to students accustomed to reading aggressively edited-down opinions. But sometimes more is ultimately less. I occasionally use curly brackets—{ }—to distinguish edits I have made in the opinions from the original opinion's use of square brackets.

If you would prefer a different format for the casebook, one more easily readable on screen, a .docx version of the casebook is available at tmcasebook.org.

The casebook remains a work in progress. I update it every summer. I'm grateful to the many professors who have adopted the book for use in their classrooms and who have written to me with corrections and suggestions. I'm also grateful to the many students who have done the same.

This is a free casebook. My hope is that this casebook shows that it is possible to produce a reasonably useful American law school casebook on standard word-processing software without the need for the traditional publishers—and their exploitative prices per copy. My further hope is that, being free and online, the casebook is more accessible to students around the world. The downside is that the book is not professionally proofread, formatted, or bluebooked. Please forgive any errors.

Finally, the book is free largely due to the support of NYU Law's students and alumni, most notably, John M. Desmarais (NYU Law '88) of Desmarais LLP, who established the professorship I hold at NYU Law. I thank all of them for their support.

–Barton Beebe

Introduction

Trademark lawyers often tell the story in one form or another of the Coca-Cola lawyer who spoke in 1986 of the value of the company's goodwill as symbolized by its brand: "The production plants and inventories of The Coca-Cola Company could go up in flames overnight. Yet, on the following morning there is not a bank in Atlanta, New York, or anywhere else, that would not lend this Company the funds necessary for rebuilding, accepting as security only the inherent good will in its trademarks 'Coca-Cola' and 'Coke.'"[1] The story was and remains no exaggeration. In 2023, Interbrand estimated the value of the Coca-Cola brand to be $57.5 billion[2]—as against fixed assets in 2023 of $9.8 billion.[3]

APPLE, GOOGLE, COKE, MICROSOFT, SAMSUNG, TOYOTA, MCDONALDS, LOUIS VUITTON, NIKE, PEPSI, FACEBOOK, VISA, CITI, STARBUCKS. Instantly recognizable by a very large proportion of humanity, these are among the most valuable and influential signs in the world, rivalling in significance many religious and national symbols. They are only the most notorious of the millions of brand names that populate the modern marketplace. Trademark law regulates these brand names, from the multi-billion dollar global brands to the name of the local shop down the street. Without trademark protection, many would cease to exist.

In this introductory chapter, we first review the early history of trademarks and trademark law, including the first great Supreme Court trademark case, the so-called *Trade-Mark Cases*. We then critically consider the varied policy justifications for trademark protection. We conclude by briefly situating trademark law within the larger scheme of intellectual property law.

A.   The History of U.S. Trademark Law

1.   The Origins of Trademarks and Trademark Law

In the excerpt that follows, Professor Mark McKenna surveys the origins of American trademark law from seventeenth-century English case law up through nineteenth-century American case law. Some of the cases he mentions may seem far removed in their facts and reasoning from the present-day world of the global internet and multi-billion dollar brands. But as you will see, the early history of trademark law implicates questions that continue to concern courts and trademark law policymakers. What is the proper rationale for trademark protection? Are trademark rights simply a form of pernicious monopoly rights? Is trademark law intellectual property law or is it unfair competition law? What should qualify for trademark protection? What role should intent or "bad faith" play in the determination of liability for trademark infringement? Should consumers have standing to sue when they are confused by one company's use of a mark similar to another company's mark?

Mark P. McKenna, *The Normative Foundations of Trademark Law*, 82 NOTRE DAME L. REV. 1839, 1849-62 (2007) (some footnotes altered or omitted)

II. A SECOND LOOK AT EARLY TRADEMARK PROTECTION

[1] Use of markings to identify and distinguish one's property dates to antiquity, and regulations regarding use of those marks almost as long . . . . Because nineteenth-century American courts explicitly drew on English law . . . , a full account necessarily begins in England.

A. Medieval Marks as Liabilities

[2] Scholars have identified a number of ways in which individuals and producers historically used distinguishing marks. Most basically, merchants used marks to demonstrate ownership of physical goods, much in the way that ranchers use cattle brands to identify their cattle. Use of marks to indicate ownership of goods was particularly important for owners whose goods moved in transit, as those

---

[1] Quoted in Thomas D. Drescher, *The Transformation and Evolution of Trademarks—From Signals to Symbols to Myth*, 82 TRADEMARK REP. 301, 301-02 (1992).

[2] *See* Interbrand, Best Global Brands, https://interbrand.com/best-global-brands/.

[3] The Coca-Cola Company, Balance Sheet, https://investors.coca-colacompany.com/financial-information/balance-sheet.

marks often allowed owners to claim goods that were lost. Producers relied on identifying marks, for example, to demonstrate ownership of goods recovered at sea.[25]

[3] Marks also were quite important to the operation of the guild system in medieval England. Local guilds often developed reputations for the quality of their products. When they did, the names of the towns or regions in which those guilds operated became repositories of goodwill. To maintain that goodwill, guilds needed to be able to restrict membership and identify and punish members who produced defective products. Guilds therefore required their members to affix distinguishing marks to their products so they could police their ranks effectively.[26]

[4] Importantly, guilds required members to display their marks for the purpose of developing and maintaining the collective goodwill of the guild; marks were *not* used for the purpose of establishing individual producer goodwill. Indeed, intraguild competition was strictly forbidden. Moreover, guild regulations were not motivated primarily by a concern for consumers. Even in the cutlers' trade, where marks seem to have been viewed most analogously to modern trademarks,[28] regulation was intended not for the protection of purchasers, but for "guidance of those exercising control or working in rivalry."[29] In fact, though it is not clear how often mark owners sought enforcement of their marks during this period, whatever enforcement mark owners did pursue seems to have been motivated by their concern about being held responsible for products they did not make.

B. English Trademark Cases

. . . .

1. Trademarks in Courts of Law and Equity

[5] The first reported English decision clearly involving a claim based on use of a party's trademark was the court of equity's 1742 decision in *Blanchard v. Hill*,[39] {in which Lord Chancellor Hardwicke declined to issue an injunction}. The plaintiff in that case, a maker of playing cards, sought an injunction

> to restrain the defendant from making use of the Great *Mogul* as a stamp upon his cards, to the prejudice of the plaintiff, upon a suggestion, that the plaintiff had the sole right to this stamp, having appropriated it to himself, conformable to the charter granted to the cardmakers' company by King Charles the First.[40]

[6] The factual context of *Blanchard* is particularly noteworthy; the plaintiff was seeking protection of a mark for playing cards pursuant to a royal charter, and charters granting exclusive rights to cardmakers had been at the center of a long political struggle between Parliament and the Crown. Marks played an important role in the contested charter scheme because cardmakers were required to use their seals so that exclusivity could be enforced,[42] a fact that clearly colored the court's view of the case. . . .

---

[25] Owners also carved identifying marks into the beaks of swans they were allowed to own by royal privilege. *See* Frank I. Schechter, The Historical Foundations Of The Law Relating To Trade-Marks 35-37 (1925).

[26] Not coincidentally, these mandatory marks also made it possible for the Crown to regulate conduct, particularly in the printing industry, where the Crown policed heresy and piracy. *See id.* at 63-77.

[28] There are some examples in the cutlers' trade of the government treating marks as property that could be passed by will and of owners advertising to suppress piracy. *See id.* at 119-20.

[29] *Id.* at 120 (quoting Robert Eadon Leader, History of the Cutlers of Hallamshire 110 (1906)).

[39] (1742) 2 Atk. 484 (Ch.), 26 Eng. Rep. 692

[40] *Id.* at 484, 26 Eng. Rep. at 692-93.

[42] *See* The Case of Monopolies, (1603) 11 Co. Rep. 84b, 88b, 77 Eng. Rep. 1260, 1266 (K.B.) (calling the playing card monopoly granted by Queen Elizabeth under her royal prerogative an "odious monopoly").

[7] The *Blanchard* decision, however, should not be read as a categorical condemnation of claims based on use of a competitor's mark. Rather, Lord Hardwicke was focused on cases in which the plaintiff's claim of exclusive rights emanated from a monopoly granted by royal charter. In fact, his decision in *Blanchard* specifically distinguished the plaintiff's claim in that case from the clothier's claim referenced in Popham's report of *Southern {v. How*, which was probably the case *J.G. v. Samford* (C.P. 1584) in which one clothier used the mark of another with the intent to deceive consumers}. Unlike the plaintiff in *Blanchard*, who claimed the exclusive right to use his Mogul mark without qualification, the clothier in *Southern* based his case on the defendant's "fraudulent design, to put off bad cloths by this means, or to draw away customers from the other clothier."[45] When the defendant intended to pass off its goods as those of the plaintiff, Lord Hardwicke implied, an injunction might well be appropriate.

[8] Despite the initial reluctance of courts of equity to recognize exclusive rights in trademarks and Lord Hardwicke's clear suggestion that claimants pursue such claims at law, the first reported trademark decision by an English common law court was the 1824 decision in *Sykes v. Sykes*.[46] In that case, the court upheld a verdict for the plaintiff against defendants who marked their shot-belts and powder-flasks with the words "Sykes Patent" in imitation of the plaintiff's use of the same mark for its shot-belts and powder-flasks.[47] After specifically noting that the plaintiff's sales had decreased after the defendants began selling their identically labeled products, the court concluded that the defendants had violated the plaintiff's rights by marking their goods so as "to denote that they were of the genuine manufacture of the plaintiff" and "[selling] them to retail dealers, for the express purpose of being resold, as goods of the plaintiff's manufacture."[48]

[9] A number of common law cases following the *Sykes* decision recognized claims in similar circumstances, imposing liability when a producer sought to pass off its goods as those of a competitor.[49] Those cases generally were brought as actions on the case, in the nature of deceit. Yet one must be careful not to read those cases through modern lenses—despite the form of action, courts in these early cases invariably described the defendant as having practiced fraud *against the plaintiff*.[51]

[10] Like their counterparts in courts of law, courts of equity became more solicitous of trademark claims in the first part of the nineteenth century. Of particular significance, courts very early on concluded that, where a claimant could demonstrate an exclusive right to use a particular mark, equity would intervene to protect a property interest and evidence of fraudulent intent was not necessary. . . .

[11] As Lord Westbury said in *Leather Cloth Co. v. American Leather Cloth Co.*[57] rejecting any contention that courts of equity based their jurisdiction on fraud,

> The true principle, therefore, would seem to be, that the jurisdiction of the Court in the protection given to trade marks rests upon property, and that the Court interferes by injunction, because that is the only mode by which property of this description can be effectually protected.[59]

Significantly, Lord Westbury reached this conclusion after noting that, even when a party held out his goods as those of another, the other had no right to complain unless the act caused him some pecuniary

---

[45] *Blanchard*, 2 Atk. at 485, 26 Eng. Rep. at 693.

[46] (1824) 3 B. & C. 541, 107 Eng. Rep. 834 (K.B.).

[47] *Sykes*, 3 B. & C. at 543, 107 Eng. Rep. at 835.

[48] *Id.*

[49] *See, e.g.*, Blofeld v. Payne, (1833) 4 B. & Ad. 410, 411-12, 110 Eng. Rep. 509, 510 (K.B.).

[51] *See Blofeld*, 4 B. & Ad. at 412, 110 Eng. Rep. at 510 (upholding the verdict for the plaintiff and holding that the defendant's use of envelopes resembling those of plaintiff's, and containing the same words, was a "fraud against the plaintiff").

[57] (1863) 4 De G.J. & S. 137, 141, 46 Eng. Rep. 868 (Ch).

[59] *Id.* at 142, 46 Eng. Rep. at 870.

loss or damage.[60] "Imposition on the public, occasioned by one man selling his goods as the goods of another, cannot be the ground of private right of action or suit."[61] The court in *Levy v. Walker*[62] was even more explicit that the protection of trademarks was intended to protect producers and not primarily for the benefit of consumers: "The Court interferes solely for the purpose of protecting the owner of a trade or business from a fraudulent invasion of that business by somebody else. It does not interfere to prevent the world outside from being misled into anything."[63]

. . . .

C. Early American Trademark Jurisprudence

1. Trademark Law Targets Dishonest Trade Diversion

[12] As noted above, I read the decisions of the English common law courts and courts of equity as reflecting the same fundamental concern. In both types of cases, courts were singularly focused on the harm to a producer from improper diversion of its trade, and they worked with existing forms of action to remedy that harm. American courts had the same focus when they began deciding trademark cases, and they repeatedly made clear that the purpose of trademark law was to protect a party from illegitimate attempts to divert its trade.[82]

[13] In *Coats v. Holbrook*,[83] for example, the court said that a person is not allowed to imitate the product of another and "thereby attract to himself the patronage that without such deceptive use of such names . . . would have inured to the benefit of that other person."[84]

[14] . . . Moreover, . . . American courts concluded very early on that this protection in many cases was based on a property right,[91] following essentially the approach of English courts of equity.

2. Trademarks and Unfair Competition

[15] Because the purpose of trademark protection traditionally was to prevent trade diversion by competitors, it has long been regarded as a species of the broader law of unfair competition, and even more broadly, as part of the law governing other fraudulent (and unfair) business practices. This view of trademark protection as a species of unfair competition was not, as some have suggested, a post hoc conflation of two branches of the law. From the very beginning, trademark cases and those only "analogous" to trademark cases were grounded in the same fundamental principle—that no person has the right to pass off his goods as those of another. . . .

---

[60] *Id.* at 140, 46 Eng. Rep. at 870.

[61] *Id.* at 141, 46 Eng. Rep. at 870.

[62] (1878) 10 Ch.D. 436.

[63] *Id.* at 448.

[82] Like its English predecessor, American trademark law was predominantly a product of judicial decision. Prior to the Act of July 8, 1870, ch. 230, 16 Stat. 198, 210, statutory protection, to the extent it existed, was at the state level and highly trade-specific. Massachusetts, for example, specifically regulated the use of marks on sailcloth. *See* Schechter, *supra* note 23, at 130-32. The Supreme Court declared the first two attempts at federal trademark legislation unconstitutional. *See* The Trade-Mark Cases, 100 U.S. 82, 99 (1879) (invalidating the trademark legislation of 1870 and the Act of Aug. 14, 1876, ch. 274, 19 Stat. 141 (which imposed criminal sanctions against one who fraudulently used, sold or counterfeited trademarks)). Even after Congress began legislating again in this area, however, trademark law remained fundamentally a creature of common law. Indeed, the Lanham Act, ch. 540, 60 Stat. 427 (1946), is widely noted to have generally codified common law.

[83] 7 N.Y. Ch. Ann. 713 (1845).

[84] *Id.* at 717.

[91] *See, e.g.*, The Trade-Mark Cases, 100 U.S. 82, 92 (1879); Blackwell v. Armistead, 3 F. Cas. 546, 548 (C.C.W.D. Va. 1872) (No. 1474); Derringer v. Plate, 29 Cal. 292, 294-95 (1865); Avery & Sons v. Meikle & Co., 4 Ky. L. Rptr. 759, 764-65 (1883);

[16] At some point in the late nineteenth century, American courts began to use the term "unfair competition" slightly differently. Those courts divided the universe of distinguishing marks into "technical trademarks," which were protected in actions for trademark infringement, and "trade names," which could only be protected in actions for unfair competition. Arbitrary or fanciful terms applied to particular products were considered technical trademarks,[99] while surnames, geographic terms, descriptive terms were considered trade names.[100] . . . .

[17] In practice, cases of trademark infringement and those of unfair competition differed primarily in terms of what the plaintiff had to prove. Use of another's technical trademark was unlikely to have a legitimate explanation and could be condemned categorically. Trademark infringement plaintiffs therefore did not have to prove intent. Use of another's trade name, on the other hand, may have had an innocent purpose, such as description of the product's characteristics or its geographic origin. As a result, in contrast to trademark infringement plaintiffs, unfair competition claimants had to prove that the defendant intended to pass off its products as those of the plaintiff. . . . .

Comments and Questions

1.   *"Technical trademarks", "trade names", and intent.* In addressing the role of intent in late nineteenth century American unfair competition law, McKenna cites *The Restatement (Third) of Unfair Competition*. The *Restatement* explains:

> In both England and the United States {in the late nineteenth century}, the property conception of trademark rights extended only to certain designations. When the defendant imitated a designation that was clearly distinctive of the plaintiff's goods, the natural inference that the defendant intended to deceive prospective purchasers eventually led to a conclusive presumption of fraud. Thus, in the case of words or other symbols invented by the plaintiff or arbitrary designations that had no apparent relation to the plaintiff's goods except as an indication of source, the courts began to protect the plaintiff's "property" interest in the mark without regard to the presence of any fraudulent intent. Such marks were characterized as "trademarks," and cases involving the unauthorized use of these marks were designated as actions for "trademark infringement." The focus of the inquiry thus shifted from an analysis of the defendant's conduct to a consideration of the nature of the plaintiff's right. Less distinctive marks that had nevertheless come to be recognized by prospective consumers as indications of source were called "trade names." Although not recognized as "property" in the same sense as technical "trademarks," protection for "trade names" remained available through the action for "unfair competition," with its historical emphasis on the fraudulent character of the defendant's conduct.
>
> . . . The initial emphasis on fraud and property rights has generally given way to a more explicit analysis of the propriety of the defendant's conduct as a means of competition, and the technical distinctions between the actions for trademark infringement and unfair competition have now been abandoned.

RESTATEMENT (THIRD) OF UNFAIR COMPETITION § 9, cmt. d (1995).

2.   *Production marks.* As the McKenna excerpt explains, local guilds required production marks not just to aid in asserting their monopoly but also to fix liability for poorly-made goods that might tarnish the reputation of the guild. An early example of quality enforcement—and of trademark

---

[99] *See* RESTATEMENT (THIRD) OF UNFAIR COMPETITION § 9 (1995); *see also* 1 MCCARTHY § 4:4, at 4-4 (defining technical trademarks as marks that were "fanciful, arbitrary, distinctive, non-descriptive in any sense and not a personal name").

[100] Trade names then cumulatively can be thought to comprise what we now think of as indicators which lack inherent distinctiveness and are protectable only with evidence of secondary meaning.

adjudication—comes to us in the remarkable story of the fourteenth-century bladesmith John Odinsay. Odinsay was accused of making a sword that broke during combat when one Sir Peter Harpdon used it to defend himself from highway brigands while travelling through Bordeaux in 1345. Sir Peter recovered from his wounds in that skirmish and went on to fight next to the Black Prince in the Battle of Crecy in 1346. But upon his return to London, he pursued the matter of the broken sword. The hallmark suggested that Odinsay had made it (and the penalties for such faulty craftsmanship would have ruined Odinsay and his family), but the mark turned out to be a forgery. The London bladesmiths' guild discovered that several of its members' marks were being forged, perhaps by smiths in nearby cities. *See* Thomas D. Drescher, *The Transformation and Evolution of Trademarks—From Signals to Symbols to Myth*, 82 TRADEMARK REPORTER 301, 313-18 (1992).

2. The Trade-Mark Cases

The Supreme Court's 1879 opinion in the *Trade-Mark Cases* is the first great Supreme Court opinion on trademarks (often written at the time as "trade-marks" or "trade marks", which latter usage British English still prefers to this day). It arose out of three criminal cases in which the defendants challenged the constitutionality of the federal trademark law in effect at the time. As you will see, it was not an auspicious start for federal trademark law.

Trade-Mark Cases
100 U.S. 82 (1879)

MR. JUSTICE MILLER delivered the opinion of the court.

[1] The three cases whose titles stand at the head of this opinion are criminal prosecutions for violations of what is known as the trade-mark legislation of Congress. The first two are indictments in the southern district of New York, and the last is an information in the southern district of Ohio. In all of them the judges of the circuit courts in which they are pending have certified to a difference of opinion on what is substantially the same question; namely, are the acts of Congress on the subject of trade-marks founded on any rightful authority in the Constitution of the United States?

[2] The entire legislation of Congress in regard to trade-marks is of very recent origin. It is first seen in sects. 77 to 84, inclusive, of the act of July 8, 1870, entitled 'An Act to revise, consolidate, and amend the statutes relating to patents and copyrights.' 16 Stat. 198. The part of this act relating to trade-marks is embodied in chap. 2, tit. 60, sects. 4937 to 4947, of the Revised Statutes.

[3] It is sufficient at present to say that they provide for the registration in the Patent Office of any device in the nature of a trade-mark to which any person has by usage established an exclusive right, or which the person so registering intends to appropriate by that act to his exclusive use; and they make the wrongful use of a trade-mark, so registered, by any other person, without the owner's permission, a cause of action in a civil suit for damages. Six years later we have the act of Aug. 14, 1876 (19 Stat. 141), punishing by fine and imprisonment the fraudulent use, sale, and counterfeiting of trade-marks registered in pursuance of the statutes of the United States, on which the informations and indictments are founded in the cases before us.

[4] The right to adopt and use a symbol or a device to distinguish the goods or property made or sold by the person whose mark it is, to the exclusion of use by all other persons, has been long recognized by the common law and the chancery courts of England and of this country, and by the statutes of some of the States. It is a property right for the violation of which damages may be recovered in an action at law, and the continued violation of it will be enjoined by a court of equity, with compensation for past infringement. This exclusive right was not created by the act of Congress, and does not now depend upon it for its enforcement. The whole system of trade-mark property and the civil remedies for its protection existed long anterior to that act, and have remained in full force since its passage.

[5] These propositions are so well understood as to require neither the citation of authorities nor an elaborate argument to prove them.

[6] As the property in trade-marks and the right to their exclusive use rest on the laws of the States, and, like the great body of the rights of person and of property, depend on them for security and

protection, the power of Congress to legislate on the subject, to establish the conditions on which these rights shall be enjoyed and exercised, the period of their duration, and the legal remedies for their enforcement, if such power exist at all, must be found in the Constitution of the United States, which is the source of all powers that Congress can lawfully exercise.

[7] In the argument of these cases this seems to be conceded, and the advocates for the validity of the acts of Congress on this subject point to two clauses of the Constitution, in one or in both of which, as they assert, sufficient warrant may be found for this legislation.

[8] The first of these is the eighth clause of sect. 8 of the first article. That section, manifestly intended to be an enumeration of the powers expressly granted to Congress, and closing with the declaration of a rule for the ascertainment of such powers as are necessary by way of implication to carry into efficient operation those expressly given, authorizes Congress, by the clause referred to, 'to promote the progress of science and useful arts, by securing for limited times, to authors and inventors, the exclusive right to their respective writings and discoveries.'*

[9] As the first and only attempt by Congress to regulate the *right of trade-marks* is to be found in the act of July 8, 1870, to which we have referred, entitled 'An Act to revise, consolidate, and amend the statutes relating to *patents* and *copyrights*,' terms which have long since become technical, as referring, the one to inventions and the other to the writings of authors, it is a reasonable inference that this part of the statute also was, in the opinion of Congress, an exercise of the power found in that clause of the Constitution. It may also be safely assumed that until a critical examination of the subject in the courts became necessary, it was mainly if not wholly to this clause that the advocates of the law looked for its support.

[10] Any attempt, however, to identify the essential characteristics of a trade-mark with inventions and discoveries in the arts and sciences, or with the writings of authors, will show that the effort is surrounded with insurmountable difficulties.

[11] The ordinary trade-mark has no necessary relation to invention or discovery. The trade-mark recognized by the common law is generally the growth of a considerable period of use, rather than a sudden invention. It is often the result of accident rather than design, and when under the act of Congress it is sought to establish it by registration, neither originality, invention, discovery, science, nor art is in any way essential to the right conferred by that act. If we should endeavor to classify it under the head of writings of authors, the objections are equally strong. In this, as in regard to inventions, originality is required. And while the word *writings* may be liberally construed, as it has been, to include original designs for engravings, prints, &c., it is only such as are *original*, and are founded in the creative powers of the mind. The writings which are to be protected are *the fruits of intellectual labor*, embodied in the form of books, prints, engravings, and the like. The trade-mark may be, and generally is, the adoption of something already in existence as the distinctive symbol of the party using it. At common law the exclusive right to it grows out of its *use*, and not its mere adoption. By the act of Congress this exclusive right attaches upon registration. But in neither case does it depend upon novelty, invention, discovery, or any work of the brain. It requires no fancy or imagination, no genius, no laborious thought. It is simply founded on priority of appropriation. We look in vain in the statute for any other qualification or condition. If the symbol, however plain, simple, old, or well-known, has been first appropriated by the claimant as his distinctive trade-mark, he may by registration secure the right to its exclusive use. While such legislation may be a judicious aid to the common law on the subject of trade-marks, and may be within the competency of legislatures whose general powers embrace that class of subjects, we are unable to see any such power in the constitutional provision concerning authors and inventors, and their writings and discoveries.

[12] The other clause of the Constitution supposed to confer the requisite authority on Congress is the third of the same section, which, read in connection with the granting clause, is as follows: 'The

---

* {Note that the Supreme Court misquoted the Constitution here. There is no comma after "limited times" or "authors and inventors."}

Congress shall have power to regulate commerce with foreign nations, and among the several States, and with the Indian tribes.'

. . . .

[13] If {a law's} main purpose be to establish a regulation applicable to all trade, to commerce at all points, especially if it be apparent that it is designed to govern the commerce wholly between citizens of the same State, it is obviously the exercise of a power not confided to Congress.

[14] We find no recognition of this principle in the chapter on trade-marks in the Revised Statutes. We would naturally look for this in the description of the class of persons who are entitled to register a trade-mark, or in reference to the goods to which it should be applied. . . . But no such idea is found or suggested in this statute. Its language is: 'Any person or firm domiciled in the United States, and any corporation created by the United States, or of any State or Territory thereof,' or any person residing in a foreign country which by treaty or convention affords similar privileges to our citizens, may be registration obtain protection for his trade-mark. Here is no requirement that such person shall be engaged in the kind of commerce which Congress is authorized to regulate. It is a general declaration that anybody in the United States, and anybody in any other country which permits us to do the like, may, by registering a trade-mark, have it fully protected. . . . The remedies provided by the act when the right of the owner of the registered trade-mark is infringed, are not confined to the case of a trade-mark used in foreign or inter-state commerce.

[15] It is therefore manifest that no such distinction is found in the act, but that its broad purpose was to establish a universal system of trade-mark registration, for the benefit of all who had already used a trade-mark, or who wished to adopt one in the future, without regard to the character of the trade to which it was to be applied or the residence of the owner, with the solitary exception that those who resided in foreign countries which extended no such privileges to us were excluded from them here.

. . . .

[16] While we have, in our references in this opinion to the trade-mark legislation of Congress, had mainly in view the act of 1870, and the civil remedy which that act provides, it was because the criminal offences described in the act of 1876 are, by their express terms, solely referable to frauds, counterfeits, and unlawful use of trade-marks which were registered under the provisions of the former act. If that act is unconstitutional, so that the registration under it confers no lawful right, then the criminal enactment intended to protect that right falls with it.

[17] The questions in each of these cases being an inquiry whether these statutes can be upheld in whole or in part as valid and constitutional, must be answered in the negative; and it will be

So certified to the proper circuit courts.

3. The Statutory Development of U.S. Trademark law and the Lanham Act of 1946

Rep. Fritz Lanham, 1880-1965
(D-Texas, 1919-1947)

Excerpt from Restatement (Third) of Unfair Competition § 9 (1995)

[1] *e. Trademark legislation.* The federal government and each of the states have enacted legislation protecting trademarks. The statutes generally provide a mechanism for the registration of trademarks, describe the types of marks that may be registered, and specify the procedural and substantive advantages afforded to the owner of a trademark registration. The statutes, however, do not ordinarily preempt the protection of trademarks at common law.

[2] Although several states had earlier enacted legislation to prevent the fraudulent use of trademarks, the first federal trademark statute was not enacted until 1870. This initial attempt at federal protection proved short-lived, however, when in 1879 the Supreme Court in the *Trade-Mark Cases*, 100 U.S. (10 Otto) 82 (1879), held that the statute had been unconstitutionally grounded on the patent and copyright clause of the Constitution. A second federal statute was enacted in 1881, but in reaction to the *Trade-Mark Cases*, registration under the act was limited to marks used in commerce with foreign nations and the Indian tribes. The first modern federal trademark registration statute was the Trademark Act of 1905, grounded on the commerce clause. In a continuation of the distinction that had developed at common law between technical "trademarks" and "trade names," the Act of 1905 limited registration to fanciful and arbitrary marks, except for marks that had been in actual use for 10 years preceding passage of the statute.

[3] To clarify and strengthen the rights of trademark owners, the Act of 1905 was replaced by the Trademark Act of 1946 (effective July 5, 1947), 15 U.S.C.A. §§ 1051-1127, commonly known as the Lanham Act. The Lanham Act is generally declarative of existing law, incorporating the principal features of common law trademark protection. However, among the major innovations of the Lanham Act were the adoption of a constructive notice rule that effectively expanded the geographic scope of trademark rights, and an attempt to provide a measure of security to trademark owners in the form of "incontestable" rights in certain trademarks. The Lanham Act in § 43(a) also added a general proscription against false designations and representations that has come to serve as a federal law of deceptive marketing.

[4] Statutes in every state also provide for the registration of trademarks. In 1949 the United States (now International) Trademark Association prepared a Model State Trademark Bill patterned after the federal registration system. The Model Bill, revised in 1964 and 1992, provides the basis for much of the current state legislation.

From Edward S. Rogers, *The Lanham Act and the Social Function of Trademarks*, 14 LAW & CONTEMP. PROBS. 173, 180-83 (1949)

. . . .

[1] The prospect of getting anything through Congress in 1937 was not encouraging. Our committee{, the Trade Mark Committee of the Patent Section of the American Bar Association,} kept notes and I had a scrapbook in which I stuck ideas that came in from all sorts of places. More as a matter of convenience than anything else, I cast those notes and ideas in the form of a draft statute.

[2] In the winter of 1937 the Commissioner of Patents asked me to come to Washington to see him. He said he had had a conference with Fritz Lanham, who was chairman of the subcommittee of the House Patent Committee dealing with trademarks, and asked me to see Mr. Lanham, which I did. Mr. Lanham said that a large number of piecemeal amendments to the 1905 Act had been proposed and that he had been studying the Act and couldn't make head or tail of it; that if it were amended piecemeal it would make incomprehensible what had hitherto been merely obscure. So he asked if anywhere around there was a skeleton draft of a new act that could be used as a sort of clotheshorse to hang things on. I told him I had such a draft and he asked me to leave it with him, which I, of course, was glad to do.

[3] I supposed that Mr. Lanham was just going to study this memorandum and skeleton—it was hardly more than that—and begin to hold hearings. I was surprised when, on January 19, 1938, he introduced it as H.R. 9041.

[4] Immediately bar associations appointed committees which did thoughtful and conscientious work, with the result that we now have a new Trade-Mark Act. Since the last Act was passed in 1905 and the new Act in 1946—forty-one years later—I suspect we are going to have to live with the Lanham Act for a long time.

. . . .

[5] Whenever there was a hearing before any committee on the trade-mark bill, sooner or later there appeared zealous men from the Department of Justice who raised all manner of objections. They asserted that trade-marks are monopolistic and any statutory protection of them plays into the hands of big business and should be discouraged. In vain it was pointed out that what is now big business started as little business—that trade-marks are not, like patents and copyrights, a government grant of an exclusive right, that trade-marks are visible reputation and symbols of good will, that trade-marks are the antithesis of monopoly, and that to protect them is to insure the one whose goods or services they distinguish against fraud and misrepresentation.

[6] No progress seemed to be made with the Department's representatives, who were against not only the protection of trade-marks but trade-marks as an institution. . . .

Comments and Questions

1.   *The long road to the Lanham Act.* In his influential treatise, J. Thomas McCarthy records the fate of legislative efforts through the war years leading to the Lanham Act of 1946:

> Hearings on the bill and the various forms in which it was reintroduced were held in March 1938, March 1939, June 1939, and passed the House and Senate in 1939 and 1940. However, the Senate moved to reconsider the bill on June 23, 1940 and it was returned to the calendar and died. In the 77th Congress a reintroduced bill passed the Senate in 1941 and the House in 1942, but the bill died upon being referred back to Committee in 1942. Hearings were held in the 78th Congress in 1943 and 1944, but the bill was not passed. Finally, the 1945 version of the bill (H.R. 1654) was passed by the 79th Congress.

MCCARTHY ON TRADEMARKS AND UNFAIR COMPETITION § 5.4 (2018). If we date the Lanham Act from its first draft in 1937 (or indeed back to the so-called Vestal Bill of 1931), then the Act is more than 80 years old. This may help to explain the existence of certain especially abstruse statutory sections that the student will confront through the course of studying U.S. trademark law.

4. Statutory Developments

The Lanham Act has been amended numerous times since its July 5, 1947 effective date. Listed here are some of the more important amendments, many of which we will refer to through the course of this casebook.

1962   The limiting phrase "purchasers as to the source of origin of such goods or services" was deleted from Lanham Act § 32. 1962 Pub. L. No. 87-772, 76 Stat. 769. This arguably significantly broadened the scope of anti-infringement protection under the Act.

1975   The following sentence was added to Lanham Act § 35: "The court in exceptional cases may award reasonable attorney fees to the prevailing party." 1975 Pub. L. No. 93-600, 88 Stat. 1955.

1975   Congress finally changed the name of the "Patent Office" to the "Patent and Trademark Office." 1975 Pub. L. No. 93-596, 88 Stat. 1949.

1982   The Court of Customs and Patent Appeals became the Court of Appeals for the Federal Circuit. Pub. L. 97-164, 96 Stat. 25.

1984   The Trademark Counterfeiting Act of 1984 was enacted, 1984 Pub. L. No. 98-473, 98 Stat. 1837, amending Lanham §§ 34, 35, and 36, and establishing criminal trademark anti-counterfeiting penalties in 18 U.S.C. § 2320.

1988   The Trademark Law Revision Act of 1988 (TLRA) was enacted, effective November 16, 1989. Pub. L. No. 100-667, 102 Stat. 3935. The TLRA established the "intent-to-use" basis for registration and federal statutory "constructive use" for purposes of priority. It also significantly rewrote Lanham Act § 43(a).

1996   The Federal Trademark Dilution Act (FTDA), enacted and effective January 16, 1996, established a federal cause of action for anti-dilution protection in Lanham Act § 43(c). Pub. L. No. 104-98, 109 Stat. 985. The FTDA has been replaced by the Trademark Dilution Revision Act of 2006.

1996   The Anticounterfeiting Consumer Protection Act of 1996 further enhanced procedures to combat and penalties for trademark counterfeiting. Pub. L. No. 104-153, 110 Stat 1386. The Act also introduced statutory damages for counterfeiting.

1999   The Anticybersquatting Consumer Protection Act (ACPA) established Lanham Act § 43(d) to combat the cybersquatting of domain names confusingly similar to or dilutive of trademarks. Pub. L. No. 106-113, 113 Stat. 1501.

2002   The Madrid Protocol Implementation Act (MPIA), enacted Nov. 2, 2002 and effective Nov. 2, 2003, established Lanham Act §§ 60-74. 116 Stat. 1758, 1913 Pub. L. No. 107-273. With the MPIA, the U.S. became a member of the Madrid System of international trademark registration.

2006   The Trademark Dilution Revision Act of 2006 (TDRA) significantly rewrote Lanham Act § 43(c). Pub. L. No. 109-312, 120 Stat. 1730. It replaced the FTDA of 1996.

2008   The Prioritizing Resources and Organization for Intellectual Property Act of 2008 (PRO-IP Act) enhanced civil damages and criminal penalties for trademark counterfeiting. Pub. L. No. 110-313, 122 Stat. 3014.

2020   The Trademark Modernization Act of 2020 (TMA) instituted various mechanisms for challenging trademark filings making inaccurate claims of use in commerce and established that a finding of a likelihood of confusion or dilution triggers a rebuttable presumption of irreparable harm. Pub. L. No. 116-260, 134 Stat. 118.

Comments and Questions

1.   *"The Last Best Place."* One of the stranger moments in the history of U.S. trademark legislation involves the phrase "The Last Best Place." Between 2001 and 2004, a Nevada business named Last Best Beef, LLC filed eight applications at the PTO to register the phrase "The Last Best Place" in connection with various goods and services. In 2005, Congress passed and the President signed into law an appropriations bill with a rider that consisted of the following language: "Notwithstanding any other provision of this Act, no funds appropriated under this Act shall be used to register, issue, transfer, or enforce any trademark of the phrase 'The Last Best Place.'" *See* Pub.L. No. 109–108, 119 Stat. 2290. Upon learning of this statutory command in an appropriations bill that covered the PTO, the PTO suspended all consideration of Last Best Beef's trademark applications and no further applications for the phrase have since been filed. What? In 1988, a Montana writer had entitled an anthology of Montana-oriented poetry and prose "The Last Best Place." The phrase was soon taken up by Montana businesses and state government. In 2005, Montana Senator Conrad Burns attached the rider to the appropriations bill on the ground that the phrase "belongs to the State of Montana." *See* John L. Welch, *Montana Senator Again Blocks "LAST BEST PLACE" Registrations*, The TTABlog, Feb. 27, 2009, http://thettablog.blogspot.com/2009/02/montana-senator-max-baucus-announced.html. *See also The Last Best Beef, LLC v. Dudas*, 506 F.3d 333 (4th Cir. 2007) (not seeing a problem with any of this).

B.   The Policy Justifications for Trademark Protection

Probably the most oft-quoted passage from the *Trade-Mark Cases* is the paragraph in which the Supreme Court compared trademarks to the two other most significant forms of intellectual property, copyrights and patents (paragraph 11 in the excerpt above). Consider whether what Justice Miller wrote in 1879 about the development of brand names is still accurate today:

> The ordinary trade-mark has no necessary relation to invention or discovery. The trade-mark recognized by the common law is generally the growth of a considerable period of use, rather than a sudden invention. It is often the result of accident rather than design, and when under the act of Congress it is sought to establish it by registration, neither originality, invention, discovery, science, nor art is in any way essential to the right conferred by that act. If we should endeavor to classify it under the head of writings of authors, the objections are equally strong. In this, as in regard to inventions, originality is required. And while the word writings may be liberally construed, as it has been, to include original designs for engravings, prints, &c., it is only such as are original, and are founded in the creative powers of the mind. The writings which are to be protected are the fruits of intellectual labor, embodied in the form of books, prints, engravings, and the like. The trade-mark may be, and generally is, the adoption of something already in existence as the distinctive symbol of the party using it. At common law the exclusive right to it grows out of its use, and not its mere adoption. By the act of Congress this exclusive right attaches upon registration. But in neither case does it depend upon novelty, invention, discovery, or any work of the brain. It requires no fancy of imagination, no genius, no laborious thought. It is simply founded on priority of appropriation.

Id. at 94.

By 1942, the Court was describing trademarks and the role of trademark law in different terms. In *Mishawaka Rubber & Woolen Mfg. Co. v. S.S. Kresge Co.*, 316 U.S. 203 (1942), Justice Frankfurter explained:

The protection of trade-marks is the law's recognition of the psychological function of symbols. If it is true that we live by symbols, it is no less true that we purchase goods by them. A trade-mark is a merchandising short-cut which induces a purchaser to select what he wants, or what he has been led to believe he wants. The owner of a mark exploits this human propensity by making every effort to impregnate the atmosphere of the market with the drawing power of a congenial symbol. Whatever the means employed, the aim is the same—to convey through the mark, in the minds of potential customers, the desirability of the commodity upon which it appears. Once this is attained, the trade-mark owner has something of value. If another poaches upon the commercial magnetism of the symbol he has created, the owner can obtain legal redress.

Id. at 205.

By the 1980s, American courts were describing trademarks and trademark law in yet different terms, terms which still resonate today. Reflecting the rise of the Chicago School economic analysis of law, Judge Easterbrook described the economic benefits of trademarks and trademark protection in *Scandia Down Corp. v. Euroquilt, Inc.*, 772 F.2d. 1423 (7th Cir. 1985):

Trademarks help consumers to select goods. By identifying the source of the goods, they convey valuable information to consumers at lower costs. Easily identified trademarks reduce the costs consumers incur in searching for what they desire, and the lower the costs of search the more competitive the market. A trademark also may induce the supplier of goods to make higher quality products and to adhere to a consistent level of quality. The trademark is a valuable asset, part of the "goodwill" of a business. If the seller provides an inconsistent level of quality, or reduces quality below what consumers expect from earlier experience, that reduces the value of the trademark. The value of a trademark is in a sense a "hostage" of consumers; if the seller disappoints the consumers, they respond by devaluing the trademark. The existence of this hostage gives the seller another incentive to afford consumers the quality of goods they prefer and expect.

Id. at 1429-30.

Which description of trademarks most accurately reflects their characteristics in the present day? Are they often adopted, in the terms of the *Trade-Mark Cases*, as "the result of accident rather than design"? Can we say of the development of trademarks, as of the legal conditions leading to their protection, that "no fancy of imagination, no genius, no laborious thought" is required? Or is it rather that, through the development of a brand name, "[t]he owner of a mark...mak[es] every effort to impregnate the atmosphere of the market with the drawing power of a congenial symbol"? Is the consumer in some sense a victim of these machinations of the trademark owner, who through the "commercial magnetism" of the trademark "induces the purchaser to select what he wants, or what he has been led to believe he wants"? Or is it finally not consumers who are victims of the trademark, but the trademark who is a "hostage" of consumers, whom it serves by enabling them to find what they desire and to insist on "the quality of goods they prefer and expect"?

1. The Economic Justification for Trademark Protection

These differing accounts of the trademark and trademark law are probably all more or less true, depending on the trademark, product, and consumer at issue. But it is well-accepted that the last account, based on the economic analysis of law, is currently by far the dominant account of trademark law. In *Qualitex Co. v. Jacobson Products Co., Inc.*, 514 U.S. 159 (U.S. 1995), Justice Breyer cited, among other sources, William Landes & Richard Posner, *The Economics of Trademark Law*, 78 TRADEMARK REP. 267, 271-272 (1988), in support of the following statement of the purposes of trademark law:

{T}rademark law, by preventing others from copying a source-identifying mark, reduces the customer's costs of shopping and making purchasing decisions, for it quickly and easily assures a potential customer that this item—the item with this mark—is made by the same producer as other similarly marked items that he or she liked (or disliked) in the past. At the same time, the law helps assure a producer that it (and not an imitating competitor)

13

will reap the financial, reputation-related rewards associated with a desirable product. The law thereby encourages the production of quality products, and simultaneously discourages those who hope to sell inferior products by capitalizing on a consumer's inability quickly to evaluate the quality of an item offered for sale.

Id. at 163-64 (citations omitted).

The current orthodox view of trademarks, then, is that they (1) minimize consumer search costs, and (2) provide incentives to producers to produce consistent levels of product quality. This latter benefit of trademarks is especially important for certain types of products. In general, products may be understood to possess three types of characteristics: "search" characteristics, such as color or price, which can be inspected prior to purchase; "experience" characteristics, such as taste, which can only be verified through use of the product; and "credence" characteristics, such as durability, which can only be confirmed over time. *See* Phillip Nelson, *Advertising as Information*, 82 J. POL. ECON. 729 (1974). For products such as medicine, automobiles or high-technology goods, the "search" characteristics of which say little about the quality of the product, consumers may rely heavily on the trademark attached to the product in making their purchasing decision. It follows that in a market without reliable source-identification for such products, producers would have little incentive to invest in the production of products of high quality. This is because they would likely be undercut by competitors who would offer cheaper products of lower quality under the same mark. *See* George A. Ackerlof, *The Market for "Lemons": Quality Uncertainty and the Market Mechanism*, 84 Q.J. OF ECON. 488 (1970).

As indications of quality, trademarks signify and allow firms to develop commercial *goodwill*, which for many firms may be by far their most valuable asset. The concept of goodwill encompasses the reputation of the firm and its products and the probability, based on this reputation, that consumers will continue to patronize the firm in the future. A nineteenth-century court described goodwill in these terms:

> When an individual or a firm or a corporation has gone on for an unbroken series of years conducting a particular business, and has been so scrupulous in fulfilling every obligation, so careful in maintaining the standard of goods dealt in, so absolutely honest and fair in all business dealings that customers of the concern have become convinced that their experience in the future will be as satisfactory as it has been in the past, while such customers' good report of their own experience tends continually to bring new customers to the same concern, there has been produced an element of value quite as important—in some cases, perhaps far more important—than the plant or machinery with which the business is carried on.

Washburn v. National Wall-Paper Co., 81 F. 17, 20 (2d Cir. 1897).

2. Criticisms of the Economic Justification for Trademark Protection

The example of Coca-Cola and brands like it may lead many readers to doubt the sufficiency of the economic account of trademark law, focused as it is on search costs and incentives to produce quality goods. After all, many trademarks, such as COKE, do more than merely indicate the source of the goods to which they are affixed, and strictly speaking, some trademarks don't even do that. A t-shirt bearing the trademark ARSENAL is not intended to indicate and is not read by consumers to indicate that Arsenal soccer players knitted the shirt themselves. The trademark primarily functions instead as a "badge of support for or loyalty or affiliation to the trademark proprietor." Arsenal Football Club Plc v. Matthew Reed, Case C-206/01, [2003] ETMR 19, ¶ 15. This same function may be attributed to many trademarks, and not simply to high-fashion marks such as POLO or PRADA, but also to more mundane marks such as PEPSI or FORD, whose owners have quite consciously sought to build "consumption communities"[1] around these brands. *See Int'l Order of Job's Daughters v. Lindeburg & Co.*, 633 F.2d 912, 918 (9th Cir. 1980) (recognizing that "[w]e commonly identify ourselves by displaying emblems expressing allegiances. Our

---

[1] DANIEL J. BOORSTIN, AMERICANS: THE DEMOCRATIC EXPERIENCE 145 (1974).

14

jewelry, clothing, and cars are emblazoned with inscriptions showing the organizations we belong to, the schools we attend, the landmarks we have visited, the sports teams we support, the beverages we imbibe"). In such situations, the mark itself is often the primary product characteristic that the consumer wishes to acquire, and the underlying material good, if any, is merely a means of conveying that characteristic and an alibi for the consumption of that characteristic.[2] We typically think of a trademark as supplementary in relation to the goods to which it is affixed, as something added to preexisting goods. But certain doctrines in trademark law may make sense only if one appreciates that for certain brands, this relation is reversed. The brand is prior and the physical goods are supplementary to it, supporting and enhancing the brand's value, so that a firm (for example, a fashion house) may first design a brand and then produce or license tangible or intangible goods consistent with that brand.

Even when the consumer is interested in the quality of the material good, the trademark may contribute to deleterious "artificial product differentiation," as when consumers pay a premium for branded versions of pharmaceuticals when lower-cost generic versions are required by government regulation to meet exactly the same quality standards as the more expensive branded versions. This argument, which associates trademarks with the purported evils of some forms of advertising, first gained significant influence with the publication in 1933 of the economist Edward Chamberlin's book *The Theory of Monopolistic Competition*, which systematically formulated the artificial product differentiation view.[3] Chamberlin's work proved to be especially influential in mid-twentieth century trademark commentary[4] and is reflected to some degree in Justice Frankfurter's discussion of trademarks in *Mishawaka Rubber*. Other courts sometimes picked up on Chamberlin's ideas. *See, e.g., Smith v. Chanel, Inc.*, 402 F.2d 562, 567 (2d Cir. 1968) (proposing that, through the trademark, "economically irrational elements are introduced into consumer choices; and the trademark owner is insulated from the normal pressures of price and quality competition. In consequence the competitive system fails to perform its function of allocating available resources efficiently.").

Since the 1980s, however, mainstream economic thought has grown increasingly hostile toward, even dismissive of, the argument that, as Landes and Posner characterize it, trademarks "promote social waste and consumer deception" through "the power of brand advertising to bamboozle the public and thereby promote monopoly."[5] Instead, economists have come to view trademarks and advertising in a much more positive light. *See* George Stigler, *The Economics of Information*, 69 J. POL. ECON. 213 (1961). The consensus view now is that advertising cheaply conveys information to consumers, particularly with respect to "experience goods." *See* Phillip Nelson, *Advertising as Information*, 82 J. POL. ECON. 729 (1974). Advertising also signals that the advertiser believes its goods to be of sufficiently high quality to benefit from advertising. "The higher quality brand will, other things being equal, have a comparative advantage in acquiring more customers by advertising—since it will retain a larger fraction of them on repeat sales." *See* Jack Hirshleifer, *Where Are We in the Theory of Information?*, 63 AM. ECON. REV. PROC. 31, 38 (1973).[6] Finally, consumers may greatly benefit even from supposedly "artificial" product

---

[2] For further discussion of the trademark "merchandising right," see Stacey L. Dogan & Mark A. Lemley, *The Merchandising Right: Fragile Theory or Fait Accompli?*, 54 EMORY L.J. 461 (2005).

[3] *See also* JOAN ROBINSON, THE ECONOMICS OF IMPERFECT COMPETITION 89 (1933).

[4] *See generally* Glynn S. Lunney, *Trademark Monopolies*, 48 EMORY L.J. 367, 367-69 (1999) (discussing the influence of Chamberlin's work on trademark commentary). *See also* Sherwin Rosen, *Advertising, Information, and Product Differentiation, in* ISSUES IN ADVERTISING: THE ECONOMICS OF PERSUASION 161-91 (David G. Tuerck ed., 1978) (summarizing the artificial product differentiation view). *See generally* Beverly W. Pattishall, *Trademarks and the Monopoly Phobia*, 50 MICH. L. REV. 967 (1952) (criticizing the artificial product differentiation view).

[5] Landes & Posner, *supra*, at 276-77.

[6] *See also* Mark Lemley, The *Modern Lanham Act and the Death of Common Sense*, 108 YALE L.J. 1687, 1690 (1999) (paraphrasing, though not necessarily endorsing, this theory as "In effect, 'we advertise,

differentiation and may enjoy—and willingly pay for—the consumption of high-performance and high-status goods. *See* Jake Linford, *Placebo Marks*, 47 PEPP. L. REV. 45 (2020).

Despite the current consensus in economic and legal thought that advertising serves important informational functions in markets, criticisms of branding and advertising remain influential in popular thought. *See, e.g.*, NAOMI KLEIN, NO LOGO: TAKING AIM AT BRAND BULLIES (2000); JULIET B. SCHOR, BORN TO BUY: THE COMMERCIALIZED CHILD AND THE NEW CONSUMER CULTURE (2005). For readers sympathetic to these criticisms, two questions arise with respect to trademarks and trademark law. First, is it fair to apply general criticisms of advertising to trademarks specifically? Though trademarks are usually central to most forms of advertising, aren't trademarks themselves mere informational devices? Second, and related, how, if at all, can trademark law be modified to limit such alleged harms as artificial product differentiation or the "bamboozle[ing]" of the public? Stated differently, how can trademark law continue to promote the ability of marks to *inform* consumers without also promoting the ability of marks to *persuade*? How practically speaking can trademark law minimize persuasion but still preserve information?[7] Any serious criticism of the role that trademark law plays in perpetuating status consumption or introducing "economically irrational elements" into purchasing decisions should be able to answer these questions. Perhaps limiting the scope of trademark rights or the kinds of commercial signifiers that can be protected as trademarks would lessen the persuasive impact of strong brands. But it may be that minor modifications to trademark law will not help to ameliorate the effects of deeply-engrained consumption practices, and efforts to reform these practices will be more effective if undertaken elsewhere.[8]

Opponents of overly expansive trademark rights (and defendants in trademark cases) may find more traction by appealing to what is arguably the true overarching goal of trademark law, one which subsumes the goals of lowering consumer search costs and incentivizing consistent levels of product quality. Trademark law's overarching goal is to foster competition, primarily by enabling the efficient communication of information in the marketplace. When trademark law overprotects, it impedes the optimal flow of information to consumers, tends to give undue market power to incumbents, and can significantly disrupt the efficient operation of the patent and copyright systems (a possibility which we will address in a moment). The argument from competition speaks the language of mainstream economics but often does so in favor of limiting rather than expanding trademark property rights.

Comments and Questions

1. *Trademark law and "property."* Critics of the expansion in the subject matter and scope of trademark protection often accuse the law of having lost its purportedly traditional focus on consumer protection and having instead embraced a property-rights rationale for trademark protection. Elsewhere in the article excerpted above in Part A, McKenna directly challenges this view:

> {T}rademark law was not traditionally intended to protect consumers. Instead, trademark law, like all unfair competition law, sought to protect producers from illegitimate diversions of their trade by competitors. Courts did focus on consumer deception in these cases, but only because deception distinguished actionable unfair competition from mere competition, which was encouraged. In fact, courts denied relief in many early trademark cases despite clear evidence that consumers were likely to be confused by the defendant's use. Invariably they did so because the plaintiff could not show

---

and therefore we must sell a good of sufficiently high quality that we can afford this high-cost expenditure.'").

[7] *See* Barton Beebe, *Search and Persuasion in Trademark Law*, 103 MICH. L. REV. 2020 (2005).

[8] For the seminal discussion that anticipates nearly all of trademark commentary on these issues since, see Ralph S. Brown, Jr., *Advertising and the Public Interest: Legal Protection of Trade Symbols*, 57 YALE L.J. 1165 (1948).

that the defendant's actions were likely to divert customers who otherwise would have gone to the plaintiff.

Moreover, American courts protected producers from illegitimately diverted trade by recognizing property rights. This property-based system of trademark protection was largely derived from the natural rights theory of property that predominately influenced courts during the time American trademark law developed in the nineteenth century . . . .

Critics cannot continue simply to claim that modern law is illegitimate because it does not seek to protect consumers. Because it never really did.

Mark P. McKenna, *The Normative Foundations of Trademark Law*, 82 NOTRE DAME L. REV. 1839, 1841, 1916 (2007). For an alternative reading of the history of American trademark law, see Robert G. Bone, *Hunting Goodwill: A History of the Concept of Goodwill in Trademark Law*, 86 B.U. L. REV. 547 (2006).

2. *Beware of the term "consumer."* Trademark talk habitually uses the term "consumer" and only that term to describe members of the public. Dustin Marlan criticizes the term for "(1) its connotation of humans as reductive market-based objects; (2) its anti-ecological bent; and (3) its nonsensical nature." Dustin Marlan, *Is "Consumer" Biasing Trademark Law?*, 8 TEX. A&M L. REV. 367, 377 (2021). He argues that "the biasing effects of *consumer* may be contributing to trademark law defining the public in a manner that is patronizing, biased, insulting, and indulgent of likelihood-of-confusion claims." *Id.* at 373. He advocates "one of two approaches: (1) take active steps to phase out use of *consumer* and replace it with more respectful and appropriate terminology such as *citizen*; or (2) simply maintain the status quo in using *consumer*, but each time be conscious of the biasing effects that the *consumer* construct may have for the law and us as its subjects." *Id.* at 373-74.

3. *Do trademarks indicate source or obscure it?* It is routinely stated that trademarks' chief function is to indicate the source of the goods to which they are affixed. But depending on how one defines "source," many trademarks arguably function to *disguise* the true source of their goods. Does the mark NIKE tell us anything more about where exactly our shoes were manufactured or who manufactured them and under what working conditions than, say, the term "imported"? When in 2001 Jonah Peretti, then a graduate student at MIT, sought to use Nike's own shoe customization program to call attention to the manufacturing conditions for Nike's shoes, Nike refused to print on the shoes he had ordered from them the word he specified: "sweatshop." Peretti's email exchange with Nike went viral and damaged Nike's brand image. *See* Kathleen Elkins, *How a Fight With Nike Led Buzzfeed's Jonah Peretti to Create a Billion-Dollar Media Empire*, CNBC.com, Aug. 3, 2017, https://www.cnbc.com/2017/08/02/how-jonah-peretti-created-buzzfeed-a-billion-dollar-media-empire.html. (Peretti went on to cofound *Huffington Post* and then found BuzzFeed.com.)

4. *Other general theories of trademark law.* The economic account of trademark law remains dominant, but students may be interested in alternative general approaches. *See, e.g.*, Barton Beebe, *The Semiotic Analysis of Trademark Law*, 51 UCLA L. REV. 621 (2004) (using semiotic theory to analyze trademark law); Jeremy Sheff, *Marks, Morals, and Markets*, 65 STAN. L. REV. 761 (2013) (using utilitarian and contractarian moral theory to analyze trademark law). For a study of a self-regulating system of designation that operates outside of formal intellectual property law, see David Fagundes, *Talk Derby to Me: Intellectual Property Norms Governing Roller Derby Pseudonyms*, 90 TEX. L. REV. 1093 (2012).

C. Trademark Law Within the Larger Scheme of Intellectual Property Law

As the excerpt above from the *Trade-Mark Cases* suggests, when seen from the perspective of trademark law, copyright law and patent law can appear to be closely similar to each other and quite different from trademark law—so much so that it is not unreasonable to ask why trademark is grouped with patent and copyright under the rubric of "intellectual property law" rather than separated out as some hybrid of competition law and intellectual property law. As the table at the conclusion of this section summarizes, both copyright and patent are based on the Intellectual Property Clause of the Constitution, which empowers Congress "{t}o promote the Progress of Science and useful Arts, by securing for limited Times to Authors and Inventors the exclusive Right to their respective Writings and Discoveries." U.S. Const. art. I, § 8, cl. 8. The Constitution thus requires copyright and patent to promote innovation, human creativity, or more generally, human "Progress," with patent focusing primarily on incentivizing the invention of new technologies, such as new pharmaceuticals, better machines, or more efficient methods of manufacture, and copyright focusing on incentivizing the production of "works of authorship," such as novels, music, and motion pictures (and this textbook).

Inventions and works of authorship share important characteristics (akin to "public goods")[9] that make intellectual property protections useful. Both tend to be expensive to develop, but once developed, they are relatively inexpensive to reproduce in copies. It can cost $1 billion to develop a successful pharmaceutical and bring it to market and potentially only a few dollars or less per copy to manufacture it. The consumption of inventions and works of authorship also tends to be "non-rivalrous." A potentially unlimited number of people can benefit equally from the same idea or listen each to his or her own copy of the same recording of the same musical work. Finally, without recourse to prohibitions established by law, it is often exceedingly difficult to exclude people from and thus charge a price for the benefit of an invention or work of authorship. This condition has only intensified with improvements in reproduction and distribution technologies, whether they take the form of ever more flexible assembly lines, automated manufacture, 3D printing, or the reproduction of digital files on a home computer or the internet.

To address these problems, patent law and copyright law provide limited terms of protection to qualifying works, with patent's term significantly shorter in duration than copyright's. In essence, the public makes a bargain with inventors and authors. To incentivize them, we give them exclusive rights in their innovations so that they can recoup the costs of and perhaps profit from their innovating activity, but in exchange, we eventually claim their innovations for the public domain, where these innovations become free for all, including subsequent inventors and authors, to use.

In contrast to copyright and patent law, trademark law is based not on the Intellectual Property Clause, but the Commerce Clause. Its goal is not to promote the progress of "Science and useful Arts" but rather to promote fair and efficient competition. Its term of protection is unlimited in time provided that the trademark owner continues to use the trademark in commerce. And the utilization of trademarks is arguably rivalrous. If two firms share the same trademark for the same type of product in the same marketplace, the utility of both trademarks will be severely diminished.

For all of the differences among copyright, patent, and trademark law, note that these separate regimes of intellectual property law can simultaneously protect the same thing. For example, a logo might qualify for both copyright and trademark protection. A particular product feature, such as the shape of a mobile phone, might qualify for trademark protection and design patent protection. A

---

[9] *See* Wendy J. Gordon, *Fair Use As Market Failure: A Structural and Economic Analysis of the Betamax Case and Its Predecessors*, 82 COLUM. L. REV. 1600 (1982). Gordon describes "public goods" as follows:

> A public good is often described as having two defining traits. First, it is virtually inexhaustible once produced, in the sense that supplying additional access to new users would not deplete the supply available to others. Second, and more important for the instant purposes, persons who have not paid for access cannot readily be prevented from using a public good. Because it is difficult or expensive to prevent "free riders" from using such goods, public goods usually will be under-produced if left to the private market. A familiar example of a public good is national defense. Since it is not possible to use a radar early-warning network in a way that discriminates between one person who has paid for defense and his neighbor who has not, a less than optimal amount of national defense will be produced if its purchase is left to the usual consensual market mechanisms of voluntary purchase. Some sort of compulsory payment, such as taxation, and central decision-making may be necessary to eliminate free riders and obtain the socially desirable amount of defense.

Id. at 1610-11 (footnotes omitted).

particular furniture design might qualify for trademark protection, design patent protection, and copyright protection as well.

These overlapping regimes of exclusive rights can create significant problems in intellectual property law, some of which we will engage later in this casebook. For example, what should happen when the term of copyright protection in a particular work of authorship expires, but that expression also functions as a trademark? Should trademark law allow the Walt Disney Company to continue to assert exclusive rights in images of Mickey Mouse after its copyright in those images has expired? More significantly, should companies be able to assert trademark rights in product features that also qualify for utility patent protection, or at least that perform some mechanical function in addition to serving as designations of source?

Comments and Questions

1. *Do we want to incentivize* more *trademarks*? We generally seek through patent and copyright law to incentivize the production of more patentable inventions and more copyrightable works of authorship. Should we similarly design trademark law to incentivize the production of more trademarks? Is there anything intrinsically valuable about trademarks? Do more trademarks indicate or themselves constitute "Progress"? Could there be situations (or market sectors) in which there are too many trademarks?

V10.0/2023-07-22

	Trademark Law	**Copyright Law**	**Utility Patent Law**	**Design Patent Law**
Protectable Subject Matter	Designations of commercial source, including brand names, logos, product packaging, and product configurations	Works of authorship, including literary, musical, sculptural, graphic, and architectural works, motion pictures, computer software, and sound recordings	Inventions, including processes, machines, manufactured articles, and compositions of matter	Ornamental designs for articles of manufacture
Constitutional Basis	Commerce Clause	Intellectual Property Clause	Intellectual Property Clause	Intellectual Property Clause
Statutory Basis	Lanham Act, 15 U.S.C. § 1051 et seq.	Copyright Act, 17 U.S.C. § 101 et seq.	Patent Act, 35 U.S.C. § 101 et seq.	Patent Act, 35 U.S.C. § 101 et seq.
Basic Requirements for Protection	Distinctive of source; used in commerce; not functional	Fixed in a tangible medium of expression; originality	Novel, non-obvious, and useful	Ornamental, novel, and non-obvious
Term of Protection	Registration lasts 10 years; perpetually renewable as long as the mark is distinctive and used in commerce	Life of the author plus 70 years; for works for hire, 95 years from date of publication	20 years from filing date of patent application	15 years from date of grant of patent for applications filed on or after May 13, 2015; 14 years from date of grant of patent for applications filed before May 13, 2015
How Rights Are Acquired	"Common law" rights through use in commerce; registered rights through registration at PTO	Through fixation; registration not required	Patent application at PTO	Patent application at PTO

V10.0/2023-07-22

I. Establishing Trademark Rights

In order to qualify for trademark protection under U.S. federal law, a trademark must meet three basic requirements: (1) the trademark must be "distinctive" of the source of the goods or services to which it is affixed, (2) the trademark must not be disqualified from protection by various statutory bars to protection, the most significant of which is that the trademark not be "functional," and (3) the trademark must be used in commerce.

Note what is missing from this list of basic requirements for trademark protection. First, in order to qualify for protection under the Lanham Act, a trademark does not need to be registered at the PTO (though, as we will discuss in Part I.D, there are significant benefits to registration). Lanham Act § 32, 15 U.S.C. § 1114, protects *registered* marks from unauthorized uses that are likely to cause consumer confusion as to the true source of the unauthorized user's goods. Lanham Act § 43(a), 15 U.S.C. § 1125(a), does the same for *unregistered* marks. (And Section 43(c), 15 U.S.C. § 1125(c), protects both registered and unregistered marks from trademark dilution). As a matter of tradition, trademark lawyers sometimes refer to unregistered mark protection under § 43(a) as "common law" protection of trademarks even though this protection is based on statutory federal law.

Second, a protectable trademark need not manifest itself in any particular form.[1] Consider the extraordinary variety of forms that trademarks (here, all registered) may take:

- Words: APPLE for computers (U.S. Reg. No. 1,078,312, Nov. 29, 1977); AMAZON for online retailing services (U.S. Reg. No. 2,832,943, April 13, 2004); NIKE for athletic shoes (U.S. Reg. No. 978,952, Feb. 19, 1974); THE for clothing (U.S. Reg. No. 6,763,118, June 21, 2022).

- Phrases: JUST DO IT for clothing (U.S. Reg. No. 1,875,307, Jan. 24, 1995).

- Two-dimensional still images: a "'wing' design" for sports bags (U.S. Reg. No. 1145473, Jan. 6, 1981)

- Two-dimensional moving images: for online entertainment services, "[t]he mark consists of a moving image of a flash of light from which rays of light are emitted against a background of sky and clouds. The scene then pans downward to a torch being held by a lady on a pedestal. The word "COLUMBIA" appears across the top running through the torch and then a circular rainbow appears in the sky encircling the lady." (U.S. Reg. No. 1,975,999, May 28, 1996).

- Colors: the color canary yellow for adhesive stationary notes (U.S. Reg. No. 2,390,667, Oct. 3, 2000); the color brown for parcel delivery services (U.S. Reg. No. 2,131,693, Jan. 27, 1988).

---

[1] *See* Jerome Gilson & Anne Gilson LaLonde, *Cinnamon Buns, Marching Ducks, and Cherry-Scented Racecar Exhaust: Protecting Nontraditional Trademarks*, 95 TRADEMARK REP. 773 (2005).

Int. Cl.: 16

Prior U.S. Cls.: 2, 5, 22, 23, 29, 37, 38 and 50

Reg. No. 2,390,667

United States Patent and Trademark Office   Registered Oct. 3, 2000

TRADEMARK
PRINCIPAL REGISTER

MINNESOTA MINING AND MANUFACTURING COMPANY (DELAWARE CORPORATION), AKA 3M
3M CENTER
SAINT PAUL, MN 551441000

FOR: STATIONERY NOTES CONTAINING ADHESIVE ON ONE SIDE FOR ATTACHMENT TO SURFACES, IN CLASS 16 (U.S. CLS. 2, 5, 22, 23, 29, 37, 38 AND 50).

FIRST USE 0-0-1978; IN COMMERCE 0-0-1978.

THE MARK IS LINED FOR CANARY YELLOW, AND THE APPLICANT CLAIMS COLOR AS THE MARK.

THE MARK CONSISTS OF THE COLOR CANARY YELLOW USED OVER THE ENTIRE SURFACE OF THE GOODS. THE MATTER SHOWN IN BROKEN LINES SHOWS THE POSITION OF THE MARK AND IS NOT CLAIMED AS PART OF THE MARK.
SEC. 2(F).

SER. NO. 75-087,575, FILED 4-5-1996.

TERESA M. RUPP, EXAMINING ATTORNEY

- Colors as used on apparel: for promotional services relating to sports events, where "[t]he mark consists of the colors green and gold where the color green is applied to the jacket and the color gold is applied to the three waist buttons and the two sleeve buttons on each arm of the jacket." (U.S. Reg. No. 6,000,045, March 3, 2020).

- Sounds: Tarzan's yell for toy action figures (U.S. Reg. No. 2,210,506, Dec. 15, 1998); for canned and frozen vegetables where the mark consists of "the sound of a deep, male, human-like voice saying 'Ho-Ho-Ho' in even intervals with each 'Ho' dropping in pitch" (U.S. Reg. No. 2,519,203, Dec. 18, 2001).

- Scents: for toy modeling compounds, where "[t]he mark is a scent of a sweet, slightly musky, vanilla fragrance, with slight overtones of cherry, combined with the smell of a salted, wheat-based dough" (U.S. Reg. No. 5,467,089, May 15, 2018).

- Textures: for wines where "[t]he mark consists of a velvet textured covering on the surface of a bottle of wine" (U.S. Reg. No. 3,155,702, Oct. 17, 2006).[2]

---

[2] *See* Christina S. Monteiro, *A Nontraditional Per-Spectrum: The Touch of Trademarks*, INTA BULL., June 15, 2010, at 4.

- Motions: for automobiles where "[t]he mark consists of the unique motion in which the door of a vehicle is opened. The doors move parallel to the body of the vehicle but are gradually raised above the vehicle to a parallel position." (U.S. Reg. No. 2,793,439, Dec. 16, 2003).

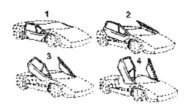

- Buildings exteriors: the design of a building for restaurant services (U.S. Reg. No. 1,045,615, Aug. 3, 1976).

- Building interiors: for retail consumer electronics services, "the mark consists of the design and layout of a retail store. The store features a clear glass storefront surrounded by a paneled facade consisting of large, rectangular horizontal panels over the top of the glass front, and two narrower panels stacked on either side of the storefront. Within the store, rectangular recessed lighting units traverse the length of the store's ceiling. There are cantilevered shelves below recessed display spaces along the side walls, and rectangular tables arranged in a line in the middle of the store parallel to the walls and extending from the storefront to the back of the store. There is multi-tiered shelving along the side walls, and a oblong table with stools located at the back of the store, set below video screens flush mounted on the back wall. The walls, floors, lighting, and other fixtures appear in dotted lines and are not claimed as individual features of the mark; however, the placement of the various items are considered to be part of the overall mark." (U.S. Reg. No. 4,277,914, Jan. 22, 2013).

- Product shapes: for mobile phones, where "the mark consists of the configuration of a rectangular handheld mobile digital electronic device with rounded corners" (U.S. Reg. No. 3,457,218, July 1, 2008); for uncooked hamburger patties, where "the mark consists of the configuration of a hamburger patty" (U.S. Reg. No. 5,742,743, May 7, 2019); for footwear, where "the mark consists of [*sic*] three-dimensional configuration of a zip tie with a substantially rectangular end, all in the color red" (U.S. Reg. No. 6,681,777, Mar. 29, 2022).

23

- Product packaging: for soft drinks, "[t]he mark consists of a three dimensional configuration of a version of the Coca Cola Contour Bottle, rendered as a two-liter bottle, having a distinctive curved shape with an inward curve or pinch in the bottom portion of the bottle and vertical flutes above and below a central flat panel portion." (U.S. Reg. No. 4,242,307, Nov. 13, 2012).

The reader may be surprised to see that trademark rights can cover such a wide array of subject matter. This Part covers how these various marks have managed to qualify for trademark protection and why various other marks have failed to qualify. Section I.A devotes a great deal of attention to what is by far the most important requirement for trademark protection: that the trademark be "distinctive." Section I.B then turns to the various statutory bars to protection, including the functionality bar, which disqualify marks from protection under the Lanham Act. Section I.C seeks to make sense of the "use in commerce" requirement for trademark protection. Section I.D reviews why it is worthwhile to register a mark at the PTO and how the registration process works. Section I.E addresses the geographic scope of the protection of registered and unregistered marks.

A.   Trademark Distinctiveness

Lanham Act § 45; 15 U.S.C. § 1127

> The term "trademark" includes any word, name, symbol, or device, or any combination thereof . . . used by a person . . . to identify and distinguish his or her goods, including a unique product, from those manufactured or sold by others and to indicate the source of the goods, even if that source is unknown.

The § 45 definition of the term "trademark" emphasizes that a protectable trademark must be distinctive of source — it must "identify and distinguish . . . goods . . . and . . . indicate the source of the goods." Note that in order to qualify for protection, a trademark need not indicate the precise manufacturing source of the goods or the corporate name of the producer of the goods. For example, the trademark TIDE for laundry detergent need not indicate in exactly which factory the particular bottle of laundry detergent was made or that Proctor & Gamble ultimately owns the TIDE brand. Instead, consumers need only know that all products bearing the same trademark originate in or are sponsored by the same source, even if that source is "anonymous" to consumers.[3] This is sometimes known as the "anonymous source" theory of trademark protection.

A trademark will qualify as distinctive if either (1) it is "inherently distinctive" of source or (2) it has developed "acquired distinctiveness" of source. A mark is inherently distinctive if "its intrinsic nature serves to identify a particular source." *Wal-Mart Stores, Inc. v. Samara Bros., Inc.*, 529 U.S. 205 210 (2000) (alterations omitted). The underlying assumption is that as a matter of consumer literacy, consumers will almost instantly recognize that an inherently distinctive mark is a designation of source, even when they encounter the mark for the first time. After all, how else would a modern consumer make sense of the word "apple" as used in the sale of electronics that have nothing to do with apples? Inherently distinctive marks "almost *automatically* tell a customer that they refer to a brand," *Qualitex*

---

[3] *See* McCarthy § 3.9 ("[T]he 'source' identified by a trademark need not be known by name to the buyer. It may be anonymous in the sense that the buyer does not know, or care about, the name of the corporation that made the product or the name of the corporation which distributes it. But the buyer is entitled to assume that all products carrying the same trademark are somehow linked with or sponsored by that single, anonymous source."). *See also* P & P Imports LLC v. Johnson Enterprises, LLC, 46 F.4th 953, 960–61 (9th Cir. 2022).

Co. v. Jacobson Products Co., Inc., 514 U.S. 159 162-63 (1995) (emphasis in original), and "immediately . . . signal a brand or a product 'source.'" *Id.* at 163.

Marks that lack inherent distinctiveness may nevertheless qualify as distinctive if they have developed "acquired distinctiveness," otherwise known as "secondary meaning," through advertising or use in the marketplace. Over time, consumers may come to identify what might have seemed merely a description of the good or service (e.g., "American Airlines") or merely a decoration on a product (e.g., three stripes on the side of an athletic shoe) as a designation of the source of that product. Indeed, consumers may come to identify the configuration of the product itself as a signifier of its source.

Here in Section I.A, we will spend considerable time reviewing how courts determine if a commercial sign qualifies as inherently distinctive or as possessing acquired distinctiveness. Before proceeding, two things should be kept in mind. First, some of the opinions below address the registrability of the marks at issue at the PTO while other opinions address the protectability under § 43(a) of marks that have never been registered. Recall that registration is not a prerequisite for trademark protection under the Lanham Act. Many significant trademark cases over past decades have involved unregistered marks. The important point for our purposes in this subsection is that the basic doctrine relating to the registrability of a mark is essentially the same as the doctrine relating to whether it may be protected regardless of its registration status. We may use opinions from either context to understand the distinctiveness requirement in trademark law.

Second, this subsection will first consider distinctiveness doctrine as it relates to verbal marks, and will then proceed to the more difficult area of distinctiveness doctrine that covers non-verbal marks, such as logos, colors, product packaging, and product configuration (i.e., the shape of the product itself).

1. Inherent Distinctiveness of Source and Acquired Distinctiveness of Source

a. Inherent Distinctiveness of Source

i. The *Abercrombie* Spectrum

The excerpt below, from *Abercrombie & Fitch Co. v. Hunting World, Inc.*, 537 F.2d 4 (2d Cir. 1976), analyzes some of the most fundamental terms and concepts in trademark law. Though *Abercrombie* is now a relatively old opinion, its influence on U.S. and even foreign trademark law cannot be overstated. It is the origin of the "*Abercrombie* spectrum" of trademark distinctiveness, a classification scheme that is used in a wide variety of areas of trademark doctrine.

The essential facts underlying the opinion are as follows. Plaintiff Abercrombie & Fitch Company ("A&F") operated various sporting goods stores in New York City and elsewhere. It had multiple PTO registrations for its trademark SAFARI. Among these was a registration for SAFARI for cotton clothing, a registration for SAFARI for hats, and a registration for SAFARI for shoes. Defendant Hunting World, Incorporated ("HW") began to sell at its New York City store sporting apparel, including hats and shoes, bearing the terms "Safari," "Minisafari," and "Safariland." A&F sued on the ground that HW's conduct would confuse consumers as to the true source of HW's goods. At the core of the case was the question of whether A&F's SAFARI trademark possessed distinctiveness of source on certain of A&F's goods.

As you read the excerpt, consider the following questions:

- To the extent that a mark's categorization somewhere along the *Abercrombie* spectrum bears directly on whether the mark will qualify for trademark protection, which borders between categories do you suspect are especially disputed?

- Where would you classify the trademark "safari" for clothing? for boots? for hats?

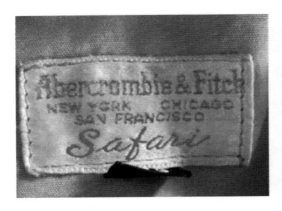 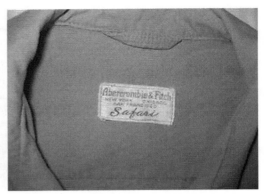

Abercrombie & Fitch Co. v. Hunting World, Inc.
537 F.2d 4, 9-11 (2d Cir. 1976)

FRIENDLY, Circuit Judge:

. . . .

[1] It will be useful at the outset to restate some basic principles of trademark law, which, although they should be familiar, tend to become lost in a welter of adjectives.

[2] The cases, and in some instances the Lanham Act, identify four different categories of terms with respect to trademark protection. Arrayed in an ascending order which roughly reflects their eligibility to trademark status and the degree of protection accorded, these classes are (1) generic, (2) descriptive, (3) suggestive, and (4) arbitrary or fanciful. The lines of demarcation, however, are not always bright. Moreover, the difficulties are compounded because a term that is in one category for a particular product may be in quite a different one for another,[6] because a term may shift from one category to another in light of differences in usage through time,[7] because a term may have one meaning to one group of users and a different one to others, and because the same term may be put to different uses with respect to a single product.

[3] A generic term is one that refers, or has come to be understood as referring, to the genus of which the particular product is a species. At common law neither those terms which were generic nor those which were merely descriptive could become valid trademarks, see Delaware & Hudson Canal Co. v. Clark, 80 U.S. (13 Wall.) 311, 323, 20 L.Ed. 581 (1872) ("Nor can a generic name, or a name merely descriptive of an article or its qualities, ingredients, or characteristics, be employed as a trademark and the exclusive use of it be entitled to legal protection"). . . . While, as we shall see, the Lanham Act makes an important exception with respect to those merely descriptive terms which have acquired secondary meaning, see § 2(f), 15 U.S.C. § 1052(f), it offers no such exception for generic marks. The Act provides for the cancellation of a registered mark if at any time it "becomes the common descriptive name of an article or substance," § 14(c). This means that even proof of secondary meaning, by virtue of which some "merely descriptive" marks may be registered, cannot transform a generic term into a subject for trademark. As explained in J. Kohnstam, Ltd. v. Louis Marx and Company, 280 F.2d 437, 440, 47 CCPA 1080 (1960), no matter how much money and effort the user of a generic term has poured into promoting the sale of its merchandise and what success it has achieved in securing public identification, it cannot deprive competing manufacturers of the product of the right to call an article by its name. We

---

[6] To take a familiar example "Ivory" would be generic when used to describe a product made from the tusks of elephants but arbitrary as applied to soap.

[7] See, e.g., Haughton Elevator Co. v. Seeberger, 85 U.S.P.Q. 80 (1950), in which the coined word 'Escalator', originally fanciful, or at the very least suggestive, was held to have become generic.

have recently had occasion to apply this doctrine of the impossibility of achieving trademark protection for a generic term, CES Publishing Corp. v. St. Regis Publications, Inc., 531 F.2d 11 (1975). The pervasiveness of the principle is illustrated by a series of well known cases holding that when a suggestive or fanciful term has become generic as a result of a manufacturer's own advertising efforts, trademark protection will be denied save for those markets where the term still has not become generic and a secondary meaning has been shown to continue. Bayer Co. v. United Drug Co., 272 F. 505 (2d Cir. 1921) (L. Hand, D. J.) {finding "aspirin" generic}; DuPont Cellophane Co. v. Waxed Products Co., 85 F.2d 75 (2d Cir.) (A. N. Hand, C. J.), cert. denied, 299 U.S. 601 (1936) {finding "cellophane" generic}; King-Seeley Thermos Co. v. Aladdin Industries, Inc., 321 F.2d 577 (2d Cir. 1963) {finding "thermos" generic}. A term may thus be generic in one market and descriptive or suggestive or fanciful in another.

[4] The term which is descriptive but not generic[11] stands on a better basis. Although § 2(e) of the Lanham Act, 15 U.S.C. § 1052, forbids the registration of a mark which, when applied to the goods of the applicant, is "merely descriptive," § 2(f) removes a considerable part of the sting by providing that "except as expressly excluded in paragraphs (a)-(d) of this section, nothing in this chapter shall prevent the registration of a mark used by the applicant which has become distinctive of the applicant's goods in commerce" and that the Commissioner may accept, as prima facie evidence that the mark has become distinctive, proof of substantially exclusive and continuous use of the mark applied to the applicant's goods for five years preceding the application. As indicated in the cases cited in the discussion of the unregistrability of generic terms, "common descriptive name," as used in §§ 14(c) and 15(4), refers to generic terms applied to products and not to terms that are "merely descriptive." In the former case any claim to an exclusive right must be denied since this in effect would confer a monopoly not only of the mark but of the product by rendering a competitor unable effectively to name what it was endeavoring to sell. In the latter case the law strikes the balance, with respect to registration, between the hardships to a competitor in hampering the use of an appropriate word and those to the owner who, having invested money and energy to endow a word with the good will adhering to his enterprise, would be deprived of the fruits of his efforts.

[5] The category of "suggestive" marks was spawned by the felt need to accord protection to marks that were neither exactly descriptive on the one hand nor truly fanciful on the other, a need that was particularly acute because of the bar in the Trademark Act of 1905, 33 Stat. 724, 726, (with an exceedingly limited exception noted above) on the registration of merely descriptive marks regardless of proof of secondary meaning. See Orange Crush Co. v. California Crushed Fruit Co., 54 U.S.App.D.C. 313, 297 F. 892 (1924). Having created the category the courts have had great difficulty in defining it. Judge Learned Hand made the not very helpful statement:

> It is quite impossible to get any rule out of the cases beyond this: That the validity of the mark ends where suggestion ends and description begins.

Franklin Knitting Mills, Inc. v. Fashionit Sweater Mills, Inc., 297 F. 247, 248 (S.D.N.Y. 1923), aff'd per curiam, 4 F.2d 1018 (2d Cir. 1925), a statement amply confirmed by comparing the list of terms held suggestive with those held merely descriptive in 3 Callmann, Unfair Competition, Trademarks and Monopolies s 71.2 (3d ed.). Another court has observed, somewhat more usefully, that:

---

[11] See, e. g., W. E. Bassett Co. v. Revlon, Inc., 435 F.2d 656 (2d Cir. 1970). A Commentator has illuminated the distinction with an example of the "Deep Bowl Spoon":

> "Deep Bowl" identifies a significant characteristic of the article. It is "merely descriptive" of the goods, because it informs one that they are deep in the bowl portion . . . . It is not, however, "the common descriptive name" of the article (since) the implement is not a deep bowl, it is a spoon . . . . "Spoon" is not merely descriptive of the article it identifies the article (and therefore) the term is generic.

Fletcher, Actual Confusion as to Incontestability of Descriptive Marks, 64 Trademark Rep. 252, 260 (1974). On the other hand, "Deep Bowl" would be generic as to a deep bowl.

A term is suggestive if it requires imagination, thought and perception to reach a conclusion as to the nature of goods. A term is descriptive if it forthwith conveys an immediate idea of the ingredients, qualities or characteristics of the goods.

Stix Products, Inc. v. United Merchants & Manufacturers Inc., 295 F.Supp. 479, 488 (S.D.N.Y. 1968). Also useful is the approach taken by this court in Aluminum Fabricating Co. of Pittsburgh v. Season-All Window Corp., 259 F.2d 314 (2d Cir. 1958), that the reason for restricting the protection accorded descriptive terms, namely the undesirability of preventing an entrant from using a descriptive term for his product, is much less forceful when the trademark is a suggestive word since, as Judge Lumbard wrote, 259 F.2d at 317:

> The English language has a wealth of synonyms and related words with which to describe the qualities which manufacturers may wish to claim for their products and the ingenuity of the public relations profession supplies new words and slogans as they are needed.

If a term is suggestive, it is entitled to registration without proof of secondary meaning. Moreover, as held in the Season-All case, the decision of the Patent Office to register a mark without requiring proof of secondary meaning affords a rebuttable presumption that the mark is suggestive or arbitrary or fanciful rather than merely descriptive.

[6] It need hardly be added that fanciful or arbitrary terms[12] enjoy all the rights accorded to suggestive terms as marks without the need of debating whether the term is "merely descriptive" and with ease of establishing infringement.

In the light of these principles we must proceed to a decision of this case.

Comments and Questions

1. *Is "SAFARI" generic as to clothing, hats, and boots?* Judge Friendly found that safari was a generic term when used in connection with certain items of clothing and hats. Here is part of his reasoning:

> It is common ground that A&F could not apply 'Safari' as a trademark for an expedition into the African wilderness. This would be a clear example of the use of 'Safari' as a generic term. What is perhaps less obvious is that a word may have more than one generic use. The word 'Safari' has become part of a family of generic terms which, although deriving no doubt from the original use of the word and reminiscent of its milieu, have come to be understood not as having to do with hunting in Africa, but as terms within the language referring to contemporary American fashion apparel. These terms name the components of the safari outfit well-known to the clothing industry and its customers: the 'Safari hat', a broad flat-brimmed hat with a single, large band; the 'Safari jacket', a belted bush jacket with patch pockets and a buttoned shoulder loop; when the jacket is accompanied by pants, the combination is called the 'Safari suit'.

Abercrombie, 537 F.2d at 11-12. Judge Friendly determined that the term "safari" was not generic, however, when used in connection with boots; it was either suggestive or merely descriptive, and because the registration of SAFARI for boots had become "incontestable" (a concept we will discuss below), the mark was found in either case to be protected. *Id.* at 12. Nevertheless, HW was deemed to be making a "fair use" (another concept we will address below) of the term safari in connection with its boots and was thus found not to be infringing. *Id.* at 12-13.

We will devote much more attention to the question of genericism in Part I.A.1.c below.

---

[12] As terms of art, the distinctions between suggestive terms and fanciful or arbitrary terms may seem needlessly artificial. Of course, a common word may be used in a fanciful sense; indeed one might say that only a common word can be so used, since a coined word cannot first be put to a bizarre use. Nevertheless, the term "fanciful", as a classifying concept, is usually applied to words invented solely for their use as trademarks. When the same legal consequences attach to a common word, i. e., when it is applied in an unfamiliar way, the use is called "arbitrary."

2.   *What* Abercrombie *borderlines are the most disputed?* Under the *Abercrombie* spectrum, suggestive, arbitrary, and fanciful marks qualify as inherently distinctive and may be protected without a showing that the mark has developed secondary meaning as a designation of source. Descriptive marks do not qualify as inherently distinctive and require a showing of secondary meaning to be protected. Generic marks may not be protected regardless of any showing of secondary meaning. Thus, there are two significantly disputed borders in the *Abercrombie* spectrum, the border between generic and descriptive marks (addressed in Part I.A.1.c) and the border between descriptive and suggestive marks (addressed in the next subsection).

In practice, it rarely makes much difference whether the inherently distinctive mark is deemed suggestive, arbitrary, or fanciful. In the context of the likelihood of confusion analysis (discussed in Part II), many courts recite the rule that fanciful marks should receive a greater scope of protection than arbitrary marks, and arbitrary marks a greater scope of protection than suggestive marks, but it is not clear that these distinctions have had any effect on litigation outcomes. Indeed, courts not uncommonly group arbitrary and fanciful marks into the same category, as *Abercrombie* itself does.

3.   *Coined terms that are not fanciful, but rather suggestive.* Not all coined terms qualify as fanciful. In *Surfvivor Media, Inc. v. Survivor Productions*, 406 F.3d 625 (9th Cir. 2005), the court analyzed the *Abercrombie* classification of the trademark SURFVIVOR for beach-themed products:

> Because "Surfvivor" is a coined term, [plaintiff] Deptula contends that it should be treated as a fanciful mark. However, the mere fact that a mark consists of a coined term does not automatically render that mark fanciful. See Interstellar Starship Servs. Ltd. v. Epix, Inc., 184 F.3d 1107, 1111 (9th Cir. 1999) (determining that the coined phrase "EPIX" for electronic pictures should not automatically be considered an arbitrary [or fanciful] mark). Fanciful marks have no commonly known connotation to the product at hand. By contrast, the term "Surfvivor" is highly evocative of the company's beach-related products.

Id. at 632. The court ultimately determined that the SURFVIVOR mark was suggestive. *See id.*

4.   *Why choose a non-inherently distinctive descriptive mark?* Lawyers may advise their clients always to choose inherently distinctive marks (and ideally only fanciful marks) because such marks do not require any showing of secondary meaning to qualify for protection. Yet clients often prefer — and the marketplace is full of — descriptive marks, particularly marks that are descriptive in a laudatory sense (e.g., BEST BUY). Why should this be the case? In an opinion involving the trademark FASHIONKNIT, Judge Learned Hand offered one persuasive explanation:

> I have always been at a loss to know why so many marks are adopted which have an aura, or more, of description about them. With the whole field of possible coinage before them, it is strange that merchants insist upon adopting marks that are so nearly descriptive. Probably they wish to interject into the name of their goods some intimation of excellence, and are willing to incur the risk.

Franklin Knitting Mills, Inc. v. Fashionit Sweater Mills, Inc., 297 F. 247 (S.D.N.Y. 1923). *See also Aloe Creme Labs., Inc. v. Milsan, Inc.*, 423 F.2d 845, 165 U.S.P.Q. 37 (9th Cir. 1970) ("Apparently entrepreneurs cannot resist the temptation to tie the name of their product to some disabling quality of description, geography, or vanity."). The Gilson treatise discusses this issue thoroughly at JEROME GILSON & ANNE GILSON LaLONDE, GILSON ON TRADEMARKS § 2.01 (2022).

5.   *Do misspellings make any difference?* In short, no. *See Restatement (Third) of Unfair Competition* (1995) § 14, cmt. a ("The misspelling or corruption of an otherwise descriptive word will not ordinarily alter the descriptive character of the designation."); *Spex, Inc. v. Joy of Spex, Inc.*, 847 F. Supp. 567 (N.D. Ill. 1994) (SPEX for eyeglasses merely descriptive); *In re Quik-Print Copy Shops, Inc.*, 616 F.2d 523, 205 U.S.P.Q. 505 (C.C.P.A. 1980) (QUIK-PRINT for photocopy services merely descriptive). *See also Flexitized, Inc. v. National Flexitized Corp.*, 335 F.2d 774, 780, 142 U.S.P.Q 334 (2d Cir. 1964) ("That the terms used to comprise a trademark are misspelled, or represent the combination of several words or parts of words, or are otherwise so formed or malformed that the mark does not appear in any

standard dictionary, will not preclude a finding of invalidity based on descriptiveness if the terms which are used, interpreted according to the basic rules of the English language, do sufficiently describe.").

ii.   Distinguishing Suggestive from Descriptive Marks

There are a number of reasons why a trademark owner would want to show that a mark on the border between descriptiveness and suggestiveness is in fact suggestive and thus inherently distinctive. First, as we will see in Part I.A.1.b, it can be difficult and costly to show that a mark deemed descriptive has developed secondary meaning as a designation of source. Second, as we will see in Part I.D, only inherently distinctive marks may be registered on an intent-to-use basis.

Where a mark falls along the continuum between suggestiveness and descriptiveness can be difficult to determine, and a court's determination of the issue difficult to predict. Courts' approaches vary, but all emphasize, as did Judge Friendly in *Abercrombie*, the question of the degree of "imagination" a consumer must use to connect the meaning of the mark to the characteristics of the goods. *See, e.g., Platinum Home Mortgage Corp. v. Platinum Financial Group, Inc.*, 149 F.3d 722, 47 U.S.P.Q.2d 1587 (7th Cir. 1998) (stating the Seventh Circuit's "degree of imagination" test as "[I]f a mark imparts information directly it is descriptive. If it stands for an idea which requires some operation of the imagination to connect it with the goods, it is suggestive", and quoting approvingly the district court's reasoning that PLATINUM MORTGAGE is descriptive because "the mental leap . . . is nearly instantaneous and . . . requires little imagination to associate 'platinum' with superiority and quality service").

Because the borderline between descriptive and suggestive marks is so important, two representative analyses are provided here for your consideration. To give you a sense of the relative importance of various opinions in the trademark law canon, it is worth noting that neither of the opinions excerpted here has been nearly as influential as *Abercrombie*. They are provided instead as everyday examples from various circuits of how courts draw (sometimes unpredictably, sometimes wrongly) the border between suggestiveness and descriptiveness.

In reading these cases, consider the following questions:

- Which factors should be the most important to a court's determination of whether a mark is either descriptive or suggestive?

- How might you design a consumer survey to aid a court in determining whether a mark is either descriptive or suggestive?

- Has the court in *Innovation Ventures* (the second opinion below) adopted a sensible approach to analyzing descriptiveness versus suggestiveness? If you were the plaintiff (i.e., the asserter of trademark rights), would you prefer the *Zatarains* or the *Innovation Ventures* approach?

Zatarains, Inc. v. Oak Grove Smokehouse, Inc.
698 F.2d 786, 792-93 (5th Cir. 1983)

{Plaintiff Zatarains, Inc. ("Zatarain's") used two registered trademarks: FISH-FRI for fried-fish batter and CHICK-FRI for fried chicken batter. Competitors, including Oak Grove Smokehouse, Inc. ("Oak Grove") and Visko's Fish Fry, Inc. ("Visco's"), used phrases like "FISH FRY" or "CHICKEN FRY" on the packaging of competing products to describe the contents of those products. Both sides of the dispute cross-appealed the outcome of the district court's bench trial.}

Goldberg, Circuit Judge:

. . . .

[1] Throughout this litigation, Zatarain's has maintained that the term "Fish-Fri" is a suggestive mark automatically protected from infringing uses by virtue of its registration in 1962. Oak Grove and Visko's assert that "fish fry" is a generic term identifying a class of foodstuffs used to fry fish; alternatively, Oak Grove and Visko's argue that "fish fry" is merely descriptive of the characteristics of the product. The district court found that "Fish-Fri" was a descriptive term identifying a function of the product being sold. Having reviewed this finding under the appropriate "clearly erroneous" standard, we affirm.

[2] We are mindful that "[t]he concept of descriptiveness must be construed rather broadly." Callman § 70.2. Whenever a word or phrase conveys an immediate idea of the qualities, characteristics, effect, purpose, or ingredients of a product or service, it is classified as descriptive and cannot be claimed as an exclusive trademark. Id. § 71.1; see Stix Products, Inc. v. United Merchants & Manufacturers, Inc., 295 F.Supp. 479, 488 (S.D.N.Y. 1968). Courts and commentators have formulated a number of tests to be used in classifying a mark as descriptive.

[3] A suitable starting place is the dictionary, for "[t]he dictionary definition of the word is an appropriate and relevant indication 'of the ordinary significance and meaning of words' to the public." American Heritage Life Insurance Co. v. Heritage Life Insurance Co., 494 F.2d 3, 11 n.5 (5th Cir. 1974). Webster's Third New International Dictionary 858 (1966) lists the following definitions for the term "fish fry": "1. a picnic at which fish are caught, fried, and eaten; . . . . 2. fried fish." Thus, the basic dictionary definitions of the term refer to the preparation and consumption of fried fish. This is at least preliminary evidence that the term "Fish-Fri" is descriptive of Zatarain's product in the sense that the words naturally direct attention to the purpose or function of the product.

[4] The "imagination test" is a second standard used by the courts to identify descriptive terms. This test seeks to measure the relationship between the actual words of the mark and the product to which they are applied. If a term "requires imagination, thought and perception to reach a conclusion as to the nature of goods," Stix Products, 295 F.Supp. at 488, it is considered a suggestive term. Alternatively, a term is descriptive if standing alone it conveys information as to the characteristics of the product. In this case, mere observation compels the conclusion that a product branded "Fish-Fri" is a prepackaged coating or batter mix applied to fish prior to cooking. The connection between this merchandise and its identifying terminology is so close and direct that even a consumer unfamiliar with the product would doubtless have an idea of its purpose or function. It simply does not require an exercise of the imagination to deduce that "Fish-Fri" is used to fry fish. Accordingly, the term "Fish-Fri" must be considered descriptive when examined under the "imagination test."

[5] A third test used by courts and commentators to classify descriptive marks is "whether competitors would be likely to need the terms used in the trademark in describing their products." Union Carbide Corp. v. Ever-Ready, Inc., 531 F.2d 366, 379 (7th Cir. 1976). A descriptive term generally relates so closely and directly to a product or service that other merchants marketing similar goods would find the term useful in identifying their own goods. Common sense indicates that in this case merchants other than Zatarain's might find the term "fish fry" useful in describing their own particular batter mixes. While Zatarain's has argued strenuously that Visko's and Oak Grove could have chosen from dozens of other possible terms in naming their coating mix, we find this position to be without merit. As this court has held, the fact that a term is not the only or even the most common name for a product is not determinative, for there is no legal foundation that a product can be described in only one fashion. There are many edible fish in the sea, and as many ways to prepare them as there are varieties to be prepared. Even piscatorial gastronomes would agree, however, that frying is a form of preparation accepted virtually around the world, at restaurants starred and unstarred. The paucity of synonyms for the words "fish" and "fry" suggests that a merchant whose batter mix is specially spiced for frying fish is likely to find "fish fry" a useful term for describing his product.

[6] A final barometer of the descriptiveness of a particular term examines the extent to which a term actually has been used by others marketing a similar service or product. This final test is closely related to the question whether competitors are likely to find a mark useful in describing their products. As noted above, a number of companies other than Zatarain's have chosen the word combination "fish fry" to identify their batter mixes. Arnaud's product, "Oyster Shrimp and Fish Fry," has been in competition with Zatarain's "Fish-Fri" for some ten to twenty years. When companies from A to Z, from Arnaud to Zatarain's, select the same term to describe their similar products, the term in question is most likely a descriptive one.

[7] The correct categorization of a given term is a factual issue; consequently, we review the district court's findings under the "clearly erroneous" standard of Fed.R.Civ.P. 52. The district court in this case found that Zatarain's trademark "Fish-Fri" was descriptive of the function of the product being sold.

Having applied the four prevailing tests of descriptiveness to the term "Fish-Fri," we are convinced that the district court's judgment in this matter is not only not clearly erroneous, but clearly correct.

{In a footnote, the court considered and rejected the argument that FISH-FRI was generic as to fish-frying batter. The court also affirmed the district court's finding that CHICK-FRI was descriptive.}

Innovation Ventures, LLC v. N.V.E., Inc.
694 F.3d 723, 729-730 (6th Cir. 2012)

{Plaintiff Innovation Ventures, LLC, d/b/a Living Essentials ("LE"), produced a beverage under the mark 5-HOUR ENERGY. Defendant NVE began to produce a similar beverage under the mark 6 HOUR POWER. Plaintiff sued and defendant claimed that plaintiff's mark was merely descriptive. The parties' cross-moved for summary judgment.}

Boggs, Circuit Judge

. . . .

[1] NVE claims that the term "5–hour ENERGY" is not a distinctive mark, but is a descriptive mark.[1] A descriptive mark, by itself, is not protectable. However, "[a] merely descriptive term . . . can, by acquiring a secondary meaning, i.e., becoming distinctive of the applicant's goods . . . , become a valid trademark." Induct–O–Matic Corp. v. Inductotherm Corp., 747 F.2d 358, 362 (6th Cir. 1984). LE counters that the "5–hour ENERGY" mark is not descriptive, but rather is distinctive, due to the mark's suggestiveness. Such a mark "suggests rather than describes an ingredient or characteristic of the goods and requires the observer or listener to use imagination and perception to determine the nature of the goods." Id. at 362.

[2] The "5–hour ENERGY" mark could be characterized as merely descriptive, in the sense that it simply describes a product that will give someone five hours of energy. But that is not the end of such an inquiry. The first question one would ask is *how* would the energy be transferred? Through food? Through drink? Through injections? Through pills? Through exercise? Also, one would ask what kind of energy is the mark referring to? Food energy (measured in Calories)? Electrical energy? Nuclear energy? With some thought, one could arrive at the conclusion that the mark refers to an energy shot. But it is

---

[1] We note that, in contrast with its position in this case, in other litigation NVE has asserted that its own mark, "6 Hour POWER," is an "inherently distinctive" mark. See Complaint at ¶ 12, N.V.E., Inc. v. N2G Distrib., Inc. & Alpha Performance Labs, No. 2:08–cv–01824 (D.N.J. Apr. 14, 2008) ("The 6 HOUR POWER mark distinguishes NVE as the source of these products, is inherently distinctive, and has also become distinctive through the acquisition of secondary meaning." (emphasis added)).

not as straightforward as NVE suggests. Such cognitive inferences are indicative of "suggestive" rather than descriptive marks.

[3] The nature of the "5–hour ENERGY" mark "shares a closer kinship with those marks previously designated as suggestive than those labeled merely descriptive because of the degree of inferential reasoning necessary for a consumer to discern" that the "5–hour ENERGY" mark relates to an energy shot. *Tumblebus v. Cranmer*, 399 F.3d 754, 763 (6th Cir. 2005). The connection between "5–hour" and "ENERGY" is "not so obvious that a consumer seeing [5–hour ENERGY] in isolation would know that the term refers to" an energy shot rather than, for example, a battery for electronics, an exercise program, a backup generator, or a snack for endurance sports. Ibid. Connecting the mark "5–hour ENERGY" with the energy-shot product requires "imagination and perception to determine the nature of the goods." *Induct–O–Matic*, 747 F.2d at 362.

[4] "The line between merely descriptive and suggestive marks is admittedly hazy and can be difficult to discern." *Tumblebus*, 399 F.3d at 763. However, we disagree with NVE's contention that the mark is not distinctive and thus not protectable. The "5–hour ENERGY" mark is "suggestive."

{The Sixth Circuit found other fact issues and remanded.}

Comments and Questions

1. *The PTO's conflicting analysis of the* 5-HOUR ENERGY *mark.* In a subsequent case, *Innovation Ventures, LLC v. N2G Distrib., Inc.*, 763 F.3d 524 (6th Cir. 2014), the Sixth Circuit noted that the PTO had initially denied registration of the 5-HOUR ENERGY mark on the ground that it was descriptive and lacked secondary meaning. In a footnote, the court simply stated: "By contrast, we have held that the '5–hour ENERGY' mark was 'suggestive and thus protectable' by at least March 2006. *Innovation Ventures, LLC v. N.V.E., Inc.*, 694 F.3d 723, 730 (6th Cir. 2012)." *Innovation Ventures, LLC v. N2G Distrib., Inc.*, 763 F.3d at 530 n.1. In September 2005, Innovation Ventures resorted to registration of the mark on the Supplemental Register. In August 2011, upon a showing of secondary meaning, the mark was finally registered on the Principal Register. (For a discussion of the difference between the Supplemental Register and the Principal Register, see Part I.D.1 below).

Here are a few further examples of marks classified either as descriptive or suggestive. You are strongly encouraged to decide for yourself how you would predict the court ruled before consulting the actual outcome (and keep in mind that the court may simply have gotten it wrong):

- COASTAL WINE for wine made near a coast. *See Callaway Vineyard & Winery v. Endsley Capital Group, Inc.*, 63 U.S.P.Q.2d 1919 (TTAB 2002) (finding the mark to be descriptive since the mark describes "a significant feature of applicant's goods, namely the place or establishment where applicant produces its wine").

- 24 HOUR FITNESS for fitness facilities. *See 24 Hour Fitness USA, Inc. v. 24/7 Tribeca Fitness, LLC*, 277 F. Supp. 2d 356 (S.D.N.Y. 2003) (finding that the mark "describe[s] a physical training-related facility that is available, if not around the clock, at least for substantial periods of time on a regular basis.").

- CROSSFIT for "fitness training and consulting." *See Crossfit, Inc. v. Quinnie*, 232 F. Supp. 3d 1295, 1306 (N.D. Ga. 2017) ("The Court finds that the CROSSFIT® mark is a suggestive mark. The mark CROSSFIT® is a combination of the terms, "cross" and "fit," which are both commonly associated with exercise and fitness. The term "cross" has been used in sports and fitness as in cross-training to refer to combining different sports or types of exercises in order to improve a person's fitness and performance. The combination of the terms into a single unique word places the mark in the "suggestive" category, requiring a leap of the imagination to get from the mark to the product. The CROSSFIT® mark is not an arbitrary term such as KODAK." (citation omitted)).

- XTREME LASHES for artificial eyelashes. *See Xtreme Lashes, LLC v. Xtended Beauty, Inc.*, 576 F.3d 221 (5th Cir. 2009) (finding the mark to be suggestive; "The consumer must exercise some imagination to associate 'xtreme lashes' with 'artificially elongated eyelashes.'").

- LITTLE MERMAID for a doll taking the form of a mermaid. *See In re United Trademark Holdings, Inc.*, 122 U.S.P.Q.2d 1796 (TTAB 2017) (finding the mark to be descriptive for a doll taking the form of a mermaid because consumers will "understand the mark to describe the public domain character in the Hans Christian Andersen fairy tale, as well as a young or little mermaid"; by contrast, "[c]onsumers reasonably expect goods and services bearing the name or image of {Superman} to emanate from, or be produced or marketed under license from, the entity which created the character and therefore owns the right to profit from commercialization of it.").

- 100% and 100% TIME RELEASE MOISTURIZER for skin moisturizer. *See Estee Lauder, Inc. v. The Gap, Inc.*, 108 F.3d 1503 (2d Cir. 1997) (affirming the district court's finding the mark to be suggestive; "The phrase '100% Time Release Moisturizer' could be read to indicate the purity of the moisturizing content of Lauder's product, or to imply an enduring effect. Or, as the district court found, it could be read as indicating that the bottle contains nothing but time-release moisturizer or that the product moisturizes continuously until removed or worn off. All of these interpretations require some stretch of the imagination. And of course, as the court found, if the term '100%' is simply viewed as the brand of time-release moisturizer, it plainly is suggestive.").

Comments and Questions

1. *Surveying for suggestiveness versus descriptiveness.* In *Rise-N-Shine, LLC v. Duner-Fenter*, No. 14 Civ. 1305, 2015 WL 876470 (S.D.N.Y. Feb. 28, 2015), the plaintiff produced a dietary supplement under the mark GO AWAY GRAY that purportedly prevents the growth of gray hair. The defendant produced a competing dietary supplement under the mark GET AWAY GREY. The defendant asserted that the plaintiff's mark was descriptive (and both parties agreed that the plaintiff's mark lacked secondary meaning). The plaintiff presented survey evidence of the mark's suggestiveness. The methodology of the survey was essentially as follows:

> First, the pool of respondents was limited—through screening questions at the beginning of the survey—to adults between the ages of 35 and 55, residing in the United States, who had purchased vitamins or supplements in the previous six months, and who reported that they would "definitely" or "probably" consider buying vitamins or supplements "to promote healthy hair" in the next six months. In all, 208 participants qualified after these screening mechanisms. Next, respondents were informed of the difference between a brand name and a product description, and given two test phrases ("ONE A DAY" and "IMMUNITY BOOSTER") to evaluate whether they understood that distinction. Respondents were then asked whether they believed the Disputed Mark—as well as two other marks, "SLIM–FAST" and "MUSCLE BUILDER," which were included to minimize potential bias—refers to a product's brand name or describes a product's function or purpose, or whether the respondent did not know. Respondents were also asked, at the conclusion of the survey, whether they had gray hair, and 176 of the 208 respondents answered affirmatively. Ultimately, 49% of survey respondents—and 51% of respondents with gray hair—answered that they believed the Disputed Mark was a brand name. {The survey expert} then excluded all those respondents who incorrectly identified either SLIM–FAST or MUSCLE BUILDER as a brand name or product description, which left 160 respondents. Of those respondents, 56% in total, and 59% of those with gray hair, answered that they believed the Disputed Mark was a brand name.

Id. at *1. Judge Sullivan rejected the defendant's motion in limine to exclude the survey expert's testimony and allowed the survey results to be presented to the jury. *Id.* at *4. Does this survey methodology for distinguishing between descriptive and suggestive marks appear valid?

2. *Is the protection of descriptive marks constitutionally sound?* *See* Lisa Ramsey, *Descriptive Trademarks and the First Amendment*, 70 TENN. L. REV. 1095 (2003) (arguing that the protection of descriptive marks violates the free speech clause of the First Amendment because it does not directly advance the government's interest in protecting consumers from confusion and is in any case more extensive than necessary).

iii. Special Rules for Classification of Certain Kinds of Trademarks

There are many special rules that guide the *Abercrombie* classification of certain kinds of trademarks. Nearly all of them are detailed in the PTO's *Trademark Manual of Examining Procedure* ("TMEP"), tmep.uspto.gov, which is an excellent resource for the trademark lawyer, particularly one who specializes in trademark "prosecution," i.e., the process of registering trademarks at the PTO. Among the most important of these special rules are the following:

◊ **Descriptiveness of Geographic Terms**

As we will see through the course of this Part, Lanham Act § 2, 15 U.S.C. § 1052, has several provisions giving special treatment to geographic terms. Consider for the moment § 2(e)(2), which provides: "No trademark by which the goods of the applicant may be distinguished from the goods of others shall be refused registration on the principal register on account of its nature unless it ... (e) Consists of a mark which ... (2) when used on or in connection with the goods of the applicant is primarily geographically descriptive of them, except as indications of regional origin may be registrable under section 1054 of this title."

Such "primarily geographically descriptive" marks may only be registered or otherwise protected upon a showing of secondary meaning (with one important exception that we will address in a moment). Lanham Act § 2(f), 15 U.S.C. § 1052(f). The TTAB has established a relatively straightforward three-part test for determining whether a mark is "primarily geographically descriptive." The mark will fall into this category if: "(1) the primary significance of the mark is a generally known geographic location; (2) the goods or services originate in the place identified in the mark; <u>and</u> (3) purchasers would be likely to believe that the goods or services originate in the geographic place identified in the mark." TMEP § 1210.01(a). *See, e.g., In re Carolina Apparel*, 48 USPQ2d 1542 (TTAB 1998) (finding CAROLINA APPAREL for clothing stores in North Carolina to be primarily geographically descriptive); *In re Brouwerij Nacional Balashi NV*, 80 U.S.P.Q.2d 1820 (TTAB 2006) (finding BALASHI BEER and BALASHI for beer made in the Balashi neighborhood of the Santa Cruz district of Aruba to be not primarily geographically descriptive where the term is "so obscure or remote that purchasers of beer in the United States would typically fail to recognize the term as indicating the geographical source of applicant's goods."). For a more problematic case, see *University Book Store v. Board of Regents of University of Wisconsin System*, 33 U.S.P.Q.2d 1385 (TTAB 1994) (finding WISCONSIN BADGERS for apparel to be not primarily geographically descriptive where consumers would not perceive the primary significance of the mark as a whole as designating a particular geographic location).

The third prong of the PGD test calls for evidence that consumers would make a "goods/place association" (or "service/place association") between (a) the geographic location referred to by the mark and (b) the goods sold under the mark. Importantly, if the geographic location is "neither obscure nor remote," TMEP § 1210.04, and the goods actually originate from that location, then this goods/place association may ordinarily be presumed. The result is that the goods/place association is almost always presumed. *See, e.g., In re Spirits of New Merced, LLC*, 85 U.S.P.Q.2d 1614 (TTAB 2007) (finding YOSEMITE BEER to be primarily geographically descriptive where the registration applicant's beer was brewed near Yosemite National Park and applicant failed to overcome presumption of goods/place association; "[s]ince the goods originate at or near [Yosemite National Park], we can presume an association of applicant's beer with the park."). *But see In re Mankovitz*, 90 USPQ2d 1246 (TTAB 2009) (finding THE MONTECITO DIET for a diet system to be not primarily geographically descriptive where evidence of goods/place association consisted only of the fact that the registration applicant lived in Montecito, California; "it would be speculation on our part to reach the conclusion that the goods or services originate there or that the public would understand that there is a goods/place relationship").

◇   **Certification Marks and Collective Marks**

"Certification marks" and "collective marks" are special forms of trademarks in the Lanham Act. Lanham Act § 45 defines a certification mark as follows:

The term "certification mark" means any word, name, symbol, or device, or any combination thereof—

(1) used by a person other than its owner, or

(2) which its owner has a bona fide intention to permit a person other than the owner to use in commerce and files an application to register on the principal register established by this Act,

to certify regional or other origin, material, mode of manufacture, quality, accuracy, or other characteristics of such person's goods or services or that the work or labor on the goods or services was performed by members of a union or other organization.

As the § 45 definition suggests, certification marks may take a variety of forms, including:

- certifications of a good's quality, e.g., SCOTCH WHISKY "to certify that the goods/services provided originate in Scotland and have met the Standards as set forth in The Scotch Whisky Regulations 2009 and The Scotch Whisky technical file", Reg. No. 6,763,223 (June 21, 2022); the UL mark of Underwriters Laboratories, Inc., Reg. No. 782,589 (Dec. 29, 1964); the U-in-a-circle mark of the Orthodox Union, Reg. No. 636,593 (Oct. 30, 1956);

- certifications of the regional origin of a product, e.g., the "Grown in Idaho" mark of the State of Idaho Potato Commission, Reg. No. 4,221,403 (July 24, 2012); the ROQUEFORT mark of the Community of Roquefort, France, Reg. No. 0571798 (Mar. 10, 1953); *but see Interprofessionel du Gruyere v. U.S. Dairy Exp. Council*, 61 F.4th 407, 425 (4th Cir. 2023) (in refusing registration of GRUYERE as a certification mark on the ground that the term is generic, finding that "the pervasive sales of non-Swiss and non-French cheese labeled as gruyere in the United States{} and the common usage of gruyere establish that when purchasers walk into retail stores and ask for gruyere, they regularly mean a type of cheese, and not a cheese that was produced in the Gruyère region of Switzerland and France" (cleaned up));

- certifications that a product was union-made e.g., the International Union of Painters and Allied Trades mark indicating that the designated services were performed by union members, Reg. No. 2,749,294 (Aug. 12, 2003)

Various specific rules apply to certification marks. First, certifying organizations may not themselves produce goods or services to which the certification mark is applied. *See* Lanham Act § 14(5)(B), 15 U.S.C. § 1064(5)(B). Rather, certifying organizations can only function as certifiers of other entities' goods or services. Second, certifying organizations must restrict the use of their mark only to certify goods or services that meet the certification standards. *See* Lanham Act § 14(5)(A) & (C), 15 U.S.C. § 1064(5)(A) & (C). Third, certifying organizations must not "discriminately refuse[] to certify or to continue to certify the goods or services of any person who maintains the standards or conditions which such mark certifies." *See* Lanham Act § 14(5) (D), 15 U.S.C. § 1064(5) (D); *see also* Jeanne C. Fromer, *The Unregulated Certification Mark(et)*, 69 STAN. L. REV. 121 (2017) (discussing examples of certification organizations' arbitrary, inconsistent, and anticompetitive application of their own certifying standards). To circumvent the constraints placed on certification marks, many certifying organizations prefer to register standard trademarks and license their use in a manner equivalent to a certification system. *See* Alexandra Mogyoros, *Attestation Marks and Pseudo-Certification Marks: A Divergence of Roles in Trademark Law*, 43 EURO. INTELL. PROP. REV. 219 (2021); C. Bradford Biddle, Frank X. Curci, Matthew Dodson & Molly Edwards, *Standards Setting Organizations and Trademark Registration: An Empirical Analysis* (working paper May 19, 2019).

In contrast to certification marks, collective marks are used by members of the collective to identify their goods and services as made by collective members. The "anti-use-by-owner" rule that applies to certification marks—i.e., the rule that the owner of the certification mark may not itself sell goods or services bearing the certification mark—does not apply to collective marks.[1] Lanham Act § 45 defines collective marks as follows:

> The term "collective mark" means a trademark or service mark–
>
> > (1) used by the members of a cooperative, an association, or other collective group or organization, or
> >
> > (2) which such cooperative, association, or other collective group or organization has a bona fide intention to use in commerce and applies to register on the principal register established by this Act,
>
> and includes marks indicating membership in a union, an association, or other organization.

When certification or collective marks take the form of geographic designations, the distinctiveness analysis of them is unique in the statutory scheme. Lanham Act § 2(e)(2) establishes that proprietors of certification or collective marks that take the form of "indications of regional origin" need not establish that the indication of regional origin has secondary meaning in order to register the indication as trademark. A mark's ability to qualify as a regional certification or collective mark turns on "whether the public understands that goods bearing the mark come only from the region named in the mark, not whether the public is expressly aware of the certification function of the mark per se." TMEP § 1306.05(a). See also *Institut Nat'l Des Appellations D'Origine v. Brown-Forman Corp.*, 47 USPQ2d 1875 (TTAB 1998).

⬦ **Surnames**

Just as it does with geographic marks, § 2 of the Lanham Act, 15 U.S.C. § 1052, also explicitly addresses the protectability of surnames and classifies them essentially as descriptive marks. It states: "No trademark by which the goods of the applicant may be distinguished from the goods of others shall be refused registration on the principal register on account of its nature unless it . . . (e) Consists of a

---

[1] The distinction between certification and collective marks is sometimes very fine, leading McCarthy to lament that "[t]he problem with collective trademarks and service marks is that they are almost indistinguishable from certification marks." MCCARTHY § 19:99. McCarthy suggests that one advantage (or disadvantage) of collective marks is that they offer a way to avoid the strict requirements for the operation of certification marks established in Lanham Act § 14(5).

mark which . . . (4) is primarily merely a surname." Surnames may be registered only upon a showing of acquired distinctiveness under § 2(f), 15 U.S.C. § 1052(f). As the TMEP explains, § 2(e)(4) "reflects the common law that exclusive rights in a surname per se cannot be established without evidence of long and exclusive use that changes its significance to the public from that of a surname to that of a mark for particular goods or services. The common law also recognizes that surnames are shared by more than one individual, each of whom may have an interest in using his surname in business; and, by the requirement for evidence of distinctiveness, the law, in effect, delays appropriation of exclusive rights in the name." TMEP § 1211.

But what qualifies as "primarily merely a surname"? "Fiore," "Hackler," and "Bird" are used as surnames, but each has been deemed not "primarily merely a surname" under trademark law. *See In re Isabella Fiore LLC*, 75 USPQ2d 1564 (TTAB 2005); *In re United Distillers plc*, 56 USPQ2d 1220 (TTAB 2000); *Fisher Radio Corp. v. Bird Elec. Corp.*, 162 USPQ 265 (TTAB 1969). The TTAB has established five factors to be considered in determining whether the relevant purchasing public perceives the primary significance of a term to be that of a surname: (1) whether the surname is rare; (2) whether the term is the surname of anyone connected with the applicant; (3) whether the term has any recognized meaning other than as a surname; (4) whether it has the "look and feel" of a surname; (5) in cases of stylized, rather than standard character marks, whether the stylization of lettering is distinctive enough to create a separate commercial impression. *In re Benthin Mgmt. GmbH*, 37 USPQ2d 1332, 1333-1334 (TTAB 1995) (finding that the mark BENTHIN in stylized lettering inside an oval design would not be perceived as primarily merely a surname). If it is determined that the relevant purchasing public does not perceive a term as a surname, then the term would likely be classified as either arbitrary or suggestive, or possibly even as fanciful. In any case, the term would qualify as inherently distinctive of source.[2]

What about historic surnames? "A term with surname significance may not be primarily merely a surname if that term also identifies a historical place or person." TMEP § 1211.01(a)(iv). *See, e.g., Lucien Piccard Watch Corp. v. Since 1868 Crescent Corp.*, 314 F. Supp. 329, 331 (S.D.N.Y. 1970) (finding that DA VINCI for jewelry and leather goods is not primarily merely a surname for purposes of Section 2(e)(4); "While defendant has demonstrated by way of the Manhattan telephone directory that the name Da Vinci is in current use as a surname (by one C. Leonardo da Vinci and one Lora Da Vinci), the name Da Vinci, even without the given name Leonardo, comes very near having as its exclusive connotation the world-renowned 15th century artist, sculptor, architect, musician, engineer and philosopher (to whom defendant refers as a 'deceased Florentine painter') and hardly suggests that he personally had something to do with the designing of plaintiff's luggage."). *But see In re Champion Int'l Corp.*, 229 USPQ 550, 551 (TTAB 1985) (finding McKINLEY to be primarily merely a surname despite being the surname of William McKinley, the 25th President of the United States).

---

[2] As for full names, the common law has long treated full names the same as it treats surnames: both require a showing of secondary meaning to merit protection. But importantly, the PTO treats full names differently from surnames for purposes of registration. It will allow the registration of a full name without any showing that the name carries secondary meaning (or is famous), provided that the applicant can show that the name is being used as an indication of commercial origin rather than as simply the applicant's own name. *See Brooks v. Calloway*, 93 U.S.P.Q.2d 18232010 WL 595585, at *8 (T.T.A.B. 2010) ("A personal name mark, unless it is primarily merely a surname, is registrable on the Principal Register without a showing of secondary meaning, and thus is deemed to be inherently distinctive under the Lanham Act if the record shows that it is used in a manner that would be perceived by purchasers as identifying the services in addition to the person."). The divergence between the common law and the registration regime with respect to full names can lead to strange outcomes. *See, e.g., Zinner v. Olenych*, 108 F. Supp. 3d 369, 381–86 (E.D. Va. 2015) (explaining the difference between the USPTO's "more lenient standard" and the common law doctrine and finding that plaintiff's mark, ED ZINNER, was a personal name, unprotectable under the common law, yet awarding it a presumption of validity, because the USPTO had granted it registration).

◇   **Non-English Words: The Doctrine of "Foreign Equivalents"**

"The foreign equivalent of a merely descriptive English word is no more registrable than the English word itself." TMEP § 1209.03(g). Thus, "lait," "leche," and "Milch" as brand names for milk would be deemed generic, and "frais," "fresca," and "frisch" as brand names for milk would likely be deemed descriptive and require secondary meaning to be protected. *See, e.g., In re Tokutake Indus. Co.*, 87 USPQ2d 1697 (TTAB 2008) (finding AYUMI, meaning "walking," and its Japanese character equivalent to be merely descriptive for footwear); *In re Oriental Daily News, Inc.*, 230 USPQ 637 (TTAB 1986) (finding Chinese characters meaning "Oriental Daily News" to be merely descriptive of newspapers); *In re Vetements Group AG*, Serial Nos. 88944198 and 88946135 (T.T.A.B. April 21, 2023) [not precedential] (finding the asserted mark VETEMENTS generic for clothing; "[T]he evidence of record indicates approximately 1.3 million {French} speakers live in the United States. While that may represent a small percentage of US citizens and residents, it nonetheless is a large number of speakers of a modern, living language that is the fifth most commonly spoken non-English language in this country.").[3]

The doctrine of foreign equivalents is riddled with limitations and exceptions, however. Among these are, first, that "[t]he doctrine should be applied only when it is likely that the ordinary American purchaser would stop and translate the foreign word into its English equivalent." *See In re Hag Aktiengesellschaft*, 155 U.S.P.Q. 598 (TTAB 1967) (finding KABA, meaning coffee in Serbian and Ukranian, to be descriptive for coffee). *But see Palm Bay Imports v. Veuve Clicquot*, 396 F.3d 1369 (Fed. Cir. 2005) (finding that VEUVE CLICQUOT is not confusingly similar to THE WIDOW, since most American consumers won't know that "veuve" means "widow" in French). Second, "foreign words from dead or obscure languages may be so unfamiliar to the American buying public that they should not be translated into English for descriptiveness purposes." TMEP § 1209.03(g). This limitation appears to be very rarely applied, however. Third, as the TMEP tries to explain, "marks comprised of a term from a foreign language used with an English term may be found registrable if the commercial impression created by the combination differs from that which would be created by two English words." *Id.* The representative case here is *In re Johanna Farms Inc.*, 8 USPQ2d 1408 (TTAB 1988) (finding LA YOGURT for yogurt to be registrable without showing of secondary meaning). *See also In re Le Sorbet, Inc.*, 228 U.S.P.Q. 27 (TTAB 1985) (finding LE SORBET for sorbet to be descriptive because it is a foreign-language term preceded by a foreign-language article); *In re Monfrere*, Serial No. 88004556 (TTAB March 2, 2020) [not precedential] (finding MONFRÈRE FASHION not confusingly similar with MY BROTHER, both for apparel). *See generally* Anne Gilson LaLonde, *Far From Fluent: Making Sense of the Doctrine of Foreign Equivalents* (LexisNexis 2021).

◇   **Acronyms**

The general rule is that an acronym will be classified as descriptive or generic if (1) the wording it stands for is merely descriptive of or generic as to the goods or services, and (2) relevant purchasers will recognize the acronym as an acronym of the merely descriptive or generic wording it represents (rather than as, say, a fanciful sequence of letters). TMEP § 1209.03(h). *See, e.g., In re Thomas Nelson, Inc.*, 97 USPQ2d 1712, 1715 (TTAB 2011) (finding NKJV to be substantially synonymous with merely descriptive term "New King James Version" and thus merely descriptive of bibles); *Baroness Small Estates, Inc. v. Am. Wine Trade, Inc.*, 104 USPQ2d 1224, 1230-31 (TTAB 2012) (finding CMS to be

---

[3] A common objection to the doctrine of foreign equivalents is that Americans don't speak "foreign" languages. In fact, according to U.S. Census Bureau data, 21.7% of Americans speak a language other than English at home. *See* https://www.census.gov/acs/www/about/why-we-ask-each-question/language/. Regardless, for the doctrine of foreign equivalents, the "ordinary American purchaser" includes "*all* American purchasers, including those proficient in a non-English language who would ordinarily be expected to translate words into English." *In re Spirits Int'l, N.V.*, 563 F.3d 1347, 1352 (Fed. Cir. 2009) (emphasis added).

inherently distinctive on the ground that it is not substantially synonymous with the grape varietals cabernet, merlot, and syrah and is thus not merely descriptive of wine).

b. Acquired Distinctiveness of Source

A descriptive, and thus non-inherently distinctive, mark may qualify for protection if it is shown to have developed "acquired distinctiveness" or "secondary meaning" (the two terms mean the same thing) as a designation of source. For example, though the term "American Airlines" is highly descriptive of an airline service based in the U.S., the term has developed enormous secondary meaning as a designation of source through use and advertising. As the Supreme Court commented in *Wal-Mart Stores, Inc. v. Samara Bros., Inc.*, 529 U.S. 205 (2000), the term "secondary meaning" is not as clear as it could be:

> The phrase "secondary meaning" originally arose in the context of word marks, where it served to distinguish the source-identifying meaning from the ordinary, or "primary," meaning of the word. "Secondary meaning" has since come to refer to the acquired, source-identifying meaning of a nonword mark as well. It is often a misnomer in that context, since nonword marks ordinarily have no "primary" meaning. Clarity might well be served by using the term "acquired meaning" in both the word-mark and the nonword-mark contexts—but in this opinion we follow what has become the conventional terminology.

Id. at 211 fn. Indeed, most trademark practitioners still continue as a matter of tradition to use the term "secondary meaning" rather than "acquired distinctiveness."

Each circuit typically uses its own multifactor test to determine if a mark has developed secondary meaning. They are generally quite similar. Here are some examples of these tests:

- Second Circuit: "(1) advertising expenditures, (2) consumer studies linking the mark to a source, (3) unsolicited media coverage of the product, (4) sales success, (5) attempts to plagiarize the mark, and (6) length and exclusivity of the mark's use." *Genesee Brewing Co. v. Stroh Brewing Co.*, 124 F.3d 137, 143 n.4 (2d Cir. 1997).

- Third Circuit: "We have identified an eleven-item, non-exhaustive list of factors relevant to the factual determination whether a term has acquired secondary meaning: (1) the extent of sales and advertising leading to buyer association; (2) length of use; (3) exclusivity of use; (4) the fact of copying; (5) customer surveys; (6) customer testimony; (7) the use of the mark in trade journals; (8) the size of the company; (9) the number of sales; (10) the number of customers; and, (11) actual confusion." *E.T. Browne Drug Co. v. Cococare Products, Inc.*, 538 F.3d 185, 199 (3d Cir. 2008).

- Ninth Circuit: "Secondary meaning can be established in many ways, including (but not limited to) direct consumer testimony; survey evidence; exclusivity, manner, and length of use of a mark; amount and manner of advertising; amount of sales and number of customers; established place in the market; and proof of intentional copying by the defendant." *Art Attacks Ink, LLC v. MGA Enter., Inc.*, 581 F.3d 1138, 1145 (9th Cir. 2009). *See also Japan Telecom, Inc. v. Japan Telecom Am., Inc.*, 287 F.3d 866, 62 U.S.P.Q.2d 1593 (9th Cir. 2002) (listing secondary meaning factors as "(1) whether actual purchasers of the product bearing the claimed trademark associate the trademark with the producer, (2) the degree and manner of advertising under the claimed trademark, (3) the length and manner of use of the claimed trademark, and (4) whether use of the claimed trademark has been exclusive.").

The three opinion excerpts that follow offer examples of courts' analyses of whether a non-inherently distinctive mark has developed sufficient secondary meaning to qualify for protection. In reading these excerpts, consider the following questions:

- What proportion of consumers in the relevant population should courts require to perceive the mark as possessing secondary meaning for the mark to qualify for protection? 25%? 50? 75%? Relatedly, how should courts determine what constitutes the relevant population of consumers?

- How would you devise a survey to test for secondary meaning?

- Why should "length and exclusivity of use" matter for purposes of establishing secondary meaning?

- Imagine a situation in which Company David, after a great deal of market research, adopts an especially good descriptive mark and initiates a small-scale launch of the descriptive mark in the marketplace. Company Goliath then becomes aware of Company David's mark, adopts the mark as its own, and immediately spends enormous resources building up secondary meaning in the mark, so that when consumers see the mark, they think of Company Goliath. Which company should be granted rights in the mark? And is this in your view an equitable or efficient outcome?

Frosty Treats Inc. v. Sony Computer Entertainment America
426 F.3d 1001, 1003-1006 (8th Cir. 2005)

Morris Sheppard Arnold, Circuit Judge

[1] A group of affiliated companies, Frosty Treats, Inc., Frosty Treats of Louisville, Inc., Frosty Treats Wholesale, Inc., and Frosty Treats of Atlanta, Inc., collectively known as "Frosty Treats," sued Sony Computer Entertainment America, Inc., (SCEA) asserting, inter alia, claims under state and federal law for trademark infringement and dilution, and for unfair competition. Frosty Treats premised these claims upon SCEA's depiction of an ice cream truck and clown character in SCEA's Twisted Metal video game series. Frosty Treats contends that because the ice cream truck . . . in the final game, is labeled with its brand identifier, "Frosty Treats," the games create a likelihood of confusion as to Frosty Treats's sponsorship of or affiliation with the games. See 15 U.S.C. § 1125(a). The district court granted SCEA's motion for summary judgment on all of Frosty Treats's claims, and Frosty Treats appeals. We affirm.

[2] Frosty Treats asserts that the district court erred by finding that there were no genuine issues of material fact and holding as a matter of law that the "Frosty Treats" mark was not protectable. . . .

[3] We review a grant of summary judgment de novo, applying the same standards as the district court. . . .

I.

[4] Frosty Treats argues first that the district court erred by holding that its "Frosty Treats" mark is not entitled to trademark protection because it is generic, or, in the alternative, descriptive without secondary meaning. Frosty Treats asserts that the mark is suggestive, or, at worst, descriptive with an acquired secondary meaning, and therefore protectible. We disagree. At best, the "Frosty Treats" mark is descriptive, and there is no basis for concluding that it has acquired secondary meaning.

[5] The stylized words "Frosty Treats" appear toward the rear of the passenger's side of plaintiffs' ice cream vans as pink capital letters with frost on the upper portion of each letter. See Figure 1 (depicting the "Frosty Treats" decal). The decal on which these words appear is approximately nine inches wide by four inches high and is surrounded by decals of the frozen products that the Frosty Treats vans sell. See Figure 2 (depicting a typical Frosty Treats van).

Figure 1.

Figure 2.

[6] To determine whether this mark is protectible, we must first categorize it. "A term for which trademark protection is claimed will fall in one of four categories: (1) generic, (2) descriptive, (3) suggestive, or (4) arbitrary or fanciful." WSM, Inc. v. Hilton, 724 F.2d 1320, 1325 (8th Cir. 1984). A generic mark refers to the common name or nature of an article, and is therefore not entitled to trademark protection. Co–Rect Prods., Inc. v. Marvy! Adver. Photography, Inc., 780 F.2d 1324, 1329 (8th Cir. 1985). A term is descriptive if it conveys an "immediate idea of the ingredients, qualities or characteristics of the goods," Stuart Hall Co., Inc. v. Ampad Corp., 51 F.3d 780, 785–86 (8th Cir. 1995), and is protectible only if shown to have acquired a secondary meaning. Co–Rect Prods., 780 F.2d at 1329. Suggestive marks, which require imagination, thought, and perception to reach a conclusion as to the nature of the goods, and arbitrary or fanciful marks, are entitled to protection regardless of whether they have acquired secondary meaning. See id.

[7] If it is not generic, the phrase "Frosty Treats" is, at best, descriptive. Frosty Treats is in the business of selling frozen desserts out of ice cream trucks. "Frosty Treats" conveys an immediate idea of the qualities and characteristics of the goods that it sells. No imagination, thought, or perception is required to reach a conclusion as to the nature of its goods. To prevail, therefore, Frosty Treats must demonstrate that the mark has acquired a secondary meaning. "Secondary meaning is an association formed in the minds of consumers between the mark and the source or origin of the product." Id. at 1330. To establish secondary meaning, Frosty Treats must show that "Frosty Treats" serves to identify its goods and distinguish them from those of others. Id. Secondary meaning does not require the consumer to identify a source by name but does require that the public recognize the mark and associate it with a single source. Stuart Hall, 51 F.3d at 789; see Heartland Bank v. Heartland Home Fin., Inc., 335 F.3d 810, 818–19 (8th Cir. 2003) (Smith, J., concurring).

[8] The record, when viewed in favor of Frosty Treats, demonstrates that SCEA is entitled to judgment as a matter of law on this issue. Frosty Treats has failed to put forth more than a scintilla of evidence that the public recognizes its "Frosty Treats" mark and associates it with a single source. Frosty Treats claims that its survey evidence demonstrates that the term "Frosty Treats" has acquired secondary meaning, but, if anything, it indicates the opposite. In the survey, respondents were shown images of the Frosty Treats ice cream van and asked, "Are you familiar with or have you ever seen or heard of this before?" Forty-seven percent responded affirmatively. They were then asked what they knew about the van. The respondents most frequently mentioned that it sold ice cream. Only one percent of the respondents in the survey mentioned Frosty Treats by name. There is no indication in the record that the survey respondents (apart from the one percent) were familiar with the vans because of the small nine-by-four-inch "Frosty Treats" decal on the rear portion of the side of the van, the only place where the phrase "Frosty Treats" appears on the vehicle. This decal, moreover, is surrounded by numerous other decals comprising the van's menu board. See Figure 2. Frosty Treats's survey provides no basis to conclude that the respondents associated the van with a single source as opposed to simply a generic ice cream truck.

[9] Although direct evidence such as consumer testimony or surveys are most probative of secondary meaning, it can also be proven by circumstantial evidence. See Heartland Bank, 335 F.3d at 819–20 (Smith, J., concurring). Circumstantial evidence such as the exclusivity, length and manner of use of the mark; the amount and manner of advertising; the amount of sales and number of customers; the plaintiff's established place in the market; and the existence of intentional copying could also establish secondary meaning. See id. (citing 2 J. Thomas McCarthy, McCarthy on Trademarks & Unfair Competition §§ 15:30, 15:60, 15:61, 15.66, 15.70 (4th ed. 1999)). But the circumstantial evidence that Frosty Treats offered to establish secondary meaning also fails to raise a genuine issue of material fact.

[10] We recognize that the application of some of these criteria to the facts of this case may militate in favor of a finding of secondary meaning in the mind of a reasonable juror. For instance, there is evidence that Frosty Treats has used the term in a continuous and substantially exclusive manner since 1991. Cf. Stuart Hall, 51 F.3d at 789–90. Furthermore, the record reflects that Frosty Treats, although a relatively small company, is nevertheless one of the largest ice cream truck street vendors in the nation.

[11] On the other hand, there is no evidence that SCEA intentionally copied the term. Most significantly, the record does not contain sufficient evidence for a juror to conclude that Frosty Treats engages in advertising or publication of the "Frosty Treats" mark to an extent that would be effective in having the public recognize it and equate it with a single source. See Co-Rect Prods., 780 F.2d at 1330; Heartland Bank, 335 F.3d at 820 (Smith, J., concurring). In fact, Frosty Treats does not even prominently display the "Frosty Treats" mark on its street-vending vans, which according to its brief is the primary way that it advertises the phrase. As mentioned earlier, the phrase appears on the vans as a nine-by-four-inch decal that is surrounded by numerous other decals of frozen desserts.

[12] Furthermore, SCEA submitted indirect evidence that the term "Frosty Treats" has not acquired secondary meaning. SCEA's expert conducted a survey of 204 children and 200 adults who had purchased ice cream from an ice cream truck in Frosty Treats's largest markets. When asked to volunteer the names of any ice cream trucks that they had purchased ice cream from, not one recalled the name "Frosty Treats." The evidence as a whole simply does not provide a sufficient basis for concluding that the phrase "Frosty Treats" has acquired a secondary meaning. Accordingly, it is not protectible under trademark law.

{The court went on to find, inter alia, that there was no likelihood of confusion as to the source or sponsorship of SCEA's video game.}

Cartier, Inc. v. Four Star Jewelry Creations, Inc.
348 F.Supp.2d 217, 228-231 (S.D.N.Y. 2004)

{Defendant Four Star Jewelry Creations produced knockoffs of certain of plaintiff Cartier's watches. Defendant argued that plaintiff's watch designs did not possess secondary meaning as designations of source and thus were unprotectable under trademark law.}

MOTLEY, District Judge

. . . .

2. Consumer Recognition: the Expert Reports

[1] Defendants and Plaintiff both conducted surveys to test the secondary meaning of the four families of Cartier watches at issue. Simply stated, the parties retained experts to poll the public as to whether they associated the Panthere, Pasha, Tank Americaine, and Tank Francaise, or more specifically, their watch designs, with Cartier.

a. Defendants' Expert: Mr. Harry O'Neill

[2] Defendants retained Mr. Harry O'Neill, Vice Chairman of Roper ASW. Mr. O'Neill's report is hereinafter referenced as the "Roper Report."

[3] The Roper Report was created by intercepting shoppers at six shopping malls throughout the country: Atlanta, Boston, Chicago, Dallas, Los Angeles and San Francisco. O'Neill attempted to pick malls with "relatively upscale stores" in order to maximize the likelihood of identifying survey participants who represented the appropriate population. O'Neill concluded that a mall that was anchored by Sears or Kmart, for example, would be unlikely to be frequented by consumers in the luxury watch market.

[4] At the malls, shoppers were intercepted and screened to determine their eligibility to participate. Shoppers who were under 18, did not have their glasses or contact lenses available but relied on them, or who worked for an advertising company, market research company, or watch retailer or manufacturer were ineligible to be surveyed. Id. Shoppers were further asked whether or not they owned a watch worth at least $2,500. If so, they were qualified to answer the survey's questions. If not, they were asked: "How likely is it that you would consider buying a fine watch—one that would cost at least $2,500—in the next couple of years—very likely, fairly likely, not very likely or not at all likely?" Those who responded indicated that they were "very likely" or "fairly likely" qualified to participate.

43

[5] Eligible participants were then shown pictures of a Cartier Tank Francaise, a Cartier Tank Americaine, a Cartier Panthere, and five other watches made by other manufacturers, namely, Chopard, Rolex, Tag Heuer, Movado and Bvlgari. With each picture, a participant was asked: "Do you associate this style or design with the watches of one or more than one company?" If so, although unnecessary to establish secondary meaning, as an "added extra attraction," participants were asked a second, follow-up question as to whether they recognized to which particular company the watch belonged.

[6] The results of the Roper study are as follows: 38% of the respondents associated the style or design of the Tank Americaine with one company (with 13% correctly identifying Cartier as that company); 34% of the respondents said that they associated the style or design of the Tank Francaise with one company (with 13% correctly identifying Cartier as that company); 31% associated the Panthere style or design with one company (with 13% correctly identifying Cartier as that company). Based on these figures in the Roper Report, O'Neill concludes that a significant portion of the purchasing public does not associate the style or design of the watches at issue with Cartier.

[7] What is noteworthy to the Court, however, is the considerable discrepancy in findings at the Atlanta mall vis a vis the results obtained in surveying shoppers at the other five malls. Of the six malls involved in creating the Roper Report, only the Atlanta mall was anchored by upscale retail establishments. Whereas the Atlanta Mall was anchored by Neiman Marcus and Bloomingdales, the Boston mall was not anchored by any high-end stores, although there was one within five minutes' walking distance, the Chicago mall was anchored by Marshall Fields and Carson Pirie Scott and the Dallas mall was anchored by a Dillar Folis and a Mervins. Further, in Atlanta, 69% of survey respondents owned a watch worth at least $2,500, compared to the 41% of respondents at the other locales. For those who did not already own a fine watch, 55% of the participants were "very likely" to purchase one in the near future, compared to 15% of the participants who answered in similar fashion at the other malls. Accordingly, the court concludes that the population of survey respondents at the Atlanta mall was the most representative of the Cartier consumer population. Here, 63% of the participants associated the style and design of the Tank Francaise with one company, 60% of respondents associated the Tank Americaine with one company, and 60% associated the style or design of the Panthere with one company.

b. Plaintiffs' Expert: Dr. Sidney Lirtzman

[8] Dr. Lirtzman criticized the Roper Report on the grounds that it surveyed the wrong population insofar as it failed to distinguish between those "very likely" to purchase an expensive, luxury timepiece in the near future, and those who were "fairly likely" to make such a purchase. He testified that the survey results from Atlanta indicate that if the Roper Report had been conducted exclusively at "high end malls" and included only those persons more resolute about their intentions of buying a fine watch, the numbers of participants identifying the style or design of the three Cartier watches with one company would have been higher.

[9] To support this conclusion, Lirtzman conducted his own survey designed to parallel O'Neill's, with the exception of two important differences: Lirtzman only interviewed individuals who either already owned a luxury watch or were "very likely" to purchase a watch in the next year, whereas the Roper Report includes respondents who were "very likely" to purchase a watch "in the near future" and persons who were "fairly likely" to purchase such a luxury watch "in the next couple of years." Further, Lirtzman intercepted individuals while they were shopping not in shopping malls, but in Tourneau Watch Company stores, two in Manhattan and one in the Roosevelt Field Mall on Long Island, NY, one in Costa Mesa, CA, and one in Century City in Los Angeles, CA. Tourneau is an authorized dealer of Cartier watches. In light of this relationship, the Tourneau stores feature prominent posters of Cartier watches as well as display cases with Cartier watches.

[10] The Lirtzman study also included a few less significant alterations from O'Neill's study. Lirtzman asked if the participants associated the watch's design with a particular source, as opposed to asking about whether the participant associated the "design or style" with a particular source. Because it is irrelevant to establishing secondary meaning, Lirtzman also did not ask O'Neill's second question as

to whether the participant could identify which company she or he associated with the watch's design. The Lirtzman study was also limited to the Tank Francaise and the Panthere because these watches were the least recognized according to the Roper Report. Lirtzman showed participants pictures of the Tag Heuer and Movado watches, like the Roper Report, achieving the same percentages for recognition of these watches among participants, but excluded the other controls. Finally, the photographs shown to survey participants in Lirtzman's study are increasingly clear and more uniform than those shown to participants in the Roper study.

[11] The results of Lirtzman's study are as follows: 61% of the survey respondents associated the Tank Francaise's design with a particular source and 63% of the survey respondents associated the Panthere with a particular source. Lirtzman concludes from this result and the Atlanta results in the Roper Report that surveying individuals who either own or are very likely to purchase a luxury watch establishes consumer recognition of the Cartier watch families at issue in the range of 50 to 60%.

[12] Defendants' principal objection to Lirtzman's report is that in light of the Cartier posters at Tourneau and the fact that its watches are among those displayed in Tourneau's cases, the result of the study are biased. The court, however, disagrees. There are a panoply of luxury watches prominently featured at Tourneau, both in the display cases and on the walls as posters and murals; Tourneau changes its displays every few months; and there are 110 brands sold at Tourneau, all of which have multiple lines or models within them. The Cartier case, for example, contains six to a dozen watch models, including the watches at issue. As such, while Cartier is sold at Tourneau and is displayed among the many images a consumer perceives while shopping there, the likelihood that a survey participant's reaction to the Tank Francaise and Panthere would have been so influenced is so minimal as to have little to no effect on the probative value of Lirtzman's report.

[13] Moreover, the court credits the testimony of Dr. Lirtzman that valid market research does not require a secondary meaning survey to be conducted in a vacuum given the nature of the questions posed to the survey participants. At Tourneau, consumers were asked questions in an environment in which one would actually purchase a luxury timepiece. Images of the products to be sold are customary in such an environment. Had the Lirtzman's pollsters asked about particular brands of the watches shown to participants surrounded by promotional images, this would raise the specter of potential bias; but here, where the question was simply whether a participant associated the watch with a particular company, without asking which one, no such concern arises.

[14] Therefore, in light of a) the results obtained by defendants' expert in Atlanta, where the survey was undoubtedly taken in a mall where higher-end merchandise is sold, meaning, an environment more consistent with Cartier's consumer population, and where the respondents were increasingly likely to either own or purchase a luxury time piece in the immediate future; b) plaintiffs' survey showing that the Atlanta results are more likely to be accurate than those obtained in other fora; and c) the Court's concerns about the absence of persons within the age group 18–34 or mistakes in tabulating their survey results in the Roper Report, the court adopts the testimony of Dr. Sidney Lirtzman, finding that the results obtained in Atlanta and in the Lirtzman Report are representative of the secondary meaning of the watches at issue.

{The court ultimately found secondary meaning in all four Cartier watch designs and infringement by defendant of those designs.}

In the following case, *Board of Supervisors for Louisiana State University Agricultural & Mechanical College v. Smack Apparel Co.*, 550 F.3d 465 (5th Cir. 2008), the plaintiffs Louisiana State University, the University of Oklahoma, Ohio State University, the University of Southern California, and Collegiate Licensing Company (the official licensing agent for the universities) brought suit against defendant Smack Apparel for its unauthorized sale of apparel bearing the universities' colors and various printed messages associated with the universities (but not bearing the universities' names or mascots). The Eastern District of Louisiana granted the plaintiffs' motion for summary judgment on the issue of trademark infringement. Excerpted below is the Fifth Circuit's discussion of whether the universities' colors carry secondary meaning as designations of source.

Note that we will soon return to the protectability of colors as trademarks in Part I.A.2.a when we consider *Qualitex Co. v. Jacobson Products Co., Inc.*, 514 U.S. 159 (1995).

Board of Supervisors for Louisiana State University Agricultural & Mechanical College v. Smack Apparel Co.
550 F.3d 465, 475-478 (5th Cir. 2008)

REAVLEY, Circuit Judge:

. . . .

[1] The parties correctly agree that a color scheme can be protected as a trademark when it has acquired secondary meaning and is non-functional. *Qualitex Co. v. Jacobson Prods. Co.*[22] Although the parties discuss color at length in their briefs, the Universities do not claim that every instance in which their team colors appear violates their respective trademarks. Instead, the claimed trademark is in the colors on merchandise that combines other identifying indicia referring to the Universities. It is appropriate therefore to consider not only the color but also the entire context in which the color and other indicia are presented on the t-shirts at issue here.

[2] Smack contends that the claimed marks are too broad to encompass a trademark because the concept of color along with other identifying indicia is not distinctive. We disagree. As noted, the statute contemplates that a trademark may include any word, name, or symbol *"or any combination thereof."*[23] The Supreme Court has recognized that the Lanham Act describes the universe of permissible marks "in the broadest of terms."[24] Because the Court recognizes that trademarks may include color, we see no reason to exclude color plus other identifying indicia from the realm of protectible marks provided the remaining requirements for protection are met. Thus, the first step here is to ask whether the Universities' claimed marks have acquired secondary meaning.

[3] Secondary meaning "occurs when, 'in the minds of the public, the primary significance of a [mark] is to identify the source of the product rather than the product itself.'" *Wal–Mart Stores, Inc. v. Samara Bros., Inc.*[25] The inquiry is one of the public's mental association between the mark and the

---

[22] 514 U.S. 159, 163–64 (1995).

[23] 15 U.S.C. § 1127 (emphasis added).

[24] *Qualitex*, 514 U.S. at 162.

[25] 529 U.S. 205, 211 (2000) (citation omitted).

alleged mark holder. *Sno–Wizard Mfg., Inc. v. Eisemann Prods. Co.*[26] A mark has acquired secondary meaning when it "has come through use to be uniquely associated with a specific source." *Pebble Beach Co. v. Tour 18 I Ltd.*[27] We have applied a multi-factor test for determining secondary meaning. The factors include: "(1) length and manner of use of the mark or trade dress, (2) volume of sales, (3) amount and manner of advertising, (4) nature of use of the mark or trade dress in newspapers and magazines, (5) consumer-survey evidence, (6) direct consumer testimony, and (7) the defendant's intent in copying the trade dress."[28] These factors in combination may show that consumers consider a mark to be an indicator of source even if each factor alone would not prove secondary meaning.[29]

[4] There is no dispute in this case that for a significant period of time the Universities have been using their color schemes along with other indicia to identify and distinguish themselves from others. Smack admits in its brief that the Universities' colors are well known among fans "as a shorthand nonverbal visual means of identifying the universities." But according to Smack, the longstanding use of the school colors to adorn licensed products is not the same as public recognition that the school colors identify the Universities as a unique source of goods. We think, however, that the factors for determining secondary meaning and an examination of the context in which the school colors are used and presented in this case support the conclusion that the secondary meaning of the marks is inescapable.

[5] The record shows that the Universities have been using their color combinations since the late 1800s.[30] The color schemes appear on all manner of materials, including brochures, media guides, and alumni materials associated with the Universities. Significantly, each university features the color schemes on merchandise, especially apparel connected with school sports teams, and such prominent display supports a finding of secondary meaning.[31] The record also shows that sales of licensed products combining the color schemes with other references to the Universities annually exceed the tens of millions of dollars.[32] As for advertising, the district court held that the Universities "advertise items with their school colors in almost every conceivable manner . . . ."[33] It is not clear from the summary judgment evidence where and how the Universities advertise their merchandise, but they certainly do use their color schemes and indicia in numerous promotional materials aimed at students, faculty, alumni, and the public in general, which strengthens the conclusion that the color schemes and indicia viewed in context of wearing apparel also serves as an indicator of the Universities as the source or sponsor of the apparel. Furthermore, the district court correctly observed that the school color schemes have been referenced multiple times in newspapers and magazines and that the schools also frequently refer to themselves using the colors.[34] The district court did not specifically refer to any consumer-survey evidence or direct consumer testimony, but it noted that Smack admitted it had incorporated the

---

[26] 791 F.2d 423, 427 (5th Cir. 1986) ("[T]he prime element of secondary meaning is 'a mental association in buyers' minds between the alleged mark and a single source of the product.'" (citation omitted)).

[27] 155 F.3d 526, 536 (5th Cir. 1998) (internal quotation marks omitted), *abrogation on other grounds recognized by Eppendorf–Netheler–Hinz GMBH v. Ritter GMBH,* 289 F.3d 351, 356 (5th Cir. 2002).

[28] *Pebble Beach,* 155 F.3d at 541.

[29] *Id.*

[30] OSU adopted its school colors in 1878, while LSU has been using its colors since 1893, and OU and USC since 1895.

[31] *See Pebble Beach,* 155 F.3d at 541–52 (prominent display of golf hole's trade dress in advertising supported finding of secondary meaning as a designator of source).

[32] For example, LSU sells between $10 and $20 million worth of goods each year, while the annual sales volume for the other schools is approximately $13 million for USC, $20 million for OU, and $50 million for OSU.

[33] *Bd. of Supervisors,* 438 F.Supp.2d at 658.

[34] For example, LSU and third parties have referred to that university as the "Purple and Gold."

Universities' color schemes into its shirts to refer to the Universities and call them to the mind of the consumer. Thus, Smack itself believed that the Universities' color schemes had secondary meaning that could influence consumers, which further supports the conclusion that there is secondary meaning here.[35] Given the longstanding use of the color scheme marks and their prominent display on merchandise, in addition to the well-known nature of the colors as shorthand for the schools themselves and Smack's intentional use of the colors and other references, there is no genuine issue of fact that when viewed in the context of t-shirts or other apparel, the marks at issue here have acquired the secondary meaning of identifying the Universities in the minds of consumers as the source or sponsor of the products rather than identifying the products themselves.

[6] We think this conclusion is consistent with the importance generally placed on sports team logos and colors by the public. We have previously noted, although not in the context of secondary meaning, that team emblems and symbols are sold because they serve to identify particular teams, organizations, or entities with which people wish to identify. *See Boston Prof'l Hockey Ass'n v. Dallas Cap & Emblem Mfg., Inc.*[36] We think this desire by consumers to associate with a particular university supports the conclusion that team colors and logos are, in the minds of the fans and other consumers, source indicators of team-related apparel. By associating the color and other indicia with the university, the fans perceive the university as the source or sponsor of the goods because they want to associate with that source.

[7] Smack argues that because photographs of businesses near the campuses of the Universities show use of school colors by those businesses, consumers in college towns merely associate school colors with "support of the home team." Smack cites no authority or supporting evidence for its contention, however. Moreover, the fact that other businesses in college towns may use the same colors as a local university does not create an issue of fact as to the secondary meaning of the colors used in merchandise that the Universities indisputably produce, especially given Smack's admission of intentional use of the colors to influence consumers.

[8] Smack also argues that because the Universities grant licenses to many licensees, a consumer may not identify a university as the *single* source of the product. The fact that the Universities may grant licenses to many licensees to sell authorized products does not negate the fact that the schools are still the sources of the marks.[37] We conclude that the record establishes secondary meaning in the marks here.

{The Fifth Circuit went on to affirm the E.D.La.'s disposition of the case in all respects.}

Comments and Questions

1. *Necessary proportion of relevant consumer population perceiving secondary meaning.* Courts generally require that a "substantial" proportion of the relevant consumer population perceive the descriptive mark as a designation of source for that mark to qualify for protection. *See, e.g., Coach*

---

[35] *See also Thomas & Betts Corp. v. Panduit Corp.*, 65 F.3d 654, 663 (7th Cir. 1995). We also note that the record does contain survey evidence compiled by the Universities indicating that approximately thirty percent of consumers interviewed believed two of Smack's t-shirts were produced or sponsored by the Universities. We have indicated that survey evidence often may be the most direct and persuasive evidence of secondary meaning. *Sugar Busters LLC v. Brennan*, 177 F.3d 258, 269 (5th Cir. 1999). Nevertheless, Smack moved in limine to exclude the Universities' survey evidence, and the district court found it unnecessary to rule on the motion because of the other evidence in the record. Because no party has raised the issue, we express no opinion on the correctness of the district court's belief and merely note the presence of the survey evidence in the record.

[36] 510 F.2d 1004, 1011 (5th Cir. 1975).

[37] *Cf. Taco Cabana Int'l, Inc. v. Two Pesos, Inc.*, 932 F.2d 1113, 1121 (5th Cir. 1991) ("An owner may license its trademark or trade dress and retain proprietary rights if the owner maintains adequate control over the quality of goods and services that the licensee sells with the mark or dress.").

Leatherware Co. v. AnnTaylor, Inc., 933 F.2d 162, 168 (2d Cir. 1991) ("The plaintiff is not required to establish that *all* consumers relate the product to its producer; it need only show that a substantial segment of the relevant consumer group makes this connection."). But what proportion is substantial? If survey evidence is presented, courts have generally been satisfied, as in the *Cartier* case above, with a proportion at or above 50%. *See, e.g., Harlequin Enterprises, Ltd. v. Gulf & Western Corp.*, 644 F.2d 946 (2d Cir. 1981) (finding 50% association to be probative of secondary meaning in book cover design); *Spraying Systems Co. v. Delavan*, 975 F.2d 387, 394 (7th Cir. 1992) ("While a 50-percent figure is regarded as clearly sufficient to establish secondary meaning, a figure in the thirties can only be considered marginal."); Boston Beer Co. Ltd. Partnership v. Slesar Bros. Brewing Co., 9 F.3d 175, 183 n.5 (1st Cir. 1993) (characterizing a 36% showing of association as "hardly overwhelming").

More generally, courts may require more compelling evidence of secondary meaning for marks that are highly descriptive. *See* MCCARTHY § 15:28 ("[A]s a general rule of thumb, the more descriptive the term, the greater the evidentiary burden to establish secondary meaning. That is, the less distinctive the term, the greater the quantity and quality of evidence of secondary meaning needed to prove the requisite degree of distinctiveness.").

2.   *The statutory mechanism for registration of descriptive marks with secondary meaning.* Lanham Act §§ 2(e) & 2(f), 15 U.S.C. §§ 1052(e) & (f), provide for the registration of descriptive marks with secondary meaning. The relevant portions of § 2 read as follows:

> No trademark by which the goods of the applicant may be distinguished from the goods of others shall be refused registration on the principal register on account of its nature unless it . . .
>
> (e) Consists of a mark which (1) when used on or in connection with the goods of the applicant is merely descriptive or deceptively misdescriptive of them.
>
> (f) Except as expressly excluded in subsections (a), (b), (c), (d), (e)(3), and (e)(5) of this section, nothing in this chapter shall prevent the registration of a mark used by the applicant which has become distinctive of the applicant's goods in commerce.

15 U.S.C. § 1052.

c.   Generic Marks

Trademarks may be deemed generic either (1) because they are born generic or (2) because they lose their source distinctiveness through a process of "genericide." The following are examples of marks born generic:

- *Schwan's IP, LLC v. Kraft Pizza Co.*, 460 F.3d 971, 79 U.S.P.Q.2d 1790 (8th Cir. 2006) (finding BRICK OVEN for frozen pizza to be generic);

- *Ale House Management, Inc. v. Raleigh Ale House, Inc.*, 205 F.3d 137, 54 U.S.P.Q.2d 1040 (4th Cir. 2000) (finding ALE HOUSE for chain of restaurants serving food and beer to be generic);

- *Continental Airlines Inc. v. United Air Lines Inc.*, 53 U.S.P.Q.2d 1385, 1999 WL 1421649 (TTAB 2000) (finding E-TICKET for electronic ticketing services to be generic);

- *Nat'l Conf. of Bar Examiners v. Multistate Legal Studies, Inc.*, 692 F.2d 478, 487 (7th Cir. 1982) (finding MULTISTATE BAR EXAMINATION for legal testing services to be generic).

The following are examples of marks that have fallen to genericide:

- *Haughton Elevator Co. v. Seeberger*, 85 U.S.P.Q. 80 (Comm'r Pat. 1950) (cancelling registration of ESCALATOR for moving staircases);

- *Duncan F. Duncan, Inc. v. Royal Tops Mfg. Co.*, 343 F.2d 655, 662 (7th Cir. 1965) (finding that the term "yo-yo" had long since become generic despite plaintiff's "herculean efforts to fasten upon the toy the generic term, 'return top'");

- *Bayer Co. v. United Drug Co.*, 272 F. 505, 510 (D.N.Y. 1921) (finding as to the mark ASPIRIN for acetyl salicylic acid that "[a]mong consumers generally the name has gone into the public domain").

The following are examples of marks that are not in fact generic and remain registered trademarks at the PTO:

- BAND-AID for "protective surgical dressing in the form of a bandage" (U.S. Reg. No. 194,123, Jan. 13, 1925);
- REALTOR for real estate brokerage services (U.S. Reg. No. 519,789, Jan. 15, 1950);
- STYROFOAM for "multicellular expanded synthetic resinous material" (U.S. Reg. No. 539,147, March 13, 1951).

There are a variety of simple rules of thumb that inform courts' determination of whether a mark is generic or descriptive. *Abercrombie* outlined a genus/species distinction: "A generic term is one that refers, or has come to be understood as referring, to the genus of which the particular product is a species." *Abercrombie & Fitch Co. v. Hunting World, Inc.*, 537 F.3d 4, 9 (2d Cir. 1976). There is also the "who-are-you/what-are-you" distinction:

> In determining whether a term is generic, we have often relied upon the "who-are-you/what-are-you" test: "A mark answers the buyer's questions 'Who are you?' 'Where do you come from?' 'Who vouches for you?' But the [generic] name of the product answers the question 'What are you?'" *Official Airline Guides, Inc. v. Goss*, 6 F.3d 1385, 1391 (9th Cir. 1993) (quoting 1 J. Thomas McCarthy, *Trademarks and Unfair Competition* § 12.01 (3d ed. 1992)). Under this test, "[i]f the primary significance of the trademark is to describe the *type of product* rather than the *producer*, the trademark [is] a generic term and [cannot be] a valid trademark." *Anti–Monopoly, Inc. v. General Mills Fun Group*, 611 F.2d 296, 304 (9th Cir. 1979) (emphases added)

Filipino Yellow Pages, Inc. v. Asian Journal Publications, Inc., 198 F.3d 1143, 1147 (9th Cir. 1999). Courts will also rely on the proposition that a mark is generic if it is the "common descriptive name" of the good or service to which it is affixed. *See, e.g.*, *San Francisco Arts & Athletics, Inc. v. U.S. Olympic Committee*, 483 U.S. 522, 532 n. 7 (1987) ("A common descriptive name of a product or service is generic. Because a generic name by definition does not *distinguish* the identity of a particular product, it cannot be registered as a trademark under the Lanham Act." (emphasis in original)).

But while the basic principles underlying the genericness analysis are straightforward, distinguishing between a highly descriptive mark and a generic mark can be exceedingly difficult in close cases, and the stakes in such cases can be exceedingly high.[1] Recall that even a "highly descriptive" mark will qualify for protection upon a showing of secondary meaning. A generic mark, by contrast, is unredeemable; it will never receive protection under any circumstances. Genericness doctrine, meanwhile, can be quite malleable.

The following three cases offer different views of trademark genericism. The first is the Supreme Court case *United States Patent and Trademark Office v. Booking.com B.V.*, __ U.S. __, 140 S.Ct. 2298 (June 30, 2020). In analyzing whether the mark BOOKING.COM is generic, the three opinions in the case engage a variety of overarching questions in genericism doctrine, such as whether the facts of consumer perception or the goals of competition policy should drive the genericism analysis. The second case emerged out of a dispute between the giant snackfood maker Frito-Lay North America, Inc. and an upstart competitor, Princeton Vanguard LLC (subsequently purchased by Snyder's Lance, Inc.), who introduced "pretzel crisps" into the market and sought to trademark the term. The *Snyder's Lance* opinion is quite lengthy but useful for our purposes because it shows the wide variety of evidence that parties may present in a hard-fought genericism dispute. It will be of special interest to students

---

[1] Is "App Store" a generic term for an online platform selling apps? *See Apple, Inc. v. Amazon.com Inc.*, No. 11 Civ. 1327, 2011 WL 2638191, at *7 (N.D. Cal. July 6, 2011) ("The court assumes without deciding that the 'App Store' mark is protectable as a descriptive mark that has arguably acquired secondary meaning." But the court found, on Apple's preliminary injunction motion, that Amazon's use of "App Store" to describe its app store did not create a likelihood of confusion.).

interested in the nuts-and-bolts of frontline genericism litigation. The third opinion, *Elliott v. Google, Inc.*, engages the question of whether the mark GOOGLE has fallen victim to genericide. Remarkably, the court reasons that even if the public uses the verb "google" in a generic sense to describe the act of "searching on the internet without regard to the search engine used," that would not support a finding that GOOGLE has become generic for internet search services.

United States Patent and Trademark Office v. Booking.com B.V.
No. 19-46, 140 S.Ct. 2298, __ U.S. __ (June 30, 2020)

Justice GINSBURG delivered the opinion of the Court.

[1] This case concerns eligibility for federal trademark registration. Respondent Booking.com, an enterprise that maintains a travel-reservation website by the same name, sought to register the mark "Booking.com." Concluding that "Booking.com" is a generic name for online hotel-reservation services, the U. S. Patent and Trademark Office (PTO) refused registration.

[2] A generic name—the name of a class of products or services—is ineligible for federal trademark registration. The word "booking," the parties do not dispute, is generic for hotel-reservation services. "Booking.com" must also be generic, the PTO maintains, under an encompassing rule the PTO currently urges us to adopt: The combination of a generic word and ".com" is generic.

[3] In accord with the first- and second-instance judgments in this case, we reject the PTO's sweeping rule. A term styled "generic.com" is a generic name for a class of goods or services only if the term has that meaning to consumers. Consumers, according to lower court determinations uncontested here by the PTO, do not perceive the term "Booking.com" to signify online hotel-reservation services as a class. In circumstances like those this case presents, a "generic.com" term is not generic and can be eligible for federal trademark registration.

I

A

. . . .

[4] The Lanham Act not only arms trademark owners with federal claims for relief; importantly, it establishes a system of federal trademark registration. The owner of a mark on the principal register enjoys "valuable benefits," including a presumption that the mark is valid. *Iancu v. Brunetti*, 588 U. S. ── , ── (2019) (slip op., at 2); see §§ 1051, 1052. The supplemental register contains other product and service designations, some of which could one day gain eligibility for the principal register. See § 1091. The supplemental register accords more modest benefits; notably, a listing on that register announces one's use of the designation to others considering a similar mark. See 3 J. McCarthy, Trademarks and Unfair Competition § 19:37 (5th ed. 2019) (hereinafter McCarthy). Even without federal registration, a mark may be eligible for protection against infringement under both the Lanham Act and other sources of law. See *Matal*, 582 U. S., at ── ── ── (slip op., at 4–5).

[5] Prime among the conditions for registration, the mark must be one "by which the goods of the applicant may be distinguished from the goods of others." § 1052; see § 1091(a) (supplemental register contains "marks capable of distinguishing . . . goods or services"). Distinctiveness is often expressed on an increasing scale: Word marks "may be (1) generic; (2) descriptive; (3) suggestive; (4) arbitrary; or (5) fanciful." *Two Pesos, Inc. v. Taco Cabana, Inc.*, 505 U.S. 763, 768 (1992).

. . . .

[6] At the lowest end of the distinctiveness scale is "the generic name for the goods or services." §§ 1127, 1064(3), 1065(4). The name of the good itself (*e.g.*, "wine") is incapable of "distinguish[ing] [one producer's goods] from the goods of others" and is therefore ineligible for registration. § 1052; see § 1091(a). Indeed, generic terms are ordinarily ineligible for protection as trademarks at all. See Restatement (Third) of Unfair Competition § 15, p. 142 (1993); *Otokoyama Co. v. Wine of Japan Import, Inc.*, 175 F.3d 266, 270 (CA2 1999) ("[E]veryone may use [generic terms] to refer to the goods they designate.").

51

B

[7] Booking.com is a digital travel company that provides hotel reservations and other services under the brand "Booking.com," which is also the domain name of its website.[1] Booking.com filed applications to register four marks in connection with travel-related services, each with different visual features but all containing the term "Booking.com."[2]

[8] Both a PTO examining attorney and the PTO's Trademark Trial and Appeal Board concluded that the term "Booking.com" is generic for the services at issue and is therefore unregistrable. "Booking," the Board observed, means making travel reservations, and ".com" signifies a commercial website. The Board then ruled that "customers would understand the term BOOKING.COM primarily to refer to an online reservation service for travel, tours, and lodgings." Alternatively, the Board held that even if "Booking.com" is descriptive, not generic, it is unregistrable because it lacks secondary meaning.

[9] Booking.com sought review in the U. S. District Court for the Eastern District of Virginia, invoking a mode of review that allows Booking.com to introduce evidence not presented to the agency. See § 1071(b). Relying in significant part on Booking.com's new evidence of consumer perception, the District Court concluded that "Booking.com"—unlike "booking"—is not generic. The "consuming public," the court found, "primarily understands that BOOKING.COM does not refer to a genus, rather it is descriptive of services involving 'booking' available at that domain name." *Booking.com B.V. v. Matal*, 278 F.Supp.3d 891, 918 (2017). Having determined that "Booking.com" is descriptive, the District Court additionally found that the term has acquired secondary meaning as to hotel-reservation services. For those services, the District Court therefore concluded, Booking.com's marks meet the distinctiveness requirement for registration.

[10] The PTO appealed only the District Court's determination that "Booking.com" is not generic. Finding no error in the District Court's assessment of how consumers perceive the term "Booking.com," the Court of Appeals for the Fourth Circuit affirmed the court of first instance's judgment. In so ruling, the appeals court rejected the PTO's contention that the combination of ".com" with a generic term like "booking" "is *necessarily* generic." 915 F. 3d 171, 184 (2019). Dissenting in relevant part, Judge Wynn concluded that the District Court mistakenly presumed that "generic.com" terms are usually descriptive, not generic.

[11] We granted certiorari, 589 U. S. --, 140 S.Ct. 489 (2019), and now affirm the Fourth Circuit's decision.

II

[12] Although the parties here disagree about the circumstances in which terms like "Booking.com" rank as generic, several guiding principles are common ground. First, a "generic" term names a "class" of goods or services, rather than any particular feature or exemplification of the class. {S}ee §§ 1127, 1064(3), 1065(4) (referring to "the generic name for the goods or services"); *Park 'N Fly*, 469 U.S. at 194 ("A generic term is one that refers to the genus of which the particular product is a species."). Second, for a compound term, the distinctiveness inquiry trains on the term's meaning as a whole, not its parts in isolation. {S}ee *Estate of P. D. Beckwith, Inc. v. Commissioner of Patents*, 252 U.S. 538, 545–546 (1920). Third, the relevant meaning of a term is its meaning to consumers. {S}ee *Bayer Co. v. United Drug Co.*, 272 F. 505, 509 (SDNY 1921) (Hand, J.) ("What do the buyers understand by the word for whose use the parties are contending?"). Eligibility for registration, all agree, turns on the mark's capacity to

---

[1] A domain name identifies an address on the Internet. The rightmost component of a domain name—".com" in "Booking.com"—is known as the top-level domain. Domain names are unique; that is, a given domain name is assigned to only one entity at a time.

[2] For simplicity, this opinion uses the term "trademark" to encompass the marks whose registration Booking.com seeks. Although Booking.com uses the marks in connection with services, not goods, rendering the marks "service marks" rather than "trademarks" under 15 U.S.C. § 1127, that distinction is immaterial to the issue before us.

"distinguis[h]" goods "in commerce." § 1052. Evidencing the Lanham Act's focus on consumer perception, the section governing cancellation of registration provides that "[t]he primary significance of the registered mark to the relevant public . . . shall be the test for determining whether the registered mark has become the generic name of goods or services." § 1064(3).[3]

[13] Under these principles, whether "Booking.com" is generic turns on whether that term, taken as a whole, signifies to consumers the class of online hotel-reservation services. Thus, if "Booking.com" were generic, we might expect consumers to understand Travelocity—another such service—to be a "Booking.com." We might similarly expect that a consumer, searching for a trusted source of online hotel-reservation services, could ask a frequent traveler to name her favorite "Booking.com" provider.

[14] Consumers do not in fact perceive the term "Booking.com" that way, the courts below determined. The PTO no longer disputes that determination. See Pet. for Cert. I; Brief for Petitioners 17–18 (contending only that a consumer-perception inquiry was unnecessary, not that the lower courts' consumer-perception determination was wrong). That should resolve this case: Because "Booking.com" is not a generic name to consumers, it is not generic.

III

[15] Opposing that conclusion, the PTO urges a nearly *per se* rule that would render "Booking.com" ineligible for registration regardless of specific evidence of consumer perception. In the PTO's view, which the dissent embraces, when a generic term is combined with a generic top-level domain like ".com," the resulting combination is generic. In other words, every "generic.com" term is generic according to the PTO, absent exceptional circumstances.[4]

[16] The PTO's own past practice appears to reflect no such comprehensive rule. See, *e.g.*, Trademark Registration No. 3,601,346 ("ART.COM" on principal register for, *inter alia*, "[o]nline retail store services" offering "art prints, original art, [and] art reproductions"); Trademark Registration No. 2,580,467 ("DATING.COM" on supplemental register for "dating services"). Existing registrations inconsistent with the rule the PTO now advances would be at risk of cancellation if the PTO's current view were to prevail. See § 1064(3). We decline to adopt a rule essentially excluding registration of "generic.com" marks. As explained below, we discern no support for the PTO's current view in trademark law or policy.

A

[17] The PTO urges that the exclusionary rule it advocates follows from a common-law principle, applied in *Goodyear's India Rubber Glove Mfg. Co.* v. *Goodyear Rubber Co.*, 128 U.S. 598 (1888), that a generic corporate designation added to a generic term does not confer trademark eligibility. In *Goodyear*, a decision predating the Lanham Act, this Court held that "Goodyear Rubber Company" was not "capable

---

[3] The U. S. Patent and Trademark Office (PTO) suggests that the primary-significance test might not govern outside the context of § 1064(3), which subjects to cancellation marks previously registered that have "become" generic. See Reply Brief 11; Tr. of Oral Arg. 19. To so confine the primary-significance test, however, would upset the understanding, shared by Courts of Appeals and the PTO's own manual for trademark examiners, that the same test governs whether a mark is registrable in the first place. See, *e.g.*, *In re Cordua Restaurants, Inc.*, 823 F.3d 594, 599 (CA Fed. 2016); *Nartron Corp. v. STMicroelectronics, Inc.*, 305 F.3d 397, 404 (CA6 2002); *Genesee Brewing Co. v. Stroh Brewing Co.*, 124 F.3d 137, 144 (CA2 1997); Trademark Manual of Examining Procedure § 1209.01(c)(i), p. 1200–267 (Oct. 2018), http://tmep.uspto.gov. We need not address today the scope of the primary-significance test's application, for our analysis does not depend on whether one meaning among several is "primary." Sufficient to resolve this case is the undisputed principle that consumer perception demarcates a term's meaning.

[4] The PTO notes only one possible exception: Sometimes adding a generic term to a generic top-level domain results in wordplay (for example, "tennis.net"). That special case, the PTO acknowledges, is not presented here and does not affect our analysis.

of exclusive appropriation." *Id.*, at 602. Standing alone, the term "Goodyear Rubber" could not serve as a trademark because it referred, in those days, to "well-known classes of goods produced by the process known as Goodyear's invention." *Ibid.* "[A]ddition of the word 'Company'" supplied no protectable meaning, the Court concluded, because adding "Company" "only indicates that parties have formed an association or partnership to deal in such goods." *Ibid.* Permitting exclusive rights in "Goodyear Rubber Company" (or "Wine Company, Cotton Company, or Grain Company"), the Court explained, would tread on the right of all persons "to deal in such articles, and to publish the fact to the world." *Id.*, at 602–603.

[18] "Generic.com," the PTO maintains, is like "Generic Company" and is therefore ineligible for trademark protection, let alone federal registration. According to the PTO, adding ".com" to a generic term—like adding "Company"—"conveys no additional meaning that would distinguish [one provider's] services from those of other providers." Brief for Petitioners 44. The dissent endorses that proposition: "Generic.com" conveys that the generic good or service is offered online "and nothing more." *Post*, at --
.

[19] That premise is faulty. A "generic.com" term might also convey to consumers a source-identifying characteristic: an association with a particular website. As the PTO and the dissent elsewhere acknowledge, only one entity can occupy a particular Internet domain name at a time, so "[a] consumer who is familiar with that aspect of the domain-name system can infer that BOOKING.COM refers to *some specific entity*." Brief for Petitioners 40. See also Tr. of Oral Arg. 5 ("Because domain names are one of a kind, a significant portion of the public will always understand a generic '.com' term to refer to a specific business. . . ."); *post*, at ---- (the "exclusivity" of "generic.com" terms sets them apart from terms like "Wine, Inc." and "The Wine Company"). Thus, consumers could understand a given "generic.com" term to describe the corresponding website or to identify the website's proprietor. We therefore resist the PTO's position that "generic.com" terms are capable of signifying only an entire class of online goods or services and, hence, are categorically incapable of identifying a source.[5]

[20] The PTO's reliance on *Goodyear* is flawed in another respect. The PTO understands *Goodyear* to hold that "Generic Company" terms "are ineligible for trademark protection *as a matter of law*"—regardless of how "consumers would understand" the term. Brief for Petitioners 38. But, as noted, whether a term is generic depends on its meaning to consumers. *Supra*, at --. That bedrock principle of the Lanham Act is incompatible with an unyielding legal rule that entirely disregards consumer perception. Instead, *Goodyear* reflects a more modest principle harmonious with Congress' subsequent enactment: A compound of generic elements is generic if the combination yields no additional meaning *to consumers* capable of distinguishing the goods or services.

[21] The PTO also invokes the oft-repeated principle that "no matter how much money and effort the user of a generic term has poured into promoting the sale of its merchandise . . . , it cannot deprive competing manufacturers of the product of the right to call an article by its name." *Abercrombie & Fitch*

---

[5] In passing, the PTO urges us to disregard that a domain name is assigned to only one entity at a time. That fact, the PTO suggests, stems from "a functional characteristic of the Internet and the domain-name system," and functional features cannot receive trademark protection. Brief for Petitioners 32. "[A] product feature is functional, and cannot serve as a trademark," we have held, "if it is essential to the use or purpose of the article or if it affects the cost or quality of the article." *TrafFix Devices, Inc. v. Marketing Displays, Inc.*, 532 U.S. 23, 32, 121 S.Ct. 1255, 149 L.Ed.2d 164 (2001) (internal quotation marks omitted); see § 1052(e) (barring from the principal registrar "any matter that, as a whole, is functional"). This case, however, does not concern trademark protection for a feature of the Internet or the domain-name system; Booking.com lays no claim to the use of unique domain names generally. Nor does the PTO contend that the particular domain name "Booking.com" is essential to the use or purpose of online hotel-reservation services, affects these services' cost or quality, or is otherwise necessary for competitors to use. In any event, we have no occasion to decide the applicability of § 1052(e)'s functionality bar, for the sole ground on which the PTO refused registration, and the sole claim before us, is that "Booking.com" is generic.

Co. v. Hunting World, Inc., 537 F.2d 4, 9 (CA2 1976). That principle presupposes that a generic term is at issue. But the PTO's only legal basis for deeming "generic.com" terms generic is its mistaken reliance on *Goodyear.*

[22] While we reject the rule proffered by the PTO that "generic.com" terms are generic names, we do not embrace a rule automatically classifying such terms as nongeneric. Whether any given "generic.com" term is generic, we hold, depends on whether consumers in fact perceive that term as the name of a class or, instead, as a term capable of distinguishing among members of the class.[6]

B

[23] The PTO, echoed by the dissent, *post*, at -- – --, objects that protecting "generic.com" terms as trademarks would disserve trademark law's animating policies. We disagree.

[24] The PTO's principal concern is that trademark protection for a term like "Booking.com" would hinder competitors. But the PTO does not assert that others seeking to offer online hotel-reservation services need to call their services "Booking.com." Rather, the PTO fears that trademark protection for "Booking.com" could exclude or inhibit competitors from using the term "booking" or adopting domain names like "ebooking.com" or "hotel-booking.com." Brief for Petitioners 27–28. The PTO's objection, therefore, is not to exclusive use of "Booking.com" as a mark, but to undue control over similar language, *i.e.*, "booking," that others should remain free to use.

[25] That concern attends any descriptive mark. Responsive to it, trademark law hems in the scope of such marks short of denying trademark protection altogether. Notably, a competitor's use does not infringe a mark unless it is likely to confuse consumers. See §§ 1114(1), 1125(a)(1)(A); 4 McCarthy § 23:1.50 (collecting state law). In assessing the likelihood of confusion, courts consider the mark's distinctiveness: "The weaker a mark, the fewer are the junior uses that will trigger a likelihood of consumer confusion." 2 *id.*, § 11:76. When a mark incorporates generic or highly descriptive components, consumers are less likely to think that other uses of the common element emanate from the mark's owner. *Ibid.* Similarly, "[i]n a 'crowded' field of look-alike marks" (*e.g.*, hotel names including the word "grand"), consumers "may have learned to carefully pick out" one mark from another. *Id.*, § 11:85. And even where some consumer confusion exists, the doctrine known as classic fair use, see *id.*, § 11:45, protects from liability anyone who uses a descriptive term, "fairly and in good faith" and "otherwise than as a mark," merely to describe her own goods. 15 U.S.C. § 1115(b)(4); see *KP Permanent Make-Up, Inc. v. Lasting Impression I, Inc.*, 543 U.S. 111, 122–123 (2004).

[26] These doctrines guard against the anticompetitive effects the PTO identifies, ensuring that registration of "Booking.com" would not yield its holder a monopoly on the term "booking." Booking.com concedes that "Booking.com" would be a "weak" mark. Tr. of Oral Arg. 66. See also *id.*, at 42–43, 55. The

---

[6] Evidence informing that inquiry can include not only consumer surveys, but also dictionaries, usage by consumers and competitors, and any other source of evidence bearing on how consumers perceive a term's meaning. Surveys can be helpful evidence of consumer perception but require care in their design and interpretation. See Brief for Trademark Scholars as *Amici Curiae* 18–20 (urging that survey respondents may conflate the fact that domain names are exclusive with a conclusion that a given "generic.com" term has achieved secondary meaning). Moreover, difficult questions may be presented when a term has multiple concurrent meanings to consumers or a meaning that has changed over time. See, *e.g.*, 2 J. McCarthy, Trademarks and Unfair Competition § 12:51 (5th ed. 2019) (discussing terms that are "a generic name to some, a trademark to others"); *id.*, § 12:49 ("Determining the distinction between generic and trademark usage of a word . . . when there are no other sellers of [the good or service] is one of the most difficult areas of trademark law."). Such issues are not here entailed, for the PTO does not contest the lower courts' assessment of consumer perception in this case. See Pet. for Cert. I; Brief for Petitioners 17–18. For the same reason, while the dissent questions the evidence on which the lower courts relied, *post*, at -- – --, --, we have no occasion to reweigh that evidence. Cf. *post*, at -- – -- (SOTOMAYOR, J., concurring).

mark is descriptive, Booking.com recognizes, making it "harder . . . to show a likelihood of confusion." *Id.*, at 43. Furthermore, because its mark is one of many "similarly worded marks," Booking.com accepts that close variations are unlikely to infringe. *Id.*, at 66. And Booking.com acknowledges that federal registration of "Booking.com" would not prevent competitors from using the word "booking" to describe their own services. *Id.*, at 55.

[27] The PTO also doubts that owners of "generic.com" brands need trademark protection in addition to existing competitive advantages. Booking.com, the PTO argues, has already seized a domain name that no other website can use and is easy for consumers to find. Consumers might enter "the word 'booking' in a search engine," the PTO observes, or "proceed directly to 'booking.com' in the expectation that [online hotel-booking] services will be offered at that address." Brief for Petitioners 32. Those competitive advantages, however, do not inevitably disqualify a mark from federal registration. All descriptive marks are intuitively linked to the product or service and thus might be easy for consumers to find using a search engine or telephone directory. The Lanham Act permits registration nonetheless. See § 1052(e), (f). And the PTO fails to explain how the exclusive connection between a domain name and its owner makes the domain name a generic term all should be free to use. That connection makes trademark protection more appropriate, not less. See *supra*, at --.

[28] Finally, even if "Booking.com" is generic, the PTO urges, unfair-competition law could prevent others from passing off their services as Booking.com's. Cf. *Genesee Brewing Co. v. Stroh Brewing Co.*, 124 F.3d 137, 149 (CA2 1997); *Blinded Veterans Assn. v. Blinded Am. Veterans Foundation*, 872 F.2d 1035, 1042–1048 (CADC 1989). But federal trademark registration would offer Booking.com greater protection. See, *e.g.*, *Genesee Brewing*, 124 F.3d at 151 (unfair-competition law would oblige competitor at most to "make more of an effort" to reduce confusion, not to cease marketing its product using the disputed term); *Matal*, 582 U. S., at -- (slip op., at 5) (federal registration confers valuable benefits); Brief for Respondent 26 (expressing intention to seek protections available to trademark owners under the Anticybersquatting Consumer Protection Act, 15 U.S.C. § 1125(d)); Brief for Coalition of .Com Brand Owners as *Amici Curiae* 14–19 (trademark rights allow mark owners to stop domain-name abuse through private dispute resolution without resorting to litigation). We have no cause to deny Booking.com the same benefits Congress accorded other marks qualifying as nongeneric.

* * *

[29] The PTO challenges the judgment below on a sole ground: It urges that, as a rule, combining a generic term with ".com" yields a generic composite. For the above-stated reasons, we decline a rule of that order, one that would largely disallow registration of "generic.com" terms and open the door to cancellation of scores of currently registered marks. Accordingly, the judgment of the Court of Appeals for the Fourth Circuit regarding eligibility for trademark registration is

Affirmed.

Justice SOTOMAYOR, concurring.

[30] The question before the Court here is simple: whether there is a nearly *per se* rule against trademark protection for a "generic.com" term. See *ante*, at -- - - --; *post*, at -- (BREYER, J., dissenting). I agree with the Court that there is no such rule, a holding that accords with how the U. S. Patent and Trademark Office (PTO) has treated such terms in the past. See *ante*, at -- (noting that the "PTO's own past practice appears to reflect no such comprehensive rule"). I add two observations.

[31] First, the dissent wisely observes that consumer-survey evidence "may be an unreliable indicator of genericness." *Post*, at ---10. Flaws in a specific survey design, or weaknesses inherent in consumer surveys generally, may limit the probative value of surveys in determining whether a particular mark is descriptive or generic in this context. But I do not read the Court's opinion to suggest that surveys are the be-all and end-all. As the Court notes, sources such as "dictionaries, usage by consumers and competitors, and any other source of evidence bearing on how consumers perceive a term's meaning" may also inform whether a mark is generic or descriptive. *Ante*, at --, n. 6.

[32] Second, the PTO may well have properly concluded, based on such dictionary and usage evidence, that Booking.com is in fact generic for the class of services at issue here, and the District Court

may have erred in concluding to the contrary. But that question is not before the Court. With these understandings, I concur in the Court's opinion.

Justice BREYER, dissenting.

[33] What is Booking.com? To answer this question, one need only consult the term itself. Respondent provides an online booking service. The company's name informs the consumer of the basic nature of its business and nothing more. Therein lies the root of my disagreement with the majority.

[34] Trademark law does not protect generic terms, meaning terms that do no more than name the product or service itself. This principle preserves the linguistic commons by preventing one producer from appropriating to its own exclusive use a term needed by others to describe their goods or services. Today, the Court holds that the addition of ".com" to an otherwise generic term, such as "booking," can yield a protectable trademark. Because I believe this result is inconsistent with trademark principles and sound trademark policy, I respectfully dissent.

I

A

. . . .

By preventing others from copying a distinctive mark, trademark law "protect[s] the ability of consumers to distinguish among competing producers" and "secure[s] to the owner of the mark the goodwill of his business." *Park 'N Fly, Inc. v. Dollar Park & Fly, Inc.*, 469 U.S. 189, 198 (1985). Ultimately, the purpose of trademark law is to "foster competition" and "suppor[t] the free flow of commerce." *Matal*, 582 U. S., at –– (slip op., at 3) (internal quotation marks omitted).

. . . .

[35] There are also "generic" terms, such as "wine" or "haircuts." They do nothing more than inform the consumer of the kind of product that the firm sells. We have called generic terms "descriptive of a class of goods." *Goodyear's India Rubber Glove Mfg. Co.* v. *Goodyear Rubber Co.*, 128 U.S. 598, 602 (1888). And we have said that they simply convey the "genus of which the particular product is a species." *Park 'N Fly*, 469 U.S. at 196. A generic term is not eligible for use as a trademark. That principle applies even if a particular generic term "ha[s] become identified with a first user" in the minds of the consuming public. *CES Publishing Corp. v. St. Regis Publications, Inc.*, 531 F.2d 11, 13 (CA2 1975) (Friendly, J.). The reason is simple. To hold otherwise "would grant the owner of the mark a monopoly, since a competitor could not describe his goods as what they are." *Ibid.*

[36] Courts have recognized that it is not always easy to distinguish generic from descriptive terms. See, *e.g., Abercrombie & Fitch Co. v. Hunting World, Inc.*, 537 F.2d 4, 9 (CA2 1976) (Friendly, J.). It is particularly difficult to do so when a firm wishes to string together two or more generic terms to create a compound term. Despite the generic nature of its component parts, the term as a whole is not necessarily generic. In such cases, courts must determine whether the combination of generic terms conveys some distinctive, source-identifying meaning that each term, individually, lacks. See 2 J. McCarthy, Trademarks and Unfair Competition § 12:39 (5th ed. June 2020 update) (McCarthy). If the meaning of the whole is no greater than the sum of its parts, then the compound is itself generic. See *Princeton Vanguard, LLC v. Frito-Lay North Am., Inc.*, 786 F.3d 960, 966–967 (CA Fed. 2015); *In re Gould Paper Corp.*, 834 F.2d 1017, 1018 (CA Fed. 1987) (registration is properly denied if "the separate words joined to form a compound have a meaning identical to the meaning common usage would ascribe to those words as a compound"); see also 2 McCarthy § 12:39 (collecting examples of compound terms held to be generic).

[37] In *Goodyear*, 128 U.S. 598, we held that appending the word "'Company'" to the generic name for a class of goods does not yield a protectable compound term. *Id.,* at 602–603. The addition of a corporate designation, we explained, "only indicates that parties have formed an association or partnership to deal in such goods." *Id.,* at 602. For instance, "parties united to produce or sell wine, or to raise cotton or grain," may well "style themselves Wine Company, Cotton Company, or Grain Company." *Ibid.* But they would not thereby gain the right to exclude others from the use of those terms "for the

57

obvious reason that all persons have a right to deal in such articles, and to publish the fact to the world." *Id.,* at 603. "[I]ncorporation of a company in the name of an article of commerce, without other specification," we concluded, does not "create any exclusive right to the use of the name." *Ibid.*

[38] I cannot agree with respondent that the 1946 Lanham Act "repudiate[d] *Goodyear* and its ilk." Brief for Respondent 39. It is true that the Lanham Act altered the common law in certain important respects. Most significantly, it extended trademark protection to descriptive marks that have acquired secondary meaning. See *Qualitex Co. v. Jacobson Products Co.*, 514 U.S. 159, 171 (1995). But it did not disturb the basic principle that *generic* terms are ineligible for trademark protection, and nothing in the Act suggests that Congress intended to overturn *Goodyear*. We normally assume that Congress did not overturn a common-law principle absent some indication to the contrary. See *Astoria Fed. Sav. & Loan Assn. v. Solimino*, 501 U.S. 104, 108 (1991). I can find no such indication here. Perhaps that is why the lower courts, the Trademark Trial and Appeal Board (TTAB), the U. S. Patent and Trademark Office's (PTO) Trademark Manual of Examining Procedure (TMEP), and leading treatises all recognize *Goodyear*'s continued validity. See, *e.g., In re Detroit Athletic Co.*, 903 F.3d 1297, 1304 (CA Fed. 2018); *In re Katch, LLC*, 2019 WL 2560528, *10 (TTAB 2019); TMEP §§ 1209.03(d) (Oct. 2018); 2 McCarthy § 12:39; 4 L. Altman & M. Pollack, Callmann on Unfair Competition, Trademarks and Monopolies § 18:11 (4th ed., June 2020 update).

[39] More fundamentally, the *Goodyear* principle is sound as a matter of law and logic. *Goodyear* recognized that designations such as "Company," "Corp.," and "Inc." merely indicate corporate form and therefore do nothing to distinguish one firm's goods or services from all others'. 128 U.S. at 602. It follows that the addition of such a corporate designation does not "magically transform a generic name for a product or service into a trademark, thereby giving a right to exclude others." 2 McCarthy § 12:39. In other words, where a compound term consists simply of a generic term plus a corporate designation, the whole is *necessarily* no greater than the sum of its parts.

B

[40] This case requires us to apply these principles in the novel context of internet domain names. Respondent seeks to register a term, "Booking.com," that consists of a generic term, "booking" (known as the second-level domain) plus ".com" (known as the top-level domain). The question at issue here is whether a term that takes the form "generic.com" is generic in the ordinary course. In my view, appending ".com" to a generic term ordinarily yields no meaning beyond that of its constituent parts. Because the term "Booking.com" is just such an ordinary "generic.com" term, in my view, it is not eligible for trademark registration.

[41] Like the corporate designations at issue in *Goodyear*, a top-level domain such as ".com" has no capacity to identify and distinguish the source of goods or services. It is merely a necessary component of any web address. See 1 McCarthy § 7:17.50. When combined with the generic name of a class of goods or services, ".com" conveys only that the owner operates a website related to such items. Just as "Wine Company" expresses the generic concept of a company that deals in wine, "wine.com" connotes only a website that does the same. The same is true of "Booking.com." The combination of "booking" and ".com" does not serve to "identify a particular characteristic or quality of some thing; it *connotes the basic nature of that thing*"—the hallmark of a generic term. *Blinded Veterans Assn. v. Blinded Am. Veterans Foundation*, 872 F.2d 1035, 1039 (CADC 1989) (Ginsburg, J. for the court) (emphasis added; internal quotation marks omitted).

[42] When a website uses an inherently distinctive second-level domain, it is obvious that adding ".com" merely denotes a website associated with that term. Any reasonably well-informed consumer would understand that "post-it.com" is the website associated with Post-its. See *Minnesota Min. & Mfg. Co. v. Taylor*, 21 F.Supp.2d 1003, 1005 (Minn. 1998). Likewise, "plannedparenthood.com" is obviously just the website of Planned Parenthood. See *Planned Parenthood Federation of Am., Inc. v. Bucci*, 1997 WL 133313, *8 (SDNY, Mar. 24, 1997). Recognizing this feature of domain names, courts generally ignore the top-level domain when analyzing likelihood of confusion. See *Brookfield Communications, Inc. v. West Coast Entertainment Corp.*, 174 F.3d 1036, 1055 (CA9 1999).

[43] Generic second-level domains are no different. The meaning conveyed by "Booking.com" is no more and no less than a website associated with its generic second-level domain, "booking." This will ordinarily be true of any generic term plus ".com" combination. The term as a whole is just as generic as its constituent parts. See 1 McCarthy § 7:17.50; 2 *id.*, § 12:39.50.

[44] There may be exceptions to this rule in rare cases where the top-level domain interacts with the generic second-level domain in such a way as to produce meaning distinct from that of the terms taken individually. See *ante,* at ––, n. 4. Likewise, the principles discussed above may apply differently to the newly expanded universe of top-level domains, such as ".guru," ".club," or ".vip," which may "conve[y] information concerning a feature, quality, or characteristic" of the website at issue. *In re North Carolina Lottery*, 866 F.3d at 1367; see also Brief for International Trademark Association as *Amicus Curiae* 10–11; TMEP § 1209.03(m). These scenarios are not presented here, as "Booking.com" conveys only a website associated with booking.

C

[45] The majority believes that *Goodyear* is inapposite because of the nature of the domain name system. Because only one entity can hold the contractual rights to a particular domain name at a time, it contends, consumers may infer that a "generic.com" domain name refers to some specific entity. *Ante,* at ––.

[46] That fact does not distinguish *Goodyear*. A generic term may suggest that it is associated with a specific entity. That does not render it nongeneric. For example, "Wine, Inc." implies the existence of a specific legal entity incorporated under the laws of some State. Likewise, consumers may perceive "The Wine Company" to refer to some specific company rather than a genus of companies. But the addition of the definite article "the" obviously does not transform the generic nature of that term. See *In re The Computer Store, Inc.*, 211 U.S.P.Q. 72, 74–75 (TTAB 1981). True, these terms do not carry the exclusivity of a domain name. But that functional exclusivity does not negate the principle animating *Goodyear*: Terms that merely convey the nature of the producer's business should remain free for all to use. See 128 U.S. at 603.

[47] This case illustrates the difficulties inherent in the majority's fact-specific approach. The lower courts determined (as the majority highlights), that consumers do not use the term "Booking.com" to refer to the class of hotel reservation websites in ordinary speech. 915 F. 3d 171, 181–183 (CA4 2019); *ante,* at ––. True, few would call Travelocity a "Booking.com." *Ibid.* But literal use is not dispositive. See 915 F. 3d, at 182; *H. Marvin Ginn Corp. v. International Assn. of Fire Chiefs, Inc.*, 782 F.2d 987, 989–990 (CA Fed. 1986). Consumers do not use the term "Wine, Incs." to refer to purveyors of wine. Still, the term "Wine, Inc." is generic because it signifies only a company incorporated for that purpose. See *Goodyear*, 128 U.S. at 602–603. Similarly, "Booking, Inc." may not be trademarked because it signifies only a booking company. The result should be no different for "Booking.com," which signifies only a booking website.

[48] More than that, many of the facts that the Court supposes may distinguish some "generic.com" marks as descriptive and some as generic are unlikely to vary from case to case. There will never be evidence that consumers literally refer to the relevant class of online merchants as "generic.coms." Nor are "generic.com" terms likely to appear in dictionaries. And the key fact that, in the majority's view, distinguishes this case from *Goodyear*—that only one entity can own the rights to a particular domain name at a time—is present in every "generic.com" case. See *ante*, at ––.

[49] What, then, stands in the way of automatic trademark eligibility for every "generic.com" domain? Much of the time, that determination will turn primarily on survey evidence, just as it did in this case. See 915 F. 3d, at 183–184.

[50] However, survey evidence has limited probative value in this context. Consumer surveys often test whether consumers associate a term with a single source. See 2 McCarthy § 12:14–12:16 (describing types of consumer surveys). But it is possible for a generic term to achieve such an association—either because that producer has enjoyed a period of exclusivity in the marketplace, *e.g., Kellogg Co. v. National Biscuit Co.*, 305 U.S. 111, 118–119 (1938), or because it has invested money and effort in securing the

59

public's identification, *e.g.*, *Abercrombie*, 537 F.2d at 9. Evidence of such an association, no matter how strong, does not negate the generic nature of the term. *Ibid.* For that reason, some courts and the TTAB have concluded that survey evidence is generally of little value in separating generic from descriptive terms. See *Schwan's IP, LLC* v. *Kraft Pizza Co.*, 460 F.3d 971, 975–976 (CA8 2006); *Hunt Masters, Inc. v. Landry's Seafood Restaurant, Inc.*, 240 F.3d 251, 254–255 (CA4 2001); *A. J. Canfield Co. v. Honickman*, 808 F.2d 291, 301–303 (CA3 1986); *Miller Brewing Co. v. Jos. Schlitz Brewing Co.*, 605 F.2d 990, 995 (CA7 1979); *In re Hikari Sales USA, Inc.*, 2019 WL 1453259, *13 (TTAB 2019). Although this is the minority viewpoint, see 2 McCarthy § 12:17.25, I nonetheless find it to be the more persuasive one.

[51] Consider the survey evidence that respondent introduced below. Respondent's survey showed that 74.8% of participants thought that "Booking.com" is a brand name, whereas 23.8% believed it was a generic name. At the same time, 33% believed that "Washingmachine.com"—which does not correspond to any company—is a brand, and 60.8% thought it was generic.

[52] What could possibly account for that difference? "Booking.com" is not *inherently* more descriptive than "Washingmachine.com" or any other "generic.com." The survey participants who identified "Booking.com" as a brand likely did so because they had heard of it, through advertising or otherwise. If someone were to start a company called "Washingmachine.com," it could likely secure a similar level of consumer identification by investing heavily in advertising. Would that somehow transform the nature of the term itself? Surely not. This hypothetical shows that respondent's survey tested consumers' association of "Booking.com" with a particular company, not anything about the term itself. But such association does not establish that a term is nongeneric. See *Kellogg*, 305 U.S. at 118–119; *Abercrombie*, 537 F.2d at 9.

[53] Under the majority's approach, a "generic.com" mark's eligibility for trademark protection turns primarily on survey data, which, as I have explained, may be an unreliable indicator of genericness. As the leading treatise writer in this field has observed, this approach "[d]iscard[s] the predictable and clear line rule of the [PTO] and the Federal Circuit" in favor of "a nebulous and unpredictable zone of generic name and top level domain combinations that somehow become protectable marks when accompanied by favorable survey results." 1 McCarthy § 7:17.50. I would heed this criticism. In my view, a term that takes the form "generic.com" is not eligible for federal trademark registration, at least not ordinarily. There being no special circumstance here, I believe that "Booking.com" is a generic term not eligible for federal registration as a trademark.

II

[54] In addition to the doctrinal concerns discussed above, granting trademark protection to "generic.com" marks threatens serious anticompetitive consequences in the online marketplace.

[55] The owners of short, generic domain names enjoy all the advantages of doing business under a generic name. These advantages exist irrespective of the trademark laws. Generic names are easy to remember. Because they immediately convey the nature of the business, the owner needs to expend less effort and expense educating consumers. See Meystedt, What Is My URL Worth? Placing a Value on Premium Domain Names, 19 Valuation Strategies 10, 12 (2015) (Meystedt) (noting "ability to advertise a single URL and convey exactly what business a company operates"); cf. Folsom & Teply, Trademarked Generic Words, 89 Yale L. J. 1323, 1337–1338 (1980) (Folsom & Teply) (noting " 'free advertising' effect"). And a generic business name may create the impression that it is the most authoritative and trustworthy source of the particular good or service. See Meystedt 12 (noting that generic domain names inspire "[i]nstant trust and credibility" and "[a]uthority status in an industry"); cf. Folsom & Teply 1337, n. 79 (noting that consumers may believe that "no other product is the 'real thing' "). These advantages make it harder for distinctively named businesses to compete.

[56] Owners of generic domain names enjoy additional competitive advantages unique to the internet—again, regardless of trademark protection. Most importantly, domain name ownership confers automatic exclusivity. Multiple brick-and-mortar companies could style themselves "The Wine Company," but there can be only one "wine.com." And unlike the trademark system, that exclusivity is world-wide.

[57] Generic domains are also easier for consumers to find. A consumer who wants to buy wine online may perform a keyword search and be directed to "wine.com." Or he may simply type "wine.com" into his browser's address bar, expecting to find a website selling wine. See Meystedt 12 (noting "ability to rank higher on search engines" and "ability to use existing type-in traffic to generate additional sales"); see also 915 F. 3d, at 189 (Wynn, J., concurring in part and dissenting in part). The owner of a generic domain name enjoys these benefits not because of the quality of her products or the goodwill of her business, but because she was fortunate (or savvy) enough to be the first to appropriate a particularly valuable piece of online real estate.

[58] Granting trademark protection to "generic.com" marks confers additional competitive benefits on their owners by allowing them to exclude others from using *similar* domain names. Federal registration would allow respondent to threaten trademark lawsuits against competitors using domains such as "Bookings.com," "eBooking.com," "Booker.com," or "Bookit.com." Respondent says that it would not do so. See Tr. of Oral Arg. 55–56. But other firms may prove less restrained.

[59] Indeed, why would a firm want to register its domain name as a trademark unless it wished to extend its area of exclusivity beyond the domain name itself? The domain name system, after all, already ensures that competitors cannot appropriate a business's actual domain name. And unfair-competition law will often separately protect businesses from passing off and false advertising. See *Genesee Brewing Co. v. Stroh Brewing Co.*, 124 F.3d 137, 149 (CA2 1997); 2 McCarthy § 12:2.

[60] Under the majority's reasoning, many businesses could obtain a trademark by adding ".com" to the generic name of their product (*e.g.*, pizza.com, flowers.com, and so forth). As the internet grows larger, as more and more firms use it to sell their products, the risk of anticompetitive consequences grows. Those consequences can nudge the economy in an anticompetitive direction. At the extreme, that direction points towards one firm per product, the opposite of the competitive multifirm marketplace that our basic economic laws seek to achieve.

[61] Not to worry, the Court responds, infringement doctrines such as likelihood of confusion and fair use will restrict the scope of protection afforded to "generic.com" marks. *Ante,* at -- – --. This response will be cold comfort to competitors of "generic.com" brands. Owners of such marks may seek to extend the boundaries of their marks through litigation, and may, at times succeed. See, *e.g., Advertise.com v. AOL, LLC*, 2010 WL 11507594 (CD Cal.) (owner of "Advertising.com" obtained preliminary injunction against competitor's use of "Advertise.com"), vacated in part, 616 F.3d 974 (CA9 2010). Even if ultimately unsuccessful, the threat of costly litigation will no doubt chill others from using variants on the registered mark and privilege established firms over new entrants to the market. See Brief for Electronic Frontier Foundation as *Amicus Curiae* 19–20.

* * *

[62] In sum, the term "Booking.com" refers to an internet booking service, which is the generic product that respondent and its competitors sell. No more and no less. The same is true of "generic.com" terms more generally. By making such terms eligible for trademark protection, I fear that today's decision will lead to a proliferation of "generic.com" marks, granting their owners a monopoly over a zone of useful, easy-to-remember domains. This result would tend to inhibit, rather than to promote, free competition in online commerce. I respectfully dissent.

Snyder's Lance, Inc. v. Frito-Lay North America, Inc.
542 F.Supp.3d 371, 2021 WL 2322931 (W.D.N.C. June 7, 2021)

Kenneth D. Bell, United States District Judge

[1] In this case the Parties zealously dispute whether Plaintiffs' asserted trademark PRETZEL CRISPS is entitled to federal trademark registration. Indeed, this quarrel between two giants of the snack food industry is now more than a decade old and includes two precedential decisions of the Trademark Trial and Appeal Board ("TTAB" or "Board") and decisions from both the Federal Circuit and Fourth Circuit Courts of Appeals. By this Final Order and Judgment, after a full *de novo* review of the entire record before the TTAB and the additional evidence offered in this action, the Court now resolves the merits of Defendant Frito-Lay North America, Inc.'s ("Frito-Lay") challenge to the mark.

[2] For the reasons discussed below, the Court will 1) deny the Parties' cross-motions for summary judgment; 2) affirm the TTAB's cancellation of the registration of the mark PRETZEL CRISPS for pretzel crackers on the Supplemental Register because the mark is generic; and 3) affirm the TTAB's denial of Plaintiff Princeton-Vanguard, LLC's ("Princeton-Vanguard")[1] application to register PRETZEL CRISPS on the Principal Register for the same reason.[2]

I. LEGAL STANDARDS, RULING ON SUMMARY JUDGMENT MOTIONS AND STIPULATION WAIVING TRIAL

[3] The fundamental threshold issue in this action is whether Plaintiffs' mark PRETZEL CRISPS is generic and therefore not eligible for trademark protection. Whether an asserted mark is generic is a question of fact. . . .

[4] In reviewing the Parties' extensive supporting, opposition and reply briefs (together with thousands of pages of exhibits and the underlying record at the TTAB), it is obvious that the issue of genericness is genuinely disputed such that entry of summary judgment for any party would be inappropriate. . . .

[5] Upon the denial of summary judgment, this matter would normally proceed to a bench trial on the merits. However, as they did before the TTAB, the Parties have waived their right to present live testimony at trial and stipulated that the Court may fully consider and rule on all the issues presented based on the written record. The Court has agreed to do so, and this Order and Judgment thus reflects the Court's final determination of the facts and resulting ruling and judgment on the merits.

---

[1] Princeton Vanguard's co-Plaintiff is Snyder's-Lance, Inc. ("Snyder's-Lance"), which is its parent company.

[2] Having determined that the mark is generic, the Court need not and does not decide the further issue of whether if the mark were found to be descriptive it has acquired distinctiveness (secondary meaning) with respect to its association with the Plaintiffs.

[6] While the Parties agree that the Court may rule on the merits based on the existing record without hearing further evidence at trial, the Parties sharply disagree on the Court's standard of review of the TTAB's decision and the applicable burden of proof. . . .

[7] {W}hile the Court will consider all the evidence *de novo*, it will also consider the TTAB's findings in weighing the evidentiary value that will be afforded the new evidence presented by the Parties. . . .

[8] The burden of proof is more easily addressed. In the Federal Circuit decision in this matter, the court expressly held that Frito-Lay bears the burden to prove genericness by a preponderance of the evidence. *Princeton Vanguard*, 786 F.3d at 965, n.2. . . . This unambiguous ruling is binding on this Court, *see Snyder's-Lance*, 991 F.3d at 522, as Frito-Lay acknowledged at oral argument. Therefore, Frito-Lay must prove that PRETZEL CRISPS is generic by a preponderance of the evidence.

II. FACTS AND PROCEDURAL HISTORY

[9] The pretzel, a simple mixture of water, flour and salt, is a well-known snack food with a long and colorful history dating back to the Middle Ages, when Catholic priests rewarded young children who learned their prayers with soft strips of baked bread dough folded to resemble arms crossed in prayer.[6] German immigrants in the 1700's brought their "bretzels" (from the Old German "brezitella" which is derived from the Latin for "arm" (*bracchiatus*)) to the United States and by 1861 a commercial pretzel bakery was making "hard" pretzels – a brittle, glazed and salted cracker-like version of the original soft pretzel – that could be shipped and stored in airtight containers. Over the ensuing years, pretzels became increasingly popular and have been baked and sold as snacks in many sizes, forms and names, including sticks, thins, crackers, chips, rods, rounds and, as at issue here, crisps. Over $500 million worth of pretzels are now sold annually in the United States, with the average American consuming about two pounds of pretzels a year. (https://positivelypa.com/pretzel-facts/ (accessed May 14, 2021)).

[10] The use of the term "pretzel crisps" dates from, at the latest, the late 1990's. For example, in April 1998, an article in *Men's Health* suggested a recipe for a low-calorie snack mix consisting of "flat pretzel crisps and crunchy pretzel sticks." In 1999, *The San Francisco Chronicle* included "Honey-mustard pretzel crisps" on its list of "Hot" grocery items. In 2001, the *Charleston Gazette* recommended serving a dip recipe "at room temperature with pretzel crisps or crackers."

[11] Princeton-Vanguard developed their pretzel snack product in 2004. Warren and Sara Wilson, experienced entrepreneurs who had launched several successful snack food brands, created a snack food product that took the middle slice of a pretzel and produced it in a flat, cracker form. Princeton-Vanguard named the product PRETZEL CRISPS and began marketing and selling their pretzels in the "deli snacks" section of the grocery stores and food markets. PRETZEL CRISPS have been a major commercial success and are a market leader among pretzel products, having enjoyed sales growth almost every year since the brand's launch.

[12] Since 2004, Plaintiffs have sold more than $1.25 billion dollars of Pretzel Crips to wholesalers and retailers (which translates into more than $2.5 billion in retail revenue). These sales are driven by an extensive marketing and advertising campaign. Snyder's-Lance has spent more than $50 million on advertising, marketing, and promoting the PRETZEL CRISPS brand through traditional marketing and advertising channels, as well as through social media, in-store demonstrations, and "seeding" events and

---

[6] In medieval Europe, monks gave away pretzels as religious symbols to the poor to provide spiritual as well as literal sustenance. Thus, the pretzel became a sign of fulfillment, good fortune and prosperity. In 1529, pretzel bakers saved Vienna from ransacking by Ottomon Turks when they heard the invaders tunneling under the city during their early morning work and alerted the city leadership (thereby earning their own coat of arms which includes angry lions holding a pretzel). By the 17th Century, the interlocking loops of the pretzel had also come to symbolize undying love when couples in Switzerland began eating a pretzel in their wedding ceremonies to seal the bond of matrimony, which is reputed to be the origin of the phrase "tying the knot." *See* foodandwine.com/lifestyle/religious-history-pretzels (Updated April 17, 2019, accessed May 5, 2021); The Pretzel: A Twisted History (History. com Jan. 30, 2020).

contests. For example, in 2016 and 2017, Snyder's-Lance estimates it had 225 million consumer impressions from its print and online advertising of PRETZEL CRISPS, and its field marketing teams travelled the country to promote PRETZEL CRISPS, distributing some 600,000 product samples at various events.[8]

{In 2005, Princeton Vanguard obtained a registration for PRETZEL CRISPS on the Supplemental Register as a descriptive mark that had not yet developed acquired distinctiveness. In late 2009, Princeton Vanguard filed to register PRETZEL CRISPS for "pretzel crackers" on the Principal Register. Frito-Lay opposed the registration on the grounds that the mark was generic for pretzel crackers and in the alternative that even if the mark was descriptive rather than generic, it lacked acquired distinctiveness. In 2014, the Trademark Trial and Appeal Board (TTAB) ruled that the mark was generic. Princeton-Vanguard appealed that ruling to the Federal Circuit, which remanded the case back to the TTAB for application of the correct legal test. In 2017, the TTAB again ruled that the mark was generic. Princeton-Vanguard then appealed this ruling to the W.D.N.C. In 2021, after a skirmish before the Fourth Circuit involving whether the W.D.N.C. had subject matter jurisdiction over a case that had previously been appealed directly to the Federal Circuit, the Fourth Circuit remanded the case back to the W.D.N.C.}

III. DISCUSSION

[13] Trademark law protects the goodwill represented by particular marks and serves the twin objectives of preventing consumer confusion between products and the sources of those products, on the one hand, and protecting the "linguistic commons" by preventing exclusive use of terms that represent their common meaning, on the other. *Booking.com B.V.*, 915 F.3d at 175 (citing *OBX-Stock, Inc. v. Bicast, Inc.*, 558 F.3d 334, 339–40 (4th Cir. 2009)). In order to be protectable, marks must be "distinctive." To determine whether a proposed mark is protectable, courts ascertain the strength of the mark by placing it into one of four categories of distinctiveness, in ascending order: (1) generic, (2) descriptive, (3) suggestive, or (4) arbitrary or fanciful. . . .

[14] Generic terms do not contain source-identifying significance—they do not distinguish the particular product or service from other products or services on the market. Accordingly, generic terms can never obtain trademark protection, as trademarking a generic term effectively grants the owner a monopoly over a common term. Registration must be refused if a mark "is the generic name of any of the goods or services for which registration is sought." McCarthy § 12:57. If protection were allowed, a competitor could not describe his goods or services as what they are. *Booking.com B.V.*, 915 F.3d at 177 (citing *CES Publ'g Corp. v. St. Regis Publ'ns, Inc.*, 531 F.2d 11, 13 (2d Cir. 1975)). Once a term is deemed generic, it cannot subsequently become non-generic. *Id.* at 180.

[15] Especially significant here, the law forbids trademarking generic terms, even when a putative mark holder engages in successful efforts to establish consumer recognition of an otherwise generic term. *Id.* at 193-94. "[N]o matter how much money and effort the user of a generic term has poured into promoting the sale of its merchandise and what success it has achieved in securing public identification, it cannot deprive competing manufacturers of the product of the right to call an article by its name." *Abercrombie & Fitch Co. v. Hunting World, Inc.*, 537 F.2d 4, 9 (2d Cir. 1976).[9] Therefore, even advertising, repeated use, and consumer association will not warrant affording trademark protection to a generic term. *See Am. Online, Inc. v. AT&T Corp.*, 243 F.3d 812, 821 (4th Cir. 2001) ("[T]he repeated use of

---

[8] In 2018, Campbell's Soup Co. bought Snyder's-Lance, combining the company with Campbell's existing Pepperidge Farm business and other brands to create Campbell Snacks, an even larger company unit with additional marketing reach and resources.

[9] The Supreme Court recently confirmed this principle in *United States Pat. & Trademark Off. v. Booking.com B. V.*, 140 S. Ct. 2298, 2306–07 (2020), emphasizing that it "presupposes that a generic term is at issue." *Id.* In other words, the determination of whether a mark is generic must be made separately and independently of the mark's commercial success and association with a particular company that results from extensive advertising and marketing (which would, of course, still be relevant to a determination of whether a descriptive mark had acquired secondary meaning).

ordinary words . . . cannot give [a single company] a proprietary right over those words, even if an association develops between the words and [that company].”). In sum, courts have long sought to foreclose companies from monopolizing common terms, holding that no single competitor has the right to “corner the market” on ordinary words and phrases. *See Booking.com B.V.*, 915 F.3d at 193.

[16] According to the test adopted long ago by the Supreme Court in *Kellogg Co. v. Nat’l Biscuit Co.*, a plaintiff seeking to establish a valid trademark as compared to a generic mark “must show that the primary significance of the term in the minds of the consuming public is not the product but the producer.” 305 U.S. 111, 118 (1938). A mark is not generic simply because it plays some role in denoting to the public what the product or service is; rather, a mark may serve a dual function—that of identifying a product [or service] while at the same time indicating its source. Thus, “the critical issue in genericness cases is whether members of the relevant public primarily use or understand the term sought to be protected to refer to the genus of goods or services in question.” *Princeton Vanguard*, 786 F.3d at 965 (citing, *H. Marvin Ginn Corp. v. Int’l Ass’n of Fire Chiefs, Inc.*, 782 F.2d 987, 989-90 (Fed. Cir. 1986)). In other words, would the mark be perceived by the purchasing public as merely a common name for the goods rather than a mark identifying the good’s source? *Id.* at 766.

[17] According to the Federal Circuit,[10] determining a mark’s genericness requires “a two-step inquiry: First, what is the genus (or class) of goods or services at issue? Second, is the term sought to be registered or retained on the register understood by the relevant public primarily to refer to that genus of goods or services?” *Id.* at 990. The Parties do not dispute either the genus of goods or the relevant public. The genus of goods at issue is “pretzel crackers” and the relevant public are “ordinary consumers who purchase and eat pretzel crackers.” *See Princeton-Vanguard*, 786 F.3d at 965.

[18] *Booking.com*, the most recent Supreme Court opinion on the question of whether a trademark is generic, provides the Court clear guidance on the process for making the factual finding on how the relevant public perceives the mark. Evidence of the public’s understanding of the mark as either a common name or a mark identifying the good’s source may be obtained from dictionaries; usage by the mark holder, consumers and others; consumer surveys;[11] publications and any other source of evidence bearing on how consumers perceive a term’s meaning. *See Booking.com B. V.*, 140 S. Ct. at 2306–07; *Princeton Vanguard*, 786 F.3d at 965. Also, the public’s primary understanding of a mark “is derived from it as a whole, not from its elements separated and considered in detail;” therefore, “it should be considered in its entirety.” *Estate of P.D. Beckwith, Inc. v. Comm’r of Patents*, 252 U.S. 538, 545–46 (1920). Although “a mark must be considered as a whole,” this “does not preclude courts from considering the meaning of individual words in determining the meaning of the entire mark.” *Hunt Masters, Inc. v. Landry’s Seafood Rest., Inc.*, 240 F.3d 251, 254 (4th Cir. 2001).

[19] Further, for an asserted trademark such as PRETZEL CRISPS that is a “compound of generic elements” (“pretzel” and “crisps”),[12] the mark “is generic if the combination yields no additional meaning

---

[10] The Fourth Circuit follows a functionally similar three-step test: (1) identify the class of product or service to which use of the mark is relevant; (2) identify the relevant consuming public; and (3) determine whether the primary significance of the mark to the relevant public is as an indication of the nature of the class of the product or services to which the mark relates, which suggests that it is generic, or an indication of the source or brand, which suggests that it is not generic. *Booking.com B.V.*, 915 F.3d at 180.

[11] With respect to consumer surveys, the Supreme Court has specifically cautioned: “surveys can be helpful evidence of consumer perception but require care in their design and interpretation. See Brief for Trademark Scholars as Amici Curiae 18–20 (urging that survey respondents may conflate the fact that domain names are exclusive with a conclusion that a given “generic.com” term has achieved secondary meaning) . . . . [McCarthy], § 12:49 (“Determining the distinction between generic and trademark usage of a word . . . when there are no other sellers of [the good or service] is one of the most difficult areas of trademark law.”).” *Booking.com B. V.*, 140 S. Ct. at 2307.

[12] At oral argument, Plaintiffs’ counsel agreed that both “pretzels” and “crisps” are generic terms.

to consumers capable of distinguishing the goods or services." *Booking.com B. V.*, 140 S. Ct. at 2306. (emphasis in original). This principle is not inconsistent with consideration of a mark in its entirety. "An inquiry into the public's understanding of a mark requires consideration of the mark as a whole. Even if each of the constituent words in a combination mark is generic, the combination is not generic unless the entire formulation does not add any meaning to the otherwise generic mark." *In re Steelbuilding.com*, 415 F.3d 1293, 1297 (Fed. Cir. 2005).

[20] To find if the combination of generic terms in an asserted trademark has "*additional*" meaning to consumers, the Court logically must first determine what meaning the generic elements would have to the relevant public. See *Booking.com*, 915 F.3d at 184-85 ("when confronted with a compound term like PRETZEL CRISPS, courts may consider as a first step the meaning of each of the term's component marks ..."). The TTAB analyzed the constituent terms "PRETZEL" and "CRISPS" at length in its two decisions. *See* TTAB Decision 2, 124 U.S.P.Q.2d at 1201-04.

[21] The Board evaluated the "meaning of each to the consuming public as indicated by dictionary definitions and other competent sources." *Id.* at 1188. Princeton-Vanguard submitted a definition of "pretzel" as "[a] glazed brittle biscuit that is salted on the outside and usually baked in the form of a loose knot or a stick." *Id.* Warren Wilson, Princeton-Vanguard's Manager and co-founder, defined the "PRETZEL CRISPS" product as being a form of pretzel: "PRETZEL CRISPS crackers possess a unique shape, based on removing the middle slice from a traditional pretzel design." *Id.* Finally, Defendant's original identification of goods for Application Serial No. 78405596, as filed on April 21, 2004, stated simply "pretzels." After receiving an office action refusing its applied-for mark as generic, Defendant submitted an amendment to the identification re-characterizing the goods as "pretzel crackers." The Trademark Rules state that an "applicant may amend the application to clarify or limit, but not to broaden, the identification of goods and/or services ..." Trademark Rule 2.71; 37 CFR § 2.71. Because the amendment to its identification was found to be acceptable, Princeton-Vanguard's identified "pretzel crackers" is by rule a subcategory of the broader product category "pretzel."

[22] As to the term "CRISPS," the Parties submitted to the Board dictionary definitions of the term as meaning, in relevant part, "(noun) Something crisp or brittle;" and "(noun) Something crisp or easily crumpled." Frito-Lay's witness Pam Forbus testified that the "generic term 'crisp' or 'crisps'" had been used by Frito-Lay and others to identify their snack food items "since at least as early as 1959." Such products include Munchos potato crisps, Baked Lay's and Baked Ruffles potato crisps, Stacy's soy crisps, TRUENORTH nut crisps and FLAT EARTH fruit crisps and veggie crisps. *Id.* Moreover, Princeton-Vanguard previously used the term "CRISPS" in the nutrition facts labels displayed on its "PRETZEL CRISPS" product, referring to the number of "crisps" in a serving size. Also, in responding to requests for admission, Princeton-Vanguard admitted that "'crisps' can be used as a term for the product that is the subject of the Application." *Id.* Finally, the definition of the word "cracker," in pertinent part, is "a dry thin crispy baked bread product that may be leavened or unleavened." "Cracker," Merriam-Webster.com; https://www.merriamwebster.com/dictionary/cracker. (Accessed 11 May. 2021). "Crisps" may therefore also be "crackers."

[23] Accordingly, based on the separate meanings of the two words, the term "pretzel" "crisps" would be perceived by a consumer to refer to a pretzel in the form of a crisp or cracker (or, alternatively, a cracker or crisp that tastes like a pretzel). So, the question is what additional meaning can consumers find in the combination of the two generic words "pretzel" and "crisps" that can serve as an indication that the combined term may refer to a single source? Unlike booking.com (the combined mark identifies a specific company at that internet address) and American Airlines (consumers understand that there are numerous separately named airlines in the United States and don't refer to them collectively as "American Airlines"), there is no additional meaning that results from the combination of the generic terms that make up PRETZEL CRISPS in the minds of consumers. "Pretzel" "crisps" are pretzels in the shape or form of a cracker and "pretzel crisps," viewed together, would be perceived as the same thing. *See Convenient Food Mart, Inc. v. 6-Twelve Convenient Mart, Inc.*, 690 F. Supp. 1457, 1464 (D. Md. 1988), *aff'd*, 870 F.2d 654 (4th Cir. 1989) (acknowledging that mark must be considered as a whole, but also finding "arrangement of the words 'Convenient Food Mart' obvious and meaning nothing more than a

convenient food mart").[14] In sum, the Court finds that the combined term PRETZEL CRISPS adds no additional meaning to consumers that suggests the mark is not primarily a generic name.

[24] The analysis of whether a combination of generic terms adds any meaning to the separate meaning of the generic words that make up the mark can also be considered from another angle, which is whether the disputed combined term can satisfy the basic elements of a "descriptive" term, which is the trademark category just beyond generic terms (and how Plaintiffs argue PRETZEL CRIPS should be categorized). "Descriptive" terms "immediately convey information concerning a feature, quality, or characteristic" of the producer's goods or services, not simply the good or service itself. *See In re North Carolina Lottery*, 866 F.3d 1363, 1367 (Fed. Cir. 2017) However, PRETZEL CRISPS does not convey any "feature, quality or characteristic" of "pretzel crackers" (the agreed genus of goods).[15] Instead, it is simply another name for the goods being sold. Accordingly, the failure of the combined term to convey any additional meaning that allows it to function as a "descriptive" term further supports a finding that the combined term is merely "a common name for the goods" which is appropriately placed in the lower category of generic goods.

[25] Although the Court concludes that the combination of the generic elements "pretzel" and "crisps" does not create any additional meaning for consumers from which they can distinguish Plaintiffs' product and thus indicates that PRETZEL CRISPS is generic, the Court does not rest its finding of genericness on that finding. Rather, after considering *de novo* all the evidence offered by the Parties which bears on consumers' perception of the mark, the Court finds that, on balance, a preponderance of the evidence supports the conclusion that the mark, considered only in its entirety, is generic.

[26] Before reviewing the evidence in detail, the Court notes two points relevant to its overall analysis. First, exercising its discretion, the Court views the more recent purported evidence of consumer perception (from both sides) as less probative than evidence closer to Princeton-Vanguard's registration applications and Frito-Lay's opposition. As discussed above, the law does not permit a generic mark to evolve into a descriptive mark or other type of non-generic mark based on the association of the product with a particular company (driven by the mark holder's marketing success). And, Plaintiffs themselves acknowledge that it "accords with [ ] common-sense reasoning that, as more consumers are exposed to PRETZEL CRISPS crackers' packaging prominently displaying the PRETZEL CRISPS mark and encounter the mark in advertisements and on social media, they will naturally come to view it as [a] brand name..." So, the farther in time the evidence is from Plaintiffs' trademark applications, the more likely it is that the cumulative effect of Plaintiffs' sales efforts will limit the ability of the evidence to establish consumer perceptions of genericness as distinguished from secondary meaning resulting from Plaintiffs' successful marketing.

[27] This is particularly true for Plaintiffs' "social media" evidence. In 2004, when the first trademark application was filed, "social media" likely referred to nothing more than the fact that journalists could often be found at a bar. Facebook was only founded the same year, with Twitter (2006), Instagram (2010) and Tik-Tok (2016) following and then later exploding in popularity. A tweet or Facebook or Instagram post in 2018, 14 years after Princeton-Vanguard's initial trademark application and 8 years after Frito-Lay's opposition, provides at best limited guidance about consumer perception

---

[14] When asked at oral argument to identify any additional meaning or source identification that the combined term adds to its generic components, Plaintiffs' counsel simply reiterated their position that the Court should not consider the meaning of the component terms in any way (notwithstanding the clear recent direction from the Supreme Court in *Boooking.com*).

[15] As with "additional meaning," when asked at oral argument why "pretzel crisps" is a descriptive term, Plaintiffs' counsel did not identify any "feature, quality or characteristic" of the goods that is reflected in the mark.

when the mark was first registered. Accordingly, the Court finds that more recent evidence has less probative value on the question of genericness.[16]

[28] Second, in making its factual determination of genericness, the Court has considered not just the "quantity" of evidence (the number of times the mark is allegedly used in some "trademark" sense) but also the "quality" of the evidence presented. In other words, the Court finds that not all bare mentions of the mark are equal. For example, many (indeed most) of the cited references to PRETZEL CRISPS appear in otherwise irrelevant financial documents or simply reflect the fact that Plaintiffs are marketing and selling the product (i.e., term appearing in the reporting of results for Snyder's-Lance's second quarter of 2013, and article noting that "media sponsors include . . . Startup Digest, Pretzel Crisps, Modern Oats,"), rather than more direct evidence of *consumer* perceptions (i.e., an article suggesting that a baked potato dip be served with "your favorite potato chips or pretzel crisps"). Thus, the Court has, as it must, not only "counted" the evidence but "weighed" it to reach the final conclusion that PRETZEL CRISPS is, on balance,[19] a generic term for the goods sold by Plaintiffs.

[29] The Court evaluates each type of supporting evidence offered by the Parties as follows:

Dictionaries

[30] As noted above, the Court may look to the dictionary for evidence of common usage to support a finding of genericness. *See* McCarthy, § 11:51 While the Parties have provided definitions of the words "pretzel" and "crisps" as discussed above, it appears that there are no dictionary definitions of the mark as a whole. Plaintiffs contend that the absence of dictionary definitions of "pretzel crisps" is "powerful evidence that the mark is not generic." The Court disagrees. First, the authority offered by Plaintiffs in support of their position, *JFJ Toys, Inc. v. Sears Holdings Corp.*, 237 F. Supp. 3d 311, 332–33 (D. Md. 2017),[20] notes that "[d]ictionary definitions are particularly helpful where a composite mark which was 'invented' by its holder is listed in the dictionary as the accepted designator for a unique product," citing *Nat'l Fed'n of the Blind, Inc. v. Loompanics Enterprises, Inc.*, 936 F. Supp. 1232, 1248 (D. Md. 1996) (in turn citing *Murphy Door Bed Co. v. Interior Sleep Systems, Inc.*, 874 F.2d 95, 101 (2d Cir. 1989)). Here, although the Court does not find that Princeton-Vanguard invented the PRETZEL CRISPS name as discussed above, Plaintiffs contend they did. Thus, by their own version of the facts, the absence of a dictionary definition would appear to cut against rather than support their arguments.

[31] More significant to the Court, while there is no dictionary definition of "pretzel crisps," there is also no dictionary definition of "pretzel crackers," "pretzel chips," or "pretzel thins," all of which Plaintiffs agree are generic terms. And, similarly, a reasonable search by the Court finds no dictionary definition of other non-pretzel generic snack food names such as "pita chips." In other words, names of particular food products, whether brand specific or generic, are unlikely to be in the dictionary, presumably because dictionary editors do not find the term noteworthy enough to warrant an entry of any type. *See* TTAB Decision 2, 124 U.S.P.Q.2d at 1193. Therefore, in the specific context of the facts presented here, dictionary definitions are not particularly helpful to either party beyond the meaning of

---

[16] However, more recent evidence would likely be more probative than earlier evidence on the issue of secondary meaning, which the Court does not reach.

[19] Plaintiffs argue that the Court should consider all such mentions (even the same article appearing in different publications) as persuasive relevant evidence because any use of the name as a brand "could . . . have [an] impact on readers' perception." This argument misses the question, which is what are *consumers'* perceptions, not how the materials published by Plaintiffs and others about their sales efforts or sales success in financial related documents might speculatively "impact" such perceptions.

[20] In *JFT Toys*, the Court agreed with the USPTO that a suggestive term, "Stomp Rocket," was not generic, finding that because of the lack of any dictionary reference to a rocket in the definition of "stomp" and no definition at all for "stomp rocket" that "the dictionary is unhelpful to Defendants." *JFJ Toys*, 237 F. Supp. 3d at 333.

the words that make up the mark as discussed above (as part of the question of whether the compound mark adds additional meaning to consumers).

Usage by Plaintiffs

[32] The Parties have also proffered examples of the Plaintiffs' use of the mark for the Court to consider on genericness. While the vast majority of Plaintiffs' uses of the mark refer to PRETZEL CRISPS as a brand, three references from high ranking executives have been cited to the Court as evidence supporting generic use. In 2010, Maureen Phelan, VP of Sales for Snack Factory, told a major potential customer (Starbucks): "I have seen your new line of healthy snack foods in the stores & think Pretzel Crisps would be a great addition. We are the *original pretzel crisp company* about to introduce a new package which is much more appealing to your demographic than our current deli line." (emphasis added). And, in 2009, Snack Factory's Vice President of Marketing Perry Abbenante asked a marketing firm for help coming up with a new name for an "umbrella brand" for the product, explaining that "Pretzel Crisps" consists of "two pretty generic words" and could be vulnerable to a challenge. ("Per our conversation, I was hoping you and PGW braintrust could mull over some creative names we might be able to use as an umbrella brand for Pretzel Crisps. Currently, we do have a copyright on the name Pretzel Crisps, but because it's a two pretty generic words [sic], there could be a challenge to it."). Finally, the founder Mr. Wilson also used the term generically in a published interview, noting, "We have been able to take the middle out of pretzel making the pretzel crisp a thin crunchy cracker-like snack."

[33] While evidence of the mark owner's generic use may be "strong evidence of genericness," McCarthy, § 12.13, there must be "repeated and consistent instances of such usage," *JFJ Toys, Inc. v. Sears Holdings Corp.*, 237 F. Supp. 3d at 331, for that use to have a significant effect. Accordingly, although these statements by Plaintiffs' executives are generally consistent with the other evidence discussed below which supports a finding of genericness and have been considered, the Court does not view these apparently isolated instances as indicative of general usage of the mark generically by Plaintiffs. Therefore, the Court does not find Plaintiffs' use of the mark generically to be "strong evidence" and gives it relatively little weight in the balance of evidence.

Usage by Competitors, Industry Insiders and Others

[34] More significant to the Court than Plaintiffs' limited generic use, the record reflects use of pretzel crisps generically by competitors and food vendors. In 2010, Kraft introduced pretzel crackers under its RITZ MUNCHABLES mark, using "pretzel crisps" as the generic descriptor.[21] The generic nature of this use is evident from the way "pretzel crisps" was set off from Kraft Food's RITZ MUNCHABLES mark in different typeface and color. Princeton-Vanguard complained to Kraft and threatened litigation.

[35] Plainly choosing to avoid a lengthy battle with an aggressive and similarly deep pocketed competitor (a decision which now may seem particularly prescient to Kraft in light of the decade long history of this case), Kraft entered into an Agreement and Mutual Release with Princeton-Vanguard in which Kraft was allowed to continue to use the mark generically for several months[22] but thereafter agreed not to use "pretzel crisps" "as a product descriptor" or a "trademark." Kraft made no concession, admission of liability or acknowledgement that Princeton-Vanguard was entitled to a registration for "pretzel crisps" or of "any fact" (but agreed that Princeton owns a registration on the Supplemental Register, which of course was true at the time).

---

[21] All food items are required to list a "statement of identity" or "generic descriptor" to describe the food. The name established by law or regulation, or in the absence thereof, the common or usual name of the food, if the food has one, should be used as the statement of identity. If there is none, then an appropriate descriptive name, that is not misleading, should be used. Brand names are not considered to be statements of identity and should not be unduly prominent compared to the statement of identity. *See 21 CFR 101.3(b) & (d).*

[22] Kraft's distributors were allowed to continue to distribute and sell the Ritz Munchables pretzel crisps indefinitely so long as they were sold and distributed by Kraft as permitted in the agreement.

[36] Significantly, Kraft was careful to both note Frito-Lay's already pending opposition to Princeton-Vanguard's efforts to obtain a principal registration and include a provision allowing Kraft to resume generic use of the term should a court or trademark office find the term to be generic. Following the settlement, Kraft changed the generic descriptor "pretzel crisps" on its packaging to "pretzel thins" and "pretzel rounds" (two terms that Plaintiffs agree are not used as trademarks), demonstrating that Kraft considers all of these terms to be generic. *See* Doc. No. 33 at 17 ("Kraft subsequently adopted the terms 'pretzel thins' and 'pretzel rounds' to describe its products"; *see also* Opp'n No. 91195552 at A1543 (declaration from Warren Wilson testifying that "pretzel thins" and "pretzel rounds" are "generic descriptors").

[37] Also in 2010, the food delivery company Diet Gourmet offered for sale on its snack menu "Pretzel crisps, grapes, . . . cheese and . . . dipping sauce" in the same generic way that it listed "Baked pita chips, roasted garlic hummus . . ." and "bagel chips." Mr. Wilson sent a letter to the Diet Gourmet food delivery company demanding that the company stop using the term "pretzel crisps" without indicating that the term is a trademarked brand. There is no evidence in the record of a response by Diet Gourmet.

[38] Similarly, in 2011, Pretzels, Inc. used "pretzel crisps" generically in promotional materials for its Trussetts "Crispy Pretzel" snack product (the information sheet for the product referenced the "pretzel crisps market" and the company was listed in a trade show program guide as selling "pretzel crisps."). Again, Princeton-Vanguard complained, and the matter was resolved without litigation when Pretzels, Inc. agreed to revise its promotional materials "notwithstanding the industry's use of the generic term 'pretzel crisps'."

[39] More recently, Plaintiffs have continued to object to other companies' ongoing generic use of the mark (even after the TTAB ruled the mark was generic and ordered the registration cancelled). For example, in 2018 Wish Farms posted a recipe on its website for "Blueberry Pretzel Crisps." The recipe did not feature Plaintiffs' product, and the term "Pretzel Crisps" was used generically to refer to the recipe itself. Claiming that PRETZEL CRISPS was at that time a "registered trademark" (ignoring the TTAB's decision that the registration should be cancelled), Snyder's-Lance demanded that the small company cease using "pretzel crisps" (unless it changed the recipe to include Plaintiffs' product). Wish Farms agreed to change the recipe name but declined to "alter the recipe" to include Plaintiffs' product, noting that "the photos were done with a different product and the quickest way that we could address your concern was to simply change the name."

[40] As another example, in 2017, Plaintiffs sent a cease-and-desist letter to Betty Jane Homemade Candies over the use of the term "Pretzel Crisps" as a generic ingredient in its "Betty's Bites" snack. "Pretzel Crisps" was listed alongside other ingredients including "Caramel," "Milk Chocolate," and "Sea Salt" and was used in the same manner as those other generic terms. In response to the letter, Betty Jane's owner stated that he "assumed [pretzel crisps] was a descriptor term for the type of pretzel item (similar to pretzel rod for example, describing the pretzel product)."

[41] All of these examples show that the third parties involved believed "pretzel crisps" was a commonly understood generic term, without any intent by the third parties to copy or trade on Plaintiffs' purported mark or goodwill. In response, Plaintiffs argue that their successful policing efforts "support the conclusion that others in the industry recognize PRETZEL CRISPS as a brand name." The Court disagrees. In the Court's view, after reviewing the particular circumstances and communications described above, the various agreements not to use "pretzel crisps" do not reflect any "recognition" that PRETZEL CRISPS is a brand name. Rather, the agreements represent the considered practical judgment of the accused companies (which in all cases but one were significantly smaller enterprises) that it wasn't worth the cost to resist Plaintiffs' threats. On the contrary, the Court finds the generic use by these unrelated companies to be a clear indication of public perception that "pretzel crisps" is a name for a type of pretzel snack rather than a brand name. Indeed, Plaintiffs' ability to successfully use its trademark registration (even after the TTAB ruling that it should be cancelled) to deny others the ability to use a common product name only emphasizes the power Plaintiffs have wielded to clear the

70

marketplace of similarly named products and the importance of not allowing generic terms to become registered trademarks.

[42] In contrast to the generic use of the mark by competitors and others who sought to use pretzel crisps to describe a product or snack, the Court does not find Plaintiffs' evidence from a few hand-picked industry insiders, who do millions of dollars a year of business with Plaintiffs, to be significantly probative of consumer perception of genericness (as distinguished from evidence of commercial success and secondary meaning). Defendant submitted declarations from four distributors, testifying that the term is not used generically in the industry. . . .

. . . .

Media References

[43] In the TTAB and this Court, Plaintiffs have offered in total approximately 1800 "media references" from 2004 to 2018 in support of their position that PRETZEL CRISPS is not generic. The Court has separately reviewed every one of these proffered references. For the reasons discussed below, after considering not only the number but also the probative nature and quality of the references (as well as some illustrative current advertisements), the Court finds that, on balance, the cited media references favor a finding that consumers primarily perceive "pretzel crisps" as a term that identifies a common name for the goods rather than a mark identifying the good's source.

[44] The "media reference" evidence comes to the Court as exhibits to the Declaration of Christopher Lauzau, who says that he is a "Senior Legal Research Analyst" employed by Plaintiffs' law firm Debevoise & Plimpton LLP. There is no evidence that Mr. Lauzau has any legal education or particular training or expertise in trademark law (although the Court expects he has received appropriate supervision as a non-attorney staff member of the law firm). And, as a member of Plaintiffs' legal team, he is (and should be in accordance with the rules of professional responsibility) inherently biased in favor of his firm's clients. Accordingly, the Court will consider the contentions of Mr. Lauzau not as settled "facts," as repeatedly portrayed by Plaintiffs, but rather as "attorney" argument as to what the documents (which the Court has independently reviewed in detail) show.

[45] Mr. Lauzau conducted two LexisNexis database searches for the terms "pretzel crisp," "pretzel crisps" and/or "pretzelcrisp." The results included articles from both print publications and Internet blogs. The first search, conducted in April 2012 for the TTAB proceedings, covered the time period from October 2004 to April 2012. Overall, there were 331 articles included in the results. Because the database did not filter out punctuation or short words such as "the" or "of," there were some results that are not applicable to the search, which he removed. He also removed entries that appeared multiple times in the same publication but included in his analysis 26 duplicate articles that appeared in different publications.

[46] Mr. Lauzau reviewed 260 references after this winnowing process. He opines that a total of 216 (83%) "clearly" referred to PRETZEL CRISPS as a brand name of snacks produced by Snack Factory or its licensees, 36 (14%) referred to that phrase "in a way that may have been a generic reference," and 8 results (3%) were unclear (but adds that he believes that "contextual clues suggest that the author was speaking about Snack Factory's PRETZEL CRISPS crackers."). However, his declaration does not reveal how he made the subjective decision to classify the references nor does it even identify which of the references he put in each category.[27]

[47] The second search covered the period from April 21, 2012 to October 23, 2018. There were 1,469 articles included in the results. After eliminating duplicated entries (including duplicated articles that appear in different publications), there were a total of 895 unique articles. Mr. Lauzau claims that

---

[27] With respect to the second search, Mr. Lauzau has at least indicated how he classified the various references but curiously has failed to do so with respect to the first search (even after being criticized for not doing so). The Court finds this lack of transparency to be a significant additional reason to discount his claims about the first search.

"786 (87.8%) used PRETZEL CRISPS as a trademark, 24 (2.7%) were false positives, and 85 (9.5%) used the term in an arguably generic fashion." Although in this second search he again did not explain how he reached his decision to place the references in the respective categories, he did include a notation on each article as to how it was categorized.[28]

[48] The Court's conclusions from its review and analysis of the references differ markedly from Mr. Lauzau's. Even if the Court were to accept Mr. Lauzau's classification of the references (which it does not), the Court finds numerous flaws in his analysis. First, and most importantly, it is misleading to simply add up the references and conclude that the highest number of "hits" reflects an accurate assessment of consumer preferences. Not all references are equal, far from it. Instead, the nature, depth and source of the references must be considered to fairly draw any conclusions from the collection of articles.

[49] After reviewing all the references individually, the Court finds that they can be grouped into several categories for analysis (in addition to duplicates which represented over 36% of the references reviewed):

Press Releases / Other Plaintiff Created References / Business References

[50] A majority of the articles (close to 60%), reflect Plaintiffs' business affairs, financial results and executive employment changes. . . . *See, e.g.,* . . . Doc. No. 41-12, p. 51 (stating that the team for First Aid Shot Therapy, a healthcare company, is comprised of executives that were responsible for the launch and success of Pretzel Crisps, as well as other products). . . .

. . . .

Lawsuit References

[51] The list of media references that Mr. Lauzau counts as equal "trademark" references also includes a number of articles (approximately 4%) that discuss the court decisions related to this dispute. . . .

. . . .

False Positive and Indeterminate References

[52] Approximately 3% of the articles were "false positives" that did not include the terms that were searched in any relevant context and, similarly, approximately 3% of the articles could not be classified by the Court for lack of information or context about the article or other reasons.

[53] Accordingly, the Court finds that adding together the business articles, lawsuit articles, false positives and indeterminate articles approximately 70% of the articles offered by Mr. Lauzau have little or no probative value with respect to the question of genericness.

Generic References

[54] The Court finds that approximately 13% of the articles reflect generic use of "pretzel crisps." *See, e.g.,* . . . 41-13, p. 32 (describing a school lunch idea that includes "[h]ummus with carrots, red peppers, green peppers, pretzel crisps and dried fruit"); 42-3, p. 121 (explaining how Skinnygirl creator Bethenny Frankel plans on offering pretzel crisps and pita chips as products); . . .;[30] *see also* TTAB Decision 2, 124 U.S.P.Q at 1190-91 (quoting numerous other generic references). In these articles, "pretzel crisps" are used without any particular reference to the term as a brand or to Plaintiffs. Many reference "homemade" or "my own" "pretzel crisps." And, in a number of the articles, including several

---

[28] The Court notes that it is some indication of the subjectiveness (and perhaps the care) with which Mr. Lauzau completed his task that in at least one case *the same article* was classified once as a "generic" reference and once as a "trademark" use.

[30] Also, Plaintiffs excluded from their generic results references to other companies providing "pretzel crisps." *See, e.g.,* [Doc 42-2] at 253 (referring to "Stacy's Pretzel Crisps"); [Doc. 42-6] at 131 (using the term "Pretzel Crisps" to refer to "Stacy's Bake Shop crisps.").]

of those cited above, "pretzel crisps" are listed in a parallel manner with other food items such as "popcorn" or "chips," further emphasizing that the term is being used generically.

[55] Further, other media articles cited by Frito-Lay reflect strong evidence of generic use, including the use of "Pretzel Crisps" as a category for the taste test among several different brands of pretzel crackers. *See* Doc. No. 28-13 at 17-18 (January 2009 San Francisco Chronicle article determining that Snack Factory came in third in a taste test comparing Pepperidge Farm, Trader Joe's other brands which are generically referenced as "pretzel chips," "pretzel crackers" and "pretzel crisps" in the article); . . . Doc. No. 28-11 at 2 (2010 Chefs Best taste test for "Pretzel Crisps" declaring Pepperidge Farm the category winner and making clear generic use of the term – "what makes a great pretzel crisp?," "the best pretzel crisps will be dark gold." "moderate saltiness will most define the basic taste profile of top-quality pretzel crisps."). In sum, the Court finds that the articles in which "pretzel crisps" is used generically provide clear affirmative evidence that consumers primarily view the term "pretzel crisps" as a type of goods rather than a brand name.

"Brand" Identification References

[56] The remaining articles (approximately 20%) can be generously described as articles in which PRETZEL CRISPS may be referred to as a brand or the use of the term appears to refer specifically to Plaintiffs' product. However, for the reasons discussed below, the Court finds, in the exercise of its judgment, that a substantial percentage of those references should be given only a limited weight.

[57] While a number of the articles use Pretzel Crisps in a way that indicates it is viewed as a brand, *see, e.g.*, 41-2, p. 11, #13 (comparing the ingredients in Tostitos and Pretzel Crisps to discover the better snack); . . . many more articles are similar to the "business" articles discussed above in that they only describe or reflect Plaintiffs' sales efforts.

[58] That is, the articles simply reflect the fact that Plaintiffs are active participants in the marketplace rather than more direct evidence of consumer perceptions. See, e.g., 41-2, p. 2, #2 (listing exhibitors, including Pretzel Crisps, at an Earth Day Fair); 41-2, p. 3, #3 (advertising Pretzel Crisps and mentioning the nutrition facts, flavors, and store placement). . . .

[59] Again, evidence that a product has become a success and associated with a particular company cannot change a generic term into a non-generic brand. Thus, the Court's judgment, considering all aspects of these articles, is that they are entitled to relatively less weight than the generic articles discussed above, even though they are more numerous.

[60] Moreover, as noted above in the Court's review of both the business and the "brand identification" articles, many of the cited articles refer to Plaintiffs' product as "Snack Factory Pretzel Crisps" rather than simply "Pretzel Crisps." The Court finds this is significant and undercuts Plaintiffs' argument that the term PRETZEL CRISPS is, *standing alone*, perceived as a brand.[31] The wide prevalence of using Snack Factory as a clear brand identifier preceding "Pretzel Crisps" makes it more likely that consumers perceive pretzel crisps as a product name rather than a second brand name.[32] Recent advertisements easily found by the Court on the internet vividly demonstrate this point.

---

[31] Indeed, in some of Plaintiff's purchasing contracts, the Product Description is "Pretzel Crips" and the "Extended product desc." is "Thin, flat pretzel crisps," while the "Trademark" is listed only as "Snack Factory."

[32] Plaintiffs' argue that "Snack Factory Pretzel Crisps" is no different than saying "Frito-Lay's cool ranch DORITOS." The Court disagrees. Beyond the absence of any evidence that DORITOS are often referred to as "Frito-Lay Doritos" in communications describing the brand, DORITOS is not even arguably the name of a class or type of food.

[61] The Costco ad pictured above is contained in an advertising circular for the period May 19, 2021 to June 13, 2021. *See* https://www.costcoinsider.com/costco-may-and-june-2021-coupon-book/ (accessed May 21, 2021). In the top two panels, Costco is offering a special price on both Snack Factory Pretzel Crisps and Stacy's Pita Chips. The ad uses both Snack Factory and Stacy's as the brand names and then "Organic," "Pretzel Crisps" and "Pita Chips" as generic product descriptors for the snacks. The Court also notes the difference in how "Cheerios" and "Sunny D" are both referred to only by their brand names in the bottom two panels. Thus, this ad is a striking example of how Snack Factory (brand name) and "pretzel crisps" (product name) are often viewed differently when used together.

[62] Similarly, in the ad for Publix supermarket pictured below, Snack Factory is used as the brand name and pretzel crisps the product name in the same way that "Ithaca" and "Whisps" are the brand names for "hummus" and "cheese crisps."

https://www.publix.com/savings/weekly-ad (Valid 5/19/2021 – 5/25/2021) (accessed May 21, 2021).

[63] In summary, for all the reasons discussed above, the Court finds, after a careful *de novo* review, that the media references offered into evidence and discussed above on balance support a finding that Frito-Lay has established by a preponderance of evidence that PRETZEL CRISPS is a generic term.

Consumer Surveys

[64] Pursuant to the Supreme Court's directive in *Booking.com* and the Federal Circuit decision in this matter,[34] the Court also considers – cautiously – the survey evidence presented by the Parties. At

---

[34] Prior to *Booking.com*, in the Fourth Circuit and elsewhere consumer survey evidence was not considered in cases where, as here, the mark was not a coined term. *See, e.g., Hunt Masters, Inc. v. Landry's*

the TTAB, Plaintiffs submitted two surveys and related expert declarations, one from Dr. E. Deborah Jay (the "Jay Survey") on genericness and the other from George Mantis (the "Mantis Survey") on secondary meaning. Frito-Lay submitted one survey and a related declaration from Dr. Alex Simonson on genericness. In this Court, Plaintiffs have filed additional declarations from both their experts and Frito-Lay has submitted an Expert Report and Declaration from Professor Isabella Cunningham on secondary meaning. None of the Parties have challenged the credentials of any of the experts, and the Court finds that all of them are well qualified to express their opinions. Accordingly, all of the expert reports and declarations have been considered *de novo*, although for the reasons discussed below the Court finds the Jay Survey and the Mantis Survey most instructive.

[65] Dr. Jay, founder and President of Field Research Corp., conducted what is commonly known as a "Teflon" survey in an attempt to test how consumers perceive the term PRETZEL CRISPS. Named after a survey performed to determine if "Teflon" was a valid trademark, a Teflon survey gives the survey participants an explanation of the generic versus trademark distinction and then asks respondents to identify whether a term refers to a brand name or a common name. *See* McCarthy § 12:16. ("A 'Teflon survey' is essentially a mini-course in the generic versus trademark distinction, followed by a test.").

[66] A randomized "double-blind" phone survey was conducted between February 16 and 25, 2010. The eligibility criteria were defined as adults who had "personally purchased salty snacks for themselves or for someone else in the past three months or think that they would do this in the next three months." As a gateway, in accordance with the Teflon format, survey respondents were given an explanation of the difference between brand and common names, and then asked both whether BAKED TOSTITOS is a brand or common name, and whether TORTILLA CHIPS is a brand or common name. Only those who answered both questions correctly were allowed to proceed with the survey. Initially 500 adults were questioned regarding their eligibility to participate in the survey. Of those, 347 of the 500 met the eligibility requirements to take the mini-test, and only 222 of the 347 answered both questions correctly on the mini-test and were thus considered "qualified respondents" who were allowed to take the survey. In describing the "representativeness" of these 222 participants to all adult U.S. consumers, Dr. Jay reported in her TTAB declaration that the participants were younger than a truly representative sample and not geographically representative in that consumers in the South were underrepresented.

[67] In the survey itself, participants were questioned about a number of terms and asked whether they are "brand" or "common" names, with the option available for participants to say that they didn't know or had not heard of a name.

[68] For the 222 respondents who participated in the Jay survey, the results were as follows:

Name	Brand	Common	Don't know/Haven't heard
SUN CHIPS	96%	3%	<1%
CHEESE NIPS	85%	13%	2%
PRETZEL CRISPS	**55%**	**36%**	**9%**
FLAVOR TWISTS	48%	34%	18%
GOURMET POPCORN	25%	72%	3%
ONION RINGS	8%	91%	1%
MACADEMIA NUT	7%	92%	<1%

Seafood Restaurant, Inc. 240 F.3d 251, 255, 57 USPQ2d 1884, 1886 (4th Cir. 2001) ("Hunt does not claim to have first coined the term 'crab house.' Therefore, it is not necessary to determine whether the term has become generic through common use, rendering Hunt's consumer survey irrelevant."); TTAB Decision 2, 124 U.S.P.Q. at 1202-04 (collecting cases). However, as discussed above, such evidence was considered by the Supreme Court in *Booking.com* and the Federal Circuit instructed the TTAB to consider survey evidence in this matter. Accordingly, the Court has considered the evidence, with due regard for the limitations of such evidence cited by the Supreme Court (which had led many courts to not consider the evidence in these circumstances as noted).

[69] Based on these results, Dr. Jay concluded in her report that "the majority of consumers understand the term PRETZEL CRISPS to function as a brand name."

[70] While the Court does not find fault with Dr. Jay's expertise, survey methodology or the execution of the survey, it does question her conclusion and confidence in the results. First, even taking the results at face value, the survey suggests only a small majority of respondents (55%) believed that PRETZEL CRISPS is a brand, as compared to the vast majority who correctly identified Sun Chips (96%) and Cheese Nips (85%).

[71] Moreover, Plaintiffs and Dr. Jay cite the 55% result without any discussion of the inherent "margin of error" in the survey. In a footnote to her initial declaration in the TTAB, Dr. Jay acknowledged that "[a]nalyses based on the overall sample of 222 completed interviews have a maximum sampling error of approximately +/-7 percentage points at the 95% confidence level." She also admitted that "there are other potential sources of error in surveys besides sampling error," but expressed her opinion that "the overall design and execution of the survey minimized the potential for other sources of error."

[72] The "margin of error" in surveys should be considered in whether and how much to rely on their results. *See vonRosenberg v. Lawrence*, 413 F.Supp.3d 437, 449 n.9 (D.S.C. 2019) (finding that a 5.6% error rate was a "wide margin of error" relevant to the weight that should be given to a trademark survey on genericness where, considering the error rate, the "rate of [survey respondents] who responded "category" rather than "trademark" would fall below 50%, thus arguably negating its ability to show that a "majority" of individuals consider the mark generic. *See* 2 McCarthy on Trademarks and Unfair Competition § 12:6 (5th ed.) (for genericness, "majority use controls")"); *Borinquen Biscuit Corp. v. M.V. Trading Corp.*, 443 F.3d 112, 120 n. 6 (1st Cir. 2006) (concluding that an expert report's "small sample size and large margin of error [10%] combined to cast considerable doubt on its statistical integrity"). . . . This seems especially important in circumstances like here in which the answers of only 222 survey respondents are purported to fairly represent the consumer perceptions of over 100 million adults in the United States.

[73] Using a 7% margin of error, the range of those who view PRETZEL CRISPS as a brand within the margin of error is 48% to 63%. In other words, without discounting the results of the Jay Survey in any manner (even for the other sources of error Dr. Jay references), a finding that fewer than a majority of respondents perceived PRETZEL CRISPS as a brand is within the survey's margin of error. Indeed, if the percentages of those who believed that the term is a brand or common name are fully adjusted up or down for the margin of error then the difference between them could be very small, 48% to 43%.

[74] However, beyond consideration of the margin of error (which still leaves a small relative but not absolute majority identifying the mark as a brand), the Court finds there are a number of reasons that suggest the survey results should be discounted in addition to considering the margin of error. First, as mentioned above, Dr. Jay acknowledges that the survey population is not representative of the relevant population, either by age or geography. However, the amount and direction of the survey error or uncertainty as a consequence of these disparities is not quantified or estimated.

[75] Moreover, the answers of the survey respondents with respect to a number of the "control" terms do not inspire confidence in the survey results and appear to reflect that the survey respondents' choices may have been driven, in significant part, by commercial success or notoriety rather than a valid assessment of the distinction between generic and trademark names. While over 90% of respondents correctly identified "macadamia nuts" and "onion rings" as generic names, 25% incorrectly identified "gourmet popcorn" as a brand. More significantly, less than half of respondents correctly identified FLAVOR TWISTS (which are twisted corn chips) as a brand. The Court finds that this failure indicates that the bulk of survey respondents did not fully understand the distinction between common names and brands. The mark FLAVOR TWISTS is plainly not a common name (TWISTS is certainly not a common name for corn chips, if it has any "common" meaning at all).

[76] So, what accounts for the vast difference in correct answers for CHEESE NIPS and SUN CHIPS, which are also brands? Simply put, the difference likely lies in marketing and commercial success. CHEESE NIPS and SUN CHIPS are more well-known and successful than FLAVOR TWISTS as a name

76

standing alone (indeed if the survey had included the full product name FRITOS FLAVOR TWISTS the Court expects the results may have been markedly different). Thus, the failure of respondents to correctly identify FLAVOR TWISTS as a brand suggests that a substantial portion of the survey results reflect secondary meaning (the association of a product with a particular source) rather than a recognition of genericness.[35]

[77] Accordingly, it is the Court's judgment – based on the fact that less than a majority of respondents may have believed PRETZEL CRISPS is a brand name (taking into account the survey's margin of error), the other limitations and concerns about the survey results discussed above and the Supreme Court's warning to be cautious in relying on consumer surveys purporting to measure genericness – that the results of the Jay Survey are, at best, inconclusive. Thus, the Court does not agree that the survey indicates that consumers "primarily" perceive PRETZEL CRISPS as a brand.[36]

. . . .

[78] In sum, considering all the available evidence, the Court, finds that, on balance, the survey evidence slightly favors[39] an affirmative finding that consumers primarily perceive PRETZEL CRISPS as a common or generic name.

Google and Social Media References

[79] Plaintiffs also offered evidence of Google searches and social media mentions on Twitter to support their position that PRETZEL CRISPS is not generic. Specifically, Plaintiffs' attorneys' employee Mr. Lauzau (whose work and conclusions the Court criticized with respect to media references above) conducted a Google search for the term "pretzel crisps" in October 2018 that he alleges shows "based on my review of results" that 87 (90%) of the first 97 results "used the term PRETZEL CRISPS as a trademark or referred directly to Princeton Vanguard's product." With respect to Twitter, another of Plaintiffs' law firm's non-attorney staff members (Elliot Beaver) conducted a subjective review of social media mentions of "Pretzel Crisps" on Twitter from April 1, 2018 through October 24, 2018 and concluded that a majority of tweets (63%) "referenced the PRETZEL CRISPS brand in a non-generic fashion."

[80] However, the Court does not find either the Google search or the Twitter analysis persuasive on the issue of genericness. First, as discussed above, these searches have only a limited usefulness in establishing whether PRETZEL CRISPS is generic due to the more than a decade (and $50 million in advertising and marketing expenditures) that has passed since the challenged registration of the mark in 2005. Again, the repeated use of ordinary words cannot give a single company a proprietary right over those words, even if an association develops between the words and that company. *Am. Online*, 243 F.3d at 821.

[81] Second, for the Google search, the same concerns that the Court expressed about Mr. Lauzau in connection with media references (that he has no training in trademark law and is plainly not an impartial witness) apply here as well. Also, as with the list of media references, Mr. Lauzau does not indicate how he determined which of the search results used PRETZEL CRISPS "as a trademark" nor does he distinguish between search results that reflect the Plaintiffs' own websites (which are 3 of the first 5

---

[35] While genericness and secondary meaning are different concepts, they are not easily disentangled, particularly for successful products. Indeed, a product may have a leading market share with a generic name. *See Kellogg*, 305 U.S. at 118 (shredded wheat).

[36] Compare, for example, the consumer survey results reported in the District Court decision in Booking.com, in which the plaintiff produced a Teflon survey which revealed that 74.8 percent of respondents identified BOOKING.COM as a brand name. *Booking.com B.V. v. Matal*, 278 F. Supp. 3d 891, 915 (E.D. Va. 2017).

[39] Even if the Court were to find that all the survey evidence was on balance inconclusive that would not affect the Court's ultimate factual determination that there is sufficient affirmative evidence to conclude that PRETZEL CRISPS is a generic mark.

results) or websites that were sponsored by Plaintiffs (*see*, e.g., Doc. 42-11 at 4 (recipe provided by Plaintiffs to Allrecipes.com) and those websites that reflect independent trademark references. Indeed, the vast bulk of the Google search results simply identify websites of large companies offering PRETZEL CRISPS for sale. (*See Id.* at 2 (Amazon.com, Walmart.com, etc.)). Again, there is no dispute that Plaintiffs have developed a very large business selling their pretzel product; however, the typical commercial sales efforts associated with that business—including the websites featured in the Plaintiffs' Google search, do not reflect *consumer* perceptions of genericness. Instead, to the extent they have relevance to this action at all, they may be mostly evidence of secondary meaning, an issue that the Court does not reach. Accordingly, the Court gives the Google results little weight.

[82] Similarly, it is undisputed that Plaintiffs have developed a large social media presence as part of their marketing efforts. As of October 2018, the PRETZEL CRISPS brand had over 47,800 followers on Twitter. Mr. Beaver, a "litigation case manager" at Plaintiffs' counsel's law firm, claims to have "personally reviewed" each of 1137 tweets and 132 hashtags but does not indicate which ones he identified as brand references, generic references, neither, or false positives or how he reached his conclusions (and like Mr. Lauzau there is no evidence that he has any training or expertise in trademark law).

[83] Moreover, Mr. Beaver counted as "brand references" all tweets posted by Plaintiffs, all tweets with Plaintiffs' twitter handle (@pretzelcrisps) or the hashtag #snackfactory and all tweets that reference "Snack Factory" or include an image of Snack Factory products. As with Plaintiffs' own press releases, none of Plaintiffs' tweets or those sponsored by Plaintiffs (which account for a substantial percentage of the tweets and over three-quarters of the hashtags), *id.*, provide any probative evidence of consumer perceptions. Rather, they simply reflect Plaintiffs' efforts to "brand" and promote their own product.

[84] Further, merely referencing Plaintiffs or their hashtag does not necessarily make the use of "pretzel crisps" in a tweet a brand reference. As with the Google search results discussed above, use of the disputed product name in the normal course of business communications, here on Twitter, does not reveal whether or not a consumer understands the product *name* primarily as a brand or a type of goods. Instead, it just reflects consumer engagement with the product,[40] which, again, may be relevant to secondary meaning but not necessarily genericness. Simply put, it is unremarkable and unconvincing that communication about a product mentions the product name. And, because consumer perception of a term may be "mixed," that is, reflecting both generic use and brand awareness, *see Booking.com*, 278 F.3d at 902, a bare reference to the product name does not answer the more difficult question before the Court of how consumers *primarily* perceive the term. So, after a *de novo* review of the evidence, the Court finds, for all the reasons discussed above, that Plaintiffs' evidence of Twitter communications is unpersuasive.

Other Available Product Names

[85] Finally, Plaintiffs argue that the availability of other product names for "pretzel cracker" snacks supports their claim that PRETZEL CRISPS is not generic. First, regardless of the availability of similar names for a product, a generic name cannot be registered as a trademark thereby granting exclusive use of the name of a product to a single company. *See Ale House Mgmt., Inc. v. Raleigh Ale House*, 205 F.3d 137, 141 (4th Cir. 2000) (affirming summary judgment finding term ALE HOUSE generic, while also noting alternative generic names like "bar," "lounge," "pub," "saloon," and "tavern"); *see also McCarthy* § 12:9 ("There is usually no one, single and exclusive generic name for a product. Any product may have many generic designations. Any one of those is incapable of trademark significance.").

[86] Second, the Court does not find that the names suggested, while generic, are necessarily "equally acceptable" alternatives. For example, Plaintiffs claim that "pretzel thins" and "pretzel rounds"

---

[40] The Court also is concerned that a focus on those relative few consumers who are most engaged with the product through Twitter would be a misleading sample in determining how the "relevant public," i.e., average or typical consumers perceive the product name.

are equivalent generic names. However, "pretzel thins" is also a name used for regularly shaped thin pretzels and "pretzel rounds" is used for small, rounded pretzel pieces as well as snacks that look more like Plaintiff's "pretzel crisps" product. Therefore, a company could reasonably conclude that "pretzel crisps" is a better description for a small, rounded pretzel product.

[87] Moreover, the absence of other companies using the name "pretzel crisps" to describe their products is neither "compelling evidence" as urged by Plaintiffs nor even surprising. As discussed above, Plaintiffs have aggressively "policed" the mark. Thus, the obvious reason no one else uses the name is they will be threatened with legal action. In such circumstances, the relative absence of competitive use of the name simply reflects a practical business judgment rather than any acknowledgement that "pretzel crisps" is not generic.

IV. CONCLUSION

[88] In conclusion, there is no dispute that Snack Factory Pretzel Crisps is a hugely successful product, due in no small part to Plaintiffs' extensive marketing efforts and the PRETZEL CRISPS trademark registration they received and have enforced to clear the field of similarly named products. However, no matter how much commercial success the product enjoys, Plaintiffs are not entitled to monopolize the common name of the product being sold. Summarizing the evidence on the genericness of the mark, considered as a whole, the Court finds that the combination of the acknowledged generic elements of the compound mark "yields no additional meaning to consumers capable of distinguishing the goods" and, independently, usage by competitors, media references and consumer surveys (as well as some use by Plaintiffs) reflects that, on balance, consumers primarily perceive "pretzel crisps" to be a common / generic name. Therefore, for all the reasons discussed above, the Court finds that Frito-Lay has carried its burden to prove by a preponderance of the evidence that PRETZEL CRISPS is a generic mark, and this Court will affirm the TTAB and order the cancellation of the registration of the mark.

. . . .

Elliott v. Google, Inc.
860 F.3d 1151 (9th Cir. 2017)

TALLMAN, Circuit Judge

I.

[1] Between February 29, 2012, and March 10, 2012, Chris Gillespie used a domain name registrar to acquire 763 domain names that included the word "google." Each of these domain names paired the word "google" with some other term identifying a specific brand, person, or product—for example, "googledisney.com," "googlebarackobama.net," and "googlenewtvs.com."

[2] Google, Inc. ("Google") objected to these registrations and promptly filed a complaint with the National Arbitration Forum ("NAF"), which has authority to decide certain domain name disputes under the registrar's terms of use. Google argued that the registrations violate the Uniform Domain Name Dispute Resolution Policy, which is included in the registrar's terms of use, and amount to domain name infringement, colloquially known as "cybersquatting." Specifically, Google argued that the domain names are confusingly similar to the GOOGLE trademark and were registered in bad faith. The NAF agreed, and transferred the domain names to Google on May 10, 2012.

[3] Shortly thereafter, David Elliott filed, and Gillespie later joined,[2] an action in the Arizona District Court. Elliott petitioned for cancellation of the GOOGLE trademark under the Lanham Act, which allows cancellation of a registered trademark if it is primarily understood as a "generic name for the goods or services, or a portion thereof, for which it is registered." 15 U.S.C. § 1064(3). Elliott petitioned for

---

[2] For the remainder of this opinion, we collectively refer to Appellants as "Elliott."

cancellation on the ground that the word "google" is primarily understood as "a generic term universally used to describe the act[ ] of internet searching."

[4] On September 23, 2013, the parties filed cross-motions for summary judgment on the issue of genericness. Elliott requested summary judgment because (1) it is an indisputable fact that a majority of the relevant public uses the word "google" as a verb—i.e., by saying "I googled it," and (2) verb use constitutes generic use as a matter of law. Google maintained that verb use does not automatically constitute generic use, and that Elliott failed to create even a triable issue of fact as to whether the GOOGLE trademark is generic. Specifically, Google argued that Elliott failed to present sufficient evidence to support a jury finding that the relevant public primarily understands the word "google" as a generic name for internet search engines. The district court agreed with Google and its framing of the relevant inquiry, and granted summary judgment in its favor.

[5] Elliott raises two arguments on appeal. First, he argues that the district court misapplied the primary significance test and failed to recognize the importance of verb use. Second, he argues that the district court impermissibly weighed the evidence when it granted summary judgment for Google. We review the district court's grant of summary judgment de novo . . . . For the reasons described below, we reject both of Elliott's arguments and affirm summary judgment for Google.

II.

. . . .

[6] Over time, the holder of a valid trademark may become a "victim of 'genericide.'" *Freecycle Network, Inc. v. Oey*, 505 F.3d 898, 905 (9th Cir. 2007) (quoting J. Thomas McCarthy, McCarthy on Trademarks and Unfair Competition § 12:1 (4th ed. 1998) [hereinafter McCarthy]). Genericide occurs when the public appropriates a trademark and uses it as a generic name for particular types of goods or services irrespective of its source. For example, ASPIRIN, CELLOPHANE, and ESCALATOR were once protectable as arbitrary or fanciful marks because they were primarily understood as identifying the source of certain goods. But the public appropriated those marks and now primarily understands aspirin, cellophane, and escalator as generic names for those same goods. *See Bayer Co. v. United Drug Co.*, 272 F. 505, 510 (S.D.N.Y. 1921); *DuPont Cellophane Co. v. Waxed Prods. Co.*, 85 F.2d 75, 82 (2d Cir. 1936); *Freecycle Network, Inc.*, 505 F.3d at 905. The original holders of the ASPIRIN, CELLOPHANE, and ESCALATOR marks are thus victims of genericide.

[7] The question in any case alleging genericide is whether a trademark has taken the "fateful step" along the path to genericness. *Ty Inc. v. Softbelly's Inc.*, 353 F.3d 528, 531 (7th Cir. 2003). The mere fact that the public sometimes uses a trademark as the name for a unique product does not immediately render the mark generic. *See* 15 U.S.C. § 1064(3). Instead, a trademark only becomes generic when the "primary significance of the registered mark to the relevant public" is as the name for a particular type of good or service irrespective of its source. *Id.*

[8] We have often described this as a "who-are-you/what-are-you" test. *See Yellow Cab Co. of Sacramento v. Yellow Cab of Elk Grove, Inc.*, 419 F.3d 925, 929 (9th Cir. 2005) (quoting *Filipino Yellow Pages, Inc.*, 198 F.3d at 1147). . . .

A.

[9] On appeal, Elliott claims that he has presented sufficient evidence to create a triable issue of fact as to whether the GOOGLE trademark is generic, and that the district court erred when it granted summary judgment for Google. First, he argues that the district court erred because it misapplied the primary significance test and failed to recognize the importance of verb use. Specifically, he argues that the district court erroneously framed the inquiry as whether the primary significance of the word "google" to the relevant public is as a generic name for internet search engines, or as a mark identifying the Google search engine in particular. Instead, Elliott argues that the court should have framed the inquiry as whether the relevant public primarily uses the word "google" as a verb.

[10] We conclude that Elliott's proposed inquiry is fundamentally flawed for two reasons. First, Elliott fails to recognize that a claim of genericide must always relate to a particular type of good or service. Second, he erroneously assumes that verb use automatically constitutes generic use. For similar

reasons, we conclude that the district court did not err in its formulation of the relevant inquiry under the primary significance test.

[11] First, we take this opportunity to clarify that a claim of genericide or genericness must be made with regard to a particular type of good or service. We have not yet had occasion to articulate this requirement because parties usually present their claims in this manner sua sponte. *See, e.g., KP Permanent Make–Up, Inc.*, 408 F.3d at 605 (claiming that "micro colors" is generic for micropigmentation services); *Filipino Yellow Pages, Inc.*, 198 F.3d at 1146 (claiming that "Filipino Yellow Pages" is generic for "telephone directories targeted at the Filipino–American community"); *Park 'N Fly, Inc.*, 718 F.2d at 330 (claiming that "Park 'N Fly" is generic for airport parking lots). But here, Elliott claims that the word "google" has become a generic name for "the act" of searching the internet, and argues that the district court erred when it focused on internet search engines. We reject Elliott's criticism and conclude that the district court properly recognized the necessary and inherent link between a claim of genericide and a particular type of good or service.

[12] This requirement is clear from the text of the Lanham Act, which allows a party to apply for cancellation of a trademark when it "becomes the generic name for the *goods or services* . . . for which it is registered." 15 U.S.C. § 1064(3) (emphasis added). The Lanham Act further provides that "[i]f the registered mark becomes the generic name for less than all of the *goods or services* for which it is registered, a petition to cancel the registration for only those *goods or services* may be filed." *Id.* (emphasis added). Finally, the Lanham Act specifies that the relevant question under the primary significance test is "whether the registered mark has become the generic name of [certain] *goods or services.*" *Id.* (emphasis added). In this way, the Lanham Act plainly requires that a claim of genericide relate to a particular type of good or service.

[13] We also note that such a requirement is necessary to maintain the viability of arbitrary marks as a protectable trademark category. By definition, an arbitrary mark is an existing word that is used to identify the source of a good with which the word otherwise has no logical connection. *See JL Beverage Co.*, 828 F.3d at 1107. If there were no requirement that a claim of genericide relate to a particular type of good, then a mark like IVORY, which is "arbitrary as applied to soap," could be cancelled outright because it is "generic when used to describe a product made from the tusks of elephants." *Abercrombie & Fitch Co. v. Hunting World, Inc.*, 537 F.2d 4, 9 n.6 (2d Cir. 1976). This is not how trademark law operates: Trademark law recognizes that a term may be unprotectable with regard to one type of good, and protectable with regard to another type of good. In this way, the very existence of arbitrary marks as a valid trademark category supports our conclusion that a claim of genericide must relate to a particular type of good or service.

[14] Second, Elliott's alternative inquiry fails because verb use does not automatically constitute generic use. Elliott claims that a word can only be used in a trademark sense when it is used as an adjective. He supports this claim by comparing the definitions of adjectives and trademarks, noting that both adjectives and trademarks serve descriptive functions.

[15] Once again, Elliott's semantic argument contradicts fundamental principles underlying the protectability of trademarks. When Congress amended the Lanham Act to specify that the primary significance test applies to claims of genericide, it specifically acknowledged that a speaker might use a trademark as the name for a product, i.e., as a noun, and yet use the mark with a particular source in mind, i.e., as a trademark. It further explained that:

> A trademark can serve a dual function—that of [naming] a product while at the same time indicating its source. Admittedly, if a product is unique, it is more likely that the trademark adopted and used to identify that product will be used as if it were the identifying name of that product. But this is not conclusive of whether the mark is generic.

S. Rep. No. 98–627, at 5 (1984). In this way, Congress has instructed us that a speaker might use a trademark as a noun and still use the term in a source-identifying trademark sense.

[16] Moreover, we have already implicitly rejected Elliott's theory that only adjective use constitutes trademark use. In *Coca-Cola Co. v. Overland, Inc.*, 692 F.2d 1250 (9th Cir. 1982), the Coca-

Cola Company sued a local restaurant for trademark infringement because its servers regularly and surreptitiously replaced customer orders for "a coke" with a non-Coca-Cola beverage. *Id.* at 1252. The restaurant defended on the basis of genericide, arguing that the COKE trademark had become a generic name for all cola beverages. *Id.* at 1254. To support its claim, the restaurant presented employee affidavits stating that the employees believed that customers who ordered "a coke" were using the term in a generic sense. *Id.* We rejected these affidavits because they were not based on personal knowledge. More significant to the issue at hand, we also noted that the mere fact that customers ordered "a coke," i.e., used the mark as a noun, failed to show "what . . . customers [were] thinking," or whether they had a particular source in mind. *Id.* at 1255.

[17] If Elliott were correct that a trademark can only perform its source-identifying function when it is used as an adjective, then we would not have cited a need for evidence regarding the customers' inner thought processes. Instead, the fact that the customers used the trademark as a noun and asked for "a coke" would prove that they had no particular source in mind. In this way, we have implicitly rejected Elliott's theory that a trademark can only serve a source-identifying function when it is used as an adjective.

[18] For these reasons, the district court correctly rejected Elliott's theory that verb use automatically constitutes generic use.[3] Moreover, the district court aptly coined the terms "discriminate verb" and "indiscriminate verb" in order to evaluate Elliott's proffered examples of verb use and determine whether they were also examples of generic use. Although novel, these terms properly frame the relevant inquiry as whether a speaker has a particular source in mind. We have already acknowledged that a customer might use the noun "coke" in an indiscriminate sense, with no particular cola beverage in mind; or in a discriminate sense, with a Coca–Cola beverage in mind. In the same way, we now recognize that an internet user might use the verb "google" in an indiscriminate sense, with no particular search engine in mind; or in a discriminate sense, with the Google search engine in mind.

[19] Because a claim of genericide must relate to a particular type of good or service and because verb use does not necessarily constitute generic use, the district court did not err when it refused to frame its inquiry as whether the relevant public primarily uses the word "google" as a verb. Moreover, the district court correctly framed its inquiry as whether the primary significance of the word "google" to the relevant public is as a generic name for internet search engines or as a mark identifying the Google search engine in particular. We therefore evaluate Elliott's claim of genericide and the sufficiency of his proffered evidence under the proper inquiry.

B.

[20] Elliott next argues that the district court must have impermissibly weighed the evidence when it granted summary judgment for Google in light of the "sheer quantity" of evidence that Elliott produced to support his claim of genericide. *See Jesinger v. Nev. Fed. Credit Union*, 24 F.3d 1127, 1131 (9th Cir. 1994) (noting that a court "must not weigh the evidence" at summary judgment). We disagree. Instead, we conclude that Elliott's admissible evidence is largely inapposite to the relevant inquiry under the primary significance test because Elliott ignores the fact that a claim of genericide must relate to a particular type of good or service.

[21] A party applying for cancellation of a registered trademark bears the burden of proving genericide by a preponderance of the evidence. *Anti–Monopoly, Inc. v. Gen. Mills Fun Grp.*, 684 F.2d 1316, 1319 (9th Cir. 1982). Moreover, the holder of a registered trademark benefits from a presumption of

---

[3] We acknowledge that if a trademark is used as an adjective, it will typically be easier to prove that the trademark is performing a source-identifying function. If a speaker asks for "a Kleenex tissue," it is quite clear that the speaker has a particular brand in mind. But we will not assume that a speaker has no brand in mind simply because he or she uses the trademark as a noun and asks for "a Kleenex." Instead, the party bearing the burden of proof must offer evidence to support a finding of generic use. *See* McCarthy § 12:8 ("The fact that buyers or users often call for or order a product by a [trademark] term does not necessarily prove that that term is being used as a 'generic name.' ").

validity and has "met its [initial] burden of demonstrating" the lack of "a genuine issue of material fact" regarding genericide. *Coca–Cola Co.*, 692 F.2d at 1254. Therefore, in light of the relevant inquiry under the primary significance test, Elliott was required to identify sufficient evidence to support a jury finding that the primary significance of the word "google" to the relevant public is as a name for internet search engines generally and not as a mark identifying the Google search engine in particular.

[22] At summary judgment, the district court assumed that a majority of the public uses the verb "google" to refer to the act of "searching on the internet without regard to [the] search engine used."[4] In other words, it assumed that a majority of the public uses the verb "google" in a generic and indiscriminate sense. The district court then concluded that this fact, on its own, cannot support a jury finding of genericide under the primary significance test. We agree.

[23] As explained above, a claim of genericide must relate to a particular type of good. Even if we assume that the public uses the verb "google" in a generic and indiscriminate sense, this tells us nothing about how the public primarily understands the word itself, irrespective of its grammatical function, with regard to internet search engines. As explained below, we also agree that Elliott's admissible evidence only supports the favorable but insufficient inference already drawn by the district court—that a majority of the public uses the verb "google" in a generic sense. Standing in isolation,[5] this fact is insufficient to support a jury finding of genericide. The district court therefore properly granted summary judgment for Google.

[24] We begin with Elliott's three consumer surveys. . . . Here, the district court properly excluded two of Elliott's consumer surveys because they were not conducted according to accepted principles. Specifically, these surveys were designed and conducted by Elliott's counsel, who is not qualified to design or interpret surveys. . . .

[25] The district court properly considered only Elliott's third survey, which was conducted by James Berger—a qualified survey expert. Elliott's third survey is a "Thermos" survey, which generally "puts the respondent in an imaginary situation . . . and asks how the respondent would ask" for the type of good for which the trademark is alleged to be generic. McCarthy § 12:15 (citing *Am. Thermos Prods. Co. v. Aladdin Indus.*, 207 F.Supp. 9, 21–22 (D. Conn. 1962), *aff'd*, 321 F.2d 577 (2d Cir. 1963)). Here, Berger asked 251 respondents: "If you were going to ask a friend to search for something on the Internet, what word or phrase would you use to tell him/her what you want him/her to do?" Over half of the 251 respondents answered this question by using the word "google" as a verb.

[26] Although verb use does not automatically constitute generic use, the district court allowed Berger to rely on the third survey to offer his expert "opinion that a majority of the public uses the word google as a [generic and indiscriminate] verb to mean search on the internet." In this way, Elliott's admissible consumer survey evidence goes no further than supporting the favorable inference already drawn by the district court.[7]

---

[4] In making this assumption, the district court drew a favorable (and generous) inference for Elliott. As discussed above, verb use does not necessarily constitute generic use, yet most of Elliott's proffered evidence relies on that theory.

[5] Contrary to our colleague's suggestion, we do not hold that generic verb use is "categorically irrelevant." However, evidence that a mark is used in a generic sense in one particular setting cannot support a finding of genericide when it is unaccompanied by evidence regarding the primary significance of the mark as a whole.

[7] The district court also considered a fourth survey. Although Google already benefits from a presumption against genericide, *see Coca–Cola Co.*, 692 F.2d at 1254, Google offered a "Teflon" survey to prove that the GOOGLE mark is not generic. A Teflon survey begins with a brief lesson explaining the difference between brand names and common names. It then asks respondents to classify a series of words, including the trademark at issue, as either brand names or common names. *E. I. DuPont de*

[27] We next consider Elliott's examples of alleged generic use by the media and by consumers. Documented examples of generic use might support a claim of genericide if they reveal a prevailing public consensus regarding the primary significance of a registered trademark.... However, if the parties offer competing examples of both generic and trademark use, this source of evidence is typically insufficient to prove genericide. *See id.*

[28] Initially, we note that Elliott's admissible examples are only examples of verb use. To repeat, verb use does not automatically constitute generic use. For instance, Elliott purports to offer an example of generic use by T–Pain, a popular rap music artist. But we will not assume that T–Pain is using the word "google" in a generic sense simply because he tells listeners to "google [his] name." T–Pain, *Bottlez*, *on* rEVOLVEr (RCA Records 2011). Without further evidence regarding T–Pain's inner thought process, we cannot tell whether he is using "google" in a discriminate or indiscriminate sense. In this way, many of Elliott's admissible examples do not even support the favorable inference that a majority of the relevant public uses the verb "google" in a generic sense.

[29] Elliott also attempted to offer clear examples of indiscriminate verb use by the media and by consumers. For example, in response to Google's motion for summary judgment, he produced a transcript from an episode of a German television show in which a character claims to have "googled at Wikipedia." Elliott also produced examples in which the media uses phrases like "googled on ebay," "googled on facebook," and "googled on pinterest." Finally, Elliott produced evidence suggesting that certain consumers claimed that they accessed a website by "googling" it, even though those consumers actually accessed the website through a non-Google search engine.

[30] The district court properly excluded these examples of indiscriminate verb use because they were not disclosed during discovery and because Elliott failed to show that his delay was "substantially justified or ... harmless." Fed. R. Civ. P. 37(c)(1). Moreover, even if these examples had been timely disclosed, they are largely irrelevant because they only support the favorable inference already drawn by the district court.

{The court then considered Elliott's proferred expert testimony and dictionary evidence and concluded that each only supports favorable inference already drawn by the district court.}

[31] Next, we consider Elliott's claim that Google has used its own trademark in a generic sense. Generic use of a mark by the holder of that mark can support a finding of genericide. *See* McCarthy § 12:13. However, Elliott has not presented an example of generic use by Google. Instead, Elliott has presented an email from Google cofounder Larry Page, which encourages recipients to "[h]ave fun and keep googling!" Once again, Elliott relies on an example of verb use. Elliott has not shown, nor is it likely that he could show, that the cofounder of Google had no particular search engine in mind when he told recipients of the "Google Friends Newsletter" to "keep googling."[10]

[32] Finally, we consider Elliott's claim that there is no efficient alternative for the word "google" as a name for "the act" of searching the internet regardless of the search engine used. Once again, a claim of genericide must relate to a particular type of good or service. In order to show that there is no efficient alternative for the word "google" as a generic term, Elliott must show that there is no way to describe "internet search engines" without calling them "googles." Because not a single competitor calls its search engine "a google," and because members of the consuming public recognize and refer to different

---

Nemours & Co. v. Yoshida Int'l, Inc., 393 F.Supp. 502, 526–27 (E.D.N.Y. 1975). In response to Google's Teflon survey, a little over 93% of respondents classified "Google" as a brand name. Most respondents also classified "Coke," "Jello," "Amazon," and "Yahoo!" as brand names, and classified "Refrigerator," "Margarine," "Browser," and "Website" as common names. Unlike Elliott's Thermos survey, Google's Teflon survey offers comparative evidence as to how consumers primarily understand the word "google" irrespective of its grammatical function.

[10] Elliott also argues that the email shows generic use because "googling" is not capitalized. As we explained with regard to verb use and noun use, we cannot rely on grammatical formalism to determine what a speaker has in mind when using a registered trademark. *See Coca–Cola Co.*, 692 F.2d at 1255.

"internet search engines," Elliott has not shown that there is no available substitute for the word "google" as a generic term. *Compare, e.g., Q–Tips, Inc. v. Johnson & Johnson*, 108 F.Supp. 845, 863 (D.N.J. 1952) (concluding that "medical swab" and "cotton-tipped applicator" are efficient alternatives for Q–Tips); *with Bayer Co.*, 272 F. at 505 (concluding that there is no efficient substitute for the generic term "aspirin" because consumers do not know the term "acetyl salicylic acid"); *see also Softbelly's Inc.*, 353 F.3d at 531 (explaining that genericide does not typically occur "until the trademark has gone so far toward becoming the exclusive descriptor of the product that sellers of competing brands cannot compete effectively without using the name").

[33] Elliott cannot survive summary judgment based on "sheer quantity" of irrelevant evidence. We agree with the district court that, at best, Elliott has presented admissible evidence to support the inference that a majority of the relevant public uses the verb "google" in a generic sense. Because this fact alone cannot support a claim of genericide, the district court properly granted summary judgment for Google.

. . . .

WATFORD, Circuit Judge, concurring:

[34] I join the court's well-reasoned opinion with one caveat. To resolve this appeal, we need not decide whether evidence of a trademark's "indiscriminate" verb use could ever tell us something about whether the public primarily thinks of the mark as the generic name for a type of good or service. Maj. op. at 1159–60. To the extent the court's opinion can be read as taking a position on that question, I decline to join that aspect of its reasoning.

[35] We don't need to resolve whether evidence of indiscriminate verb use is categorically irrelevant in an action alleging that a trademark has become generic because, on this record, no rational jury could find in the plaintiffs' favor even taking into account the flimsy evidence of indiscriminate verb use they produced. In support of its motion for summary judgment, Google produced overwhelming evidence that the public primarily understands the word "Google" as a trademark for its own search engine, not the name for search engines generally. In Google's consumer survey, 93% of respondents identified "Google" as a brand name, rather than a common name for search engines. In every dictionary in the record, the first entry for "Google" or "google" refers to Google's search engine. Google extracted concessions from the plaintiffs' expert linguists that Google functions as a trademark for Google's search engine. Google also submitted evidence showing that it uses its trademark to refer only to its own search engine, that it polices infringement by others, and that its competitors refrain from using the trademark to refer to their own search engines. Finally, Google offered evidence showing that major media outlets use "Google" to refer exclusively to Google's search engine.

[36] In response, the plaintiffs produced thousands of pages of largely irrelevant evidence showing merely that "google" is sometimes used as a verb. The sliver of potentially relevant evidence purporting to show that the public uses the verb "google" to refer to searching the Internet with any search engine (as opposed to Google's search engine in particular) is too insubstantial to save the plaintiffs' case. For example, the plaintiffs point to their Thermos survey, in which respondents were asked what word or phrase they would use to ask a friend to search for something on the Internet. Most respondents answered either "google," "google it," "google something," "google this," "google search," or "bring up google." However, those answers share the same problem that the court identifies with almost all of the plaintiffs' evidence, such as the rapper T–Pain's lyric telling his listeners to "google my name." That is, without more context, we simply can't tell whether the survey respondents were referring to searching the Internet with Google's search engine or with any search engine generally.

[37] At most, with respect to evidence that the public employs the verb "google" without regard to the search engine used, the plaintiffs have mustered secondary definitions from a few dictionaries and expert testimony from their linguists. Whatever this evidence might suggest about the use of "google" as a verb, no rational jury could rely on it to find, on this record, that the word has become the generic name for Internet search engines. As already mentioned, these dictionaries' primary definitions of the word uniformly refer to Google's own search engine. And the expert linguists conceded in their depositions

that, despite their opinion that "google" is used in verb form without regard to a specific search engine, the term has not become a generic name for search engines.

[38] There may never be a case that turns on evidence that a trademark is commonly used as a verb to refer to use of a type of good or service, as opposed to use of the particular product for which the trademark is registered. But if such a case were to arise, it's not obvious to me that a jury should be foreclosed from relying on the way the public uses the word as a verb to decide whether the public also thinks of the mark as the generic name for the type of good or service. The way we use words as verbs is often related to how we use those words as adjectives or nouns, such that evidence of indiscriminate verb use could potentially be relevant in deciding whether a trademark has become the generic name for a type of good or service. To the extent the court's opinion can be read to foreclose the consideration of such evidence as a matter of law, I decline to join it.

Comments and Questions

1. *What is the appropriate level of abstraction?* With respect to the genus/species distinction, how does one establish the appropriate level of abstraction at which one defines the genus, the species, and even the subspecies (or, for that matter, the family above the genus)? What prevents a plaintiff from claiming that the genus is, for example, beer, and the plaintiff merely wants rights in the name of a species of beer, which is "light beer"? *See Miller Brewing Co. v. G. Heileman Brewing Co.*, 561 F.2d 75 (7th Cir. 1977) (finding LIGHT and LITE for beer to be generic).

2. *Surveying for Genericism: The "*Thermos*" Survey Method.* In *American Thermos Products Co. v. Aladdin Industries, Inc.*, 207 F. Supp. 9 (D. Conn. 1962), aff'd, 321 F.2d 577 (2d Cir. 1963), the defendant argued that the term "thermos" had lost its significance as a designation of source and become a generic term for vacuum-insulated containers. To support this argument, the defendant submitted a survey whose method has been copied in many subsequent genericism cases. *See, e.g., E.T. Browne Drug Co. v. Cococare Products, Inc.*, 538 F.3d 185, 87 U.S.P.Q.2d 1655 (3d Cir. 2008) (evaluating *Thermos*-type survey). *See also* McCARTHY § 12:15. In essence, a *Thermos* survey (1) asks the survey respondent whether they are familiar with the general product at issue (e.g., "the type of container that is used to keep liquids, like soup, coffee, tea and lemonade, hot or cold for a period of time"), (2) asks the respondent to imagine him/herself walking into a store and asking for that product, and then (3) inquires "What would you ask for—that is, what would you tell the clerk you wanted?" The survey will then typically ask some form of the question "Can you think of any other words that you would use to ask for the product?" In *American Thermos Products*, 75% of the 3,300 respondents answered "Thermos" to the "what would you ask for" question. *American Thermos Products*, 207 F. Supp. at 21-22. The court found that the term "thermos" had become generic for vacuum-insulated bottles.

The *Thermos* survey method has been criticized on the ground that "for a very strong trademark, respondents with brand loyalty may answer with the trademark and drop what they consider to be a generic name, because it's so obvious to them." McCARTHY § 12:15. Imagine you walk into a fast food restaurant in order to purchase a carbonated cola-flavored beverage. What would you ask for? What do you think the results of such a survey of 100 respondents would be, and do they support McCarthy's criticism?

3. *Surveying for Genericism: The "*Teflon*" Survey Method.* In *E. I. DuPont de Nemours & Co. v. Yoshida International, Inc.*, 393 F. Supp. 502 (E.D.N.Y. 1975), Dupont, producer of TEFLON resins, brought a trademark action against the defendant Yoshida, producer of EFLON zippers. In response to Yoshida's argument that TEFLON had become generic, DuPont submitted two surveys, one of which was a telephone survey in which respondents were first given what was essentially a mini-course in the difference between "brand names" and "common names" and then asked if "teflon" was a brand name or a common name. The core of the survey script proceeded as follows:

> I'd like to read 8 names to you and get you to tell me whether you think it is a brand name
> or a common name; by *brand* name, I mean a word like *Chevrolet* which is made by one
> company; by *common* name, I mean *a word like automobile* which is made by a number of

86

different companies. So if I were to ask you, "Is Chevrolet a brand name or a common name?," what would you say?

Now, if I were to ask you, "Is washing machine a brand name or a common name?," what would you say?

[If respondent understands continue. If not understand, explain again.]

Now, would you say ——— is a brand name or a common name?

McCARTHY § 12:16. In one evening, 514 men and 517 women were surveyed in 20 cities. The survey results were as follows:

NAME	BRAND/%	COMMON/%	DON'T KNOW/%
STP	90	5	5
THERMOS	51	46	3
MARGARINE	9	91	1
TEFLON	68	31	2
JELLO	75	25	1
REFRIGERATOR	6	94	-
ASPIRIN	13	86	-
COKE	76	24	-

Interestingly, Yoshida submitted a *Thermos* survey to support its claim that TEFLON had become generic. As the court explained, this survey

> was conducted among adult women, 90.6% of whom expressed awareness of 'kitchen pots and pans that have their inside surfaces coated by chemical substances to keep grease or food from sticking to them.' Of the aware respondents, 86.1% apparently mentioned only 'TEFLON' or 'TEFLON II' [DuPont's mark for an improved means of applying its resin to metal surfaces] as their sole answer when asked, 'What is the name . . . or names of these pots and pans . . . ?' Further, 71.7% of the aware women gave only 'TEFLON' or 'TEFLON II' as the name they would use to describe the pots and pans to a store clerk or friend.

E. I. DuPont de Nemours & Co., 393 F.Supp. at 525.

The court ultimately found DuPont's brand name vs. common name survey to be the most persuasive. In Yoshida's *Thermos* survey (as in other surveys in the case not discussed here), the court found, "respondents were, by the design of the questions, more often than not focusing on supplying the inquirer a 'name', without regard to whether the principal significance of the name supplied was 'its indication of the nature or class of an article, rather than an indication of its origin.'" *Id.* at 527 (quoting *King-Seeley Thermos Co.*, 321 F.2d at 580). Only DuPont's brand name vs. common name survey

> really gets down to the critical element of the case. . . . {T}he responses of the survey reveal that the public is quite good at sorting out brand names from common names, and, for TEFLON, answers the critical question left unanswered by the ambiguities inherent in {the other surveys]—that of the principal significance of the TEFLON mark to the public. Not only have defendants failed to show that TEFLON's principal significance is as a common noun, plaintiff has succeeded in showing it to be a 'brand name'—an indicator, in the words of DuPont's questionnaire, of a product 'made by one company.'"

E. I. DuPont de Nemours & Co., 393 F.Supp. at 527.

Do you agree that the *Teflon* survey method is superior to the *Thermos* survey method for assessing whether a mark is generic?

4. *Surveying for Genericism: Secondary Meaning Surveys?* In a portion of the *Snyder's Lance* opinion not excerpted above, the district court quoted and endorsed the TTAB's analysis of a secondary meaning survey that Princeton Vanguard had submitted in an effort to prove that PRETZEL CRISPS had acquired

secondary meaning. The TTAB interpreted the survey evidence rather differently. As quoted by the Synder's Lance district court, the TTAB explained:

The {Mantis Survey} was conducted via online participation, between August 26 and August 30, 2011. There were 400 survey participants. Respondents were invited by email to participate in the survey and were told it was about "salty snack foods." Individuals were then asked prescreening questions. To be included in the survey, individuals had to, among other things, be the "primary grocery shopper," be "between the ages of 24 and 39," and "have purchased crackers and pretzels in the past month and will purchase crackers and pretzels in the next month."

Survey respondents were informed during the screening process about the difference between "brand" and "common" names and then allowed to proceed with the survey only if they correctly associated BAKED TOSTITOS with "only one company" and TORTILLA CHIPS with "more than one company." For those who proceeded with the study, two control names were given, and the same questions were asked. The results are shown as follows:

NAME	Only One Company	More	Don't Know
SUN CHIPS	96.5%	3%	.5%
ONION RINGS	23.8%	72%	4.3%
PRETZEL CRISPS	**38.7%**	**47.8%**	**13.5%**

Based on the survey, Mr. Mantis found that 38.7% of the respondents associated the name "PRETZEL CRISPS" with only one company. On that basis, he stated: "It is my opinion that the name 'PRETZEL CRISPS,' used in conjunction with a salty snack food product, has acquired secondary meaning."

Plaintiff retained Dr. Ivan Ross to rebut the findings of Mr. Mantis. Keeping in mind that the rebuttal was as to a survey offered to show acquired distinctiveness, Dr. Ross' main objection to the Mantis survey is that although Mr. Mantis said that he conducted the survey for the purpose of establishing secondary meaning, Mr. Mantis's methodology actually analyzes genericness. Plaintiff specifically argues that the Mantis survey was conducted in the manner of a Teflon-style survey, in that participants were asked whether they associate each term with one company or with more than one company. In this regard, during the initial mini-course, participants were specifically instructed as to the differences between "brand" and "common" names:

Some names are brand names. A brand name refers to a product associated with one particular company. Other names are common names. A common name refers to a type of product associated with more than one company.

As such, participants were told that if they associated a term with "one particular company" then it is a "brand name," and vice-versa. With this instruction given to all participants in the survey, we find it logical to consider all those who said they associated the term "PRETZEL CRISPS" with "one particular company" thus also found the term "PRETZEL CRISPS" to be a "brand name" rather than a "common name," and that all those who said they associated the term "PRETZEL CRISPS" with "more than one company" thus also found the term "PRETZEL CRISPS" to be a "common name" rather than a "brand name." In this regard, only 38.7% of participants, which is rather less than 50%, found the term to be a brand name.

Accordingly, we find that although the Mantis survey was conducted and offered for the purpose of showing secondary meaning, if we had considered the other two surveys on the question of genericness, the Mantis survey should also have been considered on the issue of genericness. Since substantially less than half of the Mantis survey respondents associated the term "PRETZEL CRISPS" with a single source, this survey weighs in favor of finding genericness. We note, in this regard, that even if we were to split the 13.5% percent of "don't know" responses, as suggested by Defendant with regard to the Simonson survey, then adding 6.75% to each of the "only one company" and "more than one company" tallies, we still have less than a majority who associate the term with one company, and more than half who associate the term with more than one company, and so we have the same result.

Snyder's Lance, Inc. v. Frito-Lay North America, Inc., __ F.Supp.3d __, 2021 WL 232293, at *22–23 (2021) (quoting *Frito-Lay N. Am., Inc. v. Princeton Vanguard, LLC*, 124 U.S.P.Q.2d 1184, 1191-1201 (TTAB 2017)).

5. *Is* WINDOWS *for a computer operating system generic?* On December 20, 2011, Microsoft filed suit against Lindows.com ("Lindows") alleging that Lindows' mark LINDOWS for a Linux-based operating system infringed Microsoft's WINDOWS mark. Lindows argued that WINDOWS was generic at the time that Microsoft first began to use it in 1985. In *Microsoft Corp. v. Lindows.com, Inc.*, No. 01 Civ. 2115C, 2002 WL 31499324 (W.D.Wash., Mar. 15, 2002), the district court denied Microsoft's motion for a preliminary injunction, finding that there were "serious questions regarding whether Windows is a non-generic name and thus eligible for the protections of federal trademark law." *Id.* at *18. The case eventually settled — with Microsoft agreeing to pay Lindows $20 million to change its name (to Linspire) and cease using the LINDOWS mark on any of its products.

6. *Usage policies.* Owners of very well-known marks are especially wary of their marks' falling prey to genericide through widespread generic usage. They typically develop and seek to enforce strict policies on how their marks are used. See, e.g., Google, Rules for proper usage, http://www.google.com/permissions/trademark/rules.html ("Use a generic term following the trademark, for example: GOOGLE search engine, Google search, GOOGLE web search"; "Use the trademark only as an adjective, never as a noun or verb, and never in the plural or possessive form."; "If you do not capitalize the entire mark, always spell and capitalize the trademark exactly as they are shown in the Google Trademarks and Suggested Accepted Generic Terms.").

7. *Source-denotative in American English, but generic elsewhere?* Sheepskin boots with a tanned outer surface, fleece interior, and synthetic soles are generically known as "ugg boots" or "uggs" in Australia and New Zealand, where they were originally developed and where a variety of companies use the term "ugg" to describe the boots they manufacture. In the United States, by contrast, UGG is a registered trademark for such boots, owned by Deckers Outdoor Corp. (U.S. Trademark Reg. No. 4,234,396, Oct. 30, 2012). When an Australian company sought to sell what it called "ugg boots" in the United States, Deckers sued. The Australian company argued that the term was generic. It lost. In granting summary judgment to Deckers on the issue, the court explained:

> Australian Leather has evidence that ugg is generic in Australia, but there is no evidence that Americans familiar with Australian usage (or Australian visitors to the United States) would be misled into thinking that there is only one brand of ugg-style sheepskin boots available in this country. Australian Leather needed to come forward with some evidence that would allow a jury to conclude that the term ugg has a generic meaning to buyers in the United States; its Australian and surf-shop evidence does not suffice.

Deckers Outdoor Corp. v. Australian Leather Pty. Ltd., 340 F. Supp. 3d 706, 716 (N.D. Ill. 2018).

For an interesting comparison, the Swiss and French associations representing the makers of Gruyère cheese filed in 2015 an application at the PTO to register the term GRUYERE (without the accent) as a certification mark. GRUYÈRE is a protected geographic indication in the European Union and Switzerland. Various American dairy interests opposed the registration. The TTAB refused registration on the ground that the term was generic. It found that American consumers "understand the term 'gruyere' as a designation that primarily refers to a category within the genus of cheese that can come from anywhere." *Int'l Dairy Foods Ass'n v. Interprofession Du Gruyere*, 2020 TTAB LEXIS 268, *82, 2020 U.S.P.Q.2D 10892 (TTAB August 5, 2020).

8. *Can a color be generic?* In *Milwaukee Electric Tool Corp. v. Freud America, Inc.*, Cancellation Nos. 92,059,634 & 92,059,637 (TTAB Dec. 2, 2019) [precedential], the TTAB found that the color red was generic when covering the surface of saw blades:

> This evidence overwhelmingly demonstrates that the color red on saw blades is so common in the industry that it cannot identify a single source for saw blades for power woodworking machines or saw blades for reciprocating power saws. What is more, because the evidence establishes that the color red was widely used by others at the time Freud filed the underlying applications for each of its subject registrations and third-party use continues to the present day, the color red was generic for power saw blades when Freud applied for both of its marks and remains so now.

Id. at *67. Most commentators would likely agree with the proposition that "[g]enericness seems . . . to be the wrong pigeonhole for a proposed color mark." John L. Welch, *Precedential No. 37: TTAB Rules that the Color Red is Generic for Saw Blades*, THE TTABLOG, Dec. 9, 2019, http://thettablog.blogspot.com/2019/12/precedential-no-37-ttab-rules-that.html. More appropriate would have been a finding that the mark lacked acquired distinctiveness, failed to function as a mark, or was perceived by consumers as mere decoration. However, one of the marks at issue had been registered for more than five years, so it could not likely have been challenged on these grounds. (*See* Lanham Act § 14 and Part I.D.6 below).

9. *Can a product shape be generic?* In *In re Jasmin Larian, LLC*, 2022 TTAB LEXIS 99 (TTAB Jan. 19, 2022) [precedential], the applicant sought to register as a trademark the configuration of its "Ark" handbag, shown below. The TTAB held that the configuration had long since become a commonplace design originating from multiple sources and was thus generic. It reasoned: "In the context of product design, genericness may be found where the design is so common in the industry that it cannot be said to identify a particular source." *Id.* at *8.

d.   Failure to Function as a Mark

In recent years, trademark applicants have increasingly sought to register cultural memes or other commonplace slogans as trademarks for various merchandise. The PTO has rejected such applications on the ground that the applied-for marks are not perceived by consumers as designations of source. *See, e.g.*, *In re Texas With Love, LLC*, Serial No. 87793802 (TTAB October 29, 2020) [precedential] (refusing to register TEXAS LOVE for "hats, shirts" on ground that because the phrase "only serves as an expression of a concept or sentiment, and is widely used by third parties, it would not be perceived as an indicator of source in the context of Applicant's identified goods."); *In re Gillard*, Serial No. 87469115 (TTAB Jan. 11, 2019) (not citable as precedent) (refusing application of one John Gillard to register #COVFEFE on ground that "because hashtags are commonly employed to facilitate categorization and searching of topics of public discussion, and the record makes it clear that #COVFEFE has served that purpose in promoting discussion of the mystery word in the President's tweet, the public will not understand #COVFEFE to identify one, and only one, source of clothing, and to recognize Applicant as that source, when it appears on Applicant's goods"); PTO Office Action, U.S. Application Serial No. 86,506,015, Mar. 25, 2015 (refusing registration of JE SUIS CHARLIE for various goods on ground that "[b]ecause consumers are accustomed to seeing this slogan or motto commonly used in everyday speech by many different sources, the public will not perceive the motto or slogan as a trademark that identifies the source of applicant's goods but rather only as conveying an informational message"); PTO Office Action, U.S. Application No. 88579771, Sept. 11, 2019 (refusing basketball player LeBron James's application to register TACO TUESDAY in connection with podcasting and other related goods and services); PTO Office Action, U.S. Application No. 86,479,784, Mar. 4, 2015 (refusing registration of I CAN'T BREATHE for clothing). In the opinion excerpted below, the TTAB refused country music singer Lee Greenwood's application to register the phrase GOD BLESS THE USA on failure to function grounds. Is the TTAB essentially engaging in a secondary meaning analysis or are its concerns broader?

Mr. Lee Greenwood

In re Lee Greenwood
Serial No. 87168719, 2020 WL 7074687 (TTAB Dec. 1, 2020)

[1] Applicant, Lee Greenwood, seeks registration on the Principal Register of the proposed mark GOD BLESS THE USA (in standard characters) for "accent pillows; decorative centerpieces of wood," in International Class 20 and "decorative wall hangings, not of textile" in International Class 27 {Application Serial No. 87,168,719}.

[2] The Trademark Examining Attorney has refused registration of Applicant's proposed mark under Sections 1, 2 and 45 of the Trademark Act, 15 U.S.C. §§ 1051, 1052 and 1127, on the ground that it fails to function as a trademark. When the refusal was made final, Applicant appealed and filed a brief seeking reversal of the refusal to register.

. . . .

[3] A proposed trademark is registrable only if it functions as an identifier of the source of the applicant's goods or services. *In re Yarnell Ice Cream, LLC*, 2019 USPQ2d 265039, *16 (TTAB 2019). To function as a trademark, an applicant's proposed mark must, by definition, "identify and distinguish his or her goods, . . . from those manufactured or sold by others and . . . indicate the source of the goods, even if that source is unknown." 15 U.S.C. § 1127, *quoted in In re Texas With Love, LLC*, 2020 USPQ2d 11290, *2 (TTAB 2020). *See also In re Bose Corp.*, 546 F.2d 893, 192 USPQ 213, 215 (CCPA 1976) ("[T]he classic function of a trademark is to point out distinctively the origin of the goods to which it is attached"). "Matter that does not operate to indicate the source or origin of the identified goods or services and distinguish them from those of others does not meet the statutory definition of a trademark and may not be registered, regardless of the register on which registration is sought." *In re AC Webconnecting Holding B.V.*, 2020 USPQ2d 11048, *2-3 (TTAB 2020).

[4] The critical inquiry in determining whether a proposed mark functions as a trademark is how it would be perceived by the relevant public. *In re Vox Populi Registry Ltd.*, 2020 USPQ2d 11289, *4 (TTAB 2020); *In re TracFone Wireless, Inc.*, 2019 USPQ2d 222983, *1 (TTAB 2019) ("The key question is whether the asserted mark would be perceived as a source indicator for Applicant's [goods or] services."); *D.C. One Wholesaler, Inc. v. Chien*, 120 USPQ2d 1710, 1713 (TTAB 2016). To function as a

trademark, the proposed mark must be used in a manner calculated to project to purchasers or potential purchasers a single source or origin for the goods. *In re DePorter*, 129 USPQ2d 1298, 1299 (TTAB 2019). "Thus, a threshold issue in some cases (like this one) is whether the phrase in question in fact functions to identify the source of the services recited in the application and distinguish them from the services of others or, instead, would be perceived merely as communicating the ordinary meaning of the words to consumers." *In re Wal-Mart Stores, Inc.*, 129 USPQ2d 1148, 1149 (TTAB 2019). "Where the evidence suggests that the ordinary consumer would take the words at their ordinary meaning rather than read into them some special meaning distinguishing the goods from similar goods of others, then the words fail to function as a mark." *In re Ocean Tech., Inc.*, 2019 USPQ2d 450686, *3 (TTAB 2019) (internal punctuation omitted).

[5] Consumers ordinarily take widely-used, commonplace messages at their ordinary meaning, and not as source indicators, absent evidence to the contrary. *See In re Mayweather Promotions, LLC*, 2020 USPQ2d 11298, *1 (TTAB 2020) ("Widely used commonplace messages are those that merely convey ordinary, familiar concepts or sentiments and will be understood as conveying the ordinary concept or sentiment normally associated with them, rather than serving any source-indicating function."). "Messages that are used by a variety of sources to convey social, political, religious, or similar sentiments or ideas are likely to be perceived as an expression of support for, or affiliation or affinity with, the ideas embodied in the message rather than as a mark that indicates a single source of the goods or services." *In re DePorter*, 129 USPQ2d at 1302 n.14 (quoting TMEP § 1202.04(b)). "The more commonly a phrase is used, the less likely that the public will use it to identify only one source and the less likely that it will be recognized by purchasers as a trademark." *In re Eagle Crest Inc.*, 96 USPQ2d 1227, 1229 (TTAB 2010) *quoted in In re Peace Love World Live, LLC*, 127 USPQ2d 1400, 1402 (TTAB 2018).

[6] To determine how consumers are likely to perceive the phrase sought to be registered, we look not only to the specimens, but to other evidence of record showing the phrase as used in general parlance. *In re Wal-Mart*, 129 USPQ2d at 1150. The Examining Attorney maintains that Applicant's applied-for mark, GOD BLESS THE USA, is a common patriotic message, analogous to and synonymous with "God Bless America." *See* TMEP § 1202.04(b) ("Derivatives or variations of widely used messages also fail to function as marks if they convey the same or similar type of information or sentiment as the original wording."). The wording is, in fact, commonly used by many different sources on a vast array of goods, she notes, as illustrated by evidence obtained from over three dozen third-party websites. The following are representative samples from various sources:

12

13

92

14 Zazzle.com, *Id.* at 14.

15 Shop.ColonialWilliamsburg.com, *Id.* at 22

16 SupportStore.com, *Id.* at 24.

17 CelebratingHomeDirect.com, *Id.* at 29.

18 ChristmasLoft.com, *Id.* at 36.

19 HobbyLobby.com, *Id.* at 38.

[7] Thus, the record evidence demonstrates that a variety of sources prominently display the phrase GOD BLESS THE USA on a range of household items such as mugs, trays, cutting boards, pillows, ornaments, posters, flags, and the like. This common use by third parties renders it less likely that the public would perceive the phrase as identifying a single commercial source. *In re Wal-Mart*, 129 USPQ2d at 1156. In that sense, this case is reminiscent of *D.C. One Wholesaler v. Chien*, where the phrase "I <<heart>> DC" was commonly available on a range of goods, from apparel and aprons to commuter cups and keychains. 120 USPQ2d at 1713-14. There, the Board found that the "widespread ornamental use of the phrase by third parties 'is part of the environment in which the [proposed mark] is perceived by the public and . . . may influence how the [proposed mark] is perceived.'" *Id.* at 1716 (quoting *In re Hulting*, 107 USPQ2d 1175, 1178 (TTAB 2013); *In re Tilcon Warren Inc.*, 221 USPQ 86, 88 (TTAB 1984)). Here, as there, the record indicates that the phrase GOD BLESS THE USA is displayed, not as a source indicator, but as an expression of patriotism, affection, or affiliation with the United States of America. *Id.*

[8] Applicant, a country music artist, insists that "God Bless the USA" would be commonly recognized as his signature song. He quotes Wikipedia:

> "God Bless the USA" is an American patriotic song written and recorded by country music artist Lee Greenwood, and is considered to be his signature song. The first album it appears on is 1984's You've Got a Good Love Comin'. It reached No. 7 on the Billboard magazine Hot Country Singles chart when originally released in the spring of 1984, and was played at the 1984 Republican National Convention with President Ronald Reagan and first lady Nancy Reagan in attendance, but the song gained greater prominence during the Gulf War in 1990 and 1991, as a way of boosting morale. The popularity of the song rose sharply after the September 11 attacks and during the 2003 invasion of Iraq, and the song was re-released as a single, re-entering the country music charts at No. 16 and peaking at No. 16 on the Billboard Hot 100 pop chart in 2001.

"The song 'God Bless the USA' has been downloaded at least two and half million times since reentering the Billboard Country Digital Song Sales Chart," Applicant points out. He maintains that if one searches for "God Bless the USA" on the Google search engine, the first page of results refers to Applicant's song title. In view of "Mr. Greenwood's talent and fame" and "the notoriety of his iconic song 'God Bless the USA' and his close association therewith . . .," Applicant contends that the public will regard the proposed mark GOD BLESS THE USA as his trademark.

[9] However, "[i]t is well settled that not every designation that is placed or used on a product necessarily functions as a trademark for said product and not every designation adopted with the intention that it perform a trademark function necessarily accomplishes that purpose." *D.C. One Wholesaler v. Chien*, 120 USPQ2d at 1713; *accord In re Texas With Love*, 2020 USPQ2d 11290 at *2-3. Because there are no limitations to the channels of trade or classes of consumers of the goods identified in the application, the relevant consumers are members of the general public, who may or may not be music aficionados. *CBS Inc. v. Morrow*, 708 F.2d 1579, 218 USPQ 198, 199 (Fed. Cir. 1983); *Bell's Brewery, Inc. v. Innovation Brewing*, 125 USPQ2d 1340, 1345 (TTAB 2017), *cited in In re Mayweather Promotions*, 2020 USPQ2d 11298 at *3. In any event, even if these consumers were familiar with the song and Applicant himself, they may not associate the household items identified in the involved application with Applicant or his song, when so many third parties offer household items bearing the same wording.

---

[20] Etsy.com Aug. 11, 2017 Office Action TSDR at 30.

[21] Etsy.com, *Id.* at 34.

[22] Houzz.com, *Id.* at 42.

[23] DiscountDecorativeFlags.com, *Id.* at 50.

[10] In sum, based on the record evidence, we find that Applicant's proposed mark GOD BLESS THE USA is "devoid of source-identifying significance and therefore fails to function as a trademark." *In re Hulting*, 107 USPQ2d at 1181.

Decision: The refusal to register is affirmed as to both classes.

In *In re Lizzo, LLC*, Serial Nos. 88466264 and 88466281, 2023 TTAB LEXIS 22 (TTAB Feb. 2, 2023), the trademark registration applicant is the trademark holding company owned by the famous artist known as Lizzo. It sought to register the mark 100% THAT BITCH, which is a lyrical phrase in one of Lizzo's songs entitled "Truth Hurts." The applicant's submitted specimen of use is shown below.

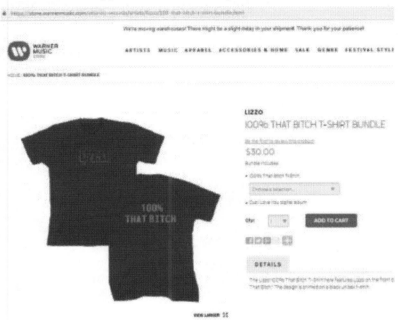

The Examining Attorney refused registration on failure to function grounds, determining that the asserted mark "is a commonplace expression widely used by a variety of sources to convey an ordinary, familiar, well-recognized sentiment." *Id.* at *2. On appeal, the Trademark Trial and Appeal Board reversed. Its opinion is lengthy with numerous images and will reward a full reading. Excerpted here is the core of the Board's reasoning:

> {T}he evidence here does not demonstrate that Applicant's proposed mark is used in general parlance or that it conveys a common social, political, patriotic, religious or other informational message such as DRIVE SAFELY, THINK GREEN or WATCH THAT CHILD. Applicant and the Examining Attorney agree that the proposed mark conveys a feeling of female strength, empowerment and independence. But more importantly, considering the entirety of the record, we find that most consumers would perceive 100% THAT BITCH used on the goods in the application as associated with Lizzo rather than as a commonplace expression.

> {T}he evidence in these appeals establishes that in 2017, the musical artist Lizzo encountered "I just took a DNA test, turns out I'm 100% that bitch" as a Twitter meme from the same year. The message in the meme resonated with her, and she used the meme as a lyric in her 2017 song "Truth Hurts," which went on to become a Billboard Number 1 hit single. Lizzo did not originate the expression she encountered as a Twitter meme, and subsequently granted a writing credit for her song "Truth Hurts" to its originator. *See Hole In 1 Drinks, Inc. v. Lajtay*, 2020 USPQ2d 10020, at *9 (TTAB 2020) ("[T]rademark rights are not gained by creating a mark, but through use of the mark."). Nonetheless, lyrics from

songs are more likely to be attributed to the artists who sing, rap or otherwise utter them, rather than the songwriters, who may be different individuals receiving varying degrees of writing credit. The evidence of record here indicates that Lizzo and her hit song "Truth Hurts" popularized the lyric and elevated 100% THAT BITCH from what may have been a lesser known phrase (the evidence of record only points to use of that phrase from the 2017 meme onward) to more memorable status.

All of the evidence of record regarding third-party use of 100% THAT BITCH is from 2017 or later. The Urban Dictionary entry for the term is dated June 12, 2019. Thus, the evidence is contemporaneous with or subsequent to the release of Lizzo's hit single "Truth Hurts." There is no evidence of use of the term 100% THAT BITCH prior to 2017, so we have no indication that the proposed mark already was "widely used, over a long period of time and by a large number of merchandisers" before Lizzo popularized it. *See D.C. One Wholesaler, Inc.*, 120 USPQ2d at 1716. And, as noted above, much of the evidence of third-party use specifically seeks to associate the goods emblazoned with 100% THAT BITCH with Lizzo, her music and the lyrics from "Truth Hurts." In addition, evidence of record indicates that third-party retailers responding to takedown notices from Applicant's counsel recognize that 100% THAT BITCH is associated with Lizzo and her music.[29]

. . . .

The record as a whole does not establish that the proposed mark is a common expression in such widespread use that it fails to function as a mark for the goods identified in this application.

In re Lizzo, LLC, Serial Nos. 88466264 and 88466281, 2023 TTAB LEXIS 22, at *22-25 (TTAB Feb. 2, 2023).

Comments and Questions

1. For more on the "failure to function as a mark" bar to protectability, see Alexandra J. Roberts, *Trademark Failure to Function*, 104 Iowa L. Rev. 1977 (2019). *See also* Lisa P. Ramsey, *Using Failure to Function Doctrine to Protect Free Speech and Competition in Trademark Law*, 104 Iowa L. Rev. Online 70, 89 (2020) ("Allowing trademark registration and protection of puns, political and social messages, culturally important terms or images, and other common words or designs for expressive merchandise can chill and suppress the speech of competing manufacturers, print-on-demand companies, and others who want to display this language on products sold to people who desire these goods because of the ideas they convey.").

e.   Further Examples of *Abercrombie* Classifications

Provided here are numerous examples of courts' classification of trademarks' distinctiveness along the *Abercrombie* spectrum. You are very strongly encouraged to determine your own view on the appropriate classification before you consult how the court ruled. Do any of the following classifications strike you as incorrect?

- TIDE for laundry detergent. *See Wal-Mart Stores, Inc. v. Samara Bros.*, 529 U.S. 205, 210 (2000) (giving TIDE for laundry detergent as an example of a suggestive mark).

- SERIAL for "entertainment in the nature of ongoing audio program featuring investigative reporting, interviews, and documentary storytelling." *See In re Serial Podcast, LLC*, 126 U.S.P.Q.2d 1061 (TTAB 2018) (finding the applied-for standard character mark to be generic

---

[29] . . . . The third parties seeking to associate their use of the phrase 100% THAT BITCH with Lizzo suggests that, for purposes of **this** failure to function refusal, the phrase currently is associated with Lizzo. We observe, nonetheless, that proliferation of unauthorized third-party use risks the mark's loss of strength as an exclusive source indicator, or even abandonment. *See, e.g., Nobelle.com, LLC v. Qwest Commc'ns Int'l, Inc.*, 66 USPQ2d 1300, 1306-07 (TTAB 2003).

but finding the applied-for logos incorporating the term to possess acquired distinctiveness and qualify for protection)

- THE STORK CLUB for a restaurant. *See Stork Restaurant v. Sahati*, 166 F.2d 348, 355 (9th Cir. 1948) (finding the stork club to be arbitrary as to a restaurant and reasoning that "[i]t is in no way descriptive of the appellant's night club, for in its primary significance it would denote a club for storks. Nor is it likely that the sophisticates who are its most publicized customers are particularly interested in the stork.").

- GOOGLE for internet search service. *See* GILSON § 2.04 (giving GOOGLE for search engine as an example of a fanciful mark).

- SNAKELIGHT for a light with a flexible neck. *See Black & Decker Corp. v. Dunsford*, 944 F. Supp. 220 (S.D.N.Y. 1996) (finding the mark to be descriptive and reasoning that "Snakelight' is just what it says: a 'snake-like' light. In this context, the word 'snake' functions as an adjective, modifying the principal term, the generic noun 'light.' Taken as a whole, the name conveys the 'immediate idea' of the 'characteristics' of the product [citing *Abercrombie*]).

- CLOROX for bleach. *See Clorox Chemical Co. v. Chlorit Mfg. Corp.*, 25 F. Supp. 702, 705 (D.N.Y. 1938) ("'Clorox' is a fanciful word, arbitrarily selected in no wise describes its ingredients.").

- STREETWISE for street maps. *See Streetwise Maps, Inc. v. VanDam, Inc.*, 159 F.3d 739, 744 (2d Cir. 1998) ("The district court ranked the Streetwise mark as suggestive, meaning that the term "suggested" the features of the product and required the purchaser to use his or her imagination to figure out the nature of the product. We agree.").

- SUPREME for vodka. *See Supreme Wine Co. v. American Distilling Co.*, 310 F.2d 888, 889 (2d Cir. 1962) (finding SUPREME for vodka to be descriptive on the ground that "[m]erely laudatory words, such as 'best', 'outstanding', or 'supreme' cannot of their own force indicate the source or origin of the labeled goods").

- PLAYBOY for a men's magazine. *See Playboy Enters., Inc. v. Chuckleberry Pub., Inc.*, 687 F.2d 563, 566-67 (2d. Cir. 1982) (finding the mark to be suggestive and reasoning that "Playboy is defined in the Random House Dictionary of the English Language (unabridged ed. 1966) as 'a wealthy, carefree man who devotes most of his time to leisure, self-amusement, and hedonistic pleasures, conventionally frequenting parties and night clubs, romancing a rapid succession of attractive young women, and racing speedboats and sports cars.' Although the word may signify the aspirations of PLAYBOY's readership, it does not describe the product or its contents.").

- NO NAME for meat and other food products. *See J&B Wholesale Distributing, Inc. v. Redux Beverages, LLC*, 85 U.S.P.Q.2d 1623, 1626 (D. Minn. 2007) ("[S]tanding alone, 'No Name' does not bear any relation to the product—that is it does not tell the consumer anything about the product. The Court thus finds that 'No Name' is an arbitrary mark that is entitled to protection.").

- BAIKALSKAYA for vodka produced in the Lake Baikal region of Russia, where "Baikalskaya" means "from Baikal" in Russian. *See In re Joint-Stock Co. "Baik,"* 80 USPQ2d 1305 (TTAB 2006) (finding BAIKALSKAYA for vodka to be primarily geographically descriptive)

- KODAK for photographic film. *See Wal-Mart Stores, Inc. v. Samara Bros.*, 529 U.S. 205, 210 (2000) (giving Kodak for film as an example of a fanciful mark).

- GLOW for fragrance, shower gel, and body lotion products. *See Glow Indus., Inc. v. Lopez*, 252 F. Supp. 2d 962, 978 (C.D. Cal. 2002) (finding GLOW suggestive as to perfume and reasoning that "[t]he mark does not directly describe the attributes of Glow, Inc.'s perfume. Indeed, words other than the GLOW mark are used on the packaging to convey the fact that the perfume is a sandalwood scent. The mark thus appears to refer suggestively to the positive feeling one will achieve by using the product."); id. at 979 (finding GLOW suggestive as to shower gel and body lotion and reasoning that "'Glow' is not descriptive of the qualities or characteristics of shower gels or body lotions. Indeed, one who hears the word does not immediately think of such products. Rather, some amount of association is required to link the concept of glowing skin to use of a particular gel or lotion.").

- BRICK OVEN PIZZA for frozen pizza. See *Schwan's IP, LLC v. Kraft Pizza Co.*, 460 F.3d 971 (8th Cir. 2006) (citing industry usage, media usage, and PTO rulings to find the term generic for pizza that is or appears to be baked in a brick oven).

- CITIBANK for banking services. *See Citibank, N.A. v. Citibanc Group, Inc.*, 724 F.2d 1540, 222 U.S.P.Q. 292 (11th Cir. 1984) (approving of the district court's finding that CITIBANK is suggestive for banking services).

- ODOL for mouthwash. See *In re Odol Chemical Corp.*, 150 U.S.P.Q. 827 (TTAB 1966) (finding ODOL for mouthwash to be fanciful).

- MORNINGSIDE for financial services. *See Morningside Group Ltd. v. Morningside Capital Group L.L.C.*, 182 F.3d 133 (2d Cir. 1999) (finding MORNINGSIDE to be arbitrary as to financial services).

- EAST END for vodka distilled in the East End of Houston, Texas. *See In re Buffalo Bayou Distilleries, LLC*, Serial No. 86,583,137 (TTAB July 30, 2018) (not citable as precedent) ("In this case, the record reflects that 'East End' can refer to numerous geographic locations, suggesting that its primary significance is not referring to the area in Houston, Texas. Also, the quantity and nature of the evidence regarding the East End of Houston does not establish that it is generally known to U.S. consumers. . . . The first prong of the inquiry under Section 2(e)(2), that the primary significance of the term in the mark sought to be registered is the name of a place generally known to the public, is not satisfied.").

- NUMBER ONE IN FLOOR CARE for vacuums. *See* Hoover *Co. v. Royal Appliance Mfg. Co.*, 238 F.3d 1357, 1360, 57 U.S.P.Q.2d 1720 (Fed. Cir. 2001) (finding the mark NUMBER ONE IN FLOOR CARE for vacuums to "generally laudatory . . . and thus . . . not inherently distinctive").

- MARCH MADNESS for annual basketball tournament. *See March Madness Athletic Ass'n, L.L.C. v. Netfire, Inc.*, 310 F. Supp. 2d 786 (N.D. Tex. 2003) (finding without analysis the mark MARCH MADNESS to be descriptive of an annual basketball tournament).

- SPEEDY for bail bond services. *See Lederman Bonding Co. v. Sweetalia*, 83 U.S.P.Q.2d 1660, 2006 WL 2949290, at *3 (D. Colo. 2006) (finding SPEEDY for bail bond services to be descriptive "because it describes the quality of the bail bond services offered").

- BEAR for cold-weather outerwear. *See Bear U.S.A., Inc. v. A.J. Sheepskin & Leather Outerwear, Inc.*, 909 F.Supp. 896, 904 (S.D.N.Y. 1995) ("The word 'bear, especially in conjunction with the image of a polar bear, is connected with the concept of cold weather and protection from the elements. It suggests that the type of outerwear and boots sold by plaintiff offer the sort of protection afforded by bears' skins. The imagination and thought process involved in this mental association supports the conclusion that plaintiff's bear marks are suggestive, particularly as used in connection with boots and cold weather outwear.").

- QUANTUM for a health club. *See Quantum Fitness Corp. v. Quantum Lifestyle Ctrs.*, 83 F. Supp. 2d 810, 820 (S.D. Tex. 1999) (finding QUANTUM to be arbitrary for health club and reasoning, in part, that "[t]he absence of a connection between the term "quantum" and the plaintiff's products is evidenced by the frequent use of the word by third parties in a variety of different, unrelated lines of business").

- VIAGRA for an erectile dysfunction drug. *See Pfizer Inc. v. Sachs*, 652 F. Supp. 2d 512, 520 (S.D.N.Y. 2009) ("The Viagra mark is fanciful, because the word "Viagra" was coined specifically for purposes of this trademark and has no meaning outside this context.").

- Each of 928, 924, 944, 911, 911S, and 911SC for automobiles. *See Porsche Cars N. Am., Inc. v. Lloyd Design Corp.*, 2002 U.S. Dist. LEXIS 9612 (N.D. Ga. Mar. 26, 2002) ("[M]ost courts have held that model numbers, whether numbers or alphanumeric designations, are generally considered descriptive for the purposes of trademark protection. Although they may be "arbitrary" in the sense that they do not refer directly to a characteristic of the products, model numbers are generally intended merely to distinguish one specific product from another by a particular source, and are not intended to distinguish products from totally different sources.").

2.   The Distinctiveness Analysis of Nonverbal Marks

We have so far discussed the concept of trademark distinctiveness only in reference to word marks. But as we saw at the beginning of this Part, contemporary trademark law offers protection to far more than words and phrases. It protects image marks, sound marks, scent marks, and perhaps someday it will protect flavor or taste marks. *See In re N.V. Organon*, 79 U.S.P.Q.2d 1639, 2006 WL 1723556 (TTAB 2006) (denying registration to a mark consisting of "an orange flavor" for "pharmaceuticals for human use, namely, antidepressants in quick-dissolving tablets and pills" on the grounds that the mark lacked distinctiveness and was functional). Trademark law also protects "trade dress," which may consist of a product's packaging or configuration as well as nearly any other aspect of the product or service.

Over the past two decades, courts have struggled with how to analyze the distinctiveness of nonverbal marks, none more so than the Supreme Court in a series of three opinions:

- *Two Pesos, Inc. v. Taco Cabana, Inc.*, 505 U.S. 763 (1992) (analyzing the source-distinctiveness of a restaurant interior),

- *Qualitex Co. v. Jacobson Products Co., Inc.*, 514 U.S. 159 (1995) (analyzing the source-distinctiveness of a single color), and

- *Wal-Mart Stores, Inc. v. Samara Bros., Inc.*, 529 U.S. 205 (2000) (analyzing the source-distinctiveness of an apparel design).

In *Two Pesos*, the Court held that inherently distinctive trade dress could be protected without a showing of secondary meaning. In other words, and contrary to lower court case law primarily from the Second Circuit, the Court held that there was no special rule requiring that trade dress always show secondary meaning. In *Qualitex*, the Court held that a single color could qualify for trademark protection (provided that it possessed acquired distinctiveness of source). Finally, in *Samara Bros.* (or *Wal-Mart*, as some courts prefer), the Court arguably rewrote *Two Pesos*. It described the universe of trade dress as consisting of at least two categories: product packaging trade dress and product configuration trade dress. Product packaging trade dress was deemed capable of being inherently distinctive and when it was, it did not require a showing of secondary meaning to receive protection. Product configuration trade dress, however, could never be inherently distinctive and must always be shown to have acquired distinctiveness in order to qualify for protection.

One area of distinctiveness doctrine that the Court has not explicitly addressed is how to analyze the inherent distinctiveness of product packaging. Should courts use the *Abercrombie* spectrum or some other scheme of classification? As we will see below, there appears to be a circuit split on this issue.

a.   Initial Supreme Court Approaches to the Analysis of Nonverbal Marks

In reading *Two Pesos*, consider the following questions:

- The jury in *Two Pesos* presented to the Court a strange set of factual findings. The trade dress at issue was inherently distinctive but it lacked secondary meaning. How is this logically possible? Or perhaps better asked, how must we define inherent distinctiveness and secondary meaning so that this can be logically possible?

- What concerns might have motivated the Second Circuit to create a rule that all trade dress must show secondary meaning to qualify for protection?

- The trade dress at issue in *Two Pesos* was unregistered and thus protected, if at all, under Section 43(a) of the Lanham Act, 15 U.S.C. § 1125(a). Should the unregistered status of the trade dress have any bearing on the court's analysis of its distinctiveness?

- If, as *Two Pesos* holds, trade dress can be inherently distinctive, how should courts determine whether a specific instance of trade dress is in fact inherently distinctive? Should they simply apply the *Abercrombie* categories? Does *Two Pesos* offer any guidance on the matter?

Two Pesos, Inc. v. Taco Cabana, Inc.
505 U.S. 763 (1992)

Justice WHITE delivered the opinion of the Court.

[1] The issue in this case is whether the trade dress[1] of a restaurant may be protected under § 43(a) of the Trademark Act of 1946 (Lanham Act), 60 Stat. 441, 15 U.S.C. § 1125(a) 1982 ed.), based on a finding of inherent distinctiveness, without proof that the trade dress has secondary meaning.

I

[2] Respondent Taco Cabana, Inc., operates a chain of fast-food restaurants in Texas. The restaurants serve Mexican food. The first Taco Cabana restaurant was opened in San Antonio in September 1978, and five more restaurants had been opened in San Antonio by 1985. Taco Cabana describes its Mexican trade dress as

---

[1] The District Court instructed the jury: "'[T]rade dress' is the total image of the business. Taco Cabana's trade dress may include the shape and general appearance of the exterior of the restaurant, the identifying sign, the interior kitchen floor plan, the decor, the menu, the equipment used to serve food, the servers' uniforms and other features reflecting on the total image of the restaurant." 1 App. 83–84. The Court of Appeals accepted this definition and quoted from *Blue Bell Bio–Medical v. Cin–Bad, Inc.,* 864 F.2d 1253, 1256 (CA5 1989): "The 'trade dress' of a product is essentially its total image and overall appearance." See 932 F.2d 1113, 1118 (CA5 1991). It "involves the total image of a product and may include features such as size, shape, color or color combinations, texture, graphics, or even particular sales techniques." *John H. Harland Co. v. Clarke Checks, Inc.,* 711 F.2d 966, 980 (CA11 1983). Restatement (Third) of Unfair Competition § 16, Comment *a* (Tent.Draft No. 2, Mar. 23, 1990).

100

"a festive eating atmosphere having interior dining and patio areas decorated with artifacts, bright colors, paintings and murals. The patio includes interior and exterior areas with the interior patio capable of being sealed off from the outside patio by overhead garage doors. The stepped exterior of the building is a festive and vivid color scheme using top border paint and neon stripes. Bright awnings and umbrellas continue the theme." 932 F.2d 1113, 1117 (CA5 1991).

[3] In December 1985, a Two Pesos, Inc., restaurant was opened in Houston. Two Pesos adopted a motif very similar to the foregoing description of Taco Cabana's trade dress. Two Pesos restaurants expanded rapidly in Houston and other markets, but did not enter San Antonio. In 1986, Taco Cabana entered the Houston and Austin markets and expanded into other Texas cities, including Dallas and El Paso where Two Pesos was also doing business.

[4] In 1987, Taco Cabana sued Two Pesos in the United States District Court for the Southern District of Texas for trade dress infringement under § 43(a) of the Lanham Act, 15 U.S.C. § 1125(a) (1982 ed.),[2] and for theft of trade secrets under Texas common law. The case was tried to a jury, which was instructed to return its verdict in the form of answers to five questions propounded by the trial judge. The jury's answers were: Taco Cabana has a trade dress; taken as a whole, the trade dress is nonfunctional; the trade dress is inherently distinctive;[3] the trade dress has not acquired a secondary meaning[4] in the Texas market; and the alleged infringement creates a likelihood of confusion on the part of ordinary customers as to the source or association of the restaurant's goods or services. Because, as the jury was told, Taco Cabana's trade dress was protected if it either was inherently distinctive or had acquired a secondary meaning, judgment was entered awarding damages to Taco Cabana. In the course of calculating damages, the trial court held that Two Pesos had intentionally and deliberately infringed Taco Cabana's trade dress.[5]

---

[2] Section 43(a) provides: "Any person who shall affix, apply, or annex, or use in connection with any goods or services, or any container or containers for goods, a false designation of origin, or any false description or representation, including words or other symbols tending falsely to describe or represent the same, and shall cause such goods or services to enter into commerce, and any person who shall with knowledge of the falsity of such designation of origin or description or representation cause or procure the same to be transported or used in commerce or deliver the same to any carrier to be transported or used, shall be liable to a civil action by any person doing business in the locality falsely indicated as that of origin or in the region in which said locality is situated, or by any person who believes that he is or is likely to be damaged by the use of any such false description or representation." 60 Stat. 441.

This provision has been superseded by § 132 of the Trademark Law Revision Act of 1988, 102 Stat. 3946, 15 U.S.C. § 1121.

[3] The instructions were that, to be found inherently distinctive, the trade dress must not be descriptive.

[4] Secondary meaning is used generally to indicate that a mark or dress "has come through use to be uniquely associated with a specific source." Restatement (Third) of Unfair Competition § 13, Comment *e* (Tent.Draft No. 2, Mar. 23, 1990). "To establish secondary meaning, a manufacturer must show that, in the minds of the public, the primary significance of a product feature or term is to identify the source of the product rather than the product itself." *Inwood Laboratories, Inc. v. Ives Laboratories, Inc.*, 456 U.S. 844, 851, n. 11, 102 S.Ct. 2182, 2187, n. 11, 72 L.Ed.2d 606 (1982).

[5] The Court of Appeals agreed: "The weight of the evidence persuades us, as it did Judge Singleton, that Two Pesos brazenly copied Taco Cabana's successful trade dress, and proceeded to expand in a manner that foreclosed several lucrative markets within Taco Cabana's natural zone of expansion." 932 F.2d, at 1127, n. 20.

[5] The Court of Appeals ruled that the instructions adequately stated the applicable law and that the evidence supported the jury's findings. In particular, the Court of Appeals rejected petitioner's argument that a finding of no secondary meaning contradicted a finding of inherent distinctiveness.

[6] In so holding, the court below followed precedent in the Fifth Circuit. In *Chevron Chemical Co. v. Voluntary Purchasing Groups, Inc.,* 659 F.2d 695, 702 (CA5 1981), the court noted that trademark law requires a demonstration of secondary meaning only when the claimed trademark is not sufficiently distinctive of itself to identify the producer; the court held that the same principles should apply to protection of trade dresses. The Court of Appeals noted that this approach conflicts with decisions of other courts, particularly the holding of the Court of Appeals for the Second Circuit in *Vibrant Sales, Inc. v. New Body Boutique, Inc.,* 652 F.2d 299 (1981), cert. denied, 455 U.S. 909 (1982), that § 43(a) protects unregistered trademarks or designs only where secondary meaning is shown. *Chevron, supra,* at 702. We granted certiorari to resolve the conflict among the Courts of Appeals on the question whether trade dress that is inherently distinctive is protectible under § 43(a) without a showing that it has acquired secondary meaning. 502 U.S. 1071 (1992). We find that it is, and we therefore affirm.

II

[7] The Lanham Act[7] was intended to make "actionable the deceptive and misleading use of marks" and "to protect persons engaged in … commerce against unfair competition." § 45, 15 U.S.C. § 1127. Section 43(a) "prohibits a broader range of practices than does § 32," which applies to registered marks, *Inwood Laboratories, Inc. v. Ives Laboratories, Inc.,* 456 U.S. 844, 858 (1982), but it is common ground that § 43(a) protects qualifying unregistered trademarks and that the general principles qualifying a mark for registration under § 2 of the Lanham Act are for the most part applicable in determining whether an unregistered mark is entitled to protection under § 43(a). See *A.J. Canfield Co. v. Honickman,* 808 F.2d 291, 299, n. 9 (CA3 1986); *Thompson Medical Co. v. Pfizer Inc.,* 753 F.2d 208, 215–216 (CA2 1985).

[8] A trademark is defined in 15 U.S.C. § 1127 as including "any word, name, symbol, or device or any combination thereof" used by any person "to identify and distinguish his or her goods, including a unique product, from those manufactured or sold by others and to indicate the source of the goods, even if that source is unknown." In order to be registered, a mark must be capable of distinguishing the applicant's goods from those of others. § 1052. Marks are often classified in categories of generally increasing distinctiveness; following the classic formulation set out by Judge Friendly, they may be (1) generic; (2) descriptive; (3) suggestive; (4) arbitrary; or (5) fanciful. See *Abercrombie & Fitch Co. v. Hunting World, Inc.,* 537 F.2d 4, 9 (CA2 1976). The Court of Appeals followed this classification and petitioner accepts it. The latter three categories of marks, because their intrinsic nature serves to identify a particular source of a product, are deemed inherently distinctive and are entitled to protection. In contrast, generic marks—those that "refe[r] to the genus of which the particular product is a species," *Park 'N Fly, Inc. v. Dollar Park & Fly, Inc.,* 469 U.S. 189, 194 (1985), citing *Abercrombie & Fitch, supra,* at 9—are not registrable as trademarks. *Park 'N Fly, supra,* 469 U.S., at 194.

. . . .

[9] The Court of Appeals determined that the District Court's instructions were consistent with the foregoing principles {of trademark doctrine} and that the evidence supported the jury's verdict. Both courts thus ruled that Taco Cabana's trade dress was not descriptive but rather inherently distinctive, and that it was not functional. None of these rulings is before us in this case, and for present purposes we assume, without deciding, that each of them is correct. In going on to affirm the judgment for respondent, the Court of Appeals, following its prior decision in *Chevron,* held that Taco Cabana's inherently distinctive trade dress was entitled to protection despite the lack of proof of secondary meaning. It is this issue that is before us for decision, and we agree with its resolution by the Court of Appeals. There is no persuasive reason to apply to trade dress a general requirement of secondary

---

[7] The Lanham Act, including the provisions at issue here, has been substantially amended since the present suit was brought. See Trademark Law Revision Act of 1988, 102 Stat. 3946, 15 U.S.C. § 1121.

meaning which is at odds with the principles generally applicable to infringement suits under § 43(a). Petitioner devotes much of its briefing to arguing issues that are not before us, and we address only its arguments relevant to whether proof of secondary meaning is essential to qualify an inherently distinctive trade dress for protection under § 43(a).

[10] Petitioner argues that the jury's finding that the trade dress has not acquired a secondary meaning shows conclusively that the trade dress is not inherently distinctive. The Court of Appeals' disposition of this issue was sound:

> "Two Pesos' argument—that the jury finding of inherent distinctiveness contradicts its finding of no secondary meaning in the Texas market—ignores the law in this circuit. While the necessarily imperfect (and often prohibitively difficult) methods for assessing secondary meaning address the empirical question of current consumer association, the legal recognition of an inherently distinctive trademark or trade dress acknowledges the owner's legitimate proprietary interest in its unique and valuable informational device, regardless of whether substantial consumer association yet bestows the additional empirical protection of secondary meaning." 932 F.2d, at 1120, n. 7.

[11] Although petitioner makes the above argument, it appears to concede elsewhere in its brief that it is possible for a trade dress, even a restaurant trade dress, to be inherently distinctive and thus eligible for protection under § 43(a). Recognizing that a general requirement of secondary meaning imposes "an unfair prospect of theft [or] financial loss" on the developer of fanciful or arbitrary trade dress at the outset of its use, petitioner suggests that such trade dress should receive limited protection without proof of secondary meaning. *Id.,* at 10. Petitioner argues that such protection should be only temporary and subject to defeasance when over time the dress has failed to acquire a secondary meaning. This approach is also vulnerable for the reasons given by the Court of Appeals. If temporary protection is available from the earliest use of the trade dress, it must be because it is neither functional nor descriptive, but an inherently distinctive dress that is capable of identifying a particular source of the product. Such a trade dress, or mark, is not subject to copying by concerns that have an equal opportunity to choose their own inherently distinctive trade dress. To terminate protection for failure to gain secondary meaning over some unspecified time could not be based on the failure of the dress to retain its fanciful, arbitrary, or suggestive nature, but on the failure of the user of the dress to be successful enough in the marketplace. This is not a valid basis to find a dress or mark ineligible for protection. The user of such a trade dress should be able to maintain what competitive position it has and continue to seek wider identification among potential customers.

[12] This brings us to the line of decisions by the Court of Appeals for the Second Circuit that would find protection for trade dress unavailable absent proof of secondary meaning, a position that petitioner concedes would have to be modified if the temporary protection that it suggests is to be recognized. In *Vibrant Sales, Inc. v. New Body Boutique, Inc.,* 652 F.2d 299 (1981), the plaintiff claimed protection under § 43(a) for a product whose features the defendant had allegedly copied. The Court of Appeals held that unregistered marks did not enjoy the "presumptive source association" enjoyed by registered marks and hence could not qualify for protection under § 43(a) without proof of secondary meaning. *Id.,* at 303, 304. The court's rationale seemingly denied protection for unregistered, but inherently distinctive, marks of all kinds, whether the claimed mark used distinctive words or symbols or distinctive product design. The court thus did not accept the arguments that an unregistered mark was capable of identifying a source and that copying such a mark could be making any kind of a false statement or representation under § 43(a).

[13] This holding is in considerable tension with the provisions of the Lanham Act. If a verbal or symbolic mark or the features of a product design may be registered under § 2, it necessarily is a mark "by which the goods of the applicant may be distinguished from the goods of others," 60 Stat. 428, and must be registered unless otherwise disqualified. Since § 2 requires secondary meaning only as a condition to registering descriptive marks, there are plainly marks that are registrable without showing secondary meaning. These same marks, even if not registered, remain inherently capable of distinguishing the goods of the users of these marks. Furthermore, the copier of such a mark may be

seen as falsely claiming that his products may for some reason be thought of as originating from the plaintiff.

[14] Some years after *Vibrant,* the Second Circuit announced in *Thompson Medical Co. v. Pfizer Inc.,* 753 F.2d 208 (1985), that in deciding whether an unregistered mark is eligible for protection under § 43(a), it would follow the classification of marks set out by Judge Friendly in *Abercrombie & Fitch,* 537 F.2d, at 9. Hence, if an unregistered mark is deemed merely descriptive, which the verbal mark before the court proved to be, proof of secondary meaning is required; however, "[s]uggestive marks are eligible for protection without any proof of secondary meaning, since the connection between the mark and the source is presumed." 753 F.2d, at 216. The Second Circuit has nevertheless continued to deny protection for trade dress under § 43(a) absent proof of secondary meaning, despite the fact that § 43(a) provides no basis for distinguishing between trademark and trade dress. See, *e.g., Stormy Clime Ltd. v. ProGroup, Inc.,* 809 F.2d, at 974; *Union Mfg. Co. v. Han Baek Trading Co.,* 763 F.2d 42, 48 (1985); *LeSportsac, Inc. v. K mart Corp.,* 754 F.2d 71, 75 (1985).

[15] The Fifth Circuit was quite right in *Chevron,* and in this case, to follow the *Abercrombie* classifications consistently and to inquire whether trade dress for which protection is claimed under § 43(a) is inherently distinctive. If it is, it is capable of identifying products or services as coming from a specific source and secondary meaning is not required. This is the rule generally applicable to trademarks, and the protection of trademarks and trade dress under § 43(a) serves the same statutory purpose of preventing deception and unfair competition. There is no persuasive reason to apply different analysis to the two. The "proposition that secondary meaning must be shown even if the trade dress is a distinctive, identifying mark, [is] wrong, for the reasons explained by Judge Rubin for the Fifth Circuit in *Chevron." Blau Plumbing, Inc. v. S.O.S. Fix–It, Inc.,* 781 F.2d 604, 608 (CA7 1986). The Court of Appeals for the Eleventh Circuit also follows *Chevron, AmBrit, Inc. v. Kraft, Inc.,* 805 F.2d 974, 979 (1986), and the Court of Appeals for the Ninth Circuit appears to think that proof of secondary meaning is superfluous if a trade dress is inherently distinctive, *Fuddruckers, Inc. v. Doc's B.R. Others, Inc.,* 826 F.2d 837, 843 (1987).

[16] It would be a different matter if there were textual basis in § 43(a) for treating inherently distinctive verbal or symbolic trademarks differently from inherently distinctive trade dress. But there is none. The section does not mention trademarks or trade dress, whether they be called generic, descriptive, suggestive, arbitrary, fanciful, or functional. Nor does the concept of secondary meaning appear in the text of § 43(a). Where secondary meaning does appear in the statute, 15 U.S.C. § 1052 (1982 ed.), it is a requirement that applies only to merely descriptive marks and not to inherently distinctive ones. We see no basis for requiring secondary meaning for inherently distinctive trade dress protection under § 43(a) but not for other distinctive words, symbols, or devices capable of identifying a producer's product.

[17] Engrafting onto § 43(a) a requirement of secondary meaning for inherently distinctive trade dress also would undermine the purposes of the Lanham Act. Protection of trade dress, no less than of trademarks, serves the Act's purpose to "secure to the owner of the mark the goodwill of his business and to protect the ability of consumers to distinguish among competing producers. National protection of trademarks is desirable, Congress concluded, because trademarks foster competition and the maintenance of quality by securing to the producer the benefits of good reputation." *Park 'N Fly,* 469 U.S., at 198, 105 S.Ct., at 663, citing S.Rep. No. 1333, 79th Cong., 2d Sess., 3–5 (1946) (citations omitted). By making more difficult the identification of a producer with its product, a secondary meaning requirement for a nondescriptive trade dress would hinder improving or maintaining the producer's competitive position.

[18] Suggestions that under the Fifth Circuit's law, the initial user of any shape or design would cut off competition from products of like design and shape are not persuasive. Only nonfunctional, distinctive trade dress is protected under § 43(a). The Fifth Circuit holds that a design is legally functional, and thus unprotectible, if it is one of a limited number of equally efficient options available to competitors and free competition would be unduly hindered by according the design trademark

protection. See *Sicilia Di R. Biebow & Co. v. Cox,* 732 F.2d 417, 426 (1984). This serves to assure that competition will not be stifled by the exhaustion of a limited number of trade dresses.

[19] On the other hand, adding a secondary meaning requirement could have anticompetitive effects, creating particular burdens on the startup of small companies. It would present special difficulties for a business, such as respondent, that seeks to start a new product in a limited area and then expand into new markets. Denying protection for inherently distinctive nonfunctional trade dress until after secondary meaning has been established would allow a competitor, which has not adopted a distinctive trade dress of its own, to appropriate the originator's dress in other markets and to deter the originator from expanding into and competing in these areas.

[20] As noted above, petitioner concedes that protecting an inherently distinctive trade dress from its inception may be critical to new entrants to the market and that withholding protection until secondary meaning has been established would be contrary to the goals of the Lanham Act. Petitioner specifically suggests, however, that the solution is to dispense with the requirement of secondary meaning for a reasonable, but brief, period at the outset of the use of a trade dress. Reply Brief for Petitioner 11–12. If § 43(a) does not require secondary meaning at the outset of a business' adoption of trade dress, there is no basis in the statute to support the suggestion that such a requirement comes into being after some unspecified time.

III

[21] We agree with the Court of Appeals that proof of secondary meaning is not required to prevail on a claim under § 43(a) of the Lanham Act where the trade dress at issue is inherently distinctive, and accordingly the judgment of that court is affirmed.

It is so ordered.

Justice SCALIA, concurring {omitted}

Justice STEVENS, concurring in the judgment.

[1] As the Court notes in its opinion, the text of § 43(a) of the Lanham Act, 15 U.S.C. § 1125(a) (1982 ed.), "does not mention trademarks or trade dress." *Ante,* at 2760. Nevertheless, the Court interprets this section as having created a federal cause of action for infringement of an unregistered trademark or trade dress and concludes that such a mark or dress should receive essentially the same protection as those that are registered. Although I agree with the Court's conclusion, I think it is important to recognize that the meaning of the text has been transformed by the federal courts over the past few decades. I agree with this transformation, even though it marks a departure from the original text, because it is consistent with the purposes of the statute and has recently been endorsed by Congress.

[2] It is appropriate to begin with the relevant text of § 43(a).... Section 43(a) provides a federal remedy for using either "a false designation of origin" or a "false description or representation" in connection with any goods or services. The full text of the section makes it clear that the word "origin" refers to the geographic location in which the goods originated, and in fact, the phrase "false designation of origin" was understood to be limited to false advertising of geographic origin. For example, the "false designation of origin" language contained in the statute makes it unlawful to represent that California oranges came from Florida, or vice versa.[3]

[3] For a number of years after the 1946 enactment of the Lanham Act, a "false description or representation," like "a false designation of origin," was construed narrowly ....

II

[4] Over time, the Circuits have expanded the categories of "false designation of origin" and "false description or representation." One treatise[6] identified the Court of Appeals for the Sixth Circuit as the

---

[3] This is clear from the fact that the cause of action created by this section is available only to a person doing business in the locality falsely indicated as that of origin. See n. 1, *supra.*

[6] McCarthy § 27:3, p. 345.

first to broaden the meaning of "origin" to include "origin of source or manufacture" in addition to geographic origin.[7] Another early case, described as unique among the Circuit cases because it was so "forward-looking,"[8] interpreted the "false description or representation" language to mean more than mere "palming off." *L'Aiglon Apparel, Inc. v. Lana Lobell, Inc.,* 214 F.2d 649 (CA3 1954) . . . . Although some have criticized the expansion as unwise,[9] it is now "a firmly embedded reality."[10] The United States Trade Association Trademark Review Commission noted this transformation with approval: "Section 43(a) is an enigma, but a very popular one. Narrowly drawn and intended to reach false designations or representations as to the geographical origin of products, the section has been widely interpreted to create, in essence, a federal law of unfair competition . . . . It has definitely eliminated a gap in unfair competition law, and its vitality is showing no signs of age."[11]

[5] Today, it is less significant whether the infringement falls under "false designation of origin" or "false description or representation"[12] because in either case § 43(a) may be invoked. The federal courts are in agreement that § 43(a) creates a federal cause of action for trademark and trade dress infringement claims. 1 J. Gilson, Trademark Protection and Practice § 2.13, p. 2–178 (1991). They are also in agreement that the test for liability is likelihood of confusion: "[U]nder the Lanham Act [§ 43(a)], the ultimate test is whether the public is likely to be deceived or confused by the similarity of the marks . . . . Whether we call the violation infringement, unfair competition or false designation of origin, the test is identical—is there a 'likelihood of confusion?'" *New West Corp. v. NYM Co. of California, Inc.,* 595 F.2d 1194, 1201 (CA9 1979) (footnote omitted). And the Circuits are in general agreement, with perhaps the exception of the Second Circuit, that secondary meaning need not be established once there is a finding of inherent distinctiveness in order to establish a trade dress violation under § 43(a).

III

[6] Even though the lower courts' expansion of the categories contained in § 43(a) is unsupported by the text of the Act, I am persuaded that it is consistent with the general purposes of the Act. For example, Congressman Lanham, the bill's sponsor, stated: "The purpose of [the Act] is to protect legitimate business and the consumers of the country."[15] 92 Cong.Rec. 7524 (1946). One way of

---

[7] Federal–Mogul–Bower Bearings, Inc. v. Azoff, 313 F.2d 405, 408 (6th Cir. 1963).

[8] Derenberg, 32 N.Y.U.L.Rev., at 1047, 1049.

[9] See, *e.g.,* Germain, Unfair Trade Practices Under § 43(a) of the Lanham Act: You've Come a Long Way Baby—Too Far, Maybe?, 64 Trademark Rep. 193, 194 (1974) ("It is submitted that the cases have applied Section 43(a) to situations it was not intended to cover and have used it in ways that it was not designed to function").

[10] 2 McCarthy § 27:3, p. 345.

[11] The United States Trademark Association Trademark Review Commission Report and Recommendations to USTA President and Board of Directors, 77 Trademark Rep. 375, 426 (1987). {In the body of his opinion, Justice Stevens appears to have misnamed the United States Trademark Association, which was the predecessor organization of the International Trademark Association.}

[12] Indeed, in count one of the complaint, respondent alleged that petitioner "is continuing to affix, apply, or use in connection with its restaurants, goods and services a false designation o[f] origin, or a false description and representation, tending to falsely describe or represent the same," and that petitioner "has falsely designated the origin of its restaurants, goods and services and has falsely described and represented the same . . . ." App. 44–45; see Tr. of Oral Arg. 37.

[15] The Senate Report elaborated on these two goals:

"The purpose underlying any trade-mark statute is twofold. One is to protect the public so it may be confident that, in purchasing a product bearing a particular trade-mark which it favorably knows, it will get the product which it asks for and wants to get. Secondly, where the owner of a trade-mark has spent energy, time, and money in presenting to the public

accomplishing these dual goals was by creating uniform legal rights and remedies that were appropriate for a national economy. Although the protection of trademarks had once been "entirely a State matter," the result of such a piecemeal approach was that there were almost "as many different varieties of common law as there are States" so that a person's right to a trademark "in one State may differ widely from the rights which [that person] enjoys in another." H.R.Rep. No. 944, 76th Cong., 1st Sess., 4 (1939). The House Committee on Trademarks and Patents, recognizing that "trade is no longer local, but ...national," saw the need for "national legislation along national lines [to] secur[e] to the owners of trademarks in interstate commerce definite rights." *Ibid.*[16]

[7] Congress has revisited this statute from time to time, and has accepted the "judicial legislation" that has created this federal cause of action. Recently, for example, in the Trademark Law Revision Act of 1988, 102 Stat. 3935, Congress codified the judicial interpretation of § 43(a), giving its *imprimatur* to a growing body of case law from the Circuits that had expanded the section beyond its original language.

[8] Although Congress has not specifically addressed the question whether secondary meaning is required under § 43(a), the steps it has taken in this subsequent legislation suggest that secondary meaning is not required if inherent distinctiveness has been established.[17] First, Congress broadened the language of § 43(a) to make explicit that the provision prohibits "any word, term, name, symbol, or device, or any combination thereof" that is "likely to cause confusion, or to cause mistake, or to deceive as to the affiliation, connection, or association of such person with another person, or as to the origin, sponsorship, or approval of his or her goods, services, or commercial activities by another person." 15 U.S.C. § 1125(a). That language makes clear that a confusingly similar trade dress is actionable under § 43(a), without necessary reference to "falsity." Second, Congress approved and confirmed the extensive judicial development under the provision, including its application to trade dress that the federal courts had come to apply.[18] Third, the legislative history of the 1988 amendments reaffirms

---

the product, he is protected in his investment from its misappropriation by pirates and cheats. This is the well-established rule of law protecting both the public and the trade-mark owner." S.Rep. No. 1333, 79th Cong., 2d Sess., 3 (1946).

By protecting trademarks, Congress hoped "to protect the public from deceit, to foster fair competition, and to secure to the business community the advantages of reputation and good will by preventing their diversion from those who have created them to those who have not. This is the end to which this bill is directed." *Id.*, at 4.

[16] Forty years later, the USTA Trademark Review Commission assessed the state of trademark law. The conclusion that it reached serves as a testimonial to the success of the Act in achieving its goal of uniformity: "The federal courts now decide, under federal law, all but a few trademark disputes. State trademark law and state courts are less influential than ever. Today the Lanham Act is the paramount source of trademark law in the United States, as interpreted almost exclusively by the federal courts." Trademark Review Commission, 77 Trademark Rep., at 377.

[17] "When several acts of Congress are passed touching the same subject-matter, subsequent legislation may be considered to assist in the interpretation of prior legislation upon the same subject." *Tiger v. Western Investment Co.*, 221 U.S. 286, 309 (1911); see *NLRB v. Bell Aerospace Co. Division of Textron, Inc.*, 416 U.S. 267, 275 (1974); *Red Lion Broadcasting Co. v. FCC*, 395 U.S. 367, 380–381 (1969); *United States v. Stafoff*, 260 U.S. 477, 480 (1923) (opinion of Holmes, J.).

[18] As the Senate Report explained, revision of § 43(a) is designed "to codify the interpretation it has been given by the courts. Because Section 43(a) of the Act fills an important gap in federal unfair competition law, the committee expects the courts to continue to interpret the section.

"As written, Section 43(a) appears to deal only with false descriptions or representations and false designations of geographic origin. Since its enactment in 1946, however, it has been widely interpreted as creating, in essence, a federal law of unfair competition. For example, it has been applied to cases involving the infringement of unregistered marks, violations of trade dress and certain nonfunctional

Congress' goals of protecting both businesses and consumers with the Lanham Act. And fourth, Congress explicitly extended to any violation of § 43(a) the basic Lanham Act remedial provisions whose text previously covered only registered trademarks.[20] The aim of the amendments was to apply the same protections to unregistered marks as were already afforded to registered marks. See S.Rep. No. 100–515, p. 40 (1988). These steps buttress the conclusion that § 43(a) is properly understood to provide protection in accordance with the standards for registration in § 2. These aspects of the 1988 legislation bolster the claim that an inherently distinctive trade dress may be protected under § 43(a) without proof of secondary meaning.

IV

[9] In light of the consensus among the Courts of Appeals that have actually addressed the question, and the steps on the part of Congress to codify that consensus, *stare decisis* concerns persuade me to join the Court's conclusion that secondary meaning is not required to establish a trade dress violation under § 43(a) once inherent distinctiveness has been established. Accordingly, I concur in the judgment, but not in the opinion, of the Court.

Justice THOMAS, concurring in the judgment {omitted}

Comments and Questions

1.   *Taco Cabana eventually purchased Two Pesos.* After winning the $3.7 million jury award in the above case, Taco Cabana again sued Two Pesos for failing to make court-ordered changes in its trade dress. As part of the settlement of this dispute, Taco Cabana eventually purchased Two Pesos. See http://en.wikipedia.org/wiki/Taco_Cabana. *See also* Ron Ruggless, *Taco Cabana Buys Rival Two Pesos*, NATION'S RESTAURANT NEWS, Jan. 25, 1993.

2.   *The advantages and disadvantages of defining trade dress broadly and narrowly.* Courts commonly claim that trade dress constitutes the "total image and overall appearance" of a product, *Blue Bell Bio-Medical v. Cin-Bad, Inc.*, 864 F.2d 1253, 1256 (5th Cir. 1989). *See also Chun King Sales, Inc. v. Oriental Foods, Inc.*, 136 F. Supp. 659, 664 (D. Cal. 1955) (analyzing "the *tout ensemble* of the article as it appears to the average buyer"). Yet courts also typically require that the plaintiff specify and even enumerate the combination of elements it is claiming as protectable trade dress. *See, e.g., Sports Traveler, Inc. v. Advance Magazine Publishers, Inc.*, 25 F. Supp. 2d 154, 162 (S.D.N.Y. 1998) ("Despite this mandate to focus on the overall appearance of the product, a plaintiff must still articulate the specific elements of the trade dress that render the trade dress unique or novel, that is, capable of being an identifier for the product's source."); *Abercrombie & Fitch Stores, Inc. v. American Eagle Outfitters, Inc.*, 280 F.3d 619, 635 (6th Cir. 2002) (stating that a plaintiff is "expected to list the elements of the designs and the unique combinations it [seeks] to protect . . . ."). *Cf. General Motors Corp. v. Lanard Toys, Inc.*, 468 F.3d 405, 415 (6th Cir. 2006) (finding sufficient plaintiff's definition of the trade dress of its hummer and humvee vehicles as "the exterior appearance and styling of the vehicle design which includes the grille, slanted and raised hood, split windshield, rectangular doors, squared edges, etc.").

What strategic considerations may come into play in how a plaintiff defines its trade dress? What are the costs and benefits of defining it too broadly or too narrowly?

---

configurations of goods and actionable false advertising claims." S.Rep. No. 100–515, p. 40 (1988) U.S.Code Cong. & Admin.News 1988, pp. 5577, 5605.

[20] See 15 U.S.C. §§ 1114, 1116–1118.

In reading *Qualitex*, consider the following questions:

- It is often remarked that the Court's holding in *Qualitex* is in significant tension with its previous holding in *Two Pesos*. Do you detect any tension between the holdings of the two cases?

- Does Justice Breyer's analysis apply as well to a combination of two or more colors?

- In light of *Qualitex*, how do you predict courts will treat smells, textures, and tastes? Are such marks capable of inherent distinctiveness?

Qualitex Co. v. Jacobson Products Co., Inc.
514 U.S. 159 (1995)

Justice BREYER delivered the opinion of the Court.

[1] The question in this case is whether the Trademark Act of 1946 (Lanham Act), 15 U.S.C. §§ 1051–1127 (1988 ed. and Supp. V), permits the registration of a trademark that consists, purely and simply, of a color. We conclude that, sometimes, a color will meet ordinary legal trademark requirements. And, when it does so, no special legal rule prevents color alone from serving as a trademark.

I

[2] The case before us grows out of petitioner Qualitex Company's use (since the 1950's) of a special shade of green-gold color on the pads that it makes and sells to dry cleaning firms for use on dry cleaning presses. In 1989, respondent Jacobson Products (a Qualitex rival) began to sell its own press pads to dry cleaning firms; and it colored those pads a similar green gold. In 1991, Qualitex registered the special green-gold color on press pads with the Patent and Trademark Office as a trademark. Registration No. 1,633,711 (Feb. 5, 1991). Qualitex subsequently added a trademark infringement count, 15 U.S.C. § 1114(1), to an unfair competition claim, § 1125(a), in a lawsuit it had already filed challenging Jacobson's use of the green-gold color.

[3] Qualitex won the lawsuit in the District Court. 1991 WL 318798 (CD Cal. 1991). But, the Court of Appeals for the Ninth Circuit set aside the judgment in Qualitex's favor on the trademark infringement claim because, in that Circuit's view, the Lanham Act does not permit Qualitex, or anyone else, to register "color alone" as a trademark. 13 F.3d 1297, 1300, 1302 (1994).

[4] The Courts of Appeals have differed as to whether or not the law recognizes the use of color alone as a trademark. Compare *NutraSweet Co. v. Stadt Corp.,* 917 F.2d 1024, 1028 (CA7 1990) (absolute prohibition against protection of color alone), with *In re Owens–Corning Fiberglas Corp.,* 774 F.2d 1116, 1128 (CA Fed. 1985) (allowing registration of color pink for fiberglass insulation), and *Master Distributors, Inc. v. Pako Corp.,* 986 F.2d 219, 224 (CA8 1993) (declining to establish *per se* prohibition against protecting color alone as a trademark). Therefore, this Court granted certiorari. 512 U.S. 1287 (1994). We now hold that there is no rule absolutely barring the use of color alone, and we reverse the judgment of the Ninth Circuit.

II

[5] The Lanham Act gives a seller or producer the exclusive right to "register" a trademark, 15 U.S.C. § 1052 (1988 ed. and Supp. V), and to prevent his or her competitors from using that trademark, § 1114(1). Both the language of the Act and the basic underlying principles of trademark law would seem to include color within the universe of things that can qualify as a trademark. The language of the Lanham Act describes that universe in the broadest of terms. It says that trademarks "includ[e] any word, name, symbol, or device, or any combination thereof." § 1127. Since human beings might use as a "symbol" or "device" almost anything at all that is capable of carrying meaning, this language, read literally, is not restrictive. The courts and the Patent and Trademark Office have authorized for use as a mark a particular shape (of a Coca–Cola bottle), a particular sound (of NBC's three chimes), and even a particular scent (of plumeria blossoms on sewing thread). See, *e.g.,* Registration No. 696,147 (Apr. 12, 1960); Registration Nos. 523,616 (Apr. 4, 1950) and 916,522 (July 13, 1971); *In re Clarke,* 17 U.S.P.Q.2d

1238, 1240 (TTAB 1990). If a shape, a sound, and a fragrance can act as symbols why, one might ask, can a color not do the same?

[6] A color is also capable of satisfying the more important part of the statutory definition of a trademark, which requires that a person "us[e]" or "inten[d] to use" the mark

> "to identify and distinguish his or her goods, including a unique product, from those manufactured or sold by others and to indicate the source of the goods, even if that source is unknown." 15 U.S.C. § 1127.

True, a product's color is unlike "fanciful," "arbitrary," or "suggestive" words or designs, which almost *automatically* tell a customer that they refer to a brand. *Abercrombie & Fitch Co. v. Hunting World, Inc.,* 537 F.2d 4, 9–10 (CA2 1976) (Friendly, J.); see *Two Pesos, Inc. v. Taco Cabana, Inc.,* 505 U.S. 763, 768 (1992). The imaginary word "Suntost," or the words "Suntost Marmalade," on a jar of orange jam immediately would signal a brand or a product "source"; the jam's orange color does not do so. But, over time, customers may come to treat a particular color on a product or its packaging (say, a color that in context seems unusual, such as pink on a firm's insulating material or red on the head of a large industrial bolt) as signifying a brand. And, if so, that color would have come to identify and distinguish the goods— *i.e.,* "to indicate" their "source"—much in the way that descriptive words on a product (say, "Trim" on nail clippers or "Car–Freshner" on deodorizer) can come to indicate a product's origin. See, *e.g., J. Wiss & Sons Co. v. W.E. Bassett Co.,* 59 C.C.P.A. 1269, 1271 (Pat.), 462 F.2d 567, 569 (1972); *Car–Freshner Corp. v. Turtle Wax, Inc.,* 268 F.Supp. 162, 164 (SDNY 1967). In this circumstance, trademark law says that the word (*e.g.,* "Trim"), although not inherently distinctive, has developed "secondary meaning." See *Inwood Laboratories, Inc. v. Ives Laboratories, Inc.,* 456 U.S. 844, 851, n. 11, (1982) ("[S]econdary meaning" is acquired when "in the minds of the public, the primary significance of a product feature . . . is to identify the source of the product rather than the product itself"). Again, one might ask, if trademark law permits a descriptive word with secondary meaning to act as a mark, why would it not permit a color, under similar circumstances, to do the same?

[7] We cannot find in the basic objectives of trademark law any obvious theoretical objection to the use of color alone as a trademark, where that color has attained "secondary meaning" and therefore identifies and distinguishes a particular brand (and thus indicates its "source"). In principle, trademark law, by preventing others from copying a source-identifying mark, "reduce[s] the customer's costs of shopping and making purchasing decisions," 1 J. McCarthy, McCarthy on Trademarks and Unfair Competition § 2.01[2], p. 2–3 (3d ed. 1994) (hereinafter McCarthy), for it quickly and easily assures a potential customer that *this* item—the item with this mark—is made by the same producer as other similarly marked items that he or she liked (or disliked) in the past. At the same time, the law helps assure a producer that it (and not an imitating competitor) will reap the financial, reputation-related rewards associated with a desirable product. The law thereby "encourage[s] the production of quality products," *ibid.,* and simultaneously discourages those who hope to sell inferior products by capitalizing on a consumer's inability quickly to evaluate the quality of an item offered for sale. See, *e.g.,* 3 L. Altman, Callmann on Unfair Competition, Trademarks and Monopolies § 17.03 (4th ed. 1983); Landes & Posner, The Economics of Trademark Law, 78 T.M. Rep. 267, 271–272 (1988); *Park 'N Fly, Inc. v. Dollar Park & Fly, Inc.,* 469 U.S. 189, 198 (1985); S.Rep. No. 100–515, p. 4 (1988) U.S.Code Cong. & Admin.News, 1988, pp. 5577, 5580. It is the source-distinguishing ability of a mark—not its ontological status as color, shape, fragrance, word, or sign—that permits it to serve these basic purposes. See Landes & Posner, Trademark Law: An Economic Perspective, 30 J.Law & Econ. 265, 290 (1987). And, for that reason, it is difficult to find, in basic trademark objectives, a reason to disqualify absolutely the use of a color as a mark.

[8] Neither can we find a principled objection to the use of color as a mark in the important "functionality" doctrine of trademark law. The functionality doctrine prevents trademark law, which seeks to promote competition by protecting a firm's reputation, from instead inhibiting legitimate competition by allowing a producer to control a useful product feature. It is the province of patent law, not trademark law, to encourage invention by granting inventors a monopoly over new product designs or functions for a limited time, 35 U.S.C. §§ 154, 173, after which competitors are free to use the innovation. If a product's functional features could be used as trademarks, however, a monopoly over

such features could be obtained without regard to whether they qualify as patents and could be extended forever (because trademarks may be renewed in perpetuity). See *Kellogg Co. v. National Biscuit Co.,* 305 U.S. 111, 119–120 (1938) (Brandeis, J.); *Inwood Laboratories, Inc., supra,* 456 U.S., at 863 (White, J., concurring in result) ("A functional characteristic is 'an important ingredient in the commercial success of the product,' and, after expiration of a patent, it is no more the property of the originator than the product itself") (citation omitted). Functionality doctrine therefore would require, to take an imaginary example, that even if customers have come to identify the special illumination-enhancing shape of a new patented light bulb with a particular manufacturer, the manufacturer may not use that shape as a trademark, for doing so, after the patent had expired, would impede competition—not by protecting the reputation of the original bulb maker, but by frustrating competitors' legitimate efforts to produce an equivalent illumination-enhancing bulb. See, *e.g., Kellogg Co., supra,* 305 U.S., at 119–120 (trademark law cannot be used to extend monopoly over "pillow" shape of shredded wheat biscuit after the patent for that shape had expired). This Court consequently has explained that, "[i]n general terms, a product feature is functional," and cannot serve as a trademark, "if it is essential to the use or purpose of the article or if it affects the cost or quality of the article," that is, if exclusive use of the feature would put competitors at a significant non-reputation-related disadvantage. *Inwood Laboratories, Inc., supra,* 456 U.S., at 850, n. 10. Although sometimes color plays an important role (unrelated to source identification) in making a product more desirable, sometimes it does not. And, this latter fact—the fact that sometimes color is not essential to a product's use or purpose and does not affect cost or quality—indicates that the doctrine of "functionality" does not create an absolute bar to the use of color alone as a mark. See *Owens–Corning,* 774 F.2d, at 1123 (pink color of insulation in wall "performs no nontrademark function").

[9] It would seem, then, that color alone, at least sometimes, can meet the basic legal requirements for use as a trademark. It can act as a symbol that distinguishes a firm's goods and identifies their source, without serving any other significant function. See U.S. Dept. of Commerce, Patent and Trademark Office, Trademark Manual of Examining Procedure § 1202.04(e), p. 1202–13 (2d ed. May, 1993) (hereinafter PTO Manual) (approving trademark registration of color alone where it "has become distinctive of the applicant's goods in commerce," provided that "there is [no] competitive need for colors to remain available in the industry" and the color is not "functional"); see also 1 McCarthy §§ 3.01[1], 7.26, pp. 3–2, 7–113 ("requirements for qualification of a word or symbol as a trademark" are that it be (1) a "symbol," (2) "use[d] . . . as a mark," (3) "to identify and distinguish the seller's goods from goods made or sold by others," but that it not be "functional"). Indeed, the District Court, in this case, entered findings (accepted by the Ninth Circuit) that show Qualitex's green-gold press pad color has met these requirements. The green-gold color acts as a symbol. Having developed secondary meaning (for customers identified the green-gold color as Qualitex's), it identifies the press pads' source. And, the green-gold color serves no other function. (Although it is important to use *some* color on press pads to avoid noticeable stains, the court found "no competitive need in the press pad industry for the green-gold color, since other colors are equally usable." 21 U.S.P.Q.2d, at 1460.) Accordingly, unless there is some special reason that convincingly militates against the use of color alone as a trademark, trademark law would protect Qualitex's use of the green-gold color on its press pads.

III

[10] Respondent Jacobson Products says that there are four special reasons why the law should forbid the use of color alone as a trademark. We shall explain, in turn, why we, ultimately, find them unpersuasive.

[11] *First,* Jacobson says that, if the law permits the use of color as a trademark, it will produce uncertainty and unresolvable court disputes about what shades of a color a competitor may lawfully use. Because lighting (morning sun, twilight mist) will affect perceptions of protected color, competitors and courts will suffer from "shade confusion" as they try to decide whether use of a similar color on a similar product does, or does not, confuse customers and thereby infringe a trademark. Jacobson adds that the "shade confusion" problem is "more difficult" and "far different from" the "determination of the similarity of words or symbols." Brief for Respondent 22.

[12] We do not believe, however, that color, in this respect, is special. Courts traditionally decide quite difficult questions about whether two words or phrases or symbols are sufficiently similar, in context, to confuse buyers. They have had to compare, for example, such words as "Bonamine" and "Dramamine" (motion-sickness remedies); "Huggies" and "Dougies" (diapers); "Cheracol" and "Syrocol" (cough syrup); "Cyclone" and "Tornado" (wire fences); and "Mattres" and "1–800–Mattres" (mattress franchisor telephone numbers). See, *e.g., G.D. Searle & Co. v. Chas. Pfizer & Co.,* 265 F.2d 385, 389 (CA7 1959); *Kimberly–Clark Corp. v. H. Douglas Enterprises, Ltd.,* 774 F.2d 1144, 1146–1147 (CA Fed. 1985); *Upjohn Co. v. Schwartz,* 246 F.2d 254, 262 (CA2 1957); *Hancock v. American Steel & Wire Co. of N.J.,* 40 C.C.P.A. (Pat.) 931, 935, 203 F.2d 737, 740–741 (1953); *Dial–A–Mattress Franchise Corp. v. Page,* 880 F.2d 675, 678 (CA2 1989). Legal standards exist to guide courts in making such comparisons. See, *e.g.,* 2 McCarthy § 15.08; 1 McCarthy §§ 11.24–11.25 ("[S]trong" marks, with greater secondary meaning, receive broader protection than "weak" marks). We do not see why courts could not apply those standards to a color, replicating, if necessary, lighting conditions under which a colored product is normally sold. See Ebert, Trademark Protection in Color: Do It By the Numbers!, 84 T.M.Rep. 379, 405 (1994). Indeed, courts already have done so in cases where a trademark consists of a color plus a design, *i.e.,* a colored symbol such as a gold stripe (around a sewer pipe), a yellow strand of wire rope, or a "brilliant yellow" band (on ampules). See, *e.g., Youngstown Sheet & Tube Co. v. Tallman Conduit Co.,* 149 U.S.P.Q. 656, 657 (TTAB 1966); *Amsted Industries, Inc. v. West Coast Wire Rope & Rigging Inc.,* 2 U.S.P.Q.2d 1755, 1760 (TTAB 1987); *In re Hodes–Lange Corp.,* 167 U.S.P.Q. 255, 256 (TTAB 1970).

[13] *Second,* Jacobson argues, as have others, that colors are in limited supply. See, *e.g., NutraSweet Co.,* 917 F.2d, at 1028; *Campbell Soup Co. v. Armour & Co.,* 175 F.2d 795, 798 (CA3 1949). Jacobson claims that, if one of many competitors can appropriate a particular color for use as a trademark, and each competitor then tries to do the same, the supply of colors will soon be depleted. Put in its strongest form, this argument would concede that "[h]undreds of color pigments are manufactured and thousands of colors can be obtained by mixing." L. Cheskin, Colors: What They Can Do For You 47 (1947). But, it would add that, in the context of a particular product, only some colors are usable. By the time one discards colors that, say, for reasons of customer appeal, are not usable, and adds the shades that competitors cannot use lest they risk infringing a similar, registered shade, then one is left with only a handful of possible colors. And, under these circumstances, to permit one, or a few, producers to use colors as trademarks will "deplete" the supply of usable colors to the point where a competitor's inability to find a suitable color will put that competitor at a significant disadvantage.

[14] This argument is unpersuasive, however, largely because it relies on an occasional problem to justify a blanket prohibition. When a color serves as a mark, normally alternative colors will likely be available for similar use by others. See, *e.g., Owens–Corning,* 774 F.2d, at 1121 (pink insulation). Moreover, if that is not so—if a "color depletion" or "color scarcity" problem does arise—the trademark doctrine of "functionality" normally would seem available to prevent the anticompetitive consequences that Jacobson's argument posits, thereby minimizing that argument's practical force.

[15] The functionality doctrine, as we have said, forbids the use of a product's feature as a trademark where doing so will put a competitor at a significant disadvantage because the feature is "essential to the use or purpose of the article" or "affects [its] cost or quality." *Inwood Laboratories, Inc.,* 456 U.S., at 850, n. 10. The functionality doctrine thus protects competitors against a disadvantage (unrelated to recognition or reputation) that trademark protection might otherwise impose, namely, their inability reasonably to replicate important non-reputation-related product features. For example, this Court has written that competitors might be free to copy the color of a medical pill where that color serves to identify the kind of medication (*e.g.,* a type of blood medicine) in addition to its source. See *id.,* at 853, 858, n. 20 ("[S]ome patients commingle medications in a container and rely on color to differentiate one from another"); see also J. Ginsburg, D. Goldberg, & A. Greenbaum, Trademark and Unfair Competition Law 194–195 (1991) (noting that drug color cases "have more to do with public health policy" regarding generic drug substitution "than with trademark law"). And, the federal courts have demonstrated that they can apply this doctrine in a careful and reasoned manner, with sensitivity to the effect on competition. Although we need not comment on the merits of specific cases, we note that

lower courts have permitted competitors to copy the green color of farm machinery (because customers wanted their farm equipment to match) and have barred the use of black as a trademark on outboard boat motors (because black has the special functional attributes of decreasing the apparent size of the motor and ensuring compatibility with many different boat colors). See *Deere & Co. v. Farmhand, Inc.,* 560 F.Supp. 85, 98 (SD Iowa 1982), aff'd, 721 F.2d 253 (CA8 1983); *Brunswick Corp. v. British Seagull Ltd.,* 35 F.3d 1527, 1532 (CA Fed. 1994), cert. pending, No. 94–1075; see also *Nor–Am Chemical v. O.M. Scott & Sons Co.,* 4 U.S.P.Q.2d 1316, 1320 (ED Pa. 1987) (blue color of fertilizer held functional because it indicated the presence of nitrogen). The Restatement (Third) of Unfair Competition adds that, if a design's "aesthetic value" lies in its ability to "confe[r] a significant benefit that cannot practically be duplicated by the use of alternative designs," then the design is "functional." Restatement (Third) of Unfair Competition § 17, Comment *c*, pp. 175–176 (1993). The "ultimate test of aesthetic functionality," it explains, "is whether the recognition of trademark rights would significantly hinder competition." *Id.,* at 176.

[16] The upshot is that, where a color serves a significant nontrademark function—whether to distinguish a heart pill from a digestive medicine or to satisfy the "noble instinct for giving the right touch of beauty to common and necessary things," G. Chesterton, Simplicity and Tolstoy 61 (1912)— courts will examine whether its use as a mark would permit one competitor (or a group) to interfere with legitimate (nontrademark-related) competition through actual or potential exclusive use of an important product ingredient. That examination should not discourage firms from creating esthetically pleasing mark designs, for it is open to their competitors to do the same. See, *e.g., W.T. Rogers Co. v. Keene,* 778 F.2d 334, 343 (CA7 1985) (Posner, J.). But, ordinarily, it should prevent the anticompetitive consequences of Jacobson's hypothetical "color depletion" argument, when, and if, the circumstances of a particular case threaten "color depletion."

. . . .

IV

[17] Having determined that a color may sometimes meet the basic legal requirements for use as a trademark and that respondent Jacobson's arguments do not justify a special legal rule preventing color alone from serving as a trademark (and, in light of the District Court's here undisputed findings that Qualitex's use of the green-gold color on its press pads meets the basic trademark requirements), we conclude that the Ninth Circuit erred in barring Qualitex's use of color as a trademark. For these reasons, the judgment of the Ninth Circuit is

Reversed.

Comments and Questions

1. Why did Qualitex bother seeking certiorari review of its single-color claim if it had already won its case against Jacobsen on its broader trade dress claim? Both the district court and the Ninth Circuit ruled that Jacobsen had infringed Qualitex's overall trade dress, consisting of "[t]he total impression of the Qualitex green-gold pad and its 'Sun Glow' name . . . or overall appearance[ ] of the Qualitex product." *Qualitex Co. v. Jacobson Prod. Co.,* 13 F.3d 1297, 1304 (9th Cir. 1994). But this judgment would likely not have enabled Qualitex to prevent competitors, including Jacobsen, from selling press pads in a green-gold color but prominently bearing a different brand name or other distinguishing feature. Qualitex sought at the Supreme Court a more abstract and much more powerful property right: the exclusive right to use the green-gold color on press pads regardless of brand name or any other distinguishing feature.

2. *Color Marks and Non-English-Speaking and Illiterate Consumers.* Perhaps it makes sense that a company like Tiffany & Co. would assert exclusive rights in the distinctive robin's-egg blue color of its packaging, *see* U.S. Reg. No. 2,359,351 (June 20, 2000) ("The mark consists of a shade of blue often referred to as robin's-egg blue which is used on boxes."), or even that 3M Corp. would assert exclusive rights in the canary yellow color of its Post-It Pads, see U.S. Reg. No. 2,390,667 (Oct. 3, 2000) ("The mark consists of the color canary yellow used over the entire surface of the goods."), but why would a manufacturer of dry cleaning press pad covers claim rights in the color of its press pad covers? Professor

Laura Heymann points to one possible explanation. *See* Laura A. Heymann, *The Reasonable Person in Trademark Law*, 52 ST. LOUIS. L.J. 781, 792 (2008). Though the Supreme Court opinion makes no mention of the issue, the *Qualitex* district court opinion noted that "many [dry cleaning businesses] are foreign speaking with limited skills in reading or speaking English." *Qualitex Co. v. Jacobson Prods. Co., Inc.*, No. 90 Civ. 1183, 1991 WL 318798, at *1 (C.D. Cal. Sep. 5,1991), aff'd in part and rev'd in part, 13 F.3d 1297 (9th Cir. 1994), rev'd, 514 U.S. 159 (1995).

b.   Product Packaging Trade Dress Versus Product Configuration Trade Dress

Between *Two Pesos* in 1992 and *Samara Bros.* in 2000, lower courts struggled to establish a workable test by which to determine whether a particular instance of trade dress was inherently distinctive. Courts had particular difficulty establishing a test to determine whether trade dress in the form of product configuration—i.e., in the form of design features of the product itself—was inherently distinctive. As we will see, in *Samara Bros.* the Supreme Court solved this problem of product configuration rather abruptly.

i.   The Differing Distinctiveness Analysis of Product Packaging and Product Configuration

In reading through *Samara Bros.*, consider the following questions:

- In *Samara Bros.*, the Supreme Court accepted certiorari on the following question: "What must be shown to establish that a product's design is inherently distinctive for purposes of Lanham Act trade-dress protection?" *Wal-Mart Stores, Inc. v. Samara Brothers, Inc.*, 528 U.S. 808 (1999). How did the Court answer this question?

- Is the court's holding in *Samara Bros.* consistent with its holding in *Two Pesos*?

An example of the apparel at issue in *Samara Bros.*

Wal-Mart Stores, Inc. v. Samara Bros., Inc.
529 U.S. 205 (2000)

Justice SCALIA delivered the opinion of the Court.

[1] In this case, we decide under what circumstances a product's design is distinctive, and therefore protectible, in an action for infringement of unregistered trade dress under § 43(a) of the Trademark Act of 1946 (Lanham Act), 60 Stat. 441, as amended, 15 U.S.C. § 1125(a).

I

Respondent Samara Brothers, Inc., designs and manufactures children's clothing. Its primary product is a line of spring/summer one-piece seersucker outfits decorated with appliques of hearts, flowers, fruits, and the like. A number of chain stores, including JCPenney, sell this line of clothing under contract with Samara.

[2] Petitioner Wal-Mart Stores, Inc., is one of the Nation's best known retailers, selling among other things children's clothing. In 1995, Wal-Mart contracted with one of its suppliers, Judy-Philippine, Inc., to manufacture a line of children's outfits for sale in the 1996 spring/summer season. Wal-Mart sent Judy-Philippine photographs of a number of garments from Samara's line, on which Judy-Philippine's garments were to be based; Judy-Philippine duly copied, with only minor modifications, 16 of Samara's garments, many of which contained copyrighted elements. In 1996, Wal-Mart briskly sold the so-called knockoffs, generating more than $1.15 million in gross profits.

[3] In June 1996, a buyer for JCPenney called a representative at Samara to complain that she had seen Samara garments on sale at Wal-Mart for a lower price than JCPenney was allowed to charge under its contract with Samara. The Samara representative told the buyer that Samara did not supply its clothing to Wal-Mart. Their suspicions aroused, however, Samara officials launched an investigation, which disclosed that Wal-Mart and several other major retailers—Kmart, Caldor, Hills, and Goody's—were selling the knockoffs of Samara's outfits produced by Judy-Philippine.

[4] After sending cease-and-desist letters, Samara brought this action in the United States District Court for the Southern District of New York against Wal-Mart, Judy-Philippine, Kmart, Caldor, Hills, and Goody's for copyright infringement under federal law, consumer fraud and unfair competition under New York law, and—most relevant for our purposes—infringement of unregistered trade dress under § 43(a) of the Lanham Act, 15 U.S.C. § 1125(a). All of the defendants except Wal-Mart settled before trial.

[5] After a weeklong trial, the jury found in favor of Samara on all of its claims. Wal-Mart then renewed a motion for judgment as a matter of law, claiming, *inter alia,* that there was insufficient evidence to support a conclusion that Samara's clothing designs could be legally protected as distinctive trade dress for purposes of § 43(a). The District Court denied the motion, 969 F.Supp. 895 (S.D.N.Y. 1997), and awarded Samara damages, interest, costs, and fees totaling almost $1.6 million, together with injunctive relief, see App. to Pet. for Cert. 56-58. The Second Circuit affirmed the denial of the motion for judgment as a matter of law, 165 F.3d 120 (1998), and we granted certiorari, 528 U.S. 808, 120 S.Ct. 308, 145 L.Ed.2d 35 (1999).

II

[6] The Lanham Act provides for the registration of trademarks, which it defines in § 45 to include "any word, name, symbol, or device, or any combination thereof [used or intended to be used] to identify and distinguish [a producer's] goods . . . from those manufactured or sold by others and to indicate the source of the goods . . . ." 15 U.S.C. § 1127. Registration of a mark under § 2 of the Lanham Act, 15 U.S.C. § 1052, enables the owner to sue an infringer under § 32, 15 U.S.C. § 1114; it also entitles the owner to a presumption that its mark is valid, see § 7(b), 15 U.S.C. § 1057(b), and ordinarily renders the registered mark incontestable after five years of continuous use, see § 15, 15 U.S.C. § 1065. In addition to protecting registered marks, the Lanham Act, in § 43(a), gives a producer a cause of action for the use by any person of "any word, term, name, symbol, or device, or any combination thereof . . . which . . . is likely to cause confusion . . . as to the origin, sponsorship, or approval of his or her goods . . . ." 15 U.S.C. § 1125(a). It is the latter provision that is at issue in this case.

[7] The breadth of the definition of marks registrable under § 2, and of the confusion-producing elements recited as actionable by § 43(a), has been held to embrace not just word marks, such as "Nike," and symbol marks, such as Nike's "swoosh" symbol, but also "trade dress"—a category that originally included only the packaging, or "dressing," of a product, but in recent years has been expanded by many Courts of Appeals to encompass the design of a product. See, *e.g., Ashley Furniture Industries, Inc. v. Sangiacomo N. A., Ltd.,* 187 F.3d 363 (C.A.4 1999) (bedroom furniture); *Knitwaves, Inc. v. Lollytogs, Ltd.,* 71 F.3d 996 (C.A.2 1995) (sweaters); *Stuart Hall Co., Inc. v. Ampad Corp.,* 51 F.3d 780 (C.A.8 1995) (notebooks). These courts have assumed, often without discussion, that trade dress constitutes a

"symbol" or "device" for purposes of the relevant sections, and we conclude likewise. "Since human beings might use as a 'symbol' or 'device' almost anything at all that is capable of carrying meaning, this language, read literally, is not restrictive." *Qualitex Co. v. Jacobson Products Co.,* 514 U.S. 159, 162 (1995). This reading of § 2 and § 43(a) is buttressed by a recently added subsection of § 43(a), § 43(a)(3), which refers specifically to "civil action[s] for trade dress infringement under this chapter for trade dress not registered on the principal register." 15 U.S.C. § 1125(a)(3) (1994 ed., Supp. V).

[8] The text of § 43(a) provides little guidance as to the circumstances under which unregistered trade dress may be protected. It does require that a producer show that the allegedly infringing feature is not "functional," see § 43(a)(3), and is likely to cause confusion with the product for which protection is sought, see § 43(a)(1)(A), 15 U.S.C. § 1125(a)(1)(A). Nothing in § 43(a) explicitly requires a producer to show that its trade dress is distinctive, but courts have universally imposed that requirement, since without distinctiveness the trade dress would not "cause confusion . . . as to the origin, sponsorship, or approval of [the] goods," as the section requires. Distinctiveness is, moreover, an explicit prerequisite for registration of trade dress under § 2, and "the general principles qualifying a mark for registration under § 2 of the Lanham Act are for the most part applicable in determining whether an unregistered mark is entitled to protection under § 43(a)." *Two Pesos, Inc. v. Taco Cabana, Inc.,* 505 U.S. 763, 768 (1992) (citations omitted).

[9] In evaluating the distinctiveness of a mark under § 2 (and therefore, by analogy, under § 43(a)), courts have held that a mark can be distinctive in one of two ways. First, a mark is inherently distinctive if "[its] intrinsic nature serves to identify a particular source." *Ibid.* In the context of word marks, courts have applied the now-classic test originally formulated by Judge Friendly, in which word marks that are "arbitrary" ("Camel" cigarettes), "fanciful" ("Kodak" film), or "suggestive" ("Tide" laundry detergent) are held to be inherently distinctive. See *Abercrombie & Fitch Co. v. Hunting World, Inc.,* 537 F.2d 4, 10-11 (C.A.2 1976). Second, a mark has acquired distinctiveness, even if it is not inherently distinctive, if it has developed secondary meaning, which occurs when, "in the minds of the public, the primary significance of a [mark] is to identify the source of the product rather than the product itself." *Inwood Laboratories, Inc. v. Ives Laboratories, Inc.,* 456 U.S. 844, 851, n. 11 (1982).[*]

[10] The judicial differentiation between marks that are inherently distinctive and those that have developed secondary meaning has solid foundation in the statute itself. Section 2 requires that registration be granted to any trademark "by which the goods of the applicant may be distinguished from the goods of others"—subject to various limited exceptions. 15 U.S.C. § 1052. It also provides, again with limited exceptions, that "nothing in this chapter shall prevent the registration of a mark used by the applicant which has become distinctive of the applicant's goods in commerce"—that is, which is not inherently distinctive but has become so only through secondary meaning. § 2(f), 15 U.S.C. § 1052(f). Nothing in § 2, however, demands the conclusion that *every* category of mark necessarily includes some marks "by which the goods of the applicant may be distinguished from the goods of others" *without* secondary meaning—that in every category some marks are inherently distinctive.

[11] Indeed, with respect to at least one category of mark—colors—we have held that no mark can ever be inherently distinctive. See *Qualitex, supra,* at 162-163,. In *Qualitex,* petitioner manufactured and sold green-gold dry-cleaning press pads. After respondent began selling pads of a similar color, petitioner brought suit under § 43(a), then added a claim under § 32 after obtaining registration for the color of its pads. We held that a color could be protected as a trademark, but only upon a showing of

---

[*] The phrase "secondary meaning" originally arose in the context of word marks, where it served to distinguish the source-identifying meaning from the ordinary, or "primary," meaning of the word. "Secondary meaning" has since come to refer to the acquired, source-identifying meaning of a nonword mark as well. It is often a misnomer in that context, since nonword marks ordinarily have no "primary" meaning. Clarity might well be served by using the term "acquired meaning" in both the word-mark and the nonword-mark contexts—but in this opinion we follow what has become the conventional terminology.

secondary meaning. Reasoning by analogy to the *Abercrombie & Fitch* test developed for word marks, we noted that a product's color is unlike a "fanciful," "arbitrary," or "suggestive" mark, since it does not "almost *automatically* tell a customer that [it] refer[s] to a brand," 514 U.S., at 162-163, and does not "immediately . . . signal a brand or a product 'source,'" *id.,* at 163. However, we noted that, "over time, customers may come to treat a particular color on a product or its packaging . . . as signifying a brand." *Ibid.* Because a color, like a "descriptive" word mark, could eventually "come to indicate a product's origin," we concluded that it could be protected *upon a showing of secondary meaning. Ibid.*

[12] It seems to us that design, like color, is not inherently distinctive. The attribution of inherent distinctiveness to certain categories of word marks and product packaging derives from the fact that the very purpose of attaching a particular word to a product, or encasing it in a distinctive packaging, is most often to identify the source of the product. Although the words and packaging can serve subsidiary functions—a suggestive word mark (such as "Tide" for laundry detergent), for instance, may invoke positive connotations in the consumer's mind, and a garish form of packaging (such as Tide's squat, brightly decorated plastic bottles for its liquid laundry detergent) may attract an otherwise indifferent consumer's attention on a crowded store shelf—their predominant function remains source identification. Consumers are therefore predisposed to regard those symbols as indication of the producer, which is why such symbols "almost *automatically* tell a customer that they refer to a brand," *id.,* at 162-163, and "immediately . . . signal a brand or a product 'source,'" *id.,* at 163. And where it is not reasonable to assume consumer predisposition to take an affixed word or packaging as indication of source—where, for example, the affixed word is descriptive of the product ("Tasty" bread) or of a geographic origin ("Georgia" peaches)—inherent distinctiveness will not be found. That is why the statute generally excludes, from those word marks that can be registered as inherently distinctive, words that are "merely descriptive" of the goods, § 2(e)(1), 15 U.S.C. § 1052(e)(1), or "primarily geographically descriptive of them," see § 2(e)(2), 15 U.S.C. § 1052(e)(2). In the case of product design, as in the case of color, we think consumer predisposition to equate the feature with the source does not exist. Consumers are aware of the reality that, almost invariably, even the most unusual of product designs—such as a cocktail shaker shaped like a penguin—is intended not to identify the source, but to render the product itself more useful or more appealing.

[13] The fact that product design almost invariably serves purposes other than source identification not only renders inherent distinctiveness problematic; it also renders application of an inherent-distinctiveness principle more harmful to other consumer interests. Consumers should not be deprived of the benefits of competition with regard to the utilitarian and esthetic purposes that product design ordinarily serves by a rule of law that facilitates plausible threats of suit against new entrants based upon alleged inherent distinctiveness. How easy it is to mount a plausible suit depends, of course, upon the clarity of the test for inherent distinctiveness, and where product design is concerned we have little confidence that a reasonably clear test can be devised. Respondent and the United States as *amicus curiae* urge us to adopt for product design relevant portions of the test formulated by the Court of Customs and Patent Appeals for product packaging in *Seabrook Foods, Inc. v. Bar-Well Foods, Ltd.,* 568 F.2d 1342 (1977). That opinion, in determining the inherent distinctiveness of a product's packaging, considered, among other things, "whether it was a 'common' basic shape or design, whether it was unique or unusual in a particular field, [and] whether it was a mere refinement of a commonly-adopted and well-known form of ornamentation for a particular class of goods viewed by the public as a dress or ornamentation for the goods." *Id.,* at 1344 (footnotes omitted). Such a test would rarely provide the basis for summary disposition of an anticompetitive strike suit. Indeed, at oral argument, counsel for the United States quite understandably would not give a definitive answer as to whether the test was met in this very case, saying only that "[t]his is a very difficult case for that purpose." Tr. of Oral Arg. 19.

[14] It is true, of course, that the person seeking to exclude new entrants would have to establish the nonfunctionality of the design feature, see § 43(a)(3), 15 U.S.C. § 1125(a)(3) (1994 ed., Supp. V)—a showing that may involve consideration of its esthetic appeal, see *Qualitex, supra,* at 170, 115 S.Ct. 1300. Competition is deterred, however, not merely by successful suit but by the plausible threat of successful suit, and given the unlikelihood of inherently source-identifying design, the game of allowing suit based

117

upon alleged inherent distinctiveness seems to us not worth the candle. That is especially so since the producer can ordinarily obtain protection for a design that *is* inherently source identifying (if any such exists), but that does not yet have secondary meaning, by securing a design patent or a copyright for the design—as, indeed, respondent did for certain elements of the designs in this case. The availability of these other protections greatly reduces any harm to the producer that might ensue from our conclusion that a product design cannot be protected under § 43(a) without a showing of secondary meaning.

[15] Respondent contends that our decision in *Two Pesos* forecloses a conclusion that product-design trade dress can never be inherently distinctive. In that case, we held that the trade dress of a chain of Mexican restaurants, which the plaintiff described as "a festive eating atmosphere having interior dining and patio areas decorated with artifacts, bright colors, paintings and murals," 505 U.S., at 765 (internal quotation marks and citation omitted), could be protected under § 43(a) without a showing of secondary meaning, see *id.,* at 776. *Two Pesos* unquestionably establishes the legal principle that trade dress can be inherently distinctive, see, *e.g., id.,* at 773, 112 S.Ct. 2753, but it does not establish that *product-design* trade dress can be. *Two Pesos* is inapposite to our holding here because the trade dress at issue, the decor of a restaurant, seems to us not to constitute product *design.* It was either product packaging—which, as we have discussed, normally *is* taken by the consumer to indicate origin— or else some *tertium quid* that is akin to product packaging and has no bearing on the present case.

[16] Respondent replies that this manner of distinguishing *Two Pesos* will force courts to draw difficult lines between product-design and product-packaging trade dress. There will indeed be some hard cases at the margin: a classic glass Coca-Cola bottle, for instance, may constitute packaging for those consumers who drink the Coke and then discard the bottle, but may constitute the product itself for those consumers who are bottle collectors, or part of the product itself for those consumers who buy Coke in the classic glass bottle, rather than a can, because they think it more stylish to drink from the former. We believe, however, that the frequency and the difficulty of having to distinguish between product design and product packaging will be much less than the frequency and the difficulty of having to decide when a product design is inherently distinctive. To the extent there are close cases, we believe that courts should err on the side of caution and classify ambiguous trade dress as product design, thereby requiring secondary meaning. The very closeness will suggest the existence of relatively small utility in adopting an inherent-distinctiveness principle, and relatively great consumer benefit in requiring a demonstration of secondary meaning.

[17] We hold that, in an action for infringement of unregistered trade dress under § 43(a) of the Lanham Act, a product's design is distinctive, and therefore protectible, only upon a showing of secondary meaning. The judgment of the Second Circuit is reversed, and the case is remanded for further proceedings consistent with this opinion.

It is so ordered.

Comments and Questions

1. *Assuming product configuration.* Does Justice Scalia's admonition that "courts should err on the side of caution and classify ambiguous trade dress as product design" make sense as a policy matter? What are the costs and benefits of this approach to trademark owners, to their competitors, and to their consumers?

2. *What about copyright infringement in* Samara Bros.*?* At the district court, "[t]he jury found that Wal–Mart had wilfully infringed Samara's rights, awarding Samara $912,856.77 on the copyright claims, $240,458.53 for the Lanham Act violation and $50 for the state law violations." *Samara Bros. v. Wal-Mart Stores, Inc.,* 165 F.3d 120, 123 (2d Cir. 1998). Decades later, Judge Denny Chin, who was the district court judge in *Samara Bros.* (and is now on the Second Circuit), reflected on the case:

> Ironically, the Supreme Court latched on to a very small part of the case. This was principally a copyright case—the copying of Samara's copyrighted designs. But Samara had included a trade dress claim, and the jury awarded some damages for the trade dress claim, although far less than for the copyright claims. The jury's award on the copyright claims remained intact, and, ultimately, the Supreme Court's reversal had little practical

impact on the case, even as it made new law. Apparently, the Supreme Court saw this case as an opportunity to clarify the law in the trade dress area, and it did so.

Hon. Denny Chin, Litigating *Copyright Cases: A View from the Bench*, 59 J. COPYRIGHT SOC'Y U.S.A. 185, 194–95 (2012).

ii. Distinguishing Product Packaging from Product Configuration

The Supreme Court's holding in *Samara Bros.* eliminated one problem—how to analyze the inherent distinctiveness of product configuration trade dress—but created another: how to determine whether a particular product feature or combination of product features qualifies as product packaging trade dress, product configuration trade dress, or perhaps some other kind of trade dress. The opinion excerpts that follow offer examples of how courts have sought to determine where along the packaging/configuration divide particular forms of trade dress fall. In reading the opinions, consider the following question: How should a court treat various forms of decoration applied to the surface of the product (e.g., stripes on the side of an athletic shoe)? Is such decoration product packaging, production configuration, or something else?

In re Slokevage
441 F.3d 957 (Fed. Cir. 2006)

LOURIE, Circuit Judge.

[1] Joanne Slokevage ("Slokevage") appeals from the decision of the United States Patent and Trademark Office, Trademark Trial and Appeal Board ("Board") sustaining the refusal of the examiner to register her trade dress mark for clothing. *In re Joanne Slokevage,* Serial No. 75602873 (TTAB Nov. 10, 2004) ("*Final Decision*"). Because the Board's finding that Slokevage's trade dress was product design and thus could not be inherently distinctive . . . we affirm.

BACKGROUND

[2] Slokevage filed an application to register a mark on the Principal Register for "pants, overalls, shorts, culottes, dresses, skirts." Slokevage described the mark in her application as a "configuration" that consists of a label with the words "FLASH DARE!" in a V-shaped background, and cut-out areas located on each side of the label. The cut-out areas consist of a hole in a garment and a flap attached to the garment with a closure device. This trade dress configuration, which is located on the rear of various garments, is depicted below:

[3] Although Slokevage currently seeks to register a mark for the overall configuration of her design, she has already received protection for various aspects of the trade dress configuration. For example, she received a design patent for the cut-out area design. She also registered on the Supplemental Register[1] a design mark for the cut-out area. In addition, she registered the word mark "FLASH DARE!" on the Principal Register.

---

[1] Pursuant to section 23 of the Lanham Act, the United States Patent and Trademark Office ("PTO") maintains a Supplemental Register for marks "capable of distinguishing applicant's goods or services and not registrable on the principal register." 15 U.S.C. § 1091(a).

[4] The trademark examiner initially refused registration of the proposed mark on the ground that it constituted a clothing configuration that is not inherently distinctive. The examiner afforded Slokevage the opportunity to submit evidence of acquired distinctiveness or to disclaim the design elements of the configuration, but Slokevage chose not to submit evidence of acquired distinctiveness or to disclaim the design elements. Rather, she argued that the trade dress was inherently distinctive. The examiner, relying on section 2(f) of the Trademark Act, 15 U.S.C. § 1052(f), made final his refusal to register the mark on the ground that the clothing configuration constitutes "product design/configuration," and pursuant to the decision of the U.S. Supreme Court in *Wal-Mart Stores, Inc. v. Samara Brothers, Inc.,* 529 U.S. 205, 120 S.Ct. 1339, 146 L.Ed.2d 182 (2000), "product design" cannot be inherently distinctive. The examiner noted that Slokevage's reference in her application to the trade dress as a "cut-away flap design" supported a determination that the configuration constitutes product design . . . .

[5] Slokevage appealed the refusal of the examiner to register the trade dress configuration, and the Board affirmed the examiner's decision. The Board found that the cut-out areas, consisting of the holes and flaps, constituted product design. Relying on *Wal-Mart,* the Board observed that a product design "will not be regarded as a source indicator at the time of its introduction." According to the Board, Slokevage's trade dress, as product design, could not be inherently distinctive, and therefore could not be registered absent a showing of acquired distinctiveness.

. . . .

DISCUSSION

. . . .

[6] As a preliminary matter, Slokevage argues that whether trade dress is product design or not is a legal determination, whereas the government asserts that it is a factual issue. The resolution of that question is an issue of first impression for this court. We conclude that the determination whether trade dress is product design is a factual finding because it is akin to determining whether a trademark is inherently distinctive or whether a mark is descriptive, which are questions of fact. . . . Inherent distinctiveness or descriptiveness involves consumer perception and whether consumers are predisposed towards equating a symbol with a source. *See In re MBNA Am. Bank, N.A.,* 340 F.3d 1328, 1332 (Fed. Cir. 2003). Such issues are determined based on testimony, surveys, and other evidence as questions of fact. Determining whether trade dress is product design or product packaging involves a similar inquiry. *Wal-Mart,* 529 U.S. at 213 (discussing product packaging and design in the context of consumers ability to equate the product with the source). We therefore will defer to the Board's finding on product design, affirming the Board if its decision is supported by substantial evidence . . . .

I. Trade Dress and Product Design

[7] On appeal, Slokevage argues that the Board erred in determining that the trade dress[2] for which she seeks protection is product design and thus that it cannot be inherently distinctive. She asserts that the Board's reliance on the Supreme Court's decision in *Wal-Mart* to support its position that Slokevage's trade dress is product design is misplaced. In particular, she contends that *Wal-Mart* does not provide guidance on how to determine whether trade dress is product design. Moreover, she maintains that the trade dress at issue in *Wal-Mart,* which was classified as product design without explanation, is different from Slokevage's trade dress because the *Wal-Mart* trade dress implicated the overall appearance of the product and was a theme made up of many unique elements. Slokevage argues that her trade dress, in contrast, involves one component of a product design, which can be used with a variety of types of clothing. Slokevage further asserts that her trade dress is located on the rear hips of garments, which is a location that consumers frequently recognize as identifying the source of the garment.

[8] The PTO responds that the Board correctly concluded that Slokevage's trade dress is product design and that it properly relied on *Wal-Mart* for support of its determination. According to the PTO, in

---

[2] Slokevage admits that the configuration she is seeking to protect is "trade dress" and thus we will accept for purposes of this appeal that the configuration is "trade dress."

the *Wal-Mart* decision the Supreme Court determined that a design of clothing is product design. The PTO further asserts that the trade dress at issue in *Wal-Mart,* which was classified as product design, is similar to Slokevage's trade dress. The trade dress in *Wal-Mart* consists of design elements on a line of garments, and Slokevage's trade dress similarly consists of a design component common to the overall design of a variety of garments. The PTO notes that Slokevage's trade dress application refers to her trade dress as a "configuration" including a "clothing feature," and that "product configuration" is synonymous with "product design." The PTO also argues that under *Wal-Mart* product design cannot be inherently distinctive, the rationale being that consumers perceive product design as making the product more useful or desirable, rather than indicating source. According to the PTO, the trade dress at issue here makes the product more desirable to consumers, rather than indicates source. Finally, the PTO notes that even if it were a close case as to whether Slokevage's trade dress constitutes product design, the Court's opinion in *Wal-Mart* states that in "close cases," trade dress should be categorized as product design, thereby requiring proof of acquired distinctiveness for protection. 529 U.S. at 215.

[9] We agree with the Board that Slokevage's trade dress constitutes product design and therefore cannot be inherently distinctive. . . .

[10] Directly relevant to our discussion of product design is the Court's discussion in *Wal-Mart.* . . . {T}he {*Wal-Mart*} Court established a bright-line rule—product design cannot be inherently distinctive, and always requires proof of acquired distinctiveness to be protected. The Court did not recite the factors that distinguish between product packaging and product design trade dress, but stated that in "close cases" courts should classify the trade dress as product design. *Id.* at 215.

[11] Both parties agree that if we determine that the trade dress at issue is product design, then it cannot be inherently distinctive under the decision in *Wal-Mart.* The issue pertinent to this appeal, however, is whether Slokevage's proposed trade dress is product design. Although the decision in *Wal-Mart* does not expressly address the issue of what constitutes product design, it is informative to this case because it provides examples of trade dress that are product design. The Court observed that a "cocktail shaker shaped like a penguin" is product design and that the trade dress at issue in that case, "a line of spring/summer one-piece seersucker outfits decorated with appliques of hearts, flowers, fruits, and the like" is product design. *Wal-Mart,* 529 U.S. at 207. These examples demonstrate that product design can consist of design features incorporated into a product. Slokevage urges that her trade dress is not product design because it does not alter the entire product but is more akin to a label being placed on a garment. We do not agree. The holes and flaps portion are part of the design of the clothing—the cut-out area is not merely a design placed on top of a garment, but is a design incorporated into the garment itself. Moreover, while Slokevage urges that product design trade dress must implicate the entire product, we do not find support for that proposition. Just as the product design in *Wal-Mart* consisted of certain design features featured on clothing, Slokevage's trade dress similarly consists of design features, holes and flaps, featured in clothing, revealing the similarity between the two types of design.

[12] In addition, the reasoning behind the Supreme Court's determination that product design cannot be inherently distinctive is also instructive to our case. The Court reasoned that, unlike a trademark whose "predominant function" remains source identification, product design often serves other functions, such as rendering the "product itself more useful or more appealing." *Wal-Mart,* 529 U.S. at 212, 213. The design at issue here can serve such utilitarian and aesthetic functions. For example, consumers may purchase Slokevage's clothing for the utilitarian purpose of wearing a garment or because they find the appearance of the garment particularly desirable. Consistent with the Supreme Court's analysis in *Wal-Mart,* in such cases when the purchase implicates a utilitarian or aesthetic purpose, rather than a source-identifying function, it is appropriate to require proof of acquired distinctiveness.

[13] Finally, the Court in *Wal-Mart* provided guidance on how to address trade dress cases that may be difficult to classify: "To the extent that there are close cases, we believe that courts should err on the side of caution and classify ambiguous trade dress as product design, thereby requiring secondary meaning." 529 U.S. at 215. Even if this were a close case, therefore, we must follow that precedent and

classify the trade dress as product design. We thus agree with the Board that Slokevage's trade dress is product design and therefore that she must prove acquired distinctiveness in order for her trade dress mark to be registered.

LVL XIII Brands, Inc. v. Louis Vuitton Malletier S.A.
209 F. Supp. 3d 612, 626 (S.D.N.Y. 2016)

In *LVL XIII Brands*, the plaintiff produced "'luxury' men's sneakers" featuring "a rectangular metal toe plate with a 'LVL XIII inscription' secured to the front outsole of the sneaker by metal screws." *Id.* at 628. (See the above image on the left). The defendant produced luxury sneakers also featuring a metal toe plate (above, right). The parties filed cross-motions for summary judgment. The district court analyzed whether the plaintiff's toe plate design was product packaging or product configuration:

> This is not a close case. Even a cursory examination of the TP {metal toe plate} discloses that it does not qualify as a trademark or product packaging.... {P}roduct packaging is generally limited to "the appearance of labels, wrappers, boxes, envelopes, and other containers used in packaging a product as well as displays and other materials used in presenting the product to prospective purchasers." Restatement (Third) of Unfair Competition § 16 cmt.a (1995).

> Tellingly, LVL XIII has not offered any admissible evidence to support its claim that the TP falls within either of these categories. And the record evidence is decidedly to the contrary.

> First, the "packag[ing]" described in LVL XIII's business plan consists solely of "distinctive branded shoe boxes" and "black cotton dust bags"—it does not include the TP.

> Second, in declining to register {LVL XIII's trademark} Application, the PTO stated that "the rectangular shape of the shoe toe plate . . . is a configuration of a feature of the *shoe design*," which "can never be inherently distinctive as a matter of law." Although the PTO's determination is not dispositive, the Court is to "accord weight" to it. *Genesee Brewing Co. v. Stroh Brewing Co.,* 124 F.3d 137, 148 n. 11 (2d Cir. 1997). Such deference is particularly appropriate where, as here, the PTO's determination is consistent with the registrant's own characterization of the claimed mark: As noted, the '102 Application sought registration for a "shoe toe *design*" (emphasis added); *see In re Slokevage,* 441 F.3d at 959 ("Slokevage's reference in her application to the trade dress as a 'cut-away flap design' supported a determination that the configuration constitutes product design."). And LVL XIII used dotted lines to identify unclaimed portions of the mark, a procedure

---

1   http://www.thefashionlaw.com/home/louis-vuitton-lvl-xiii-head-back-to-court-over-sneaker-top-plates?rq=LVL%20XIII.

required only for "trade dress marks." *See* U.S. Patent & Trademark Office, Trademark Manual of Examining Procedures ("TMEP") § 1202.02(c)(i) (Apr. 2016 ed.).

Despite this evidence, LVL XIII argues that the TP is an inherently distinctive trademark because its uniform size and placement on LVL XIII's line of sneakers renders it "arbitrary" and "fanciful," and thus apt to be an automatic indicator of source. That argument is not persuasive.... Despite LVL XIII's efforts to shoehorn the TP into the trademark category, it does not fit. Rather, like the configuration in *Slokevage*, the TP serves a primarily aesthetic function: making LVL XIII's sneakers appear more enticing. Accordingly, the TP can be classified only as a product design feature which is not inherently distinctive. To prevail on its Lanham Act claims, LVL XIII must therefore show that the TP acquired secondary meaning.

LVL XIII Brands, Inc. v. Louis Vuitton Malletier S.A., 209 F. Supp. 3d 612, 652–54 (S.D.N.Y. 2016) (footnotes and some citations omitted). The Second Circuit subsequently affirmed. *LVL XIII Brands, Inc. v. Louis Vuitton Malletier SA*, 720 F. App'x 24 (2d Cir. 2017).

McKernan's Tunnel Permit	Burek's Tunnel Permit	Sandwich Ship Supply's Tunnel Permit

McKernan v. Burek
118 F. Supp. 2d 119 (D.Mass. 2000)

In *McKernan*, the plaintiff McKernan sold a novelty bumper sticker that purported to be a "Cape Cod Canal Tunnel Permit." (This was meant to be hilarious. There is no tunnel to Cape Cod.) He brought a trademark infringement suit against Burek and others who were producing similar bumper stickers. McKernan conceded that his bumper sticker design had no secondary meaning. The parties filed cross-motions for summary judgment. Judge Lasker analyzed whether the bumper sticker was product packaging or product configuration as follows:

The Tunnel Permit presents one of the "hard cases at the margin" referred to by the Supreme Court {in *Wal-Mart*}. It is particularly difficult to try to distinguish between the packaging and the product when discussing an ornamental bumper sticker. The packaging and the product are so intertwined that distinguishing between them may be regarded as a scholastic endeavor.

Nevertheless, the Supreme Court's opinion in *Wal–Mart* provides some guidance. The example given in *Wal–Mart*, of the classic Coca–Cola bottle is instructive: an item is the product if it is the essential commodity being purchased and consumed rather than the dress which presents the product.

Here, the essential commodity being purchased is a joke on a bumper sticker. All of the visual elements contained in the Tunnel Permit are a part of this joke and indispensable to it. What is being purchased and consumed is the novelty sticker, not dress identifying the prestige or standing of its source. Because McKernan is seeking protection for the product being consumed, the proper classification of what McKernan seeks to protect is product design. This view of the matter is strengthened by the *Wal–Mart* Court's remarkably clear advice that in close cases trial courts should "err on the side of caution and classify ambiguous trade dress as product design." *Wal–Mart*, 529 U.S. at 215.

Accordingly, because McKernan seeks to protect his product design which, by definition, cannot be "inherently distinctive," his claim under § 43(a) fails.

118 F. Supp. 2d at 123-24. (McKernan did not bring a copyright claim, apparently because he falsely represented to the Copyright Office that he had drawn the image of Cape Cod appearing on the sticker when in fact he had copied it from a book. *Id.* at 122.).

Best Cellars, Inc. v. Wine Made Simple, Inc.
320 F.Supp.2d 60, 69-70 (S.D.N.Y. 2003)

In *Best Cellars*, the plaintiff, a wine retailer based in New York City, broadly claimed as its trade dress

> the total effect of the interior design of its store, which it describes as: (1) eight words differentiating taste categories; (2) eight colors differentiating taste categories; (3) eight computer manipulated images differentiating taste categories; (4) taste categories set above display fixtures by order of weight; (5) single display bottles set on stainless-steel wire pedestals; (6) square 4"x4" cards with verbal descriptions of each wine ("shelf talkers") with text arranged by template; (7) shelf talkers positioned at eye level, below each display bottle; (8) bottles vertically aligned in rows of nine; (9) storage cabinets located beneath vertically aligned bottled; (10) materials palette consisting of light wood and stainless steel; (11) mixture of vertical racks and open shelving display fixtures; (12) no fixed aisles; (13) bottles down and back-lit; and (14) limited selection (approximately 100) of relatively inexpensive wine.

Id. at 70.

Judge Lynch briefly analyzed whether this constituted product packaging trade dress or product configuration trade dress as follows:

> Unlike more traditional trade dress cases that concern product packaging (like water bottles, *see Nora Beverages, Inc. v. Perrier Group of America, Inc.*, 269 F.3d 114 (2d Cir. 2001)) or product designs (like children's clothing, *see Samara Bros.*, 529 U.S. at 213), this

---

[1] From Rockwell Group, http://www.rockwellgroup.com/projects/entry/best-cellars.

case concerns the interior decor of a retail establishment where customers purchase other products. In this, the case is similar to *Two Pesos,* which concerned the interior decor of Mexican-themed restaurants. *See Two Pesos,* 505 U.S. at 764–65 n. 1 (noting that trade dress "may include features such as size, shape, color or color combinations, texture, graphics, or even particular sales techniques" (citations and internal quotation marks omitted)). As the Supreme Court explained, the interior decor category fits awkwardly into the classifications of trade dress law, constituting either product packaging or a *"tertium quid"* akin to product packaging. *Samara Bros.,* 529 U.S. at 215. Interior decor is thus clearly *not* product design. Accordingly, it is appropriate to analyze the Best Cellars' interior decor trade dress under the product packaging standard for inherent distinctiveness . . . .

Id. at 69-70.

Fedders Corp. v. Elite Classics
268 F. Supp. 2d 1051 (S.D. Ill. 2003)

In *Fedders*, the plaintiff, a manufacturer of single room air conditioners claimed as its trade dress the "undulating curve on the left or right of the faceplate separating the portion of the faceplate on which the controls are positioned from the air intake louvers." Judge Gilbert analyzed the question of product packaging / product configuration as follows:

> In this case, the key question is whether the subject trade dress—the undulating curve on the decorative front—is part of the product design or packaging. The defendants argue that the curve is part of the product design, and that, therefore, evidence of secondary meaning is required. On the other hand, Fedders notes that the curve is not functional, but rather, purely esthetic. Moreover, Fedders argues that the curve is a unique design that is associated with its Chassis line of air conditioners. Therefore, according to Fedders, the curve is "inherently distinctive," and no evidence of secondary meaning is necessary . . . .

> In this case, the Court believes that Fedders's undulating curve is not "packaging", but rather product design. The curve serves a purpose other than to identify the maker. It serves the purpose of making the air conditioners more esthetically appealing.

Id. at 1061-62.

In re SnoWizard, Inc.
129 U.S.P.Q.2d 1001 (TTAB 2018)

The applicant sought to register the mark shown below for goods it identified as consisting of a "Concession trailer for snowball vendors to operate a viable snowball business." *Id.* at 1001. The applicant described the mark as follows: "The mark consists of a three-dimensional configuration of a snowcapped roof with the word "SNOBALLS", a snowball and associated beverage container positioned on top of a concession trailer for snowball vendors. The matter shown in broken or dotted lines is not part of the mark and serves only to show the position or placement of the mark." *Id.* at 1001-02.

The applicant presented the photograph shown below as its specimen of use:

The TTAB found: "Clearly, the product at issue in this case is the concession trailer; that is the product offered for sale, purchased by, and used by snowball vendors. It is not a container for flavored shaved ice or snowballs sold to consumers, as suggested by Applicant. Accordingly, Applicant's applied-for mark is properly characterized as a product design. Specifically, it is the design of the roof of a concession trailer. It therefore requires a showing of acquired distinctiveness in order to be registered on the Principal Register." *Id.* at 1003. (Reviewing, among other things, voluminous photographic evidence of similar concession trailers, the TTAB went on to find no secondary meaning. *See id.* at 1004-08)

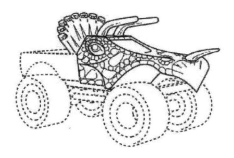

In re Frankish Enterprises Ltd.
113 U.S.P.Q.2d 1964 (TTAB 2015)

In *In Re Frankish Enterprises Ltd.*, the applicant sought to register the above-pictured three-dimensional mark for "[e]ntertainment services, namely, performing and competing in motor sports events in the nature of monster truck exhibitions." The applicant described the mark as follows: "The mark consists of a truck cab body in the design of a fanciful, prehistoric animal. The matter shown by dotted lines is not part of the mark, but serves only to show the position of the mark." The TTAB concluded that the mark was capable of inherent distinctiveness:

> Applicant does not seek registration of its design for a *product,* it seeks registration of its "fanciful, prehistoric animal" design for its monster truck exhibition *services,* and under *Two Pesos,* trade dress for services may be inherently distinctive. Indeed, Applicant's service is exhibiting its monster truck in action, such as doing wheelies, jumping over and crushing smaller vehicles and otherwise entertaining fans with the truck's size, power and sheer awesomeness, which could be performed with or without the "fanciful, prehistoric animal" design on the outside of the truck, just as Taco Cabana's service of offering Mexican food to restaurant customers could be performed without the particular interior design found to be inherently distinctive in *Two Pesos.* {T}he "fanciful, prehistoric animal" design is akin to the packaging of what is being sold, in this case Applicant's monster truck services.

In Re Frankish Enterprises Ltd., 113 U.S.P.Q.2d 1964, 2015 WL 1227728, at *4 (TTAB 2015). (For the Board's determination of whether in fact the mark was inherently distinctive, see below in Part I.A.2.c).

Comments and Questions

1. Is the three stripes design for the surface of athletic shoes shown in the registration below product configuration, product packaging, or some "tertium quid"? (The dotted lines do not constitute part of the claimed mark. The registration includes them only to show placement of the mark).

Int. Cl.: 25

Prior U.S. Cls.: 22 and 39

United States Patent and Trademark Office

Reg. No. 3,029,135
Registered Dec. 13, 2005

TRADEMARK
PRINCIPAL REGISTER

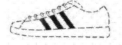

ADIDAS-SALOMON AG (FED REP GERMANY AKTIENGESELLSCHAFT (AG))
ADI-DASSLER STRASSE 1-2
D-91074 HERZOGENAURACH, FED REP GERMANY

FOR: FOOTWEAR, IN CLASS 25 (U.S. CLS. 22 AND 39).

FIRST USE 1-1-1952; IN COMMERCE 1-1-1952.

THE MARK CONSISTS OF THREE PARALLEL STRIPES WITH SERRATED EDGES APPLIED TO

FOOTWEAR. THE STRIPES ARE POSITIONED ON THE FOOTWEAR UPPER IN THE AREA BETWEEN THE LACES AND THE SOLE. THE DOTTED OUTLINE OF THE FOOTWEAR IS NOT CLAIMED AS PART OF THE MARK AND IS INTENDED ONLY TO SHOW THE POSITION OF THE MARK.

SEC. 2(F).

SER. NO. 78-539,734, FILED 12-29-2004.

ALINA MORRIS, EXAMINING ATTORNEY

c. Analyzing the Inherent Distinctiveness of Product Packaging Trade Dress

Product configuration trade dress and single colors (whether applied to the packaging of the product or the product itself) are per se incapable of inherent distinctiveness, and it is likely that courts would also find smells, tastes, and textures also to be incapable of inherent distinctiveness. But this leaves a wide array of nonverbal marks, including product packaging trade dress, that remain capable of inherent distinctiveness. The question, then, is how to determine whether a particular mark that falls into one of these categories is in fact inherently distinctive. While the *Abercrombie* spectrum works reasonably well for verbal marks, it is not clear that it is well-suited to the inherent distinctiveness analysis of nonverbal marks. Instead, as we will see below, most courts outside of the Second Circuit have adopted the so-called *Seabrook* factors, from *Seabrook Foods, Inc. v. Bar–Well Foods Ltd.*, 568 F.2d 1342 (CCPA 1977), to analyze the inherent distinctiveness of nonverbal marks.

We first consider an example of the Second Circuit's proud attempt to adapt its *Abercombie* spectrum to the question of whether a product packaging feature is inherently distinctive. We then turn to an example of the (probably far more sensible) *Seabrook* factors approach to the question.

i. Using the *Abercrombie* Spectrum to Analyze Whether Product Packaging Is Inherently Distinctive

Fun-Damental Too, Ltd. v. Gemmy Industries Corp.
111 F.3d 993, 997-998, 999-1001 (2d Cir. 1997)

{Plaintiff Fun-Damental Too, Ltd. ("Fun-Damental") brought suit for trademark infringement against defendants alleging that defendants had copied the trade dress of Fun-Damental's "Toilet Bank" (see photo below) in the sale of their own "Currency Can."

Judge Mukasey of the S.D.N.Y. granted a preliminary injunction in favor of Fun-Damental. Defendants appealed. Excerpted here are the court's description of the Toilet Bank's trade dress and the court's analysis of the inherent distinctiveness, if any, of that trade dress.}

CARDAMONE, Circuit Judge

. . . .

[1] Plaintiff's product is displayed in stores in a royal blue triangular-shaped box. The Toilet Bank itself is visible within the open-style box, which allows a consumer access to the toilet handle so that the flushing sound may be tested. The toy's bowl is covered with a clear plastic cover that includes a raised three-dimensional circle to which is affixed a gray sticker depicting a coin. The bank is held in place in its box by a 1/4 inch strap running up one side of the toilet bowl, through the plastic cover, and down the other side.

[2] The product name "TOILET BANK" appears in yellow letters on the royal blue box's lower front panel. The four inch-high upper rear panel is decorated with the product name and two pictures demonstrating how to use the product. The top picture shows a hand holding a coin over the toilet bowl, and the bottom one shows an index finger depressing the handle with the message "REAL FLUSHING SOUND" in white letters on a red bubble. In the upper right hand corner of this panel is a yellow starburst with the words "REAL FLUSHING SOUND" in red letters. Below it is a yellow arrow pointing down toward the handle with the legend in red: "TRY ME" and in smaller letters: "PRESS HANDLE." The same message appears on a red arrow sticker, affixed to the toilet tank, pointing diagonally towards the silver handle.

. . . .

[3] We ordinarily evaluate inherent distinctiveness of trade dress by applying the trademark classifications as set forth by Judge Friendly in *Abercrombie & Fitch Co. v. Hunting World, Inc.,* 537 F.2d 4, 9 (2d Cir. 1976). *See Paddington Corp. v. Attiki Importers & Distrib., Inc.,* 996 F.2d 577, 583 (2d Cir. 1993) (adopting Judge Friendly's test to evaluate the inherent distinctiveness of product packaging). Within this framework, trade dress is classified on a spectrum of increasing distinctiveness as generic, descriptive, suggestive, or arbitrary/fanciful . . . .

[4] The Supreme Court has emphasized that an inherently distinctive trade dress is one whose "intrinsic nature serves to identify a particular source of a product," *Two Pesos, Inc. v. Taco Cabana, Inc.,* 505 U.S. 763, 768 (1992), although it may not yet have widespread identification among consumers. *Id.* at 771. Consumers generally rely on packaging for information about the product and its source. But the varieties of labels and packaging available to wholesalers and manufacturers are virtually unlimited. As a consequence, a product's trade dress typically will be arbitrary or fanciful and meet the inherently distinctive requirement for § 43(a) protection. *Mana Prods., Inc. v. Columbia Cosmetics Mfg., Inc.,* 65 F.3d 1063, 1069 (2d Cir. 1995); *Chevron Chem. Co. v. Voluntary Purchasing Groups, Inc.,* 659 F.2d 695, 703 (5th Cir. 1981).

[5] Yet trade dress protection has limits. A trade dress that consists of the shape of a product that conforms to a well-established industry custom is generic and hence unprotected. For example, the cosmetics industry's common use of black, rectangular-shaped compacts renders that packaging generic. *Mana,* 65 F.3d at 1070; *see also Paddington,* 996 F.2d at 583 (soda industry practice would render green cans generic for the purpose of packaging lime-flavored soda). In short, despite the broad opportunity to design an arbitrary or fanciful trade dress, a specific trade dress must still be evaluated to determine whether it is so distinctive as to point to a single source of origin and thereby be entitled to Lanham Act protection.

[6] Defendants urge us to adopt a more stringent standard of distinctiveness than that used by the trial court. Recently we declined to use the *Abercrombie* spectrum of distinctiveness in a trade dress case that involved features of the product itself. *Knitwaves, Inc. v. Lollytogs Ltd.,* 71 F.3d 996 (2d Cir. 1995). In an attempt to extend that rationale, defendants suggest we adopt an alternative test for inherent distinctiveness of trade dress set forth in *Seabrook Foods, Inc. v. Bar–Well Foods Ltd.,* 568 F.2d 1342, 1344 (C.C.P.A. 1977). Under *Seabrook,* the inquiry is whether the design or shape of a package is a common, basic one, or whether it is unique or unusual in a particular field; whether the design is a mere refinement of a commonly-adopted and well-known form of ornamentation for a particular class of goods viewed by the public as a trade dress or ornamentation for such goods, or whether it is one capable of creating a commercial impression separate from the accompanying words. *Id.*

[7] We see no reason to abandon the *Abercrombie* distinctiveness spectrum in this case. Several reasons lead us to decline. First, we have expressly ruled that the *Abercrombie* classifications apply to packaging. *Paddington,* 996 F.2d at 583. Second, *Knitwaves* is a pure product configuration case, separate from product packaging, the category of trade dress at issue in this case. In *Knitwaves,* the trade dress lay in the product itself, rather than in a symbol—a trademark or packaging—associated with the product. It was therefore difficult to define some aspect or feature of the trade dress as "descriptive" or "arbitrary" in relation to the product. *See Knitwaves,* 71 F.3d at 1007–08 (quoting *Duraco Prods. v. Joy Plastic Enters., Ltd.,* 40 F.3d 1431, 1440–41 (3d Cir. 1994)). In contrast, a store display of a product's packaging style creates an image of the product more readily separated from the product itself. Moreover, although there may be a finite set of ways to configure a product, the variety of packaging available for a given product is limited only by the bounds of imagination. These factors render packaging more suitable than product configuration for classification under the *Abercrombie* system as arbitrary or fanciful, suggestive, descriptive, or generic.

[8] Third, use of the *Abercrombie* test tracks the purpose of the Lanham Act to identify source. That is, it is consistent with the Supreme Court's emphasis on a trade dress' capacity to "identify a particular source of the product." *Two Pesos,* 505 U.S. at 771. While a more stringent test is necessary in the product configuration context, applying *Abercrombie* to product packaging serves the aims of the Lanham Act because consumers are more likely to rely on the packaging of a product than on the product's design as

an indication of source. Restatement (Third) of Unfair Competition § 16 cmt. b (1995). In contrast, over-inclusive protection of the product design risks conferring benefits beyond the intended scope of the Lanham Act and entering what is properly the realm of patent law. *See Fabrication Enters., Inc. v. Hygenic Corp.,* 64 F.3d 53, 59 n. 4 (2d Cir. 1995). Thus, though the *Abercrombie* classifications were originally developed for analysis of word marks, we conclude that because of the endless number of product packaging options the *Abercrombie* test is appropriately applied in this trade dress case.

B. Distinctiveness in the Instant Case

[9] Defendants insist that the Toilet Bank's trade dress is not inherently distinctive, principally because the elements identified as part of that characterization are generic. Classification under the *Abercrombie* spectrum of distinctiveness is a question of fact reviewed under the clearly erroneous standard. *See Bristol–Myers Squibb Co. v. McNeil–P.P.C., Inc.,* 973 F.2d 1033, 1039–40 (2d Cir. 1992) (classification of trademarks). We evaluate trade dress distinctiveness by looking at all its elements and considering the total impression the trade dress gives to the observer. *Paddington,* 996 F.2d at 584. Concededly, a number of individual features of the Toilet Bank's trade dress are common in the toy industry; for example, the triangular shape of the box and its open styling are found everywhere on toy store shelves. The red arrows stating "Try Me," the starburst (separate from the notation "flushing sound"), and the raised blister are similarly quite usual legends in the toy business. Although some of the individual elements of a trade dress are generic or descriptive, the impression given by all of them in combination may be inherently distinctive. Such was what the district court found here; and we cannot say that this finding is clearly erroneous.

[10] Gemmy maintains that the trial court improperly considered the similarities between its product and Fun–Damental's when making the inherently distinctive determination regarding the Toilet Bank's trade dress. We disagree. Although Fun–Damental makes no claim regarding the copying of its product, it was appropriate to consider the packaging in conjunction with the product, rather than simply the empty box. "[T]rade dress today encompasses a broad concept of how a product presented to the public looks, including its color, design, container, and all the elements that make up its total appearance." *Mana,* 65 F.3d at 1069.

[11] This "total look" approach is the only workable way to consider such elements of the trade dress as the arrow sticker that is affixed to the Toilet Bank's tank. Because the box is open in order to display the product, it was proper to analyze Fun–Damental's trade dress as seen by consumers—including the Toilet Bank product. Further, there is no risk of "spillover" protection for the Toilet Bank as a product here since the injunction is limited to the sale of a similar product in a *particular* package, rather than an absolute ban on the sale of the Currency Can in an open-style box. In sum, we conclude that looking at the product itself in the context of its packaging is a proper method of analyzing open-style packaging for trade dress protection.

---

ii. Using the *Seabrook* Factors to Analyze Whether Product Packaging is Inherently Distinctive

In *Seabrook*, the plaintiff Seabrook had registered, for frozen vegetables, a mark consisting in part of a pointed loop (or "stylized leaf design", as Seabrook called it) as shown below. Seabrook opposed the registration of Bar-Well's mark, also for frozen foods, that incorporated a similar pointed loop design on the ground that Bar-Well's use of the mark would confuse consumers. The Court of Customs & Patent Appeals (the predecessor court to the Court of Appeals for the Federal Circuit) set forth various factors relevant to the question of whether consumers would perceive the pointed loop design (absent the words and image of a farm) as inherently distinctive of source:

> In determining whether a design is arbitrary or distinctive this court has looked to whether it was a 'common' basic shape or design, whether it was unique or unusual in a particular field, whether it was a mere refinement of a commonly-adopted and well-known form of

ornamentation for a particular class of goods viewed by the public as a dress or ornamentation for the goods, or whether it was capable of creating a commercial impression distinct from the accompanying words.

Id. at 1344. The CCPA ultimately determined that the design at issue would be perceived merely as decoration. *Id.* These factors soon came to inform most courts analysis of the inherent distinctiveness of all nonverbal trademarks (including, before *Samara Bros.*, product configuration trade dress).

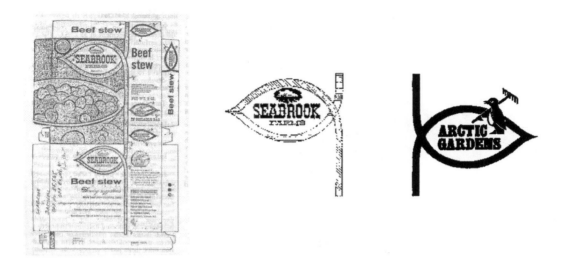

Note that the two leading treatises on trademark law disagree on whether the *Abercrombie* spectrum or the *Seabrook* factors work better for assessing the inherent distinctiveness of product packaging trade dress. McCarthy strongly endorses *Seabrook*:

> In the author's view, the *Seabrook* test is by far the preferable test to classify inherently distinctive trade dress in packaging and containers. Necessarily focusing upon the probable reaction of the ordinary consumer, it focuses upon the key issue in these cases: is the design so different in this market that it will immediately be perceived as a source identifier, not merely or solely as an attractive decoration or embellishment. The *Abercrombie* spectrum was developed specifically for word marks and does not translate into the world of shapes and designs.

MCCARTHY § 8:13. The Gilson treatise remains loyal to *Abercrombie*:

> The *Abercrombie* classifications are not an ideal fit for product packaging trade dress cases; is a squeeze bottle with a top that squirts liquid suggestive of dish soap or spring water or is it generic for those products because it is so widely used? Nevertheless, pending further clarification from the Supreme Court, lower courts should continue to use the *Abercrombie* spectrum in classifying product packaging trade dress.

GILSON § 2A.03[1][a][ii].

Note further that if a court finds a feature of product packaging to lack both inherent and acquired distinctiveness or a feature of product configuration to lack acquired distinctiveness, then the court will often (but not always) deem the feature to be "mere ornamentation."

As you read through the following opinion, consider the following questions:

- Which test is better: *Abercrombie* or *Seabrook*? On what grounds should courts prefer one or the other? Which test tends to be more plaintiff-friendly, i.e., more prone to find the trade dress at issue to be inherently distinctive?

- Could *Seabrook* be successfully modified to apply to the inherent distinctiveness analysis of verbal marks as well?

Amazing Spaces, Inc. v. Metro Mini Storage
608 F.3d 225 (5th Cir. 2010)

{The relevant facts are as follows: Plaintiff Amazing Spaces, Inc. ("Amazing Spaces") and defendant Metro Mini Storage ("Metro") are rival self-storage businesses in Houston, Texas. Amazing Spaces claims a star design as its service mark, which it registered at the PTO in 2004 (see the registration certificate below). Metro used a similar design on its storage buildings. In response to Amazing Spaces' suit for trademark infringement, Metro argued that Amazing Spaces' star design mark lacked both inherent and acquired distinctiveness and was improperly registered. The district court agreed and granted Metro's motion for summary judgment on the issue. On appeal, after considering, among other things, the weight to be accorded to the PTO registration (an issue we will discuss in Part I.D below), the Fifth Circuit turned to the question of whether the star design was inherently distinctive.}

APPENDIX

Int. Cl.: 39

Prior U.S. Cls.: 100 and 105

United States Patent and Trademark Office   Reg. No. 2,859,845
                                                 Registered July 6, 2004

SERVICE MARK
PRINCIPAL REGISTER

AMAZING SPACES (TEXAS CORPORATION)   FIRST USE 4-0-1998; IN COMMERCE 4-0-1998.
9040 LOUETTA ROAD, SUITE B
SPRING, TX 77379   SER. NO. 76-540,854, FILED 8-15-2003.

FOR: STORAGE SERVICES, IN CLASS 39 (U.S.   DOMINIC J. FERRAIUOLO, EXAMINING ATTOR-
CLS. 100 AND 105).   NEY

KING, Circuit Judge

. . . .

2. Inherent Distinctiveness

[1] As mentioned above, "a mark is inherently distinctive if 'its intrinsic nature serves to identify a particular source.'" *Wal–Mart Stores,* 529 U.S. at 210 (quoting *Two Pesos,* 505 U.S. at 768). Inherent distinctiveness is attributable to a mark when the mark "almost *automatically* tells a customer that it refers to a brand and . . . immediately signal[s] a brand or a product source." *Id.* at 212 (quoting *Qualitex Co. v. Jacobson Prods. Co.,* 514 U.S. 159, 162–63 (1995)). The parties disagree over not only the answer to whether the Star Symbol is inherently distinctive but also over the proper method for conducting the inquiry. Metro urges that the familiar *Abercrombie* test cannot be used to categorize the Star Symbol and instead asks that we apply the *Seabrook Foods* test to determine that the Star Symbol is not inherently distinctive. Amazing Spaces, by contrast, presses the application of the *Abercrombie* test, under which it claims the Star Symbol is inherently distinctive, and it argues alternatively that the Star Symbol is inherently distinctive under the *Seabrook Foods* test.

a. *Abercrombie*

[2] In *Abercrombie,* Judge Friendly sought to arrange the universe of marks into a spectrum of distinctiveness. *See* 537 F.2d at 9. . . .

[3] We agree with Metro that the Star Symbol resists categorization under the *Abercrombie* test, and we consequently do not rely on a rote application of its categories in determining whether the Star Symbol is inherently distinctive. The Supreme Court's most recent recitation of the *Abercrombie*

132

categories noted its use only in the context of marks consisting of words. *See Wal–Mart Stores,* 529 U.S. at 210 ("*In the context of word marks,* courts have applied the now-classic test originally formulated by Judge Friendly . . . ." (emphasis added) (citing *Abercrombie,* 537 F.2d at 10–11)). The Court's precedent also supports the proposition that some marks, although deserving of legal protection, do not fit within the *Abercrombie* spectrum. In *Qualitex,* the Court declined to apply the *Abercrombie* test to a mark consisting purely of a shade of color used in a product's trade dress, holding that the mark could constitute a legally protectable mark only through a showing of secondary meaning. 514 U.S. at 162–63. The Court further extended that logic when, in *Wal–Mart Stores,* it stated that "[i]t seems to us that [product] design, like color, is not inherently distinctive" and held that marks consisting of a product's design were protectable only upon proof of secondary meaning—a conclusion it could not have reached had it applied the *Abercrombie* test. *Wal–Mart Stores,* 529 U.S. at 212. Professor McCarthy, a luminary in the field of trademark law, has likewise suggested that the *Abercrombie* test may not apply to all marks, stating that "[u]se of the spectrum of descriptive, suggestive, arbitrary and fanciful is largely confined to word marks. It is usually not suitable for nonword designations such as shapes and images . . . [, which] must be judged by other guidelines." 2 MCCARTHY ON TRADEMARKS § 11:2, at 11–7. . . .

[4] As the district court discovered, the challenge of placing the Star Symbol into *Abercrombie*'s constellation of categories is a futile endeavor. We have described the *Abercrombie* categories as follows . . . .

[5] The district court briefly probed the utility of applying the *Abercrombie* test and concluded that the Star Symbol did not fit as a generic, descriptive, or suggestive mark. *See Amazing Spaces,* 665 F.Supp.2d at 737. The district court first rejected the notion that the Star Symbol was generic because "[a] five-pointed star within a circle does not refer to a product or service provided by a self-storage company" and "[t]he evidence of widespread use of a five-point star or a five-point star set within a circle by many diverse businesses and government offices supports the conclusion that the star mark is not related to or a generic symbol for self-storage goods or services." *Id.* It next determined that the Star Symbol was not descriptive because "[i]t does not identify a characteristic or quality of self-storage service, such as its function or quality." *Id.* Nor was the Star Symbol suggestive, according to the district court, because "[t]here is no basis to conclude that a five-pointed star set within a circle suggests an attribute of self-storage services." *Id.* We discern no flaws in the district court's analysis with respect to these three categories. However, the logical extension of the district court's analysis is the conclusion that the Star Symbol is arbitrary or fanciful, which under the *Abercrombie* test would render it inherently distinctive and thus entitled to protection. Yet the district court refused to so conclude, stating that "the star mark cannot be classified as arbitrary or fanciful unless it is inherently distinctive so as to serve as a source identifier for Amazing Spaces." *Id.* It then turned to the *Seabrook Foods* test in conducting its inquiry into the Star Symbol's inherent distinctiveness. *See id.*

[6] We agree that the Star Symbol—indeed, any mark—lacks inherent distinctiveness if its intrinsic nature does not serve to identify its source. *See Wal–Mart Stores,* 529 U.S. at 210 ("[A] mark is inherently distinctive if 'its intrinsic nature serves to identify a particular source.'" (quoting *Two Pesos,* 505 U.S. at 768)). Furthermore, as we have already indicated, we approve the district court's decision to apply a test other than *Abercrombie* in this case. However, we disagree somewhat with the district court's reasoning that a mark cannot be categorized as arbitrary or fanciful unless it is inherently distinctive. Under the *Abercrombie* test, it is the categorization of a mark that dictates its inherent distinctiveness, not the other way around. A rote application of the *Abercrombie* test yields the conclusion that the Star Symbol is an arbitrary or fanciful mark because it "'bear[s] no relationship to the products or services to which [it is] applied.'" *Pebble Beach,* 155 F.3d at 540 (quoting *Zatarains,* 698 F.2d at 791). Were we to apply the *Abercrombie* test mechanically to the Star Symbol, without an eye to the question the test seeks to answer, we would be left with the conclusion that the Star Symbol is inherently distinctive. The district court, aware of that result, proceeded to apply the *Seabrook Foods* test. *See Amazing Spaces,* 665 F.Supp.2d at 737.

[7] Both the Supreme Court and scholars have questioned the applicability of the *Abercrombie* test to marks other than words. *See Wal–Mart Stores,* 529 U.S. at 210–13, (noting that the *Abercrombie* test

was developed and applied "[i]n the context of word marks" and declining to apply it to a mark consisting of product design); *Qualitex*, 514 U.S. at 162–63 (referring to the *Abercrombie* test but not applying it to a mark consisting of a shade of color); .... 1 MCCARTHY ON TRADEMARKS § 8:13, at 8–58.1 ("Only in some cases does [*Abercrombie*] classification make sense [for trade dress] .... The word spectrum of marks simply does not translate into the world of shapes and images."); .... We do not go so far as to hold that the *Abercrombie* test is eclipsed every time a mark other than a word is at issue. Instead, we hold that the *Abercrombie* test fails to illuminate the fundamental inquiry in this case: whether the Star Symbol's "'intrinsic nature serves to identify'" Amazing Spaces and its storage services. *Wal–Mart Stores*, 529 U.S. at 210 (quoting *Two Pesos*, 505 U.S. at 768, 112 S.Ct. 2753). For the answer to that question, we now turn to the *Seabrook Foods* test employed by the district court.

b. *Seabrook Foods*

[8] In contrast to the *Abercrombie* test, the *Seabrook Foods* test, articulated by the U.S. Court of Customs and Patent Appeals in 1977, applies expressly to marks consisting of symbols and designs:

> In determining whether a design is arbitrary or distinctive this court has looked to [1] whether it was a "common" basic shape or design, [2] whether it was unique or unusual in a particular field, [3] whether it was a mere refinement of a commonly-adopted and well-known form of ornamentation for a particular class of goods viewed by the public as a dress or ornamentation for the goods, or [4] whether it was capable of creating a commercial impression distinct from the accompanying words.

Seabrook Foods, 568 F.2d at 1344 (footnotes omitted).[14] The first three of the *Seabrook Foods* "'questions are merely different ways to ask whether the design, shape or combination of elements is so unique, unusual or unexpected in this market that one can assume without proof that it will automatically be perceived by customers as an indicator of origin—a trademark.'" *I.P. Lund Trading ApS v. Kohler Co.*, 163 F.3d 27, 40 (1st Cir. 1998) (quoting 1 MCCARTHY ON TRADEMARKS § 8:13, at 8–58.5). As is true of the *Abercrombie* test, the *Seabrook Foods* test seeks an answer to the question whether a mark's "'intrinsic nature serves to identify a particular source.'" *Wal–Mart Stores*, 529 U.S. at 210 (quoting *Two Pesos*, 505 U.S. at 768, 112 S.Ct. 2753) ....[16]

[9] We agree with the assessment of ... Professor McCarthy that the *Seabrook Foods* factors are variations on a theme rather than discrete inquiries. In *Star Industries v. Bacardi & Co.*, the Second Circuit noted that "'[c]ommon basic shapes' or letters are, as a matter of law, not inherently distinctive ..., [but] stylized shapes or letters may qualify, provided the design is not commonplace but rather unique or unusual in the relevant market." 412 F.3d 373, 382 (2d Cir. 2005) (citing *Seabrook Foods*, 568 F.2d at 1344; *Permatex Co. v. Cal. Tube Prods., Inc.*, 175 U.S.P.Q. 764, 766 (TTAB1972)). This statement, turning on whether the symbol or design is "common," comprises, essentially, the first two *Seabrook Foods* factors. However, the third *Seabrook Foods* factor similarly asks whether a symbol or design is "common" in the sense that it is likely to be perceived by the public as ornamentation rather than a mark. *See Wiley*

---

[14] As noted above, the district court omitted discussion of the fourth factor, which by its terms applies only when a party seeks trademark protection for a background design typically accompanied by words. *See Amazing Spaces*, 665 F.Supp.2d at 736. Similarly, we will not consider the fourth *Seabrook Foods* factor.

[16] We note, of course, that the *Wal–Mart* Court was urged by the respondent in that case and by the United States as *amicus curiae* to adopt the *Seabrook Foods* test writ large for product design but declined to do so. *Id.* at 213–14, 120 S.Ct. 1339. The Court's concern was that "[s]uch a test would rarely provide the basis for summary disposition of an anticompetitive strike suit." *Id.* at 214, 120 S.Ct. 1339. However, as discussed below, we are of the opinion that the relevant portions of the *Seabrook Foods* test do provide a basis for summary disposition in this case. Because we conclude that the Star Symbol is not inherently distinctive under the *Seabrook Foods* test, we do not address whether it constitutes a "reasonably clear test," *id.* at 213, such that it would be preferable to the *Abercrombie* test in the ordinary trademark or service mark dispute.

v. Am. Greetings Corp., 762 F.2d 139, 142 (1st Cir. 1985) (equating a red heart shape on a teddy bear to "an ordinary geometric shape" because it "carrie[d] no distinctive message of origin to the consumer, . . . given the heart shape's widespread use as decoration for any number of products put out by many different companies").[17] A "common" symbol or design—lacking inherent distinctiveness—is the antithesis of a symbol or design that "'is so unique, unusual or unexpected in this market that one can assume without proof that it will automatically be perceived by customers as an indicator of origin—a trademark.'" *I.P. Lund Trading*, 163 F.3d at 40 (quoting 1 MCCARTHY ON TRADEMARKS § 8:13, at 8–58.5); *accord* RESTATEMENT § 13 cmt. d, at 107 ("Commonplace symbols and designs are not inherently distinctive since their appearance on numerous products makes it unlikely that consumers will view them as distinctive of the goods or services of a particular seller.").

[10] The district court determined that the Star Symbol was "not a plain five-pointed star" but was instead "shaded and set within a circle," rendering it "sufficient[ly] styliz[ed]" to be "more than a common geometric shape." *Amazing Spaces*, 665 F.Supp.2d at 737. It then proceeded to conclude that the Star Symbol "[wa]s not inherently distinctive and d[id] not act as an indicator of origin for any self-storage business, including Amazing Spaces." *Id.* at 738. It supported this assertion with a discussion of "[t]he ubiquitous nature of the five-pointed star set within a circle" in Texas, specifically its "use[ ] as a decoration or ornamentation on innumerable buildings, signs, roads, and products." *Id.* The court concluded that this ubiquity—including use of the same or a similar star design in 63 businesses and 28 other self-storage locations—"preclude[d] a finding that [the Star Symbol wa]s inherently distinctive or that it c[ould] serve as an indicator of origin for a particular business." *Id.*

[11] Undoubtedly, the Star Symbol is stylized relative to an unshaded five-pointed star design not set within a circle. However, we disagree that the issue of stylization revolves around comparing a design's actual appearance to its corresponding platonic form. Instead, as discussed above, asking whether a shape is stylized is merely another way of asking whether the design is "commonplace" or "unique or unusual in the relevant market," *Star Indus.*, 412 F.3d at 382 (citing *Permatex*, 175 U.S.P.Q. at 766), or whether it is "a mere refinement of a commonly-adopted and well-known form of ornamentation for a particular class of goods viewed by the public as a dress or ornamentation," *Seabrook Foods*, 568 F.2d at 1344.[18] The stylization inquiry is properly conceived of as asking whether a

---

[17] The interrelationship between these inquiries is also reflected in Professor McCarthy's discussion of common geometric shapes:

> Most common geometric shapes are regarded as not being inherently distinctive, in view of the common use of such shapes in all areas of advertising. Thus, such ordinary shapes as circles, ovals, squares, etc., either when used alone or as a background for a word mark, cannot function as a separate mark unless (1) the shape is likely to create a commercial impression on the buyer separate from the word mark or any other indicia and (2) the shape is proven to have secondary meaning . . . . The rationale is that such designs have been so widely and commonly used as mere decorative graphic elements that the origin-indicating ability of such designs has been diminished.

1 MCCARTHY ON TRADEMARKS § 7:29, at 7–73–74 (footnotes omitted).

[18] The parties dispute the scope of the "relevant market"—specifically, whether the district court correctly considered use of a similar or identical star design beyond the self-storage service industry. Amazing Spaces contends that we should limit our analysis to the self-storage services industry, while Metro argues that we may take into account uses of star designs in a larger context. The second *Seabrook Foods* factor refers to uniqueness or unusualness "in a particular field," 568 F.2d at 1344, and the Second Circuit has stated that a stylized design may be protectable when it "is not commonplace but rather unique or unusual in the relevant market," *Star Indus.*, 412 F.3d at 382. Similarly, the third factor refers to whether a mark is commonly used as ornamentation for a "particular class of goods." *Seabrook Foods*, 568 F.2d at 1344. In contrast, the First Circuit, in considering whether a red heart on the chest of a teddy

particular symbol or design is stylized such that prospective purchasers of goods or services are likely to differentiate it from other, similar symbols or designs.[19] *See Wiley*, 762 F.2d at 142 (holding that a red heart on a teddy bear "carrie[d] no distinctive message of origin to the consumer … given the heart shape's widespread use as decoration for any number of products put out by many different companies"); *Brooks Shoe Mfg. Co. v. Suave Shoe Corp.*, 716 F.2d 854, 858 (11th Cir. 1983) (holding that a design consisting of a "V," "7," or arrow on athletic shoes was common ornamentation such that it was not inherently distinctive); RESTATEMENT § 13 cmt. d, at 107 ("The manner in which a symbol or design is used is also relevant to the likelihood that it will be perceived as an indication of source. In some instances a design is likely to be viewed as mere ornamentation rather than as a symbol of identification."). The record evidence is replete with similar or identical five-pointed stars, both raised and set in circles, and used in similar manners, such that—notwithstanding the residual evidence of the presumption of validity—no reasonable jury could find that the Star Symbol is even a mere refinement of this commonly adopted and well-known form of ornamentation.[20] The Star Symbol is thus not "'so

---

bear was inherently distinctive, appeared to consider the broader use of red hearts in determining whether the use at issue was unique or unusual. *See Wiley*, 762 F.2d at 142 ("[T]he record contains so many examples of use of a red heart motif on teddy bears and other stuffed animals, *not to mention all manner of other toys and paraphernalia,* that no reasonable argument on this point can be made." (emphasis added)). The rule in the RESTATEMENT asks whether, "because of the nature of the designation and *the context in which it is used,* prospective purchasers are likely to perceive it as a designation that … identifies goods or services produced or sponsored by a particular person." RESTATEMENT § 13(a), at 104 (emphasis added). It further explains that

> [c]ommonplace symbols and designs are not inherently distinctive since their appearance on numerous products makes it unlikely that consumers will view them as distinctive of the goods or services of a particular seller. Thus, unless the symbol or design is striking, unusual, or otherwise likely to differentiate the products of a particular producer, the designation is not inherently distinctive.

Id. § 13 cmt. d, at 107. Finally, and most importantly, the Lanham Act defines "service mark" as a mark used "to identify and distinguish the services of one person … from the services of others and to indicate the source of the services." Lanham Act § 45, 15 U.S.C. § 1127. Because a mark must distinguish one person's services from another, we agree that our inquiry is whether the Star Symbol identifies and distinguishes Amazing Spaces's self-storage services from others' self-storage services. This does not mean, however, that we must blind ourselves to uses beyond the self-storage services industry: the fact that the same or a similar star is used in countless other ways certainly bears on whether it is "likely that prospective purchasers will perceive [a given star design] as an indication of source" within a particular industry because a "[c]ommonplace symbol[']s … appearance on numerous products makes it unlikely that consumers will view [it] as distinctive of the goods or services of a particular seller." RESTATEMENT § 13 cmt. d, at 107.

[19] Under this analysis, use by third parties of a design bears on whether the design is inherently distinctive, not merely whether the design "is a 'strong' or a 'weak' [ ]mark." *Exxon Corp. v. Tex. Motor Exchange of Houston, Inc.*, 628 F.2d 500, 504 (5th Cir. 1980); *cf. Union Nat'l Bank of Tex., Laredo, Tex.*, 909 F.2d at 848 n. 25 (noting that widespread industry use can render a mark not inherently distinctive, but third-party use otherwise typically affects the issue of whether there is a likelihood of confusion between marks).

[20] This is what differentiates the Star Symbol from the examples of registered marks containing stars that Amazing Spaces cites to support the protectability of five-pointed stars. The Dallas Cowboys star is stylized through the inclusion of a white border. The star in the Wal–Mart registration is a plain, five-pointed star, but the registered mark consists of more than just the star—the mark is the words "Wal" and "Mart" on either side of the star. The LanChile Airlines star is set against a circle that is 50%

unique, unusual or unexpected in this market that one can assume without proof that it will automatically be perceived by customers as an indicator of origin—a trademark,'" *I.P. Lund Trading,* 163 F.3d at 40 (quoting 1 MCCARTHY ON TRADEMARKS § 8:13, at 8–58.5), and it "does not almost *automatically* tell a customer that it refers to a brand . . . [or] immediately signal a brand or a product source," *Wal–Mart Stores,* 529 U.S. at 212, 120 S.Ct. 1339 (alterations and internal quotation marks omitted). Because the Star Symbol does not, by "'its intrinsic nature[,] serve[ ] to identify a particular source,'" *id.* at 210, it is not inherently distinctive, and it can be protected only upon a showing of secondary meaning.

{The court ultimately found that the star design lacked secondary meaning. It remanded the case, however, on the question, among others, of whether the overall appearance of Amazing Spaces' facilities, rather than simply the star design alone, was protectable trade dress.}

Fiji Water Co., LLC v. Fiji Mineral Water USA, LLC
741 F.Supp.2d 1165, 1176-77 (C.D.Cal. 2010)

{The essential facts are as follows: Plaintiff produced water bottled in Fiji under the mark FIJI and with trade dress as defined and shown below. Defendant also produced water bottled in Fiji under the mark VITI and with trade dress as shown below. Plaintiff sued for trademark (and trade dress) infringement and won a preliminary injunction. Excerpted here are the court's description of the plaintiff's trade dress and the court's analysis of the inherent distinctiveness of that trade dress.}

CORMAC J. CARNEY, District Judge

. . . .

[1] FIJI also alleges that the VITI product infringes the FIJI trade dress, which includes the following elements: the use of a bottle with a dominantly square shape, with a recessed central body portion defined by the protruding shoulders and base portions of the bottle, a blue bottle cap, a transparent outer front label with a pink accent in the lower right hand corner, a depiction of a blue background and palm tree fronds on the inside of the back label, a three-dimensional effect created by having a transparent label on the front panel of the bottle revealing the inner side of the back label, a rainwater

---

filled in, and it is adjacent to the words "LanChile Airlines." Finally, the USA Truck mark is a complex design consisting of a white star within a blue circle, set against a white rectangle with blue borders and a red stripe running across the middle. Each of these marks contains elements distinguishing it from the commonplace stars in the record. *See Union Nat'l Bank of Tex., Laredo, Tex.,* 909 F.2d at 848 n. 25 (noting that the appropriate inquiry is whether the mark as a whole is protectable, not whether its component parts are individually protectable (citing *Estate of P.D. Beckwith v. Comm'r of Patents,* 252 U.S. 538, 40 S.Ct. 414, 64 L.Ed. 705 (1919))).

drop on the front label, a statement on the front label stating "From the islands of Fiji/Natural Artesian Water," and prominent use of the four-letter, two-syllable word FIJI, in block white lettering with a metallic outline around the letters.

. . . .

[2] The second element that FIJI must establish to succeed on the merits for its trade dress infringement claim is that its trade dress is inherently distinctive or has acquired secondary meaning. Packaging such as the FIJI bottle shape and label design is inherently distinctive if "[its] intrinsic nature serves to identify a particular source." *Wal–Mart Stores, Inc. v. Samara Bros., Inc.*, 529 U.S. 205, 210, (2000); see also 1 *McCarthy on Trademarks* § 8:12.50 (4th ed. 2010) (bottle is packaging). To determine whether packaging is so "unique, unusual, or unexpected in this market that one can assume without proof that it will automatically be perceived by consumers as an indicator of origin," the court may look to {the *Seabrook* factors}. *Seabrook Foods, Inc. v. Bar–Well Foods Ltd.*, 568 F.2d 1342 (CPPA 1977). *See Wal–Mart Stores, Inc.*, 529 U.S. at 210 (noting that the *Abercrombie* spectrum of distinctiveness is properly applied to word marks); see also 1 *McCarthy on Trademarks* § 8:13 (4th ed. 2010) (commenting that *Seabrook* test is preferred for classifying inherently distinctive trade dress in packaging and containers); *DCNL, Inc. v. Almar Sales Co.*, 47 U.S.P.Q.2d 1406, 1997 WL 913941 (N.D.Cal. 1997), aff'd without opinion, 178 F.3d 1308 (9th Cir. 1998).

[3] Although the square bottle and blue cap elements may be fairly common in the bottled water industry, the stylized hibiscus, the palm fronds and the three-dimensional effect of the transparent front label with palm fronds on the inside back label are not a common design. *Contra Paddington Corp. v. Attiki Imps. & Distribs., Inc.*, 996 F.2d 577 (2d Cir. 1993) (giving examples of designs that are not inherently distinctive in certain markets, such as packaging lime soda in green cans or showing a shining car on a bottle of car wax). The stylized white block letters with metallic outline for the word "FIJI," together with the tropical foliage using hues of blue and green and the raindrop invites consumers to imagine fresh, clear water from a remote tropical island. Reviewing the 2008 Bottled Water Guide that FIJI submitted reveals no other brands that combine the elements of the square bottle, three-dimensional labeling effect, and tropical motif. FIJI has won international awards for print and packaging excellence and design innovation in the food packaging industry, which is strong evidence that its packaging is unique or unusual in the field and not simply a variation on existing bottled water designs. Finally, the transparent three-dimensional label distinguishes FIJI from the other brands, and makes the trade dress recognizable even apart from the block-letter word mark FIJI, as evidenced by some of the open-ended responses consumers gave in FIJI's consumer confusion survey. Based on this evidence, the Court concludes that FIJI's trade dress is inherently distinctive.

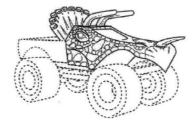

In re Frankish Enterprises Ltd.
113 U.S.P.Q.2d 1964 (TTAB 2015)

{You will recall that the applicant sought to register the above-pictured three-dimensional mark for "[e]ntertainment services, namely, performing and competing in motor sports events in the nature of monster truck exhibitions." Having concluded that the mark was capable of inherent distinctiveness as "akin to the packaging of" the applicant's monster truck services, the TTAB applied the *Seabrook* factors as follows to find that the mark was inherently distinctive:

> Here, the evidence made of record by the Examining Attorney fails to show that Applicant's "fanciful, prehistoric animal" design is either a common or a basic shape or design. Rather, it is unique among the more than 100 monster trucks depicted in the Examining Attorney's image search results. To the extent that two of the monster trucks among those results have certain characteristics in common with Applicant's mark, they are nevertheless readily distinguishable from Applicant's unique design which includes peculiar horns, scales, a protective shield and other features which neither Swamp Thing nor the "Raptors" monster trucks share. Indeed, Applicant's monster truck is "unique" and "unusual" in the monster truck field. The Examining Attorney provided scant, if any, evidence that Applicant's truck is a "mere refinement" of anything, let alone a "commonly-adopted" and "well-known form" in the monster truck field. To the contrary, the totality of the record makes clear that Applicant's truck stands alone in the quality and quantity of its distinctive traits which set it apart from the other monster trucks about which the Examining Attorney submitted evidence, as the body of Applicant's truck is cut and molded to convey the body of a dinosaur and adorned with other dinosaur elements, including horns, a protective shield and eyes bordered by scales. These elements are unique and make Applicant's truck unlike any of those included in the Examining Attorney's search results.

In Re Frankish Enterprises Ltd., 113 U.S.P.Q.2d 1964, 2015 WL 1227728, at *5 (TTAB 2015).

Though the Second Circuit apparently still subscribes to the use of *Abercrombie* in the analysis of the inherent distinctiveness of non-configuration trade dress, consider whether *Seabrook*-like factors inform the Second Circuit's analysis in the *Star Industries* case below.

Star Industries, Inc. v. Bacardi & Co. Ltd.
412 F.3d 373 (2d Cir. 2005)

{Star Industries, Inc. ("Star") developed and registered the mark as shown and described below for orange-flavored GEORGI vodka. Bacardi & Co. Ltd. ("Bacardi") then developed a similar mark for orange flavored rum. Star brought suit. Excerpted below is the court's description of Star's mark and its analysis of the inherent distinctiveness of that mark. Like the *Seabrook* plaintiff's claim that the pointed loop alone was source distinctive, Star was claiming that the "O" alone was distinctive of source.}

POOLER, Circuit Judge

. . . .

[1] In June 1996, inspired by the success of flavored vodkas introduced by leading international companies such as Stolichnaya, Star's president decided to develop an orange-flavored Georgi vodka. A new label was designed, consisting of the traditional Georgi label, which contains a coat of arms and a logo consisting of stylized capital letters spelling 'Georgi' on a white background, together with three new elements: an orange slice, the words "orange flavored," and a large elliptical letter "O" appearing below the "Georgi" logo and surrounding all of the other elements. The "O" was rendered as a vertical oval, with the outline of the "O" slightly wider along the sides (about one quarter inch thick) and narrowing at the top and bottom (about one eighth inch thick); the outline of the "O" is colored orange and decorated with two thin gold lines, one bordering the inside and one bordering the outside of the outline. Star was apparently the first company to distribute an orange-flavored alcoholic beverage packaged in a bottle bearing a large elliptical orange letter "O."

. . . .

[2] The district court erred when it described the Star "O" as a basic geometric shape or letter, and therefore rejected inherent distinctiveness and required a showing of secondary meaning. The Star "O" is not a "common basic shape" or letter, and the district court's holding to the contrary was premised on a misunderstanding of this trademark law concept. Unshaded linear representations of common shapes or letters are referred to as "basic." They are not protectable as inherently distinctive, because to protect them as trademarks would be to deprive competitors of fundamental communicative devices essential to the dissemination of information to consumers. However, stylized letters or shapes are not "basic," and are protectable when original within the relevant market. *See Courtenay Communications Corp. v. Hall*, 334 F.3d 210, 215 n.32 (2d Cir. 2003) (distinguishing case of mark consisting of word displayed with distinctive "typeface, color, and other design elements," which was protectable, from cases holding generic words not protectable); *compare W In re W.B. Roddenbery Co.*, 135 U.S.P.Q. 215, 216 (TTAB 1962) (holding design consisting of colored circle attached to differently colored rectangle protectable as inherently distinctive) *with In re Hillerich & Bradsby Co.*, 40 C.C.P.A. 990, 204 F.2d 287, 288 (1953) (noting that applicant conceded that unshaded line oval was not inherently distinctive). Star's "O" is sufficiently stylized to be inherently distinctive and therefore protectable as a trademark. It is stylized with respect to shading, border, and thickness, and each of these design elements distinguishes it from the simple or basic shapes and letters that have been held unprotectable.

[3] The Star "O" design had sufficient shape and color stylization to render it slightly more than a simply linear representation of an ellipse or the letter "O." It was, furthermore, a unique design in the alcoholic beverage industry at the time it was introduced. This suffices to establish its inherent distinctiveness and thus its protectability. Furthermore, the Star "O" design is protectable separately from the other design elements on the Georgi orange-flavored vodka label precisely because the "O" design is itself inherently distinctive. *See In re E.J. Brach & Sons*, 45 C.C.P.A. 998, 256 F.2d 325, 327 (1958); *W.B. Roddenbery*, 135 U.S.P.Q. at 216. However, the extent of stylization was marginal at best. The outline of the "O," though not uniform, is ordinary in its slightly varying width, and the interior and exterior borders are also ordinary. The result is a "thin" or weak mark, which will be entitled to only limited protection. *See Libman Co. v. Vining Indus.*, 69 F.3d 1360, 1363 (7th Cir. 1995).

{The court went on to find no likelihood of confusion.}

d. Analyzing the Acquired Distinctiveness of Nonverbal Marks

The secondary meaning analysis of nonverbal marks is largely the same as that of verbal marks. Courts tend to use essentially the same factors and considerations for both. *See, e.g., Herman Miller, Inc. v. Palazzetti Imports and Exports, Inc.*, 270 F.3d 298 (6th Cir. 2001) (reviewing seven factors to determine that Herman Miller had raised an issue of fact as to the secondary meaning of the design of its Eames chair); *Yankee Candle Co. v. Bridgewater Candle Co.*, 259 F.3d 25, 43–45, (1st Cir. 2001) (finding insufficient evidence of secondary meaning in plaintiff's label designs for scented candles).

Courts may treat one factor differently, however, in the context of product configuration. Evidence that the defendant deliberately copied from the plaintiff may not carry as much weight when the defendant copied product configuration. *See, e.g., Kaufman & Fisher Wish Co. v. F.A.O. Schwarz*, 184 F. Supp. 2d 311, 319 (S.D.N.Y. 2001) (in case involving defendant's alleged trademark infringement of plaintiff's toy doll and packaging, stating that "[t]he probative value of evidence of intentional copying is particularly limited in cases involving product design, since 'the copier may very well be exploiting a particularly desirable feature, rather than seeking to confuse consumers as to the source of the product.' *Duraco Products, Inc. v. Joy Plastic Enterprises, Ltd.*, 40 F.3d 1431, 1453 (3d Cir. 1994)").

The concept of "limping trademarks" is also relevant to determining whether nonverbal marks (and indeed some verbal marks) have developed sufficient acquired distinctiveness to merit protection. This concept comes to American trademark law from English trademark law, and in particular from the opinion of Mr. Justice Jacobs (as he then was, before becoming a Lord Justice) in *Philips Elecs. BV v. Remington Consumer Prods.*, [1998] RPC 283 (U.K.). There, Philips had claimed trademark rights in the mark PHILISHAVE and separate trademark rights in the particular configuration of the three rotating heads on its electric shaver. As to the latter, product configuration mark, Jacobs memorably explained that the three-headed configuration "has never been used by Philips as the sole means of identification of trade source. It has never been trusted by Philips to do this job on its own, a matter plainly relevant in considering acquired distinctiveness. It is at best a 'limping trade mark', needing the crutch of 'Philishave' in use." *Id.* at 290. In other words, standing on its own, the three-headed configuration fails to indicate source; it only does so when appearing with the PHILISHAVE mark. For more on the concept of limping marks, see Rebecca Tushnet, *Registering Disagreement: Registration in Modern American Trademark Law*, 130 HARV. L. REV. 867, 922-25 (2017) (urging American trademark law to recognize the phenomenon of limping marks).

B. Bars to Protection

Even if a trademark is distinctive of source, it will still be denied protection if it falls within one of the statutory bars established under Lanham Act § 2, 15 U.S.C. § 1052. We review the most important of these statutory bars here.

It is important to note that, strictly speaking, the § 2 statutory bars are bars only to the *registration* of a mark at the PTO. Recall however that the Lanham Act will protect both registered marks under § 32, 15 U.S.C. § 1114, and unregistered marks under § 43(a), 15 U.S.C. § 1125(a). This framework raises a question that the law has not yet definitively answered: if a mark is refused registration or its registration is cancelled under one of the statutory bars established in § 2, can the user of the mark nevertheless seek protection of the mark under § 43(a)? For example, if a mark consists of the flag of a foreign nation and thus is barred from registration under Lanham Act § 2(b), could the user of the mark nevertheless claim exclusive rights in the mark under § 43(a)? Though scholarly opinion remains divided, the better view would appear to be that a mark unregistrable under § 2 should be unprotectable under § 43(a). *See Two Pesos, Inc. v. Taco Cabana, Inc.*, 505 U.S. 763, 768 (1992) ("[I]t is common ground that § 43(a) protects qualifying unregistered trademarks and that the general principles qualifying a mark for registration under § 2 of the Lanham Act are for the most part applicable in determining whether an unregistered mark is entitled to protection under § 43(a)."); *Renna v. Cnty. of Union, N.J.*, 88 F.Supp.3d 310, 319 (D.N.J. 2014) ("It follows that such unregistrable marks, not actionable as registered marks under Section 32, are not actionable under Section 43, either."). *Cf. Matal v. Tam*, 582 U.S. __, 137 S.Ct. 1744, 1752 n. 1 (2017) ("We need not decide today whether respondent could bring suit under § 43(a) if his application for federal registration had been lawfully denied under the disparagement clause.").

We will not review the specifics of the registration process until Section II.D. However, in order to complete our picture of what marks qualify for protection, be they registered or unregistered, we will necessarily review opinions in this section that involve questions of registration. Thus, the reader will need to tolerate references to certain aspects of the registration process that will not become clear until Section II.D.

Lanham Act § 2; 15 U.S.C. § 1052

No trademark by which the goods of the applicant may be distinguished from the goods of others shall be refused registration on the principal register on account of its nature unless it–

(a) Consists of or comprises immoral, deceptive, or scandalous matter; or matter which may disparage[1] or falsely suggest a connection with persons, living or dead, institutions, beliefs, or national symbols, or bring them into contempt, or disrepute; or a geographical indication which, when used on or in connection with wines or spirits, identifies a place other than the origin of the goods and is first used on or in connection with wines or spirits by the applicant on or after one year after the date on which the WTO Agreement (as defined in section 3501(9) of Title 19) enters into force with respect to the United States.

(b) Consists of or comprises the flag or coat of arms or other insignia of the United States, or of any State or municipality, or of any foreign nation, or any simulation thereof.

(c) Consists of or comprises a name, portrait, or signature identifying a particular living individual except by his written consent, or the name, signature, or portrait of a deceased President of the United States during the life of his widow, if any, except by the written consent of the widow.

(d) Consists of or comprises a mark which so resembles a mark registered in the Patent and Trademark Office, or a mark or trade name previously used in the United States by another and not abandoned, as to be likely, when used on or in connection with the goods of the applicant, to cause confusion, or to cause mistake, or to deceive: Provided, That if the Director determines that confusion, mistake, or deception is not likely to result from the continued use by more than one person of the same or similar marks under conditions and limitations as to the mode or place of use of the marks or the goods on or in connection with which such marks are used, concurrent registrations may be issued to such persons when they have become entitled to use such marks as a result of their concurrent lawful use in commerce prior to (1) the earliest of the filing dates of the applications pending or of any registration issued under this chapter; (2) July 5, 1947, in the case of registrations previously issued under the Act of March 3, 1881, or February 20, 1905, and continuing in full force and effect on that date; or (3) July 5, 1947, in the case of applications filed under the Act of February 20, 1905, and registered after July 5, 1947. Use prior to the filing date of any pending application or a registration shall not be required when the owner of such application or registration consents to the grant of a concurrent registration to the applicant. Concurrent registrations may also be issued by the Director when a court of competent jurisdiction has finally determined that more than one person is entitled to use the same or similar marks in commerce. In issuing concurrent registrations, the Director shall prescribe conditions and limitations as to the mode or place of use of the mark or the goods on or in connection with which such mark is registered to the respective persons.

(e) Consists of a mark which (1) when used on or in connection with the goods of the applicant is merely descriptive or deceptively misdescriptive of them, (2) when used on or in connection with the goods of the applicant is primarily geographically descriptive of

---

[1] {Note that the prohibition on the registration of marks that "may disparage . . . persons" was held to be invalid under the Free Speech Clause of the First Amendment in *Matal v. Tam*, 582 U.S. __, 137 S.Ct. 1744 (2017) and the prohibition of the registration of marks that are "immoral . . . or scandalous" was held to be invalid under the same constitutional provision in *Iancu v. Brunetti*, No. 18-302, 2019 WL 2570622, __ U.S. __ (June 24, 2019)}.

them, except as indications of regional origin may be registrable under section 1054 of this title, (3) when used on or in connection with the goods of the applicant is primarily geographically deceptively misdescriptive of them, (4) is primarily merely a surname, or (5) comprises any matter that, as a whole, is functional.

(f) Except as expressly excluded in subsections (a), (b), (c), (d), (e)(3), and (e)(5) of this section, nothing in this chapter shall prevent the registration of a mark used by the applicant which has become distinctive of the applicant's goods in commerce. The Director may accept as prima facie evidence that the mark has become distinctive, as used on or in connection with the applicant's goods in commerce, proof of substantially exclusive and continuous use thereof as a mark by the applicant in commerce for the five years before the date on which the claim of distinctiveness is made. Nothing in this section shall prevent the registration of a mark which, when used on or in connection with the goods of the applicant, is primarily geographically deceptively misdescriptive of them, and which became distinctive of the applicant's goods in commerce before December 8, 1993.

A mark which would be likely to cause dilution by blurring or dilution by tarnishment under section 1125(c) of this title, may be refused registration only pursuant to a proceeding brought under section 1063 of this title. A registration for a mark which would be likely to cause dilution by blurring or dilution by tarnishment under section 1125(c) of this title, may be canceled pursuant to a proceeding brought under either section 1064 of this title or section 1092 of this title.

1. Functionality

Even when a product (or packaging) feature is distinctive of source, trademark law will not protect that product feature if it is "functional." *See* Lanham Act § 2(e)(5), 15 U.S.C. § 1052(e)(5) (prohibiting the registration of any mark that "comprises any matter that, as a whole, is functional"). Of course, all source-distinctive product features are functional in the lay sense that they function to indicate the source of the product to which they are attached or of which they form a part. In trademark law, however, functionality is a term of art denoting a legal conclusion about the particular nature or degree of the product feature's technical or competitive importance. The opinions excerpted in this subsection cover both categories of functionality in U.S. trademark law: "utilitarian functionality" (or as some call it, "mechanical functionality") and "aesthetic functionality." The name of the first category may sound like a redundancy, and the name of the second, an oxymoron, yet the underlying policy goals that inform utilitarian and aesthetic functionality doctrine show that the two categories have much in common.

a. Foundational Cases

The following three opinions—*In re Morton-Norwich Products, Inc.*, 671 F.2d 1322 (CCPA 1982); *Inwood Labs., Inc. v. Ives Labs., Inc.*, 456 U.S. 844 (1982); and *TrafFix Devices, Inc. v. Marketing Displays, Inc.*, 532 U.S. 23 (2001)—provide the foundation for current functionality doctrine in the federal courts. *Morton-Norwich* has given us the four "*Morton-Norwich* factors" that the Federal Circuit and consequently the PTO and TTAB use to determine functionality. *Inwood* is the source of the famous (in trademark circles) footnote number 10, which states that "a product feature is functional if it is essential to the use or purpose of the article or if it affects the cost or quality of the article." *Inwood*, 456 U.S. at 851 n. 10. By the time of the Supreme Court's *TrafFix* opinion in 2001, functionality doctrine had increasingly come to rely on competition-oriented (and plaintiff-friendly) tests for functionality. *TrafFix* sought to return functionality doctrine to *Inwood*'s "traditional" definition of functionality. In the next subsection, we will consider whether *TrafFix* has successfully done so. First, however, we must gain a grounding in the foundational cases.

i. In re Morton-Norwich Product, Inc.

In reading *In re Morton-Norwich Products, Inc.*, 671 F.2d 1322 (CCPA 1982), consider the following questions:

- When the *Morton-Norwich* opinion turns to the question of the functionality of the spray bottle design at issue, it appears to adopt several different definitions of "functionality" (e.g., a product feature is nonfunctional if competitor's have "no necessity to copy it"; a product feature is nonfunctional where there is "no evidence that it was dictated" by the functions to be performed by the product; a product feature is functional if the granting of exclusive rights in it "will hinder competition"). Are these different approaches equivalent? Which are more plaintiff-friendly or defendant-friendly?

- Of the various relevant factors that the *Morton-Norwich* court sets out to determine functionality, which do you expect have proven to be the most important?

In re Morton-Norwich Products, Inc.
671 F.2d 1332 (CCPA 1982)

RICH, Judge

[1] This appeal is from the ex parte decision of the United States Patent and Trademark Office (PTO) Trademark Trial and Appeal Board (board), 209 USPQ 437 (TTAB 1980), in application serial No. 123,548, filed April 21, 1977, sustaining the examiner's refusal to register appellant's container configuration on the principal register. We reverse the holding on "functionality" and remand for a determination of distinctiveness.

Background

[2] Appellant's application seeks to register the following container configuration as a trademark for spray starch, soil and stain removers, spray cleaners for household use, liquid household cleaners and general grease removers, and insecticides:

[3] Appellant owns U.S. Design Patent 238,655, issued Feb. 3, 1976, on the above configuration, and U.S. Patent 3,749,290, issued July 31, 1973, directed to the mechanism in the spray top.

[4] The above-named goods constitute a family of products which appellant sells under the word-marks FANTASTIK, GLASS PLUS, SPRAY 'N WASH, GREASE RELIEF, WOOD PLUS, and MIRAKILL. Each of these items is marketed in a container of the same configuration but appellant varies the color of the body of the container according to the product. Appellant manufactures its own containers and stated in its application (amendment of April 25, 1979) that:

> Since such first use (March 31, 1974) the applicant has enjoyed substantially exclusive and continuous use of the trademark (i.e., the container) which has become distinctive of the applicant's goods in commerce.

[5] The PTO Trademark Attorney (examiner), through a series of four office actions, maintained an unshakable position that the design sought to be registered as a trademark is not distinctive, that there is no evidence that it has become distinctive or has acquired a secondary meaning, that it is "merely functional," "essentially utilitarian," and non-arbitrary, wherefore it cannot function as a trademark. In the second action she requested applicant to "amplify the description of the mark with such particularity that any *portion* of the alleged mark considered to be non functional (sic) is incorporated in the description." (Emphasis ours.) She said, "The Examiner sees none." Having already furnished two affidavits to the effect that consumers spontaneously associate the package design with appellant's products, which had been sold in the container to the number of 132,502,000 by 1978, appellant responded to the examiner's request by pointing out, in effect, that it is the overall configuration of the

container rather than any particular feature of it which is distinctive and that it was intentionally designed to be so, supplying several pieces of evidence showing several other containers of different appearance which perform the same functions. Appellant also produced the results of a survey conducted by an independent market research firm which had been made in response to the examiner's demand for evidence of distinctiveness. The examiner dismissed all of the evidence as "not persuasive" and commented that there had "still not been one iota of evidence offered that the subject matter of this application has been promoted as a trademark," which she seemed to consider a necessary element of proof. She adhered to her view that the design "is no more than a non-distinctive purely functional container for the goods plus a purely functional spray trigger controlled closure * * * essentially utilitarian and non-arbitrary * * *."

[6] Appellant responded to the final rejection with a simultaneously filed notice of appeal to the board and a request for reconsideration, submitting more exhibits in support of its position that its container design was not "purely functional." The examiner held fast to all of her views and forwarded the appeal, repeating the substance of her rejections in her Answer to appellant's appeal brief. An oral hearing was held before the board.

Board Opinion

[7] The board, citing three cases, stated it to be "well-settled" that the configuration of a container "may be registrable for the particular contents thereof if the shape is non-functional in character, and is, in fact, inherently distinctive, or has acquired secondary meaning as an indication of origin for such goods." In discussing the "utilitarian nature" of the alleged trademark, the board took note of photographs of appellant's containers for FANTASTIK spray cleaner and GREASE RELIEF degreaser, the labels of which bore the words, respectively, "adjustable easy sprayer," and "NEW! Trigger Control Top," commenting that "the advertising pertaining to applicant's goods promotes the word marks of the various products and the desirable functional features of the containers."

[8] In light of the above, and after detailed review of appellant's survey evidence without any specific comment on it, the board concluded its opinion as follows:

> After a careful review of the evidence in the case before us, we cannot escape the conclusion that the container for applicant's products, *the configuration* of which it seeks to register, *is dictated primarily by functional (utilitarian) considerations*, and is therefore unregistrable despite any de facto secondary meaning which applicant's survey and other evidence of record might indicate. As stated in the case of *In re Deister Concentrator Company, Inc.* (48 CCPA 952, 289 F.2d 496, 129 USPQ 314 (1961), "not every word or configuration that has a de facto secondary meaning is protected as a trademark." (Emphasis ours.)

Issues

[9] The parties do not see the issues in the same light. Appellant and the solicitor agree that the primary issue before us is whether the subject matter sought to be registered—the configuration of the container—is "functional."

[10] Appellant states a second issue to be whether the configuration has the capacity to and does distinguish its goods in the marketplace from the goods of others.

[11] The solicitor contends that it would be "premature" for us to decide the second issue if we disagree with the PTO on the first issue and have to reach it, and that we should, in that event, remand the case so the board can "consider" it. Whether to remand is, therefore, an issue.

OPINION

[12] A trademark is defined as "any word, name, symbol, or device or any combination thereof adopted and used by a manufacturer or merchant to identify his goods and distinguish them from those manufactured or sold by others" (emphasis ours). 15 U.S.C. s 1127 (1976). Thus, it was long the rule that a trademark must be something other than, and separate from, the merchandise to which it is applied. Davis v. Davis, 27 F. 490, 492 (D.Mass.1886) . . . .

[13] Aside from the trademark/product "separateness" rationale for not recognizing the bare design of an article or its container as a trademark, it was theorized that all such designs would soon be appropriated, leaving nothing for use by would-be competitors. One court, for example, feared that "The forms and materials of packages to contain articles of merchandise * * * would be rapidly taken up and appropriated by dealers, until someone, bolder than the others, might go to the very root of things, and claim for his goods the primitive brown paper and tow string, as a peculiar property." Harrington v. Libby, 11 F.Cas. 605, 606 (C.C.S.D.N.Y.1877) (No. 6,107). Accord, Diamond Match Co. v. Saginaw Match Co., 142 F. 727, 729-30 (6th Cir. 1906).

[14] This limitation of permissible trademark subject matter later gave way to assertions that one or more features of a product or package design could legally function as a trademark. E.g., Alan Wood Steel Co. v. Watson, 150 F.Supp. 861, 863 (D.D.C. 1957); Capewell Horse Nail Co. v. Mooney, supra. It was eventually held that the entire design of an article (or its container) could, without other means of identification, function to identify the source of the article and be protected as a trademark. E.g., In re Minnesota Mining and Manufacturing Co., 335 F.2d 836, 837, 142 USPQ 366, 367 (1964).

[15] That protection was limited, however, to those designs of articles and containers, or features thereof, which were "nonfunctional." . . . . This requirement of "nonfunctionality" is not mandated by statute, but "is deduced entirely from court decisions." In re Mogen David Wine Corp., 328 F.2d 925, 932 (1964) (Rich, J., concurring).* It has as its genesis the judicial theory that there exists a fundamental right to compete through imitation of a competitor's product, which right can only be temporarily denied by the patent or copyright laws:

> If one manufacturer should make an advance in effectiveness of operation, or in simplicity of form, or in utility of color; and if that advance did not entitle him to a monopoly by means of a machine or process or a product or a design patent; and if by means of unfair trade suits he could shut out other manufacturers who plainly intended to share in the benefits of unpatented utilities * * * he would be given gratuitously a monopoly more effective than that of the unobtainable patent in the ratio of eternity to seventeen years. (Pope Automatic Merchandising Co. v. McCrum-Howell Co., 191 F. 979, 981-82 (7th Cir. 1911).)

. . . .

[16] An exception to the right to copy exists, however, where the product or package design under consideration is "nonfunctional" and serves to identify its manufacturer or seller, and the exception exists even though the design is not temporarily protectible through acquisition of patent or copyright. Thus, when a design is "nonfunctional," the right to compete through imitation gives way, presumably upon balance of that right with the originator's right to prevent others from infringing upon an established symbol of trade identification.

[17] This preliminary discussion leads to the heart of the matter—how do we define the concept of "functionality," and what role does the above balancing of interests play in that definitional process?

I. Functionality Defined

[18] Many courts speak of the protectability as trademarks of product and package configurations in terms of whether a particular design is "functional" or "nonfunctional." Without proper definition, however, such a distinction is useless for determining whether such design is registrable or protectable as a trademark, for the label "functional" has dual significance. It has been used, on the one hand, in lay fashion to indicate "the normal or characteristic action of anything," and, on the other hand, it has been used to denote a legal conclusion. Compare, In re Penthouse International Ltd., 565 F.2d 679, 681 (CCPA 1977) (If the product configuration "has a non-trademark function, the inquiry is not at an end; possession of a function and of a capability of indicating origin are not in every case mutually exclusive."), with In re Mogen David Wine Corp., 328 F.2d at 933 (Rich, J., concurring) ("The Restatement

---

* {Note that the Lanham Act has since been amended explicitly to exclude functional marks from protection. See Pub. L. No. 105-330 (1998) (amending Section 2(e)(5), 15 U.S.C. § 1152(e)(5)).}

appears to use the terms 'functional' and 'nonfunctional' as labels to denote the legal consequence: if the former, the public may copy; and if the latter, it may not. This is the way the 'law' has been but it is not of much help in deciding cases.").

[19] Accordingly, it has been noted that one of the "distinct questions" involved in "functionality" reasoning is, "In what way is (the) subject matter functional or utilitarian, factually or legally?" In re Honeywell, Inc., 497 F.2d 1344, 1350 (CCPA 1974) (Rich, J., concurring). This definitional division . . . leads to the resolution that if the designation "functional" is to be utilized to denote the *legal* consequence, we must speak in terms of de facto functionality and de jure functionality, the former being the use of "functional" in the lay sense, indicating that although the design of a product, a container, or a feature of either is directed to performance of a function, it may be legally recognized as an indication of source. De jure functionality, of course, would be used to indicate the opposite—such a design may not be protected as a trademark.

[20] This is only the beginning, however, for further definition is required to explain how a determination of whether a design is de jure functional is to be approached. We start with an inquiry into "utility."

A. "Functional" means "utilitarian"[1]

[21] From the earliest cases, "functionality" has been expressed in terms of "utility." In 1930, this court stated it to be "well settled that the configuration of *an article having utility* is not the subject of trade-mark protection." (Emphasis ours.) In re Dennison Mfg. Co., 39 F.2d 720 (1930) (Arbitrary urn or vase-like shape of reinforcing patch on a tag.). Accord, Sparklets Corp. v. Walter Kidde Sales Co., 104 F.2d 396, 399 (1939); In re National Stone-Tile Corp., 57 F.2d 382, 383 (1932). This broad statement of the "law", that the design of an article "having utility" cannot be a trademark, is incorrect and inconsistent with later pronouncements.

[22] We wish to make it clear . . . that a discussion of "functionality" is always in reference to the design of the thing under consideration (in the sense of its appearance) and not the thing itself . . . .

[23] Most designs . . . result in the production of articles, containers, or features thereof which are indeed utilitarian, and examination into the possibility of trademark protection is not to the mere existence of utility, but to the degree of design utility. . . . The configuration of a thermostat cover was . . . refused registration because a round cover was "probably * * * the most utilitarian" design which could have been selected for a round mechanism. In re Honeywell, Inc., 532 F.2d 180, 182 (CCPA 1976).

[24] Thus, it is the "utilitarian" design of a "utilitarian" object with which we are concerned, and the manner of use of the term "utilitarian" must be examined at each occurrence. The latter occurrence is, of course, consistent with the lay meaning of the term. But the former is being used to denote a legal consequence (it being synonymous with "functional"), and it therefore requires further explication.

B. "Utilitarian" means "superior in function (de facto) or economy of manufacture," which "superiority" is determined in light of competitive necessity to copy

[25] Some courts have stated this proposition in the negative. In American-Marietta Co. v. Krigsman, 275 F.2d 287, 289 (2d Cir. 1960), the court stated that "those features of the original goods

---

[1] It is well known that the law of "functionality" has been applied in both a "utilitarian" sense and in terms of "aesthetics." See e.g., Vuitton et Fils S.A. v. J. Young Enterprises, Inc., 644 F.2d 769 (9th Cir. 1981); International Order of Job's Daughters v. Lindeburg and Co., 633 F.2d 912 (9th Cir. 1980); Famolare, Inc. v. Melville Corp., 472 F.Supp. 738 (D.Hawaii 1979). Recognition of this provides an explanation for the statement that, "the term 'functional' is not to be treated as synonymous with the literal significance of the term 'utilitarian'." J.C. Penney Co. v. H.D. Lee Mercantile Co., 120 F.2d 949, 954 (8th Cir. 1941). It will be so treated, however, where the issue is one of "utilitarian functionality" and not "aesthetic functionality." The PTO does not argue in this case that appellant's container configuration is aesthetically functional, notwithstanding appellant's argument that its design was adopted, in part, for aesthetic reasons.

that are not in any way essential to their use" may be termed "nonfunctional." But what does this statement mean? In the case at bar, for example, we cannot say that it means that the subject design is "functional" merely because a hollow body, a handhold, and a pump sprayer are "essential to its use." What this phrase must mean is not that the generic parts of the article or package are essential, but, as noted above, that the particular design of the whole assembly of those parts must be essential. This, of course, leaves us to define "essential to its use," which is also the starting place for those courts which have set forth in positive fashion the reasons they believe that some product or package designs are not protectible as trademarks and thus not registrable.

. . . .

[26] Thus, it is clear that courts in the past have considered the public policy involved in this area of the law as, not the right to slavishly copy articles which are not protected by patent or copyright, but the need to copy those articles, which is more properly termed the right to compete effectively. Even the earliest cases, which discussed protectability in terms of exhaustion of possible packaging forms, recognized that the real issue was whether "the effect would be to gradually throttle trade." Harrington v. Libby, supra at 606.

[27] More recent cases also discuss "functionality" in light of competition. One court noted that the "question in each case is whether protection against imitation will hinder the competitor in competition." Truck Equipment Service Co. v. Fruehauf Corp., 536 F.2d 1210, 1218 (8th Cir. 1976). Another court, upon suit for trademark infringement (the alleged trademark being plaintiff's building design), stated that "enjoining others from using the building design (would not) inhibit competition in any way." Fotomat Corp. v. Cochran, 437 F.Supp. 1231, 1235 (D.Kan. 1977). This court has also referenced "hinderance of competition" in a number of the "functionality" cases which have been argued before it. E.g., In re Penthouse International Ltd., 565 F.2d supra at 682 (Would protection of the design "hinder competition"?); In re Mogen David Wine Corp., 328 F.2d at 933 (Rich, J., concurring, cited with approval in Penthouse International, supra, stated that, "Whether competition would in fact be hindered is really the crux of the matter.").

[28] The Restatement of Torts, s 742, designates a design of goods as "functional" if it "affects their purpose, action or performance, or the facility or economy of processing, handling or using them * * *." (Emphasis ours.) To ensure that use of the word "affects" was clear, Comment a to that section indicates that a "feature" may be found "functional" if it "contributes to" the utility, durability, effectiveness or ease of use, or the efficiency or economy of manufacture of that "feature." Excusing the fact that the design of the "feature" is not referenced, and equating "feature" with "design," this seems to take us back to where we started—with those cases that deny trademark protection to those articles "having utility." Further, it appears to us that "affects" and "contributes to" are both so broad as to be meaningless, for every design "affects" or "contributes to" the utility of the article in which it is embodied. "Affects" is broad enough to include a design which reduces the utility or the economy of manufacture.

. . . .

[29] Although the Restatement appears to ignore the policies which created the law of "functionality," it is noted at the end of the first paragraph of Comment a to s 742, in accord with the cases previously discussed, that we should examine whether prohibition of imitation by others will "deprive them of something which will substantially hinder them in competition."

II. Determining "Functionality"

A. In general

[30] Keeping in mind, as shown by the foregoing review, that "functionality" is determined in light of "utility," which is determined in light of "superiority of design," and rests upon the foundation "essential to effective competition," Ives Laboratories, Inc. v. Darby Drug Co., 601 F.2d 631, 643 (2d Cir. 1979), and cases cited supra, there exist a number of factors, both positive and negative, which aid in that determination.

[31] Previous opinions of this court have discussed what evidence is useful to demonstrate that a particular design is "superior." In In re Shenango Ceramics, Inc., 53 CCPA 1268, 1273, 362 F.2d 287, 291

(1966), the court noted that the existence of an expired utility patent which disclosed the utilitarian advantage of the design sought to be registered as a trademark was evidence that it was "functional." Accord, Best Lock Corp. v. Schlage Lock Co., 413 F.2d at 1199; Mine Safety Appliances Co. v. Storage Battery Co., 405 F.2d 901, 902 (1969); In re Deister Concentrator Co., 289 F.2d at 501; Daniel v. Electric Hose & Rubber Co., 231 F. 827, 833 (3d Cir. 1916). It may also be significant that the originator of the design touts its utilitarian advantages through advertising. Shenango, supra; Deister, supra; Mine Safety Appliances, supra; In re Pollak Steel Co., 314 F.2d 566, 567 (1963).

[32] Since the effect upon competition "is really the crux of the matter," it is, of course, significant that there are other alternatives available. Nims, Unfair Competition and Trade-Marks at 377; compare, Time Mechanisms, Inc. v. Qonaar Corp., 422 F.Supp. 905, 913 (D.N.J. 1976) ("the parking meter mechanism can be contained by housings of many different configurations") and In re World's Finest Chocolate, Inc., 474 F.2d 1012, 1014 (CCPA 1973) ("We think competitors can readily meet the demand for packaged candy bars by use of other packaging styles, and we find no utilitarian advantages flowing from this package design as opposed to others as was found in the rhomboidally-shaped deck involved in *Deister*.") and In re Mogen David Wine Corp., 328 F.2d at 933 (Rich, J., concurring. "Others can meet any real or imagined demand for wine in decanter-type bottles—assuming there is any such thing— without being in the least hampered in competition by inability to copy the Mogen David bottle design.") and In re Minnesota Mining and Mfg. Co., 335 F.2d at 840 (It was noted to be an undisputed fact of record that the article whose design was sought to be registered "could be formed into almost any shape.") and Fotomat Corp. v. Cochran, 437 F.Supp. supra at 1235 (The court noted that the design of plaintiff's building functioned "no better than a myriad of other building designs.") with In re Honeywell, Inc., 532 F.2d at 182 (A portion of the board opinion which the court adopted noted that there "are only so many basic shapes in which a thermostat or its cover can be made," but then concluded that, "The fact that thermostat covers may be produced in other forms or shapes does not and cannot detract from the functional character of the configuration here involved.").

[33] It is also significant that a particular design results from a comparatively simple or cheap method of manufacturing the article. In Schwinn Bicycle Co. v. Murray Ohio Mfg. Co., 339 F.Supp. 973, 980 (M.D.Tenn. 1971), aff'd, 470 F.2d 975 (6th Cir. 1972), the court stated its reason for refusing to recognize the plaintiff's bicycle rim surface design as a trademark:

> The evidence is uncontradicted that the various manufacturers of bicycle rims in the United States consider it commercially necessary to mask, hide or camouflage the roughened and charred appearance resulting from welding the tubular rim sections together. The evidence represented indicates that the only other process used by bicycle rim manufacturers in the United States is the more complex and more expensive process of grinding and polishing.

Accord, In re Pollak Steel Co., 314 F.2d at 570; Luminous Unit Co. v. R. Williamson & Co., supra at 269.

B. The case at bar

1. The evidence of functionality

[34] We come now to the task of applying to the facts of this case the distilled essence of the body of law on "functionality" above discussed. The question is whether appellant's plastic spray bottle is de jure functional; is it the best or one of a few superior designs available? We hold, on the basis of the evidence before the board, that it is not.

[35] The board thought otherwise but did not state a single supporting reason. In spite of her strong convictions about it, neither did the examiner. Each expressed mere opinions and it is not clear to us what either had in mind in using the terms "functional" and "utilitarian." Of course, the spray bottle is highly useful and performs its intended functions in an admirable way, but that is not enough to render the design of the spray bottle—which is all that matters here—functional.

[36] As the examiner appreciated, the spray bottle consists of two major parts, a bottle and a trigger-operated, spray-producing pump mechanism which also serves as a closure. We shall call the latter the spray top. In the first place, a molded plastic bottle can have an infinite variety of forms or

designs and still function to hold liquid. No one form is necessary or appears to be "superior." Many bottles have necks, to be grasped for pouring or holding, and the necks likewise can be in a variety of forms. The PTO has not produced one iota of evidence to show that the shape of appellant's bottle was required to be as it is for any de facto functional reason, which might lead to an affirmative determination of de jure functionality. The evidence, consisting of competitor's molded plastic bottles for similar products, demonstrates that the same functions can be performed by a variety of other shapes with no sacrifice of any functional advantage. There is no necessity to copy appellant's trade dress to enjoy any of the functions of a spray-top container.

[37] As to the appearance of the spray top, the evidence of record shows that it too can take a number of diverse forms, all of which are equally suitable as housings for the pump and spray mechanisms. Appellant acquired a patent on the pump mechanism (No. 3,749,290) the drawings of which show it embodied in a structure which bears not the slightest resemblance to the appearance of appellant's spray top. The pictures of the competition's spray bottles further illustrate that no particular housing design is necessary to have a pump-type sprayer. Appellant's spray top, seen from the side, is rhomboidal, roughly speaking, a design which bears no relation to the shape of the pump mechanism housed within it and is an arbitrary decoration—no more de jure functional than is the grille of an automobile with respect to its under-the-hood power plant. The evidence shows that even the shapes of pump triggers can and do vary while performing the same function.

[38] What is sought to be registered, however, is no single design feature or component but the overall composite design comprising both bottle and spray top. While that design must be accommodated to the functions performed, we see no evidence that it was dictated by them and resulted in a functionally or economically superior design of such a container.

[39] Applying the legal principles discussed above, we do not see that allowing appellant to exclude others (upon proof of distinctiveness) from using this trade dress will hinder competition or impinge upon the rights of others to compete effectively in the sale of the goods named in the application, even to the extent of marketing them in functionally identical spray containers. The fact is that many others are doing so. Competitors have apparently had no need to simulate appellant's trade dress, in whole or in part, in order to enjoy all of the functional aspects of a spray top container. Upon expiration of any patent protection appellant may now be enjoying on its spray and pump mechanism, competitors may even copy and enjoy all of its functions without copying the external appearance of appellant's spray top.[3]

[40] If the functions of appellant's bottle can be performed equally well by containers of innumerable designs and, thus, no one is injured in competition, why did the board state that appellant's design is functional and for that reason not registrable?

{The Court went on to remand the application for a determination of distinctiveness.}

Comments and Questions

1. The TMEP has summarized the *Morton-Norwich* factors as follows:

    A determination of functionality normally involves consideration of one or more of the following factors, commonly known as the "*Morton-Norwich* factors":

    (1) the existence of a utility patent that discloses the utilitarian advantages of the design sought to be registered;

    (2) advertising by the applicant that touts the utilitarian advantages of the design;

    (3) facts pertaining to the availability of alternative designs; and

---

[3] It is interesting to note that appellant also owns design patent 238,655 for the design in issue, which, at least presumptively, indicates that the design is not de jure functional. See In re Schilling, 421 F.2d 747, 750, 164 USPQ 576, 578 (CCPA 1970); In re Garbo, 48 CCPA 845, 848, 287 F.2d 192, 193-94, 129 USPQ 72, 73 (1961).

(4) facts pertaining to whether the design results from a comparatively simple or inexpensive method of manufacture.

TMEP § 1202.02(a)(v).

ii.   Inwood Labs., Inc. v. Ives Labs., Inc.

Inwood Labs., Inc. v. Ives Labs., Inc., 456 U.S. 844 (1982), is important for our purposes here mainly because of its brief, one-sentence footnote 10, which has had an enormous impact on functionality doctrine. Nevertheless, it is worth understanding the basic facts underlying the *Inwood* opinion—facts to which we will return when we consider secondary liability in trademark law below. Ives Laboratories, Inc. ("Ives") manufactured and marketed the patented prescription drug cyclandelate, a vasodilator, under the registered trademark CYCLOSPASMOL. After Ives' patent expired in 1972, several generic drug manufacturers, including Inwood Laboratories, Inc., began manufacturing and marketing cyclandelate capsules that copied the appearance, including the color, of Ives' capsules. Pharmacists then began placing capsules produced by the generic manufacturers into bottles labeled with Ives' CYCLOSPASMOL mark. Ives brought an action for trademark infringement against the manufacturers, alleging that the manufacturers were vicariously liable for the infringement of Ives' CYCLOSPASMOL mark by the pharmacists. The Supreme Court ultimately found that the generic manufacturers were not liable.

In the course of her opinion for the Court, Justice O'Connor noted: "Ives argued that the colors of its capsules were not functional." She appended to this statement footnote number 10:

> In general terms, a product feature is functional if it is essential to the use or purpose of the article or if it affects the cost or quality of the article. *See Sears, Roebuck & Co. v. Stiffel Co.*, 376 U.S. 225, 232 (1964); *Kellogg Co. v. National Biscuit Co.*, 305 U.S. 111, 122 (1938).

It is not clear to what exactly Justice O'Connor was citing in *Stiffel*, but the *Kellogg* court had stated that the pillow shape of Nabisco's shredded wheat was functional: "The evidence is persuasive that this form is functional—that the cost of the biscuit would be increased and its high quality lessened if some other form were substituted for the pillow-shape" *Id.* at 122.

Now nearly forgotten is that *Inwood* contained further discussion of the concept of functionality in trademark law. In a subsequent footnote, Justice O'Connor criticized the *Inwood* appellate court for failing to respond to the district court's determination that the color of Ives' capsules was functional. *Inwood*, 456 U.S. at 857 n. 20. In his concurrence joined by Justice Marshall, Justice White also took the appellate court to task for failing to respond to the district court's functionality determination. In doing so, he quoted the appellate court's definition of functionality apparently with approval: "A functional characteristic is 'an important ingredient in the commercial success of the product.'" *Id.* at 863 (White, J., concurring) (quoting *Ives Laboratories, Inc. v. Darby Drug Co., Inc.*, 601 F.2d 631 (2nd Cir. 1979)). As we will see below, this language, going to whether a product feature is "an important ingredient in the commercial success of the product," would come back to haunt functionality doctrine and aesthetic functionality doctrine in particular.

3.   TrafFix Devices, Inc. v. Marketing Displays, Inc.

Between *Inwood* (1982) and *TrafFix* (2001), functionality doctrine appeared to many to have lost its moorings. Perhaps influenced by *Morton-Norwich*, courts increasingly relied on various forms of a "competitive necessity" test to determine if a particular product feature was functional, and because alternative designs could often be found or hypothesized, the "competitive necessity" test tended to benefit plaintiffs (i.e., those asserting trademark property rights).

TrafFix attempted to return functionality doctrine to *Inwood*'s definition of functionality. But in order to do so, *TrafFix* had to explain the meaning of a statement the Court had made six years earlier in *Qualitex* (1995). This is the relevant passage from *Qualitex*:

> This Court consequently has explained that, "[i]n general terms, a product feature is functional," and cannot serve as a trademark, "if it is essential to the use or purpose of the article or if it affects the cost or quality of the article," that is, if exclusive use of the feature

would put competitors at a significant non-reputation-related disadvantage. *Inwood Laboratories, Inc.,* 456 U. S., at 850, n. 10.

Qualitex Co. v. Jacobson Products Co., Inc., 514 U.S. 159, 165 (1995). Before reading *TrafFix*, consider this question: does this passage from *Qualitex* suggest that *Inwood*'s test ("essential to the use or purpose . . . ") is interchangeable with and the equivalent of the test asking if "exclusive use of the feature would put competitors at a significant non-reputation-related disadvantage"? Would appellate courts have been justified in assuming the equivalence between these two statements of the test for functionality?

In reading *TrafFix*, consider these additional questions:

- How do we determine if a product feature is "essential to the use or purpose" of the product? What do we mean by "essential"? That the product feature is a competitive necessity? An engineering necessity? How could a product feature be "essential to the use or purpose" of the product if there are alternative designs that competitors could use and still compete effectively?

- Why not just establish a per se rule that the subject of an expired utility patent is per se functional under trademark law and cannot under any circumstances qualify for trademark protection?

- Are there any product features that do not in some way "affect[] the cost or quality of the product"?

- Why not apply the *Inwood Laboratories* test to aesthetic product features as well?

- Does *TrafFix* in any sense overrule *Morton-Norwich*?

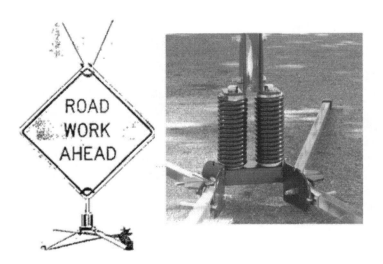

TrafFix Devices, Inc. v. Marketing Displays, Inc.
532 U.S. 23 (2001)

Justice KENNEDY delivered the opinion of the Court.

[1] Temporary road signs with warnings like "Road Work Ahead" or "Left Shoulder Closed" must withstand strong gusts of wind. An inventor named Robert Sarkisian obtained two utility patents for a mechanism built upon two springs (the dual-spring design) to keep these and other outdoor signs upright despite adverse wind conditions. The holder of the now-expired Sarkisian patents, respondent Marketing Displays, Inc. (MDI), established a successful business in the manufacture and sale of sign stands incorporating the patented feature. MDI's stands for road signs were recognizable to buyers and users (it says) because the dual-spring design was visible near the base of the sign.

[2] This litigation followed after the patents expired and a competitor, TrafFix Devices, Inc., sold sign stands with a visible spring mechanism that looked like MDI's. MDI and TrafFix products looked

alike because they were. When TrafFix started in business, it sent an MDI product abroad to have it reverse engineered, that is to say copied. Complicating matters, TrafFix marketed its sign stands under a name similar to MDI's. MDI used the name "WindMaster," while TrafFix, its new competitor, used "WindBuster."

[3] MDI brought suit under the Trademark Act of 1946 (Lanham Act), 60 Stat. 427, as amended, 15 U.S.C. § 1051 *et seq.*, against TrafFix for trademark infringement (based on the similar names), trade dress infringement (based on the copied dual-spring design), and unfair competition. TrafFix counterclaimed on antitrust theories. After the United States District Court for the Eastern District of Michigan considered cross-motions for summary judgment, MDI prevailed on its trademark claim for the confusing similarity of names and was held not liable on the antitrust counterclaim; and those two rulings, affirmed by the Court of Appeals, are not before us.

I

[4] We are concerned with the trade dress question. The District Court ruled against MDI on its trade dress claim. 971 F.Supp. 262 (E.D.Mich. 1997). After determining that the one element of MDI's trade dress at issue was the dual-spring design, *id.,* at 265, it held that "no reasonable trier of fact could determine that MDI has established secondary meaning" in its alleged trade dress, *id.,* at 269. In other words, consumers did not associate the look of the dual-spring design with MDI. As a second, independent reason to grant summary judgment in favor of TrafFix, the District Court determined the dual-spring design was functional. On this rationale secondary meaning is irrelevant because there can be no trade dress protection in any event. In ruling on the functional aspect of the design, the District Court noted that Sixth Circuit precedent indicated that the burden was on MDI to prove that its trade dress was nonfunctional, and not on TrafFix to show that it was functional (a rule since adopted by Congress, see 15 U.S.C. § 1125(a)(3) (1994 ed., Supp. V)), and then went on to consider MDI's arguments that the dual-spring design was subject to trade dress protection. Finding none of MDI's contentions persuasive, the District Court concluded MDI had not "proffered sufficient evidence which would enable a reasonable trier of fact to find that MDI's vertical dual-spring design is *non*-functional." 971 F.Supp., at 276. Summary judgment was entered against MDI on its trade dress claims.

[5] The Court of Appeals for the Sixth Circuit reversed the trade dress ruling. 200 F.3d 929 (1999). The Court of Appeals held the District Court had erred in ruling MDI failed to show a genuine issue of material fact regarding whether it had secondary meaning in its alleged trade dress, *id.,* at 938, and had erred further in determining that MDI could not prevail in any event because the alleged trade dress was in fact a functional product configuration, *id.,* at 940. The Court of Appeals suggested the District Court committed legal error by looking only to the dual-spring design when evaluating MDI's trade dress. Basic to its reasoning was the Court of Appeals' observation that it took "little imagination to conceive of a hidden dual-spring mechanism or a tri or quad-spring mechanism that might avoid infringing [MDI's] trade dress." *Ibid.* The Court of Appeals explained that "[i]f TrafFix or another competitor chooses to use [MDI's] dual-spring design, then it will have to find *some other way* to set its sign apart to avoid infringing [MDI's] trade dress." *Ibid.* It was not sufficient, according to the Court of Appeals, that allowing exclusive use of a particular feature such as the dual-spring design in the guise of trade dress would "hinde[r] competition somewhat." Rather, "[e]xclusive use of a feature must 'put competitors at a *significant* non-reputation-related disadvantage' before trade dress protection is denied on functionality grounds." *Ibid.* (quoting *Qualitex Co. v. Jacobson Products Co.,* 514 U.S. 159, 165, 115 S.Ct. 1300, 131 L.Ed.2d 248 (1995)). In its criticism of the District Court's ruling on the trade dress question, the Court of Appeals took note of a split among Courts of Appeals in various other Circuits on the issue whether the existence of an expired utility patent forecloses the possibility of the patentee's claiming trade dress protection in the product's design. 200 F.3d, at 939. Compare *Sunbeam Products, Inc. v. West Bend Co.,* 123 F.3d 246 (C.A.5 1997) (holding that trade dress protection is not foreclosed), *Thomas & Betts Corp. v. Panduit Corp.,* 138 F.3d 277 (C.A.7 1998) (same), and *Midwest Industries, Inc. v. Karavan Trailers, Inc.,* 175 F.3d 1356 (C.A.Fed. 1999) (same), with *Vornado Air Circulation Systems, Inc. v. Duracraft Corp.,* 58 F.3d 1498, 1500 (C.A.10 1995) ("Where a product configuration is a significant inventive component of an invention

covered by a utility patent . . . it cannot receive trade dress protection"). To resolve the conflict, we granted certiorari. 530 U.S. 1260 (2000).

II

[6] It is well established that trade dress can be protected under federal law. The design or packaging of a product may acquire a distinctiveness which serves to identify the product with its manufacturer or source; and a design or package which acquires this secondary meaning, assuming other requisites are met, is a trade dress which may not be used in a manner likely to cause confusion as to the origin, sponsorship, or approval of the goods. In these respects protection for trade dress exists to promote competition. As we explained just last Term, see *Wal-Mart Stores, Inc. v. Samara Brothers, Inc.,* 529 U.S. 205, 120 S.Ct. 1339, 146 L.Ed.2d 182 (2000), various Courts of Appeals have allowed claims of trade dress infringement relying on the general provision of the Lanham Act which provides a cause of action to one who is injured when a person uses "any word, term name, symbol, or device, or any combination thereof . . . which is likely to cause confusion . . . as to the origin, sponsorship, or approval of his or her goods." 15 U.S.C. § 1125(a)(1)(A). Congress confirmed this statutory protection for trade dress by amending the Lanham Act to recognize the concept. Title 15 U.S.C. § 1125(a)(3) (1994 ed., Supp. V) provides: "In a civil action for trade dress infringement under this chapter for trade dress not registered on the principal register, the person who asserts trade dress protection has the burden of proving that the matter sought to be protected is not functional." This burden of proof gives force to the well-established rule that trade dress protection may not be claimed for product features that are functional. *Qualitex, supra,* at 164-165; *Two Pesos, Inc. v. Taco Cabana, Inc.,* 505 U.S. 763, 775 (1992). And in *Wal-Mart, supra,* we were careful to caution against misuse or overextension of trade dress. We noted that "product design almost invariably serves purposes other than source identification." *Id.,* at 213.

[7] Trade dress protection must subsist with the recognition that in many instances there is no prohibition against copying goods and products. In general, unless an intellectual property right such as a patent or copyright protects an item, it will be subject to copying. As the Court has explained, copying is not always discouraged or disfavored by the laws which preserve our competitive economy. *Bonito Boats, Inc. v. Thunder Craft Boats, Inc.,* 489 U.S. 141, 160 (1989). Allowing competitors to copy will have salutary effects in many instances. "Reverse engineering of chemical and mechanical articles in the public domain often leads to significant advances in technology." *Ibid.*

[8] The principal question in this case is the effect of an expired patent on a claim of trade dress infringement. A prior patent, we conclude, has vital significance in resolving the trade dress claim. A utility patent is strong evidence that the features therein claimed are functional. If trade dress protection is sought for those features the strong evidence of functionality based on the previous patent adds great weight to the statutory presumption that features are deemed functional until proved otherwise by the party seeking trade dress protection. Where the expired patent claimed the features in question, one who seeks to establish trade dress protection must carry the heavy burden of showing that the feature is not functional, for instance by showing that it is merely an ornamental, incidental, or arbitrary aspect of the device.

[9] In the case before us, the central advance claimed in the expired utility patents (the Sarkisian patents) is the dual-spring design; and the dual-spring design is the essential feature of the trade dress MDI now seeks to establish and to protect. The rule we have explained bars the trade dress claim, for MDI did not, and cannot, carry the burden of overcoming the strong evidentiary inference of functionality based on the disclosure of the dual-spring design in the claims of the expired patents.

[10] The dual springs shown in the Sarkisian patents were well apart (at either end of a frame for holding a rectangular sign when one full side is the base) while the dual springs at issue here are close together (in a frame designed to hold a sign by one of its corners). As the District Court recognized, this makes little difference. The point is that the springs are necessary to the operation of the device. The fact that the springs in this very different-looking device fall within the claims of the patents is illustrated by MDI's own position in earlier litigation. In the late 1970's, MDI engaged in a long-running intellectual property battle with a company known as Winn-Proof. Although the precise claims of the Sarkisian

patents cover sign stands with springs "spaced apart," U.S. Patent No. 3,646,696, col. 4; U.S. Patent No. 3,662,482, col. 4, the Winn-Proof sign stands (with springs much like the sign stands at issue here) were found to infringe the patents by the United States District Court for the District of Oregon, and the Court of Appeals for the Ninth Circuit affirmed the judgment. *Sarkisian v. Winn-Proof Corp.,* 697 F.2d 1313 (1983). Although the Winn-Proof traffic sign stand (with dual springs close together) did not appear, then, to infringe the literal terms of the patent claims (which called for "spaced apart" springs), the Winn-Proof sign stand was found to infringe the patents under the doctrine of equivalents, which allows a finding of patent infringement even when the accused product does not fall within the literal terms of the claims. *Id.,* at 1321-1322; see generally *Warner-Jenkinson Co. v. Hilton Davis Chemical Co.,* 520 U.S. 17 (1997). In light of this past ruling—a ruling procured at MDI's own insistence—it must be concluded the products here at issue would have been covered by the claims of the expired patents.

[11] The rationale for the rule that the disclosure of a feature in the claims of a utility patent constitutes strong evidence of functionality is well illustrated in this case. The dual-spring design serves the important purpose of keeping the sign upright even in heavy wind conditions; and, as confirmed by the statements in the expired patents, it does so in a unique and useful manner. As the specification of one of the patents recites, prior art "devices, in practice, will topple under the force of a strong wind." U.S. Patent No. 3,662,482, col. 1. The dual-spring design allows sign stands to resist toppling in strong winds. Using a dual-spring design rather than a single spring achieves important operational advantages. For example, the specifications of the patents note that the "use of a pair of springs . . . as opposed to the use of a single spring to support the frame structure prevents canting or twisting of the sign around a vertical axis," and that, if not prevented, twisting "may cause damage to the spring structure and may result in tipping of the device." U.S. Patent No. 3,646,696, col. 3. In the course of patent prosecution, it was said that "[t]he use of a pair of spring connections as opposed to a single spring connection . . . forms an important part of this combination" because it "forc[es] the sign frame to tip along the longitudinal axis of the elongated ground-engaging members." App. 218. The dual-spring design affects the cost of the device as well; it was acknowledged that the device "could use three springs but this would unnecessarily increase the cost of the device." *Id.,* at 217. These statements made in the patent applications and in the course of procuring the patents demonstrate the functionality of the design. MDI does not assert that any of these representations are mistaken or inaccurate, and this is further strong evidence of the functionality of the dual-spring design.

III

[12] In finding for MDI on the trade dress issue the Court of Appeals gave insufficient recognition to the importance of the expired utility patents, and their evidentiary significance, in establishing the functionality of the device. The error likely was caused by its misinterpretation of trade dress principles in other respects. As we have noted, even if there has been no previous utility patent the party asserting trade dress has the burden to establish the nonfunctionality of alleged trade dress features. MDI could not meet this burden. Discussing trademarks, we have said "'[i]n general terms, a product feature is functional,' and cannot serve as a trademark, 'if it is essential to the use or purpose of the article or if it affects the cost or quality of the article.'" *Qualitex,* 514 U.S., at 165 (quoting *Inwood Laboratories, Inc. v. Ives Laboratories, Inc.,* 456 U.S. 844, 850, n. 10 (1982)). Expanding upon the meaning of this phrase, we have observed that a functional feature is one the "exclusive use of [which] would put competitors at a significant non-reputation-related disadvantage." 514 U.S., at 165. The Court of Appeals in the instant case seemed to interpret this language to mean that a necessary test for functionality is "whether the particular product configuration is a competitive necessity." 200 F.3d, at 940. See also *Vornado,* 58 F.3d, at 1507 ("Functionality, by contrast, has been defined both by our circuit, and more recently by the Supreme Court, in terms of competitive need"). This was incorrect as a comprehensive definition. As explained in *Qualitex, supra,* and *Inwood, supra,* a feature is also functional when it is essential to the use or purpose of the device or when it affects the cost or quality of the device. The *Qualitex* decision did not purport to displace this traditional rule. Instead, it quoted the rule as *Inwood* had set it forth. It is proper to inquire into a "significant non-reputation-related disadvantage" in cases of esthetic functionality, the question involved in *Qualitex.* Where the design is functional under the *Inwood* formulation there is no

need to proceed further to consider if there is a competitive necessity for the feature. In *Qualitex,* by contrast, esthetic functionality was the central question, there having been no indication that the green-gold color of the laundry press pad had any bearing on the use or purpose of the product or its cost or quality.

[13] The Court has allowed trade dress protection to certain product features that are inherently distinctive. *Two Pesos,* 505 U.S., at 774. In *Two Pesos,* however, the Court at the outset made the explicit analytic assumption that the trade dress features in question (decorations and other features to evoke a Mexican theme in a restaurant) were not functional. *Id.,* at 767, n. 6. The trade dress in those cases did not bar competitors from copying functional product design features. In the instant case, beyond serving the purpose of informing consumers that the sign stands are made by MDI (assuming it does so), the dual-spring design provides a unique and useful mechanism to resist the force of the wind. Functionality having been established, whether MDI's dual-spring design has acquired secondary meaning need not be considered.

[14] There is no need, furthermore, to engage, as did the Court of Appeals, in speculation about other design possibilities, such as using three or four springs which might serve the same purpose. 200 F.3d, at 940. Here, the functionality of the spring design means that competitors need not explore whether other spring juxtapositions might be used. The dual-spring design is not an arbitrary flourish in the configuration of MDI's product; it is the reason the device works. Other designs need not be attempted.

[15] Because the dual-spring design is functional, it is unnecessary for competitors to explore designs to hide the springs, say, by using a box or framework to cover them, as suggested by the Court of Appeals. *Ibid.* The dual-spring design assures the user the device will work. If buyers are assured the product serves its purpose by seeing the operative mechanism that in itself serves an important market need. It would be at cross-purposes to those objectives, and something of a paradox, were we to require the manufacturer to conceal the very item the user seeks.

[16] In a case where a manufacturer seeks to protect arbitrary, incidental, or ornamental aspects of features of a product found in the patent claims, such as arbitrary curves in the legs or an ornamental pattern painted on the springs, a different result might obtain. There the manufacturer could perhaps prove that those aspects do not serve a purpose within the terms of the utility patent. The inquiry into whether such features, asserted to be trade dress, are functional by reason of their inclusion in the claims of an expired utility patent could be aided by going beyond the claims and examining the patent and its prosecution history to see if the feature in question is shown as a useful part of the invention. No such claim is made here, however. MDI in essence seeks protection for the dual-spring design alone. The asserted trade dress consists simply of the dual-spring design, four legs, a base, an upright, and a sign. MDI has pointed to nothing arbitrary about the components of its device or the way they are assembled. The Lanham Act does not exist to reward manufacturers for their innovation in creating a particular device; that is the purpose of the patent law and its period of exclusivity. The Lanham Act, furthermore, does not protect trade dress in a functional design simply because an investment has been made to encourage the public to associate a particular functional feature with a single manufacturer or seller. The Court of Appeals erred in viewing MDI as possessing the right to exclude competitors from using a design identical to MDI's and to require those competitors to adopt a different design simply to avoid copying it. MDI cannot gain the exclusive right to produce sign stands using the dual-spring design by asserting that consumers associate it with the look of the invention itself. Whether a utility patent has expired or there has been no utility patent at all, a product design which has a particular appearance may be functional because it is "essential to the use or purpose of the article" or "affects the cost or quality of the article." *Inwood,* 456 U.S., at 850, n. 10, 102 S.Ct. 2182.

[17] TrafFix and some of its *amici* argue that the Patent Clause of the Constitution, Art. I, § 8, cl. 8, of its own force, prohibits the holder of an expired utility patent from claiming trade dress protection. Brief for Petitioner 33-36; Brief for Panduit Corp. as *Amicus Curiae* 3; Brief for Malla Pollack as *Amicus Curiae* 2. We need not resolve this question. If, despite the rule that functional features may not be the subject of trade dress protection, a case arises in which trade dress becomes the practical equivalent of

an expired utility patent, that will be time enough to consider the matter. The judgment of the Court of Appeals is reversed, and the case is remanded for further proceedings consistent with this opinion.

It is so ordered.

Comments and Questions

1.   *A missing "significantly"?* The *TrafFix* Court held that "a feature is also functional when it is essential to the use or purpose of the device or when it affects the cost or quality of the device." Is there any product feature that would not affect in some way the cost of the product? Would it be reasonable to read the *TrafFix* holding as implicitly requiring that, to be functional, the product feature must *significantly* affect the cost of the product—i.e., affect the cost in such a way that granting exclusive rights in the product feature would put competitors at a "significant non-reputation related disadvantage"? If this is the proper reading of the *TrafFix* holding, then how is it different from the "competitive necessity" test?

2.   *Functionality and food flavors.* Under *TrafFix*, are flavors of food protectable as trademarks? In a case in which a restaurant franchisor sued a knock-off restaurant, the court found that food flavors are functional. *See* New York Pizzeria, Inc. v. Syal, 56 F. Supp. 3d 875, 882 (S.D. Tex. 2014) ("The flavor of food undoubtedly affects its quality, and is therefore a functional element of the product.").

b.   Utilitarian Functionality Case Law after *TrafFix*

After the Supreme Court issued its opinion in *TrafFix*, the lower courts applied the teachings of the opinion in a variety of ways. Presented here are excerpts from certain of the leading lower court functionality opinions after *TrafFix*.

Note that the Second Circuit has not yet had occasion to apply *TrafFix* in a utilitarian functionality context.

In reading these opinions, consider the following questions:

- Which opinion represents the best interpretation of *TrafFix*?

- Which opinions' approaches to functionality are more pro-plaintiff (i.e., less likely to find a product feature to be functional) or pro-defendant (i.e., more likely to find a product feature to be functional) in orientation?

- Where would you place each opinion's definition of or approach to functionality on *Morton-Norwich*'s continuum from de facto to de jure functionality? In other words, for each opinion, does the opinion define functionality in a way that is closer to a de facto definition of functionality or a de jure definition of functionality?

i.   Federal Circuit

In *Valu Engineering, Inc. v. Rexnord Corp.*, 278 F.3d 1268 (Fed. Cir. 2002), the Federal Circuit was the first court of appeals to consider a functionality issue after *TrafFix*. As you will see, the Federal Circuit read *TrafFix* as license essentially to conduct business as usual. Do you agree that *TrafFix* did not "alter" the *Morton-Norwich* analysis?

Valu Engineering, Inc. v. Rexnord Corp.
278 F.3d 1268, 1275-76 (Fed. Cir. 2002)

{Valu Engineering, Inc. ("Valu") applied to register various trademarks consisting of cross-sectional designs of conveyer guide rails. Specifically, Valu sought to register three marks, one for each of its round, flat, and tee cross-sectional designs, as shown below. Valu claimed that the designs had acquired distinctiveness. Rexnord Corp. ("Rexnord") opposed the registration on the ground, among others, that Valu's conveyer guide rail designs were functional. The TTAB agreed and sustained Rexnord's opposition. The Federal Circuit affirmed. Excerpted here is the Federal Circuit's analysis of *TrafFix*.}

DYK, Circuit Judge:

. . . .

[1] The Supreme Court reversed {the Sixth Circuit in *TrafFix*}, finding that the court of appeals gave insufficient evidentiary weight to the expired utility patents in analyzing the functionality of the dual-spring design, and that it overread *Qualitex*: "the Court of Appeals . . . seemed to interpret {*Qualitex*} to mean that a necessary test for functionality is 'whether the particular product configuration is a competitive necessity.' . . . This was incorrect as a comprehensive definition." *TrafFix*, 121 S.Ct. at 1261. The Court then reaffirmed the "traditional rule" of *Inwood* that "a product feature is functional if it is essential to the use or purpose of the article or if it affects the cost or quality of the article." *Id.* The Court further held that once a product feature is found to be functional under this "traditional rule," "there is no need to proceed further to consider if there is competitive necessity for the feature," and consequently "[t]here is no need . . . to engage . . . in speculation about other design possibilities . . . . Other designs need not be attempted." *Id.* at 1262.[4]

[2] We do not understand the Supreme Court's decision in *TrafFix* to have altered the *Morton–Norwich* analysis. As noted above, the *Morton–Norwich* factors aid in the determination of whether a particular feature is functional, and the third factor focuses on the availability of "other alternatives." *Morton–Norwich*, 671 F.2d at 1341. We did not in the past under the third factor require that the opposing party establish that there was a "competitive necessity" for the product feature. Nothing in *TrafFix* suggests that consideration of alternative designs is not properly part of the overall mix, and we do not read the Court's observations in *TrafFix* as rendering the availability of alternative designs irrelevant. Rather, we conclude that the Court merely noted that once a product feature is found functional based on other considerations[5] there is no need to consider the availability of alternative designs, because the feature cannot be given trade dress protection merely because there are alternative designs available. But that does not mean that the availability of alternative designs cannot be a legitimate source of evidence to determine whether a feature is functional in the first place. We find it significant that neither party argues that *TrafFix* changed the law of functionality, and that scholarly commentary has reached exactly the same conclusion that we have:

> In the author's view, the observations by the Supreme Court in *TrafFix* do not mean that the availability of alternative designs cannot be a legitimate source of evidence to determine in the first instance if a particular feature is in fact "functional." Rather, the Court merely said that once a design is found to be functional, it cannot be given trade dress status merely because there are alternative designs available . . . .
>
> . . . .

---

[4] *TrafFix* suggests that there may be a requirement under *Qualitex* to inquire into a "significant non-reputation-related disadvantage" in aesthetic functionality cases, because aesthetic functionality was "the question involved in *Qualitex*." 121 S.Ct. at 1262. This statement has been criticized because "aesthetic functionality was not the central question in the *Qualitex* case." J. Thomas McCarthy, 1 *McCarthy on Trademarks and Unfair Competition* § 7:80, 7–198 (4th ed. 2001). We need not decide what role, if any, the determination of a "significant non-reputation-related disadvantage" plays in aesthetic functionality cases, because aesthetic functionality is not at issue here.

[5] For example, a feature may be found functional where the feature "affects the cost or quality of the device." *TrafFix*, 121 S.Ct. at 1263.

... The existence of actual or potential alternative designs that work equally well strongly suggests that the particular design used by plaintiff is not needed by competitors to effectively compete on the merits.

J. Thomas McCarthy, 1 *McCarthy on Trademarks and Unfair Competition*, § 7:75, 7–180–1 (4th ed. 2001). In sum, *TrafFix* does not render the Board's use of the *Morton–Norwich* factors erroneous.

{The court went on to affirm the TTAB's application of the *Morton-Norwich* factors, emphasizing that, "[a]s this court's predecessor noted in *Morton–Norwich*, the 'effect upon competition "is really the crux"' of the functionality inquiry, *id.* at 1341, and, accordingly, the functionality doctrine preserves competition by ensuring competitors "the right to compete effectively." *Id.* at 1339."}

ii. Fifth Circuit

Eppendorf-Netheler-Hinz GMBH v. Ritter GMBH
289 F.3d 351 (5th Cir. 2002)

{Plaintiff Eppendorf–Netheler–Hinz GMBH ("Eppendorf") manufactured disposable pipette tips and dispenser syringes to which the pipette tips can be attached for use in laboratories. Defendant Ritter GMBH ("Ritter") began to manufacture pipette tips that were interchangeable with and priced lower than Eppendorf's tips. Eppendorf brought suit against Ritter for, among other things, trade dress infringement. In June of 2000, ten months before the Supreme Court handed down *TrafFix*, Eppendorf's claims were tried before a jury, which returned a verdict in favor of Eppendorf. The district court denied Ritter's motion for judgment as a matter of law. Ritter appealed.}

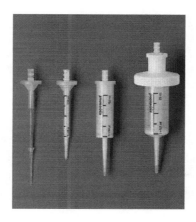

EDITH H. JONES, Circuit Judge

. . . .

[1] Eppendorf contends that Ritter infringed upon eight elements of the Combitips's trade dress: (1) the flange on top of the tip; (2) the fins connecting the flange to the body of the tip; (3) the plunger head; (4) the plunger; (5) the length of the tips; (6) the eight sizes of the tips; (7) the coloring scheme on the tips; and (8) the angle of the stump on the tips.

. . . .

[2] The crucial issue presented by this appeal is whether the eight design elements of the Eppendorf Combitips are functional as a matter of law. This case was tried in June of 2000, almost ten months before the Supreme Court decided *TrafFix*. The district court, correctly applying this circuit's utilitarian test of functionality, instructed the jury as follows:

> A design or characteristic is nonfunctional if there are reasonably effective and efficient alternatives possible. Hence, a product's trade dress is functional only, one, if competitors need to incorporate it in order to compete effectively because it is essential to the product's use, or, two, if it significantly affects the cost or quality of the article. A design is functional

159

and thus unprotectable if it is one of a limited number of equally efficient options available to competitors and free competition would be significantly disadvantaged by according the design trademark protection.

Relying on this instruction, the jury determined that the Combitips were non-functional. Ritter and RK Manufacturing moved for judgment as a matter of law on the issue of functionality, and the district court denied the motion.

. . . .

[3] Eppendorf contends that the evidence supports the jury's finding of non-functionality because "[t]he evidence clearly established that there were alternative designs to each of the eight non-functional features." *Appellee's Brief* at 20. Indeed, there is extensive testimony in the record regarding available alternative designs for each of the eight elements. For example, Eppendorf's expert testified that the number of fins under the flange "could be increased or decreased or their appearance could be changed." *Appellee's Brief* at 5. Thus, Eppendorf argues that the fins are non-functional because alternative designs are available to competitors in the marketplace.

[4] Eppendorf's argument, while consistent with this circuit's utilitarian definition of functionality, is unpersuasive in light of the Court's discussion of functionality in *TrafFix*. As explained above, the primary test for functionality is whether the product feature is essential to the use or purpose of the product or if it affects the cost or quality of the product. In *TrafFix*, the Court determined that the dual-spring design on a wind-resistant road sign was functional because the dual-spring design "provides a unique and useful mechanism to resist the force of the wind." 532 U.S. at 33, 121 S.Ct. at 1262. The Court rejected the argument that the springs were non-functional because a competitor could use three or four springs which would serve the same purpose. *Id.* The Court explained,

> There is no need, furthermore, to engage, as did the Court of Appeals, in speculation about other design possibilities, such as using three or four springs which might serve the same purpose . . . . The dual-spring design is not an arbitrary flourish in the configuration of [the road sign]; it is the reason the device works. Other designs need not be attempted.

Id. at 33–34, 121 S.Ct. at 1261. Accordingly, the design features for which Eppendorf seeks trade dress rights are functional if they are essential to the use or purpose of the Combitips or affect the cost or quality of the Combitips. The availability of alternative designs is irrelevant.

[5] In this case it is undisputed that the Combitips's fins provide necessary support for the flange. Without the fins, the flange is subject to deformation. The only testimony offered by Eppendorf to prove non-functionality of the fins related to the existence of alternative design possibilities. Eppendorf's functionality expert testified that the appearance and number of fins could be changed without affecting the function of the fins. Eppendorf did not prove, however, that the fins are an arbitrary flourish which serve no purpose in the Combitips. Rather, Eppendorf's experts concede that fins of some shape, size or number are necessary to provide support for the flange and to prevent deformation of the product. Thus, the fins are design elements necessary to the operation of the product.[5] Because the fins are essential to the operation of the Combitips, they are functional as a matter of law, and it is unnecessary to consider design alternatives available in the marketplace. *TrafFix*, 532 U.S. at 33–34.

[6] Likewise, a careful review of the record demonstrates that Eppendorf failed to prove that the remaining Combitip design elements are unnecessary, non-essential design elements. It is undisputed that: (1) The flange is necessary to connect the Combitip to the dispenser syringe; (2) The rings on the plunger head are necessary to lock the plunger into a cylinder in the dispenser syringe; (3) The plunger is necessary to push liquids out of the tip, and the ribs on the plunger stabilize its action; (4) The tips at the lower end of the Combitips are designed to easily fit into test tubes and other receptacles; (5) The

---

[5] Additionally, Eppendorf's experts concede that some of the suggested alternative designs would slightly increase the cost of the product. This provides further support for the conclusion that the fins are functional under the traditional definition of functionality.

size of the Combitip determines the dispensed volume, and size is essential to accurate and efficient dispensing; (6) The color scheme used on the Combitip—clear plastic with black lettering—enables the user easily to see and measure the amount of liquid in the Combitip, and black is standard in the medical industry; and (7) The stumps of the larger Combitips must be angled to separate air bubbles from the liquid and ensure that the full volume of liquid is dispensed. Thus, all eight design elements identified by Eppendorf are essential to the operation of the Combitips.

[7] Eppendorf's theory of non-functionality focused on the existence of alternative designs. Eppendorf's design expert summarized Eppendorf's approach to functionality: "My conclusion was that to achieve the same functional purpose, [the design elements identified by Eppendorf] can be changed significantly, considerably without affecting the overall intended purpose." Although alternative designs are relevant to the utilitarian test of functionality, alternative designs are not germane to the traditional test for functionality. Each of the eight design elements identified by Eppendorf is essential to the use or purpose of the Combitips, and is not arbitrary or ornamental features. Therefore, no reasonable juror could conclude that Eppendorf carried its burden of proving non-functionality.

. . . .

[8] Accordingly, we REVERSE the judgment of the district court and RENDER judgment for Ritter and RK Manufacturing. We likewise VACATE the injunction entered by the district court . . . .

Comments and Questions

1.   *Sixth Circuit application of* TrafFix. Just as it did with *Eppendorf* in the Fifth Circuit, *TrafFix* directly altered the outcome of a functionality case being litigated in the Sixth Circuit when *TrafFix* was handed down. In *Antioch Co. v. Western Trimming Corp.*, 196 F.Supp.2d 635 (S.D.Ohio 2002), the district court initially found that the plaintiff's scrap book design was nonfunctional in light of the availability of alternative designs, but the court invited the defendant to renew its motion for summary judgment on the issue if *TrafFix* altered the legal framework for assessing trade dress functionality. The defendant did so and the district court then ruled that the trade dress at issue was functional. The Sixth Circuit affirmed. *See Antioch Co. v. Western Trimming Corp.*, 347 F.3d 150, 156-157 (6th Cir. 2003) ("[A] a court is not *required* to examine alternative designs when applying the traditional test for functionality. That much is clear from *TrafFix Devices* . . . . The dual strap-hinge design, spine cover, padded album cover, and reinforced pages are all components that are essential to the use of Antioch's album and affect its quality. We thus agree with the district court's conclusion that there was no genuine issue of material fact regarding the functionality of Antioch's album under the traditional *Inwood* test." (emphasis in original)).

iii. Ninth Circuit

Int. Cl.: 9

Prior U.S. Cls.: 21, 23, 26, 36 and 38

United States Patent and Trademark Office

Reg. No. 3,470,983
Registered July 22, 2008

TRADEMARK
PRINCIPAL REGISTER

APPLE INC. (CALIFORNIA CORPORATION)
1 INFINITE LOOP
CUPERTINO, CA 95014

FOR: HANDHELD MOBILE DIGITAL ELECTRONIC DEVICES COMPRISED OF A MOBILE PHONE, DIGITAL AUDIO AND VIDEO PLAYER, HANDHELD COMPUTER, PERSONAL DIGITAL ASSISTANT, ELECTRONIC PERSONAL ORGANIZER, POCKET COMPUTER FOR NOTE-TAKING, ELECTRONIC CALENDAR, CALCULATOR, AND CAMERA, AND CAPABLE OF PROVIDING ACCESS TO THE INTERNET AND SENDING AND RECEIVING ELECTRONIC MAIL, DIGITAL AUDIO, VIDEO, TEXT, IMAGES, GRAPHICS AND MULTIMEDIA FILES, IN CLASS 9 (U.S. CLS. 21, 23, 26, 36 AND 38).

FIRST USE 6-29-2007; IN COMMERCE 6-29-2007.

NO CLAIM IS MADE TO THE EXCLUSIVE RIGHT TO USE "SMS", APART FROM THE MARK AS SHOWN.

THE COLOR(S) BLACK, BLUE, BROWN, BROWN-GRAY, GRAY-GREEN, GREEN, ORANGE, RED, SILVER, TAN, WHITE AND YELLOW IS/ARE CLAIMED AS A FEATURE OF THE MARK.

THE MARK CONSISTS OF THE CONFIGURATION OF A RECTANGULAR HANDHELD MOBILE DIGITAL ELECTRONIC DEVICE WITH ROUNDED SILVER EDGES, A BLACK FACE, AND AN ARRAY OF 16 SQUARE ICONS WITH ROUNDED EDGES. THE TOP 12 ICONS APPEAR ON A BLACK BACKGROUND, AND THE BOTTOM 4 APPEAR ON A SILVER BACKGROUND. THE FIRST ICON DEPICTS THE LETTERS "SMS" IN GREEN INSIDE A WHITE SPEECH BUBBLE ON A GREEN BACKGROUND; THE SECOND ICON IS WHITE WITH A THIN RED STRIPE AT THE TOP; THE THIRD ICON DEPICTS A SUNFLOWER WITH YELLOW PETALS, A BROWN CENTER, AND A GREEN STEM IN FRONT OF A BLUE SKY; THE FOURTH ICON DEPICTS A CAMERA LENS WITH A BLACK BARREL AND BLUE GLASS ON A SILVER BACKGROUND; THE FIFTH ICON DEPICTS A TAN TELEVISION CONSOLE WITH BROWN KNOBS AND A GRAY-GREEN SCREEN; THE SIXTH ICON DEPICTS A WHITE GRAPH LINE ON A BLUE BACKGROUND; THE SEVENTH ICON DEPICTS A MAP WITH YELLOW AND ORANGE ROADS, A PIN WITH A RED HEAD, AND A RED-AND-BLUE ROAD SIGN WITH THE NUMERAL "280" IN WHITE; THE EIGHTH ICON DEPICTS AN ORANGE SUN ON A BLUE BACKGROUND, WITH THE TEMPERATURE IN WHITE; THE NINTH ICON DEPICTS A WHITE CLOCK WITH BLACK AND RED HANDS AND NUMERALS ON A BLACK BACKGROUND; THE TENTH ICON DEPICTS THREE BROWN-GRAY CIRCLES AND ONE ORANGE CIRCLE ON A BLACK BACKGROUND WITH A WHITE BORDER, WITH THE MATHEMATICAL SYMBOLS FOR ADDITION, SUBTRACTION, MULTIPLICATION, AND THE EQUAL SIGN DISPLAYED IN WHITE ON THE CIRCLES; THE ELEVENTH ICON DEPICTS A PORTION OF A YELLOW NOTEPAD WITH BLUE AND RED RULING, WITH BROWN BINDING AT THE TOP; THE TWELFTH ICON DEPICTS THREE SILVER GEARS OVER A THATCHED BLACK-AND-SILVER BACKGROUND; THE THIRTEENTH ICON DEPICTS A WHITE TELEPHONE RECEIVER AGAINST A GREEN BACKGROUND; THE FOURTEENTH ICON DEPICTS A WHITE ENVELOPE OVER A BLUE SKY

WITH WHITE CLOUDS; THE FIFTEENTH ICON DEPICTS A WHITE COMPASS WITH A WHITE-AND-RED NEEDLE OVER A BLUE MAP; THE SIXTEENTH ICON DEPICTS THE DISTINCTIVE CONFIGURATION OF APPLICANT'S MEDIA PLAYER DEVICE IN WHITE OVER AN ORANGE BACKGROUND.

SEC. 2(F).

SER. NO. 77-303,282, FILED 10-12-2007.

SKYE YOUNG, EXAMINING ATTORNEY

Apple, Inc. v. Samsung Electronics Co. Ltd.
786 F.3d 983 (Fed. Cir. 2015)

PROST, Chief Judge

[1] Samsung Electronics Co., Ltd., Samsung Electronics America, Inc., Samsung Telecommunications America, LLC (collectively, "Samsung") appeal from a final judgment of the U.S. District Court for the Northern District of California in favor of Apple Inc. ("Apple").

[2] A jury found that Samsung infringed Apple's design and utility patents and diluted Apple's trade dresses. For the reasons that follow, we affirm the jury's verdict on the design patent infringements, the validity of two utility patent claims, and the damages awarded for the design and utility patent infringements appealed by Samsung. However, we reverse the jury's findings that the asserted trade dresses are protectable. We therefore vacate the jury's damages awards against the Samsung products that were found liable for trade dress dilution and remand for further proceedings consistent with this opinion.

BACKGROUND

[3] Apple sued Samsung in April 2011. On August 24, 2012, the first jury reached a verdict that numerous Samsung smartphones infringed and diluted Apple's patents and trade dresses in various combinations and awarded over $1 billion in damages.

[4] ... The diluted trade dresses are Trademark Registration No. 3,470,983 ("'983 trade dress") and an unregistered trade dress defined in terms of certain elements in the configuration of the iPhone.

[5] Following the first jury trial, the district court upheld the jury's infringement, dilution, and validity findings over Samsung's post-trial motion [and a second post-trial motion]. On March 6, 2014, the district court entered a final judgment in favor of Apple, and Samsung filed a notice of appeal ....

DISCUSSION

[6] We review the denial of Samsung's post-trial motions under the Ninth Circuit's procedural standards .... The Ninth Circuit reviews de novo a denial of a motion for judgment as a matter of law ....

I. Trade Dresses

[7] The jury found Samsung liable for the likely dilution of Apple's iPhone trade dresses under the Lanham Act. When reviewing Lanham Act claims, we look to the law of the regional circuit where the district court sits. We therefore apply Ninth Circuit law.

[8] The Ninth Circuit has explained that "[t]rade dress is the totality of elements in which a product or service is packaged or presented." *Stephen W. Boney, Inc. v. Boney Servs., Inc.*, 127 F.3d 821, 828 (9th Cir. 1997). The essential purpose of a trade dress is the same as that of a trademarked word: to identify the source of the product. 1 *McCarthy on Trademarks and Unfair Competition* § 8:1 (4th ed.) ("[L]ike a word asserted to be a trademark, the elements making up the alleged trade dress must have been used in such a manner as to denote product source."). In this respect, "protection for trade dress exists to promote competition." *TrafFix Devices, Inc. v. Mktg. Displays, Inc.*, 532 U.S. 23, 28, 121 S.Ct. 1255, 149 L.Ed.2d 164 (2001).

[9] The protection for source identification, however, must be balanced against "a fundamental right to compete through imitation of a competitor's product ...." *Leatherman Tool Grp., Inc. v. Cooper Indus., Inc.*, 199 F.3d 1009, 1011–12 (9th Cir. 1999). This "right can only be temporarily denied by the patent or copyright laws." *Id.* In contrast, trademark law allows for a perpetual monopoly and its use in the protection of "physical details and design of a product" must be limited to those that are "nonfunctional." *Id.* at 1011–12; *see also Qualitex Co. v. Jacobson Prods. Co.*, 514 U.S. 159, 164–65 (1995) ("If a product's functional features could be used as trademarks, however, a monopoly over such features could be obtained without regard to whether they qualify as patents and could be extended forever (because trademarks may be renewed in perpetuity)."). Thus, it is necessary for us to determine first whether Apple's asserted trade dresses, claiming elements from its iPhone product, are nonfunctional and therefore protectable.

[10] "In general terms, a product feature is functional if it is essential to the use or purpose of the article or if it affects the cost or quality of the article." *Inwood Labs., Inc. v. Ives Labs., Inc.*, 456 U.S. 844, 850 n. 10 (1982). "A product feature need only have some utilitarian advantage to be considered functional." *Disc Golf Ass'n v. Champion Discs, Inc.*, 158 F.3d 1002, 1007 (9th Cir. 1998). A trade dress, taken as a whole, is functional if it is "in its particular shape because it works better in this shape." *Leatherman*, 199 F.3d at 1013.

[11] "[C]ourts have noted that it is, and should be, more difficult to claim product configuration trade dress than other forms of trade dress." *Id.* at 1012–13 (discussing cases). Accordingly, the Supreme Court and the Ninth Circuit have repeatedly found product configuration trade dresses functional and therefore non-protectable. *See, e.g., TrafFix*, 532 U.S. at 26–27, 35; *Secalt S.A. v. Wuxi Shenxi Const. Mach. Co.*, 668 F.3d 677, 687 (9th Cir. 2012) (affirming summary judgment that a trade dress on a hoist design was functional); *Disc Golf*, 158 F.3d at 1006 (affirming summary judgment that a trade dress on a disc entrapment design was functional).

[12] Moreover, federal trademark registrations have been found insufficient to save product configuration trade dresses from conclusions of functionality. *See, e.g., Talking Rain Beverage Co. v. S. Beach Beverage*, 349 F.3d 601, 602 (9th Cir. 2003) (affirming summary judgment that registered trade dress covering a bottle design with a grip handle was functional); *Tie Tech, Inc. v. Kinedyne Corp.*, 296 F.3d 778, 782–83 (9th Cir. 2002) (affirming summary judgment that registered trade dress covering a handheld cutter design was functional). The Ninth Circuit has even reversed a jury verdict of non-functionality of a product configuration trade dress. *See Leatherman*, 199 F.3d at 1013 (reversing jury verdict that a trade dress on the overall appearance of a pocket tool was non-functional). Apple conceded during oral argument that it had not cited a single Ninth Circuit case that found a product configuration trade dress to be non-functional. Oral Arg. 49:0630, available at http://www.cafc.uscourts.gov/oral-argument-recordings/14–1335/all.

[13] The Ninth Circuit's high bar for non-functionality frames our review of the two iPhone trade dresses on appeal. While the parties argue without distinguishing the two trade dresses, the unregistered trade dress and the registered '983 trade dress claim different details and are afforded different evidentiary presumptions under the Lanham Act. We analyze the two trade dresses separately below.

A. Unregistered Trade Dress

[14] Apple claims elements from its iPhone 3G and 3GS products to define the asserted unregistered trade dress:

> a rectangular product with four evenly rounded corners;
>
> a flat, clear surface covering the front of the product;
>
> a display screen under the clear surface;
>
> substantial black borders above and below the display screen and narrower black borders on either side of the screen; and
>
> when the device is on, a row of small dots on the display screen, a matrix of colorful square icons with evenly rounded corners within the display screen, and an unchanging bottom dock of colorful square icons with evenly rounded corners set off from the display's other icons.

Appellee's Br. 10–11. As this trade dress is not registered on the principal federal trademark register, Apple "has the burden of proving that the claimed trade dress, taken as a whole, is not functional . . . ." *See* 15 U.S.C. § 1125(c)(4)(A).

[15] Apple argues that the unregistered trade dress is nonfunctional under each of the *Disc Golf* factors that the Ninth Circuit uses to analyze functionality: "(1) whether the design yields a utilitarian advantage, (2) whether alternative designs are available, (3) whether advertising touts the utilitarian advantages of the design, and (4) whether the particular design results from a comparatively simple or inexpensive method of manufacture." *See Disc Golf*, 158 F.3d at 1006. However, the Supreme Court has more recently held that "a feature is also functional . . . when it affects the cost or quality of the device." *See TrafFix*, 532 U.S. at 33. The Supreme Court's holding was recognized by the Ninth Circuit as "short circuiting some of the *Disc Golf* factors." *Secalt*, 668 F.3d at 686–87. Nevertheless, we explore Apple's contentions on each of the *Disc Golf* factors and conclude that there was insufficient evidence to support a jury finding in favor of non-functionality on any factor.

1. Utilitarian Advantage

[16] Apple argues that "the iPhone's physical design did not 'contribute unusually . . . to the usability' of the device." Appellee's Br. 61. Apple further contends that the unregistered trade dress was "developed . . . not for 'superior performance.'" *Id*. at 62 n. 18. Neither "unusual usability" nor "superior performance," however, is the standard used by the Ninth Circuit to determine whether there is any utilitarian advantage. The Ninth Circuit "has never held, as [plaintiff] suggests, that the product feature must provide superior utilitarian advantages. To the contrary, [the Ninth Circuit] has suggested that in order to establish nonfunctionality the party with the burden must demonstrate that the product feature

164

serves no purpose other than identification." *Disc Golf*, 158 F.3d at 1007 (internal quotation marks omitted).

[17] The requirement that the unregistered trade dress "serves no purpose other than identification" cannot be reasonably inferred from the evidence. Apple emphasizes a single aspect of its design, beauty, to imply the lack of other advantages. But the evidence showed that the iPhone's design pursued more than just beauty. Specifically, Apple's executive testified that the theme for the design of the iPhone was:

> to create a new breakthrough design for a phone that was beautiful and simple and *easy to use* and created a beautiful, smooth surface that had a touchscreen and went right to the rim with the bezel around it and looking for a look that we found was beautiful and *easy to use* and appealing.

J.A. 40722–23 (emphases added).

[18] Moreover, Samsung cites extensive evidence in the record that showed the usability function of every single element in the unregistered trade dress. For example, rounded corners improve "pocketability" and "durability" and rectangular shape maximizes the display that can be accommodated. J.A. 40869–70; J.A. 42612–13. A flat clear surface on the front of the phone facilitates touch operation by fingers over a large display. J.A. 42616–17. The bezel protects the glass from impact when the phone is dropped. J.A. 40495. The borders around the display are sized to accommodate other components while minimizing the overall product dimensions. J.A. 40872. The row of dots in the user interface indicates multiple pages of application screens that are available. J.A. 41452–53. The icons allow users to differentiate the applications available to the users and the bottom dock of unchanging icons allows for quick access to the most commonly used applications. J.A. 42560–61; J.A. 40869–70. Apple rebuts none of this evidence.

[19] Apple conceded during oral argument that its trade dress "improved the quality [of the iPhone] in some respects." Oral Arg. 56:09–17. It is thus clear that the unregistered trade dress has a utilitarian advantage. *See Disc Golf*, 158 F.3d at 1007.

2. Alternative Designs

[20] The next factor requires that purported alternative designs "offer exactly the same features" as the asserted trade dress in order to show non-functionality. *Tie Tech*, 296 F.3d at 786 (quoting *Leatherman*, 199 F.3d at 1013–14). A manufacturer "does not have rights under trade dress law to compel its competitors to resort to alternative designs which have a different set of advantages and disadvantages." *Id.*

[21] Apple, while asserting that there were "numerous alternative designs," fails to show that any of these alternatives offered exactly the same features as the asserted trade dress. Apple simply catalogs the mere existence of other design possibilities embodied in rejected iPhone prototypes and other manufacturers' smartphones. The "mere existence" of other designs, however, does not prove that the unregistered trade dress is non-functional. *See Talking Rain*, 349 F.3d at 604.

3. Advertising of Utilitarian Advantages

[22] "If a seller advertises the utilitarian advantages of a particular feature, this constitutes strong evidence of functionality." *Disc Golf*, 158 F.3d at 1009. An "inference" of a product feature's utility in the plaintiff's advertisement is enough to weigh in favor of functionality of a trade dress encompassing that feature. *Id.*

[23] Apple argues that its advertising was "[f]ar from touting any utilitarian advantage of the iPhone design . . . ." Appellee's Br. 60. Apple relies on its executive's testimony that an iPhone advertisement, portraying "the distinctive design very clearly," was based on Apple's "product as hero" approach. *Id.* (quoting J.A. 40641–42; 40644:22). The "product as hero" approach refers to Apple's stylistic choice of making "the product the biggest, clearest, most obvious thing in [its] advertisements, often at the expense of anything else around it, to remove all the other elements of communication so [the viewer] see[s] the product most predominantly in the marketing." J.A. 40641–42.

[24] Apple's arguments focusing on its stylistic choice, however, fail to address the substance of its advertisements. The substance of the iPhone advertisement relied upon by Apple gave viewers "the ability to see a bit about how it might work," for example, "how flicking and scrolling and tapping and all these multitouch ideas simply [sic]." J.A. 40644:23–40645:2. Another advertisement cited by Apple similarly displayed the message, "[t]ouching is believing," under a picture showing a user's hand interacting with the graphical user interface of an iPhone. J.A. 24896. Apple fails to show that, on the substance, these demonstrations of the user interface on iPhone's touch screen involved the elements claimed in Apple's unregistered trade dress and why they were not touting the utilitarian advantage of the unregistered trade dress.

4. Method of Manufacture

[25] The fourth factor considers whether a functional benefit in the asserted trade dress arises from "economies in manufacture or use," such as being "relatively simple or inexpensive to manufacture." *Disc Golf*, 158 F.3d at 1009.

[26] Apple contends that "[t]he iPhone design did not result from a 'comparatively simple or inexpensive method of manufacture'" because Apple experienced manufacturing challenges. Appellee's Br. 61 (quoting *Talking Rain*, 349 F.3d at 603). Apple's manufacturing challenges, however, resulted from the durability considerations for the iPhone and not from the design of the unregistered trade dress. According to Apple's witnesses, difficulties resulted from its choices of materials in using "hardened steel"; "very high, high grade of steel"; and, "glass that was not breakable enough, scratch resistant enough." *Id.* (quoting J.A. 40495–96, 41097). These materials were chosen, for example, for the iPhone to survive a drop:

> If you drop this, you don't have to worry about the ground hitting the glass. You have to worry about the band of steel surrounding the glass hitting the glass . . . . In order to, to make it work, we had to use very high, high grade of steel because we couldn't have it sort of deflecting into the glass.

J.A. 40495–96. The durability advantages that resulted from the manufacturing challenges, however, are outside the scope of what Apple defines as its unregistered trade dress. For the design elements that comprise Apple's unregistered trade dress, Apple points to no evidence in the record to show they were not relatively simple or inexpensive to manufacture. *See Disc Golf*, 158 F.3d at 1009 ("[Plaintiff], which has the burden of proof, offered no evidence that the [asserted] design was not relatively simple or inexpensive to manufacture.").

[27] In sum, Apple has failed to show that there was substantial evidence in the record to support a jury finding in favor of non-functionality for the unregistered trade dress on any of the *Disc Golf* factors. Apple fails to rebut the evidence that the elements in the unregistered trade dress serve the functional purpose of improving usability. Rather, Apple focuses on the "beauty" of its design, even though Apple pursued both "beauty" and functionality in the design of the iPhone. We therefore reverse the district court's denial of Samsung's motion for judgment as a matter of law that the unregistered trade dress is functional and therefore not protectable.

B. The Registered '983 Trade Dress

[28] In contrast to the unregistered trade dress, the '983 trade dress is a federally registered trademark. The federal trademark registration provides "prima facie evidence" of non-functionality. *Tie Tech*, 296 F.3d at 782–83. This presumption "shift[s] the burden of production to the defendant . . . to provide evidence of functionality." *Id.* at 783. Once this presumption is overcome, the registration loses its legal significance on the issue of functionality. *Id.* ("In the face of sufficient and undisputed facts demonstrating functionality, . . . the registration loses its evidentiary significance.").

[29] The '983 trade dress claims the design details in each of the sixteen icons on the iPhone's home screen framed by the iPhone's rounded-rectangular shape with silver edges and a black background:

> The first icon depicts the letters "SMS" in green inside a white speech bubble on a green background;

. . .

the seventh icon depicts a map with yellow and orange roads, a pin with a red head, and a red-and-blue road sign with the numeral "280" in white;

. . .

the sixteenth icon depicts the distinctive configuration of applicant's media player device in white over an orange background.

'983 trade dress (omitting thirteen other icon design details for brevity).

[30] It is clear that individual elements claimed by the '983 trade dress are functional. For example, there is no dispute that the claimed details such as "the seventh icon depicts a map with yellow and orange roads, a pin with a red head, and a red-and-blue road sign with the numeral '280' in white" are functional. *See id.* Apple's user interface expert testified on how icon designs promote usability. This expert agreed that "the whole point of an icon on a smartphone is to communicate to the consumer using that product, that if they hit that icon, certain functionality will occur on the phone." J.A. 41458–59. The expert further explained that icons are "[v]isual shorthand for something" and that "rectangular containers" for icons provide "more real estate" to accommodate the icon design. J.A. 41459, 41476. Apple rebuts none of this evidence.

[31] Apple contends instead that Samsung improperly disaggregates the '983 trade dress into individual elements to argue functionality. But Apple fails to explain how the total combination of the sixteen icon designs in the context of iPhone's screen-dominated rounded-rectangular shape—all part of the iPhone's "easy to use" design theme—somehow negates the undisputed usability function of the individual elements. *See* J.A. 40722–23. Apple's own brief even relies on its expert's testimony about the "instant recognizability due to highly intuitive icon usage" on "the home screen of the iPhone." J.A. 41484; Appellee's Br. 43, 70, 71 (quoting J.A. 41484). Apple's expert was discussing an analysis of the iPhone's overall combination of icon designs that allowed a user to recognize quickly particular applications to use. J.A. 41484, 25487. The iPhone's usability advantage from the combination of its icon designs shows that the '983 trade dress viewed as a whole "is nothing other than the assemblage of functional parts . . . ." *See Tie Tech*, 296 F.3d at 786 (quoting *Leatherman*, 199 F.3d at 1013). There is no "separate 'overall appearance' which is non-functional." *Id.* (quoting *Leatherman*, 199 F.3d at 1013). The undisputed facts thus demonstrate the functionality of the '983 trade dress. "In the face of sufficient and undisputed facts demonstrating functionality, as in our case, the registration loses its evidentiary significance." *See id.* at 783.

[32] The burden thus shifts back to Apple. *See id.* But Apple offers no analysis of the icon designs claimed by the '983 trade dress. Rather, Apple argues generically for its two trade dresses without distinction under the *Disc Golf* factors. Among Apple's lengthy citations to the record, we can find only two pieces of information that involve icon designs. One is Apple's user interface expert discussing other possible icon designs. The other is a citation to a print iPhone advertisement that included the icon designs claimed in the '983 trade dress. These two citations, viewed in the most favorable light to Apple, would be relevant to only two of the *Disc Golf* factors: "alternative design" and "advertising." But the cited evidence suffers from the same defects as discussed in subsections I.A.2 and I.A.3. Specifically, the expert's discussion of other icon design possibilities does not show that the other design possibilities "offer[ed] exactly the same features" as the '983 trade dress. *See Tie Tech*, 296 F.3d at 786 (quoting *Leatherman*, 199 F.3d at 1013–14). The print iPhone advertisement also fails to establish that, on the substance, it was not touting the utilitarian advantage of the '983 trade dress. The evidence cited by Apple therefore does not show the non-functionality of the '983 trade dress.

[33] In sum, the undisputed evidence shows the functionality of the registered '983 trade dress and shifts the burden of proving non-functionality back to Apple. Apple, however, has failed to show that there was substantial evidence in the record to support a jury finding in favor of non-functionality for the '983 trade dress on any of the *Disc Golf* factors. We therefore reverse the district court's denial of Samsung's motion for judgment as a matter of law that the '983 trade dress is functional and therefore not protectable.

[34] Because we conclude that the jury's findings of non-functionality of the asserted trade dresses were not supported by substantial evidence, we do not reach Samsung's arguments on the fame and likely dilution of the asserted trade dresses, the Patent Clause of the Constitution, or the dilution damages.

{The Court went on to affirm all remaining district court holdings}.

iv.   Seventh Circuit

Specialized Seating, Inc. v. Greenwich Industries, L.P.
616 F.3d 722 (7th Cir. 2010)

{Declaratory defendant Greenwich Industries, L.P., doing business under the name Clarin, owned PTO Registration No. 2,803,875 for a trademark for folding chairs consisting of "a configuration of a folding chair containing an X-frame profile, a flat channel flanked on each side by rolled edges around the perimeter of the chair, two cross bars with a flat channel and rolled edges at the back bottom of the chair, one cross bar with a flat channel and rolled edges on the front bottom, protruding feet, and a back support, the outer sides of which slant inward." An image of the folding chair configuration is provided below. Specialized Seating, Inc. ("Specialized") sought a declaratory judgment that its folding chair design did not infringe Clarin's design. Specialized argued that Clarin's mark was functional. The district court held a bench trial and agreed, ordering that the registration be cancelled. Clarin appealed.}

EASTERBROOK, Circuit Judge

. . . .

[1] The [district] judge found that [Clarin's] x-frame construction is functional because it was designed to be an optimal tradeoff between a chair's weight (and thus its cost, since lighter chairs use less steel) and its strength; an x-frame chair also folds itself naturally when knocked over (an important consideration for large auditoriums, where it is vital that chairs not impede exit if a fire or panic breaks out); the flat channel at the seat's edge, where the attachment to the frame slides so that the chair can fold, was designed for strength and attaching hooks to link a chair with its nearest neighbor; the front and back cross bars contribute strength (and allow thinner tubing to be used in the rest of the frame); and the inward-sloping frame of the back support allows the chair to support greater vertical loads than Clarin's older "a-back" design, which the "b-back" design, depicted in the trademark registration, succeeded. The a-back design is on the left and the b-back on the right:

[2] Clarin chairs with a-back designs failed when the audience at rock concerts, seeking a better view, sat on top of the chairs' backs and put their feet on the seats. The tubing buckled at the bend in the frame. The b-back design is less likely to buckle when someone sits on it, and it also produces a somewhat wider back, which concert promoters see as a benefit. (Patrons sometimes try to get closer to the stage by stepping through rows of chairs. The gap between b-back chairs is smaller, so they are more effective at keeping crowds in place.)

[3] Having concluded not only that the overall design of Clarin's chair is functional, but also that each feature is functional, the district judge added that Clarin had defrauded the Patent and Trademark Office by giving misleadingly incomplete answers to the trademark examiner's questions. The examiner initially turned down Clarin's proposal to register the design as a trademark, observing that the design appeared to be functional. Clarin replied that the design was chosen for aesthetic rather than functional reasons. (This was not a complete answer, as attractiveness is a *kind* of function. See *Jay Franco & Sons, Inc. v. Franek,* 615 F.3d 855, 860–61 (7th Cir. 2010). But we need not pursue that subject.) Clarin observed that a patent it held on an x-frame chair, No. 1,943,058, issued in 1934, did not include all of the features in the mark's design. What Clarin did not tell the examiner is that it held three other patents on x-frame designs: No. 1,600,248, issued in 1926; No. 2,137,803, issued in 1938; and No. 3,127,218, issued in 1964. The district judge concluded that the four patents collectively cover every feature of the design submitted for a trademark except the b-back, and that as the b-back is a functional improvement over the a-back Clarin should have disclosed all of these utility patents. Had it done so, the judge thought, the examiner would have refused to register the proposed mark.

. . . .

[4] The district judge started from the proposition, which the Supreme Court articulated in *TrafFix,* that claims in an expired utility patent presumptively are functional. Since utility patents are supposed to be restricted to inventions that have utility, and thus are functional, that's a sensible starting point—and since inventions covered by utility patents pass into the public domain when the patent expires, it is inappropriate to use trademark law to afford extended protection to a patented invention. See also *Jay Franco,* 615 F.3d at 857–59. Clarin itself obtained four utility patents for aspects of the x-frame folding chair. These patents disclose every aspect of the asserted trademark design except for the b-back. And the district judge did not commit a clear error by concluding that the b-back design is a functional improvement over the a-back design. This means that the trademark design is functional as a unit, and that every important aspect of it is independently functional. It looks the way it does in order to be a better chair, not in order to be a better way of identifying who made it (the function of a trademark).

[5] We do not doubt that there are many other available functional designs. Sometimes the function of the functionality doctrine is to prevent firms from appropriating basic forms (such as the circle) that go into many designs. Our contemporaneous opinion in *Jay Franco* discusses that aspect of the functionality doctrine. This does not imply that preserving basic elements for the public domain is the doctrine's *only* role.

[6] Another goal, as *TrafFix* stressed, is to separate the spheres of patent and trademark law, and to ensure that the term of a patent is not extended beyond the period authorized by the legislature. A design such as Clarin's x-frame chair is functional not because it is the only way to do things, but because it represents one of many solutions to a problem. Clarin tells us that other designs are stronger, or thinner, or less likely to collapse when someone sits on the backrest, or lighter and so easier to carry and set up. Granted. But as Clarin's '248 patent states, the x-frame design achieves a favorable strength-to-weight ratio. Plastic chairs are lighter but weaker. Y-frame chairs are stronger but use more metal (and so are heavier and more expensive); some alternative designs must be made with box-shaped metal pieces to achieve strength, and this adds to weight and the cost of fabrication. The list of alternative designs is very long, and it is easy to see why hundreds of different-looking folding chairs are on the market.

[7] What this says to us is that *all* of the designs are functional, in the sense that they represent different compromises along the axes of weight, strength, kind of material, ease of setup, ability to connect ("gang") the chairs together for maximum seating density, and so on. A novel or distinctive selection of attributes on these many dimensions can be protected for a time by a utility patent or a design patent, but it cannot be protected forever as one producer's trade dress. When the patent expires, other firms are free to copy the design to the last detail in order to increase competition and drive down the price that consumers pay. See, e.g., *Bonito Boats, Inc. v. Thunder Craft Boats, Inc.,* 489 U.S. 141(1989); *Sears, Roebuck & Co. v. Stiffel Co.,* 376 U.S. 225 (1964) . . . .

[8] Because the district court did not commit clear error in finding Clarin's design to be functional, it is unnecessary to decide whether Clarin committed fraud on the Patent and Trademark Office . . . .

AFFIRMED

c.   Aesthetic Functionality

As the Supreme Court briefly explained in *TrafFix*, a product (or packaging) feature that performs no technical, mechanical function may nevertheless be barred from protection on the ground that it is "aesthetically functional." Under *TrafFix*, the test to determine whether a product feature is aesthetically functional is not the *Inwood* test. Instead, courts should ask whether there are a limited range of alternative designs available to competitors such that exclusive rights in the product feature would put competitors at a significant non-reputation-related competitive disadvantage. What might have prompted courts to abandon the *Inwood* test in the aesthetic functionality context?

A few classic illustrations of aesthetically functional product configuration from the *Restatement (Third) of Unfair Competition* may help to convey the general idea of aesthetic functionality:

8. A is the first seller to market candy intended for Valentine's Day in heart-shaped boxes. Evidence establishes that the shape of the box is an important factor in the appeal of the product to a significant number of consumers. Because there are no alternative designs capable of satisfying the aesthetic desires of these prospective purchasers, the design of the box is functional . . . .

9. A manufactures outdoor lighting fixtures intended for mounting on the walls of commercial buildings to illuminate adjacent areas. The evidence establishes that architectural compatibility with the building is an important factor in the purchase of such fixtures and that A's product is considered to be aesthetically compatible with contemporary architecture. The evidence also establishes that only a limited number of designs are considered compatible with the type of buildings on which A's product is used. Because of the limited range of alternative designs available to competitors, a court may properly conclude that the design of the lighting fixture is functional under the rule stated in this Section.

Restatement (Third) of Unfair Competition § 17.

A few examples from the aesthetic functionality case law may also help to introduce the doctrine:

- *British Seagull Ltd. v. Brunswick Corp.*, 35 F.3d 1527 (Fed. Cir. 1994) (affirming the TTAB's refusal to register the color black for outboard marine engines and approving of the Board's reasoning that "although the color black is not functional in the sense that it makes these engines work better, or that it makes them easier or less expensive to manufacture, black is more desirable from the perspective of prospective purchasers because it is color compatible with a wider variety of boat colors and because objects colored black appear smaller than they do when they are painted other lighter or brighter colors.").

- *In re Florists' Transworld Delivery, Inc.*, Serial No. 77590475 (TTAB Mar. 28, 2013) (precedential) (affirming examiner's rejection of application to register the color black for boxes containing flowers and floral arrangements; "[c]ompetitors who, for example, want to offer flowers for bereavement purposes, Halloween or to imbue an element of elegance or luxury to their presentations through packaging therefor will be disadvantaged if they must avoid using the color black in such packaging.").

- *Deere & Co. v. Farmhand, Inc.*, 560 F. Supp. 85, 217 U.S.P.Q. 252 (S.D. Iowa 1982) (finding the color "John Deere green" to be aesthetically functional as used on farm loaders because farmers prefer to match the color of their loaders and tractors). *But see* Deere & Co. v. FIMCO Inc., 239 F.Supp.3d 964, 997-1003 (W.D. Ky. 2017) (finding John Deere's green and yellow color scheme to be non-functional and distinguishing *Farmhand* on grounds that (1) it was adjudicated before *Qualitex*, *TrafFix*, and the Sixth Circuit's establishment of the "comparable alternatives" and "effective competition" tests for aesthetic functionality, and (2) Deere sought in *Farmhand* to prevent competitors from using "John Deere green" either alone or in combination with any other color, whereas Deere seeks here merely to prevent competitors from using a combination of green and yellow).

- *In re Ferris Corp.*, 59 U.S.P.Q.2d 1587 (TTAB 2000) (not citable as precedent) (affirming examiner's refusal to register the color pink for surgical bandages; the color is "de jure functional" in that it blends well with the natural color of certain human ethnicities' skin and there are no viable alternative colors available).

Of the three opinions that follow, *Pagliero v. Wallace China Co.*, 198 F.2d 339 (9th Cir. 1952), is somewhat notorious for having proposed a definition of aesthetic functionality that, when interpreted loosely, could end up prohibiting the protection of anything that was "an important ingredient in the commercial success of the product," including the trademark itself. The Ninth Circuit no longer follows *Pagliero. See, e.g., Au-Tomotive Gold, Inc. v. Volkswagen of Am., Inc.*, 457 F.3d 1062, 1072 (9th Cir. 2006) ("In the case of a claim of aesthetic functionality, an alternative test inquires whether protection of the feature as a trademark would impose a significant non-reputation-related competitive disadvantage."). In *Wallace Int'l Silversmiths, Inc. v. Godinger Silver Art Co.*, 916 F.2d 76 (2d Cir. 1990), the Second Circuit explicitly rejected *Pagliero*. In *Christian Louboutin S.A. v. Yves Saint Laurent America Holding, Inc.*, 696 F.3d 206, 218- (2d Cir. 2012), the Second Circuit was asked to determine whether a particular color applied to the outsole (the underside) of shoes was aesthetically functional.

Two final points. First, not all circuits are receptive to the concept of aesthetic functionality. *See, e.g., Bd. of Supervisors for La. State Univ. Agric. & Mech. Coll. v. Smack Apparel Co.*, 550 F.3d 465, 487-88 (5th Cir. 2008) ("We do not believe that the Court's dictum in *TrafFix* requires us to abandon our long-settled view rejecting recognition of aesthetic functionality."). Why might these circuits refuse to consider aesthetic functionality as a special case of functionality? Second, and related, the student hoping to understand the essence of aesthetic functionality doctrine may do well not to focus too much on the term "aesthetic" or even on the term "functionality." "Aesthetic functionality" is a horribly chosen name for a doctrine that seeks to make up for one particular shortcoming of utilitarian functionality doctrine, which is that it is simply not well designed to analyze *non-utilitarian, non-mechanical* product features. Aesthetic functionality doctrine seeks to accomplish the same procompetitive goals as utilitarian functionality doctrine, but it does so precisely with respect to non-mechanical product features, be they strictly "aesthetic" or not, that all competitors must be able to include in their products in order to compete effectively. *See generally* Justin Hughes, *Cognitive and Aesthetic Functionality in Trademark Law*, 36 CARDOZO L. REV. 1227 (2015).

i. Foundational Cases

Wallace Hibiscus (L) and Tepco Hibiscus (R)

Pagliero v. Wallace China Co.
198 F.2d 339, 343-44 (9th Cir. 1952)

{Wallace China Co. ("Wallace") produced hotel china imprinted with various designs. Wallace's business model involved selling initial sets of hotel china at a relatively low price and making significant profits on selling replacement pieces (made necessary by breakage) bearing matching designs. Pagliero Brothers, doing business as Technical Porcelain and Chinaware Company ("Tepco"), produced low cost hotel china bearing designs substantially identical to Wallace's. This undercut Wallace's business model. Wallace brought federal trademark and other causes of action against Tepco for this and other conduct by Tepco. The district court found infringement and enjoined Tepco from producing china bearing designs similar to Wallace's. Excerpted here is the Ninth Circuit's discussion of the aesthetic functionality of Wallace's designs.}

ORR, Circuit Judge

. . . .

[1] Tepco's use of the designs in question cannot be enjoined even though it be assumed that Wallace can establish secondary meaning for them. Imitation of the physical details and designs of a competitor's product may be actionable, if the particular features imitated are 'non-functional' and have acquired a secondary meaning. *Crescent Tool Co. v. Kilborn & Bishop Co.*, 2d Cir., 1917, 247 F. 299. But, where the features are 'functional' there is normally no right to relief. 'Functional' in this sense might be said to connote other than a trade-mark purpose. If the particular feature is an important ingredient in the commercial success of the product, the interest in free competition permits its imitation in the absence of a patent or copyright. On the other hand, where the feature or, more aptly, design, is a mere arbitrary embellishment, a form of dress for the goods primarily adopted for purposes of identification and individuality and, hence, unrelated to basic consumer demands in connection with the product, imitation may be forbidden where the requisite showing of secondary meaning is made. Under such circumstances, since effective competition may be undertaken without imitation, the law grants protection.

[2] These criteria require the classification of the designs in question here as functional. Affidavits introduced by Wallace repeat over and over again that one of the essential selling features of hotel china, if, indeed, not the primary, is the design. The attractiveness and eye-appeal of the design sells the china. Moreover, from the standpoint of the purchaser china satisfies a demand for the aesthetic as well as for the utilitarian, and the design on china is, at least in part, the response to such demand. The granting of relief in this type of situation would render Wallace immune from the most direct and effective competition with regard to these lines of china. It seems clear that these designs are not merely indicia of source, as that one who copies them can have no real purpose other than to trade on his competitor's reputation. On the contrary, to imitate is to compete in this type of situation. Of course, Tepco can also compete by developing designs even more aesthetically satisfying, but the possibility that an alternative product might be developed has never been considered a barrier to permitting imitation competition in other types of cases. The law encourages competition not only in creativeness but in economy of manufacture and distribution as well. Hence, the design being a functional feature of the china, we find it unnecessary to inquire into the adequacy of the showing made as to secondary meaning of the designs.

{The Ninth Circuit ordered the district court's injunction to be modified to remove all reference to Tepco's use of designs similar to Wallace's.}

V10.0/2023-07-22

Wallace "Grande Baroque" Silverware

In reading *Wallace Int'l Silversmiths, Inc. v. Godinger Silver Art Co.*, 916 F.2d 76 (2d Cir. 1990), consider the following questions:

- How should a court define the relevant market for purposes of assessing competitive alternatives to the plaintiff's design? What exactly is wrong with Wallace's argument that it merely wants to claim the baroque style of silverware, and that countless other styles of silverware are still available for competitors to use?

- Even if we are able reliably to define the relevant marketplace, how many alternative designs should be available for a court to determine that the plaintiff's design is not aesthetically functional?

Wallace Int'l Silversmiths, Inc. v. Godinger Silver Art Co.
916 F.2d 76 (2d Cir. 1990)

WINTER, Circuit Judge:

[1] Wallace International Silversmiths ("Wallace") appeals from Judge Haight's denial of its motion for a preliminary injunction under Section 43(a) of the Lanham Act, 15 U.S.C. § 1125(a) (1988), prohibiting Godinger Silver Art Co., Inc. ("Godinger") from marketing a line of silverware with ornamentation that is substantially similar to Wallace's GRANDE BAROQUE line. Judge Haight held that the GRANDE BAROQUE design is "a functional feature of 'Baroque' style silverware" and thus not subject to protection as a trademark. We affirm.

BACKGROUND

[2] Wallace, a Delaware corporation, has sold sterling silver products for over one hundred years. Its GRANDE BAROQUE pattern was introduced in 1941 and is still one of the best-selling silverware lines in America. Made of fine sterling silver, a complete place setting costs several thousand dollars. Total sales of GRANDE BAROQUE silverware have exceeded fifty million dollars. The GRANDE BAROQUE pattern is fairly described as "ornate, massive and flowery [with] indented, flowery roots and scrolls and curls along the side of the shaft, and flower arrangements along the front of the shaft." Wallace owns a trademark registration for the GRANDE BAROQUE name as applied to sterling silver flatware and hollowware. The GRANDE BAROQUE design is not patented, but on December 11, 1989, Wallace filed an application for trademark registration for the GRANDE BAROQUE pattern. This application is still pending.

[3] Godinger, a New York corporation, is a manufacturer of silver-plated products. The company has recently begun to market a line of baroque-style silver-plated serving pieces. The suggested retail price of the set of four serving pieces is approximately twenty dollars. Godinger advertised its new line under the name 20TH CENTURY BAROQUE and planned to introduce it at the Annual New York Tabletop and Accessories Show, the principal industry trade show at which orders for the coming year are taken. Like Wallace's silverware, Godinger's pattern contains typical baroque elements including an indented root, scrolls, curls, and flowers. The arrangement of these elements approximates Wallace's design in

many ways, although their dimensions are noticeably different. The most obvious difference between the two designs is that the Godinger pattern extends further down the handle than the Wallace pattern does. The Wallace pattern also tapers from the top of the handle to the stem while the Godinger pattern appears bulkier overall and maintains its bulk throughout the decorated portion of the handle. Although the record does not disclose the exact circumstances under which Godinger's serving pieces were created, Godinger admits that its designers were "certainly inspired by and aware of [the Wallace] design when [they] created [the 20TH CENTURY BAROQUE] design."

[4] On the afternoon of April 23, 1990, Leonard Florence of Wallace learned from a wholesale customer, Michael C. Fina Company, that Godinger had placed an advertisement for its 20TH CENTURY BAROQUE serving pieces in an industry trade magazine. George Fina, the company's president, said that he was "confused" when he saw what he believed to be a pattern identical to GRANDE BAROQUE being advertised by another company. He asked Mr. Florence whether Wallace had licensed the design to Godinger or whether "the Godinger product was simply a 'knock-off.'" Two days after this conversation, Wallace filed the complaint in the instant matter stating various federal trademark and state unfair competition claims. Wallace also filed a motion for a temporary restraining order and sought a preliminary injunction prohibiting Godinger from using the mark 20TH CENTURY BAROQUE or infringing the trade dress of Wallace's GRANDE BAROQUE product.

[5] Due to the imminence of the trade show, the district court held a hearing on Wallace's application for preliminary relief the day after Wallace had filed its complaint. The record consisted of affidavits from Florence and Fina reciting the facts described *supra,* samples of the Wallace and Godinger pieces, and various photographs and catalogue illustrations of silverware from other manufacturers. Later that day, Judge Haight issued a Memorandum Opinion and Order in which he concluded that the GRANDE BAROQUE design was a "functional" feature of baroque-style silverware and thus ineligible for trade dress protection under Section 43(a) of the Lanham Act.

. . . .

[6] Judge Haight found that the similarities between the Godinger and Wallace designs involved elements common to all baroque-style designs used in the silverware market. He noted that many manufacturers compete in that market with such designs and found that "[t]he 'Baroque' curls, roots and flowers are not 'mere indicia of source.' Instead, they are requirements to compete in the silverware market." Judge Haight concluded that "the 'Grande Baroque' design is a functional feature of 'Baroque' style silverware," relying on *Pagliero v. Wallace China Co.,* 198 F.2d 339 (9th Cir. 1952).

[7] Although we agree with Judge Haight's decision, we do not endorse his reliance upon *Pagliero.* That decision allowed a competitor to sell exact copies of china bearing a particular pattern without finding that comparably attractive patterns were not available to the competitor. It based its holding solely on the ground that the particular pattern was an important ingredient in the commercial success of the china. *Id.* at 343–44. We rejected *Pagliero* in *LeSportsac, Inc. v. K Mart Corp.,* 754 F.2d 71 (2d Cir. 1985), and reiterate that rejection here. Under *Pagliero,* the commercial success of an aesthetic feature automatically destroys all of the originator's trademark interest in it, notwithstanding the feature's secondary meaning and the lack of any evidence that competitors cannot develop non-infringing, attractive patterns. By allowing the copying of an exact design without any evidence of market foreclosure, the *Pagliero* test discourages both originators and later competitors from developing pleasing designs. *See Keene Corp. v. Paraflex Industries, Inc.,* 653 F.2d 822, 824–25 (3d Cir. 1981).

[8] Our rejection of *Pagliero,* however, does not call for reversal. Quite unlike *Pagliero,* Judge Haight found in the instant matter that there is a substantial market for baroque silverware and that effective competition in that market requires "use [of] essentially the same scrolls and flowers" as are found on Wallace's silverware. Based on the record at the hearing, that finding is not clearly erroneous and satisfies the requirement of *Stormy Clime Ltd. v. Progroup, Inc.,* 809 F.2d 971 (2d Cir. 1987), that a design feature not be given trade dress protection where use of that feature is necessary for effective competition. *Id.* at 976–77.

. . . .

[9] Our only hesitation in holding that the functionality doctrine applies is based on nomenclature. "Functionality" seems to us to imply only utilitarian considerations and, as a legal doctrine, to be intended only to prevent competitors from obtaining trademark protection for design features that are necessary to the use or efficient production of the product. *See Keene, supra* at 825 ("inquiry should focus on the extent to which the design feature is related to the utilitarian function of the product or feature"). Even when the doctrine is referred to as "aesthetic" functionality, it still seems an apt description only of pleasing designs of utilitarian features. Nevertheless, there is no lack of language in caselaw endorsing use of the defense of aesthetic functionality where trademark protection for purely ornamental features would exclude competitors from a market. *See, e.g., Rogers, supra* at 347 ("Though a producer does not lose a design trademark just because the public finds it pleasing, there may come a point where the design feature is so important to the value of the product to consumers that continued trademark protection would deprive them of competitive alternatives [.]") (Posner, J.) . . . .

[10] We put aside our quibble over doctrinal nomenclature, however, because we are confident that whatever secondary meaning Wallace's baroque silverware pattern may have acquired, Wallace may not exclude competitors from using those baroque design elements necessary to compete in the market for baroque silverware. It is a first principle of trademark law that an owner may not use the mark as a means of excluding competitors from a substantial market. Where a mark becomes the generic term to describe an article, for example, trademark protection ceases. 15 U.S.C. § 1064(3) (1988); *see Abercrombie & Fitch Co. v. Hunting World, Inc.,* 537 F.2d 4 (2d Cir. 1976). Where granting trademark protection to the use of certain colors would tend to exclude competitors, such protection is also limited. *See First Brands Corp. v. Fred Meyer, Inc.,* 809 F.2d 1378 (9th Cir. 1987); J. McCarthy, *Trademarks and Unfair Competition,* § 7:16 *et seq.* Finally, as discussed *supra,* design features of products that are necessary to the product's utility may be copied by competitors under the functionality doctrine.

[11] In the instant matter, Wallace seeks trademark protection, not for a precise expression of a decorative style, but for basic elements of a style that is part of the public domain. As found by the district court, these elements are important to competition in the silverware market. We perceive no distinction between a claim to exclude all others from use on silverware of basic elements of a decorative style and claims to generic names, basic colors or designs important to a product's utility. In each case, trademark protection is sought, not just to protect an owner of a mark in informing the public of the source of its products, but also to exclude competitors from producing similar products. We therefore abandon our quibble with the aesthetic functionality doctrine's nomenclature and adopt the Restatement's view that, where an ornamental feature is claimed as a trademark and trademark protection would significantly hinder competition by limiting the range of adequate alternative designs, the aesthetic functionality doctrine denies such protection. *See* Third Restatement of the Law, Unfair Competition (Preliminary Draft No. 3), Ch. 3, § 17(c) at 213–14. This rule avoids the overbreadth of *Pagliero* by requiring a finding of foreclosure of alternatives[2] while still ensuring that trademark protection does not exclude competitors from substantial markets.[3]

---

[2] The Restatement's Illustrations expressly reject *Pagliero.* Illustration 6 reads as follows:

> *A* manufactures china. Among the products marketed by *A* is a set of china bearing a particular "overall" pattern covering the entire upper surface of each dish. Evidence indicates that aesthetic factors play an important role in the purchase of china, that *A*'s design is attractive to a significant number of consumers, and that the number of alternative patterns is virtually unlimited. In the absence of evidence indicating that similarly attractive "overall" patterns are unavailable to competing manufacturers, *A*'s pattern design is not functional under the rule stated in this Section.

[3] Restatement Illustrations 7 and 8 reflect this aspect of the rule. They read as follows:

> 7. The facts being otherwise as stated in Illustration 6, *A*'s design consists solely of a thin gold band placed around the rim of each dish. Evidence indicates that a significant number

[12] Of course, if Wallace were able to show secondary meaning in a precise expression of baroque style, competitors might be excluded from using an identical or virtually identical design. In such a case, numerous alternative baroque designs would still be available to competitors. Although the Godinger design at issue here was found by Judge Haight to be "substantially similar," it is not identical or virtually identical, and the similarity involves design elements necessary to compete in the market for baroque silverware. Because according trademark protection to those elements would significantly hinder competitors by limiting the range of adequate alternative designs, we agree with Judge Haight's denial of a preliminary injunction.

Affirmed.

ii. Aesthetic Functionality and the Apparel Fashion Industry

In reading the excerpt below from *Christian Louboutin S.A. v. Yves Saint Laurent America Holding, Inc.*, 696 F.3d 206 (2d Cir. 2012), consider the following question:

- Perhaps the Second Circuit is correct that there should be no per se rule against the trademark protection of individual colors with respect to apparel, but should there at least be a *TrafFix*-like "strong presumption" against such protection?

- Many followers of the *Louboutin* case were quite surprised by the Second Circuit's resolution of the dispute. Do you think the court reached the right result?

Christian Louboutin S.A. v. Yves Saint Laurent America Holding, Inc.
696 F.3d 206, 218-228 (2d Cir. 2012)

{Since 1992, designer Christian Louboutin has painted the outsoles of his high-heeled women's shoes with a high-gloss red lacquer, specifically, Pantone 18-1663 TPX Chinese Red. In 2008, based on the secondary meaning he built up in the design, Plaintiff Christian Louboutin S.A. ("Louboutin") registered the red lacquered outsole as a trademark (see the registration certificate below). In 2011, defendant Yves Saint Laurent America Holding, Inc. ("YSL") began marketing a line of monochrome shoes in, among other colors, red. YSL's red monochrome shoe bore a red insole, heel, upper, and outsole. Louboutin sued, claiming infringement of its registered mark. The district court found that the mark was aesthetically functional and, according to the Second Circuit's reading, articulated a per se rule that a single color can never serve as a trademark in the fashion industry. Louboutin appealed. Excerpted below is the court's discussion of aesthetic functionality.}

---

of consumers prefer china decorated with only a gold rim band. Because the number of alternative designs available to satisfy the aesthetic desires of these prospective purchasers is extremely limited, the rim design is functional under the rule stated in this Section.

8. *A* is the first seller to market candy intended for Valentine's Day in heart-shaped boxes. . . .

Int. Cl.: 25

Prior U.S. Cls.: 22 and 39

United States Patent and Trademark Office   Reg. No. 3,361,597
Registered Jan. 1, 2008

**TRADEMARK
PRINCIPAL REGISTER**

CHRISTIAN LOUBOUTIN (FRANCE INDIVIDUAL)
24 RUE VICTOR MASSÉ
PARIS, FRANCE 75009

FOR: WOMEN'S HIGH FASHION DESIGNER FOOTWEAR, IN CLASS 25 (U.S. CLS. 22 AND 39).

FIRST USE 0-0-1992; IN COMMERCE 0-0-1992.

THE COLOR(S) RED IS/ARE CLAIMED AS A FEATURE OF THE MARK.

THE MARK CONSISTS OF A LACQUERED RED SOLE ON FOOTWEAR. THE DOTTED LINES ARE NOT PART OF THE MARK BUT ARE INTENDED ONLY TO SHOW PLACEMENT OF THE MARK.

SEC. 2(F).

SER. NO. 77-141,789, FILED 3-27-2007.

NORA BUCHANAN WILL, EXAMINING ATTORNEY

PER CURIAM:

. . . .

III. The "Functionality" Defense

[1] As the Supreme Court observed in *Qualitex*, aspects of a product that are "functional" generally "cannot serve as a trademark." *Id.* at 165. We have observed that "[t]he doctrine of functionality prevents trademark law from inhibiting legitimate competition by giving monopoly control to a producer over a useful product." *Nora Beverages, Inc.*, 269 F.3d at 120 n. 4; *see Genesee Brewing Co.*, 124 F.3d at 145 n. 5 (it is a "fundamental principle of trademark law that a trademark . . . does not grant a monopoly of production"). This is so because functional features can be protected only through the patent system, which grants a limited monopoly over such features until they are released into general use (typically after either 14 or 20 years, depending on the type of patent). *See Fabrication Enters., Inc.*, 64 F.3d at 58–59 & n. 4 ("The Lanham Act is not concerned with protecting innovation by giving the innovator a monopoly, which is the function of patent law.") . . . .

[2] As noted above, two forms of the functionality doctrine are relevant to us today: "traditional" or "utilitarian" functionality, and "aesthetic" functionality. Both forms serve as an affirmative defense to a trademark infringement claim.

177

A. "Traditional" or "Utilitarian" Functionality

[3] According to our traditional understanding of functionality, a product feature is considered to be "functional" in a utilitarian sense[11] if it is (1) "essential to the use or purpose of the article," or if it (2) "affects the cost or quality of the article." *Inwood Labs.,* 456 U.S. at 850 n. 10, 102 S.Ct. 2182. A feature is essential "'if [it] is dictated by the functions to be performed'" by the article. *LeSportsac, Inc. v. K mart Corp.,* 754 F.2d 71, 76 (2d Cir. 1985) (quoting *Warner Bros. Inc. v. Gay Toys Inc.,* 724 F.2d 327, 331 (2d Cir. 1983)).[13] It affects the cost or quality of the article where it "'permits the article to be manufactured at a lower cost' or 'constitutes an improvement in the operation of the goods.'"[14] *Id.* (quoting *Warner Bros., Inc.,* 724 F.2d at 331). A finding that a product feature is functional according to the *Inwood* test will ordinarily render the feature ineligible for trademark protection.

B. "Aesthetic Functionality"

[4] Generally, "[w]here [a product's] design is functional under the *Inwood* formulation there is no need to proceed further." *TrafFix Devices, Inc. v. Marketing Displays, Inc.,* 532 U.S. 23, 33 (2001) ("*TrafFix* "). Nevertheless, as the Supreme Court had held in 1995 in *Qualitex,* when the aesthetic design of a product is *itself* the mark for which protection is sought, we may also deem the mark functional if giving the markholder the right to use it exclusively "would put competitors at a significant non-reputation-related disadvantage," *Qualitex,* 514 U.S. at 165. This remains true even if there is "no indication that [the mark has] any bearing on the use or purpose of the product or its cost or quality." *TrafFix,* 532 U.S. at 33; *see Landscape Forms, Inc. v. Colum. Cascade Co.,* 70 F.3d 251, 253 (2d Cir. 1995) (when evaluating design trademarks we consider whether "certain features of the design are essential to effective competition in [the] particular market").

[5] As set forth below, the test for aesthetic functionality is threefold: At the start, we address the two prongs of the *Inwood* test, asking whether the design feature is either "essential to the use or purpose" or "affects the cost or quality" of the product at issue. Next, if necessary, we turn to a third prong, which is the competition inquiry set forth in *Qualitex.* In other words, if a design feature would, from a traditional utilitarian perspective, be considered "essential to the use or purpose" of the article, or to affect its cost or quality, then the design feature is functional under *Inwood* and our inquiry ends.[15] But if the design feature is not "functional" from a traditional perspective, it must still pass the fact-intensive *Qualitex* test and be shown not to have a significant effect on competition in order to receive trademark protection.

i. The Development of the Aesthetic Functionality Doctrine

---

[11] *See Wallace Int'l Silversmiths, Inc. v. Godinger Silver Art Co.,* 916 F.2d 76, 80 (2d Cir. 1990) (noting that the term "functionality" as commonly understood seems to imply "only utilitarian considerations").

[13] In *LeSportsac,* K Mart challenged the trade dress of a backpack composed of "parachute nylon and trimmed in cotton carpet tape with matching cotton-webbing straps. The zippers used to open and close the bags [we]re color coordinated with the bags themselves, and usually [we]re pulled with hollow rectangular metal sliders." *LeSportsac,* 754 F.2d at 74.

[14] In *Warner Brothers,* we cited as examples *Kellogg Co. v. National Biscuit Co.,* 305 U.S. 111, 122, 59 S.Ct. 109, 83 L.Ed. 73 (1938), in which the pillow shape of a shredded wheat biscuit was deemed functional because the cost of the cereal would be increased and its quality lessened by any other form, and *Fisher Stoves Inc. v. All Nighter Stove Works, Inc.,* 626 F.2d 193, 195 (1st Cir. 1980), in which a two-tier woodstove design was deemed functional because it improved the operation of the stove. *See Warner Bros., Inc.,* 724 F.2d at 331.

[15] *See, e.g., Industria Arredamenti Fratelli Saporiti v. Charles Craig, Ltd.,* 725 F.2d 18, 19 (2d Cir. 1984) (interlocking design of couch cushions was a visual "label" but served a utilitarian purpose by keeping cushions in place and was therefore functional).

[6] Although the theory of aesthetic functionality was proposed as early as 1938,[16] the first court to adopt the theory as the basis for denial of protection of a design was the United States Court of Appeals for the Ninth Circuit in *Pagliero v. Wallace China Co.*, 198 F.2d 339 (9th Cir. 1952)....

[7] Despite its apparent counterintuitiveness (how can the purely aesthetic be deemed functional, one might ask?), our Court has long accepted the doctrine of aesthetic functionality. *See, e.g., Warner Bros., Inc.*, 724 F.2d at 329–32 (distinctive color and symbols on toy car were not functional, and so were protectable as trade dress).[17] We have rejected, however, the circular "important ingredient" test formulated by the *Pagliero* court, which inevitably penalized markholders for their success in promoting their product.[18] Instead, we have concluded that "Lanham Act protection does not extend to configurations of ornamental features which would *significantly* limit the range of competitive designs available." *Coach Leatherware Co. v. AnnTaylor, Inc.*, 933 F.2d 162, 171 (2d Cir. 1991) (emphasis added). Accordingly, we have held that the doctrine of aesthetic functionality bars protection of a mark that is "necessary to compete in the [relevant] market." *Villeroy & Boch Keramische Werke K.G. v. THC Sys., Inc.*, 999 F.2d 619, 622 (2d Cir. 1993).

ii. A Modern Formulation of the Aesthetic Functionality Doctrine

[8] In 1995, the Supreme Court in *Qualitex* gave its imprimatur to the aesthetic functionality doctrine, holding that "[t]he ultimate test of aesthetic functionality ... is whether the recognition of trademark rights [in an aesthetic design feature] would significantly hinder competition." *Qualitex*, 514 U.S. at 170 (quoting Restatement (Third) of Unfair Competition § 17, cmt. c, at 176 (1993)) (internal quotation marks omitted). Six years later, reiterating its *Qualitex* analysis, the Supreme Court in *TrafFix* declared that where "[a]esthetic functionality [is] the central question," courts must "inquire" as to whether recognizing the trademark "would put competitors at a significant non-reputation-related disadvantage." *TrafFix*, 532 U.S. at 32–33.

---

[16] In 1938, the Restatement of Torts stated that "[a] feature of goods is functional ... if it affects their purpose, action or performance, or the facility or economy of processing, handling or using them; it is non-functional if it does not have any of such effects." Restatement of Torts § 742 (1938). In the official comment to that Section, the Restatement explained several ways in which goods or their features might be functional. With regard to "goods [that] are bought largely for their aesthetic value," the Restatement suggested that "their features may be functional because they definitely contribute to that value and thus aid the performance of an object for which the goods are intended." *Id.* § 742, cmt. a. This was the first time that a commentator had proposed that an aesthetic product feature might be functional. *See* 1 McCarthy on Trademarks § 7:79 (4th ed.).

[17] The doctrine of aesthetic functionality remains controversial in our sister circuits, which have applied the doctrine in varying ways (and some not at all). For example, the Seventh Circuit has applied the doctrine of aesthetic functionality liberally, holding that "[f]ashion is a form of function." *See Jay Franco & Sons, Inc. v. Franek*, 615 F.3d 855, 860 (7th Cir. 2010). The Sixth Circuit recently discussed the doctrine, but made clear that it has not yet decided whether or not to adopt it. *See Maker's Mark Distillery, Inc. v. Diageo N. Am., Inc.*, 679 F.3d 410, 417–19 (6th Cir. 2012). The Ninth Circuit has applied the doctrine inconsistently. *See* 1 McCarthy on Trademarks § 7:80 (4th ed.) (collecting cases). The Fifth Circuit rejects the doctrine of aesthetic functionality entirely. *Bd. of Supervisors for La. State Univ. Agric. & Mech. Coll. v. Smack Apparel Co.*, 550 F.3d 465, 487–88 (5th Cir. 2008) (arguing that the Supreme Court has recognized the aesthetic functionality doctrine only in *dicta*, and that therefore the Fifth Circuit's long-standing rejection of the doctrine was not abrogated by *Qualitex* and *TrafFix*).

[18] *See Wallace Int'l Silversmiths*, 916 F.2d at 80 ("We rejected *Pagliero*['s 'important ingredient' formulation] in [*Le*]*Sportsac* and reiterate that rejection here." (internal citation omitted)); Mark P. McKenna, *(Dys)functionality*, 48 Hous. L.Rev. 823, 851 (2011) ("Courts that apply the aesthetic functionality doctrine today overwhelmingly rely on the test the Supreme Court endorsed in *TrafFix* [rather than the *Pagliero* test], ... asking whether exclusive use of the claimed feature put competitors at a significant non-reputation-related disadvantage.").

[9] Although we have not recently had occasion to apply the doctrine of aesthetic functionality thus enunciated by the Supreme Court, it is clear that the combined effect of *Qualitex* and *TrafFix* was to validate the aesthetic functionality doctrine as it had already been developed by this Court in cases including *Wallace International Silversmiths, Stormy Clime,* and *LeSportsac. See Yurman Design, Inc.,* 262 F.3d at 116 (confirming, five months after the *TrafFix* decision, that a putative design trademark is "aesthetic[ally] functional[ ]," and therefore barred from trademark protection, if granting "the right to use [the mark] exclusively 'would put competitors at a significant non-reputation-related disadvantage'" (quoting *TrafFix,* 532 U.S. at 32)).

[10] On the one hand, "'[w]here an ornamental feature is claimed as a trademark and trademark protection would significantly hinder competition by limiting the range of adequate alternative designs, the aesthetic functionality doctrine denies such protection.'" *Forschner Grp., Inc. v. Arrow Trading Co.,* 124 F.3d 402, 409–10 (2d Cir. 1997) (quoting *Wallace Int'l Silversmiths, Inc.,* 916 F.2d at 81). But on the other hand, "'distinctive and arbitrary arrangements of predominantly ornamental features that do *not* hinder potential competitors from entering the same market with differently dressed versions of the product are non-functional[,] and [are] hence eligible for [trademark protection].'" *Fabrication Enters., Inc.,* 64 F.3d at 59 (quoting *Stormy Clime,* 809 F.2d at 977) (emphasis added).

[11] In short, a mark is aesthetically functional, and therefore ineligible for protection under the Lanham Act, where protection of the mark *significantly* undermines competitors' ability to compete in the relevant market. *See Knitwaves, Inc. v. Lollytogs Ltd.,* 71 F.3d 996, 1006 (2d Cir. 1995) (linking aesthetic functionality to availability of alternative designs for children's fall-themed sweaters); *Landscape Forms, Inc.,* 70 F.3d at 253 (holding that "in order for a court to find a product design functional, it must first find that certain features of the design are essential to effective competition in a particular market"). In making this determination, courts must carefully weigh "the competitive benefits of protecting the source-identifying aspects" of a mark against the "competitive costs of precluding competitors from using the feature." *Fabrication Enters., Inc.,* 64 F.3d at 59.

[12] Finally, we note that a product feature's successful source indication can sometimes be difficult to distinguish from the feature's aesthetic function, if any. *See, e.g., Jay Franco & Sons, Inc. v. Franek,* 615 F.3d 855, 857 (7th Cir. 2010) (noting that "[f]iguring out which designs [produce a benefit other than source identification] can be tricky"). Therefore, in determining whether a mark has an aesthetic function so as to preclude trademark protection, we take care to ensure that the mark's very success in denoting (and promoting) its source does not itself defeat the markholder's right to protect that mark. *See Wallace Int'l Silversmiths, Inc.,* 916 F.2d at 80 (rejecting argument that "the commercial success of an aesthetic feature automatically destroys all of the originator's trademark interest in it, notwithstanding the feature's secondary meaning and the lack of any evidence that competitors cannot develop non-infringing, attractive patterns").

[13] Because aesthetic function and branding success can sometimes be difficult to distinguish, the aesthetic functionality analysis is highly fact-specific. In conducting this inquiry, courts must consider both the markholder's right to enjoy the benefits of its effort to distinguish its product and the public's right to the "vigorously competitive market [ ]" protected by the Lanham Act, which an overly broad trademark might hinder. *Yurman Design, Inc.,* 262 F.3d at 115 (internal quotation mark omitted). In sum, courts must avoid jumping to the conclusion that an aesthetic feature is functional merely because it denotes the product's desirable source. *Cf. Pagliero,* 198 F.2d at 343.

iii. Aesthetic Functionality in the Fashion Industry

[14] We now turn to the *per se* rule of functionality for color marks in the fashion industry adopted by the District Court—a rule that would effectively deny trademark protection to any deployment of a single color in an item of apparel. As noted above, the *Qualitex* Court expressly held that "sometimes [ ] a color will meet ordinary legal trademark requirements[, a]nd, when it does so, no special legal rule prevents color alone from serving as a trademark." *Qualitex,* 514 U.S. at 161, 115 S.Ct. 1300. In other words, the Supreme Court specifically forbade the implementation of a *per se* rule that would deny protection for the use of a single color as a trademark in a particular industrial context. *Qualitex* requires

an individualized, fact-based inquiry into the nature of the trademark, and cannot be read to sanction an industry-based *per se* rule. The District Court created just such a rule, on the theory that "there is something unique about the fashion world that militates against extending trademark protection to a single color." *Louboutin,* 778 F.Supp.2d at 451.

[15] Even if *Qualitex* could be read to permit an industry-specific *per se* rule of functionality (a reading we think doubtful), such a rule would be neither necessary nor appropriate here. We readily acknowledge that the fashion industry, like other industries, has special concerns in the operation of trademark law; it has been argued forcefully that United States law does not protect fashion design adequately.[19] Indeed, the case on appeal is particularly difficult precisely because, as the District Court well noted, in the fashion industry, color can serve as a tool in the palette of a designer, rather than as mere ornamentation. *Louboutin,* 778 F.Supp.2d at 452–53.

[16] Nevertheless, the functionality defense does not guarantee a competitor "the greatest range for [his] creative outlet," *id.* at 452–53, but only the ability to fairly compete within a given market.[20] *See*

---

[19] The intellectual property protection of fashion design has been for years a subject of controversy among commentators. Some have proposed working within the confines of the current intellectual property system, while others have advocated that fashion design may be an appropriate area for *sui generis* statutory protection. *See generally* C. Scott Hemphill & Jeannie Suk, *The Law, Culture, and Economics of Fashion,* 61 Stan. L.Rev. 1147 (2009); *see also id.* at 1184–90. (Indeed, suggested legislation creating such protection has been considered several times by Congress, although not adopted. *See, e.g.,* Design Piracy Prohibition Act, H.R. 2033, 110th Cong. § 2(c) (2007); Design Piracy Prohibition Act, S. 1957, 110th Cong. § 2(c) (2007).) Still other commentators have suggested that intellectual property protection of fashion design would be damaging to the industry and should be avoided. *See* Kal Raustiala & Christopher Sprigman, *The Piracy Paradox: Innovation and Intellectual Property in Fashion Design,* 92 Va. L.Rev. 1687, 1775–77 (2006).

It is arguable that, in the particular circumstances of this case, the more appropriate vehicle for the protection of the Red Sole Mark would have been copyright rather than trademark. *See generally Kieselstein–Cord v. Accessories by Pearl, Inc.,* 632 F.2d 989, 993–94 (2d Cir. 1980) (addressing the broad issue of aesthetically functional copyrights and holding that decorative belt buckles that were used principally for ornamentation could be copyrighted because the primary ornamental aspect of the buckles was conceptually separate from their subsidiary utilitarian function); Laura A. Heymann, *The Trademark/Copyright Divide,* 60 SMU L.Rev. 55 (2007). However, because Louboutin has chosen to rely on the law of trademarks to protect his intellectual property, we necessarily limit our review to that body of law and do not further address the broad and complex issue of fashion design protection.

[20] The trademark system, in this way, stands in sharp contrast to the copyright system. Copyright, unlike trademark, rewards creativity and originality even if they interfere with the rights of an existing copyright holder. In the copyright system there is a defense to infringement known as "independent creation": if a writer or musician, through the creative process, independently arrives at an arrangement of words or notes that is the subject of a copyright, he may market the result of his creativity despite the existing copyright. *See Feist Publ'ns, Inc. v. Rural Tel. Serv. Co.,* 499 U.S. 340, 346, 111 S.Ct. 1282, 113 L.Ed.2d 358 (1991) (requesting that the reader "assume that two poets, each ignorant of the other, compose identical poems. Neither work is novel, yet both are original and, hence, copyrightable"); *Procter & Gamble Co. v. Colgate–Palmolive Co.,* 199 F.3d 74, 77–78 (2d Cir. 1999). The trademark system, unlike the copyright system, aims to prevent consumer confusion even at the expense of a manufacturer's creativity: in trademark, if a branding specialist produces a mark that is identical to one already trademarked by another individual or corporation, he must "go back to the drawing board." *See Blendco, Inc. v. Conagra Foods, Inc.,* 132 Fed.Appx. 520, 523 (5th Cir. 2005) (although defendant's allegedly independent creation of infringing mark tended to show that infringement was not willful, defendant remained liable for damages); *Tuccillo v. Geisha NYC, LLC,* 635 F.Supp.2d 227 (E.D.N.Y. 2009) (same).

Wallace Int'l Silversmiths, Inc., 916 F.2d at 81 ("It is a first principle of trademark law that an owner may not use the mark as a means of *excluding* competitors from a … market." (emphasis added)). The purpose of the functionality defense "is to prevent advances in functional design from being *monopolized by the owner of* [the mark] … in order to encourage competition and the broadest dissemination of useful design features." *Fabrication Enters., Inc.,* 64 F.3d at 58 (internal quotation marks omitted) (emphasis added).

[17] In short, "[b]y focusing upon hindrances to legitimate competition, the [aesthetic] functionality test, carefully applied, can accommodate consumers' somewhat conflicting interests in being assured enough product differentiation to avoid confusion as to source and in being afforded the benefits of competition among producers." *Stormy Clime,* 809 F.2d at 978–79.

. . . .

IV. The Red Sole Mark

[18] Having determined that no per se rule governs the protection of single-color marks in the fashion industry, any more than it can do so in any other industry, we turn our attention to the Red Sole Mark. As we have explained, Part II.A, *ante,* we analyze a trademark infringement claim in two stages, asking first whether the mark "merits protection" and, second, whether the allegedly infringing use of the mark (or a similar mark) is "likely to cause consumer confusion." *Louis Vuitton Malletier,* 454 F.3d at 115. The functionality defense (including the tripartite aesthetic functionality test) is an affirmative defense that we consider at the second stage of this analysis. *Stormy Clime, Ltd.,* 809 F.2d at 974.

. . . .

[19] Although, as set forth below, we determine that the Mark as it currently stands is ineligible for protection insofar as it would preclude competitors' use of red outsoles in all situations, including the monochromatic use now before us, we conclude that the Mark has acquired secondary meaning—and thus the requisite "distinctness" to merit protection—when used as a red outsole contrasting with the remainder of the shoe. Because in this case we determine that the Red Sole Mark merits protection only as modified, and because YSL's use of a red outsole on monochromatic red shoes does not infringe on the Mark as modified, we need not, and do not, reach the issues of customer confusion and functionality at the second stage of the trademark infringement analysis described above.

A. Distinctiveness

. . . .

[20] We further hold that the record fails to demonstrate that the secondary meaning of the Red Sole Mark extends to uses in which the sole *does not* contrast with the upper—in other words, when a red sole is used on a monochromatic red shoe. As the District Court observed, "[w]hen Hollywood starlets cross red carpets and high fashion models strut down runways, and heads turn and eyes drop to the celebrities' feet, lacquered red outsoles on *high-heeled, black shoes* flaunt a glamorous statement that *pops out* at once." *Louboutin,* 778 F.Supp.2d at 448 (emphasis added). As clearly suggested by the District Court, it is the *contrast* between the sole and the upper that causes the sole to "pop," and to distinguish its creator.

[21] The evidentiary record further demonstrates that the Louboutin mark is closely associated with contrast. For example, Pinault, the chief executive of YSL's parent company, wrote that the "distinctive signature" of the Mark is in its "contrast with the general presentation of the [shoe], particularly its upper." Joint App'x 529. Of the hundreds of pictures of Louboutin shoes submitted to the District Court, only *four* were monochrome red. *Compare id.* 19, 415, 438, 587 (depicting monochrome Louboutin shoes), *with id.* 415–27, 431–47, 593–653, 680–724 (photographs and news articles depicting Louboutin shoes). And Louboutin's own consumer surveys show that when consumers were shown the YSL monochrome red shoe, of those consumers who misidentified the pictured shoes as Louboutin-made, nearly every one cited the red *sole* of the shoe, rather than its general red color. We conclude, based upon the record before us, that Louboutin has not established secondary meaning in an application of a red sole to a red shoe, but *only* where the red sole contrasts with the "upper" of the shoe. The use of a red lacquer on the outsole of a red shoe of the same color is not a use of the Red Sole Mark.

[22] Because we conclude that the secondary meaning of the mark held by Louboutin extends only to the use of a lacquered red outsole that contrasts with the adjoining portion of the shoe, we modify the Red Sole Mark, pursuant to Section 37 of the Lanham Act, 15 U.S.C. § 1119,[26] insofar as it is sought to be applied to any shoe bearing the same color "upper" as the outsole. We therefore instruct the Director of the Patent and Trade Office to limit the registration of the Red Sole Mark to only those situations in which the red lacquered outsole contrasts in color with the adjoining "upper" of the shoe. *See id.*

[23] In sum, we hold that the Red Sole Mark is valid and enforceable as modified. This holding disposes of the Lanham Act claims brought by both Louboutin and YSL because the red sole on YSL's monochrome shoes is neither a use of, nor confusingly similar to, the Red Sole Mark. We therefore affirm the denial of the preliminary injunction insofar as Louboutin could not have shown a likelihood of success on the merits in the absence of an infringing use of the Red Sole Mark by YSL.

B. Likelihood of Confusion and Functionality

[24] Having limited the Red Sole Mark as described above, and having established that the red sole used by YSL is not a use of the Red Sole Mark, it is axiomatic that we need not—and should not—address either the likelihood of consumer confusion or whether the modified Mark is functional.

. . . .

Comments and Questions

1.   *Are Louboutin's and YSL's shoes nevertheless confusingly similar?*   The Second Circuit's resolution of the dispute was unconventional, to say the least. Given the secondary meaning of Louboutin's mark, do you think the court was justified in finding, without analysis, that there would be no consumer confusion as to source between Louboutin's shoes bearing a red outsole with contrasting upper and YSL's shoes bearing both a red outsole and red upper?

2.   *Trademark placement.* Would granting one producer exclusive trademark rights in entirely red shoes put competitors at a significant non-reputation-related disadvantage? What about granting one producer exclusive trademark rights only in an entirely red upper? Why is an outsole different? Is this a case just about color or about color and the placement of the mark? On the importance of where a trademark is placed to how consumers perceive the trademark, see Thomas R. Lee, Eric D. DeRosia, & Glenn L. Christensen, *An Empirical and Consumer Psychology Analysis of Trademark Distinctiveness*, 41 ARIZ. ST. L.J. 1033 (2009). *See also* Mark A. Lemley & Mark P. McKenna, *Trademark Spaces and Trademark Law's Secret Step Zero*, 75 STAN. L. REV. 1 (2023) (discussing "locations that consumers are likely to assume are serving as trademarks").

2.   Deceptive and Deceptively Misdescriptive Marks

Lanham Act § 2; 15 U.S.C. § 1052

> No trademark by which the goods of the applicant may be distinguished from the goods of others shall be refused registration on the principal register on account of its nature unless it–
>
> (a) Consists of or comprises . . . deceptive . . . matter . . .
>
> . . . .
>
> (e) Consists of a mark which (1) when used on or in connection with the goods of the applicant is merely descriptive or deceptively misdescriptive of them, . . . (3) when used

---

[26] 15 U.S.C. § 1119 provides that "[i]n any action involving a registered mark the court may determine the right to registration, order the cancellation of registrations, *in whole or in part,* restore canceled registrations, and otherwise rectify the register with respect to the registrations of any party to the action. Decrees and orders shall be certified by the court to the Director, who shall make appropriate entry upon the records of the Patent and Trademark Office, and shall be controlled thereby." (emphasis added).

on or in connection with the goods of the applicant is primarily geographically deceptively misdescriptive of them.

(f) Except as expressly excluded in subsections (a), (b), (c), (d), (e)(3), and (e)(5) of this section, nothing in this chapter shall prevent the registration of a mark used by the applicant which has become distinctive of the applicant's goods in commerce. . . .

In determining whether marks are "deceptive" or "deceptively misdescriptive" with respect to the goods to which they are affixed, U.S. trademark law analyzes geographic marks (i.e., marks that convey a geographic meaning) differently from how it analyzes non-geographic marks. Before turning to the peculiar manner in which the law treats geographically deceptive or "primarily geographically deceptively misdescriptive" marks, Lanham Act § 2(e)(3), 15 U.S.C. § 1052(e)(3), we first consider the law's more straightforward analysis of the deceptiveness or deceptive misdescriptiveness of non-geographic marks.

a. *Non-Geographic* Deceptive and Deceptively Misdescriptive Marks

A non-geographic deceptive trademark cannot be registered or otherwise protected under federal trademark law. *See* Lanham Act § 2(a), 15 U.S.C. § 1052(a). By contrast, a non-geographic "deceptively misdescriptive" mark may be registered or otherwise protected under federal trademark law, but only if the mark is shown to have developed secondary meaning as a designation of source. *See* Lanham Act §§ 2(e)(1) & 2(f), 15 U.S.C. §§ 1052(e)(1) & 2(f).

The basic test for determining whether a non-geographic mark is deceptive or deceptively misdescriptive is relatively straightforward. In *In re Budge Mfg. Co.*, 857 F.2d 773 (Fed. Cir. 1988), the Federal Circuit affirmed the TTAB's refusal to register the mark LOVEE LAMB for automobile seat covers that were not in fact made of lambskin on the ground that the mark was deceptive. In doing so, it established a three-step test for determining whether a mark is deceptive or deceptively misdescriptive. The TMEP summarizes the three steps as follows:

> (1) Is the term misdescriptive of the character, quality, function, composition or use of the goods?
>
> (2) If so, are prospective purchasers likely to believe that the misdescription actually describes the goods?
>
> (3) If so, is the misdescription likely to affect a significant portion of the relevant consumers' decision to purchase?

TMEP § 1203.02(b). If the answer to each question is yes, then the mark is deceptive under Section 2(a) and cannot be protected. If the answer to question (2) is yes (consumers would likely believe that the misdescription actually describes the goods), but the answer to question (3) is no (the misdescription would nevertheless not affect their decision to purchase), then the mark is deceptively misdescriptive under Section 2(e)(1) and can be protected upon a showing of secondary meaning. (And if the answer to question (2) is no, then the mark is likely arbitrary and thus inherently distinctive—e.g. DIAMOND pencils).

Thus, for non-geographic marks, the question of whether the mark's misdescription would be material to consumers' decisions to purchase the good is what separates an unprotectable deceptive mark from a potentially protectable deceptively misdescriptive mark. This can be a difficult question to answer. The TMEP instructs trademark examining attorneys to focus on "objective criteria" such as whether the misdescription conveys superior quality, enhanced performance or function, difference in price, health benefits, or conformity with meritorious religious practice or social policy. See TMEP § 1203.02(d)(i). The Federal Circuit has emphasized that the misdescription must be material to a "significant portion of relevant consumers." *See In re Spirits Intern., N.V.*, 563 F.3d 1347, 1356 (Fed. Cir. 2009).

Examples of non-geographic marks found to be deceptive:

- *In re White Jasmine LLC*, 106 USPQ2d 1385 (TTAB 2013) (finding the term "white" in WHITE JASMINE to be deceptive for tea that did not include white tea, where "[t]he evidence establishes that consumers perceive that white tea has desirable health benefits. Thus, the misdescription is material to consumers interested in purchasing or drinking white tea to obtain these health benefits, and is likely to induce such purchasers to buy or drink the tea.")

- *In re Phillips-Van Heusen Corp.*, 63 USPQ2d 1047 (TTAB 2002) (finding SUPER SILK to be deceptive for clothing made of "silk-like" fabric, even where labeling indicated true fiber content of fabric).

- *In re Shapely, Inc.*, 231 USPQ 72 (TTAB 1986) (holding SILKEASE deceptive for clothing not made of silk, even where hangtag claimed that the product has "the look and feel of the finest silks with the easy care of polyester").

- *In re Organik Technologies, Inc.*, 41 USPQ2d 1690 (TTAB 1997) (holding ORGANIK deceptive for clothing and textiles made from cotton that is neither from an organically grown plant nor free of chemical processing or treatment).

Examples of non-geographic marks found to be deceptively misdescriptive:

- *Gold Seal Co. v. Weeks*, 129 F. Supp. 928 (D.D.C. 1955) (affirming TTAB's finding GLASS WAX to be deceptively misdescriptive for glass cleaner where "[t]he evidence does not show that the public has been influenced to purchase the product on account of believing that it contained wax, or that the product was simply a wax to be placed upon glass.").

- *In re Berman Bros. Harlem Furniture Inc.*, 26 U.S.P.Q.2d 1514 (TTAB 1993) (affirming examiner's determination that FURNITURE MAKERS was deceptively misdescriptive for a retail furniture store that sells, but does not make furniture)

- *In re Christopher C. Hinton*, 116 U.S.P.Q.2d 1051 (TTAB 2015) (affirming examiner's determination that THCTea was deceptively misdescriptive for tea-based beverages not containing THC (tetrahydrocannabinol), the primary psychoactive ingredient in marijuana; TTAB repeatedly noted that the question of whether the mark was deceptive under Section 2(a) was not before it, since the examiner had stopped at a finding of deceptive misdescriptiveness under Section 2(e)(1))

b. *Geographic* Deceptive and Deceptively Misdescriptive Marks

While trademark law's analysis of the deceptive misdescriptiveness and deceptiveness of *non-geographic* marks is relatively uncomplicated, the same cannot be said about the law's analysis of the deceptive misdescriptiveness and deceptiveness of *geographic* marks. American trademark law devotes special attention to geographic marks primarily because many foreign trading partners have significant economic and cultural interests in preserving the exclusivity of their geographic names (such as CHAMPAGNE, CAMEMBERT, or PARMA). In trade negotiations, particularly those leading to the North American Free Trade Agreement of 1992, the Americans agreed to amend the Lanham Act so that geographic marks that were merely deceptively misdescriptive would be treated the same as geographic marks that were outright deceptive—specifically, geographic marks that were merely deceptively misdescriptive would be unregistrable regardless of whether they possessed secondary meaning. The mechanics of this change in the Lanham Act took the form, in essence, of amending Lanham Act § 2(f) to exclude geographically deceptively misdescriptive marks from that subsection's mechanism by which certain otherwise defective marks can be registered upon a showing of secondary meaning. *See* Lanham Act § 2(f), 15 U.S.C. § 1052(f) (providing that marks that fall under the provision of § 2(e)(3), in that they are "primarily geographically deceptively misdescriptive,"[1] do not qualify for registration upon a showing of secondary meaning).

---

[1] No one likes this statutory phrase "primarily geographically deceptively misdescriptive" from Section 2(e)(3), but we appear to be stuck with it. In her opinion in *In re Miracle Tuesday, LLC*, 695 F.3d 1339 (Fed. Cir. 2012), Judge O'Malley took pains to distance her own elegant prose from the statutory

Thus, we now have a scheme in which *non-geographic* marks that are merely deceptively misdescriptive can be registered upon a showing of secondary meaning while *geographic* marks that are merely deceptively misdescriptive cannot be registered, even if they possess secondary meaning. Meanwhile, any mark that is outright deceptive, be it non-geographic or geographic, is unregistrable. America's trading partners and perhaps even American trade negotiators at the time could be forgiven for having thought that the Americans had indeed made a significant trade concession, one that limited the ability of trademark applicants at the PTO to register even merely deceptively misdescriptive geographic terms.

Enter the Federal Circuit. In *In re California Innovations, Inc.* 329 F.3d 1334, 1336–1341 (Fed. Cir. 2003), the Federal Circuit reviewed the history of the amendment to the Lanham Act and reached the following conclusion: just as the Lanham Act now treats geographically deceptively misdescriptive terms and geographically deceptive terms the same way (neither is registrable under any circumstances), so the PTO should employ exactly the same test that it uses to determine if a geographic mark is outright deceptive under Lanham Act § 2(a) also to determine if a geographic mark is merely deceptively misdescriptive under Lanham Act § 2(e)(3). Specifically, a mark may be found to be geographically deceptively misdescriptive only if its misdescription is found to be material to consumers' decision to purchase. (Recall that materiality need not be shown for a *non-geographic* mark to be found deceptively misdescriptive.) *See also In re Miracle Tuesday LLC*, 695 F.3d 1339, 1343 (Fed. Cir. 2012); *In re Spirits Int'l, N.V.*, 563 F.3d 1347, 1350–54 (Fed. Cir. 2009).

In summarizing the current test for geographic deceptive misdescriptiveness (and geographic deceptiveness), the *Trademark Manual of Examining Procedure* states that a mark will be found to be geographically deceptively misdescriptive (or geographically deceptive) if:

> (1) The primary significance of the mark is a generally known geographic location;
>
> (2) The goods or services do not originate in the place identified in the mark;
>
> (3) Purchasers would be likely to believe that the goods or services originate in the geographic place identified in the mark; and
>
> (4) The misrepresentation would be a material factor in a significant portion of the relevant consumers' decision to buy the goods or use the services.

TMEP § 1210.05(b). The result is that if all four elements of this test are met, then the mark may be geographically deceptive, geographically deceptively misdescriptive, or both geographically deceptive and geographically deceptively misdescriptive. In any of these cases the mark is unprotectable. For marks not claiming use in commerce or acquired distinctiveness prior to December 8, 1993 (the date of enactment of the NAFTA Implementation Act), the PTO will typically issue a refusal based on Section 2(e)(3) and Section 2(a).[2] *See* TMEP § 1210.05(d).

---

language: "The phrase 'primarily geographically deceptively misdescriptive' is a statutory term of art in the trademark context; we neither take responsibility for nor endorse the split infinitives or absence of necessary commas its use in this opinion requires." *Id.* at 1342 n. 2. Where possible, this casebook will drop "primarily" and simply speak of "geographically deceptively misdescriptive" marks.

[2] The Gilson treatise explains why the difference between the two categories might matter:

> The test for determining whether a mark is deceptive under Section 2(a) is now the same as that for determining whether a mark is primarily geographically deceptively misdescriptive under Section 2(e)(3). The difference comes with respect to registrability: Geographically deceptive marks cannot be registered on either the Principal or Supplemental Register, while primarily geographically deceptively misdescriptive marks may be registered on the Principal Register if the marks became distinctive of the goods or services before December 8, 1993, and they may be registered on the Supplemental Register if they have been in use in commerce since before December 8, 1993.

GILSON § 2.03[4][c][3].

Consider the strange implications of the Federal Circuit's holding in *California Innovations*. Before the NAFTA amendments in 1993, geographically deceptively misdescriptive marks could be registered upon a showing of secondary meaning. The Americans then amended the Lanham Act to provide that any terms that qualify as geographically deceptively misdescriptive may not be registered. However, by adding a materiality requirement, *California Innovations* then made it much more difficult for terms to qualify as geographically deceptively misdescriptive. As a result, at least for certain marks, the U.S. has arguably adopted an even laxer standard for registration of geographically misdescriptive terms. If the misdescriptiveness of such terms is not material to the consumer's decision to purchase, then the term may be registrable, and now *without any need to show secondary meaning*. For if such terms are not geographically deceptively misdescriptive (because the materiality requirement is not satisfied), neither are they geographically descriptive, a status which would trigger the secondary meaning requirement. Instead, in the wake of *California Innovations*, it would appear that such terms are essentially suggestive or arbitrary, i.e., inherently distinctive. For a thorough discussion of this turn of events, *see* Robert Brauneis & Roger E. Schechter, *Geographic Trademarks and the Protection of Competitor Communication*, 96 TRADEMARK REP. 782 (2006).

Comments and Questions

1. *Synthesizing the Tests*. The tests for geographic descriptiveness, geographic deceptiveness, and geographic deceptive misdescriptiveness may appear quite complicated. Experience has shown that these tests distract the student from far more important issues in trademark law. To try to aid in understanding the tests, the flowchart below attempts to synthesize the tests into a series of questions.

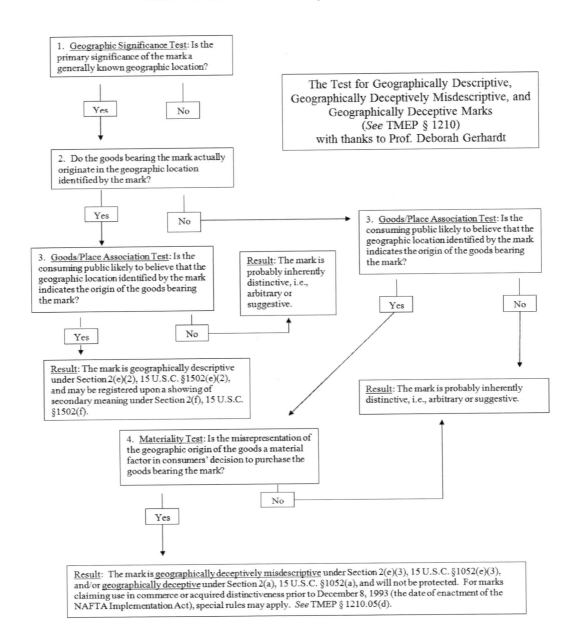

2. *Examples of marks held to be geographically deceptively misdescriptive.* There are many examples of marks held to be geographically deceptively misdescriptive. *See, e.g, In re Miracle Tuesday LLC*, 695 F3d 1339, 104 USPQ2d 1330 (Fed. Cir. 2012) (affirming the TTAB's refusal to register the composite mark consisting of JPK PARIS 75 and design as primarily geographically deceptively misdescriptive for apparel that did not originate in Paris; "Although [applicant's Miami-based designer] Mr. Klifa may still consider himself to be Parisian, the goods that applicant seeks to register are not because there is no current connection between the goods and Paris."); *In re Premiere Distillery, LLC*, 103 USPQ2d 1483 (TTAB 2012) (finding REAL RUSSIAN primarily geographically deceptively misdescriptive for vodka not made in Russia; "In view of this demonstrated fame and reputation of Russian vodka to the relevant public, we may infer that a substantial portion of consumers who encounter REAL RUSSIAN on applicant's vodka are likely to incorrectly believe that the vodka comes from Russia and that such mistaken belief would materially influence their decision to purchase the vodka"); *In re Compania de Licores Internacionales S.A.*, 102 USPQ2d 1841 (TTAB 2012) (finding OLD HAVANA primarily geographically deceptively misdescriptive for rum not made in Cuba); *Corporacion Habanos, S.A. v.*

Guantanamera Cigars Co., 102 USPQ2d 1085 (TTAB 2012) (finding GUANTANAMERA, a Spanish word literally meaning "girl from Guantanamo" or "of or from Guantanamo, Cuba," primarily geographically deceptively misdescriptive for cigars not made in Cuba).

3. *Example of a mark held not to be geographically deceptively misdescriptive*. For an example of a mark held not to be geographically deceptively misdescriptive, consider *In re Glaze Inc.*, Serial No. 76565437 (TTAB Mar. 17, 2005) (not citable as precedent). In *In re Glaze*, the applicant sought to register the mark SWISSCELL for batteries not made in Switzerland. The examing attorney refused registration and then the TTAB reversed. The Board found that because the mark incorporated the word "Swiss," the primary significance of the mark was a generally known geographic location. However, the Board found that consumers would not likely believe that the batteries originated in Switzerland:

> Even when we view the evidence that perhaps two Swiss companies make different type of batteries and that Switzerland is a country with a prosperous and stable market economy, we hold that, as in *California Innovations*, 66 USPQ2d at 1859, this is tenuous evidence that purchasers would expect batteries for lighting to come from Switzerland . . . .
>
> [H]ere the evidence of a goods/place association consists of a single battery company (Renata) and another company that makes vehicle batteries. Under the stricter *California Innovations* standards, we are constrained to find that the examining attorney has not established the required goods/place association between Switzerland and batteries for lighting.

Id. at *4. Finally, the Board found no evidence that the misrepresentation of the source of the batteries would influence consumers' decision to purchase them:

> The few references in the retailers' advertisements to "Swiss quality" and "Swiss manufacture" in relation to {another Swiss company's Swiss-made} batteries do not show that prospective purchasers' decisions would be materially influenced by the term "Swiss" when purchasing batteries for lighting . . . .
>
> The only other evidence that could indicate that the term "Swiss" may materially impact purchasing decisions is the nebulous references to "Swiss quality." There is simply insufficient evidence to hold that the term "Swiss" applied to virtually any product materially influences purchasers.

Id. at *4-5. Thus the mark was neither geographically descriptive nor geographically deceptively misdescriptive. Apparently, it therefore qualified as inherently distinctive.

3. Marks that May Falsely Suggest a Connection

Lanham Act § 2; 15 U.S.C. § 1052

> No trademark by which the goods of the applicant may be distinguished from the goods of others shall be refused registration on the principal register on account of its nature unless it–
>
> (a) Consists of or comprises . . . matter which may . . . falsely suggest a connection with persons, living or dead, institutions, beliefs, or national symbols . . . .
>
> . . . .
>
> (c) Consists of or comprises a name, portrait, or signature identifying a particular living individual except by his written consent, or the name, signature, or portrait of a deceased President of the United States during the life of his widow, if any, except by the written consent of the widow.

In re Nieves & Nieves LLC
113 U.S.P.Q.2d 1639 (TTAB 2015)

Opinion by Bergsman, Administrative Trademark Judge:

[1] Nieves & Nieves LLC ("Applicant") filed an intent-to-use application to register the mark ROYAL KATE, in standard character form, for the following goods as amended:

Cosmetics; fragrances; perfumes; . . . personal care products, namely, shampoo, body wash, conditioner, soap, shower gel, in Class 3;

Watches; cufflinks; key fobs of precious metals; jewelry; jewelry boxes, in Class 14;

Pouches, namely leather pouches, pouches for holding makeup, keys and other personal items; purses; handbags; pocketbooks; clutches; backpacks . . . in Class 18;

Bedding, namely, bed sheets . . . ; bath towels; towels, in Class 24; and

Apparel . . . ; bibs not of paper; cloth diapers, in Class 25.

The application includes a statement that "the name(s), portrait(s), and/or signature(s) shown in the mark does not identify a particular living individual."

[2] The Trademark Examining Attorney refused to register Applicant's mark under Section 2(a) of the Trademark Act of 1946, 15 U.S.C. § 1052(a), on the ground that ROYAL KATE falsely suggests a connection with Catherine, Duchess of Cambridge, also known as Kate Middleton. The Trademark Examining Attorney also refused to register Applicant's mark under Section 2(c) of the Trademark Act, 15 U.S.C. § 1052(c), on the ground that ROYAL KATE consists of a name identifying a particular living individual whose written consent to register the mark is not of record.

. . . .

II. Whether ROYAL KATE Falsely Suggests a Connection with Kate Middleton?

[3] To determine whether Applicant's ROYAL KATE mark falsely suggests a connection with Kate Middleton under Section 2(a), the Board analyzes whether the evidence of record satisfies the following four-part test:

(1)   Whether Applicant's mark ROYAL KATE is the same as or a close approximation of Kate Middleton's previously used name or identity;

(2)   Whether Applicant's mark ROYAL KATE would be recognized as such by purchasers, in that the mark points uniquely and unmistakably to Kate Middleton;

(3)   Whether Kate Middleton is not connected with the goods that will be sold by Applicant under its mark; and

(4)   Whether Kate Middleton's name or identity is of sufficient fame or reputation that when Applicant's mark is used on Applicant's goods, a connection with Kate Middleton would be presumed.

See In re Pedersen, 109 USPQ2d 1185, 1188 (TTAB 2013); *In re Jackson Int'l Trading Co.*, 103 USPQ2d 1417, 1419 (TTAB 2012). *See also Univ. of Notre Dame du Lac v. J.C. Gourmet Food Imports Co.*, 703 F.2d 1372, 217 USPQ 505, 509 (Fed. Cir. 1983) (hereinafter *"Notre Dame"*); *Bd. of Trs. of Univ. of Ala. v. Pitts*, 107 USPQ2d 2001, 2025 (TTAB 2013) (hereinafter *"Pitts"*).

A. Whether Applicant's mark ROYAL KATE is the same as or a close approximation of the name or identity of Kate Middleton?

[4] Applicant argues that ROYAL KATE is not a close approximation of Kate Middleton's previously-used name or identity because there is no evidence that Kate Middleton herself used ROYAL KATE as

190

her name or identity and because Kate Middleton is not officially a "royal."[1] Specifically, Applicant contends as follows:

> Although some may argue that ROYAL KATE may be reasonably understood as referring to Kate Middleton, Duchess of Cambridge, by some persons, it is not a close approximation of her name because ROYAL is not part of Middleton's name or title.

[5] We reject Applicant's interpretation of the first prong of the test as inappropriately narrowing the scope of Section 2(a). The creation of a false suggestion of a connection results from an applicant's use of something that is closely "associated with a particular personality or 'persona' of someone other than the applicant. *Notre Dame*, 217 USPQ at 509; *see also Pitts*, 107 USPQ2d at 2024. The reason for the statutory prohibition is that the person identified loses the right to control his/her identity. *Notre Dame*, 217 USPQ at 509 ("There may be no likelihood of such confusion as to the source of goods even under a theory of "sponsorship" or "endorsement," and, nevertheless, one's right of privacy, or the related right of publicity, may be violated.").

[6] The statutory false suggestion of a connection refusal emerged from the right to privacy and right of publicity.

> Evolving out of the rights of privacy and publicity, the false suggestion of a connection under § 2(a) of the Trademark Act was intended to preclude registration of a mark which conflicts with another's rights, even though not founded on the familiar test of likelihood of confusion. [*Notre Dame* 217 USPQ at 509]. An opposer may prevail on the false suggestion of a connection ground when its right to control the use of its identity is violated, even if the name claimed to be appropriated was never commercially exploited by the opposer as a trademark or in a manner analogous to trademark use. *See Notre Dame*, 703 F.2d at 1375, 217 USPQ at 508; *Buffett*, 226 USPQ at 429. *However, while a party's interest in its identity does not depend for its existence on the adoption and use of a technical trademark, a party must nevertheless have a protectable interest in a name (or its equivalent). Thus, we focus on the key factor in the false suggestion analysis for this case: whether applicants' mark is a close approximation of opposers' name or identity, i.e., a right in which opposers possess a protectable interest.*

Pitts, 107 USPQ2d at 2025 (emphasis supplied).

[7] The right of publicity has developed to protect the commercial interest of celebrities in their identities. Under this right, the celebrity has an interest that may be protected from the unauthorized commercial exploitation of that identity. If the celebrity's identity is commercially exploited without the consent of the celebrity, there has been an invasion of his/her right, regardless of whether his/her "name or likeness" is used. *Cf. Carson v. Here's Johnny Portable Toilets, Inc.*, 698 F.2d 831, 218 USPQ 1, 4 (6th Cir. 1983) (former late night television personality Johnny Carson's identity may be exploited even if his name or likeness is not used).

[8] The evidence reflects that Kate Middleton is a celebrity. That means her identity has value which the § 2(a) false suggestion refusal is intended to protect. *See Notre Dame*, 217 USPQ at 509 ("It is a right of this nature [that is, the right to privacy or right to publicity], a right to control the use of one's identity, which the University also asserts under § 2(a)."). Therefore, it is the right of publicity basis for the false suggestion of a connection refusal that applies in this case.

---

[1] "Royal" is defined, inter alia, as "of or pertaining to a king, queen, other sovereign" and informally as "a royal person; member of the royalty," or "a member of England's royal family." *The Random House Dictionary of the English Language (Unabridged)*, p. 1677 (2nd ed. 1977). The Board may take judicial notice of dictionary definitions., Univ. of Notre Dame du Lac v. J.C. Gourmet Food Imp. Co., 213 USPQ 594 (TTAB 1982), aff'd, 703 F.2d 1372, 217 USPQ 505 (Fed. Cir. 1983). See also Dictionary.com attached to the October 27, 2011 Office Action.

[9] The fact that Kate Middleton, the Duchess of Cambridge, has never used ROYAL KATE as her name or identity does not obviate the false suggestion of a connection refusal. A term may be considered the identity of a person even if his or her name or likeness is not used. All that is required is that the mark sought to be registered clearly identifies a specific person (*i.e.*, Kate Middleton). . . . *See also In re Urbano*, 51 USPQ2d 1776, 1779 (TTAB 1999) ("[W]hile the general public in the United States may or may not have seen the upcoming Olympic games referred to precisely as 'Sydney 2000,' we have no doubt that the general public in the United States would recognize this phrase as referring unambiguously to the upcoming Olympic Games in Sydney, Australia, in the year 2000.").

[10] We take this opportunity to make explicit what was implicit in our prior decisions in *Pitts* and *In re Urbano*, 51 USPQ2d 1776 (TTAB 1999): the first prong of the false suggestion of a connection test inquires into whether applicant's mark is the same as or a close approximation of the name or identity of a particular person other than the applicant, whether or not the person actually "used" the name or identity himself or herself. . . . Therefore, in this case, we examine the evidence of record to determine whether it establishes that Applicant's mark ROYAL KATE would be understood by the relevant public as identifying Kate Middleton.

[11] As noted above, the term "royal" refers to a member of the England's royal family. The mark ROYAL KATE creates a commercial impression that references Kate Middleton as a member of the royal family. This is corroborated by articles in the media referencing Kate Middleton as a "royal." . . . .

[12] In fact, Kate Middleton is referred to as "Her Royal Highness." Applicant submitted an excerpt from "The official website of The British Monarchy" (royal.gov.uk) which references Kate Middleton as "her Royal Highness." . . . .

[13] The Trademark Examining Attorney submitted numerous examples of media coverage referring to Kate Middleton as ROYAL KATE. . . .

[14] This evidence is sufficient to establish that the mark ROYAL KATE is a close approximation of the identity of Kate Middleton because American media uses the term ROYAL KATE to identify Kate Middleton and, therefore, the American public receives media reports identifying Kate Middleton as ROYAL KATE. In fact, because the American public receives reports that Kate Middleton will be referred to as Her Royal Highness the Duchess of Cambridge, there is a natural association between the mark ROYAL KATE and Kate Middleton regardless of whether she uses that moniker herself. *See Bd. of Trustees of the Univ. of Ala. v. BAMA-Werke Curt Baumann*, 231 USPQ 408 (TTAB 1986) ("BAMA" uniquely pointed to the identity of the University of Alabama even though the school had not adopted it as a trademark and had only sporadically referred to itself as BAMA, in large part due to the public's association of the term with the school).

B. Whether Applicant's mark ROYAL KATE would be recognized as a close approximation of Kate Middleton's identity by purchasers, in that the mark points uniquely and unmistakably to Kate Middleton?

[15] Applicant is seeking to register its mark for fashion products such as cosmetics, jewelry, handbags, bedding and clothing and Applicant characterized these products as "luxury items and home goods." The goods and services themselves serve, if anything, to reinforce that the Mark uniquely and unmistakably points to Kate Middleton. Kate Middleton, by virtue of her being a member of the British Royal family and wife of Prince William, the second in line to the English throne, has become a fashion trendsetter. As the evidence establishes, the media reports what she is wearing, where she goes and what she purchases . . . .

[16] . . . Applicant has not come forward with any evidence that the name ROYAL KATE refers to anyone other than Kate Middleton.

C. Whether Kate Middleton is connected with the goods that are sold or will be sold by Applicant under its mark?

[17] Applicant acknowledges that Kate Middleton is not connected with the goods that are or will be sold by Applicant under the mark ROYAL KATE, and that Kate Middleton has not consented to Applicant's use of her persona.

D. Whether Kate Middleton's name or identity is of sufficient fame or reputation that when Applicant's mark ROYAL KATE is used on Applicant's goods, a connection with Kate Middleton would be presumed?

[18] ... The evidence discussed in Section B ... demonstrates that Kate Middleton's identity is of sufficient renown that when Applicant's mark ROYAL KATE is used in connection with Applicant's goods, a connection with Kate Middleton will be presumed.

[19] "Applicant does not dispute that Catherine, Duchess of Cambridge, is a well-known figure, stemming from her well-publicized relationship with Prince William and her subsequent wedding." "Also, the Applicant does not dispute the ... claim that Kate Middleton's fame is not temporary." However, Applicant argues that "while the Duchess of Cambridge is well-known, there is no evidence of a presumptive connection between Catherine and the specific goods upon which Applicant's mark will be used. Simply because Catherine is believed to have style and good taste does not mean that she is publicly perceived to be involved in the industry at all." We do not require proof that Kate Middleton is well-known for cosmetics, jewelry, handbags, bedding and clothing. Our inquiry is whether Kate Middleton's renown is such that when the mark ROYAL KATE is used with those products, consumers will recognize ROYAL KATE as referring to Kate Middleton such that a connection with Kate Middleton will be presumed. As the Board held in *In re Pedersen*, 109 USPQ2d 1185, 1202 (TTAB 2013):

> [T]he key is whether the name *per se* is unmistakably associated with a particular person or institution and, as used would point uniquely to the person or institution. In short, it is the combination of: (1) a name of sufficient fame or reputation and (2) its use on or in connection with particular goods or services, that would point uniquely to a particular person or institution. [Internal citation omitted]. Thus, our inquiry is whether consumers of medicinal herbal remedies would think only of the Lakota tribes when the LAKOTA name is used on such goods. *Cf. Notre Dame*, 217 USPQ 509 ("'Notre Dame' is not a name solely associated with the University. It serves to identify a famous and sacred religious figure and is used in the names of churches dedicated to Notre Dame, such as the Cathedral of Notre Dame in Paris.").

[20] In view [of the record evidence], we find that Kate Middleton's identity is of sufficient fame or reputation that when Applicant's mark ROYAL KATE is used on Applicant's goods, a connection with Kate Middleton will be presumed.

E. Analyzing the factors.

[21] [W]e find that Applicant's mark ROYAL KATE for the goods listed in the application falsely suggests a connection with Kate Middleton.

III. Whether the mark ROYAL KATE identifies a particular living individual whose written consent to register the mark is not of record?

[22] Section 2(c) of the Trademark Act, 15 U.S.C. § 1052(c) provides the following:

> No trademark by which the goods of the applicant may be distinguished from the goods of others shall be refused registration on the principal register on account of its nature unless it ... (c) Consists of or comprises a name, portrait, or signature identifying a particular living individual except by his written consent, or the name, signature, or portrait of a deceased President of the United States during the life of his widow, if any, except by the written consent of the widow.

[23] The purpose of requiring the consent of a living individual to the registration of his or her name, signature, or portrait is to protect rights of privacy and publicity that living persons have in the designations that identify them. *In re Hoefflin*, 97 USPQ2d 1174, 1176 (TTAB 2010); *Martin v. Carter Hawley Hale Stores, Inc.*, 206 USPQ 931, 933 (TTAB 1979) (Section 2(c) was designed "to protect one who, for valid reasons, could expect to suffer damage from another's trademark use of his name.") ....

[24] Whether consent to registration is required depends on whether the public would recognize and understand the mark as identifying a particular living individual. A consent is required only if the individual bearing the name in the mark will be associated with the mark as used on the goods or

services, either because: (1) the person is so well known that the public would reasonably assume a connection between the person and the goods or services; or (2) the individual is publicly connected with the business in which the mark is used . . . .

[25] For purposes of Section 2(c), a "name" does not have to be the full name of an individual. Section 2(c) applies not only to full names, but also first names, surnames, shortened names, pseudonyms, stage names, titles, or nicknames, if there is evidence that *the name identifies a specific living individual* who is publicly connected with the business in which the mark is used, or *who is so well known that such a connection would be assumed. See In re Hoefflin*, 97 USPQ2d at 1177-78 (holding registration of the marks OBAMA PAJAMA, OBAMA BAHAMA PAJAMAS, and BARACK'S JOCKS DRESS TO THE LEFT barred under Section 2(c) in the absence of consent to register, because they create a direct association with President Barack Obama); *Krause v. Krause Publ'ns, Inc.*, 76 USPQ2d at 1909 ("the mark KRAUSE PUBLICATIONS, although it includes only the surname of petitioner, would fall within the provisions of Section 2(c) if petitioner establishes that KRAUSE, as used on or in connection with the goods or services set forth in the involved registration, points uniquely to him 'as a particular living individual.'"); *In re Sauer*, 27 USPQ2d at 1074-75 (holding registration of a mark containing BO, used in connection with a sports ball, barred under Section 2(c) in the absence of consent to register, because BO is the nickname of a well-known athlete and thus use of the mark would lead to the assumption that he was associated with the goods) . . . .

[26] *In re Steak & Ale Rest. of Am., Inc.*, 185 USPQ 447, 448 (TTAB 1975) is particularly analogous to the present case. In that decision, the Board affirmed a Section 2(c) refusal of the mark PRINCE CHARLES because the wording identifies a particular well-known living individual whose consent was not of record. The Board reasoned that "the addition of a given name or a surname to the word 'PRINCE' could well serve as a name or 'nickname' for a particular living individual who could be identified and referred to in the various walks of life with this appellation." We find that this same logic applies to the mark ROYAL KATE. *Cf. Ceccato v. Manifattura Lane Gaetano Marzotto & Figli S.p.A.*, 32 USPQ2d 1192, 1196 (TTAB 1994) (evidence shows that "Duca D'Aosta" is a title and does not refer "unequivocally to a particular living individual.")

[27] While with lesser-known figures there may have to be evidence showing that the consuming public connects them with the manufacturing or marketing of the goods at issue, well-known individuals such as celebrities and world-famous political figures are entitled to the protection of Section 2(c) without having to demonstrate a connection with the involved goods or services. *See In re Hoefflin*, 97 USPQ2d at 1177 (because Barack Obama is the President of the United States, the purchasing public will reasonably assume that marks consisting of the names BARACK and OBAMA identify President Barack Obama); *In re Masucci*, 179 USPQ 829, 830 (TTAB 1973) (in spite of any common law rights applicant may have, EISENHOWER for greeting cards was refused on the ground that it consisted of the name of the late President Eisenhower during the life of his widow, and application for registration was filed without her consent).

[28] As we found in the previous section, ROYAL KATE identifies Kate Middleton whose identity is renowned. By any measure, she is a celebrity, and thus the term ROYAL KATE points uniquely and unmistakably to Kate Middleton. Although Kate Middleton, the Duchess of Cambridge, does not use the name ROYAL KATE, it has become an expression used by the American public (and media) to identify her. We find that the mark ROYAL KATE is the name of a particular living individual, namely, Kate Middleton, and because Kate Middleton has not consented to the use and registration of that name, the Section 2(c) refusal is affirmed.

[29] *Decision*: The refusals to register under Section 2(a) & (c) are affirmed.

Comments and Questions

1. *Difference between § 2(a) false suggestion of a connection and § 2(c) identification of living individual without consent.* Lanham Act § 2(c), 15 U.S.C. § 1052(c) prohibits the registration of a mark which "consists of or comprises a name . . . identifying a particular living individual except by his written

consent . . ." This does not mean that, for example, every person bearing the surname Singh has the ability under § 2(c) to prohibit the registration of a mark incorporating the word Singh. On the contrary,

> A name is deemed to "identify" a particular living individual, for purposes of Section 2(c), only if the "individual bearing the name in question will be associated with the mark as used on the goods, either because that person is so well known that the public would reasonably assume the connection, or because the individual is publicly connected with the business in which the mark is used."

In re Sauer, 27 U.S.P.Q.2d 1073 (TTAB 1993) (quoting *Martin v. Carter Hawley Hale Stores, Inc.*, 206 USPQ 931 (TTAB 1979). In practice, for well-known celebrities, § 2(a), which tends to require a showing of general notoriety, and 2(c), which tends only to require a showing of niche notoriety, are redundant. *See, e.g., In re Sauer*, 27 U.S.P.Q.2d 1073 (TTAB 1993) (finding the composite mark consisting of BO BALL and design to be prohibited from registration under § 2(a) as falsely suggesting a connection with professional sportsmen Bo Jackson and under § 2(c) as identify a living individual so well-known that the public would reasonably assume a connection); *In re Richard M. Hoefflin*, 97 U.S.P.Q.2d 1174 (TTAB 2010) (prohibiting registration of marks, for pajamas, OBAMA PAJAMA, OBAMA BAHAMA PAJAMAS and BARACK'S JOCKS DRESS TO THE LEFT under § 2(c)). But for non-celebrities, § 2(c) can prohibit registrations that § 2(a) may not, provided that the non-celebrity is "publicly connected with the business in which the mark is used." *See, e.g., Ross v. Analytical Technology Inc.*, 51 U.S.P.Q.2d 1269 (TTAB 1999) (prohibiting registration of ROSS for equipment for electrochemical analysis where plaintiff James W. Ross, Jr., was a retired inventor well-known in the field).

2. *Deceased celebrities.* The use of famous historical names will not necessarily trigger the § 2(a) bar. *See, e.g.,* Lucien Piccard Watch Corp. v. Crescent Corp., 314 F. Supp. 329 (S.D.N.Y. 1970) (finding that mark DA VINCI on various goods, including luggage, will not falsely suggest a connection with Leonardo da Vinci because the mark "hardly suggests that he personally had something to do with the designing of plaintiff's luggage"). *But see Association Pour La Defense et La Promotion De Loeuvre De Marc Chagall Dite Comite Marc Chagall v. Bondarchuk*, 82 U.S.P.Q.2d 1838, 2007 WL 749714 (TTAB 2007) (prohibiting registration of MARC CHAGALL for vodka; "we conclude that the evidence in this record is more than adequate to establish that the mark would be recognized as the name of the painter Marc Chagall and that the name is of sufficient fame or reputation that when the respondent's mark is used on the goods a connection with the painter Marc Chagall would be presumed").

3. For a comprehensive review of section 2(a) caselaw, see Anne Gilson LaLonde, *Giving the Wrong Impression: Section 2(a)'s False Suggestion of a Connection*, 110 TRADEMARK REP. 877 (2020).

4. Confusingly-Similar Marks Under Lanham Act § 2(d)

Lanham Act § 2(d), 15 U.S.C. § 1052 (d), prohibits the registration of a mark that:

> Consists of or comprises a mark which so resembles a mark registered in the Patent and Trademark Office, or a mark or trade name previously used in the United States by another and not abandoned, as to be likely, when used on or in connection with the goods of the applicant, to cause confusion, or to cause mistake, or to deceive.

Because this particular statutory bar bears so much in common with the likelihood of confusion analysis reviewed at length below in Part II.B, we will discuss the § 2(d) bar in that section.

5. Disparaging and Scandalous Marks

The American trademark system provides the benefits of trademark protection and trademark registration to certain kinds of marks but not to others. Furthermore, the government will censor certain uses of trademarks that it deems objectionable, such as those it judges to be infringing of another person's trademark rights. How is this consistent with the Free Speech Clause of the First Amendment that "Congress shall make no law . . . abridging the freedom of speech"? The cases that follow help to answer this question.

In *Matal v. Tam*, 137 S.Ct. 1744, 582 U.S. _ (U.S. 2017), excerpted below, the Supreme Court held that the Lanham Act § 2(a) prohibition on the registration of marks that "may disparage . . . persons" was invalid under the Free Speech Clause. *Tam* is significant for a number of reasons specific to trademark law. First, it abrogated a half-century of PTO practice and federal court case law applying the § 2(a)'s "disparagement clause." Second, *Tam* also arguably raises significant questions about whether antidilution law, which we cover in Part II.C below, is constitutional. May the government restrict non-deceptive speech that "impairs the distinctiveness of the famous mark," 15 U.S.C. § 1125(c)(2)(B), or that "harms the reputation of the famous mark," 15 U.S.C. § 1125(c)(2)(C)? Third, *Tam* brought to an end the appeal to the Fourth Circuit of *Blackhorse v. Pro-Football, Inc.*, 111 U.S.P.Q.2d 1080, 2014 WL 2757516 (TTAB June 18, 2014). In *Blackhorse*, five Native Americans petitioned to cancel various trademark registrations consisting in whole or in part of the term REDSKINS for professional football-related services on the ground that at the time of their registration they were disparaging of Native Americans and thus obtained contrary to Lanham Act §§ 14(c) and 2(a), 15 U.S.C. §§ 1064(c) & 1052(a). (If you strongly support Tam's registration of THE SLANTS, what is your position on the government's registration of the term "redskins" by a professional football team in the nation's capital?)

Tam also prompted the question of whether the Lanham Act § 2(a) prohibition on the registration of any mark that "consists of or comprises . . . scandalous matter" is also unconstitutional. In *Iancu v. Brunetti*, No. 18-302, 2019 WL 2570622, 588 U.S. _ (June 24, 2019), excerpted below and involving the mark FUCT for athletic apparel, the Supreme Court found that the § 2 bar against the registration of scandalous matter is also unconstitutional. You will see, however, that the Court found *Brunetti* to be a much closer case than *Tam*.

Beware that *Tam* and *Brunetti* as presented here have been severely edited-down to focus on the Justices' statements about the trademark system. The opinion excerpts provide in some instances only the gist (and few of the subtleties) of the Justices' First Amendment analyses. Students with a special interest in First Amendment doctrine would be better served taking the time to read the full opinions.

Matal v. Tam
137 S.Ct. 1744, 582 U.S. _ (2017)

[1] Justice ALITO announced the judgment of the Court and delivered the opinion of the Court with respect to Parts I, II, and III–A, and an opinion with respect to Parts III–B, III–C, and IV, in which THE CHIEF JUSTICE, Justice THOMAS, and Justice BREYER join.

[2] This case concerns a dance-rock band's application for federal trademark registration of the band's name, "The Slants." "Slants" is a derogatory term for persons of Asian descent, and members of the band are Asian–Americans. But the band members believe that by taking that slur as the name of their group, they will help to "reclaim" the term and drain its denigrating force.

[3] The Patent and Trademark Office (PTO) denied the application based on a provision of federal law prohibiting the registration of trademarks that may "disparage . . . or bring . . . into contemp[t] or

disrepute" any "persons, living or dead." 15 U.S.C. § 1052(a). We now hold that this provision violates the Free Speech Clause of the First Amendment. It offends a bedrock First Amendment principle: Speech may not be banned on the ground that it expresses ideas that offend.

I

A

[4] "The principle underlying trademark protection is that distinctive marks—words, names, symbols, and the like—can help distinguish a particular artisan's goods from those of others." *B & B Hardware, Inc. v. Hargis Industries, Inc.*, 135 S.Ct. 1293, 1299 (2015); see also *Wal–Mart Stores, Inc. v. Samara Brothers, Inc.*, 529 U.S. 205, 212 (2000). A trademark "designate[s] the goods as the product of a particular trader" and "protect[s] his good will against the sale of another's product as his." *United Drug Co. v. Theodore Rectanus Co.*, 248 U.S. 90, 97 (1918); see also *Hanover Star Milling Co. v. Metcalf*, 240 U.S. 403, 412–413 (1916). It helps consumers identify goods and services that they wish to purchase, as well as those they want to avoid. See *Wal–Mart Stores, supra,* at 212–213; *Park 'N Fly, Inc. v. Dollar Park & Fly, Inc.*, 469 U.S. 189, 198 (1985).

[5] "[F]ederal law does not create trademarks." *B & B Hardware, supra,* at ––––, 135 S.Ct., at 1299. Trademarks and their precursors have ancient origins, and trademarks were protected at common law and in equity at the time of the founding of our country. 3 J. McCarthy, Trademarks and Unfair Competition § 19:8 (4th ed. 2017) (hereinafter McCarthy); see *Trade–Mark Cases*, 100 U.S. 82, 92 (1879). For most of the 19th century, trademark protection was the province of the States. See *Two Pesos, Inc. v. Taco Cabana, Inc.*, 505 U.S. 763, 780–782 (1992) (Stevens, J., concurring in judgment); *id.*, at 785 (THOMAS, J., concurring in judgment). Eventually, Congress stepped in to provide a degree of national uniformity, passing the first federal legislation protecting trademarks in 1870. See Act of July 8, 1870, §§ 77–84, 16 Stat. 210–212. The foundation of current federal trademark law is the Lanham Act, enacted in 1946. See Act of July 5, 1946, ch. 540, 60 Stat. 427. By that time, trademark had expanded far beyond phrases that do no more than identify a good or service. Then, as now, trademarks often consisted of catchy phrases that convey a message.

[6] Under the Lanham Act, trademarks that are "used in commerce" may be placed on the "principal register," that is, they may be federally registered. 15 U.S.C. § 1051(a)(1). And some marks "capable of distinguishing [an] applicant's goods or services and not registrable on the principal register ... which are in lawful use in commerce by the owner thereof" may instead be placed on a different federal register: the supplemental register. § 1091(a). There are now more than two million marks that have active federal certificates of registration. PTO Performance and Accountability Report, Fiscal Year 2016, p. 192 (Table 15), https://www.uspto.gov/sites/default/files/ documents/USPTOFY16PAR.pdf (all Internet materials as last visited June 16, 2017). This system of federal registration helps to ensure that trademarks are fully protected and supports the free flow of commerce. "[N]ational protection of trademarks is desirable," we have explained, "because trademarks foster competition and the maintenance of quality by securing to the producer the benefits of good reputation." *San Francisco Arts & Athletics, Inc. v. United States Olympic Comm.*, 483 U.S. 522, 531 (1987) (internal quotation marks omitted); see also *Park 'N Fly, Inc., supra,* at 198 ("The Lanham Act provides national protection of trademarks in order to secure to the owner of the mark the goodwill of his business and to protect the ability of consumers to distinguish among competing producers").

B

[7] Without federal registration, a valid trademark may still be used in commerce. See 3 McCarthy § 19:8. And an unregistered trademark can be enforced against would-be infringers in several ways. Most important, even if a trademark is not federally registered, it may still be enforceable under § 43(a) of the Lanham Act, which creates a federal cause of action for trademark infringement. See *Two Pesos, supra,* at 768 ("Section 43(a) prohibits a broader range of practices than does § 32, which applies to registered marks, but it is common ground that § 43(a) protects qualifying unregistered trademarks"

197

(internal quotation marks and citation omitted)).[1] Unregistered trademarks may also be entitled to protection under other federal statutes, such as the Anticybersquatting Consumer Protection Act, 15 U.S.C. § 1125(d). See 5 McCarthy § 25A:49, at 25A–198 ("[T]here is no requirement [in the Anticybersquatting Act] that the protected 'mark' be registered: unregistered common law marks are protected by the Act"). And an unregistered trademark can be enforced under state common law, or if it has been registered in a State, under that State's registration system. See 3 *id.,* § 19:3, at 19–23 (explaining that "[t]he federal system of registration and protection does not preempt parallel state law protection, either by state common law or state registration" and "[i]n the vast majority of situations, federal and state trademark law peacefully coexist"); *id.,* § 22:1 (discussing state trademark registration systems).

[8] Federal registration, however, "confers important legal rights and benefits on trademark owners who register their marks." *B & B Hardware,* 135 S.Ct., at 1317 (internal quotation marks omitted). Registration on the principal register (1) "serves as 'constructive notice of the registrant's claim of ownership' of the mark," *ibid.* (quoting 15 U.S.C. § 1072); (2) "is 'prima facie evidence of the validity of the registered mark and of the registration of the mark, of the owner's ownership of the mark, and of the owner's exclusive right to use the registered mark in commerce on or in connection with the goods or services specified in the certificate,'" *B & B Hardware,* 135 S.Ct., at 1300 (quoting § 1057(b)); and (3) can make a mark "'incontestable'" once a mark has been registered for five years," *ibid.* (quoting §§ 1065, 1115(b)); see *Park 'N Fly,* 469 U.S., at 193. Registration also enables the trademark holder "to stop the importation into the United States of articles bearing an infringing mark." 3 McCarthy § 19:9, at 19–38; see 15 U.S.C. § 1124.

C

[9] The Lanham Act contains provisions that bar certain trademarks from the principal register. For example, a trademark cannot be registered if it is "merely descriptive or deceptively misdescriptive" of goods, § 1052(e)(1), or if it is so similar to an already registered trademark or trade name that it is "likely . . . to cause confusion, or to cause mistake, or to deceive," § 1052(d).

[10] At issue in this case is one such provision, which we will call "the disparagement clause." This provision prohibits the registration of a trademark "which may disparage . . . persons, living or dead, institutions, beliefs, or national symbols, or bring them into contempt, or disrepute." § 1052(a).[2] This clause appeared in the original Lanham Act and has remained the same to this day. See § 2(a), 60 Stat. 428.

[11] When deciding whether a trademark is disparaging, an examiner at the PTO generally applies a "two-part test." The examiner first considers "the likely meaning of the matter in question, taking into account not only dictionary definitions, but also the relationship of the matter to the other elements in the mark, the nature of the goods or services, and the manner in which the mark is used in the marketplace in connection with the goods or services." Trademark Manual of Examining Procedure § 1203.03(b)(i) (Apr. 2017), p. 1200–150, http://tmep.uspto.gov. "If that meaning is found to refer to identifiable persons, institutions, beliefs or national symbols," the examiner moves to the second step,

---

[1] In the opinion below, the Federal Circuit opined that although "Section 43(a) allows for a federal suit to protect an unregistered trademark," "it is not at all clear" that respondent could bring suit under § 43(a) because "there is no authority extending § 43(a) to marks denied under § 2(a)'s disparagement provision." *In re Tam,* 808 F.3d 1321, 1344–1345, n. 11 (en banc), as corrected (Feb. 11, 2016). When drawing this conclusion, the Federal Circuit relied in part on our statement in *Two Pesos* that "the general principles qualifying a mark for registration under § 2 of the Lanham Act are for the most part applicable in determining whether an unregistered mark is entitled to protection under § 43(a)." 505 U.S., at 768. We need not decide today whether respondent could bring suit under § 43(a) if his application for federal registration had been lawfully denied under the disparagement clause.

[2] The disparagement clause also prevents a trademark from being registered on the supplemental register. § 1091(a).

asking "whether that meaning may be disparaging to a substantial composite[3] of the referenced group." *Ibid.* If the examiner finds that a "substantial composite, although not necessarily a majority, of the referenced group would find the proposed mark . . . to be disparaging in the context of contemporary attitudes," a prima facie case of disparagement is made out, and the burden shifts to the applicant to prove that the trademark is not disparaging. *Ibid.* What is more, the PTO has specified that "[t]he fact that an applicant may be a member of that group or has good intentions underlying its use of a term does not obviate the fact that a substantial composite of the referenced group would find the term objectionable." *Ibid.*

D

[12] Simon Tam is the lead singer of "The Slants." *In re Tam,* 808 F.3d 1321, 1331 (C.A.Fed. 2015) (en banc), as corrected (Feb. 11, 2016). He chose this moniker in order to "reclaim" and "take ownership" of stereotypes about people of Asian ethnicity. *Ibid.* (internal quotation marks omitted). The group "draws inspiration for its lyrics from childhood slurs and mocking nursery rhymes" and has given its albums names such as "The Yellow Album" and "Slanted Eyes, Slanted Hearts." *Ibid.*

[13] Tam sought federal registration of "THE SLANTS," on the principal register, but an examining attorney at the PTO rejected the request, applying the PTO's two-part framework and finding that "there is . . . a substantial composite of persons who find the term in the applied-for mark offensive." The examining attorney relied in part on the fact that "numerous dictionaries define 'slants' or 'slant-eyes' as a derogatory or offensive term." The examining attorney also relied on a finding that "the band's name has been found offensive numerous times"—citing a performance that was canceled because of the band's moniker and the fact that "several bloggers and commenters to articles on the band have indicated that they find the term and the applied-for mark offensive."

[14] Tam contested the denial of registration before the examining attorney and before the PTO's Trademark Trial and Appeal Board (TTAB) but to no avail. Eventually, he took the case to federal court, where the en banc Federal Circuit ultimately found the disparagement clause facially unconstitutional under the First Amendment's Free Speech Clause. The majority found that the clause engages in viewpoint-based discrimination, that the clause regulates the expressive component of trademarks and consequently cannot be treated as commercial speech, and that the clause is subject to and cannot satisfy strict scrutiny. See 808 F.3d, at 1334–1339. The majority also rejected the Government's argument that registered trademarks constitute government speech, as well as the Government's contention that federal registration is a form of government subsidy. See *id.,* at 1339–1355. And the majority opined that even if the disparagement clause were analyzed under this Court's commercial speech cases, the clause would fail the "intermediate scrutiny" that those cases prescribe. See *id.,* at 1355–1357.

[15] Several judges wrote separately, advancing an assortment of theories. Concurring, Judge O'Malley agreed with the majority's reasoning but added that the disparagement clause is unconstitutionally vague. See *id.,* at 1358–1363. Judge Dyk concurred in part and dissented in part. He argued that trademark registration is a government subsidy and that the disparagement clause is facially constitutional, but he found the clause unconstitutional as applied to THE SLANTS because that mark constitutes "core expression" and was not adopted for the purpose of disparaging Asian–Americans. See *id.,* at 1363–1374. In dissent, Judge Lourie agreed with Judge Dyk that the clause is facially constitutional but concluded for a variety of reasons that it is also constitutional as applied in this case. See *id.,* at 1374–1376. Judge Reyna also dissented, maintaining that trademarks are commercial speech and that the disparagement clause survives intermediate scrutiny because it "directly advances the government's substantial interest in the orderly flow of commerce." See *id.,* at 1376–1382.

[16] The Government filed a petition for certiorari, which we granted in order to decide whether the disparagement clause "is facially invalid under the Free Speech Clause of the First Amendment." Pet. for Cert. i; see *sub. nom. Lee v. Tam,* 579 U.S. ––––, 137 S.Ct. 30 (2016).

---

[3] By "composite," we assume the PTO means component.

II

{Tam argued that Lanham Act § 2(a) prohibits the registration of marks that disparage only "persons," which, Tam argued, "includes only natural and juristic persons," not "non-juristic entities such as racial and ethnic groups." The Court rejected this argument.}

III

[17] Because the disparagement clause applies to marks that disparage the members of a racial or ethnic group, we must decide whether the clause violates the Free Speech Clause of the First Amendment. And at the outset, we must consider three arguments that would either eliminate any First Amendment protection or result in highly permissive rational-basis review. Specifically, the Government contends (1) that trademarks are government speech, not private speech, (2) that trademarks are a form of government subsidy, and (3) that the constitutionality of the disparagement clause should be tested under a new "government-program" doctrine. We address each of these arguments below.

A

[18] The First Amendment prohibits Congress and other government entities and actors from "abridging the freedom of speech"; the First Amendment does not say that Congress and other government entities must abridge their own ability to speak freely. And our cases recognize that "[t]he Free Speech Clause . . . does not regulate government speech." *Pleasant Grove City v. Summum*, 555 U.S. 460, 467 (2009); see *Johanns v. Livestock Marketing Assn.*, 544 U.S. 550, 553 (2005) ("[T]he Government's own speech . . . is exempt from First Amendment scrutiny"); *Board of Regents of Univ. of Wis. System v. Southworth*, 529 U.S. 217, 235 (2000).

. . . .

[19] [I]t is far-fetched to suggest that the content of a registered mark is government speech. If the federal registration of a trademark makes the mark government speech, the Federal Government is babbling prodigiously and incoherently. It is saying many unseemly things. See App. to Brief for Pro–Football, Inc., as *Amicus Curiae*. It is expressing contradictory views.[9] It is unashamedly endorsing a vast array of commercial products and services. And it is providing Delphic advice to the consuming public.

[20] For example, if trademarks represent government speech, what does the Government have in mind when it advises Americans to "make.believe" (Sony),[10] "Think different" (Apple),[11] "Just do it" (Nike),[12] or "Have it your way" (Burger King)[13]? Was the Government warning about a coming disaster when it registered the mark "EndTime Ministries"[14]?

[21] The PTO has made it clear that registration does not constitute approval of a mark. See *In re Old Glory Condom Corp.*, 26 USPQ 2d 1216, 1220, n. 3 (T.T.A.B. 1993) ("[I]ssuance of a trademark registration . . . is not a government imprimatur"). And it is unlikely that more than a tiny fraction of the public has any idea what federal registration of a trademark means. See *Application of National Distillers & Chemical Corp.*, 49 C.C.P.A. (Pat.) 854, 863, 297 F.2d 941, 949 (1962) (Rich, J., concurring) ("The

---

[9] Compare "Abolish Abortion," Registration No. 4,935,774 (Apr. 12, 2016), with "I Stand With Planned Parenthood," Registration No. 5,073,573 (Nov. 1, 2016); compare "Capitalism Is Not Moral, Not Fair, Not Freedom," Registration No. 4,696,419 (Mar. 3, 2015), with "Capitalism Ensuring Innovation," Registration No. 3,966,092 (May 24, 2011); compare "Global Warming Is Good," Registration No. 4,776,235 (July 21, 2015), with "A Solution to Global Warming," Registration No. 3,875,271 (Nov. 10, 2010).

[10] "make.believe," Registration No. 4,342,903 (May 28, 2013).

[11] "Think Different," Registration No. 2,707,257 (Apr. 15, 2003).

[12] "Just Do It," Registration No. 1,875,307 (Jan. 25, 1995).

[13] "Have It Your Way," Registration No. 0,961,016 (June 12, 1973).

[14] "EndTime Ministries," Registration No. 4,746,225 (June 2, 2015).

purchasing public knows no more about trademark registrations than a man walking down the street in a strange city knows about legal title to the land and buildings he passes" (emphasis deleted)).

. . . .

[22] Perhaps the most worrisome implication of the Government's argument concerns the system of copyright registration. If federal registration makes a trademark government speech and thus eliminates all First Amendment protection, would the registration of the copyright for a book produce a similar transformation? See 808 F.3d, at 1346 (explaining that if trademark registration amounts to government speech, "then copyright registration" which "has identical accoutrements" would "likewise amount to government speech").

[23] The Government attempts to distinguish copyright on the ground that it is "'the engine of free expression,'" Brief for Petitioner 47 (quoting *Eldred v. Ashcroft,* 537 U.S. 186, 219, 123 S.Ct. 769, 154 L.Ed.2d 683 (2003)), but as this case illustrates, trademarks often have an expressive content. Companies spend huge amounts to create and publicize trademarks that convey a message. It is true that the necessary brevity of trademarks limits what they can say. But powerful messages can sometimes be conveyed in just a few words.

[24] Trademarks are private, not government, speech.

. . . .

{The Court further rejected the Government's government subsidy and government-program arguments.}

IV

[25] Having concluded that the disparagement clause cannot be sustained under our government-speech or subsidy cases or under the Government's proposed "government-program" doctrine, we must confront a dispute between the parties on the question whether trademarks are commercial speech and are thus subject to the relaxed scrutiny outlined in *Central Hudson Gas & Elec. Corp. v. Public Serv. Comm'n of N. Y.,* 447 U.S. 557 (1980). The Government and *amici* supporting its position argue that all trademarks are commercial speech. They note that the central purposes of trademarks are commercial and that federal law regulates trademarks to promote fair and orderly interstate commerce. Tam and his *amici,* on the other hand, contend that many, if not all, trademarks have an expressive component. In other words, these trademarks do not simply identify the source of a product or service but go on to say something more, either about the product or service or some broader issue. The trademark in this case illustrates this point. The name "The Slants" not only identifies the band but expresses a view about social issues.

[26] We need not resolve this debate between the parties because the disparagement clause cannot withstand even *Central Hudson* review.[17] Under *Central Hudson,* a restriction of speech must serve "a substantial interest," and it must be "narrowly drawn." *Id.,* at 564–565 (internal quotation marks omitted). This means, among other things, that "[t]he regulatory technique may extend only as far as the interest it serves." *Id.,* at 565. The disparagement clause fails this requirement.

[27] It is claimed that the disparagement clause serves two interests. The first is phrased in a variety of ways in the briefs. Echoing language in one of the opinions below, the Government asserts an interest in preventing "'underrepresented groups'" from being "'bombarded with demeaning messages in commercial advertising.'" Brief for Petitioner 48 (quoting 808 F.3d, at 1364 (Dyk, J., concurring in part and dissenting in part)). An *amicus* supporting the Government refers to "encouraging racial tolerance and protecting the privacy and welfare of individuals." Brief for Native American Organizations as *Amici*

---

[17] As with the framework discussed in Part III–C of this opinion, we leave open the question whether *Central Hudson* provides the appropriate test for deciding free speech challenges to provisions of the Lanham Act. And nothing in our decision should be read to speak to the validity of state unfair competition provisions or product libel laws that are not before us and differ from § 1052(d)'s disparagement clause.

Curiae 21. But no matter how the point is phrased, its unmistakable thrust is this: The Government has an interest in preventing speech expressing ideas that offend. And, as we have explained, that idea strikes at the heart of the First Amendment. Speech that demeans on the basis of race, ethnicity, gender, religion, age, disability, or any other similar ground is hateful; but the proudest boast of our free speech jurisprudence is that we protect the freedom to express "the thought that we hate." *United States v. Schwimmer,* 279 U.S. 644, 655 (1929) (Holmes, J., dissenting).

[28] The second interest asserted is protecting the orderly flow of commerce. See 808 F.3d, at 1379–1381 (Reyna, J., dissenting); Brief for Petitioner 49; Brief for Native American Organizations as *Amicus Curiae* 18–21. Commerce, we are told, is disrupted by trademarks that "involv[e] disparagement of race, gender, ethnicity, national origin, religion, sexual orientation, and similar demographic classification." 808 F.3d, at 1380–1381 (opinion of Reyna, J.). Such trademarks are analogized to discriminatory conduct, which has been recognized to have an adverse effect on commerce. See *ibid.*; Brief for Petitioner 49; Brief for Native American Organizations as *Amici Curiae* 18–20.

[29] A simple answer to this argument is that the disparagement clause is not "narrowly drawn" to drive out trademarks that support invidious discrimination. The clause reaches any trademark that disparages *any person, group, or institution*. It applies to trademarks like the following: "Down with racists," "Down with sexists," "Down with homophobes." It is not an anti-discrimination clause; it is a happy-talk clause. In this way, it goes much further than is necessary to serve the interest asserted.

[30] The clause is far too broad in other ways as well. The clause protects every person living or dead as well as every institution. Is it conceivable that commerce would be disrupted by a trademark saying: "James Buchanan was a disastrous president" or "Slavery is an evil institution"?

[31] There is also a deeper problem with the argument that commercial speech may be cleansed of any expression likely to cause offense. The commercial market is well stocked with merchandise that disparages prominent figures and groups, and the line between commercial and non-commercial speech is not always clear, as this case illustrates. If affixing the commercial label permits the suppression of any speech that may lead to political or social "volatility," free speech would be endangered.

* * *

[32] For these reasons, we hold that the disparagement clause violates the Free Speech Clause of the First Amendment. The judgment of the Federal Circuit is affirmed.

It is so ordered.

Justice GORSUCH took no part in the consideration or decision of this case.

Justice KENNEDY, with whom Justice GINSBURG, Justice SOTOMAYOR, and Justice KAGAN join, concurring in part and concurring in the judgment.

[1] The Patent and Trademark Office (PTO) has denied the substantial benefits of federal trademark registration to the mark THE SLANTS. The PTO did so under the mandate of the disparagement clause in 15 U.S.C. § 1052(a), which prohibits the registration of marks that may "disparage . . . or bring . . . into contemp[t] or disrepute" any "persons, living or dead, institutions, beliefs, or national symbols."

[2] As the Court is correct to hold, § 1052(a) constitutes viewpoint discrimination—a form of speech suppression so potent that it must be subject to rigorous constitutional scrutiny. The Government's action and the statute on which it is based cannot survive this scrutiny.

[3] The Court is correct in its judgment, and I join Parts I, II, and III–A of its opinion. This separate writing explains in greater detail why the First Amendment's protections against viewpoint discrimination apply to the trademark here. It submits further that the viewpoint discrimination rationale renders unnecessary any extended treatment of other questions raised by the parties.

I

[4] Those few categories of speech that the government can regulate or punish—for instance, fraud, defamation, or incitement—are well established within our constitutional tradition. See *United States v.*

Stevens, 559 U.S. 460, 468 (2010). Aside from these and a few other narrow exceptions, it is a fundamental principle of the First Amendment that the government may not punish or suppress speech based on disapproval of the ideas or perspectives the speech conveys. See *Rosenberger v. Rector and Visitors of Univ. of Va.,* 515 U.S. 819, 828–829 (1995).

[5] The First Amendment guards against laws "targeted at specific subject matter," a form of speech suppression known as content based discrimination. *Reed v. Town of Gilbert,* 576 U.S. ----, ----, 135 S.Ct. 2218, 2230 (2015). This category includes a subtype of laws that go further, aimed at the suppression of "particular views ... on a subject." *Rosenberger,* 515 U.S., at 829. A law found to discriminate based on viewpoint is an "egregious form of content discrimination," which is "presumptively unconstitutional." *Id.,* at 829–830.

[6] At its most basic, the test for viewpoint discrimination is whether—within the relevant subject category—the government has singled out a subset of messages for disfavor based on the views expressed. See *Cornelius v. NAACP Legal Defense & Ed. Fund, Inc.,* 473 U.S. 788, 806 (1985) ("[T]he government violates the First Amendment when it denies access to a speaker solely to suppress the point of view he espouses on an otherwise includible subject"). In the instant case, the disparagement clause the Government now seeks to implement and enforce identifies the relevant subject as "persons, living or dead, institutions, beliefs, or national symbols." 15 U.S.C. § 1052(a). Within that category, an applicant may register a positive or benign mark but not a derogatory one. The law thus reflects the Government's disapproval of a subset of messages it finds offensive. This is the essence of viewpoint discrimination.

. . . .

II

[7] The parties dispute whether trademarks are commercial speech and whether trademark registration should be considered a federal subsidy. The former issue may turn on whether certain commercial concerns for the protection of trademarks might, as a general matter, be the basis for regulation. However that issue is resolved, the viewpoint based discrimination at issue here necessarily invokes heightened scrutiny.

[8] "Commercial speech is no exception," the Court has explained, to the principle that the First Amendment "requires heightened scrutiny whenever the government creates a regulation of speech because of disagreement with the message it conveys." *Sorrell v. IMS Health Inc.,* 564 U.S. 552, 566 (2011) (internal quotation marks omitted). Unlike content based discrimination, discrimination based on viewpoint, including a regulation that targets speech for its offensiveness, remains of serious concern in the commercial context. See *Bolger v. Youngs Drug Products Corp.,* 463 U.S. 60, 65, 71–72 (1983).

[9] To the extent trademarks qualify as commercial speech, they are an example of why that term or category does not serve as a blanket exemption from the First Amendment's requirement of viewpoint neutrality. Justice Holmes' reference to the "free trade in ideas" and the "power of ... thought to get itself accepted in the competition of the market," *Abrams v. United States,* 250 U.S. 616, 630 (1919) (dissenting opinion), was a metaphor. In the realm of trademarks, the metaphorical marketplace of ideas becomes a tangible, powerful reality. Here that real marketplace exists as a matter of state law and our common-law tradition, quite without regard to the Federal Government. These marks make up part of the expression of everyday life, as with the names of entertainment groups, broadcast networks, designer clothing, newspapers, automobiles, candy bars, toys, and so on. See Brief for Pro–Football, Inc., as *Amicus Curiae* 8 (collecting examples). Nonprofit organizations—ranging from medical-research charities and other humanitarian causes to political advocacy groups—also have trademarks, which they use to compete in a real economic sense for funding and other resources as they seek to persuade others to join their cause. See *id.,* at 8–9 (collecting examples). To permit viewpoint discrimination in this context is to permit Government censorship.

[10] This case does not present the question of how other provisions of the Lanham Act should be analyzed under the First Amendment. It is well settled, for instance, that to the extent a trademark is confusing or misleading the law can protect consumers and trademark owners. See, *e.g., FTC v. Winsted*

Hosiery Co., 258 U.S. 483, 493 (1922) ("The labels in question are literally false, and ... palpably so. All are, as the Commission found, calculated to deceive and do in fact deceive a substantial portion of the purchasing public"). This case also does not involve laws related to product labeling or otherwise designed to protect consumers. See *Sorrell, supra,* at 579, ("[T]he government's legitimate interest in protecting consumers from commercial harms explains why commercial speech can be subject to greater governmental regulation than noncommercial speech" (internal quotation marks omitted)). These considerations, however, do not alter the speech principles that bar the viewpoint discrimination embodied in the statutory provision at issue here.

. . . .

*   *   *

[11] A law that can be directed against speech found offensive to some portion of the public can be turned against minority and dissenting views to the detriment of all. The First Amendment does not entrust that power to the government's benevolence. Instead, our reliance must be on the substantial safeguards of free and open discussion in a democratic society.

[12] For these reasons, I join the Court's opinion in part and concur in the judgment.

Justice THOMAS, concurring in part and concurring in the judgment.

. . . .

[1] I also write separately because "I continue to believe that when the government seeks to restrict truthful speech in order to suppress the ideas it conveys, strict scrutiny is appropriate, whether or not the speech in question may be characterized as 'commercial.'" *Lorillard Tobacco Co. v. Reilly,* 533 U.S. 525, 572 (2001) (THOMAS, J., concurring in part and concurring in judgment); see also, *e.g., 44 Liquormart, Inc. v. Rhode Island,* 517 U.S. 484, 518 (1996) (same). I nonetheless join Part IV of Justice ALITO's opinion because it correctly concludes that the disparagement clause, 15 U.S.C. § 1052(a), is unconstitutional even under the less stringent test announced in *Central Hudson Gas & Elec. Corp. v. Public Serv. Comm'n of N. Y.,* 447 U.S. 557 (1980).

(Photo credit: hafgod, grailed.com)

Iancu v. Brunetti
No. 18-302, 2019 WL 2570622, 588 U.S. __ (June 24, 2019)

Justice KAGAN delivered the opinion of the Court.

[1] Two Terms ago, in *Matal* v. *Tam*, 582 U.S. __ (2017), this Court invalidated the Lanham Act's bar on the registration of "disparag[ing]" trademarks. 15 U.S. C. § 1052(a). Although split between two non-majority opinions, all Members of the Court agreed that the provision violated the First Amendment because it discriminated on the basis of viewpoint. Today we consider a First Amendment challenge to a neighboring provision of the Act, prohibiting the registration of "immoral[ ] or scandalous" trademarks. *Ibid.* We hold that this provision infringes the First Amendment for the same reason: It too disfavors certain ideas.

I.

[2] Respondent Erik Brunetti is an artist and entrepreneur who founded a clothing line that uses the trademark FUCT. According to Brunetti, the mark (which functions as the clothing's brand name) is pronounced as four letters, one after the other: F-U-C-T. But you might read it differently and, if so, you would hardly be alone. See Tr. of Oral Arg. 5 (describing the brand name as "the equivalent of [the] past participle form of a well-known word of profanity"). That common perception caused difficulties for Brunetti when he tried to register his mark with the U.S. Patent and Trademark Office (PTO).

205

[3] Under the Lanham Act, the PTO administers a federal registration system for trademarks. See 15 U.S. C. §§ 1051, 1052. Registration of a mark is not mandatory. The owner of an unregistered mark may still use it in commerce and enforce it against infringers. But registration gives trademark owners valuable benefits. For example, registration constitutes "prima facie evidence" of the mark's validity. § 1115(a). And registration serves as "constructive notice of the registrant's claim of ownership," which forecloses some defenses in infringement actions. § 1072. Generally, a trademark is eligible for registration, and receipt of such benefits, if it is "used in commerce." § 1051(a)(1). But the Act directs the PTO to "refuse[ ] registration" of certain marks. § 1052. For instance, the PTO cannot register a mark that "so resembles" another mark as to create a likelihood of confusion. § 1052(d). It cannot register a mark that is "merely descriptive" of the goods on which it is used. § 1052(e). It cannot register a mark containing the flag or insignia of any nation or State. See § 1052(b). There are five or ten more (depending on how you count). And until we invalidated the criterion two years ago, the PTO could not register a mark that "disparage[d]" a "person[ ], living or dead." § 1052(a); see *Tam*, 582 U.S. ___.

[4] This case involves another of the Lanham Act's prohibitions on registration—one applying to marks that "[c]onsist[ ] of or comprise[ ] immoral[ ] or scandalous matter." § 1052(a). The PTO applies that bar as a "unitary provision," rather than treating the two adjectives in it separately. *In re Brunetti*, 877 F. 3d 1330, 1336 (CA Fed. 2017). To determine whether a mark fits in the category, the PTO asks whether a "substantial composite of the general public" would find the mark "shocking to the sense of truth, decency, or propriety"; "giving offense to the conscience or moral feelings"; "calling out for condemnation"; "disgraceful"; "offensive"; "disreputable"; or "vulgar." 877 F. 3d, at 1336 (internal quotation marks omitted).

[5] Both a PTO examining attorney and the PTO's Trademark Trial and Appeal Board decided that Brunetti's mark flunked that test. The attorney determined that FUCT was "a total vulgar" and "therefore[ ] unregistrable." On review, the Board stated that the mark was "highly offensive" and "vulgar," and that it had "decidedly negative sexual connotations." As part of its review, the Board also considered evidence of how Brunetti used the mark. It found that Brunetti's website and products contained imagery, near the mark, of "extreme nihilism" and "anti-social" behavior. In that context, the Board thought, the mark communicated "misogyny, depravity, [and] violence." The Board concluded: "Whether one considers [the mark] as a sexual term, or finds that [Brunetti] has used [the mark] in the context of extreme misogyny, nihilism or violence, we have no question but that [the term is] extremely offensive."

[6] Brunetti then brought a facial challenge to the "immoral or scandalous" bar in the Court of Appeals for the Federal Circuit. That court found the prohibition to violate the First Amendment. As usual when a lower court has invalidated a federal statute, we granted certiorari.

II

[7] This Court first considered a First Amendment challenge to a trademark registration restriction in *Tam*, just two Terms ago. There, the Court declared unconstitutional the Lanham Act's ban on registering marks that "disparage" any "person[ ], living or dead." § 1052(a). The eight-Justice Court divided evenly between two opinions and could not agree on the overall framework for deciding the case. (In particular, no majority emerged to resolve whether a Lanham Act bar is a condition on a government benefit or a simple restriction on speech.) But all the Justices agreed on two propositions. First, if a trademark registration bar is viewpoint-based, it is unconstitutional. And second, the disparagement bar was viewpoint-based.

[8] The Justices thus found common ground in a core postulate of free speech law: The government may not discriminate against speech based on the ideas or opinions it conveys. See *Rosenberger* v. *Rector and Visitors of Univ. of Va.*, 515 U.S. 819, 829–830 (1995) (explaining that viewpoint discrimination is an "egregious form of content discrimination" and is "presumptively unconstitutional"). In Justice Kennedy's explanation, the disparagement bar allowed a trademark owner to register a mark if it was "positive" about a person, but not if it was "derogatory." *Tam* (slip op., at 2). That was the "essence of viewpoint discrimination," he continued, because "[t]he law thus reflects the Government's disapproval

of a subset of messages it finds offensive." *Id.* (slip op., at 2–3). JUSTICE ALITO emphasized that the statute "denie[d] registration to any mark" whose disparaging message was "offensive to a substantial percentage of the members of any group." *Id.* (slip op., at 22). The bar thus violated the "bedrock First Amendment principle" that the government cannot discriminate against "ideas that offend." *Id.* (slip op., at 1–2). Slightly different explanations, then, but a shared conclusion: Viewpoint discrimination doomed the disparagement bar.

[9] If the "immoral or scandalous" bar similarly discriminates on the basis of viewpoint, it must also collide with our First Amendment doctrine. The Government does not argue otherwise. In briefs and oral argument, the Government offers a theory for upholding the bar if it is viewpoint-neutral (essentially, that the bar would then be a reasonable condition on a government benefit). But the Government agrees that under *Tam* it may not "deny registration based on the views expressed" by a mark. "As the Court's *Tam* decision establishes," the Government says, "the criteria for federal trademark registration" must be "viewpoint-neutral to survive Free Speech Clause review." Pet. for Cert. 19. So the key question becomes: Is the "immoral or scandalous" criterion in the Lanham Act viewpoint-neutral or viewpoint-based?

[10] It is viewpoint-based. The meanings of "immoral" and "scandalous" are not mysterious, but resort to some dictionaries still helps to lay bare the problem. When is expressive material "immoral"? According to a standard definition, when it is "inconsistent with rectitude, purity, or good morals"; "wicked"; or "vicious." Webster's New International Dictionary 1246 (2d ed. 1949). Or again, when it is "opposed to or violating morality"; or "morally evil." Shorter Oxford English Dictionary 961 (3d ed. 1947). So the Lanham Act permits registration of marks that champion society's sense of rectitude and morality, but not marks that denigrate those concepts. And when is such material "scandalous"? Says a typical definition, when it "giv[es] offense to the conscience or moral feelings"; "excite[s] reprobation"; or "call[s] out condemnation." Webster's New International Dictionary, at 2229. Or again, when it is "shocking to the sense of truth, decency, or propriety"; "disgraceful"; "offensive"; or "disreputable." Funk & Wagnalls New Standard Dictionary 2186 (1944). So the Lanham Act allows registration of marks when their messages accord with, but not when their messages defy, society's sense of decency or propriety. Put the pair of overlapping terms together and the statute, on its face, distinguishes between two opposed sets of ideas: those aligned with conventional moral standards and those hostile to them; those inducing societal nods of approval and those provoking offense and condemnation. The statute favors the former, and disfavors the latter. "Love rules"? "Always be good"? Registration follows. "Hate rules"? "Always be cruel"? Not according to the Lanham Act's "immoral or scandalous" bar.

[11] The facial viewpoint bias in the law results in viewpoint-discriminatory application. Recall that the PTO itself describes the "immoral or scandalous" criterion using much the same language as in the dictionary definitions recited above. The PTO, for example, asks whether the public would view the mark as "shocking to the sense of truth, decency, or propriety"; "calling out for condemnation"; "offensive"; or "disreputable." Using those guideposts, the PTO has refused to register marks communicating "immoral" or "scandalous" views about (among other things) drug use, religion, and terrorism. But all the while, it has approved registration of marks expressing more accepted views on the same topics. See generally Gilson & LaLonde, Trademarks Laid Bare, 101 Trademark Reporter 1476, 1510–1513, 1518–1522 (2011); Brief for Barton Beebe et al. as *Amici Curiae* 28–29.

[12] Here are some samples. The PTO rejected marks conveying approval of drug use (YOU CAN'T SPELL HEALTHCARE WITHOUT THC for pain-relief medication, MARIJUANA COLA and KO KANE for beverages) because it is scandalous to "inappropriately glamoriz[e] drug abuse." PTO, Office Action of Aug. 28, 2010, Serial No. 85038867; see Office Action of Dec. 24, 2009, Serial No. 77833964; Office Action of Nov. 17, 2009, Serial No. 77671304. But at the same time, the PTO registered marks with such sayings as D.A.R.E. TO RESIST DRUGS AND VIOLENCE and SAY NO TO DRUGS—REALITY IS THE BEST TRIP IN LIFE. See PTO, Reg. No. 2975163 (July 26, 2005); Reg. No. 2966019 (July 12, 2005). Similarly, the PTO disapproved registration for the mark BONG HITS 4 JESUS because it "suggests that people should engage in an illegal activity [in connection with] worship" and because "Christians would be morally outraged by a statement that connects Jesus Christ with illegal drug use." Office Action of Mar. 15, 2008,

Serial No. 77305946. And the PTO refused to register trademarks associating religious references with products (AGNUS DEI for safes and MADONNA for wine) because they would be "offensive to most individuals of the Christian faith" and "shocking to the sense of propriety." *Ex parte Summit Brass & Bronze Works*, 59 USPQ 22, 23 (Dec. Com. Pat. 1943); *In re Riverbank Canning Co.*, 95 F. 2d 327, 329 (CCPA 1938). But once again, the PTO approved marks—PRAISE THE LORD for a game and JESUS DIED FOR YOU on clothing—whose message suggested religious faith rather than blasphemy or irreverence. See Reg. No. 5265121 (Aug. 15, 2017); Reg. No. 3187985 (Dec. 19, 2006). Finally, the PTO rejected marks reflecting support for al-Qaeda (BABY AL QAEDA and AL-QAEDA on t-shirts) "because the bombing of civilians and other terrorist acts are shocking to the sense of decency and call out for condemnation." Office Action of Nov. 22, 2004, Serial No. 78444968; see Office Action of Feb. 23, 2005, Serial No. 78400213. Yet it approved registration of a mark with the words WAR ON TERROR MEMORIAL. Reg. No. 5495362 (Jun. 19, 2018). Of course, all these decisions are understandable. The rejected marks express opinions that are, at the least, offensive to many Americans. But as the Court made clear in *Tam*, a law disfavoring "ideas that offend" discriminates based on viewpoint, in violation of the First Amendment. *Tam* (opinion of ALITO, J.) (slip op., at 2); see *id.* (slip op., at 22–23); *id.* (opinion of Kennedy, J.) (slip op., at 2–3).

[13] How, then, can the Government claim that the "immoral or scandalous" bar is viewpoint-neutral? The Government basically asks us to treat decisions like those described above as PTO examiners' mistakes. Still more, the Government tells us to ignore how the Lanham Act's language, on its face, disfavors some ideas. In urging that course, the Government does not dispute that the statutory language—and words used to define it—have just that effect. At oral argument, the Government conceded: "[I]f you just looked at the words like 'shocking' and 'offensive' on their face and gave them their ordinary meanings[,] they could easily encompass material that was shocking [or offensive] because it expressed an outrageous point of view or a point of view that most members" of society reject. Tr. of Oral Arg. 6. But no matter, says the Government, because the statute is "susceptible of" a limiting construction that would remove this viewpoint bias. *Id.*, at 7 (arguing that the Court should "attempt to construe [the] statute in a way that would render it constitutional"). The Government's idea, abstractly phrased, is to narrow the statutory bar to "marks that are offensive [or] shocking to a substantial segment of the public because of their *mode* of expression, independent of any views that they may express." *Id.*, at 11 (emphasis added). More concretely, the Government explains that this reinterpretation would mostly restrict the PTO to refusing marks that are "vulgar"—meaning "lewd," "sexually explicit or profane." *Id.*, at 27, 30. Such a reconfigured bar, the Government says, would not turn on viewpoint, and so we could uphold it.

[14] But we cannot accept the Government's proposal, because the statute says something markedly different. This Court, of course, may interpret "ambiguous statutory language" to "avoid serious constitutional doubts." *FCC* v. *Fox Television Stations, Inc.*, 556 U.S. 502, 516 (2009). But that canon of construction applies only when ambiguity exists. "We will not rewrite a law to conform it to constitutional requirements." *United States* v. *Stevens*, 559 U.S. 460, 481 (2010) (internal quotation marks and alteration omitted). So even assuming the Government's reading would eliminate First Amendment problems, we may adopt it only if we can see it in the statutory language. And we cannot. The "immoral or scandalous" bar stretches far beyond the Government's proposed construction. The statute as written does not draw the line at lewd, sexually explicit, or profane marks. Nor does it refer only to marks whose "mode of expression," independent of viewpoint, is particularly offensive. It covers the universe of immoral or scandalous—or (to use some PTO synonyms) offensive or disreputable—material. Whether or not lewd or profane. Whether the scandal and immorality comes from mode or instead from viewpoint. To cut the statute off where the Government urges is not to interpret the statute Congress enacted, but to fashion a new one.[*]

---

[*] We reject the dissent's statutory surgery for the same reason. Although conceding that the term "immoral" cannot be saved, the dissent thinks that the term "scandalous" can be read as the Government

[15] And once the "immoral or scandalous" bar is interpreted fairly, it must be invalidated. The Government just barely argues otherwise. In the last paragraph of its brief, the Government gestures toward the idea that the provision is salvageable by virtue of its constitutionally permissible applications (in the Government's view, its applications to lewd, sexually explicit, or profane marks). In other words, the Government invokes our First Amendment overbreadth doctrine, and asks us to uphold the statute against facial attack because its unconstitutional applications are not "substantial" relative to "the statute's plainly legitimate sweep." *Stevens*, 559 U.S., at 473. But to begin with, this Court has never applied that kind of analysis to a viewpoint-discriminatory law. In *Tam*, for example, we did not pause to consider whether the disparagement clause might admit some permissible applications (say, to certain libelous speech) before striking it down. The Court's finding of viewpoint bias ended the matter. And similarly, it seems unlikely we would compare permissible and impermissible applications if Congress outright banned "offensive" (or to use some other examples, "divisive" or "subversive") speech. Once we have found that a law "aim[s] at the suppression of " views, why would it matter that Congress could have captured some of the same speech through a viewpoint-neutral statute? *Tam* (opinion of Kennedy, J.) (slip op., at 2). But in any event, the "immoral or scandalous" bar is substantially overbroad. There are a great many immoral and scandalous ideas in the world (even more than there are swearwords), and the Lanham Act covers them all. It therefore violates the First Amendment.

[16] We accordingly affirm the judgment of the Court of Appeals.

[17] It is so ordered.

Justice ALITO, concurring.

[1] For the reasons explained in the opinion of the Court, the provision of the Lanham Act at issue in this case violates the Free Speech Clause of the First Amendment because it discriminates on the basis of viewpoint and cannot be fixed without rewriting the statute. Viewpoint discrimination is poison to a free society. But in many countries with constitutions or legal traditions that claim to protect freedom of speech, serious viewpoint discrimination is now tolerated, and such discrimination has become increasingly prevalent in this country. At a time when free speech is under attack, it is especially important for this Court to remain firm on the principle that the First Amendment does not tolerate viewpoint discrimination. We reaffirm that principle today.

[2] Our decision is not based on moral relativism but on the recognition that a law banning speech deemed by government officials to be "immoral" or "scandalous" can easily be exploited for illegitimate ends. Our decision does not prevent Congress from adopting a more carefully focused statute that precludes the registration of marks containing vulgar terms that play no real part in the expression of ideas. The particular mark in question in this case could be denied registration under such a statute. The term suggested by that mark is not needed to express any idea and, in fact, as commonly used today, generally signifies nothing except emotion and a severely limited vocabulary. The registration of such marks serves only to further coarsen our popular culture. But we are not legislators and cannot substitute a new statute for the one now in force.

---

proposes. See *post,* at 1–2 (SOTOMAYOR, J., concurring in part and dissenting in part). But that term is not "ambiguous," as the dissent argues, *post,* at 3; it is just broad. Remember that the dictionaries define it to mean offensive, disreputable, exciting reprobation, and so forth. See *supra,* at 5–6; *post,* at 3 (accepting those definitions). Even if hived off from "immoral" marks, the category of scandalous marks thus includes *both* marks that offend by the ideas they convey *and* marks that offend by their mode of expression. And its coverage of the former means that it discriminates based on viewpoint. We say nothing at all about a statute that covers only the latter—or, in the Government's more concrete description, a statute limited to lewd, sexually explicit, and profane marks. Nor do we say anything about how to evaluate viewpoint-neutral restrictions on trademark registration, see *post,* at 14–17—because the "scandalous" bar (whether or not attached to the "immoral" bar) is not one.

Chief Justice ROBERTS, concurring in part and dissenting in part.

[1] The Lanham Act directs the Patent and Trademark Office to refuse registration to marks that consist of or comprise "immoral, deceptive, or scandalous matter." 15 U.S.C. § 1052(a). Although the statute lists "immoral" and "scandalous" separately, the PTO has long read those terms together to constitute a unitary bar on "immoral or scandalous" marks.

[2] The Government concedes that the provision so read is broad enough to reach not only marks that offend because of their mode of expression (such as vulgarity and profanity) but also marks that offend because of the ideas they convey. The Government urges, however, that the provision can be given a narrowing construction—it can be understood to cover only marks that offend because of their mode of expression.

[3] The Court rejects that proposal on the ground that it would in effect rewrite the statute. I agree with the majority that the "immoral" portion of the provision is not susceptible of a narrowing construction that would eliminate its viewpoint bias. As JUSTICE SOTOMAYOR explains, however, the "scandalous" portion of the provision is susceptible of such a narrowing construction. Standing alone, the term "scandalous" need not be understood to reach marks that offend because of the ideas they convey; it can be read more narrowly to bar only marks that offend because of their mode of expression—marks that are obscene, vulgar, or profane. That is how the PTO now understands the term, in light of our decision in *Matal v. Tam*, 582 U.S. __ (2017). I agree with JUSTICE SOTOMAYOR that such a narrowing construction is appropriate in this context.

[4] I also agree that, regardless of how exactly the trademark registration system is best conceived under our precedents—a question we left open in *Tam*—refusing registration to obscene, vulgar, or profane marks does not offend the First Amendment. Whether such marks can be registered does not affect the extent to which their owners may use them in commerce to identify goods. No speech is being restricted; no one is being punished. The owners of such marks are merely denied certain additional benefits associated with federal trademark registration. The Government, meanwhile, has an interest in not associating itself with trademarks whose content is obscene, vulgar, or profane. The First Amendment protects the freedom of speech; it does not require the Government to give aid and comfort to those using obscene, vulgar, and profane modes of expression. For those reasons, I concur in part and dissent in part.

Justice BREYER, concurring in part and dissenting in part.

. . . .

[5] I would conclude that the prohibition on registering "scandalous" marks does not "wor[k] harm to First Amendment interests that is disproportionate in light of the relevant regulatory objectives." *Reed*, 576 U.S., at __ (opinion of BREYER, J.) (slip op., at 4). I would therefore uphold this part of the statute. I agree with the Court, however, that the bar on registering "immoral" marks violates the First Amendment. Because JUSTICE SOTOMAYOR reaches the same conclusions, using roughly similar reasoning, I join her opinion insofar as it is consistent with the views set forth here.

Justice SOTOMAYOR, with whom Justice BREYER joins, concurring in part and dissenting in part.

[1] The Court's decision today will beget unfortunate results. With the Lanham Act's scandalous-marks provision, 15 U.S.C. § 1052(a), struck down as unconstitutional viewpoint discrimination, the Government will have no statutory basis to refuse (and thus no choice but to begin) registering marks containing the most vulgar, profane, or obscene words and images imaginable.

[2] The coming rush to register such trademarks—and the Government's immediate powerlessness to say no—is eminently avoidable. Rather than read the relevant text as the majority does, it is equally possible to read that provision's bar on the registration of "scandalous" marks to address only obscenity, vulgarity, and profanity. Such a narrowing construction would save that duly enacted legislative text by rendering it a reasonable, viewpoint-neutral restriction on speech that is permissible in the context of a beneficial governmental initiative like the trademark-registration system. I would apply that narrowing construction to the term "scandalous" and accordingly reject petitioner Erik Brunetti's facial challenge.

I

. . . .

[3] Here, Congress used not only the word "scandalous," but also the words "immoral" and "disparage," in the same block of statutory text—each as a separate feature that could render a mark unregistrable. See § 1052(a). *Tam* already decided that "disparage" served to prohibit marks that were offensive because they derided a particular person or group. See 582 U.S., at ___ (opinion of ALITO, J.) (slip op., at 22) ("It denies registration to any mark that is offensive to a substantial percentage of the members of any group"); *id.,* at ___ (opinion of Kennedy, J.) (slip op., at 2) ("[A]n applicant may register a positive or benign mark but not a derogatory one"). That defines one of the three words. Meanwhile, as the majority explains, the word "immoral" prohibits marks that are offensive because they transgress widely held moral beliefs. See *ante*, at 5. That defines a second of the three words.

[4] With marks that are offensive because they are disparaging and marks that are offensive because they are immoral already covered, what work did Congress intend for "scandalous" to do? A logical answer is that Congress meant for "scandalous" to target a third and distinct type of offensiveness: offensiveness in the mode of communication rather than the idea. The other two words cover marks that are offensive because of the ideas they express; the "scandalous" clause covers marks that are offensive because of the mode of expression, apart from any particular message or idea.

[5] To be sure, there are situations in which it makes sense to treat adjoining words as expressing the same or highly similar concepts (even at the risk of some redundancy). Cf. *Swearingen* v. *United States*, 161 U.S. 446, 450 (1896) (construing "'obscene, lewd or lascivious'" to have a unified meaning). That is essentially the approach that the majority takes. See *ante,* at 6.[2] But that is not the approach that Congress appears to have intended here. For example, "scandalous" does not serve as a broader catchall at the end of a list of similar words that all point in one direction. *E.g., Washington State Dept. of Social and Health Servs.* v. *Guardianship Estate of Keffeler*, 537 U.S. 371, 384 (2003). Nor is "scandalous" simply grouped among a number of closely related terms that help define its meaning. *E.g., Gustafson* v. *Alloyd Co.*, 513 U.S. 561, 575 (1995).

[6] The text of § 1052, instead, is a grab bag: It bars the registration of marks featuring "immoral, deceptive, or scandalous matter," as well as, *inter alia*, disparaging marks, flags, insignias, mislabeled wines, and deceased Presidents. See §§ 1052(a)–(e). This is not, in other words, a situation in which Congress was simply being "verbos[e] and proli[x]," *Bruesewitz* v. *Wyeth LLC*, 562 U.S. 223, 236 (2011), using two synonyms in rapid-fire succession when one would have done fine. Instead, "scandalous" and "immoral" are separated by an unrelated word ("deceptive") and mixed in with a lengthy series of other, unrelated concepts. The two therefore need not be interpreted as mutually reinforcing under the Court's precedents. See *Graham County Soil and Water Conservation Dist.* v. *United States ex rel. Wilson*, 559 U.S. 280, 288 (2010).

[7] For that reason, while the majority offers a reasonable reading of "scandalous," it also unnecessarily and ill-advisedly collapses the words "scandalous" and "immoral." Instead, it should treat them as each holding a distinct, nonredundant meaning, with "immoral" covering marks that are offensive because they transgress social norms, and "scandalous" covering marks that are offensive because of the mode in which they are expressed.

[8] What would it mean for "scandalous" in § 1052(a) to cover only offensive modes of expression? The most obvious ways—indeed, perhaps the only conceivable ways—in which a trademark can be expressed in a shocking or offensive manner are when the speaker employs obscenity, vulgarity, or profanity. Obscenity has long been defined by this Court's decision in *Miller* v. *California*, 413 U.S. 15 (1973). See *id.*, at 24–26. As for what constitutes "scandalous" vulgarity or profanity, I do not offer a list,

---

[2] That interpretive move appears to accord with the Federal Circuit and the PTO's past practice. *Ante,* at 2–3. Nevertheless, it is by no means the only reasonable way to read this text, and indeed some courts have suggested that "scandalous" can and should be applied independently of "immoral," see, *e.g., In re McGinley*, 660 F. 2d 481, 485, n. 6 (CCPA 1981).

but I do interpret the term to allow the PTO to restrict (and potentially promulgate guidance to clarify) the small group of lewd words or "swear" words that cause a visceral reaction, that are not commonly used around children, and that are prohibited in comparable settings.[4] Cf. 18 U.S. C. § 1464 (prohibiting "obscene, indecent, or profane language" in radio communications); *FCC v. Pacifica Foundation*, 438 U.S. 726, 746, and n. 22 (1978) (opinion of Stevens, J.) (regulator's objection to a monologue containing various "four-letter words" was not to its "point of view, but to the way in which it [wa]s expressed"); 46 CFR § 67.117(b)(3) (2018) (Coast Guard regulation prohibiting vessel names that "contain" or are "phonetically identical to obscene, indecent, or profane language, or to racial or ethnic epithets"); see also Jacobs, The Public Sensibilities Forum, 95 Nw. U. L. Rev. 1357, 1416–1417, and n. 432 (2001) (noting that "swear words" are "perhaps more than any other categor[y] capable of specific articulation" and citing one state agency's list). Of course, "scandalous" offers its own limiting principle: if a word, though not exactly polite, cannot be said to be "scandalous"—*e.g.,* "shocking" or "extremely offensive," 8 Century Dictionary 5374—it is clearly not the kind of vulgarity or profanity that Congress intended to target. Everyone can think of a small number of words (including the apparent homonym of Brunetti's mark) that would, however, plainly qualify.[5]

B

[9] A limiting construction like the one just discussed is both appropriate in this context and consistent with past precedent. First, while a limiting construction must always be at least reasonable, there are contexts in which imposing such a construction is more appropriate than others. The most obvious example of a setting where more caution is required is in the realm of criminal statutes, where considerations such as the prohibition against vagueness and the rule of lenity come into play . . . . Here, however, the question is only whether the Government must be forced to provide the ancillary benefit of trademark registration to pre-existing trademarks that use even the most extreme obscenity, vulgarity, or profanity. The stakes are far removed from a situation in which, say, Brunetti was facing a threat to his liberty, or even his right to use and enforce his trademark in commerce.

. . . .

[10] Taking the word "scandalous" to target only those marks that employ an offensive mode of expression follows a similar practice. To be sure, the word could be read more broadly, thereby sweeping unconstitutionally into viewpoint discrimination. And imposing a limiting construction is, of course, "not a license for the judiciary to rewrite language enacted by the legislature." *United States* v. *Albertini*, 472 U.S. 675, 680 (1985). But where the Court can reasonably read a statute like this one to save it, the Court should do so. See *Stern v. Marshall*, 564 U.S. 462, 477–478 (2011); *NLRB* v. *Jones & Laughlin Steel Corp.*, 301 U.S. 1, 30 (1937).

---

[4] Although the Government represents, and case law and scholarship appear to confirm, that "scandalous" in § 1052(a) has often been applied to cover this kind of content, see Brief for United States 27; *In re Boulevard Entertainment, Inc.*, 334 F. 3d 1336, 1340 (CA Fed. 2003); Snow, Denying Trademark for Scandalous Speech, 51 U. C. D. L. Rev. 2331, 2339 (2018) (Snow), the majority notes that the PTO has hardly amassed a perfect track record of consistency, see *ante*, at 6–8. Be that as it may, the Government undeniably receives a large volume of trademark applications that easily would fit under this rubric (examples of which I will spare the reader). See *In re Brunetti*, 877 F. 3d 1330, 1355 (CA Fed. 2017) (noting an appendix containing marks denied registration "whose offensiveness cannot be reasonably questioned"). As a result of today's ruling, all of those marks will now presumably have to be registered.

[5] There is at least one particularly egregious racial epithet that would fit this description as well. While *Matal v. Tam*, 582 U. S. __ (2017), removed a statutory basis to deny the registration of racial epithets in general, the Government represented at oral argument that it is holding in abeyance trademark applications that use that particular epithet. See Tr. of Oral Arg. 61. As a result of today's ruling, the Government will now presumably be compelled to register marks containing that epithet as well rather than treating it as a "scandalous" form of profanity under § 1052(a).

II

[11] Adopting a narrow construction for the word "scandalous"—interpreting it to regulate only obscenity, vulgarity, and profanity—would save it from unconstitutionality. Properly narrowed, "scandalous" is a viewpoint-neutral form of content discrimination that is permissible in the kind of discretionary governmental program or limited forum typified by the trademark-registration system.

. . . .

III

[12] "The cardinal principle of statutory construction is to save and not to destroy." *Jones & Laughlin Steel Corp.*, 301 U.S., at 30; see also *Hooper* v. *California*, 155 U.S. 648, 657 (1895) ("The elementary rule is that every reasonable construction must be resorted to, in order to save a statute from unconstitutionality"). In directing the PTO to deny the ancillary benefit of registration to trademarks featuring "scandalous" content, Congress used a word that is susceptible of different meanings. The majority's reading would render the provision unconstitutional; mine would save it. Under these circumstances, the Court ought to adopt the narrower construction, rather than permit a rush to register trademarks for even the most viscerally offensive words and images that one can imagine.[13]

[13] That said, I emphasize that Brunetti's challenge is a facial one. That means that he must show that "'a substantial number of [the scandalous-marks provision's] applications are unconstitutional, judged in relation to the [provision's] plainly legitimate sweep.'" *United States* v. *Stevens*, 559 U.S. 460, 473 (2010). With "scandalous" narrowed to reach only obscene, profane, and vulgar content, the provision would not be overly broad. Cf. *Frisby*, 487 U.S., at 488 (rejecting a facial challenge after adopting a limiting construction); *Boos*, 485 U.S., at 331 (same). Even so, hard cases would remain, and I would expect courts to take seriously as-applied challenges demonstrating a danger that the provision had been used to restrict speech based on the views expressed rather than the mode of expression.[14] Cf. *Finley*, 524 U.S., at 587 (reserving the possibility of as-applied challenges).

[14] Freedom of speech is a cornerstone of our society, and the First Amendment protects Brunetti's right to use words like the one at issue here. The Government need not, however, be forced to confer on Brunetti's trademark (and some more extreme) the ancillary benefit of trademark registration, when "scandalous" in § 1052(a) can reasonably be read to bar the registration of only those marks that are obscene, vulgar, or profane. Though I concur as to the unconstitutionality of the term "immoral" in § 1052(a), I respectfully dissent as to the term "scandalous" in the same statute and would instead uphold it under the narrow construction discussed here.

Comments and Questions

1. *The saga continues: Lanham Act § 2(c).* Lanham Act § 2(c) prohibits the registration of a trademark that "[c]onsists of or comprises a name . . . identifying a particular living individual" without the individual's "written consent." In 2018, Steve Elster applied to register the mark TRUMP TOO SMALL for use on t-shirts. In a brief, routine opinion, The Trademark Trial and Appeal Board affirmed the examiner's refusal to register the mark on the ground that it was prohibited by Lanham Act § 2(c). *In re Steve Elster*, Serial No. 87749230 (TTAB July 2, 2020) [not precedential]. On appeal, the Federal Circuit held that § 2(c) is unconstitutional as applied to Elster:

---

[13] As noted above, I agree with the majority that § 1052(a)'s bar on the registration of "immoral" marks is unconstitutional viewpoint discrimination. See *supra*, at 2. I would simply sever that provision and uphold the bar on "scandalous" marks. See *Reno* v. *American Civil Liberties Union*, 521 U. S. 844, 882–883 (1997); *Brockett* v. *Spokane Arcades, Inc.*, 472 U. S. 491, 504–507 (1985); see also *Tam*, 582 U. S., at ___ (slip op., at 26) (striking down only the disparagement clause).

[14] The majority adverts to details in the record that could call into question whether the PTO engaged in viewpoint discrimination in this very case. See *ante*, at 3. Because a facial challenge is the only challenge before the Court, I do not address whether an as-applied challenge could have merit here.

In short, whether we apply strict scrutiny and the compelling government interest test, or *Central Hudson's* intermediate scrutiny and the substantial government interest test, "the outcome is the same." *Sorrell v. IMS Health Inc.*, 564 U.S. 552, 571 (2011). The PTO's refusal to register Elster's mark cannot be sustained because the government does not have a privacy or publicity interest in restricting speech critical of government officials or public figures in the trademark context—at least absent actual malice, which is not alleged here.

In re Elster, 26 F.4th 1328, 1338–39 (Fed. Cir. 2022). On June 5, 2023, the Supreme Court granted certiorari review. *Vidal v. Elster*, No. 22-704, 2023 WL 3800017 (U.S. June 5, 2023).

2. *Marijuana marks*. To qualify for federal registration, a mark must be used in commerce for goods or services that are legal under federal law. For this reason, the T.T.A.B. has affirmed the refusal of registration of the mark HERBAL ACCESS for "retail store services featuring herbs" when such services consisted of the sale of marijuana in Washington state, under whose law such sales are legal. *In re Brown*, 119 USPQ2d 1350 (TTAB 2016). *See also In re Stanley Bros. Social Enterprises, LLC*, 2020 U.S.P.Q.2d 10658 (TTAB 2020); *In re JJ206, LLC, dba JuJu Joints*, 120 USPQ2d 1568 (TTAB 2016); *In re Canopy Growth Corp.*, Serial Nos. 86475885 & 86475899 (TTAB 2019). For a critique of the PTO's application of a "lawful use" requirement, see Robert A. Mikos, *Unauthorized and Unwise: The Lawful Use Requirement in Trademark Law*, 75 VAND. L. REV. 161 (2022).

C. Use in Commerce as a Prerequisite for Trademark Rights

As stated at the beginning of this Part, a trademark must be used in commerce to qualify for protection. *See Lucent Info. Mgmt. v. Lucent Techs., Inc.*, 186 F.3d 311, 319 (3d Cir. 1999) ("It is axiomatic that if there is 'no trade — no trademark.'" (quoting *La Societe Anonyme des Parfums le Galion v. Jean Patou, Inc.*, 495 F.2d 1265, 1274 (2d Cir. 1974)). In this subsection, we consider the nature of this "use in commerce" requirement.

To avoid ambiguity, it may be useful to recognize from the start the several different aspects of the concept of "use in commerce" in U.S. trademark law, only one of which we will focus on in this subsection.

- *"Use in Commerce" as Implementing the Commerce Clause Limitation on the Reach of Congressional Power*: As the Lanham Act § 45 definition of "commerce" indicates ("The word 'commerce' means all commerce which may lawfully be regulated by Congress."), federal trademark law will regulate only those uses that fall within the Congress's Commerce Clause power. Thus, if a trademark owner does not use its trademark in a manner that affects interstate commerce, federal trademark law will not protect that trademark. The trademark owner must instead rely on state law. This is very rarely an issue given current Commerce Clause jurisprudence. *See, e.g., Christian Faith Fellowship Church v. adidas AG*, 841 F.3d 986, 995 (Fed. Cir. 2016) (holding that plaintiff's single intrastate sale of two hats bearing the mark at issue to an out-of-state resident was regulable by Congress under the Commerce Clause and thus satisfied the Lanham Act's "use in commerce" requirement).

- *"Use in Commerce" for Purposes of Establishing Trademark Rights*: This is the focus of this subsection.

- *"Use in Commerce" for Purposes of Determining Whether a Trademark Owner Has Abandoned Its Rights*: If a trademark owner ceases to use its trademark in commerce without an intent to resume use, it may be deemed to have "abandoned" its mark. *See* Lanham Act § 45, 15 U.S.C. § 1127 (defining when a mark shall be deemed "abandoned"). We will address the doctrine of trademark abandonment in Part III.D below.

- *"Use in Commerce" for Purposes of Determining Whether a Defendant Has Made an Infringing "Actionable Use" of the Plaintiff's Mark*: In several high-profile internet-related cases in the early years of the century, defendants argued that the terms of each of the infringement sections of the Lanham Act—Lanham Act §§ 32, 43(a), and 43(c)—require a showing that the defendant is making a "use in commerce" to be liable. These defendants argued that they were not making a "use in commerce" as that term is specifically defined under Lanham Act § 45 and should thus not be found liable. We will address the case law on this issue, which has ultimately largely come to reject this argument, in Part II.A.1 below.

- *"Commercial Use" of a Mark for Purposes of Determining Whether a Defendant Has Made an Infringing "Actionable Use" of the Plaintiff's Mark*: Finally, Lanham Act §§ 32, 43(a), and 43(c) appear to require that for a defendant's conduct to be infringing, the defendant must be using the mark "in connection with the sale, distribution, or advertising of any goods or services." Lanham Act § 32(1)(a), 15 U.S.C. § 1114(1)(a). Defendants engaged in non-profit, expressive uses of marks (such as internet gripe sites that do not sell any goods) have argued that their conduct does not constitute "commercial use" and is thus not infringing. We will address this issue in Part II.A.2 below.

The student is strongly advised to distinguish between these various aspects of "use in commerce" as we proceed, particularly the difference between (a) "use in commerce" by the *plaintiff* for purposes of establishing the plaintiff's trademark rights and (b) "use in commerce" (or "commercial use") by the *defendant* for purposes of establishing the defendant's trademark infringement.

With respect to the *plaintiff's* use in commerce for purposes of establishing trademark rights, a further distinction should be drawn from the start. Though the two areas of law are closely related, there are nevertheless important differences between (1) the extent of "use in commerce" that a mark owner must make for the mark to qualify for federal registration, and (2) the extent of "use in commerce" that a mark owner must make of a mark to establish unregistered, "common law" priority over subsequent users of the same mark. In general, the quantum of use necessary for registration is a stricter requirement than that necessary for purposes of establishing unregistered common law priority. *See* McCarthy § 16:12–16:14.

In Part I.C.1, we address the use in commerce requirement for federal registration. As you will see, *Aycock Engineering, Inc. v. Airflite, Inc.*, 560 F.3d 1350 (Fed. Cir. 2009), and *Couture v. Playdom, Inc.*, 778 F.3d 1379 (Fed. Cir. 2015), make clear that the owner of a mark must actually complete the sale of goods or services bearing the mark to customers for the mark to qualify for federal registration.[1] Mere advertising or other promotional conduct without actual sales will not support federal registration. By contrast, in Part I.C.2, *Planetary Motion, Inc. v. Techsplosion, Inc.*, 261 F.3d 1188 (11th Cir. 2001), shows that for purposes of establishing unregistered, common law priority in a mark, advertising and other promotional conduct prior to actual sales may be sufficient to support a priority claim.

In reading through these two subsections, consider whether the distinction between use for purposes of registration and use for purposes of common law priority makes sense as a matter of sound policy.

1. Use in Commerce as a Prerequisite for Federal Trademark Registration

Lanham Act § 45, 15 U.S.C. § 1127

> The term "use in commerce" means the bona fide use of a mark in the ordinary course of trade, and not made merely to reserve a right in a mark. For purposes of this chapter, a mark shall be deemed to be in use in commerce–
>
> (1) on goods when–
>
> > (A) it is placed in any manner on the goods or their containers or the displays associated therewith or on the tags or labels affixed thereto, or if the nature of the goods

---

[1] There is a minor exception to the general rule that a trademark owner must make use in commerce of its mark in order for the mark to qualify for federal registration. As discussed more fully in Part II.D below, Lanham Act § 44(e), 15 U.S.C. § 1126(e), provides that foreign applicants applying under a § 44 filing basis need not show actual use in commerce prior to obtaining registration. *See* McCarthy § 29:14.

makes such placement impracticable, then on documents associated with the goods or their sale, and

(B) the goods are sold or transported in commerce, and

(2) on services when it is used or displayed in the sale or advertising of services and the services are rendered in commerce, or the services are rendered in more than one State or in the United States and a foreign country and the person rendering the services is engaged in commerce in connection with the services.

The word "commerce" means all commerce which may lawfully be regulated by Congress.

United States Patent Office
983,064
Registered Apr. 30, 1974

SUPPLEMENTAL REGISTER
Service Mark

Ser. No. 367,571, filed P.R. Aug. 10, 1970;
Am. S.R. Apr. 27, 1973

AIRFLITE

Aycock Engineering, Inc. (North Carolina corporation)
492 Rayconda
Fayetteville, N.C. 28304

For: ARRANGING FOR INDIVIDUAL RESERVA-TIONS FOR FLIGHTS ON AIRPLANES, in CLASS 105 (INT. CL. 39).
First use at least as early as June 23, 1969; in commerce at least as early as Mar. 3, 1970.

Aycock Engineering, Inc. v. Airflite, Inc.
560 F.3d 1350 (Fed. Cir. 2009)

O'GRADY, District Judge:

[1] In 1970, Respondent–Appellant Aycock Engineering, Inc. ("Aycock Engineering") applied for a service mark, which was registered at the United States Patent and Trademark Office ("USPTO") in 1974 after examination. In 2007, however, the USPTO Trademark Trial and Appeal Board ("TTAB") declared the registration void because it failed to meet the "use in commerce" element of the Lanham Act. Aycock Engineering now appeals the TTAB's ruling. The question presented herein is whether the use in commerce requirement is met when an applicant uses a service mark in the preparatory stages of a service's development, but never offers the service to the public. We hold that it is not.

I. BACKGROUND

[2] In the late 1940s, William Aycock conceived of and began work on a service involving chartering flights in the air taxi industry. At that time, the common practice for air taxi companies was to lease entire airplanes, not individual seats. Consequently, individual passengers not belonging to a larger party faced more difficulty and expense in chartering a flight. Mr. Aycock intended, through his service, to allow solo passengers to arrange flights on chartered aircraft for less cost.

[3] Mr. Aycock did not plan on operating the chartered air taxi services himself. Instead, his goal was to develop a system where he would serve his customers by acting as the middleman, or "communication link," between the customer and one of the air taxi service operators he contracted with to provide flights on an individual seat basis. Mr. Aycock planned to advertise his service, which he called the AIRFLITE service, to the public and to have those interested in using the service call a toll-free phone number to schedule reservations. After learning of customers' travel plans, Mr. Aycock would then arrange for the air taxi service to fly his customers with similar travel plans to their destinations. Mr.

Aycock believed that in order for his service to become operational, he needed at least 300 air taxi operators in the United States to agree to participate in his air-taxi-operator network.[2]

[4] In the years after conceiving of the idea for his service, Mr. Aycock worked toward offering the service to the public. In the mid–1960s, he formed Aycock Engineering—the corporate entity under which his service would operate. He also sought and obtained two toll-free telephone numbers that the public could use to make reservations. In March of 1970, Mr. Aycock invited virtually all air taxi operators certified by the Federal Aviation Administration ("FAA") to join his operation by, inter alia, distributing flyers with in-depth information about his AIRFLITE service. He eventually entered into contracts with some of those air taxi service operators.[3] Under these contracts, air taxi operators agreed to participate in the AIRFLITE service and even paid modest initiation fees to Mr. Aycock. Furthermore, Mr. Aycock filed a service mark application on August 10, 1970 for the term AIRFLITE.

[5] Despite his efforts, Mr. Aycock's operation never got off the ground. While he estimated that he needed at least 300 air service operators under contract to make his service operational, Mr. Aycock never had more than twelve (4% of his minimum goal) under contract at any time throughout his company's history. And while Mr. Aycock advertised to air taxi operators, he never marketed the AIRFLITE service to the general public. More specifically, the record does not suggest that Mr. Aycock ever gave the public an opportunity to use the toll-free phone numbers to book reservations, or that he ever spoke with a member of the general public about making a reservation. Finally, and most notably, Mr. Aycock never arranged for a single passenger to fly on a chartered flight.[4]

[6] Mr. Aycock's AIRFLITE mark, which he applied for on August 10, 1970, was registered by the USPTO on April 30, 1974 on the Supplemental Register[*] after a prosecution that involved considerable negotiation between Mr. Aycock and the trademark examining attorney . . . . The recitation of services for the AIRFLITE service mark eventually agreed upon by the USPTO and Mr. Aycock was "[a]rranging for individual reservations for flights on airplanes." *Id.* at 729. Mr. Aycock's application to renew his AIRFLITE service mark was granted by the USPTO on April 27, 1994.

[7] In 2001, Airflite, Inc., the Petitioner–Appellee, filed a petition for cancellation alleging, inter alia, that Aycock Engineering did not use its AIRFLITE mark prior to registration in connection with the services identified in its registration. In that proceeding, the TTAB agreed with Airflite, Inc. and cancelled the AIRFLITE registration, finding that Mr. Aycock failed to render the service described in its registration in commerce. *Airflite, Inc. v. Aycock Eng'g, Inc.,* Cancellation 92032520, 2007 WL 2972237, at *7 (TTAB Oct. 4, 2007) ("*TTAB Decision* ").

. . . .

D. Use Requirement

[8] Under § 45 of the Lanham Act, a service mark is any "word, name, symbol or device, or any combination thereof used by a person, or which a person has a bona fide intention to use in commerce . . . to identify and distinguish the services of one person . . . from the services of others." 15 U.S.C. § 1127 (2006). The definition of "service mark" is virtually identical to the definition of "trademark." But while service marks apply to intangible services, trademarks are used to distinguish tangible goods. *See Chance v. Pac–Tel Teletrac Inc.,* 242 F.3d 1151, 1156 (9th Cir. 2001).

---

[2] Mr. Aycock stated in his deposition, "We start this when 300 air taxi operators in the United States have signed on to provide the transportation." J.A. 1942.

[3] Some of the contracts originated in the 1970s, and some came as late as 2001.

[4] When asked at his deposition whether he had ever arranged for an individual to fly on an airplane, Mr. Aycock stated, "I had never made a—any arrangement . . . I had never had a talk with the customer then talked with the air taxi operator and reached any agreement on them carrying the customer."

[*] {The Supplemental Register is reserved for marks that are capable of, but have not yet developed, source distinctiveness—i.e., marks that are descriptive and do not yet possess acquired distinctiveness. *See* Lanham Act § 23, 15 U.S.C. § 1091.}

[9] "It is clear from the wording of the Lanham Act that applications for service mark registrations are subject to the same statutory criteria as are trademarks." 3 J. Thomas McCarthy, *McCarthy on Trademarks and Unfair Competition* § 19:82 (4th ed. 2008) [hereinafter McCarthy]; see 15 U.S.C. § 1053 (2006). One such statutory criterion that applies to both trademarks and service marks is the "use in commerce" requirement. . . . The registration of a mark that does not meet the use requirement is void ab initio. *See Gay Toys, Inc. v. McDonald's Corp.*, 585 F.2d 1067, 1068 (CCPA 1978); 3 McCarthy § 19:112.

[10] Despite the seeming harmony and simplicity in the application of the use requirement to trademarks and service marks, opportunity exists for confusion in this area of the law. Different statutory requirements apply to applications filed before November 16, 1989, as compared to those filed after. This is because in 1988, Congress passed the Trademark Law Revision Act ("TLRA"). The TLRA altered the burden that applicants must meet before satisfying the use element by requiring an applicant to make a "bona fide use of [the] mark in the ordinary course of trade." Trademark Law Revision Act of 1988, Pub.L. No. 100–667, 102 Stat. 3935 (effective November 16, 1989) (codified at 15 U.S.C. § 1127 (2006)).

[11] This "bona fide use" language was intended to eliminate "token uses," which occurred when applicants used marks in conjunction with selling goods or offering services for the sole purpose of obtaining registration, and with no intention of legitimately using the mark in commerce until a later date. See *Blue Bell, Inc. v. Jaymar–Ruby, Inc.*, 497 F.2d 433, 437 (2d Cir. 1974). Before 1989, a "token use" was sufficient to satisfy the use requirement and qualify a mark for registration. *See Id.*

[12] In addition to eliminating token uses, the 1988 TLRA made other changes to the use requirement. Before 1989, an applicant only qualified for registration if he was using his mark in commerce at the time he filed his application at the USPTO. *WarnerVision Entm't Inc. v. Empire of Carolina, Inc.*, 101 F.3d 259, 260 (2d Cir. 1996). But after 1989, an applicant could begin the registration process even when his mark was not in use in commerce at the time of the filing, so long as he had a "bona fide intention to use the mark in commerce" at a later date. 15 U.S.C. § 1051(b) (2006). Applicants filing these "intent to use" applications are only granted registration, however, if they file a verified statement of commercial use proving eventual use of the mark in commerce. *Id.* § 1051(d).

[13] Because the mark at issue here is a service mark, the use requirement relating to service mark applications, as opposed to trademark applications, guides our analysis. Furthermore, the application at issue in this case was filed in 1970. Therefore, this case must be decided according to the service mark use requirement that appeared in the Lanham Act in 1970 (i.e., the pre–1989 version). *See* 3 McCarthy § 19:112. However, for the reasons stated below, our holding in this case also applies to the current (and post–1989) service mark use requirement.

E. Use Requirement for Service Marks

[14] With the exception of the 1988 TLRA statutory language eliminating token uses and permitting intent-to-use applications, the service mark use requirement as it appeared in 1970 is materially identical to the post–1989 version. The use provision of the Lanham Act in force in 1970 stated that a service mark was in use in commerce "when it is used or displayed in the sale or advertising of services, and the services are rendered in commerce, or the services are rendered in more than one State or in this and a foreign country and the person rendering the services is engaged in commerce in connection therewith." Pub.L. No. 87–772, 76 Stat. 769 (1962). Therefore, like the current use requirement, a service mark applicant seeking to meet the pre–1989 version had to (1) use the mark in the sale or advertising of a service and (2) show that the service was either rendered in interstate commerce or rendered in more than one state or in this and a foreign country by a person engaged in commerce.

[15] Courts, as well as the TTAB, have interpreted the pre–1989 statutory language in analogous cases. Without question, advertising or publicizing a service that the applicant intends to perform in the future will not support registration. *In re Cedar Point, Inc.*, 220 USPQ 533, 536 (TTAB 1983) (quoting *Intermed Commc'ns, Inc. v. Chaney*, 197 USPQ 501, 507–08 (TTAB 1977)); *Greyhound Corp. v. Armour Life Ins. Co.*, 214 USPQ 473, 474 (TTAB 1982). Instead, the advertising or publicizing must relate to "an existing service which has already been offered to the public." *Greyhound*, 214 USPQ at 474.

Furthermore, "[m]ere adoption (selection) of a mark accompanied by preparations to begin its use are insufficient . . . for claiming ownership of and applying to register the mark." *Intermed,* 197 USPQ at 507; *see Blue Bell,* 497 F.2d at 437. "At the very least," in order for an applicant to meet the use requirement, "there must be an open and notorious public offering of the services to those for whom the services are intended." *Intermed,* 197 USPQ at 507.

[16] In *Intermed,* the TTAB rejected a service mark application for failing to meet the use in commerce requirement even where the applicant had performed many pre-application service-oriented activities involving the public. *Id.* at 508–09. The applicant in that case sought to register a mark intended to identify an international medical services operation. *Id.* at 502. The applicant's plan was to build the international service from an already operating United States-based medical service. *Id.* at 503. The applicant intended to, and did use the United States-based operation as a fundraising affiliate of the new international operation. *Id.* at 504. Additionally, the applicant communicated with and solicited the support of the Iranian government regarding the service before the application was filed. *Id.* The applicant also issued a detailed announcement using the service mark term before the filing date designed to inform and update individuals about the service's status. *Id.* Finally, and also before the date of application, the applicant hired a fundraising firm to raise money for the service. *Id.* at 508.

[17] Despite these activities, the TTAB held that the applicant failed to meet the use requirement because the services described in the application were not "offered, promoted, advertised or rendered . . . in commerce." *Intermed,* 197 USPQ at 504. The TTAB stated that "[t]he statute requires not only the display of the mark in the sale or advertising of services but also the rendition of those services in order to constitute use of the service mark in commerce." *Id.* At 507–08. The TTAB further explained that adopting a mark accompanied by mere "preparations to begin its use" is insufficient for service mark registration, and that in order for the use requirement to be met, there must be "an open and notorious public offering of the services to those for whom the services are intended." *Id.* at 507.

[18] In 1983, the TTAB again rejected a service mark application because it failed to meet the use requirement. *Cedar Point,* 220 USPQ at 533. In *Cedar Point,* the Cedar Point amusement park, which had been in business for decades, was preparing to open a new water park addition in mid-May of 1980. *Id.* at 535. One preparatory step taken by Cedar Point before opening day was the filing of a service mark application to register the mark "OCEANA" for its new water park service. *Id.* Cedar Point also distributed nearly 700,000 water park advertisement brochures containing the OCEANA mark during the months preceding the grand opening. *Id.*

[19] The TTAB emphasized the fact that Cedar Point filed its service mark application with the USPTO before it opened the water park's doors and offered those services to the public. *Id.* at 535–36. The TTAB then explained that the use of a mark in connection with the advertising of services intended to be "available at some time in the future, but not yet available at the time of filing" does not qualify the mark for registration. *Id.* at 535. Therefore, Cedar Point's water park advertising campaign, which was ongoing at the time the application was filed, was insufficient on its own to support registration. *Id.* As a result, the TTAB held that the "applicant's mark 'OCEANA' was not in 'use in commerce' . . . at the time of the filing of [the] application" and that the application was thus void ab initio. *Id.* at 537.

[20] Interestingly, Cedar Point filed for its service mark roughly one month before the scheduled opening of the new water park. *Id.* at 535. With the application date being so close to the opening date, it is indisputable that Cedar Point had taken numerous steps toward constructing the water park by the time the application was filed. Nevertheless, the TTAB found none of these preparatory steps sufficient to satisfy the use in commerce requirement.

. . . .

[21] We find the reasoning of these cases persuasive. The language of the statute, by requiring that the mark be "used or displayed in the sale or advertising of services, and the services are rendered in commerce," makes plain that advertisement and actual use of the mark in commerce are required; mere preparations to use that mark sometime in the future will not do. Thus, we hold that an applicant's

preparations to use a mark in commerce are insufficient to constitute use in commerce. Rather, the mark must be actually used in conjunction with the services described in the application for the mark.

F. Analysis

. . . .

[22] But [Aycock's] activities, even taken together, do not constitute a service that falls within the scope of our definition of the recitation of services. As mentioned earlier, it is our view that the service described in Mr. Aycock's service mark application covers only the arranging of flights between an air taxi operator and a passenger, and not preparatory efforts to arrange a network of air taxi operators. The activities described above, however, were merely preparatory steps that Mr. Aycock took toward his goal of one day, as he described, operating a "communication service between persons desiring to charter aircraft" that "put[ ] individuals desiring air transportation in contact with people rendering that service." J.A. 736, 749.

[23] In order for Mr. Aycock to satisfy the use requirement, more was required. Mr. Aycock had to develop his company to the point where he made an open and notorious public offering of his AIRFLITE service to intended customers. *See Intermed*, 197 USPQ at 507. However, at no point in time did Mr. Aycock give a potential customer the chance to use his AIRFLITE service. He never arranged for a single flight between a customer and an air taxi operator. This is because Mr. Aycock, as stated in his deposition, believed he needed at least 300 air taxi operators under contract before his service could become operational. Reasonably, because he never had more than twelve air taxi operators under contract at any one time, Mr. Aycock chose not to open his doors to the public.

{The court affirmed the TTAB's cancellation of Aycock's mark. Judge Newman dissented on the ground that, notwithstanding the description of services listed in the registration that was finally agreed to by Aycock, "it is inappropriate now to construe the registration so as to exclude the actual use of the mark as was explained in the examination, shown in the specimens, and fully explored in the public record of the prosecution." Aycock Eng'g, 560 F.3d at 1365 (Newman, J., dissenting).}

Comments and Questions

1. *Use of a mark "merely to reserve a right in a mark."* In *Social Technologies LLC v. Apple Inc.*, 4 F.4th 811 (9th Cir. 2021), Social Technologies filed an intent to use application for the mark MEMOJI in connection with a mobile phone application, but it had not yet launched the application and thus had not yet made actual use of the mark in commerce. Apple then announced that it was adopting the mark also for a mobile phone application. Social Technologies then had one job. All it needed to do was launch its application as planned and thus make a legitimate use of its mark in commerce, which, as we will discuss further in sections I.D and I.E below, would complete the registration process and enable it to claim its intent to use application date as its priority date. But in the process of preparing to make actual use of the mark, Social Technologies' co-founder and president wrote a series of disastrous emails to his employees. The Ninth Circuit cited these emails to conclude that Social Technologies had ultimately launched its product merely to reserve a right in the MEMOJI mark and hold Apple hostage. For example, the co-founder made clear that they should now design the application purely to support the trademark application. He insisted to his engineers that "*the editing feature [was] vital*" to "*satisfy the 'editing' requirement of the trademark.*" *Id.* at 815 (emphasis in original). As the Ninth Circuit noted, he also emailed his employees: "*We are lining up all of our information, in preparation for a nice lawsuit against Apple, Inc! We are looking REALLY good. Get your Lamborghini picked out!*" *Id.* (emphasis in original). The Ninth Circuit affirmed summary judgment in favor of Apple on the ground that Social Technologies failed to satisfy the Lanham Act § 45 requirement that its use be a "bona fide use of a mark in the ordinary course of trade, and not made merely to reserve a right in a mark." 15 U.S.C. § 1125.

———————————

Couture v. Playdom, Inc.
778 F.3d 1379 (Fed. Cir. 2015)

DYK, Circuit Judge:

[1] David Couture ("appellant") appeals from a decision of the Trademark Trial and Appeal Board (the "Board") granting a petition by Playdom, Inc. ("appellee") to cancel appellant's PLAYDOM service mark. We affirm.

BACKGROUND

[2] On May 30, 2008, appellant filed an application to register the service mark PLAYDOM pursuant to Lanham Act § 1(a), 15 U.S.C. § 1051(a). As a specimen showing use of the mark, appellant submitted a "[s]creen capture of [a] website offering Entertainment Services in commerce." Also on May 30, 2008, appellant had created the website, which was hosted at www.playdominc.com. As of May 30, 2008, the website included only a single page, which stated: "[w]elcome to PlaydomInc.com. We are proud to offer writing and production services for motion picture film, television, and new media. Please feel free to contact us if you are interested:playdominc@gmail.com." The webpage included the notice: "Website Under Construction." No services under the mark were provided until 2010, well after the application was filed. The PLAYDOM mark was registered by the United States Patent and Trademark Office ("PTO") on January 13, 2009, as registration no. 3,560,701.

[3] On February 9, 2009, appellee filed an application to register the identical mark—PLAYDOM. Appellant's registered mark was cited by the examining attorney as a ground for rejecting appellee's application under Lanham Act § 2(d), 15 U.S.C. § 1052(d). On June 15, 2009, appellee filed a petition to cancel the registration of appellant's mark, arguing, inter alia, that appellant's registration was void ab initio because appellant had not used the mark in commerce as of the date of the application. On February 3, 2014, the Board granted the cancellation petition, stating that appellant "had not rendered his services as of the filing date of his application" because he had "merely posted a website advertising his readiness, willingness and ability to render said services," and the registration was therefore void ab initio.

DISCUSSION

. . . .

I

. . . .

[4] We have not previously had occasion to directly address whether the offering of a service, without the actual provision of a service, is sufficient to constitute use in commerce under Lanham Act § 45, 15 U.S.C. § 1127. In *Aycock,* we stated that, "[a]t the very least, in order for an applicant to meet the use requirement, there must be an open and notorious public offering of the services to those for whom the services are intended." 560 F.3d at 1358 (internal quotation marks and citation omitted). The applicant in *Aycock* had not made such an "open and notorious public offering of his . . . service to intended customers," and the registration was therefore void *ab initio. Id.* at 1361–62 (citation omitted). But we did not suggest in *Aycock* that an open and notorious public offering alone is sufficient to establish use in commerce. And appellant does not point to any decision by the Board which found mere offering of a service to be sufficient.

[5] On its face, the statute is clear that a mark for services is used in commerce only when *both* [1] "it is used or displayed in the sale or advertising of services *and* [2] the services are rendered . . . ." 15 U.S.C. § 1127 (emphasis added). This statutory language reflects the nature of trademark rights:

> There is no such thing as property in a trademark except as a right appurtenant to an established business or trade in connection with which the mark is employed . . . . [T]he right to a particular mark grows out of its use, not its mere adoption . . . .

United Drug Co. v. Theodore Rectanus Co., 248 U.S. 90, 97, 39 S.Ct. 48, 63 L.Ed. 141 (1918).

[6] Other circuits have interpreted Lanham Act § 45 as requiring actual provision of services. For example, in *International Bancorp, LLC v. Societe des Bains de Mer et du Cercle des Etrangers a Monaco*, 329 F.3d 359, 361–66 (4th Cir. 2003), the Fourth Circuit held that, absent evidence of actual bookings made by a New York office for the Monte Carlo casino in Monaco, the activities of the New York office, including trade shows, advertising campaigns, partnering with charities, mail and telephone marketing, and soliciting media coverage, were insufficient to establish use in commerce of the "Casino de Monte Carlo" service mark. However, apart from the activities of the New York office, evidence that United States citizens had gone to the casino in Monaco established trade with a foreign nation and thus use in commerce. *Id.* at 365–66; *see Sensient Techs. Corp. v. SensoryEffects Flavor Co.*, 613 F.3d 754, 759–63 (8th Cir. 2010) (analogizing to service marks and holding no use in commerce where alleged infringer issued press release, made announcement, gave presentations, and constructed website with "under construction" notice where there was no evidence of any sale or transport of goods bearing the mark at issue); *Buti v. Impressa Perosa, S.R.L.*, 139 F.3d 98, 100–03 (2d Cir. 1998) (promotion of Italian cafe in the United States, including distributing promotional materials offering free meals, did not constitute use in commerce where restaurant services were only provided in Italy and not in the United States and where it was conceded that "the food and drink services . . . form[ed] no part of the trade between Italy and the United States").[2]

. . . .

[7] Here, there is no evidence in the record showing that appellant rendered services to any customer before 2010, and the cancellation of appellant's registration was appropriate.

II

[8] Appellant also argues that the Board erred in failing to allow him to amend the basis of the application to Lanham Act § 1(b), which provides for requesting registration where "[a] person . . . has a bona fide intention, under circumstances showing the good faith of such person, to use a trademark in commerce . . . ." 15 U.S.C. § 1051(b)(1).

[9] 37 C.F.R. § 2.35(b) provides procedures for substitution of a basis in an application either before or after publication. 37 C.F.R. § 2.35(b)(1)-(2). But that provision contemplates substitution during the pendency of an application, not after registration. *See* TMEP § 806.03(j) (Jan. 2015) ("Any petition to change the basis must be filed before issuance of the registration."). Therefore, the Board did not err in not granting appellant's request to amend the basis of the application.

AFFIRMED

Comments and Questions

1. *Amending the application to seek registration under section 1(b)'s intent to use provision*. In *In re Alessandra Suuberg*, Serial No. 88234650, 2021 TTAB LEXIS 459 (TTAB 2021) [precedential], the Board, citing *Couture*, affirmed the examiner's refusal to register the mark where "the applicant's activities were preliminary and had not resulted in any use of the mark in commerce prior to the filing of the application." *Id.* at *8–9. In a footnote, the Board took pains to point out that "[t]he Examining Attorney suggested on two occasions that Applicant amend her application to seek registration under the intent-to-use provisions of Section 1(b) of the Trademark Act, 15 U.S.C. § 1051(b). . . . Had Applicant done so, she would have had the chance to preserve her application and its filing date, and at a later date, if bona fide use of her mark had begun, make the necessary showing of use to obtain a registration. Id." *Id.* at *11 n. 13. In contrast, because Mr. Couture had already completed registration of the mark, he could not amend the basis of the registration.

---

[2] Although these other circuit cases involve infringement, they address the same language in Lanham Act § 45.

2.   Use in Commerce as a Prerequisite for Unregistered "Common Law" Priority

Planetary Motion, Inc. v. Techsplosion, Inc.
261 F.3d 1188 (11th Cir. 2001)

RESTANI, Judge:

[1] Planetary Motion, Inc. ("Planetary Motion" or "Appellee") sued Techsplosion, Inc. and Michael Gay a/k/a Michael Carson (respectively "Techsplosion" and "Carson"; collectively "Appellants") for infringement and dilution of an unregistered trademark under Section 43(a) and (c) of the Federal Trademark Act, 15 U.S.C. § 1051 *et seq.* (1994) ("Lanham Act"), and for violation of Florida's unfair competition law. Fla. Stat. Ann. § 495.151 (West 2000). Finding that Planetary Motion had established priority of use and a likelihood of confusion, the United States District Court for the Southern District of Florida entered summary judgment in favor of Planetary Motion. We affirm the judgment . . . .

Facts

I. Development and Distribution of the "Coolmail" Software

[2] In late 1994, Byron Darrah ("Darrah") developed a UNIX-based program (the "Software") that provides e-mail users with notice of new e-mail and serves as a gateway to the users' e-mail application. On December 31, 1994, Darrah distributed the Software over the Internet by posting it on a UNIX user site called "Sunsite," from which it could be downloaded for free. Darrah had named the Software "Coolmail" and this designation appeared on the announcement sent to the end-users on Sunsite as well as on the Software user-manual, both of which accompanied the release.

[3] The Software was distributed without charge to users pursuant to a GNU General Public License that also accompanied the release. A GNU General Public License allows users to copy, distribute and/or modify the Software under certain restrictions, e.g., users modifying licensed files must carry "prominent notices" stating that the user changed the files and the date of any change. After the release of the Software, Darrah received correspondence from users referencing the "Coolmail" mark and in some cases suggesting improvements. In 1995, Darrah released two subsequent versions of the Software under the same mark and also pursuant to the GNU General Public License.

[4] In early 1995, a German company named S.u.S.E. GmbH sought permission from Darrah to include the Software in a CD-ROM package sold as a compilation of Unix-based programs. Darrah consented and, pursuant to the GNU licensing agreement, S.u.S.E. distributed the Software in its compilation product and in subsequent versions thereof. S.u.S.E. sold and continues to sell the software compilation in stores in the United States and abroad, as well as over the Internet.

II. Launch of Techsplosion's "CoolMail" E-mail Service

[5] In 1998, Appellant Carson formed Techsplosion, for the purpose of operating a business based on an e-mail service that he had developed. On April 16, 1998, Techsplosion began offering the e-mail service on the Internet under the mark "CoolMail." Two days later, Techsplosion activated the domain name "coolmail.to". Techsplosion delivered an e-mail solicitation under the "CoolMail" mark to approximately 11,000 members of the Paramount Banner Network, an Internet advertising network, also created and operated by Carson. Techsplosion charged no fee to subscribe to the service and generated revenues through the sale of banner advertisements on its web site.

III. Planetary Motion's E-mail Service & Application for Trademark Registration

[6] Appellee Planetary Motion is a computer software and telecommunications company that developed and owns an electronic mail service called "Coolmail." As part of its service, Planetary Motion enables a person to check e-mail via telephone without logging onto a computer. On April 24, 1998, Planetary Motion filed three intent-to-use applications to register the mark "Coolmail" with the United States Patent and Trademark Office. Though Planetary Motion was aware that Darrah's Software also bore the mark "Coolmail," it represented in its applications that it was not aware of any mark upon which its proposed registered mark would infringe. Planetary Motion launched its Coolmail e-mail service to subscribers on June 8, 1998.

IV. Planetary Motion's Complaint and Subsequent Acquisition of Darrah's Rights

[7] On April 22, 1999, Planetary Motion filed a complaint against Techsplosion. In the complaint, Planetary Motion alleged infringement of the alleged mark "Coolmail" for use in connection with e-mail services. Planetary alleged federal trademark infringement and unfair competition under Section 43(a) of the Lanham Act, 15 U.S.C. § 1125(a), as well as injury to business reputation and dilution under Florida Statute § 495.151.

[8] On June 10, 1999, Techsplosion filed an Answer, Affirmative Defenses, and Counterclaims. The counterclaims alleged infringement of the mark "Coolmail" for use in connection with e-mail services. Techsplosion alleged unfair competition, false designation, description, and representation under the Lanham Act, common trademark infringement, common law unfair competition, and injury to business reputation and dilution.

[9] In July of 1999, Planetary Motion purchased from Darrah all rights, title, and interest to the Software including all copyrights, trademarks, patents and other intellectual property rights.[1] On August 31, 1999, Planetary filed an Amended Verified Complaint, adding a claim for dilution under Section 43(c) of the Lanham Act, 15 U.S.C. § 1125(c), and alleging violation of trademark rights assigned from Darrah.

V. Disposition of Planetary Motion's Complaint

[10] On January 31, 2000, the district court entered an Order granting Planetary Motion's motion for summary judgment and denying Carson's and Techsplosion's motion for summary judgment. The district court based the Order on two findings: (1) that the alleged mark was affixed to Darrah's software, and that Darrah's distribution of the software over the Internet constituted a "transport in commerce," resulting in the creation of trademark rights and priority, and (2) there was a likelihood of confusion because the marks "are essentially the same." The district court did not reach the issue of whether Techsplosion's use of "CoolMail" in connection with its e-mail service diluted Planetary Motion's mark.

[11] On the same date, the district court entered final judgment granting Planetary Motion permanent injunctive relief. *See* 15 U.S.C. § 1116. The order also awarded Planetary Motion profits and damages, as well as attorney fees and costs, pursuant to section 35 of the Lanham Act, 15 U.S.C. § 1117. {Techsplosion appealed.}

Discussion

. . . .

I. Prior Use in Commerce

[12] Under common law, trademark ownership rights are "appropriated only through actual prior use in commerce." *Tally-Ho, Inc. v. Coast Community College Dist.,* 889 F.2d 1018, 1022 (11th Cir. 1989) (citation omitted). Under the Lanham Act,[5] the term "use in commerce" is defined in . . . 15 U.S.C. § 1127.[6]

---

[1] The assignee of a trade name or service mark "steps into the shoes of the assignor." *Premier Dental Prods. Co. v. Darby Dental Supply Co.,* 794 F.2d 850, 853 (3d Cir.), *cert. denied,* 479 U.S. 950 (1986). Appellants do not contest the validity of the assignment from Darrah, nor do they dispute that in purchasing rights to Darrah's software, Planetary Motion succeeded to all rights possessed by Darrah.

[5] "In the absence of registration, rights to a mark traditionally have depended on the very same elements that are now included in the statutory definition: the bona fide use of a mark in commerce that was not made merely to reserve a mark for later exploitation." *Allard Enters., Inc. v. Advanced Programming Res., Inc.,* 146 F.3d 350, 357 (6th Cir. 1998). Common law and statutory trademark infringements are merely specific aspects of unfair competition. *New West Corp. v. NYM Co. of Cal., Inc.,* 595 F.2d 1194, 1201 (9th Cir. 1979) (citing, *inter alia, Dresser Indus., Inc. v. Heraeus Engelhard Vacuum, Inc.,* 395 F.2d 457, 461 (3d Cir.), *cert. denied,* 393 U.S. 934, 89 S.Ct. 293, 21 L.Ed.2d 270 (1968)).

[6] Appellants appear to have conceded that if Darrah sent out original programs and related manuals, this would satisfy the affixation requirement:

The district court found that because the statute is written in the disjunctive (i.e., "sale *or* transport"), Darrah's wide distribution of the Coolmail software over the Internet, even absent any sales thereof, was sufficient to establish ownership rights in the "CoolMail" mark. Appellants contend that "transport in commerce" alone—here, Darrah's free distribution of software over the Internet "with no existing business, no intent to form a business, and no sale under the mark"—is insufficient to create trademark rights. Appellants' Brief at 13. Appellants' argument lacks merit.

[13] The parties do not make clear the two different contexts in which the phrase "use in commerce" is used. The term "use in commerce" as used in the Lanham Act "denotes Congress's authority under the Commerce Clause rather than an intent to limit the [Lanham] Act's application to profit making activity." *United We Stand Am., Inc. v. United We Stand, Am. N.Y., Inc.,* 128 F.3d 86, 92-93 (2d Cir. 1997) (citation omitted), *cert. denied,* 523 U.S. 1076 (1998); U.S. Const., Art. I, § 8, cl. 3. Because Congress's authority under the Commerce Clause extends to activity that "substantially affects" interstate commerce, *United States v. Lopez,* 514 U.S. 549, 559 (1995), the Lanham Act's definition of "commerce" is concomitantly broad in scope: "all commerce which may lawfully be regulated by Congress." 15 U.S.C. § 1127. *See also Steele v. Bulova Watch Co.,* 344 U.S. 280, 283-84 (1952); *Larry Harmon Pictures Corp. v. Williams Rest. Corp.,* 929 F.2d 662, 666 (Fed. Cir.) (allowing registration for an intrastate provider of restaurant services with an undefined interstate clientele), *cert. denied,* 502 U.S. 823 (1991). The distribution of the Software for end-users over the Internet satisfies the "use in commerce" jurisdictional predicate. *See, e.g., Planned Parenthood Fed'n of Am., Inc. v. Bucci,* 42 U.S.P.Q.2d 1430, 1434 (S.D.N.Y. 1997) ("The nature of the Internet indicates that establishing a typical home page on the Internet, for access to all users, would satisfy the Lanham Act's 'in commerce' requirement."), *aff'd,* 152 F.3d 920 (2d Cir.), *cert. denied,* 525 U.S. 834 (1998).

[14] Nevertheless, the use of a mark in commerce also must be sufficient to establish *ownership rights* for a plaintiff to recover against subsequent users under section 43(a). *See New England Duplicating Co. v. Mendes,* 190 F.2d 415, 417-18 (1st Cir. 1951) (after finding "use in commerce" jurisdiction predicate satisfied, court noted that "[t]he question remains whether the plaintiff has established that he was the 'owner' of the mark, for under [15 U.S.C. § 1051] only the 'owner' of a mark is entitled to have it registered."). The court in *Mendes* set forth a two part test to determine whether a party has established "prior use" of a mark sufficient to establish ownership:

> [E]vidence showing, first, adoption,[7] and, second, use in a way sufficiently public to identify or distinguish the marked goods in an appropriate segment of the public mind as those of

---

> MR. GIGLIOTTI [counsel for Techsplosion]: [The mark] has to be on the product or on the associated documentation. It is on neither.
>
> THE COURT: It is not on the associated documentation[?] How about the original programs Darrah sent out and manuals that went with it, and all that material, wasn't that enough for affixation?
>
> MR. GIGLIOTTI: Yes, Your Honor, that is affixation; however, he did not meet the sale requirement.
>
> R3-85-19 to 20.

In any case, the affixation requirement is met because the Software was distributed under a filename that is also the claimed mark, was promoted under the same mark, was accompanied by a user manual bearing the mark, and was sold in a compilation under the mark.

[7] It is uncontested that Darrah adopted the mark "Coolmail" before Appellants' use of the mark in connection with their e-mail service.

the adopter of the mark, is competent to establish ownership, even without evidence of actual sales.[8]

Id. at 418. *See also New West,* 595 F.2d at 1200.[9]

[15] Courts generally must inquire into the activities surrounding the prior use of the mark to determine whether such an association or notice is present. *See, e.g., Johnny Blastoff, Inc. v. L.A. Rams Football Co.,* 188 F.3d 427, 433 (7th Cir. 1999) ("The determination of whether a party has established protectable rights in a trademark is made on a case by case basis, considering the totality of the circumstances."), *cert. denied,* 528 U.S. 1188, (2000). Under the "totality of circumstances" analysis, a party may establish "use in commerce" even in the absence of sales. "[A]lthough evidence of sales is highly persuasive, the question of use adequate to establish appropriation remains one to be decided on the facts of each case . . . ." *New West,* 595 F.2d at 1200 (quoting *Mendes,* 190 F.2d at 418). The court in *New West* recognized that "mere advertising by itself may not establish priority of use," but found that promotional mailings coupled with advertiser and distributor solicitations met the *Mendes* "public identification" ownership requirement. *Id.* at 1200. Thus, contrary to Appellants' assertions, the existence of sales or lack thereof does not by itself determine whether a user of a mark has established ownership rights therein.[10] *Compare Marvel Comics Ltd. v. Defiant,* 837 F.Supp. 546, 549 (S.D.N.Y. 1993) (finding announcement of "Plasmer" title to 13 million comic book readers and promotion at annual trade convention sufficient to establish trademark ownership rights, notwithstanding lack of any sales) *with WarnerVision Entm't Inc. v. Empire of Carolina Inc.,* 915 F.Supp. 639, 645-46 (S.D.N.Y.) (finding toy manufacturer's promotional efforts insufficient to establish priority of use where only a few presentations were made to industry buyers, even though one resulted in a sale to a major toy retailer), *aff'd in part, vacated in part,* 101 F.3d 259 (2d Cir. 1996).[11]

---

[8] This ownership test is not for the purpose of establishing the "use in commerce" jurisdictional predicate of the Lanham Act. *See, e.g., Univ. of Fla. v. KPB, Inc.,* 89 F.3d 773, 776 n. 4 (11th Cir. 1996). *See supra* discussion in text.

[9] This ownership requirement parallels the statutory definition of "trademark": "any word, name, symbol, or device, or any combination thereof . . . used by a person . . . to identify and distinguish his or her goods . . . from those manufactured or sold by others . . . ." 15 U.S.C. § 1127. The Seventh Circuit has held that a higher quantum of use may be necessary to establish ownership rights under common law than under the statute because the notice function of registration is lacking. *See Zazu Designs v. L'Oreal, S.A.,* 979 F.2d 499, 503-04 (7th Cir. 1992). In addition, the continuity of a user's commercial activities in connection with the mark is also relevant to determining whether use is sufficient to establish common law ownership. *Circuit City Stores, Inc. v. CarMax, Inc.,* 165 F.3d 1047, 1054-55 (6th Cir. 1999) ("A party establishes a common law right to a trademark only by demonstrating that its use of the mark was 'deliberate and continuous, not sporadic, casual or transitory.'").

[10] Appellants cite *Future Domain Corp. v. Trantor Sys. Ltd.,* 27 U.S.P.Q.2d 1289, 1293, 1993 WL 270522 (N.D.Cal. 1993) for the proposition that there must be a sale in order to satisfy the "use in commerce" requirement. *Future Domain,* however, turned not on the *existence* of sales but whether the extent of the purported mark owner's activities created a public association between the mark and the product. There, the court determined that a computer software manufacturer's promotion of a mark at a trade show—where at most 7,000 persons actually received or requested information about the mark and where no orders were taken—was not sufficient to create such an association. *Id.* at 1293-95.

[11] Courts applying the "totality of circumstances" approach routinely have found evidence of a few sales of goods to which the mark had been affixed insufficient to establish trademark ownership. For example, in *Zazu Designs,* 979 F.2d at 503-04, the plaintiff hair salon had sold a few bottles of shampoo bearing the mark "Zazu" both over the counter and mailed over state lines. The court found that such limited sales "neither link the Zazu mark with [the plaintiff's] product in the minds of consumers nor put other producers on notice." *Id.* at 503.

[16] Similarly, not every transport of a good is sufficient to establish ownership rights in a mark. To warrant protection, use of a mark "need not have gained wide public recognition," but "[s]ecret, undisclosed internal shipments are generally inadequate." *Blue Bell, Inc. v. Farah Mfg. Co.,* 508 F.2d 1260, 1265 (5th Cir. 1975).[12] In general, uses that are *de minimis* may not establish trademark ownership rights. *See, e.g., Paramount Pictures Corp. v. White,* 31 U.S.P.Q.2d 1768, 1772-73, 1994 WL 484936 (Trademark Tr. & App. Bd. 1994) (finding no bona fide use in ordinary course of trade where mark was affixed to a game consisting of three pieces of paper and distributed for the purpose of promoting musical group).

[17] We find that, under these principles, Darrah's activities under the "Coolmail" mark constitute a "use in commerce" sufficiently public to create ownership rights in the mark. First, the distribution was widespread, and there is evidence that members of the targeted public actually associated the mark Coolmail with the Software to which it was affixed. Darrah made the software available not merely to a discrete or select group (such as friends and acquaintances, or at a trade show with limited attendance), but to numerous end-users via the Internet. The Software was posted under a filename bearing the "Coolmail" mark on a site accessible to anyone who had access to the Internet. End-users communicated with Darrah regarding the Software by referencing the "Coolmail" mark in their e-mails. Appellants argue that only technically-skilled UNIX-users made use of the Software, but there is no evidence that they were so few in number to warrant a finding of *de minimis* use.

[18] Third,* the mark served to identify the source of the Software. The "Coolmail" mark appeared in the subject field and in the text of the announcement accompanying each release of the Software, thereby distinguishing the Software from other programs that might perform similar functions available on the Internet or sold in software compilations.[13] The announcements also apparently indicated that Darrah was the "Author/Maintainer of Coolmail" and included his e-mail address. The user manual also indicated that the Software was named "Coolmail."[14] The German company S.u.S.E. was able to locate Darrah in order to request permission to use his Software in its product under the mark "Coolmail."

---

[12] In *Bonner v. City of Prichard,* 661 F.2d 1206 (11th Cir. 1981) (en banc), the Eleventh Circuit adopted as binding precedent all decisions handed down by the former Fifth Circuit prior to October 1, 1981.

* {Note: The court apparently miscounted. There is no "second" in the unedited opinion.}

[13] Darrah testified that "[m]ost of the source files ... have [the mark] in them. Also there's a copyright notice included with the software that has the name Coolmail. And the name of the executable file itself is Coolmail." R2-47-Exh. 3 at 67.

[14] Darrah: The Coolmail name always comes with the documentation that comes with the software.

* * *

Q: What documentation are you talking about?

A: There's a user manual that comes with it.

* * *

Q: Does it say "Coolmail" on page 1?

A. Yes.

Q: Where does it say "Coolmail" on page 1?

A: At the top.

... and on the header of every page.

Q: What does it say, exactly?

A: I'm not sure if it says this verbatim, it's "Coolmail," space, then the version number.

R2-47-Exh. 3 at 68, 72 to 73.

Appellants do not assert that S.u.S.E. was unaware that the Software was called "Coolmail" when it contacted Darrah.

[19] Fourth, other potential users of the mark had notice that the mark was in use in connection with Darrah's Software. In investigating whether the mark Coolmail existed before submitting its trademark registration application for its e-mail service, Planetary Motion was able to discover that Darrah was using the mark to designate his Software product.

[20] Fifth, the Software was incorporated into several versions of a product that was in fact sold worldwide and specifically attributed ownership of the Software to Darrah under the "Coolmail" mark. Any individual using the S.u.S.E. product, or competitor of S.u.S.E., that wanted to know the source of the program that performed the e-mail notification function, could do so by referring to the user manual accompanying the product. There is no support for the argument that for a trademark in software to be valid, the mark must appear on the box containing the product incorporating it, that the mark must be displayed on the screen when the program is running, or that the software bearing the mark be a selling point for the product into which it is incorporated. There is no requirement that the public come to associate a mark with a product in any particular way or that the public be passive viewers of a mark for a sufficient public association to arise.

[21] Sixth, software is commonly distributed without charge under a GNU General Public License. The sufficiency of use should be determined according to the customary practices of a particular industry. *See* S. Rep. 100-515 at 44 (1988) ("The committee intends that the revised definition of 'use in commerce' [see note 13, *supra*] be interpreted to mean commercial use *which is typical in a particular industry.*") (emphasis added). That the Software had been distributed pursuant to a GNU General Public License does not defeat trademark ownership, nor does this in any way compel a finding that Darrah abandoned his rights in trademark. Appellants misconstrue the function of a GNU General Public License. Software distributed pursuant to such a license is not necessarily ceded to the public domain and the licensor purports to retain ownership rights, which may or may not include rights to a mark.[16]

. . . .

[22] Appellants also rely on *DeCosta v. Columbia Broad. Sys., Inc.,* 520 F.2d 499, 513 (1st Cir. 1975), *cert. denied,* 423 U.S. 1073 (1976), to argue that Darrah is an eleemosynary individual and therefore unworthy of protection under unfair competition laws. The *DeCosta* court did not hold that the that the absence of a profit-oriented enterprise renders one an eleemosynary individual, nor did it hold that such individuals categorically are denied protection. Rather, the *DeCosta* court expressed "misgivings" of extending common law unfair competition protection, clearly available to eleemosynary organizations, to eleemosynary individuals.[18] *Id.* The court's reluctance to extend protection to eleemosynary individuals was based on an apparent difficulty in establishing a line of demarcation between those eleemosynary individuals engaged in commerce and those that are not. But as the sufficiency of use to establish trademark ownership is inherently fact-driven, the court need not have based its decision on such a consideration. *Mendes,* 190 F.2d at 418. Common law unfair competition protection extends to non-profit organizations because they nonetheless engage in *competition* with other organizations. *See Girls Clubs of Am., Inc. v. Boys Clubs of Am., Inc.,* 683 F.Supp. 50 (S.D.N.Y. 1988), *aff'd,* 859 F.2d 148 (2d Cir.). Thus, an eleemosynary individual that uses a mark in connection with a good or service may nonetheless acquire ownership rights in the mark if there is sufficient evidence of competitive activity.

---

[16] Because a GNU General Public License requires licensees who wish to copy, distribute, or modify the software to include a copyright notice, the license itself is evidence of Darrah's efforts to control the use of the "CoolMail" mark in connection with the Software.

[18] It is unlikely that the plaintiff's activities in *De Costa*—costumed performances and distribution of his picture at local rodeos, parades, hospitals, etc.—would generate a "public association" sufficient to confer him common law trademark ownership rights. The court assumed *arguendo,* however, that the plaintiff's activities did warrant protection, and went on to find that the evidence did not support a finding of likelihood of confusion.

[23] One individual can invest time, effort and money in developing software or other technologically-based goods or services that would be of interest to a multitude of users, other developers, and retail establishments. In fact, the program was of sufficient interest for S.u.S.E. to put effort into including it in its own software which was sold for profit, including the effort of obtaining Darrah's permission under the GNU General Public License.

[24] Here, Darrah's activities bear elements of competition, notwithstanding his lack of an immediate profit-motive. By developing and distributing software under a particular mark, and taking steps to avoid ceding the Software to the public domain, Darrah made efforts to retain ownership rights in his Software and to ensure that his Software would be distinguishable from other developers who may have distributed similar or related Software. Competitive activity need not be fueled solely by a desire for direct monetary gain. Darrah derived value from the distribution because he was able to improve his Software based on suggestions sent by end-users. Just as any other consumers, these end-users discriminate among and share information on available software. It is logical that as the Software improved, more end-users used his Software, thereby increasing Darrah's recognition in his profession and the likelihood that the Software would be improved even further.

[25] In light of the foregoing, the use of the mark in connection with the Software constitutes significant and substantial public exposure of a mark sufficient to have created an association in the mind of public.

{The court went on to find a likelihood of confusion between Planetary Motion's and Techsplosion's marks. The court affirmed the terms of the permanent injunction but found the award of attorney fees to be an abuse of discretion.}

Comments and Questions

1. *"Analogous Use" of a Trademark.* As a terminological matter, trademark lawyers and courts will sometimes refer to pre-sales activity that may form the basis for common law priority as "use analogous" to trademark use, or "analogous use." *See, e.g., American Express Co. v. Goetz*, 515 F.3d 156, 161 (2d Cir. 2008) ("[T]he analogous use doctrine, where it applies, eases the technical requirements for trademarks and services marks in favor of a competing claimant who asserts priority on the basis of earlier analogous use of the mark."); *id.* at 161-62 ("At the very least analogous use must be use that is open and notorious. In other words, analogous use must be of such a nature and extent that the mark has become popularized in the public mind so that the relevant segment of the public identifies the marked goods with the mark's adopter." (citations and quotation marks omitted)).

2. *The "totality of the circumstances" test.* What kind and degree of pre-sales and/or sales activity can satisfy the use in commerce requirement for purposes of common law priority? Most courts have adopted some form of a "totality of the circumstances" test, sometimes heavily influenced by the equities of the case. *See La Societe Anonyme des Parfums Le Galion v. Jean Patou, Inc.*, 495 F.2d 1265, 1274 n. 11 (2d Cir. 1974) ("[T]he balance of the equities plays an important role in deciding whether defendant's use is sufficient to warrant trademark protection."). In *Chance v. Pac-Tel Teletrac Inc.*, 242 F.3d 1151 (9th Cir. 2001), for example, the Ninth Circuit summarized the factors that might be relevant to a totality of the circumstances analysis of use in commerce sufficient to justify rights:

> Accordingly, we hold that the totality of the circumstances must be employed to determine whether a service mark has been adequately used in commerce so as to gain the protection of the Lanham Act. In applying this approach, the district courts should be guided in their consideration of non-sales activities by factors we have discussed, such as the genuineness and commercial character of the activity, the determination of whether the mark was sufficiently public to identify or distinguish the marked service in an appropriate segment of the public mind as those of the holder of the mark, the scope of the non-sales activity relative to what would be a commercially reasonable attempt to market the service, the degree of ongoing activity of the holder to conduct the business using the mark, the amount of business transacted, and other similar factors which might distinguish whether a service has actually been "rendered in commerce".

Id. at 1159. Applying these factors, the Ninth Circuit found that the October 1989 mailing by Allen Chance ("Chance") of 35,000 postcards promoting his TELETRAC tracking service that led to 128 telephone responses but no sales was not sufficient to establish use in commerce. Meanwhile,

> Pac–Tel, in contrast, had significant activities even prior to [Chance's] post card mailing. The record demonstrates that as early as June 1989, Pac–Tel began using the mark on a continuous basis. As early as 1984, a Pac–Tel predecessor company was using the mark as part of its business name. Pac–Tel began a public relations campaign using the mark to introduce its new service in July 1989. In September 1989, it sent out brochures to potential customers. In early fall 1989, it conducted interviews with major newspapers including the *Wall Street Journal, Washington Post* and *Chicago Tribune* which resulted in a number of stories that mentioned the service mark. During this time the service was marketed to potential customers who managed large vehicle fleets through a slide presentation using the mark. While the district court found that Pac–Tel's first use was in April 1990, when it began making its service available on a commercial basis for the first time on the Los Angeles school buses, the totality of the record demonstrates that its first use of the mark was significantly earlier and clearly predated [Chance]'s first use

Id. at 1160.

Another example of the application of the totality of the circumstances test, along with a strong grounding in the balance of the equities, is *Johnny Blastoff, Inc. v. Los Angeles Rams Football Co.*, 188 F.3d 427 (7th Cir. 1999). When the Los Angeles Rams announced that they were moving to St. Louis, Rodney Rigsby, proprietor of Johnny Blastoff, Inc., had the bright idea somehow to claim ownership of the ST. LOUIS RAMS mark before the football team could. He filed a State of Wisconsin trademark application on February 22, 1995, and two federal intent-to-use registration applications on March 10, 1995. The court found that the football team's use in commerce preceded these dates. Here is the core of the court's analysis:

> On January 17, 1995, Georgia Frontiere, the owner of the Rams, and St. Louis Mayor Freeman Bosley held a press conference at which they announced the Rams' intention to relocate from Los Angeles to St. Louis. The press conference story received extensive national and local press, including the *St. Louis Dispatch's* publication, on January 18, 1995, of a sixteen-page pullout section of the newspaper entitled "St. Louis Rams." Vendors sold unlicensed "St. Louis Rams" merchandise in the St. Louis area in January of 1995, and by February of 1995, more than 72,000 personal seat licenses for the St. Louis Rams' home games had been received. By the time Blastoff registered the "St. Louis Rams" mark in Wisconsin in February of 1995, a significant portion of the public associated the mark with the Rams football club. However, Blastoff asserts that the defendants had not sufficiently used the mark "St. Louis Rams" to be given priority. Blastoff argues that at the January 17, 1995, press conference, none of the defendants used the words "St. Louis Rams," and thus, this term was rendered an "unarticulated idea for a team name," which is not protectable. Blastoff also states that newspaper and media coverage is insufficient to establish priority. Finally, Blastoff contends that the football club "operated publicly and exclusively as [the] 'L.A. Rams'" as late as February 8, 1995.
>
> For the purpose of establishing public identification of a mark with a product or service, the fact-finder may rely on the use of the mark in "advertising brochures, catalogs, newspaper ads, and articles in newspapers and trade publications," *T.A.B. Systems v. Pactel Teletrac*, 77 F.3d 1372, 1375 (Fed. Cir. 1996), as well as in media outlets such as television and radio. *See In re Owens–Corning Fiberglas Corp.*, 774 F.2d 1116, 1125 (Fed. Cir. 1985). In addition, courts have recognized that "abbreviations and nicknames of trademarks or names used *only* by the public give rise to protectable rights in the owners of the trade name or mark which the public modified." *Nat'l Cable Television Assoc. v. Am. Cinema Editors, Inc.*, 937 F.2d 1572, 1577 (Fed. Cir. 1991). Such public use of a mark is deemed to be on behalf of the mark's owners. *See id.* Blastoff has failed to demonstrate any equivalent

use of the mark "St. Louis Rams" by February of 1995, when the defendants established, by use and public association, their priority in the mark. Blastoff's insignificant and very limited use of the mark prior to February of 1995, consisting of the development of the "Tower City Rams" design, along with the production of a swatch of material with "St. Louis Rams" embroidery, is insufficient to establish a link between the mark and its products. Furthermore, the owner's use of a trademark is relevant in establishing public identification of a mark with a product or service. Georgia Frontiere, owner of the Rams, in announcing her intention to move the franchise to St. Louis from Los Angeles, implicitly adopted the exact phrase "St. Louis Rams" on the date of her press conference. This Court's decision in *Indianapolis Colts, Inc. v. Metropolitan Baltimore Football Club Ltd.*, 34 F.3d 410, 413 (7th Cir. 1994), is strong support for the proposition that the Rams organization and the NFL had a long-established priority over the use of the "Rams" name in connection with the same professional football team, regardless of urban affiliation.

Id. at 435.

3. *"Stealing" someone else's idea for a trademark.* Because use, rather than invention, is the basis for trademark rights under the Lanham Act, there is no remedy under the Act for the "theft" of an idea for a trademark. In *American Express Co. v. Goetz*, 515 F.3d 156 (2d Cir. 2008), cert. denied, 129 S. Ct. 176 (U.S. 2008), the declaratory defendant Stephen Goetz developed the slogan "My Life. My Card." for a credit card and sought to interest various credit card providers in using it and his consulting services. On July 30, 2004, Goetz mailed a proposal to American Express urging American Express to adopt the mark. American Express never responded. In November, 2004, however, American Express launched a global campaign based on the phrase "My Life. My Card."

When Goetz threatened suit, American Express filed for a declaration of non-infringement. Documents produced in the litigation showed that the advertising firm Ogilvy Group first proposed the mark to American Express on July 22, 2004, and Goetz eventually conceded that Ogilvy had developed and American Express had adopted the mark without any knowledge of his proposal.

The district court granted summary judgment to American Express and the Second Circuit affirmed. What drove the outcome of the litigation was not the priority of invention issue, however. Instead, it was the simple fact that Goetz never made a qualifying use in commerce of the mark: "[C]onstruing all the facts in Goetz's favor, the only reasonable conclusion that can be drawn is that My Life, My Card was a component of Goetz's business proposal to the credit card companies rather than a mark designating the origin of any goods or services he offered to them." *Id.* at 160.

4. *Trademark trolls and the use in commerce requirement.* The use in commerce prerequisite for trademark rights has the salutary effect of limiting the ability of bad faith agents to exploit the trademark registration system in the way that some "non-practicing entities" arguably exploit the patent system. In *Central Mfg., Inc. v. Brett*, 492 F.3d 876 (9th Cir. 2007), the defendant George Brett (and brothers) manufactured a hybrid wood-metal bat under the trademark STEALTH. Plaintiff Central Mfg., of which the then-notorious trademark troll Leo Stoller was president and sole shareholder, sued for infringement of its own mark STEALTH, which it had registered in 1985 for "[s]porting goods, specifically, tennis rackets, golf clubs, tennis balls, basketballs, baseballs, soccer balls, golf balls, cross bows, tennis racket strings and shuttle cocks." When Brett challenged Stoller to produce any evidence of use in commerce of the mark, Stoller's documents failed to persuade the district court. For example: "Plaintiffs produced a table of 'Stealth Brand Baseball Sales' between 1996 and 2003, but could provide absolutely no information to justify the lump sum 'sales' figures listed. There is no way for this Court to know that this alleged sales sheet bears any relation to reality and is not simply something Plaintiffs generated on a home computer for the purposes of this litigation." *Id.* at 883 (quoting Central Mfg. Co. v. Brett, 2006 WL 681058 (N.D.Ill. Mar 15, 2006)). The Seventh Circuit affirmed:

Stoller has repeatedly sought ways to get around trademark law's prohibition on the stockpiling of unused marks, and this case is no different. It is unfathomable that a company claiming to have engaged in thousands of dollars of sales of a product for more than a decade would be unable to produce even a single purchase order or invoice as proof. Self-serving deposition testimony is not enough to defeat a motion for summary judgment. By exposing Central's failure to make bona fide use of the "Stealth" mark for baseballs, Brett Brothers met its burden to overcome the presumption afforded by the 1985 registration, and summary judgment in its favor was the appropriate course.

Id. at 883. Brett was also awarded attorney fees. In December 2010, Stoller was indicted on fraud charges related to statements made in his bankruptcy filings. In November 2014, he was sentenced to 20 months in a federal prison. *See* http://en.wikipedia.org/wiki/Leo_Stoller.

For a more recent example of behavior possibly akin to trademark trolling, see Eric Goldman, *My Declaration Identifying Emoji Co. GmbH as a Possible Trademark Troll*, TECH. & MARKETING L. BLOG, Sept. 20, 2021, https://blog.ericgoldman.org/archives/2021/09/my-declaration-identifying-emoji-co-gmbh-as-a-possible-trademark-troll.htm (https://perma.cc/L4YN-X89U) (discussing the high-volume litigation behavior of Emoji Co. GmbH).

D.   The Trademark Registration Process

Use, rather than registration, is the basis of federal trademark rights in the United States. *See In re Int'l Flavors & Fragrances, Inc.*, 183 F.3d 1361, 1366 (Fed. Cir. 1999) ("The federal registration of a trademark does not create an exclusive property right in the mark. The owner of the mark already has the property right established by prior use. However, those trademark owners who register their marks with the PTO are afforded additional protection not provided by the common law."). As explained previously in this Part, the Lanham Act will protect a trademark owner's exclusive rights in any trademark it is using in commerce regardless of whether the mark is registered provided that the unregistered mark meets the various substantive requirements for registration established by the Act. In other words, if the mark as used in commerce could be registered, it will be protected even if it is not registered. Conversely, the Lanham Act will not protect a trademark registrant's exclusive rights in its registered mark if it no longer uses its mark in commerce and cannot prove an intent to resume use in the near future. On this basis, it is often said that the U.S. trademark system is a "use-based" system in contrast to the "registration-based" systems more common around the world.[1] In the United States, registration merely records the preexistence of externally established rights.[2]

The U.S. registration system is different in another significant respect. Unlike many foreign registration systems, which review applications only for compliance with formal requirements, the PTO reviews applications to ensure that they meet both formal requirements (which are largely set forth in Lanham Act § 1) and substantive requirements (largely found in Lanham Act § 2). These substantive requirements include both "absolute grounds" for refusal of registration, such as that the mark is deceptive, and "relative grounds" for refusal, such as that the mark is confusingly similar with a previously registered mark.

A trademark applicant at the PTO must claim at least one "filing basis" for its application among the five that are provided by the Lanham Act. These filing bases are:

---

[1] *See, e.g.*, Graeme B. Dinwoodie, *(National) Trademark Laws and the (Non-National) Domain Name System*, 21 U. PA. J. INT'L ECON. L. 495, 496 (2000) ("[F]or over a century the United States has steadfastly resisted adoption of a registration-based system of trademark priority and has adhered instead to a use-based philosophy."); *see also* William M. Landes & Richard A. Posner, *Trademark Law: An Economic Perspective*, 30 J.L. & Econ. 265, 282 (1987) (comparing the American use-based system to other nations' registration-based systems and concluding that the former is more economically efficient).

[2] *See, e.g.*, Keebler Co. v. Rovira Biscuit Corp., 624 F.2d 366, 372 (1st Cir. 1980) ("[F]ederal registration . . . does not create the underlying right in a trademark. That right, which accrues from the use of a particular name or symbol, is essentially a common law property right . . . .").

1. Lanham Act § 1(a): the applicant is already making actual use of the mark in commerce;

2. Lanham Act § 1(b): the applicant has a bona fide intent to use the mark in commerce in the near future;

3. Lanham Act § 44(d): the applicant filed a foreign application to register the mark within six months prior to its application to the PTO and claims the priority date of that prior foreign application;

4. Lanham Act § 44(e): the applicant possesses a registration of the mark in the applicant's country of origin;

5. Lanham Act § 66(a): the applicant requests extension of protection of an international registration under the Madrid System for the international registration of trademarks.

The first four filing bases are not mutually exclusive; the § 66(a) filing basis, by contrast, may not be combined with other filing bases. While the §§ 1(a), 44(d), and 44(e) filing bases have been available since the effective date of the original Lanham Act on July 5, 1947, the § 1(b), or "ITU," filing basis became available with the effective date of the Trademark Law Revision Act (TLRA) on November 16, 1989,[3] and the § 66(a) filing basis became available with the effective date of the Madrid Protocol Implementation Act on November 2, 2003.[4] Most trademark applications at the PTO are now filed under the Lanham Act § 1(b) intent to use basis.

Lanham Act §§ 44 & 66(a), 15 U.S.C. §§ 1126 & 1141f, set forth important though relatively obscure exceptions to the general rule that a trademark must be used in commerce for it to be federally registered. *See, e.g.*, Lanham Act § 44(e), 15 U.S.C. § 1126(e) ("The application must state the applicant's bona fide intention to use the mark in commerce, but use in commerce shall not be required prior to registration."). As noted in *In re Cyber-Blitz Trading Services*, 47 U.S.P.Q.2d 1638 (Comm'r Pats. 1998),

> [o]ne significant difference between Section 1(b) and 44 of the Trademark Act is that Applicants who rely on Section 1(b) as a filing basis must establish use of the mark prior to registration, or the application will become abandoned. In contrast, Applicants who rely solely on Section 44 are not required to demonstrate use in order to obtain registration. *Crocker National Bank v. Canadian Imperial Bank of Commerce*, 223 USPQ 909 (TTAB 1984). In fact, the first time evidence of use usually is required for Section 44 Applicants is upon the filing of an Affidavit of Continued Use under Section 8 of the Trademark Act, 15 U.S.C. § 1058. This does not occur until five to six years after registration.

Id. at 1639-40. *See also* TMEP § 1009. The reasoning of *Cyber-Blitz* also applies to § 66(a) applications.[5] *See also Lodestar Anstalt v. Bacardi & Co. Ltd.*, 31 F.4th 1228, 1245–51 (9th Cir. 2022).

For a sense of scale, the figure below shows the number of trademark applications at the PTO per year for each filing basis from 1981 through 2020. What might explain the spike in applications in the period 1999–2000? As for why Lanham Act § 1(a) use-based applications have increased in number so dramatically since 2017, see USPTO, *Trademarks and Patents in China: The Impact of Non-Market Factors on Filing Trends and IP Systems* (January 2021) (discussing numerous Chinese-government subsidy measures encouraging Chinese nationals to procure foreign trademark registrations). *See also* Barton

---

[3] Trademark Law Revision Act of 1988, Pub. L. No. 100-667, 102 Stat. 3935 (codified as amended in scattered sections of the U.S.C.).

[4] Madrid Protocol Implementation Act, Pub. L. No. 107-273, 116 Stat. 1913 (2002) (codified as amended at 15 U.S.C. §§ 1141–1141 (2006)).

[5] However, as is suggested by *Dragon Bleu (SARL) v. VENM*, LLC, 112 U.S.P.Q.2d 1925 (TTAB 2014), which dealt with § 66(a) registrations, if the § 44 or § 66(a) registrant is accused of having abandoned its mark in the U.S., the registrant may be required to present evidence of use sooner than five years after the date of registration. On the issue of trademark abandonment, see Part III.D.

Beebe & Jeanne Fromer, *Fake Trademark Specimens: An Empirical Study*, 121 Colum. L. Rev. Forum 217 (2020).

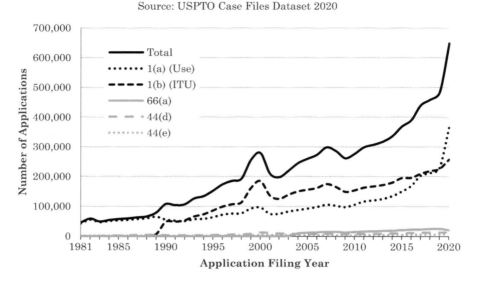

Applications Per Year By Filing Basis, 1981-2020
Source: USPTO Case Files Dataset 2020

For marks already being used in commerce, a successful application proceeds though at least five basic stages: (1) application, (2) examination, (3) publication in the PTO's Official Gazette, (4) opposition, and (5) registration.

Intent-to-use applications proceed through certain additional substages, thus: (1) application, (2) examination, (3) publication in the PTO's Official Gazette, (4.a) opposition, (4.b) the issuance by the PTO of a Notice of Allowance, (4.c) the filing by the applicant of a Statement of Use showing that the applicant has begun to make actual use of the mark in commerce; and (5) registration.

We review each of these stages below. But first we consider why a trademark owner should federally register its mark.

Comments and Questions

1. *The phenomenon of "submarine trademarks."* Below is the registration certificate for the IPHONE mark. Note the priority date claimed: "Priority claimed under Sec. 44(d) on Trinidad/Tobago Application No. 37090, filed 3-27-2006." Rather than file an application for the mark at the USPTO on March 27, 2006, Apple instead filed on that date in Trinidad & Tobago through a shell company. As the registration certificate indicates, on September 26, 2006 (six months after March 27, 2006 minus a day), Apple then took advantage of Lanham Act § 44(d) to assert the priority date of their Trinidad & Tobago application in the U.S. Why would Apple, like many other consumer-oriented high-technology and fashion companies, engage in such a circuitous route to registration? Consider that at the time Apple filed its applications, Trinidad & Tobago did not provide a searchable online database of trademark applications filed at its Intellectual Property Office. *See* Carsten Fink, Andrea Fosfuri, Christian Helmers, & Amanda Myers, *Submarine Trademarks*, 31 J. Econ. & Management Strategy 818 (2022).

Int. Cl.: 9

Prior U.S. Cls.: 21, 23, 26, 36 and 38

United States Patent and Trademark Office

Reg. No. 3,669,402

Registered Aug. 18, 2009

TRADEMARK
PRINCIPAL REGISTER

iPhone

APPLE INC. (CALIFORNIA CORPORATION)
1 INFINITE LOOP
CUPERTINO, CA 95014

FOR: HANDHELD MOBILE DIGITAL ELECTRO-
NIC DEVICES FOR THE SENDING AND RECEIV-
ING OF TELEPHONE CALLS, ELECTRONIC MAIL,
AND OTHER DIGITAL DATA, FOR USE AS A
DIGITAL FORMAT AUDIO PLAYER, AND FOR
USE AS A HANDHELD COMPUTER, PERSONAL
DIGITAL ASSISTANT, ELECTRONIC ORGANIZER,
ELECTRONIC NOTEPAD, AND CAMERA, IN
CLASS 9 (U.S. CLS. 21, 23, 26, 36 AND 38).

FIRST USE 1-9-2007; IN COMMERCE 1-29-2007.

THE MARK CONSISTS OF STANDARD CHAR-
ACTERS WITHOUT CLAIM TO ANY PARTICULAR
FONT, STYLE, SIZE, OR COLOR.

PRIORITY CLAIMED UNDER SEC. 44(D) ON
TRINIDAD/TOBAGO APPLICATION NO. 37090,
FILED 3-27-2006.

SEC. 2(F).

SER. NO. 77-975,076, FILED 9-26-2006.

LINDA ESTRADA, EXAMINING ATTORNEY

1. Benefits and Costs of Trademark Registration

a. Registration on the Principal Register

Registration on the Principal Register confers significant, substantive advantages on the registered mark. First and perhaps most importantly, under Lanham Act § 7(c), 15 U.S.C. § 1057, registration confers on the registrant nationwide priority in the mark as of the date of application. Section 7(c) reads as follows:

> (c) *Application to register mark considered constructive use.* Contingent on the registration of a mark on the principal register provided by this Act, the filing of the application to register such mark shall constitute constructive use of the mark, conferring a right of priority, nationwide in effect, on or in connection with the goods or services specified in the registration against any other person except for a person whose mark has not been abandoned and who, prior to such filing–
>
> (1) has used the mark;
>
> (2) has filed an application to register the mark which is pending or has resulted in registration of the mark; or
>
> (3) has filed a foreign application to register the mark on the basis of which he or she has acquired a right of priority, and timely files an application under section 44(d) [15 USC 1126(d)] to register the mark which is pending or has resulted in registration of the mark.

15 U.S.C § 1057. This right of priority extends nationwide even if, as is often the case, the registrant has not itself used the mark throughout the nation. And in the case of ITU applications, the intent to use applicant enjoys nationwide priority as of its ITU application date even if several years pass before the applicant finally makes an actual use of its mark and completes its registration. (We will address the geographic scope of trademark rights in more detail in Part I.E).

Second, registration confers on the mark a prima facie presumption of the validity of the mark and the registrant's ownership of the mark. Lanham Act §§ 7(b) & 33(a), 15 U.S.C. §§ 1057(b) & 1115(a). In practice, however, it is not clear how much weight courts place on the § 33 presumption of validity. *Compare, e.g., Christian Louboutin S.A. v. Yves Saint Laurent America Holdings, Inc.*, 696 F.3d 206, 216 n.10 (2d Cir. 2012) ("In order to rebut the presumption of validity, the allegedly infringing party must show, by a preponderance of the evidence, . . . that the mark is ineligible for protection.") *with Custom Vehicles, Inc. v. Forest River, Inc.*, 476 F.3d 481, 486 (7th Cir. 2007) ("[T]he presumption of validity that

235

registration creates is easily rebuttable, since it merely shifts the burden of production to the alleged infringer."), *and Door Systems, Inc. v. Pro-Line Door Systems, Inc.*, 83 F.3d 169, 172 (7th Cir. 1996) ("The presumption of validity that federal registration confers evaporates as soon as evidence of invalidity is presented. Its only function is to incite such evidence and when the function has been performed the presumption drops out of the case.").

Third, only marks registered on the Principal Register may achieve incontestable status, which confers a significant benefit on descriptive marks. Lanham Act §§ 15 and 33, 15 U.S.C. §§ 1065 & 1115, set out the main requirements a registrant must meet to file a Declaration of Incontestability of a Mark Under Section 15: (1) the mark must have been in continuous use for any period of five consecutive years after the date of registration and must still be in use at the time of filing, (2) there has been no final decision adverse to the registrant's ownership of or validity of the registration of the mark, and (3) there is no proceeding involving the registrant's ownership of or validity of the registration of the mark pending at the PTO or in any court. Lanham Act § 15, 15 U.S.C. § 1065.

Incontestable status limits the grounds on which the registered mark's validity may be contested for the remaining life of the registration (which may be renewed in perpetuity). Lanham Act §§ 15 and 33(b) explicitly list out these grounds; any that are not listed are foreclosed. One ground not listed is that the mark lacks secondary meaning. Thus, the validity of descriptive marks that have achieved incontestable status may not be challenged on the ground that they lack secondary meaning—though they may be challenged on the ground that they are generic.[6] Another ground not listed is that the mark fails to function as a mark. *See* Lisa P. Ramsey, *Using Failure to Function Doctrine to Protect Free Speech and Competition in Trademark Law*, 104 IOWA L. REV. ONLINE 70 (2020) (advocating that § 14 and § 15 be amended to allow any mark to be cancelled at any time on the ground that it fails to function as a mark).

In the notorious case of *Park 'N Fly, Inc. v. Dollar Park and Fly, Inc.*, 469 U.S. 189 (1985), which is excerpted in Part I.D.8 below, the Supreme Court confirmed the rule that incontestable marks may not be challenged on the ground that they lack secondary meaning. In *Park 'N Fly*, the Court held that the incontestable—and clearly descriptive—mark "Park 'N Fly" for airport parking services could not be challenged on the ground that it lacked secondary meaning, notwithstanding that the record below strongly suggested that the mark lacked secondary meaning at the time of registration in 1971 and still lacked secondary meaning when the case was being litigated in the early 1980s. *See id.* at 211 (Stevens, J., dissenting).[7]

Registrants may also use incontestable status "defensively" in situations in which their registered mark is accused of infringing another mark. *See* McCARTHY § 31:141. Together, Lanham Act §§ 15 and 33(b) establish that in the case of registrations granted incontestable status, the right of the registrant to use its registered mark in commerce on the goods specified in the registration is incontestable (even

---

[6] Furthermore, even if the statute forces the court to find that the incontestable mark possesses secondary meaning, a court may nevertheless find that the mark's secondary meaning is so weak that as a practical matter no consumers would be confused by a similar mark. *See* Rebecca Tushnet, *Registering Disagreement: Registration in Modern American Trademark Law*, 130 HARV. L. REV. 867, 903-04 (2017).

[7] In his lengthy dissent, Justice Stevens expressed his dismay that the decision of a single trademark examiner in an ex parte proceeding a decade earlier, followed by the registrant's perfunctory filing of a declaration of incontestability, could somehow prevent the Court from striking from the Principal Register an "inherently unregistrable" mark. *See Park 'N Fly*, 469 U.S. at 206–07 (Stevens, J., dissenting). He also added his own opinion of trademark quality at the PTO for good measure. *See id.* at 212 ("No matter how dedicated and how competent administrators may be, the possibility of error is always present, especially in nonadversary proceedings."). In a footnote to this statement, Justice Stevens quoted a PTO official who testified to Congress that "at any one time, about 7 percent of our 25 million documents are either missing or misfiled." *Id.* at 212 n.12 (quoting Hearing Before the Subcomm. on Patents, Copyrights & Trademarks of the S. Comm. on the Judiciary, 98th Cong. 5 (1983) (statement of Gerald J. Mossinghoff, Assistant Secretary and Comm'r of Patents and Trademarks)).

if the use causes confusion). For example, in *Garcoa, Inc. v. Sierra Sage Herbs LLC*, No. 21 Civ. 4672, 2022 WL 16548874 (C.D. Cal. October 4, 2022), the plaintiff used the registered mark BLUE GOO for pain relief products and claimed that the defendant's registered mark GREEN GOO, also for pain relief products, infringed. Wisely, the defendant had previously applied for and received incontestable status for its registration. The court granted the defendant's motion for summary judgment purely on the basis that by operation of Lanham Act §§ 15 and 33(b), the defendant's right to use its mark in commerce on the goods specified in the registration was incontestable. The court never reached the issue of likelihood of confusion.

Registration confers additional benefits on the trademark owner:

- Owners of registered marks may obtain statutory damages against counterfeiters. *See* Lanham Act § 35(c) (statutory damages available in "cases involving the use of a counterfeit mark"), 15 U.S.C. 1117(c), and Lanham Act § 34(d)(1)(B)(i) (defining "counterfeit mark" as "counterfeit of a mark that is registered on the principal register"), 15 U.S.C. § 1116(d)(1)(B)(i). Owners of registered marks may also benefit from criminal prosecution of trademark counterfeiters. *See* 18 U.S.C. § 2320.

- Owners of registered marks enjoy the right to request customs officials to bar the importation of goods bearing infringing trademarks under Lanham Act § 42, 15 U.S.C. § 1124.

- In the case of registered trade dress, owners do not bear the burden of establishing the non-functionality of their trade dress. Under Lanham Act § 43(a)(3), 15 U.S.C. § 1125(a)(3), owners of unregistered trade dress bear this burden.

Note that it is often still said, incorrectly, that only owners of *registered* marks may seek treble damages and attorney fees in exceptional cases under Lanham Act § 35(a). In fact, the TLRA of 1988 amended Section § 35(a) to reference any "violation under section 43(a)," thus providing enhanced damages and attorney fees in exceptional cases to owners of unregistered marks.

b. Registration on the Supplemental Register

Marks that fail to qualify for Principal Register registration because they are determined to lack secondary meaning may nevertheless seek registration on the Supplemental Register. Specifically, Lanham Act Section 23(a), 15 U.S.C. § 1091(a), provides in part:

> All marks capable of distinguishing applicant's goods or services and not registerable on the principal register provided in this chapter, except those declared to be unregisterable under subsections (a), (b), (c), (d), and (e)(3) of section 1052 [Lanham Act § 2] of this title, which are in lawful use in commerce by the owner thereof, on or in connection with any goods or services may be registered on the supplemental register upon the payment of the prescribed fee and compliance with the provisions of subsections (a) and (e) of section 1051 [Lanham Act § 1] of this title so far as they are applicable.

Id. Principal Register applicants typically seek Supplemental Register registration (by amending their application) only after the PTO has refused registration on the Principal Register on the ground that the applied-for mark is descriptive and lacks secondary meaning. As the language of § 23(a) establishes ("which are in lawful use in commerce"), only use-based applications can be converted into supplemental registrations; intent to use applications do not have this option.

There are several benefits to Supplemental Register registration:

- Examiners may cite the supplemental registration against future applications for either Principal or Supplement Register registration where the future applied-for mark would be confusingly similar under § 2(d) with the supplemental registration mark. *See* Application of Clorox Co., 578 F.2d 305, 307 (C.C.P.A. 1978). *See also* MCCARTHY § 19:37 (calling the result in *Clorox* "strange and unsettling"); Anne Gilson LaLond & Jerome Gilson, *The U.S. Supplemental Register: Solace, Substance or Just Extinct?*, 103 TRADEMARK REP. 828, 892 (2013) (criticizing *Clorox* on ground that "from a public policy standpoint, these non-marks should not prevent registration of actual trademarks.").

- Relatedly, the mark registered on the Supplemental Register is more likely to be detected in search reports prepared for others contemplating the registration of similar marks.

- Supplemental registration may form the basis for registration of certain marks (particularly those that are descriptive or take the form of product configuration or packaging) in certain foreign countries and regions. The Supplemental Register was originally established for this purpose. *See* Armstrong Paint & Varnish Works v. Nu-Enamel Corp., 305 U.S. 315, 334 n. 21 (1938); In re the Pepsi-Cola Co., 120 U.S.P.Q. 468 (T.T.A.B. Mar. 4, 1959).

Note, however, that supplemental registration does not provide any of the important advantages gained by principal registration. It has no evidentiary or remedial significance. It does not establish constructive use under § 7(c), 15 U.S.C. § 1057(c), or constructive notice of ownership under § 22, 15 U.S.C. § 1072, nor can a mark registered on the supplemental register gain incontestable status under § 15, 15 U.S.C. § 1065.

c. Costs of Trademark Registration

Current PTO fees for the registration of a trademark range from $250 to $500 per Nice class. Experienced trademark prosecutors will generally estimate that the cost to register a trademark at the PTO, including both filing fees and attorney's fees, starts at approximately $1,500 for a simple use-based single-class word mark application, with the addition of perhaps $500 per additional Nice class. Attorney's fees may vary by the quality of counsel. More complex applications, including those filed on an intent to use basis or for non-verbal marks, may cost considerably more.

2. Lanham Act § 1(b) Intent to Use Applications and the Bona Fide Intent to Use Requirement

As the figure above shows, by 1993, over half of all trademark applications filed annually at the PTO were filed on a § 1(b) intent to use filing basis. The ITU filing basis allows an applicant to begin the trademark registration process before it has used its mark in commerce provided that it has a "a bona fide intention, under circumstances showing the good faith of such person, to use [the] trademark in commerce." Lanham Act § 1(b)(1), 15 U.S.C. § 1051(b)(1). The ITU filing basis greatly benefits firms that wish to establish the registrability of and priority rights in their marks before actually using their marks in commerce. However, the ITU system is also open to abuse from firms who have at the time of filing no real intention to use the mark, but rather wish merely to establish an option to use the mark sometime in the future. It is also open to abuse from "meme mark" filers who rush to file a § 1(b) application for the latest cultural catchphrase but have at the time of filing no reasonably well-developed plan actually to use that phrase on or in connection with goods or services. *See* Barton Beebe, *Is the Trademark Office a Rubber Stamp?*, 48 HOUSTON L. REV. 751, 757 (2011) (discussing "meme mark" filings associated with September 11 such as "Let's Roll" and "Seal Team 6").

The following opinion grew out of a priority battle between two claimants to the trademark WORKWIRE.

Kelly Services, Inc. v. Creative Harbor, LLC
846 F.3d 857 (6th Cir. 2017)

CLAY, Circuit Judge.

[1] Defendant Creative Harbor, LLC ("Creative Harbor") appeals the judgment entered by the district court on February 1, 2016, voiding Creative Harbor's trademark applications numbered 86198230 and 86198309, respectively. Creative Harbor challenges the district court's determinations that: (1) Creative Harbor lacked a *bona fide* intention to use its requested mark in commerce with respect to some of the goods and services identified in its trademark applications, in violation of § 1(b) of the Lanham Act, 15 U.S.C. § 1051(b); and (2) if Creative Harbor lacked such intent with respect to any of the goods and services, the applications must be voided in their entirety. We have jurisdiction over this appeal pursuant to 28 U.S.C. § 1291. For the reasons set forth below, we AFFIRM IN PART and VACATE

IN PART the district court's judgment. We REMAND for further proceedings consistent with this opinion.

BACKGROUND

I. Factual History

[2] We present the facts in the light most favorable to Creative Harbor, against whom the district court entered summary judgment.

[3] Defendant Creative Harbor is a California-based technology startup purportedly "engaged in the business of original content creation and concept development for all media, including but not limited to, internet, mobile, photography, film, and TV." (Answer.) Creative Harbor was founded in 2014 by Christian Jurgensen ("Jurgensen"), who serves as Creative Harbor's owner, sole manager, and CEO.

[4] Plaintiff Kelly Services, Inc. is a Michigan-based company that is allegedly "one of the world's largest providers of personnel and managed business services – staffing 99% of Fortune 100 companies and 90% of Fortune 500 companies." (Complaint.) Plaintiff Kelly Properties, LLC, is an affiliated entity of Kelly Services, Inc. Because Plaintiffs do not assert separate claims or arguments, and have identical interests for the purposes of this appeal, we refer to them collectively as "Kelly Services."

[5] In essence, the parties dispute which of them should have priority to the trademark WORKWIRE ("the Mark"), which both wish to use in connection with their competing employment-based software applications. In September 2013, Jurgensen allegedly developed an idea for a mobile application designed to connect employers with prospective employees. Jurgensen decided to call the application "WorkWire," and formed Creative Harbor in February 2014 to develop the WorkWire application. In early 2014, Creative Harbor hired an intellectual property attorney to explore obtaining the WORKWIRE trademark. That attorney allegedly advised Creative Harbor that the Mark was available.

[6] However, in early 2013, Kelly Services allegedly began developing its own employment-based iPad application, which it intended to distribute through the Apple App Store. Kelly Services also decided to name its application "WorkWire." Kelly Services allegedly completed this iPad application on February 4, 2014, and submitted the application to Apple for its approval and eventual distribution. On February 17, 2014, Apple approved Kelly Services' application, but did not release it on the App Store immediately.

[7] On February 19, 2014, Creative Harbor filed two trademark applications seeking rights to the Mark with the United States Patent and Trademark Office at 6:28 p.m. and 7:56 p.m. Eastern Standard Time, respectively ("the Applications"). The Applications sought the right to use the Mark in connection with thirty-six individually identified goods and services. Creative Harbor affirmed under penalty of perjury that it possessed a *bona fide* intention to use the Mark in commerce on or in connection with each of the goods and services listed in the Applications. On the same day, at approximately 8:11 p.m. Eastern Standard Time, Kelly Services' iPad application became available on the Apple App Store. A customer first downloaded the Kelly Services application on February 20, 2014.

[8] On March 10, 2014, Creative Harbor sent Kelly Services a cease and desist letter asserting its right to use the Mark, and demanding that Kelly Services cease using the WORKWIRE name in connection with Kelly Services' Apple App Store iPad application. Sixteen days later, Kelly Services responded to that letter by bringing suit against Creative Harbor in the United States District Court for the Eastern District of Michigan. In its complaint, Kelly Services sought a declaratory judgment, *inter alia*, that: (1) it possessed superior rights to the Mark; (2) it had not infringed on Creative Harbor's rights to the Mark; and (3) Creative Harbor's rights to the Mark were invalid.

[9] On May 2, 2014, Creative Harbor answered the complaint and filed counterclaims against Kelly Services. Relevant to this appeal, Creative Harbor sought a declaratory judgment that it had priority rights to the Mark over Kelly Services because it filed the Applications before Kelly Services began using the Mark in commerce.

. . . .

II. Procedural History

[10] Kelly Services sought discovery related to various issues in the case, including Creative Harbor's intent to use the Mark in commerce with respect to each of the goods and services listed in the Applications. In response to Kelly Services' document requests, Creative Harbor produced a PowerPoint presentation that included mock-up "wireframes" (a concept map outlining the elements of a software application) for a potential iPhone application.

[11] Kelly Services also deposed Jurgensen as Creative Harbor's representative pursuant to Federal Rule of Civil Procedure 30(b)(6). During the deposition, Kelly Services asked Jurgensen a number of questions related to Creative Harbor's plans to use the Mark in connection with the thirty-six goods and services identified in the Applications. In response to these questions, Jurgensen testified that Creative Harbor's outside attorney, David Sharifi, prepared the Applications under Jurgensen's instructions to "protect the mark" as to different products and services for which the Mark "could" eventually be used "in case the brand got bigger." (Deposition transcript.) Accordingly, Jurgensen testified that he was not personally aware of the particular reasons why Sharifi included particular goods and services in the Applications. Jurgensen elaborated that "some of these services might be of future importance. Some of these terms might protect my endeavors in the future that I have . . . with the brand . . . . We can go through every single [item], but I can also say to some of them this would have been a future use." (*Id.*)

[12] Additionally, Jurgensen made several statements concerning the goods and services identified in the Applications. {These statements are discussed below}.

[13] On May 14, 2015, Creative Harbor moved for partial summary judgment seeking a declaration that it had priority to the Mark based on the Applications. Kelly Services opposed Creative Harbor's motion on the ground that the Applications were invalid because Creative Harbor lacked *bona fide* intent to use the Mark on some of the goods and services listed in the Applications, as required by § 1(b) of the Lanham Act. The district court construed Kelly Services' opposition as a cross-motion for summary judgment on the priority issue.

. . . .

[14] On October 16, 2015, the district court granted Kelly Services' cross-motion for summary judgment, voiding the Applications in their entirety. *Kelly Servs. II*, 140 F.Supp.3d at 623. The district court concluded that there was no genuine issue of material fact that Creative Harbor lacked a *bona fide* intent to use the Mark as to some of the goods and services listed in its Applications. *Id.* at 618–19. After surveying TTAB precedent, the district court concluded that Creative Harbor's lack of *bona fide* intent as to some of the goods and services necessitated voiding the Applications in their entirety. *Id.* at 622.

. . . .

DISCUSSION

[15] On appeal, Creative Harbor argues that: (1) the district court erred in concluding that it lacked a *bona fide* intent to use the Mark in commerce with respect to some of the goods and services listed in the Applications at the time the Applications were filed; and (2) even if Creative Harbor did lack *bona fide* intent as to certain goods and services, the Applications should not have been voided in their entirety. We address each of these arguments in turn.

I. *Bona Fide* Intent

A. Standard of Review

[16] We review *de novo* the district court's partial grant of summary judgment . . . .

B. Applicable Legal Principles

. . . .

[17] Two of our sister Circuits and the TTAB have held that "lack of a bona fide intent is proper statutory grounds on which to challenge a trademark application." *M.Z. Berger*, 787 F.3d at 1375; *Aktieselskabet AF 21. Nov. 2001 v. Fame Jeans Inc.*, 525 F.3d 8, 21 (D.C. Cir. 2008); *L'Oreal S.A. v. Marcon*, 102 U.S.P.Q.2d 1434, 2012 WL 1267956, at *11 (T.T.A.B. 2012). The parties do not contest that premise.

More importantly, § 1(b) explicitly requires that an ITU applicant have a *bona fide* intent to use the mark in commerce as to the goods and services listed in the application. 15 U.S.C. § 1051(b)(1). We therefore join the Federal and D.C. Circuits and hold that a lack of *bona fide* intent is a proper ground on which to oppose an ITU application. *M.Z. Berger*, 787 F.3d at 1375; *Aktieselskabet*, 525 F.3d at 21.

[18] Although the Lanham Act does not define what constitutes a *bona fide* intent to later use a mark in commerce, the Federal Circuit has explained "that the applicant's intent must be demonstrable and more than a mere subjective belief." *M.Z. Berger*, 787 F.3d at 1375; 3 *McCarthy on Trademarks* § 19.14, at 19.48 ("Congress did not intend the issue to be resolved simply by an officer of the applicant later testifying, 'Yes, indeed, at the time we filed that application, I did truly intend to use the mark at some time in the future.'"). Accordingly, "whether an applicant had a 'bona fide intent' to use the mark in commerce at the time of the application requires *objective* evidence of intent." *M.Z. Berger*, 787 F.3d at 1376 (emphasis added). "Although the evidentiary bar is not high, the circumstances must indicate that the applicant's intent to use the mark was firm *and not merely intent to reserve a right in the mark*." *Id.* (emphasis added). This determination must be made on a "case-by-case basis considering the totality of the circumstances," and may be assessed as of the time the application was filed. *Id* . . . .

[19] "Neither the [Lanham Act] nor [its] legislative history indicates the specific quantum or type of objective evidence required to meet the bar" to show *bona fide* intent. *M.Z. Berger*, 787 F.3d at 1376. Drawing from the relevant legislative history, however, the TTAB has provided "several specific examples of objective circumstances which, if proven, 'may cast doubt on the bona fide nature of the intent or even disprove it entirely.'" *Lane*, 1994 WL 740491, at *6 (quoting S. Rep. No. 100-515, at 23 (1988)).

> For example, the applicant may have filed numerous intent-to-use applications to register the same mark for many more new products than are contemplated, numerous intent-to-use applications for a variety of desirable trademarks intended to be used on [a] single new product, numerous intent-to-use applications to register marks consisting of or incorporating descriptive terms relating to a contemplated new product, numerous intent-to-use applications to replace applications which have lapsed because no timely declaration of use has been filed, an excessive number of intent-to-use applications to register marks which ultimately were not actually used, an excessive number of intent-to-use applications in relation to the number of products the applicant is likely to introduce under the applied-for marks during the pendency of the applications, or applications unreasonably lacking in specificity in describing the proposed goods. Other circumstances may also indicate the absence of genuine bona fide intent to actually use the mark.

Id. (quoting S. Rep. No. 100-515, at 23–24).

[20] Further, one prominent practitioner has recently compiled a list of "affirmative activities that have been deemed indicative of the *presence* of a bona fide intent to use," including:

- conducting a trademark availability search;
- performing preparatory graphic design work or labeling on sales material for a product;
- using a mark in test marketing;
- testimony regarding informal, unwritten business plans or market research;
- obtaining necessary regulatory permits;
- obtaining a correlative domain name for the mark or setting up a website;
- making contacts with individuals who might help develop a business;
- correspondence mentioning the planned use of the mark;
- attempts to find licensees, including ones outside of the U.S.; [and]
- obtaining commercial space in which to perform the services.

See Sandra Edelman, *Proving Your Bona Fides—Establishing Bona Fide Intent to Use Under the U.S. Trademark (Lanham) Act*, 99 TRADEMARK RPTR. 763, 781–82 (2009) (footnotes omitted) (emphasis in original).

[21] On a motion for summary judgment in an action challenging an ITU application for lack of *bona fide* intent, the party opposing the application ("opposing party" or "opposer") "has the initial burden of demonstrating by a preponderance of the evidence that [the] applicant lacked a bona fide intent to use the mark on the identified goods." *Bos. Red Sox Baseball Club LP v. Sherman*, 88 U.S.P.Q.2d 1581, 2008 WL 4149008, at *6 (T.T.A.B. 2007). Once this showing is made, the applicant must either come forward with objective documentary evidence demonstrating *bona fide* intent, or else provide "other facts … which adequately explain or outweigh [the] applicant's failure to provide such documentary evidence." *Honda Motor Co.*, 2009 WL 962810, at *2. Without a valid excuse, the "absence of any documentary evidence on the part of an applicant regarding [bona fide intent] constitutes objective proof sufficient to prove that the applicant lack[ed] a bona fide intention to use its mark in commerce." *Bos. Red Sox*, 2008 WL 4149008, at *6. "While the burden to produce evidence shifts, the burden of persuasion by a preponderance of the evidence remains with the party asserting a lack of a bona fide intention to use." *Intel Corp.*, 2007 WL 1520948, at *4.

C. Analysis

[22] Creative Harbor argues that the evidence in the record shows that it had a *bona fide* intent to use the Mark in connection with each and every one of the thirty-six goods and services listed in the Applications at the time they were filed. We disagree.

1. *Prime Facie* Showing of Lack of *Bona Fide* Intent

[23] As the party challenging Creative Harbor's Applications, Kelly Services bore "the initial burden of demonstrating by a preponderance of the evidence that [Creative Harbor] lacked a bona fide intent to use the mark on the identified goods." *Bos. Red Sox*, 2008 WL 4149008, at *6. We hold that Kelly Services met this initial burden.

[24] As the district court correctly found, Jurgensen's deposition testimony on behalf of Creative Harbor was sufficient to demonstrate by a preponderance of the evidence that Creative Harbor lacked *bona fide* intent to use the Mark as to at least some of the goods and services identified in the Applications at the time the Applications were filed. The district court and Kelly Services specifically reference the following portions of Jurgensen's deposition:

- Mr. Jurgensen testified that he asked his attorney to file the [Applications] in order 'to protect this brand … *in case the brand got bigger; in case it diversifies a little bit*.' (Deposition testimony.);

- Mr. Jurgensen said that the services and goods listed on the [Applications] 'were defined with the idea of protecting my present and *future exploration of this name—of this brand*.' (*Id.*);

- Mr. Jurgensen conceded that at the time his attorney drafted the [Application] he (Jurgensen) 'had clear ideas for some of them, and *some of them were meant for future exploration*.' (*Id.*);

- Mr. Jurgensen acknowledged that some of the listed 'services *might* be of future importance' and that they '*might* protect my endeavors in the future that I have … .' (*Id.*);

- In the [Applications], Creative Harbor stated that it intended to use the Mark with 'computer game software,' but Mr. Jurgensen testified that Creative Harbor did 'not' intend to use the Mark 'with a game.' (*Id.*);

- In the [Applications], Creative Harbor said that it intended to use the Mark in connection with 'professional credentialing verification services … on behalf of others,' but Mr. Jurgensen acknowledged that he simply 'wanted *to keep the option open to at some point do that*.' (*Id.*);

- In the [Applications], Creative Harbor said that it intended to use the Mark in connection with 'employee relations information services,' but when asked about that listing, Mr. Jurgensen did not know what it 'refers to.' (*Id.*);

242

- In the [Applications], Creative Harbor said that it intended to use the Mark in connection with 'employment staffing consultation services,' and Mr. Jurgensen explained that Creative Harbor included this service because '*maybe at some point* [the WorkWire application] would have consulting in there, *maybe some kind of career advisor*, something like this.' (*Id.*);

- In the [Applications], Creative Harbor said that it intended to use the Mark in connection with 'business consulting' services, but Mr. Jurgensen conceded that he 'wanted to make sure [that] was there included' because the company 'could' perhaps perform those services 'at some point' in the future. (*Id.*)

Kelly Servs. II, 140 F.Supp.3d at 617–18 (emphasis in original) (record citations altered).

[25] These excerpts establish that Creative Harbor did not have a "firm" intention to use the Mark in connection with computer software games, professional credentialing verification services, employee relations information services, employment staffing consultation services, and business consulting services—all goods and services listed in the Applications. *See M.Z. Berger*, 787 F.3d at 1376. Moreover, several of Jurgensen's other statements strongly suggest that Creative Harbor included some goods and services in the Applications merely to "reserve a right in the mark" in case it ever decided to expand its commercial activities into those areas. *Id.* Jurgensen's statement that, at the time the Applications were filed, Creative Harbor "had clear ideas for some of [the goods and services], and *some of them were meant for future exploration*" is particularly indicative of Creative Harbor's lack of firm intent. Creative Harbor was not permitted to claim the Mark for uses that might only materialize after some unspecified "future exploration"—it was required to have firm plans to use the Mark at the time the Applications were filed. *M.Z. Berger*, 787 F.3d at 1376. Taking all of Jurgensen's statements together, we are persuaded that the district court was correct in concluding that Kelly Services carried its initial burden in showing that it was more likely than not that Creative Harbor lacked *bona fide* intent as to some of the goods and services listed in the Applications.

. . . .

[26] Accordingly, we hold that Kelly Services met its initial burden of production to show that Creative Harbor lacked *bona fide* intent as to some of the goods and services listed in the Applications.

2. Rebuttal Evidence

[27] Once Kelly Services met its initial burden of production, Creative Harbor was required to come forward with either objective documentary evidence establishing its *bona fide* intent, or facts supporting a sound explanation as to why such evidence was lacking. *Honda Motor Co.*, 2009 WL 962810, at *2. We hold that Creative Harbor provided sufficient objective evidence as to some of the goods and services listed in the Applications, but not others.

[28] In its summary judgment briefing, and again on appeal, Creative Harbor marshals significant evidence demonstrating its *bona fide* intent. A representative sample of Creative Harbor's evidence includes:

- Its hiring of a computer program development firm to develop an employment-based software application for Apple's "App Store." (App Developer Agreement);

- A trademark search it purportedly conducted to determine whether the WORKWIRE name was available. (Deposition testimony);

- The wireframes it developed for its proposed employment-based software application. (*Id.*);

- Its business plans for the proposed application. (5 Year Business Plan);

- Its obtaining of the www.work-wire.com domain name. (Domain Registration); and

- Its press release regarding its employment-based software application. (Press Release.)

[29] The district court correctly acknowledged that Creative Harbor's evidence "makes clear" that Creative Harbor had a *bona fide* intent as to some of the goods and services listed in the Applications. *Kelly Servs. II*, 140 F.Supp.3d at 618. For example, the district court noted "that Creative Harbor had a 'firm' intent to use the Mark in connection with an iPhone application that connected job seekers with

employers." *Id.* We agree with the district court, however, that Creative Harbor's evidence ultimately "misses the mark." *Id.*

[30] As the district court correctly noted, "evidence that Creative Harbor intended to use the Mark with respect to *some* of the goods and services listed in the [Applications] does not contradict Kelly [Services'] evidence that Creative Harbor *lacked* a firm intent to use the Mark on several of the *other* services and goods listed in the [Applications.]" *Id.* (emphasis in original). Creative Harbor, for example, failed to come forward with any objective evidence showing a *bona fide* intent to use the Mark in connection with computer software games, professional credentialing verification services, employee relations information services, employment staffing consultation services, and business consulting services—the goods and services most fatally undermined by Jurgensen's deposition testimony. Nor did Creative Harbor offer any reasons excusing its failure to come forward with such objective evidence . . . .

[31] Accordingly, we hold that Creative Harbor lacked a *bona fide* intent to use the Mark in connection with at least some of the goods and services listed in the Applications.

II. Remedy

. . . .

[32] Finally, the district court's interpretation {of *Spirits International, B.V. v. S.S. Taris Zeytin Ve Zeytinyagi Tarim Satis Kooperatifleri Birligi*, 99 U.S.P.Q.2d 1545, 2011 WL 2909909 (T.T.A.B. 2011)} would lead to perverse results. Imagine a hypothetical § 1(b) ITU applicant who submits an application listing 100 goods associated with the requested mark with a subjective intention to use the mark in connection with all of the goods. The hypothetical applicant has at least some objective documentary evidence supporting its *bona fide* intent as to all 100 goods, but a competitor nevertheless challenges the applicant's *bona fide* intent as to ten of the goods in a declaratory action in federal district court. Under the district court and Kelly Services' interpretation of *Spirits International*, the applicant is put in quite a quandary: he must either (1) voluntarily delete the challenged goods, even if the challenges lack merit; or (2) risk having his entire application voided if the district court determines that he lacked *bona fide* intent for even a single item. If the applicant lacks ironclad documentary evidence for even one item— which is likely in circumstances where the application lists a large number of goods and services—his incentive is to delete the challenged goods rather than risk losing the entire application. Similarly, his competitor is incentivized to bring *bona fide* intent challenges to all of the applicant's future applications, because the competitor can likely bully the applicant into at least some concessions, and the only consequence for the competitor if it loses is legal fees, which may be a relative pittance depending on the industry and the value of the mark . . . .

. . . .

[33] Accordingly, we hold that when a § 1(b) ITU applicant lacks *bona fide* intent as to some, but not all, of the goods and services listed in her application, the application should not be voided in its entirety absent fraud or other egregious conduct. *Grand Canyon*, 2006 WL 802407, at *1–3. Rather, the court should determine as to which goods and services the applicant lacked *bona fide* intent, and excise the overbroad portions of the application. We thus hold that the district court erred in voiding Creative Harbor's Applications in their entirety.

III. Remand

. . . .

[34] On remand, the district court should evaluate each of the thirty-six goods and services listed in the Applications, and make individualized determinations as to whether Creative Harbor's objective documentary evidence establishes a *bona fide* intention to eventually use those items in commerce. The district court may wish to conduct an evidentiary hearing in service of this inquiry, although we do not require it to do so.

. . . .

ALICE M. BATCHELDER, Circuit Judge, concurring in part and dissenting in part and dissenting from the judgment.

. . . .

[35] TTAB precedent suggests that it is incumbent upon the applicant to amend its application to eliminate portions of its § 1(b) ITU application for which it cannot demonstrate bona fide intent, or else risk having the entire application voided. Creative Harbor refused to take advantage of this remedy. The district court therefore correctly voided both of Creative Harbor's applications *ab initio*. Because my colleagues reach the opposite conclusion, I respectfully dissent.

3.   Process of Registration

The PTO provides excellent annotated flowcharts of the registration process for each of the five filing bases on its website at: https://www.uspto.gov/trademark/trademark-timelines/trademark-application-and-post-registration-process-timelines. The reader is very strongly encouraged to consult these flow charts while reviewing the following information.

a.   Application

As of February 15, 2020, all trademark applications must be filed electronically. As of August 3, 2019, foreign-domiciled entities must file their applications through a U.S.-licensed attorney. U.S.-domiciled entities may continue to file their applications without an attorney— though, as discussed in Comment 2 at the end of this section, applications filed by specialist trademark attorneys tend to do significantly better.

The application is relatively simple. *See* Lanham Act §§ 1(a) & 1(b) (setting out the required contents of use-based and intent-to-use applications, respectively). The following are the most important elements of the application:

- *Filing Basis*: As mentioned above, the applicant must specify at least one of the five filing bases provided for in the Lanham Act.

- *Designation of Goods and Services*: The applicant must identify the particular goods or services on or in connection with which it uses or intends to use the mark. The *U.S. Acceptable Identification of Goods and Services Manual*, available online, provides a listing of acceptable identifications of goods and services. The applicant should also identify the international class number(s) of the identified goods or services as established by the *Nice International Classification of Goods and Services for the Purposes of the Registration of Trademarks*. ("Nice" after the French city where the *Nice Agreement* was reached, and pronounced to rhyme with "peace"). The 45 classes of the *Nice Classification* are listed below. In principle, the identification of goods or services does not limit the breadth of the applicant's registered exclusive rights. The sole purpose of the identification of goods and services is to aid the PTO in internal administration and review of applications. However, litigants sometimes cite a registered mark's identification of goods and services to support their particular view of the scope of the registered rights at issue—and courts sometimes treat the identification as relevant, though not binding, on the question.

- *Drawing*: The applicant must submit a drawing of the trademark. As of 2003, if the mark consists of colors, the drawing must as well. For word marks, a typed representation of the mark is sufficient. For nonvisual marks, such as sound or scent marks, the applicant need not submit a drawing. The PTO relies instead on the applicant's description of the mark given elsewhere in the application and on the applicant's specimen of use. TMEP § 807.09.

- *Specimen of Use*: Applicants filing a "1(a)" use-based application must submit one specimen of use of the mark in commerce for each international class in which the applicant seeks registration. This specimen typically takes the form of digital photographs of the mark attached to goods or .pdf images of materials promoting services. Applicants filing a "1(b)" intent-to-use application need not (because they very likely cannot) submit a specimen of use with their application, but must do so instead when they file their Statement of Use. *See* Lanham Act § 1(d)(1) (15 U.S.C. 1051(d)(1)).

See Lanham Act § 1, 15 U.S.C. § 1051.

The 45 Classes of the Nice Classification

Goods	Services
001 - Chemicals	035 - Advertising and Business Services
002 - Paints	036 - Insurance and Finance Services
003 - Cleaning Substances	037 - Construction and Repair Services
004 - Industrial Oils	038 - Telecommunications Services
005 - Pharmaceuticals	039 - Shipping and Travel Services
006 - Common Metals	040 - Material Treatment Services
007 - Machines	041 - Education and Entertainment Services
008 - Hand Tools	042 - Science and Technology Services
009 - Computers and Scientific Devices	043 - Food Services
010 - Medical Supplies	044 - Medical and Vet Services
011 - Appliances	045 - Legal and Security Services
012 - Vehicles	
013 - Firearms	
014 - Precious Metals	
015 - Musical Instruments	
016 - Paper Goods	
017 - Rubber Products	
018 - Leather Goods	
019 - Building Materials	
020 - Furniture	
021 - Household Utensils	
022 - Ropes and Textile Products	
023 - Yarns and Threads	
024 - Textiles	
025 - Clothing	
026 - Lace and Embroidery	
027 - Carpets	
028 - Games and Sporting Goods	
029 - Meat, Fish, Poultry	
030 - Coffee, Flour, Rice	
031 - Grains, Agriculture	
032 - Beers and Beverages	
033 - Alcoholic Beverages	
034 - Tobacco Products	

For applications filed under Lanham Act § 1 or § 44, the PTO will grant a filing date to the application according to the date on which all of the following "minimum requirements" are received at the PTO: (1) name of the applicant, (2) name and address for correspondence, (3) a clear drawing of the mark; (4) a listing of the goods or services; and (5) the filing fee for at least one class of goods or services. *See* TMEP §§ 201-02. For Madrid System applications filed under Lanham Act § 66(a), compliance with minimum filing requirements is established by the International Bureau at the World Intellectual Property Organization. (We will discuss the Madrid System in more detail in Part I.D.6 below).

b. Examination

Typically within about six to eight months from the application's filing date, an examining attorney will engage in a substantive examination of the application to determine if there are any absolute or relative grounds for refusal. *See* Lanham Act § 12(a), 15 U.S.C. § 1062(a). With respect to relative grounds for refusal, the examining attorney will search the PTO's X-Search and TESS databases (the latter of which is available online at no charge) to determine if any marks have already been filed that may be confusingly similar with the applied-for mark under Lanham Act §2(d), 15 U.S.C. § 1052(d).[8]

---

[8] At the examination stage, an examiner may not refuse registration on the ground that the applied-for mark will dilute another mark. *See* Lanham Act § 2(f), 15 U.S.C. § 1052(f) ("A mark which when used would cause dilution under section 43(c) may be refused registration only pursuant to a[n opposition] proceeding brought under section 13.").

Estimates based on data from the mid-2010s indicate that almost half of applications receive such § 2(d) refusals.[9] If the examining attorney finds no grounds for refusal, the attorney will approve the mark for publication in the PTO's Official Gazette. One study suggests that only about 15% of use-based applications and 21% of ITU applications proceed directly from application to approval for publication without any grounds for refusal being identified by an examining attorney.[10]

If the examining attorney finds grounds for refusal, the attorney will send an "office action" to the applicant to explain the grounds for refusal. Effective December 3, 2022, the applicant has a maximum of three months to respond (applicants previously had six months) and, if appropriate, to amend the application to satisfy the examiner's objections.[11] If the applicant fails to respond, the application will be deemed abandoned. *See* Lanham Act § 12(b), 15 U.S.C. § 1062(b). Correspondence between the office and the applicant will continue until either (1) the examining attorney approves the application for publication, (2) the examining attorney issues a final office action refusing registration of the mark, or (3) the applicant abandons the application. *See id.* The applicant may appeal the final office action to the Trademark Trial and Appeal Board.

c. Publication

Marks approved for publication are published in the PTO's Official Gazette (OG), a weekly online publication. *See* Lanham Act § 12(a), 15 U.S.C. § 1062(a). Publication in the OG gives notice to the public that the PTO plans to register the mark. For a 30-day period following the date of the mark's publication in the OG, any party that believes it would be harmed by the registration, including as a result of dilution, may file an opposition to the registration of the mark. *See* Lanham Act § 13, 15 U.S.C. § 1063.

d. Opposition and the Trademark Trial and Appeal Board

Oppositions are rare. *See* Barton Beebe & Jeanne Fromer, *Are We Running Out of Trademarks? An Empirical Study of Trademark Depletion & Congestion*, 131 HARV. L. REV. 945, 971 n. 128 (2018) (reporting that "[f]or applications filed from 1985 through 2014, only 2.10% were opposed and only 0.90% were opposed successfully"). Those few oppositions that are filed are heard by the Trademark Trial and Appeal Board. The TTAB is an administrative board within the PTO that acts in the capacity of a trial court of first instance in opposition, cancellation, interference, and concurrent use proceedings and in the capacity of an appellate body in ex parte appeals from final office actions. Created in 1958, the TTAB consists of the Director of the PTO, the Commissioner for Patents, the Commissioner for Trademarks, and Administrative Judges appointed by the Secretary of Commerce in consultation with the Director. The Director and Commissioners rarely sit on TTAB panels. At this writing, there are 25 Administrative Judges on the TTAB, all of whom are highly experienced in trademark matters. The TTAB sits in panels of three judges. The Trademark Trial and Appeal Board Manual of Procedure, available online, details all aspects of TTAB procedure. Proceedings before the TTAB are conducted in writing (though counsel may request oral argument). There is no live testimony, though transcribed testimony, taken under oath and subject to cross-examination, may be submitted. Note that only those TTAB opinions that are explicitly labeled as "citable as precedent" should be cited to the TTAB in subsequent proceedings.

Under the terms of Lanham Act § 21, 15 U.S.C. § 1071, TTAB judgments may be appealed either to a federal district court or to the Court of Appeals for the Federal Circuit. There are two advantages of the district court route. First, the record in the case may be supplemented with additional evidence. Second, the district court's rulings may be appealed to its reviewing appellate court, thus making it possible to

---

[9] See Barton Beebe & Jeanne Fromer, *Are We Running Out of Trademarks? An Empirical Study of Trademark Depletion & Congestion*, 131 HARV. L. REV. 945, 1005 (2018)

[10] *See* Barton Beebe, *Is the Trademark Office a Rubber Stamp?: Trademark Registration Rates at the PTO, 1981-2010*, 48 HOUSTON L. REV. 752 (2012).

[11] Applicants whose filing basis is §66(a) under the Madrid Protocol continue to have six months to respond to an office action.

avoid the Federal Circuit; for example, if the applicant appeals the PTO's decision to the Eastern District of Virginia, Fourth Circuit case law would control.[12]

If the applicant prevails in the opposition proceeding, then the mark proceeds to registration.

The TTAB and Issue Preclusion. TTAB proceedings may gain substantially increased importance in certain situations in light of the Supreme Court opinion in *B & B Hardware, Inc. v. Hargis Indus., Inc.*, 135 S. Ct. 1293 (2015). In 1993, B & B registered the mark SEALTIGHT in connection with metal fasteners for use in the aerospace industry. In 1996, Hargis sought to register the mark SEALTITE in connection with metal fasteners for use in building construction. B & B opposed on the ground that Hargis's mark was confusingly similar to B & B's mark. The TTAB found a likelihood of confusion and refused registration. Hargis did not appeal this decision. While the TTAB opposition proceeding was pending, B & B sued Hargis in federal district court, arguing that Hargis's mark infringed B & B's. Before the district court could rule, the TTAB announced its finding of a likelihood of confusion. B & B argued to the district court that the TTAB's decision should be given preclusive effect. The district court disagreed and the jury ultimately found no likelihood of confusion. The Eight Circuit affirmed.

The Supreme Court reversed and remanded. It held: "So long as the other ordinary elements of issue preclusion are met, when the usages adjudicated by the TTAB are materially the same as those before the district court, issue preclusion should apply." *Id*. at 1310. For an example of the effect of *B & B* outside of the likelihood of confusion context, see *Ashe v. PNC Financial Services Group, Inc.*, 165 F. Supp. 3d 357 (D. Md. 2015) (holding that TTAB's prior determination that defendant had priority of use of mark SPENDOLOGY collaterally estopped plaintiff from asserting that defendant's use infringed on plaintiff's identical mark).

Standing to Oppose. Lanham Act § 13, 15 U.S.C. § 1063, states that "[a]ny person who believes that he would be damaged by the registration of a mark upon the principal register" may file an opposition. In *Ritchie v. Simpson*, 170 F.3d 1092 (Fed. Cir. 1999), the Federal Circuit interpreted this language liberally: "an opposer must meet two judicially-created requirements in order to have standing—the opposer must have a 'real interest' in the proceedings and must have a 'reasonable' basis for his belief of damage." *Id*. at 1095. "In no case has this court ever held that one must have a specific commercial interest, not shared by the general public, in order to have standing as an opposer . . . . The crux of the matter is not how many others share one's belief that one will be damaged by the registration, but whether that belief is reasonable and reflects a real interest in the issue." *Id*. at 1096-97. In *Ritchie*, the Federal Circuit held that Mr. Ritchie, who "described himself as a 'family man' who believes that the 'sanctity of marriage requires a husband and wife who love and nurture one another,'" *id*. at 1097, had standing to oppose O.J. Simpson's application to register the marks O.J. SIMPSON, O.J., and THE JUICE.

However, in *Rebecca Curtin v. United Trademark Holdings Inc.*, Opposition No. 91241083 (TTAB May 4, 2023) [precedential], the TTAB overrode a 2018 opinion of a previous TTAB panel to find that Professor Curtin did not have standing to oppose the registration of RAPUNZEL for dolls. Professor Curtin stated that she "is a professor of law teaching trademark law, and is also a consumer who participates amongst other consumers in the marketplace for dolls and toy figures of fairytale characters, including Rapunzel." *Id*. at 3. She argued that the asserted mark failed to function as a mark, was generic, and would

---

[12] Formerly, a disadvantage of the district court route was that the applicant was required to pay the government's expenses in defending any ex parte PTO decision before the district court, including prorated salaries of the government attorneys, regardless of whether the applicant prevailed. This rule was based on Lanham Act § 21(b)(3), 15 U.S.C. § 1071(b)(3): "[U]nless the court finds the expenses to be unreasonable, all the expenses of the proceeding shall be paid by the [appealing] party bringing the case, whether the final decision is in favor of such party or not." However, in *Peter v. NantKwest*, 140 S.Ct. 365 (2019), the Supreme Court determined that similar language from the Patent Act did not override "the bedrock principle known as the '"American Rule"': Each litigant pays his own attorney's fees, win or lose, unless a statute or contract provides otherwise." *Id*. at 370. Thus, applicants challenging ex parte PTO decisions at a district court need not pay the government's attorney's fees.

deny to consumers the benefit of healthy competition in the market for dolls depicting the public domain Rapunzel character. Dismissing her opposition, the TTAB quoted Lanham Act § 1127 ("The intent of this chapter is to regulate commerce within the control of Congress . . . to protect persons engaged in such commerce against unfair competition") to conclude that "the Trademark Act regulates commerce and protects plaintiffs with commercial interests"—and apparently does not intend to do anything more than that. *Curtin*, at 7. Citing *Lexmark Int'l, Inc. v. Static Control Components, Inc.*, 572 U.S. 118 (2014), the TTAB explained:

> The Supreme Court's review of this statement of purpose led it to hold, in *Lexmark*, that "to come within the zone of interests in a suit" under Section 43(a)(1) of the Trademark Act, 15 U.S.C. § 1125(a)(1) – which, similar to Section 13, may be invoked only by a plaintiff "who believes that he or she is or is likely to be damaged" by the challenged act – "a plaintiff must allege an injury to a commercial interest in reputation or sales." *Lexmark*, 109 USPQ2d at 2069 (emphasis added). The Court specifically stated that while consumers "may well have an injury-in-fact" caused by violations of the Trademark Act, they "cannot invoke the protection" of the statute based solely on injuries suffered as consumers, "a conclusion reached by every Circuit to consider the question." *Id.*

Because Professor Curtin had not alleged that any commercial interests of her own would be injured, the TTAB refused to consider the merits of her opposition. "Put simply, the Trademark Act does not provide 'consumer standing.' That is, it does not entitle mere consumers to a statutory cause of action; a statutory cause of action is reserved for those with commercial interests." *Curtin*, at 11.

e.   Registration

With respect to use-based applications, if no opposition is filed within thirty days or if the opposition fails, then the PTO issues a certificate of registration and notice of the registration is published in the Official Gazette. With respect to intent-to-use applications that are either unopposed or unsuccessfully opposed, the PTO issues a Notice of Allowance. The applicant then has six months (extendable for a total of three years) to file a Statement of Use showing that it is making use of the mark in commerce. *See* Lanham Act § 2(d), 15 U.S.C. § 1052(d); TMEP § 1106.

4.   Post-Registration Maintenance of the Registration

The term of registration is ten years. Lanham Act § 8, 15 U.S.C. § 1058. The registration may be renewed indefinitely provided that the registrant complies with the requirements of Lanham Act §§ 8 & 9, 15 U.S.C. §§ 1058 & 1059. Section 8 requires the registrant to file an Affidavit of Continuing Use "(1) on or after the fifth anniversary and no later than the sixth anniversary of the date of registration . . . and (2) within the year before the end of every ten-year period after the date of registration." TMEP § 1604.04. Thus, the registrant must file a "Section 8 affidavit" in the sixth year of the registration, the tenth year, the twentieth year, the thirtieth year, etc. Section 8 adds a six-month grace period to this deadline. *See* Lanham Act § 8(c), 15 U.S.C. § 1058(c). *See also* TMEP § 1604.04 ("*Example*: For a registration issued on Nov. 1, 2005, a six-year affidavit or declaration may be filed as early as Nov. 1, 2010, and may be filed as late as Nov. 1, 2011, before entering the six-month grace period.").

Section 9 requires the registrant to file a Renewal Application every tenth year following the date of registration. Registrants typically file the Section 8 Affidavit of Continuing Use and the Section 9 Renewal Application as a single document. Section 9 also adds a sixth-month grace period. *See* Lanham Act § 9(a), 15 U.S.C. § 1059(a). *See also* TMEP § 1606.03 ("*Example*: For a registration issued on November 5, 1998, an application for renewal may be filed as early as November 5, 2007, and as late as November 5, 2008, before entering the six-month grace period.").

Registrants are also strongly advised to file an Affidavit of Incontestability under Lanham Act § 15 (15 U.S.C. § 1065) within one year after any five-year period of continuous use of the mark. In practice, sophisticated trademark owners typically combine their first § 8 Affidavit of Continuing Use (filed in the sixth year following registration) with a § 15 Affidavit of Incontestability. A § 15 affidavit may be filed at any time during the duration of the registration of the mark, however, provided that it is filed within the year following five years' continuous use of the mark. See TMEP § 1605.03.

5. Notice of Federal Registration

Lanham Act § 29, 15 U.S.C. § 1111, provides:

> Notwithstanding the provisions of section 22 hereof {15 USC § 1072}, a registrant of a mark registered in the Patent and Trademark Office, may give notice that his mark is registered by displaying with the mark the words "Registered in U.S. Patent and Trademark Office" or "Reg. U.S. Pat. & Tm. Off." or the letter R enclosed within a circle, thus ®; and in any suit for infringement under this Act by such a registrant failing to give such notice of registration, no profits and no damages shall be recovered under the provisions of this Act unless the defendant had actual notice of the registration.

Id. The latter part of § 29 is generally understood to establish that in situations where the registrant has not provided statutory notice of the registration of its mark, that registrant may only win profits and damages from a period *after* the defendant had actual notice of the registration status of the mark. *See* McCarthy § 19:144.[13]

The ® or "r in a circle" designation indicates that the mark is registered on either the Principal or Supplemental Register. A "TM" or "SM" designation indicates that the mark is unregistered, but that the owner is claiming property rights in the mark. Firms may sometimes use the "TM" or "SM" designations in an attempt to educate consumers that the mark at issue is a designation of source rather than simply a description, decoration, or feature of the product.

6. Cancellation of Registration

Lanham Act § 14, 15 U.S.C. § 1064, addresses the circumstances under which a third party may petition to cancel a registration. It provides, in essence, that for the five year period following the date of registration, a third party may petition to cancel the registration for any reason. *See* Lanham Act § 14(1), 15 U.S.C. § 1064(1). After five years have passed from the date of registration, a third party may petition to cancel a registration for only a limited number of reasons expressly enumerated in Lanham Act § 14(3), 15 U.S.C. § 1064(3). Here is the relevant statutory language:

> A petition to cancel a registration of a mark, stating the grounds relied upon, may, upon payment of the prescribed fee, be filed as follows by any person who believes that he is or will be damaged, including as a result of a likelihood of dilution by blurring or dilution by tarnishment under section 1125(c) of this title, by the registration of a mark on the principal register established by this chapter, or under the Act of March 3, 1881, or the Act of February 20, 1905:

> (1) Within five years from the date of the registration of the mark under this chapter.

---

[13] May registrants take advantage of their rights under Lanham Act § 43(a), dealing with unregistered marks, to claim profits and damages even where the registrant did not provide statutory notice? McCarthy suggests that the answer is no:

> The more problematic question is whether a registrant who proves infringement under both § 32(1) (registered mark) and § 43(a) (unregistered mark) can avoid the notice limitation imposed by § 29 by claiming all of its damages fall under the § 43(a) count. A strict reading of the statutory language of § 29 would, in the author's opinion, lead to the conclusion that such a registrant cannot avoid the § 29 damage limitation by using § 43(a). Section 29 does not distinguish between the kind of statutory infringement that a registrant proves. Rather, § 29 simply states that no profits and damages shall be recovered "under the provisions of this Act" unless statutory or actual notice was given.

McCarthy § 19:144.

. . . .

(3) At any time if the registered mark becomes the generic name for the goods or services, or a portion thereof, for which it is registered, or is functional, or has been abandoned, or its registration was obtained fraudulently or contrary to the provisions of section 1054 of this title or of subsection (a), (b), or (c) of section 1052 of this title for a registration under this chapter, or contrary to similar prohibitory provisions of such prior Acts for a registration under such Acts, or if the registered mark is being used by, or with the permission of, the registrant so as to misrepresent the source of the goods or services on or in connection with which the mark is used. If the registered mark becomes the generic name for less than all of the goods or services for which it is registered, a petition to cancel the registration for only those goods or services may be filed. A registered mark shall not be deemed to be the generic name of goods or services solely because such mark is also used as a name of or to identify a unique product or service. The primary significance of the registered mark to the relevant public rather than purchaser motivation shall be the test for determining whether the registered mark has become the generic name of goods or services on or in connection with which it has been used.

Lanham Act § 14, 15 U.S.C. § 1064. Note what is missing from § 14(3). Most significantly, after five years have passed since the date of registration, a third party cannot petition to cancel the registration on the ground that the mark is merely descriptive without secondary meaning (this ground is not included in § 14(3)) or on the ground that the registered mark is confusingly similar with a previously used mark (§ 2(d) is not included in § 14(3)). Nor can the registration be cancelled on the ground that the mark fails to function as a mark. This five-year time limit on grounds for cancellation petitions at the PTO applies even if the registrant has not applied for incontestable status.[14]

Ex parte expungement and ex parte reexamination. In 2020, the Trademark Modernization Act (TMA) added Lanham Act § 16A, which provides that third parties (or the PTO itself) may seek *ex parte* expungement of a registration, in whole or part, for any goods or services listed in the registration in connection with which the registrant has never in fact made a use of the mark in commerce. The challenger may seek *ex parte* expungement at any time from the fourth year through the tenth year of the registration. The TMA also added Lanham Act § 16B, which provides that third parties (or the PTO itself) may seek *ex parte* reexamination of a registration to verify that the registered mark has been used on all the goods or services listed in the registration as of the filing date of a use-based application or the filing date of the Statement of Use following an ITU application. An *ex parte* reexamination request must be filed within the first five years of the challenged registration. Both § 16A and § 16B are effective as of December 27, 2021.

Lanham Act § 37. Lanham Act § 37, 15 U.S.C. § 1119, provides federal courts with broad powers over registrations:

In any action involving a registered mark the court may determine the right to registration, order the cancelation of registrations, in whole or in part, restore canceled registrations, and otherwise rectify the register with respect to the registrations of any party to the action. Decrees and orders shall be certified by the court to the Director, who shall make appropriate entry upon the records of the Patent and Trademark Office, and shall be controlled thereby.

Id. The Fourth Circuit has determined, however, that § 37 does not allow federal courts to override the time limits built in to § 14. *See Shakespeare Co. v. Silstar Corp. of Am.*, 9 F.3d 1091 (4th Cir. 1993).

---

[14] Note that Lanham Act § 14 can be read only to apply to cancellation petitions brought before *the PTO*. If the registrant has not obtained incontestable status for the mark, challengers *in federal court* are arguably not limited by Lanham Act § 14 in the grounds on which they can challenge the validity—or at least the enforceability—of the mark. *But see* McCarthy § 30:112 (arguing that § 14's five-year limit on grounds for cancellation applies to federal courts as well).

7. The Madrid System

The United States has been a member of the "Madrid System" for the international registration of trademarks since November 2, 2003, which was the effective date of the Madrid Protocol Implementation Act ("MPIA"), 116 Stat. 1758, 1913 Pub. L. 107-273.[15] The Madrid System provides an efficient means by which trademark applicants or registrants may apply to register their marks at multiple foreign trademark offices through a single application filed at (and a single fee paid to) their home trademark office. For example, a trademark applicant or registrant at the PTO may file a single application and pay a single fee to register its trademark at any or all of the 130 countries[16] within the Madrid Union; the fee increases with the number of countries. The PTO will forward any such application to the International Bureau administering the Madrid System (based in Geneva at the World Intellectual Property Organization ("WIPO")), which will then forward the application in turn to all countries selected by the applicant. This can result in significant cost savings for the applicant because it need not hire foreign local counsel to prosecute its application unless the local trademark office rejects or otherwise demands some response relating to the application. Furthermore, the Madrid registrant need only file a single form and pay a single fee to renew its mark across multiple foreign countries.

For U.S. applicants, there are certain drawbacks to using Madrid. First, many foreign trademark offices permit relatively broad definitions of the goods or services with which the mark will be used. The PTO, however, does not. As a result, the U.S. applicant must file a narrow definition of the applied-for mark's goods in order to satisfy the PTO but will then be required to use that definition when it seeks to extend its protection abroad. For this reason, some U.S. applicants seek to file in foreign countries locally rather than through Madrid.

A second disadvantage of Madrid is that all international trademark registrations filed through Madrid remain dependent on the applicant's home (or "basic") registration for five years from the date of that home registration. If the home registration fails during that five year period (as a result of a "central attack" from a third party opposer or for any other reason), then all international registrations will fail as well. However, within three months from the date of the cancellation of its home registration, the Madrid registrant may file to "transform" its international registrations into local registrations.

Comments and Questions

1.   *Trademark registration rates at the PTO.* The PTO's release of data concerning the registration process has made it possible to estimate the overall trademark registration rate at the PTO, i.e., the proportion of trademark applications that result in registration. For use-based applications filed at the PTO from 1981 through 2007, the overall registration rate was .75. *See* Barton Beebe, *Is the Trademark Office a Rubber Stamp?*, 48 HOUSTON L. REV. 751, 762 (2011). For ITU-based applications filed from November 16, 1989 through 2007, the registration rate was .37. *Id.* What might explain this significant difference in registration rates between use-based and ITU-based applications? Consider the publication rates of such applications, i.e., the proportion of applications that the PTO approved for publication. For use-based applications filed at the PTO from 1981 through 2007, the publication rate was .76. *Id.* at 770. For ITU-based applications filed from November 16, 1989 through 2007, the publication rate was also .76. *Id.* Recall that after an ITU-based application is approved for publication, the applicant must then submit a Statement of Use in order to complete the registration process.

---

[15] The Madrid System functions under two international instruments, the Madrid Agreement Concerning the International Registration of Marks of 1891, which the U.S. has never joined, and the 1989 Protocol Relating to the Madrid Agreement Concerning the International Registration of Marks (generally referred to as the "Madrid Protocol"), which was developed primarily to bring the U.S. and other major economies (such as the U.K. and Japan), into the Madrid System. Both the Agreement and the Protocol are filing treaties rather than substantive harmonization treaties.

[16] As of June 2023. *See* http://www.wipo.int/madrid/en/members/. Canada became a party to the Madrid Protocol in June 2019, and Brazil did so in October 2019.

The figure below shows trademark publication and registration rates at the PTO over time. What might explain the pronounced dip in registration rates in 1999-2000?

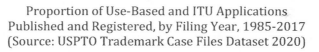

Proportion of Use-Based and ITU Applications
Published and Registered, by Filing Year, 1985-2017
(Source: USPTO Trademark Case Files Dataset 2020)

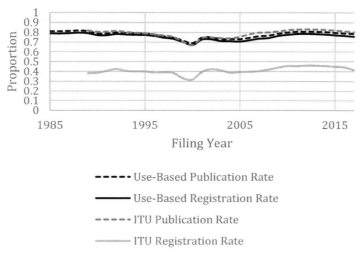

----- Use-Based Publication Rate

—— Use-Based Registration Rate

-- -- ITU Publication Rate

▒▒▒▒▒ ITU Registration Rate

2.   *Do trademark lawyers matter?* Deborah Gerhardt and John McClanahan have presented compelling evidence that trademark applications filed by attorneys do significantly better than applications filed by non-attorneys. *See* Deborah R. Gerhardt & Jon P. McClanahan, *Do Trademark Lawyers Matter?*, 16 STAN. TECH. L. REV. 583 (2013). They note in particular that for the period 1984 through 2012, the publication rate for applications filed by attorneys was 82% while the publication rate for applications filed by non-attorneys was 60%. *Id.* at 606. They also reported significant differences in the publication rates of applications depending on the experience of the attorney filing the application. *Id.* at 610. See the article for a consideration of factors that may explain these differences.

3.   *Trademark registrations as an index of innovation?* Scholarship has focused on the question of whether trademark registration data may be used to measure the rate of "non-technological" innovation, specifically, innovation in the service and marketing sectors (sectors about which patent data often has very little to say). *See, e.g.*, Valentine Millot, Trademarks as an Indicator of Product and Marketing Innovations, OECD Science, Technology and Industry Working Papers 2009/06 (2009), http://dx.doi.org/10.1787/224428874418. *See also* Dev Saif Gangjee, *Trade Marks and Innovation?*, TRADEMARK LAW AND THEORY II (G.B. Dinwoodie & M.D. Janis eds., 2021).

4.   *Do state trademark regsitrations have any value?* In general, no they do not. Scholars have even gone so far as to call for their abolition. *See* Lee Ann W. Lockridge, *Abolishing State Trademark Registrations*, 29 CARDOZO ARTS & ENT. L.J. 597 (2011). Lockridge reports:

> Under the law of forty-five states, registrations provide registrants with no significant, enforceable substantive rights beyond those awarded under state common law or under the federal statute protecting unregistered common law trademarks. In five states certain substantive rights can accrue to an owner through state registration, although those rights are limited by competing rights held by certain common law owners or federal registrants.

Id. at 598-99. Lockridge observes that in five states (Massachusetts, Minnesota, Rhode Island, Texas, and Washington), state law provides that a state trademark registration will create constructive notice of the registrant's claim of ownership as of the date of state registration, which impairs the ability of a common law adopter of the mark to claim good faith adoption of the mark after that date (or good faith geographic expansion within the state of its prior continuing use). *Id.* at 624. This benefit arises only under state law, however, and has no bearing on claims brought under federal law. *Id.* In the face of a subsequent third party federal registration, a state trademark registrant is typically treated no better than a § 7(c) prior "common law" user.

McCarthy proposes one way in which state registration may provide a slight advantage in federal litigation:

> State registrations in most states have little legal significance other than serving as proof that on a certain date the registrant filed a claim that it was using a certain mark. This gives a slight procedural advantage of proving priority compared to merely relying upon a trademark owner's inherent common-law right of priority as proven by business records.

McCarthy at § 22:1 (footnote omitted). Note, however, that before the TTAB, state trademark registrations are not competent evidence of use by the state registrant of the mark. *See, e.g., Visa International Service Ass'n v. Visa Realtors*, 208 U.S.P.Q. 462 (TTAB 1980).

For a broader historical discussion of the relation between state trademark law and federal trademark law, see Mark P. McKenna, *Trademark Law's Faux Federalism*, in INTELLECTUAL PROPERTY AND THE COMMON LAW 288 (Shyamkrishna Balganesh ed. 2013). McKenna argues that "the persistent sense that federal and state law regulate concurrently has masked a significant federalization of trademark and unfair competition law over the last forty to fifty years." *Id*. at 289. McKenna goes so far as to call for the explicit federal preemption of state trademark and unfair competition law. *Id*. at 298.

8. Incontestable Status and *Park 'N Fly*

Park 'N Fly, Inc. v. Dollar Park and Fly, Inc.
469 U.S. 189 (1985)

Justice O'CONNOR delivered the opinion of the Court.

[1] In this case we consider whether an action to enjoin the infringement of an incontestable trade or service mark may be defended on the grounds that the mark is merely descriptive. We conclude that neither the language of the relevant statutes nor the legislative history supports such a defense.

I

[2] Petitioner operates long-term parking lots near airports. After starting business in St. Louis in 1967, petitioner subsequently opened facilities in Cleveland, Houston, Boston, Memphis, and San Francisco. Petitioner applied in 1969 to the United States Patent and Trademark Office (Patent Office) to register a service mark consisting of the logo of an airplane and the words "Park 'N Fly." The registration issued in August 1971. Nearly six years later, petitioner filed an affidavit with the Patent Office to establish the incontestable status of the mark. As required by § 15 of the Trademark Act of 1946 (Lanham Act), 60 Stat. 433, as amended, 15 U.S.C. § 1065, the affidavit stated that the mark had been registered and in continuous use for five consecutive years, that there had been no final adverse decision to petitioner's claim of ownership or right to registration, and that no proceedings involving such rights were pending. Incontestable status provides, subject to the provisions of § 15 and § 33(b) of the Lanham Act, "conclusive evidence of the registrant's exclusive right to use the registered mark . . . ." § 33(b), 15 U.S.C. § 1115(b).

[3] Respondent also provides long-term airport parking services, but only has operations in Portland, Oregon. Respondent calls its business "Dollar Park and Fly." Petitioner filed this infringement action in 1978 in the United States District Court for the District of Oregon and requested the court permanently to enjoin respondent from using the words "Park and Fly" in connection with its business. Respondent counterclaimed and sought cancellation of petitioner's mark on the grounds that it is a generic term. See § 14(c), 15 U.S.C. § 1064(c). Respondent also argued that petitioner's mark is unenforceable because it is merely descriptive. See § 2(e), 15 U.S.C. § 1052(e) . . . .

[4] After a bench trial, the District Court found that petitioner's mark is not generic and observed that an incontestable mark cannot be challenged on the grounds that it is merely descriptive . . . . The District Court permanently enjoined respondent from using the words "Park and Fly" and any other mark confusingly similar to "Park 'N Fly."

[5] The Court of Appeals for the Ninth Circuit reversed. 718 F.2d 327 (1983). The District Court did not err, the Court of Appeals held, in refusing to invalidate petitioner's mark. *Id.,* at 331. The Court of Appeals noted, however, that it previously had held that incontestability provides a defense against the cancellation of a mark, but it may not be used offensively to enjoin another's use. *Ibid.* Petitioner, under this analysis, could obtain an injunction only if its mark would be entitled to continued registration without regard to its incontestable status. Thus, respondent could defend the infringement action by showing that the mark was merely descriptive. Based on its own examination of the record, the Court of Appeals then determined that petitioner's mark is in fact merely descriptive, and therefore respondent should not be enjoined from using the name "Park and Fly." *Ibid.*

[6] The decision below is in direct conflict with the decision of the Court of Appeals for the Seventh Circuit in *Union Carbide Corp. v. Ever-Ready Inc.,* 531 F.2d 366, cert. denied, 429 U.S. 830, 97 S.Ct. 91, 50 L.Ed.2d 94 (1976). We granted certiorari to resolve this conflict, 465 U.S. 1078, 104 S.Ct. 1438, 79 L.Ed.2d 760 (1984), and we now reverse.

II

[7] Congress enacted the Lanham Act in 1946 in order to provide national protection for trademarks used in interstate and foreign commerce. S.Rep. No. 1333, 79th Cong., 2d Sess., 5 (1946). Previous federal legislation, such as the Federal Trademark Act of 1905, 33 Stat. 724, reflected the view that protection of trademarks was a matter of state concern and that the right to a mark depended solely on the common law. S.Rep. No. 1333, at 5. Consequently, rights to trademarks were uncertain and subject to variation in different parts of the country. Because trademarks desirably promote competition and the maintenance of product quality, Congress determined that "a sound public policy requires that trademarks should receive nationally the greatest protection that can be given them." *Id.,* at 6. Among the new protections created by the Lanham Act were the statutory provisions that allow a federally registered mark to become incontestable. §§ 15, 33(b), 15 U.S.C. §§ 1065, 1115(b).

[8] The provisions of the Lanham Act concerning registration and incontestability distinguish a mark that is "the common descriptive name of an article or substance" from a mark that is "merely descriptive." §§ 2(e), 14(c), 15 U.S.C. §§ 1052(e), 1064(c). Marks that constitute a common descriptive name are referred to as generic. A generic term is one that refers to the genus of which the particular product is a species. *Abercrombie & Fitch Co. v. Hunting World, Inc.,* 537 F.2d 4, 9 (CA2 1976). Generic terms are not registrable, and a registered mark may be canceled at any time on the grounds that it has become generic. See §§ 2, 14(c), 15 U.S.C. §§ 1052, 1064(c). A "merely descriptive" mark, in contrast, describes the qualities or characteristics of a good or service, and this type of mark may be registered only if the registrant shows that it has acquired secondary meaning, *i.e.,* it "has become distinctive of the applicant's goods in commerce." §§ 2(e), (f), 15 U.S.C. §§ 1052(e), (f).

[9] This case requires us to consider the effect of the incontestability provisions of the Lanham Act in the context of an infringement action defended on the grounds that the mark is merely descriptive. Statutory construction must begin with the language employed by Congress and the assumption that the ordinary meaning of that language accurately expresses the legislative purpose. See *American Tobacco Co. v. Patterson,* 456 U.S. 63, 68, 102 S.Ct. 1534, 1537, 71 L.Ed.2d 748 (1982). With respect to incontestable trade or service marks, § 33(b) of the Lanham Act states that "registration shall be conclusive evidence of the registrant's exclusive right to use the registered mark" subject to the conditions of § 15 and certain enumerated defenses. Section 15 incorporates by reference subsections (c) and (e) of § 14, 15 U.S.C. § 1064. An incontestable mark that becomes generic may be canceled at any time pursuant to § 14(c). That section also allows cancellation of an incontestable mark at any time if it has been abandoned, if it is being used to misrepresent the source of the goods or services in connection with which it is used, or if it was obtained fraudulently or contrary to the provisions of § 4, 15 U.S.C. § 1054, or §§ 2(a)–(c), 15 U.S.C. §§ 1052(a)–(c).

[10] One searches the language of the Lanham Act in vain to find any support for the offensive/defensive distinction applied by the Court of Appeals. The statute nowhere distinguishes between a registrant's offensive and defensive use of an incontestable mark. On the contrary, § 33(b)'s

255

declaration that the registrant has an "exclusive right" to use the mark indicates that incontestable status may be used to enjoin infringement by others. A conclusion that such infringement cannot be enjoined renders meaningless the "exclusive right" recognized by the statute. Moreover, the language in three of the defenses enumerated in § 33(b) clearly contemplates the use of incontestability in infringement actions by plaintiffs. See §§ 33(b)(4)–(6), 15 U.S.C. §§ 1115(b)(4)–(6).

[11] The language of the Lanham Act also refutes any conclusion that an incontestable mark may be challenged as merely descriptive. A mark that is merely descriptive of an applicant's goods or services is not registrable unless the mark has secondary meaning. Before a mark achieves incontestable status, registration provides prima facie evidence of the registrant's exclusive right to use the mark in commerce. § 33(a), 15 U.S.C. § 1115(a). The Lanham Act expressly provides that before a mark becomes incontestable an opposing party may prove any legal or equitable defense which might have been asserted if the mark had not been registered. *Ibid.* Thus, § 33(a) would have allowed respondent to challenge petitioner's mark as merely descriptive if the mark had not become incontestable. With respect to incontestable marks, however, § 33(b) provides that registration is *conclusive* evidence of the registrant's exclusive right to use the mark, subject to the conditions of § 15 and the seven defenses enumerated in § 33(b) itself.* Mere descriptiveness is not recognized by either § 15 or § 33(b) as a basis for challenging an incontestable mark.

[12] The statutory provisions that prohibit registration of a merely descriptive mark but do not allow an incontestable mark to be challenged on this ground cannot be attributed to inadvertence by Congress. The Conference Committee rejected an amendment that would have denied registration to any descriptive mark, and instead retained the provisions allowing registration of a merely descriptive mark that has acquired secondary meaning. See H.R.Conf.Rep. No. 2322, 79th Cong., 2d Sess., 4 (1946) (explanatory statement of House managers). The Conference Committee agreed to an amendment providing that no incontestable right can be acquired in a mark that is a common descriptive, *i.e.*, generic, term. *Id.*, at 5. Congress could easily have denied incontestability to merely descriptive marks as well as to generic marks had that been its intention.

[13] The Court of Appeals in discussing the offensive/defensive distinction observed that incontestability protects a registrant against cancellation of his mark. 718 F.2d, at 331. This observation is incorrect with respect to marks that become generic or which otherwise may be canceled at any time pursuant to §§ 14(c) and (e). Moreover, as applied to marks that are merely descriptive, the approach of the Court of Appeals makes incontestable status superfluous. Without regard to its incontestable status, a mark that has been registered five years is protected from cancellation except on the grounds stated in §§ 14(c) and (e). Pursuant to § 14, a mark may be canceled on the grounds that it is merely descriptive only if the petition to cancel is filed within five years of the date of registration. § 14(a), 15 U.S.C. § 1064(a). The approach adopted by the Court of Appeals implies that incontestability adds nothing to the protections against cancellation already provided in § 14. The decision below not only lacks support in the words of the statute; it effectively emasculates § 33(b) under the circumstances of this case.

III

[14] Nothing in the legislative history of the Lanham Act supports a departure from the plain language of the statutory provisions concerning incontestability. Indeed, a conclusion that incontestable status can provide the basis for enforcement of the registrant's exclusive right to use a trade or service mark promotes the goals of the statute. The Lanham Act provides national protection of trademarks in order to secure to the owner of the mark the goodwill of his business and to protect the ability of consumers to distinguish among competing producers. See S.Rep. No. 1333, at 3, 5. National protection of trademarks is desirable, Congress concluded, because trademarks foster competition and the maintenance of quality by securing to the producer the benefits of good reputation. *Id.*, at 4. The incontestability provisions, as the proponents of the Lanham Act emphasized, provide a means for the registrant to quiet title in the ownership of his mark. See Hearings on H.R. 82 before the Subcommittee

---

* {Lanham Act § 33(b) has since been amended to list nine defenses.}

of the Senate Committee on Patents, 78th Cong., 2d Sess., 21 (1944) (remarks of Rep. Lanham); *id.*, at 21, 113 (testimony of Daphne Robert, ABA Committee on Trade Mark Legislation); Hearings on H.R. 102 et al. before the Subcommittee on Trade-Marks of the House Committee on Patents, 77th Cong., 1st Sess., 73 (1941) (remarks of Rep. Lanham). The opportunity to obtain incontestable status by satisfying the requirements of § 15 thus encourages producers to cultivate the goodwill associated with a particular mark. This function of the incontestability provisions would be utterly frustrated if the holder of an incontestable mark could not enjoin infringement by others so long as they established that the mark would not be registrable but for its incontestable status.

. . . .

IV

[15] Respondent argues that the decision by the Court of Appeals should be upheld because trademark registrations are issued by the Patent Office after an *ex parte* proceeding and generally without inquiry into the merits of an application. This argument also unravels upon close examination. The facts of this case belie the suggestion that registration is virtually automatic. The Patent Office initially denied petitioner's application because the examiner considered the mark to be merely descriptive. Petitioner sought reconsideration and successfully persuaded the Patent Office that its mark was registrable.

[16] More generally, respondent is simply wrong to suggest that third parties do not have an opportunity to challenge applications for trademark registration. If the Patent Office examiner determines that an applicant appears to be entitled to registration, the mark is published in the Official Gazette. § 12(a), 15 U.S.C. § 1062(a). Within 30 days of publication, any person who believes that he would be damaged by registration of the mark may file an opposition. § 13, 15 U.S.C. § 1063. Registration of a mark provides constructive notice throughout the United States of the registrant's claim to ownership. § 22, 15 U.S.C. § 1072. Within five years of registration, any person who believes that he is or will be damaged by registration may seek to cancel a mark. § 14(a), 15 U.S.C. § 1064(a). A mark may be canceled at any time for certain specified grounds, including that it was obtained fraudulently or has become generic. § 14(c), 15 U.S.C. § 1064(c).

[17] The Lanham Act, as the dissent notes, *post*, at 673 – 674, authorizes courts to grant injunctions "according to principles of equity." § 34, 15 U.S.C. § 1116. Neither respondent nor the opinion of the Court of Appeals relies on this provision to support the holding below. Whatever the precise boundaries of the courts' equitable power, we do not believe that it encompasses a substantive challenge to the validity of an incontestable mark on the grounds that it lacks secondary meaning. To conclude otherwise would expand the meaning of "equity" to the point of vitiating the more specific provisions of the Lanham Act.[7] Similarly, the power of the courts to cancel registrations and "to otherwise rectify the register," § 37, 15 U.S.C. § 1119, must be subject to the specific provisions concerning incontestability. In effect, both respondent and the dissent argue that these provisions offer insufficient protection against improper registration of a merely descriptive mark, and therefore the validity of petitioner's mark may be challenged notwithstanding its incontestable status. Our responsibility, however, is not to evaluate the wisdom of the legislative determinations reflected in the statute, but instead to construe and apply the provisions that Congress enacted.

V

[18] The Court of Appeals did not attempt to justify its decision by reference to the language or legislative history of the Lanham Act. Instead, the court relied on its previous decision in *Tillamook County Creamery v. Tillamook Cheese & Dairy Assn.*, 345 F.2d 158, 163 (CA9), cert. denied, 382 U.S. 903 (1965), for the proposition that a registrant may not rely on incontestability to enjoin the use of the mark

---

[7] We note, however, that we need not address in this case whether traditional equitable defenses such as estoppel or laches are available in an action to enforce an incontestable mark. See generally Comment, Incontestable Trademark Rights and Equitable Defenses in Infringement Litigation, 66 Minn.L.Rev. 1067 (1982).

by others. Examination of *Tillamook,* however, reveals that there is no persuasive justification for the judicially created distinction between offensive and defensive use of an incontestable mark . . . .

VI

[19] We conclude that the holder of a registered mark may rely on incontestability to enjoin infringement and that such an action may not be defended on the grounds that the mark is merely descriptive. Respondent urges that we nevertheless affirm the decision below based on the "prior use" defense recognized by § 33(b)(5) of the Lanham Act. Alternatively, respondent argues that there is no likelihood of confusion and therefore no infringement justifying injunctive relief. The District Court rejected each of these arguments, but they were not addressed by the Court of Appeals. 718 F.2d, at 331–332, n. 4. That court may consider them on remand. The judgment of the Court of Appeals is reversed, and the case is remanded for further proceedings consistent with this opinion.

It is so ordered.

Justice STEVENS, dissenting.

[1] In trademark law, the term "incontestable" is itself somewhat confusing and misleading because the Lanham Act expressly identifies over 20 situations in which infringement of an allegedly incontestable mark is permitted.[1] Moreover, in § 37 of the Act, Congress unambiguously authorized judicial review of the validity of the registration "in any action involving a registered mark." The problem in this case arises because of petitioner's attempt to enforce as "incontestable" a mark that Congress has plainly stated is inherently unregistrable.

[2] The mark "Park 'N Fly" is at best merely descriptive in the context of airport parking. Section 2 of the Lanham Act plainly prohibits the registration of such a mark unless the applicant proves to the Commissioner of the Patent and Trademark Office that the mark "has become distinctive of the applicant's goods in commerce," or to use the accepted shorthand, that it has acquired a "secondary meaning." See 15 U.S.C. §§ 1052(e), (f). Petitioner never submitted any such proof to the Commissioner, or indeed to the District Court in this case. Thus, the registration plainly violated the Act.

[3] The violation of the literal wording of the Act also contravened the central purpose of the entire legislative scheme. Statutory protection for trademarks was granted in order to safeguard the goodwill that is associated with particular enterprises. A mark must perform the function of distinguishing the producer or provider of a good or service in order to have any legitimate claim to protection. A merely descriptive mark that has not acquired secondary meaning does not perform that function because it simply "describes the qualities or characteristics of a good or service." *Ante,* at 662. No legislative purpose is served by granting anyone a monopoly in the use of such a mark.

[4] Instead of confronting the question whether an inherently unregistrable mark can provide the basis for an injunction against alleged infringement, the Court treats the case as though it presented the same question as *Union Carbide Corp. v. Ever-Ready, Inc.,* 531 F.2d 366 (CA7), cert. denied, 429 U.S. 830, 97 S.Ct. 91, 50 L.Ed.2d 94 (1976), a case in which the merely descriptive mark had an obvious and well-established secondary meaning. In such a case, I would agree with the Court that the descriptive character of the mark does not provide an infringer with a defense. In this case, however, the provisions of the Act dealing with incontestable marks do not support the result the Court has reached. I shall first

---

[1] Section 33(b) enumerates seven categories of defenses to an action to enforce an incontestable mark. See 15 U.S.C. § 1115(b), quoted *ante,* at 662, n. 3. In addition, a defendant is free to argue that a mark should never have become incontestable for any of the four reasons enumerated in § 15. 15 U.S.C. § 1065. Moreover, § 15 expressly provides that an incontestable mark may be challenged on any of the grounds set forth in subsections (c) and (e) of § 14, 15 U.S.C. § 1064, and those sections, in turn, incorporate the objections to registrability that are defined in §§ 2(a), 2(b), and 2(c) of the Act. 15 U.S.C. §§ 1052(a), (b), and (c).

explain why I agree with the conclusion that the Court of Appeals reached; I shall then comment on each of the three arguments that the Court advances in support of its contrary conclusion.

I

[5] The word "incontestable" is not defined in the Act. Nor, surprisingly, is the concept explained in the Committee Reports on the bill that was enacted in 1946. The word itself implies that it was intended to resolve potential contests between rival claimants to a particular mark. And, indeed, the testimony of the proponents of the concept in the Committee hearings that occurred from time to time during the period when this legislation was being considered reveals that they were primarily concerned with the problem that potential contests over the ownership of registrable marks might present. No one ever suggested that any public purpose would be served by granting incontestable status to a mark that should never have been accepted for registration in the first instance.

[6] In those hearings the witnesses frequently referred to incontestability as comparable to a decree quieting title to real property. Such a decree forecloses any further contest over ownership of the property, but it cannot create the property itself. Similarly the incontestability of a trademark precludes any competitor from contesting the registrant's ownership, but cannot convert unregistrable subject matter into a valid mark. Such a claim would be clearly unenforceable.

. . . .

[7] The legislative history of the incontestability provisions indicates that Congress did not intend to prevent the use of mere descriptiveness as a substantive defense to a claim of infringement if the mark has not acquired secondary meaning . . . .

[8] . . . In light of this legislative history, it is apparent that Congress could not have intended that incontestability should preserve a merely descriptive trademark from challenge when the statutory procedure for establishing secondary meaning was not followed and when the record still contains no evidence that the mark has ever acquired a secondary meaning.

[9] If the registrant of a merely descriptive mark complies with the statutory requirement that prima facie evidence of secondary meaning must be submitted to the Patent and Trademark Office, it is entirely consistent with the policy of the Act to accord the mark incontestable status after an additional five years of continued use. For if no rival contests the registration in that period, it is reasonable to presume that the initial prima facie showing of distinctiveness could not be rebutted. But if no proof of secondary meaning is ever presented, either to the Patent and Trademark Office or to a court, there is simply no rational basis for leaping to the conclusion that the passage of time has transformed an inherently defective mark into an incontestable mark.

[10] No matter how dedicated and how competent administrators may be, the possibility of error is always present,[12] especially in nonadversary proceedings. For that reason the Court normally assumes that Congress intended agency action to be subject to judicial review unless the contrary intent is expressed in clear and unambiguous language. In this statute Congress has expressed no such intent. On the contrary, it has given the courts the broadest possible authority to determine the validity of trademark registrations "in any action involving a registered mark." § [37, 15 U.S.C. § 1119]. The exercise of that broad power of judicial review should be informed by the legislative purposes that motivated the enactment of the Lanham Act.

---

[12] Recently, Gerald J. Mossinghoff, Assistant Secretary and Commissioner of Patents and Trademarks, gave the following testimony before Congress: "[O]ne of the biggest problems we have had is that, at any one time, about 7 percent of our 25 million documents are either missing or misfiled. The paper system was set up in 1836 and has remained virtually unchanged since then. During that time it simply has deteriorated to the point where 7 percent of the documents are missing." Hearing before the Subcommittee on Patents, Copyrights and Trademarks of the Senate Committee on the Judiciary, 98th Cong., 1st Sess., 5 (1983).

[11] Congress enacted the Lanham Act "to secure trade-mark owners in the goodwill which they have built up." [S.Rep. No. 1333, at 5] But without a showing of secondary meaning, there is no basis upon which to conclude that petitioner has built up any goodwill that is secured by the mark "Park 'N Fly." In fact, without a showing of secondary meaning, we should presume that petitioner's business appears to the consuming public to be just another anonymous, indistinguishable parking lot. When enacting the Lanham Act, Congress also wanted to "protect the public from imposition by the use of counterfeit and imitated marks and false trade descriptions." [*Ibid.*] Upon this record there appears no danger of this occurrence, and as a practical matter, without any showing that the public can specifically identify petitioner's service, it seems difficult to believe that anyone would imitate petitioner's marks, or that such imitation, even if it occurred, would be likely to confuse anybody.

[12] On the basis of the record in this case, it is reasonable to infer that the operators of parking lots in the vicinity of airports may make use of the words "park and fly" simply because those words provide a ready description of their businesses, rather than because of any desire to exploit petitioner's goodwill. There is a well-recognized public interest in prohibiting the commercial monopolization of phrases such as "park and fly." When a business claims the exclusive right to use words or phrases that are a part of our common vocabulary, this Court should not depart from the statutorily mandated authority to "rectify the register," 15 U.S.C. § 1119, absent a clear congressional mandate. Language, even in a commercial context, properly belongs to the public unless Congress instructs otherwise. In this case we have no such instruction; in fact, the opposite command guides our actions: Congress' clear insistence that a merely descriptive mark, such as "Park 'N Fly" in the context of airport parking, remain in the public domain unless secondary meaning is proved.

[13] The basic purposes of the Act, the unambiguous congressional command that no merely descriptive mark should be registered without prior proof that it acquired secondary meaning, and the broad power of judicial review granted by § 37 combine to persuade me that the registrant of a merely descriptive mark should not be granted an injunction against infringement without ever proving that the mark acquired secondary meaning.

II

[14] The Court relies on three different, though not unrelated, arguments to support its negative answer to the question "whether an action to enjoin the infringement of an incontestable mark may be defended on the grounds that the mark is merely descriptive," *ante,* at 660: (1) the language of § 33(b) is too plain to prevent any other conclusion; (2) the legislative history indicates that Congress decided not to deny incontestable status to merely descriptive marks; and (3) the practical value of incontestable status would be nullified if the defense were recognized. Each of these arguments is unpersuasive.

The Plain Language

[15] After the right to use a registered mark has become incontestable, § 33(b) provides that "the registration shall be conclusive evidence of the registrant's exclusive right to use the registered mark." 15 U.S.C. § 1115(b). Read in isolation, this provision surely does lend support to the Court's holding. Indeed, an isolated and literal reading of this language would seem to foreclose any nonstatutory defense to an action to enjoin the infringement of an incontestable mark. The Court, however, wisely refuses to adopt any such rigid interpretation of § 33(b).

[16] An examination of other provisions of the Act plainly demonstrates that no right to injunctive relief against infringement automatically follows from the achievement of incontestable status. Thus, § 34 states that courts with proper jurisdiction "shall have power to grant injunctions, according to the principles of equity and upon such terms as the court may deem reasonable." 15 U.S.C. § 1116. If a registrant establishes the violation of any right, § 35 additionally emphasizes that any recovery shall be "subject to the principles of equity." 15 U.S.C. § 1117. These sections are in addition to the broad power that § 37 grants to courts in "any action involving a registered mark" to "determine the right to registration, order the cancelation of registrations, in whole or in part, restore canceled registrations, and otherwise rectify the register with respect to the registrations of any party to the action." 15 U.S.C. § 1119. Moreover, it is well established that injunctions do not issue as a matter of course, and that "the

essence of equity jurisdiction has been the power of the Chancellor to do equity," [*Hecht Co. v. Bowles*, 321 U.S. 321, 329 (1944),] particularly when an important public interest is involved.

[17] In exercising its broad power to do equity, the federal courts certainly can take into account the tension between the apparent meaning of § 33(b) and the plain command in §§ 2(e), (f) of the Act prohibiting the registration of a merely descriptive mark without any proof of secondary meaning. Because it would be { }demonstrably at odds with the intent of [Congress]{ } to grant incontestable status to a mark that was not eligible for registration in the first place, the Court is surely authorized to require compliance with § 2(f) before granting relief on the basis of § 33(b).

The Legislative History

[18] The language of §§ 2(e), (f) expressly demonstrates Congress' concern over granting monopoly privileges in merely descriptive marks. However, its failure to include mere descriptiveness in its laundry list of grounds on which incontestability could be challenged is interpreted by the Court today as evidence of congressional approval of incontestable status for all merely descriptive marks.

[19] This history is unpersuasive because it is perfectly clear that the failure to include mere descriptiveness among the grounds for challenging incontestability was based on the understanding that such a mark would not be registered without a showing of secondary meaning. See *supra*, at 618. To read Congress' failure as equivalent to an endorsement of incontestable status for merely descriptive marks without secondary meaning can only be described as perverse.

The Practical Argument

[20] The Court suggests that my reading of the Act "effectively emasculates § 33(b) under the circumstances of this case." *Ante*, at 663. But my reading would simply require the owner of a merely descriptive mark to prove secondary meaning before obtaining any benefit from incontestability. If a mark is in fact "distinctive of the applicant's goods in commerce" as § 2(f) requires, that burden should not be onerous. If the mark does not have any such secondary meaning, the burden of course could not be met. But if that be the case, the purposes of the Act are served, not frustrated, by requiring adherence to the statutory procedure mandated by Congress.

[21] In sum, if petitioner had complied with § 2(f) at the time of its initial registration, or if it had been able to prove secondary meaning in this case, I would agree with the Court's disposition. I cannot, however, subscribe to its conclusion that the holder of a mark which was registered in violation of an unambiguous statutory command "may rely on incontestability to enjoin infringement." *Ante,* at 667; see also *ante,* at 663. Accordingly, I respectfully dissent.

E. The Geographic Extent of Trademark Rights

We consider in this section the geographical extent of trademark rights within the territorial borders of the United States. Under the common law, priority of usage has long been the basis of the geographic extent of a claimant's rights; first in time is first in right. The Lanham Act provides registered marks with the benefit of very important exceptions to this common law principle. We begin first with the geographic extent of rights in unregistered, common law marks. We then turn to the geographic extent of rights in federally registered marks.

1. The Geographic Extent of Rights in *Unregistered* Marks

A classic hypothetical in American trademark law involves the question of whether the owner of an unregistered mark used in, say, Anchorage, Alaska, can assert exclusive rights in that mark beyond the borders of Anchorage. Can the proprietor of the unregistered mark ARCTIC COFFEE for a cafe in Anchorage, Alaska prevent someone in Miami, Florida from later opening a cafe under the same name? And should it make a difference if the proprietor of the Miami coffee shop knew of the existence of the ARCTIC COFFEE cafe in Anchorage when she opened her cafe in Miami?

In the cases *Hanover Star Milling Co. v. Metcalf*, 240 U.S. 403 (1916) (commonly known as the *Tea Rose* case), and *United Drug Co. v. Theodore Rectanus*, 248 U.S. 90 (1918), the Supreme Court established the so-called "*Tea Rose-Rectanus* rule," which holds that:

(1) The territorial scope of an unregistered mark is limited to the territory in which the mark is known and recognized by relevant consumers in that territory.

(2) The senior user of an unregistered mark cannot stop the use of a territorially remote good faith junior user who was first to use the mark in that remote territory.

MCCARTHY § 26.2. The result of the *Tea Rose-Rectanus* rule is that, for unregistered marks, the first person to adopt the mark in the United States and subsequent good faith remote junior users may end up coexisting in the national marketplace, with each entity claiming exclusive rights in the mark in the geographic area in which each was the first to use the mark. Thus, the Anchorage and Miami cafes both using the mark ARCTIC COFFEE may coexist, provided that the Miami cafe adopted its mark in good faith (the standard for which we will consider below). Furthermore, barring federal registration by either the Anchorage or the Miami cafe, the two firms' exclusive rights will expand across the country only in those areas in which each firm is the first to use the mark in good faith.

The case below, *Nat'l Ass'n for Healthcare Commc'ns, Inc. v. Cent. Arkansas Area Agency on Aging, Inc.*, 257 F.3d 732, 734 (8th Cir. 2001), offers a relatively straightforward example of the application of the *Tea Rose-Rectanus* doctrine.

a. The *Tea Rose-Rectanus* Doctrine Applied

The six counties where Central Arkansas Area Agency on Aging, Inc. uses its mark.

National Association for Healthcare Communications, Inc. v. Central Arkansas Area Agency on Aging, Inc.
257 F.3d 732 (8th Cir. 2001)

LOKEN, Circuit Judge.

[1] This is an action under the Lanham Act and state law to determine which party has the superior right to use the service mark "CareLink" in Arkansas. The National Association for Healthcare Communications, Inc. ("Healthcom") was the first to use the mark nationally. It has a federal service mark registration pending but must rely in this case on its common law trademark rights as enforced under the Lanham Act. *See* 15 U.S.C. § 1125(a). The Central Arkansas Area Agency on Aging, Inc. ("CA") was the first to use the mark in six counties in central Arkansas and has registered its mark under the Arkansas trademark statutes. *See* Ark.Code Ann. Tit. 4, Ch. 71 (Michie Supp. 1999). The district court held that CA as first user prevailed in its six-county trade area and that CA's state registration entitled it to statewide relief. Accordingly, the court enjoined Healthcom from using the CareLink mark anywhere in Arkansas. *National Ass'n for Healthcare Commun., Inc. v. Central Ark. Area Agency on Aging, Inc.*, 119 F.Supp.2d 884 (E.D.Ark. 2000). Healthcom appeals. Agreeing that CA is entitled to injunctive relief, but

limited to the six Arkansas counties where it has used the mark, we remand to the district court with instructions to modify the injunction.

I.

[2] *The Parties' Use of the CareLink Mark.* Healthcom is an Illinois corporation that provides remote electronic monitoring devices and emergency response services for at-home clients in twenty-five States, including Arkansas. Healthcom solicits local hospitals and home health care agencies to become members of Healthcom's National Association for Emergency Response, Inc. Each member's subscribers (individual clients or patients) are then offered a variety of CareLink at-home emergency response services. A CareLink program typically consists of monitoring equipment, usually leased by Healthcom to the member health care provider or directly to the subscriber, plus a round-the-clock support center operated by Healthcom, which responds to the subscriber's emergency calls in a prearranged fashion and may monitor medical equipment in the subscriber's home or monitor the whereabouts of an at-risk subscriber, such as one suffering from Alzheimer's disease. Each provider-member markets CareLink programs and equipment to its patients, bills the patients, and pays Healthcom a monthly fee for each patient using CareLink services.

[3] CA is a private, nonprofit Arkansas corporation organized in 1979 to provide a broad range of support services to elderly and disabled persons in a six-county region in central Arkansas. CA's mission is to provide cost-effective, community-based alternatives to nursing home care. CA has 750 employees and 300 volunteers who assist some 10,000 elderly persons in the region. CA has never provided personal emergency response services, but it has occasionally paid for such services being provided to CA clients. In January 1995, CA adopted the trade name "CareLink" to use in lieu of its corporate name, which had proved awkward and hard to remember, and which created the mis-impression that CA is a government agency.

[4] *Facts relating to first usage.* Healthcom began marketing emergency response services under the CareLink service mark in 1991 or early 1992. From 1992 to 1995, Healthcom spent an estimated $50,000 attempting to sell its services in Arkansas. Despite these efforts, during this period Healthcom made only one $385 sale in Arkansas, to an end user who stopped using its CareLink service in April 1994. Healthcom had no Arkansas customers from April 1994 to September 1995, when it entered into a contract with North Arkansas Regional Medical Center in Harrison. By July 1999, Healthcom had contracts with seven Arkansas health care providers and served 350 individual subscribers. Healthcom estimated that its total Arkansas revenues in 1999 would be just over $82,000. Healthcom has *never* had a customer for its CareLink services located within the six-county region served by CA. Healthcom applied for federal trademark registration on May 4, 1999, and its application is pending.

[5] CA adopted the CareLink trade name and logo in early 1995 and has prominently displayed the logo on stationery, business cards, client information materials, and other publicity materials. CA registered its CareLink mark with the Arkansas Secretary of State on March 23, 1995, and has used the mark in promoting all of its services, except hospice care. CA's annual revenues grew from $5,000,000 to $12,000,000 from early 1995 to mid–1999. Although CA derives most of its revenues from government grants, in 1999 it received approximately $138,000 in private donations and an estimated $250,000 from clients able to pay for its services. All of CA's clients reside in its six-county region, but its activities are publicized beyond central Arkansas through news coverage, telephone listings, advertisements, and a monthly column in an Arkansas newspaper for the elderly.

[6] CA did not know of Healthcom's prior usage when it adopted the CareLink name and logo and received a state registration in early 1995. When CA learned that the North Arkansas Regional Medical Center was using Healthcom's CareLink mark for emergency response services in northern Arkansas, CA sent a cease-and-desist letter to that provider. The parties were unable to resolve the resulting dispute. Healthcom then commenced this action, alleging common law trademark infringement and unfair competition in violation of the Lanham Act, 15 U.S.C. § 1125(a), and seeking an injunction barring CA from using the mark and cancellation of CA's state registration. CA counterclaimed, alleging unfair competition under the Lanham Act and trademark infringement under Ark.Code Ann. § 4–71–212, and

seeking an injunction prohibiting Healthcom from using its CareLink mark in Arkansas or, alternatively, in CA's six-county region.

[7] Deciding the case on cross motions for summary judgment, the district court dismissed Healthcom's claims because its use of the CareLink mark in Arkansas prior to CA's state registration was *de minimis*. The court granted CA a permanent injunction prohibiting Healthcom from using the mark anywhere in Arkansas because CA's use of the mark has been substantial, because a statewide injunction is necessary "to prevent confusion among consumers and to prevent Healthcom from passing off its services as those of [CA]," and because CA's state registration entitles it to a statewide injunction. Healthcom appeals, arguing that its common law trademark is entitled to priority because it first used the mark in Arkansas. Alternatively, Healthcare argues the district court abused its discretion in granting CA an overly broad injunction.

II.

[8] Nearly a century ago, the Supreme Court established what is now called the *Tea Rose/Rectanus* doctrine—the first user of a common law trademark may not oust a later user's good faith use of an infringing mark in a market where the first user's products or services are not sold. *See United Drug Co. v. Theodore Rectanus Co.,* 248 U.S. 90, 100–01 (1918); *Hanover Star Milling Co. v. Metcalf,* 240 U.S. 403, 415 (1916). The rationale is a core principle of trademark law: the owner of a mark may not "monopolize markets that his trade has never reached and where the mark signifies not his goods but those of another." *Hanover Star Milling,* 240 U.S. at 416. That essential principle applies even when the first user has federally registered its mark under the Lanham Act, with one important modification: the owner of a *registered* mark has the right to expand its use into a new market unless an infringing user had penetrated that market *prior to registration. See Natural Footwear Ltd. v. Hart, Schaffner & Marx,* 760 F.2d 1383, 1395 (3d Cir.); 15 U.S.C. § 1072.

[9] In this case we must apply the *Tea Rose/Rectanus* doctrine in resolving two distinct inquiries. First, we must determine whether Healthcom, as the first user of a CareLink common law mark elsewhere in the country, is entitled by reason of its own market penetration to oust CA from any area in Arkansas. Second, to the extent Healthcom failed to prove first use in Arkansas, we must determine whether CA, as owner of a state-registered mark used only in six counties, is entitled to statewide injunctive relief against Healthcom's present use of its mark.

A.

[10] It is undisputed that, in early 1995, CA adopted the CareLink mark in good faith, without knowledge of Healthcom's prior use. To be entitled to injunctive relief against CA's subsequent good faith use, Healthcom must prove that its prior use of the mark penetrated the geographic market in question. In determining whether Healthcom achieved the necessary market penetration, we apply the factors identified in our often-cited *Sweetarts* cases:

> [Healthcom's] dollar value of sales at the time [CA] entered the market, number of customers compared to the population of the state, relative and potential growth of sales, and length of time since significant sales. Though the market penetration need not be large to entitle [Healthcom] to protection, it must be significant enough to pose the real likelihood of confusion among the consumers in that area.

Sweetarts v. Sunline, Inc., 380 F.2d 923, 929 (8th Cir. 1967); *Sweetarts v. Sunline, Inc.,* 436 F.2d 705, 708 (8th Cir. 1971) (citation omitted). Where the first user's activities in a remote area are "so small, sporadic, and inconsequential" that its market penetration is *de minimis,* the first user is not entitled to protection against a later user's good faith adoption of the mark in that area. *Sweetarts,* 380 F.2d at 929.

[11] Healthcom argues that it penetrated the Arkansas market through its one sale to an end user in 1992, its seven provider-member contracts and 350 subscribers since the fall of 1995, and its continuous advertising and marketing efforts beginning in 1992. Healthcom errs in assuming without proof that the entire State of Arkansas is a single geographic market for these purposes. CA adopted its CareLink mark for use in six counties in central Arkansas, not the entire State. Healthcom has *never* made a sale in that area, nor has it even attempted to prove that CA's use of the mark in its region is causing a

likelihood of confusion elsewhere in the State. For this reason alone, Healthcom has not penetrated CA's six-county trade area, and the district court properly denied Healthcom injunctive relief against CA's use in that area.

[12] This leaves the question whether Healthcom is entitled to injunctive relief as a prior user with market penetration in any other part of Arkansas. We agree with the district court that Healthcom's one $385 sale long before CA's adoption of its mark was *de minimis* market penetration. That leaves Healthcom's reliance on later sales and continuous advertising. CA argues that sales in Arkansas after CA began using the mark are irrelevant, and that Healthcom's prior advertising may not be used to satisfy the *Sweetarts* market penetration test. Those are strong arguments. The issue is whether they warrant summary judgment.

[13] *Sweetarts* expressly recognized that the market penetration issue is focused on the time when the later user entered the market. However, subsequent sales by the first user *may* establish a trend of increased sales justifying a finding of market penetration. *See Natural Footwear,* 760 F.2d at 1401. Likewise, while "advertising alone is not sufficient to satisfy the significant market penetration test of *Sweetarts,*" *Flavor Corp. of Am. v. Kemin Indus., Inc.,* 493 F.2d 275, 284 (8th Cir. 1974), we are not prepared to say as a matter of law that a first user's highly focused local advertising, followed by initial sales shortly after a later user enters the market, may never satisfy the *Sweetarts* test. *Compare Natural Footwear,* 760 F.2d at 1402–03; *Nutri/System, Inc. v. Con–Stan Indus., Inc.,* 809 F.2d 601, 604 (9th Cir. 1987). Nevertheless, we need not decide whether CA is entitled to summary judgment on the market penetration issue statewide because Healthcom presented no evidence that CA is presently likely to enter areas of Arkansas beyond its six-county region, and no evidence that any customers or potential customers of Healthcom are actually confused, or likely to be confused, by CA's use of its CareLink mark in serving a six-county region where Healthcom does no business. In these circumstances, the district court properly dismissed all of Healthcom's claims for relief. *See generally Gaston's White River Resort v. Rush,* 701 F.Supp. 1431, 1435 (W.D.Ark. 1988).

B.

[14] Having concluded that Healthcom is not entitled to injunctive relief, we turn to CA's counterclaim for injunctive relief and the district court's grant of a statewide injunction. As we have explained, CA has superior common law rights in its six-county region, and it is a state-registered user of the CareLink mark. Therefore, under both the Lanham Act and the Arkansas trademark statute, CA is entitled to an injunction against an infringing use that is likely to cause confusion as to origin. *See* 15 U.S.C. § 1125(a)(1)(A); Ark.Code Ann. § 4–71–212(1). . . .

. . . .

[15] In summary, the absence of concrete evidence of likelihood of confusion outside of CA's six-county region makes it improvident to grant a statewide injunction on this record. Healthcom is now enjoined from using its CareLink mark in CA's trade area. If CA never expands beyond that area, this injunction may be all the judicial action that is required. If CA does decide to expand, its statewide registration puts Healthcom at risk of being ousted. But any future prayer by CA for a broader injunction may raise issues that would be better resolved on a fuller fact record, such as whether Healthcom was the first user in any local market; whether the CareLink mark is descriptive and, if so, whether CA's mark has become incontestable or has acquired secondary meaning; precisely what services CA claims its registration covers; and whether there is likelihood of confusion between users of those services and users of Healthcom's emergency response services. . . . Additional issues would be raised if Healthcom's mark is granted federal registration. *See Spartan Food Sys., Inc. v. HFS Corp.,* 813 F.2d 1279, 1284 (4th Cir. 1987); *Burger King of Fla., Inc. v. Hoots,* 403 F.2d 904, 906–07 (7th Cir. 1968).

[16] We affirm the dismissal of Healthcom's claims and the grant of a permanent injunction barring Healthcom's use of its CareLink mark in CA's six-county trade area. We reverse the grant of a statewide injunction and remand to the district court for an appropriate modification of its Judgment dated January 31, 2000.

Comments and Questions

1. *The geographic scope of rights in unregistered descriptive marks.* If the senior user's unregistered mark is a non-inherently distinctive mark, then the geographic scope of the senior's rights are limited to the area in which the mark possesses secondary meaning. A junior user will be enjoined from using the mark in areas in which the senior user has already established secondary meaning. *See, e.g., Katz Drug Co. v. Katz*, 188 F.2d 696 (8th Cir. 1951). More generally, competitors using unregistered confusingly-similar descriptive marks may end up in a "race to secondary meaning," MCCARTHY § 26:25, in which each competitor seeks to be the first to establish secondary meaning—and thus exclusive rights—in the descriptive term in any particular area where the competitors are competing.

2. *What about internet use of the mark?* Does the commercial use of a mark on an internet website accessible anywhere in the country establish national geographic common law rights for the mark? Courts have reasoned that common law rights based only on internet use should extend geographically only so far as the mark owner can show actual market penetration. The owner can do so through evidence consisting of the internet protocol addresses of website visitors, the geographic location of online buyers of goods or services bearing the mark, and other evidence that the website is not merely accessible, but has been accessed by consumers in any geographic areas at issue. *See, e.g., Optimal Pets, Inc. v. Nutri-Vet, LLC*, 877 F. Supp. 2d 953, 962 (C.D. Cal. 2012) ("In considering the adequacy of {the plaintiff's} proof of sufficient market penetration, evidence regarding internet sales and internet advertising will be considered together with the evidence of sales and advertising in geographic areas. Thus, a sale to a customer through the internet will be considered a sale in the geographical area in which the customer is located."); *id.* at 964 (granting judgment as a matter of law to defendant on ground that "[t]here could be no reasonable finding that [the plaintiff] has proven legally sufficient market penetration to establish a common law trademark as to the entire United States or any geographical area").

3. *Tacking.* Can a trademark owner modify the mark over time without loss of priority? If a newly modified mark continues to create the "same, continuing commercial impression" as the previous mark (be it registered or unregistered) such that "consumers generally would regard them as essentially the same," then the mark owner may claim the priority date of the previous mark. *Brookfield Communications, Inc. v. West Coast Entertainment Corp.*, 174 F.3d 1036, 1048 (9th Cir. 1999). In such a situation, the priority date of the previous mark is "tacked" on to the new mark. The standard for tacking is "exceedingly strict." *Id. See also Quiksilver, Inc. v. Kymsta Corp.*, 466 F.3d 749, 760 (9th Cir. 2006) (holding that the plaintiff cannot tack earlier use of QUIKSILVER ROXY onto later use of ROXY because the marks did not create the same continuing commercial impression). In *Hana Financial, Inc. v. Hana Bank*, 135 S. Ct. 907 (2015), the Supreme Court held that the question of whether an earlier mark may be tacked on to a later mark is an issue of fact to be determined by the jury.

b.   **The Good Faith Standard in the *Tea Rose-Rectanus* Doctrine**

When a mark is being used on an unregistered basis by a common law senior user, what constitutes good faith adoption of the same mark (for the same or confusingly-similar goods) by a junior user? All courts agree that if, as in the *Central Arkansas* case above, the junior user of an unregistered mark had no knowledge of the senior user's use at the time that the junior user adopted its mark, then the junior user adopted its mark in good faith. But what if the junior user *did* have knowledge of the senior user's use? As discussed below in *Stone Creek, Inc. v. Omnia Italian Design, Inc.*, 875 F.3d 426 (9th Cir. 2017), the circuits are split on this question.

Stone Creek, Inc. v. Omnia Italian Design, Inc.
875 F.3d 426 (9th Cir. 2017)

{Stone Creek manufactured furniture and sold directly to consumers in five showrooms in the Phoenix, Arizona area. It adopted the mark STONE CREEK in a red oval for furniture in 1990 and obtained federal registration of the mark in 2012. In 2003, Stone Creek and Omnia agreed that Omnia would manufacture leather furniture branded with the STONE CREEK mark for sale in Stone Creek's showrooms. In 2008, without Stone Creek's knowledge or authorization, Omnia began to supply furniture under the STONE CREEK mark to Bon-Ton furniture stores in portions of Illinois, Indiana, Iowa, Michigan, Ohio, Pennsylvania, and Wisconsin. For this purpose, Omnia copied the STONE CREEK logo directly from Stone Creek's materials and used the logo in a variety of sales materials and on warranty cards. In 2013, Stone Creek learned of Omnia's conduct and filed suit.

The district court found no likelihood of confusion largely on the basis that the parties operated in geographically separate marketing channels. Reversing, the Ninth Circuit found a likelihood of confusion. It then turned to the issue of good faith under the *Tea Rose-Rectanus* doctrine.

Note that, in essence, Omnia was an "intermediate junior user" of the mark—i.e., it adopted the mark at a time intermediate between Stone Creek's first use of the mark and its eventual registration of the mark. As we will discuss further in the next section, Lanham Act § 33(b)(5), 15 U.S.C. § 1115(b)(5), allows such intermediate junior users to continue to use their mark after the senior user has registered it, but only if the intermediate junior user adopted the mark "without knowledge of the registrant's prior use." Because Omnia clearly had knowledge of Stone Creek's prior unregistered use, it could not take advantage of § 33(b)(5) and instead sought to retreat back to the residual common law *Tea Rose-Rectanus* doctrine (through Lanham Act § 33(a), 15 U.S.C. § 1115(a)). This forced the Ninth Circuit to decide if the *Tea Rose-Rectanus* doctrine applied only to those remote junior users who lacked knowledge of the senior user's use.}

McKEOWN, Circuit Judge:

. . . .

II. The Tea Rose–Rectanus Doctrine

[1] Our determination of a likelihood of confusion with respect to the STONE CREEK mark does not end the infringement analysis. The *Tea Rose–Rectanus* doctrine is an affirmative defense separate and apart from the underlying infringement claim. 5 McCarthy, *supra*, § 26:4. Omnia asserts that its use of Stone Creek's mark is protected under that doctrine and argues that we may affirm the district court's judgment of no liability on this alternative basis.

[2] The *Tea Rose–Rectanus* doctrine has its roots in the common law: it is named for a pair of Supreme Court cases, *Hanover Star Milling Co. v. Metcalf*, 240 U.S. 403 (1916) ("*Tea Rose*"), and *United Drug Co. v. Theodore Rectanus Co.*, 248 U.S. 90 (1918). The central proposition underlying the two cases is that common-law trademark rights extend only to the territory where a mark is known and recognized, so a later user may sometimes acquire rights in pockets geographically remote from the first user's territory. The question we address is whether Omnia acquired common-law rights in the Midwest under the *Tea Rose–Rectanus* doctrine.

[3] Omnia's common-law rights, if they exist, are not wiped out merely because Stone Creek later filed a federal registration. Although federal registration presumptively entitles the senior user to nationwide protection, 15 U.S.C. § 1057(b), the Lanham Act preserves legal and equitable defenses that could have been asserted prior to registration, *id.* § 1115(a). Under this rule, already-established common-law rights are carved out of the registrant's scope of protection. *Id.* § 1115(b)(5); *Johnny Blastoff, Inc. v. L.A. Rams Football Co.*, 188 F.3d 427, 435 (7th Cir. 1999). In other words, the geographic scope of a senior user's rights in a registered trademark looks like Swiss cheese: it stretches throughout the United States with holes cut out where others acquired common-law rights prior to the registration.

Because Omnia began using the mark in 2008, well before Stone Creek's federal registration in 2012, the *Tea Rose–Rectanus* defense is available to Omnia if it is applicable.

[4] To take advantage of the *Tea Rose–Rectanus* doctrine, the junior user must establish good faith use in a geographically remote area. *See Rectanus*, 248 U.S. at 100, 39 S.Ct. 48; *cf. Grupo Gigante SA De CV v. Dallo & Co.*, 391 F.3d 1088, 1096 & n.26 (9th Cir. 2004). Like the district court, we limit our discussion to the question of good faith because it is dispositive.

[5] The varying descriptions of good faith in the leading Supreme Court cases have spawned a circuit split, and our circuit has not yet weighed in. *See Grupo Gigante*, 391 F.3d at 1096 n.26. On one side, some circuits have held that the junior user's knowledge of the senior user's prior use of the mark destroys good faith. *See, e.g., Nat'l Ass'n for Healthcare Commc'ns, Inc. v. Cent. Ark. Area Agency on Aging, Inc.*, 257 F.3d 732, 735 (8th Cir. 2001); *Money Store v. Harriscorp Fin., Inc.*, 689 F.2d 666, 674–75 (7th Cir. 1982). In contrast, other circuits have held that knowledge is a factor informing good faith, but the "focus is on whether the [junior] user had the intent to benefit from the reputation or goodwill of the [senior] user." *GTE Corp. v. Williams*, 904 F.2d 536, 541 (10th Cir. 1990); *see C.P. Interests, Inc. v. Cal. Pools, Inc.*, 238 F.3d 690, 700 (5th Cir. 2001). We conclude that the better view is that there is no good faith if the junior user had knowledge of the senior user's prior use.

[6] Looking back to the origins of the *Tea Rose–Rectanus* doctrine informs why knowledge defeats a claim of good faith use. In *Tea Rose*, the senior user began selling "Tea Rose" flour in approximately 1872; many years later, the junior user began selling "Tea Rose" flour without any knowledge of the senior user's prior use. 240 U.S. at 407–08. At the time that the trademark infringement action was filed, the senior user had made sales in Massachusetts, Ohio, and Pennsylvania, while the junior user's sales had reached Mississippi, Alabama, Georgia, and Florida. *Id.* at 408–10. *Rectanus* arose on similar facts: the senior user began selling "Rex" drugs around 1877 and operated in New England, while the junior user began selling "Rex" drugs around 1883 and operated in Kentucky, with neither party being aware of the other's use of the "Rex" mark for more than twenty years. 248 U.S. at 94–96. In both cases, the Supreme Court held that the senior user could not enjoin the junior user's use of the same mark because the junior user adopted the mark in good faith and had developed a local reputation in an area where the mark was not recognized as designating the senior user. *See id.* at 103–04; *Tea Rose*, 240 U.S. at 415–16.

[7] When describing good faith, the Supreme Court emphasized that the junior user had no awareness of the senior user's use of the mark. The Court in *Tea Rose* states that the junior user "adopted and used [the trademark] in good faith without knowledge or notice that the name 'Tea Rose' had been adopted or used . . . by anybody else." 240 U.S. at 410. The Court also refers to the situation as one where the two parties "independently" employ the same mark. *Id.* at 41. And the Court's reasoning concentrates on knowledge:

> Under the circumstances that are here presented, to permit the [senior user] to use the mark in Alabama, to the exclusion of the [junior user], would take the trade and good will of the latter company—built up at much expense and *without notice of the former's rights*—and confer it upon the former, to the complete perversion of the proper theory of trademark rights.

Id. at 420 (emphasis added).

[8] The same focus on notice emerges in *Rectanus*, which grants protection for an "innocent" junior user who has "hit upon" the same mark and avers that the parties acted "in perfect good faith; neither side having any knowledge or notice of what was being done by the other." 248 U.S. at 96, 103. The Court also relies on a case that says that the defendants there acted in good faith because they "believ[ed] [their] use to be original with them." *Richter v. Anchor Remedy Co*, 52 F. 455, 455 (C.C.W.D. Pa. 1892), *aff'd sub nom. Richter v. Reynolds*, 59 F. 577 (3d Cir. 1893). Seventy years later, Justice Brennan stressed that application of the *Tea Rose–Rectanus* doctrine requires an absence of knowledge. *See K Mart Corp. v. Cartier, Inc.*, 486 U.S. 281, 314 n.8 (1988) (Brennan, J., concurring in part and dissenting in part) ("[A]

firm can develop a trademark that is identical to a trademark already in use in a geographically distinct and remote area if the firm is unaware of the identity.").

[9] The Seventh and Eighth Circuits and the Trademark Trial and Appeal Board ("TTAB") agree with this reading. The Seventh Circuit put it explicitly: "A good faith junior user is one who begins using a mark with no knowledge that someone else is already using it." *Money Store*, 689 F.2d at 674. The court went on to analyze whether the junior user in that case had constructive or actual knowledge of the senior user's use. *Id.* at 675. The Eighth Circuit follows the same approach, parroting the language from *Tea Rose* and *Rectanus*. *See Nat'l Ass'n for Healthcare Commc'ns*, 257 F.3d at 735 ("adopted the [mark] in good faith, without knowledge of [the] prior use"). And the TTAB, the administrative board charged with deciding certain trademark disputes and appeals, similarly holds that "appropriat[ing] a mark with knowledge that it is actually being used by another" means "that use is not believed to be a good faith use." *Woman's World Shops Inc. v. Lane Bryant Inc.*, 5 U.S.P.Q.2d 1985, 1988 (T.T.A.B. 1988).

[10] The courts that have ruled the other way have latched on to one line in the *Tea Rose* case which reads:

> [W]here two parties independently are employing the same mark upon goods of the same class, but in separate markets wholly remote the one from the other, the question of prior appropriation is legally insignificant; unless, at least, it appear that the second adopter has selected the mark *with some design inimical to the interests of the [senior] user, such as to take the benefit of the reputation of his goods, to forestall the extension of his trade, or the like.*

240 U.S. at 415 (emphasis added). But this brief reference to "design inimical" does not override the central focus on knowledge; it is not without significance that "design inimical" does not appear anywhere else in the opinion. The Court in *Rectanus* repeats the "design inimical" language as a direct quote of the language from the *Tea Rose* case and mentions offhand that the junior user did not have a "sinister purpose." 248 U.S. at 101. More salient are the various points in the leading opinions that draw a close connection between "good faith" and "knowledge" or "notice." *See, e.g., id.* at 96 ("in perfect good faith; neither side having any knowledge or notice of what was being done by the other"); *id.* at 103 ("in good faith, and without notice of any prior use by others, selected and used the 'Rex' mark"); *Tea Rose*, 240 U.S. at 410 ("trademark was adopted and used [by the junior user] in good faith without knowledge or notice that the name 'Tea Rose' had been adopted or used by the [senior user]"); *id.* at 419 ("in good faith and without notice of the [senior user's] mark").

[11] Tying good faith to knowledge makes sense in light of the policy underlying the doctrinal framework. As the Supreme Court explained, the *Tea Rose–Rectanus* doctrine operates to protect a junior user who unwittingly adopted the same mark and invested time and resources into building a business with that mark. *Rectanus*, 248 U.S. at 103; *Tea Rose*, 240 U.S. at 419. A junior user like Omnia who has affirmative knowledge of the senior user's mark has not serendipitously chosen the same mark and independently built up its own brand. Instead, a user like Omnia knows that its actions come directly at the expense of the senior user, potentially blocking the senior user from entering into the new market. Viewed in this light, the junior user has acted in bad faith, which "serve[s] as evidence that the [senior] user's mark, at least in reputation, has extended to the new area." *Developments in the Law Trade-Marks and Unfair Competition*, 68 Harv. L. Rev. 814, 859 (1955); 5 McCarthy, *supra*, § 26:12.

[12] The knowledge standard also better comports with the Lanham Act. The statutory section preserving the *Tea Rose–Rectanus* defense for junior users acting pre-registration requires that the junior user's mark "was adopted *without knowledge* of the registrant's prior use." 15 U.S.C. § 1115(b)(5) (emphasis added). More broadly, one major change effected by the Lanham Act is that securing federal registration affords nationwide rights regardless of where the registrant has used the mark, a result accomplished by a provision that puts would-be users on constructive notice. *See id.* §§ 1057(b), 1072; 5 McCarthy, *supra*, § 26:32. In other words, the Lanham Act displaces the *Tea Rose–Rectanus* defense by charging later users with knowledge of a mark listed on the federal register. If constructive notice is sufficient to defeat good faith, it follows that actual notice should be enough too.

[13] Once knowledge is accepted as a determinative factor in deciding good faith, the *Tea Rose–Rectanus* doctrine has no applicability here. The district court found that "[Omnia] was a non-innocent remote user" who "acquired no common law trademark rights in the [Midwest]." That conclusion flows from the parties' agreement that Omnia adopted Stone Creek's mark with knowledge of Stone Creek's previous use. The *Tea Rose–Rectanus* doctrine provides no shelter to Omnia for infringement of Stone Creek's mark.

{The Ninth Circuit then held, among other things, that Stone Creek must show intentional or willful infringement before disgorgement of Omnia's profits could be awarded. The Ninth Circuit remanded the case back to the district court to determine whether Omnia willfully infringed.}

Comments and Questions

1. *Is* Stone Creek *bad policy?* Consider the following oft-quoted language from the Supreme Court's *Rectanus* opinion:

> There is no such thing as property in a trade-mark except as a right appurtenant to an established business or trade in connection with which the mark is employed. The law of trade-marks is but a part of the broader law of unfair competition; the right to a particular mark grows out of its use, not its mere adoption; its function is simply to designate the goods as the product of a particular trader and to protect his good will against the sale of another's product as his; and it is not the subject of property except in connection with an existing business. *Hanover Milling Co. v. Metcalf*, 240 U. S. 403, 412-414.

> The owner of a trade-mark may not, like the proprietor of a patented invention, make a negative and merely prohibitive use of it as a monopoly. *See United States v. Bell Telephone Co.*, 167 U. S. 224, 250; *Bement v. National Harrow Co.*, 186 U. S. 70, 90; *Paper Bag Patent Case*, 210 U. S. 405, 424.

> . . . .

> It results that the adoption of a trade-mark does not, at least in the absence of some valid legislation enacted for the purpose, project the right of protection in advance of the extension of the trade, or operate as a claim of territorial rights over areas into which it thereafter may be deemed desirable to extend the trade. And the expression, sometimes met with, that a trade-mark right is not limited in its enjoyment by territorial bounds, is true only in the sense that wherever the trade goes, attended by the use of the mark, the right of the trader to be protected against the sale by others of their wares in the place of his wares will be sustained.

United Drug Co. v. Theodore Rectanus, 248 U.S. 90, 97-98 (1918). In effect, under *Stone Creek*, the senior user of an unregistered mark enjoys exclusive rights in the mark against any other person in the nation who is aware of the senior user's use, even if the senior user has not yet used the mark in that person's particular remote location. Is this outcome consistent with the principles articulated in *Rectanus*? Imagine you wish to open a cafe in New York City under the service mark ARCTIC COFFEE. You google the term and discover that a cafe in Anchorage, Alaska is already using the mark. You then search the mark on the PTO's Trademark Electronic Search System and learn that the Anchorage cafe has not applied to register the mark. Under *Stone Creek*, you cannot adopt the mark in good faith, and if the Anchorage cafe eventually expands into New York City, it may assert priority over your use. Is this sound policy?

2. The Geographic Extent of Rights in *Registered* Marks

Unless the Lanham Act states otherwise, the common law norms of *Tea Rose-Rectanus* apply as much to registered marks as they do to unregistered marks. But crucially, the Lanham Act states otherwise extensively, primarily through the operation of Lanham Act §§ 7(c), 15, 22, and 33, 15 U.S.C. §§ 1057(c), 1065, 1072, & 1115. Indeed, these sections depart so dramatically from the common law norms that it is easy to forget that at least in theory they form merely an overlay on those underlying norms, one that grants registered marks important privileges in the form of exceptions to the *Tea Rose-Rectanus* doctrine. We consider these exceptions here.

a. **Applications Filed on or after November 16, 1989: Constructive Use Priority as of Date of Application**

The Trademark Law Revision Act of 1988 (TLRA) created Lanham Act § 7(c), 15 U.S.C. § 1057(c), which applies to all applications filed on or after the November 16, 1989 effective date of the TLRA.[1] Section 7(c) reads as follows:

> (c) *Application to register mark considered constructive use.* Contingent on the registration of a mark on the principal register provided by this Act, the filing of the application to register such mark shall constitute constructive use of the mark, conferring a right of priority, nationwide in effect, on or in connection with the goods or services specified in the registration against any other person except for a person whose mark has not been abandoned and who, prior to such filing–
>
> (1) has used the mark;
>
> (2) has filed an application to register the mark which is pending or has resulted in registration of the mark; or
>
> (3) has filed a foreign application to register the mark on the basis of which he or she has acquired a right of priority, and timely files an application under section 44(d), 15 USC § 1126(d), to register the mark which is pending or has resulted in registration of the mark.

Id. Section 7(c) thus confers on the successful registrant nationwide "constructive use" priority in the registered mark as of the date of application, and does so regardless of whether the registrant has in fact made or is in fact making actual nationwide use of the mark. *See Humanoids Group v. Rogan*, 375 F.3d 301, 305 n.3 (4th Cir. 2004) ("Constructive use establishes a priority date with the same legal effect as the earliest actual use of a trademark at common law." (citation omitted)). Note that until the registration issues, this priority is merely "contingent" nationwide priority. The applicant may not use § 7(c) to enjoin others' conduct until the registration issues, at which time the registrants' constructive use priority is the date of application.

To appreciate the practical significance of § 7(c), imagine the following course of events:

- Time 1: A files a § 1(b) intent-to-use application for registration of the mark.
- Time 2: B subsequently begins to make actual use of the mark throughout the U.S.
- Time 3: A begins to make actual use of the mark throughout the U.S. and files a Statement of Use.
- Time 4: A's application matures into registration.

Under the terms of § 7(c), registration confers on A nationwide priority as of Time 1 even though A did not make actual use of the mark until Time 3. At Time 4, A may enjoin B's use. Meanwhile, even though B was the first to make actual use of the mark, B cannot on that basis enjoin A from making its own actual use and thereby completing the ITU process. *See WarnerVision Entertainment Inc. v. Empire of Carolina Inc.*, 101 F.3d 259, 262 (2d Cir. 1996) ("The ITU provisions permit the holder of an ITU application to use the mark in commerce, obtain registration, and thereby secure priority retroactive to the date of

---

[1] The Lanham Act does not explicitly state that the benefits of § 7(c) should be available only to applications filed on or after the effective date of the TLRA. However, as McCarthy notes, "Lanham Act § 33(b)(5), 15 U.S.C. § 1115(b)(5) distinguishes between the application date creating constructive use on the one hand and the registration date creating constructive notice [under § 22] on the other hand, limiting the later to a case where "the application for registration is filed before the effective date of the Trademark Law Revision Act of 1988." This indicates a legislative intent to restrict the benefits of § 7(c) constructive use to registrations resulting from applications filed after the effective date of the revision." McCarthy § 26.38 fn 1.10.

filing of the ITU application. Of course, this right or privilege is not indefinite; it endures only for the time allotted by the statute. But as long as an ITU applicant's privilege has not expired, a court may not enjoin it from making the use necessary for registration on the grounds that another party has used the mark subsequent to the filing of the ITU application. To permit such an injunction would eviscerate the ITU provisions and defeat their very purpose.").

i. The Senior Common Law User Scenario

As the statutory language makes clear, § 7(c) nationwide constructive use priority is subject to certain important limitations. Most significantly, constructive use priority does not apply to any entity that began use of the mark at issue somewhere in the United States prior to the registrant's own use and date of application. For example:

- Time 1: A begins actual use of the mark in Area A.
- Time 2: B begins actual use of the mark in Area B.
- Time 3: B applies to register the mark.
- Time 4: B's registration issues.

On these simple facts, A qualifies as a "senior common law user" of the mark, because its unregistered use preceded B's unregistered use and date of application for registration. Once B has registered its mark, A may continue to use its mark, but this raises a difficult question: exactly *where* may A continue to do so?

The answer is that A may continue to use its mark anywhere it was using the mark at the date of B's *registration* (not the date of B's application). In the senior common law user scenario, the statutory basis for A's frozen area of use is not § 7(c) and its provision of nationwide constructive use *at the date of application*, because by the clear terms of the section, nationwide constructive use priority does not apply to senior common law users. So what provision does apply to such users? It is Lanham Act § 22, 15 U.S.C. § 1072, that freezes the senior common law user. Section 22 provides that "Registration of a mark on the principal register provided by this chapter or under the Act of March 3, 1881, or the Act of February 20, 1905, shall be constructive notice of the registrant's claim of ownership thereof." *See also* Lanham Act § 15, 15 U.S.C. § 1065 (providing incontestable marks with incontestable rights "except to the extent, if any, to which the use of a mark registered on the principal register infringes a valid right acquired under the law of any State or Territory by use of a mark or trade name continuing from a date prior to the date of registration under this chapter of such registered mark"). Section 22's constructive notice *at the date of registration* is understood to be nationwide in effect and strips the senior common law user of any claim to good faith expansion in the use of its mark after that date. *See Allard Enterprises v. Advanced Programming Res., Inc.* 249 F.3d 564 (6th Cir. 2001). *See also Geisha LLC v. Tuccillo*, No. 05 Civ. 5529, 2009 U.S. Dist. LEXIS 20300 (N.D. Ill. March 13, 2009) (citing *Allard*) (stating that rights are frozen at registration but finding that the senior user had actual notice of junior's federal trademark application before expansion, which prevented the senior user's rights from expanding).

ii. The Intermediate Junior User Scenario

Lanham Act § 33(b)(5), 15 U.S.C. § 1115(b)(5), establishes a so-called "intermediate junior user" defense against registered marks that are incontestable and, through § 33(a), registered marks that are contestable. Section 33(b)(5) provides that the registrant's rights are subject to the defense

> (5) That the mark whose use by a party is charged as an infringement was adopted without knowledge of the registrant's prior use and has been continuously used by such party or those in privity with him from a date prior to (A) the date of constructive use of the mark established pursuant to section 7(c) {15 USC § 1057(c)}, (B) the registration of the mark under this Act if the application for registration is filed before the effective date of the Trademark Law Revision Act of 1988, or (C) publication of the registered mark under subsection (c) of section 12 of this Act {15 USC § 1062(c)}: Provided, however, That this defense or defect shall apply only for the area in which such continuous prior use is proved.

15 U.S.C. § 1115(b)(5).

The practical significance of § 33(b)(5) may be demonstrated with the following set of facts:

- Time 1:   A begins actual use of the mark in Area A.
- Time 2:   B begins actual use of the mark in Area B without knowledge of A's use.
- Time 3:   A applies to register the mark.
- Time 4:   A's registration issues.

In this set of facts, A is the senior user (i.e., the first user within the United States) and B is the junior user (somewhere in the United States) who began its use at a time intermediate between A's first use and A's application to register. Registrant A may enjoin B's use anywhere in the United States except where B was using the mark at Time 3 (in other words, if B has been expanding its use, B is frozen to the extent of its expansion at the date of A's application). *See* § 33(b)(5), 15 U.S.C. § 1115(b)(5) ("from a date prior to (A) the date of constructive use of the mark established pursuant to section 7(c) .... [T]his defense or defect shall apply only for the area in which such continuous prior use is proved."). *See also* Gilson on Trademarks § 11.08. Note that A may seek an injunction only once its registration has issued.

But what if the intermediate junior user adopted the mark at issue *with knowledge* of the registrant's senior common law use? Section 33(b)(5) would not apply (because it explicitly requires adoption "without knowledge"), but is § 7(c) any help? In contrast with § 33(b)(5), § 7(c) makes no mention of knowledge, nor does it explicitly limit itself only to senior common law users or exclude intermediate junior users. Instead, § 7(c) simply refers to any person who "prior to such filing ... has used the mark." Can an intermediate junior user who adopted *with knowledge* before the registrant's application date thus retreat back to § 7(c) and claim the same right as a senior common law user to continue to use its mark in an area frozen as of the date of the registrant's registration?

The law is not clear on this question, and it was never raised in the *Stone Creek* case above, but experience has shown that especially attentive students tend to ask it. The answer is almost certainly that the intermediate junior user *with knowledge* cannot work around § 33(b)(5) by resorting to § 7(c). For prior common law users of the registrant's mark, be they senior common law users or intermediate junior (common law) users, Section 7(c) provides no independent basis for freezing any such user's prior rights. It states only that the registrant's nationwide constructive use as of the date of application does not apply to anyone who used the mark before the registrant's date of application. Instead, in general, § 22 would freeze the rights of all such prior users at the latest at the date of the registrant's registration, with the exception that under the more specific provisions of § 33(b)(5), the rights of good faith intermediate junior users in particular are frozen earlier at the registrant's date of application. What then of intermediate junior users who did not adopt in good faith (i.e., who adopted with knowledge of the registrant's prior use)? It would be at odds with the purposes of the Lanham Act (among them, to promote good faith conduct) to leave bad faith intermediate junior users better off than good faith intermediate junior users by treating the former as if they were senior common law users under § 7(c) and § 22. Instead, once the registrant's registration issues, the intermediate junior user who adopted with knowledge of the registrant's prior use would almost certainly be required to cease all use of its mark (subject to the *Dawn Donut* rule, discussed below).

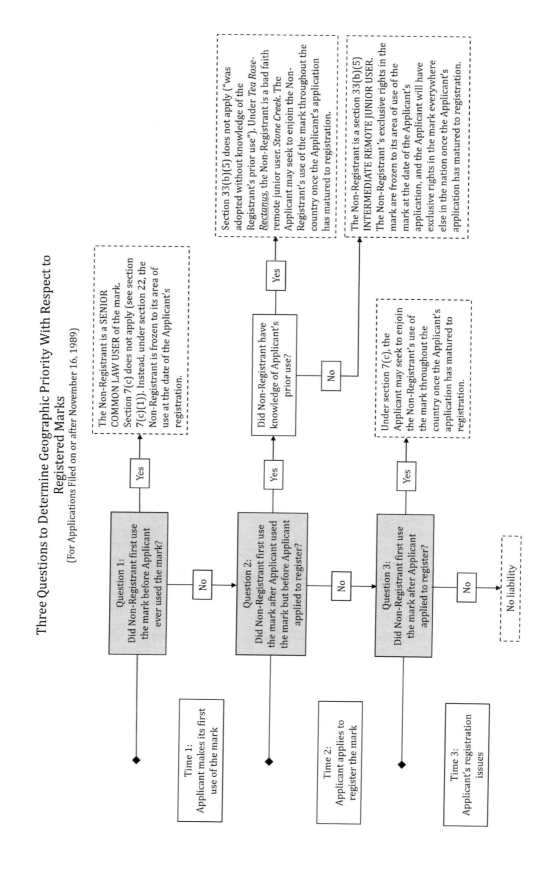

Three Questions to Determine Geographic Priority With Respect to Registered Marks

(For Applications Filed on or after November 16, 1989)

b. Applications Filed before November 16, 1989: Constructive Notice Priority as of Date of Registration

Applications filed before November 16, 1989 must rely on § 22, 15 U.S.C. § 1072:

> Registration of a mark on the principal register provided by this Act or under the Act of March 3, 1981, or the Act of February 20, 1905, shall be constructive notice of the registrant's claim of ownership thereof.

This "constructive notice" disables any person who adopts the mark after the registrant's date of registration from claiming that it did so in good faith. *See* McCARTHY § 26:32.

With respect to applications filed before November 16, 1989, senior common law users (those who adopted the mark before the registrant began actual use of the mark) are frozen to their area of use as of the date of registration. *See* Lanham Act §§ 15 & 22, 15 U.S.C. §§ 1065 & 1072. Section 33(b)(5) applies to intermediate junior users. *See, e.g., Burger King of Fla., Inc. v. Hoots*, 403 F.2d 904 (7th Cir. 1968) (limiting intermediate junior user of BURGER KING for restaurant services to 25-mile radius around Mattoon, Illinois).

c. Concurrent Use and Registration

Lanham Act § 2(d), 15 U.S.C. § 1052(d), provides that two or more parties may use or register similar or identical marks for similar or identical goods provided that their respective uses of the marks will be sufficiently geographically distinct as not to cause consumer confusion. The text of § 2(d) provides as follows:

> No trademark by which the goods of the applicant may be distinguished from the goods of others shall be refused registration on the principal register on account of its nature unless it—
>
> . . . .
>
> (d) Consists of or comprises a mark which so resembles a mark registered in the Patent and Trademark Office, or a mark or trade name previously used in the United States by another and not abandoned, as to be likely, when used on or in connection with the goods of the applicant, to cause confusion, or to cause mistake, or to deceive: Provided, That if the Director determines that confusion, mistake, or deception is not likely to result from the continued use by more than one person of the same or similar marks under conditions and limitations as to the mode or place of use of the marks or the goods on or in connection with which such marks are used, concurrent registrations may be issued to such persons when they have become entitled to use such marks as a result of their concurrent lawful use in commerce prior to (1) the earliest of the filing dates of the applications pending or of any registration issued under this chapter; (2) July 5, 1947, in the case of registrations previously issued under the Act of March 3, 1881, or February 20, 1905, and continuing in full force and effect on that date; or (3) July 5, 1947, in the case of applications filed under the Act of February 20, 1905, and registered after July 5, 1947. Use prior to the filing date of any pending application or a registration shall not be required when the owner of such application or registration consents to the grant of a concurrent registration to the applicant. Concurrent registrations may also be issued by the Director when a court of competent jurisdiction has finally determined that more than one person is entitled to use the same or similar marks in commerce. In issuing concurrent registrations, the Director shall prescribe conditions and limitations as to the mode or place of use of the mark or the goods on or in connection with which such mark is registered to the respective persons.

15 U.S.C. § 1052(d). *See also* TMEP § 1207.

Thus, the first applicant for a mark may be granted a registration covering the entirety of the United States except for the limited area in which an intermediate junior user or senior common law user is entitled to use the mark. *See, e.g., Terrific Promotions, Inc. v. Vanlex, Inc.*, 36 U.S.P.Q.2d 1349 (TTAB 1995) ("TPI is entitled to a concurrent use registration for the mark DOLLAR BILLS and design for discount variety goods store services for the area comprising the entire United States except for the counties of Essex, Bergen, Hudson, Union and Middlesex in New Jersey, the five Boroughs of New York City and the counties of Suffolk, Nassau, Westchester, Rockland and Putnam in New York, the county of Fairfield in Connecticut and the county of Allegheny in Pennsylvania." (see registration certificate below)); *Weiner King, Inc. v. Wiener King Corp.*, 615 F.2d 512 (C.C.P.A. 1980) (limiting junior user-registrant's registration to the entirety of the U.S. except for certain areas of New Jersey in which senior user had been using its mark). Meanwhile, the intermediate junior user or senior common law user may seek to register the mark for the limited area in which it is allowed still to use the mark. *See, e.g., Ole' Taco, Inc. v. Tacos Ole, Inc.*, 221 U.S.P.Q. 912 (TTAB 1984) (limiting senior user's registration to entirety of U.S. except for area consisting of 180-mile radius around Grand Rapids, Michigan; limiting junior user's registration to Grand Rapids, Michigan (see registration certificates below)).

Though concurrent registrations are an interesting phenomenon, they are exceedingly rare. The PTO's data indicate that among all 2.65 million live trademark registrations on the Principal Register in 2020, only 332 consisted of registrations subject to concurrent use. *See* USPTO, *Case Files Dataset*, https://www.uspto.gov/ip-policy/economic-research/research-datasets/trademark-case-files-dataset (concur_use_in).

Int. Cl.: 42

Prior U.S. Cl.: 101

United States Patent and Trademark Office Reg. No. 1,926,806
Registered Oct. 17, 1995

SERVICE MARK
PRINCIPAL REGISTER
CONCURRENT USE

TPI OF ILLINOIS, INC. (ILLINOIS CORPORATION)
4611 WEST 136TH STREET
CRESTWOOD, IL 60445 , BY MERGER WITH TERRIFIC PROMOTIONS, INC. (MARYLAND CORPORATION) ALEXANDRIA, VA 22312

FOR: DISCOUNT VARIETY GOODS STORE SERVICES, IN CLASS 42 (U.S. CL. 101).
FIRST USE 11–15–1986; IN COMMERCE 11–15–1986.
REGISTRATION LIMITED TO THE AREA COMPRISING THE ENTIRE UNITED STATES EXCEPT FOR THE COUNTIES OF ESSEX,

BERGEN, HUDSON, UNION AND MIDDLESEX IN NEW JERSEY, THE FIVE BOROUGHS OF NEW YORK CITY AND THE COUNTIES OF SUFFOLK, NASSAU, WESTCHESTER, ROCKLAND AND PUTNAM IN NEW YORK, THE COUNTY OF FAIRFIELD IN CONNECTICUT AND THE COUNTY OF ALLEGHENY IN PENNSYLVANIA, CONCURRENT USE PROCEEDING NO. 853 WITH SERIAL NO. 73/725611.

SER. NO. 73–725,611, FILED 5-2-1988.

WAI BUI ZEE, EXAMINING ATTORNEY

Int. Cl.: 42

Prior U.S. Cl.: 100

United States Patent and Trademark Office   Reg. No. 1,376,369
Registered Dec. 17, 1985

SERVICE MARK
PRINCIPAL REGISTER

Olé Tacos

OLE' TACO INC. (MICHIGAN CORPORATION)
2417 EASTERN AVE. SE.
GRAND RAPIDS, MI 49507

FOR: RESTAURANT SERVICES, IN CLASS
42 (U.S. CL. 100).
FIRST USE 9-0-1969; IN COMMERCE
9-0-1969.
SUBJECT TO CONCURRENT USE PRO-
CEEDING WITH SERIAL NO. 89,563. APPLI-
CANT CLAIMS THE AREA COMPRISING THE
STATE OF MICHIGAN, AND SUCH PORTIONS
OF INDIANA, ILLINOIS, AND OHIO AS DO

NOT EXTEND BEYOND A 180-MILE RADIUS
WHOSE CENTRAL POINT IS GRAND RAPIDS,
MICHIGAN.
NO CLAIM IS MADE TO THE EXCLUSIVE
RIGHT TO USE "TACOS", APART FROM THE
MARK AS SHOWN.
THE TERM "OLE" AS USED IN THE MARK
IS A SPANISH EXPRESSION MEANING
"BRAVO!".

SER. NO. 93,243, FILED 7-12-1976.

MARC BERGSMAN, EXAMINING ATTORNEY

Int. Cl.: 42

Prior U.S. Cl.: 100

United States Patent and Trademark Office   Reg. No. 1,135,911
Registered May 20, 1980
OG Date Aug. 18, 1987

Restricted

SERVICE MARK
PRINCIPAL REGISTER

TACOS OLE'

TACOS OLE, INC. (FLORIDA CORPO-
RATION)
4142 SW. 70TH CT.
MIAMI, FL 33155

REGISTRATION LIMITED TO THE
AREA COMPRISING THE ENTIRE
UNITED STATES EXCEPT THE STATE
OF MICHIGAN AND SUCH PORTIONS
OF ILLINOIS, INDIANA AND OHIO AS
DO NOT EXTEND A 180-MILE RADIUS
WHOSE CENTRAL POINT IS GRAND
RAPIDS, MICHIGAN. CONCURRENT

USE PROCEEDING NO. 498 WITH, OLE'
TACO INC.
WITHOUT DISCLAIMING ANY
COMMON LAW RIGHTS OR RIGHTS IN
THE MARK AS A WHOLE, THE WORD
"TACOS" IS DISCLAIMED. APART
FROM THE MARK AS SHOWN.
FOR: RESTAURANT AND CATERING
SERVICES, IN CLASS 42 (U.S. CL. 100).
FIRST USE 1-20-1969; IN COMMERCE
1-20-1969.

SER. NO. 89,563, FILED 6-7-1976.

Comments and Questions

1. *Consent to use agreements.* Two users of similar marks may reach an agreement in which they promise not to sue each other for trademark infringement provided that each complies with the limitations on use set forth in the agreement. These limitations may limit use to, among other things, specific geographical areas, specific goods or services, or specific mark formats. *See Brennan's Inc. v. Dickie Brennan & Co. Inc.*, 376 F.3d 356, 364 (5th Cir. 2004) (discussing consent to use agreements);

277

McCarthy § 18:79 (same). *See also* Eric Pfanner, *British Judge Allows Apple to Keep Logo on iTunes*, NY Times, May 9, 2006, https://www.nytimes.com/2006/05/09/technology/09apple.html (discussing litigation between Apple Computer and Apple Corps, the Beatles' corporate entity, concerning the former's alleged breach of the 1991 consent to use agreement between the two firms). Courts (and examiners) typically give great weight to consent to use agreements, but they sometimes nevertheless find a likelihood of confusion. See, for example, *In Re 8-Bit Brewing LLC*, Serial No. 86760527, 2017 WL 5885609, (Oct. 30, 2017), in which the TTAB affirmed the examiner's section 2(d) refusal to register the applied-for mark 8-BIT ALEWORKS in light of the registered mark 8 BIT BREWING COMPANY:

> Ultimately, in view of the identity of the involved goods, beer, and their trade channels, as well as the overall strong similarity of the marks, we conclude there is a likelihood of confusion between Applicant's applied-for mark 8-Bit Aleworks and the registered marks, 8 bit Brewing Company (with and without design). We make this conclusion bearing in mind that "consent agreements are frequently entitled to great weight." *Bay State Brewing Co.*, 117 USPQ2d at 1967. In this case, however, Registrant's consent is ambiguous and outweighed by the several other relevant *du Pont* factors. In other words, the shortcomings in the consent agreement are such that consumer confusion remains likely.

In Re 8-Bit Brewing LLC, 2017 WL 5885609, at *8. *But see In re American Cruise Lines, Inc.*, 128 U.S.P.Q.2d 1157 (TTAB 2018) (reversing examiner's Lanham Act § 2(d) refusal even though consent agreement between CONSTELLATION and AMERICAN CONSTELLATION for cruise ships contained no provisions requiring parties to seek to avoid confusion, reasoning that "[w]hile the inclusion of provisions to avoid any potential confusion are preferred and probative in consent agreements, they are not mandatory.").

2. *Secondary meaning in only one part of the United States*. To register a non-inherently distinctive mark, the mark owner need only show that the mark has secondary meaning in some part of the United States. *But see* McCarthy 15:72 (citing a 1963 TTAB opinion for the proposition that "the law is unclear [on this issue], with a hint that proving secondary meaning in only a small part of the United States might not be sufficient."). Yet the priority rights that stem from registration are nationwide in scope. Does this make sense as a policy matter? *Cf. Société des produits Nestlé v. Mondelez UK Holdings & Services*, C-84/17 P, C-85/17 P and C-95/17 P, ECLI:EU:C:2018:596, ¶ 83 (CJEU, July 25, 2018) (holding that for purposes of registering an EU trademark that is not inherently distinctive anywhere in the European Union, the applicant must show that the mark has acquired secondary meaning throughout the European Union).

d. The *Dawn Donut* Rule

In *Dawn Donut Co. v. Hart's Food Stores, Inc.*, 267 F.2d 358 (2d Cir. 1959), the Second Circuit established a significant geographic limitation on a federal registrant's ability to enjoin confusingly-similar uses by those over whom the registrant has priority. The *Dawn Donut* court held that though registration confers on the registrant nationwide priority, mere registration without more does not entitle the registrant to nationwide injunctive relief. Instead, the registrant must show that it is likely to make (or is already making) an actual use of the mark in a post-registration junior user's area of trade before the registrant will be entitled to enjoin the junior use. The *Dawn Donut* rule does not present a problem for a registrant making nationwide use of its mark. But for a registrant making only a local or regional use of its mark, the registrant cannot enjoin uses in different geographic areas until it can show that it is actually using or is likely imminently to use its mark in those areas or its reputation has spread to those areas.

In the *Dawn Donut* case itself, the plaintiff was the senior user and registrant of the mark DAWN for doughnuts, which it had registered in 1927 and renewed under the Lanham Act in 1947. In 1951, the defendant began to use the same mark for doughnuts in Rochester, New York. At the time of the suit, the plaintiff was not using its mark in the Rochester area. The Second Circuit held that if the plaintiff was not making actual use of its mark in the Rochester area, then the defendant's use of the mark would not create a likelihood of confusion that could form the basis of injunctive relief:

> [I]f the use of the marks by the registrant and the unauthorized user are confined to geographically separate markets, with no likelihood that the registrant will expand his use

into the defendant's market, so that no public confusion is possible, then the registrant is not entitled to enjoin the junior user's use of the mark.

Dawn Donut, 267 F. 2d at 364. The plaintiff could seek relief at a later date if it could show an intent to expand into the defendant's area of use:

> [B]ecause of the effect we have attributed to the constructive notice provision of the Lanham Act, the plaintiff may later, upon a proper showing of an intent to use the mark at the retail level in defendant's market area, be entitled to enjoin defendant's use of the mark.

Id. at 365. The strange effect of the *Dawn Donut* rule is that the defendant would have to stop its use of the mark and yield to the plaintiff at some point in the future when the plaintiff could show expansion into defendant's area of trade.

Dawn Donut remains good law. In the remarkable case of *What-A-Burger Of Virginia, Inc. v. Whataburger, Inc. Of Corpus Christi, Texas*, 357 F.3d 441 (4th Cir. 2004), the declaratory defendant Whataburger-Texas registered the mark WHATABURGER for restaurant services in September, 1957. By the time of the suit, Whataburger-Texas was using the mark in connection with over 500 locations in various southern states but not in Virginia. The declaratory plaintiff What-A-Burger-Virginia began to use the mark WHAT-A-BURGER in Newport News, Virginia in August, 1957, and subsequently expanded its use to various other locations in Virginia in the following years. In 1970, Whataburger-Texas became aware of What-A-Burger-Virginia's use in Virginia and proposed a licensing arrangement. There was no further communication between the parties until 2002, when Whataburger-Texas contacted What-A-Burger-Virginia to determine if What-A-Burger-Virginia's use was infringing on Whataburger-Texas's registered mark. What-A-Burger-Virginia asserted, among other things, that Whataburger-Texas was barred by the doctrine of laches from asserting infringement because it had waited nearly thirty years to do so. Whataburger-Texas successfully argued that laches could not apply because, under the principles established in *Dawn Donut*, Whataburger-Texas could not have sought during that thirty year period to enjoin What-A-Burger-Virginia's use of the mark in Virginia. The Fourth Circuit explained: "There is nothing in this case to indicate a likelihood of entry into the local Virginia market by {Whataburger-Texas} (in fact, {Whataburger-Texas} specifically disavows any such intention) or that the likelihood of confusion otherwise looms large, triggering the obligation for {Whataburger-Texas} to initiate an action for trademark infringement." *Id.* at 451.

Dawn Donut is not without its critics, however. At least one judge has criticized the *Dawn Donut* rule as obsolete:

> The *Dawn Donut* Rule was enunciated in 1959. Entering the new millennium, our society is far more mobile than it was four decades ago. For this reason, and given that recent technological innovations such as the Internet are increasingly deconstructing geographical barriers for marketing purposes, it appears to me that a re-examination of precedents would be timely to determine whether the *Dawn Donut* Rule has outlived its usefulness.

Circuit City Stores, Inc. v. CarMax, Inc., 165 F.3d 1047, 1057 (6th Cir. 1999) (Jones, J., concurring). More recently, the Second Circuit aggressively distinguished away *Dawn Donut* in *Guthrie Healthcare Sys. v. ContextMedia, Inc.*, 826 F.3d 27, 48 (2d Cir. 2016) ("*Dawn Donuts*, {sic} did not present the problem, like this case, of a plaintiff who has shown entitlement to an injunction in one geographic area and seeks to have the injunction extend beyond as well. It therefore has no pertinence to the question at issue here.").

For an excellent (and brief) practical overview of the *Dawn Donut* rule, see Christopher P. Bussert, *Trademark Enforcement in Distinct Geographic Territories: Is the Infringement Case "Ripe"?*, FRANCHISE LAWYER, Summer 2019, at 3.

3. National Borders and Trademark Rights

We have focused so far on trademark uses *within* the territorial borders of the U.S. and the geographical extent of rights established by such uses. We turn now to trademark uses *outside* the territorial borders of the U.S. and to the question of whether such uses can form the basis for exclusive rights within the U.S.

As set forth below in Part I.E.3.a and as exemplified in *Person's Co., Ltd. v. Christman*, 900 F.2d 1565 (Fed. Cir. 1990), the traditional view has long been that trademark rights are generally limited to national borders and that foreign uses of trademarks generally do not confer exclusive rights within the U.S. However, as discussed in Part I.E.3.b, the "well-known marks doctrine" holds that foreign uses of trademarks that become very well-known in the U.S. may form the basis for exclusive rights within the U.S. even when the foreign user is not making any actual use of the mark within the U.S. Finally, as presented in Part I.E.3.c, a more recent opinion from the Fourth Circuit, *Belmora LLC v. Bayer Consumer Care AG*, 819 F.3d 697 (4th Cir. 2016), *cert. denied*, 137 S. Ct. 1202 (U.S. 2017), has the potential profoundly to change our traditional understanding of the national limits of trademark rights (and of the relation between Lanham Act §§ 32 and 43(a)). *Belmora* was denied certiorari review. If its reasoning is adopted by other circuits, it may significantly lessen the importance of much of the doctrine discussed in Parts I.E.3.a & b.

a. National-Border Limits on Trademark Rights

The opinion below, *Person's Co., Ltd. v. Christman*, 900 F.2d 1565 (Fed. Cir. 1990), is frequently cited as standing for the proposition that foreign uses do not establish exclusive rights within the U.S. In reading through the opinion, consider the following questions:

- Does the outcome in *Person's* strike you as fair?

- Alternatively, has the Federal Circuit chosen the economically efficient outcome? If not, what would that outcome be?

- Is the *Person's* holding still viable in a globalized, internet-based economy?

Person's Co., Ltd. v. Christman
900 F.2d 1565 (Fed. Cir. 1990)

EDWARD S. SMITH, Senior Circuit Judge.

[1] Person's Co., Ltd. appeals from the decision of the Patent and Trademark Office Trademark Trial and Appeal Board (Board) which granted summary judgment in favor of Larry Christman and ordered the cancellation of appellant's registration[2] for the mark "PERSON'S" for various apparel items. Appellant Person's Co. seeks cancellation of Christman's registration[3] for the mark "PERSON'S" for wearing apparel on the following grounds: likelihood of confusion based on its prior foreign use, abandonment, and unfair competition within the meaning of the Paris Convention. We affirm the Board's decision.

Background

[2] The facts pertinent to this appeal are as follows: In 1977, Takaya Iwasaki first applied a stylized logo bearing the name "PERSON'S" to clothing in his native Japan. Two years later Iwasaki formed Person's Co., Ltd., a Japanese corporation, to market and distribute the clothing items in retail stores located in Japan.

[3] In 1981, Larry Christman, a U.S. citizen and employee of a sportswear wholesaler, visited a Person's Co. retail store while on a business trip to Japan. Christman purchased several clothing items bearing the "PERSON'S" logo and returned with them to the United States. After consulting with legal counsel and being advised that no one had yet established a claim to the logo in the United States, Christman developed designs for his own "PERSON'S" brand sportswear line based on appellant's products he had purchased in Japan. In February 1982, Christman contracted with a clothing manufacturer to produce clothing articles with the "PERSON'S" logo attached. These clothing items were

---

[2] Registration No. 1,354,062, issued August 13, 1985.

[3] Registration No. 1,297,698, issued September 25, 1984.

sold, beginning in April 1982, to sportswear retailers in the northwestern United States. Christman formed Team Concepts, Ltd., a Washington corporation, in May 1983 to continue merchandising his sportswear line, which had expanded to include additional articles such as shoulder bags. All the sportswear marketed by Team Concepts bore either the mark "PERSON'S" or a copy of appellant's globe logo; many of the clothing styles were apparently copied directly from appellant's designs.

[4] In April 1983, Christman filed an application for U.S. trademark registration in an effort to protect the "PERSON'S" mark. Christman believed himself to be the exclusive owner of the right to use and register the mark in the United States and apparently had no knowledge that appellant soon intended to introduce its similar sportswear line under the identical mark in the U.S. market. Christman's registration issued in September 1984 for use on wearing apparel.

[5] In the interim between Christman's first sale and the issuance of his registration, Person's Co., Ltd. became a well known and highly respected force in the Japanese fashion industry. The company, which had previously sold garments under the "PERSON'S" mark only in Japan, began implementing its plan to sell goods under this mark in the United States. According to Mr. Iwasaki, purchases by buyers for resale in the United States occurred as early as November 1982. This was some seven months subsequent to Christman's first sales in the United States. Person's Co. filed an application for U.S. trademark registration in the following year, and, in 1985, engaged an export trading company to introduce its goods into the U.S. market. The registration for the mark "PERSON'S" issued in August 1985 for use on luggage, clothing and accessories. After recording U.S. sales near 4 million dollars in 1985, Person's Co. granted California distributor Zip Zone International a license to manufacture and sell goods under the "PERSON'S" mark in the United States.

[6] In early 1986, appellant's advertising in the U.S. became known to Christman and both parties became aware of confusion in the marketplace. Person's Co. initiated an action to cancel Christman's registration on the following grounds: (1) likelihood of confusion; (2) abandonment; and (3) unfair competition within the meaning of the Paris Convention. Christman counterclaimed and asserted prior use and likelihood of confusion as grounds for cancellation of the Person's Co. registration.

[7] After some discovery, Christman filed a motion with the Board for summary judgment on all counts. In a well reasoned decision, the Board held for Christman on the grounds that Person's use of the mark in Japan could not be used to establish priority against a "good faith" senior user in U.S. commerce. The Board found no evidence to suggest that the "PERSON'S" mark had acquired any notoriety in this country at the time of its adoption by Christman. Therefore, appellant had no reputation or goodwill upon which Christman could have intended to trade, rendering the unfair competition provisions of the Paris Convention inapplicable. The Board also found that Christman had not abandoned the mark, although sales of articles bearing the mark were often intermittent. The Board granted summary judgment to Christman and ordered appellant's registration cancelled.

[8] The Board held in its opinion on reconsideration that Christman had not adopted the mark in bad faith despite his appropriation of a mark in use by appellant in a foreign country. The Board adopted the view that copying a mark in use in a foreign country is not in bad faith unless the foreign mark is famous in the United States or the copying is undertaken for the purpose of interfering with the prior user's planned expansion into the United States. Person's Co. appeals and requests that this court direct the Board to enter summary judgment in its favor.

Issues

[9] 1. Does knowledge of a mark's use outside U.S. commerce preclude good faith adoption and use of the identical mark in the United States prior to the entry of the foreign user into the domestic market?

[10] 2. Did the Board properly grant summary judgment in favor of Christman on the issue of abandonment?

Cancellation

[11] The Board may properly cancel a trademark registration within five years of issue when, e.g. (1) there is a valid ground why the trademark should not continue to be registered and (2) the party petitioning for cancellation has standing. Such cancellation of the marks' registrations may be based

upon any ground which could have prevented registration initially. The legal issue in a cancellation proceeding is the right to register a mark, which may be based on either (1) ownership of a foreign registration of the mark in question or (2) use of the mark in United States commerce.

Priority

[12] The first ground asserted for cancellation in the present action is § 2(d) of the Lanham Act; each party claims prior use of registered marks which unquestionably are confusingly similar and affixed to similar goods.

[13] Section 1 of the Lanham Act[10] states that "[t]he owner of a trademark *used in commerce* may register his trademark . . . ." The term "commerce" is defined in Section 45 of the Act as ". . . all commerce which may be lawfully regulated by Congress." No specific Constitutional language gives Congress power to regulate trademarks, so the power of the federal government to provide for trademark registration comes only under its commerce power. The term "used in commerce" in the Lanham Act refers to a sale or transportation of goods bearing the mark in or having an effect on: (1) United States interstate commerce; (2) United States commerce with foreign nations; or (3) United States commerce with the Indian Tribes.

[14] In the present case, appellant Person's Co. relies on its use of the mark in Japan in an attempt to support its claim for priority in the United States. Such foreign use has no effect on U.S. commerce and cannot form the basis for a holding that appellant has priority here. The concept of territoriality is basic to trademark law; trademark rights exist in each country solely according to that country's statutory scheme. Christman was the first to use the mark in United States commerce and the first to obtain a federal registration thereon. Appellant has no basis upon which to claim priority and is the junior user under these facts.[16]

Bad Faith

[15] Appellant vigorously asserts that Christman's adoption and use of the mark in the United States subsequent to Person's Co.'s adoption in Japan is tainted with "bad faith" and that the priority in the United States obtained thereby is insufficient to establish rights superior to those arising from Person's Co.'s prior adoption in a foreign country. Relying on *Woman's World Shops, Inc. v. Lane Bryant, Inc.,* 5 USPQ2d 1985 (TTAB 1988), Person's Co. argues that a "remote junior user" of a mark obtains no right superior to the "senior user" if the "junior user" has adopted the mark with knowledge of the "senior user's" prior use.[18] In *Woman's World,* the senior user utilized the mark within a limited geographical area. A junior user from a different geographical area of the United States sought unrestricted federal registration for a nearly identical mark, with the exception to its virtually exclusive rights being those of the known senior user. The Board held that such an appropriation with knowledge failed to satisfy the good faith requirements of the Lanham Act and denied the concurrent use rights

---

[10] The case at bar is decided under the provisions of the Act in force prior to the enactment of the Trademark Law Revision Act of 1988.

[16] Section 44 of the Lanham Act, 15 U.S.C. § 1126 (1982), permits qualified foreign applicants who own a registered mark in their country of origin to obtain a U.S. trademark registration without alleging actual use in U.S. commerce. If a U.S. application is filed within six months of the filing of the foreign application, such U.S. registration will be accorded the same force and effect as if filed in the United States on the same date on which the application was first filed in the foreign country. The statutory scheme set forth in § 44 is in place to lower barriers to entry and assist foreign applicants in establishing business goodwill in the United States. Person's Co. does not assert rights under § 44, which if properly applied, might have been used to secure priority over Christman.

[18] Appellant repeatedly makes reference to a "world economy" and considers Christman to be the remote junior user of the mark. Although Person's did adopt the mark in Japan prior to Christman's use in United States commerce, the use in Japan cannot be relied upon to acquire U.S. trademark rights. Christman is the senior user as that term is defined under U.S. trademark law.

sought by the junior user. 5 USPQ2d at 1988. Person's Co. cites *Woman's World* for the proposition that a junior user's adoption and use of a mark with knowledge of another's prior use constitutes bad faith. It is urged that this principle is equitable in nature and should not be limited to knowledge of use within the territory of the United States.

[16] While the facts of the present case are analogous to those in *Woman's World,* the case is distinguishable in one significant respect. In *Woman's World,* the first use of the mark by both the junior and senior users was in United States commerce. In the case at bar, appellant Person's Co., while first to adopt the mark, was not the first user in the United States. Christman is the senior user, and we are aware of no case where a senior user has been charged with bad faith. The concept of bad faith adoption applies to remote junior users seeking concurrent use registrations; in such cases, the likelihood of customer confusion in the remote area may be presumed from proof of the junior user's knowledge.[20] In the present case, when Christman initiated use of the mark, Person's Co. had not yet entered U.S. commerce. The Person's Co. had no goodwill in the United States and the "PERSON'S" mark had no reputation here. Appellant's argument ignores the territorial nature of trademark rights.

[17] Appellant next asserts that Christman's knowledge of its prior use of the mark in Japan should preclude his acquisition of superior trademark rights in the United States. The Board found that, at the time of registration, Christman was not aware of appellant's intention to enter the U.S. clothing and accessories market in the future. Christman obtained a trademark search on the "PERSON'S" mark and an opinion of competent counsel that the mark was "available" in the United States. Since Appellant had taken no steps to secure registration of the mark in the United States, Christman was aware of no basis for Person's Co. to assert superior rights to use and registration here. Appellant would have us infer bad faith adoption because of Christman's awareness of its use of the mark in Japan, but an inference of bad faith requires something more than mere knowledge of prior use of a similar mark in a foreign country.

[18] As the Board noted below, Christman's prior use in U.S. commerce cannot be discounted solely because he was aware of appellant's use of the mark in Japan. While adoption of a mark with knowledge of a prior actual *user* in U.S. commerce may give rise to cognizable equities as between the parties, no such equities may be based upon knowledge of a similar mark's existence or on a problematical intent to use such a similar mark in the future. Knowledge of a foreign use does not preclude good faith adoption and use in the United States. While there is some case law supporting a finding of bad faith where (1) the foreign mark is famous here[23] or (2) the use is a nominal one made solely to block the prior foreign user's planned expansion into the United States,[24] as the Board correctly found, neither of these circumstances is present in this case.

[19] We agree with the Board's conclusion that Christman's adoption and use of the mark were in good faith. Christman's adoption of the mark occurred at a time when appellant had not yet entered U.S. commerce; therefore, no prior user was in place to give Christman notice of appellant's potential U.S. rights. Christman's conduct in appropriating and using appellant's mark in a market where he believed the Japanese manufacturer did not compete can hardly be considered unscrupulous commercial conduct. Christman adopted the trademark being used by appellant in Japan, but appellant has not identified any aspect of U.S. trademark law violated by such action. Trademark rights under the Lanham Act arise solely out of use of the mark in U.S. commerce or from ownership of a foreign registration thereon; "[t]he law pertaining to registration of trademarks does not regulate all aspects of business morality." [citation omitted] When the law has been crafted with the clarity of crystal, it also has the

---

[20] *See* 2 J. McCarthy, *Trademarks and Unfair Competition* § 26:4 (2d ed. 1984); Restatement of Torts § 732 comment a (1938).

[23] See, e.g., Vaudable v. Montmartre, Inc., 20 Misc.2d 757, 193 N.Y.S.2d 332, 123 USPQ 357 (N.Y.Sup.Ct. 1959); Mother's Restaurants, Inc. v. Mother's Other Kitchen, Inc., 218 USPQ 1046 (TTAB 1983).

[24] See Davidoff Extension, S.A. v. Davidoff Int'l., 221 USPQ 465 (S.D.Fla. 1983).

qualities of a glass slipper: it cannot be shoe-horned onto facts it does not fit, no matter how appealing they might appear.

. . . .

Conclusion

[20] In *United Drug Co. v. Rectanus Co.*, 248 U.S. 90 (1918), the Supreme Court of the United States determined that "[t]here is no such thing as property in a trademark except as a right appurtenant to an established business or trade in connection with which the mark is employed . . . . [I]ts function is simply to designate the goods as the product of a particular trader and to protect his goodwill against the sale of another's product as his; and it is not the subject of property except in connection with an existing business."[36] In the present case, appellant failed to secure protection for its mark through use in U.S. commerce; therefore, no established business or product line was in place from which trademark rights could arise. Christman was the first to use the mark in U.S. commerce. This first use was not tainted with bad faith by Christman's mere knowledge of appellant's prior foreign use, so the Board's conclusion on the issue of priority was correct . . . . Accordingly, the grant of summary judgment was entirely in order, and the Board's decision is affirmed.

AFFIRMED.

b. The Well-Known Marks Doctrine

Though it is rarely invoked, the well-known marks doctrine constitutes an important exception to—or variation on—the territoriality principle in trademark law. It is also the source of a basic split between the Ninth and Second Circuits on whether U.S. federal trademark law incorporates well-known marks protection. As you read through the opinions below, consider the following questions:

- As a policy matter, for a foreign mark not used in the U.S., how well-known should such a mark be in the U.S. for it to qualify for protection in the U.S.? Should mere secondary meaning in a particular geographic location be sufficient? "Secondary meaning plus"? Nationwide fame?

- What is the particular statutory or common law basis for the Ninth Circuit's application of the well-known marks doctrine?

- Is the New York Court of Appeals approach to the issue persuasive?

- Is the well-known marks doctrine simply a transnational extension of the *Tea Rose-Rectanus* doctrine? Is there any way in which the well-known marks doctrine is different?

i. The Well-Known Marks Doctrine in the Ninth Circuit

Grupo Gigante SA De CV v. Dallo & Co., Inc. 391 F.3d 1088 (9th Cir. 2004)

KLEINFELD, Circuit Judge.

[1] This is a trademark case. The contest is between a large Mexican grocery chain that has long used the mark, but not in the United States, and a small American chain that was the first to use the mark in the United States, but did so, long after the Mexican chain began using it, in a locality where shoppers were familiar with the Mexican mark.

Facts

[2] Grupo Gigante S.A. de C.V. ("Grupo Gigante") operates a large chain of grocery stores in Mexico, called "Gigante," meaning "Giant" in Spanish. Grupo Gigante first called a store "Gigante" in Mexico City in 1962. In 1963, Grupo Gigante registered the "Gigante" mark as a trade name in Mexico, and has kept its registration current ever since. The chain was quite successful, and it had expanded into Baja

---

[36] 248 U.S. at 97. It goes without saying that the underlying policy upon which this function is grounded is the protection of the public in its purchase of a service or product. *See, e.g. In re Canadian Pacific Ltd.*, 754 F.2d 992, 994 (Fed.Cir. 1985).

California, Mexico by 1987. By 1991, Grupo Gigante had almost 100 stores in Mexico, including six in Baja, all using the mark "Gigante." Two of the Baja stores were in Tijuana, a city on the U.S.-Mexican border, just south of San Diego.

[3] As of August 1991, Grupo Gigante had not opened any stores in the United States. That month, Michael Dallo began operating a grocery store in San Diego, using the name "Gigante Market." In October 1996, Dallo and one of his brothers, Chris Dallo, opened a second store in San Diego, also under the name Gigante Market. The Dallo brothers—who include Michael, Chris, and their two other brothers, Douray and Rafid—have since controlled the two stores through various limited liability corporations.

[4] In 1995, which was after the opening of the Dallos' first store and before the opening of their second, Grupo Gigante began exploring the possibility of expanding into Southern California. It learned of the Dallos' Gigante Market in San Diego. Grupo Gigante decided against entering the California market at that time. It did nothing about the Dallos' store despite Grupo Gigante's knowledge that the Dallos were using "Gigante" in the store's name.

[5] In 1998, Grupo Gigante decided that the time had come to enter the Southern California market. It arranged a meeting with Michael Dallo in June 1998 to discuss the Dallos' use of the name "Gigante." Grupo Gigante was unsuccessful at this meeting in its attempt to convince Dallo to stop using the "Gigante" mark. Also in June 1998, Grupo Gigante registered the "Gigante" mark with the state of California. The Dallos did likewise in July 1998. Neither has registered the mark federally.

[6] About one year later, in May 1999, Grupo Gigante opened its first U.S. store. That store was followed by a second later that year, and then by a third in 2000. All three stores were in the Los Angeles area. All were called "Gigante," like Grupo Gigante's Mexican stores.

[7] In July 1999, after learning of the opening of Grupo Gigante's first U.S. store, the Dallos sent Grupo Gigante a cease-and-desist letter, making the same demand of Grupo Gigante that Grupo Gigante had made of them earlier: stop using the name Gigante. Grupo Gigante responded several days later by filing this lawsuit. Its claim was based on numerous federal and state theories, including trademark infringement under the Lanham Act.[3] It sought compensatory and punitive damages, a declaratory judgment that it had the superior right to the Gigante mark, and an injunction against the Dallos' use of the mark. The Dallos counterclaimed, on similar theories, asserting it had the superior right to the mark in Southern California.[4] The Dallos sought a declaratory judgment, injunctive relief, damages, and cancellation of Grupo Gigante's California registration of the mark.

[8] The district court disposed of the case in a published decision on cross motions for summary judgment.[5] The court recognized that under the "territoriality principle," use of a mark in another country generally does not serve to give the user trademark rights in the United States. Thus, the territoriality principle suggests that the Dallos' use of the mark, which was the first in the United States, would entitle them to claim the mark. But it held that because Grupo Gigante had already made Gigante

---

[3] Specifically, Grupo Gigante asserted the following causes of action: (1) improper use of a well-known mark, under Article 6 *bis* of the Paris Convention; (2) unfair competition, under Article 10 *bis* of the Paris Convention; (3) trademark infringement, under § 43(a) of the Lanham Act, 15 U.S.C. § 1125(a); (4) false designation of origin, misrepresentation, and unfair competition, under § 43(a) of the Lanham Act, 15 U.S.C. § 1125(a); (5) violation of the Federal Trademark Dilution Act of 1996, 15 U.S.C. § 1125(c); (6) common law unfair competition; (7) unfair competition under California law; (8) dilution under California law; and (9) common law misappropriation.

[4] The Dallos asserted the following causes of action: (1) trademark infringement, under § 43(a) of the Lanham Act, 15 U.S.C. § 1125(a); (2) false designation of origin, misrepresentation, and unfair competition, under § 43(a) of the Lanham Act, 15 U.S.C. § 1125(a); (3) common law unfair competition; (4) trademark infringement and unfair competition under California law; (5) dilution under California law; and (6) common law misappropriation.

[5] Grupo Gigante S.A. de C.V. v. Dallo & Co., Inc., 119 F.Supp.2d 1083 (C.D.Cal. 2000).

a well-known mark in Southern California by the time the Dallos began using it, an exception to the territoriality principle applied. As the district court interpreted what is known as the "famous-mark" or "well-known mark" exception to the territoriality principle, Grupo Gigante's earlier use in Mexico was sufficient to give it the superior claim to the mark in Southern California. The court held, therefore, that Grupo Gigante was entitled to a declaratory judgment that it had a valid, protectable interest in the Gigante name. Nevertheless, the court held that laches barred Grupo Gigante from enjoining the Dallos from using the mark at their two existing stores. The Dallos appeal the holding that Grupo Gigante has a protectable right to use the mark in Southern California. Grupo Gigante appeals the laches holding. We agree in large part with the district court's excellent opinion, but some necessary qualifications to it require a remand.

Analysis

The exception for famous and well-known foreign marks

[9] We review the summary judgment decision de novo.

[10] A fundamental principle of trademark law is first in time equals first in right. But things get more complicated when to time we add considerations of place, as when one user is first in time in one place while another is first in time in a different place. The complexity swells when the two places are two different countries, as in the case at bar.

[11] Under the principle of first in time equals first in right, priority ordinarily comes with earlier *use* of a mark in commerce. It is "not enough to have invented the mark first or even to have registered it first." If the first-in-time principle were all that mattered, this case would end there. It is undisputed that Grupo Gigante used the mark in commerce for decades before the Dallos did. But the facts of this case implicate another well-established principle of trademark law, the "territoriality principle." The territoriality principle, as stated in a treatise, says that "[p]riority of trademark rights in the United States depends solely upon priority of use in the United States, not on priority of use anywhere in the world."[9] Earlier use in another country usually just does not count.[10] Although we have not had occasion to address this principle, it has been described by our sister circuits as "basic to trademark law," in large part because "trademark rights exist in each country solely according to that country's statutory scheme."[11] While Grupo Gigante used the mark for decades before the Dallos used it, Grupo Gigante's use was in Mexico, not in the United States. Within the San Diego area, on the northern side of the border, the Dallos were the first users of the "Gigante" mark. Thus, according to the territoriality principle, the Dallos' rights to use the mark would trump Grupo Gigante's.

[12] Grupo Gigante does not contest the existence of the territoriality principle. But like the first-in-time, first-in-right principle, it is not absolute. The exception, as Grupo Gigante presents it, is that when foreign use of a mark achieves a certain level of fame for that mark within the United States, the territoriality principle no longer serves to deny priority to the earlier foreign user. The Dallos concede that there is such an exception, but dispute what it takes for a mark to qualify for it. Grupo Gigante would interpret the exception broadly, while the Dallos would interpret it narrowly.

[13] Grupo Gigante does not argue to this court that it used the mark *in the United States* in a way that qualifies for protection regardless of the territoriality principle and any exception to it. While the district court opinion suggests that Grupo Gigante made an alternative argument of this sort below, its argument on appeal is limited to whether the mark has become well-known enough to overcome the territoriality principle. For example, while the statement of facts in Grupo Gigante's brief claims that

---

[9] J. Thomas McCarthy, *McCarthy on Trademarks and Unfair Competition,* § 29:2, at 29–6 (4th ed. 2002) (internal footnote omitted).

[10] See Person's Co., Ltd. v. Christman, 900 F.2d 1565, 1569–70 (Fed.Cir. 1990); Buti v. Perosa, S.R.L., 139 F.3d 98, 103–05 (2d Cir. 1998); Fuji Photo Film Co., Inc. v. Shinohara Shoji Kabushiki Kaisha, 754 F.2d 591, 599 (5th Cir. 1985).

[11] *Fuji Photo,* 754 F.2d at 599; *see also Person's,* 900 F.2d at 1569.

Grupo Gigante engaged in advertising in Mexico that reached United States consumers, Grupo Gigante does not assert that this advertising, combined with other activities, constitutes domestic use of the mark.[13] Thus, while Grupo Gigante does not appear to concede explicitly that application of the famous-mark exception is necessary to its success on appeal, the structure of its argument suggests as much. Since the district court based its holding on an interpretation of the exception, and since Grupo Gigante does not urge us to consider alternative ways it might be eligible for protection, we have no occasion to decide, and do not decide, whether Grupo Gigante could establish protection for its mark apart from application of the famous-mark exception to the territoriality principle.

[14] There is no circuit-court authority—from this or any other circuit—applying a famous-mark exception to the territoriality principle. At least one circuit judge has, in a dissent, called into question whether there actually is any meaningful famous-mark exception.[14] We hold, however, that there is a famous mark exception to the territoriality principle. While the territoriality principle is a long-standing and important doctrine within trademark law, it cannot be absolute. An absolute territoriality rule without a famous-mark exception would promote consumer confusion and fraud. Commerce crosses borders. In this nation of immigrants, so do people. Trademark is, at its core, about protecting against consumer confusion and "palming off."[15] There can be no justification for using trademark law to fool immigrants into thinking that they are buying from the store they liked back home.

[15] It might not matter if someone visiting Fairbanks, Alaska from Wellington, New Zealand saw a cute hair-salon name—"Hair Today, Gone Tomorrow," "Mane Place," "Hair on Earth," "Mary's Hair'em," or "Shear Heaven"—and decided to use the name on her own salon back home in New Zealand. The ladies in New Zealand would not likely think they were going to a branch of a Fairbanks hair salon. But if someone opened a high-end salon with a red door in Wellington and called it Elizabeth Arden's, women might very well go there because they thought they were going to an affiliate of the Elizabeth Arden chain, even if there had not been any other Elizabeth Ardens in New Zealand prior to the salon's opening. If it was not an affiliate, just a local store with no connection, customers would be fooled. The real Elizabeth Arden chain might lose business if word spread that the Wellington salon was nothing special.

[16] The most cited case for the famous-mark exception is *Vaudable v. Montmartre, Inc.,* a 1959 trial court decision from New York.[16] A New York restaurant had opened under the name "Maxim's," the same name as the well-known Parisian restaurant in operation since 1893, and still in operation today. The New York Maxim's used similar typography for its sign, as well as other features likely to evoke the Paris Maxim's—particularly among what the court called "the class of people residing in the cosmopolitan city of New York who dine out"[17] (by which it apparently meant the sort of people who spend for dinner what some people spend for a month's rent). The court enjoined the New York use, even though the Paris restaurant did not operate in New York, or in the United States, because the Maxim's mark was "famous."[18]

[17] While *Vaudable* stands for the principle that even those who use marks in other countries can sometimes—when their marks are famous enough—gain exclusive rights to the marks in this country, the case itself tells us little about just how famous or well-known the foreign mark must be. The opinion states in rather conclusory terms that the Paris Maxim's "is, of course, well known in this country," and that "[t]here is *no doubt* as to its unique and eminent position as a restaurant of international fame and

---

[13] See, e.g., Int'l Bancorp, LLC v. Societe des Bains de Mer, 329 F.3d 359, 370 (4th Cir. 2003).

[14] *Int'l Bancorp,* 329 F.3d at 389 n. 9 (Motz, J., dissenting) ("Nor does the 'famous marks' doctrine provide SBM any refuge. That doctrine has been applied so seldom (never by a federal appellate court and only by a handful of district courts) that its viability is uncertain.").

[15] See Thane Int'l, Inc. v. Trek Bicycle Corp., 305 F.3d 894, 901 (9th Cir. 2002).

[16] *Vaudable v. Montmartre, Inc.,* 20 Misc.2d 757, 193 N.Y.S.2d 332 (N.Y.Sup.Ct. 1959).

[17] *Id.* at 334.

[18] *Id.* at 335.

prestige."[19] This language suggests that Maxim's had achieved quite a high degree of fame here, and certainly enough to qualify for the exception to the territoriality principle, but it suggests nothing about just how much fame was necessary. It does not suggest where the line is between "Shear Heaven" and Maxim's.

[18] The Patent and Trademark Office's Trademark Trial and Appeal Board, whose expertise we respect and whose decisions create expectations, has recognized the validity of the famous-mark exception.[20] But as with *Vaudable,* none of these cases helps us to establish a clear threshold for just how famous a mark must be to qualify for the exception.

[19] Grupo Gigante urges us to adopt the approach the district court took. The district court held that the correct inquiry was to determine whether the mark had attained secondary meaning in the San Diego area. Secondary meaning refers to a mark's actual ability to trigger in consumers' minds a link between a product or service and the source of that product or service. That is, a mark has secondary meaning "when, in the minds of the public, the primary significance of a mark is to identify the source of the product rather than the product itself."[21] Determining whether a mark has secondary meaning requires taking into account at least seven considerations, which the district court did in this case.[22]

[20] Applying its interpretation of the famous-mark exception, the district court concluded that Grupo Gigante's use of the mark had achieved secondary meaning in the San Diego area by the time the Dallos opened their first store, and thus the court held that Grupo Gigante's use was eligible for the exception to the territoriality principle. Grupo Gigante asserts that we, too, should adopt secondary meaning as the definition of the exception. We decline to go quite this far, however, because following the district court's lead would effectively cause the exception to eclipse the territoriality rule entirely.

[21] Secondary meaning has two functions. First, it serves to determine whether certain marks are distinctive enough to warrant protection. Some marks—those that are arbitrary, fanciful, or suggestive—are deemed inherently distinctive. Others—including those that are descriptive of some feature of the products or services to which they are attached—require some indication of distinctiveness before trademark protection is available. That required indication is that the mark have acquired secondary meaning. Thus, before Grupo Gigante (or for that matter the Dallos) could have a protectable interest in "Gigante" at all, Grupo Gigante would have to show that the mark has acquired secondary meaning by demonstrating that it has come to identify to consumers Grupo Gigante's particular brand of store, not merely a characteristic of Grupo Gigante's stores and others like them.

[22] Second, and most relevant to this case, secondary meaning defines the geographic area in which a user has priority, regardless of who uses the mark first. Under what has become known as the *Tea Rose–Rectanus* doctrine, priority of use in one geographic area within the United States does not necessarily suffice to establish priority in another area. Thus, the first user of a mark will not necessarily be able to stop a subsequent user, where the subsequent user is in an area of the country "remote" from the first user's area.[26] The practical effect is that one user may have priority in one area, while another

---

[19] *Id.* at 334 (emphasis added).

[20] See, e.g., The All England Lawn Tennis Club (Wimbledon) Ltd. v. Creations Aromatiques, Inc., 220 U.S.P.Q. 1069, 1072, 1983 WL 51903 (TTAB 1983); Mother's Rests. Inc. v. Mother's Other Kitchen, Inc., 218 U.S.P.Q. 1046, 1048, 1983 WL 51992 (TTAB 1983).

[21] *Wal–Mart Stores, Inc. v. Samara Bros., Inc.,* 529 U.S. 205, 211 (2000) (internal quotation and editing omitted).

[22] See Filipino Yellow Pages, Inc. v. Asian Journal Publ'ns, Inc., 198 F.3d 1143 (9th Cir. 1999).

[26] Good faith may also be an issue in such cases. *See Hanover Star,* 240 U.S. at 415, 36 S.Ct. 357 (excepting from the general *Tea Rose–Rectanus* principle cases in which "the second adopter has selected the mark with some design inimical to the interests of the first user, such as to take the benefit of the reputation of his goods, to forestall the extension of his trade, or the like."). Good faith is not raised in

user has priority over the very same mark in a different area. The point of this doctrine is that in the remote area, where no one is likely to know of the earlier user, it is unlikely that consumers would be confused by the second user's use of the mark. Secondary meaning comes into play in determining just how far each user's priority extends. Courts ask whether the first, geographically limited use of the mark is well-known enough that it has gained secondary meaning not just within the area where it has been used, but also within the remote area, which is usually the area where a subsequent user is claiming the right to use the mark.

[23] Assume, for example, that Grupo Gigante had been using the mark in Arizona as well as in various parts of Mexico, and that it had met all the other requirements of having a protectable interest in the mark, including having established secondary meaning throughout Arizona. If the Dallos later began using the same mark in San Diego without knowledge of Grupo Gigante's earlier "remote" use in Arizona, whether Grupo Gigante could stop them would depend on what the mark meant to consumers in San Diego. Under the *Tea Rose–Rectanus* doctrine, Grupo Gigante would have priority in San Diego, and thus be able to stop the Dallos' use of the mark, only if the secondary meaning from Grupo Gigante's use of the mark in Arizona extended to San Diego as well. If, on the other hand, the secondary meaning from Grupo Gigante's use were limited to Arizona, then the Dallos might be free to continue using the mark in San Diego.

[24] Thus, if the dispute before us were between a Mexican and Arizonan Grupo Gigante on the one hand, and the Dallos on the other, we would analyze, under the *Tea Rose–Rectanus* doctrine, whether Grupo Gigante's use of the mark had achieved secondary meaning in San Diego. This is how the district court analyzed the actual dispute, as a result of having defined the exception to the territoriality principle in terms of secondary meaning. In other words, the district court treated Grupo Gigante's use of the mark exactly as it would have had Grupo Gigante used the mark not only in Mexico, but also in another part of the United States. Under the district court's interpretation of the exception to the territoriality principle, the fact that Grupo Gigante's earlier use of the mark was entirely outside of the United States becomes irrelevant.

[25] The problem with this is that treating international use differently is what the territoriality principle does. This interpretation of the exception would effectively eliminate the territoriality principle by eliminating any effect of international borders on protectability. We would end up treating foreign uses of the mark just as we treat domestic uses under the *Tea Rose–Rectanus* doctrine, asking in both cases whether the use elsewhere resulted in secondary meaning in the local market.

[26] We would go too far if we did away with the territoriality principle altogether by expanding the famous-mark exception this much. The territoriality principle has a long history in the common law,[30] and at least two circuits have described it as "basic to trademark law."[31] That status reflects the lack of a uniform trademark regime across international borders. What one must do to acquire trademark rights in one country will not always be the same as what one must do in another. And once acquired, trademark rights gained in other countries are governed by each country's own set of laws.[32]

---

this appeal (perhaps because the appeal comes up on summary judgment) and is irrelevant to our analysis.

[30] As McCarthy has noted, traces of the territoriality principle appear in Justice Holmes's opinion for the U.S. Supreme Court in *A. Bourjois & Co. v. Katzel,* 260 U.S. 689, 692 (1923). McCarthy, *supra,* at § 29:1, p. 29–4; *see also Philip Morris Inc. v. Allen Distribs., Inc.,* 48 F.Supp.2d 844, 850 (S.D.Ind. 1999) (identifying *Bourjois* as marking the shift from "the 'universality' principle [to] a 'territoriality principle' that recognizes a separate legal existence for a trademark in each country whose laws afford protection to the mark").

[31] *Fuji Photo,* 754 F.2d at 599; *Person's,* 900 F.2d at 1569.

[32] *See Ingenohl v. Walter E. Olsen & Co., Inc.,* 273 U.S. 541, 544, (1927) ("A trademark started elsewhere would depend for its protection in Hongkong upon the law prevailing in Hongkong and would

Furthermore, we are arguably required by the Paris Convention, of which the United States is a signatory, to preserve the territoriality principle in some form.[33] Thus, we reject Grupo Gigante's argument that we should define the well-known mark exception as merely an inquiry into whether the mark has achieved secondary meaning in the area where the foreign user wishes to assert protection.

[27] To determine whether the famous-mark exception to the territoriality rule applies, the district court must determine whether the mark satisfies the secondary meaning test. The district court determined that it did in this case, and we agree with its persuasive analysis. But secondary meaning is not enough.

[28] In addition, where the mark has not before been used in the American market, the court must be satisfied, by a preponderance of the evidence, that a *substantial* percentage of consumers in the relevant American market is familiar with the foreign mark. The relevant American market is the geographic area where the defendant uses the alleged infringing mark. In making this determination, the court should consider such factors as the intentional copying of the mark by the defendant, and whether customers of the American firm are likely to think they are patronizing the same firm that uses the mark in another country. While these factors are not necessarily determinative, they are particularly relevant because they bear heavily on the risks of consumer confusion and fraud, which are the reasons for having a famous-mark exception.

[29] Because the district court did not have the benefit of this additional test, we vacate and remand so that it may be applied. We intimate no judgment on whether further motion practice and some additions to what the district court has already written in its published opinion will suffice, or whether trial will be needed to apply this new test. Nor do we intimate what the result should be. The concurring opinion is incorrect in its suggestion that the case necessarily must go to trial because distinctiveness of a mark is a question of fact and defendants have contested the reliability of plaintiffs' survey evidence. That conclusion flies in the face of the 1986 triumvirate of summary judgment cases.[34] Regardless of whether questions are factual, there is nothing to try unless there is a genuine issue of material fact. One survey that is impeachable, but still good enough to get to a jury, weighed against no survey evidence at all on the other side, along with all the other evidence in the record, does not necessarily add up to a genuine issue of fact. . . .

VACATED AND REMANDED.

GRABER, Circuit Judge, concurring:

[30] I concur in the majority's opinion because I agree that a foreign owner of a supposedly famous or well-known foreign trademark must show a higher level of "fame" or recognition than that required to establish secondary meaning. Ultimately, the standard for famous or well-known marks is an intermediate one. To enjoy extraterritorial trademark protection, the owner of a foreign trademark need not show the level of recognition necessary to receive nation-wide protection against trademark dilution. On the other hand, the foreign trademark owner who does not use a mark in the United States must show more than the level of recognition that is necessary in a domestic trademark infringement case.

---

confer no rights except by the consent of that law."); *Fuji Photo*, 754 F.2d at 599 ("[T]rademark rights exist in each country solely according to that country's statutory scheme.").

[33] *Paris Convention for the Protection of Industrial Property*, Mar. 20, 1883, as revised at Stockholm, July 14, 1967, art. 6(3), 21 U.S.T. 1583, § 6(3) ("A mark duly registered in a country of the Union shall be regarded as independent of marks registered in the other countries of the Union, including the country of origin.").

[34] See Celotex Corp. v. Catrett, 477 U.S. 317 (1986); Anderson v. Liberty Lobby, Inc., 477 U.S. 242 (1986); Matsushita Elec. Indus. Co. v. Zenith Radio, 475 U.S. 574 (1986).

[31] Nonetheless, I write separately to express my view that the evidence that Plaintiffs have presented thus far is insufficient as a matter of law to establish that their mark is famous or well-known. The survey population and the survey's results establish little more than the fact that Plaintiffs' customers are familiar with Plaintiffs' stores. In an abundance of caution, the majority does not intimate whether that evidence is sufficient to warrant a grant of summary judgment in Plaintiffs' favor on the issue of the famous mark exception. I would go beyond intimation and hold directly that Plaintiffs' evidence is insufficient to support a grant of summary judgment in its favor. I would further hold that, unless the district court entertains a renewed motion for summary judgment on a considerably expanded record, this case should proceed to trial.

[32] The district court, relying entirely on survey evidence, concluded that Plaintiffs' trademark had acquired secondary meaning and was thus entitled to protection from domestic users.[1] The survey population consisted of only 78 people in San Diego County who were "Spanish-speaking, and had recently purchased Mexican-style food at a supermarket or other food store." *Grupo Gigante S.A. de C.V. v. Dallo & Co., Inc.,* 119 F.Supp.2d 1083, 1093 (C.D.Cal. 2000). Twenty-four respondents from that population "(1) had recently shopped at a Gigante store in Mexico; (2) believed that the Gigante name was affiliated with an entity that had at least one store located in Mexico; or (3) were aware of a Gigante supermarket located in Mexico." *Id.* However, the survey was conducted in 2000, nine years *after* Defendants first began using the Gigante name in the United States. When testing for awareness of the Gigante mark *before* Defendants' entry into the San Diego market in 1991, the awareness level dropped to 20 to 22 percent of the respondents. *Id.* That is, the district court based its conclusion that Plaintiffs' mark was well known on a survey that turned up just *seventeen people* who had heard of Gigante before 1991.

[33] That evidence is insufficient in two important respects. First, the survey result is highly questionable in view of its narrowly defined survey population. Plaintiffs' own description of their stores makes clear that the goods sold are little different from those available in any large retail grocery store: "Product offerings in the Gigante stores generally include a complete selection of perishable and non-perishable foods and a wide selection of general merchandise, as well as clothing and fashion items." Further, Plaintiffs admit in their briefs that the clientele of their Mexican stores includes "both Hispanic and non-Hispanic" customers. Consequently, nothing about *either* the nature of the goods sold by Plaintiffs *or* its customer base warrants limiting the relevant public to Mexican–Americans.

. . . .

[34] Because Plaintiffs sell widely-available, non-specialized goods to the general public, it is uninformative to focus exclusively on Mexican–Americans living in San Diego County. The district court's reliance on Plaintiffs' survey is especially problematic because its population was limited to Mexican–Americans who had recently purchased Mexican-style food at a supermarket or grocery store. That survey is only very slightly more informative than the study whose probative value we dismissed entirely in *Avery Dennison Corp. v. Sumpton,* 189 F.3d 868 (9th Cir. 1999), because it focused exclusively on the plaintiff's existing customers: "Avery Dennison's marketing reports are comparable to a survey we discussed in *Anti–Monopoly, Inc. v. General Mills Fun Group, Inc.,* 684 F.2d 1316 (9th Cir. 1982), proving only the near tautology that consumers already acquainted with Avery and Avery Dennison products are familiar with Avery Dennison." 189 F.3d at 879.

[35] Because a conclusion that Plaintiffs have a protectable interest would prohibit Defendants from selling groceries under that mark to *any* residents of San Diego County—not just to Mexican–Americans—it makes little sense to define the relevant public so narrowly. Comprised of all grocery

---

[1] Expert surveys can provide the most persuasive evidence of secondary meaning. *Comm. for Idaho's High Desert, Inc. v. Yost,* 92 F.3d 814, 822 (9th Cir. 1996). "However, survey data is not a requirement and secondary meaning can be, and often is, proven by circumstantial evidence." 5 J. Thomas McCarthy, *McCarthy on Trademarks and Unfair Competition,* § 32:190, at 32–319 to 32–320 (4th ed. 2002).

shoppers, the "relevant sector of the public" in this case is the very antithesis of a specialized market; because everyone eats, the relevant sector of the public consists of all residents of San Diego County, without qualification.

[36] Second, in view of the standard we announce today, I do not believe that a showing that 20 to 22 percent of the relevant market is familiar with the foreign mark establishes that a "significant" or "substantial" percentage of that market is familiar with the foreign mark. On that ground alone, I would conclude that Plaintiffs have failed, so far, to show that their mark is famous or well-known.

[37] In terms of the level of fame, trademark dilution cases often speak of a "significant percentage of the defendant's market." *Mead Data Cent., Inc. v. Toyota Motor Sales, U.S.A., Inc.*, 875 F.2d 1026, 1031 (2d Cir. 1989). Discussing the level of recognition required to establish "niche fame," McCarthy argues that "a mark should not be categorized as 'famous' unless it is known to more than 50 percent of the defendant's potential customers." 4 J. Thomas McCarthy, *McCarthy on Trademarks and Unfair Competition*, § 24:112, at 24–271 (4th ed. 2002).

[38] I would adopt a similar standard for the exception for famous or well-known foreign marks. When a foreign mark has not been used in the United States, I would require the owner of the foreign mark to show, through surveys and other evidence, that a majority of the defendant's customers and potential customers, on aggregate, were familiar with the foreign mark when the defendant began its allegedly infringing use. Admittedly, that is a high standard. However, I believe that a stringent standard is required when conferring trademark protection to a mark that has never been, and perhaps never may be, used in this country. A conclusion that Plaintiffs' mark is well-known in the relevant sector brings with it the right to oust Defendants from their own market, notwithstanding the fact that they have established priority of use. A bare showing of acquired distinctiveness should not suffice to invert the ordinary allocation of trademark rights.

[39] Of course, I recognize that the doctrine of "niche fame" has received heavy, and in the context of *domestic* trademark law, deserved criticism. However, the niche fame cases may provide the district court with an instructive benchmark against which to measure an intermediate standard of fame.[2]

[40] In summary, I agree with the majority's conclusion that this case must be remanded and the evidence reevaluated under a heightened standard for the famous or well-known marks exception. However, I would hold directly that the evidence presented thus far does not meet that standard and thus does not suffice to warrant protection for Plaintiff's mark. Finally, in determining whether a foreign mark has met the standard for famous or well-known foreign trademarks, I would look to precedent from this court and others addressing whether a mark has become famous in its market niche.

ii.   The Well-Known Marks Doctrine in the Second Circuit

ITC Ltd. v. Punchgini, Inc.
482 F.3d 135 (2d Cir. 2007)

RAGGI, Circuit Judge.

[1] This case requires us to decide, among other things, the applicability of the "famous marks" doctrine to a claim for unfair competition under federal and state law. Plaintiffs ITC Limited and ITC Hotels Limited (collectively "ITC") held a registered United States trademark for restaurant services: "Bukhara." They sued defendants, Punchgini, Inc., Bukhara Grill II, Inc., and certain named individuals associated with these businesses, in the United States District Court for the Southern District of New

---

[2] There are no other cases that directly guide us here. Although international trademark law has recognized both the territoriality principle and the exception for famous and well-known marks since 1925, remarkably, no case addressed meaningfully the exception before the district court's decision below. Since that decision, only one case has confronted the issue. *Empresa Cubana del Tabaca v. Culbro Corp.*, 70 U.S.P.Q.2d 1650, 2004 WL 602295 (S.D.N.Y. 2004). *Empresa Cubana* adhered closely to the reasoning and conclusion of the district court in this case. *Id.* at 1676–77.

York (Gerard E. Lynch, *Judge*) claiming that defendants' use of a similar mark and related trade dress constituted trademark infringement, unfair competition, and false advertising in violation of federal and state law. ITC now appeals from the district court's award of summary judgment in favor of defendants on all claims. *See ITC Ltd. v. Punchgini, Inc.,* 373 F.Supp.2d 275 (S.D.N.Y. 2005).

[2] Having reviewed the record *de novo*, we affirm the award of summary judgment on ITC's infringement claim, concluding, as did the district court, that ITC abandoned its Bukhara mark for restaurant services in the United States. To the extent ITC insists that the "famous marks" doctrine nevertheless permits it to sue defendants for unfair competition because its continued international use of the mark led to a federally protected right, we conclude that Congress has not yet incorporated that doctrine into federal trademark law.[2] Therefore, we affirm the award of summary judgment on ITC's federal unfair competition claim. Whether the famous marks doctrine applies to a New York common law claim for unfair competition and, if so, how famous a mark must be to trigger that application, are issues not easily resolved by reference to existing state law. Accordingly, we certify questions relating to these issues to the New York Court of Appeals, reserving our decision on this part of ITC's appeal pending the state court's response.

I. Factual Background

A. The Bukhara Restaurant in New Delhi

[3] ITC Limited is a corporation organized under the laws of India. Through its subsidiary, ITC Hotels Limited, it owns and operates the Maurya Sheraton & Towers, a five-star hotel in New Delhi, India. One of the restaurants in the Maurya Sheraton complex is "Bukhara." Named after a city in Uzbekistan on the legendary Silk Road between China and the West, Bukhara offers a cuisine and decor inspired by the northwest frontier region of India. Since its opening in 1977, the New Delhi Bukhara has remained in continuous operation, acquiring a measure of international renown.[4]

[4] Over the past three decades, ITC has sought to extend the international reach of the Bukhara brand. At various times, it has opened or, through franchise agreements, authorized Bukhara restaurants in Hong Kong, Bangkok, Bahrain, Montreal, Bangladesh, Singapore, Kathmandu, Ajman, New York, and Chicago. As of May 2004, however, ITC-owned or -authorized Bukhara restaurants were in operation only in New Delhi, Singapore, Kathmandu, and Ajman.

B. ITC's Use of the Bukhara Mark in the United States

1. ITC's Use and Registration of the Mark for Restaurants

[5] In 1986, an ITC-owned and -operated Bukhara restaurant opened in Manhattan. In 1987, ITC entered into a franchise agreement for a Bukhara restaurant in Chicago. Shortly after opening its New York restaurant, ITC sought to register the Bukhara mark with the United States Patent and Trademark Office ("Patent and Trademark Office"). On October 13, 1987, ITC obtained United States trademark registration for the Bukhara mark in connection with "restaurant services." *See* United States Trademark Registration No. 1,461,445 (Oct. 13, 1987). The Manhattan restaurant remained in operation for only five years, closing on December 17, 1991. On August 28, 1997, after a decade in business, ITC cancelled its Chicago franchise. Notwithstanding its registration, ITC concedes that it has not owned, operated, or

---

[2] Although the term "famous marks" is often used to describe marks that qualify for protection under the federal anti-dilution statute, *see* 15 U.S.C. § 1125(c), the "famous marks" doctrine is, in fact, a different and distinct "legal concept under which a trademark or service mark is protected within a nation if it is well known in that nation even though the mark is not actually used or registered in that nation," 4 J. Thomas McCarthy, *McCarthy on Trademarks and Unfair Competition,* § 29.2, at 29–164 (4th ed. 2002). Thus, the famous marks doctrine might more aptly be described as the famous foreign marks doctrine. It is in this latter sense that we reference the famous marks doctrine on this appeal.

[4] The record indicates that in 2002 and 2003, the New Delhi Bukhara was named one of the world's fifty best restaurants by London-based "Restaurant" magazine.

licensed any restaurant in the United States using the Bukhara mark since terminating the Chicago restaurant franchise.

2. Use of the Mark for Packaged Foods

[6] Over three years later, in 2001, ITC commissioned a marketing study to determine the viability of selling packaged food products in the United States under the Bukhara label, including "Dal Bukhara."[5] In that same year, ITC filed an application with the Patent and Trademark Office to register a "Dal Bukhara" mark in connection with packaged, ready-to-serve foods. In May 2003, ITC sold packaged Dal Bukhara food products to two distributors, one in California and the other in New Jersey. One month later, in June 2003, ITC exhibited Dal Bukhara products at the International Fancy Foods Show in New York City.

C. The Opening of "Bukhara Grill"

[7] Meanwhile, in 1999, named defendants Raja Jhanjee, Vicky Vij, Dhandu Ram, and Paragnesh Desai, together with Vijay Roa, incorporated "Punchgini, Inc." for the purpose of opening an Indian restaurant in New York City. Jhanjee, Vij, and Ram had all previously worked at the New Delhi Bukhara, and Vij had also previously worked at ITC's New York Bukhara. In selecting a name for their restaurant, the Punchgini shareholders purportedly considered "Far Pavilions" and "Passage to India" before settling on "Bukhara Grill." As Vij candidly acknowledged at his deposition, there was then "no restaurant Bukhara in New York, and we just thought we will take the name." Vij Dep. 25:7–11, May 5, 2004. After some initial success with "Bukhara Grill," several Punchgini shareholders, with the support of two additional partners, defendants Mahendra Singh and Bachan Rawat, organized a second corporation, "Bukhara Grill II, Inc.," in order to open a second New York restaurant, "Bukhara Grill II."

[8] When the record is viewed in the light most favorable to ITC, numerous similarities suggestive of deliberate copying can readily be identified between the defendants' Bukhara Grill restaurants and the Bukhara restaurants owned or licensed by ITC. Quite apart from the obvious similarity in name, defendants' restaurants mimic the ITC Bukharas' logos, decor, staff uniforms, wood-slab menus, and red-checkered customer bibs. Indeed, the similarities were sufficiently obvious to be noted in a press report, wherein defendant Jhanjee is quoted acknowledging that the New York Bukhara Grill restaurant "is quite like Delhi's Bukhara."

D. Plaintiffs' Cease and Desist Letter

[9] By letter dated March 22, 2000, ITC, through counsel, demanded that defendants refrain from further use of the Bukhara mark. The letter accused defendants of unlawfully appropriating the reputation and goodwill of ITC's Bukhara restaurants in India and the United States by adopting a virtually identical name for their New York Bukhara Grill restaurants. It further demanded, under threat of legal action, that defendants acknowledge ITC's exclusive rights to the Bukhara mark, disclose the period for which defendants had used the mark, and remit to ITC any profits derived therefrom.

[10] In a response dated March 30, 2000, defendants' counsel expressed an interest in avoiding litigation. Nevertheless, counsel observed that ITC appeared to have abandoned the Bukhara mark by not using it in the United States for several years. Receiving no reply, defendants' counsel sent a second letter to ITC dated June 22, 2000, stating that, if no response was forthcoming "by June 28, 2000, we will assume that ITC Limited has abandoned rights it may have had in the alleged mark and any alleged claim against our client." Marsh Letter to Horwitz, June 22, 2000. The record indicates no timely reply.

[11] Instead, almost two years later, on April 15, 2002, ITC's counsel wrote to defendants reiterating the demands made in March 2000 and complaining of defendants' failure formally to respond to that initial letter. Defendants' counsel promptly challenged the latter assertion; faulted ITC for failing to reply to his March 22, 2000 letter; and reasserted his abandonment contention, a position that he claimed was now bolstered by the passage of additional time. There was apparently no further communication among the parties until this lawsuit.

---

[5] This product takes its name from a lentil dish served at the New Delhi Bukhara restaurant.

E. The Instant Lawsuit

[12] On February 26, 2003, ITC filed the instant lawsuit. In the amended complaint that is the controlling pleading for purposes of our review, ITC charged defendants with trademark infringement under section 32(1)(a) of the Lanham Act, *see* 15 U.S.C. § 1114(1)(a), as well as unfair competition and false advertising under sections 43(a) and 44(h) of the Lanham Act, *see* 15 U.S.C. §§ 1125(a), 1126(h). ITC also pursued parallel actions under New York common law.[6] As an affirmative defense, defendants charged ITC with abandonment of its United States rights to the Bukhara mark and, on that ground, they filed a counterclaim seeking cancellation of the ITC registration.

[13] Following discovery, defendants successfully moved for summary judgment. In a detailed published decision, the district court ruled that ITC could not pursue an infringement claim because the record conclusively demonstrated its abandonment of the Bukhara mark as applied to restaurants in the United States. *See ITC Ltd. v. Punchgini, Inc.*, 373 F.Supp.2d at 285. To the extent ITC asserted that its continued operation of Bukhara restaurants outside the United States allowed it to sue defendants for unfair competition under the famous marks doctrine, the district court was not convinced. It observed that, even if it were to assume the applicability of the famous marks doctrine, ITC had failed to adduce sufficient evidence to permit a reasonable jury to conclude that the name or trade dress of its foreign restaurants had attained the requisite level of United States recognition to trigger the doctrine. *See id.* at 291. Finally, the district court found that ITC lacked standing to pursue its false advertising claim. *See id.* at 291–92. This appeal followed.

[14] Before this court, ITC advances essentially three arguments. It submits that (1) the record does not conclusively establish its abandonment of United States rights in the Bukhara mark, (2) the district court misapplied applicable federal and state law regarding the famous marks doctrine, and (3) it has standing to sue defendants for false advertising.

II. Discussion

{The court determined that ITC had abandoned its registered Bukhara mark. We will address abandonment in Part III of the casebook below.}

C. Unfair Competition

1. Federal Claim Under Section 43(a)(1)(A) of the Lanham Act

[15] ITC claims that defendants violated section 43(a)(1)(A) of the Lanham Act by engaging in unfair competition in the use of its Bukhara mark and its related trade dress. Section 43(a)(1)(A) allows the producer of a product or service to initiate a cause of action against a person who uses "any word, term name, symbol, or device, or any combination thereof . . . which . . . is likely to cause confusion . . . as to the origin, sponsorship, or approval of [the producer's] . . . services." 15 U.S.C. § 1125(a)(1)(A). This protection is broader than that afforded by section 32(1)(a), which prohibits only infringement of marks actually registered with the Patent and Trademark Office. *See Two Pesos v. Taco Cabana*, 505 U.S. 763, 768 (1992) ("Section 43(a) prohibits a broader range of practices than does § 32, which applies to registered marks, but it is common ground that § 43(a) protects qualifying unregistered trademarks" (internal citations and quotation marks omitted)); *accord Chambers v. Time Warner, Inc.*, 282 F.3d 147, 155 (2d Cir. 2002).

[16] To succeed on a section 43(a)(1)(A) claim, a plaintiff must prove (1) that the mark or dress is distinctive as to the source of the good or service at issue, and (2) that there is the likelihood of confusion between the plaintiff's good or service and that of the defendant. *See Yurman Design, Inc. v. PAJ, Inc.*, 262 F.3d 101, 115 (2d Cir. 2001) (citing *Wal–Mart Stores, Inc. v. Samara Bros.*, 529 U.S. 205, 210 (2000)); *see also Two Pesos v. Taco Cabana*, 505 U.S. at 768; *Louis Vuitton Malletier v. Dooney & Bourke, Inc.*, 454 F.3d

---

[6] ITC's amended complaint also charged defendants with false designation of origin in violation of the Lanham Act, 15 U.S.C. § 1125(a), and deceptive acts and practices in violation of New York General Business Law § 349, but it appears to have abandoned those claims in otherwise opposing defendants' motion for summary judgment. *See ITC Ltd. v. Punchgini, Inc.*, 373 F.Supp.2d at 278.

108, 115 (2d Cir. 2006). Preliminary to making this showing, however, a plaintiff must demonstrate its own right to use the mark or dress in question. . . .

[17] In light of our conclusion that, as a matter of law, ITC abandoned its registered Bukhara mark as of August 28, 2000, ITC confronts a high hurdle in demonstrating that, at the time of defendants' challenged actions, it possessed a priority right to the use of the Bukhara mark and related trade dress for restaurants in the United States. *See Vais Arms, Inc. v. Vais*, 383 F.3d at 292 n. 8 (noting that "abandonment results in a break in the chain of priority") (quoting 2 McCarthy, supra, § 17:4); *Emergency One, Inc. v. American Fire Eagle Engine Co.*, 332 F.3d 264, 268 (4th Cir. 2003) ("The priority to use a mark . . . can be lost through abandonment."). To clear this hurdle, ITC invokes the famous marks doctrine. It submits that, because (1) since 1977, it has continuously used its Bukhara mark and trade dress outside the United States; and (2) that mark was renowned in the United States before defendants opened their first Bukhara Grill restaurant in New York in 1999, it has a priority right to the mark sufficient to claim section 43(a)(1)(A) protection in this country.

[18] To explain why we disagree, we begin by discussing the principle of trademark territoriality. We then discuss the famous marks exception to this principle and the international treaties, implementing legislation, and policy concerns relied on by ITC in urging the application of this exception to this case.

a. The Territoriality Principle

[19] The principle of territoriality is basic to American trademark law. *See American Circuit Breaker Corp. v. Or. Breakers, Inc.*, 406 F.3d 577, 581 (9th Cir. 2005); *Kos Pharms., Inc. v. Andrx Corp.*, 369 F.3d 700, 714 (3d Cir. 2004); *Buti v. Impressa Perosa, S.R.L.*, 139 F.3d 98, 103 (2d Cir. 1998); *Person's Co. v. Christman*, 900 F.2d 1565, 1568–69 (Fed.Cir. 1990). As our colleague, Judge Leval, has explained, this principle recognizes that

> a trademark has a separate legal existence under each country's laws, and that its proper lawful function is not necessarily to specify the origin or manufacture of a good (although it may incidentally do that), but rather to symbolize the domestic goodwill of the domestic markholder so that the consuming public may rely with an expectation of consistency on the domestic reputation earned for the mark by its owner, and the owner of the mark may be confident that his goodwill and reputation (the value of the mark) will not be injured through use of the mark by others in domestic commerce.

Osawa & Co. v. B & H Photo, 589 F.Supp. 1163, 1171–72 (S.D.N.Y. 1984).[14]

[20] Precisely because a trademark has a separate legal existence under each country's laws, ownership of a mark in one country does not automatically confer upon the owner the exclusive right to use that mark in another country. Rather, a mark owner must take the proper steps to ensure that its rights to that mark are recognized in any country in which it seeks to assert them. Cf. *Barcelona.com, Inc. v. Excelentisimo Ayuntamiento De Barcelona*, 330 F.3d 617, 628 (4th Cir. 2003) ("United States courts do not entertain actions seeking to enforce trademark rights that exist only under foreign law."); *E. Remy Martin & Co., S.A. v. Shaw–Ross Int'l Imports, Inc.*, 756 F.2d 1525, 1531 (11th Cir. 1985) ("Our concern must be the business and goodwill attached to United States trademarks, not French trademark rights under French law." (internal quotation marks omitted)).

---

[14] The "territoriality principle" stands in contrast to the so-called "universality principle," which posits that "if a trademark [is] lawfully affixed to merchandise in one country, the merchandise would carry that mark lawfully wherever it went and could not be deemed an infringer although transported to another country where the exclusive right to the mark was held by someone other than the owner of the merchandise." *Osawa & Co. v. B & H Photo*, 589 F.Supp. at 1171. The universality principle has been rejected in American trademark law. *See American Circuit Breaker Corp. v. Or. Breakers, Inc.*, 406 F.3d at 581 (citing *A. Bourjois & Co. v. Katzel*, 260 U.S. 689 (1923)).

[21] As we have already noted, United States trademark rights are acquired by, and dependent upon, priority of use. *See supra* at 146–47. The territoriality principle requires the use to be in the United States for the owner to assert priority rights to the mark under the Lanham Act. *See Buti v. Impressa Perosa, S.R.L.,* 139 F.3d at 103 (noting that "Impressa's registration and use of the Fashion Café name in Italy has not, given the territorial nature of trademark rights, secured it any rights in the name under the Lanham Act"); *La Societe Anonyme des Parfums le Galion v. Jean Patou, Inc.,* 495 F.2d at 1271 n. 4 ("It is well-settled that foreign use is ineffectual to create trademark rights in the United States."); . . . *cf. Grupo Gigante S.A. De C.V. v. Dallo & Co.,* 391 F.3d 1088, 1093 (9th Cir. 2004) (stating general proposition that "priority of trademark rights in the United States depends solely upon priority of use in the United States, not on priority of use anywhere in the world," although recognizing famous marks doctrine as an exception to territoriality principle (quoting 4 McCarthy, *supra,* § 29:2, at 29–6)). *But see International Bancorp, LLC v. Societe des Bains de Mer et du Cercle des Etrangers a Monaco,* 329 F.3d 359, 381 (4th Cir. 2003) (concluding that United States trademark rights can be acquired merely through advertising in the United States combined with rendering of services abroad to American customers). Thus, absent some use of its mark in the United States, a foreign mark holder generally may not assert priority rights under federal law, even if a United States competitor has knowingly appropriated that mark for his own use. *See Person's Co. v. Christman,* 900 F.2d at 1569–70 (holding that foreign use is not sufficient to establish priority rights even over a United States competitor who took mark in bad faith).

b. The Famous Marks Doctrine as an Exception to the Territoriality Principle

[22] ITC urges us to recognize an exception to the territoriality principle for those foreign marks that, even if not used in the United States by their owners, have achieved a certain measure of fame within this country.

(1) Origin of the Famous Marks Doctrine

[23] The famous marks doctrine is no new concept. It originated in the 1925 addition of Article *6bis* to the Paris Convention for the Protection of Industrial Property, Mar. 20, 1883, as rev. at Stockholm, July 14, 1967, 21 U.S.T. 1583, 828 U.N.T.S. 305 ("Paris Convention"). Article *6bis,* which by its terms applies only to trademarks, requires member states

> ex officio if their legislation so permits, or at the request of an interested party, to refuse or to cancel the registration, and to prohibit the use, of a trademark which constitutes a reproduction, an imitation, or a translation, liable to create confusion, of a mark considered by the competent authority of the country of registration or use to be well known in that country as being already the mark of a person entitled to the benefits of this Convention and used for identical or similar goods. These provisions shall also apply when the essential part of the mark constitutes a reproduction of any such well-known mark or an imitation liable to create confusion therewith.

Paris Convention, art. *6bis.*[15] One commentator has observed that the "purpose" of Article *6bis* "is to avoid the registration and use of a trademark, liable to create confusion with another mark already well known in the country of such registration or use, although the latter well-known mark is not, or not yet, protected in that country by a registration which would normally prevent the registration or use of the conflicting mark." G.H.C. Bodenhausen, *Guide to the Application of the Paris Convention for the Protection of Industrial Property* 90 (1968).

---

[15] The reach of Article *6bis* was extended to service marks by Article 16(2) of the Agreement on Trade–Related Aspects of Intellectual Property Rights ("TRIPs"), *see generally* Uruguay Round Agreements Act, Pub.L. No. 103–465, 108 Stat. 4809 (1994) (codified as amended at scattered sections of the United States Code), which states that "Article *6bis* of the Paris Convention shall apply, *mutatis mutandis,* to services."

(2) The Famous Marks Doctrine in the United States

(a) State Common Law

[24] The famous marks doctrine appears first to have been recognized in the United States by a New York trial court in a common law action for unfair competition in the use of a trademark. *See Maison Prunier v. Prunier's Rest. & Café*, 159 Misc. 551, 557–58, 288 N.Y.S. 529, 535–36 (N.Y.Sup.Ct. 1936). The owner of "Maison Prunier," a Paris restaurant with a branch in London, sought to enjoin defendants' operation of a New York City restaurant named "Prunier's Restaurant and Café." The New York restaurant had apparently adopted both the Paris restaurant's name and slogan ("*Tout ce qui vient de la mer*"[16]) and boldly advertised itself as "The Famous French Sea Food Restaurant." While the French plaintiff conceded that it had never operated a restaurant in the United States, it nevertheless sought relief for the unauthorized use of its name and mark under the common law of unfair competition.

[25] In ruling in favor of the plaintiff, the trial court first observed that "the right of a French corporation to sue here for protection against unfair competition was expressly granted in [Article *10bis* of] the [Paris] convention between the United States and various other powers for the protection of industrial property." *Id.* at 554, 288 N.Y.S. at 532.[17] It then ruled that "actual competition in a product is not essential to relief under the doctrine of unfair competition." *Id.* at 555, 288 N.Y.S. at 533. The plaintiff was entitled to protection from "'any injury which might result to it from the deception of the public through the unauthorized use of its trade name, or a trade name which would lead the public to believe that it was in some way connected with the plaintiff.'" *Id.* at 556, 288 N.Y.S. at 534 (quoting *Long's Hat Stores Corp. v. Long's Clothes, Inc.*, 224 A.D. 497, 498, 231 N.Y.S. 107, 107 (1st Dep't 1928)). Although the court acknowledged the general rule of territoriality, *see id.* at 557, 288 N.Y.S. 529, 288 N.Y.S. at 535 (noting no "right to protection against the use of a trade-mark or trade name beyond the territory in which it operates"), it recognized an exception to the rule where the second user was guilty of bad faith, *see id.* at 557–58, 288 N.Y.S. at 536–37. The court identified the fame of the mark as a factor relevant to deciding whether the second user had, in good faith, made use of a mark without knowing of its prior use by another party. *See id.* at 559, 288 N.Y.S. at 537. The *Prunier* court concluded that the French plaintiff was entitled to protection against unfair competition because its trademark enjoyed "wide repute" and the facts of the case indicated a total lack of good faith on the part of the defendants. *Id.* at 559, 288 N.Y.S. at 537. The basis of this holding, it should be noted, was not Article *6bis* of the Paris Convention. Instead, the holding was based entirely on New York common law principles of unfair competition.

[26] More than twenty years later, in *Vaudable v. Montmartre, Inc.*, 20 Misc.2d 757, 193 N.Y.S.2d 332 (N.Y.Sup.Ct. 1959), another New York trial court granted a different Paris restaurant, "Maxim's," injunctive relief against a New York City restaurant that had appropriated its name, decor, and distinctive script style, all without permission. The court concluded that the lack of direct competition between the two restaurants was "immaterial" to a common law claim for unfair competition. *Id.* at 759, 193 N.Y.S.2d at 335. The only relevant question was whether "there had been a misappropriation, for the advantage of one person, of a property right belonging to another." *Id.* at 759, 193 N.Y.S.2d at 335. Noting that the Paris Maxim's had been in continuous operation since 1946, when it reopened after World War II, the court concluded that its owners had priority rights as against the junior American user by virtue of (1) their uninterrupted use of the mark abroad, and (2) the fame of the "Maxim's" mark among "the class of people residing in the cosmopolitan city of New York who dine out." *Id.* at 758, 193 N.Y.S.2d at 334.

---

[16] "Everything that comes from the sea."

[17] Article *10bis* of the Paris Convention requires member states to "assure to nationals [of other member states] effective protection against unfair competition." Paris Convention, art. *10bis*.

(b) Federal Actions

(i) Trademark Board Rulings

[27] A quarter century later, the federal Trademark Trial and Appeal Board ("Trademark Board") invoked *Vaudable's* recognition of the famous marks doctrine in several *inter partes* proceedings.[18] In *Mother's Rests., Inc. v. Mother's Other Kitchen, Inc.,* the Trademark Board stated in *dictum* that:

> [I]t is our view that prior use and advertising of a mark in connection with goods or services marketed in a foreign country (whether said advertising occurs inside or outside the United States) creates no priority rights in said mark in the United States as against one who, in good faith, has adopted the same or similar mark for the same or similar goods or services in the United States prior to the foreigner's first use of the mark on goods or services sold and/or offered in the United States at least unless it can be shown that the foreign party's mark was, at the time of the adoption and first use of a similar mark by the first user in the United States, a "famous" mark within the meaning of *Vaudable v. Montmartre, Inc.*

218 U.S.P.Q 1046, at *8 (TTAB 1983) (concluding that customers would be likely to confuse the "Mother's Pizza Parlour" trademark with the "Mother's Other Kitchen" trademark) (internal citation omitted).

[28] That same year, the Trademark Board applied the same reasoning in *All England Lawn Tennis Club, Ltd. v. Creations Aromatiques,* 220 U.S.P.Q. 1069 (1983), granting plaintiff's request to block registration of a trademark for "Wimbledon Cologne" even though plaintiff was not itself using the Wimbledon mark on any product sold in the United States. The Trademark Board observed that the Wimbledon mark had "acquired fame and notoriety as used in association with the annual championships within the meaning of Vaudable" and that "purchasers of applicant's cologne would incorrectly believe that said product was approved by or otherwise associated with the Wimbledon tennis championships and that allowance of the application would damage opposer's rights to the mark." *Id.* at *10.

[29] Recently, the Trademark Board has reiterated in dicta that owners of well known foreign marks need not use those marks in the United States to challenge the registration of marks likely to promote confusion on the part of consumers. *See, e.g., First Niagara Ins. Brokers, Inc. v. First Niagara Fin. Group, Inc.,* 77 U.S.P.Q.2d 1334, *30–31 (2005), overruled on other grounds by *First Niagara Ins. Brokers, Inc. v. First Niagara Fin. Group, Inc.,* 476 F.3d 867 (Fed.Cir. Jan. 9, 2007), 2007 U.S.App. LEXIS 367.

[30] As this court has frequently observed, Trademark Board decisions, "while not binding on courts within this Circuit, are nevertheless 'to be accorded great weight'" under general principles of administrative law requiring deference to an agency's interpretation of the statutes it is charged with administering. *Buti v. Impressa Perosa S.R.L.,* 139 F.3d at 105 (quoting *Murphy Door Bed Co. v. Interior Sleep Sys., Inc.,* 874 F.2d 95, 101 (2d Cir. 1989)); *see also In re Dr Pepper Co.,* 836 F.2d 508, 510 (Fed.Cir. 1987). In applying this principle to this case, however, we identify a significant concern: nowhere in the three cited rulings does the Trademark Board state that its recognition of the famous marks doctrine derives from any provision of the Lanham Act or other federal law. Indeed, the federal basis for the Trademark Board's recognition of the famous marks doctrine is never expressly stated. Its reliance on *Vaudable* suggests that recognition derives from state common law. At least one Trademark Board member, however, has questioned whether state common law can support recognition of the famous marks doctrine as a matter of federal law:

> [I]t seems to me that the *Vaudable* decision according protection to the famous Maxim's restaurant in the United States . . . is inapplicable in this case since that decision was based on a theory of unfair competition, namely misappropriation, under the law of the State of

---

[18] The Trademark Board's primary function is to determine whether trademarks are registerable and to conduct opposition and cancellation proceedings by which interested parties can dispute the claims of applicants and registrants. *See* 15 U.S.C. §§ 1051, 1063–64.

New York. Under Federal law, it seems to me that application of the well-known marks doctrine depends on whether the applicable text of the Paris Convention … and, in particular, Article *6bis* of that Convention, is self-executing [so as to become part of federal law].

Mother's Rests., Inc. v. Mother's Other Kitchen, Inc., 218 U.S.P.Q 1046, at *21 (Allen, concurring in part, dissenting in part) (internal citations omitted). Because we conclude that the Trademark Board's reliance on state law to recognize the famous marks doctrine falls outside the sphere to which we owe deference, we consider *de novo* the question of that doctrine's existence within federal trademark law.

(ii) Federal Case Law

[31] To date, the Ninth Circuit Court of Appeals is the only federal appeals court to have recognized the famous marks doctrine as a matter of federal law. *See Grupo Gigante S.A. De C.V. v. Dallo & Co.,* 391 F.3d at 1088; *cf. International Bancorp, LLC v. Societe des Bains de Mer et du Cercle des Estrangers a Monaco,* 329 F.3d at 389 n. 9 (Motz, J., dissenting) (noting that the famous marks doctrine has been applied so infrequently that its viability is uncertain). In *Grupo Gigante,* 391 F.3d at 1088, the Ninth Circuit considered whether the "Gigante" mark—registered and used by a large chain of grocery stores in Mexico since 1963—was sufficiently well known among Mexican–Americans in Southern California to afford it priority over a competing "Gigante" mark used by a separate chain of Los Angeles grocery stores. In resolving this question, the court ruled:

> [T]here is a famous mark exception to the territoriality principle. While the territoriality principle is a long-standing and important doctrine within trademark law, it cannot be absolute. An absolute territoriality rule without a famous-mark exception would promote consumer confusion and fraud. Commerce crosses borders. In this nation of immigrants, so do people. Trademark is, at its core, about protecting against consumer confusion and "palming off." There can be no justification for using trademark law to fool immigrants into thinking that they are buying from the store they liked back home.

Id. at 1094 (footnotes omitted).

[32] In *Grupo Gigante,* the Ninth Circuit did not reference either the language of the Lanham Act nor Article *6bis* of the Paris Convention to support recognition of the famous marks doctrine. Indeed, elsewhere in its opinion, the court specifically stated that the Paris Convention creates no "additional substantive rights" to those provided by the Lanham Act. *Id.* at 1100. The court also acknowledged that the famous marks doctrine is not recognized by California state law. *See id.* at 1101 (observing that cases cited by plaintiff "provide no support for the conclusion that use anywhere in the world suffices to establish priority in California"). Thus, it appears that the Ninth Circuit recognized the famous marks doctrine as a matter of sound policy: "An absolute territoriality rule without a famous marks exception would promote customer confusion and fraud." *Id.* at 1094.

[33] This court has twice referenced the famous marks doctrine, but on neither occasion were we required to decide whether it does, in fact, provide a legal basis for acquiring priority rights in the United States for a foreign mark not used in this country. *See Buti v. Impressa Perosa, S.R.L.,* 139 F.3d at 104 n. 2 (referencing Mother's Restaurant and Vaudable but, in the end, concluding that famous marks doctrine "has no application here given that Impressa has made no claim under that doctrine"); *see also Empresa Cubana del Tabaco v. Culbro Corp.,* 399 F.3d at 481 (declining to decide whether famous marks doctrine should be recognized because "even assuming that the famous marks doctrine is otherwise viable and applicable, the [Cuban] embargo bars [plaintiff] from acquiring property rights in the … mark through the doctrine").[19]

---

[19] In *Empresa Cubana,* however, we did observe, in *dictum,* that "[t]o the extent that a foreign entity attempts to utilize the famous marks doctrine as [a] basis for its right to a U.S. trademark and seeks to prevent another entity from using the mark in the United States, the claim should be brought under Section 43(a)." *Id.* at 480 n. 10.

. . . .

(c) Treaties Protecting Famous Marks and United States Implementing Legislation

[34] ITC insists that Article *6bis* of the Paris Convention, together with Article 16(2) of the Agreement on Trade–Related Aspects of Intellectual Property Rights ("TRIPs"), *see* Uruguay Round Agreements Act, Pub.L. No. 103–465, 108 Stat. 4809 (1994) (codified as amended at scattered sections of United States Code), provides legal support for its claim to famous marks protection. . . . Further, TRIPs Article 16(2) extends Article *6bis* to service marks, *see supra* at 156 n. 15.

[35] At the outset, we observe that ITC does not specifically contend that these two treaty articles are self-executing. While *Vanity Fair Mills v. T. Eaton Co.,* 234 F.2d 633 (2d Cir. 1956), might support such an argument with respect to Article *6bis* protection of trademarks, *see id.* at 640 (observing in *dictum* that, upon ratification by Congress, the Paris Convention required "no special legislation in the United States . . . to make [it] effective here"), no similar conclusion can extend to Article 16(2) protection of service marks because TRIPs is plainly not a self-executing treaty. *See In re Rath,* 402 F.3d 1207, 1209 n. 2 (Fed.Cir. 2005); *see also* S.Rep. No. 103–412, at 13 (1994) (accompanying the Uruguay Round Agreements Act, Pub.L. No. 103–465, 108 Stat. 4809 (1994)) (stating that TRIPs and other GATT agreements "are not self-executing and thus their legal effect in the United States is governed by implementing legislation"). While Congress has amended numerous federal statutes to implement specific provisions of the TRIPs agreement, it appears to have enacted no legislation aimed directly at Article 16(2).[23]

[36] ITC nevertheless submits that Lanham Act sections 44(b) and (h) effectively incorporate the protections afforded famous marks by the Paris Convention and TRIPs.

{In a lengthy analysis, the court concluded that §§ 44(b) & (h) do not provide a basis for famous marks protection.}

(d) Policy Rationales Cannot, by Themselves, Support Judicial Recognition of the Famous Marks Doctrine Under Federal Law

[37] Even if the Lanham Act does not specifically incorporate Article *6bis* and Article 16(2) protections for famous foreign marks, ITC urges this court to follow the Ninth Circuit's lead and to recognize the famous marks doctrine as a matter of sound policy. *See Grupo Gigante S.A. De C.V. v. Dallo & Co.,* 391 F.3d at 1094 (recognizing famous marks doctrine because "[t]here can be no justification for using trademark law to fool immigrants into thinking that they are buying from the store they liked back home"). ITC argues that the United States cannot expect other nations to protect famous American trademarks if United States courts decline to afford reciprocal protection to famous foreign marks.

[38] We acknowledge that a persuasive policy argument can be advanced in support of the famous marks doctrine. *See, e.g., De Beers LV Trademark Ltd. v. DeBeers Diamond Syndicate, Inc.,* 2005 U.S. Dist. LEXIS 9307, at *25 (noting that "[r]ecognition of the famous marks doctrine is particularly desirable in a world where international travel is commonplace and where the Internet and other media facilitate the rapid creation of business goodwill that transcends borders") . . . . The fact that a doctrine may promote sound policy, however, is not a sufficient ground for its judicial recognition, particularly in an area regulated by statute. *See, e.g., Badaracco v. Comm'r,* 464 U.S. 386, 398 (1984) ("The relevant

---

[23] *See, e.g.,* Pub.L. No. 103–465, 514, 108 Stat. 4809, 4976 (amending 17 U.S.C. § 104A, governing copyrights in restored works, to comport with TRIPs); Pub.L. No. 103–465, 532, 108 Stat. 4809, 4983 (amending 35 U.S.C. § 154, governing United States patents, to comport with TRIPs). Significantly, Congress has enacted legislation to implement TRIPs Article 16(3), which contemplates the extension of anti-dilution protection to certain famous marks. *See* Federal Trademark Dilution Act of 1995, Pub.L. No. 104–98, 109 Stat. 985 (1995) (codified at 15 U.S.C. § 1125(c)); *see* H. Rep. 104–374, reprinted in 1995 U.S.C.C.A.N. 1029 (indicating that anti-dilution act was intended to make United States law consistent with terms of TRIPs and Paris Convention). No comparable legislation exists with respect to Article 16(2).

question is not whether, as an abstract matter, the rule advocated by petitioners accords with good policy. The question we must consider is whether the policy petitioners favor is that which Congress effectuated by its enactment of [the statute]."). In light of the comprehensive and frequently modified federal statutory scheme for trademark protection set forth in the Lanham Act, we conclude that any policy arguments in favor of the famous marks doctrine must be submitted to Congress for it to determine whether and under what circumstances to accord federal recognition to such an exception to the basic principle of territoriality. *See Almacenes Exito S.A. v. El Gallo Meat Mkt., Inc.,* 381 F.Supp.2d at 326–28. Absent such Congressional recognition, we must decline ITC's invitation to grant judicial recognition to the famous marks doctrine simply as a matter of sound policy.

[39] For all these reasons, we affirm the district court's award of summary judgment in favor of defendants on ITC's federal unfair competition claim.

2. State Common Law Claim for Unfair Competition

a. ITC's Reliance on the Famous Marks Doctrine to Sue for Unfair Competition Under New York Law

[40] ITC submits that, even if we affirm the district court's dismissal of its federal unfair competition claim, we must reverse the dismissal of its parallel state law claim. As it correctly observes, New York common law allows a plaintiff to sue for unfair competition where a "property right or a commercial advantage" has been "misappropriated." *Flexitized, Inc. v. National Flexitized Corp.,* 335 F.2d 774, 781–82 (2d Cir. 1964). Nevertheless, in light of ITC's abandonment of the Bukhara mark and dress for restaurants in the United States, its common law assertion of a "property right or a commercial advantage" in these designations based on their foreign use depends on whether New York recognizes the famous marks doctrine in the circumstances here at issue.

[41] As we have already noted, at least two New York cases indicate such recognition as a general matter: *Vaudable v. Montmartre, Inc.,* 20 Misc.2d 757, 193 N.Y.S.2d 332, and *Maison Prunier v. Prunier's Rest. & Café,* 159 Misc. 551, 288 N.Y.S. 529. Neither the New York Court of Appeals nor any intermediate New York appellate court, however, has ever specifically adopted the views expressed in *Prunier* and *Vaudable* to accord common law protection to the owners of famous marks. Moreover, no New York court has clearly delineated a standard for determining when a mark becomes sufficiently famous to warrant protection. "In the absence of authoritative law from the state's highest court, we must either (1) predict how the New York Court of Appeals would resolve the state law question, or, if state law is so uncertain that we can make no reasonable prediction, (2) certify the question to the New York Court of Appeals for a definitive resolution." *DiBella v. Hopkins,* 403 F.3d 102, 111 (2d Cir. 2005). In this case, we opt for certification.

b. Certifying the Question of New York's Common Law Recognition of the Famous Marks Doctrine

(1) Standard for Certification

[42] New York law and Second Circuit Local Rule § 0.27 permit us to certify to the New York Court of Appeals "determinative questions of New York law [that] are involved in a case pending before [us] for which no controlling precedent of the Court of Appeals exists." N.Y. Comp.Codes R. & Regs. tit. 22, § 500.27(a). In deciding whether to certify a question, we consider, *inter alia,* "(1) the absence of authoritative state court interpretations of the [law in question]; (2) the importance of the issue to the state, and whether the question implicates issues of state public policy; and (3) the capacity of certification to resolve the litigation." *Morris v. Schroder Capital Mgmt. Int'l,* 445 F.3d 525, 531 (2d Cir. 2006) (internal quotation marks omitted).

(2) Certified Question 1: Does New York Recognize the Famous Marks Doctrine?

[43] In this case, we conclude that these factors weigh in favor of certifying the question of New York's recognition of the famous marks doctrine. First, the only New York cases to address the question of whether state common law recognizes the famous marks doctrine, *Vaudable* and *Prunier,* are decades-old trial court decisions. While these decisions are routinely cited by non-New York courts as accurate

statements of the state's common law of unfair competition,[28] and while commentators routinely identify the cases as foundational in the development of the famous marks doctrine,[29] the lack of authoritative adoption of the famous marks doctrine by New York's highest court weighs in favor of certification. Second, recognition of the famous marks doctrine as part of New York common law is plainly an important policy issue for a state that plays a pivotal role in international commerce. This factor strongly counsels in favor of our soliciting the views of the New York Court of Appeals. *See generally Board of Regents v. Roth*, 408 U.S. 564, 577, 92 S.Ct. 2701, 33 L.Ed.2d 548 (1972) (observing that property interests "are created and their dimensions are defined by existing rules or understandings that stem from an independent source such as state law"). Finally, certification will conclusively resolve the question of whether ITC's state unfair competition claim was, in fact, properly dismissed.

[44] Accordingly, we certify the following question to the New York Court of Appeals: "Does New York common law permit the owner of a famous mark or trade dress to assert property rights therein by virtue of the owner's prior use of the mark or dress in a foreign country?"

(3) Certified Question 2: How Famous Must a Mark Be to Come Within the Famous Marks Doctrine?

[45] If the New York Court of Appeals were to answer the first certified question in the affirmative, we ask it to consider a second query: "How famous must a foreign mark or trade dress be to permit its owner to sue for unfair competition?"[30] Although we have had no prior occasion to address this question, we note the availability of a number of possible standards.

(a) Secondary Meaning

[46] If New York were inclined to recognize a broad famous marks doctrine, the Court of Appeals might conclude that a foreign mark's acquisition of "secondary meaning" in the state was sufficient to accord it common law protection. "Secondary meaning" is a term of art referencing a trademark's ability to "'identify the source of the product rather than the product itself.'" *Two Pesos, Inc. v. Taco Cabana, Inc.*, 505 U.S. at 766 n. 4 (quoting *Inwood Labs., Inc., v. Ives Labs., Inc.*, 456 U.S. 844, 851 n. 11 (1982)); *see Allied Maint. Corp. v. Allied Mech. Trades, Inc.*, 42 N.Y.2d 538, 545 (1977) (explicating "secondary meaning" under New York law); *see also Genesee Brewing Co. v. Stroh Brewing Co.*, 124 F.3d 137, 143 n. 4 (2d Cir. 1997) (identifying factors relevant to determining secondary meaning). Under this standard, a court deciding whether to accord famous marks protection would consider only whether the source of the foreign mark is well known in New York. *See generally Grupo Gigante S.A. De C.V. v. Dallo & Co.*, 391 F.3d at 1097.

[47] The Court of Appeals might note, however, that in *Grupo Gigante* the Ninth Circuit specifically rejected "secondary meaning" as the appropriate standard for application of the famous marks doctrine. That federal court explained that such an interpretation of the famous marks doctrine went "too far" because it effectively eliminated the territoriality principle that itself "has a long history in the common law." *Id.* at 1097–98.

---

[28] See, e.g., Grupo Gigante S.A. De C.V. v. Dallo & Co., 391 F.3d at 1095; Buti v. Impressa Perosa, S.R.L., 139 F.3d at 104; Person's Co. v. Christman, 900 F.2d at 1570; Almacenes Exito S.A. v. El Gallo Meat Mkt., Inc., 381 F.Supp.2d at 328; De Beers LV Trademark Ltd. v. DeBeers Diamond Syndicate, Inc., 2005 U.S. Dist. LEXIS 9307 at *21–22.

[29] *See, e.g.,* 4 McCarthy, *supra*, § 29:4, at 29–12; Graeme B. Dinwoodie et al., *International Intellectual Property Law and Policy* 108 (2001).

[30] In formulating both certified questions, we do not intend to limit the Court of Appeals' analysis or its response. That court may expand or modify the certified questions as it deems appropriate to indicate whether state common law recognizes the famous marks doctrine and the scope of that recognition.

(b) Secondary Meaning Plus

[48] Instead, the Court of Appeals might consider the Ninth Circuit's compromise standard, which can be described as "secondary meaning plus." *See id.* at 1098 (holding that "secondary meaning is not enough"). Under this test, "where the mark has not before been used in the American market,[31] the court must be satisfied, by a preponderance of the evidence, that a *substantial* percentage of consumers in the relevant American market is familiar with the foreign mark." *Id.* (emphasis added); *see also* 4 McCarthy, *supra*, § 29:4, at 29–17 (suggesting that a "substantial" percentage of consumers in the relevant American market would be at least 50%).

[49] Judge Graber, concurring in *Grupo Gigante,* emphasized the intermediate character of this standard:

> I agree that a foreign owner of a supposedly famous or well-known foreign trademark must show a higher level of "fame" or recognition than that required to establish secondary meaning. Ultimately, the standard for famous or well-known marks is an intermediate one. To enjoy extraterritorial trademark protection, the owner of a foreign trademark need not show the level of recognition necessary to receive nation-wide protection against trademark dilution. On the other hand, the foreign trademark owner who does not use a mark in the United States must show more than the level of recognition that is necessary in a domestic trademark infringement case.

391 F.3d at 1106 (Graber, J., concurring).

(c) The Anti–Dilution Statute Standard

[50] Precisely because "secondary meaning plus" is an intermediate standard, the Court of Appeals might also consider the high standard of recognition established by section 43(c) of the Lanham Act, the federal anti-dilution statute. *See* 15 U.S.C. § 1125(c). Under that federal law, four non-exclusive factors are relevant when determining whether a mark is sufficiently famous for anti-dilution protection:

> (i) The duration, extent, and geographic reach of advertising and publicity of the mark, whether advertised or publicized by the owner or third parties;
>
> (ii) The amount, volume, and geographic extent of sales of goods or services offered under the mark;
>
> (iii) The extent of actual recognition of the mark;
>
> (iv) Whether the mark was registered under the Act of March 3, 1881, or the Act of February 20, 1905, or on the principal register.

Id. § 1125(c)(2).

[51] Under the federal anti-dilution statute, the holder of a mark deemed famous under this test may seek an injunction against another person who, "at any time after the owner's mark has become famous, commences use of a mark or trade name in commerce that is likely to cause dilution by blurring or dilution by tarnishment of the famous mark, regardless of the presence or absence of actual or likely confusion, of competition, or of actual economic injury." *Id.* § 1125(c)(1). ITC does not sue for dilution in this case. Nevertheless, the Court of Appeals might consider whether the factors set out in the statute provide a useful guide for defining famous marks generally.

(d) Recommendation of the World Intellectual Property Organization

[52] Finally, should the Court of Appeals decide to articulate an entirely new and different standard of recognition for the application of the famous marks doctrine, among the factors it might consider are those identified as relevant in the non-binding "Joint Recommendation Concerning Provisions on the Protection of Well–Known Marks," adopted by the World Intellectual Property Organization in 1999:

---

[31] New York could, of course, conclude that a "secondary meaning plus" standard also applied to a foreign mark or dress that had previously been used in the United States where, as in this case, such domestic use had been abandoned.

(1) the degree of knowledge or recognition of the mark in the relevant sector of the public;

(2) the duration, extent and geographical area of any use of the mark;

(3) the duration, extent and geographical area of any promotion of the mark, including advertising or publicity and the presentation, at fairs or exhibitions, or the goods and/or services to which the mark applies;

(4) the duration and geographical area of any registrations, and/or any application for registration, of the mark, to the extent that they reflect use or recognition of the mark;

(5) the record of successful enforcement of rights in the mark, in particular, the extent to which the mark was recognized as well known by competent authorities; [and]

(6) the value associated with the mark.

World Intellectual Property Organization, Joint Recommendation Concerning Provisions on the Protection of Well–Known Marks (Sept. 1999), *available at* http:// www. wipo. int/ about- ip/ en/ development iplaw/ pub 833.htm.

[53] We express no view as to how New York should define its state common law. We simply reserve decision on ITC's challenge to the district court's dismissal of its state common law claim for unfair competition pending the New York Court of Appeals response to our certified questions.

ITC Ltd. v. Punchgini, Inc.
880 N.E.2d 852 (N.Y. 2007)

Read, J.

. . . .

II.

Certified Question No. 1

[1] "Does New York common law permit the owner of a famous mark or trade dress to assert property rights therein by virtue of the owner's prior use of the mark or dress in a foreign country?"

[2] The Second Circuit's first certified question calls upon us to define property rights in the context of a common-law unfair competition claim grounded on a theory of misappropriation. Thus, we must consider whether a famous foreign mark constitutes property or a commercial advantage protected from unfair competition under New York law.

[3] We have long recognized two theories of common-law unfair competition: palming off and misappropriation (*see Electrolux Corp. v Val-Worth, Inc.*, 6 NY2d 556, 567-568 [1959] {discussing the acceptance of these theories of unfair competition in New York courts and collecting cases}). "Palming off"—that is, the sale of the goods of one manufacturer as those of another—was the first theory of unfair competition endorsed by New York courts, and "has been extended . . . to situations where the parties are not even in competition" (*Electrolux*, 6 NY2d at 567).

[4] After the United States Supreme Court sanctioned the misappropriation theory of unfair competition in *International News Service v Associated Press* (248 US 215 [1918]), "[t]he principle that one may not misappropriate the results of the skill, expenditures and labors of a competitor has . . . often been implemented in [New York] courts" (*Electrolux*, 6 NY2d at 567). Indeed, the New York cases cited by the District Court and the Second Circuit as embodying the famous or well-known marks doctrine in New York common law—*Prunier* and *Vaudable*—were, in fact, decided wholly on misappropriation theories.

[5] In *Prunier*, the plaintiff operated celebrated haute cuisine restaurants in Paris and London, but none in the United States. The defendants opened a restaurant in New York and

"appropriated to themselves the plaintiff's name. . . . Indeed, it was admitted . . . that the name was intentionally selected because of plaintiff's well-known reputation and good will which has been built up as the result of decades of honest business effort.

"The defendants den[ied], however, that they ever held themselves out as being Prunier's of Paris" (159 Misc at 553).

The court upheld the legal viability of an unfair competition claim by the plaintiff—even though the two restaurants were not in direct competition—so long as "plaintiff['s] conten[tion] that its reputation extends far beyond the territorial limits of Paris and London and that it has a substantial following *in New York city* and in other parts of the world" was proved (*id.* at 559 [emphasis added]).

[6] In *Vaudable*, the plaintiff's restaurant in Paris—Maxim's—was internationally famous "in the high-class restaurant field" (20 Misc 2d at 758-759). The defendants "appropriate[d] the good will plaintiffs [had] created in the name Maxim's as a restaurant," and were therefore held liable for unfair competition based on misappropriation even though the parties were "not in present actual competition" (*id.* at 759). "The trend of the law, both statutory and decisional," the court opined, "has been to extend the scope of the doctrine of unfair competition, whose basic principle is that commercial unfairness should be restrained whenever it appears that there has been a misappropriation, for the advantage of one person, of a property right belonging to another" (*id.* at 759 [citations omitted]; *see also Roy Export Co. v Columbia Broadcasting Sys.*, 672 F2d 1095, 1105 [2d Cir 1982] [with decline of general federal common law after inception of misappropriation branch of unfair competition tort in *International News Service*, "the doctrine was developed by the states, New York in particular; there it has flourished in a variety of factual settings"]).

[7] While expositors of the famous marks doctrine point to *Prunier* and *Vaudable* (*see* 5 McCarthy on Trademarks and Unfair Competition § 29:4 n 2 [4th ed 2007] [citing *Prunier* and *Vaudable* as "(p)erhaps the most famous examples" of the "well known" marks doctrine]), *Prunier* and *Vaudable* themselves in no way explain or proclaim—let alone rely on—any famous or well-known marks doctrine for their holdings. Instead, *Prunier* and *Vaudable* fit logically and squarely within our time-honored misappropriation theory, which prohibits a defendant from using a plaintiff's property right or commercial advantage—in *Prunier* and *Vaudable*, the goodwill attached to a famous name—to compete unfairly against the plaintiff in New York.

[8] Under New York law, "[a]n unfair competition claim involving misappropriation usually concerns the taking and use of the plaintiff's property to compete against the plaintiff's own use of the same property" (*Roy Export*, 672 F2d at 1105). The term "commercial advantage" has been used interchangeably with "property" within the meaning of the misappropriation theory (*see Flexitized, Inc. v National Flexitized Corp.*, 335 F2d 774, 781-782 [2d Cir 1964]). What *Prunier* and *Vaudable* stand for, then, is the proposition that for certain kinds of businesses (particularly cachet goods/services with highly mobile clienteles), goodwill can, and does, cross state and national boundary lines.

[9] Accordingly, while we answer "Yes" to the first certified question, we are not thereby recognizing the famous or well-known marks doctrine, or any other new theory of liability under the New York law of unfair competition. Instead, we simply reaffirm that when a business, through renown in New York, possesses goodwill constituting property or a commercial advantage in this state, that goodwill is protected from misappropriation under New York unfair competition law. This is so whether the business is domestic or foreign.

III.

Certified Question No. 2

[10] "How famous must a foreign mark or trade dress be to permit its owner to sue for unfair competition?"

[11] Protection from misappropriation of a famous foreign mark presupposes the existence of actual goodwill in New York (*see e.g. Roy Export*, 672 F2d at 1105 [misappropriation under New York law usually requires use in state of plaintiff's property or commercial advantage to compete against plaintiff]). If a foreign plaintiff has no goodwill in this state to appropriate, there can be no viable claim

for unfair competition under a theory of misappropriation. At the very least, a plaintiff's mark, when used in New York, must call to mind its goodwill. Otherwise, a plaintiff's property right or commercial advantage based on the goodwill associated with its mark is not appropriated in this state when its unregistered mark is used here. Thus, at a minimum, consumers of the good or service provided under a certain mark by a defendant in New York must primarily associate the mark with the foreign plaintiff (*cf. Allied Maintenance Corp. v Allied Mech. Trades*, 42 NY2d 538, 545 [1977]).

[12] Whether consumers of a defendant's goods or services primarily associate such goods or services with those provided by a foreign plaintiff is an inquiry that will, of necessity, vary with the facts of each case. Accordingly, we cannot—and do not—provide an exhaustive list of the factors relevant to such an inquiry. That said, some factors that would be relevant include evidence that the defendant intentionally associated its goods with those of the foreign plaintiff in the minds of the public, such as public statements or advertising stating or implying a connection with the foreign plaintiff; direct evidence, such as consumer surveys, indicating that consumers of defendant's goods or services believe them to be associated with the plaintiff; and evidence of actual overlap between customers of the New York defendant and the foreign plaintiff.

[13] If the customers of a New York defendant do not identify a mark with the foreign plaintiff, then no use is being made of the plaintiff's goodwill, and no cause of action lies under New York common law for unfair competition. As a result, to prevail against defendants on an unfair competition theory under New York law, ITC would have to show first, as an independent prerequisite, that defendants appropriated (i.e., deliberately copied), ITC's Bukhara mark or dress for their New York restaurants. If they successfully make this showing, plaintiffs would then have to establish that the relevant consumer market for New York's Bukhara restaurant primarily associates the Bukhara mark or dress with those Bukhara restaurants owned and operated by ITC.

[14] Accordingly, the certified questions should be answered in accordance with this opinion.

Comments and Questions

1. *The final disposition of* ITC v. Punchgini. The case returned to the Second Circuit, which affirmed the district court's initial grant of summary judgment to the defendant on the ground, among others, that BUKARA for restaurant services had no secondary meaning in New York. *ITC Ltd. v. Punchgini, Inc.*, 518 F.3d 159 (2d Cir. 2008), *aff'g* 373 F.Supp.2d 275 (S.D.N.Y. 2005).

2. *"Well-known marks doctrine" or "famous marks doctrine"?* In a footnote in a portion of the New York Court of Appeals opinion not included in the excerpt above, the court addressed the terminological ambiguity over the correct name of the doctrine at issue:

> There is some ambiguity regarding the proper name for what has been variously called the "famous marks doctrine," the "well-known marks doctrine" and the "famous mark doctrine" (*see e.g.* 5 McCarthy on Trademarks and Unfair Competition § 29:4 [4th ed 2007] [using the above names interchangeably]). Apparently, the use of "well-known" in place of "famous" took hold after the Lanham Act was amended by passage of the Federal Trademark Anti-Dilution Act of 2006, which uses "famous" as a term of art (*see* 15 USC § 1125 [c]). At any rate, "famous" and "well-known," "mark" and "marks," have been used interchangeably to describe the putative doctrine, and no distinction is intended by our choice of words here.

ITC Ltd. v. Punchgini, Inc., 880 N.E.2d 852, 856 n.1 (N.Y. 2007).

c. *Belmora* and the End of Territorial Limits on Trademark Rights?

As stated above, the Fourth Circuit's opinion in *Belmora LLC v. Bayer Consumer Care AG*, 819 F.3d 697 (4th Cir. 2016), *cert. denied*, 137 S. Ct. 1202, (U.S. 2017), represents a significant break with much of our traditional understanding of the national limits of trademark rights and with the requirement that a plaintiff use a mark in commerce in the U.S. (or otherwise own a mark that qualifies as a well-known mark in the U.S.) in order to assert exclusive rights in the mark.

Two noteworthy cases form the basis of *Belmora*. The first is *International Bancorp, LLC v. Societe des Bains de Mer et du Cercle des Estrangers a Monaco*, 329 F.3d 359 (4th Cir. 2003). The mark at issue was CASINO DE MONTE CARLO. The declaratory plaintiffs operated various websites whose domain names and content incorporated at least "some portion", *id.* at 361, of the term CASINO DE MONTE CARLO and various images of the declaratory defendant's casino in Monte Carlo, which has operated under the CASINO DE MONTE CARLO mark since 1863. The defendant advertised its casino in the U.S. but rendered its services only abroad. In a controversial opinion, the Fourth Circuit found infringement. Judge Luttig reasoned, in short, that the defendant had shown "use in commerce" because (1) U.S. consumers' purchase of casino services from the defendant constituted trade with a foreign nation that Congress was empowered to regulate, and (2) the defendant's advertising of its mark in the U.S. had made the mark distinctive as a designation of source in the U.S. In a thorough and well-reasoned opinion, Judge Motz dissented. *Id.* at 383-398 (Motz, J., dissenting).

The second is *Lexmark International, Inc. v. Static Control Components, Inc.*, 134 S. Ct. 1377 (2014). Static Control Components (SCC) produced components that various companies employed in the remanufacture and refurbishing of used toner cartridges for Lexmark printers. Such remanufacturers were significantly disrupting Lexmark's own sales of replacement toner cartridges for its printers. SCC alleged that Lexmark engaged in false advertising (1) by informing certain Lexmark toner cartridge end-users that they were contractually required to return used cartridges to Lexmark and (2) by informing remanufacturing companies that it was illegal to refurbish certain Lexmark toner cartridges and to use SCC's components in doing so. *Id.* at 1384-85. The district court granted Lexmark's motion to dismiss on the ground that SCC lacked standing. *Id.* at 1385. The Sixth Circuit reversed. *Id.* As explained in *Belmora*, the Supreme Court clarified in *Lexmark* what the plaintiff must show to have standing to sue for false advertising.

Two final notes: First, the *Belmora* opinion makes no reference whatsoever to the well-known marks doctrine. As you will see, *Belmora*'s facts cry out for application of the doctrine. But early on in the litigation, the TTAB determined that Article 6bis of the Paris Convention "do[es] not afford an independent cause of action for parties in Board proceedings," nor does any section of the Lanham Act establish such a cause of action. *Bayer Consumer Care AG v. Belmora LLC*, 90 U.S.P.Q.2d 1587, 2009 WL 962811, *5 (TTAB 2009).

Second, *Meenaxi Enterprise, Inc. v. Coca-Cola Company*, 38 F.4th 1067 (Fed. Cir. 2022) engages facts and arguments comparable to those in *Belmora*. Students wishing to dig deeper into the implications—and limits—of the *Belmora* decision should begin with *Meenaxi*.

Belmora LLC v. Bayer Consumer Care AG
819 F.3d 697 (4th Cir. 2016), *cert. denied*, 137 S. Ct. 1202 (2017)

AGEE, Circuit Judge:

[1] In this unfair competition case, we consider whether the Lanham Act permits the owner of a foreign trademark and its sister company to pursue false association, false advertising, and trademark cancellation claims against the owner of the same mark in the United States. Bayer Consumer Care AG ("BCC") owns the trademark "FLANAX" in Mexico and has sold naproxen sodium pain relievers under that mark in Mexico (and other parts of Latin America) since the 1970s. Belmora LLC owns the FLANAX trademark in the United States and has used it here since 2004 in the sale of its naproxen sodium pain relievers. BCC and its U.S. sister company Bayer Healthcare LLC ("BHC," and collectively with BCC, "Bayer") contend that Belmora used the FLANAX mark to deliberately deceive Mexican–American consumers into thinking they were purchasing BCC's product.

[2] BCC successfully petitioned the U.S. Trademark Trial and Appeal Board ("TTAB") to cancel Belmora's registration for the FLANAX mark based on deceptive use. Belmora appealed the TTAB's decision to the district court. In the meantime, BCC filed a separate complaint for false association against Belmora under § 43 of the Lanham Act, 15 U.S.C. § 1125, and in conjunction with BHC, a claim for false advertising. After the two cases were consolidated, the district court reversed the TTAB's cancellation order and dismissed the false association and false advertising claims.

[3] Bayer appeals those decisions. For the reasons outlined below, we vacate the judgment of the district court and remand this case for further proceedings consistent with this opinion.

I. Background

[4] This appeal comes to us following the district court's grant of Belmora's Federal Rule of Civil Procedure 12(b)(6) motion to dismiss Bayer's complaint and Belmora's Rule 12(c) motion for judgment on the pleadings on the trademark cancellation claim. . . .

A. The FLANAX Mark

[5] BCC registered the trademark FLANAX in Mexico for pharmaceutical products, analgesics, and anti-inflammatories. It has sold naproxen sodium tablets under the FLANAX brand in Mexico since 1976. FLANAX sales by BCC have totaled hundreds of millions of dollars, with a portion of the sales occurring in Mexican cities near the United States border. BCC's FLANAX brand is well-known in Mexico and other Latin American countries, as well as to Mexican–Americans and other Hispanics in the United States, but BCC has never marketed or sold its FLANAX in the United States. Instead, BCC's sister company, BHC, sells naproxen sodium pain relievers under the brand ALEVE in the United States market.

[6] Belmora LLC began selling naproxen sodium tablets in the United States as FLANAX in 2004. The following year, Belmora registered the FLANAX mark in the United States. Belmora's early FLANAX packaging (below, left) closely mimicked BCC's Mexican FLANAX packaging (right), displaying a similar color scheme, font size, and typeface.

Belmora later modified its packaging (below), but the color scheme, font size, and typeface remain similar to that of BCC's FLANAX packaging.

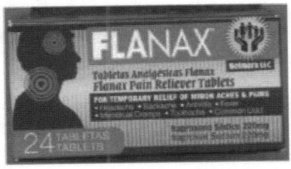

[7] In addition to using similar packaging, Belmora made statements implying that its FLANAX brand was the same FLANAX product sold by BCC in Mexico. For example, Belmora circulated a brochure to prospective distributors that stated,

> For generations, Flanax has been a brand that Latinos have turned to for various common ailments. Now you too can profit from this highly recognized topselling brand among Latinos. Flanax is now made in the U.S. and continues to show record sales growth everywhere it is sold. Flanax acts as a powerful attraction for Latinos by providing them with products they know, trust and prefer.

Belmora also employed telemarketers and provided them with a script containing similar statements. This sales script stated that Belmora was "the direct producers of FLANAX in the US" and that "FLANAX is a very well known medical product in the Latino American market, for FLANAX is sold successfully in Mexico." Belmora's "sell sheet," used to solicit orders from retailers, likewise claimed that "Flanax products have been used [for] many, many years in Mexico" and are "now being produced in the United States by Belmora LLC."

[8] Bayer points to evidence that these and similar materials resulted in Belmora's distributors, vendors, and marketers believing that its FLANAX was the same as or affiliated with BCC's FLANAX. For instance, Belmora received questions regarding whether it was legal for FLANAX to have been imported from Mexico. And an investigation of stores selling Belmora's FLANAX "identified at least 30 [purchasers] who believed that the Flanax products ... were the same as, or affiliated with, the Flanax products they knew from Mexico."

B. Proceedings Below

1.

[9] In 2007, BCC petitioned the TTAB to cancel Belmora's registration for the FLANAX mark, arguing that Belmora's use and registration of the FLANAX mark violated Article 6bis of the Paris Convention "as made applicable by Sections 44(b) and (h) of the Lanham Act." BCC also sought cancellation of Belmora's registration under § 14(3) of the Lanham Act because Belmora had used the FLANAX mark "to misrepresent the source of the goods ... [on] which the mark is used." Lanham Act § 14(3), 15 U.S.C. § 1064(3).

[10] The TTAB dismissed BCC's Article 6bis claim, concluding that Article 6bis "is not self-executing" and that § 44 of the Lanham Act did not provide "an independent basis for cancellation." However, the TTAB allowed Bayer's § 14(3) claim to proceed. In 2014, after discovery and a hearing, the TTAB ordered cancellation of Belmora's FLANAX registration, concluding that Belmora had misrepresented the source of the FLANAX goods and that the facts "d[id] not present a close case." The TTAB noted that Belmora 1) knew the favorable reputation of Bayer's FLANAX product, 2) "copied" Bayer's packaging, and 3) "repeatedly invoked" that reputation when marketing its product in the United States.

2.

[11] Shortly after the TTAB's ruling, Bayer filed suit in the Southern District of California, alleging that 1) BCC was injured by Belmora's false association with its FLANAX product in violation of Lanham Act § 43(a)(1)(A), and 2) BCC and BHC were both injured by Belmora's false advertising of FLANAX under § 43(a)(1)(B). The complaint also alleged three claims under California state law.

[12] Belmora meanwhile appealed the TTAB's cancellation order and elected to proceed with the appeal as a civil action in the Eastern District of Virginia. It argued that the TTAB erred in concluding that Bayer "had standing and/or a cause of action" under § 14(3) and in finding that Belmora had misrepresented the source of its goods. Belmora also sought a declaration that its actions had not violated the false association and false advertising provisions of Lanham Act § 43(a), as Bayer had alleged in the California district court proceeding. Bayer filed a counterclaim challenging the TTAB's dismissal of its Paris Convention treaty claims.

[13] The California case was transferred to the Eastern District of Virginia and consolidated with Belmora's pending action. Belmora then moved the district court to dismiss Bayer's § 43(a) claims under Rule 12(b)(6) and for judgment on the pleadings under Rule 12(c) on the § 14(3) claim. On February 6, 2015, after two hearings, the district court issued a memorandum opinion and order ruling in favor of Belmora across the board.

[14] The district court acknowledged that "Belmora's FLANAX ... has a similar trade dress to Bayer's FLANAX and is marketed in such a way that capitalizes on the goodwill of Bayer's FLANAX." It nonetheless "distilled" the case "into one single question":

> Does the Lanham Act allow the owner of a foreign mark that is not registered in the United
> States and further has never used the mark in United States commerce to assert priority

310

rights over a mark that is registered in the United States by another party and used in United States commerce?

The district court concluded that "[t]he answer is no" based on its reading of the Supreme Court's decision in *Lexmark International, Inc. v. Static Control Components, Inc.*, 134 S.Ct. 1377 (2014). Accordingly, the district court dismissed Bayer's false association and false advertising claims for lack of standing. At the same time, it reversed the TTAB's § 14(3) cancellation order.

[15] Bayer filed a timely notice of appeal, and we have jurisdiction under 28 U.S.C. § 1291. The U.S. Patent and Trademark Office ("USPTO") intervened to defend the TTAB's decision to cancel Belmora's registration and to argue that the Lanham Act conforms to the United States' commitments in Article 6bis of the Paris Convention.[3]

II. Discussion

[16] We review de novo the district court's decision to dismiss a proceeding under Rules 12(b)(6) and 12(c), accepting as true all well-pleaded allegations in the plaintiff's complaint and drawing all reasonable factual inferences in the plaintiff's favor. . . .

A. False Association and False Advertising Under Section 43(a)

[17] The district court dismissed Bayer's false association[4] and false advertising claims because, in its view, the claims failed to satisfy the standards set forth by the Supreme Court in *Lexmark*. At the core of the district court's decision was its conclusion that 1) Bayer's claims fell outside the Lanham Act's "zone of interests"—and are not cognizable—"because Bayer does not possess a protectable interest in the FLANAX mark in the United States," and 2) that a "cognizable economic loss under the Lanham Act" cannot exist as to a "mark that was not used in United States commerce."

[18] On appeal, Bayer contends these conclusions are erroneous as a matter of law because they conflict with the plain language of § 43(a) and misread *Lexmark*.

1.

[19] "While much of the Lanham Act addresses the registration, use, and infringement of trademarks and related marks, § 43(a) . . . goes beyond trademark protection." *Dastar Corp. v. Twentieth Century Fox Film Corp.*, 539 U.S. 23, 28–29 (2003). Written in terms of the putative defendant's conduct, § 43(a) sets forth unfair competition causes of action for false association and false advertising:

> Any person who, on or in connection with any goods or services, or any container for goods, uses in commerce any word, term, name, symbol, or device, or any combination thereof, or any false designation of origin, false or misleading description of fact, or false or misleading representation of fact, which—
>
> (A) [False Association:] is likely to cause confusion, or to cause mistake, or to deceive as to the affiliation, connection, or association of such person with another person, or as to the origin, sponsorship, or approval of his or her goods, services, or commercial activities by another person, or
>
> (B) [False Advertising:] in commercial advertising or promotion, misrepresents the nature, characteristics, qualities, or geographic origin of his or her or another person's goods, services, or commercial activities,

---

[3] The district court had agreed with the TTAB that Article 6bis does not create an independent cause of action for the cancellation of Belmora's FLANAX registration. Because Bayer appears to have abandoned its treaty claims on appeal and their resolution is not necessary to our decision, we do not address any issue regarding the Paris Convention arguments.

[4] As the district court pointed out, we have sometimes denominated Lanham Act § 43(a)(1)(A) claims as "false designation" claims. We think it preferable to follow the Supreme Court's terminology in *Lexmark* and instead refer to such claims as those of "false association," although the terms can often be used interchangeably.

311

shall be liable in a civil action by any person who believes that he or she is or is likely to be damaged by such act.

Lanham Act § 43(a)(1), 15 U.S.C. § 1125(a)(1). Subsection A, which creates liability for statements as to "affiliation, connection, or association" of goods, describes the cause of action known as "false association." Subsection B, which creates liability for "misrepresent[ing] the nature, characteristics, qualities, or geographic origin" of goods, defines the cause of action for "false advertising."

[20] Significantly, the plain language of § 43(a) does not require that a plaintiff possess or have used a trademark in U.S. commerce as an element of the cause of action. Section 43(a) stands in sharp contrast to Lanham Act § 32, which is titled as and expressly addresses "infringement." 15 U.S.C. § 1114 (requiring for liability the "use in commerce" of "any reproduction, counterfeit, copy, or colorable imitation *of a registered mark* " (emphasis added)). Under § 43(a), it is the defendant's use in commerce—whether of an offending "word, term, name, symbol, or device" or of a "false or misleading description [or representation] of fact"—that creates the injury under the terms of the statute. And here the alleged offending "word, term, name, symbol, or device" is Belmora's FLANAX mark.

[21] What § 43(a) does require is that Bayer was "likely to be damaged" by Belmora's "use[ ] in commerce" of its FLANAX mark and related advertisements. The Supreme Court recently considered the breadth of this "likely to be damaged" language in *Lexmark,* a false advertising case arising from a dispute in the used-printer-cartridge market. 134 S.Ct. at 1383, 1388. The lower courts in *Lexmark* had analyzed the case in terms of "prudential standing"—that is, on grounds that are "prudential" rather than constitutional. *Id.* at 1386. The Supreme Court, however, observed that the real question in *Lexmark* was "whether Static Control has a cause of action under the statute." *Id.* at 1387. This query, in turn, hinged on "a straightforward question of statutory interpretation" to which it applied "traditional principles" of interpretation. *Id.* at 1388. As a threshold matter, the Supreme Court noted that courts must be careful not to import requirements into this analysis that Congress has not included in the statute:

> We do not ask whether in our judgment Congress *should* have authorized Static Control's suit, but whether Congress in fact did so. Just as a court cannot apply its independent policy judgment to recognize a cause of action that Congress has denied, it cannot limit a cause of action that Congress has created merely because 'prudence' dictates.

Id. The Court concluded that § 43(a)'s broad authorization—permitting suit by "any person who believes that he or she is or is likely to be damaged"—should not be taken "literally" to reach the limits of Article III standing, but is framed by two "background principles," which may overlap. *Id.*

[22] First, a plaintiff's claim must fall within the "zone of interests" protected by the statute. *Id.* The scope of the zone of interests is not "especially demanding," and the plaintiff receives the "benefit of any doubt." *Id.* at 1389. Because the Lanham Act contains an "unusual, and extraordinarily helpful" purpose statement in § 45, identifying the statute's zone of interests "requires no guesswork." *Id.* Section 45 provides:

> The intent of this chapter is to regulate commerce within the control of Congress by making actionable the deceptive and misleading use of marks in such commerce; to protect registered marks used in such commerce from interference by State, or territorial legislation; to protect persons engaged in such commerce against unfair competition; to prevent fraud and deception in such commerce by the use of reproductions, copies, counterfeits, or colorable imitations of registered marks; and to provide rights and remedies stipulated by treaties and conventions respecting trademarks, trade names, and unfair competition entered into between the United States and foreign nations.

Lanham Act § 45, 15 U.S.C. § 1127.[5]

---

[5] In the same section, the Lanham Act defines "commerce" as "all commerce which may lawfully be regulated by Congress." Lanham Act § 45, 15 U.S.C. § 1127. We have previously construed this phrase to

[23] The Supreme Court observed that "[m]ost of the enumerated purposes are relevant to a false-association case," while "a typical false-advertising case will implicate only the Act's goal of 'protecting persons engaged in commerce within the control of Congress against unfair competition.'" *Lexmark*, 134 S.Ct. at 1389. The Court concluded "that to come within the zone of interests in a suit for false advertising under [§ 43(a)], a plaintiff must allege an injury to a commercial interest in reputation or sales." *Id.* at 1390.

[24] The second *Lexmark* background principle is that "a statutory cause of action is limited to plaintiffs whose injuries are proximately caused by violations of the statute." *Id.* The injury must have a "sufficiently close connection to the conduct the statute prohibits." *Id.* In the § 43(a) context, this means "show[ing] economic or reputational injury flowing directly from the deception wrought by the defendant's advertising; and that that occurs when deception of consumers causes them to withhold trade from the plaintiff." *Id.* at 1391.

[25] The primary lesson from *Lexmark* is clear: courts must interpret the Lanham Act according to what the statute says. To determine whether a plaintiff, "falls within the class of plaintiffs whom Congress has authorized to sue," we "apply traditional principles of statutory interpretation." *Id.* at 1387. The outcome will rise and fall on the "meaning of the congressionally enacted provision creating a cause of action." *Id.* at 1388.

[26] We now turn to apply these principles to the case before us.

2.

a.

[27] We first address the position, pressed by Belmora and adopted by the district court, that a plaintiff must have initially used its own mark in commerce within the United States as a condition precedent to a § 43(a) claim. In dismissing BCC's § 43(a) claims, the district court found dispositive that "Bayer failed to plead facts showing that it used the FLANAX mark in commerce in [the] United States." Upon that ground, the district court held "that Bayer does not possess a protectable interest in the [FLANAX] mark."

[28] As noted earlier, such a requirement is absent from § 43(a)'s plain language and its application in *Lexmark*. Under the statute, the *defendant* must have "use[d] in commerce" the offending "word, term, name, [or] symbol," but the *plaintiff* need only "believe[ ] that he or she is or is likely to be damaged by such act." Lanham Act § 43(a), 15 U.S.C. § 1125(a).

[29] It is important to emphasize that this is an unfair competition case, not a trademark infringement case. Belmora and the district court conflated the Lanham Act's infringement provision in § 32 (which authorizes suit only "by the registrant," and thereby requires the plaintiff to have used its own mark in commerce) with unfair competition claims pled in this case under § 43(a). Section 32 makes clear that Congress knew how to write a precondition of trademark possession and use into a Lanham Act cause of action when it chose to do so. It has not done so in § 43(a). *See Russello v. United States*, 464 U.S. 16, 23 (1983) ("[W]here Congress includes particular language in one section of a statute but omits it in another section of the same Act, it is generally presumed that Congress acts intentionally and purposely in the disparate inclusion or exclusion.").

[30] Given that *Lexmark* advises courts to adhere to the statutory language, "apply[ing] traditional principles of statutory interpretation," *Lexmark*, 134 S.Ct. at 1388, we lack authority to introduce a requirement into § 43(a) that Congress plainly omitted. Nothing in *Lexmark* can be read to suggest that

---

mean that the term is "coterminous with that commerce that Congress may regulate under the Commerce Clause of the United States Constitution." *Int'l Bancorp, LLC v. Societe des Bains de Mer et du Cercle des Etrangers a Monaco*, 329 F.3d 359, 363–64 (4th Cir. 2003). "Commerce" in Lanham Act context is therefore an expansive concept that "necessarily includes all the explicitly identified variants of interstate commerce, foreign trade, and Indian commerce." *Id.* at 364 (citing U.S. Const. art. I, § 8, cl. 3); *see also infra* n. 6.

§ 43(a) claims have an unstated requirement that the plaintiff have first used its own mark (word, term, name, symbol, or device) in U.S. commerce before a cause of action will lie against a defendant who is breaching the statute.

[31] The district court thus erred in requiring Bayer, as the plaintiff, to have pled its prior use of its own mark in U.S. commerce when it is the defendant's use of a mark or misrepresentation that underlies the § 43(a) unfair competition cause of action. Having made this foundational error, the district court's resolution of the issues requires reversal.[6]

[32] Admittedly, some of our prior cases appear to have treated a plaintiff's use of a mark in United States commerce as a prerequisite for a false association claim. *See Lamparello v. Falwell,* 420 F.3d 309, 313 (4th Cir. 2005) ("Both infringement [under § 32] and false designation of origin [under § 43(a)] have [the same] five elements."); *People for the Ethical Treatment of Animals v. Doughney,* 263 F.3d 359, 364 (4th Cir. 2001) (same); *Int'l Bancorp,* 329 F.3d at 361 n. 2 ("[T]he tests for trademark infringement and unfair competition . . . are identical."); *Lone Star Steakhouse & Saloon v. Alpha of Va., Inc.,* 43 F.3d 922, 930 (4th Cir. 1995) ("[T]o prevail under §§ 32(1) and 43(a) of the Lanham Act for trademark infringement and unfair competition, respectively, a complainant must demonstrate that it has a valid, protectible trademark[.]"). However, none of these cases made that consideration the *ratio decidendi* of its holding or analyzed whether the statute in fact contains such a requirement. *See, e.g.,* 5 J. Thomas McCarthy, Trademarks and Unfair Competition § 29:4 (4th ed. 2002) (observing that *International Bancorp* merely "assumed that to trigger Lanham Act § 43(a), the plaintiff's mark must be 'used in commerce'"). Moreover, all of these cases predate *Lexmark,* which provides the applicable Supreme Court precedent interpreting § 43(a). *See U.S. Dep't of Health & Human Servs. v. Fed. Labor Relations Auth.,* 983 F.2d 578, 581 (4th Cir. 1992) ("A decision by a panel of this court, or by the court sitting en banc, does not bind subsequent panels if the decision rests on authority that subsequently proves untenable.").

[33] Although the plaintiffs' use of a mark in U.S. commerce was a fact in common in the foregoing cases, substantial precedent reflects that § 43(a) unfair competition claims come within the statute's protectable zone of interests without the preconditions adopted by the district court and advanced by Belmora. As the Supreme Court has pointed out, § 43(a) "goes beyond trademark protection." *Dastar Corp.,* 539 U.S. at 29. For example, a plaintiff whose mark has become generic—and therefore not protectable—may plead an unfair competition claim against a competitor that uses that generic name and "fail[s] adequately to identify itself as distinct from the first organization" such that the name causes "confusion or a likelihood of confusion." *Blinded Veterans Ass'n v. Blinded Am. Veterans Found.,* 872 F.2d 1035, 1043 (D.C.Cir. 1989); *see also Kellogg Co. v. Nat'l Biscuit Co.,* 305 U.S. 111, 118–19 (1938) (requiring the defendant to "use reasonable care to inform the public of the source of its product" even though the plaintiff's "shredded wheat" mark was generic and therefore unprotectable); *Singer Mfg. Co. v. June Mfg. Co.,* 163 U.S. 169, 203–04 (1896) (same, for "Singer" sewing machines).

---

[6] Even though the district court's error in transposing § 43(a)'s requirements for a defendant's actions upon the plaintiff skews the entire analysis, the district court also confused the issues by ill-defining the economic location of the requisite unfair competition acts. As noted earlier, *supra* n. 5, a defendant's false association or false advertising conduct under § 43(a) must occur in "commerce within the control of Congress." Such commerce is not limited to purchases and sales within the territorial limits of the United States as the district court seems to imply at times with regard to § 43(a) and § 14(3) claims. *See* J.A. 483, 506 (as to § 14(3), stating that "Bayer did not use the FLANAX mark in the United States"); J.A. 487 (as to § 43(a), stating that "Bayer failed to plead facts showing that it used the FLANAX mark in commerce in [the] United States"). Instead, as we explained in *International Bancorp,* Lanham Act "commerce" includes, among other things, "foreign trade" and is not limited to transactions solely within the borders of the United States. *Int'l Bancorp,* 329 F.3d at 364. Of course, any such "foreign trade" must satisfy the *Lexmark* "zone of interests" and "proximate cause" requirements to be cognizable for Lanham Act purposes.

[34] Likewise, in a "reverse passing off" case, the plaintiff need not have used a mark in commerce to bring a § 43(a) action.[7] A reverse-passing-off plaintiff must prove four elements: "(1) that the work at issue originated with the plaintiff; (2) that origin of the work was falsely designated by the defendant; (3) that the false designation of origin was likely to cause consumer confusion; and (4) that the plaintiff was harmed by the defendant's false designation of origin." *Universal Furniture Int'l, Inc. v. Collezione Europa USA, Inc.,* 618 F.3d 417, 438 (4th Cir. 2010). Thus, the plaintiff in a reverse passing off case must plead and prove only that the work "originated with" him—not that he used the work (which may or may not be associated with a mark) in U.S. commerce. *Id.*

[35] The generic mark and reverse passing off cases illustrate that § 43(a) actions do not require, implicitly or otherwise, that a plaintiff have first used its own mark in United States commerce. If such a use were a condition precedent to bringing a § 43(a) action, the generic mark and reverse passing off cases could not exist.

[36] In sum, the Lanham Act's plain language contains no unstated requirement that a § 43(a) plaintiff have used a U.S. trademark in U.S. commerce to bring a Lanham Act unfair competition claim. The Supreme Court's guidance in *Lexmark* does not allude to one, and our prior cases either only assumed or articulated as dicta that such a requirement existed. Thus, the district court erred in imposing such a condition precedent upon Bayer's claims.[8]

[37] As Bayer is not barred from making a § 43(a) claim, the proper *Lexmark* inquiry is twofold. Did the alleged acts of unfair competition fall within the Lanham Act's protected zone of interests? And if so, did Bayer plead proximate causation of a cognizable injury? We examine the false association and false advertising claims in turn.

b.

i.

[38] As to the zone of interests, *Lexmark* advises that "[m]ost of the [Lanham Act's] enumerated purposes are relevant to false-association cases." 134 S.Ct. at 1389. One such enumerated purpose is "making actionable the deceptive and misleading use of marks" in "commerce within the control of Congress." Lanham Act § 45, 15 U.S.C. § 1127; *see also Two Pesos, Inc. v. Taco Cabana, Inc.,* 505 U.S. 763, 784 n. 19 (1992) (Stevens, J., concurring) ("Trademark law protects the public by making consumers confident that they can identify brands they prefer and can purchase those brands without being confused or misled."). As pled, BCC's false association claim advances that purpose.

[39] The complaint alleges Belmora's misleading association with BCC's FLANAX has caused BCC customers to buy the Belmora FLANAX in the United States instead of purchasing BCC's FLANAX in

---

[7] Reverse passing off occurs when a "producer misrepresents someone else's goods or services as his own," in other words, when the defendant is selling the plaintiff's goods and passing them off as originating with the defendant. *Universal Furniture Int'l, Inc. v. Collezione Europa USA, Inc.,* 618 F.3d 417, 438 (4th Cir. 2010) (quoting *Dastar Corp.,* 539 U.S. at 28 n. 1).

[8] A plaintiff who relies only on foreign commercial activity may face difficulty proving a cognizable false association injury under § 43(a). A few isolated consumers who confuse a mark with one seen abroad, based only on the presence of the mark on a product in this country and not other misleading conduct by the mark holder, would rarely seem to have a viable § 43(a) claim.

The story is different when a defendant, as alleged here, has—as a cornerstone of its business—intentionally passed off its goods in the United States as the same product commercially available in foreign markets in order to influence purchases by American consumers. *See M. Kramer Mfg. Co. v. Andrews,* 783 F.2d 421, 448 (4th Cir. 1986) ("[E]vidence of intentional, direct copying establishes a prima facie case of secondary meaning sufficient to shift the burden of persuasion to the defendant on that issue."). Such an intentional deception can go a long way toward establishing likelihood of confusion. *See Blinded Veterans,* 872 F.2d at 1045 ("Intent to deceive … retains potency; when present, it is probative evidence of a likelihood of confusion.").

Mexico. For example, the complaint alleges that BCC invested heavily in promoting its FLANAX to Mexican citizens or Mexican–Americans in border areas. Those consumers cross into the United States and may purchase Belmora FLANAX here before returning to Mexico. And Mexican–Americans may forego purchasing the FLANAX they know when they cross the border to visit Mexico because Belmora's alleged deception led them to purchase the Belmora product in the United States.

[40] In either circumstance, BCC loses sales revenue because Belmora's deceptive and misleading use of FLANAX conveys to consumers a false association with BCC's product. Further, by also deceiving distributors and vendors, Belmora makes its FLANAX more available to consumers, which would exacerbate BCC's losses.... In each scenario, the economic activity would be "within the control of Congress" to regulate. Lanham Act § 45, 15 U.S.C. § 1127.

[41] We thus conclude that BCC has adequately pled a § 43(a) false association claim for purposes of the zone of interests prong. Its allegations reflect the claim furthers the § 45 purpose of preventing "the deceptive and misleading use of marks" in "commerce within the control of Congress."

ii.

[42] Turning to *Lexmark's* second prong, proximate cause, BCC has also alleged injuries that "are proximately caused by [Belmora's] violations of the [false association] statute." 134 S.Ct. at 1390. The complaint can fairly be read to allege "economic or reputational injury flowing directly from the deception wrought by the defendant's" conduct. *Id.* at 1391. As previously noted, BCC alleges "substantial sales in major cities near the U.S.-Mexico border" and "millions of dollars promoting and advertising" its FLANAX brand in that region. (Compl. ¶¶ 11–12). Thus, BCC may plausibly have been damaged by Belmora's alleged deceptive use of the FLANAX mark in at least two ways. As reflected in the zone of interests discussion, BCC FLANAX customers in Mexico near the border may be deceived into foregoing a FLANAX purchase in Mexico as they cross the border to shop and buy the Belmora product in the United States. Second, Belmora is alleged to have targeted Mexican–Americans in the United States who were already familiar with the FLANAX mark from their purchases from BCC in Mexico. We can reasonably infer that some subset of those customers would buy BCC's FLANAX upon their return travels to Mexico if not for the alleged deception by Belmora. Consequently, BCC meets the *Lexmark* pleading requirement as to proximate cause.

[43] BCC may ultimately be unable to prove that Belmora's deception "cause[d] [these consumers] to withhold trade from [BCC]" in either circumstance, *Lexmark*, 134 S.Ct. at 1391, but at the initial pleading stage we must draw all reasonable factual inferences in BCC's favor. *Priority Auto Grp.*, 757 F.3d at 139. Having done so, we hold BCC has sufficiently pled a § 43(a) false association claim to survive Belmora's Rule 12(b)(6) motion. The district court erred in holding otherwise.

c.

[44] BCC and BHC both assert § 43(a)(1)(B) false advertising claims against Belmora. BHC's claim represents a "typical" false advertising case: it falls within the Act's zone of interests by "protecting persons engaged in commerce within the control of Congress against unfair competition." *Lexmark*, 134 S.Ct. at 1389 (quoting 15 U.S.C. § 1127). As a direct competitor to Belmora in the United States, BHC sufficiently alleges that Belmora engaged in Lanham Act unfair competition by using deceptive advertisements that capitalized on BCC's goodwill.... If not for Belmora's statements that its FLANAX was the same one known and trusted in Mexico, some of its consumers could very well have instead purchased BHC's ALEVE brand. These lost customers likewise satisfy Lexmark's second prong: they demonstrate an injury to sales or reputation proximately caused by Belmora's alleged conduct.

[45] BCC's false advertising claim is perhaps not "typical" as BCC is a foreign entity without direct sales in the territorial United States. Nonetheless, BCC's claim advances the Act's purpose of "making actionable the deceptive and misleading use of marks." Lanham Act § 45, 15 U.S.C. § 1127. As alleged, Belmora's advertising misrepresents the nature of its FLANAX product in that Belmora implies that product is the same as consumers purchased in Mexico from BCC and can now buy here.

[46] To be sure, BCC's false advertising claim overlaps to some degree with its false association claim, but the two claims address distinct conduct within the two subsections of § 43(a). Belmora's

316

alleged false statements go beyond mere claims of false association; they parlay the passed-off FLANAX mark into misleading statements about the product's "nature, characteristics, qualities, or geographic origin," all hallmarks of a false advertising claim. Lanham Act 43(a)(1)(B), 15 U.S.C. 1125(a)(1)(B).

[47] Belmora's alleged false statements intertwine closely with its use of the FLANAX mark. The FLANAX mark denotes history: Belmora claims its product has been "used [for] many, many years in Mexico" and "Latinos have turned to" it "[f]or generations." FLANAX also reflects popularity: Belmora says the product is "highly recognized [and] top-selling." And FLANAX signifies a history of quality: Belmora maintains that Latinos "know, trust and prefer" the product. Each of these statements by Belmora thus directly relates to the "nature, characteristics, qualities, or geographic origin" of its FLANAX as being one and the same as that of BCC. Lanham Act § 43(a)(1)(B), 15 U.S.C. § 1125(a)(1)(B). Because these statements are linked to Belmora's alleged deceptive use of the FLANAX mark, we are satisfied that BCC's false advertising claim, like its false association claim, comes within the Act's zone of interests. As we can comfortably infer that the alleged advertisements contributed to the lost border sales pled by BCC, the claim also satisfies *Lexmark's* proximate cause prong (for the same reasons discussed above regarding the false association claim).

d.

[48] We thus conclude that the Lanham Act permits Bayer to proceed with its claims under § 43(a)—BCC with its false association claim and both BCC and BHC with false advertising claims. It is worth noting, as the Supreme Court did in *Lexmark,* that "[a]lthough we conclude that [Bayer] has *alleged* an adequate basis to proceed under [§ 43(a)], it cannot obtain relief without *evidence* of injury proximately caused by [Belmora's alleged misconduct]. We hold only that [Bayer] is entitled to a chance to prove its case." 134 S.Ct. at 1395.

[49] In granting Bayer that chance, we are not concluding that BCC has any specific trademark rights to the FLANAX mark in the United States. Belmora owns that mark. But trademark rights do not include using the mark to deceive customers as a form of unfair competition, as is alleged here. Should Bayer prevail and prove its § 43(a) claims, an appropriate remedy might include directing Belmora to use the mark in a way that does not sow confusion. *See* Lanham Act § 34(a), 15 U.S.C. § 1116(a) (authorizing injunctions based on "principles of equity"). Of course, the precise remedy would be a determination to be made by the district court in the first instance upon proper evidence.[11] We leave any potential remedy to the district court's discretion should this case reach that point. We only note that any remedy should take into account traditional trademark principles relating to Belmora's ownership of the mark.

B. Cancellation Under Section 14(3)

[50] The TTAB ordered the cancellation of Belmora's FLANAX trademark under § 14(3), finding that the preponderance of the evidence "readily establishe[d] blatant misuse of the FLANAX mark in a manner calculated to trade in the United States on the reputation and goodwill of petitioner's mark created by its use in Mexico." In reversing that decision and granting Belmora's motion for judgment on the pleadings, the district court found that BCC, as the § 14(3) complainant, "lack[ed] standing to sue pursuant to *Lexmark* " under both the zone of interests and the proximate cause prongs. The district court also reversed the TTAB's holding that Belmora was using FLANAX to misrepresent the source of its goods "because Section 14(3) requires use of the mark in United States commerce and Bayer did not use the FLANAX mark in the United States."

---

[11] For example, a remedy might include altering the font and color of the packaging or the "ready remedy" of attaching the manufacturer's name to the brand name. *Blinded Veterans,* 872 F.2d at 1047. Another option could be for the packaging to display a disclaimer—to correct for any deliberately created actual confusion. *See id.* ("The district court could, however, require [Blinded American Veterans Foundation] to attach a prominent disclaimer to its name alerting the public that it is not the same organization as, and is not associated with, the Blinded Veterans Association.").

[51] On appeal, Bayer argues that the district court erred in overturning the TTAB's § 14(3) decision because it "read a use requirement into the section that is simply not there." Appellants' Br. 49. For reasons that largely overlap with the preceding § 43(a) analysis, we agree with Bayer.

. . . .

III.

[52] For the foregoing reasons, we conclude that Bayer is entitled to bring its unfair competition claims under Lanham Act § 43(a) and its cancellation claim under § 14(3). The district court's judgment is vacated and the case remanded for further proceedings consistent with this opinion.

VACATED AND REMANDED

Comments and Questions

1. Belmora*'s implications for trademark prosecution and litigation strategy.* For a comprehensive account of *Belmora*'s practical implications for trademark prosecution and litigation strategy, see Christine Haight Farley, *No Trademark, No Problem*, 23 B.U. J. Sci. & Tech. L. 304 (2017). *See also* Martin B. Schwimmer & John L. Welch, *U.S. Law Inches Towards Protecting Trademark Reputation Without Use*, World Trademark Rev., Oct. 1, 2019. For a subsequent application of *Belmora*, see *The Coca-Cola Company v. Meenaxi Enterprises, Inc.*, Cancellation Nos. 92063353 & 92064398, 2021 WL 2681898 (TTAB June 28, 2021) [precedential].

2. *The ongoing saga of* Belmora. After the Supreme Court denied certiorari review of the 2016 Fourth Circuit opinion in *Belmora*, the case returned to the Eastern District of Virginia. In September, 2016, the district court affirmed the PTO's cancellation of Belmora's registration but granted Belmora's motion for summary judgment on Bayer's unfair competition claim on the ground that Bayer had waited too long to file suit. *See Belmora, LLC v. Bayer Consumer Care AG*, 338 F. Supp. 3d 477, 484 (E.D. Va. 2018) ("Whether a three or four-year statute of limitations is applied in this case is immaterial. That is because Bayer's filing of this action misses the statute of limitations by almost a decade."). In May, 2021, the Fourth Circuit reversed the district court's grant of summary judgment to Belmora on Bayer's unfair competition claim, holding that the district court should have applied laches rather than any state-law statute of limitations. *See Belmora LLC v. Bayer Consumer Care AG*, 987 F.3d 284 (4th Cir. 2021). The Fourth Circuit once again remanded the case back to the district court. *Id.*

II. Trademark Infringement

In this Part, we consider the infringement of trademark rights under certain sections of the Lanham Act:

- § 32, 15 U.S.C. § 1114 (likelihood of confusion with respect to registered marks)
- § 43(a), 15 U.S.C. § 1125(a) (likelihood of confusion with respect to registered or unregistered marks)
- § 43(c), 15 U.S.C. § 1125(c) (likelihood of dilution with respect to registered or unregistered marks)
- § 43(d), 15 U.S.C. § 1125(d) ("cybersquatting" of registered or unregistered marks)

The test for likelihood of confusion under § 32 is now essentially the same as the test for likelihood of confusion under § 43(a), and courts often cite to case law under one section interchangeably with case law under the other. When owners of registered marks plead likelihood of confusion, they typically do so under both § 32 and § 43(a) in the event that some defect is discovered in their registration. Such plaintiffs may also plead under both sections in order to avail themselves of the slightly broader language of § 43(a), though, again, courts have come to treat § 32 and § 43(a) as essentially interchangeable.

Courts have set forth the elements of a trademark infringement claim in a variety of ways. For example, with respect to a claim based on a likelihood of confusion under either or both of § 32 and § 43(a), courts have stated:

- "[T]o succeed in a Lanham Act suit for trademark infringement, a plaintiff has two obstacles to overcome: the plaintiff must prove that its mark is entitled to protection and, even more important, that the defendant's use of its own mark will likely cause confusion with plaintiff's mark." *Gruner + Jahr USA Publ'g v. Meredith Corp.*, 991 F.2d 1072, 1074 (2d Cir. 1993).

- "To prevail on a claim of trademark infringement under the Lanham Act, 15 U.S.C. § 1114, a party must prove: (1) that it has a protectible ownership interest in the mark; and (2) that the defendant's use of the mark is likely to cause consumer confusion." *Network Automation, Inc. v. Advanced Systems Concepts, Inc.*, 638 F.3d 1137, 1144 (9th Cir. 2011) (citations omitted).

- "To establish trademark infringement under the Lanham Act, a plaintiff must prove: (1) that it owns a valid mark; (2) that the defendant used the mark 'in commerce' and without plaintiff's authorization; (3) that the defendant used the mark (or an imitation of it) 'in connection with the sale, offering for sale, distribution, or advertising' of goods or services; and (4) that the defendant's use of the mark is likely to confuse consumers." *Rosetta Stone Ltd. v. Google, Inc.*, 676 F.3d 144, 152 (4th Cir. 2012) (citations omitted).

- "Both infringement and false designation of origin have five elements. To prevail under either cause of action, the trademark holder must prove: (1) that it possesses a mark; (2) that the [opposing party] used the mark; (3) that the [opposing party's] use of the mark occurred 'in commerce'; (4) that the [opposing party] used the mark 'in connection with the sale, offering for sale, distribution, or advertising' of goods or services; and (5) that the [opposing party] used the mark in a manner likely to confuse consumers." *Lamparello v. Falwell*, 420 F.3d 309, 313 (4th Cir. 2005) (citations omitted).

Though the enumerations vary in their level of detail, these statements of the elements of a likelihood of confusion claim are all essentially the same. The plaintiff must prove that (1) it possesses exclusive rights in a mark and (2) the defendant has infringed those exclusive rights. Our focus in Part I was on the first of these two basic elements—whether there is a property right. Our focus in this Part is on the second of these elements—whether that right has been infringed.

We begin in Part II.A by reviewing the requirement that, in order to be liable for trademark infringement, a defendant must "use in commerce" the plaintiff's mark "in connection with the sale . . .

of any goods or services." We then turn in Part II.B to forms of infringement that are based on the likelihood of consumer confusion as to the source or sponsorship of the defendant's goods. In Part II.C, we consider forms of infringement that are not based on consumer confusion, most notably trademark dilution. In Part II.D, we turn to forms of relief for cybersquatting. Finally, in Part II.E, we review the doctrine of secondary liability in trademark law.

Comments and Questions

1. *Do individual consumers or groups of consumers have standing to sue under the Lanham Act?* In short, no. Lanham Act § 32(1), 15 U.S.C. § 1114(1), which applies to registered marks, provides that an infringing party "shall be liable in a civil action *by the registrant* for the remedies hereafter provided" (emphasis added). Lanham Act § 43(a), 15 U.S.C. § 1125(a), which applies to both registered and unregistered marks, provides that an infringing party "shall be liable in a civil action *by any person* who believes that he or she is or is likely to be damaged by such act" (emphasis added). Though broad, this language has been construed to exclude consumers. *See Lexmark Int'l, Inc. v. Static Control Components, Inc.*, 572 U.S. 118, 132 (2014) ("A consumer who is hoodwinked into purchasing a disappointing product may well have an injury-in-fact cognizable under Article III, but he cannot invoke the protection of the Lanham Act—a conclusion reached by every Circuit to consider the question . . . . Even a business misled by a supplier into purchasing an inferior product is, like consumers generally, not under the Act's aegis."). *See also id.* at 140 ("To invoke the Lanham Act's cause of action for false advertising, a plaintiff must plead (and ultimately prove) an injury to a commercial interest in sales or business reputation proximately caused by the defendant's misrepresentations."). Does this make sense as a matter of sound policy? *See also Rebecca Curtin v. United Trademark Holdings Inc.*, Opposition No. 91241083 (TTAB May 4, 2023).

A.   The Actionable Use Requirement

In Part I.C above, we addressed the requirement that a trademark owner "use in commerce" the mark in order to establish rights in the mark. Here, we consider the "use in commerce" requirement as applied not to owners, but to unauthorized users. We do so because of the statutory language, shown in italics, in Lanham Act § 32 and § 43(a):

> Lanham Act § 32, 15 U.S.C. § 1114
>
> (1) Any person who shall, without the consent of the registrant (a) *use in commerce* any reproduction, counterfeit, copy, or colorable imitation of a registered mark *in connection with the sale, offering for sale, distribution, or advertising of any goods or services* on or in connection with which such use is likely to cause confusion, or to cause mistake, or to deceive . . . shall be liable in a civil action by the registrant for the remedies hereinafter provided.

> Lanham Act § 43(a), 15 U.S.C. § 1125(a)
>
> (1) Any person who, *on or in connection with any goods or services, or any container for goods, uses in commerce* any word, term, name, symbol, or device, or any combination thereof, or any false designation of origin, false or misleading description of fact, or false or misleading representation of fact, which–(A) is likely to cause confusion, or to cause mistake, or to deceive . . . shall be liable in a civil action by any person who believes that he or she is or is likely to be damaged by such act.

Thus, for a defendant to be found liable, § 32 requires a showing that the defendant made a "use in commerce" of the plaintiff's mark "in connection with the sale, offering for sale, distribution, or advertising of any goods or services," and § 43(a) requires that the defendant "use[] in commerce" the plaintiff's mark "in connection with any goods or services, or any container for goods." (Lanham Act

§ 43(c), addressing trademark dilution, similarly requires a showing that the defendant made a "use of a mark or trade name in commerce." 15 U.S.C. § 1125(c)(1). See Comment 2 at the conclusion of Part II.A.2 for a discussion of this language).

Courts have analyzed the "use in commerce" language differently from how they've analyzed the "in connection with" language. We turn first to the question of defendant's "use in commerce."

1. Defendant's "Use in Commerce"

It is clear enough that the various infringement sections of the Lanham Act all require a showing that the defendant has made a "use in commerce," if only to satisfy the constitutional limitation on Congressional power, but what constitutes such a "use in commerce"? As we discussed in Part I.C, Lanham Act § 45, 15 U.S.C. § 1127, offers a definition of this phrase:

> The term "use in commerce" means the bona fide use of a mark in the ordinary course of trade, and not made merely to reserve a right in a mark. For purposes of this Act, a mark shall be deemed to be in use in commerce—
>
> (1) on goods when–
>
>> (A) it is placed in any manner on the goods or their containers or the displays associated therewith or on the tags or labels affixed thereto, or if the nature of the goods makes such placement impracticable, then on documents associated with the goods or their sale, and
>>
>> (B) the goods are sold or transported in commerce, and
>
> (2) on services when it is used or displayed in the sale or advertising of services and the services are rendered in commerce, or the services are rendered in more than one State or in the United States and a foreign country and the person rendering the services is engaged in commerce in connection with the services.

The obvious problem, however, is that this definition appears to describe the kind of "use in commerce" necessary to *establish* trademark rights rather than the kind of "use in commerce" necessary to *infringe* those rights. In the opinion below, *Rescuecom Corp. v. Google Inc.*, 562 F.3d 123 (2d Cir. 2009), the Second Circuit went to great lengths to arrive at this rather straightforward understanding of the § 45 definition of "use in commerce." It felt the need thoroughly to consider the issue because in a previous opinion, *1–800 Contacts, Inc. v. WhenU.Com, Inc.*, 414 F.3d 400 (2d Cir. 2005), it had somehow failed to recognize that § 45 was designed to address only the conduct of trademark owners rather than that of trademark infringers. *Rescuecom* became one long, extended effort in trying to maintain appearances. In reading through *Rescuecom*, consider the following questions:

- What is the underlying policy concern that is animating this technical, even rather pedantic debate about the meaning of "use in commerce"?

- Has the Second Circuit explicitly overruled its previous decision in *1-800 Contacts*? What is the status of *Rescuecom*'s Appendix? What does it mean that, as the *Rescuecom* opinion explains, "[t]he judges of the *1–800* panel have read this Appendix and have authorized us to state that they agree with it"?

- If a search engine user enters the word "Apple" and receives advertisements for Android phones, has the search engine itself made a "use in commerce" of Apple's mark? Asked perhaps another way, if a restaurant has given written instructions to its employees to respond to a consumer's order for Pepsi with the statement "We offer Coke", has the restaurant made a "use in commerce" of the Pepsi mark that could be the basis for an infringement cause of action?

Rescuecom Corp. v. Google Inc.
562 F.3d 123 (2d Cir. 2009)

LEVAL, Circuit Judge:

[1] Appeal by Plaintiff Rescuecom Corp. from a judgment of the United States District Court for the Northern District of New York (Mordue, *Chief Judge*) dismissing its action against Google, Inc., under

Rule 12(b)(6) for failure to state a claim upon which relief may be granted. Rescuecom's Complaint alleges that Google is liable under §§ 32 and 43 of the Lanham Act, 15 U.S.C. §§ 1114 & 1125, for infringement, false designation of origin, and dilution of Rescuecom's eponymous trademark. The district court believed the dismissal of the action was compelled by our holding in *1–800 Contacts, Inc. v. WhenU.Com, Inc.,* 414 F.3d 400 (2d Cir. 2005) ("*1–800*"), because, according to the district court's understanding of that opinion, Rescuecom failed to allege that Google's use of its mark was a "use in commerce" within the meaning of § 45 of the Lanham Act, 15 U.S.C. § 1127. We believe this misunderstood the holding of *1–800.* While we express no view as to whether Rescuecom can prove a Lanham Act violation, an actionable claim is adequately alleged in its pleadings. Accordingly, we vacate the judgment dismissing the action and remand for further proceedings.

BACKGROUND

[2] As this appeal follows the grant of a motion to dismiss, we must take as true the facts alleged in the Complaint and draw all reasonable inferences in favor of Rescuecom. *Lentell v. Merrill Lynch & Co., Inc.,* 396 F.3d 161, 165 (2d Cir. 2005). Rescuecom is a national computer service franchising company that offers on-site computer services and sales. Rescuecom conducts a substantial amount of business over the Internet and receives between 17,000 to 30,000 visitors to its website each month. It also advertises over the Internet, using many web-based services, including those offered by Google. Since 1998, "Rescuecom" has been a registered federal trademark, and there is no dispute as to its validity.

[3] Google operates a popular Internet search engine, which users access by visiting www.google.com. Using Google's website, a person searching for the website of a particular entity in trade (or simply for information about it) can enter that entity's name or trademark into Google's search engine and launch a search. Google's proprietary system responds to such a search request in two ways. First, Google provides a list of links to websites, ordered in what Google deems to be of descending relevance to the user's search terms based on its proprietary algorithms . . . .

[4] The second way Google responds to a search request is by showing context-based advertising. When a searcher uses Google's search engine by submitting a search term, Google may place advertisements on the user's screen. Google will do so if an advertiser, having determined that its ad is likely to be of interest to a searcher who enters the particular term, has purchased from Google the placement of its ad on the screen of the searcher who entered that search term. What Google places on the searcher's screen is more than simply an advertisement. It is also a link to the advertiser's website, so that in response to such an ad, if the searcher clicks on the link, he will open the advertiser's website, which offers not only additional information about the advertiser, but also perhaps the option to purchase the goods and services of the advertiser over the Internet. Google uses at least two programs to offer such context-based links: AdWords and Keyword Suggestion Tool.

[5] AdWords is Google's program through which advertisers purchase terms (or keywords). When entered as a search term, the keyword triggers the appearance of the advertiser's ad and link. An advertiser's purchase of a particular term causes the advertiser's ad and link to be displayed on the user's screen whenever a searcher launches a Google search based on the purchased search term.[1] Advertisers pay Google based on the number of times Internet users "click" on the advertisement, so as to link to the advertiser's website. For example, using Google's AdWords, Company Y, a company engaged in the business of furnace repair, can cause Google to display its advertisement and link whenever a user of Google launches a search based on the search term, "furnace repair." Company Y can also cause its ad and link to appear whenever a user searches for the term "Company X," a competitor of Company Y in the furnace repair business. Thus, whenever a searcher interested in purchasing furnace repair services from Company X launches a search of the term X (Company X's trademark), an ad and link would appear on the searcher's screen, inviting the searcher to the furnace repair services of X's competitor, Company Y. And if the searcher clicked on Company Y's link, Company Y's website would

---

[1] Although we generally refer to a single advertiser, there is no limit on the number of advertisers who can purchase a particular keyword to trigger the appearance of their ads.

open on the searcher's screen, and the searcher might be able to order or purchase Company Y's furnace repair services.

[6] In addition to AdWords, Google also employs Keyword Suggestion Tool, a program that recommends keywords to advertisers to be purchased. The program is designed to improve the effectiveness of advertising by helping advertisers identify keywords related to their area of commerce, resulting in the placement of their ads before users who are likely to be responsive to it. Thus, continuing the example given above, if Company Y employed Google's Keyword Suggestion Tool, the Tool might suggest to Company Y that it purchase not only the term "furnace repair" but also the term "X," its competitor's brand name and trademark, so that Y's ad would appear on the screen of a searcher who searched Company X's trademark, seeking Company X's website.

[7] Once an advertiser buys a particular keyword, Google links the keyword to that advertiser's advertisement. The advertisements consist of a combination of content and a link to the advertiser's webpage. Google displays these advertisements on the search result page either in the right margin or in a horizontal band immediately above the column of relevance-based search results. These advertisements are generally associated with a label, which says "sponsored link." Rescuecom alleges, however, that a user might easily be misled to believe that the advertisements which appear on the screen are in fact part of the relevance-based search result and that the appearance of a competitor's ad and link in response to a searcher's search for Rescuecom is likely to cause trademark confusion as to affiliation, origin, sponsorship, or approval of service. This can occur, according to the Complaint, because Google fails to label the ads in a manner which would clearly identify them as purchased ads rather than search results. The Complaint alleges that when the sponsored links appear in a horizontal bar at the top of the search results, they may appear to the searcher to be the first, and therefore the most relevant, entries responding to the search, as opposed to paid advertisements.

[8] Google's objective in its AdWords and Keyword Suggestion Tool programs is to sell keywords to advertisers. Rescuecom alleges that Google makes 97% of its revenue from selling advertisements through its AdWords program. Google therefore has an economic incentive to increase the number of advertisements and links that appear for every term entered into its search engine.

[9] Many of Rescuecom's competitors advertise on the Internet. Through its Keyword Suggestion Tool, Google has recommended the Rescuecom trademark to Rescuecom's competitors as a search term to be purchased. Rescuecom's competitors, some responding to Google's recommendation, have purchased Rescuecom's trademark as a keyword in Google's AdWords program, so that whenever a user launches a search for the term "Rescuecom," seeking to be connected to Rescuecom's website, the competitors' advertisement and link will appear on the searcher's screen. This practice allegedly allows Rescuecom's competitors to deceive and divert users searching for Rescuecom's website. According to Rescuecom's allegations, when a Google user launches a search for the term "Rescuecom" because the searcher wishes to purchase Rescuecom's services, links to websites of its competitors will appear on the searcher's screen in a manner likely to cause the searcher to believe mistakenly that a competitor's advertisement (and website link) is sponsored by, endorsed by, approved by, or affiliated with Rescuecom.

[10] The District Court granted Google's 12(b)(6) motion and dismissed Rescuecom's claims. The court believed that our *1-800* decision compels the conclusion that Google's allegedly infringing activity does not involve use of Rescuecom's mark in commerce, which is an essential element of an action under the Lanham Act. The district court explained its decision saying that even if Google employed Rescuecom's mark in a manner likely to cause confusion or deceive searchers into believing that competitors are affiliated with Rescuecom and its mark, so that they believe the services of Rescuecom's competitors are those of Rescuecom, Google's actions are not a "use in commerce" under the Lanham Act because the competitor's advertisements triggered by Google's programs did not exhibit Rescuecom's trademark. The court rejected the argument that Google "used" Rescuecom's mark in recommending and selling it as a keyword to trigger competitor's advertisements because the court read *1-800* to compel the conclusion that this was an internal use and therefore cannot be a "use in commerce" under the Lanham Act.

DISCUSSION

[11] "This Court reviews *de novo* a district court's grant of a motion to dismiss pursuant to Federal Rules of Civil Procedure 12(b)(6)." *PaineWebber Inc. v. Bybyk,* 81 F.3d 1193, 1197 (2d Cir. 1996). When reviewing a motion to dismiss, a court must "accept as true all of the factual allegations set out in plaintiff's complaint, draw inferences from those allegations in the light most favorable to plaintiff, and construe the complaint liberally." *Gregory v. Daly,* 243 F.3d 687, 691 (2d Cir. 2001) (citations omitted).

I. Google's Use of Rescuecom's Mark Was a "Use in Commerce"

[12] Our court ruled in *1–800* that a complaint fails to state a claim under the Lanham Act unless it alleges that the defendant has made "use in commerce" of the plaintiff's trademark as the term "use in commerce" is defined in 15 U.S.C. § 1127. The district court believed that this case was on all fours with *1–800,* and that its dismissal was required for the same reasons as given in *1–800.* We believe the cases are materially different. The allegations of Rescuecom's complaint adequately plead a use in commerce.

[13] In *1–800,* the plaintiff alleged that the defendant infringed the plaintiff's trademark through its proprietary software, which the defendant freely distributed to computer users who would download and install the program on their computer. The program provided contextually relevant advertising to the user by generating pop-up advertisements to the user depending on the website or search term the user entered in his browser. *Id.* at 404–05. For example, if a user typed "eye care" into his browser, the defendant's program would randomly display a pop-up advertisement of a company engaged in the field of eye care. Similarly, if the searcher launched a search for a particular company engaged in eye care, the defendant's program would display the pop-up ad of a company associated with eye care. *See id.* at 412. The pop-up ad appeared in a separate browser window from the website the user accessed, and the defendant's brand was displayed in the window frame surrounding the ad, so that there was no confusion as to the nature of the pop-up as an advertisement, nor as to the fact that the defendant, not the trademark owner, was responsible for displaying the ad, in response to the particular term searched. *Id.* at 405.

[14] Sections 32 and 43 of the Act, which we also refer to by their codified designations, 15 U.S.C. §§ 1114 & 1125, *inter alia,* impose liability for unpermitted "use in commerce" of another's mark which is "likely to cause confusion, or to cause mistake, or to deceive," § 1114, "as to the affiliation . . . or as to the origin, sponsorship or approval of his or her goods [or] services . . . by another person." § 1125(a)(1)(A). The *1–800* opinion looked to the definition of the term "use in commerce" provided in § 45 of the Act, 15 U.S.C. § 1127. That definition provides in part that "a mark shall be deemed to be in use in commerce . . . (2) on services when it is used or displayed in the sale or advertising of services and the services are rendered in commerce." 15 U.S.C. § 1127.[2] Our court found that the plaintiff failed to show that the defendant made a "use in commerce" of the plaintiff's mark, within that definition.

[15] At the outset, we note two significant aspects of our holding in *1–800,* which distinguish it from the present case. A key element of our court's decision in *1–800* was that under the plaintiff's allegations, the defendant did not use, reproduce, or display the plaintiff's mark *at all.* The search term that was alleged to trigger the pop-up ad was the plaintiff's *website address. 1–800* noted, notwithstanding the similarities between the website address and the mark, that the website address was not used or claimed by the plaintiff as a trademark. Thus, the transactions alleged to be infringing were not transactions involving use of the plaintiff's trademark. *Id.* at 408–09.[3] *1–800* suggested in dictum that is highly

---

[2] The Appendix to this opinion discusses the applicability of § 1127's definition of "use in commerce" to sections of the Lanham Act proscribing infringement.

[3] We did not imply in *1–800* that a website can never be a trademark. In fact, the opposite is true. *See* Trademark Manual of Examining Procedures § 1209.03(m) (5th ed. 2007) ("A mark comprised of an Internet domain name is registrable as a trademark or service mark only if it functions as an identifier of the source of goods or services."); *see also Two Pesos, Inc. v. Taco Cabana, Inc.,* 505 U.S. 763, 768, 112 S.Ct. 2753, 120 L.Ed.2d 615 (1992) (Section 43(a) of the Lanham Act protects unregistered trademarks

relevant to our case that had the defendant used the plaintiff's *trademark* as the trigger to pop-up an advertisement, such conduct might, depending on other elements, have been actionable. 414 F.3d at 409 & n. 11.

[16] Second, as an alternate basis for its decision, *1–800* explained why the defendant's program, which might randomly trigger pop-up advertisements upon a searcher's input of the plaintiff's website address, did not constitute a "use in commerce," as defined in § 1127. *Id.* at 408–09. In explaining why the plaintiff's mark was not "used or displayed in the sale or advertising of services," *1–800* pointed out that, under the defendant's program, advertisers could not request or purchase keywords to trigger their ads. *Id.* at 409, 412. Even if an advertiser wanted to display its advertisement to a searcher using the plaintiff's trademark as a search term, the defendant's program did not offer this possibility. In fact, the defendant "did not disclose the proprietary contents of [its] directory to its advertising clients . . . ." *Id.* at 409. In addition to not selling trademarks of others to its customers to trigger these ads, the defendant did not "otherwise manipulate which category-related advertisement will pop up in response to any particular terms on the internal directory." *Id.* at 411. The display of a particular advertisement was controlled by the category associated with the website or keyword, rather than the website or keyword itself. The defendant's program relied upon categorical associations such as "eye care" to select a pop-up ad randomly from a predefined list of ads appropriate to that category. To the extent that an advertisement for a competitor of the plaintiff was displayed when a user opened the plaintiff's website, the trigger to display the ad was not based on the defendant's sale or recommendation of a particular trademark.

[17] The present case contrasts starkly with those important aspects of the *1–800* decision. First, in contrast to *1–800,* where we emphasized that the defendant made no use whatsoever of the plaintiff's trademark, here what Google is recommending and selling to its advertisers is Rescuecom's trademark. Second, in contrast with the facts of *1–800* where the defendant did not "use or display," much less sell, trademarks as search terms to its advertisers, here Google displays, offers, and sells Rescuecom's mark to Google's advertising customers when selling its advertising services. In addition, Google encourages the purchase of Rescuecom's mark through its Keyword Suggestion Tool. Google's utilization of Rescuecom's mark fits literally within the terms specified by 15 U.S.C. § 1127. According to the Complaint, Google uses and sells Rescuecom's mark "in the sale . . . of [Google's advertising] services . . . rendered in commerce." § 1127.

[18] Google, supported by amici, argues that *1–800* suggests that the inclusion of a trademark in an internal computer directory cannot constitute trademark use. Several district court decisions in this Circuit appear to have reached this conclusion. *See e.g., S & L Vitamins, Inc. v. Australian Gold, Inc.,* 521 F.Supp.2d 188, 199–202 (E.D.N.Y. 2007) (holding that use of a trademark in metadata did not constitute trademark use within the meaning of the Lanham Act because the use "is strictly internal and not communicated to the public"); *Merck & Co., Inc. v. Mediplan Health Consulting, Inc.,* 425 F.Supp.2d 402, 415 (S.D.N.Y. 2006) (holding that the internal use of a keyword to trigger advertisements did not qualify as trademark use). This over-reads the *1–800* decision. First, regardless of whether Google's use of Rescuecom's mark in its internal search algorithm could constitute an actionable trademark use, Google's recommendation and sale of Rescuecom's mark to its advertising customers are not internal uses. Furthermore, *1–800* did not imply that use of a trademark in a software program's internal directory precludes a finding of trademark use. Rather, influenced by the fact that the defendant was not using the plaintiff's trademark at all, much less using it as the basis of a commercial transaction, the court asserted that the particular use before it did not constitute a use in commerce. *See 1–800,* 414 F.3d at 409–12. We did not imply in *1–800* that an alleged infringer's use of a trademark in an internal software program insulates the alleged infringer from a charge of infringement, no matter how likely the use is to

---

as long as the mark could qualify for registration under the Lanham Act.); *Thompson Med. Co., Inc. v. Pfizer Inc.,* 753 F.2d 208, 215–216 (2d Cir. 1985) (same). The question whether the plaintiff's website address was an unregistered trademark was never properly before the *1–800* court because the plaintiff did not claim that it used its website address as a trademark.

cause confusion in the marketplace. If we were to adopt Google and its amici's argument, the operators of search engines would be free to use trademarks in ways designed to deceive and cause consumer confusion.[4] This is surely neither within the intention nor the letter of the Lanham Act.

[19] Google and its amici contend further that its use of the Rescuecom trademark is no different from that of a retail vendor who uses "product placement" to allow one vender to benefit from a competitors' name recognition. An example of product placement occurs when a store-brand generic product is placed next to a trademarked product to induce a customer who specifically sought out the trademarked product to consider the typically less expensive, generic brand as an alternative. *See 1–800*, 414 F.3d at 411. Google's argument misses the point. From the fact that proper, non-deceptive product placement does not result in liability under the Lanham Act, it does not follow that the label "product placement" is a magic shield against liability, so that even a deceptive plan of product placement designed to confuse consumers would similarly escape liability. It is not by reason of absence of a use of a mark in commerce that benign product placement escapes liability; it escapes liability because it is a benign practice which does not cause a likelihood of consumer confusion. In contrast, if a retail seller were to be paid by an off-brand purveyor to arrange product display and delivery in such a way that customers seeking to purchase a famous brand would receive the off-brand, believing they had gotten the brand they were seeking, we see no reason to believe the practice would escape liability merely because it could claim the mantle of "product placement." The practices attributed to Google by the Complaint, which at this stage we must accept as true, are significantly different from benign product placement that does not violate the Act.

[20] Unlike the practices discussed in *1–800*, the practices here attributed to Google by Rescuecom's complaint are that Google has made use in commerce of Rescuecom's mark. Needless to say, a defendant must do more than use another's mark in commerce to violate the Lanham Act. The gist of a Lanham Act violation is an unauthorized use, which "is likely to cause confusion, or to cause mistake, or to deceive as to the affiliation, … or as to the origin, sponsorship, or approval of … goods [or] services." *See* 15 U.S.C. § 1125(a); *Estee Lauder Inc. v. The Gap, Inc.*, 108 F.3d 1503, 1508–09 (2d Cir. 1997). We have no idea whether Rescuecom can prove that Google's use of Rescuecom's trademark in its AdWords program causes likelihood of confusion or mistake. Rescuecom has alleged that it does, in that would-be purchasers (or explorers) of its services who search for its website on Google are misleadingly directed to the ads and websites of its competitors in a manner which leads them to believe mistakenly that these ads or websites are sponsored by, or affiliated with Rescuecom. This is particularly so, Rescuecom alleges, when the advertiser's link appears in a horizontal band at the top of the list of search results in a manner which makes it appear to be the most relevant search result and not an advertisement. What Rescuecom alleges is that by the manner of Google's display of sponsored links of competing brands in response to a search for Rescuecom's brand name (which fails adequately to identify the sponsored link as an advertisement, rather than a relevant search result), Google creates a likelihood of consumer confusion as to trademarks. If the searcher sees a different brand name as the top entry in response to the search for "Rescuecom," the searcher is likely to believe mistakenly that the different name which appears is affiliated with the brand name sought in the search and will not suspect, because the fact is not adequately signaled by Google's presentation, that this is not the most relevant response to the search. Whether Google's actual practice is in fact benign or confusing is not for us to judge at this time. We consider at the 12(b)(6) stage only what is alleged in the Complaint.

---

[4] For example, instead of having a separate "sponsored links" or paid advertisement section, search engines could allow advertisers to pay to appear at the top of the "relevance" list based on a user entering a competitor's trademark—a functionality that would be highly likely to cause consumer confusion. Alternatively, sellers of products or services could pay to have the operators of search engines automatically divert users to their website when the users enter a competitor's trademark as a search term. Such conduct is surely not beyond judicial review merely because it is engineered through the internal workings of a computer program.

[21] We conclude that the district court was mistaken in believing that our precedent in *1–800* requires dismissal.

CONCLUSION

[22] The judgment of the district court is vacated and the case is remanded for further proceedings.

APPENDIX

On the Meaning of "Use in Commerce" in Sections 32 and 43 of the Lanham Act[5]

[23] In *1–800 Contacts, Inc. v. WhenU.Com, Inc.,* 414 F.3d 400 (2d Cir. 2005) ("*1–800*"), our court followed the reasoning of two district court opinions from other circuits, *U–Haul Int'l, Inc. v. WhenU.com, Inc.,* 279 F.Supp.2d 723 (E.D.Va. 2003) and *Wells Fargo & Co., v. WhenU.com, Inc.,* 293 F.Supp.2d 734 (E.D.Mich. 2003), which dismissed suits on virtually identical claims against the same defendant. Those two district courts ruled that the defendant's conduct was not actionable under §§ 32 & 43(a) of the Lanham Act, 15 U.S.C. §§ 1114 & 1125(a), even assuming that conduct caused likelihood of trademark confusion, because the defendant had not made a "use in commerce" of the plaintiff's mark, within the definition of that phrase set forth in § 45 of the Lanham Act, 15 U.S.C. § 1127. In quoting definitional language of § 1127 that is crucial to their holdings, however, *U–Haul* and *Wells Fargo* overlooked and omitted portions of the statutory text which make clear that the definition provided in § 1127 was not intended by Congress to apply in the manner that the decisions assumed.

[24] Our court's ruling in *1–800* that the Plaintiff had failed to plead a viable claim under §§ 1114 & 1125(a) was justified by numerous good reasons and was undoubtedly the correct result. In addition to the questionable ground derived from the district court opinions, which had overlooked key statutory text, our court's opinion cited other highly persuasive reasons for dismissing the action—among them that the plaintiff did not claim a trademark in the term that served as the basis for the claim of infringement; nor did the defendant's actions cause any likelihood of confusion, as is crucial for such a claim.

[25] We proceed to explain how the district courts in *U–Haul* and *Wells Fargo* adopted reasoning which overlooked crucial statutory text that was incompatible with their ultimate conclusion . . . .

{Deleted here is the court's lengthy discussion of the history of the phrase "use in commerce" in the Lanham Act and, in particular, of the 1988 amendment to § 1127's definition of "use in commerce".}

The Interpretation of § 1127's Definition of "Use in Commerce " with Respect to Alleged Infringers

[26] In light of the preceding discussion, how should courts today interpret the definition of "use in commerce" set forth in 15 U.S.C. § 1127, with respect to acts of infringement prescribed by §§ 1114 and 1125(a)? The foregoing review of the evolution of the Act seems to us to make clear that Congress did not intend that this definition apply to the sections of the Lanham Act which define infringing conduct. The definition was rather intended to apply to the sections which used the phrase in prescribing eligibility for registration and for the Act's protections. However, Congress does not enact intentions. It enacts statutes. And the process of enacting legislation is of such complexity that understandably the words of statutes do not always conform perfectly to the motivating intentions. This can create for courts difficult problems of interpretation. Because pertinent amendments were passed in 1962 and in 1988, and because the 1988 amendment did not change the pre-existing parts of the definition in § 1127, but merely added a sentence, it seems useful to approach the question of the current meaning in two steps. First, what did this definition mean between 1962 and 1988—prior to the 1988 amendment? Then, how was the meaning changed by the 1988 amendment?

[27] Between 1962 and 1988, notwithstanding the likelihood shown by the legislative history that Congress *intended* the definition to apply only to registration and qualification for benefits and not to infringement, a court addressing the issue nonetheless would probably have concluded that the section

---

[5] In this discussion, all iterations of the phrase "use in commerce" whether in the form of a noun (a "use in commerce"), a verb ("to use in commerce"), or adjective ("used in commerce"), are intended without distinction as instances of that phrase.

applied to alleged infringement, as well. Section 1127 states that its definitions apply "unless the contrary is plainly apparent from the context." One who considered the question at the time might well have wondered why Congress would have provided this restrictive definition for acts of trademark infringement with the consequence that deceptive and confusing uses of another's mark with respect to goods would escape liability if the conduct did not include the placement of the mark on goods or their containers, displays, or sale documents, and with respect to services if the conduct did not include the use or display of the mark in the sale or advertising of the services. It is easy to imagine perniciously confusing conduct involving another's mark which does not involve placement of the mark in the manner specified in the definition. Nonetheless, in spite of those doubts, one could not have said it was "plainly apparent from the context" that those restrictions did not apply to sections defining infringement. In all probability, therefore, a court construing the provision between 1962 and 1988 would have concluded that in order to be actionable under §§ 1114 or 1125(a) the allegedly infringing conduct needed to include placement of the mark in the manner specified in the definition of "use in commerce" in § 1127.

[28] The next question is how the meaning of the § 1127 definition was changed by the 1988 amendment, which, as noted, left the preexisting language about placement of the mark unchanged, but added a prior sentence requiring that a "use in commerce" be "a bona fide use in the ordinary course of trade, and not made merely to reserve a right in a mark." While it is "plainly apparent from the context" that the new first sentence cannot reasonably apply to statutory sections defining infringing conduct, the question remains whether the addition of this new sentence changed the meaning of the second sentence of the definition without changing its words.

[29] We see at least two possible answers to the question, neither of which is entirely satisfactory. One interpretation would be that, by adding the new first sentence, Congress changed the meaning of the second sentence of the definition to conform to the new first sentence, without altering the words. The language of the definition, which, prior to the addition of the new first sentence, would have been construed to apply both to sections defining infringement, and to sections specifying eligibility for registration, would change its meaning, despite the absence of any change in its words, so that the entire definition now no longer applied to the sections defining infringement. Change of meaning without change of words is obviously problematic.

[30] The alternative solution would be to interpret the two sentences of the statutory definition as of different scope. The second sentence of the definition, which survived the 1988 amendment unchanged, would retain its prior meaning and continue to apply as before the amendment to sections defining infringement, as well as to sections relating to a mark owner's eligibility for registration and for enjoyment of the protections of the Act. The new first sentence, which plainly was not intended to apply to infringements, would apply only to sections in the latter category—those relating to an owner's eligibility to register its mark and enjoy the Act's protection. Under this interpretation, liability for infringement under §§ 1114 and 1125(a) would continue, as before 1988, to require a showing of the infringer's placement of another's mark in the manner specified in the second sentence of the § 1127 definition. It would not require a showing that the alleged infringer made "bona fide use of the mark in the ordinary course of trade, and not merely to reserve a right in the mark." On the other hand, eligibility of mark owners for registration and for the protections of the Act would depend on their showing compliance with the requirements of both sentences of the definition.

[31] We recognize that neither of the two available solutions is altogether satisfactory. Each has advantages and disadvantages. At least for this Circuit, especially given our prior *1–800* precedent, which applied the second sentence of the definition to infringement, the latter solution, according a different scope of application to the two sentences of the definition, seems to be preferable.[12]

---

[12] We express no view which of the alternative available solutions would seem preferable if our Circuit had not previously applied the second sentence to sections of the Act defining infringement.

[32] The judges of the *1–800* panel have read this Appendix and have authorized us to state that they agree with it. At the same time we note that the discussion in this Appendix does not affect the result of this case. We assumed in the body of the opinion, in accordance with the holding of *1–800*, that the requirements of the second sentence of the definition of "use in commerce" in § 1127 apply to infringing conduct and found that such use in commerce was adequately pleaded. The discussion in this Appendix is therefore dictum and not a binding opinion of the court. It would be helpful for Congress to study and clear up this ambiguity.

Questions and Comments

1.   The tamasha surrounding the question of the meaning of "use in commerce" when applied to the defendant's conduct, particularly in the search engine context, appears to have abated. In *Network Automation Inc. v. Advanced Systems Concepts Inc.*, 638 F.3d 1137 (9th Cir. 2011), the plaintiff sought a declaration of non-infringement for its purchase of search engine keywords, among them the defendant's trademark, that triggered sponsored links advertising the plaintiff's services. The Ninth Circuit devoted one short paragraph to the issue of "use in commerce" by the declaratory plaintiff. The *Network Automation* court simply held: "We now agree with the Second Circuit that such use is a "use in commerce" under the Lanham Act. *See Rescuecom Corp. v. Google Inc.*, 562 F.3d 123, 127 (2d Cir. 2009) (holding that Google's sale of trademarks as search engine keywords is a use in commerce)." *Id.* at 1145. However, lower court opinions still occasionally dredge up the argument that the defendant is not making a use in commerce under Lanham Act § 45. For example, in *Naked Cowboy v. CBS*, 844 F. Supp. 2d 510, 515 (S.D.N.Y. 2012), the court ignored *Rescuecom* and granted the defendant's motion to dismiss in part on the ground that the defendant's reference to Times Square's Naked Cowboy did not constitute "use in commerce" as defined in § 45.

2.   Defendant's Use "in Connection with the Sale . . . of any Goods or Services"

We now turn to what has proven to be a far more significant threshold requirement for liability in U.S. trademark law, often called the "commercial use" requirement. This is the requirement that to be found liable the defendant must make a use of the plaintiff's mark "in connection with the sale, distribution, or advertising of any goods or services", Lanham Act § 32(1)(a), 15 U.S.C. § 1114(1)(a), or "in connection with any goods or services," Lanham Act § 43(a)(1), 15 U.S.C. § 1125(a)(1). This requirement can play an important role in infringement litigation because if the defendant can show that it did not make a use "in connection with the sale" of goods or services, then the court can rule in favor of the defendant on that basis alone without needing to address the potentially messy, fact-intensive issue of whether the defendant's conduct confuses consumers. This requirement can thus be especially helpful (perhaps even at the motion to dismiss stage) for defendants who are engaging in political speech or expressive uses of others' trademarks but who are not selling goods or services.

As the following opinion explains, previous courts had expanded the reach of the "in connection with the sale" requirement in order to enjoin the conduct of clearly bad faith internet defendants. For example, in *People for Ethical Treatment of Animals, Inc. v. Doughney*, 263 F.3d 359 (4th Cir. 2001), the defendant owned a wide variety of domain names, including many that resembled others' trademarks. He registered peta.org and created a website entitled "People Eating Tasty Animals." The organization People for the Ethical Treatment of Animals sued for trademark infringement. The defendant claimed no use of the mark "in connection with the sale" of goods or services because he sold no goods or services on his website. The Fourth Circuit found such a connection on the ground that the defendant's use interfered with internet users' efforts to reach PETA's website. *Id.* at 365. Furthermore, the defendant's website linked to "more than 30 commercial operations offering goods and services." *Id.* at 366. *See also Planned Parenthood Federation of America, Inc. v. Bucci*, No. 97 Civ. 0629, 1997 WL 133313 (S.D.N.Y. 1997), aff'd without opinion, 152 F.3d 920 (2d Cir. 1998) (reasoning similarly with respect to defendant's domain name plannedparenthood.com); *Jews For Jesus v. Brodsky*, 993 F. Supp. 282, 46 U.S.P.Q.2d 1652 (D.N.J. 1998), judgment aff'd, 159 F.3d 1351 (3d Cir. 1998) (reasoning similarly with respect to defendant's domain names jewsforjesus.org and jews-for-jesus.org).

Radiance Foundation, Inc. v. National Association for the Advancement of Colored People, 786 F.3d 316 (4th Cir. 2015), finally presented circumstances that forced a retreat from this previous case law's overly expansive reading of the "in connection with the sale" requirement.

Radiance Foundation, Inc. v. National Association for the Advancement of Colored People
786 F.3d 316 (4th Cir. 2015)

WILKINSON, Circuit Judge:

[1] The Radiance Foundation published an article online entitled "NAACP: National Association for the Abortion of Colored People" that criticized the NAACP's stance on abortion. In response to a cease-and-desist letter from the NAACP, Radiance sought a declaratory judgment that it had not infringed any NAACP trademarks. The NAACP then filed counterclaims alleging trademark infringement and dilution.

[2] The Lanham Act protects against consumer confusion about the source or sponsorship of goods or services. Persons may not misappropriate trademarks to the detriment of consumers or of the marks themselves. However, the Act's reach is not unlimited. To find Lanham Act violations under these facts risks a different form of infringement—that of Radiance's expressive right to comment on social issues under the First Amendment. Courts have taken care to avoid Lanham Act interpretations that gratuitously court grave constitutional concerns, and we shall do so here. We hold that Radiance is not liable for trademark infringement or dilution of defendant's marks by tarnishment. We vacate the injunction against Radiance entered by the district court and remand with instructions that defendant's counterclaims likewise be dismissed.

I.

[3] The National Association for the Advancement of Colored People, better known by its acronym "NAACP," is this country's "oldest and largest civil rights organization," *Radiance Found., Inc. v. NAACP*, 25 F.Supp.3d 865, 872 (E.D.Va. 2014), and one that holds a place of honor in our history. It champions "political, educational, social, and economic equality of all citizens" while working to eliminate racial and other forms of prejudice within the United States. *Id.* Since its formation, it has pursued these objectives not only through litigation but also through community outreach, informational services, and educational activities on issues of significance to the African American community. *See id.* The NAACP owns several trademarks, among them "NAACP" (federally registered) and "National Association for the Advancement of Colored People."

[4] The Radiance Foundation, established by Ryan Bomberger, is also a non-profit organization focused on educating and influencing the public about issues impacting the African American community. Radiance addresses social issues from a Christian perspective. It uses as its platform two websites, TheRadianceFoundation.org and TooManyAborted.com, where it posts articles on topics such as race relations, diversity, fatherlessness, and the impact of abortion on the black community. *Id.* at 873. Radiance also runs a billboard campaign for TooManyAborted.com; individuals may sponsor these billboards, licensing the artwork from Radiance. In addition to its billboard campaign, Radiance funds its endeavors through donations from visitors to its websites, which are facilitated by "Donate" buttons on the webpages that link to a PayPal site.

[5] In January 2013, Bomberger authored an article criticizing the NAACP's annual Image Awards, entitled "NAACP: National Association for the Abortion of Colored People." The piece lambasted the NAACP for sponsoring an awards event to recognize Hollywood figures and products that Radiance alleged defied Christian values and perpetuated racist stereotypes. The article then criticized other of the NAACP's public stances and actions. It particularly targeted the NAACP's ties to Planned Parenthood and its position on abortion. Though the NAACP has often claimed to be neutral on abortion, Radiance maintains that the NAACP's actions actually demonstrate support for the practice.

[6] The article appeared on three websites: the two owned by Radiance—TheRadianceFoundation.com and TooManyAborted.com—and a third-party site called LifeNews.com. Though the text of the article was identical across the sites, the headlines and presentation varied slightly. On TheRadianceFoundation.com, directly below the headline was an image of a TooManyAborted billboard with the headline "NAACP: National Association for the Abortion of Colored

People" repeated next to it. The TooManyAborted.com site posted the headline "The National Association for the Abortion of Colored People" with a graphic below of a red box with the words "CIVIL WRONG" followed by the modified NAACP name. Adjacent to the article on both pages was an orange button with "CLICK HERE TO GIVE ONE-TIME GIFT TO THE RADIANCE FOUNDATION" printed around the word "DONATE." Finally on LifeNews.com, the third-party site, the NAACP's Scales of Justice appeared as a graphic underneath the headline.

[7] The NAACP sent Radiance a cease-and-desist letter on January 28, 2013, after a Google alert for the "NAACP" mark unearthed the LifeNews.com article. Radiance thereupon brought a declaratory action seeking a ruling that it had not infringed or diluted any of the NAACP's marks and that its use of the marks, or similar ones, was protected under the First Amendment. The NAACP counterclaimed for trademark infringement under 15 U.S.C. §§ 1114(1) and 1125(a) and Virginia state law, and trademark dilution under 15 U.S.C. § 1125(c).

[8] After a bench trial, the district court found for the NAACP on all counterclaims and denied declaratory relief to Radiance. It held that Radiance had used the marks "in connection with" goods and services and that its use of the "NAACP" and "National Association for the Advancement of Colored People" marks, or a colorable imitation, created a likelihood of confusion among consumers. *Radiance Found.,* 25 F.Supp.3d at 878–79.

. . . .

[9] The district court issued a permanent injunction "against any use [by Radiance] of 'National Association for the Abortion of Colored People' that creates a likelihood of confusion or dilution." *Id.* at 902. However, it declined to award any damages or attorney's fees, as it found the NAACP had failed to make the case that they were warranted. *Id.* at 899–901.

[10] Radiance now appeals . . . .

II.

. . . .

B.

[11] The first element of trademark infringement at issue is . . . whether Radiance's use of the NAACP's marks was "in connection with the sale, offering for sale, distribution, or advertising of any goods or services." 15 U.S.C. § 1114(1)(a); *see also id.* § 1125(a)(1) (requiring mark be used "in connection with any goods or services"). The NAACP urges us to give this requirement a "broad construction," but that construction would expose to liability a wide array of noncommercial expressive and charitable activities. Such an interpretation would push the Lanham Act close against a First Amendment wall, which is incompatible with the statute's purpose and stretches the text beyond its breaking point. We decline to reach so far.

[12] At least five of our sister circuits have interpreted this element as protecting from liability all noncommercial uses of marks. *Farah v. Esquire Magazine,* 736 F.3d 528, 541 (D.C. Cir. 2013); *Utah Lighthouse Ministry v. Found. for Apologetic Info. & Research,* 527 F.3d 1045, 1052–54 (10th Cir. 2008); *Bosley Med. Inst., Inc. v. Kremer,* 403 F.3d 672, 676–77 (9th Cir. 2005); *Taubman Co. v. Webfeats,* 319 F.3d 770, 774 (6th Cir. 2003); *Porous Media Corp. v. Pall Corp.,* 173 F.3d 1109, 1120 (8th Cir. 1999). *But see United We Stand Am., Inc. v. United We Stand, Am. New York, Inc.,* 128 F.3d 86, 89–90 (2d Cir. 1997). We have not taken a position on whether "in connection with" goods or services indicates a commercial use. *Lamparello v. Falwell,* 420 F.3d 309, 313-14 (4th Cir. 2005).

[13] At the very least, reading the "in connection with" element to take in broad swaths of noncommercial speech would be an "overextension" of the Lanham Act's reach that would "intrude on First Amendment values." *Rogers v. Grimaldi,* 875 F.2d 994, 998 (2d Cir. 1989); *see also Taubman,* 319 F.3d at 774 (stating that the "Lanham Act is constitutional because it only regulates commercial speech"). It is true that neither of the Lanham Act's infringement provisions explicitly mentions commerciality. *Lamparello,* 420 F.3d at 314. Still, this provision must mean something more than that the mark is being used in commerce in the constitutional sense, because the infringement provisions in § 1114(1)(a) and § 1125(a)(1) include a separate Commerce Clause hook. *Bosley,* 403 F.3d at 677; *Int'l Bancorp, LLC v.*

Societe des Bains de Mer et du Cercle des Estrangers a Monaco, 329 F.3d 359, 363–64 (4th Cir. 2003); *United We Stand,* 128 F.3d at 92–93.

[14] Although this case does not require us to hold that the commercial speech doctrine is in all respects synonymous with the "in connection with" element, we think that doctrine provides much the best guidance in applying the Act. The "in connection with" element in fact reads very much like a description of different types of commercial actions: "in connection with the *sale, offering for sale, distribution,* or *advertising* of any goods or services." 15 U.S.C. § 1114(1)(a) (emphasis added).

[15] Use of a protected mark as part of "speech that does no more than propose a commercial transaction" thus plainly falls within the Lanham Act's reach. *United States v. United Foods, Inc.,* 533 U.S. 405, 409 (2001). Courts also look to the factors outlined in *Bolger v. Youngs Drug Products Corp.,* 463 U.S. 60, 66–67 (1983): whether the speech is an advertisement; whether the speech references a particular good or service; and whether the speaker (the alleged infringer) has a demonstrated economic motivation for his speech. *Greater Balt. Ctr. for Pregnancy Concerns, Inc. v. Mayor of Balt.,* 721 F.3d 264, 285 (4th Cir. 2013) (en banc). These are not exclusive factors, and the presence or absence of any of them does not necessitate a particular result.

[16] In the context of trademark infringement, the Act's purpose . . . is to protect consumers from misleading uses of marks by competitors. Thus if in the context of a sale, distribution, or advertisement, a mark is used as a source identifier, we can confidently state that the use is "in connection with" the activity. Even the Second Circuit, which rejected noncommerciality as an invariable defense to Lanham Act liability, conceded that a "crucial" factor is that the infringer "us[ed] the Mark not as a commentary on its owner, but instead as a source identifier." *United We Stand,* 128 F.3d at 92. The danger of allowing the "in connection with" element to suck in speech on political and social issues through some strained or tangential association with a commercial or transactional activity should thus be evident. Courts have uniformly understood that imposing liability under the Lanham Act for such speech is rife with the First Amendment problems.

[17] Finally, in order to determine whether the use is "in connection with" goods or services, we must consider what qualifies as a good or service. The Lanham Act does not directly define either term, but we can deduce their meaning from other defined terms and common usage. A "good" is best understood as a valuable product, physical or otherwise, that the consumer may herself employ. *See* 15 U.S.C. § 1127 (noting that a mark may be used in commerce in relation to a good when placed on a good, its container, its tag, or its associated documents); Black's Law Dictionary 809 (10th ed. 2014) (defining "goods" as "[t]hings that have value, whether tangible or not"). A service is a more amorphous concept, "denot[ing] an intangible commodity in the form of human effort, such as labor, skill, or advice." Black's Law Dictionary 1576. Because Congress intended the Lanham Act to protect consumers from confusion in the marketplace, it is probable that the Act is meant to cover a wide range of products, whether "goods" or "services." *See Yates v. United States,* --- U.S. ----, 135 S.Ct. 1074, 1082 (2015) ("Ordinarily, a word's usage accords with its dictionary definition. In law as in life, however, the same words, placed in different contexts, sometimes mean different things.").

[18] It is clear, therefore, that despite the need to reconcile the reach of the Lanham Act with First Amendment values, "goods or services" remains a broad and potentially fuzzy concept. That is yet another reason why the "in connection with" language must denote a real nexus with goods or services if the Act is not to fatally collide with First Amendment principles.

III.

. . . .

A.

[19] In finding that Radiance's use of the NAACP's marks was "in connection with" goods or services, the district court erred in several respects. To begin, the court held that because the Radiance article appeared in a Google search for the term "NAACP," it diverted "Internet users to Radiance's article as opposed to the NAACP's websites," which thereby created a connection to the NAACP's goods and services. *Radiance Found., Inc. v. NAACP,* 25 F.Supp.3d 865, 884 (E.D.Va. 2014). But typically the use of

332

the mark has to be in connection with the infringer's goods or services, not the trademark holder's. *See Utah Lighthouse Ministry v. Found. for Apologetic Info. & Research*, 527 F.3d 1045, 1053–54 (10th Cir. 2008) (stating that "the defendant in a trademark infringement . . . case must use the mark in connection with the goods or services of a competing producer, not merely to make a comment on the trademark owner's goods or services").

[20] If the general rule was that the use of the mark merely had to be in connection with the trademark holder's goods or services, then even the most offhand mention of a trademark holder's mark could potentially satisfy the "in connection with" requirement. That interpretation would expand the requirement to the point that it would equal or surpass the scope of the Lanham Act's "in commerce" jurisdictional element. This would not only make the jurisdictional element superfluous, but would hamper the ability of the "in connection with" requirement to hold Lanham Act infractions within First Amendment limits.

[21] In *People for the Ethical Treatment of Animals v. Doughney*, we stated that an infringer "need only have prevented users from obtaining or using [the trademark holder's] goods or services, or need only have connected the [infringing] website to other's goods or services" in order to satisfy the "in connection with" requirement. 263 F.3d 359, 365 (4th Cir. 2001). But that rule applies specifically where the infringer has used the trademark holder's mark in a *domain name. Id.* at 365–66. Neither of Radiance's websites used an NAACP mark in its domain name. Rather, Radiance used the NAACP's marks only in the title and body of an article criticizing the NAACP. Nothing in *PETA* indicates that the use of a mark in the course of disseminating such an idea is on that account sufficient to establish the requisite relationship to goods or services. *PETA* simply does not govern the application of the "in connection with" element in this case.

[22] The district court proceeded to find that Radiance's use of the NAACP's marks was also in connection with *Radiance's* goods or services. *Radiance Found.*, 25 F.Supp.3d at 884–85. But the court's analysis failed to demonstrate a sufficient nexus between the specific use of the marks and the sale, offer for sale, distribution, or advertisement of any of the goods or services that the court invoked. The court first found that there was a sufficient nexus "with Radiance's own information services" because Radiance "provided information" on its website. *Id.* at 884. That ruling, however, neuters the First Amendment. The provision of mere "information services" without any commercial or transactional component is speech—nothing more.

[23] In the alternative, the court held that Radiance's use of the NAACP's marks was in connection with goods or services, because the use was "part of social commentary or criticism for which they solicit donations and sponsorship." *Id.* The NAACP echoes the district court, arguing that the transactional nature of the billboard campaign and Radiance's fundraising efforts place Radiance's use of the marks "comfortably within" the reach of the "in connection with" element. Appellee's Br. at 24–26.

[24] We need not address this point with absolute pronouncements. Suffice it to say that the specific use of the marks at issue here was too attenuated from the donation solicitation and the billboard campaign to support Lanham Act liability. Although present on the article page, the Donate button was off to the side and did not itself use the NAACP's marks in any way. The billboard campaign was displayed on a different page altogether. A visitor likely would not perceive the use of the NAACP's marks in the article as being in connection with those transactional components of the website. It is important not to lose perspective. The article was just one piece of each Radiance website's content, which was comprised of articles, videos, and multimedia advocacy materials. That the protected marks appear somewhere in the content of a website that includes transactional components is not alone enough to satisfy the "in connection with" element. To say it was would come too close to an absolute rule that any social issues commentary with any transactional component in the neighborhood enhanced the commentator's risk of Lanham Act liability.

[25] The Supreme Court has warned "that charitable appeals for funds . . . involve a variety of speech interests . . . that are within the protection of the First Amendment." *Vill. of Schaumburg v. Citizens for a Better Env't*, 444 U.S. 620, 632 (1980). Such solicitation, the Court stated, is not a "variety of purely commercial speech." *Id.* Courts are thus well-advised to tread cautiously when a trademark holder

invokes the Lanham Act against an alleged non-profit infringer whose use of the trademark holder's marks may be only tenuously related to requests for money. Again, this is not to say that in all instances a solicitation by a non-profit is immune from Lanham Act liability. A solicitation may satisfy the "in connection with" element if the trademark holder demonstrates a sufficient nexus between the unauthorized use of the protected mark and clear transactional activity. Such a nexus may be present, for example, where the protected mark seems to denote the recipient of the donation. However, where, as here, the solicitations are not closely related to the specific uses of the protected marks, we are compelled to conclude that the district court erred in ruling that the "in connection element" was met.

. . . .

Questions and Comments

1.   *The difference in the language of Lanham Act § 32 and § 43(a).* You may have noticed that the two likelihood of confusion sections formulate the commercial use requirement slightly differently. *Compare* Lanham Act § 32(1)(a), 15 U.S.C. § 1114(1)(a) (establishing liability for "[a]ny person who shall use in commerce" the plaintiff's mark "in connection with the sale, offering for sale, distribution, or advertising of any goods or services" in a manner that is confusing) *to* Lanham Act § 43(a)(1), 15 U.S.C. § 1125(a)(1) (establishing liability for "[a]ny person who, on or in connection with any goods or services, or any container for goods, uses in commerce" the plaintiff's mark in a manner that is confusing). In practice, courts have read both statements of the commercial use requirement to mean the same thing.

B.   Confusion-Based Infringement

The overriding question in most federal trademark infringement litigation is a simple one: is the defendant's trademark, because of its similarity to the plaintiff's trademark, causing or likely to cause consumer confusion as to the source or sponsorship of the defendant's goods? Each of the circuits requires that, in answering this question, the district court conduct a multifactor analysis of the likelihood of consumer confusion according to the factors set out by that circuit. As the Seventh Circuit has explained, the multifactor test operates "as a heuristic device to assist in determining whether confusion exists." *Sullivan v. CBS Corp.*, 385 F.3d 772, 778 (7th Cir. 2004). In Section II.B.1, we will briefly review the peculiar history of the multifactor test approach to the likelihood of confusion (or "LOC") question. In Section II.B.2, we will focus on a particularly rich application of the multifactor test in *Virgin Enterprises Ltd. v. Nawab*, 335 F.3d 141 (2d Cir. 2003). Section II.B.4 will address the use of survey evidence in the LOC context. Sections II.B.5 through II.B.9 will address various modes of consumer confusion such as "sponsorship or affiliation" confusion, "initial interest" confusion, "post-sale" confusion, and "reverse" confusion. Section II.B.10 will return briefly to the Lanham Act § 2(d) bar to registration of a mark that is confusingly-similar to a previously registered mark.

1.   The History of the Confusion-Based Cause of Action for Trademark Infringement

a.   The Early-Twentieth Century Approach to the Likelihood of Confusion

In the following opinion, *Borden Ice Cream Co. v. Borden's Condensed Milk Co.*, 201 F. 510 (7th Cir. 1912), the appellee Borden Condensed Milk Co. was the well-known manufacturer of, among other things, milk products under the trademark BORDEN. However, the only ice cream appellee had ever made was a specialized product made from malted milk and sold only to hospitals. The appellant Borden Ice Cream Co. commenced use of the BORDEN mark for ice cream – after finding someone named Borden to join its application for a corporate charter in Illinois. Under current trademark law, this would be a clear case of trademark infringement. As you will see, the *Borden Ice Cream* court saw things differently at the time.

Borden Ice Cream Co. v. Borden's Condensed Milk Co.
201 F. 510 (7th Cir. 1912)

[1] This is an appeal from an interlocutory order of injunction entered in the District Court, restraining the appellants 'from the use of the name 'Borden' in the manufacture or sale of ice cream and

like articles, and the manufacture or sale of milk products in any of their forms, without plainly and in written or printed form attached to all cartons of such commodities, and upon all wagons or other vehicles used in the delivery of such commodities, and on all letter heads and other stationery going out to customers and to the public, and in all places where the name 'Borden's Ice Cream Company' may hereafter appear in the transaction of any business by the defendants, advising purchasers and the public in an unmistakable manner that the product of the defendants is not that of the complainant, 'Borden's Condensed Milk Company."

[2] The word 'Borden' in the corporate name of the appellee was taken from the name of Gail Borden, who founded the business in the year 1857, and since that time it has been and is now a trade-name of great value, identified almost universally with the business of milk and milk products of the appellee and its predecessors. The trade-name 'Borden,' or the word 'Borden,' constitutes one of the principal assets of the appellee, and is widely known and identified with the good will and public favor enjoyed by it throughout the United States.

[3] On May 31, 1899, the appellee was incorporated under the laws of the state of New Jersey, with broad corporate powers, and specifically authorized 'to manufacture, sell and otherwise deal in condensed, preserved and evaporated milk and all other manufactured forms of milk; to produce, purchase and sell fresh milk, and all products of milk; to manufacture, purchase and sell all food products; to raise, purchase and sell all garden, farm and dairy products; to raise, purchase and sell, and otherwise deal in, cattle and all other live stock; to manufacture, lease, purchase and sell all machinery, tools, implements, apparatus and all other articles and appliances used in connection with all or any of the purposes aforesaid, or with selling and transporting the manufactured or other products of the company; and to do any and all things connected with or incidental to the carrying on of such business, or any branch or part thereof.'

[4] It may be stated in this connection that the charter of the company contains no express authority to manufacture or sell what is known commercially as ice cream.

. . . .

[5] Appellee has developed in the state of Illinois and the city of Chicago, and elsewhere, a large business in the sale of fresh milk and cream and evaporated milk to confectioners for use by them in making commercial ice cream. It has expended large sums of money in promoting and advertising its business, and particularly in extending the sale of the so-called 'Borden's Peerless Brand Evaporated Milk, Confectioners' Size,' a high quality of evaporated milk inclosed [sic] in cans, especially designed for use in the manufacture of ice cream.

[6] For more than two years prior to the filing of the bill in the District Court, the appellee had been manufacturing a form of ice cream known as 'Borden's Malted Milk Ice Cream,' which product is, as the name implies, an ice cream made with malted milk as its basic element, and is especially adapted for use in hospitals. This malted milk ice cream, which hitherto has been used only in hospitals, the appellee is about to place on the market for general use in competition with commercial ice cream.

[7] On May 25, 1911, the appellants Charles F. Borden, George W. Brown, and Edgar V. Stanley applied to the Secretary of State of the state of Illinois for a license to incorporate under the name of 'Borden Ice Cream Company.' On July 31, 1911, the appellee notified the individual appellants that the term 'Borden' had become so firmly established in connection with the products of the appellee the use of that word in connection with any company dealing in milk products would lead to the presumption that they were the products of the appellee, and demanded that the word 'Borden' be eliminated from appellants' company name.

[8] On the same day appellee protested to the Secretary of State of the state of Illinois against the issuance of any charter under the name of 'Borden Ice Cream Company,' but on the 16th of August, 1911, a charter was duly issued to the 'Borden Ice Cream Company,' by which it was authorized 'to manufacture and sell ice cream, ices and similar products.'

[9] The appellant Charles F. Borden had never before been engaged in the ice cream business, or in buying or selling milk or milk products, or in any similar business, and is not the principal person

335

connected with the appellant Borden Ice Cream Company. The appellant Lawler is an ice cream manufacturer, and has subscribed to 47 out of a total of 50 shares of stock of the Borden Ice Cream Company. Charles F. Borden has subscribed to one share of stock, and has not paid for that.

[10] The bill charges, upon information and belief, that it is the intention of appellant Borden Ice Cream Company to use the word 'Borden' for the purpose of trading upon the reputation of appellee's goods and products, and for the purpose of deceiving and defrauding the public into the belief that such product is the product of the appellee; that such 'improper, deceitful and fraudulent use of the name 'Borden' will be a great and irreparable injury to the complainant's (appellee's) property right in its trade-name; and that the reputation of the products of complainant (appellee) will be greatly injured thereby; and that the business of complainant (appellee) will be injured;' and that there will be great confusion in the business carried on by the original company because of such improper use; and that it will be impossible for present and prospective customers to know that the product of the Borden Ice Cream Company is not the product of Borden's Condensed Milk Company.

[11] The bill and the affidavits on file do not show any facts tending to sustain the allegation of irreparable injury to the old company or its business, or showing or tending to show that the old company has been or will be injured in any way in the business which it is now engaged in. Moreover, it does not appear that the malted milk ice cream manufactured by the old company will in any way come into competition with the commercial ice cream proposed to be put on the market by the new company.

[12] The bill was filed before the defendant had started to do any business. The answer admits most of the material allegations, but denies all fraudulent purpose.

CARPENTER, District Judge (after stating the facts as above).

[13] A personal name, such as 'Borden,' is not susceptible of exclusive appropriation, and even its registration in the Patent Office cannot make it a valid trade-mark. *Howe Scale Co. v. Wyckoff*, 198 U.S. 134; *Elgin Natl. Watch Co. v. Illinois Watch Case Co.*, 179 U.S. 665; *Singer Mfg. Co. v. June Mfg. Co.*, 163 U.S. 169; *Brown Chemical Co. v. Meyer*, 139 U.S. 540.

[14] There is no charge made in the bill that the appellants are infringing, or propose to infringe, upon any technical trade-mark of the appellee, so we may dismiss any claim for relief upon that score.

[15] The only theory upon which the injunction in this case can be sustained is upon that known as unfair competition. Relief against unfair competition is granted solely upon the ground that one who has built up a good will and reputation for his goods or business is entitled to all of the resultant benefits. Good will or business popularity is property, and, like other property, will be protected against fraudulent invasion.

. . . .

[16] It has been said that the universal test question in cases of this class is whether the public is likely to be deceived as to the maker or seller of the goods. This, in our opinion, is not the fundamental question. The deception of the public naturally tends to injure the proprietor of a business by diverting his customers and depriving him of sales which otherwise he might have made. This, rather than the protection of the public against imposition, is the sound and true basis for the private remedy. That the public is deceived may be evidence of the fact that the original proprietor's rights are being invaded. If, however, the rights of the original proprietor are in no wise interfered with, the deception of the public is no concern of a court of chancery. *American Washboard Co. v. Saginaw Mfg. Co.*, 103 Fed. 281.

[17] Doubtless it is morally wrong for a person to proclaim, or even intimate, that his goods are manufactured by some other and well-known concern; but this does not give rise to a private right of action, unless the property rights of that concern are interfered with. The use by the new company of the name 'Borden' may have been with fraudulent intent; and, even assuming that it was, the trial court had no right to interfere, unless the property rights of the old company were jeopardized. Nothing else being shown, a court of equity cannot punish an unorthodox or immoral, or even dishonest, trader; it cannot enforce as such the police power of the state.

[18] In the case now under our consideration the old company (the appellee) never has manufactured what is known as commercial ice cream. The new company (the appellant) was incorporated for the sole purpose of manufacturing and putting on the market such an article.

. . . .

[19] The secondary meaning of a name . . . has no legal significance, unless the two persons make or deal in the same kind of goods. Clearly the appellants here could make gloves, or plows, or cutlery, under the name 'Borden' without infringing upon any property right of the old company. If that is true, they can make anything under the name 'Borden' which the appellee has not already made and offered to the public. George v. Smith (C.C.) 52 Fed. 830.

[20] The name 'Borden,' until appellants came into the field, never had been associated with commercial ice cream. By making commercial ice cream the appellants do not come into competition with the appellee. In the absence of competition, the old company cannot assert the rights accruing from what has been designated as the secondary meaning of the word 'Borden.' The phrase 'unfair competition' presupposes competition of some sort. In the absence of competition the doctrine cannot be invoked.

[21] There being no competition between the appellants and appellee, we are confronted with the proposition that the appellee, in order to succeed on this appeal, has and can enforce a proprietary right to the name 'Borden' in any kind of business, to the exclusion of all the world.

[22] It is urged that appellee has power, under its charter, to make commercial ice cream, and that it intends some day to do so. If such intention can be protected at this time, it might well be that appellee, having enjoined appellants from making commercial ice cream, would rest content with selling its evaporated milk to ice cream dealers, and never itself manufacture the finished product. But, as was well stated by Judge Coxe, in George v. Smith, supra:

> 'It is the party who uses it first as a brand for his goods, and builds up a business under it, who is entitled to protection, and not the one who first thought of using it on similar goods, but did not use it. The law deals with acts and not intentions.'

[23] Appellee also urges that it makes and sells large quantities of evaporated or condensed milk to manufacturers of ice cream, and that if the appellants are permitted to use the name 'Borden' in the ice cream business dealers probably will believe that its ice cream is made by appellee, and will in consequence buy the finished product rather than the component parts, and that appellee's sales of evaporated or condensed milk will fall off, to its manifest damage. Such result would be too speculative and remote to form the basis of an order restraining men from using in their business any personal name, especially their own.

[24] Appellee is in this position: If it bases its right to an injunction upon the doctrine of unfair competition, no competition of any kind has been shown by the record. If it relies upon some supposed damage which may result from appellants' use of the name 'Borden' in connection with inferior goods, the action is premature, because the appellants, as yet, have neither sold nor made anything.

[25] The order of the District Court must be reversed; and it is so ordered.

b. The Development of the Modern Multifactor Test

The idiosyncrasies of tradition rather than of reason drove the development of the multifactor tests across the circuits. Each of the circuits' current multifactor tests originated either directly or indirectly from the 1938 *Restatement (First) of the Law of Torts*. The *Restatement (First)* failed to set forth a single, unified multifactor test for trademark infringement. Instead, it proposed four factors that courts should consider in all cases and nine more factors that courts should additionally consider only when the parties goods were noncompeting with each other, i.e., not substitutable for each other. Section 729 of the *Restatement (First)* set out the four factors courts should always consider:

> In determining whether the actor's designation is confusingly similar to the other's trade-mark or trade name, the following factors are important:

(a) the degree of similarity between the designation and the trade-mark or trade name in

>   (i) appearance;
>
>   (ii) pronunciation of the words used;
>
>   (iii) verbal translation of the pictures or designs involved;
>
>   (iv) suggestion;

(b) the intent of the actor in adopting the designation;

(c) the relation in use and manner of marketing between the goods or services marketed by the actor and those marketed by the other;

(d) the degree of care likely to be exercised by purchasers.

RESTATEMENT FIRST OF TORTS § 729 (1939). Section 731 set out the additional nine factors that courts should additionally consider only in cases involving noncompetitive goods:

> In determining whether one's interest in a trade-mark or trade name is protected, under the rules stated in §§ 717 and 730, with reference to the goods, services or business in connection with which the actor uses his designation, the following factors are important:
>
>   (a) the likelihood that the actor's goods, services or business will be mistaken for those of the other;
>
>   (b) the likelihood that the other may expand his business so as to compete with the actor;
>
>   (c) the extent to which the goods or services of the actor and those of the other have common purchasers or users;
>
>   (d) the extent to which the goods or services of the actor and those of the other are marketed through the same channels;
>
>   (e) the relation between the functions of the goods or services of the actor and those of the other;
>
>   (f) the degree of distinctiveness of the trademark or trade name;
>
>   (g) the degree of attention usually given to trade symbols in the purchase of goods or services of the actor and those of the other;
>
>   (h) the length of time during which the actor has used the designation;
>
>   (i) the intent of the actor in adopting and using the designation.

Id. at § 731.

Through the course of the mid-twentieth century, the federal courts lost track of the distinction between the two sets of factors, and the circuits each began to use a single, unified multifactor test regardless of whether the parties' goods were competing. Each circuit developed its own test, and for the most part, the peculiarities of the particular cases in which the circuit's multifactor test first coalesced determined which factors are still considered in that circuit today. A good example of this is found in the following opinion, *Polaroid Corp. v. Polarad Electronics Corp.*, 287 F.2d 402 (2d Cir. 1961), which is the origin of the Second Circuit's "*Polaroid* Factors." Despite Judge Friendly's clear statement that his test was meant for situations "[w]here the products are different," *id.* at 495, Second Circuit courts routinely apply the *Polaroid* factors in competing goods cases. The opinion is presented here primarily for its historical significance as one of the most influential opinions in U.S. trademark law, but also to show, in the final paragraph of the opinion excerpt, how much trademark infringement doctrine had evolved since *Borden's Ice Cream*.

Polaroid Corp. v. Polarad Electronics Corp.
287 F.2d 492 (2d Cir. 1961)

FRIENDLY, Circuit Judge.

[1] Plaintiff, Polaroid Corporation, a Delaware corporation, owner of the trademark Polaroid and holder of 22 United States registrations thereof granted between 1936 and 1956 and of a New York registration granted in 1950, brought this action in the Eastern District of New York, alleging that defendant's use of the name Polarad as a trademark and as part of defendant's corporate title infringed plaintiff's Federal and state trademarks and constituted unfair competition. It sought a broad injunction and an accounting. Defendant's answer, in addition to denying the allegations of the complaint, sought a declaratory judgment establishing defendant's right to use Polarad in the business in which defendant was engaged, an injunction against plaintiff's use of Polaroid in the television and electronics fields, and other relief. Judge Rayfiel, in an opinion reported in D.C. 1960, 182 F.Supp. 350, dismissed both the claim and the counterclaims, concluding that neither plaintiff nor defendant had made an adequate showing with respect to confusion and that both had been guilty of laches. Both parties appealed but defendant has withdrawn its cross-appeal. We find it unnecessary to pass upon Judge Rayfiel's conclusion that defendant's use of Polarad does not violate any of plaintiff's rights. For we agree that plaintiff's delay in proceeding against defendant bars plaintiff from relief so long as defendant's use of Polarad remains as far removed from plaintiff's primary fields of activity as it has been and still is.

. . . .

[2] Conceding that the bulk of its business is in optics and photography, lines not pursued by defendant, plaintiff nevertheless claims to be entitled to protection of its distinctive mark in at least certain portions of the large field of electronics. Plaintiff relies on its sales of Schmidt corrector plates, used in certain types of television systems, first under government contracts beginning in 1943 and to industry commencing in 1945; on its sale, since 1946, of polarizing television filters, which serve the same function as the color filters that defendant supplies as a part of the television apparatus sold by it; and, particularly, on the research and development contracts with the government referred to above. Plaintiff relies also on certain instances of confusion, predominantly communications intended for defendant but directed to plaintiff. Against this, defendant asserts that its business is the sale of complex electronics equipment {consisting of microwave devices and television studio equipment} to a relatively few customers; that this does not compete in any significant way with plaintiff's business, the bulk of which is now in articles destined for the ultimate consumer; that plaintiff's excursions into electronics are insignificant in the light of the size of the field; that the instances of confusion are minimal; that there is no evidence that plaintiff has suffered either through loss of customers or injury to reputation, since defendant has conducted its business with high standards; and that the very nature of defendant's business, sales to experienced industrial users and the government, precludes any substantial possibility of confusion. Defendant also asserts plaintiff's laches to be a bar.

[3] The problem of determining how far a valid trademark shall be protected with respect to goods other than those to which its owner has applied it, has long been vexing and does not become easier of solution with the years. Neither of our recent decisions so heavily relied upon by the parties, *Harold F. Ritchie, Inc. v. Chesebrough-Pond's, Inc.*, 2 Cir., 1960, 281 F.2d 755, by plaintiff, and *Avon Shoe Co., Inc. v. David Crystal, Inc.*, 2 Cir., 1960, 279 F.2d 607 by defendant, affords much assistance, since in the Ritchie case there was confusion as to the identical product and the defendant in the Avon case had adopted its mark 'without knowledge of the plaintiffs' prior use,' at page 611. Where the products are different, the prior owner's chance of success is a function of many variables: the strength of his mark, the degree of similarity between the two marks, the proximity of the products, the likelihood that the prior owner will bridge the gap, actual confusion, and the reciprocal of defendant's good faith in adopting its own mark, the quality of defendant's product, and the sophistication of the buyers. Even this extensive catalogue does not exhaust the possibilities—the court may have to take still other variables into account. American Law Institute, Restatement of Torts, §§ 729, 730, 731. Here plaintiff's mark is a strong one and the similarity between the two names is great, but the evidence of actual confusion, when analyzed, is not impressive. The filter seems to be the only case where defendant has sold, but not manufactured, a

product serving a function similar to any of plaintiff's, and plaintiff's sales of this item have been highly irregular, varying, e.g., from $2,300 in 1953 to $303,000 in 1955, and $48,000 in 1956.

[4] If defendant's sole business were the manufacture and sale of microwave equipment, we should have little difficulty in approving the District Court's conclusion that there was no such likelihood of confusion as to bring into play either the Lanham Act, 15 U.S.C.A. § 1114(1), or New York General Business Law, § 368-b, or to make out a case of unfair competition under New York decisional law, see *Avon Shoe Co. v. David Crystal, Inc.*, supra, at page 614, footnote 11. What gives us some pause is defendant's heavy involvement in a phase of electronics that lies closer to plaintiff's business, namely, television. Defendant makes much of the testimony of plaintiff's executive vice president that plaintiff's normal business is 'the interaction of light and matter.' Yet, although television lies predominantly in the area of electronics, it begins and ends with light waves. The record tells us that certain television uses were among the factors that first stimulated Dr. Land's interest in polarization, see *Marks v. Polaroid Corporation*, supra, 129 F.Supp. at page 246, plaintiff has manufactured and sold at least two products for use in television systems, and defendant's second counterclaim itself asserts likelihood of confusion in the television field. We are thus by no means sure that, under the views with respect to trademark protection announced by this Court in such cases as *Yale Electric Corp. v. Robertson*, 2 Cir., 1928, 26 F.2d 972 (locks vs. flashlights {finding confusion}); *L. E. Waterman Co. v. Gordon*, 2 Cir., 1934, 72 F.2d 272 (mechanical pens and pencils vs. razor blades {finding confusion}); *Triangle Publications, Inc. v. Rohrlich*, 2 Cir., 1948, 167 F.2d 969, 972 (magazines vs. girdles {finding confusion}); and *Admiral Corp. v. Penco, Inc.*, 2 Cir., 1953, 203 F.2d 517 (radios, electric ranges and refrigerators vs. sewing machines and vacuum cleaners {finding confusion}), plaintiff would not have been entitled to at least some injunctive relief if it had moved with reasonable promptness. However, we are not required to decide this since we uphold the District Court's conclusion with respect to laches.

{The court went on to reject the plaintiff's attempts to overcome the defendant's defense of laches.}

Questions and Comments

1. *Laches in federal trademark law.* There is no statute of limitations provision in the Lanham Act. Instead, the analogous state statute of limitations period in the forum state will typically apply in order to fill the gap in federal law. *Tandy Corp. v. Malone & Hyde, Inc.*, 769 F.2d 362 (6th Cir. 1985). "The limitations period is often used to shift the initial burden of proof for the laches defense. If the case was filed within the relevant statute of limitations, the burden will be on the defendant to show that laches applies, but if the case was filed after the limitations period expired, then the burden will be on the plaintiff to show why it would be inequitable to apply laches." 3 GILSON ON TRADEMARKS § 13.21 (2019). Different state's limitations periods can run anywhere from about two to six years. *See* 6 MCCARTHY ON TRADEMARKS AND UNFAIR COMPETITION § 31:33 (5th ed. 2019).

For an impressive application of the laches defense, see *Dropbox, Inc. v. Thru Inc.*, No. 15 Civ. 01741, 2016 WL 6696042 (N.D. Cal. Nov. 15, 2016), supplemented, 15 Civ. 01741, 2016 WL 7116717 (N.D. Cal. Dec. 7, 2016), aff'd, 728 F. App'x 717 (9th Cir. 2018), and aff'd, 728 F. App'x 717 (9th Cir. 2018). The case involved litigation between the Dropbox file hosting service and a company that probably had a reasonable claim of seniority in the DROPBOX mark. Dropbox's laches defense was so strong and Thru's litigation conduct so abusive (it waited until Dropbox's IPO announcement to file suit) that Dropbox eventually won attorney's fees and costs in the total amount of $2.3 million.

2. *"His Mark is His Authentic Seal."* In *Yale Elec. Corp. v. Robertson*, 26 F.2d 972 (2d Cir. 1928), which Judge Friendly cites in the final paragraph of *Polaroid*, Judge Hand set forth his oft-quoted description of the plaintiff's interest in preventing the use of its mark on noncompeting goods:

> However, it has of recent years been recognized that a merchant may have a sufficient economic interest in the use of his mark outside the field of his own exploitation to justify interposition by a court. His mark is his authentic seal; by it he vouches for the goods which bear it; it carries his name for good or ill. If another uses it, he borrows the owner's reputation, whose quality no longer lies within his own control. This is an injury, even though the borrower does not tarnish it, or divert any sales by its use; for a reputation, like

a face, is the symbol of its possessor and creator, and another can use it only as a mask. And so it has come to be recognized that, unless the borrower's use is so foreign to the owner's as to insure against any identification of the two, it is unlawful.

Id. at 974. If the defendant's conduct "does not tarnish [the plaintiff's reputation], or divert any sales by its use," then what exactly is the harm to the plaintiff?

2. Contemporary Applications of the Multifactor Test for the Likelihood of Consumer Confusion

Each circuit has developed its own multifactor test for the likelihood of consumer confusion. Here are the multifactor tests from certain leading circuits. As you will see, they are roughly similar:

- The Second Circuit's "*Polaroid* Factors": Polaroid Corp. v. Polarad Elecs. Corp., 287 F.2d 492, 495 (2d Cir. 1961) ("Where the products are different, the prior owner's chance of success is a function of many variables: the strength of his mark, the degree of similarity between the two marks, the proximity of the products, the likelihood that the prior owner will bridge the gap, actual confusion, and the reciprocal of defendant's good faith in adopting its own mark, the quality of defendant's product, and the sophistication of the buyers. Even this extensive catalogue does not exhaust the possibilities—the court may have to take still other variables into account. American Law Institute, Restatement of Torts, §§ 729, 730, 731.").

- The Seventh Circuit's "*Helene Curtis* Factors": Helene Curtis Indus., Inc. v. Church & Dwight Co., 560 F.2d 1325, 1330 (7th Cir. 1977) (In determining 'likelihood of confusion' several factors are important: 'the degree of similarity between the marks in appearance and suggestion; the similarity of the products for which the name is used; the area and manner of concurrent use; the degree of care likely to be exercised by consumers; the strength of the complainant's mark; actual confusion; and an intent on the part of the alleged infringer to palm off his products as those of another'. Carl Zeiss Stiftung v. VEB Carl Zeiss Jena, 433 F.2d 686, 705 (2d Cir. 1970).").

- The Ninth Circuit's "*Sleekcraft* Factors": AMF Inc. v. Sleekcraft Boats, 599 F.2d 341, 348–49 (9th Cir. 1979) ("In determining whether confusion between related goods is likely, the following factors are relevant: 1. strength of the mark; 2. proximity of the goods; 3. similarity of the marks; 4. evidence of actual confusion; 5. marketing channels used; 6. type of goods and the degree of care likely to be exercised by the purchaser; 7. defendant's intent in selecting the mark; and 8. likelihood of expansion of the product lines. *See, e.g.*, Sleeper Lounge Co. v. Bell Manufacturing Co., 253 F.2d at 722; Restatement of Torts s 731 (1938).").

In *Virgin Enterprises Ltd. v. Nawab*, 335 F.3d 141 (2d Cir. 2003), the Second Circuit applied its *Polaroid* test to determine if consumers would likely mistake the goods and services of the defendant, operating under the mark VIRGIN WIRELESS, for the those of the plaintiff, the owner of the VIRGIN mark for a wide variety of goods and services. The opinion is exceptional for its thorough analysis of the factors. In reading through *Virgin Enterprises*, consider the following questions:

- Which of the *Polaroid* factors are likely the most important to courts' adjudication of the likelihood of confusion question?

- In practice, is intent likely as unimportant to courts' determinations as the *Virgin Enterprises* opinion suggests?

- Why should strong marks receive a wider scope of protection than weak marks?

- Why should inherent strength be more important to the multifactor inquiry than acquired strength? Relatedly, why should fanciful marks receive a wider scope of protection that arbitrary or suggestive marks?

- Does the court make any basic mistakes of doctrine in its discussion of the *Abercrombie* spectrum?

Int. Cls.: 35, 39, and 42

Prior U.S. Cls.: 100, 101, 104, and 105

United States Patent and Trademark Office Reg. No. 1,851,817
Registered Aug. 30, 1994

SERVICE MARK
PRINCIPAL REGISTER

VIRGIN

VIRGIN ENTERPRISES LIMITED (UNITED KINGDOM CORPORATION)
120, CAMPDEN HILL ROAD
LONDON, W8 7AR, ENGLAND

FOR: DIRECT MAIL ADVERTISING FOR OTHERS; DISSEMINATION OF ADVERTISING MATERIALS FOR OTHER; PREPARING ADVERTISING, PROMOTIONS, AND PUBLIC RELATIONS MATERIALS FOR OTHERS; MANAGEMENT OF PROMOTIONAL AND INCENTIVE PLANS AND SERVICES FOR OTHERS; BUSINESS ORGANIZATION PROMOTIONAL CONSULTING FOR OTHERS; DEMONSTRATION OF THE GOODS AND SERVICES OF OTHERS AND THE PROMOTION THEREOF; PROMOTING AND ADVERTISING THE GOODS AND SERVICES OF OTHERS BY AIRCRAFT, AIRSHIPS AND AIR BALLOONS; OUTDOOR ADVERTISING SUCH AS BY BILLBOARDS; AND DISTRIBUTION OF ADVERTISING, PROMOTIONAL MATERIALS AND SAMPLE MATERIALS OF OTHERS, IN CLASS 35 (U.S. CLS. 101 AND 104).
FIRST USE 2-13-1993; IN COMMERCE 2-13-1993.
FOR: TRANSPORTATION OF GOODS AND PASSENGERS BY ROAD, RAIL, AIR AND SEA; FREIGHT TRANSPORTATION SERVICES; TOURIST AGENCY SERVICES; TRAVEL AGENCY SERVICES; ARRANGING TRAVEL TOURS; AND TRANSPORTATION RESERVATION SERVICES, IN CLASS 39 (U.S. CL. 105).
FIRST USE 6-0-1984; IN COMMERCE 6-0-1984.
FOR: CLUBS; NIGHTCLUBS; BARS; HOTELS; RESORTS; HOTEL RESERVATION SERVICES;

HOTEL AND RESORT MANAGEMENT FOR OTHERS; CARRY-OUT RESTAURANT AND RESTAURANT SERVICES; CATERING; COMPUTER PROGRAMMING FOR OTHERS; COMPUTER SOFTWARE DESIGN SERVICES FOR OTHERS; ARTWORK AND GRAPHIC DESIGN SERVICES FOR OTHERS; AND RETAIL STORE SERVICES IN THE FIELDS OF COSMETICS AND LAUNDRY PREPARATIONS, METAL HARDWARE, CAMERAS, RECORDS, AUDIO AND VIDEO TAPES, AUDIO AND VIDEO RECORDERS, COMPUTERS AND ELECTRONIC APPARATUS, JEWELRY, CLOCKS AND WATCHES, MUSICAL INSTRUMENTS, STATIONERY, SHEET MUSIC, BOOKS AND PHOTOGRAPHY, HANDBAGS, PURSES, LUGGAGE AND LEATHER GOODS, CLOTHING, LACE, EMBROIDERY, GIFTS AND SEWING MATERIALS, TOYS, GAMES, VIDEO GAME MACHINES AND VIDEO GAME CARTRIDGES, PROCESSED FOODS, JELLIES AND JAMS, COFFEE, TEA, BAKERY ITEMS AND CANDY, BEER, ALE, MINERAL AND AERATED WATERS AND OTHER NON-ALCOHOLIC DRINKS, WINES, SPIRITS AND LIQUEURS, AND TOBACCO AND SMOKERS' ARTICLES, IN CLASS 42 (U.S. CL. 100).

FIRST USE 11-28-1990; IN COMMERCE 11-28-1990.

OWNER OF U.S. REG. NOS. 1,469,618, 1,597,386, AND OTHERS.

SN 74-162,592, FILED 5-1-1991.

ELEANOR MELTZER, EXAMINING ATTORNEY

Virgin Enterprises Ltd. v. Nawab
335 F.3d 141 (2d Cir. 2003)

LEVAL, Circuit Judge.

[1] Plaintiff Virgin Enterprises Limited ("VEL" or "plaintiff") appeals from the denial of its motion for a preliminary injunction. This suit, brought under § 32 of the Lanham Act, 15 U.S.C. § 1114(1), alleges that defendants infringed plaintiff's rights in the registered mark VIRGIN by operating retail stores selling wireless telephones and related accessories and services under the trade name VIRGIN WIRELESS. The United States District Court for the Eastern District of New York (Sifton, J.) denied plaintiff's motion for a preliminary injunction, based upon its finding that plaintiff's registration did not cover the retail sale of wireless telephones and related products, and that plaintiff failed to show a likelihood of consumer confusion.

BACKGROUND

[2] Plaintiff VEL, a corporation with its principal place of business in London, owns U.S. Registration No. 1,851,817 ("the 817 Registration"), filed on May 5, 1991, and registered on August 30, 1994, for the VIRGIN mark as applied to *retail store services* in the fields of . . . computers and *electronic apparatus* " (emphasis added). . . . Plaintiff also owns U.S. Registration No. 1,852,776 ("the 776 Registration"), filed on May 9, 1991, and registered on September 6, 1994, for a stylized version of the VIRGIN mark for use in connection with "retail store services in the fields of . . . computers and electronic apparatus," and U.S. Registration No. 1,863,353 ("the 353 Registration"), filed on May 19, 1992, and registered on November

342

15, 1994, for the VIRGIN MEGASTORE mark. It is undisputed that these three registrations have become incontestable pursuant to 15 U.S.C. § 1065.

[3] VEL, either directly or through corporate affiliates, operates various businesses worldwide under the trade name VIRGIN, including an airline, large-scale record stores called Virgin Megastores, and an internet information service. Plaintiff or its affiliates also market a variety of goods branded with the VIRGIN name, including music recordings, computer games, books, and luggage. Three of plaintiff's megastores are located in the New York area. According to an affidavit submitted to the district court in support of plaintiff's application for preliminary injunction, Virgin Megastores sell a variety of electronic apparatus, including video game systems, portable CD players, disposable cameras, and DVD players. These stores advertise in a variety of media, including radio.

[4] Defendants Simon Blitz and Daniel Gazal are the sole shareholders of defendants Cel-Net Communications, Inc. ("Cel-Net"); The Cellular Network Communications, Inc., doing business as CNCG ("CNCG"); and SD Telecommunications, Inc. ("SD Telecom"). Blitz and Gazal formed Cel-Net in 1993 to sell retail wireless telephones and services in the New York area. Later, they formed CNCG to sell wireless phones and services on the wholesale level. CNCG now sells wireless phones and services to more than 400 independent wireless retailers. In 1998, Cel-Net received permission from New York State regulators to resell telephone services within the state.

[5] Around 1999, Andrew Kastein, a vice-president of CNCG, began to develop a Cel-Net brand of wireless telecommunications products. In early 1999, Cel-Net entered into negotiations with the Sprint PCS network to provide telecommunications services for resale by Cel-Net. In August 1999, Cel-Net retained the law firm Pennie & Edmonds to determine the availability of possible service marks for Cel-Net. Pennie & Edmonds associate Elizabeth Langston researched for Kastein a list of possible service marks; among the marks Cel-Net asked to have researched was VIRGIN. Defendants claim that Langston told Cel-Net officer Simon Corney that VIRGIN was available for use in the telecommunications field. Plaintiff disputed this, offering an affidavit from Langston that she informed defendants that she would not search the VIRGIN mark because her firm represented plaintiff.

[6] According to defendants, in December 1999, Cel-Net retained Corporate Solutions, LLC and its principals Nathan Erlich and Tahir Nawab as joint venture partners to help raise capital to launch Cel-Net's wireless telephone service. On December 2, 1999, Erlich and Nawab filed four intent-to-use applications with the U.S. Patent and Trademark Office ("PTO") to register the marks VIRGIN WIRELESS, VIRGIN MOBILE, VIRGIN COMMUNICATIONS, and VIRGIN NET in the field of telecommunications services, class 38. On December 24, 1999, Corporate Solutions incorporated defendant Virgin Wireless, Inc. ("VWI") and licensed to VWI the right to use the marks VIRGIN WIRELESS and VIRGIN MOBILE. Meanwhile, one of plaintiff's affiliates had begun to offer wireless telecommunication services bearing the VIRGIN mark in the United Kingdom. A press release dated November 19, 1999, found on plaintiff's website, stated that its Virgin Mobile wireless services were operable in the United States.

[7] On June 23, 2000, defendant Blitz signed a lease under the name Virgin Wireless for a kiosk location in South Shore Mall in Long Island from which to re-sell AT&T wireless services, telephones, and accessories under the retail name Virgin Wireless. Defendants Cel-Net and VWI later expanded their telecommunications re-sale operations to include two retail stores and four additional retail kiosks in malls in the New York area and in Pennsylvania. All of these stores have been run by VWI under the trade name VIRGIN WIRELESS. VWI also has leases and bank accounts in its name, and has shown evidence of actual retail transactions and newspaper advertisements.

[8] In August 2000, plaintiff licensed Virgin Mobile USA, LLC, to use the VIRGIN mark for wireless telecommunications services in the United States. On August 10, 2000, plaintiff filed an intent-to-use application with the PTO for use of the VIRGIN mark in the United States on telecommunications services and mobile telephones. On October 11, 2001, the PTO suspended this mark's registration in international class 9, which covers wireless telephones, and class 38, which covers telecommunications services, because the VIRGIN mark was already reserved by a prior filing, presumably defendants'. On August 16, 2001, plaintiff filed another intent-to-use application for the mark VIRGIN MOBILE to brand telecommunications services. The PTO issued a non-final action letter for both of plaintiff's pending new

registrations on October 31, 2001, which stated that defendant Corporation Solutions' pending applications for similar marks in the same class could give rise to "a likelihood of confusion." The PTO suspended action on plaintiff's application pending the processing of Corporation Solutions' applications.

[9] In October 2001, plaintiff issued a press release announcing that it was offering wireless telecommunications services and mobile telephones in the United States.

[10] Plaintiff became aware of Corporation Solutions' application for registration of the VIRGIN WIRELESS and VIRGIN MOBILE marks by May 2000. In October 2001 and December 2001, defendant VWI filed suits against plaintiff in the federal district courts in Arizona and Delaware, alleging that plaintiff was using VWI's mark. Plaintiff maintains (and the district court found) that it learned in January 2002 that VWI and Cel-Net were operating kiosks under the VIRGIN WIRELESS name and two days later filed the present suit seeking to enjoin defendants from selling mobile phones in VIRGIN-branded retail stores.

[11] On May 2, 2002, the district court considered plaintiff's application for a preliminary injunction. It found that no essential facts were in dispute, and therefore no evidentiary hearing was required. It was uncontested (and the district court accordingly found) that plaintiff sold "electronic apparatus" in its stores, including "various video game systems, portable cassette tape, compact disc, mp3, and mini disc players, portable radios, and disposable cameras," but not including telephones or telephone service, and that the only products the defendants sold in their stores were wireless telephones, telephone accessories, and wireless telephone services . . . .

[12] Arguing against plaintiff's likelihood of success, the court noted that plaintiff's registrations did not claim use of the VIRGIN mark "in telecommunications services or in the associated retail sale of wireless telephones and accessories." While plaintiff's 817 and 776 Registrations covered the retail sale of "computers and electronic apparatus," they did not extend to telecommunications services and wireless phones.

[13] The court noted that the defendants were the first to use the VIRGIN mark in telecommunications, and the first to attempt to register VIRGIN for telecommunications and retail telephone sales . . . .

DISCUSSION

. . . .

II.

[14] A claim of trademark infringement, whether brought under 15 U.S.C. § 1114(1) (for infringement of a registered mark) or 15 U.S.C. § 1125(a) (for infringement of rights in a mark acquired by use), is analyzed under the familiar two-prong test described in *Gruner + Jahr USA Publ'g v. Meredith Corp.*, 991 F.2d 1072 (2d Cir. 1993). *See Time, Inc. v. Petersen Publ'g Co. L.L.C.*, 173 F.3d 113, 117 (2d Cir. 1999) (noting that *Gruner* test is applicable to claims brought under § 1114(1) and § 1125(a)). The test looks first to whether the plaintiff's mark is entitled to protection, and second to whether defendant's use of the mark is likely to cause consumers confusion as to the origin or sponsorship of the defendant's goods. *Gruner*, 991 F.2d at 1074. Examining the question as the test dictates, we have no doubt that plaintiff was entitled to a preliminary injunction.

[15] We believe the district court accorded plaintiff too narrow a scope of protection for its famous, arbitrary, and distinctive mark. There could be no dispute that plaintiff prevailed as to the first prong of the test—prior use and ownership. For years, plaintiff had used the VIRGIN mark on huge, famous stores selling, in addition to music recordings, a variety of consumer electronic equipment. At the time the defendants began using VIRGIN, plaintiff owned rights in the mark. The focus of inquiry thus turns to the second prong of the test—whether defendants' use of VIRGIN as a mark for stores selling wireless telephone services and phones was likely to cause confusion. There can be little doubt that such confusion was likely.

[16] The landmark case of *Polaroid Corp. v. Polarad Electronics Corp.*, 287 F.2d 492 (2d Cir. 1961) (Friendly, J.), outlined a series of nonexclusive factors likely to be pertinent in addressing the issue of likelihood of confusion, which are routinely followed in such cases. . .

[17] Six of the *Polaroid* factors relate directly to the likelihood of consumer confusion. These are the strength of the plaintiff's mark; the similarity of defendants' mark to plaintiff's; the proximity of the products sold under defendants' mark to those sold under plaintiff's; where the products are different, the likelihood that plaintiff will bridge the gap by selling the products being sold by defendants; the existence of actual confusion among consumers; and the sophistication of consumers. Of these six, all but the last (which was found by the district court to be neutral) strongly favor the plaintiff. The remaining two *Polaroid* factors, defendants' good or bad faith and the quality of defendants' products, are more pertinent to issues other than likelihood of confusion, such as harm to plaintiff's reputation and choice of remedy. We conclude that the *Polaroid* factors powerfully support plaintiff's position.

[18] *Strength of the mark.* The strength of a trademark encompasses two different concepts, both of which relate significantly to likelihood of consumer confusion. The first and most important is inherent strength, also called "inherent distinctiveness." This inquiry distinguishes between, on the one hand, inherently distinctive marks—marks that are arbitrary or fanciful in relation to the products (or services) on which they are used—and, on the other hand, marks that are generic, descriptive or suggestive as to those goods. The former are the strong marks. *Abercrombie & Fitch Co. v. Hunting World, Inc.*, 537 F.2d 4, 9 (2d Cir. 1976). The second sense of the concept of strength of a mark is "acquired distinctiveness," i.e., fame, or the extent to which prominent use of the mark in commerce has resulted in a high degree of consumer recognition. *See TCPIP Holding Co. v. Haar Communications Inc.*, 244 F.3d 88, 100 (2d Cir. 2001) (describing these two concepts of strength).

[19] Considering first *inherent distinctiveness,* the law accords broad, muscular protection to marks that are arbitrary or fanciful in relation to the products on which they are used, and lesser protection, or no protection at all, to marks consisting of words that identify or describe the goods or their attributes. The reasons for the distinction arise from two aspects of market efficiency. The paramount objective of the trademark law is to avoid confusion in the marketplace. The purpose for which the trademark law accords merchants the exclusive right to the use of a name or symbol in their area or commerce is *identification,* so that the merchants can establish goodwill for their goods based on past satisfactory performance, and the consuming public can rely on a mark as a guarantee that the goods or services so marked come from the merchant who has been found to be satisfactory in the past. *See Estee Lauder Inc. v. The Gap, Inc.*, 108 F.3d 1503, 1510 (2d Cir. 1997) (quoting *Restatement (Third) of Unfair Competition* § 21 comment i (1995)); *Power Test Petroleum Distribs., Inc. v. Calcu Gas, Inc.*, 754 F.2d 91, 97 (2d Cir. 1985); *McGregor-Doniger Inc. v. Drizzle Inc.*, 599 F.2d 1126, 1131 (2d Cir. 1979). At the same time, efficiency and the public interest require that every merchant trading in a class of goods be permitted to refer to the goods by their name, and to make claims about their quality. Thus, a merchant who sells pencils under the trademark *Pencil* or *Clear Mark,* for example, and seeks to exclude other sellers of pencils from using those words in their trade, is seeking an advantage the trademark law does not intend to offer. To grant such exclusivity would deprive the consuming public of the useful market information it receives where every seller of pencils is free to call them pencils. *Abercrombie*, 537 F.2d at 9; *CES Publ'g Corp. v. St. Regis Publ'ns, Inc.*, 531 F.2d 11, 13 (2d Cir. 1975). The trademark right does not protect the exclusive right to an advertising message—only the exclusive right to an identifier, to protect against confusion in the marketplace. Thus, as a matter of policy, the trademark law accords broader protection to marks that serve exclusively as identifiers and lesser protection where a grant of exclusiveness would tend to diminish the access of others to the full range of discourse relating to their goods. *See TCPIP*, 244 F.3d at 100; *Nabisco, Inc. v. PF Brands, Inc.*, 191 F.3d 208, 215 (2d Cir. 1999); *Otokoyama Co. Ltd. v. Wine of Japan Import, Inc.*, 175 F.3d 266, 270 (2d Cir. 1999).

[20] The second aspect of efficiency that justifies according broader protection to marks that are inherently distinctive relates directly to the likelihood of confusion. If a mark is arbitrary or fanciful, and makes no reference to the nature of the goods it designates, consumers who see the mark on different objects offered in the marketplace will be likely to assume, because of the arbitrariness of the choice of

mark, that they all come from the same source. For example, if consumers become familiar with a toothpaste sold under an unusual, arbitrary brand name, such as *ZzaaqQ,* and later see that same inherently distinctive brand name appearing on a different product, they are likely to assume, notwithstanding the product difference, that the second product comes from the same producer as the first. The more unusual, arbitrary, and fanciful a trade name, the more unlikely it is that two independent entities would have chosen it. In contrast, every seller of foods has an interest in calling its product "delicious." Consumers who see the word *delicious* used on two or more different food products are less likely to draw the inference that they must all come from the same producer. *Cf. Streetwise Maps,* 159 F.3d at 744 (noting that several map producers use "street" in product names; thus plaintiff's mark using "street" was not particularly distinctive); *W. Publ'g,* 910 F.2d at 61 (noting numerous registrations of marks using word "golden"). In short, the more distinctive the mark, the greater the likelihood that the public, seeing it used a second time, will assume that the second use comes from the same source as the first. The goal of avoiding consumer confusion thus dictates that the inherently distinctive, arbitrary, or fanciful marks, i.e., strong marks, receive broader protection than weak marks, those that are descriptive or suggestive of the products on which they are used. *See Abercrombie,* 537 F.2d at 9-11; *TCPIP,* 244 F.3d at 100-01.

[21] The second sense of trademark strength, fame, or "acquired distinctiveness," also bears on consumer confusion. *See TCPIP,* 244 F.3d at 100-01; *Streetwise Maps,* 159 F.3d at 744. If a mark has been long, prominently and notoriously used in commerce, there is a high likelihood that consumers will recognize it from its prior use. Widespread consumer recognition of a mark previously used in commerce increases the likelihood that consumers will assume it identifies the previously familiar user, and therefore increases the likelihood of consumer confusion if the new user is in fact not related to the first. *See Nabisco,* 191 F.3d at 216-17. A mark's fame also gives unscrupulous traders an incentive to seek to create consumer confusion by associating themselves in consumers' minds with a famous mark. The added likelihood of consumer confusion resulting from a second user's use of a famous mark gives reason for according such a famous mark a broader scope of protection, at least when it is also inherently distinctive. *See McGregor,* 599 F.2d at 1132 (noting that secondary meaning may further enlarge the scope of protection accorded to inherently distinctive marks).

[22] Plaintiff's VIRGIN mark undoubtedly scored high on both concepts of strength. In relation to the sale of consumer electronic equipment, the VIRGIN mark is inherently distinctive, in that it is arbitrary and fanciful; the word "virgin" has no intrinsic relationship whatsoever to selling such equipment. Because there is no intrinsic reason for a merchant to use the word "virgin" in the sale of consumer electronic equipment, a consumer seeing VIRGIN used in two different stores selling such equipment will likely assume that the stores are related.

[23] Plaintiff's VIRGIN mark was also famous. The mark had been employed with world-wide recognition as the mark of an airline and as the mark for megastores selling music recordings and consumer electronic equipment. The fame of the mark increased the likelihood that consumers seeing defendants' shops selling telephones under the mark VIRGIN would assume incorrectly that defendants' shops were a part of plaintiff's organization. *See Lois Sportswear, U.S.A., Inc. v. Levi Strauss & Co.,* 799 F.2d 867, 873 (2d Cir. 1986).

[24] There can be no doubt that plaintiff's VIRGIN mark, as used on consumer electronic equipment, is a strong mark, as the district court found. It is entitled as such to a broad scope of protection, precisely because the use of the mark by others in connection with stores selling reasonably closely related merchandise would inevitably have a high likelihood of causing consumer confusion.

[25] *Similarity of marks.* When the secondary user's mark is not identical but merely similar to the plaintiff's mark, it is important to assess the degree of similarity between them in assessing the likelihood that consumers will be confused. *See McGregor,* 599 F.2d at 1133. Plaintiff's and defendants' marks were not merely similar; they were identical to the extent that both consisted of the same word, "virgin."

[26] The district court believed this factor did not favor plaintiff because it found some differences in appearance. Defendants' logo used a different typeface and different colors from plaintiff's. While

those are indeed differences, they are quite minor in relation to the fact that the name being used as a trademark was the same in each case.

[27] Advertisement and consumer experience of a mark do not necessarily transmit all of the mark's features. Plaintiff, for example, advertised its Virgin Megastores on the radio. A consumer who heard those advertisements and then saw the defendants' installation using the name VIRGIN would have no way of knowing that the two trademarks looked different. *See Sports Auth., Inc. v. Prime Hospitality Corp.*, 89 F.3d 955, 962 (2d Cir. 1996). A consumer who had visited one of plaintiff's Virgin Megastores and remembered the name would not necessarily remember the typeface and color of plaintiff's mark. The reputation of a mark also spreads by word of mouth among consumers. One consumer who hears from others about their experience with Virgin stores and then encounters defendants' Virgin store will have no way knowing of the differences in typeface. *See Hills Bros. Coffee, Inc. v. Hills Supermarkets, Inc.*, 428 F.2d 379, 381 (2d Cir. 1970) (per curiam).

[28] In view of the fact that defendants used the same name as plaintiff, we conclude the defendants' mark was sufficiently similar to plaintiff's to increase the likelihood of confusion. This factor favored the plaintiff as a matter of law. We conclude that the district court erred in concluding otherwise on the basis of comparatively trivial and often irrelevant differences.

[29] *Proximity of the products and likelihood of bridging the gap.* The next factor is the proximity of the products being sold by plaintiff and defendant under identical (or similar) marks. *See Arrow Fastener*, 59 F.3d at 396. This factor has an obvious bearing on the likelihood of confusion. When the two users of a mark are operating in completely different areas of commerce, consumers are less likely to assume that their similarly branded products come from the same source. In contrast, the closer the secondary user's goods are to those the consumer has seen marketed under the prior user's brand, the more likely that the consumer will mistakenly assume a common source. *See Cadbury Beverages, Inc. v. Cott Corp.*, 73 F.3d 474, 480-81 (2d Cir. 1996).

[30] While plaintiff had not sold telephones or telephone service prior to defendant's registration evincing intent to sell those items, plaintiff had sold quite similar items of consumer electronic equipment. These included computer video game systems, portable cassette-tape players, compact disc players, MP3 players, mini-disc players, and disposable cameras. Like telephones, many of these are small consumer electronic gadgets making use of computerized audio communication. They are sold in the same channels of commerce. Consumers would have a high expectation of finding telephones, portable CD players, and computerized video game systems in the same stores. We think the proximity in commerce of telephones to CD players substantially advanced the risk that consumer confusion would occur when both were sold by different merchants under the same trade name, VIRGIN.

[31] Our classic *Polaroid* test further protects a trademark owner by examining the likelihood that, even if the plaintiff's products were not so close to the defendants' when the defendant began to market them, there was already a likelihood that plaintiff would in the reasonably near future begin selling those products. *See Cadbury Beverages*, 73 F.3d at 482. VEL's claim of proximity was further strengthened in this regard because, as the district court expressly found, "plans had been formulated [for VEL] to enter [the market for telecommunications products and services] shortly in the future." VEL had already begun marketing telephone service in England which would operate in the United States, and, as the district court found, had made plans to sell telephones and wireless telephone service under the VIRGIN name from its retail stores.

[32] The district court, nonetheless, found in favor of the defendants with respect to the proximity of products and services. We would ordinarily give considerable deference to a factual finding on this issue. Here, however, we cannot do so because it appears the district court applied the wrong test. The court did not assess the *proximity* of defendants' VIRGIN-branded retail stores selling telephone products to plaintiff's VIRGIN-branded retail stores selling other consumer electronic products. It simply concluded that, because defendants were selling exclusively telephone products and services, and plaintiff's electronic products did not include telephones or related services, the defendants must prevail as to the proximity factor.

[33] This represents a considerable misunderstanding of the *Polaroid* test. The famous list of factors of likely pertinence in assessing likelihood of confusion in *Polaroid* was specially designed for a case like this one, in which the secondary user is not in direct competition with the prior user, but is selling a somewhat different product or service. In *Polaroid*, the plaintiff sold optical and camera equipment, while the defendant sold electronic apparatus. The test the court discussed was expressly addressed to the problem "how far a valid trademark shall be protected with respect to goods *other than those to which its owner has applied it.*" 287 F.2d at 495 (emphasis added); *see also Arrow Fastener*, 59 F.3d at 396 (noting that products need not actually compete with each other). The very fact that the test includes the "proximity" between the defendant's products and the plaintiff's and the likelihood that the plaintiff will "bridge the gap" makes clear that the trademark owner does not lose, as the district court concluded, merely because it has not previously sold the precise good or service sold by the secondary user.

[34] In our view, had the district court employed the proper test of proximity, it could not have failed to find a high degree of proximity as between plaintiff VEL's prior sales of consumer electronic audio equipment and defendants' subsequent sales of telephones and telephone services, which proximity would certainly contribute to likelihood of consumer confusion. And plaintiff was all the more entitled to a finding in its favor in respect of these matters by virtue of the fact, which the district court *did* find, that at the time defendants began using the VIRGIN mark in the retail sale of telephones and telephone services, plaintiff already had plans to bridge the gap by expanding its sales of consumer electronic equipment to include sales of those very goods and services in the near future. Consumer confusion was more than likely; it was virtually inevitable.

[35] *Actual confusion.* It is self-evident that the existence of actual consumer confusion indicates a likelihood of consumer confusion. *Nabisco*, 191 F.3d at 228. We have therefore deemed evidence of actual confusion "particularly relevant" to the inquiry. *Streetwise Maps*, 159 F.3d at 745.

[36] Plaintiff submitted to the district court an affidavit of a former employee of defendant Cel-Net, who worked at a mall kiosk branded as Virgin Wireless, which stated that individuals used to ask him if the kiosk was affiliated with plaintiff's VIRGIN stores. The district court correctly concluded that this evidence weighed in plaintiff's favor.

[37] *Sophistication of consumers.* The degree of sophistication of consumers can have an important bearing on likelihood of confusion. Where the purchasers of products are highly trained professionals, they know the market and are less likely than untrained consumers to be misled or confused by the similarity of different marks. The district court recognized that "[r]etail customers, such as the ones catered to by both the defendants and [plaintiff], are not expected to exercise the same degree of care as professional buyers, who are expected to have greater powers of discrimination." On the other hand, it observed that purchasers of cellular telephones and the service plans were likely to give greater care than self-service customers in a supermarket. Noting that neither side had submitted evidence on the sophistication of consumers, the court made no finding favoring either side. We agree that the sophistication factor is neutral in this case.

[38] *Bad faith and the quality of the defendants' services or products.* Two factors remain of the conventional *Polaroid* test: the existence of bad faith on the part of the secondary user and the quality of the secondary user's products or services. *Polaroid*, 287 F.2d at 495. Neither factor is of high relevance to the issue of likelihood of confusion. A finding that a party acted in bad faith can affect the court's choice of remedy or can tip the balance where questions are close. It does not bear directly on whether consumers are likely to be confused. *See TCPIP*, 244 F.3d at 102. The district court noted some evidence of bad faith on the defendants' part, but because the evidence on the issue was scant and equivocal, the court concluded that such a finding "at this stage [would be] speculative." The court therefore found that this factor favored neither party.

[39] The issue of the quality of the secondary user's product goes more to the harm that confusion can cause the plaintiff's mark and reputation than to the likelihood of confusion. *See Arrow Fastener*, 59 F.3d at 398 (noting that first user's reputation may be harmed if secondary user's goods are of poor

quality). In any event, the district court found this factor to be "neutral" with respect to likelihood of confusion.

* * * * * *

[40] In summary we conclude that of the six *Polaroid* factors that pertain directly to the likelihood of consumer confusion, all but one favor the plaintiff, and that one—sophistication of consumers—is neutral. The plaintiff is strongly favored by the strength of its mark, both inherent and acquired; the similarity of the marks; the proximity of the products and services; the likelihood that plaintiff would bridge the gap; and the existence of actual confusion. None of the factors favors the defendant. The remaining factors were found to be neutral. Although we do not suggest that likelihood of confusion may be properly determined simply by the number of factors in one party's favor, the overall assessment in this case in our view admits only of a finding in plaintiff's favor that defendants' sale of telephones and telephone-related services under the VIRGIN mark was likely to cause substantial consumer confusion.

[41] One issue remains. Defendants argue that plaintiff should be barred by laches from seeking injunctive relief. They contend that because of plaintiff's delay after learning of the defendants' applications to register the VIRGIN marks, they expended considerable sums and developed goodwill in their use of the VIRGIN marks before plaintiff brought suit. Because the district court ruled in the defendants' favor it made no express finding on the issue of laches. But the district court explicitly found that plaintiff first learned of defendants' use of the name VIRGIN in commerce only two days before plaintiff instituted this suit. Given that finding, plaintiff could not be chargeable with laches.

[42] We conclude that, as a matter of law, plaintiff demonstrated irreparable harm and likelihood of success on the merits and was entitled to a preliminary injunction.

CONCLUSION

REVERSED and REMANDED.

Questions and Comments

1. *The* Abercrombie *spectrum.* In its discussion of inherent distinctiveness, the court divides the *Abercrombie* spectrum into inherently and non-inherently distinctive marks: "This inquiry distinguishes between, on the one hand, inherently distinctive marks—marks that are arbitrary or fanciful in relation to the products (or services) on which they are used—and, on the other hand, marks that are generic, descriptive or suggestive as to those goods." Do you detect an error in this division?

Later in the opinion, the court refers to the *Virgin* mark as "arbitrary and fanciful." Should we treat these two *Abercrombie* categories as indistinguishable for purposes of the inherent distinctiveness analysis? Why might we seek to accord a greater scope of protection to fanciful marks than to arbitrary marks?

2. *Are all factors equally important?* In order to prevail in the overall likelihood of confusion multifactor test, must a plaintiff win all of the factors, a majority of them, some of them? Is the outcome of any particular factor necessary or sufficient to trigger a particular overall test outcome?

Empirical work offers some insight into these questions. *See* Barton Beebe, *An Empirical Study of the Multifactor Tests for Trademark Infringement*, 94 Calif. L. Rev. 1581 (2006). The author's evidence suggests that the plaintiff must win the similarity factor in order to win the overall test. Of the 192 preliminary injunction and bench trial opinions studied, 65 opinions found that the marks were not similar, and each of these 65 opinions found in favor of the defendant in the overall likelihood of confusion test. Notwithstanding the *Virgin* court's assertion that the intent factor is not "of high relevance" and may only "tip the balance where the questions are close," the study also suggests that the outcome of the intent factor correlates very strongly with the outcome of the overall test. Sixty-seven of the 192 preliminary injunction and bench trial opinions found that the intent factor favored the plaintiff. Of these 67 opinions, 65 found in favor of the plaintiff in the overall test (and in the two outlying opinions, the court found that the similarity factor favored the defendant). Overall, across the circuits, five core factors appear to drive the outcome of the likelihood of confusion test. In order of importance, these factors are the similarity of the marks, the defendant's intent, the proximity of the goods, evidence of actual confusion, and the strength of the plaintiff's mark. The remaining factors appear, in practice, to be largely irrelevant to the outcome of the test. *See also* Daryl Lim, *Trademark Confusion Revealed: An Empirical Analysis*, 71 AM. U. L. REV. 1285 (2022).

3. *Why should strong marks receive more protection?* The conventional rationale for according a greater scope of protection to strong marks is that, due to their notoriety, they are more easily called to mind by similar marks. *See* Jacob Jacoby, *The Psychological Foundations of Trademark Law: Secondary Meaning, Genericism, Fame, Confusion and Dilution*, 91 TRADEMARK REP. 1013, 1038-42 (2001). But shouldn't strong marks actually require *less* protection? Consider the example of COKE. Having been exposed to the COKE mark countless times throughout their lives, are American consumers more or less likely to detect slight differences between the COKE mark and other similar marks? Some foreign courts have had the temerity to suggest that exceptionally strong marks are less likely to be confused with other marks. *See, e.g., Baywatch Production Co. Inc. v The Home Video Channel*, High Court of Justice, Chancery Division, 31 July 1996 (Crystal J.) (citing *BASF Plc v CEP (UK) Plc* (Knox J.), 16 October 1995)); *Uprise Product Yugen Kaisha v. Commissioner of Japan Patent Office*, Heisei 22 (gyo-ke) 10274 Intellectual Property High Court of Japan (2010). Australian courts have been particularly receptive to this line of argument. *See* ROBERT BURRELL & MICHAEL HANDLER, AUSTRALIAN TRADEMARK LAW 253-55, 403-06 (2d ed. 2016). *See generally* Barton Beebe & C. Scott Hemphill, *The Scope of Strong Marks: Should Trademark Law Protect the Strong More than the Weak?*, 92 NYU L. REV. 1339 (2017).

4. *Sophistication of the relevant consumers.* Courts assess the likelihood of confusion by the "reasonably prudent" consumer of the goods or services at issue. Consumers of more expensive or more technically sophisticated goods are understood to exercise greater care in their purchasing decisions, and thus to be comparatively less likely to be confused. *See, e.g., Florida Int'l Univ. Bd. of Trustees v. Florida Nat'l Univ., Inc.*, 830 F.3d 1242, 1256 (11th Cir. 2016) (in finding no likelihood of confusion between FLORIDA INTERNATIONAL UNIVERSITY and FLORIDA NATIONAL UNIVERSITY, observing that "students looking for a college to attend are likely to be relatively sophisticated and knowledgeable because of the nature, importance, and size of the investment in a college education"); *Heartsprings, Inc. v. Heartspring, Inc.*, 143 F.3d 550, 557 (10th Cir. 1998) (finding that consumers would not likely confuse defendant's mark HEARTSPRING for a residential school for physically disabled children with plaintiff's mark HEARTSPRINGS for printed materials teaching children to resolve conflicts non-violently where tuition for defendant's school ranged from $90,000 to $150,000 per year). *See also M Welles & Assocs., Inc. v. Edwell, Inc.*, 69 F.4th 723, 736 (10th Cir. 2023) (citing *Heartsprings* in support of and affirming magistrate judge's bench trial ruling that EDWELL for nonprofit organization dedicated to improving schoolteachers' mental health was not confusingly similar with EDWEL for provider of classes and certification workshops for project management professionals); *but see id.* at 737 (Thmokovich, J., dissenting) ("The majority . . . overlooks the likelihood of confusion as to affiliation between the two.").

A Canadian case captured this aspect of consumer sophistication doctrine quite memorably. In *Atomic Energy of Canada Limited v. Areva NP Canada Ltd.*, 2009 FC 980 (2009), the plaintiff used a stylized "A" (shown below on the left) as its trademark for services relating to the design and construction of nuclear reactors while the defendant also used a stylized "A" (shown below on the right) in connection with the sale of nuclear reactor parts and components. The court noted: "All of [the plaintiff's] experts acknowledged in cross-examination that the relevant consumers would not be confused into purchasing the wrong nuclear reactor." *Id.* at ¶19. Citing English case law, the court recognized that "[I]t is not sufficient that the only confusion would be to a very small, unobservant section of society; or as Foster J. put it recently, if the only person who would be misled was a 'moron in a hurry.'" *Id.* at ¶28. Mr. Justice Zinn added: "In this industry, the fact that Homer Simpson may be confused is insufficient to find confusion." *Id.*

Are relatively poor individuals less sophisticated consumers and thus more easily confused? One S.D.N.Y. judge seemed to think so. Se*e Schieffelin & Co. v. The Jack Co.*, 1994 WL 144884 at *55 (S.D.N.Y. 1994) ("Even if some of the prospective purchasers of Dom Perignon are from low income groups, and are therefore less sophisticated shoppers than wealthier purchasers, . . ."). A later court took exception to the *Shieffelin* Court's assumption. S*ee Reebok Intern. Ltd. v. K-Mart Corp.*, 849 F.Supp. 252, 268 (S.D.N.Y. 1994) ("[T]he court expressly disagrees with this statement's implication that there is a direct relationship between income and consumer intelligence. Careless shopping habits are not a necessary by-product of a low income."). Indeed, couldn't an argument be made that low income groups would give more care to their purchases?

5. *What about the interests of consumers who are not confused?* In Michael Grynberg, *Trademark Litigation as Consumer Conflict*, 83 N.Y.U. L. Rev. 60 (2008), Grynberg argues:

> Trademark litigation typically unfolds as a battle between competing sellers who argue over whether the defendant's conduct is likely to confuse consumers. This is an unfair fight. In the traditional narrative, the plaintiff defends her trademark while simultaneously protecting consumers at risk for confusion. The defendant, relatively speaking, stands alone. The resulting "two-against-one" storyline gives short shrift to the interests of nonconfused consumers who may have a stake in the defendant's conduct. As a result, courts are too receptive to nontraditional trademark claims where the case for consumer harm is questionable. Better outcomes are available by appreciating trademark litigation's parallel status as a conflict between consumers. This view treats junior and senior trademark users as proxies for different consumer classes and recognizes that remedying likely confusion among one group of consumers may cause harm to others. Focusing on the interests of benefited and harmed consumers also minimizes the excessive weight given to moral rhetoric in adjudicating trademark cases. Consideration of trademark's consumer-conflict dimension is therefore a useful device for critiquing trademark's expansion and assessing future doctrinal developments.

Id. at 60. Should courts be more solicitous of the interests of sophisticated consumers who are in fact not confused and may benefit from the information provided by the defendant's conduct?

6. *Is it necessary for courts explicitly to consider each factor?* District courts are generally required explicitly to address each of the factors listed in their circuit's multifactor test. If a factor is irrelevant, the court must explain why. Failure to do so can result in remand. See, for example, *Sabinsa Corp. v. Creative Compounds*, 609 F.3d 175 (3d Cir. 2010), which reviewed a district court opinion that addressed only three of the ten *Lapp* factors used by the Third Circuit. The Third Circuit explained: "[W]hile it is true that a district court may find that certain of the *Lapp* factors are inapplicable or unhelpful in a particular case, the court must still explain its choice not to employ those factors. Here, the District Court failed to explain whether it viewed these remaining factors as neutral or irrelevant or how it weighed and balanced the combined factors." *Id.* at 183. Finding that the facts were "largely undisputed," *id.*, the Third Circuit declined to remand. Instead, it considered each of the ten *Lapp* factors and reversed.

7. *A two-dimensional model of trademark scope.* Trademark lawyers typically speak of trademarks in two dimensions, as in the trademark "FORD for cars" or the trademark "ACE for hardware, but not for bandages." From this we can derive a simple two-dimensional model of trademark infringement, as in the figure below. *See* Barton Beebe, *The Semiotic Analysis of Trademark Law*, 51 UCLA L. Rev. 621, 654-655 (2004). This model conceives of any given trademark as forming a point in a two-dimensional features space consisting of a trademark dimension and a goods/services dimension. The trademark dimension consists of a collapsed, one-dimensional continuum of all possible marks arranged according to similarities of "sound, sight, and meaning." The goods/services dimension similarly consists of a one-dimensional continuum of all possible goods and services arranged according to their degree of similarity.

V10.0/2023-07-22

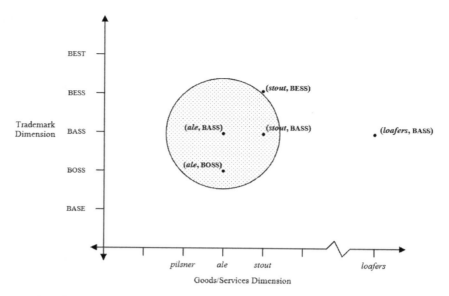

Distance in this features space is a measure of two concepts. First, distance is a measure of difference. The distance between any two points represents the degree of difference between them. Second, and related, distance is a measure of the likelihood of consumer confusion. The closer two points are in features space, the greater the proportion of consumers in the relevant consumer population who will likely confuse them.

As we have seen, in order to prevent consumer confusion as to source, trademark law invests a trademark-product combination with some broader scope of protection extending out from the point the combination forms in this features space. Otherwise, a competitor could come very near to that point, as in (*stout*, BASS) or (*ale*, BOSS) in the above figure and, by confusing some proportion of consumers as to source, unfairly appropriate as to those consumers the goodwill of the BASS ale brand. The closer a junior user's trademark-product combination comes to the trademark-product combination of a senior user, the greater the proportion of consumers who will confuse the junior's with the senior's use. At some proximity to the senior's use, trademark law declares that too high a proportion of consumers are or will be confused, and establishes a border, a property line, inside of which no competitor may come. This border, enveloping any given trademark, describes the scope of that trademark's protection and the extent of the producer's property right.

For exceptionally well-known marks, what might be the shape of the mark's scope in this features space? Would it matter where the mark falls on the *Abercrombie* spectrum? What would be the shape of the scope of protection for COCA-COLA? Can any other firm reasonably use that mark on any other good or service? What would be the shape of the scope of FORD for automobiles or APPLE for high technology goods and services?

3. Further Examples of the Application of the Multifactor Test for the Likelihood of Consumer Confusion Test

The application of the multifactor test for the likelihood of confusion is often highly fact-specific. String citations of cases finding confusion and other seemingly similar cases finding no confusion may give the impression that the test is unpredictable. *See, e.g., Bank of Texas v. Commerce Southwest, Inc.,* 741 F.2d 785, 223 U.S.P.Q. 1174 (Fed. Cir. 1984) (BANK OF TEXAS and BANC TEXAS found not confusing); *Laurel Capital Group, Inc. v. BT Fin. Corp.,* 45 F. Supp. 2d 469 (W.D. Pa. 1999) (LAUREL SAVINGS BANK and LAUREL BANK found confusing); *Popular Bank of Fla. v. Banco Popular de Puerto Rico,* 9 F. Supp. 2d 1347 (S.D. Fla. 1998) (POPULAR BANK and BANCO POPULAR found confusing); *Wachovia Bank and Trust Co. v. Crown National Bancorp.,* 27 U.S.P.Q.2d 1698 (W.D.N.C. 1993) (WACHOVIA CROWN ACCOUNT and CROWN ACCOUNT found not confusing). However, close attention to the facts of each case would show no significant inconsistencies in the courts' rulings.

Adding to the difficulty is that there are no clear rules for when marks are too similar or not similar enough to trigger liability. Good trademark lawyers tend to build up over time a feel for what courts will likely find infringing in light of all the facts of the case. Provided below are brief summaries of a few more cases in which courts found or did not find confusion to try to impart to those new to trademark law some further sense of the diverse variety of considerations that can enter into a court's application of the multifactor test.

1. In *Hero Nutritionals LLC v. Nutraceutical Corp.*, No. 11 Civ. 1195, 2013 WL 4480674 (C.D. Cal. Aug. 16, 2013), the plaintiff produced nutritional supplements for children under the registered marks YUMMI and YUMMI BEARS. The defendant began to produce vitamin supplements labelled "Vitamin C-Rex Yummy Gummy." The trade dresses of the competing products are shown below.

In finding no confusion after a bench trial, the court summarized its multifactor analysis:

> The balance of the *Sleekcraft* factors does not demonstrate a likelihood of confusion between Hero's marks and Nutraceutical's use of "Yummy Gummy." Hero's marks are weak and entitled only to a narrow scope of protection. Although the words "Yummy" and "yummi" are similar, the overall impression of the marks, including the packaging, labeling, designs, and house marks, are dissimilar. Consumers of children's vitamins at health food stores tend to be more careful and discriminating than the average shopper. Despite years of coexistence in the market, there was no showing of actual confusion, nor has Hero offered a survey to show actual confusion. Other than knowledge of the YUMMI BEARS mark, Hero has made no showing that Nutraceutical's use of "Yummy Gummy" was done in bad faith with an intent to trade off of Hero's good will. Although the products at issue are competitive and are generally sold in the same trade channel, these factors do not outweigh the other considerations leading to the ultimate conclusion that there is no likelihood of confusion.

Id. at *8.

2. In *Spangler Candy Co. v. Tootsie Roll Indus.*, LLC, 2019 WL 1170749, 372 F. Supp. 3d 588 (N.D. Ohio 2019), the defendant Tootsie Roll developed a new, red trade dress for its CHARMS MINI POPS lollipops product, shown immediately below on the right. This new trade dress was suspiciously similar to the red trade dress of the plaintiff Spangler's DUM DUMS, which had been gaining market share, shown immediately below on the left. The defendant Tootsie Roll's previous trade dress was yellow, shown below. The court found a likelihood of confusion and summarized its reasoning as follows:

> The Dum Dums trade dress is not strong and there is no evidence of actual confusion. But the two companies used the same marketing channels to sell the same product. While the Charms Mini Pops trade dress is distinguishable when seen alone, Tootsie intends the product to be sold side-by-side on the shelf with Dum Dums, which would increase the

likelihood of confusion due to the low degree of purchaser care. This intent along with other evidence also supports a conclusion that Tootsie acted with the intent to deceive. Therefore, considering all the factors, I find the evidence suggests the red Charms Mini Pops packaging is confusingly similar to the Dum Dums trade dress.

Id. at *12.

3. In *Eli Lilly & Co. v. Nat. Answers, Inc.*, 86 F. Supp. 2d 834 (S.D. Ind.), aff'd, 233 F.3d 456 (7th Cir. 2000), the plaintiff produced an antidepressant under the registered mark PROZAC. The defendant produced an herbal drug under the name HERBROZAC that it claimed promoted "mood elevation." In finding a likelihood of confusion and granting the plaintiff's motion for a preliminary injunction, the district court summarized its multifactor analysis:

Considering all the factors as set forth above, the court concludes that Lilly has shown an unusually strong case on the issue of likelihood of confusion. Most important here are the unusual strength of Lilly's PROZAC® mark, the strong similarity between PROZAC® and HERBROZAC, and defendant's intentional selection of the HERBROZAC name precisely because of its similarity to PROZAC® for the purpose of suggesting an association or affiliation between the products. Add to this mixture the fairly close "competitive proximity" of the two products, especially as pharmaceutical companies expand into the herbal and dietary supplement business, and Lilly has made a powerful showing of likelihood of success on its claim for trademark infringement.

Id. at 846.

4. In *Kate Spade LLC v. Saturdays Surf LLC*, 950 F. Supp. 2d 639 (S.D.N.Y. 2013), the plaintiff produced primarily men's apparel under the mark SATURDAYS SURF NYC. The defendant launched a line of women's apparel under the mark KATE SPADE SATURDAY. Examples of the parties' respective uses of their marks are shown below.

In finding no likelihood of confusion after a bench trial, the court summarized its multifactor analysis:

> After considering and weighing each of the *Polaroid* factors, I conclude that Saturdays Surf NYC has not shown a likelihood of confusion by a preponderance of the credible evidence. I am particularly persuaded by the relative weakness of the word that the two marks share, the significant distance between the men's and women's products, and the consistent inclusion of the famous house mark, Kate Spade, in its Kate Spade Saturday mark.

Id. at 648

5. In the relatively straightforward case of *Nikon, Inc. v. Ikon Corp.*, 987 F.2d 91 (2d Cir. 1993), the plaintiff was a world-famous producer of high-quality cameras under the mark NIKON. The defendant was a lesser known seller of low-cost cameras under the mark IKON. The court found confusion: "Applying the facts found by the court, each factor, with the exception of actual confusion, weighs heavily in favor of Nikon. And there was some evidence of actual confusion." *Id.* at 96.

6. In *Alliance for Good Gov't v. Coalition for Better Gov't*, 901 F.3d 498 (5th Cir. 2018), the plaintiff had been using the mark below on the left since the 1960s to promote political candidates in Louisiana. The defendant organization subsequently developed its own logo, below on the right, in the early 1980s or 1990s to promote political candidates in New Orleans. The district court found a likelihood of confusion and the Fifth Circuit affirmed.

Of special interest is the Fifth Circuit's analysis of the similarity of the marks, and in particular its reference to the defendant's attorney's ignoble attempt (basically a failed con) to distinguish the marks:

> Finally, we observe that Coalition attempted to distinguish the two logos—not by appearance, design, color, or font—but by the birds' species:
>
> DISTRICT COURT: They look exactly alike to me, the two birds.
>
> COUNSEL: [. . .] [N]o, they really aren't, your Honor, if you look at the wing span. The wing span of the eagle is different from the hawk. It's much larger and it fans out, and that's just the way the hawk looks.
>
> COURT: I'll tell you, unless my eyes are deceiving me, . . . those two look exactly alike. They even look like the same feathers, same number of feathers, same arrangement, head is facing the same way, the same beak. I don't know if you call them—I don't know technically what kind of bird it is, but whatever they are, they look exactly alike to me.
>
> COUNSEL: Well, they're both birds of prey; one is an eagle and one is a hawk.
>
> COURT: Okay.

COUNSEL: And when we filed with the Secretary of State to get our font, we said it was a hawk. We were represented by a hawk, not an eagle.

We agree with the district court: the birds are identical. Whether that bird is a haliaeetus leucocephalus (bald eagle), a buteo jamaicensis (red-tailed hawk), or some other bird, we need not determine.

Id. at 511–12. The plaintiff was subsequently awarded attorney's fees in the dispute, though there have been continuing skirmishes over the amount. *See Alliance for Good Gov't v. Coalition for Better Gov't*, 919 F.3d 291 (5th Cir. 2019). (For more on fee shifting in trademark disputes, see Part VI).

4. Survey Evidence and the Likelihood of Confusion

It is often said that survey evidence is routinely submitted in trademark litigation, particularly on the issue of consumer confusion. In a statement before Congress, the American Bar Association offered a typical expression of this view: "survey evidence is traditionally one of the most classic and most persuasive and most informative forms of trial evidence that trademark lawyers utilize in both prosecuting and defending against trademark claims of various sorts." *Committee Print to Amend the Federal Trademark Dilution Act: Hearing Before the Subcomm. on Courts, the Internet, and Intellectual Property of the Comm. on the Judiciary*, 108th Cong. 14 (2004) (statement of Robert W. Sacoff, Chair, Section of Intellectual Property Law, American Bar Association). In fact, empirical work suggests that survey evidence plays a surprisingly small role in deciding most trademark cases. *See* Barton Beebe, *An Empirical Study of the Multifactor Tests for Trademark Infringement*, 94 Calif. L. Rev. 1581, 1641-42 (2006). The author studied all federal court opinions applying a likelihood of confusion multifactor test over a five-year period from 2000 to 2004 and found that only 65 (20%) of the 331 opinions addressed survey evidence, 34 (10%) credited the survey evidence, and 24 (7%) ultimately ruled in favor of the outcome that the credited survey evidence itself favored. Eleven (24%) of the 46 bench trial opinions addressed survey evidence (with eight crediting it), while 24 (16%) of the 146 preliminary injunction opinions addressed survey evidence (with 12 crediting it). *Id. See also* Robert C. Bird & Joel H. Steckel, *The Role of Consumer Surveys in Trademark Infringement: Empirical Evidence from the Federal Courts*, 14 Penn. J. Bus. L. 1013 (2012) (finding that survey evidence is infrequently used in trademark litigation and suggesting that "the mere submission of a survey by a defendant appears to help its case, while a plaintiff-submitted survey can potentially hurt its case if the court deems it flawed"). *But see* Dan Sarel & Howard Marmorstein, *The Effect of Consumer Surveys and Actual Confusion Evidence in Trademark Litigation: An Empirical Assessment*, 99 Trademark Rep. 1416 (2009) (finding survey evidence presented in one-third of the opinions studied and that survey evidence had a substantial impact in cases involving dissimilar goods). *Cf.* Shari Seidman Diamond & David Franklyn, *Trademark Surveys: An Undulating Path*, 92 Texas L. Rev. 2029 (2014) (concluding based on a survey of trademark practitioners that surveys can perform a significant role in settlement negotiations).

Nevertheless, in the small subset of trademark cases involving high-stakes litigation or one or more well-funded parties, survey evidence is customary, so much so that courts will sometimes draw an "adverse inference" against a party for failing to present it. *See, e.g., Eagle Snacks, Inc. v. Nabisco Brands, Inc.*, 625 F. Supp. 571, 583 (D.N.J. 1985) ("Failure of a trademark owner to run a survey to support its claims of brand significance and/or likelihood of confusion, where it has the financial means of doing so, may give rise to the inference that the contents of the survey would be unfavorable, and may result in the court denying relief."); *but see, e.g., Tools USA and Equipment Co. v. Champ Frame Straightening Equipment Inc.*, 87 F.3d 654, 661 (4th Cir. 1996) ("Actual confusion can be demonstrated by survey evidence, but contrary to [defendant's] suggestion, survey evidence is not necessarily the best evidence of actual confusion and surveys are not required to prove likelihood of confusion.").

When litigants do present survey evidence, courts' analysis of this evidence can be painstaking, especially when the litigants present dueling survey experts. In the following opinion, *Smith v. Wal-Mart Stores, Inc.*, 537 F.Supp.2d 1302 (N.D.Ga. 2008), the declaratory plaintiff Charles Smith sought to criticize Wal-Mart's effect on American communities and workers by likening the retailer to the Nazi regime and, after Wal-Mart sent Smith two cease and desist letters, to Al Qaeda. Smith created and sold online through CafePress.com t-shirts and other merchandise incorporating the term "Walocaust" and various Nazi insignia (shown below) or the term "Wal-Qaeda" and various slogans and images (shown below). Wal-Mart produced survey evidence to support the proposition that American consumers would believe that Wal-Mart was selling the t-shirts or had otherwise authorized their sale, or that in any case, Smith's conduct tarnished Wal-Mart's trademark. Both parties moved for summary judgment. Excerpted below is Judge Timothy Batten, Sr.'s extraordinarily fine analysis of the surveys before him, which he conducted under the "actual confusion" factor of the multifactor test for the likelihood of consumer confusion. The analysis is lengthy and very detailed, but it addresses a variety of survey-related issues with which a serious student of trademark litigation should be familiar.

A few additional preliminary comments. First, the surveys at issue are modified forms of the "*Eveready* format" for likelihood of confusion surveys, based on the case *Union Carbide Corp. v. Ever-Ready, Inc.*, 531 F.2d 366 (7th Cir. 1976), in which the Seventh Circuit credited two surveys as strong evidence of the likelihood of confusion. (Despite the spelling of "Ever-Ready" in the caption of the case, most commentators, including McCarthy, refer to the survey format as the "*Eveready* format.") Second, the excerpt below addresses, in addition to the likelihood of confusion issue, a cause of action for dilution by tarnishment of Wal-Mart's mark. We will address dilution more fully in Part II.C.

In reading through the excerpt, consider the following question:

- Do you find the *Eveready* format persuasive? How else might you design a likelihood of confusion survey?

- The "third set of questions" in the surveys, "aimed at testing for confusion as to authorization or sponsorship, asked whether the company that 'put out' the shirt needed permission from another company to do so, and if so, which company." Is this an appropriate survey question to ask consumers?

Appendix B: Challenged Wal-Qaeda Images

Smith v. Wal-Mart Stores, Inc.
537 F.Supp.2d 1302 (N.D.Ga. 2008)

Timothy C. Batten, Sr., District Judge:

. . . .

II. Analysis

C. Trademark Infringement, Unfair Competition, Cybersquatting and Deceptive Trade Practices Claims

1. Actual Confusion

[1] Proof of actual confusion is considered the best evidence of likelihood of confusion. *Roto–Rooter Corp. v. O'Neal,* 513 F.2d 44, 45–46 (5th Cir. 1975). A claimant may present anecdotal evidence of marketplace confusion, and surveys, when appropriately and accurately conducted and reported, are also widely and routinely accepted as probative of actual confusion. *See, e.g., AmBrit, Inc. v. Kraft, Inc.,* 812 F.2d 1531, 1544 (11th Cir. 1986) (considering the proffered survey but giving it little weight); *SunAmerica Corp. v. Sun Life Assurance Co. of Canada,* 890 F.Supp. 1559, 1576 (N.D.Ga. 1994) (viewing the proffered survey as confirmation of consistent anecdotal evidence).

[2] Wal–Mart concedes that it has no marketplace evidence of actual consumer confusion. Instead, it presents two consumer research studies conducted by Dr. Jacob Jacoby that purport to prove that consumer confusion and damage to Wal–Mart's reputation are likely.

358

a. The Jacoby Report

[3] Jacoby developed two surveys for Wal–Mart that both purported to measure consumer confusion and dilution by tarnishment. Specifically, the stated objectives of the research were (1) "To determine whether (and if so, to what extent), when confronted with merchandise bearing Mr. Smith's designs either in person or via the Internet, prospective consumers would be confused into believing that these items either came from Wal–Mart, came from a firm affiliated with Wal–Mart, or had been authorized by Wal–Mart," and (2) "To determine whether (and if so, to what extent) exposure to Mr. Smith's designs would generate dilution via tarnishment."

[4] Deeming it impractical to test all of Smith's designs, Jacoby chose instead to test two products as representative of all of Smith's allegedly infringing products—the white t-shirt with the word "WAL*OCAUST" in blue font over the Nazi eagle clutching a yellow smiley face, and another white t-shirt that depicted the word "WAL–QAEDA" in a blue font as part of the phrase "SUPPORT OUR TROOPS. BOYCOTT WAL–QAEDA."

[5] He also tested consumer reactions to "control" designs, which he compared to consumer responses to the Walocaust and Wal–Qaeda designs. To develop the control for the Walocaust design, Jacoby replaced the star with a hyphen and removed the smiley face from the yellow circle, and for both the Walocaust and Wal–Qaeda controls, he substituted "Z" for "W." These substitutions resulted in control concepts entitled "Zal-ocaust" and "Zal–Qaeda."

[6] Jacoby engaged a market research firm to test each of the t-shirt designs in (1) a "product" study intended to test for post-purchase confusion and tarnishment, and (2) a "website" study intended to test for point-of-sale confusion and tarnishment.[15]

[7] The market research company conducted the studies in a mall-intercept format. The company's researchers would approach people who appeared to be thirteen years old or older and ask a series of screening questions.[16] To qualify for either survey, the respondent was required to be at least thirteen years old[17] and must have in the past year bought, or would in the coming year consider buying, bumper stickers, t-shirts or coffee mugs with words, symbols or designs on them. To qualify for the "website" study, the respondent must also have (1) used the Internet in the past month to search for information about products or services and (2) either (a) in the past year used the Internet to buy or to search for information about bumper stickers, t-shirts or coffee mugs with words, symbols or designs on them, or (b) in the coming year would consider buying over the Internet bumper stickers, t-shirts or coffee mugs

---

[15] This resulted in eight test cells:

	Test cells		Control cells	
Post-purchase confusion/tarnishment	Wal★ocaust t-shirt	Wal-Qaeda t-shirt	Zal-ocaust t-shirt	Zal-Qaeda t-shirt
Point-of-sale confusion/tarnishment	Wal★ocaust website	Wal-Qaeda website	Zal-ocaust website	Zal-Qaeda website

[16] The research company conducted the surveys in malls in Trumbull, Connecticut; Philadelphia, Pennsylvania; Youngstown, Ohio; Chicago Ridge, Illinois; Louisville, Kentucky; San Antonio, Texas; Colorado Springs, Colorado; and Northridge, California. The website survey was also conducted in Portland, Oregon.

[17] Because CafePress allowed only consumers over the age of thirteen to purchase from its site, Jacoby similarly limited his universe of respondents.

with words, symbols or designs on them.[18] If the respondent met the qualifications, he or she was asked to go with the researcher to the mall's enclosed interviewing facility for a five-minute interview.[19]

[8] For the "product" study, the interviewers presented to each respondent one of the four t-shirts described above and asked the respondent to imagine seeing someone wearing the shirt. The interviewer then asked a series of questions.

[9] The first three sets of questions were designed to test for consumer confusion. The interviewers were directed to ask each of the "likelihood of confusion" questions sequentially unless the respondent answered "Sears," "Wal–Mart," "Youngblood's" or "K–Mart," in which case the interviewer was to record the answer, skip the remaining confusion questions, and go directly to the tarnishment questions.

[10] In the consumer confusion series, the first set of questions tested for confusion as to source. The interviewer would ask "which company or store" the respondent thought "put out" the shirt, and if the respondent named a company or store, the interviewer then asked what about the shirt made the respondent think the shirt was "put out" by that company or store. The second set of questions, which dealt with confusion as to connection or relationship, asked the respondent whether the company or store that "put out" the shirt had some "business connection or relationship with another company" and if so, with what company. The respondent was then asked why he or she believed the companies had a business connection or relationship. A third set of questions, aimed at testing for confusion as to authorization or sponsorship, asked whether the company that "put out" the shirt needed permission from another company to do so, and if so, which company.

[11] Finally, if the respondent had not yet answered "Sears," "Wal–Mart," "Youngblood's" or "K–Mart" to any of the first three sets of questions, he or she was then asked what the shirt made him or her "think of" and then "which company or store" the shirt brought to mind.

[12] The fifth set of questions, which tested for dilution by tarnishment, were asked in reference to any company or store the respondent mentioned in his or her answers to the first four sets of questions. The first question asked whether seeing the shirt made the respondent more or less likely to shop at the store he or she had named, and the second question asked whether the perceived association with the store made the respondent more or less likely to buy the shirt.

[13] The interviews for the website study were much like those for the product study, except that instead of being shown the actual shirts, the respondents were exposed to a simulation of Smith's Walocaust CafePress homepage, his Wal–Qaeda CafePress homepage or the associated control homepage.[20] In each of the simulations, all of the hyperlinks were removed from the homepages except for the one hyperlink associated with the t-shirt that Jacoby had decided to test.

[14] Jacoby directed the interviewers to begin each website interview by providing a URL to the respondent and asking the respondent to imagine that the URL was a search term the respondent had heard or seen somewhere and wanted to look up on the Internet. The interviewer would then have the respondent sit at a computer and type the URL into the browser. The URL would take the respondent to the simulated home page for testing.

[15] The interviewer would then direct the respondent to look at the screen and scroll down the page "as [he or she] normally would" and click through to the first t-shirt on the screen. The respondent was then directed to click on the "view larger" box and look at the shirt as though he or she "found it

---

[18] Respondents who worked at an advertising agency, a market research firm or a business located in the mall (or had an immediate family member who did) were excluded, as were people who normally wore eyeglasses or contact lenses but were not wearing them at the time of the screening.

[19] The screening questionnaire provided to the Court indicates that the respondents who then participated in the surveys were given a monetary reward. Neither Jacoby's report nor any of the supporting survey documents disclosed the amount of the reward.

[20] The simulations were reproduced on a compact disc; the respondents did not view Smith's actual web pages on the Internet.

interesting and [was] considering whether or not to order it . . . ." The interviewer would then ask the respondent exactly the same series of questions posed in the product study, including the same skip pattern to be applied in the event that the respondent mentioned Sears, Wal–Mart, Youngblood's or K–Mart in response to any of the consumer confusion questions.

[16] In order to be tallied as "confused," the respondent had to meet two tests. First, the respondent had to indicate either that the shirt came from Wal–Mart (first confusion series), came from a company that had some business connection or relationship with Wal–Mart (second confusion series), or came from a source that required or obtained permission from Wal–Mart (third confusion series). Second, the respondent had to indicate that his or her reason for that understanding was either because of the prefix "Wal," the name (or equivalent), the smiley face, or the star after the prefix "Wal." Thus, a respondent who believed that there was a connection between Wal–Mart and the t-shirt that he or she was shown but who did not mention the prefix "Wal," the name (or equivalent), the smiley face, or the star, would not be counted as "confused."

[17] Any respondent who perceived an association between Wal–Mart and the t-shirt that he or she was shown and reported that the perceived association either made the respondent less likely to shop at Wal–Mart or more likely to buy that t-shirt was deemed to satisfy the requirement for dilution.

[18] The field interviewers returned 322 completed interviews for the product study and 335 for the website study. Three responses were eliminated from the sample after the research company conducted a review to ensure that each respondent was qualified to participate in the study and that the questionnaires had been completed properly. The research company then sent the name and phone number of each of the interview respondents to an independent telephone interviewing service for validation, which consisted of calling each mall-intercept respondent to ensure that the respondent had actually participated in the study and that his or her answers were accurately recorded.

[19] In the product study, 181 respondents (fifty-six percent of the usable sample) were positively validated, and sixteen respondents (about five percent) reported either different answers to the survey questions or claimed not to have participated in the study. The remainder either could not be reached during the twenty days Jacoby allocated for the validation or refused to respond to the validation survey.

[20] Jacoby reported the results of those respondents who were positively validated plus the results from the respondents who could not be reached or would not respond to the validation survey, and he eliminated the results of the respondents who provided non-affirming answers during the validation process. This resulted in 305 reported responses to the product study: seventy-three for the Wal*ocaust concept, seventy-six for the Wal–Qaeda concept, seventy-nine for the Zal-ocaust concept, and seventy-seven for the Zal–Qaeda concept.

[21] In the website study, 169 respondents (fifty-one percent of the usable sample) were positively validated, and forty-six respondents (about fourteen percent) reported either different answers to the survey questions or claimed not to have participated in the study. The remainder either could not be reached during the twenty days Jacoby allocated for the validation or refused to respond to the validation survey.

[22] As he did in the product study, Jacoby reported the results of those respondents who were positively validated plus the results from the respondents who could not be reached or would not respond to the validation survey, and he eliminated the results of the respondents who provided non-affirming answers during the validation process. This resulted in 287 reported responses to the {website} study: seventy for the Wal*ocaust concept, seventy-eight for the Wal–Qaeda concept, sixty-nine for the Zal-ocaust concept, and seventy for the Zal–Qaeda concept.

[23] Jacoby reported that the survey reflected high levels of consumer confusion and dilution by tarnishment. He claimed that the post-purchase confusion "product study" indicated a likelihood of confusion in nearly forty-eight percent of the respondents and that the point-of-sale confusion "website"

study indicated a likelihood of confusion in almost forty-one percent of the respondents.[21] Jacoby also claimed that the "dilution" study indicated that almost twelve percent of the respondents were less likely to shop at Wal–Mart after seeing Smith's designs.

b. Evidentiary Objections

[24] Smith moves to exclude Wal–Mart's expert report. He claims that Jacoby did not have the requisite Internet expertise to conduct the web-based "point-of-sale" portion of this particular study and that several aspects of Jacoby's methodology affecting both portions of the study were faulty; thus, he contends, Jacoby's study is "too deeply flawed to be considered . . . ."

[25] Wal–Mart argues that the Jacoby test was performed by a competent expert according to industry standards and therefore is valid. Wal–Mart further contends that the expert witnesses Smith presents in rebuttal are not experts in the area of consumer-goods "likelihood of confusion" trademark studies, and therefore *their* testimony is irrelevant and should be excluded.

[26] Whether a given survey constitutes acceptable evidence depends on the survey's ability to satisfy the demands of Federal Rule of Evidence 703, which requires consideration of the "validity of the techniques employed." 233–34 FED. JUD. CTR., REFERENCE MANUAL ON SCI. EVIDENCE (2d ed. 2002) (explaining that in the context of surveys for litigation purposes, "[t]he inquiry under Rule 703[, which] focuses on whether facts or data are 'of a type reasonably relied upon by experts in the particular field in forming opinions or inferences upon the subject' . . . becomes, 'Was the . . . survey conducted in accordance with generally accepted survey principles, and were the results used in a statistically correct way?'"). *See also BFI Waste Sys. of N. Am. v. Dekalb County,* 303 F.Supp.2d 1335,1346 (N.D.Ga. 2004) (noting that the opposing party could have challenged an expert witness's reference to a recent survey by questioning whether the survey methodology satisfied Rule 703).

[27] The Eleventh Circuit has held that alleged technical deficiencies in a survey presented in a Lanham Act action affect the weight to be accorded to the survey and not its admissibility. *Jellibeans, Inc. v. Skating Clubs of Ga., Inc.,* 716 F.2d 833, 844 (11th Cir. 1983). Other courts have held that a significantly flawed survey may be excludable as evidence under either Rule 403 (the rule barring evidence that is more prejudicial than probative) or Rule 702 (the rule barring unreliable expert testimony). *Citizens Fin. Group, Inc. v. Citizens Nat'l Bank,* 383 F.3d 110, 188–21 (3d Cir. 2004) (finding that the district court properly excluded survey evidence under Rules 702 and 403 where the survey contained flaws that were not merely technical, but were so damaging to the reliability of the results as to be "fatal": the survey relied on an improper universe and its questions were imprecise); *Malletier v. Dooney & Bourke, Inc.,* 525 F.Supp.2d 558, 562–63 (S.D.N.Y. 2007). Even when a party presents an admissible survey purporting to show consumer confusion, however, the survey "does not itself create a triable issue of fact." *Mattel, Inc. v. MCA Records, Inc.,* 28 F.Supp.2d 1120, 1133 (C.D.Cal. 1998) (citing *Universal City Studios, Inc. v. Nintendo Co.,* 746 F.2d 112, 118 (2d Cir. 1984), which found a survey "so badly flawed that it cannot be used to demonstrate the existence of a question of fact of the likelihood of consumer confusion"). . . .

[28] To ground a survey as trustworthy, its proponent must establish foundation evidence showing that

(1) the 'universe' was properly defined, (2) a representative sample of that universe was selected, (3) the questions to be asked of interviewees were framed in a clear, precise and non-leading manner, (4) sound interview procedures were followed by competent interviewers who had no knowledge of the litigation or the purpose for which the survey was conducted, (5) the data gathered was accurately reported, (6) the data was analyzed in accordance with accepted statistical principles and (7) objectivity of the entire process was assured.

---

[21] Jacoby arrived at these numbers by averaging the net survey results for the Walocaust and Wal–Qaeda t-shirts.

Toys R Us, Inc. v. Canarsie Kiddie Shop, 559 F.Supp. 1189, 1205 (D.C.N.Y. 1983) (citing MANUAL FOR COMPLEX LITIG., 116 (5th ed. 1981), 4 LOUISELL & MUELLER, FED. EVIDENCE § 472 (1979), and J. THOMAS MCCARTHY, TRADEMARKS & UNFAIR COMPETITION § 32:53 (1973)); *accord Rush Indus., Inc. v. Garnier LLC,* 496 F.Supp.2d 220, 227 (E.D.N.Y. 2007). Failure to satisfy any of the listed criteria may seriously compromise the survey's impact on a court's likelihood of confusion evaluation. *Id.*

[29] Smith cites several grounds for excluding the Jacoby survey. He argues that the survey is inadmissible because it (1) failed to identify the relevant consumer universe or used a consumer universe that was substantially overbroad; (2) failed to replicate shopping conditions as consumers would encounter them in the marketplace; (3) was improperly leading; (4) violated the survey structure protocol necessary to comply with double-blind standards; and (5) failed to establish a relevant factual basis for Wal–Mart's dilution by tarnishment claims. Smith further argues that even if the Court admits the survey, its consideration should be limited to only the two tested designs, despite Jacoby's claim that they are representative of all the designs Wal–Mart seeks to enjoin.

[30] As an initial matter, the Court observes that Smith does not take issue with Jacoby's qualifications to design and conduct a consumer confusion survey and to analyze its results. It is undisputed that Jacoby is a nationally renowned trademark survey expert who has testified hundreds of times. Smith contends, however, that Jacoby was unqualified to conduct this particular survey because he "lacks knowledge, experience, [and] sophistication" with regard to products marketed exclusively over the Internet and that as a result Jacoby's survey protocol contained significant flaws.

[31] Based upon its own review of Jacoby's education and experience, the Court concludes that Jacoby is qualified to design and conduct a consumer survey and to testify about its results. To the extent that Jacoby's purported lack of experience with surveys concerning goods sold exclusively online may have led him to test the wrong universe or to fail to replicate the shopping experience, as Smith has alleged, these factors will be examined when the Court evaluates the trustworthiness of the survey.

i. Web–Related Challenges

[32] In undertaking to demonstrate likelihood of confusion in a trademark infringement case by use of survey evidence, the "appropriate universe should include a fair sampling of those purchasers most likely to partake of the alleged infringer's goods or services." *Amstar Corp. v. Domino's Pizza, Inc.,* 615 F.2d 252, 264 (5th Cir. 1980). Selection of the proper universe is one of the most important factors in assessing the validity of a survey and the weight that it should receive because "the persons interviewed must adequately represent the opinions which are relevant to the litigation." *Id.* . . . .

[33] Similarly, "[a] survey that fails to adequately replicate market conditions is entitled to little weight, if any." *Leelanau Wine Cellars, Ltd. v. Black & Red, Inc.,* 452 F.Supp.2d 772, 783 (W.D.Mich. 2006), *aff'd,* 502 F.3d 504 (6th Cir. 2007) (quoting *Wells Fargo & Co.,* 293 F.Supp.2d at 766). Although "[n]o survey model is suitable for every case . . . a survey to test likelihood of confusion must attempt to replicate the thought processes of consumers encountering the disputed mark or marks as they would in the marketplace." . . . .

[34] Smith hired Dr. Alan Jay Rosenblatt as a rebuttal witness to point out Internet-related deficiencies in Jacoby's survey methodology—particularly deficiencies in universe selection and replication of marketplace conditions—that he claims resulted from Jacoby's erroneous assumptions about how people reach and interact with websites.

. . . .

(a) Survey Universe

[35] . . . . Wal–Mart maintains that Jacoby's universe selection was proper. Smith counters that it was overly broad.

[36] Although the universe Jacoby selected would include purchasers of Smith's Walocaust or Wal–Qaeda merchandise, the Court finds that it is significantly overbroad. Because Smith's merchandise was available only through his CafePress webstores and the links to his CafePress webstores from his Walocaust and Wal–Qaeda websites, it is likely that only a small percentage of the consumers in the universe selected by Jacoby would be potential purchasers of Smith's products. A survey respondent

who purchases bumper stickers, t-shirts or coffee mugs with words, symbols or designs on them may buy such merchandise because the imprint represents his or her school, company, favorite sports team, cartoon character, social group, or any of hundreds of other interests or affiliations; he or she may have no interest at all in purchasing merchandise containing messages about Wal–Mart, pro or con. The respondent may buy from brick-and-mortar stores or well-known retailers with Internet storefronts without being aware of Smith's website or CafePress, or may have little interest in buying such merchandise over the Internet at all. Therefore, a respondent who clearly falls within Jacoby's survey universe may nevertheless have no potential to purchase Smith's imprinted products. *See Leelanau Wine Cellars,* 452 F.Supp.2d at 782.

[37] Other courts have similarly criticized surveys—including surveys Jacoby conducted in other trademark infringement cases—that failed to properly screen the universe to ensure that it was limited to respondents who were potential purchasers of the alleged infringer's product.

[38] For example, in *Weight Watchers Int'l, Inc. v. Stouffer Corp.,* 744 F.Supp. 1259 (S.D.N.Y. 1990), Weight Watchers sued Stouffer for trademark infringement after Stouffer launched an advertising campaign that suggested that new exchange listings on Stouffer's Lean Cuisine packages would allow adherents to the Weight Watchers program to use Lean Cuisine entrees in their diets. *Id.* at 1262. Stouffer's likelihood of confusion survey, also conducted by Jacoby, identified the universe as "women between the ages of 18 and 55 who have purchased frozen food entrees in the past six months and who have tried to lose weight through diet and/or exercise in the past year." *Id.* at 1272. The court found that the universe was overbroad because the screener had not limited it to dieters, but also had included respondents who may have tried to lose weight by exercise only. The court concluded that as a result the survey likely included respondents who were not potential consumers, and because "[r]espondents who are not potential consumers may well be less likely to be aware of and to make relevant distinctions when reading ads than those who are potential consumers," that portion of the survey universe may have failed to make "crucial" distinctions in the likelihood of confusion testing. *Id.* at 1273.

. . . .

(b) Shopping Experience

[39] To be valid for the purposes of demonstrating actual confusion in a trademark infringement suit, it is necessary for a survey's protocol to take into account marketplace conditions and typical consumer behavior so that the survey may as accurately as possible measure the relevant "thought processes of consumers encountering the disputed mark . . . as they would in the marketplace." *Simon Prop. Group,* 104 F.Supp.2d at 1038; *accord WE Media, Inc. v. Gen. Elec. Co.,* 218 F.Supp.2d 463, 474 (S.D.N.Y. 2002).

[40] Smith contends that Jacoby's point-of-purchase study, which purported to measure consumer confusion over merchandise that Smith sold exclusively online, was improperly designed because it failed to take into account typical consumer Internet behavior. Wal–Mart does not contradict the expert testimony Smith proffers regarding consumer Internet behavior but instead maintains that it is irrelevant.

[41] Jacoby's point-of-purchase survey called for interviewers to provide each respondent with specific "search terms" that would take the respondent to a simulation of one of Smith's websites. The respondent was asked to pretend that the resulting web page was of interest and to act accordingly (looking at the page and scrolling through it as the respondent would "normally" do), and then was directed to scroll down the page, below the first screen, and click on a specific t-shirt link. The respondent was not asked what message he or she took from the website or whether the website was in fact of interest. The survey protocol also gave the respondent no choice but to scroll down to the next screen and click on the t-shirt link, the only live link in the simulation.

[42] In presenting Smith's website and directing the survey respondents to click on one specific t-shirt link, Jacoby's survey design presumed that all consumers who might be interested in a printed t-shirt, mug or bumper sticker would be equally likely to happen across Smith's designs, regardless of the respondent's level of interest in the messages on Smith's webpage.

[43] Although, as Wal–Mart points out, it is possible that some consumers may view web pages randomly and may scroll through and clink on links on pages that are not of interest to them, the Court finds that the survey protocol did not sufficiently reflect actual marketplace conditions or typical consumer shopping behavior and therefore was unlikely to have elicited a shopping mindset that would have allowed Jacoby to accurately gauge actual consumer confusion.

[44] Because Smith's merchandise was available only through his CafePress webstores and the links to his CafePress webstores from his Walocaust and Wal–Qaeda websites, it is unlikely that many consumers randomly happen across Smith's products. According to Rosenblatt's uncontroverted testimony, people do not come to websites randomly, and they do not move within websites randomly. A great majority of Internet users arrive at a particular website after searching specific terms via an Internet search engine or by following links from another website. The user makes a judgment based on contextual cues—what is shown about a prospective website from the text of a search result or what is said about a prospective website in the hyperlinked words and surrounding text of the website currently being viewed—in determining where to surf next. He moves from website to website, he moves within websites, and he performs actions such as signing a petition—or buying a product—by making choices based on what he sees and whether what he sees leads him to believe that going to the next page or following a link to another website will bring him to something he is interested in seeing, doing or buying.

[45] In the marketplace, the visitor would be presented with a screen full of Smith's anti-Wal-Mart messages. Consumers who were interested in the messages on Smith's web pages would be motivated to choose the links that would eventually lead to his products, while those who were uninterested in Smith's messages would simply leave the page. Because the survey protocol directed the respondents to "pretend" to be interested in Smith's anti-Wal-Mart homepages and then directed them to click on a specific link, there is no assurance that the respondent actually read the homepage or would have been interested enough in it to be motivated to click on the t-shirt link. *See Gen. Motors Corp. v. Cadillac Marine & Boat Co.*, 226 F.Supp. 716, 737 (D.C.Mich. 1964) (observing that because survey respondents had little interest the allegedly infringing product, it followed that their inspection of the advertisement shown to them as part of the survey protocol was "casual, cursory and careless" and therefore of little probative value).

[46] Other courts have similarly criticized surveys that failed to adequately replicate the shopping experience. In *Gen. Motors Corp.*, 226 F.Supp. at 737, the court criticized the proffered survey because it did not take into account typical consumer behavior:

> Actual purchasers of a boat would not hastily read an advertisement, nor would a potential purchaser read it carelessly. A reasonable man, anticipating the purchase of a boat, would peruse the material at least well enough to note the manufacturer as being "Cadillac Marine & Boat Company, 406 Seventh Street, Cadillac, Michigan." Also, most buyers would want to see the boat itself before making a purchase.

Although the purchase of a t-shirt obviously does not involve the same level of financial consideration a consumer typically makes when buying a boat, a consumer is likely to consider the meaning of an imprinted t-shirt such as Smith's before wearing it in public. A reasonable person who was considering buying a t-shirt that references Al–Qaeda or the Holocaust would likely read the associated webpage at least well enough to see the harsh criticism of Wal–Mart and the prominent disclaimer dispelling any notion of a possible association with the company.

(c) Impact of Internet–Related Flaws on Survey's Evidentiary Value

[47] For all of these reasons, the survey Jacoby conducted for Wal–Mart is of dubious value as proof of consumer confusion both because its survey universe was overinclusive and because its design failed to approximate real-world marketplace conditions. Jacoby's survey is subject to the same criticisms as his *Weight Watchers* survey . . . : Jacoby failed to screen the respondents to ensure that they would likely be aware of and make relevant distinctions concerning the specific product. *See Weight Watchers*, 744 F.Supp. at 1273. By failing to approximate actual market conditions, Jacoby further ensured that the

survey would not "replicate the thought processes of [likely] consumers [of the junior user's merchandise] encountering the disputed mark . . . as they would in the marketplace." *See Simon Prop. Group,* 104 F.Supp.2d at 1038; *accord Gen. Motors Corp.,* 226 F.Supp. at 737. Therefore, the Court must consider these flaws in determining whether the survey is admissible and, if so, what evidentiary weight to afford it.

ii. Structural Flaws

[48] Smith further alleges that the Jacoby study suffers from several structural flaws that diminish the trustworthiness of the results of both the web-based point-of-sale portion and the post-purchase t-shirt portion of the survey. He contends that (1) both the structure of the survey and the wording of several questions suggested the answers Wal–Mart wanted, and (2) the survey results should not be presumed to represent consumer reaction to any of the challenged merchandise that was not actually tested.

[49] Smith hired Dr. Richard Teach as a rebuttal witness to point out deficiencies in Jacoby's website study survey methodology. Teach is an emeritus marketing professor and former dean at the Georgia Tech School of Business who has designed and conducted over one hundred surveys, including about fifty buyer surveys, and has taught survey methodology, statistics and related courses. Teach testifies that he agrees with Rosenblatt's testimony and also offers criticisms of his own. Smith uses Teach's survey expertise to support his *Daubert* argument that because the survey protocol contains multiple technical flaws, the results are unreliable and hence should be afforded very light evidentiary value if not completely excluded from evidence.

[50] Wal–Mart moves to exclude Teach's testimony, supporting its motion with arguments much like those it used in its motion to exclude Rosenblatt's testimony . . . .

[51] The Court finds . . . that his extensive experience designing and evaluating surveys qualifies him to provide testimony about technical flaws in the design of Jacoby's study and the impact of those flaws on the trustworthiness of Jacoby's reported results.

[52] [T]o the extent that Teach's testimony focuses on general survey methodology, whether Jacoby's survey protocol deviated from standard methodology, and what impact any deviations may have had on the trustworthiness of Jacoby's reported results, Wal–Mart's motion to exclude it is DENIED.

(a) Leading Survey Structure and Questions

[53] Smith argues that both the structure of the survey and the wording of several questions suggested the answers Wal–Mart wanted. Wal–Mart, of course, contends that Jacoby's survey presented no such risk.

(i) Double–Blind Survey Design

[54] To ensure objectivity in the administration of the survey, it is standard practice to conduct survey interviews in such a way as to ensure that "both the interviewer and the respondent are blind to the sponsor of the survey and its purpose." REFERENCE MANUAL at 266. The parties agree that double-blind conditions are essential because if the respondents know what the interviewer wants, they may try to please the interviewer by giving the desired answer, and if the interviewer knows what his employer wants, he may consciously or unconsciously bias the survey through variations in the wording or the tone of his questions. *See id.*

[55] Smith argues that the skip pattern included in Jacoby's survey hinted to the interviewers that Wal–Mart was the survey's sponsor. The survey protocol directed the interviewers to skip to the final tarnishment question, question five, if the respondent gave any one of four specific store names—Sears, Wal–Mart, K–Mart or Youngblood's—to any of the first three questions. Similarly, if the respondent did not give any of those four names in response to the first three questions, the interviewer was directed to ask "what other companies or stores" the stimulus t-shirt brought to mind, and only if the respondent answered with one of the four names was the interviewer to ask question five, the dilution question. The text on both of the tested t-shirts began with the prefix "Wal," and Wal–Mart was the only one of the four listed names that began with that prefix.

[56] Smith argues that this series of questions combined with the t-shirt stimulus subtly informed the interviewers not only that a store name was desired, but also that a particular store name—Wal–Mart—was sought. Thus, Smith contends, because the survey failed to meet the double-blind requirement, it was not conducted in an objective manner and must be excluded for what must therefore be biased results. *See* REFERENCE MANUAL at 248 (noting that poorly formed questions may lead to distorted responses and increased error and therefore may be the basis for rejecting a survey).

[57] Wal–Mart argues that the skip patterns followed proper protocol and that even if the interviewers guessed that Wal–Mart was involved, there could be no risk of bias because (1) interviewers are professionally trained and adhere to extremely high ethical standards, and (2) it was impossible to determine from the design of the study who sponsored the study and for which side of a dispute the survey evidence was to be proffered.

[58] Based on the facts that (1) both of the tested t-shirts include the prefix "Wal" and (2) the only store on the specified list of four that included that same prefix was Wal–Mart, it is safe to surmise that the interviewers at least suspected that Wal–Mart was involved in the survey in some manner. Aside from a common sense assumption that the party with deep pockets and reason to be insulted by the tested concepts was likely to have sponsored the research, however, the interviewers had no way to know who was the proponent of the research and who was the opponent. Thus, although the survey design may have breached generally accepted double-blind protocol to some degree, because the breach offered little risk of bias toward one party or the other the Court finds this issue to be of little import in its trustworthiness determination.

(ii) Leading Questions

[59] Smith also argues that the wording of Jacoby's confusion questions was improperly leading. Although the challenged t-shirts were created and offered for sale by Charles Smith, an individual, via his CafePress webstore, the survey asked about sponsorship only in the context of companies or stores, such as in the survey's lead question, which asked, "[W]hich company or store do you think puts out this shirt?" Smith contends that this wording suggested to the respondent that the interviewer was looking for the name of a company or store, which would lead the respondent away from the answer that the shirt was put out by an individual who was criticizing a company. Wal–Mart counters that because Smith's merchandise was sold through his CafePress webstores, the questions were accurately worded and thus not misleading.

[60] The Court agrees with Smith that the disputed questions improperly led respondents to limit their answers to companies or stores. Though Smith did offer his merchandise through his CafePress webstore, as Wal–Mart argues, the Court finds this characterization disingenuous; the party Wal–Mart sued for offering the Walocaust and Wal–Qaeda merchandise for sale is not a company or a store, but instead Charles Smith, an individual. Furthermore, Wal–Mart has failed to point to any authority supporting the use of the "company or store" language in a consumer "likelihood of confusion" apparel survey or any such surveys previously conducted by Jacoby. Thus, the Court must consider this weakness in determining the admissibility or evidentiary weight to be accorded the survey.

(b) Representativeness
(i) Testing Stimuli

[61] Smith also argues that the Jacoby survey results should not be presumed to represent consumer reaction to any of the challenged merchandise that was not actually tested. Jacoby limited his surveys to testing two specific t-shirts (the Wal*ocaust smiley eagle shirt and the "SUPPORT OUR TROOPS" Wal–Qaeda shirt), and the conclusions stated in his report were narrowly drawn to refer to the tested t-shirts. At his deposition, however, he stated that because the tested shirts were "reasonably representative" of all the shirts that included the prefix "Wal" and the star, as in Wal*ocaust, or the prefix "Wal" and a hyphen, as in Wal–Qaeda, his results could be extrapolated from the tested t-shirts to all of the challenged t-shirts that shared those features.

[62] Jacoby's own deposition testimony supplies a fitting framework for analyzing this issue. When declining to offer an opinion about whether consumers would also be confused over the sponsorship of

Smith's Walocaust website, Jacoby stated that consumers respond differently to a given stimulus depending on the context in which is it presented, and because his survey tested only Smith's CafePress webstores, his survey provided him with no data upon which to answer the question about consumer confusion regarding Smith's website.

[63] Applying the same reasoning, the Court finds that test results from one Walocaust or Wal–Qaeda t-shirt provide no data upon which to estimate consumer confusion regarding another Walocaust or Wal–Qaeda t-shirt. A consumer confused about the sponsorship of a shirt that says "SUPPORT OUR TROOPS [.] BOYCOTT WAL–QAEDA" may easily grasp the commentary in the more straightforwardly derogatory "WAL–QAEDA[.] Freedom Haters ALWAYS" concept. Similarly, a consumer confused over the sponsorship of a "Walocaust" shirt paired with an eagle and a smiley face might have a crystal clear understanding of the word's meaning when it is superimposed over a drawing of a Wal–Mart–like building paired with a sign that advertises family values and discounted alcohol, firearms, and tobacco or when it is presented along with the additional text "The World is Our Labor Camp. Walmart Sucks." As a result, this weakness will also impact the Court's assessment of the survey's evidentiary value.

(ii) Sample Size and Selection

[64] Smith also challenges the survey's small sample size; the Court additionally notes that Jacoby's study employed mall-intercept methodology, which necessarily results in a non-random survey sample.

[65] It is true that the majority of surveys presented for litigation purposes do, in fact, include small and non-random samples that are not projectible to the general population or susceptible to evaluations of statistical significance. 6 MCCARTHY ON TRADEMARKS AND UNFAIR COMPETITION § 32:165 (4th ed. 2006). Courts have found that "nonprobability 'mall intercept' surveys are sufficiently reliable to be admitted into evidence," reasoning that because "nonprobability surveys are of a type often relied upon by marketing experts and social scientists in forming opinions on customer attitudes and perceptions," they may be admitted into evidence under Federal Rule of Evidence 703 as being "of a type reasonably relied upon by experts in the particular field in forming opinions or inferences upon the subject." *Id.*

[66] However, probability surveys are preferred to non-probability surveys. *Id.* (citing Jacob Jacoby, *Survey & Field Experimental Evidence,* in SAUL KASSIN & LAWRENCE S. WRIGHTSMAN, JR., 185–86 THE PSYCHOLOGY OF EVIDENCE AND TRIAL PROCEDURE (1985)). Jacoby himself has written that "behavioral science treatises on research methodology are in general agreement that, all other things being equal, probability sampling is preferred to non-probability sampling." Jacob Jacoby & Amy H. Handlin, *Non–Probability Sampling Designs for Litig. Surveys,* 81 TRADEMARK REP. 169, 170 (Mar.-Apr. 1991) (citing KUL B. RAI AND JOHN C. BLYDENBURGH, POL. SCI. STATS.. 99 (Holbrook Press Inc. 1973) and quoting its comment that "nonprobability samples do not represent the population truly, and the inapplicability of probability models as well as the impossibility of measuring or controlling random sampling error makes them even less attractive for scientific studies."). Jacoby has similarly noted that although the vast majority of in-person surveys conducted for marketing purposes employ non-probability design, marketers more typically use telephone interviews, a "sizable proportion" of which employ probability designs. Jacoby & Handlin, 81 TRADEMARK REP. at 172 & Table 1 (estimating that sixty-nine percent of commercial marketing and advertising research is conducted by telephone).

[67] Although courts typically admit nonprobability surveys into evidence, many recognize that "the results of a nonprobability survey cannot be statistically extrapolated to the entire universe," and they consequently discount the evidentiary weight accorded to them. *Id.; accord Am. Home Prods. Corp. v. Barr Labs., Inc.,* 656 F.Supp. 1058, 1070 (D.N.J. 1987) (criticizing a Jacoby survey and noting, "While non-probability survey results may be admissible, they are weak evidence of behavior patterns in the test universe.") Similarly, "[c]onducting a survey with a number of respondents too small to justify a reasonable extrapolation to the target group at large will lessen the weight of the survey." 6 MCCARTHY ON TRADEMARKS AND UNFAIR COMPETITION § 32:171.

[68] This Court finds troubling the Jacoby survey's implicit assumption that a study protocol insufficient for many marketing purposes and heavily criticized for behavioral science purposes is

nevertheless sufficient to aid a factfinder in a legal action challenging free speech. Therefore, this factor will also affect the Court's assessment of the survey's evidentiary value.

c. Admissibility

[69] Having identified numerous substantial flaws in Jacoby's survey, the Court must now determine whether the flaws limit the survey's evidentiary weight or are so substantial as to render the survey irrelevant or unreliable and therefore inadmissible under Federal Rule of Evidence 403, 702, or 703. *See Starter Corp. v. Converse, Inc.,* 170 F.3d 286, 297 (2d Cir. 1999) (excluding a survey under Rule 403 because the probative value of the survey was outweighed by potential prejudice and further noting that "a survey may be kept from the jury's attention entirely by the trial judge if it is irrelevant to the issues") (citing *C.A. May Marine Supply Co. v. Brunswick Corp.,* 649 F.2d 1049 (5th Cir. 1981)); *accord Ramdass v. Angelone,* 530 U.S. 156, 173, 120 S.Ct. 2113, 147 L.Ed.2d 125 (2000) (listing numerous cases in which courts have excluded or minimized survey evidence as unreliable).

[70] Courts in the Eleventh Circuit typically decline to exclude likelihood of confusion surveys and instead consider a survey's technical flaws when determining the amount of evidentiary weight to accord the survey. *See, e.g., Jellibeans,* 716 F.2d at 845; *Nightlight Sys., Inc. v. Nitelites Franchise Sys., Inc.,* 2007 WL 4563873 at *5 (N.D.Ga. Jul.17, 2007). Consequently, although this is a close case, the Court concludes that the better option is to admit the survey evidence and to consider the survey's flaws in determining the evidentiary weight to assign the survey in the likelihood of confusion analysis.

[71] The Court finds, however, that because the survey tested only the "SUPPORT OUR TROOPS[.] BOYCOTT WAL–QAEDA" t-shirt and the Walocaust eagle t-shirt, it has no relevance to any of Smith's other Wal–Mart–related concepts. The Court agrees with Jacoby that context matters—a lot—and therefore will not consider Jacoby's survey as evidence of likelihood of confusion with regard to the words "Walocaust" and "Wal–Qaeda" in general; the study is admissible only as to the two concepts that Jacoby actually tested. *See* Fed.R.Evid. 702 (limiting expert testimony to that "based upon sufficient facts or data").

[72] Even with regard to the tested concepts, the Court finds that the survey was so flawed that it does not create a genuine issue of material fact. *See Spraying Sys. Co. v. Delavan, Inc.,* 975 F.2d 387, 394 (7th Cir. 1992) (recognizing that if a proffered survey is severely and materially flawed, it may not be sufficient to establish a genuine issue of material fact even if it purports to show evidence of actual confusion). Jacoby surveyed an overbroad universe, failed to adequately replicate the shopping experience, and asked leading questions. He also surveyed a non-random sample that in any case was too small to allow the results to be projected upon the general market. Thus, the Court finds that the Jacoby survey is so flawed that it does not establish a genuine issue of material fact with regard to actual confusion, much less *prove* actual confusion.

[73] Lack of survey evidence showing consumer confusion is not dispositive, however; the Eleventh Circuit has moved away from relying on survey evidence. *Frehling Enters. v. Int'l Select Group, Inc.,* 192 F.3d 1330, 1341 n. 5 (11th Cir. 1999). In fact, a court may find a likelihood of confusion in the absence of any evidence of actual confusion, even though actual confusion is the best evidence of likelihood of confusion. *E. Remy Martin & Co. v. Shaw–Ross Int'l Imps., Inc.,* 756 F.2d 1525, 1529 (11th Cir. 1985). Accordingly, the Court will now consider the remaining likelihood of confusion factors.

{The court ultimately granted summary judgment to Smith on Walmart's confusion and dilution claims.}

Questions and Comments

1. *The authorization or permission question.* You will recall that the third group of questions in the surveys at issue in *Smith v. Wal-Mart* asked respondents if they thought the company that "put out" the defendant's products needed permission from another company to do so, and if so, which company. Isn't this the very question that the judge is trying to decide in the case? Why should we ask survey respondents for their view on what is in essence a legal question?

2. *Confusion by whom?* What is the appropriate consumer population to survey, the defendant's and/or the plaintiff's? McCarthy sets forth the conventional wisdom: "In a traditional case claiming 'forward' confusion, not 'reverse' confusion, the proper universe to survey is composed of the potential buyers of the *junior* user's goods or services. However, in a 'reverse confusion' case, the relevant group to be surveyed is the *senior* user's customer base." McCARTHY, at § 32:159 (citations omitted).

3. *Alternative survey formats.* Two other methods of surveying for the likelihood of consumer confusion are of particular interest.

- The "*Squirt* format". In *Squirt Co. v. Seven-Up Co.*, 628 F.2d 1086 (8th Cir. 1980), survey respondents were played radio advertisements for SQUIRT and QUIRST soft drinks and two other products. The respondents were then asked: (1) "Do you think SQUIRT and QUIRST are put out by the same company or by different companies?", and (2) "What makes you think that?" This method, consisting of either seriatim or simultaneous exposure to the plaintiff's and defendant's marks, is especially beneficial for a plaintiff whose mark may not be well-known to the survey respondents. However, some courts have rejected this survey method on the ground that it makes the respondents "artificially aware" of the plaintiff's mark and does not approximate market conditions. *See, e.g., Kargo Global, Inc. v. Advance Magazine Publishers, Inc.*, No. 06 Civ. 550, 2007 WL 2258688, at *8 (S.D. N.Y. 2007).

- The "*Exxon* format". In *Exxon Corp. v. Texas Motor Exchange of Houston, Inc.*, 628 F2d 500 (5th Cir. 1980), survey respondents were shown a photograph of one of the defendant's signs bearing its TEXON trademark. The respondents were then asked: "What is the first thing that comes to mind when looking at this sign?", and "What was there about the sign that made you say that?" If the respondents did not name a company in response to the first set of questions, they were then asked: "What is the first *company* that comes to mind when you look at this sign?" (emphasis in original survey script) and "What was there about the sign that made you mention (COMPANY)?" Courts have proven to be less receptive to this "word association" method of surveying for consumer confusion. *See, e.g., Major League Baseball Properties v. Sed Non Olet Denarius, Ltd.*, 817 F. Supp. 1103, 1122 (S.D.N.Y. 1993) ("[T]he issue here is not whether defendants' name brings to mind any other name . . . . Rather, the issue here is one of actual confusion. Plaintiff's survey questions regarding association are irrelevant to the issue of actual confusion.").

In Itamar Simonson, *The Effect of Survey Method on Likelihood of Confusion Estimates: Conceptual Analyses and Empirical Test*, 83 TRADEMARK REP. 364 (1993), Simonson compared the results of five methods of surveying for the likelihood of confusion, including a simple form of the *Eveready* format, the *Squirt* format, and the *Exxon* format. He found that the *Exxon* format "tends to overestimate the likelihood of confusion, often by a significant amount," *id.* at 385, and that the *Squirt* format, as expected, "can have a significant effect on confusion estimates when the awareness level of the senior mark is low." *Id.* at 386.

4. *What percentage of confusion is enough?* "Figures in the range of 25% to 50% have been viewed as solid support for a finding of a likelihood of confusion." McCARTHY § 32:188. Still often cited by plaintiffs with especially weak cases, *Jockey International, Inc. v. Burkard*, No 74 Civ. 123, 1975 WL 21128 (S.D. Cal. 1975), found that survey evidence of 11.4 percent supported a likelihood of confusion. *But see Georgia-Pacific Consumer Product LP v. Myers Supply, Inc.*, No. 08 Civ. 6086, 2009 WL 2192721 (W.D. Ark. 2009) (survey evidence of 11.4 percent confusion does not support a likelihood of confusion).

5. *Outside of the world of trademark law, should survey evidence be used to interpret contractual terms?* See Omri Ben-Shahar & Lior Jacob Strahilevitz, *Interpreting Contracts via Surveys and Experiments*, 92 NYU L. REV. 1753 (2017) (proposing and testing a "survey interpretation method" of contractual interpretation in which "interpretation disputes are resolved through large surveys of representative respondents, by choosing the meaning that a majority supports").

5. "Sponsorship or Affiliation" Confusion

As the surveys at issue in *Smith v. Wal-Mart Stores* suggested, trademark law may find infringement when the defendant's conduct leads consumers mistakenly to believe that there is a relation of "sponsorship" or "affiliation" between the plaintiff and the defendant. In this excerpt from *Int'l Info. Sys. Sec. Certification Consortium, Inc. v. Sec. Univ.*, LLC, 823 F.3d 153 (2d Cir. 2016), the Second Circuit strongly endorsed this expansive understanding of what constitutes actionable consumer confusion.

Int'l Info. Sys. Sec. Certification Consortium, Inc. v. Sec. Univ., LLC
823 F.3d 153, 161-163 (2d Cir. 2016)

{The plaintiff developed a certification program and the certification mark CISSP to denote a "Certified Information Systems Security Professional" who has passed the plaintiff's certification exam. The defendant offered various courses to prepare individuals for the plaintiff's exam. It was undisputed that the defendant could use the plaintiff's mark to indicate that the courses were directed towards preparing students to take the plaintiff's exam. However, the defendant advertised its courses as taught by "Master CISSP Clement Dupuis", allegedly suggesting that Mr. Dupuis had obtained some higher, "Master" level of certification from the plaintiff. Both parties moved for summary judgment.}

. . . .

A. Types of Confusion Relevant to Infringement Claims

[1] The district court held that the only type of confusion relevant in determining infringement is confusion as to *source.* This is incorrect; protection is not exclusively limited for any type of mark to cases in which there may be confusion as to source. Rather, "[t]he modern test of infringement is whether the defendant's use [is] likely to cause confusion *not just as to source,* but also as to sponsorship, affiliation or connection." 4 McCarthy on Trademarks and Unfair Competition [hereinafter "McCarthy"] § 23:76 (4th ed.) (emphasis added). Indeed, our Court has previously observed that in 1962 Congress amended 15 U.S.C. § 1114, the Lanham Act provision that provides penalties for infringement, to "broaden liability" from the prior "statutory requirement [that] confusion, mistake, or deception applied only with respect to purchasers as to the source of origin of such goods or services." *Rescuecom Corp. v. Google Inc.,* 562 F.3d 123, 136 (2d Cir. 2009) (internal quotation marks omitted). That provision now penalizes a person who

> use[s] in commerce any reproduction, counterfeit, copy, or colorable imitation of a registered mark in connection with the sale, offering for sale, distribution, or advertising of any goods or services on or in connection with which such use *is likely to cause confusion, or to cause mistake, or to deceive . . . .*

15 U.S.C. § 1114(1)(a) (emphasis added). As is plain from this statutory text, the Act's protection against infringement is not limited to any particular type of consumer confusion, much less exclusively to confusion as to source. Rather, the Lanham Act protects against numerous types of confusion, including confusion regarding affiliation or sponsorship. *See . . . Dall. Cowboys Cheerleaders, Inc. v. Pussycat Cinema, Ltd.,* 604 F.2d 200, 204–05 (2d Cir. 1979) ("Appellants read the confusion requirement too narrowly. In order to be confused, a consumer need not believe that the owner of the mark actually produced the item and placed it on the market. The public's belief that the mark's owner sponsored or otherwise approved the use of the trademark satisfies the confusion requirement." (citations omitted)); *see also Team Tires Plus, Ltd. v. Tires Plus, Inc.,* 394 F.3d 831, 835 (10th Cir. 2005) ("[T]he relevant confusion under trademark law is not limited to confusion of consumers as to the source of the goods, but also includes confusion as to sponsorship or affiliation, such as a consumer's mistaken belief that a retailer is part of a larger franchising operation.") . . . .

[2] This broader prohibition on consumer confusion as to sponsorship or approval is also made explicit in Section 43 of the Lanham Act, which prohibits false advertising and false designation of origin by providing for civil penalties to a person injured by:

> Any person who, on or in connection with any goods or services, . . . uses in commerce any word, term, name, symbol, or device, or any combination thereof, or any false

designation of origin, false or misleading description of fact, or false or misleading representation of fact, which—

>   (A) is likely to cause confusion, or to cause mistake, or to deceive as to the *affiliation, connection, or association* of such person with another person, or as to the origin, *sponsorship, or approval* of his or her goods, services, or commercial activities by another person, or

>   (B) in commercial advertising or promotion, misrepresents the nature, characteristics, qualities, or geographic origin of his or her or another person's goods, services, or commercial activities . . . .

15 U.S.C. § 1125(a)(1) (emphases added).

[3] Indeed, our case law demonstrates that consumer confusion is plainly not limited to source confusion. For example, in *Weight Watchers International, Inc. v. Luigino's, Inc.,* 423 F.3d 137 (2d Cir. 2005), we recognized that Weight Watchers was likely to succeed on its claim that a frozen food manufacturer had infringed its registered trademark in the term "Points" by prominently displaying the Weight Watchers points value on the packages of its frozen meals. In that case, it was clear from the packaging that Luigino's was the source of the actual goods—i.e. the frozen meals. Nonetheless, Weight Watchers could succeed on its claim for trademark infringement by showing "that the use of the term 'Points' on the front of the package was likely to confuse consumers into believing that Weight Watchers had determined the point values or *otherwise endorsed* the Luigino's products." *Id.* at 144 (emphasis added). Moreover, we have held that there may be consumer confusion based on the misuse of a trademark, even where it is conceded that the plaintiff's mark accurately designated the source of goods. *See Original Appalachian Artworks, Inc. v. Granada Electronics, Inc.,* 816 F.2d 68, 73 (2d Cir. 1987) (holding unauthorized importation and sale of Cabbage Patch dolls manufactured in Spain with the foreign language adoption papers and birth certificate infringed the plaintiff's trademark in Cabbage Patch dolls "even though the goods do bear [plaintiff's] trademark and were manufactured under license with [the plaintiff]," because plaintiff's "domestic good will is being damaged by consumer confusion caused by the importation of the [Spanish] dolls," which were materially different from American dolls). The district court therefore erred in applying its narrow conception of confusion relevant to infringement claims.

. . . .

{As excerpted further in Part III.B, the district court went on to find that the defendant engaged in nominative fair use of the plaintiff's mark.}

Questions and Comments

1.   *"Signifier confusion" and "affiliation confusion."* Barton Beebe and Scott Hemphill propose the following:

>   [I]t is helpful to distinguish between two fundamentally different and mutually exclusive forms of consumer confusion, which we term *signifier confusion* and *affiliation confusion.* Signifier confusion denotes those situations in which a consumer fails to detect the difference between two different marks and perceives each mark to be identical to the other. For example, a consumer may be exposed to the mark STARLUCKS and simply mistakenly read or hear the mark as STARBUCKS.

>   By contrast, affiliation confusion denotes those situations in which a consumer detects the difference between two different marks (so there is no signifier confusion), but the consumer nevertheless concludes that due to the similarity of the marks, there must be some commercial connection between the users of the marks. For example, a consumer thinks STARLUCKS represents a brand extension, sponsorship or endorsement relationship, or some other form of commercial affiliation. The consumer perceives the plaintiff as the source of or somehow responsible for the defendant's goods.

Barton Beebe & C. Scott Hemphill, *The Scope of Strong Marks: Should Trademark Law Protect the Strong More Than the Weak?*, 93 N.Y.U. L. REV. 1339, 1361 (2017). Are these two forms of consumer confusion in fact mutually exclusive? Is this distinction helpful?

Trademark scholars have been highly critical of "sponsorship or affiliation" confusion. Presented below is an excerpt from Mark A. Lemley & Mark McKenna, *Irrelevant Confusion*, 62 STAN. L. REV. 413, 417–422 (2010), which collects some of the most egregious examples up to that time of plaintiffs' threats to sue and of courts' finding of "sponsorship or affiliation" confusion. In reading through Lemley & McKenna's account, consider the extent to which trademark law should passively take consumer perceptions as given or proactively seek to shape those perceptions. In other words, should trademark law assert in some cases that as a descriptive matter it may well be that consumers are in fact confused as to source or affiliation by the defendant's conduct, but as a prescriptive matter they simply should *not* be? Should the law allow some degree of confusion in the short term so that consumers can learn in the long term not to be confused? And are federal judges and federal trademark litigation properly suited to this task? *See* Graeme B. Dinwoodie, *Trademark Law and Social Norms* (2006) (discussing courts' "reactive" and "proactive" approaches to the development of trademark law); Alfred C. Yen, *The Constructive Role of Confusion in Trademark Law*, 93 N.C. L. Rev. 77 (2014) (criticizing trademark law's absolute "eradicate confusion norm" and arguing that some degree of consumer confusion may encourage consumers to develop the cognitive skills needed to navigate complex marketplaces).

From **Mark A. Lemley & Mark McKenna, *Irrelevant Confusion*, 62 STAN. L. REV. 413, 417-422 (2010)**

[1] In 2006, back when it was good, NBC's hit show *Heroes* depicted an indestructible cheerleader sticking her hand down a kitchen garbage disposal and mangling it (the hand quickly regenerated). It was an Insinkerator brand garbage disposal, though you might have had to watch the show in slow motion to notice; the brand name was visible for only a couple of seconds. Emerson Electric, owner of the Insinkerator brand, sued NBC, alleging the depiction of its product in an unsavory light was both an act of trademark dilution and was likely to cause consumers to believe Emerson had permitted the use.

373

NBC denied any wrongdoing, but it obscured the Insinkerator name when it released the DVD and Web versions of the episode.[8] And not just television shows but also movies have provoked the ire of trademark owners: Caterpillar sued the makers of the movie Tarzan on the theory that the use of Caterpillar tractors in the movie to bulldoze the forest would cause consumers to think Caterpillar was actually anti-environment,[9] and the makers of *Dickie Roberts: Former Child Star* were sued for trademark infringement for suggesting that the star of the absurdist comedy was injured in a Slip 'N Slide accident.[10] Even museums aren't immune: Pez recently sued the Museum of Pez Memorabilia for displaying an eight-foot Pez dispenser produced by the museum's owners.[11] And forget about using kazoos on your duck tours: Ride the Ducks, a tour company in San Francisco that gives out duck-call kazoos to clients on its ducks, sued Bay Quackers, a competing duck tour company that also facilitated quacking by its clients.[12]

[2] Most of these examples involve threats of suit, and they could be dismissed simply as overreaching by a few aggressive trademark owners. But these threats were not isolated incidents, and they shouldn't be quickly ignored. The recipients of all of these threats, like many others who receive similar objections,[13] knew well that they had to take the asserted claims seriously because courts have sometimes been persuaded to shut down very similar uses. In 1998, for instance, New Line Productions was set to release a comedy about a beauty pageant that took place at a farm-related fair in Minnesota. New Line called the movie *Dairy Queens* but was forced to change the name to *Drop Dead Gorgeous* after the franchisor of Dairy Queen restaurants obtained a preliminary injunction.[14] The owners of a restaurant called the "Velvet Elvis" were forced to change its name after the estate of Elvis Presley sued for trademark infringement.[15] A humor magazine called Snicker was forced to pull a parody "ad" for a mythical product called "Michelob Oily," not because people thought Michelob was actually selling such

---

[8] *See* Paul R. La Monica, *NBC Sued over 'Heroes' Scene by Garbage Disposal Maker*, CNNMoney.com, Oct. 17, 2006, http:// money.cnn.com/2006/10/17/commentary/ mediabiz/index.htm.

[9] Caterpillar Inc. v. Walt Disney Co., 287 F. Supp. 2d 913, 917 (C.D. Ill. 2003).

[10] Wham-O, Inc. v. Paramount Pictures Corp., 286 F. Supp. 2d 1254, 1255-58 (N.D. Cal. 2003).

[11] *Museum Faces Legal Battle over Giant Pez Dispenser*, KTVU.com, July 1, 2009, http://www.ktvu.com/print/19911637/detail.html. The museum was originally called the Pez Museum, but the owners changed the name in response to a previous objection from Pez.

[12] Jesse McKinley, *A Quacking Kazoo Sets Off a Squabble*, N.Y. TIMES, June 3, 2009, at A16. Ducks are open-air amphibious vehicles that can be driven on streets and operated in the water.

[13] The Chilling Effects Clearinghouse collects letters from trademark owners that make aggressive assertions of trademark (and other intellectual property) rights. See Chilling Effects Clearinghouse, http:// www.chillingeffects.org (last visited Sept. 9, 2009). As of February 25, 2009, the Chilling Effects database contained 378 such letters. Among the many specious objections are an objection from the National Pork Board (owner of the trademark "THE OTHER WHITE MEAT") to the operator of a breastfeeding advocacy site called "The Lactivist" for selling T-shirts with the slogan "The Other White Milk," *Pork Board Has a Cow over Slogan Parody*, Chilling Effects Clearinghouse, Jan. 30, 2007, http:// www.chillingeffects.org/trademark/notice.cgi?NoticeID=6418; from Kellogg to the registrant of the domain name "evilpoptarts.com," *Kelloggs Poops on Evilpoptarts.com*, Chilling Effects Clearinghouse, June 5, 2006, http:// www.chillingeffects.org/acpa/notice.cgi?NoticeID=4377; from Nextel to the registrants of the domain name "nextpimp.com," *Nextel Says "Don't Pimp My Mark"*, Chilling Effects Clearinghouse, June 22, 2005, http:// www.chillingeffects.org/acpa/notice.cgi?NoticeID=2322; and from the owners of the Marco Beach Ocean Resort to the operators of "urinal.net," a website that collects pictures of urinals in various public places, for depicting urinals at the Resort and identifying them as such, *Mark Owner Pissed About Urinals*, Chilling Effects Clearinghouse, Jan. 4, 2005, http:// www.chillingeffects.org/trademark/notice.cgi?NoticeID=1576.

[14] Am. Dairy Queen Corp. v. New Line Prods., Inc., 35 F. Supp. 2d 727, 728 (D. Minn. 1998).

[15] Elvis Presley Enters., Inc. v. Capece, 141 F.3d 188 (5th Cir. 1998)

a beer (only six percent did[16]), but because a majority of consumers surveyed thought that the magazine needed to receive permission from Anheuser-Busch to run the ad.[17] And Snicker might face more trouble than that; another court enjoined a furniture delivery company from painting its truck to look like a famous candy bar.[18]

[3] The Mutual of Omaha Insurance Company persuaded a court to stop Franklyn Novak from selling T-shirts and other merchandise bearing the phrase "Mutant of Omaha" and depicting a side view of a feather-bonneted, emaciated human head.[19] No one who saw Novak's shirts reasonably could have believed Mutual of Omaha sold the T-shirts, but the court was impressed by evidence that approximately ten percent of all the persons surveyed thought that Mutual of Omaha "[went] along" with Novak's products.[20] The creators of Godzilla successfully prevented the author of a book about Godzilla from titling the book *Godzilla*, despite clear indications on both the front and back covers that the book was not authorized by the creators.[21]

[4] The Heisman Trophy Trust prevented a T-shirt company called Smack Apparel from selling T-shirts that used variations of the word HEISMAN, such as "HE.IS.the.MAN," to promote particular players for the Heisman Trophy.[22] This was not Smack Apparel's first trademark lesson: a court previously ordered it to stop selling T-shirts that used university colors and made oblique references to those universities' football teams because the court believed the designs created "a link in the consumer's mind between the T-shirts and the Universities" and demonstrated that Smack Apparel "inten[ded] to directly profit [from that link]."[23] Respect Sportswear was denied registration of "RATED R SPORTSWEAR" for men's and women's clothing on the ground that consumers would be confused into thinking the Motion Picture Association of America sponsored the clothes.[24] A street musician who plays guitar in New York while (nearly) naked was permitted to pursue his claim against Mars on the theory consumers would assume he sponsored M&Ms candies, since Mars advertised M&Ms with a (naked) blue M&M playing a guitar.[25] A legitimate reseller of dietary supplements lost its motion for summary judgment in a suit by the supplements' brand owner because the court concluded the reseller might have confused consumers into thinking it was affiliated with the brand owner when it purchased ad space on

---

[16] Anheuser-Busch, Inc. v. Balducci Publ'ns, 28 F.3d 769, 772-73 (8th Cir. 1994). That any consumers were confused was remarkable, and perhaps a statement about the reliability of consumer confusion surveys rather than the stupidity of 6% of the population.

[17] *Id.*

[18] Hershey Co. v. Art Van Furniture, Inc., No. 08-14463, 2008 WL 4724756 (E.D. Mich. Oct. 24, 2008). Hershey has also sued Reese's Nursery. Complaint at 1, Hershey Chocolate & Confectionery Corp. v. Reese's Nursery and Landscaping, No. 3:09-CV-00017-JPB (N.D. W. Va. Mar. 19, 2009).

[19] Mutual of Omaha Ins. Co. v. Novak, 836 F.2d 397, 397 (8th Cir. 1987).

[20] *Id.* at 400.

[21] See Toho Co. v. William Morrow & Co., 33 F. Supp. 2d 1206, 1206, 1212 (C.D. Cal. 1998).

[22] Heisman Trophy Trust v. Smack Apparel Co., No. 08 Civ. 9153(VM), 2009 WL 2170352, at *5 (S.D.N.Y. July 17, 2009). Smack Apparel produced several such T-shirts, including one that substituted the number 15 for "IS" in the word HEISMAN and was printed in the colors of the University of Florida, clearly to promote Florida quarterback Tim Tebow's candidacy. *See* Smack Apparel Lawsuit, LSU Tiger Tailer Newsletter (LSU Trademark Licensing, Baton Rouge, La.), Jan. 30, 2009, at 6.

[23] Bd. of Supervisors for La. State Univ. Agric. & Mech. Coll. v. Smack Apparel Co., 550 F.3d 465, 484 (5th Cir. 2008).

[24] Motion Picture Ass'n of Am. Inc. v. Respect Sportswear Inc., 83 U.S.P.Q.2d (BNA) 1555, 1564 (T.T.A.B. 2007).

[25] Burck v. Mars, Inc., 571 F. Supp. 2d 446 (S.D.N.Y. 2008) (denying Mars' motion to dismiss plaintiff's false endorsement claim).

Google and truthfully advertised the availability of the supplements.[26] Amoco persuaded a court that consumers might believe it sponsored Rainbow Snow's sno-cones, mostly because Rainbow Snow's shops were located in the same area as some of Amoco's Rainbo gas stations.[27] The National Football League successfully sued the state of Delaware for running a lottery based on point spreads in NFL games, even though the Lottery never used the NFL name or any of its marks for the purpose of identifying or advertising its games.[28] The court was persuaded that the betting cards' references to NFL football games by the names of the cities whose teams were playing might cause consumers to believe the NFL sponsored the lottery game.[29] And the owners of a Texas golf course that replicated famous golf holes from around the world were forced to change their course because one of the holes was, in the view of the Fifth Circuit, too similar to the corresponding South Carolina golf hole it mimicked.[30]

[5] Whatever fraction of the total universe of trademark cases these cases constitute, there are enough of them that recipients of cease and desist letters from mark owners have to take the objections seriously. Indeed many simply cave in and change their practices rather than face the uncertainty of a lawsuit. The producers of the TV show *Felicity* changed the name of the university attended by characters on the show after New York University, the school originally referenced, objected to the depiction of those students as sexually active.[31] The producers of a movie originally titled *Stealing Stanford* changed the title of their movie after Stanford University objected to the movie's storyline, which centered on a student who stole money to pay tuition.[32] It's possible that the producers of the show and the movie would have had legitimate defenses had they decided to use the real universities' names despite the objections, but in light of the case law outlined above, neither was willing to defend

---

[26] Standard Process, Inc. v. Total Health Discount, Inc., 559 F. Supp. 2d 932, 941 (E.D. Wis. 2008).

[27] Amoco Oil Co. v. Rainbow Snow, 748 F.2d 556, 559 (10th Cir. 1984). Rainbow Snow sold its snow cones from fourteen round, ten-by-six-foot booths, which were blue with a 180-degree, red-orange-yellow-green rainbow appearing on the upper half of the face of the booth and prominently displayed the name "Rainbow Snow" in white letters below the rainbow. Id. at 557. Signs at Amoco's Rainbo gas stations displayed the word "Rainbo" in white, with the word appearing against a black background and below a red-orange-yellow-blue truncated rainbow logo. *Id.*

[28] NFL v. Governor of Del., 435 F. Supp. 1372, 1376, 1380-81 (D. Del. 1977). The lottery game was called "Scoreboard" and the individual games were identified as "Football Bonus," "Touchdown," and "Touchdown II." *Id.* at 1380.

[29] The cards on which the customers of the Delaware Lottery marked their betting choices identified the next week's NFL football games by the names of the cities whose NFL teams were scheduled to compete against each other (e.g., Washington v. Baltimore). *Id.* The parties stipulated that, in the context in which they appeared, these geographic names were intended to refer to, and consumers understood them to refer to, particular NFL football teams. Id. This was enough for the court to find sponsorship or affiliation confusion because, "[a]pparently, in this day and age when professional sports teams franchise pennants, teeshirts, helmets, drinking glasses and a wide range of other products, a substantial number of people believe, if not told otherwise, that one cannot conduct an enterprise of this kind without NFL approval." *Id.* at 1381. The court therefore entered a limited injunction "requiring the Lottery Director to include on Scoreboard tickets, advertising and any other materials prepared for public distribution a clear and conspicuous statement that Scoreboard [was] not associated with or authorized by the National Football League." *Id.*

[30] Pebble Beach Co. v. Tour 18 I Ltd., 155 F.3d 526, 526 (5th Cir. 1998).

[31] Sara Lipka, *PG-13? Not This College. Or That One. Or . . .*, CHRON. HIGHER EDUC., June 26, 2009, at 1; William McGeveran, *Trademarks, Movies, and the Clearance Culture*, Info/Law, July 2, 2009, http://blogs.law.harvard.edu/infolaw/2009/07/02/tm-movie-clearance/.

[32] McGeveran, *supra*. Apparently Harvard was less troubled about a student being depicted as having stolen money to pay its tuition: the movie was retitled *Stealing Harvard*.

its right to refer to real places in their fictional storylines.[33] And anecdotes like these are becoming depressingly common. Production of the film *Moneyball*, which was based on Michael Lewis's best-selling profile of Oakland Athletics General Manager Billy Beane, was halted just days before shooting was set to begin in part because Major League Baseball disapproved of the script's depiction of baseball and therefore objected to use of its trademarks in the film.[34] Apparently Major League Baseball believes it can control the content of any film that refers to real baseball teams.

[6] What unifies all the cases that have given these creators such pause is that courts found actionable confusion notwithstanding the fact that consumers couldn't possibly have been confused about the actual source of the defendants' products . . . .

Though many of the examples provided in the Lemley & McKenna excerpt show severe overreach by trademark owners, there are of course counterexamples in which most would agree that trademark owners should have every right to seek to prevent association or affiliation confusion. For example, consumers might care strongly about whether a company is truthfully declaring itself to be an "Official Sponsor of the United States Olympic Team" or an "Official Sponsor of the United States Women's National Team."

In the following case, *Board of Supervisors for Louisiana State University Agricultural & Mechanical College v. Smack Apparel Co.*, 550 F.3d 465 (5th Cir. 2008), parts of which were excerpted in Part I.A.1.b, the Fifth Circuit addressed the argument that consumers do not care if the merchandise they purchase is authorized. The plaintiffs Louisiana State University, the University of Oklahoma, Ohio State University, the University of Southern California, and Collegiate Licensing Company (the official licensing agent for the universities) brought suit against defendant Smack Apparel for its unauthorized sale of apparel bearing the universities' colors and various printed messages associated with the universities. The Eastern District of Louisiana granted the plaintiffs' motion for summary judgment on the issue of trademark infringement. The Fifth Circuit affirmed. Excerpted here is the Fifth Circuit's discussion of sponsorship confusion and whether consumers prefer authorized merchandise in certain situations. Do you find it persuasive?

Note that the apparel at issue, further examples of which are given below, did not bear the universities' full names or mascots.

---

[33] *See also* Vince Horiuchi, *HBO Disputes Trademark Infringement in 'Big Love,'* SALT LAKE TRIB., July 8, 2009 (discussing a lawsuit filed by the University of Utah over the three-second depiction of a fictional research report bearing the University of Utah logo).

[34] Michael Cieply, *Despite Big Names, Prestige Film Falls Through*, N.Y. TIMES, July 2, 2009, at B1.

Board of Supervisors for Louisiana State University Agricultural & Mechanical College v. Smack Apparel Co.
550 F.3d 465, 478-488 (5th Cir. 2008)

REAVLEY, Circuit Judge:

. . . .

B. Likelihood of confusion

[1] Once a plaintiff shows ownership in a protectible trademark, he must next show that the defendant's use of the mark "creates a likelihood of confusion in the minds of potential customers as to the 'source, affiliation, or sponsorship' " of the product at issue. *Westchester Media v. PRL USA Holdings, Inc.*[38] When assessing the likelihood of confusion, we consider a nonexhaustive list of so-called "digits of confusion," including: "(1) the type of mark allegedly infringed, (2) the similarity between the two marks, (3) the similarity of the products or services, (4) the identity of the retail outlets and purchasers, (5) the identity of the advertising media used, (6) the defendant's intent, and (7) any evidence of actual confusion."[40] Courts also consider (8) the degree of care exercised by potential purchasers.[41] No single factor is dispositive, and a finding of a likelihood of confusion need not be supported by a majority of the factors.[42]

[2] Smack argues that there were genuine issues of material fact whether its t-shirt designs were likely to cause confusion among consumers. We disagree. The first digit, the type of mark, refers to the strength of the mark. Generally, the stronger the mark, the greater the likelihood that consumers will be confused by competing uses of the mark. We agree with the district court that the plaintiffs' marks, which have been used for over one hundred years, are strong. As noted above, Smack concedes that the Universities' color schemes are well-known and are used to identify the plaintiff Universities. It argues, however, that the district court disregarded evidence of third-party use of the Universities' team colors in a non-trademark manner, and it cites *Sun Banks of Florida, Inc. v. Sun Federal Savings and Loan Association*[46] in support of its argument.

[3] In *Sun Banks*, we held that "extensive" third-party use can weaken a mark and negate a likelihood of confusion. In that case there were "over 4400 businesses" in Florida that were using the

---

[38] 214 F.3d 658, 663 (5th Cir. 2000) (citation omitted).

[40] *Id.* at 664.

[41] *Am. Rice*, 518 F.3d at 329.

[42] *Id.*

[46] 651 F.2d 311 (5th Cir. 1981).

378

word "Sun" in their names, and we noted that "a significant number" fell within the same category of financial institutions as the plaintiff.[48]

[4] Smack presented photographs of three businesses in Louisiana, eight businesses in Ohio, and approximately 20 businesses in Oklahoma that incorporated in their signage color schemes similar to the school colors of LSU, OSU, and OU, respectively. The businesses included several restaurants and bars, a driving school, a pain management clinic, a theater, a furniture store, a dry cleaners, a motel, a donut shop, an apartment complex, and a car care company. All third-party use of a mark, not just use in the same industry as a plaintiff, may be relevant to whether a plaintiff's mark is strong or weak.[49] But the key is whether the third-party use diminishes in the public's mind the association of the mark with the plaintiff—surely lacking where colors are shown on a store wall. *See Univ. of Ga. Athletic Ass'n v. Laite.*[50] Smack's evidence falls far below that of extensive use, and the specific photographs of third-party use here fail to create an issue of fact concerning the public's association between the plaintiffs and color schemes and other indicia that clearly reference the Universities. We conclude that the Universities possess strong marks in their use of color schemes and other identifying indicia on college sports-themed merchandise.

[5] The second digit is the similarity of the marks. This factor requires consideration of the marks' appearance, sound, and meaning. The district court held that the marks at issue are virtually identical. Smack argues that there was no evidence that any of its shirts were identical to any shirts licensed by the Universities and that its t-shirt designs are not at all similar to any of the Universities' licensed products. Smack's contention is belied by the record, and even a cursory comparison of Smack's designs with the plaintiffs' licensed products reveals striking similarity.

[6] For example, one of Smack's shirt designs in purple and gold is referred to as the "sundial" shirt and was targeted toward LSU fans. The front of the shirt proclaims "2003 National Champions," and the back contains the scores from twelve games won by LSU. The scores are arranged in a circle with a short phrase poking fun at each opponent. The shirt also contains the final score of the 2004 Sugar Bowl, which LSU won, and the phrase "Sweet as Sugar!" Although the shirt does not use the initials "LSU" anywhere, its identification of LSU as the national champion is unmistakable from the colors and from the references to the games in which LSU played. This shirt is strikingly similar to LSU's own merchandise that also uses the purple and gold colors and proclaims LSU as the national champion. Several of the official designs contain the scores of the games from LSU's season and at least two designs present those scores in a circular arrangement. The official designs also contain the phrases "Ain't It Sweet!" and "Pour It On!"

[7] Another Smack shirt directed at LSU fans is the "Beat Oklahoma" shirt. It states, "Bring it Back to the Bayou." This is very similar to two official designs that state in part "Bring It Home" and "We'll Have Big Fun on the Bayou."

[8] The evidence of similarity is not limited to the shirts targeted toward LSU fans. For example, the "Bourbon Street or Bust!" shirt directed at OU fans highlights the letters "OU" in a different type face in the words "Bayou" and "your." It also states "Sweet as Sugar," references beads, and contains a picture of a mardi gras mask. OU presented evidence of official t-shirt designs that also highlight the letters "OU," contain phrases such as "Ain't Nothin' Sweeter" and "100% Pure Sugar," and contain depictions of mardi gras masks and beads. Another Smack OU design encourages, "Let's Make it Eight," while official designs proclaim "Sugar is Sweet But . . . 8 is Great!"

---

[48] *Sun Banks,* 651 F.2d at 316.

[49] *Union Nat'l Bank of Tex.,* 909 F.2d at 848 n. 24; *see also* 2 J. THOMAS MCCARTHY, MCCARTHY ON TRADEMARKS AND UNFAIR COMPETITION § 11:88 (4th ed.) ("[E]vidence of extensive third party use on a wide range of goods and services does tend to weaken strength and narrow the scope of protection.").

[50] 756 F.2d 1535, 1545 n. 27 (11th Cir. 1985).

[9] In the district court, Smack presented the affidavit of its principal, Wayne Curtiss, who explained that Smack uses humor and creative language to distinguish its t-shirt designs from those of the purportedly more conservative licensed or school-endorsed apparel. Curtiss asserted that the "got seven?" and "got eight?" shirts directed toward OSU and USC fans, respectively, are parodies of the "got milk" campaign. He further averred that he has used a similar design on shirts for LSU and OU fans. It is clear from the record, however, that use of creative language is not unique to Smack and does not make Smack's shirts dissimilar to the Universities' own products. For example, LSU presented evidence of a school-endorsed design that included the phrase "got sugar?" We conclude that Smack's shirts and the Universities' products are similar in look, sound, and meaning, and contain very similar color schemes, words, and images. The similarities in design elements are overwhelming and weigh heavily in favor of a likelihood of confusion. The district court correctly held there is no genuine issue of material fact with respect to this digit of confusion.[54]

[10] The third digit in the likelihood of confusion analysis is the similarity of the products or services. We disagree with Smack's assertion that the district court did not find a great deal of similarity between the plaintiffs' products and the t-shirts at issue, as the district court specifically held that "[i]t is undisputed that both Smack and the universities market shirts bearing the same color schemes, logos, and designs."[55] The district court went on to reject Smack's argument that its t-shirts differed from the Universities' products because of the use of irreverent phrases or slang language, reasoning that Smack's use of such phrases and language was a misuse of the Universities' good will in its marks. Smack denies that it appropriated the Universities' good will, but it does not make an argument here that its shirts are distinguishable from those of the Universities because of particular language on its shirts. We therefore find this factor weighs in favor of a likelihood of confusion.

[11] Smack concedes that the fourth factor of the analysis—identity of retail outlets and purchasers—weighs in favor of a likelihood of confusion because the Universities' licensed products are often sold wholesale to the same retailers who purchase Smack's products.

[12] The fifth digit is the identity of advertising media. The district court found that Smack used the Universities' color schemes, logos, and designs in advertising its shirts at the same or similar venues as those used by the Universities. The court based its finding on Smack's admission that it participated in the same trade shows as the Universities and that it displayed its shirts at the trade shows. The Universities do not point us to evidence that trade shows are a significant advertising channel for the kinds of products at issue in this case. Although the t-shirts are sold to the public at the same retail outlets as officially licensed merchandise, Curtiss testified that beside limited sales on Smack's web site, Smack does not sell directly to the public and does not advertise. Curtiss testified that Smack sells mainly to wholesalers. Some of these wholesalers may include Smack's shirts in advertisements that promote their own business, but Curtiss was unable to provide much information about these ads. We conclude that this digit, based on trade show advertising, is minimally probative.

[13] The sixth digit of confusion further supports a likelihood of confusion. Although not necessary to a finding of likelihood of confusion, a defendant's intent to confuse may alone be sufficient to justify an inference that there is a likelihood of confusion. As noted by the district court, Smack admitted that it "'used school colors and "other indicia" with the intent of identifying the university plaintiffs as the subject of the message expressed in the shirt design.'" Curtiss testified that it was "no coincidence" that

---

[54] Because we conclude that there is no issue of fact as to the similarity of the use of the marks in the t-shirt designs, we need not consider Smack's contention that the district court erroneously stated there had been instances where consumers actually believed Smack's shirts were affiliated with or sponsored by the Universities. Smack points to a stipulation by the parties at the summary judgment stage that there was no evidence any consumer purchased a Smack shirt believing it to be licensed by one of the Universities. Actual confusion on the part of a consumer is not required to find a likelihood of confusion, however. *Elvis Presley Enters.*, 141 F.3d at 203.

[55] *Bd. of Supervisors*, 438 F.Supp.2d at 660.

Smack's shirts incorporated the color schemes of the plaintiff Universities and that he designed the shirts to make people think of the particular school that each shirt targeted. Smack asserts that its intent to copy is not the same as an intent to confuse. The circumstances of this case show, however, that Smack intended to capitalize on the potential for confusion. Smack knew that its shirts were sold in the same venues as and sometimes alongside officially licensed merchandise, and it intentionally incorporated color marks to create the kind of association with the Universities that would influence purchasers.

[14] The Eleventh Circuit found a likelihood of confusion based on a similar intent by the defendant to capitalize on the popularity of a college sports team. *Univ. of Ga. Athletic Ass'n v. Laite.*[59] In *Laite*, the defendant used school colors and a mark strikingly similar to the University of Georgia's bulldog mascot on cans to sell "Battlin' Bulldog Beer." After concluding that the defendant's bulldog mark was similar to the university's mark, the court turned to the defendant's intent, concluding "there can be no doubt that Laite hoped to sell 'Battlin' Bulldog Beer' not because the beer tastes great, but because the cans would catch the attention of University of Georgia football fans."[61] Significantly, the court found "the defendant's intent and the similarity of design between the two marks sufficient to support the district court's finding of a 'likelihood of confusion . . . .'"[62] The same is true here. Smack did not hope to sell its t-shirts because of some competitive difference in quality or design compared with the Universities' licensed products, but rather it intended to take advantage of the popularity of the Universities' football programs and the appearance of the school teams in the college bowl games. We have previously said that when a "mark was adopted with the intent of deriving benefit from the reputation of [the mark holder] that fact alone 'may be sufficient to justify the inference that there is confusing similarity.'" *Amstar Corp. v. Domino's Pizza, Inc.*[63] We believe that Smack's admitted intent and the similarity in appearance between Smack's shirts and the Universities' licensed products is strong evidence of a likelihood of confusion.

[15] Smack argues that an intent to confuse is negated by its use of its own logo and the words "Talkin' the Talk," which it maintains identifies it as the source of the shirt. We are not persuaded. Smack's logo appears in a space that is only 2.5 inches wide. We cannot conclude, without more, that this small and inconspicuous placement of the logo would disabuse consumers of a mistaken belief that the Universities sponsored, endorsed or were otherwise affiliated with the t-shirts.[64] Smack has not pointed to evidence that its own logo is recognizable by consumers or that it was acting to trade off its own reputation as a producer of specialty t-shirts. Nor are we convinced that Smack's logo on the shirts acts as a disclaimer. The Universities point out that they require all licensed products to contain the licensee's name. Therefore, a consumer could believe that Smack's logo merely indicated that it was a licensee.[66] We conclude that the intent digit weighs in favor of a conclusion that there is a likelihood of confusion.

[16] The seventh digit is evidence of actual confusion. Evidence that consumers have been actually confused in identifying the defendant's use of a mark as that of the plaintiff may be the best evidence of a likelihood of confusion. It is well established, however, that evidence of actual confusion is not necessary for a finding of a likelihood of confusion. The district court did not resolve whether there was

---

[59] 756 F.2d 1535 (11th Cir. 1985).

[61] *Id.* at 1545 (footnote omitted).

[62] *Id.* at 1545.

[63] 615 F.2d 252, 263 (5th Cir. 1980) (quoting RESTATEMENT OF TORTS § 729, comment f (1938)).

[64] *See Pebble Beach*, 155 F.3d at 552 (noting that "conspicuous disclaimers that disclaim affiliation may reduce or eliminate confusion").

[66] *See A.T. Cross Co. v. Jonathan Bradley Pens, Inc.*, 470 F.2d 689, 692 (2d Cir. 1972) (defendant's placement of its own name on pen also bearing mark similar to plaintiff's mark "does not save the day; a purchaser could well think plaintiff had licensed defendant as a second user and the addition is thus 'an aggravation, and not a justification' " (citation omitted)).

sufficient evidence of actual confusion, and because such evidence is not required we also find it unnecessary to pass on the question further.[69]

[17] With respect to the eighth digit of confusion—the degree of care exercised by potential purchasers—the district court held that the t-shirts at issue are relatively inexpensive impulse items that are not purchased with a high degree of care. Where items are relatively inexpensive, a buyer may take less care in selecting the item, thereby increasing the risk of confusion. Smack contends there was insufficient evidence for the district court's conclusion. In response, the Universities note Curtiss' testimony that he hoped customers' decisions to purchase Smack's shirts would be "quick," and they point out that the shirts sell for less than $18. Smack cites no evidence to demonstrate an issue of fact on this point, and we agree with the district court that this digit weighs in favor of a likelihood of confusion.

[18] After reviewing the record, we conclude that there is no genuine issue of fact that Smack's use of the Universities' color schemes and other identifying indicia creates a likelihood of confusion as to the source, affiliation, or sponsorship of the t-shirts. As noted above, the digits of confusion—particularly the overwhelming similarity of the marks and the defendant's intent to profit from the Universities' reputation—compel this conclusion. This is so, we have noted, because Smack's use of the Universities' colors and indicia is designed to create the illusion of affiliation with the Universities and essentially obtain a "free ride" by profiting from confusion among the fans of the Universities' football teams who desire to show support for and affiliation with those teams.[72] This creation of a link in the consumer's mind between the t-shirts and the Universities and the intent to directly profit therefrom results in "an unmistakable aura of deception" and likelihood of confusion.

[19] Smack contends that there is no evidence that consumers care one way or the other whether t-shirts purchased for wear at a football game are officially licensed and that, absent evidence that consumers prefer licensed merchandise, it was error for the district court to conclude there was a likelihood of confusion. Smack relies in part on our decision in *Supreme Assembly, Order of Rainbow for Girls v. J.H. Ray Jewelry Company*.[74] The context of that case is different from the instant case.

[20] In *Rainbow for Girls,* a fraternal organization and its official jeweler sued a retailer for trademark infringement based on the retailer's sale of jewelry bearing the organization's registered mark. Purchasers in the fraternal-organization jewelry market bought jewelry to show membership and status in the organization. We upheld the district court's finding of no likelihood of confusion, concluding that "[t]he fact that purchasers purchased Rainbow jewelry as a direct result of the presence of the Rainbow emblem does not compel the conclusion that they did so believing that the jewelry was in any way endorsed, sponsored, approved or otherwise associated with Rainbow, *given the court's findings.*"[76] The district court had held that there was no historic custom or practice specific to Rainbow jewelry or to the fraternal jewelry industry that Rainbow jewelry could be manufactured only with Rainbow's sponsorship or approval. Instead, the court noted that fraternal organizations exercised little control over the manufacture of jewelry bearing their emblems. Furthermore, the court had held that because Rainbow's "official jeweler" was itself well-advertised and used its own distinctive mark on the jewelry, any jewelry without that distinctive mark could not cause confusion. We noted that the district court's

---

[69] The Universities contend that there was evidence of actual confusion consisting of consumer surveys concerning two of the six t-shirt designs and testimony from Curtiss that "I have had people come up and go-at the booth and go, 'Are these licensed?' " The evidence is arguably minimal, *see Amstar,* 615 F.2d at 263, but as discussed we need not resolve the matter.

[72] *See Boston Athletic Ass'n v. Sullivan,* 867 F.2d 22, 33 (1st Cir. 1989) ("Defendants' shirts are clearly designed to take advantage of the Boston Marathon and to benefit from the good will associated with its promotion by plaintiffs. Defendants thus obtain a 'free ride' at plaintiffs' expense.").

[74] 676 F.2d 1079 (5th Cir. 1982).

[76] *Id.* at 1084 (emphasis added).

findings distinguished the case from our decision in *Boston Professional Hockey Association v. Dallas Cap & Emblem Manufacturing.*

[21] In *Boston Hockey,* we held that the defendant infringed the plaintiff's trademark rights by selling embroidered patches containing the emblems of professional hockey teams.[81] There, the emblems were sold for use by the public to show "allegiance to or identification with the teams."[82] We held that the likelihood of confusion requirement was met because the defendant duplicated and sold the emblems "knowing that the public would identify them as being the teams' trademarks" and because the public's "certain knowledge . . . that the source and origin of the trademark symbols were in plaintiffs satisfies the requirements of the act."[83]

[22] Subsequently, in *Kentucky Fried Chicken Corporation v. Diversified Packaging Corporation*, we recognized that *Boston Hockey* might be read to dispose of the confusion issue when buyers undoubtedly know that the plaintiff is the source and origin of a mark.[84] We reiterated that a showing of likelihood of confusion was still required. But we noted that the circumstances in *Boston Hockey* supported the likelihood of confusion there insofar as the sale of products "universally associated" with the hockey team "supported the inescapable inference that many would believe that the product itself originated with or was somehow endorsed by Boston Hockey." In *Rainbow for Girls,* the district court opinion, which we upheld, also recognized in reference to *Boston Hockey* that "'(i)t is not unreasonable to conclude, given the degree to which sports emblems are used to advertise teams and endorse products, that a consumer seeing the emblem or name of a team on or associated with a good or service would assume some sort of sponsorship or association between the product's seller and the team.'"[87]

[23] We agree with this reasoning as applied to this case, which is more like *Boston Hockey* than *Rainbow for Girls.* We hold that given the record in this case and the digits of confusion analysis discussed above—including the overwhelming similarity between the defendant's t-shirts and the Universities' licensed products, and the defendant's admitted intent to create an association with the plaintiffs and to influence consumers in calling the plaintiffs to mind—that the inescapable conclusion is that many consumers would likely be confused and believe that Smack's t-shirts were sponsored or endorsed by the Universities. The Universities exercise stringent control over the use of their marks on apparel through their licensing program. It is also undisputed that the Universities annually sell millions of dollars worth of licensed apparel. We further recognize the public's indisputable desire to associate with college sports teams by wearing team-related apparel. We are not persuaded that simply because some consumers might not care whether Smack's shirts are officially licensed the likelihood of confusion is negated. Whether or not a consumer *cares* about official sponsorship is a different question from whether that consumer would likely *believe* the product is officially sponsored. For the foregoing reasons, we conclude that a likelihood of confusion connecting the presence of the Universities' marks and the Universities' themselves was demonstrated in this case.

. . . .

Questions and Comments

1.   *Materiality and Consumer Confusion.* How might courts constrain the enormous expansion of "sponsorship or affiliation" confusion? Lemley & McKenna:

> [W]e argue that courts can begin to rein in some of these excesses by focusing their attention on confusion that is actually relevant to purchasing decisions. Uses of a trademark that cause confusion about actual source or about responsibility for quality will

---

[81] 510 F.2d 1004 (5th Cir. 1975).

[82] Id. at 1011.

[83] *Id.* at 1012.

[84] 549 F.2d 368, 389 (5th Cir. 1977).

[87] *Rainbow for Girls*, 676 F.2d at 1085.

383

often impact purchasing decisions, so courts should presume materiality and impose liability when there is evidence such confusion is likely. Uses alleged to cause confusion about more nebulous relationships, on the other hand, are more analogous to false advertising claims, and those uses should be actionable only when a plaintiff can prove the alleged confusion is material to consumers' decision making.

Mark A. Lemley & Mark McKenna, *Irrelevant Confusion*, 62 STAN. L. REV. 413, 416 (2010).

2. *The "Circularity" Problem in Trademark Law.* Trademark commentators have long identified a fundamental problem with basing the subject matter and scope of trademark rights on consumer perception. The problem is that consumer perception is itself based at least in part on what the law allows to occur in the marketplace—and even more problematically, on what consumers *think* the law allows to occur in the marketplace. McCarthy explains:

> Th[e] reality of modern brand extensions raises the "circularity" question. If consumers think that most uses of a trademark require authorization, then in fact they will require authorization because the owner can enjoin consumer confusion caused by unpermitted uses or charge for licenses. And if owners can sue to stop unauthorized uses, then only authorized uses will be seen by consumers, creating or reinforcing their perception that authorization is necessary. This is a "chicken and the egg" conundrum. Which comes first? The trademark right on far-flung items or the license? Licensing itself may affect consumer perception if consumers see a plethora of items with the mark perhaps accompanied by an "authorized by" label.

McCARTHY § 24:9. *See also* Mark A. Lemley, *The Modern Lanham Act and the Death of Common Sense*, 108 YALE L.J. 1687, 1708 (1999) ("Ironically, having accepted the merchandising rationale for certain sorts of trademarks, we may find it hard to undo. It is possible that consumers have come to expect that "Dallas Cowboys" caps are licensed by the Cowboys, not because they serve a trademark function, but simply because the law has recently required such a relationship. If this expectation exits, consumers may be confused if the law changes."). *Cf. Vornado Air Circulation Sys., Inc. v. Duracraft Corp.*, 58 F.3d 1498, 1509 (10th Cir. 1995) ("We recognize also that consumer confusion resulting from the copying of product features is, in some measure, a self-fulfilling prophecy. To the degree that useful product configurations are protected as identifiers, consumers will come to rely on them for that purpose, but if copying is allowed, they will depend less on product shapes and more on labels and packaging.").

3. *Trademark rights in fictional elements of expressive works?* In *Lucasfilm Ltd. LLC v. Ren Ventures Ltd.*, No. 17 Civ. 07249, 2018 WL 2392963 (N.D. Cal. Apr. 24, 2018), the defendants produced a mobile game app entitled "Sabacc—The High Stakes Card Game," which was based on the card game Sabacc described in several novels from the fictional *Star Wars* universe (and which was featured in the *Star Wars* film *Solo: A Star Wars Story*). The plaintiff asserted trademark rights in the name. In denying the defendants' motion to dismiss, the Northern District of California cited several previous cases in which courts recognized trademark rights in fictional elements of expressive works:

> Defendants next contend that the name of a fictional good or service in an expressive work does not function as a mark for the expressive work in which the fictional good or service appears. On the contrary, courts have long held that fictional elements of expressive works can function as trademarks when those elements symbolize the plaintiff or its product to the consuming public. *See DC Comics, Inc. v. Filmation Assocs.*, 486 F. Supp. 1273, 1277 (S.D.N.Y. 1980). Following this principal, courts have extended trademark protection to the "General Lee" car from the television series "The Dukes of Hazzard," *see Warner Bros., Inc. v. Gay Toys, Inc.*, 658 F.2d 76, 78 (2d Cir. 1981), the fictional restaurant "The Krusty Krab" from the "SpongeBob SquarePants" television series, *see Viacom Int'l Inc. v. IJR Capital Invs., LLC*, 242 F. Supp. 3d 563, 569 (S.D. Tex. 2017), the "Hobbit" characters from J.R.R. Tolkien's works, *see Warner Bros. Entm't v. Glob. Asylum, Inc.*, No. CV 12-9547, 2012 WL 6951315 at *3-5 (C.D. Cal. Dec. 10, 2012), the fictional element "Kryptonite" associated with Superman comics, *see DC Comics v. Kryptonite Corp.*, 336 F. Supp. 2d 324, 332, 35 (S.D.N.Y. 2004), and the physical appearance of the E.T. character

from its titular motion picture film, *see Universal City Studios, Inc. v. J.A.R. Sales, Inc.*, No. 82-4892, 1982 WL 1279 at *4 (C.D. Cal. Oct. 20, 1982).

In the face of this weight of authority, defendants point to several administrative decisions from the Trademark Trial and Appeal Board (TTAB) where the Board refused to recognize certain fictional elements as being trademarks. *See* Mot. to Dismiss at 17-18. Yet these decisions merely suggest that fanciful elements do not *always* function as marks for the expressive works in which they appear, not that they may *never* do so. For example, in *Paramount Pictures Corp. v. Romulan Invasions*, 7 U.S.P.Q.2d 1897 (T.T.A.B. Mar. 31, 1988), Paramount sought to enjoin a rock band from registering "The Romulans" as the group's name, on the grounds that "Romulans" are a fictional alien race appearing in the *Star Trek* franchise. While the Board provided no explanatory reasoning for its conclusion that Paramount's use of the name did not confer trademark rights, a reasonable consumer would not likely assume the rock band was affiliated with the *Star Trek* franchise on account of its name alone. Thus, the Board concluded Paramount's use of "Romulans" should not preclude registration of the rock band's name.

Lucasfilm Ltd. LLC, 2018 WL 2392963, at *3–4. *See also* Lisa Pearson, *The Real Life of Fictional Trademarks*, 100 TRADEMARK REP. 839 (2020).

6. Initial Interest Confusion

Virgin Enterprises focused on "point of sale" confusion, i.e., consumer confusion as to source at the moment when the consumer purchases the defendant's goods or services. We turn now to other modes of confusion. We consider first "initial interest confusion," which "occurs when a customer is lured to a product by the similarity of the mark, even if the customer realizes the true source of the goods before the sale is consummated." *Promatek Indus., Ltd. v. Equitrac Corp.*, 300 F.3d 808, 812 (7th Cir. 2002), as amended (Oct. 18, 2002) (citation omitted). *See also Grotrian, Helfferich, Schulz, Th. Steinweg Nachf. v. Steinway & Sons*, 523 F.2d 1331, 1342 (2d Cir. 1975) (finding "initial confusion" when the declaratory plaintiff used the mark GROTRIAN-STEINWEG for pianos even if no consumers ultimately purchased the plaintiff's pianos believing them to be STEINWAY pianos).

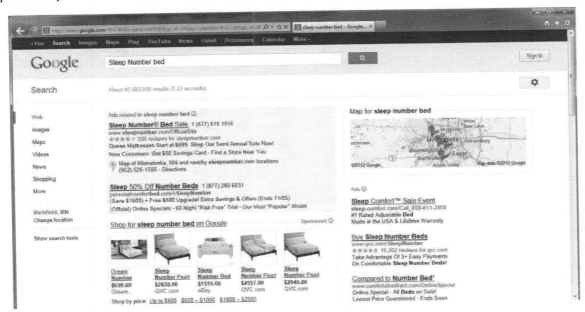

Select Comfort Corporation v. Baxter
996 F.3d 925 (8th Cir. 2021)

MELLOY, Circuit Judge.

[1] Plaintiffs and Defendants sell competing adjustable air mattresses and related products. Plaintiffs' registered trademarks include "SLEEP NUMBER", "WHAT'S YOUR SLEEP NUMBER", "SELECT COMFORT", and "COMFORTAIRE". Plaintiffs allege Defendants used similar and identical marks in several different capacities online to sell competing products. . . . At summary judgment the district court rejected as a matter of law an infringement theory based on presale or initial-interest confusion. 4 J. McCarthy, *Trademarks and Unfair Competition*, § 23:6 (4th Ed. 2010) (hereinafter *McCarthy*) (initial-interest confusion is "confusion that creates initial customer interest, even though no actual sale is finally completed as a result of the confusion"). The case proceeded to a trial on trademark infringement and dilution claims and on unfair competition and false advertising claims. Consistent with the summary judgment ruling, the district court instructed the jury that infringement liability depended on a showing of a likelihood of confusion at the time of purchase. The trial resulted in a mixed verdict.

[2] Both sides appeal. . . . Because we conclude the district court erred by finding as a matter of law that the relevant consumers were sophisticated and that a theory of initial-interest confusion could not apply, we reverse. . . .

I. Background

[3] Plaintiffs are the owners of the heavily advertised Select Comfort and Sleep Number brands of adjustable air mattresses sold online, over the phone, and (primarily) through hundreds of company-owned stores nationwide. Defendant Dires, LLC, and its principals and predecessor or affiliated companies, actually made adjustable air beds at an earlier date. Defendants have evolved into an online retailer ("personalcomfortbed.com") that utilizes internet advertising and a call-center-based sales model to sell their own brand of lower-priced adjustable air beds. The individual defendants are executives or owners of Dires or related companies, all of whom had input into marketing strategy and advertising design. Defendants are a distant second to Plaintiffs in adjustable-bed sales volume.

[4] Plaintiffs' overall theory of the case alleges Defendants employed words or phrases identical or confusingly similar to Plaintiffs trademarks in various online advertising formats including: website urls; search inquiry paid terms; embedded links in third-party sites; and general use of identical or similar phrases in text advertisements or combined graphic-and-text advertisements that could be viewed by users or detected organically by search engines. According to Plaintiffs, Defendants used these means to divert customers to their own website and phone lines where Defendants (1) failed to dispel consumer confusion or made statements that caused further source confusion and (2) made false representations about their own products and Plaintiffs' products in order to promote their own products. In this way, Plaintiffs assert trademark infringement, trademark dilution, and false-advertising theories that rely upon common facts.

[5] As relevant to claims on appeal, Plaintiffs asserted federal trademark infringement and dilution claims based on their registered trademarks, federal unfair competition and false advertising claims, and a state law deceptive trade practices claim. In a declaratory judgment counterclaim, Defendants . . . argued Plaintiffs could not maintain an infringement claim based on presale or initial-interest confusion. Both parties sought summary judgment.

[6] In summary judgment rulings, the district court found . . . [r]egarding trademark infringement . . that outstanding questions of fact precluded summary judgment. Regarding the specific question of trademark infringement in the form of initial-interest confusion, the district court first noted that Plaintiffs expressly disavowed any theory of trademark infringement that relied exclusively on Defendants' use of Plaintiffs' trademarks as paid search terms with search engine providers such as Google. Rather, Plaintiffs alleged infringement based on that use coupled with Defendants' several and varied other uses of similar and identical trademarks in multiple forms of online advertising. The district court then relied on our case, *Sensient Techs. Corp. v. SensoryEffects Flavor Co.*, 613 F.3d 754 (8th Cir. 2010), noting that the Eighth Circuit had neither expressly adopted nor rejected a theory of initial-

interest confusion as a general matter, but had refused to apply the theory in a case where consumers were sophisticated.

[7] The District Court next held as a matter of law that retail purchasers of mattresses were sophisticated consumers because mattresses are expensive. As a result, the District Court held as a matter of law that a claim alleging initial-interest confusion could not proceed and Plaintiffs would have to show a likelihood of confusion at the time of purchase. . . .

[8] At trial, Plaintiffs presented evidence which showed Defendants had used Plaintiffs' actual trademarks as paid search terms and as identical phrases in their own web-based advertising in text pages, combined text and graphical pages, as terms embedded in linked internet address urls, and in other fashions. Examples included website links that presented Plaintiffs' trademarks as identical phrases (e.g. personalcomfortbed.com/vSleepNumber or www.personalcomfortbed.com/cComfortaire). In addition, Defendants used phrases similar to Plaintiffs' trademarks, often with words broken up in a grammatically non-sensical fashion. Examples included the use of terms such as "Sleep 55% Off Number Beds" and "Comfort Air Beds on Sale" in online advertisements. Survey evidence demonstrated actual consumer confusion, although the parties disputed the relevancy and value of the survey evidence based on percentages of participants who were confused, whether the survey participants were actual or potential consumers, and how the questions were presented. Evidence also included instances of actual confusion, often from transcripts of call-center interactions, messages from customers, or messages from call-center employees. The transcripts and recordings of call-center interactions appeared to show that Defendants' call-center employees at times attempted to promote confusion and at other times attempted to dispel confusion. Finally, evidence included statements from Defendants' principals in which they described confusion as between Plaintiffs' and Defendants' brands as a "good thing" and, in response to reports of confusion, indicated that their advertisements were "working."

[9] At the end of the day, the district court submitted the case to the jury. Based on the summary judgment ruling, the district court instructed the jury that a likelihood of confusion must exist at the time of purchase to support a trademark infringement claim. . . .

[10] The jury rejected the trademark infringement claims as to the registered trademarks based on the jury instruction that limited the possibility of a likelihood of confusion to the time of purchase. . . .

II. Discussion

A. Initial-Interest Confusion

[11] The primary issue in this appeal is the availability of a theory of initial-interest confusion on the trademark infringement claim and the resulting limitation in the instruction requiring any likelihood of confusion to exist at the time of purchase. As noted, initial-interest confusion is "confusion that creates initial customer interest, even though no actual sale is finally completed as a result of the confusion." 4 *McCarthy* § 23:6. Most circuits that have addressed the question "recognize the initial interest confusion theory as a form of likelihood of confusion which can trigger a finding of infringement." *Id.* (collecting cases). In general, the theory of initial-interest confusion recognizes that a senior user's goodwill holds value at all times, not merely at the moment of purchase. The theory protects against the threat of a competitor "receiving a 'free ride on the goodwill' of [an] established mark." *Checkpoint Systems, Inc. v. Check Point Software Technologies, Inc.*, 269 F.3d 270, 295 (3d Cir. 2001) (quoting *Mobil Oil Corp. v. Pegasus Petroleum Corp.*, 818 F.2d 254, 260 (2d Cir. 1987)). This free ride may result in the consumer falsely inferring an affiliation between the junior and senior users, provide the junior user with an opportunity it otherwise would not have achieved, or deprive the senior user of an actual opportunity. *Id.* at 293–95. At least one circuit has "equated initial interest confusion to a 'bait and switch scheme.'" *Id.* at 294 (quoting *Dorr-Oliver, Inc. v. Fluid Quip, Inc.*, 94 F.3d 376, 382 (7th Cir. 1996)).

[12] In the present case, the parties dispute as a general matter whether a theory of initial-interest confusion is a viable theory of infringement in our circuit. They also dispute whether the relevant consumers—consumers investigating mattresses and online shoppers in general—are so sophisticated that the issue of consumer sophistication could properly be removed from the jury. To address these

questions, it is necessary first to review more generally the test for confusion and what our Court has said about *when* confusion must exist.

. . . .

[13] To assess the likelihood of confusion as required for a showing of infringement, our circuit employs a list of nonexclusive factors for addressing a core inquiry: whether the relevant average consumers for a product or service are likely to be confused as to the source of a product or service or as to an affiliation between sources based on a defendant's use. . . . The factors we consider come from *SquirtCo v. Seven–Up Co.*, 628 F.2d 1086, 1091 (8th Cir. 1980). . . .

[14] This flexible, context-specific, and relative-rather-than-mechanical approach makes sense because the general function of the likelihood-of-confusion factors is to guide the finder of fact towards considerations generally thought to be material to the consuming public's understanding of product source or affiliation. . . .

[15] Although our test for a likelihood of confusion is well-developed, some uncertainty remains as to *when* confusion must exist in order to support a trademark infringement claim. *Sensient*, 613 F.3d at 766. Although not addressing initial-interest confusion specifically, our Court has clearly established that claims of infringement are *not limited* solely to a likelihood of confusion at the time of purchase. *See Insty*Bit, Inc. v. Poly-Tech Indus.*, 95 F.3d 663, 671–72 (8th Cir. 1996). In *Insty*Bit*, our Court recognized that a 1962 amendment to the Lanham Act eliminated reference to "purchasers" when describing actionable confusion. *Id.* (quoting Pub. L. No. 87–772, 76 Stat. 769, 773 (1962)). We interpreted this statutory amendment as permitting claims for post-sale confusion among nonpurchasers—generally "consumers"— who witnessed a confusingly marked product. *Id.*

[16] Fourteen years later, however, our Court indicated that it was unclear as a general matter whether initial-interest or *presale* confusion was actionable. *See Sensient Tech.*, 613 F.3d at 766. There, over a dissent, our circuit identified the theory, but neither rejected nor adopted it for general application. Instead, we held that the theory did not apply on the facts of the case because the consumers at issue were sophisticated commercial purchasers of inputs for industrial food production who purchased goods with a high degree of care "after a collaborative process." *Id.* at 769.

[17] The general question of whether presale, initial-interest confusion is actionable, therefore, seemingly pits two opposing views of trademark law against one another. On the one hand, through our application and review of the likelihood of confusion factors, we recognize the varied landscape of commercial transactions and leave the jury to sort through the details. Our factors provide guidance but do not draw bright lines that might constrain the general test for confusion. Similarly, the Court in *Insty*Bit* refused to place firm constraints on the question of *when* confusion must exist. On the other hand, in *Sensient*, our Court acknowledged the possibility of cabining the likelihood-of-confusion test to a particular moment in time, at least under certain circumstances.

[18] We now address the issue left open in *Sensient* and hold that a theory of initial-interest confusion may apply in our circuit. We are, of course, bound by *Sensient*. But, when the particular conditions of *Sensient* are not present, i.e., when a jury question exists as to the issue of consumer sophistication, a plaintiff should not be barred from proving presale, initial-interest confusion. In reaching this conclusion we find the Lanham Act itself and amendments to its language as cited in *Insty*Bit* particularly compelling. Other courts addressing the question of initial-interest confusion have relied on this language. *Checkpoint*, 269 F.3d at 295 (noting that as originally enacted, "the Lanham Act only applied where the use of similar marks was 'likely to cause confusion or mistake or to deceive purchasers as to the source of origin of such goods or services' " (quoting 1946 Lanham Act) (accord *Esercizio v. Roberts*, 944 F.2d 1235, 1244 (6th Cir. 1991))); *see generally*, 4 McCarthy § 23:7 (collecting cases) (noting that several courts have interpreted this amendment as expanding trademark protection beyond point-of-sale confusion to reach presale confusion (including initial-interest confusion) and post-sale confusion). And, in general, adoption of the theory is consistent with the overall practice of recognizing the varied nature of commercial interactions and the importance of not cabining the jury's analysis of the likelihood of confusion factors. If we do not generally impose strict constraints on the

jury's nuanced assessment of how or whether the consuming public might be confused, it would be odd to presume that all commercial interactions are alike or that, in all settings, trademarks are worthy of protection only in the few moments before the consummation of a transaction.

[19] Of course, as per *Sensient*, the theory of initial-interest confusion cannot apply in our Circuit where the relevant average consumers are sophisticated at the level of the careful professional purchasers who were at issue in *Sensient*. In this regard, however, we find several comments by the dissent in *Sensient* compelling, and we note that a finding of customer sophistication typically will rest with the jury.

[20] In reaching its conclusion, the Court in *Sensient* relied upon *Checkpoint Systems* for the proposition that "courts look to factors such as product relatedness and the level of care exercised by customers to determine whether initial interest confusion exists." *Sensient*, 613 F.3d at 766. *Sensient* was an appeal from a grant of summary judgment, and on the summary judgment record, our Court indicated that the parties agreed the relevant consumers were sophisticated. The dissent in *Sensient* accurately noted, however, that in *Checkpoint Systems*, the Third Circuit had been reviewing the issue after trial, not making a determination as to consumer sophistication as a matter of law (or making any likelihood of confusion determinations) at the summary judgment stage. *Id.* at 773 (Colloton, J, dissenting). The dissent described the theory of initial-interest confusion and emphasized that, even if customers are sophisticated, that fact alone should not automatically defeat the theory. In advocating for this no-blanket-rule point, the dissent cited a Second Circuit case involving professional buyers in a lawsuit between Mobil Oil and an entity that was marketing products under the name "Pegasus Petroleum." The dissent noted that "[w]hether or not a sophisticated customer eventually would sort out the difference, the doctrine of initial interest confusion prevents an infringer from using another's mark to gain 'crucial credibility during the *initial* phases of a deal.'" *Id.* at 773 (quoting *Mobil Oil Corp. v. Pegasus Petroleum Corp.*, 818 F.2d 254, 258 (2d Cir. 1987)). And, the dissent also emphasized that the Third Circuit in *Checkpoint* specifically disclaimed any categorical rule, stating instead that the "significance [of customer sophistication] will vary, and must be determined on a case-by-case basis." *Sensient*, 613 F.3d at 773 (quoting *Checkpoint*, 269 F.3d at 297).

[21] Regardless of the relative merits of the positions reflected in *Sensient*, our general adoption of the theory of initial-interest confusion forecloses summary judgment where a question of fact exists as to the level of consumer sophistication. Here, the parties dispute the issue of consumer sophistication both in reference to shopping for mattresses and shopping online. They also dispute whether consumer sophistication should be measured at the "point of click" for an online shopper, at the point of sale upon final purchase, or at points in between. For the reasons previously discussed, we do not believe it is appropriate to cabin the analysis to any one point in time. And, in any event, authority is mixed as to whether mattress shoppers and online shoppers should be deemed careful, sophisticated consumers.

[22] On the one hand, mattresses are relatively expensive among most consumers' purchases. *See Sleepmaster Prods. Co. v. Am. Auto-Felt Corp.*, 241 F.2d 738, 741 (C.C.P.A. 1957) ("[T]he average purchaser will exercise such care in the selection of a mattress as to minimize the possibility of confusion as to the origin of the goods."). On the other hand, most people buy mattresses infrequently, so they enter the marketplace uneducated and susceptible to fast-talking sales people and brand confusion. *See Friedman v. Sealy, Inc.*, 274 F.2d 255, 261–62 (10th Cir. 1959) ("[S]ince a mattress or box spring requires an investment . . ., the degree of care which a customer might be expected to exercise is somewhat greater than if he were buying 5-cent candies. [But] the construction of sleep equipment is not a matter of common knowledge and the consumer buys infrequently. He is thus forced to rely on his memory, more than his inspection, for the recall of names, guarantees, and endorsements. Under such circumstances, confusion can easily arise.").

[23] Authority is also mixed as to the level of sophistication web-based shoppers bring to the table and how this potentially separate question should influence the general assessment of sophistication. *Compare Coca-Cola Co. v. Purdy*, No. 02-1782 ADM/JGL, 2005 WL 212797, at *4 (D. Minn. Jan. 28, 2005) ("[T]he quick and effortless nature of 'surfing' the Internet makes it unlikely that consumers can avoid confusion through the exercise of due care.") *and GoTo.com, Inc. v. Walt Disney Co.*, 202 F.3d 1199, 1209

(9th Cir. 2000) ("Navigating amongst web sites involves practically no effort whatsoever, and arguments that Web users exercise a great deal of care before clicking on hyperlinks are unconvincing.") *with Toyota Motor Sales, U.S.A., Inc. v. Tabari*, 610 F.3d 1171, 1179 (9th Cir. 2010) ("[I]n the age of [the internet], reasonable, prudent and experienced internet consumers are accustomed to such exploration by trial and error. They skip from site to site, ready to hit the back button whenever they're not satisfied with a site's contents. They fully expect to find some sites that aren't what they imagine based on a glance at the domain name or search engine summary."). *See also Network Automation, Inc. v. Advanced Systems Concepts, Inc.*, 638 F.3d 1137, 1152 (9th Cir. 2011) (noting that although "'there is generally a low degree of care exercised by Internet consumers' . . . the degree of care analysis cannot begin and end at the marketing channel. We still must consider the nature and cost of the goods, and whether 'the products being sold are marketed primarily to expert buyers.'" (quoting *Brookfield Comm'ns, Inc. v. West Coast Ent. Corp.*, 174 F.3d 1036, 1060 (9th Cir. 1999))).

[24] At the end of the day, this mix of authority regarding consumer confusion in the context of internet shopping and mattress purchases demonstrates well why a jury rather than a judge should assess the level of consumer sophistication. This point is particularly strong in a case which, like the present case, enjoys a full record including highly detailed descriptions of Plaintiffs' and Defendants' customers' experience and ample evidence of (1) *actual confusion* including transcripts of potential customers who called Defendants' call centers and believed they were calling Plaintiffs, and (2) statements by Defendants' principals describing the actual confusion as evidence that their own advertising was working. *See Kemp*, 398 F.3d at 1058 (evidence of actual confusion, while not required, is strong evidence of a likelihood of confusion); *SquirtCo*, 628 F.2d at 1091 ("Likewise, actual confusion is not essential to a finding of trademark infringement, although it is positive proof of likelihood of confusion.").

[25] Against this backdrop, we conclude a jury question existed as to the issue of consumer sophistication and summary judgment on the theory of initial-interest confusion was error. For the same reasons, and based on *Insty*Bit*, we conclude that limiting the infringement instruction to require confusion at the time of purchase was error. Finally, given the strength of the Plaintiffs' evidence on the issue of confusion, we cannot conclude that the summary judgment and instructional errors were harmless. <u>See</u> Fed. R. Civ. P. 61. In so ruling, we make no comment as to how a finding of confusion at times other than the moment of purchase might affect the analysis of remedies and the determination of damages.

. . . .

A Jim Adler & Associates TV Commercial Incorporating a Variation on the TEXAS HAMMER *Mark*

Jim S. Adler, P.C. v. McNeil Consultants, L.L.C.
10 F.4th 422 (5th Cir. 2021)

Leslie H. Southwick, Circuit Judge:

[1] Plaintiffs allege that Defendants purchased trademark terms as keywords for search-engine advertising, then placed generic advertisements that confused customers as to whether the advertisements belonged to or were affiliated with the Plaintiffs. The district court dismissed the complaint for failure to state a claim and denied Plaintiffs' motion for leave to amend the complaint. We REVERSE the dismissal, VACATE the denial of leave to amend, and REMAND for further proceedings.

FACTUAL AND PROCEDURAL BACKGROUND

[2] Because this is an appeal from a Rule 12(b)(6) dismissal, we recount the facts as alleged in Plaintiffs' complaint. Plaintiffs are Jim S. Adler P.C., a personal injury law firm in Texas, and Jim Adler, the firm's founder and lead attorney (collectively, "Adler"). Adler has offices in Houston, Dallas, San Antonio, and Channelview and employs approximately 300 people, including 27 lawyers.

[3] Adler spends significant amounts of money to market his law practice. In his marketing on television, radio, and billboards, Adler has consistently used several trademarks, including JIM ADLER, THE HAMMER, TEXAS HAMMER, and EL MARTILLO TEJANO (collectively, the "Adler marks").

[4] Adler also uses these marks in internet advertisements. Adler purchases Google "keyword ads" using the Adler marks as search terms. When a consumer performs a Google search using an Adler mark as a search term, Adler's advertisements appear alongside the results produced by the search engine's algorithm.

[5] The Defendants are two entities, McNeil Consultants, LLC and Quintessa Marketing, LLC, both of which do business as Accident Injury Legal Center, and their sole owner, Lauren Von McNeil (collectively, "McNeil"). McNeil operates a lawyer-referral website and call center. McNeil solicits and refers personal injury cases to lawyers with whom McNeil has a referral agreement that provides for compensation for referrals.

[6] Like Adler, McNeil advertises on the internet. Also like Adler, McNeil purchases Google keyword ads for the Adler marks. This ensures that an advertisement for McNeil's services appears when a user performs a Google search using an Adler mark as a search term. McNeil bids increasingly higher amounts to ensure that her advertisements appear next to or before Adler's advertisements. McNeil's advertisements "do not identify a particular lawyer or law firm as the source of the advertisement. Instead, the advertisements are designed to display generic terms that consumers might associate with any personal injury firm."

[7] McNeil purchases what is known as a "click-to-call" advertisement. If a user clicks on the advertisement using a mobile phone, the advertisement causes the user's phone to make a call rather

than visit a website. McNeil's representatives answer the telephone using a generic greeting. The complaint alleges that the ads "keep confused consumers, who were specifically searching for Jim Adler and the Adler Firm, on the phone and talking to [McNeil's] employees as long as possible in a bait-and-switch effort to build rapport with the consumer and ultimately convince [the consumer] to engage lawyers referred through [McNeil] instead."

[8] Adler sued McNeil, alleging claims for trademark infringement in violation of the Lanham Act and claims under Texas law. McNeil moved to dismiss the complaint for failure to state a claim.

[9] A magistrate judge recommended granting McNeil's motion. The magistrate judge construed Adler's claims as based solely on McNeil's purchase of the Adler marks as keywords for search-engine advertisements. He found that the allegations regarding the bait-and-switch scheme were "conclusory."

[10] The magistrate judge also concluded that Adler could not plead a likelihood of confusion as a matter of law because McNeil's advertisements are generic and do not incorporate the Adler marks. He recommended that the district court decline to exercise supplemental jurisdiction over Adler's state law claims.

[11] Adler objected to the magistrate judge's findings, conclusions, and recommendation. Adler also filed a motion for leave to amend the complaint and a proposed second amended complaint. In that motion, Adler explained that he commissioned a double-blind survey of 400 Texas residents. That survey purportedly shows that "between 34% and 44% of participants clicked McNeil's ad believing it to be put out by, affiliated or associated with, or approved by Adler."

[12] The district court adopted the findings, conclusions, and recommendation of the magistrate judge and dismissed the complaint. The court denied Adler's motion for leave to amend the complaint on the grounds of futility. The court concluded that the Lanham Act claims in the proposed second amended complaint would fail as a matter of law, even if amended, because they would be "based solely on the purchase of [Adler's] trademarks as keywords for search engine advertising" and because they did not visibly incorporate Adler's trademarks. Adler appealed.

DISCUSSION

I. Dismissal

[13] We review *de novo* a district court's ruling on a motion to dismiss under Rule 12(b)(6). *Wampler v. S.W. Bell Tel. Co.*, 597 F.3d 741, 744 (5th Cir. 2010). In our review, we "accept all well-pleaded facts as true and draw all reasonable inferences in favor of the nonmoving party." *Morgan v. Swanson*, 659 F.3d 359, 370 (5th Cir. 2011) (*en banc*). To survive a motion to dismiss, a complaint must "contain sufficient factual matter, accepted as true, to state a claim to relief that is plausible on its face." *Ashcroft v. Iqbal*, 556 U.S. 662, 678, 129 S.Ct. 1937, 173 L.Ed.2d 868 (2009) (quotation marks and citation omitted).

[14] Adler has alleged claims for trademark infringement in violation of Sections 32 and 43 of the Lanham Act, which are codified at 15 U.S.C. § 1114(1) and 15 U.S.C. § 1125(a). . . .

[15] For purposes of the motion to dismiss, McNeil does not dispute the ownership or validity of the Adler marks, nor does McNeil dispute the use of the Adler marks. The sole issue is whether Adler adequately alleged a likelihood of confusion.

A. Likelihood of confusion and search-engine advertising

. . . .

[16] For trademark infringement claims in the context of internet searches, plaintiffs often allege a specific type of confusion known as initial interest confusion, as Adler has done here. Initial interest confusion is confusion that "creates initial consumer interest, even though no actual sale is finally completed as a result of the confusion." *Elvis Presley Enters., Inc. v. Capece*, 141 F.3d 188, 204 (5th Cir. 1998). We have held that initial interest confusion is actionable under the Lanham Act. *Id.* at 193, 204.

392

[17] We have not yet had an opportunity to analyze initial interest confusion in the context of search-engine advertising, but we find some useful guidance. In one nonprecedential opinion,[1] we analyzed initial interest confusion in the context of so-called "meta tags," which are "essentially programming code instructions given to on-line search engines." *Southwest Recreational Indus., Inc. v. FieldTurf, Inc.*, No. 01-50073, 2002 WL 32783971, at *7 & n.27 (5th Cir. Aug. 13, 2002). Meta tags are "normally invisible to the Internet user," but they "are detected by search engines and increase the likelihood that a user searching for a particular topic will be directed to that Web designer's page." *Id.* at *7 n.27 (quoting *Nat'l A-1 Adver., Inc. v. Network Sols., Inc.*, 121 F. Supp. 2d 156, 164 (D.N.H. 2000)). Because meta tags direct internet traffic and are invisible to the internet user (absent the user taking additional steps), meta tags are similar to keyword advertising. *See Playboy Enters., Inc. v. Netscape Commc'ns Corp.*, 354 F.3d 1020, 1034 (9th Cir. 2004) (Berzon, J., concurring).

[18] The claim in *Southwest Recreational* was that the defendant's use of trademark terms in meta tags on its website violated the Lanham Act because such use created initial interest confusion. *Southwest Recreational Indus., Inc.*, 2002 WL 32783971, at *7. A jury found against the plaintiff on this claim, and the district court denied the plaintiff's request for a permanent injunction. *Id.* at *2. On appeal, the plaintiff argued that the district court erred because "meta tagging another company's trademark necessarily constitutes trademark infringement." *Id.* at *7. We rejected that argument. In support, we cited Ninth Circuit cases and explained that "[t]he meta tag cases in which our sister circuits have found trademark infringement involve either evidence of customer confusion or evidence that the meta tags were used illegitimately." *Id.* (discussing *Brookfield Commc'ns, Inc. v. W. Coast Ent. Corp.*, 174 F.3d 1036, 1061–65 (9th Cir. 1999) and *Playboy Enters., Inc. v. Welles*, 279 F.3d 796, 804 (9th Cir. 2002)). Finding no evidence of either, a panel of this court held that "the district court's refusal to find trademark infringement was not clearly erroneous." *Id.* at *8.

[19] Since then, the Ninth Circuit has continued to refine its understanding of confusion in the context of internet-search cases. In one opinion, that court held that the use of trademarks as keywords for search-engine advertisements could create initial interest confusion if consumers searching for trademark terms initially believe that "unlabeled banner advertisements" are links to sites that belong to or are affiliated with the trademark owner. *Playboy Enters., Inc.*, 354 F.3d at 1025–27. A separate concurrence urged the court to distinguish between claims alleging confusion and those alleging distraction:

> There is a big difference between hijacking a customer to another website by making the customer think he or she is visiting the trademark holder's website (even if only briefly), which is what may be happening in this case when the banner advertisements are not labeled, and just distracting a potential customer with another choice, when it is clear that it is a choice.

Id. at 1035 (Berzon, J., concurring).

[20] The Ninth Circuit eventually adopted Judge Berzon's concurrence, concluding that "it would be wrong to expand the initial interest confusion theory of infringement beyond the realm of the misleading and deceptive to the context of legitimate comparative and contextual advertising." *Network Automation, Inc. v. Advanced Sys. Concepts, Inc.*, 638 F.3d 1137, 1148 (9th Cir. 2011). The author of a leading treatise also agrees with this approach. *See* J. THOMAS MCCARTHY, MCCARTHY ON TRADEMARKS AND UNFAIR COMPETITION § 25A:8 (5th ed. 2021 Update). That author offered an analogy:

> [A]ssume that [a] person shopping for a car types in a search engine the word TOYOTA and finds on the search results web page a clearly labeled advertisement for VOLKSWAGEN.

---

[1] We discuss *Southwest Recreational* here notwithstanding its nonprecedential value. We do so because of the dearth of relevant cases — published or unpublished — in this circuit, and the nuances of the opinion's discussion of the issues are informative. For similar reasons, we also discuss a few Ninth Circuit opinions.

> This occurred because, hypothetically, Volkswagen purchased from the search engine the keyword "Toyota." If that computer user then ultimately decides to buy a VOLKSWAGEN instead of a TOYOTA, that is not a purchase made by mistake or as a result of confusion. If that ad and link is clearly labeled as an advertisement for VOLKSWAGEN, it is hard to see how the web user and potential car buyer is likely to be confused by the advertising link.

Id. Conversely, "[i]nitial interest confusion could occur only if the web user mistakenly thought she was going to a web site about TOYOTA cars when she clicked on the keyword link for VOLKSWAGEN. That would depend on how clearly labeled was the advertising link for VOLKSWAGEN." *Id.*

[21] We agree with *Southwest Recreational*, the Ninth Circuit opinions, and the treatise author that in the context of internet searches and search-engine advertising in particular, the critical issue is whether there is consumer confusion. Distraction is insufficient.

B. Adler's claims

[22] We now turn to Adler's trademark infringement claims.... Where the factual allegations regarding consumer confusion are implausible ... a district court may dismiss a complaint on the basis that a plaintiff failed to allege a likelihood of confusion. *See, e.g., Eastland Music Grp., LLC v. Lionsgate Ent., Inc.*, 707 F.3d 869, 871 (7th Cir. 2013).

[23] This is not such a case. Adler alleges that McNeil's advertisements use generic text and are not clearly labeled as belonging to McNeil. When McNeil's advertisements appear in response to an internet search of the Adler marks, Adler alleges that a consumer is likely to believe that the unlabeled advertisements belong to or are affiliated with Adler.

[24] Adler further alleges that McNeil's use of click-to-call advertisements exacerbates this confusion. Instead of being directed to a clearly labeled website, users who click on McNeil's advertisement are connected by telephone to a call center. McNeil employees answer the phone without identifying who they are, then seek to build a rapport with the customer before disclosing McNeil's identity. Thus, for the initial portion of the conversation, callers are unaware that they are not talking to an Adler representative.

[25] In determining that Adler's claims failed, the district court first concluded that Adler's claims were based "solely on the purchase of Plaintiffs' trademarks as keywords for search engine advertising." The court determined that the allegations regarding the bait-and-switch scheme were conclusory and, apparently for that reason, declined to consider them. We disagree and find that Adler made specific factual allegations describing how the use of the Adler marks as keyword terms — combined with generic, unlabeled advertisements and misleading call-center practices — caused initial interest confusion. This pleading included factual matter beyond the mere purchase of trademarks as keywords for search-engine advertising, and the district court should have considered those allegations.

[26] Second, the district court concluded that Adler could not plead a likelihood of confusion as a matter of law because McNeil's advertisements were generic. It is true that the Lanham Act does not protect generic terms against infringement. *See Small Bus. Assistance Corp. v. Clear Channel Broad., Inc.*, 210 F.3d 278, 279 (5th Cir. 2000). Adler, though, has not alleged trademark infringement solely on the basis of the generic text of the advertisements. Instead, he has alleged trademark infringement based on McNeil's use of the Adler marks, the ownership and validity of which is not disputed. The generic nature of McNeil's advertisements is relevant because it enhances rather than dispels the likelihood of initial interest confusion.

[27] Third, the district court concluded that Adler's claims fail as a matter of law because McNeil's use of the Adler marks is not visible to the consumer. We find no Fifth Circuit authority for such a rule of law, and we disagree with it. Such a rule would undermine the requirement that, in evaluating whether use of a trademark creates a likelihood of confusion, no single factor is dispositive. *See Xtreme Lashes, LLC*, 576 F.3d at 227.

[28] In support of its conclusion that the use of a trademark must be visible to a consumer, the district court relied on *1-800 Contacts, Inc. v. Lens.com, Inc.*, 722 F.3d 1229, 1242–49 (10th Cir. 2013). In that case, though, the Tenth Circuit explicitly avoided deciding whether a Lanham Act claim requires

that the use of a trademark be visible to the consumer. The district court in the case had observed that a user who sees sponsored advertisements has no way of knowing whether the defendant reserved a trademark or a generic term. *Id.* at 1242–43. The district court explained that "it would be anomalous to hold a competitor liable simply because it purchased a trademarked keyword when the advertisement generated by the keyword is the exact same from a consumer's perspective as one generated by a generic keyword." *Id.* at 1243.

[29] The Tenth Circuit noted that the argument had "some attraction" but then stated that "if confusion does indeed arise, the advertiser's choice of keyword may make a difference to the infringement analysis even if the consumer cannot discern that choice." *Id.* The Tenth Circuit's reasoning reflects that the absence of the trademark could be one but not the only factor to consider in evaluating the likelihood of confusion. Ultimately, that court concluded that it "need not resolve the matter because 1–800's direct-infringement claim fails for lack of adequate evidence of initial-interest confusion." *Id.*

[30] We conclude that whether an advertisement incorporates a trademark that is visible to the consumer is a relevant but not dispositive factor in determining a likelihood of confusion in search-engine advertising cases.

[31] Adler's complaint contains sufficient factual matter, accepted as true, to state a Lanham Act claim that is plausible on its face. *See Iqbal*, 556 U.S. at 678, 129 S.Ct. 1937. We express no opinion on the merits of Adler's claims, which would require, among other things, an evaluation of the digits of confusion and any other relevant factors. *See Xtreme Lashes, LLC*, 576 F.3d at 227.

. . . .

[32] We REVERSE the order dismissing the complaint under Rule 12(b)(6), VACATE the order denying leave to amend, and REMAND for further proceedings.

Questions and Comments

1. *Initial interest confusion and trade dress.* In *Gibson Guitar Corp. v. Paul Reed Smith Guitars, LP*, 423 F.3d 539 (6th Cir. 2005), Gibson and Paul Reed Smith both manufactured single cutaway guitars, the shape of which is shown below in Gibson's trademark registration for its product configuration. Gibson conceded that there was no likelihood of point-of-sale confusion due to Paul Reed Smith's prominent labelling, but argued that there was a likelihood of initial interest confusion in that consumers would see a PRS single cutaway guitar from across a store and believe it to be a Gibson guitar. The Sixth Circuit declined to apply initial interest confusion to trade dress. It reasoned:

> The potential ramifications of applying this judicially created doctrine to product-shape trademarks are different from the ramifications of applying the doctrine to trademarks on a product's name, a company's name, or a company's logo. *Cf. Versa Prods. Co. v. Bifold Co.*, 50 F.3d 189, 201–03, 207, 209, 212–13, 215 (3rd Cir. 1995) (discussing the related context of product-configuration trade dress). Specifically, there are only a limited number of shapes in which many products can be made. A product may have a shape which is neither functional nor generic (and hence which can be trademarked) but nonetheless is still likely to resemble a competing product when viewed from the far end of a store aisle. Thus, many legitimately competing product shapes are likely to create some initial interest in the competing product due to the competing product's resemblance to the better-known product when viewed from afar. In other words, application of the initial-interest-confusion doctrine to product shapes would allow trademark holders to protect not only the actual product shapes they have trademarked, but also a "penumbra" of more or less similar shapes that would not otherwise qualify for trademark protection.

Id. at 551.

(In ruling in favor of Paul Reed Smith on all surviving claims brought against it, the court ruled that Paul Reed Smith's functionality objection to the validity of Gibson's mark was moot).

Int. Cl.: 15

Prior U.S. Cl.: 36

United States Patent and Trademark Office   Reg. No. 1,782,606
Registered July 20, 1993

TRADEMARK
PRINCIPAL REGISTER

GIBSON GUITAR CORP. (DELAWARE CORPO-
RATION)
P.O. BOX 10087
641 MASSMAN DRIVE
NASHVILLE, TN 37210

FOR: GUITARS, IN CLASS 15 (U.S. CL. 36).
FIRST USE 12-0-1952; IN COMMERCE
12-0-1952.
THE LINING OF THE DRAWING IS NOT IN-
TEDED TO INDICATE COLOR.

THE MARK CONSISTS OF A UNIQUELY
SHAPED CONFIGURATION FOR THE BODY
PORTION OF THE GUITAR AS ILLUSTRATED
IN THE DRAWING BY THE SOLID LINES.

SEC. 2(F).

SER. NO. 73-675,665, FILED 7-31-1987.

MARY FRANCES BRUCE, EXAMINING AT-
TORNEY

2. *When do courts find initial interest confusion?* Initial interest confusion remains a highly controversial basis for a finding of infringement, one which courts typically resort to only in a limited set of contexts. Courts appear to be more likely to find initial interest confusion if the defendant has engaged in patently bad faith "bait and switch" sales practices or in conduct akin to intentional cybersquatting, if the relevant consumers are unsophisticated, or if the defendant competes directly with the plaintiff. *See, e.g., Epic Sys. Corp. v. YourCareUniverse, Inc.,* 244 F. Supp. 3d 878, 902 (W.D. Wisc. 2017) ("Courts are most likely to apply the doctrine of initial interest confusion doctrine in circumstances involving directly competing products, particularly when the potential purchasers are lay consumers making decisions in a relatively short amount of time with limited information."). Furthermore, in reviewing the initial interest confusion case law, Gilson concludes that to prevail on an initial interest confusion basis, the plaintiff must show that it has been economically damaged by the defendant's conduct. *See* GILSON § 5.14[01][1][a]. *See also Lamparello v. Falwell,* 420 F.3d 309, 317 (4th Cir. 2005) ("The few appellate courts that have . . . imposed liability under [the initial interest confusion] theory for using marks on the Internet have done so only in cases involving . . . one business's use of another's mark for its own financial gain. . . . Profiting financially from initial interest confusion is . . . a key element for imposition of liability under this theory."). In general, it appears that courts have developed initial interest confusion doctrine to provide them with some degree of flexibility to reach what they deem to be the right result as a matter of equity in situations where there is no consumer confusion at the point of sale.

3. *Critiquing initial interest confusion.* For a thorough critique of initial interest confusion doctrine, see Jennifer E. Rothman, *Initial Interest Confusion: Standing at the Crossroads of Trademark Law,* 27 CARDOZO L. REV. 105 (2005). Rothman observes: "The courts' initial motivation for adopting initial interest confusion was a legitimate effort to prevent baiting and switching practices. However, since then courts have unreasonably stretched the doctrine to cover many circumstances which should be considered fair competition or which are better addressed by other existing statutes." *Id.* at 113.

7.   Post-Sale Confusion

*Mastercrafters' clock (left) and LeCoultre's clock (right)**

While initial interest confusion addresses the likelihood of confusion before the point of sale, post-sale confusion, as its name suggests, addresses confusion after the point of sale. One of the first cases to recognize some form of post-sale confusion was *Mastercrafters Clock & Radio Co. v. Vacheron & Constantin-LeCoultre Watches, Inc.*, 221 F.2d 464 (2d Cir. 1955). In *Mastercrafters*, the declaratory plaintiff Mastercrafters produced an electric clock made to look like the declaratory defendant's expensive and prestigious Atmos table clock, a non-electric clock that wound itself from changes in atmospheric pressure. Mastercrafters sold its clock for about $30; LeCoultre sold the Atmos clock for not less than $175 (about $1,700 in today's money). Mastercrafters sought a declaration that its conduct did not constitute unfair competition. Judge Frank held in favor of LeCoultre. Though there was no point-of-sale confusion, there was nevertheless unfair competition:

> True, a customer examining plaintiff's clock would see from the electric cord, that it was not an 'atmospheric' clock. But, as the {district} judge found, plaintiff copied the design of the Atmos clock because plaintiff intended to, and did, attract purchasers who wanted a "luxury design" clock. This goes to show at least that some customers would buy plaintiff's cheaper clock for the purpose of acquiring the prestige gained by displaying what many visitors at the customers' homes would regard as a prestigious article. Plaintiff's wrong thus consisted of the fact that such a visitor would be likely to assume that the clock was an Atmos clock. Neither the electric cord attached to, nor the plaintiff's name on, its clock would be likely to come to the attention of such a visitor; the likelihood of such confusion suffices to render plaintiff's conduct actionable.

Id. at 464.

The post-sale confusion theory has been controversial, as the dissent in the following case suggests. In reading through *Ferrari S.P.A. v. Roberts*, 944 F.2d 1235 (6th Cir. 1991), which involves the unauthorized production of "Fauxrraris", consider the following questions:

- Should courts take into account the confusion as to source of consumers who would never actually purchase the plaintiff's goods (or the defendant's goods for that matter)?

- Should trademark law be used to protect the exclusivity of status goods? If it should not be so used, how can we make sure we do not throw out the baby with the bathwater? In other words, how can we design trademark law so that it will not protect the exclusivity of status goods but will nevertheless continue to protect the traditional source-denoting function of trademarks for non-status goods? Who decides which goods are status goods? Is a pickup truck a status good?

---

* Courtesy of Rebecca Tushnet & Georgetown Law Library, *Intellectual Property Teaching Resources* (2020).

Ferrari S.P.A. v. Roberts
944 F.2d 1235 (6th Cir. 1991)

1971 Ferrari 365 GTS4 Daytona Spyder*

Ferrari Testarossa

RYAN, Circuit Judge.

[1] This is a trademark infringement action brought pursuant to the Lanham Act, 15 U.S.C. § 1051, *et seq.* The principal issue is whether the district court correctly concluded that plaintiff Ferrari enjoyed unregistered trademark protection in the exterior shape and appearance of two of its automobiles and, if so, whether defendant Roberts' replicas of Ferrari's designs infringed that protection, in violation of section 43(a) of the Lanham Act . . . .

[2] We hold that the district court properly decided all of the issues and, therefore, we shall affirm.

I. The Facts

[3] Ferrari is the world famous designer and manufacturer of racing automobiles and upscale sports cars. Between 1969 and 1973, Ferrari produced the 365 GTB/4 Daytona. Because Ferrari intentionally limits production of its cars in order to create an image of exclusivity, only 1400 Daytonas were built; of these, only 100 were originally built as Spyders, soft-top convertibles. Daytona Spyders currently sell for one to two million dollars. Although Ferrari no longer makes Daytona Spyders, they have continuously produced mechanical parts and body panels, and provided repair service for the cars.

[4] Ferrari began producing a car called the Testarossa in 1984. To date, Ferrari has produced approximately 5000 Testarossas. Production of these cars is also intentionally limited to preserve exclusivity: the entire anticipated production is sold out for the next several years and the waiting period

---

* http://blog.hemmings.com/index.php/tag/ferrari-365-gts4-daytona-spyder/.

to purchase a Testarossa is approximately five years. A new Testarossa sells for approximately $230,000.

[5] Roberts is engaged in a number of business ventures related to the automobile industry. One enterprise is the manufacture of fiberglass kits that replicate the exterior features of Ferrari's Daytona Spyder and Testarossa automobiles. Roberts' copies are called the Miami Spyder and the Miami Coupe, respectively. The kit is a one-piece body shell molded from reinforced fiberglass. It is usually bolted onto the undercarriage of another automobile such as a Chevrolet Corvette or a Pontiac Fiero, called the donor car. Roberts marketed the Miami Spyder primarily through advertising in kit-car magazines. Most of the replicas were sold as kits for about $8,500, although a fully accessorized "turnkey" version was available for about $50,000.

[6] At the time of trial, Roberts had not yet completed a kit-car version of the Miami Coupe, the replica of Ferrari's Testarossa, although he already has two orders for them. He originally built the Miami Coupe for the producers of the television program "Miami Vice" to be used as a stunt car in place of the more expensive Ferrari Testarossa.

[7] The district court found, and it is not disputed, that Ferrari's automobiles and Roberts' replicas are virtually identical in appearance.

[8] Ferrari brought suit against Roberts in March 1988 alleging trademark infringement, in violation of section 43(a) of the Lanham Act, and obtained a preliminary injunction enjoining Roberts from manufacturing the replica cars. The injunction was later amended to permit Roberts to recommence production of the two models.

[9] Five months later, Roberts filed a voluntary petition in bankruptcy. Despite the Chapter 11 proceedings, the bankruptcy court, in a carefully limited order, lifted the automatic stay and permitted Ferrari to continue to prosecute this action. Prior to trial, the district court denied Roberts' request for a jury, and the case was tried to the court resulting in a verdict for Ferrari and a permanent injunction enjoining Roberts from producing the Miami Spyder and the Miami Coupe.

II.

. . . .

[10] The protection against infringement provided by section 43(a) is not limited to "goods, services or commercial activities" protected by registered trademarks. It extends as well, in certain circumstances, to the unregistered "trade dress" of an article. "Trade dress" refers to "the image and overall appearance of a product." *Allied Mktg. Group, Inc. v. CDL Mktg., Inc.,* 878 F.2d 806, 812 (5th Cir. 1989) . . . .

[11] Ferrari's Lanham Act claim in this case is a "trade dress" claim. Ferrari charges, and the district court found, that the unique and distinctive exterior shape and design of the Daytona Spyder and the Testarossa are protected trade dress which Roberts has infringed by copying them and marketing his replicas.

[12] Roberts asserts that there has been no infringement under section 43(a) for a number of reasons: (1) the design of Ferrari's vehicles are protected only under design patent law, *see* 35 U.S.C. § 171, and not the Lanham Act; (2) there is no actionable likelihood of confusion between Ferrari's vehicles and Roberts' replicas at the point of sale; and (3) the "aesthetic functionality doctrine" precludes recovery.

[13] We shall take up each argument in turn.

III.

[14] To prove a violation of section 43(a), Ferrari's burden is to show, by a preponderance of the evidence:

1) that the trade dress of Ferrari's vehicles has acquired a "secondary meaning,"

2) that there is a likelihood of confusion based on the similarity of the exterior shape and design of Ferrari's vehicles and Roberts' replicas, and

3) that the appropriated features of Ferrari's trade dress are primarily nonfunctional.

See Kwik-Site Corp. v. Clear View Mfg. Co., Inc., 758 F.2d 167, 178 (6th Cir. 1985).

A. Secondary Meaning

. . . .

[15] Ferrari's vehicles would not acquire secondary meaning merely because they are unique designs or because they are aesthetically beautiful. The design must be one that is instantly identified in the mind of the informed viewer as a Ferrari design. The district court found, and we agree, that the unique exterior design and shape of the Ferrari vehicles are their "mark" or "trade dress" which distinguish the vehicles' exterior shapes not simply as distinctively attractive designs, but as Ferrari creations.

[16] We also agree with the district court that Roberts' admission that he intentionally copied Ferrari's design, the survey evidence introduced by Ferrari, and the testimony of {various witnesses} amount to abundant evidence that the exterior design features of the Ferrari vehicles are "trade dress" which have acquired secondary meaning.

. . . .

B. Likelihood of Confusion

1. District Court's Findings

. . . .

[17] The district court found, based upon an evaluation of the eight *Frisch* factors, that the similarity of the exterior design of the Ferrari vehicles and the Roberts replicas was likely to confuse the public. The court noted that while no evidence was offered on two of the factors, evidence of actual confusion and likelihood of expansion of the product lines, two others, marketing channels and purchaser care, favored Roberts and the remaining factors "radically favor[ed] Ferrari." Summarized, the district court's findings on the *Frisch* "likelihood of confusion" factors are as follows:

	Factors	Favor
1.	Strength of the mark	Ferrari
2.	Relatedness of the goods	Ferrari
3.	Similarity of the marks	Ferrari
4.	Evidence of actual confusion	No evidence
5.	Marketing channels used	Roberts
6.	Likely degree of purchaser care	Roberts
7.	Roberts' intent in selecting "mark"	Ferrari
8.	Likelihood of expansion of product lines.	No evidence

[18] Recalling that the claimed mark involved here is the trade dress—the exterior shape and design of the Ferrari vehicles—it is clear that Ferrari's mark is very strong. The strength of the mark is its distinctiveness and Ferrari's designs are unquestionably distinctive. The survey evidence we have discussed, as well as the testimony that the shape of the plaintiff's vehicles "says Ferrari," is evidence of that distinctiveness. Indeed, Roberts' purposeful effort to copy the Ferrari designs is strong circumstantial evidence of the distinctiveness of the originals.

[19] There is no dispute about the relatedness of the goods factor. The products produced by both parties are sports cars.

[20] Likewise, the similarity of the marks—the exterior designs of the vehicles—is indisputable. Ferrari offered survey evidence which showed that 68% of the respondents could not distinguish a photograph of the McBurnie replica, upon which Roberts' Miami Spyder is based, from a photograph of

the genuine Ferrari Daytona Spyder. In these photographs, the cars were shown without identifying insignia. Drawings for Roberts' cars show identifying insignia, an "R" on the parking lens and vent window, but the cars produced at the time of trial did not include the "R". Because the survey respondents saw photographs of the McBurnie cars, and because all of the identifying insignia were removed, the survey has limited value in showing the likelihood of confusion between the Roberts and Ferrari vehicles if displayed with identifying emblems. The survey, however, does show that the trade dress of the two car designs, the shapes and exteriors, were quite similar. An examination of the photographs of the cars which are in evidence confirms the striking similarity of the dress of the originals and the replicas. They are virtually indistinguishable.

[21] Finally, Roberts conceded that his intent in replicating the exterior design of Ferrari's vehicles was to market a product that looked as much as possible like a Ferrari original, although Roberts made no claim to his customers that his replicas were Ferraris. "'[The] intent of [a party] in adopting [another's mark] is a critical factor, since if the mark was adopted with the intent of deriving benefit from the reputation of [the plaintiff,] *that fact alone may be sufficient to justify the inference that there is confusing similarity.'*" *Frisch's Restaurants*, 670 F.2d at 648 (emphasis in original) (quoting *Amstar Corp. v. Domino's Pizza, Inc.*, 615 F.2d 252, 263 (5th Cir.), *cert. denied*, 449 U.S. 899, 101 S.Ct. 268, 66 L.Ed.2d 129 (1980)); *see also Mastercrafters*, 221 F.2d at 467. This is especially true in cases, such as this one, where the defendant sold a comparatively cheap imitation of an expensive, exclusive item. As the court in *Rolex Watch* explained:

> By selling the bogus watches, only one inference may be drawn: the Defendants intended to derive benefit from the Plaintiff's reputation. This inference is no less reasonable when weighed against the Defendants' assertion that in selling these watches, they did not fail to inform the recipients that they were counterfeits.

Rolex Watch, U.S.A., Inc. v. Canner, 645 F.Supp. 484, 492 (S.D.Fla. 1986). Intentional copying, however, is not actionable under the Lanham Act "absent evidence that the copying was done with the intent to derive a benefit from the reputation of another." *Zin-Plas Corp. v. Plumbing Quality AGF Co.*, 622 F.Supp. 415, 420 (W.D.Mich. 1985). "Where the copying by one party of another's product is not done to deceive purchasers and thus derive a benefit from another's name and reputation, but rather to avail oneself of a design which is attractive and desirable, a case of unfair competition is not made out." *West Point Mfg.*, 222 F.2d at 586. In this case, where Ferrari's design enjoyed strong secondary meaning and Roberts admitted that he designed his cars to look like Ferrari's, the intent to copy was clear.

[22] We conclude that aside from the presumption of likelihood of confusion that follows from intentional copying, Ferrari produced strong evidence that the public is likely to be confused by the similarity of the exterior design of Ferrari's vehicles and Roberts' replicas.

2. Roberts' Objections

[23] Roberts disagrees with the legal significance of the district court's findings of likelihood of confusion. He argues that for purposes of the Lanham Act, the requisite likelihood of confusion must be confusion at the point of sale—purchaser confusion—and not the confusion of nonpurchasing, casual observers. The evidence is clear that Roberts assured purchasers of his replicas that they were not purchasing Ferraris and that his customers were not confused about what they were buying.

. . . .

b. Confusion at Point of Sale

[24] Roberts argues that his replicas do not violate the Lanham Act because he informed his purchasers that his significantly cheaper cars and kits were not genuine Ferraris and thus there was no confusion at the point of sale. The Lanham Act, however, was intended to do more than protect consumers at the point of sale. When the Lanham Act was enacted in 1946, its protection was limited to the use of marks "likely to cause confusion or mistake or to deceive purchasers as to the source of origin of such goods or services." In 1967 {*recte* 1962}, Congress deleted this language and broadened the Act's protection to include the use of marks "likely to cause confusion or mistake or to deceive." Thus, Congress intended "to regulate commerce within [its control] by making actionable the deceptive and

misleading use of marks in such commerce; [and] ... to protect persons engaged in such commerce against unfair competition ...." 15 U.S.C. § 1127. Although, as the dissent points out, Congress rejected an anti-dilution provision when recently amending the Lanham Act, it made no effort to amend or delete this language clearly protecting the confusion of goods *in commerce*. The court in *Rolex Watch* explicitly recognized this concern with regulating commerce:

> The real question before this Court is whether the alleged infringer has placed a product *in commerce* that is "likely to cause confusion, or to cause mistake, or to deceive." ... The fact that an immediate buyer of a $25 counterfeit watch does not entertain any notions that it is the real thing has no place in this analysis. Once a product is injected into commerce, there is no bar to confusion, mistake, or deception occurring at some future point in time.

Rolex Watch, 645 F.Supp. at 492-93 (emphasis in original). The *Rolex Watch* court noted that this interpretation was necessary to protect against the cheapening and dilution of the genuine product, and to protect the manufacturer's reputation. *Id.* at 495; *see also Mastercrafters,* 221 F.2d at 466. As the court explained:

> Individuals examining the counterfeits, believing them to be genuine Rolex watches, might find themselves unimpressed with the quality of the item and consequently be inhibited from purchasing the real time piece. Others who see the watches bearing the Rolex trademarks on so many wrists might find themselves discouraged from acquiring a genuine because the items have become too common place and no longer possess the prestige once associated with them.

Rolex Watch, 645 F.Supp. at 495; *see also Mastercrafters,* 221 F.2d at 466. Such is the damage which could occur here. As the district court explained when deciding whether Roberts' former partner's Ferrari replicas would be confused with Ferrari's cars:

> Ferrari has gained a well-earned reputation for making uniquely designed automobiles of quality and rarity. The DAYTONA SPYDER design is well-known among the relevant public and exclusively and positively associated with Ferrari. If the country is populated with hundreds, if not thousands, of replicas of rare, distinct, and unique vintage cars, obviously they are no longer unique. Even if a person seeing one of these replicas driving down the road is not confused, Ferrari's exclusive association with this design has been diluted and eroded. If the replica Daytona looks cheap or in disrepair, Ferrari's reputation for rarity and quality could be damaged ....

Ferrari, 11 U.S.P.Q.2d at 1848. The dissent argues that the Lanham Act requires proof of confusion at the point of sale because the eight factor test used to determine likelihood of confusion focuses on the confusion of the purchaser, not the public. The dissent submits that three of the factors, marketing channels used, likely degree of purchaser care and sophistication, and evidence of actual confusion, specifically relate to purchasers. However, evidence of actual confusion is not limited to purchasers. The survey evidence in this case showed that members of the public, but not necessarily purchasers, were actually confused by the similarity of the products. Moreover, the other five factors, strength of the mark, relatedness of the goods, similarity of the marks, defendant's intent in selecting the mark, and likelihood of product expansion, do not limit the likelihood of confusion test to purchasers.

[25] Since Congress intended to protect the reputation of the manufacturer as well as to protect purchasers, the Act's protection is not limited to confusion at the point of sale. Because Ferrari's reputation in the field could be damaged by the marketing of Roberts' replicas, the district court did not err in permitting recovery despite the absence of point of sale confusion.

    ....

KENNEDY, Circuit Judge, dissenting.

[26] I respectfully dissent because the majority opinion does more than protect consumers against a likelihood of confusion as to the source of goods; it protects the source of the goods, Ferrari, against plaintiff's copying of its design even if the replication is accompanied by adequate labelling so as to

prevent consumer confusion. I believe the majority commits two errors in reaching this result. The majority first misconstrues the scope of protection afforded by the Lanham Act by misapplying the "likelihood of confusion" test and reading an anti-dilution provision into the language of section 43(a). The majority then affirms an injunction that is overbroad . . . .

I. Section 43(a) and Trade Dress Protection

[27] The majority invokes the appropriate test to determine whether protection is available for an unregistered trademark pursuant to section 43(a) of the Lanham Act. *Kwik-Site Corp. v. Clear View Mfg. Co.,* 758 F.2d 167 (6th Cir. 1985) (secondary meaning; likelihood of confusion; and nonfunctionality of trade dress). While I agree that Ferrari's designs have acquired secondary meaning and are primarily nonfunctional, I disagree with the majority's construction and application of the likelihood of confusion test and their conclusion that the Lanham Act protects against dilution of a manufacturer's goods.

[28] This Circuit applies an eight-factor test to determine whether relevant consumers in the marketplace will confuse one item with another item. *Frisch's Restaurants, Inc. v. Elby's Big Boy, Inc.,* 670 F.2d 642 (6th Cir.), *cert. denied,* 459 U.S. 916 (1982). The majority correctly points out one purpose this test is *not* designed to accomplish: "Where the copying by one party of another's product is not done to *deceive purchasers* and thus derive a benefit from another's name and reputation, but rather to avail oneself of a design which is attractive and desirable, a case of unfair competition is not made out." *West Point Mfg. v. Detroit Stamping Co.,* 222 F.2d 581, 586 (6th Cir.) (emphasis added), *cert. denied,* 350 U.S. 840 (1955). This passage properly notes that the statute is triggered when a copier attempts to "palm off" his replica as an original. In other words, the protection afforded by the Lanham Act is primarily to potential purchasers. The protection accruing to a producer is derivative of and only incidental to this primary protection: a producer can market his goods with the assurance that another may not market a replica in a manner that will allow potential purchasers to associate the replica with the producer of the original. Unfortunately, the majority merely pays lip service to this fundamental tenet in its application of the eight-factor test.

[29] The majority never clearly defines the target group that is likely to be confused. Although *West Point* counsels that purchasers must be deceived, the majority concludes that the target group is the "public." The majority errs to the extent that its analysis shifts from potential purchasers to the broader more indefinite group of the "public."

[30] The eight-factor test contemplates that the target group is comprised of potential purchasers. For example, the importance of one factor—evidence of actual confusion—is determined by the kinds of persons confused and degree of confusion. "Short-lived confusion or confusion of individuals casually acquainted with a business is worthy of little weight . . . ." *Homeowners Group, Inc. v. Home Marketing Specialists, Inc.,* 931 F.2d 1100, 1110 (6th Cir. 1991) (quoting *Safeway Stores, Inc. v. Safeway Discount Drugs, Inc.,* 675 F.2d 1160, 1167 (11th Cir. 1982)). Two other factors obviously refer to potential purchasers: the marketing channels used and the likely degree of purchaser care and sophistication. Thus, three of the eight factors expressly focus on the likelihood of confusion as to potential purchasers.

[31] Other courts have made clear that section 43(a) is concerned with the welfare of potential purchasers in the marketplace. *See Kwik-Site,* 758 F.2d at 178 (referring to "intending purchasers" when discussing likelihood of confusion); *see also Coach Leatherware Co. v. AnnTaylor, Inc.,* 933 F.2d 162, 168 (2d Cir. 1991) (stating that plaintiff must prove that "purchasers are likely to confuse the imitating goods with the originals"); *West Point,* 222 F.2d at 592 (referring to "purchasers exercising ordinary care to discover whose products they are buying . . . ." (quoting *Reynolds & Reynolds Co. v. Norick,* 114 F.2d 278 (10th Cir. 1940))).

[32] Plaintiff's replicas are not likely to confuse potential purchasers. Plaintiff's vehicles display an "R" on the parking lenses and vent windows. No symbols or logos affiliated with Ferrari are displayed. Roberts informs all purchasers that his product is not affiliated with Ferrari. In light of these distinctions, and the high degree of customer care and sophistication that normally accompanies such a purchase—defendant's vehicles at issue sell for a minimum of $230,000, as well as the distinctly different marketing

403

channels employed by the parties, I find the evidence insufficient to prove a likelihood of confusion by potential purchasers in the marketplace.

[33] To be sure, some courts have expanded the application of the likelihood of confusion test to include individuals other than point-of-sale purchasers. These courts have included potential purchasers who may contemplate a purchase in the future, reasoning that in the pre-sale context an "observer would identify the [product] with the [original manufacturer], and the [original manufacturer]'s reputation would suffer damage if the [product] appeared to be of poor quality." *Polo Fashions, Inc. v. Craftex, Inc.*, 816 F.2d 145, 148 (4th Cir. 1987); *see Mastercrafters Clock & Radio Co. v. Vacheron & Constantin-Le Coultre Watches, Inc.*, 221 F.2d 464 (2d Cir.), *cert. denied*, 350 U.S. 832 (1955); *Rolex Watch, U.S.A., Inc. v. Canner*, 645 F.Supp. 484 (S.D.Fla. 1986).

[34] In applying the test in this manner, these courts appear to recognize that the deception of a consumer under these circumstances could dissuade such a consumer from choosing to buy a particular product, thereby foreclosing the possibility of point-of-sale confusion but nevertheless injuring the consumer based on this confusion. The injury stems from the consumer's erroneous conclusion that the "original" product is poor quality based on his perception of a replica that he thinks is the original. These cases protect a potential purchaser against confusion as to the source of a particular product. Hence, even when expanding the scope of this test, these courts did not lose sight of the focus of section 43(a): the potential purchaser. The majority applies the likelihood of confusion test in a manner which departs from this focus.

[35] The cases which have expanded the scope of the target group are distinguishable from the instant case, however. In *Rolex*, the counterfeit watches were labelled "ROLEX" on their face. Similarly, the *Mastercrafters* court found that the clock was labelled in a manner that was not likely to come to the attention of an individual. It is also noteworthy that the Second Circuit has limited *Mastercrafters* "by pointing out that '[i]n that case there was abundant evidence of actual confusion, palming off and an intent to deceive.'" *Bose Corp. v. Linear Design Labs, Inc.*, 467 F.2d 304, 310 n. 8 (2d Cir. 1972) (quoting *Norwich Pharmacal Co. v. Sterling Drug, Inc.*, 271 F.2d 569 (2d Cir. 1959), *cert. denied*, 362 U.S. 919 (1960)). No evidence was introduced in the instant case to show actual confusion, palming off or an intent to deceive and, as previously noted, plaintiff does not use any name or logo affiliated with Ferrari on its replicas.

[36] Further, these cases conclude that the proper remedy is to require identification of the source of the replica, not prohibit copying of the product. *See West Point*, 222 F.2d at 589 (stating that under such circumstances "the only obligation of the copier is to identify its product lest the public be mistaken into believing that it was made by the prior patentee"); *see also Coach Leatherware*, 933 F.2d at 173 (Winter, J., dissenting in part) (stating that "[a copier] thus has every right to copy [a product] so long as consumers know they are buying [the copied product]"). Accordingly, even if I were to conclude that plaintiff's copies created confusion in the pre-sale context, I would tailor the remedy to protect only against such confusion; this would best be accomplished through adequate labelling. The majority's remedy goes well beyond protection of consumers against confusion as to a product's source. It protects the design itself from being copied. *See supra* at 1239.

[37] In sum, the relevant focus of the eight-factor test should be upon potential purchasers in the marketplace. Plaintiff's replicas present no likelihood of confusion because plaintiff provides adequate labelling so as to prevent potential purchasers, whether in the pre-sale or point-of-sale context, from confusing its replicas with Ferrari's automobiles. The majority errs by expanding the target group to include the "public," an expansion unsupported by the language and purpose of the Lanham Act. To the extent that the majority expands the target group, the test increasingly protects the design from replication and the producer from dilution, rather than the potential purchaser from confusion.[1]

---

[1] I also note that the survey relied upon by the majority to prove a likelihood of confusion is fatally flawed. Generally, "[i]n assessing the likelihood of confusion, a court's concern is 'the performance of the

[38] The majority does more than implicitly recognize a dilution cause of action by its misapplication of the eight-factor test; it expressly reads such a cause of action into the statute. To justify this interpretation, the majority points out that Congress deleted the word "purchasers" from the statutory language in 1967 {*recte* 1962}. According to the majority, this congressional act demonstrates that Congress intended "to protect against the cheapening and dilution of the genuine product, and to protect the manufacturer's reputation." I fail to see how this one congressional act leads to such a conclusion.

[39] As an initial matter, the majority's method of reasoning should compel it to reach a different conclusion. In 1989, Congress specifically considered and rejected adding an anti-dilution provision to the Lanham Act.[2] This action, it can be asserted, demonstrates that Congress does not now consider the protection of the Lanham Act to encompass injuries to a manufacturer based on dilution. The majority cannot look to one action of Congress to bolster its position, but ignore other actions which undercut its position.

[40] More importantly, the language of the Lanham Act does not afford such protection to producers of goods. As noted in the previous section, the Lanham Act's protection runs to relevant consumers in the marketplace; its protection to producers is incidental to this primary protection. Requiring adequate labelling ensures that a producer will not have the poor quality of a replica imputed to its product by a confused potential purchaser. This is the only benefit accruing to a producer. Trademark dilution is not a cause of action under the Lanham Act. *See Eveready Battery Co. v. Adolph Coors Co.*, 765 F.Supp. 440 (N.D.Ill. 1991).

. . . .

Questions and Comments

1. *Are the Ferrari exterior designs functional?* The district court found that they were not and the Sixth Circuit affirmed:

> The district court found that Ferrari proved, by a preponderance of the evidence, that the exterior shapes and features of the Daytona Spyder and Testarossa were nonfunctional. The court based this conclusion on the uncontroverted testimony of Angelo Bellei, who

---

marks in the commercial context.'" *Homeowners Group, Inc. v. Home Marketing Specialists, Inc.*, 931 F.2d 1100, 1106 (6th Cir. 1991) (quoting *Frisch's Restaurants, Inc. v. Shoney's, Inc.*, 759 F.2d 1261, 1266 (6th Cir. 1985)). "It is the overall impression of the mark, not an individual feature, that counts." *Id.* at 1109. Applied to the instant case, this means that the analysis must be based on the products as they appear in the marketplace. The ultimate question is "whether relevant consumers are likely to believe that the products or services offered by the parties are affiliated in some way." *Id.* at 1107.

The survey lacks any probative value on the issue of consumer confusion because of the manner in which it was conducted. The survey was conducted by showing photographs of Ferrari's cars and Roberts' replicas *stripped of their identifying badges.* By conducting the survey in this manner, no assessment could be made of the likelihood of confusion in the "commercial context." Purchasers of plaintiff's cars are not purchasing from photographs. Accordingly, the survey is meaningless as to the likelihood of confusion.

[2] The most recent amendment to the Lanham Act, the Trademark Law Revision Act of 1988, Pub.L. No. 100-667, 102 Stat. 3935 (1988) (effective Nov. 16, 1989), as originally introduced in both houses of Congress, permitted separate causes of action for dilution, disparagement and tarnishment. All of these provisions were deleted from the legislation which eventually was enacted. House Rep. 100-1028 (Oct. 3, 1988), *reprinted in* United States Trademark Ass'n, The Trademark Law Revision Act of 1988, The Legislative History, Reports, Testimony, and Annotated Statutory Text 277, 278 (1989); Cong.Rec. H10411, H10421 (Oct. 19, 1988). {As Part II.C discusses, Congress eventually created Lanham Act § 43(c) in 1995 to provide for federal antidilution protection and amended § 43(c) in 2006.}

developed Ferrari's grand touring cars from 1964-75, that the company chose the exterior designs for beauty and distinctiveness, not utility.

Ferrari S.P.A., 944 F.2d at 1246.

8. Reverse Confusion

Consider a quick example of a claim of "reverse confusion." In *Dreamwerks Production, Inc. v. SKG Studio*, 142 F.3d 1127 (9th Cir. 1998), the plaintiff had been using the mark DREAMWERKS since 1984 in connection with services for organizing science fiction conventions in the Northeast and Midwest of the U.S. In 1994, Steven Spielberg, Jeffrey Katzenberg and David Geffen established the massive Hollywood studio known as DreamWorks SKG. The plaintiff sued for "reverse confusion." It argued that consumers would now believe that the plaintiff's services somehow originated in the defendant. In the *Dreamwerks* case, the Ninth Circuit reversed the district court's summary judgment in favor of the defendant and held that the matter should go to trial. The court observed: "Dreamwerks notes that whatever goodwill it has built now rests in the hands of DreamWorks; if the latter should take a major misstep and tarnish its reputation with the public, Dreamwerks too would be pulled down." *Id.* at 1130. The case eventually settled.

In many typical "forward confusion" cases, such as in the *Virgin Wireless* case above, the senior user of the mark is a much larger company than the junior user of the mark. Thus, the senior Goliath claims that the junior David's use of the mark will likely confuse consumers into believing that the junior's goods are coming from the senior user, the company with which consumers are much more familiar.

By contrast, reverse confusion typically involves a situation in which the junior user of the mark is an enormous company with the resources extensively to advertise its use of the mark. The risk is that the junior Goliath will overwhelm the meaning of the senior David's mark, so that consumers will believe that the senior users goods are coming from the junior user. This was exactly the claim the plaintiff made in the following opinion, *Wreal, LLC v. Amazon.com, Inc.*

Note, importantly, how certain of the factors in the multifactor test for the likelihood of consumer confusion change in a reverse confusion analysis. (And incidentally, do you agree with the court's treatment of the plaintiff's evidence of actual confusion?)

Wreal, LLC v. Amazon.com, Inc.
38 Fed.4th 114 (11th Cir. 2022)

Lagoa, Circuit Judge:

[1] This appeal asks us to address the doctrine of reverse-confusion trademark infringement. Reverse confusion is not a standalone claim in trademark law; rather, it is a theory of how trademark infringement can occur. In reverse-confusion cases, the plaintiff is usually a commercially smaller, but more senior, user of the mark at issue. The defendant tends to be a commercially larger, but more junior, user of the mark. The plaintiff thus does not argue that the defendant is using the mark to profit off plaintiff's goodwill; instead, the plaintiff brings suit because of the fear that consumers are associating the plaintiff's mark with the defendant's corporate identity. It is this false association and loss of product control that constitutes the harm in reverse-confusion cases.

[2] In this case, the plaintiff is Wreal, LLC, a Miami-based pornography company, which has been using the mark "FyreTV" in commerce since 2008. The defendant is Amazon.com, Inc., the largest online purveyor of goods and services in the United States, which has been using the mark "Fire TV" (or "fireTV") in commerce since 2012. Wreal does not claim that Amazon, by using the "Fire TV" mark, is attempting to profit off Wreal's good name, as would be typical in a forward-confusion case. Instead, Wreal contends that Amazon's allegedly similar mark is causing consumers to associate its mark—"FyreTV"—with Amazon.

[3] The resolution of this appeal turns on the likelihood of confusing Amazon's "Fire TV" with Wreal's "FyreTV." In forward-confusion cases, we determine likelihood of confusion by applying a well-established seven-factor test. *See Welding Servs., Inc. v. Forman*, 509 F.3d 1351, 1360 (11th Cir. 2007).

Applying those seven factors, the district court found that consumers were unlikely to confuse "Fire TV" with "FyreTV" and granted summary judgment to Amazon on Wreal's trademark infringement claims.

[4] We have not had the opportunity to delineate how this seven-factor test applies in reverse-confusion cases. As discussed below, there are several important differences in how the seven likelihood-of-confusion factors apply in reverse-confusion cases versus forward-confusion cases. When applied specifically to the issues presented here, we conclude that the district court erred in granting summary judgment and should have allowed the case to proceed to trial. We therefore reverse the district court's order.

I. FACTUAL AND PROCEDURAL BACKGROUND

A. Wreal, LLC, and FyreTV

[5] Wreal is a "Miami-based technology company that was formed in 2006 with the goal of developing a platform for streaming [pornographic] video content over the internet." *Wreal, LLC, v. Amazon.com, Inc.* (*Wreal I*), 840 F.3d 1244, 1246 (11th Cir. 2016). In 2007, Wreal launched "FyreTV," an online streaming service that Wreal markets as the "Netflix of Porn," "The Ultimate Adult Video On Demand Experience," and a "porn pay per view service." That same year, Wreal began using in commerce the marks "FyreTV" and "FyreTV.com"[1]—the latter of which represents the website where users can access the FyreTV service. *See id.* In order to access the FyreTV service, potential consumers must first go to FyreTV.com to sign up for an account. Once on the website, potential consumers must first verify they are at least eighteen years old and interested in viewing adult content before accessing the homepage, which displays several rows of pornographic images.

[6] In order to make accessing its FyreTV service easier, Wreal also sells a set-top box,[2] called the FyreBoXXX, which allows consumers to access FyreTV on their television sets. To purchase a FyreBoXXX, a potential consumer must first travel to the FyreTV.com site and set up an account. In fact, the FyreBoXXX has never been sold in any store or website save for the online store at FyreTV.com. Between October 2012 and April 2014, Wreal suspended sales of the FyreBoXXX on its website. Indeed, by the end of 2012, Wreal had suspended all forms of print, radio, trade show, and television advertising for either the FyreBoXXX or FyreTV— Wreal's only two products. As of today, Wreal advertises its products only on other adult websites.

[7] Apart from the FyreBoXXX and FyreTV.com, Wreal's customers also have other methods available to access the FyreTV service. For example, both Apple TV and Roku—two commercial set-top boxes that offer a host of general interest channels and media— support FyreTV. Thus, after signing up for an account at FyreTV.com, Wreal's customers can watch its content from their television set through a computer, a smartphone, a FyreBoXXX, an Apple TV, or a Roku.

B. Amazon and "fireTV"

[8] Amazon is the largest online purveyor of goods in the United States. In 2011, Amazon "started using the mark 'Fire' in connection with its Kindle tablets ... to highlight the new model's ability to stream video over the internet." *Id.* at 1247. In late 2012 and early 2013, Amazon was gearing up to launch several new products, including a phone, a new tablet, and a set-top box. *Id.* It decided to use the "Fire" brand, as well as its housemark, "amazon," on these products, with the set-top box being called "fireTV."[3] *Id.* During its branding discussions for the set-top box, Amazon learned about Wreal and its

---

[1] On October 14, 2008, Wreal registered both of its marks—"FyreTV" and "FyreTV.com"—with the U.S. Patent and Trademark Office. Wreal I, 840 F.3d at 1246.

[2] A "set-top box" is "a device that is connected to a television so that the television can receive digital signals." *Set-top Box, Merriam-Webster Online Dictionary,* https://www.merriam-webster.com/dictionary/set-top% 20box (last visited June 19, 2022).

[3] The record shows that Amazon has alternatively used "Fire TV" or "fireTV" in its graphics and advertisements for its set-top box. For purposes of this opinion, we use the stylization of "fireTV,"

FyreTV products, but it never contacted Wreal about the set-top box's name and decided to use the "Fire" mark without Wreal's knowledge. *Id.*

[9] Amazon launched fireTV in April 2014 with a nationwide advertising campaign covered by major magazines and television networks. The fireTV is a streaming-only set-top box; it does not contain a DVD tray and cannot play DVDs. Amazon markets the product as a set-top box for general interest content, including "instant access to Netflix, Prime Instant Video, WatchESPN," and more. It is not marketed as a device for streaming pornography. Amazon advertises the device on amazon.com, as well as on television, in print media, and using in-store displays at retailers like Best Buy and Staples. When Amazon began its search-engine-optimization efforts (to help fireTV appear on the internet), it bought ads for keywords related to fireTV, but not for FyreTV or anything related to pornography. Often—but not always—Amazon will market its "Fire" products with its housemark, "amazon." In the graphics and advertisements for the device, the device is sometimes referred to as one word, i.e., "fireTV," and sometimes it appears as two words, i.e., "Fire TV."

[10] Amazon's fireTV does not broadcast any hardcore pornographic material.[4] But the fireTV does have apps for Showtime and HBO GO, and both of those content providers broadcast softcore pornography as part of their after-hours programming. It is unclear, however, whether those providers had any such material on their apps that link to fireTV at the time of the lawsuit.

[11] It is undisputed that Amazon's policies for Amazon Prime Instant Video, which is Amazon's own streaming service and streams on the fireTV, prohibit the sale and consumption of hardcore pornography on the set-top box. However, the record evidence suggests that hardcore pornographic DVDs are available for purchase on amazon.com. The record evidence also suggests that two films with highly suggestive names were available for streaming on the fireTV through Amazon Prime Instant Video, though the record does not establish whether those films would be categorized as hardcore or softcore pornography.

[12] Moreover, Amazon does not advertise the fireTV on any pornographic websites and, as such, there is no overlap between the marketing schemes for FyreTV and fireTV. Nor does Amazon sell the fireTV on any pornographic websites. Thus, there is no overlap of the sales outlets utilized by Amazon and Wreal.

C. Evidence of Confusion

[13] In order to prevail on its trademark claims, Wreal must show a "likelihood of confusion." *Forman*, 509 F.3d at 1360. We therefore summarize the record evidence relevant to this issue, as presented by Wreal at the preliminary injunction hearing and by both parties as part of their summary judgment briefing. Below are screenshots of the marks at issue as they appear in internet advertising for the set-top boxes:

---

because Wreal highlighted the inconsistency in its response disputing Amazon's statement of undisputed facts. However, we emphasize that we make no ultimate conclusion on whether Amazon's mark is stylized as "Amazon Fire TV" or "fireTV."

[4] Generally, hardcore pornography refers to "scenes of actual sex acts." *Hardcore, Merriam-Webster Online Dictionary,* https://www.merriam-webster.com/dictionary/hard-core (last visited June 19, 2022). Softcore pornography refers to "scenes of sex acts that are less explicit than hard-core material." *Soft-core, Merriam-Webster Online Dictionary,* https://www.merriam-webster.com/dictionary/soft-core (last visited June 19, 2022).

[14] As noted above, the two products are neither advertised nor sold in the same outlets. A consumer cannot buy a fireTV at the same place where he could buy a FyreTV, and vice versa. Thus, no consumer will come across the products or marks in the same location—whether over the internet or in person at a brick-and-mortar location—save for an internet search engine like google.com. Additionally, Wreal's own evidence supports the proposition that mine-run internet consumers would not confuse Amazon's amazon.com website with Wreal's FyreTV.com website.

[15] Over the course of the litigation, both Wreal and Amazon sought to present evidence relevant to the issue of actual consumer confusion. Amazon, for its part, produced in discovery "tens of thousands" of customer service inquiries related to the fireTV. In one of those inquiries, an Amazon customer asked whether he could access adult content on the Amazon "fyreTV."[6] Wreal points to record evidence showing a number of customer service inquiries it received in which customers asked Wreal if the FyreTV streaming service would be available on Amazon's fireTV set-top box. Significantly, Wreal also produced in discovery a tweet directed to Wreal's Twitter account in which the sender asked, "Did you guys just merge with Amazon?"

[16] Both parties also presented expert testimony regarding the level of confusion between the marks—Wreal at the preliminary injunction hearing and Amazon at the summary judgment stage. Amazon's expert, Dr. Dan Sarel, conducted a consumer survey that showed a "confusion rate of one

---

[6] The district court adopted the magistrate judge's determination that, while this inquiry appears to show confusion, the sender was not confused. The magistrate judge based its conclusion solely on the text of the inquiry itself, and not on any other record evidence. In other words, the magistrate judge (and, by adoption, the district court) did not believe that the sender was confused. Credibility determinations like this, however, are inappropriate at the summary judgment stage. . . . Here, for example, a reasonable juror could view the same evidence and come to the opposite conclusion reached by the magistrate judge and the district court. Because this credibility determination improperly invaded the province of the jury, it must be disregarded.

percent," which he described as "statistically insignificant" and "nonexistent." That conclusion was bolstered by Wreal's own expert—Dr. Thomas Maronick—who conducted his own consumer surveys in April 2014 and testified at the preliminary injunction hearing that he found "very low" levels of consumer confusion.[7]

D. Procedural History

[17] Wreal filed this lawsuit against Amazon about two weeks after the fireTV's product launch. In its complaint, Wreal sought treble damages and injunctive relief for reverse-confusion trademark infringement under the Lanham Act, the Florida Deceptive and Unfair Trade Practices Act, and Florida common law.[8] Five months after filing suit, Wreal moved for a preliminary injunction, which the district court referred to the magistrate judge and ultimately denied. We affirmed that denial. *See Wreal I*, 840 F.3d at 1246.

[18] After the close of discovery, Amazon moved for summary judgment. The district court again referred the motion to the magistrate judge for a report and recommendation, and the magistrate judge recommended granting the motion. Over Wreal's objections, the district court adopted the report and recommendation and granted summary judgment to Amazon. Wreal then timely appealed.

. . . .

III. ANALYSIS

[19] Wreal argues that Amazon's use of the mark fireTV infringed its trademark FyreTV under a reverse-confusion theory— the resolution of which boils down to the likelihood of confusion between the two marks.

. . . .

[20] In order to resolve this appeal, we must determine how these seven likelihood-of-confusion factors {from *Welding Servs., Inc. v. Forman*, 509 F.3d 1351, 1360 (11th Cir. 2007)} apply in the context of reverse-confusion trademark infringement. The "paradigm case [of reverse confusion] is that of a knowing junior user with much greater economic power who saturates the market with advertising of a confusingly similar mark, overwhelming the marketplace power and value of the senior user's mark." 4 J. Thomas McCarthy, *McCarthy on Trademarks and Unfair Competition* § 23:10 (5th ed.); *see also Sands, Taylor & Wood Co. v. Quaker Oats Co.*, 978 F.2d 947, 957 (7th Cir. 1992) ("Reverse confusion occurs when a large junior user saturates the market with a trademark similar or identical to that of a smaller, senior user. In such a case, the junior user does not seek to profit from the good will associated with the senior user's mark.") Because both the harm and the theory of infringement in a reverse-confusion case differ from what is claimed in a forward-confusion case, the analysis and application of the seven likelihood-of-confusion factors differ as well.

[21] In a reverse-confusion case, the harms that can occur are varied. For example, consumers may come to believe the smaller, senior user of the mark is itself a trademark infringer, *see Banff, Ltd. v. Federated Dep't Stores, Inc.*, 841 F.2d 486, 490 (2d Cir. 1988), or that the defendant's use of the mark diminishes the value of the plaintiff's mark as a source indicator, *see Checkpoint Sys., Inc. v. Check Point Software Techs., Inc.*, 269 F.3d 270, 301–02 (3d Cir. 2001). As our sister court, the Sixth Circuit has stated in a reverse confusion case:

---

[7] Wreal complains about both studies, arguing that the Amazon study was conducted too early to be relevant to the issue of consumer confusion and that its own study was conducted for a separate purpose altogether. Absence of evidence for a proposition, however, is not affirmative evidence to the contrary. And the only survey evidence available to us is not in dispute—both surveys show that there was no consumer confusion. Nevertheless, we accord this evidence relatively little weight, as "[t]his Circuit . . . has moved away from relying on survey evidence" in trademark cases. *Frehling Enters., Inc. v. Int'l Select Grp., Inc.*, 192 F.3d 1330, 1341 n.5 (11th Cir. 1999).

[8] As noted by the district court, the protection that these three bodies of law provide is coextensive. . . .

[t]he public comes to assume the senior user's products are really the junior user's or that the former has become somehow connected to the latter. The result is that the senior user loses the value of the trademark—its product identity, corporate identity, control over its goodwill and reputation, and ability to move into new markets.

Ameritech, Inc. v. Am. Info. Techs. Corp., 811 F.2d 960, 964 (6th Cir. 1987). In this case, Wreal contends that "Amazon's use of Wreal's mark creates a likelihood that consumers will believe that Amazon is the *source* of Wreal's FyreTV service."

[22] With these principles in mind, we turn to the seven-factor test for likelihood of confusion and analyze each of the factors and their application in a reverse-confusion case. . . .

A. Distinctiveness of the Mark

[23] In the typical forward-confusion case, this factor focuses only on the conceptual strength of the plaintiff's mark. *See Frehling Enters., Inc. v. Int'l Select Grp., Inc.*, 192 F.3d 1330, 1335 (11th Cir. 1999) ("Classifying the type of mark Plaintiff has determines whether it is strong or weak."). This is because in a forward-confusion case, the plaintiff's theory is that the defendant—a newer user of the mark at issue—is attempting to profit off the plaintiff's goodwill and reputation. And here, the district court did assess the conceptual strength of Wreal's "FyreTV" mark and found it distinctive and strong.

[24] But in a reverse-confusion case, the plaintiff is not arguing that the defendant is attempting to profit off the plaintiff's goodwill. Rather, the plaintiff asserts that the defendant—the junior but more powerful mark user—has been able to commercially overwhelm the market and saturate the public conscience with its own use of the mark, thereby weakening and diminishing the value of the senior user's mark. *See, e.g., Checkpoint Sys.*, 269 F.3d at 302–03. Thus, in this situation, the conceptual strength of the plaintiff's mark is necessarily less important to the analysis. *See Com. Nat'l Ins. Servs., Inc. v. Com. Ins. Agency, Inc.*, 214 F.3d 432, 444 (3d Cir. 2000) (noting that "it is the strength of the larger, junior user's mark which results in reverse confusion"). Accordingly, when assessing the distinctiveness of the mark in a reverse-confusion case, the district court should consider both the conceptual strength of the plaintiff's mark and the relative commercial strength of the defendant's mark. *See . . . A & H Sportswear, Inc. v. Victoria's Secret Stores, Inc.*, 237 F.3d 198, 231 (3d Cir. 2000) (noting that a plaintiff is more likely to succeed when "pitted against a defendant with a far stronger mark" in reverse confusion cases); *Checkpoint Sys.*, 269 F.3d at 303 ("But in a reverse confusion situation, the senior user's claim may be strengthened by a showing that the junior user's mark is commercially relatively strong. The greater relative strength of the junior mark allows the junior user to 'overwhelm' the marketplace, diminishing the value of the senior user's mark."). . . .

[25] Here, the district court did not consider the commercial strength of Amazon's mark because it found that Wreal waived the argument by failing to raise it in its response to Amazon's motion for summary judgment and instead raised it for the first time in its objections to the magistrate judge's report and recommendation.[12] The district court erred in that finding. At the summary judgement stage, it was Amazon's burden, as the movant, to show that it was entitled to judgment as a matter of law, and the parties cannot "waive the application of the correct law or stipulate to an incorrect legal test." *Jefferson v. Sewon Am., Inc.*, 891 F.3d 911, 923 (11th Cir. 2018).

[26] The commercial strength of Amazon's mark is manifest and appears in the record. Amazon admitted in its answer that the fireTV was launched with a major advertising campaign, was covered by major magazines and television networks, and that it was a bestseller. Amazon also admits that it advertises the fireTV in multiple brick-and-mortar locations, as well as on amazon.com, one of the most visited online shopping sites in the United States. In short, Amazon's overwhelming commercial success

---

[12] The district court also noted that the presence of Amazon's "amazon" housemark alongside "fireTV" in advertisements pushed the distinctiveness-of-the-mark factor further in Amazon's favor. As we discuss below, however, the presence of a housemark should be assessed in reference to the second factor in the analysis—the similarity of the marks. *See A & H Sportswear*, 237 F.3d at 229–30.

with the fireTV mark, coupled with the conceptual strength of Wreal's mark, pushes this factor firmly in Wreal's favor.

B. Similarity of the Marks

[27] The similarity-of-the-marks analysis is, with one exception related to housemarks noted below, the same in both forward-confusion and reverse-confusion cases. We compare "the marks and consider[ ] the overall impressions that the marks create, including the sound, appearance, and manner in which they are used." *Frehling*, 192 F.3d at 1337. In doing so, we determine similarity based on "the total effect of the designation, rather than on a comparison of individual features." *Amstar Corp. v. Domino's Pizza, Inc.*, 615 F.2d 252, 260–61 (5th Cir. 1980).... Similarity in any of these elements— appearance, sound, connotation, and commercial impression—may be sufficient to find the marks similar. *See Stone Lion Cap. Partners, L.P. v. Lion Capital LLP*, 746 F.3d 1317, 1321 (Fed. Cir. 2014).

[28] The district court concluded that the marks at issue—fireTV and FyreTV—were not similar. It reached this conclusion mainly by focusing on the fact that the marks were spelled differently and used different fonts, as well as the fact that they were used differently in commerce. The district court also noted that one of Wreal's experts, Dr. Linda Williams, testified that visitors to FyreTV.com would not confuse it with amazon.com. The inquiry under this factor, however, is the similarity of the *marks*, not the similarity of the *services* or the similarity of the *sales methods*— each of which has their own factor and should thus be considered separately.

[29] When the focus is on the similarity of the marks themselves, the result is clear—FyreTV and fireTV are nearly identical. "Fire" is the first and only dominant word in both marks, and it is presented in a phonetically and connotatively identical fashion. It is also an abstract term, and thus the only term in either mark that gives the mark meaning. *See Palm Bay Imps., Inc. v. Veuve Clicquot Ponsardin Maison Fondee en 1772*, 396 F.3d 1369, 1372 (Fed. Cir. 2005) (finding similarity between "VEUVE ROYALE" and "VEUVE CLICQUOT" because "VEUVE ... remains a 'prominent feature' as the first word in the mark and the first word to appear on the label"); *Century 21 Real Estate Corp. v. Century Life of Am.*, 970 F.2d 874, 876 (Fed Cir. 1992) (finding similarity between "CENTURY 21" and "CENTURY LIFE OF AMERICA" in part because "consumers must first notice th[e] identical lead word").... By contrast, the secondary word in the marks—"TV"—is merely descriptive of or generic for the goods and services sold—i.e., streaming services. *See Frehling*, 192 F.3d at 1337 (noting that "a mark may be surrounded by additional words of lesser importance and not have its strength diluted").

[30] Moreover, the marks need not be identical, as the "purpose in considering the similarity of marks as an indicator of likelihood of confusion is that the closer the marks are, the more likely reasonable consumers will mistake the source of the product that each mark represents." *Id.* Thus, while "Fyre" and "fire" are spelled differently, and one is capitalized, the words have the same connotation and pronunciation, and the differences in font, color, and capitalization are not dispositive.

[31] The Ninth Circuit's decision in *Dreamwerks Production Group, Inc. v. SKG Studio*, 142 F.3d 1127, 1130 (9th Cir. 1998) is instructive on this point. In that case, the court had to assess the similarity of the marks "Dreamwerks" and "DreamWorks," which, like the marks at issue here, utilized different spellings and capitalization. *Id.* The Ninth Circuit concluded that the marks were similar, noting the obvious "perfect similarity of sound" and "similarity of meaning" while determining that even the similarity of sight *also* weighed in favor of a finding of similarity, as consumers "might shrug off the difference [in spelling and capitalization] as an intentional modification." *Id.* at 1131. Our decision in *Frehling* is also instructive. There, we said that the marks "BELL' OGGETTI" and "Tavola Collection by OGGETTI" were similar because the presence of the dominant and protected "OGGETTI" in both was likely to be confusing. *Frehling*, 192 F.3d at 1337. Each of these conclusions applies here.

[32] Amazon's pervasive use of its "amazon" housemark alongside "fireTV" in advertisements warrants separate discussion. In forward-confusion cases—where a commercially superior plaintiff with a strong conceptual mark sues a defendant for attempting to profit off its goodwill—the presence of a housemark is indeed likely to dispel confusion in ordinarily prudent consumers. *See, e.g., Custom Mfg.*, 508 F.3d at 652 n.10. But in reverse-confusion cases, this presumption is reversed; because the

harm is false association of the plaintiff's mark with the defendant's corporate identity, the defendant's use of a housemark alongside the mark is more likely to *cause* confusion. *See, e.g., A & H Sportswear*, 237 F.3d at 230 (noting that there is a "possibility that the [housemark] will *aggravate*, rather than mitigate, reverse confusion, by reinforcing the association of the [trademark] exclusively with [the housemark]") (emphasis added); *Attrezzi, LLC v. Maytag Corp.*, 436 F.3d 32, 39 (1st Cir. 2006) ("Yet since the alleged harm is *reverse* confusion, to the extent [the defendant's housemark] is itself the more recognized label the linkage could actually aggravate the threat to [the plaintiff].") . . .

[33] Amazon's use of its housemark alongside advertisements for the "fireTV" does exactly what one might expect it to do: it causes consumers to associate Amazon with fireTV. Because this is a reverse-confusion case asserting that Amazon's use of fireTV causes consumers to associate FyreTV with Amazon instead of Wreal, Amazon's use of the housemark supports Wreal's theory of recovery. The district court erred in concluding otherwise.

[34] In short, the parties' marks are nearly identical. Both use the same words, are pronounced the same, and have the same meaning. While they are spelled slightly differently and use different fonts, this is not enough to conclude that the marks are dissimilar. Moreover, Amazon's pervasive use of its housemark alongside "fireTV" pushes this factor even further in favor of Wreal, as it is likely to confuse consumers into believing that Amazon is the origin of the FyreTV mark. Thus, the similarity-of-the-marks factor weighs heavily in favor of Wreal.

C. Similarity of the Products

[35] The analysis of this factor is the same regardless of the theory of confusion, and "requires a determination as to whether the products are the kind that the public attributes to a single source, not whether or not the purchasing public can readily distinguish between the products of the respective parties." *Frehling*, 192 F.3d at 1338 . . . . In reverse-confusion cases, it also is relevant to ask whether consumers might expect the defendant to "bridge the gap" and enter the plaintiff's market. *See Fisons Horticulture, Inc. v. Vigoro Indus., Inc.*, 30 F.3d 466, 480 (3d Cir. 1994).

[36] Here, many pieces of record evidence are relevant to the question of whether the fireTV set-top box is similar to the FyreBoXXX. The record evidence presented in the district court established that consumers were already able to stream softcore pornography on Amazon's fireTV through content providers like HBO GO and Showtime. The record evidence also established that Amazon Prime Instant Video—Amazon's own streaming service, which, like HBO GO and Showtime, is available on the fireTV—offered consumers softcore pornography. And the record evidence also established that: (1) Amazon already offered the sale of hardcore pornographic DVDs and magazines on its related consumer website, amazon.com; (2) the parties' devices are visually similar— both are plain black set-top boxes that come with a small remote; and (3) Amazon's direct competitors in the mainstream set-top box market—Roku and Apple TV—already provided access to hardcore pornography, including FyreTV.

[37] The question therefore is whether this record evidence would suggest to an ordinarily prudent consumer that a do-it-all giant like Amazon—which already sells a set-top box that streams softcore pornography and which competes against other set-top boxes that stream hardcore pornography—would "bridge the gap" to hardcore pornography streaming and release a set-top box that streams exclusively pornographic content. We answer that question in the affirmative. Amazon is a company that already sells hardcore pornography on its website and offers softcore pornography on its set-top box. And it competes in a market in which its direct competitors offer hardcore pornography streaming directly on their set-top boxes. Given this information, a reasonable juror could conclude that Amazon decided to "bridge the gap" and offer a standalone set-top box dedicated to streaming hardcore pornography. *See id.* The two products at issue therefore "are the kind the public attributes to a single source." *E. Remy Martin*, 756 F.2d at 1530.

[38] Our caselaw provides ample support for this conclusion. In *E. Remy Martin*, a trademark dispute between a wine company and a liquor company, this Court concluded that cognac and brandy—the products sold by the liquor company—were distilled from wine and that, as a result, it was "quite likely that, even assuming a sophisticated consumer from the drinking world, such a consumer could

easily conclude that [the liquor company] had undertaken the production and sale of wine and that its name and goodwill therefore attached to [the wine company's] product." 756 F.2d at 1530. . . .

[39] Decisions from our sister circuits in reverse-confusion cases lend further support to our conclusion here. In *Attrezzi*, the First Circuit held that the products of two "small electric appliance" manufacturers were similar even though one manufacturer also used the mark on its gourmet foods and dinnerware. 436 F.3d at 39. In *Dreamwerks*, the Ninth Circuit concluded that a movie studio and a convention holder had similar products because it would not be unreasonable for consumers to presume that the production company behind Star Trek decided to bridge the gap to convention holding and had begun to host Star Trek conventions. *See* 142 F.3d at 1131 ("[M]ovies and sci-fi merchandise are now as complementary as baseball and hot dogs. The main products sold at Dreamwerks conventions are movie and TV collectibles and memorabilia; the lectures, previews and appearances by actors which attract customers to Dreamwerks conventions are all dependent, in one way or another, on the output of entertainment giants like DreamWorks.").

[40] Here, as in *E. Remy Martin* and *Dreamwerks*, a reasonable juror could conclude that Amazon was likely to market and sell a product like Wreal's. Indeed, to see a do-it-all giant like Amazon enter the pornographic streaming industry requires no more of an inferential leap than seeing a movie studio begin holding public conventions (as in *Dreamwerks*) or a liquor company begin selling wine (as in *E. Remy Martin*). Amazon already offers at least some softcore pornography on its streaming services and competes with other general-interest set-top boxes that offer hardcore pornography content on theirs, including the FyreTV streaming service at issue here. Amazon also sells hardcore pornographic materials on its website. It would not be unreasonable for a reasonable consumer to see FyreTV and think Amazon was the source.

[41] Finally, we note that "the more similar the marks are, the less necessary it is that the products themselves be very similar to create confusion." *Attrezzi*, 436 F.3d at 39. Accordingly, we conclude that this factor favors Wreal.

D. Similarity of Sales Outlets and Customer Bases

[42] As for the "similarity of sales outlets" factor, we have held:

> This factor takes into consideration where, how, and to whom the parties' products are sold. Direct competition between the parties is not required for this factor to weigh in favor of a likelihood of confusion, though evidence that the products are sold in the same stores is certainly strong. The parties' outlets and customer bases need not be identical, but some degree of overlap should be present.

Frehling, 192 F.3d at 1339 (citations omitted). The analysis of this factor is the same in forward-confusion and reverse-confusion cases.

[43] Here, the district court concluded that the "similarity of sales outlets" factor weighs in favor of Amazon. Amazon's fireTV is available everywhere—on multiple internet sites and in brick-and-mortar locations around the world. Wreal's FyreTV, on the other hand, is available in only one place and can only be purchased one way—a consumer must make his way to FyreTV.com, navigate through an eighteen-year-olds-only banner, certify that he is interested in purchasing pornography, and find the product on the website. And crucially, Amazon's fireTV is unavailable on FyreTV.com. Both *where* the products are sold and *how* the products are sold are thus different. Only to *whom* the products are sold is arguably similar, as the record evidence shows that both companies target twenty- to fifty-year-old men with disposable income. The difference, however, is that Wreal targets only individuals who "are interested in purchasing pornography"—a uniquely identifiable subset of Amazon's customer base. *Cf. Amstar*, 615 F.2d at 262 (noting that Domino Sugar and Domino's Pizza had different sales outlets and customer bases because they were distributed through different outlets despite the fact both were "in the restaurant business"). We therefore conclude that this factor favors Amazon.

E. Similarity of Advertising

[44] This similarity of advertising "factor looks to each party's method of advertising." *Frehling*, 192 F.3d at 1339. "[T]he standard is whether there is likely to be significant enough overlap in the readership of the publications in which the parties advertise that a possibility of confusion could result." *Id.* at 1340. This inquiry is the same in both forward- and reverse-confusion cases.

[45] There is no dispute in this case that the parties advertise in completely different media. Amazon advertises the fireTV on the amazon.com homepage, on television, in print media, and on in-store displays. Wreal stopped advertising on television and in print in 2012, two years before Amazon launched the fireTV. In fact, at all times relevant to the lawsuit, Wreal advertised the FyreTV and FyreBoXXX only through pornographic websites, social media, and newsletters—i.e., only on the internet or other media dedicated to similarly prurient content.

[46] Wreal nonetheless argues that this factor favors it because, very broadly speaking, both the fireTV and the FyreBoXXX advertise through search engines, word of mouth, and social media. But Wreal presented no record evidence of audience overlap. Nor does Wreal identify any website (outside of search engines like Google) where both the fireTV and the FyreBoXXX are advertised. As we explained in *Tana*, rejecting a similar argument: "[T]he only similarity in the advertising channels used by the two parties is their maintenance of websites on the World Wide Web. This similarity would dispel rather than cause confusion, however, because the websites are separate and distinct, suggesting two completely unrelated business entities." 611 F.3d at 778; *see also Therma-Scan, Inc. v. Thermoscan, Inc.*, 295 F.3d 623, 637 (6th Cir. 2002) (noting that the availability of information about the parties' goods on the internet does not lead to the conclusion that they use the same marketing channels).

[47] We therefore conclude that this factor weighs heavily in Amazon's favor.

F. Amazon's Intent

[48] In the forward-confusion context, the intent factor asks whether the "defendant adopted [the] plaintiff's mark with the intention of deriving a benefit from the plaintiff's business reputation." *Frehling*, 192 F.3d at 1340. This is because in forward-confusion cases, "customers mistakenly think that the junior user's goods or services are from the same source as or are connected with the senior user's goods or services." 4 McCarthy, *supra*, § 23:10. Without precedent pointing in any other direction, the district court understandably applied this test for intent and found that Amazon did not adopt the fireTV mark with any intent to derive a benefit from Wreal's FyreTV mark.

[49] But reverse-confusion cases are different. In this context, the concern is that customers will "purchase the senior user's goods under the mistaken impression that they are getting the goods of the junior user." *Id.* In other words, that "the junior user's advertising and promotion so swamps the senior user's reputation in the market that customers are likely to be confused into thinking that the senior user's goods are those of the junior user." *Id.* In this case, Wreal is not suggesting that Amazon chose the fireTV mark with the intention of siphoning Wreal's goodwill; instead, Wreal claims that, by Amazon's use of the fireTV mark, Wreal has lost control over its own, more senior mark.

[50] Courts have responded to this problem in varying ways. The Seventh Circuit, for example, has eliminated the intent element from its likelihood-of-confusion test in reverse-confusion cases. *See Sands*, 978 F.2d at 961. The Third Circuit has acknowledged that evidence of intent to infringe is not expected in reverse-confusion cases, but continues to consider such evidence if it exists. *See A & H Sportswear*, 237 F.3d at 232. And the Tenth Circuit, while similarly discounting the importance of the intent factor in reverse-confusion cases, has continued to apply it in the same manner in both forward- and reverse-confusion cases. *See Universal Money Ctrs., Inc. v. Am. Tel. & Tel. Co.*, 22 F.3d 1527, 1531–32 (10th Cir. 1994). Finally, the Ninth Circuit applies a modified version of the intent factor in reverse-confusion cases, under which indicia of intent may come from a variety of sources:

> At one extreme, intent could be shown through evidence that a defendant deliberately intended to push the plaintiff out of the market by flooding the market with advertising to create reverse confusion. Intent could also be shown by evidence that, for example, the defendant knew of the mark, should have known of the mark, intended to copy the plaintiff,

failed to conduct a reasonably adequate trademark search, or otherwise culpably disregarded the risk of reverse confusion. The tenor of the intent inquiry shifts when considering reverse confusion due to the shift in the theory of confusion, but no specific type of evidence is necessary to establish intent, and the importance of intent and evidence presented will vary by case.

Marketquest Grp., Inc. v. BIC Corp., 862 F.3d 927, 934–35 (9th Cir. 2017) (citations omitted).

[51] We agree with and adopt the Ninth Circuit's approach. Evidence of a specific intent to deceive is not a prerequisite to establish intent in reverse-confusion cases, as it is in forward-confusion cases. Indicia of intent can come from a wide variety of sources, including a more generalized intent to obtain market saturation or to proceed with the adoption of a mark in circumstances where the defendant had constructive knowledge of the plaintiff's mark. The facts of each case will vary, and district courts should accord the intent factor whatever weight it is due under the circumstances.

[52] Here, applying this standard, the evidence of intent is strong. First, Amazon has admitted that, before launching the fireTV, it had actual knowledge of both the FyreBoXXX and Wreal's FyreTV trademark registration. *Wreal I*, 840 F.3d at 1247 ("Amazon was aware of Wreal's FyreTV mark when it launched Fire TV but did not contact Wreal before launching Fire TV."). Amazon's Vice President of Marketing further testified in his deposition that Amazon not only chose to proceed with its usage of the fireTV mark after becoming aware of the FyreTV registration, but that his "goal was customers . . . if they search for Amazon Fire TV, if they search for our product I did not want them to first come across a porn site and have that experience." The district court, upon reviewing that testimony, concluded that no reasonable juror could view it and conclude that Amazon had any "bad faith (or other) intent to deceive consumers or drive Wreal out of the market." That conclusion was erroneous. The record evidence established that when Amazon launched the fireTV, it specifically tried to flood the market with advertising in an attempt to lower awareness of Wreal's similarly named mark. We take Amazon at its word, and we therefore conclude that the intent factor weighs heavily in favor of Wreal.

G. Actual Confusion

[53] "[E]vidence of actual confusion is the best evidence of a likelihood of confusion." *Frehling* 192 F.3d at 1340. But the presence of such evidence is obviously not a prerequisite to a finding of likelihood of confusion, as it is one of seven factors considered in the likelihood-of-confusion determination. *Id.* Indeed, "it is not necessary to show actual confusion. One merely has to show that the likelihood of confusion exists." *World Carpets, Inc. v. Dick Littrell's New World Carpets*, 438 F.2d 482, 489 (5th Cir. 1971). But in assessing the quantum of actual confusion required for a finding in the plaintiff's favor, even a "very little" amount of actual confusion is highly probative. *See id.*

[54] "The strength of such evidence depends on 'the number of instances of confusion,' 'the kinds of persons confused' and the 'degree of confusion.' " *Sovereign Mil. Hospitaller v. Fla. Priory of the Knights*, 809 F.3d 1171, 1189 (11th Cir. 2015). But even more important than the *number* of persons confused is the *type* of person confused; our "caselaw makes plain that the consumers of the relevant product or service, especially the mark holder's customers, turn the key." *Caliber Auto. Liquidators, Inc. v. Premier Chrysler, Jeep, Dodge, LLC*, 605 F.3d 931, 936 (11th Cir. 2010). Indeed, we have accorded "substantial weight" to any instances of "evidence that actual customers were confused by the use of a mark as opposed to other categories of people." *Aronowitz v. Health-Chem Corp.*, 513 F.3d 1229, 1240 (11th Cir. 2008).

[55] In reverse-confusion cases, evidence of forward confusion will usually be probative. *See Freedom Card, Inc. v. JPMorgan Chase & Co.*, 432 F.3d 463, 473 (3d Cir. 2005). But even more relevant is direct evidence of *reverse* confusion—i.e., evidence that consumers of the plaintiff's more senior mark became confused as to its source following the launch of the defendant's more junior mark. *See Sterling Drug, Inc. v. Bayer AG*, 14 F.3d 733, 741 (2d Cir. 1994) (noting that, in a reverse-confusion claim, "the relevant issue is whether consumers mistakenly believe that the senior user's products actually originate with the junior user" and that "it is appropriate to survey the senior user's customers"). Survey

evidence—while perhaps more accurately described as circumstantial evidence of confusion[16] rather than direct evidence—is, of course, admissible. But because the theory of reverse confusion depends on market saturation by the defendant's mark, a reliable survey "cannot be run in a reverse confusion case prior to the junior user's saturation of the market with its mark because, until that time, consumers have not been exposed to the relatively large advertising and promotion of the junior user that is the hallmark of a reverse confusion case." 4 McCarthy, *supra*, § 23:10.

[56] The record evidence here contains some evidence of actual confusion. For example, Wreal introduced evidence that one of its customers asked over Twitter, "Did you guys just merge with Amazon?" And one of Amazon's customers communicated with Amazon to ask whether he could access "adult content" on his Amazon "fyre" TV. Both instances directly suggest reverse confusion; the first consumer believed Amazon had purchased Wreal's trademark, and the second consumer contacted Amazon to inquire about Wreal's product.[17] But these are the only two true instances of confusion present in the record.[18]

[57] Amazon and Wreal both also introduced survey evidence regarding the rate of confusion. Dr. Thomas Maronick, who testified for Wreal at the preliminary injunction hearing, conducted a preliminary survey in April 2014 and found "very low consumer confusion" between FyreTV and fireTV. Dr. Maronick also testified that awareness of the FyreTV mark was "very low." In a similar vein, Dr. Dan Sarel, Amazon's expert, conducted a consumer survey and found a confusion rate of one percent, which he testified was "nonexistent" and "statistically insignificant."

[58] We hesitate to give significant weight to either the specifically identified instances of actual confusion or the surveys. Amazon introduced evidence from an expert witness, Peter Lehman, that tended to suggest that watching pornography is an inherently shameful act, and that consumers of pornography are less likely to report their consumption than consumers of other media. With this testimony in mind, we turn first to the first two instances of actual confusion.

[59] Our caselaw is clear that the "the quantum of evidence needed to show actual confusion is relatively small." *Jellibeans, Inc.*, 716 F.2d at 845. But our caselaw imposes no hard-and-fast rule regarding the number of instances required to prevail. *See Caliber Auto. Liquidators*, 605 F.3d at 937. "Rather, the court must evaluate the evidence of actual confusion in the light of the totality of the circumstances involved." *AmBrit*, 812 F.2d at 1543; *accord World Carpets*, 438 F.2d at 489 (5th Cir. 1971) ("[R]eason tells us that while very little proof of actual confusion would be necessary to prove the likelihood of confusion, an almost overwhelming amount of proof would be necessary to refute such proof.").

[60] Our previous decisions serve as guides. In *Safeway Stores*, when reviewing a district court's findings following a bench trial, we held that a mere two instances of confusion from relevant consumers was worthy of consideration. 675 F.2d at 1166–67, *abrogation recognized on other grounds, PlayNation Play Sys., Inc. v. Velex Corp.*, 924 F.3d 1159, 1166 (11th Cir. 2019). Additionally, in *Caliber Automotive*, we

---

[16] *See* Harvey S. Perlman, *The Restatement of the Law of Unfair Competition: A Work in Progress*, 80 Trademark Rep. 461, 472 (1990) ("Most surveys do not measure actual confusion. Surveys only give us information about a controlled and artificial world from which we are asked to draw inferences about the real world.").

[17] The magistrate judge (and, by its adoption, the district court) discounted both pieces of evidence, concluding that neither consumer was *actually* confused. As already discussed in footnote 5, *supra*, this amounted to an improper credibility determination that invaded the province of the jury.

[18] Wreal identified other pieces of evidence to the district court, but our review of the record indicates that they do not represent direct evidence of actual confusion. For example, one of Wreal's customers said, "I plan to buy the new Amazon FireTV box (I know it is NOT related to you guys— although confusion over the name may bring Fyretv some more customers and maybe a domain name sale windfall—more power to you!) Will this new Amazon streaming device have a private channel installation of FyreTV in the near future?"

stated that two instances of confusion among professional buyers weighed in the plaintiff's favor at the summary judgment stage. 605 F.3d at 937–38. In contrast, in *Frehling*, when reversing the district court's entry of judgment for the defendant following a bench trial, we concluded that a single instance of actual confusion from a "professional buyer" while "sufficient to raise an inference of actual confusion" was "not sufficiently dispositive so as to favor either side in an appreciable fashion." 192 F.3d at 1341.

[61] Perhaps most analogous are our decisions in *AmBrit* and *PlayNation*. In *AmBrit* as in this case, the relevant products (ice cream novelties there and set-top boxes, here) were sold to the general public, not professional buyers, and had a "high volume of sales" (at least, such is the case for the fireTV here). *See* 812 F.2d at 1544. The district court in *AmBrit*, after a bench trial, found that four instances of actual confusion supported a finding of actual confusion in favor of the plaintiff. *See id.* And we, reviewing for clear error, affirmed. *See id.* at 1544–45. Similarly, in *PlayNation*, the products at issue were playground equipment and pull-up bars which, like ice cream novelties and set-top boxes, are sold to the general public rather than to professional buyers. *See* 924 F.3d at 1164. Following a bench trial, the district court found that just two instances of actual confusion—in which the plaintiff's customers contacted the defendant for customer support—were sufficient to support a finding of actual confusion. *See id.* at 1167. On appeal, we affirmed the ruling. *See id.* at 1167–68.

[62] As in *AmBrit* and *PlayNation*, the reported instances of confusion in this case are relatively few. Even after years of litigation, Wreal is able to identify only two instances of potential or actual Wreal consumers being confused as to the source of its product. But the record also contains expert testimony that consumers of pornography are less likely to report their consumption than consumers of other media. Given that we are obliged to "evaluate the evidence of actual confusion in the light of the totality of the circumstances involved," *AmBrit*, 812 F.2d at 1543, we find it appropriate here to take that expert testimony into account when considering the number of reported instances of actual confusion. Although a close call, we conclude that the two reported instances of actual confusion here are sufficient to make the issue one of triable fact and thus weighs in Wreal's favor.

[63] Turning to the survey evidence, both parties advance a number of arguments either for or against the consideration of the surveys. But given that we conclude that the instances of actual confusion present in the record are sufficient to push this factor in Wreal's favor, we conclude that it is unnecessary to also address the issue of survey evidence especially as a plaintiff need not present survey evidence in a trademark claim in order to escape summary judgment. *See PlayNation*, 924 F.3d at 1169 ("Lack of survey evidence does not weigh against the plaintiff when determining likelihood of confusion.") . . . . And, as already noted above, at least in our circuit, survey evidence in trademark actions has always been viewed with a skeptical eye. *See Frehling*, 192 F.3d at 1341 n.5 ("This Circuit . . . has moved away from relying on survey evidence [in trademark cases]."); *Safeway Stores*, 675 F.2d at 1167 n.10 (noting that our circuit has "followed the trend of cases in the former Fifth Circuit, in which market surveys have not fared well as evidence in trademark cases").

IV. CONCLUSION

[64] This case addresses the application of the seven likelihood-of-confusion factors to a reverse-confusion trademark infringement case. Although some of those factors are analyzed and applied in the same way in both reverse-confusion cases and the more familiar forward-confusion cases, there are important differences in how other factors are analyzed and applied that stem from the fact that the harm and the theory of infringement differ between forward and reverse confusion.

[65] Here, the record evidence establishes that Amazon acquired actual knowledge of Wreal's registered trademark and still launched a product line with a phonetically similar name. The two marks at issue are nearly identical, the commercial strength of Amazon's mark is consistent with Wreal's theory of recovery, the parties' services are the kind that a reasonable consumer could attribute to a single source, and the record establishes that Amazon intended to swamp the market with its advertising campaign. Furthermore, Wreal has identified two consumers who a reasonable juror could conclude were confused by Amazon's chosen mark.

[66] As noted throughout our decision, there is no mechanical formula for applying the seven factors relating to likelihood of confusion. But when considering all seven factors as they apply to a theory of reverse confusion and taking all the circumstances of this case into account on the record before us, we conclude that they weigh heavily in favor of Wreal and that the district court erred when it entered summary judgment in Amazon's favor. We therefore reverse the district court's order. This is not to say that Amazon may not ultimately prevail on the merits; rather, it must do so before a jury.

REVERSED AND REMANDED.

Comments and Questions

1. *Trademark strength and reverse confusion*. In *A & H Sportswear, Inc. v. Victoria's Secret Stores, Inc.*, 237 F.3d 198, 231-32 (3d Cir. 2000), the Third Circuit discussed the relation between commercial and conceptual strength in the context of a reverse confusion claim. This discussion is excerpted below. Is the court's reasoning persuasive?

a. Commercial Strength

Where the greater advertising originates from the senior user, we are more likely to see a case of direct confusion; if the greater advertising originates from the junior user, reverse confusion is more likely . . . .

Logically, then, in a direct confusion claim, a plaintiff with a commercially strong mark is more likely to prevail than a plaintiff with a commercially weak mark. Conversely, in a reverse confusion claim, a plaintiff with a commercially weak mark is more likely to prevail than a plaintiff with a stronger mark, and this is particularly true when the plaintiff's weaker mark is pitted against a defendant with a far stronger mark . . . . "[T]he lack of commercial strength of the smaller senior user's mark is to be given less weight in the analysis because it is the strength of the larger, junior user's mark which results in reverse confusion." *Commerce Nat'l Ins. Servs., Inc. v. Commerce Ins. Agency, Inc.*, 214 F.3d 432, 444 (3d Cir. 2000) . . . .

Therefore, in a reverse confusion claim, a court should analyze the "commercial strength" factor in terms of (1) the commercial strength of the junior user as compared to the senior user; and (2) any advertising or marketing campaign by the junior user that has resulted in a saturation in the public awareness of the junior user's mark.

b. Distinctiveness or Conceptual Strength

. . . .

As stated above, in the paradigmatic reverse confusion case, the senior user has a commercially weak mark when compared with the junior user's commercially strong mark. When it comes to conceptual strength, however, we believe that, just as in direct confusion cases, a strong mark should weigh in favor of a senior user . . . .

In *H. Lubovsky, Inc. v. Esprit de Corp.*, 627 F.Supp. 483 (S.D.N.Y. 1986), the court explained that conceptual distinctiveness was relevant in the same way for a reverse confusion claim because "if a customer saw a doll in a toy store bearing a strong familiar trademark like 'Exxon,' he might well assume that the oil company had gone into the toy business; if, on the other hand, he saw a doll bearing a familiar but weak laudatory trademark like Merit, he would be unlikely to assume that it is connected with the similarly named gasoline or cigarettes." *Id.* at 487; *see also* Long & Marks, *supra*, at 22.

The *H. Lubovsky* logic resonates, for it makes more sense to hold that conceptual strength, unlike commercial strength, works in the plaintiff's favor. That is, if we were to apply the rule stated above for commercial strength, i.e., weighing weakness in the plaintiff's favor, we would bring about the perverse result that less imaginative marks would be more likely to win reverse confusion claims than arbitrary or fanciful ones. We therefore hold that, as in direct confusion claims, a district court should weigh a conceptually strong mark in the plaintiff's favor, particularly when the mark is of such a

419

distinctive character that, coupled with the relative similarity of the plaintiff's and defendant's marks, a consumer viewing the plaintiff's product is likely to assume that such a mark would only have been adopted by a single source—i.e., the defendant.

2. *Other Examples of Reverse Confusion Found. See, e.g.,* Fleet Feet, Inc. v. Nike Inc., 419 F.Supp.3d 919 (M.D.N.C. 2019), *appeal dismissed and remanded*, 986 F.3d 458 (4th Cir. 2021), and *vacated*, No. 19 Civ. 885, 2021 WL 4067544 (M.D.N.C. Apr. 6, 2021) (finding that defendant's use of the phrase "Sport Changes Everything" would cause reverse confusion with plaintiff, seller of running and fitness merchandise, in light of plaintiff's prior use of the phrases "Change Everything" and "Running Changes Everything"); *H. Lubovsky, Inc. v. Esprit De Corp.*, 627 F. Supp. 483, 228 U.S.P.Q. (BNA) 814 (S.D.N.Y. 1986) (defendant's extension of ESPRIT brand to women's shoes created reverse confusion with plaintiff's prior use of same mark for same products); *Tanel Corp. v. Reebok Intern., Ltd.*, 774 F. Supp. 49 (D. Mass. 1990) (defendant's junior use of 360 DEGREES for shoes created reverse confusion with small company's senior use of same mark for same products).

3. *Examples of Reverse Confusion Not Found. See, e.g,* Surfvivor Media, Inc. v. Survivor Productions, 406 F.3d 625 (9th Cir. 2005) (SURVIVOR television show did not create reverse confusion with SURFVIVOR for beach-themed products); *Harlem Wizards Entertainment Basketball, Inc. v. NBA Properties, Inc.*, 952 F. Supp. 1084 (D.N.J. 1997) (NBA team's adoption of name WASHINGTON WIZARDS would not create reverse confusion with HARLEM WIZARDS trick basketball team); *Pump, Inc. v. Collins Management, Inc.*, 746 F. Supp. 1159 (D. Mass. 1990) (Rock band Aerosmith's album entitled "Pump" did not create confusion with little-known rock band by same name where visual displays of marks and contexts in which they were used were different); *Lobo Enterprises, Inc. v. Tunnel, Inc.*, 693 F. Supp. 71 (S.D.N.Y. 1988) (large nightclub TUNNEL did not create reverse confusion with small gay bar TUNNEL BAR where clienteles of club and bar were sufficiently different to preclude reverse confusion); *Andy Warhol Enterprises, Inc. v. Time Inc.*, 700 F. Supp. 760 (S.D.N.Y. 1988) (*People Magazine*'s use of "Interview" as the descriptive heading of its interview section did not create reverse confusion with magazine of same name where consumers would not believe that defendant published plaintiff's magazine).

9. Reverse Passing Off

"Reverse passing off" generally involves situations in which a "defendant falsely takes credit for another's goods or services," MCCARTHY § 25.6. More specifically, reverse passing off occurs when the defendant unauthorizedly passes off as its own product (or service) what was in fact made (or performed) by the plaintiff, perhaps to gain the goodwill that the plaintiff's product might generate for the defendant, perhaps to charge a higher price to unsuspecting consumers, or perhaps simply to meet a production deadline. For example, a defendant who unauthorizedly rebottles (or simply relabels) a plaintiff's shampoo under a new brand name could be liable for reverse passing off. Who does this sort of thing? See, for a recent example, *DJ Direct, Inc. v. Margaliot*, 512 F. Supp. 3d 396 (E.D.N.Y. 2021), in which the defendant hot glued a metallic "Amasing" label directly over the plaintiff's KARAOKING mark on karaoke machines and then listed those rebranded machines on Amazon:

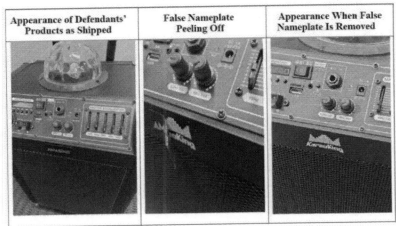

Appearance of Defendants' Products as Shipped	False Nameplate Peeling Off	Appearance When False Nameplate Is Removed

The court found reverse passing off and granted the plaintiff's motion for a preliminary injunction. *Id.* at 414–417. *Cf. id.* at 415 ("Although, as Defendants argue, Plaintiff's supplier manufactured the tangible goods offered for sale in this case, the fact that Plaintiff ordered the machines in question to be built to its specifications and to bear the KaraoKing mark, and that it provided customer service and support through its website, www.karaoking.net, supports the conclusion that Plaintiff commissioned the machines and stood behind their production."). For another example, see *Industria de Diseo Textil SA. v. Thiliko LLC*, No. 23 Civ. 47 (S.D.N.Y.) (complaint filed Jan. 4, 2023), in which the global fast-fashion retailer Zara sued the defendant Thilikó for, among other things, purchasing Zara's goods, replacing all Zara labelling with defendant's own labelling, and reselling those goods as its own (at significantly higher prices). The defendant also used on its webpage Zara's copyrighted images, as shown below.

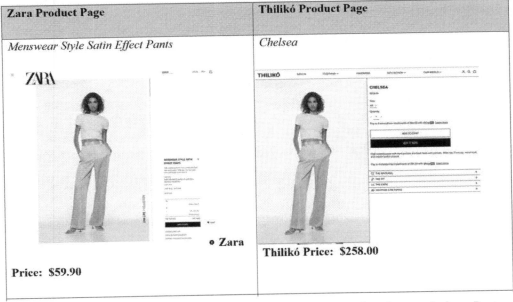

Zara Product Page	Thilikó Product Page
Menswear Style Satin Effect Pants	*Chelsea*
Price: $59.90	Thilikó Price: $258.00

Reverse passing off is a very rare cause of action, even more so after the case below, *Dastar Corp. v. Twentieth Century Fox Film Corp.*, 539 U.S. 23 (2003). We consider reverse passing off and the *Dastar* case because of the profound policy questions implicated by the cause of action and the facts of the *Dastar* case. It is one thing to provide a reverse passing off cause of action when someone unauthorizedly rebottles or relabels someone else's shampoo without attribution, but what about when someone unauthorizedly restates someone else's ideas or expression without attribution? Should trademark law and specifically the concept of "reverse passing off" provide a cause of action for plagiarism? If not, why should we treat ideas and expression differently?

Consider a related problem. One advantage that trademark protection enjoys over copyright or patent protection is that trademark protection is unlimited in time, provided that the trademark owner continue to use the mark in commerce. Thus, when patent or copyright protection of a product feature expires, the patent or copyright owner may continue to exert control over that feature through trademark law (if the feature satisfies the various requirements of trademark protection). This raises significant concerns. For example, Disney owns the Mickey Mouse image mark, whose registration is shown below:

Int. Cl.: 28

Prior U.S. Cls.: 22, 23, 38, and 50

United States Patent and Trademark Office

Reg. No. 3,619,662
Registered May 12, 2009

TRADEMARK
PRINCIPAL REGISTER

DISNEY ENTERPRISES, INC. (DELAWARE COR-
PORATION)
500 SOUTH BUENA VISTA STREET
BURBANK, CA 91521

FOR: GAMES, NAMELY, ACTION SKILL
GAMES, BOARD GAMES, MANIPULATIVE
GAMES; PLAYTHINGS, NAMELY, ACTION FIG-
URES AND ACCESSORIES THEREFOR, BEAN BAG
DOLLS, PLUSH TOYS, BATH TOYS, BUILDING
BLOCKS, DOLLS AND DOLL CLOTHING, DOLL
PLAYSETS, CRIB TOYS, ELECTRIC ACTION TOYS,
PARTY FAVORS IN THE NATURE OF SMALL
TOYS, MULTIPLE ACTIVITY TOYS, WIND-UP
TOYS, TOY VEHICLES, TOY CARS, TOY TRUCKS,

TOY ROCKETS, MUSICAL TOYS, TOY FIGURINES,
PUPPETS, FACE MASKS, HAND-HELD UNITS FOR
PLAYING ELECTRONIC GAMES, IN CLASS 28 (U.S.
CLS. 22, 23, 38 AND 50).

FIRST USE 3-28-2008; IN COMMERCE 3-28-2008.

OWNER OF U.S. REG. NOS. 2,461,981, 2,781,641,
AND OTHERS.

SN 76-588,173, FILED 4-19-2004.

TEJBIR SINGH, EXAMINING ATTORNEY

At some point, Disney's copyright rights in the countless cartoons in which Mickey Mouse is depicted will begin to expire. *See* Brooks Barnes, *Mickey's Copyright Adventure: Early Disney Creation Will Soon Be Public Property*, N.Y. TIMES, Dec. 27, 2022 (discussing the legal aspects of the expiration beginning in 2024 of Disney's copyright rights in Steamboat Willie and subsequent incarnations of Mickey Mouse). But can Disney then use its trademark rights in the image of the character to prevent others from reproducing these cartoons? With copyright law, the public agrees to grant short-term exclusive rights to the author of a work in order to incentivize authorship, but an exceedingly important part of that bargain is that these rights will eventually expire and the work will be dedicated to the public domain, free for anyone to use in any way. Should trademark rights be allowed to trump this basic bargain? For an analysis of this question with respect to the Disney-owned intellectual property Winnie the Pooh, the earliest publications of which have already begun to join the public domain, see Jennifer Jenkins, *This Bear's For You! (Or, Is It?): Can Companies Use Copyright and Trademark To Claim Rights to Public Domain Works?*, DUKE CENTER FOR THE STUDY OF THE PUBLIC DOMAIN, Jan. 1, 2022, https://web.law.duke.edu/cspd/publicdomainday/2022/bcvpd/#fn6ref (https://perma.cc/W48P-3UK2).

As you read through the *Dastar* opinion, consider whether it resolves the question of whether Disney may continue to assert exclusive rights through trademark law after its copyright rights have expired.

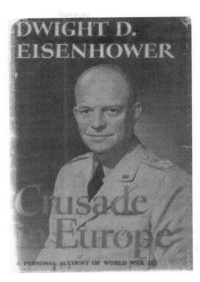

Dastar Corp. v. Twentieth Century Fox Film Corp.
539 U.S. 23 (2003)

Justice SCALIA delivered the opinion of the Court.

[1] In this case, we are asked to decide whether § 43(a) of the Lanham Act, 15 U.S.C. § 1125(a), prevents the unaccredited copying of a work, and if so, whether a court may double a profit award under § 1117(a), in order to deter future infringing conduct.

I

[2] In 1948, three and a half years after the German surrender at Reims, General Dwight D. Eisenhower completed Crusade in Europe, his written account of the allied campaign in Europe during World War II. Doubleday published the book, registered it with the Copyright Office in 1948, and granted exclusive television rights to an affiliate of respondent Twentieth Century Fox Film Corporation (Fox). Fox, in turn, arranged for Time, Inc., to produce a television series, also called Crusade in Europe, based on the book, and Time assigned its copyright in the series to Fox. The television series, consisting of 26 episodes, was first broadcast in 1949. It combined a soundtrack based on a narration of the book with film footage from the United States Army, Navy, and Coast Guard, the British Ministry of Information and War Office, the National Film Board of Canada, and unidentified "Newsreel Pool Cameramen." In 1975, Doubleday renewed the copyright on the book as the "'proprietor of copyright in a work made for hire.'" App. to Pet. for Cert. 9a. Fox, however, did not renew the copyright on the Crusade television series, which expired in 1977, leaving the television series in the public domain.

[3] In 1988, Fox reacquired the television rights in General Eisenhower's book, including the exclusive right to distribute the Crusade television series on video and to sublicense others to do so. Respondents SFM Entertainment and New Line Home Video, Inc., in turn, acquired from Fox the exclusive rights to distribute Crusade on video. SFM obtained the negatives of the original television series, restored them, and repackaged the series on videotape; New Line distributed the videotapes.

[4] Enter petitioner Dastar. In 1995, Dastar decided to expand its product line from music compact discs to videos. Anticipating renewed interest in World War II on the 50th anniversary of the war's end, Dastar released a video set entitled World War II Campaigns in Europe. To make Campaigns, Dastar purchased eight beta cam tapes of the *original* version of the Crusade television series, which is in the public domain, copied them, and then edited the series. Dastar's Campaigns series is slightly more than half as long as the original Crusade television series. Dastar substituted a new opening sequence, credit page, and final closing for those of the Crusade television series; inserted new chapter-title sequences and narrated chapter introductions; moved the "recap" in the Crusade television series to the beginning and retitled it as a "preview"; and removed references to and images of the book. Dastar created new packaging for its Campaigns series and (as already noted) a new title.

[5] Dastar manufactured and sold the Campaigns video set as its own product. The advertising states: "Produced and Distributed by: *Entertainment Distributing* " (which is owned by Dastar), and makes no reference to the Crusade television series. Similarly, the screen credits state "DASTAR CORP presents" and "an ENTERTAINMENT DISTRIBUTING Production," and list as executive producer, producer, and associate producer employees of Dastar. Supp.App. 2–3, 30. The Campaigns videos themselves also make no reference to the Crusade television series, New Line's Crusade videotapes, or the book. Dastar sells its Campaigns videos to Sam's Club, Costco, Best Buy, and other retailers and mail-order companies for $25 per set, substantially less than New Line's video set.

[6] In 1998, respondents Fox, SFM, and New Line brought this action alleging that Dastar's sale of its Campaigns video set infringes Doubleday's copyright in General Eisenhower's book and, thus, their exclusive television rights in the book. Respondents later amended their complaint to add claims that Dastar's sale of Campaigns "without proper credit" to the Crusade television series constitutes "reverse passing off"[1] in violation of § 43(a) of the Lanham Act, 15 U.S.C. § 1125(a), and in violation of state unfair-competition law. App. to Pet. for Cert. 31a. On cross-motions for summary judgment, the District Court found for respondents on all three counts, *id.,* at 54a–55a, treating its resolution of the Lanham Act claim as controlling on the state-law unfair-competition claim because "the ultimate test under both is whether the public is likely to be deceived or confused," *id.,* at 54a. The court awarded Dastar's profits to respondents and doubled them pursuant to § 35 of the Lanham Act, 15 U.S.C. § 1117(a), to deter future infringing conduct by petitioner.

[7] The Court of Appeals for the Ninth Circuit affirmed the judgment for respondents on the Lanham Act claim, but reversed as to the copyright claim and remanded. 34 Fed.Appx. 312, 316 (2002). (It said nothing with regard to the state-law claim.) With respect to the Lanham Act claim, the Court of Appeals reasoned that "Dastar copied substantially the entire *Crusade in Europe* series created by Twentieth Century Fox, labeled the resulting product with a different name and marketed it without attribution to Fox[, and] therefore committed a 'bodily appropriation' of Fox's series." *Id.,* at 314. It concluded that "Dastar's 'bodily appropriation' of Fox's original [television] series is sufficient to establish the reverse passing off." *Ibid.*[2] The court also affirmed the District Court's award under the Lanham Act of twice Dastar's profits. We granted certiorari. 537 U.S. 1099 (2003).

II

[8] The Lanham Act was intended to make "actionable the deceptive and misleading use of marks," and "to protect persons engaged in . . . commerce against unfair competition." 15 U.S.C. § 1127. While much of the Lanham Act addresses the registration, use, and infringement of trademarks and related marks, § 43(a), 15 U.S.C. § 1125(a) is one of the few provisions that goes beyond trademark protection. As originally enacted, § 43(a) created a federal remedy against a person who used in commerce either "a false designation of origin, or any false description or representation" in connection with "any goods or services." 60 Stat. 441. As the Second Circuit accurately observed with regard to the original enactment, however—and as remains true after the 1988 revision—§ 43(a) "does not have boundless application as a remedy for unfair trade practices," *Alfred Dunhill, Ltd. v. Interstate Cigar Co.,* 499 F.2d

---

[1] Passing off (or palming off, as it is sometimes called) occurs when a producer misrepresents his own goods or services as someone else's. See, *e.g., O. & W. Thum Co. v. Dickinson,* 245 F. 609, 621 (C.A.6 1917). "Reverse passing off," as its name implies, is the opposite: The producer misrepresents someone else's goods or services as his own. See, *e.g., Williams v. Curtiss-Wright Corp.,* 691 F.2d 168, 172 (C.A.3 1982).

[2] As for the copyright claim, the Ninth Circuit held that the tax treatment General Eisenhower sought for his manuscript of the book created a triable issue as to whether he intended the book to be a work for hire, and thus as to whether Doubleday properly renewed the copyright in 1976. See 34 Fed.Appx., at 314. The copyright issue is still the subject of litigation, but is not before us. We express no opinion as to whether petitioner's product would infringe a valid copyright in General Eisenhower's book.

232, 237 (C.A.2 1974). "[B]ecause of its inherently limited wording, § 43(a) can never be a federal 'codification' of the overall law of 'unfair competition,'" 4 J. McCarthy, Trademarks and Unfair Competition § 27:7, p. 27–14 (4th ed. 2002) (McCarthy), but can apply only to certain unfair trade practices prohibited by its text.

. . . .

[9] Thus, as it comes to us, the gravamen of respondents' claim is that, in marketing and selling Campaigns as its own product without acknowledging its nearly wholesale reliance on the Crusade television series, Dastar has made a "false designation of origin, false or misleading description of fact, or false or misleading representation of fact, which . . . is likely to cause confusion . . . as to the origin . . . of his or her goods." § 43(a). That claim would undoubtedly be sustained if Dastar had bought some of New Line's Crusade videotapes and merely repackaged them as its own. Dastar's alleged wrongdoing, however, is vastly different: It took a creative work in the public domain—the Crusade television series—copied it, made modifications (arguably minor), and produced its very own series of videotapes. If "origin" refers only to the manufacturer or producer of the physical "goods" that are made available to the public (in this case the videotapes), Dastar was the origin. If, however, "origin" includes the creator of the underlying work that Dastar copied, then someone else (perhaps Fox) was the origin of Dastar's product. At bottom, we must decide what § 43(a)(1)(A) of the Lanham Act means by the "origin" of "goods."

III

[10] The dictionary definition of "origin" is "[t]he fact or process of coming into being from a source," and "[t]hat from which anything primarily proceeds; source." Webster's New International Dictionary 1720–1721 (2d ed. 1949). And the dictionary definition of "goods" (as relevant here) is "[w]ares; merchandise." *Id.,* at 1079. We think the most natural understanding of the "origin" of "goods"—the source of wares—is the producer of the tangible product sold in the marketplace, in this case the physical Campaigns videotape sold by Dastar. The concept might be stretched . . . to include not only the actual producer, but also the trademark owner who commissioned or assumed responsibility for ("stood behind") production of the physical product. But as used in the Lanham Act, the phrase "origin of goods" is in our view incapable of connoting the person or entity that originated the ideas or communications that "goods" embody or contain. Such an extension would not only stretch the text, but it would be out of accord with the history and purpose of the Lanham Act and inconsistent with precedent.

[11] Section 43(a) of the Lanham Act prohibits actions like trademark infringement that deceive consumers and impair a producer's goodwill. It forbids, for example, the Coca-Cola Company's passing off its product as Pepsi-Cola or reverse passing off Pepsi-Cola as its product. But the brand-loyal consumer who prefers the drink that the Coca-Cola Company or PepsiCo sells, while he believes that that company produced (or at least stands behind the production of) that product, surely does not necessarily believe that that company was the "origin" of the drink in the sense that it was the very first to devise the formula. The consumer who buys a branded product does not automatically assume that the brand-name company is the same entity that came up with the idea for the product, or designed the product—and typically does not care whether it is. The words of the Lanham Act should not be stretched to cover matters that are typically of no consequence to purchasers.

[12] It could be argued, perhaps, that the reality of purchaser concern is different for what might be called a communicative product—one that is valued not primarily for its physical qualities, such as a hammer, but for the intellectual content that it conveys, such as a book or, as here, a video. The purchaser of a novel is interested not merely, if at all, in the identity of the producer of the physical tome (the publisher), but also, and indeed primarily, in the identity of the creator of the story it conveys (the author). And the author, of course, has at least as much interest in avoiding passing off (or reverse passing off) of his creation as does the publisher. For such a communicative product (the argument goes) "origin of goods" in § 43(a) must be deemed to include not merely the producer of the physical item (the publishing house Farrar, Straus and Giroux, or the video producer Dastar) but also the creator of the content that the physical item conveys (the author Tom Wolfe, or—assertedly—respondents).

[13] The problem with this argument according special treatment to communicative products is that it causes the Lanham Act to conflict with the law of copyright, which addresses that subject specifically. The right to copy, and to copy without attribution, once a copyright has expired, like "the right to make [an article whose patent has expired]—including the right to make it in precisely the shape it carried when patented—passes to the public." *Sears, Roebuck & Co. v. Stiffel Co.,* 376 U.S. 225, 230 (1964); *see also Kellogg Co. v. National Biscuit Co.,* 305 U.S. 111, 121–122 (1938). "In general, unless an intellectual property right such as a patent or copyright protects an item, it will be subject to copying." *TrafFix Devices, Inc. v. Marketing Displays, Inc.,* 532 U.S. 23, 29 (2001). The rights of a patentee or copyright holder are part of a "carefully crafted bargain," *Bonito Boats, Inc. v. Thunder Craft Boats, Inc.,* 489 U.S. 141, 150–151 (1989), under which, once the patent or copyright monopoly has expired, the public may use the invention or work at will and without attribution. Thus, in construing the Lanham Act, we have been "careful to caution against misuse or over-extension" of trademark and related protections into areas traditionally occupied by patent or copyright. *TrafFix,* 532 U.S., at 29. "The Lanham Act," we have said, "does not exist to reward manufacturers for their innovation in creating a particular device; that is the purpose of the patent law and its period of exclusivity." *Id.,* at 34. Federal trademark law "has no necessary relation to invention or discovery," *In re Trade–Mark Cases,* 100 U.S. 82, 94 (1879), but rather, by preventing competitors from copying "a source-identifying mark," "reduce[s] the customer's costs of shopping and making purchasing decisions," and "helps assure a producer that it (and not an imitating competitor) will reap the financial, reputation-related rewards associated with a desirable product," *Qualitex Co. v. Jacobson Products Co.,* 514 U.S. 159, 163–164 (1995) (internal quotation marks and citation omitted). Assuming for the sake of argument that Dastar's representation of itself as the "Producer" of its videos amounted to a representation that it originated the creative work conveyed by the videos, allowing a cause of action under § 43(a) for that representation would create a species of mutant copyright law that limits the public's "federal right to 'copy and to use'" expired copyrights, *Bonito Boats, supra,* at 165, 109 S.Ct. 971.

[14] When Congress has wished to create such an addition to the law of copyright, it has done so with much more specificity than the Lanham Act's ambiguous use of "origin." The Visual Artists Rights Act of 1990, § 603(a), 104 Stat. 5128, provides that the author of an artistic work "shall have the right . . . to claim authorship of that work." 17 U.S.C. § 106A(a)(1)(A). That express right of attribution is carefully limited and focused: It attaches only to specified "work[s] of visual art," § 101, is personal to the artist, §§ 106A(b) and (e), and endures only for "the life of the author," § 106A(d)(1). Recognizing in § 43(a) a cause of action for misrepresentation of authorship of noncopyrighted works (visual or otherwise) would render these limitations superfluous. A statutory interpretation that renders another statute superfluous is of course to be avoided. *E.g., Mackey v. Lanier Collection Agency & Service, Inc.,* 486 U.S. 825, 837, and n. 11 (1988).

[15] Reading "origin" in § 43(a) to require attribution of uncopyrighted materials would pose serious practical problems. Without a copyrighted work as the basepoint, the word "origin" has no discernable limits. A video of the MGM film Carmen Jones, after its copyright has expired, would presumably require attribution not just to MGM, but to Oscar Hammerstein II (who wrote the musical on which the film was based), to Georges Bizet (who wrote the opera on which the musical was based), and to Prosper Merimee (who wrote the novel on which the opera was based). In many cases, figuring out who is in the line of "origin" would be no simple task. Indeed, in the present case it is far from clear that respondents have that status. Neither SFM nor New Line had anything to do with the production of the Crusade television series—they merely were licensed to distribute the video version. While Fox might have a claim to being in the line of origin, its involvement with the creation of the television series was limited at best. Time, Inc., was the principal, if not the exclusive, creator, albeit under arrangement with Fox. And of course it was neither Fox nor Time, Inc., that shot the film used in the Crusade television series. Rather, that footage came from the United States Army, Navy, and Coast Guard, the British Ministry of Information and War Office, the National Film Board of Canada, and unidentified "Newsreel Pool Cameramen." If anyone has a claim to being the *original* creator of the material used in both the Crusade television series and the Campaigns videotapes, it would be those groups, rather than Fox. We do not think the Lanham Act requires this search for the source of the Nile and all its tributaries.

[16] Another practical difficulty of adopting a special definition of "origin" for communicative products is that it places the manufacturers of those products in a difficult position. On the one hand, they would face Lanham Act liability for *failing* to credit the creator of a work on which their lawful copies are based; and on the other hand they could face Lanham Act liability for *crediting* the creator if that should be regarded as implying the creator's "sponsorship or approval" of the copy, 15 U.S.C. § 1125(a)(1)(A). In this case, for example, if Dastar had simply "copied [the television series] as Crusade in Europe and sold it as Crusade in Europe," without changing the title or packaging (including the original credits to Fox), it is hard to have confidence in respondents' assurance that they "would not be here on a Lanham Act cause of action," Tr. of Oral Arg. 35.

[17] Finally, reading § 43(a) of the Lanham Act as creating a cause of action for, in effect, plagiarism—the use of otherwise unprotected works and inventions without attribution—would be hard to reconcile with our previous decisions. For example, in *Wal–Mart Stores, Inc. v. Samara Brothers, Inc.,* 529 U.S. 205 (2000), we considered whether product-design trade dress can ever be inherently distinctive. Wal–Mart produced "knockoffs" of children's clothes designed and manufactured by Samara Brothers, containing only "minor modifications" of the original designs. *Id.,* at 208. We concluded that the designs could not be protected under § 43(a) without a showing that they had acquired "secondary meaning," *id.,* at 214, so that they "'identify the source of the product rather than the product itself,'" *id.,* at 211 (quoting *Inwood Laboratories, Inc. v. Ives Laboratories, Inc.,* 456 U.S. 844, 851, n. 11 (1982)). This carefully considered limitation would be entirely pointless if the "original" producer could turn around and pursue a reverse-passing-off claim under exactly the same provision of the Lanham Act. Samara would merely have had to argue that it was the "origin" of the designs that Wal–Mart was selling as its own line. It was not, because "origin of goods" in the Lanham Act referred to the producer of the clothes, and not the producer of the (potentially) copyrightable or patentable designs that the clothes embodied.

[18] Similarly under respondents' theory, the "origin of goods" provision of § 43(a) would have supported the suit that we rejected in *Bonito Boats,* 489 U.S. 141, where the defendants had used molds to duplicate the plaintiff's unpatented boat hulls (apparently without crediting the plaintiff). And it would have supported the suit we rejected in *TrafFix,* 532 U.S. 23: The plaintiff, whose patents on flexible road signs had expired, and who could not prevail on a trade-dress claim under § 43(a) because the features of the signs were functional, would have had a reverse-passing-off claim for unattributed copying of his design.

[19] In sum, reading the phrase "origin of goods" in the Lanham Act in accordance with the Act's common-law foundations (which were *not* designed to protect originality or creativity), and in light of the copyright and patent laws (which *were*), we conclude that the phrase refers to the producer of the tangible goods that are offered for sale, and not to the author of any idea, concept, or communication embodied in those goods. Cf. 17 U.S.C. § 202 (distinguishing between a copyrighted work and "any material object in which the work is embodied"). To hold otherwise would be akin to finding that § 43(a) created a species of perpetual patent and copyright, which Congress may not do. See *Eldred v. Ashcroft,* 537 U.S. 186, 208 (2003).

[20] The creative talent of the sort that lay behind the Campaigns videos is not left without protection. The original film footage used in the Crusade television series could have been copyrighted, see 17 U.S.C. § 102(a)(6), as was copyrighted (as a compilation) the Crusade television series, even though it included material from the public domain, see § 103(a). Had Fox renewed the copyright in the Crusade television series, it would have had an easy claim of copyright infringement. And respondents' contention that Campaigns infringes Doubleday's copyright in General Eisenhower's book is still a live question on remand. If, moreover, the producer of a video that substantially copied the Crusade series were, in advertising or promotion, to give purchasers the impression that the video was quite different from that series, then one or more of the respondents might have a cause of action—not for reverse passing off under the "confusion ... as to the origin" provision of § 43(a)(1)(A), but for misrepresentation under the "misrepresents the nature, characteristics [or] qualities" provision of § 43(a)(1)(B). For merely saying it is the producer of the video, however, no Lanham Act liability attaches to Dastar.

* * *

[21] Because we conclude that Dastar was the "origin" of the products it sold as its own, respondents cannot prevail on their Lanham Act claim. We thus have no occasion to consider whether the Lanham Act permitted an award of double petitioner's profits. The judgment of the Court of Appeals for the Ninth Circuit is reversed, and the case is remanded for further proceedings consistent with this opinion.

It is so ordered.

Justice BREYER took no part in the consideration or decision of this case.

Comments and Questions

1. Dastar *on remand*. On remand back to the Central District of California, the district court dismissed with prejudice Twentieth Century Fox's § 43(a) and state law unfair competition claims, and with that the litigation apparently ended. *See Twentieth Century Fox Film Corp. v. Dastar Corp.*, No. 98 Civ. 07189, 2003 WL 22669587 (C.D. Cal. Oct. 14, 2003).

2. Dastar *and the reverse passing off of "any idea, concept, or communication"*. In the wake of *Dastar*, courts have uniformly held that the "origin of goods" provision of Lanham Act § 43(a) cannot prevent the unattributed use of someone else's ideas or expression. Consider, for example, *LaPine v. Seinfeld*, 92 U.S.P.Q.2d 1428, 2009 WL 2902584 (S.D.N.Y. 2009), judgment aff'd, 375 Fed. Appx. 81, 96 U.S.P.Q.2d 1130 (2d Cir. 2010). The plaintiff Missy Chase Lapine, a trained chef, wrote a cook book entitled *The Sneaky Chef: Simple Strategies for Hiding Healthy Food in Kids' Favorite Meals*, which was published in April 2007 to mild success. The defendant Jessica Seinfeld, wife of Jerry Seinfeld, subsequently authored—or was credited as the author of—the book *Deceptively Delicious: Simple Secrets to Get Your Kids Eating Good Food*, which was published in October 2007 and reached number one on the *New York Times* bestseller list.

Lapine sued for, among other things, copyright infringement and reverse passing off. The court found no copyright infringement on the ground that the "total concept and feel" of the two cookbooks was dissimilar. *Id.* at *12. On the reverse passing off claim, the court explained:

> Plaintiffs' third claim for relief alleges unfair competition in violation of section 43(a) of the Lanham Act. Section 43(a)(1) prohibits any "misleading representation of fact which (A) is likely to cause confusion ... as to the origin ... of ... goods ... or (B) in commercial advertising or promotion, misrepresents the nature, characteristics, [or] qualities ... of his or her or another person's goods." 15 U.S.C.A. § 1125(a)(1) (West 1998). This claim, too, fails as a matter of law.

In *Dastar Corp. v. Twentieth Century Fox Film Corp.*, 539 U.S. 23, 123 S.Ct. 2041, 156 L.Ed.2d 18 (2003), the Supreme Court defined the "origin of goods" for section 43(a) purposes, holding that the phrase "refers to the producer of the tangible goods that are offered for sale, and not to the author of any idea, concept, or communication embodied in those goods." *Id.* at 37.[9] To do otherwise would place the Lanham Act in conflict with the copyright [and patent] law and "be akin to finding that § 43(a) created a species of perpetual patent and copyright, which Congress may not do." *Id.* The Court recognized that the Lanham Act was not intended to protect originality or creativity. *Id.*

Following *Dastar*, a plaintiff may be able to bring a section 43(a) violation based on a defendant's repackaging of plaintiff's material as its own. *Id.* at 31 (the claim "would undoubtedly be sustained if Dastar had bought some of New Line's Crusade videotapes and merely repackaged them as its own"); *see also Flaherty v. Filardi*, No. 03 Civ. 2167, 2009 WL 749570, at *9 (S.D.N.Y. Mar. 20, 2009) ("Had [Defendant] merely changed the cover page of the script to list himself as author and provide a new title, Plaintiff might have had a Lanham Act claim."). However, "the mere act of publishing a written work without proper attribution to its creative source is not actionable under the Lanham Act." *Wellnx Life Sciences Inc. v. Iovate Health Sciences Research Inc.*, 516 F.Supp.2d 270, 285 (S.D.N.Y. 2007). Plaintiffs have not alleged that Defendants took Plaintiffs' cookbook and repackaged it as their own, nor could the evidentiary record sustain such a claim because, as explained above, the works are not substantially similar.

Although Plaintiffs did not identify in the Complaint the Section 43 subdivision under which they assert their Lanham Act unfair competition claim, Plaintiffs argue that they are asserting a claim under Section 43(a)(1)(B), the false advertising subsection, and that *Dastar* does not foreclose that claim. This argument is unavailing. Plaintiffs' Lanham Act unfair competition claim is, at its core, the same as Plaintiffs' copyright claim—that Defendants took Plaintiff Lapine's ideas and used them in *Deceptively Delicious* without Plaintiffs' permission and without any attribution as to the source of the ideas and the work.

Plaintiffs' Section 43(a) claim is premised on their allegations that Seinfeld misappropriated Lapine's work in preparing *Deceptively Delicious* and that, consequently, Seinfeld's statements that *Deceptively Delicious* is the product of her own work and Defendants' claim of a copyright in that work constitute falsities because they "assign the entire credit for [*Deceptively Delicious*] and Lapine's property contained therein, to themselves, and fail to credit Lapine or her Book." (Compl.¶¶ 73–75.) Plaintiffs assert that the alleged misrepresentations that are likely to cause confusion or deception "*as to the origin* of [*Deceptively Delicious*] and Lapine's property contained therein." (*Id.* ¶ 76 (emphasis supplied).) This is precisely the type of claim that is precluded by *Dastar*, and the Court finds persuasive those decisions holding that "a failure to attribute authorship to Plaintiff does not amount to misrepresentation of the nature, characteristics, qualities, or geographic origin of ... [Defendant's] goods." *Thomas Publishing Company, LLC v. Technology Evaluation Centers, Inc.*, No. 06 Civ.14212, 2007 WL 2193964, at * 3 (S.D.N.Y. July 27, 2007) (alteration in original); *see also Wellnx Life Sciences Inc. v. Iovate Health Sciences Research Inc.*, 516 F.Supp.2d 270, 286 (S.D.N.Y. 2007) ("[A] Lanham Act claim cannot be based on false designation of authorship in [Defendant's] publications."); *Antidote International Films v. Bloomsbury Publishing, PLC*, 467 F.Supp.2d 394, 399–400 (S.D.N.Y. 2006) ("the holding in *Dastar* that the word 'origin' in § 43(a)(1)(A) refers to producers, rather than authors, necessarily implies that the words 'nature, characteristics,

---

[9] Although *Dastar* involved copying of uncopyrighted work, subsequent decisions have recognized its applicability to copyrighted work as well. *See, e.g., Atrium Group De Ediciones Y Publicaciones, S.L. v. Harry N. Abrams, Inc.*, 565 F.Supp.2d 505, 512–13 (S.D.N.Y. 2008) (discussing cases).

[and] qualities' in § 43(a)(1)(B) cannot be read to refer to authorship. If authorship were a 'characteristic[ ]' or 'qualit[y]' of a work, then the very claim *Dastar* rejected under § 43(a)(1)(A) would have been available under § 43(a)(1)(B)" (alterations in original)). Thus, Plaintiffs' claims of unfair competition under the Lanham Act are dismissed.

Id. at *14-15.

3. Dastar *and products other than "communicative products"*. Courts have similarly held that short of the mere "repackaging" of another's products as one's own, the "origin of goods" provision of Lanham Act § 43(a) will not prevent the unattributed use of someone else's products as components in one's own products. Consider, for example, *Bretford Mfg., Inc. v. Smith System Mfg. Corp.*, 419 F.3d 576 (7th Cir. 2005). The plaintiff and defendant were competing table manufacturers. When one of its suppliers failed to produce satisfactory parts, the defendant incorporated some of the plaintiff's hardware in its sample table that it showed to purchasing officials from a school district, who placed an order. The tables the defendant ultimately delivered to the school district contained none of the plaintiff's hardware. Judge Easterbrook held for the defendant:

Passing off or palming off occurs when a firm puts someone else's trademark on its own (usually inferior) goods; reverse passing off or misappropriation is selling someone else's goods under your own mark. See *Roho, Inc. v. Marquis*, 902 F.2d 356, 359 (5th Cir. 1990). It is not clear what's wrong with reselling someone else's goods, if you first buy them at retail. If every automobile sold by DeLorean includes the chassis and engine of a Peugeot, with DeLorean supplying only the body shell, Peugeot has received its asking price for each car sold and does not suffer any harm. Still, the Supreme Court said in *Dastar* that "reverse passing off" can violate the Lanham Act if a misdescription of goods' origin causes commercial injury. Our opinion in *Peaceable Planet, Inc. v. Ty, Inc.*, 362 F.3d 986 (7th Cir. 2004), shows how this could occur.

Dastar added that the injury must be a *trademark* loss—which is to say, it must come from a misrepresentation of the goods' origin. Dastar thus had the right (so far as the Lanham Act is concerned) to incorporate into its videos footage taken and edited by others, provided that it manufactured the finished product and did not mislead anyone about who should be held responsible for shortcomings. No one makes a product from scratch, with trees and iron ore entering one end of the plant and a finished consumer product emerging at the other. Ford's cars include Fram oil filters, Goodyear tires, Owens-Corning glass, Bose radios, Pennzoil lubricants, and many other constituents; buyers can see some of the other producers' marks (those on the radio and tires for example) but not others, such as the oil and transmission fluid. Smith System builds tables using wood from one supplier, grommets (including Teflon from du Pont) from another, and vinyl molding and paint and bolts from any of a hundred more sources—the list is extensive even for a simple product such as a table. If Smith System does not tell du Pont how the Teflon is used, and does not inform its consumers which firm supplied the wood, has it violated the Lanham Act? Surely not; the statute does not condemn the way in which all products are made.

Legs are a larger fraction of a table's total value than grommets and screws, but nothing in the statute establishes one rule for "major" components and another for less costly inputs. The right question, *Dastar* holds, is whether the consumer knows who has produced the finished product. In the *Dastar* case that was Dastar itself, even though most of the product's economic value came from elsewhere; just so when Smith System includes components manufactured by others but stands behind the finished product. The portion of § 43(a) that addresses reverse passing off is the one that condemns false designations of origin. "Origin" means, *Dastar* holds, "the producer of the tangible product sold in the marketplace". 539 U.S. at 31. As far as Dallas was concerned, the table's "origin" was Smith System, no matter who made any component or subassembly.

Much of Bretford's argument takes the form that it is just "unfair" for Smith System to proceed as it did, making a sale before its subcontractor could turn out acceptable leg

430

assemblies. Businesses often think competition unfair, but federal law encourages wholesale copying, the better to drive down prices. Consumers rather than producers are the objects of the law's solicitude. If Smith System misled Dallas into thinking that it could supply high-quality tables, when its subcontractor could not match Bretford's welds and other attributes of Bretford's V-shaped leg assemblies, then the victim would be the Dallas school system. (As far as we are aware, however, Dallas is happy with the quality of the tables it received; it has not complained about a bait and switch.) As the Court observed in *Dastar*, creators of certain artistic works are entitled (along the lines of the European approach to moral rights) to control how their work is presented or altered by others. See 539 U.S. at 34-35, citing 17 U.S.C. § 106A. See also *Lee v. A.R.T. Co.*, 125 F.3d 580 (7th Cir. 1997). Bretford's table is not a "work of visual art" under § 106A (and the definition in 17 U.S.C. § 101). Once Bretford sold its goods, it had no control over how customers used their components: the Lanham Act does not include any version of the "derivative work" right in copyright law. See 17 U.S.C. § 106(2).

Id. at 580-81.

4. *Non-attribution versus misattribution*. In *Gilliam v. American Broadcasting Companies, Inc.*, 538 F.2d 14 (2d Cir. 1976), the plaintiffs were a highly successful British comedy group known as "Monty Python." They sought to enjoin the ABC television network from broadcasting edited versions of three 30-minute Monty Python programs. Though ABC had validly obtained the rights to broadcast the programs, ABC replaced approximately 24 minutes of the total of 90 minutes of Monty Python material with television commercials. Some of ABC's edits destroyed the comedic content of the work. The plaintiffs argued among other things that, in essence, their Monty Python trademark was being placed on work that should no longer be attributed to them. The Ninth Circuit explained:

> {T}he appellants claim that the editing done for ABC mutilated the original work and that consequently the broadcast of those programs as the creation of Monty Python violated the Lanham Act § 43(a), 15 U.S.C. § 1125(a). This statute, the federal counterpart to state unfair competition laws, has been invoked to prevent misrepresentations that may injure plaintiff's business or personal reputation, even where no registered trademark is concerned. It is sufficient to violate the Act that a representation of a product, although technically true, creates a false impression of the product's origin. . . . We find that the truncated version at times omitted the climax of the skits to which appellants' rare brand of humor was leading and at other times deleted essential elements in the schematic development of a story line. We therefore agree with {the district court's} conclusion that the edited version broadcast by ABC impaired the integrity of appellants' work and represented to the public as the product of appellants what was actually a mere caricature of their talents.

Id. at 24-25 (citations and footnotes omitted).[1]

Is a claim akin to the plaintiffs' claim in *Gilliam* still viable after *Dastar*? (To be clear, *Gilliam* was *not* a reverse passing off case, but what about its facts makes it problematic in light of *Dastar*?)

5. *Do data or computer software qualify as protectable tangible goods or unprotectable intangible ideas under* Dastar? The answer to this question appears to be highly fact-specific. See, for example,

---

[1] The specifics of the injunctive relief granted to the plaintiffs are more complicated. The plaintiffs filed their complaint on December 15, 1976, seeking to prevent the airing of the episodes eleven days later on December 26. For various reasons, the district court ordered ABC only to broadcast a disclaimer during the December 26 broadcast stating that the plaintiffs disassociated themselves form the program because of their editing. By the time it heard the appeal of the case in April, 1977, the Ninth Circuit was left to preliminarily enjoin ABC from any further airing of the episodes in their mutilated form.

Laura Laaman & Assocs., LLC v. Davis, No. 16 Civ. 00594, 2017 U.S. Dist. LEXIS 194175 (D. Conn. Nov. 27, 2017), in which the court reviewed recent case law:

> The question of where to draw the line between protected goods and unprotected ideas, however, has divided courts in the aftermath of *Dastar. Compare Cvent, Inc. v. Eventbrite, Inc.*, 739 F. Supp. 2d 927, 935-936 (E.D. Va. 2010) (holding that defendant's repackaging and sale of information stripped from plaintiff's computer database provided basis for cognizable reverse passing off claim); *Experian Marketing Solutions, Inc. v. U.S. Data Corp.*, No. 8:09CV24, 2009 U.S. Dist. LEXIS 82075, 2009 WL 2902957, at *10 (D. Neb. Sept. 9, 2009) (holding that defendant's unauthorized acquisition of and sale of plaintiff's consumer data files gave rise to viable reverse passing off claim) *with Smartix Intern. Corp. v. MasterCard Intern. LLC*, No. 06 CV 5174 (GBD), 2008 U.S. Dist. LEXIS 108548, 2008 WL 4444554, at *6-7 (S.D.N.Y. Sept. 30, 2008) (dismissing reverse passing off claim alleging defendant had stolen and reproduced plaintiff's software); *Bob Creeden & Associates, LTD. v. Infosoft, Inc.*, 326 F. Supp. 2d 876, 879-80 (N.D. Ill. 2004) (dismissing reverse passing off claim based on defendant's purported theft and distribution of plaintiff's software to its competitors).

Laura Laaman & Assocs., 2017 U.S. Dist. LEXIS 194175 at *13-14. For a full consideration of the problems that intangible digital goods present for trademark law, see Mark P. McKenna & Lucas Osborn, *Trademarks and Digital Goods*, 92 NOTRE DAME L. REV. 1425 (2017).

6. *What about "forward passing off"? Dastar* may be read to establish the proposition that there is no liability for reverse passing off under the Lanham Act when a defendant reproduces the plaintiff's "communicative products" and relabels those non-physical products as originating in the defendant. But does *Dastar* go too far? Does it further establish the proposition that there is no liability when a defendant places on its own "communicative products" a trademark confusingly similar with the plaintiff's mark (the standard "forward passing off" scenario)? For example, if an entity creates non-fungible tokens that explicitly reference a famous trademark and then sells those NFTs, is the entity liable for trademark infringement? Aren't the NFTs (and any images they may link to) non-physical "comunicative products" akin to those at issue in *Dastar*, the origin of which "are typically of no consequence to purchasers"? Apparently not, at least according to *Hermès Int'l v. Rothschild*, 590 F. Supp. 3d 647, 654 (S.D.N.Y. 2022) (finding that "*Dastar* said nothing at all about the general applicability of the Lanham Act to intangible goods").

10. Lanham Act § 2(d) Confusion

Recall that a registration application at the PTO may be rejected on the basis that the applied-for mark will create a likelihood of confusion with an already registered mark. The PTO's test for determining whether Lanham Act § 2(d) bars a registration is essentially the same as the multifactor test for the likelihood of confusion in the federal court litigation context. *See B&B Hardware, Inc. v. Hargis Industries, Inc.*, 135 S.Ct. 1293 (2015). Excerpted below is the discussion of the § 2(d) bar in the Trademark Manual of Examining Procedure.

TMEP § 1207.01 Likelihood of Confusion

[1] In the ex parte examination of a trademark application, a refusal under § 2(d) is normally based on the examining attorney's conclusion that the applicant's mark, as used on or in connection with the specified goods or services, so resembles a *registered* mark as to be likely to cause confusion. See TMEP § 1207.02 concerning application of the § 2(d) provision relating to marks that so resemble another mark as to be likely to deceive, and TMEP § 1207.03 concerning § 2(d) refusals based on unregistered marks (which generally are not issued in ex parte examination).

[2] The examining attorney must conduct a search of USPTO records to determine whether the applicant's mark so resembles any registered mark(s) as to be likely to cause confusion or mistake, when used on or in connection with the goods or services identified in the application. The examining attorney

also searches pending applications for conflicting marks with earlier effective filing dates . . . . The examining attorney must place a copy of the search strategy in the record.

[3] If the examining attorney determines that there is a likelihood of confusion between applicant's mark and a previously registered mark or marks, the examining attorney refuses registration of the applicant's mark under § 2(d). Before citing a registration, the examining attorney must check the automated records of the USPTO to confirm that any registration that is the basis for a § 2(d) refusal is an active registration . . . .

[4] In the seminal case involving § 2(d), *In re E. I. du Pont de Nemours & Co.*, the U.S. Court of Customs and Patent Appeals discussed the factors relevant to a determination of likelihood of confusion. 476 F.2d 1357, 177 USPQ 563 (C.C.P.A. 1973) . . . .

[5] Although the weight given to the relevant *du Pont* factors may vary, the following two factors are key considerations in any likelihood of confusion determination:

- The similarity or dissimilarity of the marks in their entireties as to appearance, sound, connotation and commercial impression.

- The relatedness of the goods or services as described in the application and registration(s).

See, e.g., Federated Foods, Inc. v. Fort Howard Paper Co., 544 F.2d 1098, 1103, 192 USPQ 24, 29 (C.C.P.A. 1976); *In re Iolo Techs., LLC*, 95 USPQ2d 1498, 1499 (TTAB 2010); *In re Max Capital Grp. Ltd.*, 93 USPQ2d 1243, 1244 (TTAB 2010); *In re Thor Tech, Inc.*, 90 USPQ2d 1634, 1635 (TTAB 2009).

[6] The following factors may also be relevant in an ex parte likelihood-of-confusion determination and must be considered if there is pertinent evidence in the record:

- The similarity or dissimilarity of established, likely-to-continue trade channels.

- The conditions under which and buyers to whom sales are made, i.e., "impulse" vs. careful, sophisticated purchasing (see TMEP § 1207.01(d)(vii)).

- The number and nature of similar marks in use on similar goods (see TMEP § 1207.01(d)(iii)).

- The existence of a valid consent agreement between the applicant and the owner of the previously registered mark (see TMEP § 1207.01(d)(viii)).

See, e.g., du Pont, 476 F.2d at 1362-63, 177 USPQ at 568-69; *In re Davey Prods. Pty Ltd.*, 92 USPQ2d 1198, 1203-04 (TTAB 2009); *In re Toshiba Med. Sys. Corp.*, 91 USPQ2d 1266, 1272-74 (TTAB 2009); *Ass'n of the U.S. Army*, 85 USPQ2d at 1271-73.

[7] As should be clear from the foregoing, there is no mechanical test for determining likelihood of confusion and "each case must be decided on its own facts." *Du Pont*, 476 F.2d at 1361, 177 USPQ at 567. In some cases, a determination that there is no likelihood of confusion may be appropriate, even where the marks are similar and the goods/services are related, because these factors are outweighed by other factors, such as differences in the relevant trade channels of the goods/services, the presence in the marketplace of a significant number of similar marks in use on similar goods/services, the existence of a valid consent agreement between the parties, or another established fact probative of the effect of use. For example, in *In re Strategic Partners, Inc.*, 102 USPQ2d 1397 (TTAB 2012), the Board reversed a refusal to register the mark ANYWEAR (in stylized text), for "footwear," finding no likelihood of confusion with the registered mark ANYWEAR BY JOSIE NATORI (and design), for "jackets, shirts, pants, stretch T-tops and stoles." Given the similarity in the marks and the relatedness of the goods, the Board stated that "under usual circumstances" it would conclude that confusion is likely to occur; however, an "unusual situation" compelled the Board "to balance the similarities between the marks and goods against the facts that applicant already owns a registration for a substantially similar mark for the identical goods, and that applicant's registration and the cited registration have coexisted for over five years." *Id.* at 1399. Applicant's prior registration of ANYWEARS for goods including footwear was substantially similar to the applied-for mark ANYWEAR for the same goods, and the registration had achieved incontestable status. *Id.* Basing its decision on the thirteenth *du Pont* factor, which "relates to 'any other established fact probative of the effect of use,'" the Board determined that this factor

outweighed the others and confusion was unlikely. *Id.* at 1399-1400 (quoting *du Pont*, 476 F.2d at 1361, 177 USPQ at 567).

[8] The decision in *Strategic Partners* may be applied and weighed against a § 2(d) refusal in the limited situation where: (1) an applicant owns a prior registration for the same mark or a mark with no meaningful difference from the applied-for-mark; (2) the identifications of goods/services in the application and applicant's prior registration are identical or identical in relevant part; and (3) the applicant's prior registration has co-existed for at least five years with the registration being considered as the basis for the Section 2(d) refusal. See *Id.* at 1400.

[9] The determination of likelihood of confusion under § 2(d) in an intent-to-use application under § 1(b) of the Trademark Act does not differ from the determination in any other type of application.

TMEP § 1207.03 Marks Previously Used in United States but Not Registered

As a basis for refusal, § 2(d) refers not only to registered marks but also to "a mark or trade name previously used in the United States by another and not abandoned." Refusal on the basis of an unregistered mark or trade name has sometimes been referred to as refusal on the basis of a "known mark." This provision is not applied in ex parte examination because of the practical difficulties with which an examining attorney is faced in locating "previously used" marks, and determining whether anyone has rights in them and whether they are "not abandoned."

Comments and Questions

1.   *Lanham Act § 2(d) and unregistered marks.* Note that § 2(d) not only prohibits the registration of a mark that is confusingly similar with any previously registered mark, but also prohibits the registration of a mark that is confusingly similar with an unregistered "mark or tradename previously used in the United States by another and not abandoned." Lanham Act § 2(d), 15 U.S.C. § 1052 (d). In practice, "[t]his provision is not applied in ex parte examination because of the practical difficulties with which an examining attorney is faced in locating 'previously used' marks, and determining whether anyone has rights in them and whether they are 'not abandoned.'" TMEP § 1207.03 (Jan. 2015).

C.   Trademark Dilution

Lanham Act § 43(c)[1] provides protection for trademarks against "dilution," which is probably the single most muddled concept in all of trademark doctrine. Of the many reasons for this, perhaps the most significant—and avoidable—is that trademark courts and commentators tend to speak of several different species of trademark dilution without identifying them any more specifically than by the generic name "dilution." From the very beginning of your study of dilution, it may be worthwhile to distinguish among three specific species of dilution: (1) dilution of uniqueness, (2) dilution by "blurring," and (3) dilution by "tarnishment." Because dilution is so easily misunderstood, each form of dilution is briefly discussed below before we turn to the representative case law. Note that, strictly speaking, U.S. trademark law protects against only dilution by blurring and dilution by tarnishment. A brief description of dilution of a trademark's uniqueness is offered because it is arguably what the trademark practitioner and scholar Frank Schechter had in mind when he first spoke of the concept of trademark dilution in the 1920s.

Dilution of Uniqueness. In his seminal 1927 article *The Rational Basis of Trademark Protection*, 40 HARV. L. REV. 813 (1927), Schechter introduced to American law the concept of trademark dilution. Schechter used the term "dilution" to refer to the impairment of a trademark's *uniqueness*, or what

---

[1] The current version of § 43(c) is sometimes referred to as the Trademark Dilution Revision Act or "TDRA," which became effective on October 6, 2006 (and which replaced the old language of § 43(c) that was established by the Federal Trademark Dilution Act of 1995 or "FTDA").

modern marketing doctrine would term its "brand differentiation."[2]   His primary concern was to preserve what he variously termed a mark's "arresting uniqueness," its "singularity," "identity," and "individuality," its quality of being "unique and different from other marks." Schechter was not so much concerned with a trademark's distinctiveness *of source*, but with a trademark's distinctiveness *from other marks*, not its "source distinctiveness," but its "differential distinctiveness."[3] In Schechter's view, trademark uniqueness was worth protecting because it generated "selling power." Certain very strong marks were not simply a means of identifying and advertising source. In a new age of mass production, they were also a means of endowing the goods to which they were attached with the characteristic of uniqueness as against the crowds of other mass-produced goods in the marketplace, a characteristic for which consumers would pay a premium.

Schechter believed, quite rightly at the time, that antidilution protection was necessary because anti-infringement protection, based on consumer confusion as to source, would not fully preserve the uniqueness of famous marks. In situations where a defendant used a famous mark on goods unrelated to those on which the famous mark normally appeared (e.g., NIKE pianos, ROLLS-ROYCE chewing gum, CHANEL waste disposal services), consumers would not likely assume that the defendant's product had the plaintiff as its source. Thus, no cause of action for consumer confusion as to source would lie.

The beauty of Schechter's original conception of antidilution protection was that it was relatively easy to put into practice. Uniqueness is an absolute concept. A mark is either unique or it is not. If a senior mark is unique in the marketplace and a junior mark appears that is identical to it, then the junior mark will destroy the senior mark's uniqueness. Thus, the test for dilution was an essentially formal one. The judge need only consider the identity or close similarity of the parties' marks. If they were identical or closely similar, then the loss of uniqueness could be presumed. *See Eli Lilly & Co. v. Natural Answers, Inc.* 233 F.3d 456, 468-69 (7th Cir. 2000) (considering only similarity of the parties' marks and the "renown" of the senior mark in finding a likelihood of dilution); *Ringling Bros-Barnum & Bailey Combined Shows, Inc. v. Utah Division of Travel Development*, 170 F.3d 449, 464 (4th Cir. 1999) ("[O]nly mark similarity and, possibly, degree of 'renown' of the senior mark would appear to have trustworthy relevance under the federal Act."). Where the consumer confusion test was a messy and unpredictable empirical analysis centered on the *consumer*, the trademark dilution test was a simple and relatively predictable analysis centered on the *trademark*.

Note that Schechter's original conception has never been enacted into law, and the language of Lanham Act § 43(c) is careful to steer clear of it. Indeed, in the early stages of the drafting of the Act, a form of antidilution protection based on "uniqueness" was proposed and rejected.[4]

Dilution by Blurring. The idea underlying the concept of trademark "blurring" is that the defendant's use of a mark similar or identical to the plaintiff's mark, though perhaps not confusing as to source, will nevertheless "blur" the link between the plaintiff's mark and the plaintiff or between the plaintiff's mark and the goods or services to which the plaintiff's mark is traditionally attached. In modern marketing parlance, anti-blurring protection seeks to preserve a brand's "typicality," the brand's "ability to conjure up a particular product category." Alexander F. Simonson, *How and When Do*

---

[2] For an important alternative reading of Schechter, which asserts that he sought to provide antidilution protection only to marks which are "synonymous with a single product or product class," see Sara Stadler Nelson, *The Wages of Ubiquity in Trademark Law*, 88 Iowa L. Rev. 731 (2003).

[3] *See* Barton Beebe, *The Semiotic Analysis of Trademark Law*, 51 UCLA L. Rev. 621 (2004) (distinguishing between source distinctiveness, or in semiotic terms, "signification," and differential distinctiveness, or in semiotic terms, "value").

[4] *See* Trademark Dilution Revision Act of 2005: Hearing Before the Subcomm. on Courts, the Internet, and Intellectual Property of the House Judiciary Comm., 109th Cong. 12-13 (2005) [hereinafter 2005 Hearing] (statement of Anne Gundelfinger, President, International Trademark Association). *See also id.* at 22-23 (testimony of William G. Barber on behalf of the American Intellectual Property Law Association).

Trademarks Dilute: A Behavioral Framework to Judge "Likelihood of Dilution", 83 TRADEMARK REP. 149, 152-53 (1993). In *Ty Inc. v. Perryman*, 306 F.3d 509 (7th Cir. 2002), Judge Posner provided a hypothetical example of blurring:

> [T]here is concern that consumer search costs will rise if a trademark becomes associated with a variety of unrelated products. Suppose an upscale restaurant calls itself "Tiffany." There is little danger that the consuming public will think it's dealing with a branch of the Tiffany jewelry store if it patronizes this restaurant. But when consumers next see the name "Tiffany" they may think about both the restaurant and the jewelry store, and if so the efficacy of the name as an identifier of the store will be diminished. Consumers will have to think harder—incur as it were a higher imagination cost—to recognize the name as the name of the store. So "blurring" is one form of dilution.

Id. at 511 (citations omitted). As Judge Posner's description suggests, the increase in "imagination cost" that blurring is thought to cause forms the basis of the economic rationale underlying antidilution protection. As Judge Posner explained, "[a] trademark seeks to economize on information costs by providing a compact, memorable and unambiguous identifier of a product or service. The economy is less when, because the trademark has other associations, a person seeing it must think for a moment before recognizing it as the mark of the product or service." Richard Posner, *When Is Parody Fair Use?*, 21 J. LEGAL STUDIES 67, 75 (1992).[5]

The blurring theory of dilution is highly empirical in orientation. For the judge to find that a junior mark "blurs" a senior mark, the judge must find that the junior mark is causing consumers to "think for a moment" before recognizing that the senior mark refers to the goods of the senior mark's owner.[6] A merely formal analysis of the similarity of the marks is insufficient. The judge must evaluate the likely effect of the junior mark on the perceptions of actual consumers and must in the process take into account such factors as the degree of distinctiveness—or typicality—of the senior mark. The analysis is once again centered on the *consumer*.

The concept of trademark blurring is controversial. In his treatise, Tom McCarthy memorably observes:

> Commentators almost uniformly contend that dilution by blurring is a purely theoretical hypothesis and rarely, if ever, happens in the real world. That is, the argument is that impairment of the distinctiveness of a trademark by blurring is like Bigfoot, the Himalayan Yeti or the Loch Ness Monster: a theoretical construct never proven to exist by incontrovertible evidence.

McCARTHY, § 24:15. For example, Christine Haight Farley defies proponents of the blurring theory to provide even one concrete (and not hypothetical) example of a famous mark that has been significantly damaged through blurring. *See* Christine Haight Farley, *Why We Are Confused about the Trademark*

---

[5] *The Restatement (Third) of Unfair Competition* provides an alternative account of dilution by blurring, one that the student may find more persuasive:

> [A] mark may be so highly distinctive and so well advertised that it acts as a powerful selling tool. Such a mark may evoke among prospective purchasers a positive response that is associated exclusively with the goods or services of the trademark owner. To the extent that others use the trademark to identify different goods, services, or businesses, a dissonance occurs that blurs this stimulant effect of the mark. The antidilution statutes protect against this dilution of the distinctiveness and selling power of the mark.

RESTATEMENT (THIRD) OF UNFAIR COMPETITION § 25 (1995). However, Judge Posner's "imagination cost" account of blurring has proven to be far more influential in the courts and commentary, for better or worse.

[6] For a strong critique of this conception of blurring, see Rebecca Tushnet, *Gone in 60 Milliseconds: Trademark Law and Cognitive Science*, 86 TEXAS L. REV. 507 (2008).

Dilution Law, 16 Fordham Intell. Prop. Media & Enter. L. J. 1175, 1184-85 (2006). Yet as we will see, courts continue to rule in favor of blurring plaintiffs, particularly when the defendant has acted in clear bad faith.

Dilution by Tarnishment. Dilution by tarnishment is fundamentally different from dilution by blurring (and arguably has nothing to do with "dilution" as Schechter originally formulated the concept). Tarnishment describes damage to the positive associations or connotations of a trademark. *See Deere & Co. v. MTD Prods., Inc.*, 41 F.3d 39, 43 (2d Cir. 1994) ("'Tarnishment' generally arises when the plaintiff's trademark is linked to products of shoddy quality, or is portrayed in an unwholesome or unsavory context likely to evoke unflattering thoughts about the owner's product[s]."). For example, in *New York Stock Exchange, Inc. v. New York, New York Hotel, LLC*, 293 F.3d 550 (2d Cir. 2002), a Las Vegas casino called its players club the "New York $lot Exchange." Owners of the NEW YORK STOCK EXCHANGE trademark took offense at the suggestion that their stock exchange was in some sense a venue for gambling, if not also for stacked odds, and sued. The district court granted summary judgment to the casino. *New York Stock Exch., Inc. v. New York, New York Hotel, LLC*, 69 F. Supp. 2d 479, 482 (S.D.N.Y. 1999). On appeal, the Second Circuit reversed and remanded on certain of the dilution claims. Among other things it found, with respect to the plaintiff's New York state law tarnishment claim, that "[a] reasonable trier of fact might . . . find that the Casino's humorous analogy would injure NYSE's reputation." *New York Stock Exch., Inc. v. New York, New York Hotel LLC*, 293 F.3d 550, 558 (2d Cir. 2002) (analyzing the issue under New York state anti-tarnishment law).

The Difference Between Trademark Confusion and Trademark Dilution. In principle, trademark confusion and trademark dilution are starkly different. When a consumer experiences trademark confusion, the similarity of the plaintiff's and the defendant's marks leads the consumer to believe that both the plaintiff's and the defendant's products are coming from the *same company*. The consumer believes that *one company* is the source of both parties' marks and products. By contrast, when a consumer experiences dilution, the similarity between the parties' marks leads the consumer to associate the two marks with each other, but the consumer does not believe that they are coming from the same company. She knows that there are *two different companies*. (e.g., Four Seasons for hotel services and Four Seasons for landscaping services). The harm in dilution by blurring is that whenever the consumer sees either the plaintiff's or the defendant's mark, she is compelled to think for a moment to determine to which of those two different companies the mark is referring. The harm in dilution by tarnishment is that any negative connotations of one of the marks may damage by association the reputation of the other mark, even when the consumer knows that the two companies are commercially unrelated. Though trademark confusion and trademark dilution are different, a population of relevant consumers may contain some consumers who are confused as to source and some other consumers (perhaps the more sophisticated in the population) who are not confused as to source but rather experience dilution. *See* McCarthy § 24:72 ("A given unauthorized use by defendant can cause confusion in some people's minds and in other people's minds cause dilution by blurring, but in no one person's mind can both perceptions occur at the same time.").

Though distinct in theory, the processes of trademark confusion and trademark dilution are sometimes treated as interchangeable by careless lawyers and courts. This can be frustrating. *See* McCarthy § 24:72.

The Elements of a Dilution Claim. In *Louis Vuitton Malletier S.A. v. Haute Diggity Dog, LLC*, 507 F.3d 252 (4th Cir. 2007), the Fourth Circuit set forth the main elements of a federal claim for dilution by blurring or dilution by tarnishment. The plaintiff must show:

> (1) that the plaintiff owns a famous mark that is distinctive;
>
> (2) that the defendant has commenced using a mark in commerce that allegedly is diluting the famous mark;
>
> (3) that a similarity between the defendant's mark and the famous mark gives rise to an association between the marks; and

(4) that the association is likely to impair the distinctiveness of the famous mark or likely to harm the reputation of the famous mark.

Id. at 264-65. Not made explicit in this listing of the elements is the important detail that the plaintiff's mark must have become famous *before* the defendant began use of its allegedly diluting mark. *See* Lanham Act § 43(c)(1), 15 U.S.C. § 1125(c)(1) ("at any time after the owner's mark has become famous").

In light of the above, the statutory language of § 43(c) excerpted below will reward a close reading. We then turn first, in section II.C.1, to the fame requirement for antidilution protection and then, in section II.C.2, to anti-blurring protection and, in section II.C.3, to anti-tarnishment protection.[7]

Lanham Act § 43(c), 15 U.S.C. § 1125(c)

(c) Dilution by blurring; dilution by tarnishment

(1) Injunctive relief. Subject to the principles of equity, the owner of a famous mark that is distinctive, inherently or through acquired distinctiveness, shall be entitled to an injunction against another person who, at any time after the owner's mark has become famous, commences use of a mark or trade name in commerce that is likely to cause dilution by blurring or dilution by tarnishment of the famous mark, regardless of the presence or absence of actual or likely confusion, of competition, or of actual economic injury.

(2) Definitions

(A) For purposes of paragraph (1), a mark is famous if it is widely recognized by the general consuming public of the United States as a designation of source of the goods or services of the mark's owner. In determining whether a mark possesses the requisite degree of recognition, the court may consider all relevant factors, including the following:

(i) The duration, extent, and geographic reach of advertising and publicity of the mark, whether advertised or publicized by the owner or third parties.

(ii) The amount, volume, and geographic extent of sales of goods or services offered under the mark.

(iii) The extent of actual recognition of the mark.

(iv) Whether the mark was registered under the Act of March 3, 1881, or the Act of February 20, 1905, or on the principal register.

(B) For purposes of paragraph (1), "dilution by blurring" is association arising from the similarity between a mark or trade name and a famous mark that impairs the distinctiveness of the famous mark. In determining whether a mark or trade name is likely to cause dilution by blurring, the court may consider all relevant factors, including the following:

(i) The degree of similarity between the mark or trade name and the famous mark.

(ii) The degree of inherent or acquired distinctiveness of the famous mark.

(iii) The extent to which the owner of the famous mark is engaging in substantially exclusive use of the mark.

(iv) The degree of recognition of the famous mark.

(v) Whether the user of the mark or trade name intended to create an association with the famous mark.

---

[7] The student wishing to avoid madness may do well to avoid the term "dilution" altogether and simply refer to these two forms of protection as "anti-blurring protection" and "anti-tarnishment" protection.

(vi) Any actual association between the mark or trade name and the famous mark.

(C) For purposes of paragraph (1), "dilution by tarnishment" is association arising from the similarity between a mark or trade name and a famous mark that harms the reputation of the famous mark.

(3) Exclusions. The following shall not be actionable as dilution by blurring or dilution by tarnishment under this subsection:

(A) Any fair use, including a nominative or descriptive fair use, or facilitation of such fair use, of a famous mark by another person other than as a designation of source for the person's own goods or services, including use in connection with—

(i) advertising or promotion that permits consumers to compare goods or services; or

(ii) identifying and parodying, criticizing, or commenting upon the famous mark owner or the goods or services of the famous mark owner.

(B) All forms of news reporting and news commentary.

(C) Any noncommercial use of a mark.

. . . .

1.   The Fame Requirement for Antidilution Protection

To qualify for federal anti-blurring and anti-tarnishment protection under § 43(c), a mark must be "widely recognized by the general consuming public of the United States as a designation of source of the goods or services of the mark's owner." Lanham Act § 43(c)(2)(A), 15 U.S.C. § 1125(c)(2)(A). Furthermore, the mark must have become famous before the defendant began its allegedly diluting use. Lanham Act § 43(c)(1), 15 U.S.C. § 1125(c)(1). Among the marks that have failed to meet the fame requirement are the "longhorn" logo of the University of Texas, *Board of Regents v. KST Elec., Ltd.*, 550 F. Supp. 2d 657, 678 (W.D. Tex. 2008), and the red dripping wax seal of the Maker's Mark whiskey bottle, *Maker's Mark Distillery, Inc. v. Diageo North America, Inc.*, 703 F. Supp. 2d 671, 698 (W.D. Ky. 2010) ("Congress intended for dilution to apply only to a small category of extremely strong marks."). Among the marks that have met the fame requirement are JUST DO IT, CHANEL, AUDI, and AMERICA'S TEAM. *See respectively Nike, Inc. v. Peter Maher and Patricia Hoyt Maher*, 100 U.S.P.Q.2d 1018, 1027 (T.T.A.B. 2011); *Chanel, Inc. v. Makarczyk*, 110 U.S.P.Q.2d 2013 (T.T.A.B. 2014); *Audi AG v. Shokan Coachworks, Inc.*, 592 F. Supp. 2d 246, 280 (N.D. N.Y. 2008); *Dallas Cowboys Football Club, Ltd. v. America's Team Properties, Inc.*, 616 F. Supp. 2d 622 (N.D. Tex. 2009).

In the opinion excerpt that follows, the Federal Circuit considered the fame of the mark COACH. Coach Services, Inc. ("CSI"), the proprietor of COACH leather goods stores, opposed Triumph Learning, LLC's application to register the mark COACH for educational materials used to prepare students for standardized tests. (Does CSI's opposition strike you as a reasonable assertion of CSI's rights in their COACH mark?) In affirming the TTAB's finding of no likelihood of confusion or dilution, the Federal Circuit found that CSI had failed to establish that its mark was "widely recognized by the general consuming public of the United States" at the time that Triumph Learning adopted its mark. Triumph filed its applications to register the COACH word mark, a stylized COACH mark, and a COACH mark and design (shown below) in December 2004. The applications were published for opposition on September 20, 2005.

Coach Servs., Inc. v. Triumph Learning LLC
668 F.3d 1356 (Fed. Cir. 2012)

O'MALLEY, Circuit Judge.

. . . .

C. Dilution

1. Fame for Dilution

[1] A threshold question in a federal dilution claim is whether the mark at issue is "famous." Under the TDRA, a mark is famous if it "is widely recognized by the general consuming public of the United States as a designation of source of the goods or services of the mark's owner." 15 U.S.C. § 1125(c)(2)(A). By using the "general consuming public" as the benchmark, the TDRA eliminated the possibility of "niche fame," which some courts had recognized under the previous version of the statute. *See Top Tobacco, LP v. N. Atl. Operating Co.,* 509 F.3d 380, 384 (7th Cir. 2007) (noting that the reference to the general public "eliminated any possibility of 'niche fame,' which some courts had recognized before the amendment"). The TDRA lists four non-exclusive factors for courts to consider when determining whether a mark is famous . . . . Whether a mark is famous under the TDRA is a factual question reviewed for substantial evidence.

. . . .

[2] It is well-established that dilution fame is difficult to prove . . . . This is particularly true where, as here, the mark is a common English word that has different meanings in different contexts. Importantly, the owner of the allegedly famous mark must show that its mark became famous "prior to the filing date of the trademark application or registration against which it intends to file an opposition or cancellation proceeding." *See Toro Co. v. ToroHead Inc.,* 61 U.S.P.Q.2d 1164, 1174 (T.T.A.B. 2001).

[3] As noted, fame for dilution requires widespread recognition by the general public. 15 U.S.C. § 1125(c)(2)(A). To establish the requisite level of fame, the "mark's owner must demonstrate that the common or proper noun uses of the term and third-party uses of the mark are now eclipsed by the owner's use of the mark." *Toro,* 61 U.S.P.Q.2d at 1180. An opposer must show that, when the general public encounters the mark "in almost any context, it associates the term, at least initially, with the mark's owner." *Id.* at 1181. In other words, a famous mark is one that has become a "household name." *Nissan Motor Co. v. Nissan Computer Corp.,* 378 F.3d 1002, 1012 (9th Cir. 2004) (quoting *Thane Int'l, Inc. v. Trek Bicycle Corp.,* 305 F.3d 894, 911 (9th Cir. 2002)). With this framework in mind, we turn to CSI's evidence of fame.

2. CSI Failed to Introduce Sufficient Evidence of Fame for Dilution

[4] The Board found that CSI's evidence of fame was insufficient to support a dilution claim. On appeal, CSI argues that the same evidence establishing fame for likelihood of confusion also establishes fame for dilution purposes. Specifically, CSI argues that the Board disregarded: (1) sales and advertising figures for years 2000–2008; (2) its sixteen federal trademark registrations; (3) unsolicited media attention; (4) joint marketing efforts; (5) two Second Circuit decisions finding the Coach hangtag, which features the COACH mark, to be famous; and (6) CSI's internal brand awareness survey showing awareness among 18–24 year old consumers. We address each category of evidence in turn. For the

440

reasons set forth below, we find substantial evidence supporting the Board's decision that CSI failed to show the requisite level of fame for dilution.

[5] Turning first to CSI's evidence of sales and advertising expenditures, CSI argues that the Board erred when it ignored the annual reports that were attached to a Notice of Reliance. As previously discussed, however, the Board correctly held that these reports were unauthenticated and thus inadmissible. The only sales and advertising figures in the record via Ms. Sadler's testimony were for one year—2008—which, notably, is after Triumph filed its use-based applications in December 2004. We agree with the Board that this limited evidence of sales and advertising is insufficient to show fame. Even if the Board had considered the annual reports, moreover, such evidence, standing alone, would be insufficient. *See Toro*, 61 U.S.P.Q.2d at 1181 ("Merely providing evidence that a mark is a top-selling brand is insufficient to show this general fame without evidence of how many persons are purchasers.").

[6] With respect to CSI's registrations, the Board found that the mere existence of federally registered trademarks is insufficient to show that the mark is famous for purposes of dilution because ownership of a registration is not proof of fame. On appeal, CSI argues that the Board erred in this determination because one of the statutory factors a court can consider in the fame analysis is whether the mark is registered on the principal register. *See* 15 U.S.C. § 1125(c)(2)(A)(iv). As Triumph points out, however, "[o]ne cannot logically infer fame from the fact that a mark is one of the millions on the Federal Register." 4 *McCarthy*, § 24:106 at 24–310. While ownership of a trademark registration *is* relevant to the fame inquiry, and—to the extent the Board decision implies otherwise—the Board erred on this point, proof of registration is not *conclusive* evidence of fame.

[7] With respect to media attention, the Board found that CSI's evidence fell short of showing "widespread recognition of opposer's mark [by] the general population." *Board Decision*, 96 U.S.P.Q.2d at 1611. Specifically, the Board found that:

> the vast majority of unsolicited media recognition for opposer's COACH mark comprises a reference to one of opposer's products as one of many different fashion buys or trends, and the news articles noting opposer's renown are too few to support a finding that opposer's mark has been transformed into a household name.

Id. On appeal, CSI argues that the Board ignored hundreds of unsolicited articles mentioning the COACH mark over the years. CSI points to several examples, including the following:

- "In fact, Coach's growth … has been phenomenal. When Sara Lee acquired the firm in 1985, its volume was about $18 million. In Sara Lee's latest fiscal year, which ended last June 30, Coach's sales exceeded $500 million. The name also resonates with consumers. The brand ranked eighth among the top 10 in accessories firms in the latest Fairchild 100 consumer survey of fashion labels, in 1995." J.A. 3607 (Women's Wear Daily, May 5, 1997).

- "Coach, one of the top makers of status handbags in the United States …" J.A. 3598 (The New York Times, Jan. 27, 1999).

- "Coach's creative director has helped transform the 60–year old company into a must-have American icon." J.A. 3156 (Women's Wear Daily, June 2001).

- "Will Coach Become Too Popular? … Coach, the maker and retailer of stylish handbags, just had a blowout season…. Clearly Coach has recorded some of the best growth numbers of any retailer or accessories maker in recent years." J.A. 3543 (Business Week, Jan. 24, 2007).

[8] Looking at the media attention in the record, there is certainly evidence that CSI's COACH mark has achieved a substantial degree of recognition. That said, many of the articles submitted are dated *after* Triumph filed its registration applications and thus do not show that CSI's mark was famous *prior* to the filing date. *See Toro*, 61 U.S.P.Q.2d at 1174 ("an owner of an allegedly famous mark must establish that its mark had become famous prior to the filing date of the trademark application" which it opposes). And, there is substantial evidence supporting the Board's determination that many of the references are limited to mentioning one of CSI's COACH products among other brands. Accordingly, even though there

is some evidence of media attention, substantial evidence supports the Board's conclusion that the media evidence submitted fails to show widespread recognition.

[9] With respect to joint marketing efforts, CSI argued that other popular brands, including LEXUS and CANON, have used the COACH mark in connection with their products. The Board found that CSI "failed to provide any testimony regarding the success of the joint marketing efforts and the effect of those efforts in promoting opposer's mark." *Board Decision*, 96 U.S.P.Q.2d at 1611, n. 37. We agree. Without evidence as to the success of these efforts or the terms of any contracts involved, they have little value here.

[10] Next, the Board found that CSI's 2008 brand awareness study was "of dubious probative value" because it did not offer a witness with first-hand knowledge of the study to explain how it was conducted. *Id.* at 1611. The Board further noted that, although the study showed a high level of brand awareness among women ages 13–24, it provided no evidence of brand awareness among women generally, or among men. *See Top Tobacco*, 509 F.3d at 384 (noting that the TDRA eliminated the possibility of "niche fame" as a basis for finding a mark famous). And, the survey was conducted in 2007, several years after Triumph filed its applications. Given these circumstances, we find no error in the Board's decision to give this survey limited weight.

[11] CSI also argues that the Board failed to adequately consider two Second Circuit decisions finding that the hangtag attached to its various handbags, which features the COACH mark, is distinctive. *See Coach Leatherware Co., Inc. v. AnnTaylor, Inc.*, 933 F.2d 162, 166 (2d Cir. 1991) (finding that Coach's lozenge-shaped leather tags embossed with the name "Coach Leatherware," which are attached to Coach's handbags by beaded brass chains, "have become distinctive and valuable through Coach's promotional efforts and by virtue of its upscale reputation"); *see also Coach, Inc. v. We Care Trading Co., Inc.*, 67 Fed.Appx. 626, 630 (2d Cir. 2002) (affirming the jury's dilution verdict on grounds that "the jury's determination that the hang tag was famous and distinctive was not unreasonable" and "the substantial similarity of the two marks here coupled with the use of Coach's very distinctive hang tag shape amply justified the jury's verdict"). Although the Board did not specifically address these cases, we agree with Triumph that they are unrelated and irrelevant, particularly because: (1) the 1991 case did not involve a dilution claim; and (2) both cases focus on the hangtag feature on CSI's handbags, not on the alleged fame of the COACH mark generally.

[12] Based on the foregoing, we agree with the Board that CSI failed to provide sufficient evidence of fame for dilution purposes. Absent a showing of fame, CSI's dilution claim fails, and we need not address the remaining statutory factors for dilution by blurring.

[13] Before moving on, we pause to emphasize the fact-specific nature of our holding today. While the burden to show fame in the dilution context is high—and higher than that for likelihood of confusion purposes—it is not insurmountable. We do not hold that CSI could never establish the requisite level of fame for dilution purposes. We hold only that, on the record presented to it, the Board had substantial support for its conclusion that CSI's evidentiary showing was just too weak to do so here.

Comments and Questions

1.   *The importance of the timing of fame evidence.* Courts appear to be applying quite strictly the requirement that the plaintiff show fame *before* defendant began use. Consider the case of *Inter IKEA Systems B.V. v. Akea, LLC*, 110 U.S.P.Q.2d 1734 (TTAB 2014). In June 2009, Akea filed an intent-to-use application for the mark AKEA for nutritional supplements in international class 5, retail services in class 35, and advice and information services relating to diet in class 44. Ikea opposed under § 2(d), claiming likelihood of confusion, and under § 13 and § 43(c), claiming likelihood of dilution. Almost all of Ikea's evidence of fame was dated after June 2009. "For example, opposer's evidence that the IKEA brand was ranked No. 28 on the Business Week/Interbrand 2012 list of the Top 100 Brands worldwide, with an estimated brand value of $12,808,000,000 is subsequent to the filing date of applicant's application and, therefore, is not relevant." *Id.* at 1745. Ikea's dilution claim therefore failed. What result? Akea's registration was refused in class 35 for retail services where the TTAB found a likelihood of confusion, but allowed in classes 5 and 44, for nutritional supplements and for information services relating to diet

respectively, where the TTAB found no likelihood of confusion (but might very well have found a likelihood of dilution had Ikea's lawyers submitted, for example, evidence that in 2008, Interbrand ranked Ikea as the 35th most valuable brand in the world worth $10.9 billion).

2. *Fame surveys.* What level of fame must a mark be shown to have achieved in survey evidence to qualify for federal antidilution protection? Consider McCarthy's proposal, which he provides in an "Author's Opinion" section of his treatise:

> I think that the extraordinary scope of the federal antidilution law requires proof of a relatively high level of recognition . . . . I believe that a minimum threshold survey response should be in the range of 75% of the general consuming public of the United States. I do not propose that a mark that obtained such a reading on a survey would automatically qualify as "famous": surveys are not indisputably accurate measures of public perception. It is no secret that survey percentages can vary widely depending on which group of people are asked questions phrased in various ways. My 75% proposal assumes that the fact finder is satisfied that the data reasonably reflects actual public perception of the entire general consuming public of the United States.

McCarthy § 24:106 (*cited in* T-Mobile US, Inc. v. AIO Wireless LLC, 991 F. Supp. 2d 888, 931 (S.D. Tex. 2014)). What would be the appropriate question to ask survey respondents?

3. *Mark fame and unauthorized parodic uses of a mark.* When sending cease and desist letters against unauthorized expressive users of their marks (such as parodists or appropriationist artists), trademark owners frequently assert that the law requires them to enforce their exclusive rights or they will lose those rights. Owners resort to this reasoning to defend often dubious and overreaching threat letters. In an effort to align owners' incentives with free speech, Mark Lemley has proposed that "[c]ourts should consider the existence, number, and prominence of unauthorized parodies, satires, or other expressive and referential uses of a mark directed at the general public as evidence tending to show that the mark is famous for both dilution and likelihood of confusion purposes, and the absence of such uses as tending to show that the mark is not famous and not as strong . . . . My proposal should encourage trademark lawyers to advise their clients to let such uses be. Trademark owners don't need to police expressive uses even today, and my approach would give them a reason not to." Mark A. Lemley, *Fame, Parody, and Policing in Trademark Law*, 2019 MICH. ST. L. REV. 1 (2019). Does this strike you as a salutary doctrinal innovation? Are courts likely to adopt it?

4. *State antidilution law as an alternative for marks that are not nationally famous.* As the table below indicates, 38 states provides state statutory antidilution protection. *See* McCarthy §24.77. Importantly, none of these states require that the mark be nationally famous to qualify for state antidilution protection. Some, such as Connecticut, Illinois, Minnesota, and New Jersey, provide protection only to a "mark which is famous in this state." *See, e.g.*, 765 Ill. Comp. Stat. 1036/65. Other state statutes, such as New York's, have been interpreted to require that the mark is "truly distinctive" to qualify for state antidilution protection. *See Allied Maint. Corp. v. Allied Mech. Trades, Inc.*, 42 N.Y.2d 538, 546 (1977). *See also Sally Gee, Inc. v. Myra Hogan, Inc.*, 699 F.2d 621, 625 (2d Cir. 1983) ("In *Allied* the majority indicated that the anti-dilution statute protects only extremely strong marks."); *Moore Bus. Forms, Inc. v. Rite Aid Corp.*, No. 90 Civ.1211E, 1991 U.S. Dist. LEXIS 18599, at *25 (W.D.N.Y. Dec. 6, 1991) ("*Allied Maintenance* requires that only truly distinctive marks be afforded the protection of New York's anti-dilution statute."). Though federal antidilution law requires a substantially higher level of fame for marks to qualify for federal antidilution protection, it does not preempt state antidilution law. *See, e.g.*, *Viacom, Inc. v. Ingram Enterprises, Inc.*, 141 F.3d 886 (8th Cir. 1998) (holding that the 1996 federal antidilution law does not preempt Missouri state antidilution law). This follows from the "general principle of federal-state trademark relations that while the states cannot subtract from the exclusive rights of trademark given by federal law, they can add to those rights." McCarthy § 24:80. A limitation of state antidilution protection, however, is that in certain instances injunctive relief may be limited only to the state covered by the statute or even to a part of that state. *See* McCarthy § 24.82.

State Statutory Antidilution Protection

Ala. Code § 8-12-17
Alaska Stat. § 45.50.180(d)
Ariz. Rev. Stat. § 44-1448.01
Ark. Code Ann. § 4-71-213
Cal. Bus. & Prof. Code § 14330
Conn. Gen. Stat. § 35-11i(c)
Del. Code Ann. tit. 6, § 3313
Fla. Stat. § 495.151
Ga. Code Ann. § 10-1-451(b)
Haw. Rev. Stat. § 482-32
Idaho Code § 48-513
765 Ill. Comp. Stat. 1036/65
Ind. Code § 24-2-1-13.5
Iowa Code § 548.113
Kan. Stat. Ann. § 81-214
La. Rev. Stat. § 51:223.1
Me. Rev. Stat. Ann. tit. 10, § 1530
Mass. Ann. Laws ch. 110B, § 12
Minn. Stat. § 333.285

Miss. Code Ann. § 75-25-25
Mo. Rev. Stat. § 417.061(1)
Mont. Code Ann. § 30-13-334
Neb. Rev. Stat. § 87-140
Nev. Rev. Stat. Ann. § 600.435
N.H. Rev. Stat. Ann. § 350-A:12
N.J. Stat. § 56:3-13.20
N.M. Stat. Ann. § 57-3B-15
N.Y. Gen. Bus. Law § 360-l
Ore. Rev. Stat. § 647.107
54 Pa. Cons. Stat. § 1124
R.I. Gen. Laws § 6-2-12
S.C. Code Ann. § 39-15-1165
Tenn. Code Ann. § 47-25-513
Tex. Bus. & Com. Code § 16.29
Utah Code Ann. § 70-3a-403
Wash. Rev. Code § 19.77.160
W. Va. Code § 47-2-13
Wyo. Stat. § 40-1-115

2. Dilution by Blurring

The following opinion, *Nike, Inc. v. Nikepal Intern., Inc.*, 84 U.S.P.Q.2d 1820 (E.D. Cal. 2007), was one of the first opinions thoroughly to analyze a claim of dilution by blurring under the new § 43(c) established by the TDRA. In reading *Nikepal*, consider the following questions;

- What is the nature of the harm to the NIKE mark? Is it reasonable to argue that Nikepal's use of the NIKEPAL mark could harm in any significant way a mark as strong as NIKE?

- Does the survey method described in the opinion strike you as valid?

- Though the opinion never addresses the likelihood of consumer confusion as to source, do you think some consumers might be confused as to source by the NIKEPAL mark? Could Nike have prevailed on a simple likelihood of confusion claim?

Nike, Inc. v. Nikepal Intern., Inc.
84 U.S.P.Q.2d 1820 (E.D. Cal. 2007)

GARLAND E. BURRELL, JR., United States District Judge.

[1] The following findings of fact and conclusions of law issue as a result of a bench trial conducted in this trademark action. Plaintiff Nike, Inc. ("Nike"), a company headquartered in Beaverton, Oregon which uses the mark NIKE, contests the use of the mark NIKEPAL by Defendant Nikepal International, Inc. ("Nikepal"), a company located in Sacramento, California. Nike initially contested Nikepal's registration of the NIKEPAL mark at the Trademark Trial and Appeal Board ("TTAB") of the United States Patent and Trademark Office ("PTO"); however, the TTAB denied Nike's opposition to Nikepal's registration of the NIKEPAL mark. Nike subsequently appealed the TTAB's ruling to this court under 15 U.S.C. § 1071 and brought additional claims for federal and state trademark dilution under 15 U.S.C. § 1125(c) and California Business and Professions Code section 14330; for trademark infringement under 15 U.S.C. § 1114; and for unfair competition under 15 U.S.C. § 1125(a).[2]

[2] Nike seeks an injunction preventing Nikepal from using the term "Nike" (or any term confusingly similar thereto) alone or as part of any trademark, domain name or business name under

---

[2] For the reasons stated herein, Nike prevails on its federal and state dilution claims. Therefore, Nike's claims for trademark infringement and unfair competition need not be reached.

which Nikepal offers goods or services in commerce. Nike also seeks a reversal of the TTAB's ruling allowing Nikepal to register the NIKEPAL mark. Nikepal seeks an affirmation of the TTAB's April 21, 2005 order. (TTAB's April 21, 2005 Order ("TTAB Decision").)

Findings of Fact

I. The Parties and their Businesses

A. Nike

[3] Nike was incorporated in 1968 under the original company name Blue Ribbon Sports. In 1971, it adopted the NIKE mark to brand its footwear products and in May 1978, the company's name was officially changed to "Nike, Inc." Today, Nike is the largest seller of athletic footwear and apparel in the world. Nike sells around 180 million pairs of shoes annually in the United States alone. Nike's principal business activity is the design, development, and worldwide marketing and distribution of high quality and technologically advanced footwear, apparel, equipment, and accessories. Nike has continuously used the NIKE mark on and in connection with the various products offered by the company since the 1970s. Sometimes, the word mark NIKE is the only brand used; sometimes, Nike's Swoosh design mark (i.e. the logo which frequently appears on products along with NIKE, and in some instances alone) is also placed on the product.

B. Nikepal

[4] Nikepal was incorporated on May 18, 1998 by the company's founder and president, Palminder Sandhu ("Mr. Sandhu"), who then began using the NIKEPAL mark in commerce. Nikepal provides services and products to analytical, environmental, and scientific laboratories. Nikepal's trademark application to the PTO requested registration for: "import and export agencies and wholesale distributorships featuring scientific, chemical, pharmaceutical, biotechnology testing instruments and glassware for laboratory use, electrical instruments, paper products and household products and cooking appliances." (Application Serial No. 76123346, filed September 6, 2000) Nikepal distributes glass syringes in varying volumes and other laboratory products to testing and power companies and also distributes paper boxes (syringe carrying cases) and nylon valves and caps for use with the syringes. Nikepal only distributes its products to laboratories, not to individuals.

[5] Nikepal does not have a retail office, but operates its business through its website (located at www.nikepal.com), via email, and via telephone. Nikepal is run by Mr. Sandhu, who also works as a transportation engineer. Currently, Nikepal has one other part-time employee. Nikepal has only a few hundred customers, but it has a list of thousands of prospective customers, some of whom receive materials from Nikepal advertising its product and service offerings under the mark NIKEPAL.

II. The Parties' Marks

A. NIKE

[6] Nike first registered the NIKE mark with the PTO in February 1974. Nike owns ten federal trademark registrations for the NIKE mark alone, covering footwear, clothing, bags, timepieces, paper products such as notebooks and binders, sport balls, swim accessories, and retail store services, all of which related to pre-May 1998 uses of the mark. By May 1998, Nike was also using and applied for trademark registrations covering the use of the NIKE mark in combination with other terms or designs for footwear, clothing, bags, timepieces, posters, sport balls, swim accessories, weights, gloves, headgear, and retail store services. For example, Nike owns nineteen federal registrations for NIKE composite marks such as: NIKE and the Swoosh design which has been in use since 1971; NIKE AIR which has been in use since 1987; NIKE-FIT which has been in use since 1990; NIKE TOWN which has been in use since 1990; NIKE SHOP which has been in use since 1991; and NIKE GOLF which has been in use since 1993. From 1998 to the present, Nike has continued to use the mark NIKE alone and in combination with other terms or designs.

B. NIKEPAL

[7] Mr. Sandhu testified that he conceived of the term Nikepal when he wanted to create a vanity license plate for his car. He testified that he selected the word "Nike" by opening a dictionary to a random

page and choosing the first word he saw, and then combined it with the first three letters of his first name "Pal." "Pal" means friend or benefactor. Mr. Sandhu admits he knew of the existence of the company Nike and its use of the NIKE mark at the time he devised the term NIKEPAL. Despite Mr. Sandhu's trial testimony concerning the manner in which he conceived of the term NIKEPAL, the court does not find it to be credible.

[7] The "Nike" portion of the NIKEPAL mark is pronounced the same way as the NIKE mark is pronounced: with a hard "i" (like bike) in the first syllable and a hard "e" (like in "key") in the second syllable.[3] The articles of incorporation signed by Mr. Sandhu for Nikepal in 1998 display the company name as "NikePal International, Inc.," with the first word of the company name spelled "NikePal," with a capital "N" and a capital "P."[4]

[8] In addition to using Nikepal as the company name, NIKEPAL appears directly on some of Nikepal's products, including on its syringe products, and on its marketing materials. Nikepal also places www.nikepal.com on its syringes to identify the source of the syringe. Nikepal also uses the NIKEPAL mark in a vanity phone number (1-877-N-I-K-E-P-A-L), on its website, and in its domain names, including nikepal.com, nikepal.biz, nikepal.us, nikepal.tv, nikepal.info, and nikepal.net.

III. Nike's Sales

[9] By the late 1980s, United States sales of NIKE branded products were over one billion dollars per year. Starting in 1991 and through the mid 1990s, sales of NIKE products in the United States were approximately two billion dollars per year, and were above five billion dollars per year by 1997. By 1997, Nike was the largest seller of athletic footwear and apparel in the world. The geographic area of Nike's sales includes the United States and 140 countries throughout the world. Since 1997, Nike has sold over 100,000,000 pairs of NIKE shoes each year.

IV. Advertising and Promotion of the NIKE Mark

[10] Nike has undertaken significant expense to promote the NIKE mark. Nike advertises in various types of media, including traditional print advertising, such as magazines (of both special and general interest), newspapers (of general circulation), leaflets, and billboards. Nike also advertises in electronic media, including radio, television, cable and internet, on sides of buildings, on taxi cabs, and through direct mailings. Nike's television advertisements have run on network channels and have reached national audiences. Nike has also promoted its mark by associating with athletes through endorsement arrangements. By 1991, Nike was spending in excess of one hundred million dollars per year in the United States alone to advertise products bearing the NIKE mark. By 1997, Nike had spent at least $1,567,900,000.00 to promote the NIKE mark in the United States.

V. Notoriety of NIKE

[11] The NIKE mark has been consistently ranked as a top brand in publications that survey the top brands each year. Since at least 1990, Nike has been named one of the top forty brands in the United States based on the EquiTrend and other studies published in BrandWeek and Financial World Magazine. Other brands ranked in such studies include FRITO LAY, LEVI'S, CAMPBELLS', HEWLETT-PACKARD, SONY, PEPSI, and VISA. One story printed in Forbes magazine, reported a survey conducted

---

[3] Nikepal's attorney attempted to convince the court that there is a pronunciation difference between NIKE and NIKEPAL. In her questions during trial, for example, she pronounced Nikepal's mark as "nik-a-pal." However, in answering her questions at trial, Mr. Sandhu, the president of Nikepal, alternated between the pronunciation of NIKEPAL as "nik-a-pal" and as "Ny-key-pal." Further, Nike's witness, Joseph Sheehan, a former FBI agent and now a private investigator, provided a tape recording of the outgoing message heard on Nikepal's answering machine which clearly pronounced the term "Nike" with long, or hard, vowels, that is an "i" like in "bike" and "e" like in "key" identical to the pronunciation of the Nike's trademark.

[4] However, since both parties refer to "Nikepal" with a lowercase "p" in this action, the court adopts this spelling for the purposes of this order.

by Young & Rubicam that ranked the NIKE brand among the top ten in the United States in 1996 with COKE, DISNEY, and HALLMARK.

VI. Evidence of Actual Association

[12] A survey conducted by Phillip Johnson of Leo J. Shapiro and Associates ("Mr. Johnson's survey"), a Chicago-based market research firm, determined that a significant number of Nikepal's potential laboratory customers actually associated NIKE with NIKEPAL. Mr. Johnson is an expert at designing surveys that measure consumer behavior. The primary business of Shapiro and Associates is to explore consumer behavior through the use of surveys for businesses such as Toys-R-Us, Target, and Petsmart in order to help them better understand their marketplace when developing new retail concepts. Nike retained Mr. Johnson to design a survey to measure, *inter alia*, the likelihood of dilution of the NIKE brand as a result of Nikepal's use of the NIKEPAL mark.

[13] In designing his study, Mr. Johnson used a universe of survey participants randomly selected from lists of companies that Mr. Sandhu's deposition testimony identified as the sources for Nikepal's current and prospective customers. Mr. Johnson conducted the survey by phone and asked respondents about their perception of a website called nikepal.com. In designing his survey, Mr. Johnson chose one of the ways that the NIKEPAL mark is used in commerce which allowed him to reasonably recreate a purchasing context while obtaining a controlled and accurate measurement. Mr. Johnson testified that this survey replicated the circumstances in which people typically encountered the NIKEPAL mark.

[14] Once survey respondents were screened to confirm that they were the persons most responsible for ordering laboratory equipment at their business, they were asked: "What if anything, came to your mind when I first said the word Nikepal?" Many survey respondents who were not actually confused about the source of the Nikepal website nonetheless identified Nike. Mr. Johnson testified that his survey revealed that the vast majority of respondents, 87%, associated Nikepal with Nike; that is, when they encounter the mark NIKEPAL, they think of Nike and/or its offerings.

[15] Evidence of actual association of the NIKEPAL mark with the NIKE mark also exists beyond the results demonstrated in Mr. Johnson's survey. Mr. Sandhu registered the domain names nikepal.biz, nikepal.us, nikepal.tv, nikepal.net, and nikepal.info with Network Solution, and until just prior to trial, those websites were inactive. Mr. Sandhu testified that at the time he registered those domains he chose not to link them to an active website. As a result, Network Solutions assigned those domains an "under construction" page and then associated with that page promotions and advertisement links to product and service offerings of its choice. These promotions and advertisements all referred to NIKE products or those of one of its competitors. Thus, when accessing Nikepal's NIKEPAL domain names (other than nikepal.com), users received information about Nike or its competitors, but not Nikepal.

Conclusions of Law

I. Dilution

[16] Under the Federal Trademark Dilution Revision Act,[6] . . . 15 U.S.C. § 1125(c)(1) ("TDRA"){, t}o prevail on its dilution claim, Nike must prove 1) that its mark was famous as of a date prior to the first use of the NIKEPAL mark and 2) that Nikepal's use of its allegedly diluting mark creates a likelihood of dilution by blurring or tarnishment.[7]

---

[6] The TDRA, signed into law on October 6, 2006, amended the previous federal anti-dilution statute (the Federal Trademark Dilution Act ("FTDA")). The TDRA revises the FTDA in three ways: it establishes that likelihood of dilution, and not actual dilution, is a prerequisite to establish a dilution claim; it sets forth four relevant factors courts may consider in determining famousness; and it also lists six relevant factors that courts may consider in determining whether a likelihood of dilution exists. *Century 21 Real Estate LLC v. Century Surety Co.*, 2007 WL 433579, at *1 (D.Ariz. Feb.6, 2007).

[7] California's anti-dilution statute, under which Nike also brings a claim, prescribes:

A. Whether NIKE Was Famous Prior to the First Use of NIKEPAL

[17] . . . Since Nikepal's first use of NIKEPAL commenced in May 1998, Nike must show that NIKE was famous before that date.

{The court applied the four factors listed in Lanham Act § 43(c)(2)(A), 15 U.S.C. 1125(c)(2)(A), to find that the NIKE mark was famous before May 1998}.

B. Likelihood of Dilution by Blurring

[18] The TDRA defines dilution by blurring as an "association arising from the similarity between a mark or trade name and a famous mark that impairs the distinctiveness of the famous mark." 15 U.S.C. § 1125(c)(2)(A) {*sic*} {*recte* 15 U.S.C. § 1125(c)(2)(B)}.

> In determining whether a mark or trade name is likely to cause dilution by blurring, the court may consider all relevant factors, including the following:
>
> (i) The degree of similarity between the mark or trade name and the famous mark.
>
> (ii) The degree of inherent or acquired distinctiveness of the famous mark.
>
> (iii) The extent to which the owner of the famous mark is engaging in substantially exclusive use of the mark.
>
> (iv) The degree of recognition of the famous mark.
>
> (v) Whether the user of the mark or trade name intended to create an association with the famous mark.
>
> (vi) Any actual association between the mark or trade name and the famous mark.

Id.

(i) The Degree of Similarity

[19] Marks in a dilution analysis must be "identical" or "nearly identical."[8] *Thane Int'l, Inc. v. Trek Bicycle Corp.,* 305 F.3d 894, 906 (9th Cir. 2002). "For marks to be nearly identical to one another, they 'must be similar enough that a significant segment of the target group of customers sees the two marks as essentially the same.'" *Playboy Enters., Inc. v. Welles,* 279 F.3d 796, 806 n. 41 (9th Cir. 2002) (internal citation omitted).

[20] The parties' marks are nearly identical. The NIKEPAL mark is a composite of the word "Nike" with the term of affinity, "pal." The composite nature of the NIKEPAL mark is evident in the logo selected by the company which clearly features an "N" and a "P." In each case the dominant feature of the mark is the term "Nike." In addition, the term "Nike" in both marks is pronounced identically with an "i" like in "bike" and an "e" like in "key." *See Porsche Cars N. Am., Inc.,* 2000 WL 641209, at *3, (finding that the

---

> Likelihood of injury to business reputation or a dilution of the distinctive quality of a mark registered under this chapter, or a mark valid at common law, or a trade name valid at common law, shall be a ground for injunctive relief notwithstanding the absence of competition between parties or the absence of confusion as to the source of goods or services.

Cal. Bus. & Prof.Code § 14330. If Nike prevails on its federal dilution claim, it will also prevail on its dilution claim under California law. *See Jada Toys, Inc. v. Mattel, Inc.,* 496 F.3d 974 (9th Cir. Aug.2, 2007); *see also Panavision Int'l v. Toeppen,* 141 F.3d 1316, 1324 (9th Cir. 1998) ("[Plaintiff's] state law dilution claim [under California Business and Professions Code section 14330] is subject to the same analysis as its federal [dilution] claim.").

[8] Nike argues that the TDRA does not require that the marks be identical or nearly identical. However, the enactment of the TDRA did "not eliminate the requirement that the mark used by the alleged diluter be 'identical,' or 'nearly identical,' or 'substantially similar,' to the protected mark." *Century 21 Real Estate LLC,* 2007 WL 433579, at *2 (citing House Report on Trademark Dilution Act of 2005 at 8, 25). {Note that the Ninth Circuit subsequently explicitly rejected this "identical or nearly identical" standard. See the casebook note following the opinion.}

trademark PORSCHE was diluted by PORCHESOURCE.COM); *see also Jada Toys, Inc.,* 496 F.3d 974, 2007 WL 2199286, at *4 (concluding "that a reasonable trier of fact could find that the HOT WHEELS and HOT RIGZ marks are nearly identical.").

[21] Further, as shown by Mr. Johnson's survey, the vast majority of the survey respondents, representing a significant segment of Nikepal's target customer group, associate Nike and/or its products and services when they encounter the mark NIKEPAL, thus perceiving the two marks as essentially the same. *See Thane Int'l, Inc.,* 305 F.3d at 906 ("The marks must be of sufficient similarity so that, in the mind of the consumer, the junior mark will conjure an association with the senior.") (citing *Nabisco, Inc. v. PF Brands,* 191 F.3d 208 (2d Cir. 1999)). Accordingly, this factor favors Nike.

(ii) Distinctiveness

. . . .

[22] Nikepal does not dispute that NIKE is, at the very least, suggestive. (*See* Nikepal's Proposed Findings and Recommendations at 42 ("[Nike's] mark is suggestive when used in connection with Plaintiff's products.").) Accordingly, NIKE is inherently distinctive and this factor favors Nike.

(iii) Substantially Exclusive Use

[23] The law does not require that use of the famous mark be absolutely exclusive, but merely "substantially exclusive." *See L.D.Kichler Co. v. Davoil Inc.,* 192 F.3d 1349, 1352 (Fed.Cir. 1999) (holding that in the trademark context, "substantially exclusive" use does not mean totally exclusive use). Therefore, a limited amount of third party use is insufficient to defeat a showing of substantially exclusive use. *See Avery Dennison Corp. v. Sumpton,* 189 F.3d 868, 878 (9th Cir. 1999) (finding that use of the mark was not substantially exclusive when the words "Avery" and "Dennison" were *"commonly* used as trademarks, both on and off of the Internet, by parties other than Avery Dennison." (emphasis added)).

[24] Nike asserts that its use of the NIKE mark is substantially exclusive. Nikepal introduced evidence of use of the term "Nike" in the company name "Nike Hydraulics, Inc.," through a bottle jack purchased from the company and a 1958 trademark registration for "Nike" owned by Nike Hydraulics. However, this evidence is insufficient to disprove Nike's claim that its use of NIKE is substantially exclusive. Even Nikepal's witness, Roger Smith, admitted that he had not encountered Nike Hydraulics before hearing that name in connection with this action. Accordingly, the court finds that Nike's use of the NIKE mark is substantially exclusive and this factor therefore favors Nike.[10]

(iv) Degree of Recognition

[25] The degree of recognition of NIKE is quite strong. Millions of NIKE products are sold in the United States annually and the evidence demonstrates that NIKE is readily recognized. This factor therefore favors Nike.

(v) Intent to Create Association

[26] Mr. Sandhu admitted that he was aware of the existence of the NIKE mark before he adopted the company name. Although he testified at trial that he came up with the term Nikepal by opening the dictionary to a random page and essentially finding that word by "fate," his testimony was not credible. Therefore, this factor favors Nike.

(vi) Actual Association

---

[10] Nikepal also introduced evidence that the term "Nike" appears in dictionaries referring to the Greek goddess of victory, that the image of Nike the goddess appeared on some Olympic medals, and that the United States Government named one of its missile programs "Nike." However, Nikepal did not show that these uses were made in commerce in association with the sale or marketing of goods or services as required under the TDRA. (*See* 15 U.S.C. § 1125(c) (1) (providing that under the TDRA, only "use of a mark or trade name in commerce" is actionable as diluting a famous mark.).)

[27] Nikepal registered the domain names nikepal.biz, nikepal.net, nikepal.us, nikepal.info and nikepal.tv. The evidence shows that the domain registrar assigned the domain names an "under construction" page and then associated with that page promotions and advertisement links to a number of web pages that offered NIKE products (or products of Nike's competitors in the shoe and apparel field). Thus, in the internet context, there is actual association between NIKEPAL and NIKE.

[28] Further, Mr. Johnson's survey also evinced that there is a strong degree of association between NIKEPAL and NIKE. Mr. Johnson's survey showed over 87% of the people in Nikepal's own customer pool associated the stimulus "Nikepal" with NIKE. The survey presents ample proof of association between the marks to support a finding that such exists in the general public. Accordingly, the court finds that there is actual association between the NIKEPAL and NIKE marks and this factor favors Nike.

[29] In conclusion, since the six factors considered in the likelihood of dilution analysis favor Nike, there is a likelihood that NIKE will suffer dilution if Nikepal is allowed to continue its use of NIKEPAL. Accordingly, Nike prevails on its federal and state dilution claims.

. . . .

CONCLUSION

[30] For the reasons stated, Nike prevails on its federal and state dilution claims, the decision of the TTAB is reversed, and the opposition to Nikepal's registration of the NIKEPAL mark is sustained. Further, Nikepal is permanently enjoined from using NIKEPAL in connection with the offering of goods or services in commerce, including its use in domain names, on web pages, in printed matter, and on products, and shall cease any such uses of NIKEPAL within sixty days of the date on which this order is filed. Nikepal may continue to use its numeric telephone number, but may not advertise or associate it with the designation "1-877-NIKEPAL."

IT IS SO ORDERED.

In reading the following opinion, consider how the *Wolfe's Borough* analysis of the blurring issue differs from the analysis undertaken by the *Nikepal* court. Does the *Wolfe's Borough* court simply assume, as does the *Nikepal* court, that association necessarily impairs the distinctiveness of the plaintiff's mark, or does the *Wolfe's Borough* court require an additional showing of impairment?

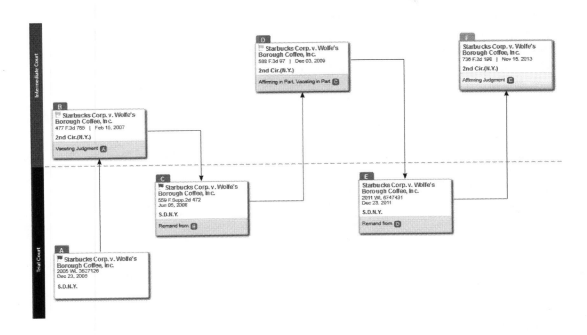

Starbucks Corp. v. Wolfe's Borough Coffee, Inc.
736 F.3d 198 (2d Cir. 2013)

LOHIER, Circuit Judge:

[1] Starbucks Corporation and Starbucks U.S. Brands LLC (together, "Starbucks") appeal from a judgment of the United States District Court for the Southern District of New York (Swain, J.) denying Starbucks' request for an injunction pursuant to the Federal Trademark Dilution Act of 1995 ("FTDA"), 15 U.S.C. § 1125(c), prohibiting Wolfe's Borough Coffee, Inc., doing business as Black Bear Micro Roastery ("Black Bear"), from using Black Bear's "Mister Charbucks," "Mr. Charbucks," and "Charbucks Blend" marks (the "Charbucks Marks"). After a bench trial followed by additional briefing from the parties upon remand from this Court, the District Court concluded that Starbucks failed to prove that the Charbucks Marks are likely to dilute Starbucks' famous "Starbucks" marks (the "Starbucks Marks") and denied Starbucks' request for an injunction.

[2] On appeal, Starbucks argues that the District Court erred in finding only minimal similarity and weak evidence of actual association between the Charbucks Marks and the Starbucks Marks. Starbucks also contends that the District Court erred in balancing the statutory dilution factors by giving no weight at all to three of the factors—the strong distinctiveness, exclusive use, and high degree of recognition of the Starbucks Marks—and placing undue weight on the minimal similarity between the marks.

[3] For the following reasons, we conclude that the District Court did not err in its factual findings, and, balancing the statutory factors *de novo*, we agree with the District Court that Starbucks failed to prove a likelihood of dilution. We therefore affirm.

BACKGROUND

[4] We assume familiarity with the underlying facts and long procedural history of the case, which are set forth in our previous opinions, *Starbucks Corp. v. Wolfe's Borough Coffee, Inc.*, 477 F.3d 765 (2d Cir. 2007) ("*Starbucks II* "), and *Starbucks Corp. v. Wolfe's Borough Coffee, Inc.*, 588 F.3d 97 (2d Cir. 2009) ("*Starbucks IV* "). We recount them here only as necessary to explain our disposition of this appeal.

[5] As of 2005, when the bench trial occurred, Starbucks had grown from a single coffee shop in Seattle in 1971 to a singularly prominent global purveyor of specialty coffee and coffee products, with

451

8,700 retail locations worldwide and revenues of $5.3 billion for fiscal year 2004. Starbucks U.S. Brands is the owner, and Starbucks Corporation a licensee, of at least 56 valid United States trademark registrations that include the Starbucks Marks. The Starbucks Marks are displayed on signs and at multiple locations in each Starbucks store, as well as on the Starbucks website.

[6] Starbucks has devoted substantial time, effort, and money to advertising and promoting the Starbucks Marks. From fiscal year 2000 to 2003, Starbucks spent over $136 million on advertising, promotion, and related marketing activities, essentially all of which featured the Starbucks Marks. Starbucks actively polices the Starbucks Marks, demanding that infringing uses be terminated and, where necessary, commencing litigation. Well before Black Bear used the term "Charbucks" as part of any product name, the Starbucks Marks were "famous" within the meaning of the FTDA. *See* 15 U.S.C. § 1125(c)(2)(A).

[7] Black Bear manufactures and sells roasted coffee beans and related goods via mail and internet order, at a limited number of New England supermarkets, and at a single New Hampshire retail outlet. In 1997 Black Bear developed a coffee blend named "Charbucks Blend"; it now sells a dark-roast coffee called "Mister Charbucks" or "Mr. Charbucks." When Black Bear began manufacturing coffee using the Charbucks Marks, it was aware of the Starbucks Marks. One of the reasons Black Bear used the term "Charbucks" was the public perception that Starbucks roasted its beans unusually darkly. Soon after Black Bear began to sell Charbucks Blend, Starbucks demanded that it cease using the Charbucks Marks. Black Bear nevertheless continued to sell coffee under the Charbucks Marks, and in 2001 Starbucks started this action claiming, among other things, trademark dilution in violation of 15 U.S.C. §§ 1125(c), 1127.[3]

[8] The District Court held a two-day bench trial in March 2005. At trial, two matters of significance to this appeal occurred. First, Black Bear's founder, James O. Clark III, testified that the name "Charbucks" had previously been used during "the coffee wars in Boston between Starbucks and the Coffee Connection," a Boston-based company. Second, Starbucks introduced the testimony of Warren J. Mitofsky, a scientist in the field of consumer research and polling. Mitofsky explained the results of a telephone survey he had conducted of six hundred participants, designed to be representative of the United States population. The survey found that when asked, "What is the first thing that comes to your mind when you hear the name 'Charbucks,' spelled C–H–A–R–B–U–C–K–S?," 30.5 percent of participants answered "Starbucks," while 9 percent answered "coffee."[5] When the participants were asked, "Can you name any company or store that you think might offer a product called 'Charbucks'?," 3.1 percent responded "Starbucks," and another 1.3 percent responded "coffee house."[6] Mitofsky concluded that "[t]he number one association of the name 'Charbucks' in the minds of consumers is with the brand 'Starbucks.'" Commenting on the scope of his survey, Mitofsky also stated: "[I]f you want to know the reaction to the name Charbucks, then the telephone is perfectly adequate. If you want to measure the reaction or the familiarity with other visual cues, then it's not the right method." *Starbucks IV*, 588 F.3d at 104.

---

[3] Starbucks also asserted claims of trademark infringement in violation of 15 U.S.C. § 1114(1); unfair competition in violation of 15 U.S.C. § 1125(a); trademark dilution in violation of New York General Business Law § 360–*l*; deceptive acts and business practices and false advertising in violation of New York General Business Law §§ 349, 350; and unfair competition in violation of New York common law. All of these claims were dismissed during the course of this suit and are not the subject of this appeal.

[5] Other common responses included "barbeque" or "charcoal" (7.9 percent); "restaurant" or "grill" (7.5 percent); "meat," "steak," or "hamburger" (4.6 percent); and "money" (3.9 percent).

[6] More popular responses to this second question included: "grocery store" (18.3 percent); "discount store" (16.9 percent); "restaurant" (7.0 percent); "department store" (4.8 percent); and "hardware store" or "home improvement store" (3.7 percent).

[9] In December 2005 the District Court ruled in favor of Black Bear and dismissed Starbucks' complaint. *See Starbucks Corp. v. Wolfe's Borough Coffee, Inc.,* No. 01 Civ. 5981, 2005 WL 3527126 (S.D.N.Y. Dec. 23, 2005) (*"Starbucks I "*). The District Court determined that there was neither actual dilution, which would establish a violation of federal trademark law,[7] nor a likelihood of dilution, which would establish a violation of New York trademark law.

[10] Starbucks appealed. While the appeal was pending, Congress passed the Trademark Dilution Revision Act of 2006 ("TDRA"), which amended the FTDA to clarify that the owner of a famous mark seeking an injunction need prove only that the defendant's mark "is likely to cause dilution ... of the famous mark, regardless of the presence or absence of actual or likely confusion, of competition, or of actual economic injury." 15 U.S.C. § 1125(c)(1). The TDRA further redefined "dilution by blurring" as "association arising from the similarity between a mark or trade name and a famous mark that impairs the distinctiveness of the famous mark." *Id.* § 1125(c)(2)(B). . . . In light of this change in the governing law, we vacated the judgment of the District Court and remanded for further proceedings. *Starbucks II,* 477 F.3d at 766.

[11] On remand, after further briefing, the District Court again ruled in Black Bear's favor for substantially the same reasons set forth in its earlier opinion, but it also analyzed the federal dilution claim in light of the TDRA. *See Starbucks Corp. v. Wolfe's Borough Coffee, Inc.,* 559 F.Supp.2d 472, 475–79 (S.D.N.Y. 2008) (*"Starbucks III "*). In particular, the District Court considered the six non-exclusive factors listed in the statute and made the following findings: (1) the marks were minimally similar, which the court deemed alone sufficient to defeat Starbucks' claim; (2) (a) the distinctiveness of the Starbucks Marks, (b) the exclusivity of their use by Starbucks, and (c) their high degree of recognition, all weighed in favor of Starbucks; (3) the intent factor weighed in Black Bear's favor because Black Bear's intent to create an association with the Starbucks Marks did not constitute bad faith; and (4) evidence from Mitofsky's survey was "insufficient to make the actual confusion factor weigh in [Starbucks'] favor to any significant degree." *Id.* at 477–78 (quotation marks omitted). Balancing all six factors, the District Court held that the record was "insufficient to demonstrate the requisite likelihood that the association arising from the similarity of the core terms is likely to impair the distinctiveness of Starbucks' mark, and Plaintiff is not entitled to injunctive relief under that statute." *Id.* at 478.

[12] Starbucks appealed again, arguing that the District Court erred in finding that the Charbucks Marks are not likely to dilute the Starbucks Marks. In *Starbucks IV,* we examined the District Court's findings as to the first, fifth, and sixth factors, as well as its balancing of the statutory factors that bear on the likelihood of dilution by blurring. We held that "the District Court did not clearly err in finding that the Charbucks Marks were minimally similar to the Starbucks Marks," 588 F.3d at 106, because the context of the Charbucks Marks (on Black Bear's packaging, on its website, and in the phrases "Charbucks Blend" and "Mister Charbucks") differentiated them from the famous marks. We concluded, however, that "the District Court erred to the extent it required 'substantial' similarity between the marks," *id.* at 107, and we suggested that the District Court had overemphasized the similarity factor. In particular, we stated that the inclusion of "the degree of similarity" as only one of six factors in the revised statute indicates that even a low degree of similarity would not categorically bar a dilution-by-blurring claim. *Id.* at 108.

[13] Turning to the fifth and sixth factors—intent to associate and actual association—we held that the District Court had erred by requiring "bad faith" to find that the intent to associate factor favored Starbucks. *Id.* at 109 (quotation marks omitted). Noting the survey results, which demonstrated some degree of association between "Charbucks" and "Starbucks," we also held that the District Court erred by relying on evidence supporting the absence of "actual *confusion* " to conclude that the actual *association* factor did not weigh in Starbucks' favor "to any significant degree." *Id.* (quotation marks

---

[7] At the time, federal law provided: "The owner of a famous mark shall be entitled ... to an injunction against another person's commercial use in commerce of a mark or trade name, if such use begins after the mark has become famous and *causes dilution of the distinctive quality of the mark* . . . ." 15 U.S.C. § 1125(c)(1) (1999) (amended 2006) (emphasis added).

omitted). The absence of actual or likely confusion, we reasoned, does not bear directly on whether dilution is likely. *Id.*

[14] Emphasizing that the analysis of a dilution by blurring claim must ultimately focus on "whether an *association,* arising from the similarity between the subject marks, 'impairs the distinctiveness of the famous mark,'" *id.* (quoting 15 U.S.C. § 1125(c)(2)(B)), we vacated the judgment of the District Court and remanded for reconsideration of the claim in light of our discussions of the first, fifth, and sixth statutory factors, *id.* at 109–10.

[15] In its opinion and order following that remand, *see Starbucks Corp. v. Wolfe's Borough Coffee, Inc.,* No. 01 Civ. 5981, 2011 WL 6747431 (S.D.N.Y. Dec. 23, 2011) ("*Starbucks V* "), the District Court recognized that the second through fifth statutory factors[8] favored Starbucks. *Id.* at *3 (citing *Starbucks IV,* 588 F.3d at 106–10). But the court again found that the first factor (the similarity of the marks) favored Black Bear because the marks were only minimally similar when presented in commerce—that is, when the Charbucks Marks are viewed on the packaging, which includes the phrases "Charbucks Blend" or "Mister Charbucks." *Id.*

[16] As for the sixth factor (actual association), the District Court acknowledged that the results of the Mitofsky survey "constitute evidence of actual association," *id.* at *4, but it then significantly discounted those results on the ground that the survey inquired into associations only with the isolated word "Charbucks" and failed to present the Charbucks Marks in full context, *id.* The court also compared the survey results in this case with those in other cases. Here, it noted, only 30.5 percent of respondents associated "Charbucks" with "Starbucks," while in other trade dilution cases 70 percent to 90 percent of survey respondents associated the relevant marks. *Id.* The District Court also compared the 3.1 percent of respondents who thought a product called "Charbucks" would be made by Starbucks to the 28 percent of respondents who made a similar origin association in a Ninth Circuit trademark dilution case. *Id.* (citing *Jada Toys, Inc. v. Mattel, Inc.,* 518 F.3d 628, 636 (9th Cir. 2008)). With the benefit of these comparisons, the District Court found that the actual association factor weighs "no more than minimally" in Starbucks' favor. *Id.*

[17] In evaluating the likelihood of dilution, the District Court emphasized the "association" and "similarity" factors. Citing the TDRA's definition of dilution by blurring as "*association arising from the similarity* between a mark or trade name and a famous mark that impairs the distinctiveness of the famous mark," the District Court explained that "[t]he statutory language leaves no doubt" that these two factors are "obviously important." *Id.* at *5 (quoting 15 U.S.C. § 1125(c)(2)(B)). 1 After balancing all six factors, the District Court held that Starbucks had failed to meet its burden of showing that it was entitled to injunctive relief:

> [T]he Charbucks marks are only weakly associated with the minimally similar Starbucks marks and, thus, are not likely to impair the distinctiveness of the famous Starbucks marks. In other words, [Starbucks] has failed to carry its burden of proving that [Black Bear's] use of its marks, as evidenced on the record before the Court, is likely to cause dilution by blurring.

Id. at *6.

[18] On appeal, Starbucks challenges both the factual findings of minimal similarity and weak association and the conclusion that it failed to demonstrate a likelihood of dilution.

---

[8] For convenience, we repeat those factors here: (ii) the distinctiveness of the Starbucks Marks; (iii) the exclusivity of Starbucks' use of its marks; (iv) the high degree of recognition of the Starbucks Marks; and (v) Black Bear's intent to associate the Charbucks Marks with the Starbucks Marks.

DISCUSSION

. . . .

B. Standard of Review

[19] After a bench trial on a claim for trademark dilution by blurring, where the district court evaluates and balances the factors listed in the TDRA, we review the court's determinations as to each factor for clear error and its balancing of those factors *de novo. See Tiffany*, 600 F.3d at 101; *Starbucks IV*, 588 F.3d at 105.[10] . . . .

. . . .

[20] We previously have declined to treat the factors pertinent to a trademark dilution analysis as an inflexible, mechanical test, suggesting instead that the importance of each factor will vary with the facts. *Nabisco, Inc. v. PF Brands, Inc.*, 191 F.3d 208, 227–28 (2d Cir. 1999), *abrogated on other grounds by Moseley*, 537 U.S. at 433, 123 S.Ct. 1115. Accordingly, we need not consider all six statutory factors listed in 15 U.S.C. § 1125(c)(2)(B)(i)-(vi) if some are irrelevant to the ultimate question; nor are we limited to those six factors. *See Louis Vuitton Malletier S.A. v. Haute Diggity Dog, LLC*, 507 F.3d 252, 266 (4th Cir. 2007) ("Not every factor will be relevant in every case, and not every blurring claim will require extensive discussion of the factors."). Instead, we employ a "cautious and gradual approach," which favors the development of a nonexclusive list of trademark dilution factors over time. *Nabisco*, 191 F.3d at 217.

C. Factual Findings: The Statutory Factors

[21] On appeal, Starbucks challenges two of the District Court's findings: (1) that there is only a minimal degree of similarity between the Starbucks Marks and the Charbucks Marks; and (2) that Starbucks demonstrated only a weak association between the marks. The District Court did not clearly err with regard to either finding.

1. Degree of Similarity

[22] In *Starbucks IV* we held that "[w]ith respect to the first factor—the degree of similarity between the marks—the District Court did not clearly err in finding that the Charbucks Marks were minimally similar to the Starbucks Marks." 588 F.3d at 106. We highlighted the difference between the Starbucks Marks and Charbucks Marks when the latter are placed in the context of Black Bear's packaging and the word "Charbucks" is incorporated into the phrases "Charbucks Blend" and "Mister Charbucks." *Id.* "The law of the case ordinarily forecloses relitigation of issues expressly or impliedly decided by the appellate court." *United States v. Quintieri*, 306 F.3d 1217, 1229 (2d Cir. 2002). Although not binding, the doctrine "counsels a court against revisiting its prior rulings in subsequent stages of the same case absent 'cogent' and 'compelling' reasons such as 'an intervening change of controlling law, the availability of new evidence, or the need to correct a clear error or prevent manifest injustice.'" *Ali v. Mukasey*, 529 F.3d 478, 490 (2d Cir. 2008) (quoting *United States v. Tenzer*, 213 F.3d 34, 39 (2d Cir. 2000)). Starbucks advances no compelling reason for us to revisit our ruling on the issue of similarity. It urges that the holding in *Starbucks IV* applied only to our "likelihood of confusion" analysis, and that the District Court erred by considering the contexts in which consumers encounter the Charbucks Marks.[11]

---

[10] We employ the same standard here that we use in the context of trademark infringement, where a district court evaluates and then balances the eight factors set forth in *Polaroid Corp. v. Polarad Electronics Corp.*, 287 F.2d 492, 495 (2d Cir. 1961), to determine whether there is a likelihood of confusion. *See, e.g., Star Indus. v. Bacardi & Co.*, 412 F.3d 373, 384 (2d Cir. 2005). The statutory factors enumerated in § 1125(c)(2)(B) are similar in kind to the *Polaroid* factors. For example, both lists include the "similarity between" the two marks; "strength" of the mark in *Polaroid* is akin to "distinctiveness" in § 1125; and "actual confusion" in *Polaroid* mirrors "actual association" in § 1125. *See Polaroid*, 287 F.2d at 495.

[11] At oral argument, Starbucks' counsel conceded that our earlier decision on minimal similarity is the law of the case.

We reject such a crabbed view of the holding and adhere to our prior ruling that the District Court did not clearly err in finding minimal similarity.

2. Actual Association

[23] Starbucks next contends that the District Court's finding that actual association "weighs no more than minimally" in Starbucks' favor, *Starbucks V*, 2011 WL 6747431, at *4, was error for two reasons. First, Starbucks argues, Black Bear's admitted intent to create an association—the fifth statutory factor—raises a "presumption of association," or at least is strong evidence of actual association—the sixth statutory factor. Second, it argues that the District Court improperly discounted the Mitofsky survey evidence, which, in Starbucks' view, proves a high degree of actual association. We reject both arguments.

a. Intent to Create an Association

[24] As an initial matter, an intent to create an association is a separate factor under the TDRA and does not constitute *per se* evidence that the actual association factor weighs in favor of the owner of the famous mark. In support of its argument to the contrary, Starbucks quotes McCarthy's treatise, which states, "If the junior [user] intended to create an association, the law may assume that it succeeded." McCarthy § 24:119. Starbucks similarly relies on *Federal Express Corp. v. Federal Espresso, Inc.*, 201 F.3d 168 (2d Cir. 2000), a dilution case in which we stated that the trier of fact "may well find that the marks are of sufficient similarity so that, in the mind of the consumer, the junior mark will conjure an association with the senior, especially in light of the testimony of [Federal Espresso's founder] that she chose the name Federal Espresso, in part, precisely because it would call to mind Federal Express." *Id.* at 177 (quotation marks omitted).

[25] Both *Federal Espresso* and McCarthy's treatise acknowledge the importance of the intent factor in determining likelihood of dilution. This makes sense, as district courts must evaluate whether a junior mark is "likely to cause" "association arising from the similarity" between the marks "that impairs the distinctiveness of the famous mark," 15 U.S.C. §§ 1125(c)(1), (c)(2)(B), and the intent to associate may bear directly on the likelihood that the junior mark will cause such an association.

[26] That said, "we interpret statutes to give effect, if possible, to every clause and word and to avoid statutory interpretations that render provisions superfluous." *United States v. Al Kassar*, 660 F.3d 108, 124–25 (2d Cir. 2011) (quotation marks omitted). Adopting Starbucks' presumption argument would effectively merge the intent to associate and the actual association factors, by making the former determinative of the latter, rather than treating them as distinct but related considerations. We therefore conclude that the District Court did not clearly err in finding that Clark's testimony concerning the origin of the Charbucks Marks was not an "admission" of actual association and that his intentions were not definitive proof of an actual association between the marks.

b. Mitofsky Survey

[27] Nor did the District Court err when it discounted the Mitofsky survey evidence because the survey measured only how respondents reacted to the isolated word "Charbucks," rather than to the Charbucks Marks in context, and because the share of respondents who indicated an association between the marks was "relatively small." *Starbucks V*, 2011 WL 6747431, at *4. We arrive at this conclusion for two reasons.

[28] First, it coheres with our decision in *Starbucks IV*, in which we discerned no clear error in the District Court's consideration of context—including the addition of "Mister" or "Blend" to "Charbucks" and Black Bear's packaging—in assessing the marks' similarity, as consumers are likely to experience the product only in the context of those full phrases and Black Bear's packaging or website. *Starbucks IV*, 588 F.3d at 106. In our analysis of Starbucks' infringement claim, we similarly determined that the District Court did not clearly err when it found (1) that the survey failed to demonstrate significant actual confusion, "[p]articularly in light of the fact that the survey was administered by telephone and did not present the term 'Charbucks' in the context in which Black Bear used it," *id.* at 117, and (2) that the survey should have examined the effects of "a hypothetical coffee named either 'Mister Charbucks' or

'Charbucks Blend'" on the respondents' impressions of Starbucks coffee as a measure of dilution by tarnishment, *id.* at 110.

[29] Second, our conclusion also comports with our prior precedents and other cases unrelated to Starbucks. In *Playtex Products, Inc. v. Georgia–Pacific Corp.*, 390 F.3d 158 (2d Cir. 2004), a case interpreting the pre-revision FTDA, we held that the results of a consumer survey showing an association between the marks "Moist–Ones" and "Wet Ones" were inadmissible as evidence of actual dilution because the defendant's product was "presented and packaged" as "*Quilted Northern* Moist–Ones." *Id.* at 168 (emphasis added). District courts within our Circuit have applied the same reasoning in evaluating surveys in the infringement context. *See, e.g., THOIP v. Walt Disney Co.*, 690 F.Supp.2d 218, 235–40 (S.D.N.Y. 2010); *Juicy Couture, Inc. v. L'Oreal USA, Inc.*, No. 04 Civ. 7203, 2006 WL 1012939, at *25–27 (S.D.N.Y. Apr. 19,2006); *WE Media, Inc. v. Gen. Elec. Co.*, 218 F.Supp.2d 463, 474 (S.D.N.Y. 2002) ("Germane survey evidence should make some effort to compare the impressions the marks have on potential customers under marketplace conditions."). In the dilution context, the language of the FTDA, which requires a plaintiff to show the defendant's "*use of a mark . . . in commerce* that is likely to cause dilution by blurring . . . ," 15 U.S.C. § 1125(c)(1) (emphasis added), clarifies that the way the defendant's mark is used in commerce is central to the dilution inquiry. As in *Playtex*, the District Court was within its rights to conclude that the Mitofsky survey had limited probative value because the defendant's marks were not presented to survey respondents as they are actually "presented and packaged" in commerce.

[30] Citing our decision in *Nabisco*, Starbucks nevertheless argues that consumers are likely to hear and view the term "Charbucks" outside the context of Black Bear's packaging and without the full phrases "Mister Charbucks" and "Charbucks Blend." *Nabisco*, 191 F.3d at 218 (rejecting an argument under the pre-revision FTDA that packaging made two marks dissimilar, because many consumers would see the marks outside of the packaging). But Starbucks presented no record evidence that "Charbucks" is ever read or heard in isolation,[13] and in the absence of such evidence, we are not persuaded by the argument. To the contrary, as we noted in *Starbucks IV*, "it is unlikely that 'Charbucks' will appear to consumers outside the context of its normal use," 588 F.3d at 106, and "it was not clearly erroneous for the District Court to find that the 'Mister' prefix or 'Blend' suffix lessened the similarity between the [marks]," *id.* at 107.

[31] Starbucks also challenges the District Court's finding that the association between "Charbucks" and Starbucks was "relatively small." It contends that the Mitofsky survey in fact provided evidence of substantial actual association. We disagree.

[32] It is true that in response to Mitofsky's question most probative of actual association—"What is the FIRST THING that comes to your mind when you hear the name 'Charbucks,' spelled C–H–A–R–B–U–C–K–S?"—30.5 percent of respondents said "Starbucks," and 9 percent said "coffee." Both of these responses suggest an association between "Charbucks" and the Starbucks Marks. In *Jada Toys*, 518 F.3d at 636, for example, the Ninth Circuit held that a survey demonstrated actual association because it showed that 28 percent of respondents thought Jada's product was made by Mattel when asked who they thought produced the item. Here, however, the equivalent question in Mitofsky's survey was: "Can you name any company or store that you think might offer a product called 'Charbucks'?"[14] In response to that question concerning source on the Mitofsky survey, however, only 3.1 percent of respondents answered "Starbucks" and 1.3 percent answered "coffee house." These percentages are far below that

---

[13] Although the name "Mr. Charbucks" is presented in plain text on at least one page of Black Bear's website, all other record uses of the Charbucks Marks situate them in Black Bear's distinct color scheme, font, and layout.

[14] Both that question and the question discussed in *Jada Toys* test not merely *association* but also source *confusion*. Source confusion may be probative of association, because to confuse Charbucks with Starbucks, the word "Charbucks" must call "Starbucks" to mind. *See Nabisco*, 191 F.3d at 221 ("Confusion lessens distinction.").

for the equivalent question in Jada Toys and fail to demonstrate anything more than minimal actual association.[15] *See Starbucks V*, 2011 WL 6747431, at *4.

[33] Ultimately, on this factor, we consider only whether the District Court clearly erred when it found that the Mitofsky survey tilts the "actual association" factor "no more than minimally in [Starbucks'] favor." *Id.* Had the Mitofsky survey presented the Charbucks Marks as they appear in commerce, we might well conclude that the District Court erred. But the word "Charbucks" was presented outside of its marketplace context, and Starbucks, which bears the burden of proof, *see Jada Toys*, 518 F.3d at 634, failed to show that this flaw did not materially impact the survey results. We therefore conclude that the record supports the District Court's decision to discount the survey and consider the actual association factor as weighing only minimally in Starbucks' favor.

D. Balancing

[34] We next balance the factors enumerated in § 1125(c)(2)(B), along with any other factors that bear on a likelihood of dilution, *de novo*. In balancing these factors, we are again mindful that the test is not an inflexible one, and that the ultimate question is whether the Charbucks Marks are likely to cause an association arising from their similarity to the Starbucks Marks, which impairs the Starbucks Marks' tendency to identify the source of Starbucks products in a unique way.

[35] We have already affirmed the District Court's finding of minimal similarity between the Charbucks Marks and the Starbucks Marks. That finding weighs heavily in Black Bear's favor. Certainly, a plaintiff may show a likelihood of dilution notwithstanding only minimal similarity. But here, minimal similarity strongly suggests a relatively low likelihood of an association diluting the senior mark . . . . {I}n *Starbucks IV*, we stated that "'similarity' is an integral element in the definition of 'blurring'" under the TDRA and suggested that, without *any* similarity, there could be no dilution by blurring. 588 F.3d at 108–09.[17]

[36] The next three factors—the degrees of distinctiveness, exclusive use, and recognition—are features of the senior mark itself that do not depend on the use of the junior mark . . . .

[37] Although the three factors of distinctiveness, recognition, and exclusivity favor Starbucks and bear to some degree on our assessment of the likelihood of dilution by blurring, the more important factors in the context of this case are the similarity of the marks and actual association. We agree with the District Court that the distinctiveness, recognition, and exclusive use of the Starbucks Marks do not overcome the weak evidence of actual association between the Charbucks and Starbucks marks. To the contrary, viewed in light of Starbucks' fame, both globally and among the Mitofsky survey participants more particularly, the fact that more survey participants did not think of "Starbucks" upon hearing "Charbucks" reinforces the District Court's finding that the marks are only minimally similar, and therefore unlikely to prompt an association that impairs the Starbucks Marks. Likewise, although the distinctiveness and exclusive use of the Starbucks Marks help Starbucks prove *susceptibility* to dilution by association arising from similarity between the Charbucks and Starbucks marks, they do not demonstrate that such an association is likely to arise, as Starbucks needed to show to obtain an injunction. Accordingly, these factors weigh only weakly in Starbucks' favor.

---

[15] Although some other respondents gave answers consistent with an association with Starbucks—18.3 percent answered "grocery store," 16.9 percent answered "discount store," 7 percent answered "restaurant," and 4.8 percent answered "department store"—these responses are also consistent with other views of what "Charbucks" could be, including meat or a charcoal grilling product, as 38.5 percent of respondents suggested.

[17] Of course, in *Starbucks IV*, we rejected a *per se* or threshold requirement of "substantial similarity" between the marks at issue in federal dilution actions. 588 F.3d at 108–09. In doing so, however, we did not suggest that a finding of *minimal* similarity could not be highly probative of the likelihood of dilution.

[38] In this case, we attribute a moderate amount of significance to the fifth factor, intent to create an association . . . .

[39] The final, disputed factor, actual association, is highly relevant to likelihood of association. In the analogous context of determining the "likelihood of confusion" for trademark infringement claims, we have noted that "[t]here can be no more positive or substantial proof of the likelihood of confusion than proof of actual confusion," even though a showing of actual confusion is not necessary to prevail on such a claim. *Savin Corp. v. Savin Grp.*, 391 F.3d 439, 459 (2d Cir. 2004). The same principle obtains with respect to proof of actual association in dilution claims. And as noted, the Mitofsky survey demonstrated weak actual association, at best.

[40] Weighing the factors above *de novo*, we agree with the District Court that Starbucks did not demonstrate a likelihood of dilution by blurring. Ultimately what tips the balance in this case is that Starbucks bore the burden of showing that it was entitled to injunctive relief on this record. Because Starbucks' principal evidence of association, the Mitofsky survey, was fundamentally flawed, and because there was minimal similarity between the marks at issue, we agree with the District Court that Starbucks failed to show that Black Bear's use of its Charbucks Marks in commerce is likely to dilute the Starbucks Marks.

CONCLUSION

[41] We have considered all of Starbucks' contentions on this appeal and have concluded that they are without merit. For the foregoing reasons, we AFFIRM the judgment of the District Court.

Comments and Questions

1. *How similar must the parties marks be to show dilution?* The *Nikepal* court applied an "identical or nearly identical" standard of similarity in its blurring analysis, following *Thane Int'l, Inc. v. Trek Bicycle Corp.*, 305 F.3d 894 (9th Cir. 2002). The Second Circuit, however, has rejected this approach. In *Starbucks Corp. v. Wolfe's Borough Coffee, Inc.*, 588 F.3d 97 (2d Cir. 2009), it emphasized that the new statute "does not use the words 'very' or 'substantial' in connection with the similarity factor," *id.* at 108, and reasoned that if courts were to impose a heightened similarity standard, this would give undue weight to the similarity factor—by turning the heightened similarity requirement into a threshold requirement that would short-circuit the six-factor multifactor balancing test for blurring. (The Second Circuit found that New York state anti-dilution law, by contrast, does impose a requirement that the marks be "'substantially' similar," *id.* at 114). In *Levi Strauss & Co. v. Abercrombie & Fitch Trading Co.*, 633 F.3d 1158 (9th Cir. 2011), the Ninth Circuit subsequently followed the Second Circuit's reasoning:

> Turning to the language of subsection (c)(2)(B), the TDRA defines "dilution by blurring" as the "association arising from the similarity between a mark and a trade name and a famous mark that impairs the distinctiveness of the famous mark." Id. § 1125(c)(2)(B) (emphasis added). Congress did not require an association arising from the "substantial" similarity, "identity" or "near identity" of the two marks. The word chosen by Congress, "similarity," sets forth a less demanding standard than that employed by many courts under the FTDA.

Id. at 1171. Do you find the Second and Ninth Circuits' reasoning persuasive? As a matter of sound policy, should courts require a heightened standard of similarity when analyzing a blurring claim? And in any case, are you persuaded that Nike and Nikepal are nearly identical?

2. *Mere association or association that impairs distinctiveness?* Recall that the TDRA defines dilution by blurring as "association. . .that impairs the distinctiveness of the famous mark." The *Nikepal* court found evidence of association, but it never addressed the question of whether this association "impairs the distinctiveness of the famous mark." Can we assume, as the *Nikepal* court appears to do, that any association necessarily impairs the distinctiveness of the plaintiff's mark? Consider what the Supreme Court said in *Moseley*:

> We do agree, however, with {the} conclusion that, at least where the marks at issue are not identical, the mere fact that consumers mentally associate the junior user's mark with a famous mark is not sufficient to establish actionable dilution. {S}uch mental association

will not necessarily reduce the capacity of the famous mark to identify the goods of its owner, the statutory requirement for dilution under the FTDA. For even though Utah drivers may be reminded of the circus when they see a license plate referring to the "greatest *snow* on earth," it by no means follows that they will associate "the greatest show on earth" with skiing or snow sports, or associate it less strongly or exclusively with the circus. "Blurring" is not a necessary consequence of mental association. (Nor, for that matter, is "tarnishing.")

Moseley v. V Secret Catalogue, 537 U.S. 418, 433-34 (2003). On remand, the *Moseley* district court took the Supreme Court's teaching very much to heart. *See V Secret Catalogue, Inc. v. Moseley*, 558 F. Supp. 2d 734 (W.D. Ky. 2008). It found all six blurring factors to favor the plaintiff, but nevertheless found no blurring: "The choice of name and presentation by the Moseleys being just slightly different from the VICTORIA'S SECRET mark, conjured the association with the famous mark, but fell short of blurring its distinctiveness in this instance." *Id.* at 748. (The *Moseley* district court found tarnishment instead, *id.* at 750).

How can the plaintiff prove that association impairs the distinctiveness of its mark? Compare *Louis Vuitton Malletier, S.A. v. Hyundai Motor Am.*, 2012 WL 1022247 (S.D.N.Y. 2012) (finding proof of association conclusive evidence of dilution), with *Louis Vuitton Malletier, S.A. v. My Other Bag, Inc.*, 156 F.Supp.3d 425, 436 n.4 (S.D.N.Y. 2016), *aff'd*, 2016 WL 7436489 (2d Cir. 2016) (rejecting the *Hyundai* reasoning, stating "association is a necessary, but not sufficient, condition for a finding of dilution by blurring"). *See also* Barton Beebe, Roy Germano, Christopher Jon Sprigman, & Joel Steckel, *Testing for Trademark Dilution in Court and the Lab*, 86 U. CHI. L. REV. 611 (2019) (presenting experimental evidence that "even when consumers associate a junior mark with a famous senior mark, this association does not necessarily result in any impairment of the ability of the senior mark to identify its source and associations").

3. *Are some trademarks so strong as to be immune to blurring?* In 2000, Professors Maureen Morrin and the late Jacob Jacoby, the latter of whom was a highly regarded trademark survey expert, reported the results of two studies they conducted to detect the effects of diluting stimuli on brand recognition and recall in test subjects. *See* Maureen Morrin & Jacob Jacoby, *Trademark Dilution: Empirical Measures for an Elusive Concept*, 19 J. Pub. Pol. & Marketing 265 (2000). Among other findings, they reported: "It appears that very strong brands are immune to dilution because their memory connections are so strong that it is difficult for consumers to alter them or create new ones with the same brand name." *Id.* at 274. Does this make sense to you? What are the implications of such a finding for anti-dilution protection, a form of protection granted only to brands "widely recognized by the general consuming public of the United States"?

4. *Does dilution protection make any difference in practice?* Commentators have long asserted that the very marks that qualify for dilution protection rarely need it. This is because such marks will likely win the conventional likelihood of confusion cause of action both because of their enormous fame and because the scope of the likelihood of confusion cause of action has expanded dramatically in the past few decades. *See, e.g.*, Mark P. McKenna, *The Normative Foundations of Trademark Law*, 82 NOTRE DAME L. REV. 1839, 1913-14 (2007). For example, if a defendant were to begin to sell Coca-Cola brand bicycles, how likely is it that Coca-Cola's lawyers would be able to prove some degree of confusion?

Empirical evidence suggests that when courts consider both confusion and dilution, their dilution determinations are usually redundant of their confusion determinations. One study found that in the year following the October 6, 2006, effective date of the TDRA, no reported federal court opinion that considered both confusion and dilution found the latter but not the former. *See* Barton Beebe, *The Continuing Debacle of U.S. Antidilution Law: Evidence from the First Year of Trademark Dilution Revision Act Case Law*, 24 Santa Clara Computer & High Tech. L.J. 449 (2008). This trend appears to have continued. In the three and a half years following the effective date of the TDRA, two reported federal court opinions have analyzed both confusion and dilution and found the latter but not the former, and one of these opinions was a dissent. *See* Hershey Co. v. Art Van Furniture, Inc., No. 08 Civ. 14463, 2008

WL 4724756 (E.D. Mich. Oct. 24, 2008); American Century Proprietary Holdings, Inc. v. American Century Casualty Co., 295 Fed. Appx. 630 (5th Cir. Oct. 3, 2008) (Garwood, J., dissenting).

This is not to say that the dilution case of action never provides relief not already provided by a confusion cause of action. As in *Nikepal*, courts may decline to consider confusion at all in their opinions and move directly to a finding of dilution. *See, e.g., V Secret Catalogue, Inc. v. Moseley*, 558 F. Supp. 2d 734 (W.D. Ky. 2008). Furthermore, a mark may be opposed in T.T.A.B. proceedings solely on the basis that it dilutes the opposer's mark. *See* 15 U.S.C. § 1052(f).

In the registration context, it appears that antidilution law has been largely irrelevant. In 2014, Jeremy Sheff reported the results of a wide-ranging empirical study of the effect of antidilution law on registration practice at the PTO. *See* Jeremy N. Sheff, *Dilution at the Patent and Trademark Office*, 21 MICH. TELECOMM. & TECH. L. REV. 79 (2014). Among other things, Sheff developed and hand-coded a dataset of all 453 TTAB dispositions of dilution claims from the January 16, 1996 effective date of the FTDA through June 30, 2014. He found only three TTAB cases over that 18-year period in which anti-dilution claims made any difference to the outcome of a TTAB adjudication. In one of these, Sheff argues, a likelihood of confusion claim could have been used to reach the same outcome, but having found dilution, the board declined to consider the confusion claim. *See Chanel, Inc. v. Jerzy Makarczyk*, 110 U.S.P.Q.2d 2013 (TTAB 2014) (CHANEL for real estate development and construction services diluting of CHANEL). The other two cases were free speech cases with highly controversial findings of dilution. *See Research in Motion Ltd. v. Defining Presence Mktg. Grp. Inc.*, 102 U.S.P.Q.2d 1187 (TTAB 2012) (CRACKBERRY for apparel diluting of BLACKBERRY); *Nat'l Pork Bd. v. Supreme Lobster & Seafood Co.*, 96 U.S.P.Q.2d 1479 (TTAB 2010) (THE OTHER RED MEAT for salmon diluting of THE OTHER WHITE MEAT).

5. *Dilution and misappropriation.* The European Trade Mark Directive explicitly provides for protection against the taking of "unfair advantage of . . . the distinctive character or repute of the trade mark." Directive (EU) 2015/2436 of the European Parliament and of the Council of 16 December 2015 to Approximate the Laws of the Member States Relating to Trade Marks, art. 10(2)(c), [2015] O.J. L 336/1 553, 567. The TDRA contains no such prohibition against the misappropriation of a mark's "selling power." David Franklyn has argued that dilution is essentially a form of "free-riding", that courts often hold in favor of plaintiffs alleging dilution in an effort to punish free-riding, and that "it would be better to scrap dilution altogether and replace it with an independent cause of action that explicitly prevents free-riding in appropriate circumstances." David J. Franklyn, Debun*king Dilution Doctrine: Toward a Coherent Theory of the Anti-Free-Rider Principle in American Trademark Law*, 56 HASTINGS L.J. 117 (2004). Do you support this proposal?

As a historical matter, Schechter himself based nearly all of his theory of dilution on a 1924 German court opinion known as the *Odol* opinion. See *Odol darf auch für gänzlich verschiedene Waren wie Mundwasser nicht verwendet werden; Entscheidung des Landgerichts Elberfeld vom 14. Sept. 1924 13. O. 89/24*, GEWERBLICHER RECHTSSCHUTZ UND URHEBERRECHT [GRUR] 204 (1924). But in attempting to sell his theory of dilution to American readers, Schechter apparently deliberately excluded from his translation of the *Odol* opinion the court's core holding, that the defendant sought "to appropriate thus the fruits of another's labor." Why might Schechter have suppressed the misappropriation nature of trademark dilution when writing to American lawyers in the 1920s, at the height of American Legal Realism? For an answer, see Barton Beebe, *The Suppressed Misappropriation Origins of Trademark Antidilution Law: the Landgericht Elberfeld's* Odol *Opinion and Frank Schechter's The Rational Basis of Trademark Protection*, in INTELLECTUAL PROPERTY AT THE EDGE: THE CONTESTED CONTOURS OF IP (Rochelle Dreyfuss & Jane Ginsburg eds, 2013) ("What Schechter sought to obscure in *Rational Basis* is that the *Odol* case was not, strictly speaking, a trademark case. Rather, it was a misappropriation case that happened to involve a trademark."). *But see* Robert Bone, *Schechter's Ideas in Historical Context and Dilution's Rocky Road*, 24 SANTA CLARA COMPUTER & HIGH TECH. L.J. 469 (2008).

3.   Dilution by Tarnishment

Which do you find more persuasive in what follows: the majority opinion or the dissenting opinion?

V Secret Catalogue, Inc. v. Moseley
605 F.3d 382 (6th Cir. 2010)

MERRITT, Circuit Judge.

[1] In this trademark "dilution by tarnishment" case, brought under the Trademark Dilution Revision Act of 2006, the question is whether the plaintiff, an international lingerie company that uses the trade name designation "Victoria's Secret" has a valid suit for injunctive relief against the use of the name "Victor's Little Secret" or "Victor's Secret" by the defendants, a small retail store in a mall in Elizabethtown, Kentucky, that sells assorted merchandise, including "sex toys" and other sexually oriented products. The District Court issued the injunction. Since then the shop has been operating under the name of "Cathy's Little Secret." The District Court concluded that even though the two parties do not compete in the same market, the "Victor's Little Secret" mark—because it is sex related— disparages and tends to reduce the positive associations and the "selling power" of the "Victoria's Secret" mark. The question is whether the plaintiff's case meets the definitions and standards for "dilution by tarnishment" set out in the new Act which amended the old Act, *i.e.*, the Federal Trademark Dilution Act of 1995.

[2] The new Act was expressly intended to overrule the Supreme Court interpretation of the old Act in this very same case, *Moseley v. V Secret Catalogue, Inc.,* 537 U.S. 418 (2003), *rev'g* 259 F.3d 464 (6th Cir. 2001), *aff'g* 54 U.S.P.Q.2d 1092 (W.D.Ky. 2000). The Supreme Court reversed a panel of this Court that had affirmed an injunction against "Victor's Little Secret" issued by the District Court. On remand to the District Court from the Supreme Court after the 2003 reversal, no new evidence was introduced, and the District Court reconsidered the case based on the same evidence but used the new language in the new Act which overrules the Supreme Court in this case. We will first brief the Supreme Court opinion and the reasons Congress overruled the Supreme Court in this case. We will then outline our understanding of the new standards for measuring trademark "dilution by tarnishment" and apply them to this case. We conclude that the new Act creates a kind of rebuttable presumption, or at least a very strong inference, that a new mark used to sell sex related products is likely to tarnish a famous mark if there is a clear semantic association between the two. That presumption has not been rebutted in this case.

I. The Supreme Court Opinion and the New Act

[3] The Supreme Court explained that this case started when an Army Colonel at Fort Knox saw an ad for "Victor's Secret" in a weekly publication. It advertised that the small store in Elizabethtown sold adult videos and novelties and lingerie.[3] There was no likelihood of confusion between the two

---

[3] The Supreme Court explained:

businesses or the two marks, but the Army Colonel was offended because the sexually-oriented business was semantically associating itself with "Victoria's Secret." The Court explained that the concepts of "dilution by blurring" and "dilution by tarnishment" originated with an article in the Harvard Law Review, Frank Schechter, "Rational Basis of Trademark Protection," 40 HARV. L. REV. 813 (1927), and that the history and meaning of the concepts were further well explained in Restatement (Third) of Unfair Competition, Section 25 (1995). The Restatement section referred to by the Supreme Court explains this new intellectual property tort and contains in § 25 a comprehensive statement of "Liability Without Proof of Confusion: Dilution and Tarnishment." "Tarnishment," as distinguished from "dilution by blurring" was the only claim before the Supreme Court and is the only claim before us in this new appeal. We quote at length the relevant Restatement explanation of "tarnishment" in the footnote below.[4]

> In the February 12, 1998, edition of a weekly publication distributed to residents of the military installation at Fort Knox, Kentucky, petitioners advertised the "GRAND OPENING just in time for Valentine's Day!" of their store "VICTOR'S SECRET" in nearby Elizabethtown. The ad featured "Intimate Lingerie *for every woman*," "Romantic Lighting"; "Lycra Dresses"; "Pagers"; and "Adult Novelties/Gifts." An army colonel, who saw the ad and was offended by what he perceived to be an attempt to use a reputable company's trademark to promote the sale of "unwholesome, tawdry merchandise," sent a copy to respondents. Their counsel then wrote to petitioners stating that their choice of the name "Victor's Secret" for a store selling lingerie was likely to cause confusion with the well-known VICTORIA'S SECRET mark and, in addition, was likely to "dilute the distinctiveness" of the mark. They requested the immediate discontinuance of the use of the name "and any variations thereof." In response, petitioners changed the name of their store to "Victor's Little Secret." Because that change did not satisfy respondents, they promptly filed this action in Federal District Court.

537 U.S. at 426 (internal citations omitted).

[4] c. *Interests protected.* The antidilution statutes have been invoked against two distinct threats to the interests of a trademark owner. First, a mark may be so highly distinctive and so well advertised that it acts as a powerful selling tool. Such a mark may evoke among prospective purchasers a positive response that is associated exclusively with the goods or services of the trademark owner. To the extent that others use the trademark to identify different goods, services or businesses, a dissonance occurs that blurs this stimulant effect of the mark. The antidilution statutes protect against this dilution of the distinctiveness and selling power of the mark.

The selling power of a trademark also can be undermined by a use of the mark with goods or services such as illicit drugs or pornography that "tarnish" the mark's image through inherently negative or unsavory associations, or with goods or services that produce a negative response when linked in the minds of prospective purchasers with the goods or services of the prior user, such as the use on insecticide of a trademark similar to one previously used by another on food products.

Tarnishment and dilution of distinctiveness, although conceptually distinct, both undermine the selling power of a mark, the latter by disturbing the conditioned association of the mark with the prior user and the former by displacing positive with negative associations. Thus, tarnishment and dilution of distinctiveness reduce the value of the mark to the trademark owner.

. . . .

g. *Tarnishment.* The antidilution statutes have also been invoked to protect the positive associations evoked by a mark from subsequent uses that may disparage or tarnish those associations. The rule stated in Subsection (1)(b) applies to cases in which the tarnishment results from a subsequent use of the mark or a substantially similar mark in a manner that associates the mark with different goods, services, or businesses. Use of another's mark by the actor, not as a trademark or trade name, but in

[4] After reviewing a number of secondary sources other than the Harvard Law Review article and the Restatement, including state statutes on dilution and a Fourth Circuit case, the Supreme Court held that "actual harm" rather than merely the "likelihood of tarnishment" is necessary and stated its conclusion as follows:

> Noting that consumer surveys and other means of demonstrating actual dilution are expensive and often unreliable, respondents [Victoria's Secret] and their *amici* argue that evidence of *an actual* "lessening of the capacity of a famous mark to identify and distinguish goods or services," may be difficult to obtain. It may well be, however, that direct evidence of dilution such as consumer surveys will not be necessary *if actual dilution can reliably be proved* through circumstantial evidence—the obvious case is one where the junior and senior marks are identical. *Whatever difficulties of proof may be entailed, they are not an acceptable reason for dispensing with proof of an essential element of a statutory violation.* The evidence in the present record is not sufficient to support the summary judgment on the dilution count. The judgment is therefore reversed, and the case is remanded for further proceedings consistent with this opinion.

537 U.S. at 434, 123 S.Ct. 1115 (emphasis added).

[5] Thus, the Court held that "actual harm" rather than merely a "likelihood" of harm must be shown by Victoria's Secret in order to prevail and that this means that Victoria's Secret carries the burden of proving an actual "lessening of the capacity of the Victoria's Secret mark to identify and distinguish goods or services sold in Victoria's Secret stores or advertised in its catalogs." *Id.* In the new law Congress rejected the Court's view that a simple "likelihood" of an association in the consumer's mind of the Victoria's Secret mark with the sexually-oriented videos and toys of "Victor's Secret" is insufficient for liability.

[6] The House Judiciary Committee Report states the purpose of the new 2006 legislation as follows:

> The *Moseley* standard *creates an undue burden* for trademark holders who contest diluting uses and should be revised.
>
> . . . .
>
> The new language in the legislation [provides] . . . specifically that the standard for proving a dilution claim is "likelihood of dilution" and that both dilution by blurring and dilution by tarnishment are actionable.

(Emphasis added.) U.S. Code Cong. & Adm. News, 109th Cong.2d Sess. 2006, Vol. 4, pp. 1091, 1092, 1097. . . . The drafters of the Committee Report also called special attention to the "burden" of proof or

---

other ways that may disparage or tarnish the prior user's goods, services, business, or mark is governed by the rule stated in Subsection (2).

Any designation that is distinctive under the criteria established in § 13 is eligible for protection against disparaging or tarnishing use by others. Whenever the subsequent use brings to mind the goods, services, business, or mark of the prior user, there is potential for interference with the positive images associated with the mark. To prove a case of tarnishment, the prior user must demonstrate that the subsequent use is likely to come to the attention of the prior user's prospective purchasers and that the use is likely to undermine or damage the positive associations evoked by the mark.

Illustration:

3. *A*, a bank, uses the designation "Cookie Jar" to identify its automatic teller machine. *B* opens a topless bar across the street from *A* under the trade name "Cookie Jar." Although prospective customers of *A* are unlikely to believe that *A* operates or sponsors the bar, *B* is subject to liability to *A* for tarnishment under an applicable antidilution statute if the customers are likely to associate *A's* mark or *A's* business with the images evoked by *B's* use.

persuasion placed on "trademark holders" by the Supreme Court's opinion in *Moseley,* suggesting a possible modification in the burden of proof. The question for us then is whether "Victor's Little Secret" with its association with lewd sexual toys creates a "likelihood of dilution by tarnishment" of Victoria's Secret mark.

II. Application of Statutory Standard

[7] The specific question in this case is whether, without consumer surveys or polls or other evidence, a semantic "association" is equivalent to a liability-creating mental "association" of a junior mark like "Victor's Little Secret" with a famous mark like "Victoria's Secret" that constitutes dilution by tarnishment when the junior mark is used to sell sexual toys, videos and similar soft-core pornographic products. There appears to be a clearly emerging consensus in the case law, aided by the language of § 25 of the Restatement of Trademarks 3d, quoted in footnote 4, *supra,* that the creation of an "association" between a famous mark and lewd or bawdy sexual activity disparages and defiles the famous mark and reduces the commercial value of its selling power. This consensus stems from an economic prediction about consumer taste and how the predicted reaction of conventional consumers in our culture will affect the economic value of the famous mark.

[8] There have been at least eight federal cases in six jurisdictions that conclude that a famous mark is tarnished when its mark is semantically associated with a new mark that is used to sell sex-related products. We find no exceptions in the case law that allow such a new mark associated with sex to stand. *See Pfizer Inc. v. Sachs,* 652 F.Supp.2d 512, 525 (S.D.N.Y. 2009) (defendants' display at an adult entertainment exhibition of two models riding a VIAGRA-branded missile and distributing condoms would likely harm the reputation of Pfizer's trademark); *Williams–Sonoma, Inc. v. Friendfinder, Inc.,* No. C 06–6572 JSW (MEJ), 2007 WL 4973848, at *7 (N.D.Cal. Dec. 6, 2007) (defendants' use of POTTERY BARN mark on their sexually-oriented websites likely to tarnish "by associating those marks for children and teenager furnishings"); *Kraft Foods Holdings, Inc. v. Helm,* 205 F.Supp.2d 942, 949–50 (N.D.Ill. 2002) (pornographic website's use of "VelVeeda" tarnishes VELVEETA trademark); *Victoria's Cyber Secret Ltd. P'ship v. V Secret Catalogue, Inc.,* 161 F.Supp.2d 1339, 1355 (S.D.Fla. 2001) (defendants' internet trade names likely to tarnish famous mark when websites "will be used for entertainment of a lascivious nature suitable only for adults"); *Mattel, Inc. v. Internet Dimensions Inc.,* 2000 WL 973745, 55 U.S.P.Q.2d 1620, 1627 (S.D.N.Y. July 13, 2000) (linking BARBIE with pornography will adversely color the public's impressions of BARBIE); *Polo Ralph Lauren L.P. v. Schuman,* 46 U.S.P.Q.2d 1046, 1048 (S.D.Tex. 1998) (defendants' use of "The Polo Club" or "Polo Executive Retreat" as an adult entertainment club tarnished POLO trademark); *Pillsbury Co. v. Milky Way Prods., Inc.,* 1981 WL 1402, 215 U.S.P.Q. 124, 135 (N.D.Ga. Dec. 24, 1981) (defendant's sexually-oriented variation of the PILLSBURY DOUGHBOY tarnished plaintiff's mark); *Dallas Cowboys Cheerleaders, Inc. v. Pussycat Cinema, Ltd.,* 467 F.Supp. 366, 377 (S.D.N.Y. 1979) (pornographic depiction of a Dallas Cowboys Cheerleader-style cheerleader in an adult film tarnished the professional mark of the Dallas Cowboys).

[9] The phrase "likely to cause dilution" used in the new statute . . . significantly changes the meaning of the law from "causes actual harm" under the preexisting law. The word "likely" or "likelihood" means "probably," WEBSTER'S THIRD NEW INTERNATIONAL DICTIONARY 1310 (1963); BLACK'S LAW DICTIONARY 1076 (1968). It is important to note also that the Committee Report quoted above seeks to reduce the "burden" of evidentiary production on the trademark holder. The burden-of-proof problem, the developing case law, and the Restatement (Third) of Trademarks in § 25 (particularly subsection g) should now be interpreted, we think, to create a kind of rebuttable presumption, or at least a very strong inference, that a new mark used to sell sex-related products is likely to tarnish a famous mark if there is a clear semantic association between the two. This *res ipsa loquitur*-like effect is not conclusive but places on the owner of the new mark the burden of coming forward with evidence that there is no likelihood or probability of tarnishment. The evidence could be in the form of expert testimony or surveys or polls or customer testimony.

[10] In the present case, the Moseleys have had two opportunities in the District Court to offer evidence that there is no real probability of tarnishment and have not done so. They did not offer at oral argument any suggestion that they could make such a showing or wanted the case remanded for that

purpose. The fact that Congress was dissatisfied with the *Moseley* result and the *Moseley* standard of liability, as well as apparently the *Moseley* burden of proof, supports the view of Victoria's Secret that the present record—in the eyes of the legislative branch—shows a likelihood of tarnishment. Without evidence to the contrary or a persuasive defensive theory that rebuts the presumption, the defendants have given us no basis to reverse the judgment of the District Court. We do not find sufficient the defendants' arguments that they should have the right to use Victor Moseley's first name and that the effect of the association is *de minimis.* The Moseleys do not have a right to use the word "secret" in their mark. They use it only to make the association with the Victoria's Secret mark. We agree that the tarnishing effect of the Moseley's mark on the senior mark is somewhat speculative, but we have no evidence to overcome the strong inference created by the case law, the Restatement, and Congressional dissatisfaction with the burden of proof used in this case in the Supreme Court. The new law seems designed to protect trademarks from any unfavorable sexual associations. Thus, any new mark with a lewd or offensive-to-some sexual association raises a strong inference of tarnishment. The inference must be overcome by evidence that rebuts the probability that some consumers will find the new mark both offensive and harmful to the reputation and the favorable symbolism of the famous mark.

[11] Our dissenting colleague, in relying on the Supreme Court treatment of the proof in this case—for example, the long quotation from the Supreme Court concerning the legal effect of the evidence—fails to concede what seems obvious: Congress overruled the Supreme Court's view of the burden of proof. As quoted above, it said, "the Moseley standard creates an undue burden for trademark holders who contest diluting uses." It seems clear that the new Act demonstrates that Congress intended that a court should reach a different result in this case if the facts remain the same. We do not necessarily disagree with our dissenting colleague that the policy followed by the Supreme Court in such cases may be better. We simply believe that the will of Congress is to the contrary with regard to the proof in this case and with regard to the method of allocating the burden of proof.

. . . .

JULIA SMITH GIBBONS, Circuit Judge, concurring.

[12] I fully concur in the majority opinion with the exception of one small quibble. I would not use the term "rebuttable presumption" to describe the inference that a new mark used to sell sex-related products is likely to tarnish a famous mark if there is a clear semantic association between the two. Practically speaking, what the inference is called makes little difference. I agree with the majority opinion that the inference is a strong one and that, to counter it, some evidence that there is no likelihood or probability of tarnishment is required. But because we are endeavoring to interpret a new law and because the legislative history is not explicit on the point of modification of the burden of proof, I think it best to end our analysis by characterizing the inference as an inference.

KAREN NELSON MOORE, Circuit Judge, dissenting.

[13] Because I believe that Victoria's Secret has failed to produce sufficient evidence to show that the Moseleys' use of the name "Victor's Little Secret" is likely to tarnish the VICTORIA'S SECRET mark, I would reverse the judgment of the district court and must respectfully dissent.

[14] Under the Trademark Dilution Revision Act of 2006 ("TDRA"), Victoria's Secret is entitled to injunctive relief if the Moseleys' use of "Victor's Little Secret" as the name of their adult-oriented novelty store[1] "is likely to cause dilution ... by tarnishment of the" VICTORIA'S SECRET mark. 15 U.S.C. § 1125(c)(1). "[D]ilution by tarnishment" is defined as an "association arising from the similarity between a mark or trade name and a famous mark that harms the reputation of the famous mark." *Id.* § 1125(c)(2)(C). Thus, under the terms of the statute, to determine whether the VICTORIA'S SECRET

---

[1] Victor's Little Secret "sell[s] a wide variety of items, including adult videos, adult novelties, and lingerie." *Moseley v. v. Secret Catalogue, Inc.,* 537 U.S. 418, 424, 123 S.Ct. 1115, 155 L.Ed.2d 1 (2003) (internal quotation marks omitted); *see also id.* at 424 n. 4, 123 S.Ct. 1115 (listing numerous other items sold). "Victor Moseley stated in an affidavit that women's lingerie represented only about five percent of their sales." *Id.* at 424, 123 S.Ct. 1115.

mark is likely to be tarnished by the Moseleys' use, this court must inquire as to both the "association" between the two marks and the "harm" that the association causes to the senior mark.

[15] Because I agree that there is a clear association between the two marks, the determinative inquiry in this dilution-by-tarnishment case is whether that association is likely to harm Victoria's Secret's reputation. *See id.* § 1125(c)(2)(C) ("that harms the reputation of the famous mark"). Contrary to the majority's conclusion, however, given the record before the panel, I would hold that Victoria's Secret has failed to meet its burden to show that the Moseleys' use of "Victor's Little Secret" is likely to dilute Victoria's Secret's mark.[2]

[16] Victoria's Secret's evidence of tarnishment includes nothing more than the following: (1) an affidavit from Army Colonel John E. Baker stating that he "was ... offended by [the] defendants' use of [Victoria's Secret's] trademark to promote ... unwholesome, tawdry merchandise," such as "'adult' novelties and gifts," and that since his "wife ... and ... daughter ... shop at Victoria's Secret, [he] was further dismayed by [the] defendants' effort to associate itself with, trade off on the image of, and in fact denigrate a store frequented by members of [his] family," Record on Appeal ("ROA") at 267 (Baker Aff.); and (2) a statement from one of Victoria's Secret's corporate officers that Victoria's Secret strives to "maintain[ ] an image that is sexy and playful" and one that "avoid[s] sexually explicit or graphic imagery." *Id.* at 90 (Kriss Aff.).

[17] Reviewing Baker's affidavit, I believe that it is plain that Baker made a "mental association" between "Victor's Little Secret" and "Victoria's Secret." *Moseley v. V Secret Catalogue, Inc.*, 537 U.S. 418, 434, 123 S.Ct. 1115, 155 L.Ed.2d 1 (2003); *see also* ROA at 266 (Baker Aff.). It is also clear that Baker held a negative impression of "Victor's Little Secret." *See Moseley*, 537 U.S. at 434, 123 S.Ct. 1115; *see also* ROA at 267 (Baker Aff.). But despite the clear negative association of this *one* individual when confronted with "Victor's Little Secret," Victoria's Secret has presented *no* evidence that Baker's, or anyone else's, distaste or dislike of "Victor's Little Secret" is likely to taint their positive opinion or perception of Victoria's Secret. Yet evidence that the junior mark is likely to undermine or alter the positive associations of the senior mark—i.e., evidence that the junior mark is likely to harm the reputation of the senior mark—is precisely the showing required under the plain language of 15 U.S.C. § 1125(c)(2)(C) to prove dilution by tarnishment. As the Second Circuit recently noted in *Starbucks Corp. v. Wolfe's Borough Coffee, Inc.*, 588 F.3d 97 (2d Cir. 2009):

> That a consumer may associate a negative-sounding junior mark with a famous mark says little of whether the consumer views the junior mark as harming the reputation of the famous mark. The more relevant question, for purposes of tarnishment, would have been how a hypothetical coffee [with a negative-sounding name] would affect the positive impressions about the coffee sold by Starbucks.

Starbucks Corp., 588 F.3d at 110; *see also* J. Thomas McCarthy, 4 McCarthy on Trademarks and Unfair Competition § 24:89 (4th ed.) [hereinafter McCarthy on Trademarks] (discussing tarnishment claims as being premised on the notion that "positive associations" of the senior mark will be displaced or degraded by the negative associations of the junior mark); Restatement (Third) of Unfair Competition

---

[2] I respectfully disagree with the majority's conclusion that in dilution-by-tarnishment cases involving new marks "with lewd or offensive-to-some sexual association[s]" the TDRA establishes a presumption or inference of tarnishment that the Moseleys must rebut. Maj. Op. at 389, 390. To be sure, the House Judiciary Committee Report highlights Congress's concern with the pre-TDRA actual-dilution standard, but I do not read its concern that the previous standard created "an undue burden" to mean that Congress envisioned a modification of the party that bears the burden of proof as opposed to simply a lightening of the evidentiary showing. *See* H.R.Rep. No. 109–23, at 5 (2005) ("Witnesses at the [ ] [legislative] hearings focused on the standard of harm threshold articulated in *Moseley* [sic] .... The *Moseley* [sic] standard creates an undue burden for trademark holders who contest diluting uses and should be revised."). The burden to show tarnishment remains with Victoria's Secret.

§ 25 cmt. g (1995) ("To prove a case of tarnishment, the prior user must demonstrate that the subsequent use is likely to ... undermine or damage the positive associations evoked by the mark."). In fact, when reviewing the exact same evidentiary record, the Supreme Court explicitly noted that Victoria's Secret's offer of proof included no evidence that "Victor's Little Secret" affected Baker's positive impressions of Victoria's Secret:

> The record in this case establishes that an army officer ... did make the mental association with "Victoria's Secret," but it also shows that *he did not therefore form any different impression of the store that his wife and daughter had patronized.* There is a complete absence of evidence of any lessening of the capacity of the VICTORIA'S SECRET mark to identify and distinguish goods or services sold in Victoria's Secret stores or advertised in its catalogs. The officer was offended by the ad, *but it did not change his conception of Victoria's Secret.* His offense was directed entirely at [the Moseleys], not at [Victoria's Secret]. Moreover, the expert retained by respondents had nothing to say about the impact of [the Moseleys'] name on the strength of [Victoria's Secret's] mark.

Moseley, 537 U.S. at 434, 123 S.Ct. 1115 (emphases added).[3]

---

[3] The majority mischaracterizes my citation to the Supreme Court's decision as evidencing a refusal to follow the "will of Congress" and a desire to follow the pre-TDRA "policy [of the] ... Supreme Court." Maj. Op. at 389. My citation to the Supreme Court's decision, however, does no such thing. First, as stated previously, I believe that the majority's conclusion that Congress intended to change which party has the burden of proof—i.e., the framework governing which party must put forth evidence in support of its position—as opposed to the standard of harm—i.e., actual harm versus a likelihood of harm—is not supported by the statute or the legislative history. In fact, the only evidence that the majority cites in support of its belief that Congress intended to place the burden of proof on the defendant is the House Committee Report, but even that Report undercuts the majority's argument. The full paragraph from which the majority draws its quotation states:

> Witnesses at the[ ] [legislative] hearings focused on the *standard of harm threshold* articulated in *Moseley* [sic]. For example, a representative of the International Trademark Association observed that "[b]y the time measurable, provable damage to the mark has occurred much time has passed, the damage has been done, and the remedy, which is injunctive relief, is far less effective." The Committee endorses this position. The *Moseley* [sic] standard creates an undue burden for trademark holders who contest diluting uses and should be revised.

H.R.Rep. No. 109–23, at 5 (internal footnote omitted and emphasis added). It was the "standard of harm threshold," i.e., the showing of actual harm that the Supreme Court employed, that was Congress's concern, not the party bearing the burden of proof. This conclusion is supported by the hearings to which the Committee Report refers. During those hearings, the focus of both the House Representatives and the witnesses was whether Congress should "maintain an actual dilution standard, as the Supreme Court held in the Victoria's Secret case," or adopt a "likelihood of dilution standard." *Trademark Dilution Revision Act of 2005: Hearing Before the Subcomm. on Courts, the Internet, and Intellectual Property of the H. Comm. on the Judiciary,* 109th Cong. 4 (2005) (statement of Rep. Berman); *see generally id.* at 1–54.

I certainly recognize that Congress changed the law concerning dilution in response to the Supreme Court's decision in *Moseley*, but the Supreme Court in *Moseley* said nothing about changing the party bearing the burden of proof and neither does the amended statute. Instead, the statute explicitly states that "dilution by tarnishment" is an "association arising from the similarity between a mark or trade name and a famous mark *that harms the reputation of the famous mark.*" 15 U.S.C. § 1125(c)(2)(C) (emphasis added). In concluding that Victoria's Secret has failed to prove a likelihood of tarnishment because it has failed to present evidence that Victor's Little Secret is likely to harm the reputation of its mark, I am doing nothing more than applying the plain language of the statute that Congress enacted

[18] In short, Victoria's Secret has presented *no* probative evidence that anyone is likely to think less of Victoria's Secret as a result of "Victor's Little Secret" and cannot therefore prevail on its claim of dilution by tarnishment. *See Hormel Foods Corp. v. Jim Henson Prods., Inc.,* 73 F.3d 497, 507 (2d Cir. 1996) ("Absent any showing that Henson's use [of a puppet named Spa'am] will create negative associations with the SPAM mark, there [is] little likelihood of dilution."). Instead of developing a record on remand that contains at least some evidence that Victoria's Secret's reputation is likely to suffer because of the negative response that "Victor's Little Secret" engendered, the record before the panel indicates only that a single individual thinks poorly of "Victor's Little Secret." *See Moseley,* 537 U.S. at 434, 123 S.Ct. 1115. On this record, it is simply no more probable that Victoria's Secret will suffer reputational harm as a result of the Moseleys' use of "Victor's Little Secret" than it is probable that those who are offended by "Victor's Little Secret" will limit their negative impressions to the Moseleys and refrain from projecting those negative associations upon Victoria's Secret. Baker's affidavit does nothing to contradict this conclusion, and given the absence of any indication that his or his family's opinion of Victoria's Secret changed following the Moseleys' use of "Victor's Little Secret," his affidavit may, in fact, provide evidence that individuals are likely to confine their distaste to the Moseleys. *See id.* ("The officer was offended by the ad, but it did not change his conception of Victoria's Secret. His offense was directed entirely at [the Moseleys], not at [Victoria's Secret].").

[19] Certainly, it is *possible* that the Moseleys' use of "Victor's Little Secret" to sell adult-oriented material and other novelties could reflect poorly on the VICTORIA'S SECRET mark and could cause Victoria's Secret to suffer damage to its "sexy and playful" reputation, but the evidentiary standard set forth in the statute is one of likelihood *not* mere possibility. Likelihood is based on probable consequence and amounts to more than simple speculation as to what might possibly happen. *See McCarthy on Trademarks* § 24:115 n. 2 (indicating that "'likelihood' in the dilution part of the Lanham Act has the same meaning as it does in the traditional infringement sections of the Lanham Act: as synonymous with 'probability'"); *see also Parks v. LaFace Records,* 329 F.3d 437, 446 (6th Cir. 2003) ("A 'likelihood' means a 'probability' rather than a 'possibility' of confusion."). Yet, as the majority notes, on the instant record, the "tarnishing effect of the Moseley's mark on the senior mark" is nothing more than "speculative." Maj. Op. at 388–89.

[20] Despite the absence of evidence, the majority is willing to assume that Victoria's Secret has met its burden to prove the essential element of "harm to reputation" based on the fact that numerous cases from other jurisdictions conclude, without much inquiry, "that a famous mark is tarnished when its mark is semantically associated with a new mark that is used to sell sex-related products." *Id.* at 388. I do not agree. Although it is true that courts have concluded that a finding of tarnishment is likely when a mark's "likeness is placed in the context of sexual activity, obscenity, or illegal activity," *Hormel Foods Corp.,* 73 F.3d at 507, a court cannot ignore the showing of reputational harm that the statute requires.[4]

---

after the Supreme Court's decision. This approach certainly reflects the "will of Congress." Maj. Op. at 389.

[4] Nor can the court ignore the character of the senior mark when applying the majority's "rule." Victoria's Secret sells women's lingerie, and, as Victoria's Secret readily admits, its own mark is already associated with sex, albeit not with sex novelties. *See* ROA at 90 (Kriss Aff.) (noting that Victoria's Secret attempts to maintain a "sexy and playful" image); *see also, e.g., id.* at 156–57 (depicting Victoria's Secret advertisements for "sexy little things" lingerie, which urge customers to "[b]e bad for goodness sake[ ] [i]n peek-a-boo's, bras and sexy Santa accessories," to "[g]ive flirty panties" as gifts, and participate in the store's "panty fantasy," which it describes as "Very racy. Very lacy"); *id.* at 209 (reproducing an article in Redbook magazine entitled "46 Things to Do to a Naked Man," which highlights Victoria's Secret's role in the sexual activities of one of the contributors).

In essence, the VICTORIA'S SECRET mark is not entirely separate from the sexual context within which the junior mark, "Victor's Little Secret," operates. This fact makes the instant case unlike many of

[21] Even assuming that "Victor's Little Secret" is plainly unwholesome when compared to Victoria's Secret and that this case is completely analogous to those cases on which the majority relies, I still maintain that it is improper simply to assume likelihood of harm to the reputation of a senior mark when dealing with a junior mark of sexual character. As recounted above, there is *no* evidence connecting Victor's Little Secret's "unwholesome" or "tawdry" sexual character to the senior mark's reputation, and there is nothing in the language of the TDRA that would allow the court to forgive a party's obligation to present proof as to an element of the tarnishment cause of action—i.e., the likelihood of harm to reputation.[5] *See* McCarthy on Trademarks § 24:115 ("Even after the 2006 revision when only a likelihood of dilution is required, ... judges should demand persuasive evidence that dilution is likely to occur. Even the probability of dilution should be proven by evidence, not just by theoretical assumptions about what possibly could occur or might happen.").

[22] With its conclusion that there is sufficient evidence of harm to the reputation of the VICTORIA'S SECRET mark based solely on the sexual nature of the junior mark, the majority sanctions an almost non-existent evidentiary standard and, in the process, essentially eliminates the requirement that a plaintiff provide some semblance of proof of likelihood of reputational harm in order to prevail on a tarnishment claim, despite the plain language of 15 U.S.C. § 1125(c)(2). Because I believe that Victoria's Secret has not met its burden to show that "Victor's Little Secret" is likely to dilute the famous mark by way of tarnishment, I respectfully dissent.

Questions and Comments

1. *Is antidilution law constitutional?* In *Matal v. Tam*, , 137 S. Ct. 1744, 582 U.S. _ (U.S. June 19, 2017), excerpted above in Part I.B.5, the Supreme Court ruled that the Lanham Act § 2(a) prohibition on the registration of marks that "may disparage ... persons" was invalid under the Free Speech Clause of

---

the cases that the majority cites. *Cf. Williams–Sonoma, Inc. v. Friendfinder, Inc.,* No. C 06–6572 JSW (MEJ), 2007 WL 4973848, at *7 (N.D.Cal. Dec. 6, 2007) (likelihood of tarnishment where "marks for children and teenager furnishings" were associated "with pornographic websites"); *Kraft Foods Holdings, Inc. v. Helm,* 205 F.Supp.2d 942, 949 (N.D.Ill. 2002) (likelihood of dilution where the mark for cheese products was associated with websites that "depict[ ] graphic sexuality and nudity, as well as illustrations of drug use and drug paraphernalia"); *Mattel Inc. v. Internet Dimensions Inc.,* 2000 WL 973745, 55 U.S.P.Q.2d (BNA) 1620, 1627 (S.D.N.Y. July 13, 2000) (likelihood of tarnishment when the BARBIE mark was linked to adult-entertainment websites); *Polo Ralph Lauren L.P. v. Schuman,* 1998 WL 110059, 46 U.S.P.Q.2d (BNA) 1046, 1048 (S.D.Tex. Feb. 9, 1998) (dilution likely where Polo Ralph Lauren's mark was associated with "an adult entertainment business"); *Toys "R" Us Inc. v. Akkaoui,* 1996 WL 772709, 40 U.S.P.Q.2d (BNA) 1836, 1838 (N.D.Cal. Oct. 29, 1996) (likelihood of tarnishment where children's toy store was associated with "a line of sexual products"); *Hasbro, Inc. v. Internet Entm't Group Ltd.,* 1996 WL 84853, 40 U.S.P.Q.2d (BNA) 1479, 1480 (W.D.Wash. Feb. 9, 1996) (dilution likely where the children's game Candyland was linked to "a sexually explicit Internet site"); *Am. Express Co. v. Vibra Approved Labs. Corp.,* 10 U.S.P.Q.2d (BNA) 2006, 2014 (S.D.N.Y. 1989) (tarnishment likely where an American Express charge card was linked to condoms and a sex-toy store); *Pillsbury Co. v. Milky Way Prods., Inc.,* 1981 WL 1402, 215 U.S.P.Q. (BNA) 124, 126, 135 (N.D.Ga. Dec. 24, 1981) (likelihood of dilution where the Pillsbury dough figures were portrayed as "engaging in sexual intercourse and fellatio"); *Dallas Cowboys Cheerleaders, Inc. v. Pussycat Cinema, Ltd.,* 467 F.Supp. 366, 377 (S.D.N.Y. 1979), *affirmed by* 604 F.2d 200, 205 (2d Cir. 1979) (tarnishment likely where NFL cheerleaders were portrayed in a pornographic film).

[5] The potential problem with simply assuming tarnishment when the junior mark places the senior mark in a sexual context becomes apparent if one considers a different case. What if the holder of a sex-related senior mark levied a claim of dilution by tarnishment against the holder of a junior mark that was similarly associated with sex? Would the court be willing to assume without further proof that despite their similar sexual origins the junior mark necessarily tarnishes the senior mark? Under the majority's reasoning, such an assumption would be appropriate. This cannot be the law.

the First Amendment. What are the implications of the Court's reasoning in *Tam* for antidilution law, and particularly for anti-tarnishment law?

2. *Tarnishment or "burnishment"? See* Jake Linford, Justin Sevier & Allyson Willis, *Trademark Tarnishmyths*, 55 ARIZ. ST. L.J. ___ (2023) (forthcoming) (reporting the results of a series of experiments that suggest that purportedly tarnishing conduct associating a targeted mark with sex, narcotics, or sacrilege does not harm the reputation and may even result in the "burnishment" of the mark).

D. Cybersquatting

There are three main methods by which a trademark owner may seek to prevent third-party unauthorized uses of its trademark as part of an internet domain name: (1) the trademark owner can pursue a traditional trademark infringement cause of action by claiming that the domain name creates a likelihood of confusion under Lanham Act § 32 or § 43(a) or a likelihood of dilution under Lanham Act § 43(c); (2) the trademark owner can bring a cause of action for "cybersquatting" under Lanham Act § 43(d); and (3) the trademark owner can seek cancellation of the domain name or the transfer of the domain name to the trademark owner under the Uniform Dispute Resolution Policy (UDRP) or the Uniform Rapid Suspension System (URS). In Part II.D.1, we will consider the first two options. We will then turn in Part II.D.2 to the UDRP and URS.

1. The Section 43(d) Prohibition Against Cybersquatting

Sporty's Farm L.L.C. v. Sportsman's Market, Inc.
202 F.3d 489 (2d Cir. 2000)

CALABRESI, Circuit Judge:

[1] This case originally involved the application of the Federal Trademark Dilution Act ("FTDA") to the Internet. *See* Federal Trademark Dilution Act of 1995, Pub.L. No. 104-98, 109 Stat. 985 (codified at 15 U.S.C. §§ 1125, 1127 (Supp. 1996)). While the case was pending on appeal, however, the Anticybersquatting Consumer Protection Act ("ACPA"), Pub.L. No. 106-113 (1999), *see* H.R.Rep. No. 106-479 (Nov. 18, 1999), was passed and signed into law. That new law applies to this case.

[2] Plaintiff-Counter-Defendant-Appellant-Cross-Appellee Sporty's Farm L.L.C. ("Sporty's Farm") appeals from a judgment, following a bench trial, of the United States District Court for the District of Connecticut (Alfred V. Covello, *Chief Judge*) dated March 13, 1998. Defendant-Third-Party-Plaintiff-Counter-Claimant-Appellee-Cross-Appellant Sportsman's Market, Inc. ("Sportsman's") cross-appeals from the same judgment.

[3] The district court held: (1) that the Sportsman's trademark ("*sporty's*") was a *famous* mark entitled to protection under the FTDA; (2) that Sporty's Farm and its parent company, Third-Party-Defendant-Appellee Omega Engineering, Inc. ("Omega"), diluted the *sporty's* mark by using the Internet domain name "sportys.com" to sell Christmas trees and by preventing Sportsman's from using its trademark as a domain name; (3) that applying the FTDA to Sporty's Farm through an injunction requiring it to relinquish sportys.com was both equitable and not a retroactive application of the statute; (4) that Sportsman's was limited to injunctive relief since the conduct of Sporty's Farm and Omega did not constitute a willful intent to dilute under the FTDA; and (5) that Sporty's Farm and Omega did not violate the Connecticut Unfair Trade Practices Act ("CUTPA"), Conn. Gen.Stat. Ann. §§ 42-110a to 42-110q (West 1992 & Supp. 1999). We apply the new anticybersquatting law and affirm the judgment in all respects, but, given the new law, on different grounds from those relied upon by the district court.

BACKGROUND

I

[4] Although the Internet is on its way to becoming a familiar aspect in our daily lives, it is well to begin with a brief explanation of how it works. The Internet is a network of computers that allows a user to gain access to information stored on any other computer on the network. Information on the Internet

is lodged on files called web pages, which can include printed matter, sound, pictures, and links to other web pages. An Internet user can move from one page to another with just the click of a mouse.[1]

[5] Web pages are designated by an address called a domain name. A domain name consists of two parts: a top level domain and a secondary level domain. The top level domain is the domain name's suffix. Currently, the Internet is divided primarily into six top level domains: (1) .edu for educational institutions; (2) .org for non-governmental and non-commercial organizations; (3) .gov for governmental entities; (4) .net for networks; (5) .com for commercial users, and (6) a nation-specific domain, which is .us in the United States. The secondary level domain is the remainder of the address, and can consist of combinations of letters, numbers, and some typographical symbols.[2] To take a simple example, in the domain name "cnn.com," cnn ("Cable News Network") represents the secondary level domain and .com represents the top level domain. Each domain name is unique.

[6] Over the last few years, the commercial side of the Internet has grown rapidly. Web pages are now used by companies to provide information about their products in a much more detailed fashion than can be done through a standard advertisement. Moreover, many consumers and businesses now order goods and services directly from company web pages. Given that Internet sales are paperless and have lower transaction costs than other types of retail sales, the commercial potential of this technology is vast.

[7] For consumers to buy things or gather information on the Internet, they need an easy way to find particular companies or brand names. The most common method of locating an unknown domain name is simply to type in the company name or logo with the suffix .com.[3] If this proves unsuccessful, then Internet users turn to a device called a search engine.[4] A search engine will find all web pages on the Internet with a particular word or phrase. Given the current state of search engine technology, that search will often produce a list of hundreds of web sites through which the user must sort in order to find what he or she is looking for. As a result, companies strongly prefer that their domain name be comprised of the company or brand trademark and the suffix .com. *See* H.R.Rep. No. 106-412, at 5 (1999).

[8] Until recently, domain names with the .com top level domain could only be obtained from Network Solutions, Inc. ("NSI"). Now other registrars may also assign them. But all these registrars grant such names primarily on a first-come, first-served basis upon payment of a small registration fee. They do not generally inquire into whether a given domain name request matches a trademark held by someone other than the person requesting the name. *See id.*

[9] Due to the lack of any regulatory control over domain name registration, an Internet phenomenon known as "cybersquatting" has become increasingly common in recent years.[5] *See, e.g., Panavision Int'l, L.P. v. Toeppen*, 141 F.3d 1316 (9th Cir. 1998). Cybersquatting involves the registration as domain names of well-known trademarks by non-trademark holders who then try to sell the names back to the trademark owners. Since domain name registrars do not check to see whether a domain name request is related to existing trademarks, it has been simple and inexpensive for any person to

---

[1] A mouse is a device that allows a computer user to issue commands by moving a marker across the screen and then clicking on the symbol, word, or icon that represents the particular information that the user wants to access.

[2] Certain symbols, such as apostrophes ('), cannot be used in a domain name.

[3] Nothing prevents an American commercial entity from seeking to use the .org or .us top level domains, but, especially in the United States, it has become customary for commercial web pages to use .com.

[4] Undoubtedly, there are many people who use a search engine before typing in a company name plus .com. The manner in which users search the Internet depends on how quickly they think the search engine is likely to locate the desired web page.

[5] "Cyber" is the prefix used to denote Internet-related things. The realm of the Internet is often referred to as "cyberspace."

register as domain names the marks of established companies. This prevents use of the domain name by the mark owners, who not infrequently have been willing to pay "ransom" in order to get "their names" back. *See* H.R.Rep. No. 106-412, at 5-7; S.Rep. No. 106-140, at 4-7 (1999).

II

[10] Sportsman's is a mail order catalog company that is quite well-known among pilots and aviation enthusiasts for selling products tailored to their needs. In recent years, Sportsman's has expanded its catalog business well beyond the aviation market into that for tools and home accessories. The company annually distributes approximately 18 million catalogs nationwide, and has yearly revenues of about $50 million. Aviation sales account for about 60% of Sportsman's revenue, while non-aviation sales comprise the remaining 40%.

[11] In the 1960s, Sportsman's began using the logo "*sporty* " to identify its catalogs and products. In 1985, Sportsman's registered the trademark *sporty's* with the United States Patent and Trademark Office. Since then, Sportsman's has complied with all statutory requirements to preserve its interest in the *sporty's* mark. *Sporty's* appears on the cover of all Sportsman's catalogs; Sportsman's international toll free number is 1-800-4*sportys;* and one of Sportsman's domestic toll free phone numbers is 1-800-*Sportys.* Sportsman's spends about $10 million per year advertising its *sporty's* logo.

[12] Omega is a mail order catalog company that sells mainly scientific process measurement and control instruments. In late 1994 or early 1995, the owners of Omega, Arthur and Betty Hollander, decided to enter the aviation catalog business and, for that purpose, formed a wholly-owned subsidiary called Pilot's Depot, LLC ("Pilot's Depot"). Shortly thereafter, Omega registered the domain name sportys.com with NSI. Arthur Hollander was a pilot who received Sportsman's catalogs and thus was aware of the *sporty's* trademark.

[13] In January 1996, nine months after registering sportys.com, Omega formed another wholly-owned subsidiary called Sporty's Farm and sold it the rights to sportys.com for $16,200. Sporty's Farm grows and sells Christmas trees, and soon began advertising its Christmas trees on a sportys.com web page. When asked how the name Sporty's Farm was selected for Omega's Christmas tree subsidiary, Ralph S. Michael, the CEO of Omega and manager of Sporty's Farm, explained, as summarized by the district court, that

> in his own mind and among his family, he always thought of and referred to the Pennsylvania land where Sporty's Farm now operates as *Spotty's farm.* The origin of the name . . . derived from a childhood memory he had of his uncle's farm in upstate New York. As a youngster, Michael owned a dog named Spotty. Because the dog strayed, his uncle took him to his upstate farm. Michael thereafter referred to the farm as Spotty's farm. The name Sporty's Farm was . . . a subsequent derivation.

Joint Appendix ("JA") at 277 (emphasis added). There is, however, no evidence in the record that Hollander was considering starting a Christmas tree business when he registered sportys.com or that Hollander was ever acquainted with Michael's dog Spotty.

[14] In March 1996, Sportsman's discovered that Omega had registered sportys.com as a domain name. Thereafter, and before Sportsman's could take any action, Sporty's Farm brought this declaratory action seeking the right to continue its use of sportys.com. Sportsman's counterclaimed and also sued Omega as a third-party defendant for, *inter alia,* (1) trademark infringement, (2) trademark dilution pursuant to the FTDA, and (3) unfair competition under state law. Both sides sought injunctive relief to force the other to relinquish its claims to sportys.com. While this litigation was ongoing, Sportsman's used "sportys-catalogs.com" as its primary domain name.

[15] After a bench trial, the court rejected Sportsman's trademark infringement claim and all related claims that are based on a "likelihood of [consumer] confusion" since "the parties operate wholly

unrelated businesses [and t]herefore, confusion in the marketplace is not likely to develop."[6] *Id.* at 282-83. But on Sportsman's trademark dilution action, where a likelihood of confusion was not necessary, the district court found for Sportsman's. The court concluded (1) that *sporty's* was a *famous* mark entitled to protection under the FTDA since "the '*Sporty's*' mark enjoys general name recognition in the consuming public," *id.* at 288, and (2) that Sporty's Farm and Omega had diluted *sporty's* because "registration of the 'sportys.com' domain name effectively compromises Sportsman's Market's ability to identify and distinguish its goods on the Internet . . . [by] preclud[ing] Sportsman's Market from using its 'unique identifier,'" *id.* at 289. The court also held, however, that Sportsman's could only get injunctive relief and was not entitled to "punitive damages . . . profits, and attorney's fees and costs" pursuant to the FTDA since Sporty Farm and Omega's conduct did not constitute willful dilution under the FTDA.[7] *Id.* at 292-93.

. . . .

[16] The district court then issued an injunction forcing Sporty's Farm to relinquish all rights to sportys.com. And Sportsman's subsequently acquired the domain name. Both Sporty's Farm and Sportsman's appeal.[8] Specifically, Sporty's Farm appeals the judgment insofar as the district court granted an injunction in favor of Sportsman's for the use of the domain name. Sportsman's, on the other hand, in addition to urging this court to affirm the district court's injunction, cross-appeals, quite correctly as a procedural matter, the district court's denial of damages under . . . the FTDA . . . . *See* 16A Charles Alan Wright, Arthur R. Miller, Edward H. Cooper, *Federal Practice and Procedure* § 3974.4 (3d ed. 1999) ("[A] cross-appeal is required to support modification of the judgment . . . .").

III

[17] As we noted above, while this appeal was pending, Congress passed the ACPA. That law was passed "to protect consumers and American businesses, to promote the growth of online commerce, and to provide clarity in the law for trademark owners by prohibiting the bad-faith and abusive registration of distinctive marks as Internet domain names with the intent to profit from the goodwill associated with such marks—a practice commonly referred to as 'cybersquatting'." S.Rep. No. 106-140, at 4. In particular, Congress viewed the legal remedies available for victims of cybersquatting before the passage of the ACPA as "expensive and uncertain." H.R.Rep. No. 106-412, at 6. The Senate made clear its view on this point:

> While the [FTDA] has been useful in pursuing cybersquatters, cybersquatters have become increasingly sophisticated as the case law has developed and now take the necessary precautions to insulate themselves from liability. For example, many cybersquatters are now careful to no longer offer the domain name for sale in any manner that could implicate liability under existing trademark dilution case law. And, in cases of warehousing and trafficking in domain names, courts have sometimes declined to provide assistance to trademark holders, leaving them without adequate and effective judicial remedies. This uncertainty as to the trademark law's application to the Internet has produced inconsistent judicial decisions and created extensive monitoring obligations, unnecessary legal costs, and uncertainty for consumers and trademark owners alike.

S.Rep. No. 106-140, at 7. In short, the ACPA was passed to remedy the perceived shortcomings of applying the FTDA in cybersquatting cases such as this one.

[18] The new act accordingly amends the Trademark Act of 1946, creating a specific federal remedy for cybersquatting. New 15 U.S.C. § 1125(d)(1)(A) reads:

---

[6] The district court also rejected Sportsman's federal actions for false designation and unfair competition on the same rationale. These rulings have not been appealed.

[7] The FTDA does not provide for punitive damages. It does, however, contemplate treble damages. *See* 15 U.S.C. § 1125(c)(2); § 1117(b).

[8] Omega has not appealed since it prevailed on all the claims made against it by Sportsman's.

A person shall be liable in a civil action by the owner of a mark, including a personal name which is protected as a mark under this section, if, without regard to the goods or services of the parties, that person-

(i) has a bad faith intent to profit from that mark, including a personal name which is protected as a mark under this section; and

(ii) registers, traffics in, or uses a domain name that—

> (I) in the case of a mark that is distinctive at the time of registration of the domain name, is identical or confusingly similar to that mark;

> (II) in the case of a famous mark that is famous at the time of registration of the domain name, is identical or confusingly similar to or dilutive of that mark; . . .

[19] The Act further provides that "a court may order the forfeiture or cancellation of the domain name or the transfer of the domain name to the owner of the mark," 15 U.S.C. § 1125(d)(1)(C), if the domain name was "registered before, on, or after the date of the enactment of this Act," Pub.L. No. 106-113, § 3010. It also provides that damages can be awarded for violations of the Act,[9] but that they are not "available with respect to the registration, trafficking, or use of a domain name that occurs before the date of the enactment of this Act." *Id.*

DISCUSSION

[20] This case has three distinct features that are worth noting before we proceed further. First, our opinion appears to be the first interpretation of the ACPA at the appellate level. Second, we are asked to undertake the interpretation of this new statute even though the district court made its ruling based on the FTDA. Third, the case before us presents a factual situation that, as far as we can tell, is rare if not unique: A Competitor X of Company Y has registered Y's trademark as a domain name and then transferred that name to Subsidiary Z, which operates a business wholly unrelated to Y. These unusual features counsel that we decide no more than is absolutely necessary to resolve the case before us.

A. Application of the ACPA to this Case

[21] . . . . Because the ACPA became law while this case was pending before us, we must decide how its passage affects this case. As a general rule, we apply the law that exists at the time of the appeal. . . .

[22] But even if a new law controls, the question remains whether in such circumstances it is more appropriate for the appellate court to apply it directly or, instead, to remand to the district court to enable that court to consider the effect of the new law. We therefore asked for additional briefing from the parties regarding the applicability of the ACPA to the case before us. After receiving those briefs and fully considering the arguments there made, we think it is clear that the new law was adopted specifically to provide courts with a preferable alternative to stretching federal dilution law when dealing with cybersquatting cases. Indeed, the new law constitutes a particularly good fit with this case. Moreover, the findings of the district court, together with the rest of the record, enable us to apply the new law to the case before us without difficulty. Accordingly, we will do so and forego a remand.

B. "Distinctive" or "Famous"

[23] Under the new Act, we must first determine whether *sporty's* is a distinctive or famous mark and thus entitled to the ACPA's protection. *See* 15 U.S.C. § 1125(d)(1)(A)(ii)(I), (II). The district court concluded that *sporty's* is both distinctive and famous. We agree that *sporty's* is a "distinctive" mark. As

---

[9] The new Act permits a plaintiff to "elect, at any time before final judgment is rendered by the trial court, to recover, instead of actual damages and profits, an award of statutory damages in the amount of not less than $1,000 and not more than $100,000 per domain name, as the court considers just." Pub.L. No. 106-113, § 3003. If the plaintiff does not so elect, the court may award damages under 15 U.S.C. § 1117(a) and (b), based on damages, profits, and the cost of the action. *See id.*

a result, and without casting any doubt on the district court's holding in this respect, we need not, and hence do not, decide whether *sporty's* is also a "famous" mark.[10]

[24] More vexing is the question posed by the criterion that focuses on "the degree of recognition of the mark in the trading areas and channels of trade used by the marks' owner and the person against whom the injunction is sought." *Id.* at § 1125(c)(1)(F). Sporty's Farm contends that, although *sporty's* is a very well-known mark in the pilot and aviation niche market, Sportsman's did not (and could not) prove that the mark was well-known to *Sporty's Farm's* customers. We need not reach this question, as we would have had to do under the FTDA, since the ACPA provides protection not only to famous marks but also to distinctive marks regardless of fame.

[25] Distinctiveness refers to inherent qualities of a mark and is a completely different concept from fame. A mark may be distinctive before it has been used—when its fame is nonexistent. By the same token, even a famous mark may be so ordinary, or descriptive as to be notable for its lack of distinctiveness. *See Nabisco, Inc. v. PF Brands, Inc.,* 191 F.3d 208, 215-26 (2d Cir. 1999). We have no doubt that *sporty's,* as used in connection with Sportsman's catalogue of merchandise and advertising, is inherently distinctive. Furthermore, Sportsman's filed an affidavit under 15 U.S.C. § 1065 that rendered its registration of the *sporty's* mark incontestable, which entitles Sportsman's "to a presumption that its registered trademark is inherently distinctive." *Equine Technologies, Inc. v. Equitechnology, Inc.,* 68 F.3d 542, 545 (1st Cir. 1995). We therefore conclude that, for the purposes of § 1125(d)(1)(A)(ii)(I), the *sporty's* mark is distinctive.

C. "Identical and Confusingly Similar"

[26] The next question is whether domain name sportys.com is "identical or confusingly similar to" the *sporty's* mark.[11] 15 U.S.C. § 1125(d)(1)(A)(ii)(I). As we noted above, apostrophes cannot be used in domain names. *See supra* note 2. As a result, the secondary domain name in this case (sportys) is indistinguishable from the Sportsman's trademark (*sporty's*). *Cf. Brookfield Communications, Inc. v. West Coast Entertainment Corp.,* 174 F.3d 1036, 1055 (9th Cir. 1999) (observing that the differences between the mark "MovieBuff" and the domain name "moviebuff.com" are "inconsequential in light of the fact that Web addresses are not caps-sensitive and that the '.com' top-level domain signifies the site's commercial nature"). We therefore conclude that, although the domain name sportys.com is not precisely identical to the *sporty's* mark, it is certainly "confusingly similar" to the protected mark under § 1125(d)(1)(A)(ii)(I). *Cf. Wella Corp. v. Wella Graphics, Inc.* 874 F.Supp. 54, 56 (E.D.N.Y. 1994) (finding the new mark "Wello" confusingly similar to the trademark "Wella").

D. "Bad Faith Intent to Profit"

[27] We next turn to the issue of whether Sporty's Farm acted with a "bad faith intent to profit" from the mark *sporty's* when it registered the domain name sportys.com. 15 U.S.C. § 1125(d)(1)(A)(i). The statute lists nine factors to assist courts in determining when a defendant has acted with a bad faith intent to profit from the use of a mark.[12] But we are not limited to considering just the listed factors

---

[10] In most respects, *sporty's* meets the rigorous criteria laid out in § 1125(c)(1), requiring both fame and distinctiveness for protection under the FTDA. *See Nabisco Brands, Inc., v. PF Brands, Inc.,* 191 F.3d 208, 216 (2d Cir. 1999). The mark (1) is sufficiently distinctive (as we discuss in the text), (2) has been used by Sportsman's for an extended period of time, (3) has had millions of dollars in advertising spent on it, (4) is used nationwide, and (5) is traded in a wide variety of retail channels. *See* 15 U.S.C. § 1125(c)(1)(A)-(E). Moreover, the record does not indicate that anyone else besides Sportsman's uses *sporty's,* and the mark is, of course, registered with federal authorities. *See id.* at § 1125(c)(1)(G)-(H).

[11] We note that "confusingly similar" is a different standard from the "likelihood of confusion" standard for trademark infringement adopted by this court in *Polaroid Corp. v. Polarad Electronics Corp.,* 287 F.2d 492 (2d Cir. 1961). *See Wella Corp. v. Wella Graphics, Inc.,* 37 F.3d 46, 48 (2d Cir. 1994).

[12] These factors are:

when making our determination of whether the statutory criterion has been met. The factors are, instead, expressly described as indicia that "may" be considered along with other facts. *Id.* § 1125(d)(1)(B)(i).

[28] We hold that there is more than enough evidence in the record below of "bad faith intent to profit" on the part of Sporty's Farm (as that term is defined in the statute), so that "no reasonable factfinder could return a verdict against" Sportsman's. *Norville v. Staten Island Univ. Hosp.,* 196 F.3d 89, 95 (2d Cir. 1999). First, it is clear that neither Sporty's Farm nor Omega had any intellectual property rights in sportys.com at the time Omega registered the domain name. *See id.* § 1125(d)(1)(B)(i)(I). Sporty's Farm was not formed until nine months after the domain name was registered, and it did not begin operations or obtain the domain name from Omega until after this lawsuit was filed. Second, the domain name does not consist of the legal name of the party that registered it, Omega. *See id.* § 1125(d)(1)(B)(i)(II). Moreover, although the domain name does include part of the name of Sporty's Farm, that entity did not exist at the time the domain name was registered.

[29] The third factor, the prior use of the domain name in connection with the bona fide offering of any goods or services, also cuts against Sporty's Farm since it did not use the site until after this litigation began, undermining its claim that the offering of Christmas trees on the site was in good faith. *See id.* § 1125(d)(1)(B)(i)(III). Further weighing in favor of a conclusion that Sporty's Farm had the requisite statutory bad faith intent, as a matter of law, are the following: (1) Sporty's Farm does not claim that its

---

(I) the trademark or other intellectual property rights of the person, if any, in the domain name;

(II) the extent to which the domain name consists of the legal name of the person or a name that is otherwise commonly used to identify that person;

(III) the person's prior use, if any, of the domain name in connection with the bona fide offering of any goods or services;

(IV) the person's bona fide noncommercial or fair use of the mark in a site accessible under the domain name;

(V) the person's intent to divert consumers from the mark owner's online location to a site accessible under the domain name that could harm the goodwill represented by the mark, either for commercial gain or with the intent to tarnish or disparage the mark, by creating a likelihood of confusion as to the source, sponsorship, affiliation, or endorsement of the site;

(VI) the person's offer to transfer, sell, or otherwise assign the domain name to the mark owner or any third party for financial gain without having used, or having an intent to use, the domain name in the bona fide offering of any goods or services, or the person's prior conduct indicating a pattern of such conduct;

(VII) the person's provision of material and misleading false contact information when applying for the registration of the domain name, the person's intentional failure to maintain accurate contact information, or the person's prior conduct indicating a pattern of such conduct;

(VIII) the person's registration or acquisition of multiple domain names which the person knows are identical or confusingly similar to marks of others that are distinctive at the time of registration of such domain names, or dilutive of famous marks of others that are famous at the time of registration of such domain names, without regard to the goods or services of the parties; and

(IX) the extent to which the mark incorporated in the person's domain name registration is or is not distinctive and famous within the meaning of subsection(c)(1) of section 43.

15 U.S.C. § 1125(d)(1)(B)(i).

use of the domain name was "noncommercial" or a "fair use of the mark," *see id.* § 1125(d)(1)(B)(i)(IV), (2) Omega sold the mark to Sporty's Farm under suspicious circumstances, *see Sporty's Farm v. Sportsman's Market,* No. 96CV0756 (D.Conn. Mar. 13, 1998), *reprinted in* Joint Appendix at A277 (describing the circumstances of the transfer of sportys.com); 15 U.S.C. § 1125(d)(1)(B)(i)(VI), and, (3) as we discussed above, the *sporty's* mark is undoubtedly distinctive, *see id.* § 1125(d)(1)(B)(i)(IX).

[30] The most important grounds for our holding that Sporty's Farm acted with a bad faith intent, however, are the unique circumstances of this case, which do not fit neatly into the specific factors enumerated by Congress but may nevertheless be considered under the statute. We know from the record and from the district court's findings that Omega planned to enter into direct competition with Sportsman's in the pilot and aviation consumer market. As recipients of Sportsman's catalogs, Omega's owners, the Hollanders, were fully aware that *sporty's* was a very strong mark for consumers of those products. It cannot be doubted, as the court found below, that Omega registered sportys.com for the primary purpose of keeping Sportsman's from using that domain name. Several months later, and after this lawsuit was filed, Omega created another company in an unrelated business that received the name Sporty's Farm so that it could (1) use the sportys.com domain name in some commercial fashion, (2) keep the name away from Sportsman's, and (3) protect itself in the event that Sportsman's brought an infringement claim alleging that a "likelihood of confusion" had been created by Omega's version of cybersquatting. Finally, the explanation given for Sporty's Farm's desire to use the domain name, based on the existence of the dog Spotty, is more amusing than credible. Given these facts and the district court's grant of an equitable injunction under the FTDA, there is ample and overwhelming evidence that, as a matter of law, Sporty's Farm's acted with a "bad faith intent to profit" from the domain name sportys.com as those terms are used in the ACPA.[13] *See Luciano v. Olsten Corp.,* 110 F.3d 210, 214 (2d Cir. 1997) (stating that, as a matter of law, judgment may be granted where "the evidence in favor of the movant is so overwhelming that 'reasonable and fair minded [persons] could not arrive at a verdict against [it].'" (quoting *Cruz v. Local Union No. 3,* 34 F.3d 1148, 1154 (2d Cir. 1994) (alteration in original))).

E. Remedy

[31] Based on the foregoing, we hold that under § 1125(d)(1)(A), Sporty's Farm violated Sportsman's statutory rights by its use of the sportys.com domain name. The question that remains is what remedy is Sportsman's entitled to. The Act permits a court to "order the forfeiture or cancellation of the domain name or the transfer of the domain name to the owner of the mark," § 1125(d)(1)(C) for any "domain name [ ] registered before, on, or after the date of the enactment of [the] Act," Pub.L. No. 106-113, § 3010. That is precisely what the district court did here, albeit under the pre-existing law, when it directed a) Omega and Sporty's Farm to release their interest in sportys.com and to transfer the name to Sportsman's, and b) permanently enjoined those entities from taking any action to prevent and/or hinder Sportsman's from obtaining the domain name. That relief remains appropriate under the ACPA. We therefore affirm the district court's grant of injunctive relief.

{The court then determined that Sportsman's was not entitled to damages under the ACPA because the Act states that damages are not "available with respect to the registration, trafficking, or use of a domain name that occurs before the date of the enactment of this Act." The court also affirmed as not clearly in error the district court's determination that Sporty's Farm had not sought willfully to dilute Sportsman's mark and thus that Sportsman's was not entitled to damages under the antidilution provisions of Lanham Act § 43(c).}

---

[13] We expressly note that "bad faith intent to profit" are terms of art in the ACPA and hence should not necessarily be equated with "bad faith" in other contexts.

Lamparello v. Falwell
420 F.3d 309 (4th Cir. 2005)

DIANA GRIBBON MOTZ, Circuit Judge.

[1] Christopher Lamparello appeals the district court's order enjoining him from maintaining a gripe website critical of Reverend Jerry Falwell. For the reasons stated below, we reverse.

I.

[2] Reverend Falwell is "a nationally known minister who has been active as a commentator on politics and public affairs." *Hustler Magazine v. Falwell,* 485 U.S. 46, 47, 108 S.Ct. 876, 99 L.Ed.2d 41 (1988). He holds the common law trademarks "Jerry Falwell" and "Falwell," and the registered trademark "Listen America with Jerry Falwell." Jerry Falwell Ministries can be found online at "www.falwell.com," a website which receives 9,000 hits (or visits) per day.

[3] Lamparello registered the domain name "www.fallwell.com" on February 11, 1999, after hearing Reverend Falwell give an interview "in which he expressed opinions about gay people and homosexuality that [Lamparello] considered . . . offensive." Lamparello created a website at that domain name to respond to what he believed were "untruths about gay people." Lamparello's website included headlines such as "Bible verses that Dr. Falwell chooses to ignore" and "Jerry Falwell has been bearing false witness (Exodus 20:16) against his gay and lesbian neighbors for a long time." The site also contained in-depth criticism of Reverend Falwell's views. For example, the website stated:

> Dr. Falwell says that he is on the side of truth. He says that he will preach that homosexuality is a sin until the day he dies. But we believe that if the reverend were to take another thoughtful look at the scriptures, he would discover that they have been twisted around to support an anti-gay political agenda . . . at the expense of the gospel.

[4] Although the interior pages of Lamparello's website did not contain a disclaimer, the homepage prominently stated, "This website is NOT affiliated with Jerry Falwell or his ministry"; advised, "If you would like to visit Rev. Falwell's website, you may click here"; and provided a hyperlink to Reverend Falwell's website.

[5] At one point, Lamparello's website included a link to the Amazon.com webpage for a book that offered interpretations of the Bible that Lamparello favored, but the parties agree that Lamparello has never sold goods or services on his website. The parties also agree that "Lamparello's domain name and web site at www.fallwell.com," which received only 200 hits per day, "had no measurable impact on the quantity of visits to [Reverend Falwell's] web site at www.falwell.com."

[6] Nonetheless, Reverend Falwell sent Lamparello letters in October 2001 and June 2003 demanding that he cease and desist from using www.fallwell.com or any variation of Reverend Falwell's name as a domain name. Ultimately, Lamparello filed this action against Reverend Falwell and his ministries (collectively referred to hereinafter as "Reverend Falwell"), seeking a declaratory judgment of noninfringement. Reverend Falwell counter-claimed, alleging trademark infringement under 15 U.S.C. § 1114 (2000), false designation of origin under 15 U.S.C. § 1125(a), unfair competition under 15 U.S.C. § 1126 and the common law of Virginia, and cybersquatting under 15 U.S.C. § 1125(d).

[7] The parties stipulated to all relevant facts and filed cross-motions for summary judgment. The district court granted summary judgment to Reverend Falwell, enjoined Lamparello from using Reverend Falwell's mark at www.fallwell.com, and required Lamparello to transfer the domain name to Reverend Falwell. *Lamparello,* 360 F.Supp.2d at 773, 775. However, the court denied Reverend Falwell's request for statutory damages or attorney fees, reasoning that the "primary motive" of Lamparello's website was "to put forth opinions on issues that were contrary to those of [Reverend Falwell]" and "not to take away monies or to profit." *Id.* at 775.

[8] Lamparello appeals the district court's order; Reverend Falwell cross-appeals the denial of statutory damages and attorney fees. We review *de novo* a district court's ruling on cross-motions for summary judgment. *See People for the Ethical Treatment of Animals v. Doughney,* 263 F.3d 359, 364 (4th Cir. 2001) [hereinafter "*PETA* "].

II.

{In analyzing Falwell's likelihood of confusion claims under Lanham Act §§ 32 and 43(a), the court addressed without deciding the issue of whether Lamparello was engaging in commercial speech or using Falwell's mark "in connection with the sale, offering for sale, distribution, or advertising of any goods or services." Instead, the court simply found no likelihood of confusion as to the true source of Lamparello's website, explaining that "to determine whether a likelihood of confusion exists as to the source of a gripe site like that at issue in this case, a court must look not only to the allegedly infringing domain name, but also to the underlying content of the website." As for the issue of initial interest confusion, the court stated that "even if we did endorse the initial interest confusion theory, that theory would not assist Reverend Falwell here because it provides no basis for liability in circumstances such as these. The few appellate courts that have followed the Ninth Circuit and imposed liability under this theory for using marks on the Internet have done so only in cases involving a factor utterly absent here—one business's use of another's mark for its own financial gain .... This critical element—use of another firm's mark to capture the markholder's customers and profits—simply does not exist when the alleged infringer establishes a gripe site that criticizes the markholder."}

III.

[9] We evaluate Reverend Falwell's cybersquatting claim separately because the elements of a cybersquatting violation differ from those of traditional Lanham Act violations. To prevail on a cybersquatting claim, Reverend Falwell must show that Lamparello: (1) "had a bad faith intent to profit from using the [www.fallwell.com] domain name," and (2) the domain name www.fallwell.com "is identical or confusingly similar to, or dilutive of, the distinctive and famous [Falwell] mark." *PETA*, 263 F.3d at 367 (citing 15 U.S.C. § 1125(d)(1)(A)).

[10] "The paradigmatic harm that the ACPA was enacted to eradicate" is "the practice of cybersquatters registering several hundred domain names in an effort to sell them to the legitimate owners of the mark." *Lucas Nursery & Landscaping, Inc. v. Grosse*, 359 F.3d 806, 810 (6th Cir. 2004). The Act was also intended to stop the registration of multiple marks with the hope of selling them to the highest bidder, "distinctive marks to defraud consumers" or "to engage in counterfeiting activities," and "well-known marks to prey on consumer confusion by misusing the domain name to divert customers from the mark owner's site to the cybersquatter's own site, many of which are pornography sites that derive advertising revenue based on the number of visits, or 'hits,' the site receives." S.Rep. No. 106-140, 1999 WL 594571, at *5-6. The Act was not intended to prevent "noncommercial uses of a mark, such as for comment, criticism, parody, news reporting, etc.," and thus they "are beyond the scope" of the ACPA. *Id.* at *9.

[11] To distinguish abusive domain name registrations from legitimate ones, the ACPA directs courts to consider nine nonexhaustive factors ....

[12] These factors attempt "to balance the property interests of trademark owners with the legitimate interests of Internet users and others who seek to make lawful uses of others' marks, including for purposes such as comparative advertising, *comment, criticism,* parody, news reporting, fair use, etc." H.R. Rep. No. 106-412, 1999 WL 970519, at *10 (emphasis added). "The first four [factors] suggest circumstances that may tend to indicate an absence of bad-faith intent to profit from the goodwill of a mark, and the others suggest circumstances that may tend to indicate that such bad-faith intent exists." *Id.* However, "[t]here is no simple formula for evaluating and weighing these factors. For example, courts do not simply count up which party has more factors in its favor after the evidence is in." *Harrods Ltd. v. Sixty Internet Domain Names*, 302 F.3d 214, 234 (4th Cir. 2002). In fact, because use of these listed factors is permissive, "[w]e need not ... march through" them all in every case. *Virtual Works, Inc. v. Volkswagen of Am., Inc.*, 238 F.3d 264, 269 (4th Cir. 2001). "The factors are given to courts as a guide, not as a substitute for careful thinking about whether the conduct at issue is motivated by a bad faith intent to profit." *Lucas Nursery & Landscaping*, 359 F.3d at 811.

[13] After close examination of the undisputed facts involved in this case, we can only conclude that Reverend Falwell cannot demonstrate that Lamparello "had a bad faith intent to profit from using the

[www.fallwell.com] domain name." *PETA,* 263 F.3d at 367. Lamparello clearly employed www.fallwell.com simply to criticize Reverend Falwell's views. Factor IV of the ACPA, 15 U.S.C. § 1125(d)(1)(B)(i)(IV), counsels against finding a bad faith intent to profit in such circumstances because "use of a domain name for purposes of . . . comment, [and] criticism," H.R.Rep. No. 106-412, 1999 WL 970519, at *11, constitutes a "bona fide noncommercial or fair use" under the statute, 15 U.S.C. § 1125(d)(1)(B)(i)(IV).[7] That Lamparello provided a link to an Amazon.com webpage selling a book he favored does not diminish the communicative function of his website. The use of a domain name to engage in criticism or commentary "even where done for profit" does not alone evidence a bad faith intent to profit, H.R.Rep. No. 106-412, 1999 WL 970519, at *11, and Lamparello did not even stand to gain financially from sales of the book at Amazon.com. Thus factor IV weighs heavily in favor of finding Lamparello lacked a bad faith intent to profit from the use of the domain name.

[14] Equally important, Lamparello has not engaged in the type of conduct described in the statutory factors as typifying the bad faith intent to profit essential to a successful cybersquatting claim. First, we have already held, *supra* Part III.B, that Lamparello's domain name does not create a likelihood of confusion as to source or affiliation. Accordingly, Lamparello has not engaged in the type of conduct— "creating a likelihood of confusion as to the source, sponsorship, affiliation, or endorsement of the site," 15 U.S.C. § 1125(d)(1)(B)(i)(V) —described as an indicator of a bad faith intent to profit in factor V of the statute.

[15] Factors VI and VIII also counsel against finding a bad faith intent to profit here. Lamparello has made no attempt—or even indicated a willingness—"to transfer, sell, or otherwise assign the domain name to [Reverend Falwell] or any third party for financial gain." 15 U.S.C. § 1125(d)(1)(B)(i)(VI). Similarly, Lamparello has not registered "multiple domain names," 15 U.S.C. § 1125(d)(1)(B)(i)(VIII); rather, the record indicates he has registered only one. Thus, Lamparello's conduct is not of the suspect variety described in factors VI and VIII of the Act.

[16] Notably, the case at hand differs markedly from those in which the courts have found a bad faith intent to profit from domain names used for websites engaged in political commentary or parody. For example, in *PETA* we found the registrant of www.peta.org engaged in cybersquatting because www.peta.org was one of *fifty* to *sixty* domain names Doughney had registered, *PETA,* 263 F.3d at 362, and because Doughney had evidenced a clear intent to sell www.peta.org to PETA, stating that PETA should try to "'settle' with him and 'make him an offer.'" *Id.* at 368. *See also Virtual Works,* 238 F.3d at 269-70. Similarly, in *Coca-Cola Co. v. Purdy,* 382 F.3d 774 (8th Cir. 2004), the Eighth Circuit found an anti-abortion activist who had registered domain names incorporating famous marks such as "Washington Post" liable for cybersquatting because he had registered almost *seventy* domain names, had offered to stop using the Washington Post mark if the newspaper published an opinion piece by him on its editorial page, and posted content that created a likelihood of confusion as to whether the famous markholders sponsored the anti-abortion sites and "ha[d] taken positions on hotly contested issues." *Id.* at 786. In contrast, Lamparello did not register multiple domain names, he did not offer to transfer them for valuable consideration, and he did not create a likelihood of confusion.

[17] Instead, Lamparello, like the plaintiffs in two cases recently decided by the Fifth and Sixth Circuits, created a gripe site. Both courts expressly refused to find that gripe sites located at domain names nearly identical to the marks at issue violated the ACPA. In *TMI, Inc. v. Maxwell,* 368 F.3d 433,

---

[7] We note that factor IV does not protect a faux noncommercial site, that is, a noncommercial site created by the registrant for the sole purpose of avoiding liability under the FTDA, which exempts noncommercial uses of marks, *see* 15 U.S.C. § 1125(c)(4)(B), or under the ACPA. As explained by the Senate Report discussing the ACPA, an individual cannot avoid liability for registering and attempting to sell a hundred domain names incorporating famous marks by posting noncommercial content at those domain names. *See* S.Rep. No. 106-140, 1999 WL 594571, at *14 (citing *Panavision Int'l v. Toeppen,* 141 F.3d 1316 (9th Cir. 1998)). But Lamparello's sole purpose for registering www.fallwell.com was to criticize Reverend Falwell, and this noncommercial use was not a ruse to avoid liability. Therefore, factor IV indicates that Lamparello did not have a bad faith intent to profit.

434-35 (5th Cir. 2004), Joseph Maxwell, a customer of homebuilder TMI, registered the domain name "www.trendmakerhome.com," which differed by only one letter from TMI's mark, TrendMaker Homes, and its domain name, "www.trendmakerhomes.com." Maxwell used the site to complain about his experience with TMI and to list the name of a contractor whose work pleased him. After his registration expired, Maxwell registered "www.trendmakerhome.info." TMI then sued, alleging cybersquatting. The Fifth Circuit reversed the district court's finding that Maxwell violated the ACPA, reasoning that his site was noncommercial and designed only "to inform potential customers about a negative experience with the company." *Id.* at 438-39.

[18] Similarly, in *Lucas Nursery & Landscaping,* a customer of Lucas Nursery registered the domain name "www.lucasnursery.com" and posted her dissatisfaction with the company's landscaping services. Because the registrant, Grosse, like Lamparello, registered a single domain name, the Sixth Circuit concluded that her conduct did not constitute that which Congress intended to proscribe—i.e., the registration of multiple domain names. *Lucas Nursery & Landscaping,* 359 F.3d at 810. Noting that Grosse's gripe site did not create any confusion as to sponsorship and that she had never attempted to sell the domain name to the markholder, the court found that Grosse's conduct was not actionable under the ACPA. The court explained: "One of the ACPA's main objectives is the protection of consumers from slick internet peddlers who trade on the names and reputations of established brands. The practice of informing fellow consumers of one's experience with a particular service provider is surely not inconsistent with this ideal." *Id.* at 811.

[19] Like Maxwell and Grosse before him, Lamparello has not evidenced a bad faith intent to profit under the ACPA. To the contrary, he has used www.fallwell.com to engage in the type of "comment[ ][and] criticism" that Congress specifically stated militates against a finding of bad faith intent to profit. *See* S. Rep. No. 106-140, 1999 WL 594571, at *14. And he has neither registered multiple domain names nor attempted to transfer www.fallwell.com for valuable consideration. We agree with the Fifth and Sixth Circuits that, given these circumstances, the use of a mark in a domain name for a gripe site criticizing the markholder does not constitute cybersquatting.

IV.

[20] For the foregoing reasons, Lamparello, rather than Reverend Falwell, is entitled to summary judgment on all counts.[8] Accordingly, the judgment of the district court is reversed and the case is remanded for entry of judgment for Lamparello.

REVERSED AND REMANDED.

2. The Uniform Dispute Resolution Policy and the Uniform Rapid Suspension System

a. The Uniform Dispute Resolution Policy

WIPO Guide to the Uniform Domain Name Dispute Resolution Policy (UDRP)

(http://www.wipo.int/amc/en/domains/guide/)

What is the Uniform Domain Name Dispute Resolution Policy?

The Uniform Domain Name Dispute Resolution Policy (the UDRP Policy) sets out the legal framework for the resolution of disputes between a domain name registrant and a third party (i.e., a party other than the registrar) over the abusive registration and use of an Internet domain name in the generic top level domains or gTLDs (e.g., .biz, .com, .info, .mobi, .name, .net, .org), and those country code top level domains or ccTLDs that have adopted the UDRP Policy on a voluntary basis. At its meetings on August 25 and 26, 1999 in Santiago, Chile, the ICANN* Board of Directors adopted the UDRP Policy, based

---

[8] Given our resolution of Lamparello's appeal, Reverend Falwell's cross-appeal with respect to statutory damages and attorney fees is moot.

* {The Internet Corporation for Assigned Names and Numbers (ICANN) is a non-profit, non-governmental organization that, among other things, administers the internet domain name system.

largely on the recommendations contained in the Report of the WIPO Internet Domain Name Process, as well as comments submitted by registrars and other interested parties. All ICANN-accredited registrars that are authorized to register names in the gTLDs and the ccTLDs that have adopted the Policy have agreed to abide by and implement it for those domains. Any person or entity wishing to register a domain name in the gTLDs and ccTLDs in question is required to consent to the terms and conditions of the UDRP Policy.

What are the advantages of the UDRP Administrative Procedure?

The main advantage of the UDRP Administrative Procedure is that it typically provides a faster and cheaper way to resolve a dispute regarding the registration and use of an Internet domain name than going to court. In addition, the procedures are considerably more informal than litigation and the decision-makers are experts in such areas as international trademark law, domain name issues, electronic commerce, the Internet and dispute resolution. It is also international in scope: it provides a single mechanism for resolving a domain name dispute regardless of where the registrar or the domain name holder or the complainant are located.

What are the WIPO Center's fees for a domain name dispute?

For a case involving between 1 and 5 domain names, the fee for a case that is to be decided by a single Panelist is USD1500 and USD4000 for a case that is to be decided by 3 Panelists.

For a case involving between 6 and 10 domain names, the fee for a case that is to be decided by a single Panelist is USD2000 and USD5000 for a case that is to be decided by 3 Panelists.

The Complainant is responsible for paying the total fees. The only time the Respondent has to share in the fees is when the Respondent chooses to have the case decided by 3 Panelists and the Complainant had chosen a single Panelist.

In exceptional circumstances, either the Panel or the WIPO Center may ask the parties to make additional payments to defray the costs of the administrative procedure.

Uniform Domain Name Dispute Resolution Policy

(As Approved by ICANN on October 24, 1999)

1. **Purpose**. This Uniform Domain Name Dispute Resolution Policy (the "Policy") has been adopted by the Internet Corporation for Assigned Names and Numbers ("ICANN"), is incorporated by reference into your Registration Agreement, and sets forth the terms and conditions in connection with a dispute between you and any party other than us (the registrar) over the registration and use of an Internet domain name registered by you. Proceedings under Paragraph 4 of this Policy will be conducted according to the Rules for Uniform Domain Name Dispute Resolution Policy (the "Rules of Procedure"), which are available at http://www.icann.org/en/dndr/udrp/uniform-rules.htm, and the selected administrative-dispute-resolution service provider's supplemental rules.

2. **Your Representations**. By applying to register a domain name, or by asking us to maintain or renew a domain name registration, you hereby represent and warrant to us that (a) the statements that you made in your Registration Agreement are complete and accurate; (b) to your knowledge, the registration of the domain name will not infringe upon or otherwise violate the rights of any third party; (c) you are not registering the domain name for an unlawful purpose; and (d) you will not knowingly use the domain name in violation of any applicable laws or regulations. It is your responsibility to determine whether your domain name registration infringes or violates someone else's rights.

3. **Cancellations, Transfers, and Changes**. We will cancel, transfer or otherwise make changes to domain name registrations under the following circumstances:

ICANN accredits private companies and organizations that wish to provide domain name registration services.}

a. subject to the provisions of Paragraph 8, our receipt of written or appropriate electronic instructions from you or your authorized agent to take such action;

b. our receipt of an order from a court or arbitral tribunal, in each case of competent jurisdiction, requiring such action; and/or

c. our receipt of a decision of an Administrative Panel requiring such action in any administrative proceeding to which you were a party and which was conducted under this Policy or a later version of this Policy adopted by ICANN. (See Paragraph 4(i) and (k) below.)

We may also cancel, transfer or otherwise make changes to a domain name registration in accordance with the terms of your Registration Agreement or other legal requirements.

4. Mandatory Administrative Proceeding.

This Paragraph sets forth the type of disputes for which you are required to submit to a mandatory administrative proceeding. These proceedings will be conducted before one of the administrative-dispute-resolution service providers listed at www.icann.org/en/dndr/udrp/approved-providers.htm (each, a "Provider").

a. Applicable Disputes. You are required to submit to a mandatory administrative proceeding in the event that a third party (a "complainant") asserts to the applicable Provider, in compliance with the Rules of Procedure, that

(i) your domain name is identical or confusingly similar to a trademark or service mark in which the complainant has rights; and

(ii) you have no rights or legitimate interests in respect of the domain name; and

(iii) your domain name has been registered and is being used in bad faith.

In the administrative proceeding, the complainant must prove that each of these three elements are present.

b. Evidence of Registration and Use in Bad Faith. For the purposes of Paragraph 4(a)(iii), the following circumstances, in particular but without limitation, if found by the Panel to be present, shall be evidence of the registration and use of a domain name in bad faith:

(i) circumstances indicating that you have registered or you have acquired the domain name primarily for the purpose of selling, renting, or otherwise transferring the domain name registration to the complainant who is the owner of the trademark or service mark or to a competitor of that complainant, for valuable consideration in excess of your documented out-of-pocket costs directly related to the domain name; or

(ii) you have registered the domain name in order to prevent the owner of the trademark or service mark from reflecting the mark in a corresponding domain name, provided that you have engaged in a pattern of such conduct; or

(iii) you have registered the domain name primarily for the purpose of disrupting the business of a competitor; or

(iv) by using the domain name, you have intentionally attempted to attract, for commercial gain, Internet users to your web site or other on-line location, by creating a likelihood of confusion with the complainant's mark as to the source, sponsorship, affiliation, or endorsement of your web site or location or of a product or service on your web site or location.

c. How to Demonstrate Your Rights to and Legitimate Interests in the Domain Name in Responding to a Complaint. When you receive a complaint, you should refer to Paragraph 5 of the Rules of Procedure in determining how your response should be prepared. Any of the following circumstances, in particular but without limitation, if found by the Panel to be proved based on its evaluation of all evidence presented, shall demonstrate your rights or legitimate interests to the domain name for purposes of Paragraph 4(a)(ii):

(i) before any notice to you of the dispute, your use of, or demonstrable preparations to use, the domain name or a name corresponding to the domain name in connection with a bona fide offering of goods or services; or

(ii) you (as an individual, business, or other organization) have been commonly known by the domain name, even if you have acquired no trademark or service mark rights; or

(iii) you are making a legitimate noncommercial or fair use of the domain name, without intent for commercial gain to misleadingly divert consumers or to tarnish the trademark or service mark at issue.

d. Selection of Provider. The complainant shall select the Provider from among those approved by ICANN by submitting the complaint to that Provider. The selected Provider will administer the proceeding, except in cases of consolidation as described in Paragraph 4(f).

e. Initiation of Proceeding and Process and Appointment of Administrative Panel. The Rules of Procedure state the process for initiating and conducting a proceeding and for appointing the panel that will decide the dispute (the "Administrative Panel").

f. Consolidation. In the event of multiple disputes between you and a complainant, either you or the complainant may petition to consolidate the disputes before a single Administrative Panel. This petition shall be made to the first Administrative Panel appointed to hear a pending dispute between the parties. This Administrative Panel may consolidate before it any or all such disputes in its sole discretion, provided that the disputes being consolidated are governed by this Policy or a later version of this Policy adopted by ICANN.

g. Fees. All fees charged by a Provider in connection with any dispute before an Administrative Panel pursuant to this Policy shall be paid by the complainant, except in cases where you elect to expand the Administrative Panel from one to three panelists as provided in Paragraph 5(b)(iv) of the Rules of Procedure, in which case all fees will be split evenly by you and the complainant.

h. Our Involvement in Administrative Proceedings. We do not, and will not, participate in the administration or conduct of any proceeding before an Administrative Panel. In addition, we will not be liable as a result of any decisions rendered by the Administrative Panel.

i. Remedies. The remedies available to a complainant pursuant to any proceeding before an Administrative Panel shall be limited to requiring the cancellation of your domain name or the transfer of your domain name registration to the complainant.

j. Notification and Publication. The Provider shall notify us of any decision made by an Administrative Panel with respect to a domain name you have registered with us. All decisions under this Policy will be published in full over the Internet, except when an Administrative Panel determines in an exceptional case to redact portions of its decision.

k. Availability of Court Proceedings. The mandatory administrative proceeding requirements set forth in Paragraph 4 shall not prevent either you or the complainant from submitting the dispute to a court of competent jurisdiction for independent resolution before such mandatory administrative proceeding is commenced or after such proceeding is concluded. If an Administrative Panel decides that your domain name registration should be canceled or transferred, we will wait ten (10) business days (as observed in the location of our principal office) after we are informed by the applicable Provider of the Administrative Panel's decision before implementing that decision. We will then implement the decision unless we have received from you during that ten (10) business day period official documentation (such as a copy of a complaint, file-stamped by the clerk of the court) that you have commenced a lawsuit against the complainant in a jurisdiction to which the complainant has submitted under Paragraph 3(b)(xiii) of the Rules of Procedure. (In general, that jurisdiction is either the location of our principal office or of your address as shown in our Whois database. See Paragraphs 1 and 3(b)(xiii) of the Rules of Procedure for details.) If we receive such documentation within the ten (10) business day period, we will not implement the Administrative Panel's decision, and we will take no further action, until we receive (i) evidence satisfactory to us of a resolution between the parties; (ii) evidence satisfactory to us that your lawsuit has been dismissed or withdrawn; or (iii) a copy of an order

485

from such court dismissing your lawsuit or ordering that you do not have the right to continue to use your domain name.

5. All Other Disputes and Litigation. All other disputes between you and any party other than us regarding your domain name registration that are not brought pursuant to the mandatory administrative proceeding provisions of Paragraph 4 shall be resolved between you and such other party through any court, arbitration or other proceeding that may be available.

6. Our Involvement in Disputes. We will not participate in any way in any dispute between you and any party other than us regarding the registration and use of your domain name. You shall not name us as a party or otherwise include us in any such proceeding. In the event that we are named as a party in any such proceeding, we reserve the right to raise any and all defenses deemed appropriate, and to take any other action necessary to defend ourselves.

7. Maintaining the Status Quo. We will not cancel, transfer, activate, deactivate, or otherwise change the status of any domain name registration under this Policy except as provided in Paragraph 3 above.

8. Transfers During a Dispute.

. . . .

9. Policy Modifications. We reserve the right to modify this Policy at any time with the permission of ICANN. We will post our revised Policy at <URL> at least thirty (30) calendar days before it becomes effective. Unless this Policy has already been invoked by the submission of a complaint to a Provider, in which event the version of the Policy in effect at the time it was invoked will apply to you until the dispute is over, all such changes will be binding upon you with respect to any domain name registration dispute, whether the dispute arose before, on or after the effective date of our change. In the event that you object to a change in this Policy, your sole remedy is to cancel your domain name registration with us, provided that you will not be entitled to a refund of any fees you paid to us. The revised Policy will apply to you until you cancel your domain name registration.

Comments and Questions

1.   *Appealing a UDRP decision.* As paragraph 4(k) of the UDRP makes clear, litigants unsatisfied with the outcome of the UDRP process may "submit[] the dispute to a court of competent jurisdiction for independent resolution." U.S. courts afford no deference to UDRP decisions. *See, e.g., Barcelona.com, Inc. v. Excelentisimo Ayntamiento De Barcelona*, 330 F.3d 617, 626 (4th Cir. 2003) ("[A]ny decision made by a panel under the UDRP is no more than an agreed-upon administration that is *not* given any deference under the ACPA." (emphasis in original)).

The following UDRP panel decision engages a recent controversy among UDRP panelists concerning a fundamental limitation of the UDRP. Under the terms of UDRP paragraph 4(a)(iii), the complainant must show, among other things, that the domain name was registered in bad faith *and* is being used in bad faith. In a standard UDRP proceeding, it is often not difficult to establish current bad faith use. But what if a domain name, though currently being used in bad faith, was initially registered in good faith? In such situations, UDRP paragraph 4(a)(iii) would apparently fail to trigger transfer of the domain name, even in cases of extreme bad faith use. For a brief period starting in 2009, a number of UDRP panel decisions sought to work around this problem by means of theories of retroactive bad faith registration or bad faith renewal. *See, e.g., Octogen Pharmacal Company, Inc. v. Domains By Proxy, Inc. / Rich Sanders and Octogen e-Solutions*, Case No. D2009-0786 (WIPO Aug. 29, 2009); *Eastman Sport Group LLC v. Jim and Kenny*, Case No. D2009-1688 (WIPO March 1, 2010). Other panel decisions rejected these efforts to reconfigure the UDRP. *See, e.g., Camon S.p.A. v. Intelli-Pet, LLC*, Case No. D2009-1716 (WIPO March 12, 2010). The following decision reports that some degree of consensus has now been reached on the issue.

Pinterest, Inc. v. Pinerest.com c/o Whois Privacy Svcs Pty Ltd/Ian Townsend
Case No. D2015-1873 (WIPO Dec. 21, 2015)

1. The Parties

[1] The Complainant is Pinterest, Inc. of San Francisco, California, United States of America ("United States"), represented by Baker & McKenzie, United Kingdom of Great Britain and Northern Ireland ("United Kingdom").

[2] The Respondent is Pinerest.com c/o Whois Privacy Services Pty Ltd of Fortitude Valley, Queensland, Australia / Ian Townsend of Madrid, Spain.

2. The Domain Name and Registrar

[3] The disputed domain name <pinerest.com> is registered with Fabulous.com (the "Registrar").

3. Procedural History

[4] The Complaint was filed with the WIPO Arbitration and Mediation Center (the "Center") on October 20, 2015. On October 21, 2015, the Center transmitted by email to the Registrar a request for registrar verification in connection with the disputed domain name. On October 27, 2015, the Registrar transmitted by email to the Center its verification response disclosing registrant and contact information for the disputed domain name which differed from the named Respondent and contact information in the Complaint. The Center sent an email communication to the Complainant on October 27, 2015, providing the registrant and contact information disclosed by the Registrar, and inviting the Complainant to submit an amended Complaint. The Complainant filed an amended Complaint on October 29, 2015.

[5] The Center verified that the Complaint together with the amended Complaint satisfied the formal requirements of the Uniform Domain Name Dispute Resolution Policy (the "Policy" or "UDRP"), the Rules for Uniform Domain Name Dispute Resolution Policy (the "Rules"), and the WIPO Supplemental Rules for Uniform Domain Name Dispute Resolution Policy (the "Supplemental Rules").

[6] In accordance with the Rules, paragraphs 2 and 4, the Center formally notified the Respondent of the Complaint, and the proceedings commenced on November 5, 2015. In accordance with the Rules, paragraph 5, the due date for Response was November 25, 2015. The Respondent did not submit any response. Accordingly, the Center notified the Respondent's default on November 26, 2015.

[7] The Center appointed Andrew D. S. Lothian as the sole panelist in this matter on December 2, 2015. The Panel finds that it was properly constituted. The Panel has submitted the Statement of Acceptance and Declaration of Impartiality and Independence, as required by the Center to ensure compliance with the Rules, paragraph 7.

4. Factual Background

[8] To the Panel's knowledge (on which subject see section 6A below), the Complainant is a provider of online services via its website and mobile applications under the PINTEREST trademark, providing a facility whereby Internet users may gather images and content and organize this into themed collections on a "pinboard".

[9] The Complainant is the owner of a variety of registered trademarks for the word mark PINTEREST in a range of different jurisdictions including, for example, United States registered trademark No. 4145087 registered on May 22, 2012 in international classes 42 and 45.

[10] According to WhoIs records the disputed domain name was created on February 25, 1998. Little is known regarding the Respondent, who appears from the WhoIs to be an individual with an address in Spain. The Complainant submits that the Respondent is not the original registrant of the disputed domain name and notes that, according to historic WhoIs records, that entity was a memorial park and funeral home in Alabama, United States. The Complainant says that the disputed domain name has more recently been transferred to the Respondent. The probable date for such transfer, according to the Complainant, is August 24, 2015, which is the "last updated" date shown on the WhoIs record of October 13, 2015.

[11] Screenshots produced by the Complainant illustrate its assertion that the disputed domain name cycles through to a number of different unconnected websites, one of which invites users to participate in a survey purporting to be run by the Complainant, which produces a popup window on entry stating "Congratulations Pinterest Visitor!", and another of which directs users to malware.

5. Parties' Contentions

A. Complainant

[12] The Complainant contends that the disputed domain name is confusingly similar to a trademark in which the Complainant owns rights; that the Respondent has no rights or legitimate interests in the disputed domain name; and that the disputed domain name has been registered and is being used in bad faith.

[13] The Complainant submits that it satisfies the threshold requirement of having trademark rights under the Policy and that its PINTEREST trademark is incorporated in the disputed domain name with the omission of a single character. The Complainant asserts that its mark is well known and that the omission of a single character from such mark constitutes "type squatting" [sic] and renders the disputed domain name confusingly similar to such mark.

[14] The Complainant contends that it has not authorized the Respondent to register or use its PINTEREST mark or any confusingly similar variant thereof, that the Respondent has not been commonly known by the disputed domain name and that the Respondent is not making a noncommercial or fair use of the disputed domain name. The Complainant asserts that as the disputed domain name cycles through unconnected websites or popups and directs users to malware this cannot be described as a *bona fide* offering of goods or services. The Complainant submits that the purpose of the disputed domain name is to capture users who mistakenly enter it when attempting to visit the Complainant's website for the Respondent's commercial gain and that accordingly the Respondent cannot claim rights or legitimate interests therein.

[15] The Complainant submits that the Respondent acquired the disputed domain name from the original registrant in bad faith in order to use the disputed domain name in bad faith by creating confusion with the Complainant's PINTEREST mark. The Complainant contends that the *Octogen* trio of cases (*City Views Limited v. Moniker Privacy Services / Xander, Jeduyu, ALGEBRALIVE*, WIPO Case No. D2009-0643; *Phillip Securities Pte Ltd v. Yue Hoong Leong*, ADNDRC Decision DE-0900226; and *Octogen Pharmacal Company, Inc. v. Domains By Proxy, Inc. / Rich Sanders and Octogen e-Solutions*, WIPO Case No. D2009-0786) are applicable in the scenario where the Respondent is not the original registrant of the disputed domain name but subsequently acquired this in bad faith and demonstrably uses it in bad faith. The Complainant also asserts that the date of registration for the purposes of the Complaint should be the date of acquisition of the disputed domain name by the Respondent and not the original creation date.

[16] The Complainant asserts that the date of acquisition of the disputed domain name by the Respondent is August 2015 and that the Respondent would have been aware of the Complainant's rights by that date. The Complainant also argues that the Respondent must have been fully aware of such rights by virtue of its use of its PINTEREST mark on the surveys to which the disputed domain name points. The Complainant also describes and illustrates the use of the disputed domain name to point to sale items on a popular auction website together with popup advertisements stating that users have downloaded malware. The Complainant asserts that the use of the disputed domain name in this manner constitutes use in bad faith within the meaning of the Policy.

B. Respondent

[17] The Respondent did not reply to the Complainant's contentions.

6. Discussion and Findings

[18] To succeed, the Complainant must demonstrate that all of the elements listed in paragraph 4(a) of the Policy have been satisfied:

(i) the disputed domain name is identical or confusingly similar to a trademark or service mark in which the Complainant has rights;

(ii) the Respondent has no rights or legitimate interests in respect of the disputed domain name; and

(iii) the disputed domain name has been registered and is being used in bad faith.

. . . .

B. Identical or Confusingly Similar

[19] The Complainant has produced a series of screenshots from the website "www.tmview.org" as evidence of its various registered trademarks. This website provides data directly from the official trademark offices of its various members and the Panel thus has no reason to doubt the authenticity of the information provided. However, the Complainant's screenshots are in tabular format and do not show a detailed view of any of the marks listed. In order to obtain such a view, the Panel verified the details of the Complainant's mark described in the factual background section above by visiting the official website of the United States Patent and Trademark Office ("USPTO") and inputting the registration number disclosed on the Complainant's screenshot (see paragraph 4.5 of the WIPO Overview 2.0 regarding a panel's discretionary referencing of trademark online databases).

[20] While the Panel is content that the information provided by the Complainant, as supplemented by its visit to the USPTO website, is sufficient to allow it to make a finding that the Complainant has rights in the PINTEREST trademark, the Panel notes that complainants and their representatives would do well to consider providing the greater detail that lies behind the initial tabular view produced by a search on "www.tmview.org", at least in respect of any one mark which is being relied upon for the purposes of paragraph 4(a)(i) of the Policy.

[21] Having found that the Complainant has rights in the PINTEREST trademark, the Panel observes that the disputed domain name is identical to such mark, subject to the omission of the initial letter "t" in the disputed domain name. The Panel accepts the Complainant's submission that the omission of a single letter in the disputed domain name is insufficient to distinguish it from the Complainant's mark and accordingly finds that the disputed domain name is confusingly similar thereto. Accordingly, the Panel finds that the requirements of paragraph 4(a)(i) of the Policy have been satisfied.

C. Rights or Legitimate Interests

[22] Paragraph 4(c) of the Policy lists several ways in which the Respondent may demonstrate rights or legitimate interests in the disputed domain name . . . .

[23] As paragraph 2.1 of the WIPO Overview 2.0 notes, a consensus view among panelists in cases under the Policy has emerged that a complainant is required to make out a *prima facie* case that the respondent has no rights or legitimate interests in a domain name and that once such *prima facie* case is made, the burden of production shifts to the respondent to come forward with appropriate allegations or evidence demonstrating such rights or legitimate interests.

[24] In the present proceeding, the Panel is satisfied that the Complainant has made out the requisite *prima facie* case by way of its submissions that the Respondent was not authorized by the Complainant to use the Complainant's PINTEREST mark or a confusingly similar variant, that the Respondent has not been commonly known by the disputed domain name and that the Respondent is not making a noncommercial or fair use thereof. Furthermore, the Complainant's evidence regarding the use to which the disputed domain name has been put, which appears to target the Complainant's PINTEREST trademark by way of a survey addressed to the "Pinterest Visitor" is also supportive of the notion that the Respondent lacks rights or legitimate interests in the disputed domain name, which is itself a close typographical variant of such mark.

[25] In these circumstances the burden of production shifts to the Respondent to bring forward evidence or allegations demonstrating rights or legitimate interests in the disputed domain name. The Respondent, however, has chosen not to file a Response in these proceedings or otherwise to communicate anything which might point towards it having such rights or legitimate interests. The

Panel does note that the disputed domain name might also be read as the two words "pine" and "rest", which might well have been the intent of the original registrant of the disputed domain name but the Panel accepts the Complainant's contention that the Respondent is not the original registrant and is a more recent acquirer. In contrast to the original registrant, the Respondent has used the disputed domain name not in connection with any meaning of the words "pine" and "rest" but rather to address the viewer of the associated website as "Pinterest Visitor", that is, the typographical variant representing the Complainant's trademark, and thereafter to deliver to such viewer a variety of unrelated websites or malware. In the Panel's opinion, no rights or legitimate interests can vest in the Respondent by virtue of such activity.

[26] Accordingly, the Panel finds that the Respondent has no rights or legitimate interests in the disputed domain name and therefore that the requirements of paragraph 4(a)(ii) of the Policy have been met.

D. Registered and Used in Bad Faith

[27] Paragraph 4(b) of the Policy states that any of the following circumstances, in particular but without limitation, shall be considered evidence of the registration and use of a domain name in bad faith . . . .

[28] Typically, a complainant would not prevail on this aspect of the Policy if its trademark rights post-date the creation date of the disputed domain name because the registrant could not have contemplated the complainant's then non-existent right and thus could not have registered the domain name in bad faith (see the discussion at paragraph 3.1 of the WIPO Overview 2.0). In the present case, the Complainant anticipates that difficulty by referencing the *Octogen* line of decisions, *supra*, in order to assert that the Policy does not require a complainant to show the conjunctive requirement of both bad faith registration and bad faith use. This Panel subscribes to the traditional and generally accepted view of the conjunctive requirement within this element of the Policy and, rather than rehearsing at length the arguments for and against the alternative interpretation provided by the *Octogen* trio, simply notes for the sake of brevity that it endorses the detailed analysis on this topic provided by the panel in *Camon S.p.A. v. Intelli-Pet, LLC*, WIPO Case No. D2009-1716.

[29] Despite this, there are exceptions to the general rule regarding a post-dating trademark, including the circumstance where a domain name has been transferred between unrelated registrants after its creation date, as is alleged here. In such a circumstance, UDRP panels typically assess the registration in bad faith requirement as at the date when the respondent took possession of the disputed domain name and not at its original creation date. In the present matter, the Complainant asserts that the Respondent acquired the disputed domain name in August 2015, thus post-dating the registration of the Complainant's trademark by almost three years. The Complainant bases its assertion on the fact that this is the "last updated" date shown on the corresponding WhoIs record.

[30] The Panel is aware that while a change in the "last updated" date on a WhoIs record might indicate a registrant transfer of a domain name, such changes can also be triggered by a renewal or indeed by the making of a variety of different types of amendments to the WhoIs data. Accordingly, the Complainant's case would have been better served by producing entries from historic WhoIs records which might have shown a change of registrants on successive records and thus have placed the matter beyond doubt. In the absence of such records, the Panel has come to the conclusion that it may nevertheless accept the Complainant's assertion on the following basis: First, the Panel considers that it is not wholly improbable that the "last updated" date on a WhoIs record represents the date of transfer to the present holder and, as such, it is not unreasonable to accept that allegation in the absence of countervailing evidence, the majority of which would necessarily be in the hands of the Respondent in its capacity as holder of the disputed domain name. In other words, once such an allegation has been made and the matter is clearly placed in issue by a complainant, the respondent is the party best able to bring forward evidence, which may come from a wide variety of sources, supporting a contrary proposition that it has been the holder of the domain name concerned for a longer period (as this Panel encountered in *Qwalify, Inc. v. Domain Administrator, Fundacion Private Whois / Gregory Ricks*, WIPO Case No. D2014-0313).

[31] Secondly, while the present Complaint lacks the detailed evidence which historic WhoIs records would have provided, the Complainant's averments regarding the identity of the original registrant of the disputed domain name and its past use are also supportive, albeit to a limited degree, of the notion that a transfer has taken place. Taking these two aspects together, the Panel finds on the balance of probabilities, and in particular on the basis of the present record, that the Respondent received a transfer of the disputed domain name after the Complainant's rights in its trademark came into being, notwithstanding the original date of creation of the disputed domain name. While the disputed domain name may have been created by its original registrant for purposes unrelated to the Complainant or its trademark, the Panel is satisfied on the balance of probabilities that the transferee and present Respondent knew of the Complainant's online fame when taking a transfer of the disputed domain name and took such transfer with intent to target the Complainant's trademark.

[32] Turning to the present use of the disputed domain name, there is little doubt in the Panel's mind that this constitutes use in bad faith within the meaning of the Policy. In the Panel's opinion, the disputed domain name is being used to capture Internet traffic generated by users of the Complainant's services, in order to deploy malware and gain customer data through confusion generated by the typographical variant of the Complainant's trademark contained within the disputed domain name. That the Respondent deliberately intended to target the Complainant by taking advantage of such typographical variant is demonstrated by its use of the correct spelling of the Complainant's trademark in the legend "Congratulations Pinterest Visitor!" displayed on the associated website. Accordingly, there can be no suggestion that the Respondent acquired the disputed domain name with a good faith motivation associated with the dictionary words "pine" and "rest" which are contained therein. Furthermore, the Respondent has chosen not to answer the Complainant's allegations or provide evidence of any alleged good faith motivation in taking a transfer of or using the disputed domain name.

[33] In all of these circumstances, the Panel finds that the disputed domain name has been registered and is being used in bad faith and therefore that the requirements of paragraph 4(a)(iii) of the Policy have been met.

7. Decision

[34] For the foregoing reasons, in accordance with paragraphs 4(i) of the Policy and 15 of the Rules, the Panel orders that the disputed domain name <pinerest.com> be transferred to the Complainant.

Andrew D. S. Lothian

Sole Panelist

Date: December 21, 2015

b. The Uniform Rapid Suspension System

In 2011, ICANN's Board of Directors approved an enormous expansion of the generic top-level domain (gTLD) system beyond the 22 gTLDs[1] then operating. In January, 2012, ICANN began accepting applications from private companies or organizations that wished to administer new gTLDs consisting essentially of any string of characters, including non-Latin characters. In October, 2013, ICANN "delegated" the first new gTLDs: شبكة (Arabic for "web/network", International Domain Registry Pty. Ltd), онлайн (Cyrillic for "online", CORE Association), сайт (Cyrillic for "site", CORE Association) and 游戏 (Chinese for "game(s)", Spring Fields, LLC). From October 2013 through 2022, ICANN delegated over 1,200 new gTLDs.[2]

ICANN has established a sophisticated process very much akin to a national trademark registration process for the evaluation of new gTLD applications (which cost $185,000 per gTLD). Objections can be

---

[1] These were: .aero, .arpa, .asia, .biz, .cat, .com, .coop, .edu, .gov, .info, .int, .jobs, .mil, .mobi, .names, .net, .org, .post, .pro, .tel, .travel and .xxx. *See* Jacqueline Lipton & Mary Wong, *Trademark and Freedom of Expression in ICANN's New gTLD Process*, 38 Monash U. L. Rev. 188, 192 (2012).

[2] See http://newgtlds.icann.org/en/program-status/delegated-strings.

raised against a new gTLD application on the ground, among others, that it conflicts with preexisting trademark rights. Students wishing to know more about this process should consult the ICANN *gTLD Applicant Guidebook.*

Our focus here, however, is not on the implications for trademark owners of the ICANN new gTLD delegation process (though those implications can be profound), but rather on a new system by which trademark owners can oppose the registration of second-level domains *within* these new gTLDs. For example, if a third-party seeks to register the second-level domain "microsoft" within the شبكة gTLD, (thus microsoft.شبكة), Microsoft may avail itself of a new means of opposing the registration that is even faster and less expensive that the UDRP. This new process is the Uniform Rapid Suspension System (URS), which largely applies only to second-level domains within new gTLDs established since 2013 and to ccTLDs (country code top-level domains such as .us) that have adopted some variation of the URS. *Cf. ECR European Consumer Rights GmbH v. WhoisGuard, Inc.*, Claim No. FA2012001924132 (Nat'l Arb. Forum, Dec. 30, 2020) (applying the URS to the .org TLD and suspending the domain name verbraucherritter.org). Students wishing to read the URS Procedure may find the document at http://newgtlds.icann.org/en/applicants/urs.

The URS is designed for especially clear, essentially "slam-dunk" cases of bad faith second-level domain registration. The URS specifies that the complainant must show:

[1] that the registered domain name is identical or confusingly similar to a word mark: (i) for which the Complainant holds a valid national or regional registration and that is in current use; or (ii) that has been validated through court proceedings; or (iii) that is specifically protected by a statute or treaty in effect at the time the URS complaint is filed.

a. Use can be shown by demonstrating that evidence of use — which can be a declaration and one specimen of current use in commerce — was submitted to, and validated by, the Trademark Clearinghouse.

b. Proof of use may also be submitted directly with the URS Complaint.

and

[2] that the Registrant has no legitimate right or interest to the domain name; and

[3] that the domain was registered and is being used in bad faith.

URS, 1.2.6.1-1.2.6.3. Note that the URS Procedure explicitly states that "[t]he burden of proof shall be clear and convincing evidence." *Id.* at 8.2

The URS process is very fast. The URS provider (such as the National Arbitration Forum) must review the complaint within two business days from the filing of the complaint. If the complaint complies with all filing requirements, the URS provider notifies the relevant registry operator, who must "lock" the targeted domain within 24 hours (locking a domain in this context merely means that the registrant cannot make any changes to registration data; the domain still resolves to a website). Within 24 hours of locking the domain, the registry operator must notify the registrant of the complaint. The registrant then has 14 days to file a response of no more than 2,500 words. If the registrant defaults on that 14 day period, the registrant still has six months from the date of a Notice of Default to reopen proceedings de novo.

The remedy available to the successful complainant is suspension of the domain name and resolution of the domain to an informational page stating that the domain name has been suspended after a URS proceeding. Unlike the UDRP, the successful complainant cannot win transfer of the domain.

The fee for a URS proceeding, which is conducted entirely electronically and only in English, is $375 to $500, depending on the number of domain names complained of. By comparison, UDRP filing fees start at $1500.

Below is the first URS decision ever issued, with respect to the domain name facebok.pw. (.pw is the TLD of the Pacific nation of Palau and was the first TLD to adopt the URS).

Facebook Inc. v. Radoslav
Claim No. FA1308001515825 (Nat'l Arb. Forum, Sept. 27, 2013)

DOMAIN NAME

<facebok.pw>

PARTIES

Complainant: Facebook Inc. of Menlo Park, California, United States of America.

Complainant Representative: Hogan Lovells (Paris) LLP of Paris, France.

Respondent: Radoslav of Presov, California, SK.

Respondent Representative:

REGISTRIES and REGISTRARS

Registries:

Registrars: Dynadot, LLC

EXAMINER

[1] The undersigned certifies that he has acted independently and impartially and to the best of his knowledge has no known conflict in serving as the Examiner in this proceeding.

Darryl C. Wilson, as Examiner.

PROCEDURAL HISTORY

Complainant submitted: August 21, 2013

Commencement: September 11, 2013

Default Date: September 26, 2013

[2] Having reviewed the communications records, the Examiner finds that the National Arbitration Forum has discharged its responsibility under URS Procedure Paragraphs 3 and 4 and Rule 4 of the Rules for the Uniform Rapid Suspension System (the "Rules").

RELIEF SOUGHT

[3] Complainant requests that the domain name be suspended for the life of the registration.

STANDARD OF REVIEW

[4] Clear and convincing evidence.

FINDINGS and DISCUSSION

[5] Complainant is Facebook Inc. which lists its address as Menlo Park, CA, USA. Complainant states that since it began doing business in 2004 it has become the world's leading provider of online social networking services with more than 1.11 billion registered users around the world. Complainant also asserts that "it is ranked as the first most visited website in the world, and has the second highest traffic in Slovakia (where the Respondent is based)." Complainant owns numerous domestic and international registrations for its FACEBOOK mark including; FACEBOOK - Community Trade Mark No. 006455687 registered on 07 October 2008.

[6] Complainant contends that Respondent's domain name, <facebok.pw>, is confusingly similar to its FACEBOOK mark, and was registered and is being used in bad faith by the Respondent who has no rights or legitimate interests in the domain name.

[7] Respondent is Radoslav Stach whose address is listed as Presnov, Slovakia. Respondent registered the disputed domain name on or about March 26, 2013. Respondent did not provide a response to the Complaint in accordance with the URS rules of procedure; however Respondent did provide correspondence which stated, "Im was offline, could you pleas tell me what I have doing ? I want removed this domain from my account!"

IDENTICAL OR CONFUSINGLY SIMILAR

[8] The only difference between the Domain Name, <facebok.pw>, and the Complainant's FACEBOOK mark is the absence of one letter ("o") in the Domain Name. In addition, it is well accepted that the top level domain is irrelevant in assessing identity or confusing similarity, thus the ".pw" is of no consequence here. The Examiner finds that the Domain Name is confusingly similar to Complainant's FACEBOOK mark.

NO RIGHTS OR LEGITIMATE INTERESTS

[9] To the best of the Complainant's knowledge, the Respondent does not have any rights in the name FACEBOOK or "facebok" nor is the Respondent commonly known by either name. Complainant has not authorized Respondent's use of its mark and has no affiliation with Respondent. The Domain Name points to a web page listing links for popular search topics which Respondent appears to use to generate click through fees for Respondent's personal financial gain. Such use does not constitute a bona fide offering of goods or services and wrongfully misappropriates Complainant's mark's goodwill. The Examiner finds that the Respondent has established no rights or legitimate interests in the Domain Name.

BAD FAITH REGISTRATION AND USE

[10] The Domain Name was registered and is being used in bad faith.

[11] The Domain Name was registered on or about March 26, 2013, nine years after the Complainant's FACEBOOK marks were first used and began gaining global notoriety.

[12] The Examiner finds that the Respondent has engaged in a pattern of illegitimate domain name registrations (See Complainant's exhibit URS Site Screenshot) whereby Respondent has either altered letters in, or added new letters to, well-known trademarks. Such behavior supports a conclusion of Respondent's bad faith registration and use. Furthermore, the Complainant submits that the Respondent is using the Domain Name in order to attract for commercial gain Internet users to its parking website by creating a likelihood of confusion as to the source, sponsorship or affiliation of the website. The Examiner finds such behavior to further evidence Respondent's bad faith registration and use.

DETERMINATION

[13] After reviewing the Complainant's submissions, the Examiner determines that the Complainant has demonstrated all three elements of the URS by a standard of clear and convincing evidence; the Examiner hereby Orders the following domain names be SUSPENDED for the duration of the registration.

<facebok.pw>

Darryl C. Wilson, Examiner

Dated: September 27, 2013

Questions and Comments

1. *The Trademark Clearinghouse.* To help trademark owners cope with the challenges presented by a greatly expanded domain name system, ICANN oversaw the development of the Trademark Clearinghouse, www.trademark-clearinghouse.com. Trademark owners that register their trademarks with the Clearinghouse (and pay the associated fees) may benefit from two main services. First, the Clearinghouse gives Clearinghouse registrants access to the "Sunrise period" for every new gTLD. During this period (which must last at least 30 days), Clearinghouse registrants enjoy priority registration of their marks as domain names within the new gTLD before that gTLD's domain name registration process is opened up to the general public. To qualify for the Sunrise Service, Clearinghouse registrants must submit proof that they are actually using the mark they have registered with the Clearinghouse. Second, the Clearinghouse will notify Clearinghouse registrants on an ongoing basis of any third-party attempt to register (or eventual success in registering) within a new gTLD a domain name that matches the Clearinghouse registrant's trademark. It is then left to the trademark owner to decide whether to pursue an infringement claim against the third-party domain name applicant or registrant.

E.   **Secondary Liability**

1.   **Service Provider Secondary Liability**

The Lanham Act does not explicitly provide for secondary liability. Instead, as the court in *Tiffany (NJ) Inc. v. eBay Inc.* explains, secondary liability in trademark law is an entirely judge-made doctrine. Both of the opinions that follow address secondary liability for providers of services. The first, *Tiffany (NJ) Inc. v. eBay Inc.*, 600 F.3d 93 (2d Cir. 2010), has essentially become the law of the land for online auction site liability for infringing conduct occurring on those sites. It focuses on the nature of the knowledge requirement in contributory liability doctrine. The second, *Gucci America, Inc. v. Frontline Processing Corp.*, 721 F.Supp.2d 228 (S.D.N.Y. 2010), involved providers of credit card services. It is a decidedly less influential case, but engages the important issue of how much control a service provider must have over the direct infringer's conduct to be liable for contributory infringement.

In reading through *Tiffany v. eBay*, consider the following question:

- As a policy matter, has the court chosen the most efficient result? Who can more efficiently bear the burden of policing eBay's website for counterfeit Tiffany merchandise?

- Are you persuaded that eBay was not willfully blind to the sale of counterfeits on its auction site?

Tiffany (NJ) Inc. v. eBay Inc.
600 F.3d 93 (2d Cir. 2010)

Sack, Circuit Judge:

[1] eBay, Inc. ("eBay"), through its eponymous online marketplace, has revolutionized the online sale of goods, especially used goods. It has facilitated the buying and selling by hundreds of millions of people and entities, to their benefit and eBay's profit. But that marketplace is sometimes employed by users as a means to perpetrate fraud by selling counterfeit goods.

[2] Plaintiffs Tiffany (NJ) Inc. and Tiffany and Company (together, "Tiffany") have created and cultivated a brand of jewelry bespeaking high-end quality and style. Based on Tiffany's concern that some use eBay's website to sell counterfeit Tiffany merchandise, Tiffany has instituted this action against eBay, asserting various causes of action—sounding in trademark infringement, trademark dilution and false advertising—arising from eBay's advertising and listing practices. For the reasons set forth below, we affirm the district court's judgment with respect to Tiffany's claims of trademark infringement and dilution but remand for further proceedings with respect to Tiffany's false advertising claim.

BACKGROUND

[3] By opinion dated July 14, 2008, following a week-long bench trial, the United States District Court for the Southern District of New York (Richard J. Sullivan, *Judge*) set forth its findings of fact and conclusions of law. *Tiffany (NJ) Inc. v. eBay, Inc.*, 576 F.Supp.2d 463 (S.D.N.Y. 2008) ("*Tiffany*"). When reviewing a judgment following a bench trial in the district court, we review the court's findings of fact for clear error and its conclusions of law *de novo. Giordano v. Thomson*, 564 F.3d 163, 168 (2d Cir. 2009). Except where noted otherwise, we conclude that the district court's findings of fact are not clearly erroneous. We therefore rely upon those non-erroneous findings in setting forth the facts of, and considering, this dispute.

eBay

[4] eBay[1] is the proprietor of www.ebay.com, an Internet-based marketplace that allows those who register with it to purchase goods from and sell goods to one another. It "connect[s] buyers and sellers

---

[1] eBay appears to be short for Echo Bay—the name of eBay's founder's consulting firm was Echo Bay Technology Group. The name "EchoBay" was already in use, so eBay was employed as the name for the website. *See* http:// en. wikipedia. org/ wiki/ EBay# Origins_ and_ history (last visited Feb. 26,

and [ ] enable[s] transactions, which are carried out directly between eBay members." *Tiffany,* 576 F.Supp.2d at 475.[2] In its auction and listing services, it "provides the venue for the sale [of goods] and support for the transaction[s], [but] it does not itself sell the items" listed for sale on the site, *id.* at 475, nor does it ever take physical possession of them, *id.* Thus, "eBay generally does not know whether or when an item is delivered to the buyer." *Id.*

[5] eBay has been enormously successful. More than six million new listings are posted on its site daily. *Id.* At any given time it contains some 100 million listings. *Id.*

[6] eBay generates revenue by charging sellers to use its listing services. For any listing, it charges an "insertion fee" based on the auction's starting price for the goods being sold and ranges from $0.20 to $4.80. *Id.* For any completed sale, it charges a "final value fee" that ranges from 5.25% to 10% of the final sale price of the item. *Id.* Sellers have the option of purchasing, at additional cost, features "to differentiate their listings, such as a border or bold-faced type." *Id.*

[7] eBay also generates revenue through a company named PayPal, which it owns and which allows users to process their purchases. PayPal deducts, as a fee for each transaction that it processes, 1.9% to 2.9% of the transaction amount, plus $0.30. *Id.* This gives eBay an added incentive to increase both the volume and the price of the goods sold on its website. *Id.*

Tiffany

[8] Tiffany is a world-famous purveyor of, among other things, branded jewelry. *Id.* at 471-72. Since 2000, all new Tiffany jewelry sold in the United States has been available exclusively through Tiffany's retail stores, catalogs, and website, and through its Corporate Sales Department. *Id.* at 472-73. It does not use liquidators, sell overstock merchandise, or put its goods on sale at discounted prices. *Id.* at 473. It does not—nor can it, for that matter—control the "legitimate secondary market in authentic Tiffany silvery jewelry," i.e., the market for second-hand Tiffany wares. *Id.* at 473. The record developed at trial "offere[d] little basis from which to discern the actual availability of authentic Tiffany silver jewelry in the secondary market." *Id.* at 474.

[9] Sometime before 2004, Tiffany became aware that counterfeit Tiffany merchandise was being sold on eBay's site. Prior to and during the course of this litigation, Tiffany conducted two surveys known as "Buying Programs," one in 2004 and another in 2005, in an attempt to assess the extent of this practice. Under those programs, Tiffany bought various items on eBay and then inspected and evaluated them to determine how many were counterfeit. *Id.* at 485. Tiffany found that 73.1% of the purported Tiffany goods purchased in the 2004 Buying Program and 75.5% of those purchased in the 2005 Buying Program were counterfeit. *Id.* The district court concluded, however, that the Buying Programs were "methodologically flawed and of questionable value," *id.* at 512, and "provide[d] limited evidence as to the total percentage of counterfeit goods available on eBay at any given time," *id.* at 486. The court nonetheless decided that during the period in which the Buying Programs were in effect, a "significant portion of the 'Tiffany' sterling silver jewelry listed on the eBay website . . . was counterfeit," *id.,* and that eBay knew "that some portion of the Tiffany goods sold on its website might be counterfeit," *id.* at 507. The court found, however, that "a substantial number of authentic Tiffany goods are [also] sold on eBay." *Id.* at 509.

[10] Reducing or eliminating the sale of all second-hand Tiffany goods, including genuine Tiffany pieces, through eBay's website would benefit Tiffany in at least one sense: It would diminish the competition in the market for genuine Tiffany merchandise. *See id.* at 510 n. 36 (noting that "there is at least some basis in the record for eBay's assertion that one of Tiffany's goals in pursuing this litigation is to shut down the legitimate secondary market in authentic Tiffany goods"). The immediate effect

---

2010); http:// news. softpedia. com/ news/ eBay- Turns- Ten- Happy- Birthday- 7502. shtml (last visited Feb. 26, 2010).

[2] In addition to providing auction-style and fixed-priced listings, eBay is also the proprietor of a traditional classified service. *Id.* at 474.

would be loss of revenue to eBay, even though there might be a countervailing gain by eBay resulting from increased consumer confidence about the bona fides of other goods sold through its website.

Anti-Counterfeiting Measures

[11] Because eBay facilitates many sales of Tiffany goods, genuine and otherwise, and obtains revenue on every transaction, it generates substantial revenues from the sale of purported Tiffany goods, some of which are counterfeit. "eBay's Jewelry & Watches category manager estimated that, between April 2000 and June 2004, eBay earned $4.1 million in revenue from completed listings with 'Tiffany' in the listing title in the Jewelry & Watches category." *Id.* at 481. Although eBay was generating revenue from all sales of goods on its site, including counterfeit goods, the district court found eBay to have "an interest in eliminating counterfeit Tiffany merchandise from eBay . . . to preserve the reputation of its website as a safe place to do business." *Id.* at 469. The buyer of fake Tiffany goods might, if and when the forgery was detected, fault eBay. Indeed, the district court found that "buyers . . . complain[ed] to eBay" about the sale of counterfeit Tiffany goods. *Id.* at 487. "[D]uring the last six weeks of 2004, 125 consumers complained to eBay about purchasing 'Tiffany' items through the eBay website that they believed to be counterfeit." *Id.*

[12] Because eBay "never saw or inspected the merchandise in the listings," its ability to determine whether a particular listing was for counterfeit goods was limited. *Id.* at 477-78. Even had it been able to inspect the goods, moreover, in many instances it likely would not have had the expertise to determine whether they were counterfeit. *Id.* at 472 n. 7 ("[I]n many instances, determining whether an item is counterfeit will require a physical inspection of the item, and some degree of expertise on the part of the examiner.").

[13] Notwithstanding these limitations, eBay spent "as much as $20 million each year on tools to promote trust and safety on its website." *Id.* at 476. For example, eBay and PayPal set up "buyer protection programs," under which, in certain circumstances, the buyer would be reimbursed for the cost of items purchased on eBay that were discovered not to be genuine. *Id.* at 479. eBay also established a "Trust and Safety" department, with some 4,000 employees "devoted to trust and safety" issues, including over 200 who "focus exclusively on combating infringement" and 70 who "work exclusively with law enforcement." *Id.* at 476.

[14] By May 2002, eBay had implemented a "fraud engine," "which is principally dedicated to ferreting out illegal listings, including counterfeit listings." *Id.* at 477. eBay had theretofore employed manual searches for keywords in listings in an effort to "identify blatant instances of potentially infringing . . . activity." *Id.* "The fraud engine uses rules and complex models that automatically search for activity that violates eBay policies." *Id.* In addition to identifying items actually advertised as counterfeit, the engine also incorporates various filters designed to screen out less-obvious instances of counterfeiting using "data elements designed to evaluate listings based on, for example, the seller's Internet protocol address, any issues associated with the seller's account on eBay, and the feedback the seller has received from other eBay users." *Id.* In addition to general filters, the fraud engine incorporates "Tiffany-specific filters," including "approximately 90 different keywords" designed to help distinguish between genuine and counterfeit Tiffany goods. *Id.* at 491. During the period in dispute,[3] eBay also "periodically conducted [manual] reviews of listings in an effort to remove those that might be selling counterfeit goods, including Tiffany goods." *Id.*

[15] For nearly a decade, including the period at issue, eBay has also maintained and administered the "Verified Rights Owner ('VeRO') Program"—a "'notice-and-takedown' system" allowing owners of intellectual property rights, including Tiffany, to "report to eBay any listing offering potentially infringing items, so that eBay could remove such reported listings." *Id.* at 478. Any such rights-holder

---

[3] In its findings, the district court often used the past tense to describe eBay's anticounterfeiting efforts. We do not take this usage to suggest that eBay has discontinued these efforts, but only to emphasize that its findings are issued with respect to a particular period of time prior to the completion of trial and issuance of its decision.

with a "good-faith belief that [a particular listed] item infringed on a copyright or a trademark" could report the item to eBay, using a "Notice Of Claimed Infringement form or NOCI form." *Id.* During the period under consideration, eBay's practice was to remove reported listings within twenty-four hours of receiving a NOCI, but eBay in fact deleted seventy to eighty percent of them within twelve hours of notification. *Id.*

[16] On receipt of a NOCI, if the auction or sale had not ended, eBay would, in addition to removing the listing, cancel the bids and inform the seller of the reason for the cancellation. If bidding had ended, eBay would retroactively cancel the transaction. *Id.* In the event of a cancelled auction, eBay would refund the fees it had been paid in connection with the auction. *Id.* at 478-79.

[17] In some circumstances, eBay would reimburse the buyer for the cost of a purchased item, provided the buyer presented evidence that the purchased item was counterfeit. *Id.* at 479.[4] During the relevant time period, the district court found, eBay "never refused to remove a reported Tiffany listing, acted in good faith in responding to Tiffany's NOCIs, and always provided Tiffany with the seller's contact information." *Id.* at 488.

[18] In addition, eBay has allowed rights owners such as Tiffany to create an "About Me" webpage on eBay's website "to inform eBay users about their products, intellectual property rights, and legal positions." *Id.* at 479. eBay does not exercise control over the content of those pages in a manner material to the issues before us.

[19] Tiffany, not eBay, maintains the Tiffany "About Me" page. With the headline "**BUYER BEWARE**," the page begins: "**Most of the purported TIFFANY & CO. silver jewelry and packaging available on eBay is counterfeit.**" Pl.'s Ex. 290 (bold face type in original). It also says, *inter alia*:

> The only way you can be certain that you are purchasing a genuine TIFFANY & CO. product is to purchase it from a Tiffany & Co. retail store, via our website (www. tiffany. com) or through a Tiffany & Co. catalogue. Tiffany & Co. stores do not authenticate merchandise. A good jeweler or appraiser may be able to do this for you.

Id.

[20] In 2003 or early 2004, eBay began to use "special warning messages when a seller attempted to list a Tiffany item." *Tiffany*, 576 F.Supp.2d at 491. These messages "instructed the seller to make sure that the item was authentic Tiffany merchandise and informed the seller that eBay 'does not tolerate the listing of replica, counterfeit, or otherwise unauthorized items' and that violation of this policy 'could result in suspension of [the seller's] account.'" *Id.* (alteration in original). The messages also provided a link to Tiffany's "About Me" page with its "buyer beware" disclaimer. *Id.* If the seller "continued to list an item despite the warning, the listing was flagged for review." *Id.*

[21] In addition to cancelling particular suspicious transactions, eBay has also suspended from its website "'hundreds of thousands of sellers every year,' tens of thousands of whom were suspected [of] having engaged in infringing conduct." *Id.* at 489. eBay primarily employed a "'three strikes rule'" for suspensions, but would suspend sellers after the first violation if it was clear that "the seller 'listed a number of infringing items,' and '[selling counterfeit merchandise] appears to be the only thing they've come to eBay to do.'" *Id.* But if "a seller listed a potentially infringing item but appeared overall to be a legitimate seller, the 'infringing items [were] taken down, and the seller [would] be sent a warning on the first offense and given the educational information, [and] told that . . . if they do this again, they will be suspended from eBay.'" *Id.* (alterations in original).[5]

---

[4] We note, however, that, Tiffany's "About Me" page on the eBay website states that Tiffany does not authenticate merchandise. Pl.'s Ex. 290.

[5] According to the district court, "eBay took appropriate steps to warn and then to suspend sellers when eBay learned of potential trademark infringement under that seller's account." *Tiffany*, 576 F.Supp.2d at 489. The district court concluded that it was understandable that eBay did not have a "hard-

[22] By late 2006, eBay had implemented additional anti-fraud measures: delaying the ability of buyers to view listings of certain brand names, including Tiffany's, for 6 to 12 hours so as to give rights-holders such as Tiffany more time to review those listings; developing the ability to assess the number of items listed in a given listing; and restricting one-day and three-day auctions and cross-border trading for some brand-name items. *Id.* at 492.

[23] The district court concluded that "eBay consistently took steps to improve its technology and develop anti-fraud measures as such measures became technologically feasible and reasonably available." *Id.* at 493.

eBay's Advertising

[24] At the same time that eBay was attempting to reduce the sale of counterfeit items on its website, it actively sought to promote sales of premium and branded jewelry, including Tiffany merchandise, on its site. *Id.* at 479-80. Among other things,

> eBay "advised its sellers to take advantage of the demand for Tiffany merchandise as part of a broader effort to grow the Jewelry & Watches category." *Id.* at 479. And prior to 2003, eBay advertised the availability of Tiffany merchandise on its site. eBay's advertisements trumpeted "Mother's Day Gifts!," Pl.'s Exs. 392, 1064, a "Fall FASHION BRAND BLOWOUT," Pl.'s Ex. 392, "Jewelry Best Sellers," *id.,* "GREAT BRANDS, GREAT PRICES," Pl.'s Ex. 1064, or "Top Valentine's Deals," Pl.'s Ex. 392, among other promotions. It encouraged the viewer to "GET THE FINER THINGS." Pl.'s Ex. 392. These advertisements provided the reader with hyperlinks, at least one of each of which was related to Tiffany merchandise—"Tiffany," "Tiffany & Co. under $150," "Tiffany & Co," "Tiffany Rings," or "Tiffany & Co. under $50." Pl.'s Exs. 392, 1064.

eBay also purchased sponsored-link advertisements on various search engines to promote the availability of Tiffany items on its website. *Tiffany,* 576 F.Supp.2d at 480. In one such case, in the form of a printout of the results list from a search on Yahoo! for "tiffany," the second sponsored link read "**Tiffany** on eBay. Find **tiffany** items at low prices. With over 5 million items for sale every day, you'll find all kinds of unique [unreadable] Marketplace. www.ebay.com." Pl.'s Ex. 1065 (bold face type in original). Tiffany complained to eBay of the practice in 2003, and eBay told Tiffany that it had ceased buying sponsored links. *Tiffany,* 576 F.Supp.2d at 480. The district court found, however, that eBay continued to do so indirectly through a third party. *Id.*

Procedural History

[25] By amended complaint dated July 15, 2004, Tiffany initiated this action. It alleged, *inter alia,* that eBay's conduct—i.e., facilitating and advertising the sale of "Tiffany" goods that turned out to be counterfeit—constituted direct and contributory trademark infringement, trademark dilution, and false advertising. On July 14, 2008, following a bench trial, the district court, in a thorough and thoughtful opinion, set forth its findings of fact and conclusions of law, deciding in favor of eBay on all claims.

[26] Tiffany appeals from the district court's judgment for eBay.

DISCUSSION

[27] We review the district court's findings of fact for clear error and its conclusions of law *de novo. Giordano v. Thomson,* 564 F.3d 163, 168 (2d Cir. 2009).

---

and-fast, one-strike rule" of suspending sellers because a NOCI "did not constitute a definitive finding that the listed item was counterfeit" and because "suspension was a very serious matter, particularly to those sellers who relied on eBay for their livelihoods." *Id.* The district court ultimately found eBay's policy to be "appropriate and effective in preventing sellers from returning to eBay and re-listing potentially counterfeit merchandise." *Id.*

I. Direct Trademark Infringement

{The court found that eBay did not directly infringe Tiffany's trademark when it used the mark on its website "to describe accurately the genuine Tiffany goods offered for sale on its website" and when it purchased sponsored links on Google and Yahoo! triggered by the Tiffany mark.}

II. Contributory Trademark Infringement

[28] The more difficult issue, and the one that the parties have properly focused our attention on, is whether eBay is liable for contributory trademark infringement—i.e., for culpably facilitating the infringing conduct of the counterfeiting vendors. Acknowledging the paucity of case law to guide us, we conclude that the district court correctly granted judgment on this issue in favor of eBay.

A. Principles

[29] Contributory trademark infringement is a judicially created doctrine that derives from the common law of torts. *See, e.g., Hard Rock Cafe Licensing Corp. v. Concession Servs., Inc.,* 955 F.2d 1143, 1148 (7th Cir. 1992); *cf. Metro-Goldwyn-Mayer Studios Inc. v. Grokster, Ltd.,* 545 U.S. 913, 930 (2005) ("[T]hese doctrines of secondary liability emerged from common law principles and are well established in the law.") (citations omitted). The Supreme Court most recently dealt with the subject in *Inwood Laboratories, Inc. v. Ives Laboratories, Inc.,* 456 U.S. 844 (1982). There, the plaintiff, Ives, asserted that several drug manufacturers had induced pharmacists to mislabel a drug the defendants produced to pass it off as Ives'. *See id.* at 847-50. According to the Court, "if a manufacturer or distributor intentionally induces another to infringe a trademark, or if it continues to supply its product to one whom it knows or has reason to know is engaging in trademark infringement, the manufacturer or distributor is contributorially responsible for any harm done as a result of the deceit." *Id.* at 854.[8] The Court ultimately decided to remand the case to the Court of Appeals after concluding it had improperly rejected factual findings of the district court favoring the defendant manufacturers. *Id.* at 857-59.

[30] *Inwood*'s test for contributory trademark infringement applies on its face to manufacturers and distributors of goods. Courts have, however, extended the test to providers of services.

[31] The Seventh Circuit applied *Inwood* to a lawsuit against the owner of a swap meet, or "flea market," whose vendors were alleged to have sold infringing Hard Rock Café T-shirts. *See Hard Rock Café,* 955 F.2d at 1148-49. The court "treated trademark infringement as a species of tort," *id.* at 1148, and analogized the swap meet owner to a landlord or licensor, on whom the common law "imposes the same duty . . . [as *Inwood*] impose[s] on manufacturers and distributors," *id.* at 1149; *see also Fonovisa, Inc. v. Cherry Auction, Inc.,* 76 F.3d 259 (9th Cir. 1996) (adopting *Hard Rock Cafe*'s reasoning and applying *Inwood* to a swap meet owner).

---

[8] The Supreme Court cited two cases in support of this proposition: *William R. Warner & Co. v. Eli Lilly & Co.,* 265 U.S. 526 (1924), and *Coca-Cola Co. v. Snow Crest Beverages, Inc.,* 64 F.Supp. 980 (D.Mass. 1946) (Wyzanski, J.), *aff'd,* 162 F.2d 280 (1st Cir.), *cert. denied,* 332 U.S. 809 (1947).

Like *Inwood, Eli Lilly* involved an allegation by a plaintiff drug manufacturer that a defendant drug manufacturer had intentionally induced distributors to pass off the defendant's drug to purchasers as the plaintiff's. 265 U.S. at 529-30. The Supreme Court granted the plaintiff's request for an injunction, stating that "[o]ne who induces another to commit a fraud and furnishes the means of consummating it is equally guilty and liable for the injury." *Id.* at 530-31.

In *Snow Crest,* the Coca-Cola Company claimed that a rival soft drink maker had infringed Coca-Cola's mark because bars purchasing the rival soft drink had substituted it for Coca-Cola when patrons requested a "rum (or whiskey) and Coca-Cola." 64 F.Supp. at 982, 987. Judge Wyzanski entered judgment in favor of the defendant primarily because there was insufficient evidence of such illicit substitutions taking place. *Id.* at 990. In doing so, the court stated that "[b]efore he can himself be held as a wrongdoer o[r] contributory infringer one who supplies another with the instruments by which that other commits a tort, must be shown to have knowledge that the other will or can reasonably be expected to commit a tort with the supplied instrument." *Id.* at 989.

[32] Speaking more generally, the Ninth Circuit concluded that *Inwood*'s test for contributory trademark infringement applies to a service provider if he or she exercises sufficient control over the infringing conduct. *Lockheed Martin Corp. v. Network Solutions, Inc.,* 194 F.3d 980, 984 (9th Cir. 1999); *see also id.* ("Direct control and monitoring of the instrumentality used by a third party to infringe the plaintiff's mark permits the expansion of *Inwood Lab.*'s 'supplies a product' requirement for contributory infringement.").

[33] We have apparently addressed contributory trademark infringement in only two related decisions, *see Polymer Tech. Corp. v. Mimran,* 975 F.2d 58, 64 (2d Cir. 1992) ("*Polymer I*"); *Polymer Tech. Corp. v. Mimran,* 37 F.3d 74, 81 (2d Cir. 1994) ("*Polymer II*"), and even then in little detail. Citing *Inwood,* we said that "[a] distributor who intentionally induces another to infringe a trademark, or continues to supply its product to one whom it knows or has reason to know is engaging in trademark infringement, is contributorially liable for any injury." *Polymer I,* 975 F.2d at 64.

[34] The limited case law leaves the law of contributory trademark infringement ill-defined. Although we are not the first court to consider the application of *Inwood* to the Internet, *see, e.g., Lockheed,* 194 F.3d 980, *supra* (Internet domain name registrar), we are apparently the first to consider its application to an online marketplace.[9]

B. Discussion

1. Does Inwood Apply?

[35] In the district court, the parties disputed whether eBay was subject to the *Inwood* test. *See Tiffany,* 576 F.Supp.2d at 504. eBay argued that it was not because it supplies a service while *Inwood* governs only manufacturers and distributors of products. *Id.* The district court rejected that distinction. It adopted instead the reasoning of the Ninth Circuit in *Lockheed* to conclude that *Inwood* applies to a service provider who exercises sufficient control over the means of the infringing conduct. *Id.* at 505-06. Looking "to the extent of the control exercised by eBay over its sellers' means of infringement," the district court concluded that *Inwood* applied in light of the "significant control" eBay retained over the transactions and listings facilitated by and conducted through its website. *Id.* at 505-07.

[36] On appeal, eBay no longer maintains that it is not subject to *Inwood.*[10] We therefore assume without deciding that *Inwood*'s test for contributory trademark infringement governs.

---

[9] European courts have done so. A Belgian court declined to hold eBay liable for counterfeit cosmetic products sold through its website. *See Lancôme v. eBay,* Brussels Commercial Court (Aug. 12, 2008), Docket No. A/07/06032. French courts, by contrast, have concluded that eBay violated applicable trademark laws. *See, e.g., S.A. Louis Vuitton Malletier v. eBay, Inc.,* Tribunal de Commerce de Paris, Premiere Chambre B. (Paris Commercial Court), Case No. 200677799 (June 30, 2008); *Hermes v. eBay,* Troyes High Court (June 4, 2008), Docket No. 06/0264; *see also* Max Colchester, "EBay to Pay Damages To Unit of LVMH," *The Wall Street Journal,* Feb. 12, 2010, http:// online. wsj. com/ article_ email/ SB 1000142405 274870433700 457505952301 8541764- l My Q j Ax MTAw MDEw M j Ex NDIy Wj. html (last visited Mar. 1, 2010) ("A Paris court Thursday ordered eBay to pay Louis Vuitton Q200,000 ($275,000) in damages and to stop paying search engines to direct certain key words to the eBay site."); *see generally,* Valerie Walsh Johnson & Laura P. Merritt, *TIFFANY v. EBAY:* A Case of Genuine Disparity in International Court Rulings on Counterfeit Products, 1 No. 2 Landslide 22 (2008) (surveying decisions by European courts in trademark infringement cases brought against eBay).

[10] Amici do so claim. *See* Electronic Frontier Foundation et al. Amici Br. 6 (arguing that *Inwood* should "not govern where, as here, the alleged contributory infringer has no direct means to establish whether there is any act of direct infringement in the first place"). We decline to consider this argument. "Although an *amicus* brief can be helpful in elaborating issues properly presented by the parties, it is normally not a method for injecting new issues into an appeal, at least in cases where the parties are competently represented by counsel." *Universal City Studios, Inc. v. Corley,* 273 F.3d 429, 445 (2d Cir. 2001).

2. Is eBay Liable Under Inwood?

[37] The question that remains, then, is whether eBay is liable under the *Inwood* test on the basis of the services it provided to those who used its website to sell counterfeit Tiffany products. As noted, when applying *Inwood* to service providers, there are two ways in which a defendant may become contributorily liable for the infringing conduct of another: first, if the service provider "intentionally induces another to infringe a trademark," and second, if the service provider "continues to supply its [service] to one whom it knows or has reason to know is engaging in trademark infringement." *Inwood*, 456 U.S. at 854. Tiffany does not argue that eBay induced the sale of counterfeit Tiffany goods on its website—the circumstances addressed by the first part of the *Inwood* test. It argues instead, under the second part of the *Inwood* test, that eBay continued to supply its services to the sellers of counterfeit Tiffany goods while knowing or having reason to know that such sellers were infringing Tiffany's mark.

[38] The district court rejected this argument. First, it concluded that to the extent the NOCIs that Tiffany submitted gave eBay reason to know that particular listings were for counterfeit goods, eBay did not continue to carry those listings once it learned that they were specious. *Tiffany*, 576 F.Supp.2d at 515-16. The court found that eBay's practice was promptly to remove the challenged listing from its website, warn sellers and buyers, cancel fees it earned from that listing, and direct buyers not to consummate the sale of the disputed item. *Id.* at 516. The court therefore declined to hold eBay contributorily liable for the infringing conduct of those sellers. *Id.* at 518. On appeal, Tiffany does not appear to challenge this conclusion. In any event, we agree with the district court that no liability arises with respect to those terminated listings.

[39] Tiffany disagrees vigorously, however, with the district court's further determination that eBay lacked sufficient knowledge of trademark infringement by sellers behind other, non-terminated listings to provide a basis for *Inwood* liability. Tiffany argued in the district court that eBay knew, or at least had reason to know, that counterfeit Tiffany goods were being sold ubiquitously on its website. *Id.* at 507-08. As evidence, it pointed to, *inter alia*, the demand letters it sent to eBay in 2003 and 2004, the results of its Buying Programs that it shared with eBay, the thousands of NOCIs it filed with eBay alleging its good faith belief that certain listings were counterfeit, and the various complaints eBay received from buyers claiming that they had purchased one or more counterfeit Tiffany items through eBay's website. *Id.* at 507. Tiffany argued that taken together, this evidence established eBay's knowledge of the widespread sale of counterfeit Tiffany products on its website. Tiffany urged that eBay be held contributorily liable on the basis that despite that knowledge, it continued to make its services available to infringing sellers. *Id.* at 507-08.

[40] The district court rejected this argument. It acknowledged that "[t]he evidence produced at trial demonstrated that eBay had *generalized* notice that some portion of the Tiffany goods sold on its website might be counterfeit." *Id.* at 507 (emphasis in original). The court characterized the issue before it as "whether eBay's *generalized* knowledge of trademark infringement on its website was sufficient to meet the 'knowledge or reason to know' prong of the *Inwood* test." *Id.* at 508 (emphasis in original). eBay had argued that "such generalized knowledge is insufficient, and that the law demands more specific knowledge of individual instances of infringement and infringing sellers before imposing a burden upon eBay to remedy the problem." *Id.*

[41] The district court concluded that "while eBay clearly possessed general knowledge as to counterfeiting on its website, such generalized knowledge is insufficient under the *Inwood* test to impose upon eBay an affirmative duty to remedy the problem." *Id.* at 508. The court reasoned that *Inwood*'s language explicitly imposes contributory liability on a defendant who "continues to supply its product [—in eBay's case, its service—] to *one* whom it knows or has reason to know is engaging in trademark infringement." *Id.* at 508 (emphasis in original). The court also noted that plaintiffs "bear a high burden in establishing 'knowledge' of contributory infringement," and that courts have

been reluctant to extend contributory trademark liability to defendants where there is some uncertainty as to the extent or the nature of the infringement. In *Inwood*, Justice White emphasized in his concurring opinion that a defendant is not "require[d] . . . to refuse to sell to dealers who merely *might* pass off its goods."

Id. at 508-09 (quoting *Inwood,* 456 U.S. at 861, 102 S.Ct. 2182) (White, J., concurring) (emphasis and alteration in original).[11]

[42] Accordingly, the district court concluded that for Tiffany to establish eBay's contributory liability, Tiffany would have to show that eBay "knew or had reason to know of specific instances of actual infringement" beyond those that it addressed upon learning of them. *Id.* at 510. Tiffany failed to make such a showing.

[43] On appeal, Tiffany argues that the distinction drawn by the district court between eBay's general knowledge of the sale of counterfeit Tiffany goods through its website, and its specific knowledge as to which particular sellers were making such sales, is a "false" one not required by the law. Appellants' Br. 28. Tiffany posits that the only relevant question is "whether all of the knowledge, when taken together, puts [eBay] on notice that there is a substantial problem of trademark infringement. If so and if it fails to act, [eBay] is liable for contributory trademark infringement." *Id.* at 29.

[44] We agree with the district court. For contributory trademark infringement liability to lie, a service provider must have more than a general knowledge or reason to know that its service is being used to sell counterfeit goods. Some contemporary knowledge of which particular listings are infringing or will infringe in the future is necessary.

[45] We are not persuaded by Tiffany's proposed interpretation of *Inwood.* Tiffany understands the "lesson of *Inwood*" to be that an action for contributory trademark infringement lies where "the evidence [of infringing activity]—direct or circumstantial, taken as a whole— . . . provide[s] a basis for finding that the defendant knew or should have known that its product or service was being used to further illegal counterfeiting activity." Appellants' Br. 30. We think that Tiffany reads *Inwood* too broadly. Although the *Inwood* Court articulated a "knows or has reason to know" prong in setting out its contributory liability test, the Court explicitly declined to apply that prong to the facts then before it. *See Inwood,* 456 U.S. at 852 n. 12, 102 S.Ct. 2182 ("The District Court also found that the petitioners did not continue to provide drugs to retailers whom they knew or should have known were engaging in trademark infringement. The Court of Appeals did not discuss that finding, and we do not address it.") (internal citation omitted). The Court applied only the inducement prong of the test. *See id.* at 852-59.

[46] We therefore do not think that *Inwood* establishes the contours of the "knows or has reason to know" prong. Insofar as it speaks to the issue, though, the particular phrasing that the Court used—that a defendant will be liable if it "continues to supply its product to *one* whom it knows or has reason to know is engaging in trademark infringement," *id.* at 854, 102 S.Ct. 2182 (emphasis added)—supports the district court's interpretation of *Inwood,* not Tiffany's.

[47] We find helpful the Supreme Court's discussion of *Inwood* in a subsequent *copyright* case, *Sony Corp. of America v. Universal City Studios, Inc.,* 464 U.S. 417 (1984). There, defendant Sony manufactured and sold home video tape recorders. *Id.* at 419. Plaintiffs Universal Studios and Walt Disney Productions held copyrights on various television programs that individual television-viewers had taped using the defendant's recorders. *Id.* at 419-20. The plaintiffs contended that this use of the recorders constituted copyright infringement for which the defendants should be held contributorily liable. *Id.* In ruling for the defendants, the Court discussed *Inwood* and the differences between contributory liability in trademark versus copyright law.

> If *Inwood's narrow standard* for contributory trademark infringement governed here, [the plaintiffs'] claim of contributory infringement would merit little discussion. Sony certainly does not 'intentionally induce[ ]' its customers to make infringing uses of [the plaintiffs'] copyrights, nor does it supply its products to *identified individuals known by it* to be engaging in continuing infringement of [the plaintiffs'] copyrights.

Id. at 439 n. 19 (quoting *Inwood,* 456 U.S. at 855; emphases added).

---

[11] The district court found the cases Tiffany relied on for the proposition that general knowledge of counterfeiting suffices to trigger liability to be inapposite. *Id.* at 510.

[48] Thus, the Court suggested, had the *Inwood* standard applied in *Sony*, the fact that Sony might have known that some portion of the purchasers of its product used it to violate the copyrights of others would not have provided a sufficient basis for contributory liability. *Inwood*'s "narrow standard" would have required knowledge by Sony of "identified individuals" engaging in infringing conduct. Tiffany's reading of *Inwood* is therefore contrary to the interpretation of that case set forth in *Sony*.

[49] Although the Supreme Court's observations in *Sony*, a copyright case, about the "knows or has reason to know" prong of the contributory trademark infringement test set forth in *Inwood* were dicta, they constitute the only discussion of that prong by the Supreme Court of which we are aware. We think them to be persuasive authority here.[12]

[50] Applying *Sony*'s interpretation of *Inwood*, we agree with the district court that "Tiffany's general allegations of counterfeiting failed to provide eBay with the knowledge required under *Inwood*." *Tiffany*, 576 F.Supp.2d at 511. Tiffany's demand letters and Buying Programs did not identify particular sellers who Tiffany thought were then offering or would offer counterfeit goods. *Id.* at 511-13.[13] And although the NOCIs and buyer complaints gave eBay reason to know that certain sellers had been selling counterfeits, those sellers' listings were removed and repeat offenders were suspended from the eBay site. Thus Tiffany failed to demonstrate that eBay was supplying its service to individuals who it knew or had reason to know were selling counterfeit Tiffany goods.

[51] Accordingly, we affirm the judgment of the district court insofar as it holds that eBay is not contributorially liable for trademark infringement.

3. Willful Blindness.

[52] Tiffany and its amici express their concern that if eBay is not held liable except when specific counterfeit listings are brought to its attention, eBay will have no incentive to root out such listings from its website. They argue that this will effectively require Tiffany and similarly situated retailers to police eBay's website—and many others like it—"24 hours a day, and 365 days a year." Council of Fashion Designers of America, Inc. Amicus Br. 5. They urge that this is a burden that most mark holders cannot afford to bear.

[53] First, and most obviously, we are interpreting the law and applying it to the facts of this case. We could not, even if we thought it wise, revise the existing law in order to better serve one party's interests at the expense of the other's.

[54] But we are also disposed to think, and the record suggests, that private market forces give eBay and those operating similar businesses a strong incentive to minimize the counterfeit goods sold on their websites. eBay received many complaints from users claiming to have been duped into buying counterfeit Tiffany products sold on eBay. *Tiffany*, 576 F.Supp.2d at 487. The risk of alienating these users gives eBay a reason to identify and remove counterfeit listings.[14] Indeed, it has spent millions of dollars in that effort.

[55] Moreover, we agree with the district court that if eBay had reason to suspect that counterfeit Tiffany goods were being sold through its website, and intentionally shielded itself from discovering the offending listings or the identity of the sellers behind them, eBay might very well have been charged

---

[12] In discussing *Inwood*'s "knows or has reason to know" prong of the contributory infringement test, *Sony* refers to a defendant's knowledge, but not to its constructive knowledge, of a third party's infringing conduct. *Sony*, 464 U.S. at 439 n. 19, 104 S.Ct. 774. We do not take the omission as altering the test *Inwood* articulates.

[13] The demand letters did say that eBay should presume that sellers offering five or more Tiffany goods were selling counterfeits, *id.* at 511, but we agree with the district court that this presumption was factually unfounded, *id.* at 511-12.

[14] At the same time, we appreciate the argument that insofar as eBay receives revenue from undetected counterfeit listings and sales through the fees it charges, it has an incentive to permit such listings and sales to continue.

with knowledge of those sales sufficient to satisfy *Inwood*'s "knows or has reason to know" prong. *Tiffany*, 576 F.Supp.2d at 513-14. A service provider is not, we think, permitted willful blindness. When it has reason to suspect that users of its service are infringing a protected mark, it may not shield itself from learning of the particular infringing transactions by looking the other way. *See, e.g., Hard Rock Café*, 955 F.2d at 1149 ("To be willfully blind, a person must suspect wrongdoing and deliberately fail to investigate."); *Fonovisa*, 76 F.3d at 265 (applying *Hard Rock Café*'s reasoning to conclude that "a swap meet can not disregard its vendors' blatant trademark infringements with impunity").[15] In the words of the Seventh Circuit, "willful blindness is equivalent to actual knowledge for purposes of the Lanham Act." *Hard Rock Café*, 955 F.2d at 1149.[16]

[56] eBay appears to concede that it knew as a general matter that counterfeit Tiffany products were listed and sold through its website. *Tiffany*, 576 F.Supp.2d at 514. Without more, however, this knowledge is insufficient to trigger liability under *Inwood*. The district court found, after careful consideration, that eBay was not willfully blind to the counterfeit sales. *Id.* at 513. That finding is not clearly erroneous.[17] eBay did not ignore the information it was given about counterfeit sales on its website.

{The Court went on to find that eBay was not diluting Tiffany's marks and did not engage in false advertising.}

In *Perfect 10, Inc. v. Visa Intern. Service Ass'n*, 494 F.3d 788 (9th Cir. 2007), the Ninth Circuit declined to hold credit card providers liable for providing payment services to websites that infringed the plaintiff's copyrights in pornographic images. Judge Kozinski dissented. *See id.* at 810 (Kozinski, J., "dissenting for the most part"). In the following opinion, the S.D.N.Y. had to decide whether to hold credit card processors liable for providing payment services to website operators that sold counterfeit merchandise.

---

[15] To be clear, a service provider is not contributorially liable under *Inwood* merely for failing to anticipate that others would use its service to infringe a protected mark. *Inwood*, 456 U.S. at 854 n. 13, 102 S.Ct. 2182 (stating that for contributory liability to lie, a defendant must do more than "reasonably anticipate" a third party's infringing conduct (internal quotation marks omitted)). But contributory liability may arise where a defendant is (as was eBay here) made aware that there was infringement on its site but (unlike eBay here) ignored that fact.

[16] The principle that willful blindness is tantamount to knowledge is hardly novel. *See, e.g. Harte-Hanks Commc'ns, Inc. v. Connaughton*, 491 U.S. 657, 659, 692, 109 S.Ct. 2678, 105 L.Ed.2d 562 (1989) (concluding in public-official libel case that "purposeful avoidance of the truth" is equivalent to "knowledge that [a statement] was false or [was made] with reckless disregard of whether it was false" (internal quotation marks omitted)); *United States v. Khorozian*, 333 F.3d 498, 504 (3d Cir. 2003) (acting with willful blindness satisfies the intent requirement of the federal bank fraud statute) . . . .

[17] Tiffany's reliance on the "flea market" cases, *Hard Rock Café* and *Fonovisa*, is unavailing. eBay's efforts to combat counterfeiting far exceeded the efforts made by the defendants in those cases. *See Hard Rock Café*, 955 F.2d at 1146 (defendant did not investigate any of the seizures of counterfeit products at its swap meet, even though it knew they had occurred); *Fonovisa*, 76 F.3d at 265 (concluding that plaintiff stated a claim for contributory trademark infringement based on allegation that swap meet "disregard[ed] its vendors' blatant trademark infringements with impunity"). Moreover, neither case concluded that the defendant was willfully blind. The court in *Hard Rock Café* remanded so that the district court could apply the correct definition of "willful blindness," 955 F.2d at 1149, and the court in *Fonovisa* merely sustained the plaintiff's complaint against a motion to dismiss, 76 F.3d at 260-61, 265.

Gucci America, Inc. v. Frontline Processing Corp.
721 F. Supp. 2d 228 (S.D.N.Y. June 23, 2010)

HAROLD BAER, JR., District Judge:

[1] Gucci America, Inc. is a well-known manufacturer of luxury goods. The company holds a variety of trademarks in its products and designs, and invests substantial capital in ensuring that the marks maintain a reputation for quality. Seeking to capitalize on the popularity of Gucci products, certain internet merchants have sold "replica," counterfeit Gucci products that infringe Gucci marks at significantly lower prices and of lower quality. Gucci recently concluded a successful litigation against one such merchant that operated a website called TheBagAddiction.com. The owners of the website admitted that they sold counterfeit Gucci products to customers across the country through the website. In its continuing effort to root out and prevent infringement of its trademarks, Gucci now brings suit against three entities, which while a step down in the "food chain," allegedly ensured that TheBagAddiction.com was able to sell these counterfeit products. These defendants allegedly established the credit card processing services used to complete the online sales of fake Gucci items. The three defendants have jointly moved to dismiss the case for lack of personal jurisdiction and for failure to state a claim. For the reasons that follow, the defendants' motion to dismiss is DENIED.

I. BACKGROUND

[2] Gucci America, Inc. ("Plaintiff" or "Gucci") is a New York company, with its principal place of business in New York City. Compl. ¶ 11. It is the sole, exclusive distributor in the United States of items labeled with the "Gucci Marks," including leather goods, jewelry, home products, and clothing. *Id.* The Gucci Marks are a series of marks—the Gucci name, the Gucci crest, the "non-interlocking GG monogram," the "repeating GG design," etc.—registered by Gucci with the United States Patent and Trademark Office. *See* Compl. ¶¶ 24–25 (reproduction of marks), Ex. 1 (Patent Office registration certificates). According to Plaintiff, the marks are well-known and recognizable in the United States and around the world. Gucci promotes the marks widely, and relies on "strict quality control standards" for its products, and as a result has achieved and retains a reputation for quality. *Id.* ¶ 28. The company spends hundreds of millions of dollars to advertise and promote its products and marks, and enjoys billions in sales of the Gucci products. "Based on the extensive sales of the Gucci [p]roducts and such products' wide popularity," claims Plaintiff, "the Gucci Marks have developed a secondary meaning and significance in the minds of the purchasing public, and the services and products utilizing and/or bearing such marks and names are immediately identified by the purchasing public with Plaintiff." *Id.* ¶ 30.

[3] This case arises out of Plaintiff's attempts to eliminate online sales of counterfeit products and the unauthorized use of the Gucci Marks. In *Gucci America, Inc., et al. v. Laurette Company, Inc., et al.*, No. 08 Civ. 5065(LAK), Gucci brought suit in this District against certain defendants, collectively known as the "Laurette Counterfeiters" or "Laurette," for the sale of counterfeit Gucci products on a website called "TheBagAddiction.com."[1] Through this website, the Laurette Counterfeiters sold a variety of "replica" luxury products, and, in particular, sold replica Gucci products under the Gucci name, with the various Gucci registered trademarks, and at fractions of the retail price for an authentic version. *See* Compl. ¶¶ 33–36 (describing and providing images of counterfeit Gucci products sold on TheBagAddiction.com). The website itself was replete with the use of the Gucci name and trademarks. *See id.* ¶ 41 (image of TheBagAddiction.com website). According to Plaintiff, the Laurette Counterfeiters "openly boasted" about the sale of counterfeit products, because the website expressly noted that the products were not authentic but rather "mirror images" of Gucci products. *See id.* ¶ 32. Though they are inferior in quality and workmanship, they appear to the naked eye to be similar if not identical to Gucci products. Gucci claims that, as a result of the sale of these counterfeit products, customers were deceived and misled

---

[1] *See* TheBagAddiction.com, http:// www. The Bag Addiction. com. This site can [no] longer be accessed because it was shut down following Gucci's lawsuit, but archived versions of the website can be browsed at The Internet Archive Wayback Machine. *See* http:// web. archive. org/ web/*/ http:// the bag addiction. com (last visited May 23, 2010).

"into believing that the products sold by the Laurette Counterfeiters on TheBagAddiction.com were authorized or sponsored by the Plaintiff." *Id.* ¶ 40. Eventually, Laurette consented to the entry of judgment and admitted liability for counterfeiting activities. According to Plaintiff, "the Laurette [c]ounterfeiters admitted … that, without authorization or license … they willfully and intentionally used, reproduced and/or copied the Gucci [m]arks in connection with their manufacturing, distributing, exporting, importing, advertising, marketing, selling and/or offering to sell their [c]ounterfeit [p]roducts." *Id.* ¶ 31.

[4] Plaintiff now seeks to bring the present action against three companies, Durango Merchant Services, Frontline Processing Corporation, and Woodforest National Bank,[2] who allegedly assisted the Laurette Counterfeiters and other similar website operators. Durango Merchant Services ("Durango") is a Wyoming corporation with its business address in Durango, Colorado…. Durango's business is predicated on assisting merchants in setting up credit card processing services with institutions that provide credit card merchant accounts…. Frontline Processing Corporation ("Frontline") is a Nevada corporation with its principal place of business in Bozeman, Montana. Frontline is a "nationwide provider of credit card processing and electronic payment services for merchants, banks, and sales agents," and is an "Independent Service Organization" and "Merchant Service Provider" with Visa and MasterCard, respectively. Compl. ¶ 58…. Finally, Woodforest National Bank ("Woodforest") is a bank organized under the laws of the United States, with its business address in The Woodlands, Texas. Similar to Frontline, Woodforest also "provides certain credit card processing services." *Id.* ¶ 14….

[5] To understand the roles of the three defendants and their alleged liability, a summary explanation of the credit card transaction process is necessary. A customer will initiate the process when he or she purchases a product from the merchant with a credit card. Once the credit card information is "swiped" on a terminal, or entered on a website, the merchant terminal transmits an authorization request to the merchant's "acquiring bank," who in this case was Frontline and Woodforest. The acquiring bank sends the credit card request through an electronic network to the cardholder's issuing bank. Based on the cardholder's credit limit or other factors, the issuing bank will send a message back through the network to the acquiring bank, who forwards it back to the merchant, which states that the merchant should either approve or decline the transaction. If approved, the merchant will complete the transaction and the acquiring bank will credit the merchant's account with the appropriate amount of funds. This entire process typically takes a matter of seconds. Some days to months after the sale is completed, the acquiring bank will submit the transaction information to the issuing bank, which will seek payment from the cardholder and settle with the acquiring bank.

[6] Gucci's overarching theory of the case is that Durango arranged for web companies that sold counterfeit Gucci products to establish credit card processing services with companies like Woodforest and Frontline. These processors then provided the credit card services necessary for the sale of the faux Gucci items. The complaint focuses largely on the allegedly representative conduct of Defendants with the Laurette Counterfeiters. According to Plaintiff, Durango acted as an agent for the defendant credit card processing companies[3] to locate potential customers, including the Laurette Counterfeiters and other similar infringing online operations. Durango collected a referral fee for bringing together these online merchants with banks and companies like Frontline and Woodforest. Durango's website billed the company as specializing in services for "High Risk Merchant Accounts," including those who sell "Replica Products." Compl. ¶ 48. Gucci alleges that the Laurette Counterfeiters entered into a "Merchant

---

[2] Gucci also brings suit against certain other "ABC Companies," unknown companies who engaged with the known defendants "in the manufacture, distribution, sale, and advertisement of [c]ounterfeit [p]roducts," Compl. ¶ 17, and "John Does," unknown individuals who also participated with the named defendants in the infringement and counterfeiting of Gucci products. *Id.* ¶ 18.

[3] Neither party has provided sufficiently clear terminology to describe Woodforest or Frontline. For the purposes of this opinion, terms like "acquiring bank" and "credit card processors" are intended to have the same meaning and do not imply anything about their services beyond what is alleged in the complaint.

Service Agreement" with Durango through one of its sales representatives, Nathan Counley and, through this relationship, "procur[ed] merchant accounts with credit card processing agencies, including Defendants Frontline and Woodforest." *Id.* ¶ 51. Gucci asserts that, through email and other documents, Durango was aware that TheBagAddiction.com sold counterfeit "replica" Gucci products and nevertheless chose to do business with them.

. . . .

[7] Gucci maintains that the credit card processing services established by these three defendants was essential to the Laurette Counterfeiters' sale of counterfeit Gucci products. These services "facilitated the Laurette Counterfeiters ability to quickly and efficiently transact sales for [c]ounterfeit [p]roducts through their website by enabling customers to use personal credit cards to pay for purchases on TheBagAddiction.com." Compl. ¶ 87. Without credit card processing, Plaintiff claims, websites like TheBagAddiction.com could not operate or functionally exist. As such, Gucci believes that Durango, Frontline, and Woodforest are equally responsible for the infringement and counterfeiting engaged in by Laurette through their website. Based on these allegations, Plaintiff brings causes of action for (1) trademark infringement and counterfeiting under the Lanham Act, 15 U.S.C. §§ 1114, 1125, 1116, 1117; (2) contributory trademark infringement and counterfeiting pursuant to the Lanham Act; (3) vicarious liability for trademark infringement and counterfeiting under the Lanham Act; and (4) trademark infringement and unfair competition under New York state law, *see* N.Y. Gen. Bus. Law §§ 360–k, 360–o. Defendants jointly moved to dismiss these claims based on a purported lack of personal jurisdiction, and because Plaintiff has failed to state a claim, pursuant to Rule 12(b)(2) and (6) of the Federal Rules of Civil Procedure.

II. DISCUSSION

A. Personal Jurisdiction

{The court found personal jurisdiction over the defendants.}

B. Trademark Infringement Liability

1. Standard of review

[8] To survive a motion to dismiss, a plaintiff must "plead enough facts to state a claim to relief that is plausible on its face." *Bell Atl. Corp. v. Twombly*, 550 U.S. 544, 570, 127 S.Ct. 1955, 167 L.Ed.2d 929 (2007). A facially plausible claim is one where "the plaintiff pleads factual content that allows the court to draw the reasonable inference that the defendant is liable for the misconduct alleged." *Ashcroft v. Iqbal*, ––– U.S. ––––, 129 S.Ct. 1937, 1949 (2009). . . .

[9] . . . Gucci offers three theories of liability to hold Defendants accountable for the infringing sales of counterfeit products by others: direct, vicarious, and contributory liability.[6]

2. Direct and Vicarious Liability

[10] Gucci has not put forth sufficient factual allegations to support trademark infringement claims based on either direct or vicarious theories of liability. . . . The problem for Gucci is that there is no indication that any of the defendants actually "used the mark in commerce." Knowledge alone of another party's sale of counterfeit or infringing items is insufficient to support direct liability, *see eBay*, 600 F.3d at 103, and there are otherwise no factual allegations that Durango, Woodforest, or Frontline themselves advertised or sold infringing goods.

[11] Gucci's allegations are also unable to support a claim for vicarious liability. Vicarious trademark infringement, a theory of liability considered elsewhere but not yet the subject of a decision by this Circuit, "requires a finding that the defendant and the infringer have an apparent or actual partnership, have authority to bind one another in transactions with third parties or exercise joint ownership or control over the infringing product." *Hard Rock Cafe Licensing Corp. v. Concession Servs., Inc.*, 955 F.2d 1143, 1150 (7th Cir. 1992); *Perfect 10, Inc. v. Visa Intern. Serv. Ass'n*, 494 F.3d 788, 807 (9th

---

[6] Federal law and state common law infringement claims are analyzed identically. *See, e.g., eBay*, 600 F.3d at 102 n. 6.

Cir. 2007) . . . . Though Gucci has raised a number of factual allegations that indicate that Defendants' services were crucial to a website like TheBagAddiction.com's sale of infringing goods, there is insufficient evidence to plausibly infer an actual or apparent partnership. The vague, puffery-like references to a "partnership" between these companies and website merchants are not enough to support vicarious liability. *See Louis Vuitton Malletier, S.A. v. Akanoc Solutions, Inc.,* 591 F.Supp.2d 1098, 1113 (N.D.Cal. 2008) ("off-hand references to customers as 'partners' is insufficient to exhibit the type of behavior and relationship that can be considered an actual or apparent partnership."). While Defendants may have sufficient control over the sale of counterfeit goods to support contributory liability, *see infra,* the facts alleged do not support an inference that they had the type of control over a company like Laurette as a whole, i.e. akin to joint ownership, necessary for vicarious liability.

3. Contributory Liability

[12] Gucci's only plausible theory of liability here is contributory trademark infringement. The Supreme Court has determined that liability can extend "beyond those who actually mislabel goods with the mark of another." *Inwood Lab., Inc. v. Ives Lab., Inc.,* 456 U.S. 844, 853 (1982) . . . . As the Seventh Circuit noted, however, the Supreme Court's test for contributory liability is not as easily applied to service providers as it is to a manufacturer. *See Hard Rock,* 955 F.2d at 1148 ("it is not clear how the doctrine applies to people who do not actually manufacture or distribute the good that is ultimately palmed off as made by someone else"); *see also Tiffany Inc. v. eBay, Inc.,* 576 F.Supp.2d 463, 504 (S.D.N.Y. 2008) (reversed on other grounds). While the "intentional inducement" prong of the *Inwood* test still applies, *see eBay,* 600 F.3d at 106, courts have crafted a slightly different test for service providers that "continue [ ] to supply its [services] to one whom it knows or has reason to know is engaging in trademark infringement." *Inwood,* 456 U.S. at 853. To avoid imputing liability on truly ancillary figures like a "temporary help service" that may set up a flea market stand for a counterfeiting merchant, *see Hard Rock,* 955 F.2d at 1148, courts in other circuits have determined that a plaintiff must also show "direct control and monitoring of the instrumentality used by a third party to infringe the plaintiff's mark." *See, e.g., Perfect 10,* 494 F.3d at 807; *Lockheed Martin Corp. v. Network Solutions, Inc.,* 194 F.3d 980, 984 (9th Cir. 1999). While the Second Circuit has yet to directly contemplate the validity of this modified part of the *Inwood* test, I concur with Judge Sullivan that this is a "persuasive synthesis." *See eBay,* 576 F.Supp.2d at 505–06. As such, Gucci can proceed with its action against Defendants if it can show that they (1) intentionally induced the website to infringe through the sale of counterfeit goods or (2) knowingly supplied services to websites and had sufficient control over infringing activity to merit liability.

(a) Intentional Inducement

[13] A party can be held liable for trademark infringement if it intentionally induces another to engage in trademark infringement. With regards to the role played by Durango, Plaintiff's inducement theory is supported by sufficient factual allegations. Durango's website reaches out to "high risk merchant accounts," including those who sell "replica products." *Id.* ¶ 48. The website further boasts that 95% of merchant accounts are approved and that Durango "specialize[s] in hard to acquire accounts." *See* Coyle Decl., Ex. 10 (printed copies of Durango website pages). Similar to the companies that promise the extension of credit or loans to those who are rejected by traditional lending institutions for having bad credit, Gucci's complaint suggests that Durango bills itself as a company that sets up a certain quality of business with credit card processing services that accept these "high risk" clients. These allegations can fairly be construed as Durango's attempt to induce less savory businesses, like those who sell counterfeit "replicas" of luxury goods. Moreover, Gucci alleges that Durango's sales representative, Nathan Counley, specifically discussed Laurette's difficulty in finding a credit card processor because they were "replica" merchants, which Gucci argues was synonymous on the internet for a counterfeiter.[7]

---

[7] Defendants challenge the meaning of both "replica" and "high risk," and claim that both are much more innocuous terms than Gucci suggests. First, "replica" is in fact often used in conjunction, or interchangeably, with the term "counterfeit" in case law on trademark infringement. *See, e.g., Hermes*

Durango "communicated an inducing message to [its] . . . users," and while there is of yet no evidence that they expressly sought out counterfeiters, Gucci has pled sufficient facts to infer that Durango crafted "advertisement[s] or solicitation[s] that broadcast[ ] a message designed to stimulate others to commit violations." *Perfect 10,* 494 F.3d at 801 (discussing contributory copyright infringement, but suggesting later that the analysis applies to trademark infringement as well). Finally, Gucci alleges that Counley and Durango helped the Laurette Counterfeiters set up a system to avoid chargebacks, which required customers to check a box that said "I understand these are replicas." This suggests "affirmative steps taken to foster infringement" or "that Defendants promoted their payment system as a means to infringe." *Id.* at 800–01.

[14] On the other hand, Gucci has failed to plausibly support a claim that either Woodforest or Frontline intentionally induced Laurette to sell counterfeit products. Durango, not Woodforest or Frontline, helped set up the Laurette Counterfeiters with credit card processing services. Though both companies allegedly advertised for high risk merchants, they did not bring Laurette to the table the way Durango allegedly did. Gucci notes that they both charged higher fees for processing high risk merchants, and that Frontline reviewed the language of the aforementioned acknowledgement of receipt of a replica product. These claims, however, are not enough to suggest that either Woodforest or Frontline took the affirmative steps necessary to foster infringement. *See Perfect 10,* 494 F.3d at 801.

(b) Control and knowledge

[15] Even if a defendant does not seek out and intentionally induce a third-party to commit trademark infringement, it may still be held liable for the infringement if it supplied services with knowledge or by willfully shutting its eyes to the infringing conduct, while it had sufficient control over the instrumentality used to infringe. *See eBay,* 576 F.Supp.2d at 505–06; *Perfect 10,* 494 F.3d at 807. Knowledge in this context means that "a service provider must have more than a general knowledge or reason to know that its service is being used to sell counterfeit goods . . . [s]ome contemporary knowledge of which particular listings are infringing or will infringe in the future is necessary." *eBay,* 600 F.3d at 107. A showing of willful blindness to this information is also sufficient. *Id.* at 109–10 ("When [a service provider] has reason to suspect that users of its service are infringing a protected mark, it may not shield itself from learning of the particular infringing transactions by looking the other way.").

[16] Here, Gucci has made substantial factual allegations about the knowledge of all three defendants. These allegations at the very least provide a strong inference that each knew that Laurette traded in counterfeit products, or were willfully blind to that fact. As described previously, Durango allegedly held itself out to high risk replica merchants. Its sales agent, Counley, traded emails with the Laurette Counterfeiters who expressly told him that they were unable to get credit card services because they sold "replica" items. Counley later wrote back to say he had found a U.S. bank that "can do replica accounts now." Compl. ¶ 54. Surely, a connection between an inability to get the services needed to transact goods online and the sale of replicas should have attracted Durango's attention.

[17] Frontline likewise is alleged to have sufficient knowledge of trademark infringement by the Laurette Counterfeiters. According to Gucci, Laurette completed an application to obtain Frontline's services, and Nathan Counley, though a Durango employee, is listed as Frontline's sales agent. Counley "acted as Frontline's agent in soliciting and directing credit card processing business from replica merchants like the Laurette Counterfeiters" and therefore Frontline may be charged with his knowledge, including his understanding of Laurette's difficulty to obtain services for selling replicas. Compl. ¶ 56. Gucci alleges that the "replica acknowledgment" described above that was created for the Laurette

---

Int'l v. Lederer de Paris Fifth Ave., Inc., 219 F.3d 104, 106 (2d Cir. 2000) ("Appellees Lederer and Artbag sell replicas of various Hermès products"); *eBay,* 600 F.3d at 100 (Defendant internet auction house has disclaimer that it "does not tolerate" replicas); *Akanoc,* 591 F.Supp.2d at 1103 ("Plaintiff believes that each of them is a counterfeit replica of Plaintiff's products which infringe Plaintiff's copyrights and trademarks."). Second, the precise meaning of the term is a fact-specific issue that can be dealt with through discovery, and I may rely on Gucci's pleadings at this stage of the litigation.

website with Counley's assistance was also reviewed by Frontline, who made suggestions as to where they should place this warning on the website. Even more significantly, Frontline allegedly performed its own investigation of products sold through TheBagAddiction.com as part of Frontline's chargeback reviews. When faced with a chargeback, Gucci claims that Frontline received supporting documentation from Laurette that included information about the specific item ordered, including a description of the item purchased. Not only did Frontline allegedly review the specific item description, Plaintiff also claims that the relatively small price tag for the item, as well as specific complaints from customers who made chargebacks about not receiving what the website purported to sell, e.g. a product made of genuine leather, should have alerted Frontline that these were infringing products. These fact-specific claims are enough to at least infer that Frontline knew or consciously avoided knowing that the counterfeit products were sold on TheBagAddiction.com

[18] Gucci claims that Woodforest's situation is similar to Frontline. As was the case with Frontline, Counley represented himself on Laurette's application as Woodforest's sales agent. *See* Compl. ¶ 72. The application itself said that Laurette was a "wholesale/retail designer [of] handbags," and listed the supplier as a Chinese bag manufacturer rather than Gucci. *See* Compl., Ex. 6. Gucci also claims that Woodforest specifically reviewed the website and the products listed on it as part of its initial decision to do business with Laurette. A Woodforest employee allegedly completed an "Internet Merchant Review Checklist," which required him or her to review the website and confirm whether it contained a complete description of the goods offered. *See* Compl. ¶ 75. Based on these claims and the website images provided by Plaintiff, even a cursory review of the TheBagAddiction.com would indicate that they claimed to sell replica Gucci products. Indeed, Plaintiff alleges that Woodforest printed out a number of pages that displayed goods that were for sale, including counterfeit Gucci products, and maintained these pages as part of their business records. Woodforest would also perform a second-level review, performed repeatedly after it accepted the business, where an employee would complete a purchase and request a refund. Finally, like Frontline, Woodforest investigated chargeback disputes and received supporting documentation that allegedly should have tipped them off to the infringing conduct. These claims are more than sufficient to suggest, at this stage of the litigation, that Woodforest knew or shielded themselves from the knowledge that Laurette was selling counterfeit Gucci products with their credit card processing system.

[19] The most significant dispute between the parties with regard to contributory liability is whether any or all of the Defendants had sufficient control over Laurette and TheBagAddiction.com website to render them liable for the web merchant's counterfeiting practices. As noted above, the control element was incorporated by the Seventh Circuit to establish a limiting principle that would exclude those service providers that do not really contribute to the infringing conduct; this Circuit has yet to directly consider the merits or contours of this modified form of the *Inwood* test. *See eBay,* 600 F.3d at 105–06 (noting control element but "assum[ing] without deciding that *Inwood* 's test for contributory trademark infringement governs"). Although the concept of control arose out of the flea market context and is based on common law landlord-tenant tort principles, *see Hard Rock,* 955 F.2d at 1149–50, the concept of control is not limited to that context. *Inwood* "laid down no limiting principle that would require defendant to be a manufacturer or distributor," and "whether the venue is online or in brick and mortar is immaterial." *eBay,* 576 F.Supp.2d at 505; *see also Fonovisa, Inc. v. Cherry Auction, Inc.,* 76 F.3d 259, 265 (9th Cir. 1996); *Lockheed Martin,* 194 F.3d at 984. The only relevant inquiry is the "extent of control . . . over the third party's means of infringement," *eBay,* 576 F.Supp.2d at 505; *Lockheed Martin,* 194 F.3d at 984, and courts have found sufficient control in an array of service contexts. *See, e.g., eBay,* 576 F.Supp.2d at 505 (online auction house); *Cartier Intern. B.V. v. Liu,* No. 02 Civ. 7926, 2003 WL 1900852, at *3 (S.D.N.Y. 2003) (company that shipped goods for counterfeiter); *Akanoc,* 591 F.Supp.2d at 1112 (internet service provider).

[20] Here, Plaintiff provides sufficient factual allegations to establish a claim that Woodforest and Frontline had some control over the directly infringing third-party, but fails to provide enough facts to show control on the part of Durango. Though Gucci has made an adequate showing of intentional inducement by Durango, there is little indication that they had much control over the website's sales

process. Durango appears to be the veritable middleman in this case. Though there allegedly was an ongoing relationship between Durango and the Laurette Counterfeiters, Gucci provides little indication that once Laurette received services from Frontline and Woodforest, Durango had any particular ability to stop or prohibit sales. Plaintiff's allegations suggest both inducement and knowledge, but "procuring merchant accounts with credit card processing agencies," Compl. ¶ 51, does not demonstrate that Durango could thereafter prevent the sale of any or all of the counterfeit products.

[21] In contrast, Gucci's complaint indicates that Frontline and Woodforest's credit card processing services are a necessary element for the transaction of counterfeit goods online, and were essential to sales from TheBagAddiction.com. Although other methods of online payment exist, such as online escrow-type services like PayPal, generally speaking "credit cards serve as the primary engine of electronic commerce." *Perfect 10,* 494 F.3d at 794. Indeed, Gucci points out that Durango's website claims that "9 out of 10 people use a credit card for their online orders." Compl. ¶ 3. As such, without the credit card processing operation set up by these two defendants, Gucci alleges that TheBagAddiction.com would largely have been unable to sell its counterfeit Gucci products. They further support this claim with an affidavit by one of the website owners, who states that "[a]pproximately 99% of payments from my customers were made using credit cards." Kirk Decl. ¶ 1. Both Frontline and Woodforest processed transactions for cardholders with major credit card institutions—Visa, MasterCard, and so forth—and, according to Gucci, Laurette sold over $500,000 in counterfeit products "during the time they utilized Defendants' merchant bankcard services." Compl. ¶ 44. By processing these transactions, both companies allegedly earned significant revenue from the transaction fees they charged. Put another way, "[t]hey knowingly provide a financial bridge between buyers and sellers of [counterfeit products], enabling them to consummate infringing transactions, while making a profit on every sale." *Perfect 10,* 494 F.3d at 810–11 (Kozinski, J., dissenting).[9] Though both Frontline and Woodforest insist they are middlemen with no ability to prevent a transaction, they do not dispute that they could have simply refused to do business with "replica" internet merchants, just like the flea market purveyor who refuses to provide a booth to a counterfeiter. *See* Compl. ¶¶ 87–89 (Woodforest and Frontline "facilitated the Laurette Counterfeiters ability to quickly and efficiently transact sales for Counterfeit Products through their website by enabling customers to use personal credit cards to pay for purchases on TheBagAddiction.com"). According to one of the website operators, "[i]f I did not receive an approval for a credit card charge, I would not ship the customer's order." Kirk Decl. ¶ 2. These allegations indicate that the infringing products "are delivered to the buyer only after defendants approve the transaction . . . This is not just an economic incentive for infringement; it's an essential step in the infringement process." *Perfect 10,* 494 F.3d at 811–12 (Kozinski, J., dissenting).

[22] Frontline and Woodforest insist that these allegations are insufficient because they do not allege direct or complete control over the website itself. However, the ability to literally shut down the website is not needed given the facts of this case. The circuits that have considered this issue look for control and monitoring over the "instrumentality used . . . to infringe the plaintiff's mark." *Perfect 10,* 494 F.3d at 807. Based on Gucci's claims, the instrumentality in this case is the combination of the website and the credit card network, since both are allegedly necessary elements for the infringing act— the sale and distribution of the counterfeit good.[10] Defendants' rely on the fact that, in *Perfect 10,* the Ninth Circuit declined to hold certain credit card processors liable for a website's trademark infringement. There, however, the infringing conduct was the publication *on the website* of trademarked images of nude models, and the distribution occurred via individuals viewing and taking the image directly from the website. *See Perfect 10,* 494 F.3d at 796 ("the infringement rests on the reproduction,

---

[9] Judge Kozinski's analysis, like that of the majority in *Perfect 10,* is largely set in the context of copyright infringement. However, he later states that his dissent on trademark infringement is based on "precisely the same reasons." *Perfect 10,* 494 F.3d at 822.

[10] Indeed, Frontline and Woodforest's credit card processing system were likely integrated to some degree, since some sort of credit card "portal" necessarily had to be embedded in the website for a customer to make a purchase.

alteration, display and distribution of Perfect 10's images over the internet"); *Perfect 10, Inc. v. Visa Inter. Serv. Assoc.,* No. C 04–00371, 2004 WL 3217732 (N.D.Cal. Dec. 3, 2004) ("Plaintiff alleges that a number of websites routinely and illicitly publish Plaintiff's images-and thereby infringe."). Plaintiff in that case failed or perhaps was unable to allege that the credit card service providers had the "power to remove infringing material" or "directly stop their distribution" because the infringement occurred on the website itself and a credit card transaction was not needed for the website to continue to infringe. *See Perfect 10,* 494 F.3d at 807. This is not the case here.

[23] Rather, Gucci's allegations indicate that they are concerned primarily with the sale of tangible counterfeit goods to customers around the country, which allegedly could not be accomplished without Woodforest and Frontline's ability to process the credit card-based purchases. In the words of the Supreme Court, these defendants "furnish[ed] the means of consummating" the trademark infringement. *See eBay,* 600 F.3d at 104 (quoting *William R. Warner & Co. v. Eli Lilly & Co.,* 265 U.S. 526, 530, 44 S.Ct. 615, 68 L.Ed. 1161 (1924)). While in *Perfect 10* the credit card services may not have been needed for a website to display infringing photographs, the infringement here occurred through the sale of the counterfeit products. "It's not possible to distribute by sale without receiving compensation, so payment is in fact part of the infringement process." *Perfect 10,* 494 F.3d at 814 (Kozinski, J., dissenting). This action resembles cases with defendants who helped consummate infringing transactions by delivering the counterfeit or infringing goods to the customer. In *Getty Petroleum Corp. v. Aris Getty, Inc.,* the First Circuit found a defendant common carrier contributorily liable because it delivered unbranded gasoline to gas stations it knew would re-sell the gasoline under the Getty brand name. *See* 55 F.3d 718, 719 (1st Cir. 1995). Lack of title to the gasoline did not matter; the defendant "supplied[ ] an essential factor—physical possession of the property to which the trademark was to be attached." *Id.* at 720. Similarly, these defendants allegedly provided an "essential factor" to the infringement because the goods could not be sold and shipped without their credit card services. "[I]t makes no difference that defendants control only the means of payment, not the mechanics of transferring the material . . . In a commercial environment, distribution and payment are . . . like love and marriage—you can't have one without the other. If cards don't process payments, pirates don't deliver booty." *Perfect 10,* 494 F.3d at 818 (Kozinski, J., dissenting). If, as Gucci alleges, the Laurette website was functionally dependent upon Woodforest and Frontline's credit card processing services to sell counterfeit Gucci products, it would be sufficient to demonstrate the control needed for liability.

* * *

[24] Gucci has sufficiently alleged facts to support personal jurisdiction and its trademark claims against Durango, Woodforest, and Frontline. Although Plaintiff has not sufficiently pled facts to support either direct or vicarious theories of liability, claims against all three defendants may proceed based on a contributory liability theory. The factual allegations are sufficient to infer that Durango intentionally induced trademark infringement, and that Woodforest and Frontline exerted sufficient control over the infringing transactions and knowingly provided its services to a counterfeiter.

III. CONCLUSION

[25] For the foregoing reasons, Defendant's motion to dismiss is DENIED.

SO ORDERED.

2. Landlord-Tenant Secondary Liability

Since *Tiffany v. eBay*, non-internet, brick-and-mortar defendants have sought to take advantage of *Tiffany v. eBay*'s defendant-friendly reformulation of contributory liability doctrine in trademark law. As the following case demonstrates, they have not been successful.

The exterior and interior of the mall at issue

Luxottica Group, S.P.A. v. Airport Mini Mall, LLC
932 F.3d 1303 (11th Cir. 2019)

JILL PRYOR, Circuit Judge:

[1] Luxury eyewear manufacturers holding registered trademarks brought a contributory trademark infringement action under the Lanham Act against owners of a discount mall whose subtenants were selling counterfeit eyewear. At trial, the jury returned a verdict in the plaintiffs' favor. After careful review and with the benefit of oral argument, we conclude that none of the issues the defendants raise on appeal demonstrates reversible error, so we affirm the jury's verdict.

I. FACTUAL AND PROCEDURAL BACKGROUND

[2] Plaintiffs Luxottica Group, S.p.A. and its subsidiary Oakley, Inc. (collectively and individually "Luxottica") manufacture and sell luxury eyewear and own registered trademarks for the Ray-Ban and Oakley brands. Defendants Jerome and Jenny Yeh own defendant Yes Assets, LLC. In 2004, Yes Assets purchased the Old National Village Shopping Center in College Park, Georgia. The Shopping Center included about 30 store fronts as well as an approximately 79,000-square-foot indoor space (the "Mall"), which contained between 120 and 130 booths to lease to individual vendors. Defendant Alice Jamison, the Yehs' daughter, managed the Shopping Center. Her responsibilities included reviewing leases, collecting rent, and visiting the Shopping Center and Yes Assets' tenants, including the lessee of the Mall.

[3] Until December 1, 2009, Yes Assets leased the Mall to a tenant, who assigned it to a subtenant, who subleased it to former Georgia congressman Pat Swindall, who in turn subleased the booths to vendors. From December 1, 2009 forward, Yes Assets leased the Mall to defendant Airport Mini Mall, LLC ("AMM"), a company Jerome and Jenny created and later gave to their son, defendant Donald Yeh, and the Mall became known as the International Discount Mall, AMM's tradename. Under the lease agreement, Yes Assets provided AMM and its subtenants (the vendors in the 120 to 130 booths) with a variety of services—including lighting, water, sewerage, maintenance and repairs, painting, and cleaning—and a parking area for customers. Greg Dickerson, whom Jerome hired as AMM's property manager, subleased the booths to vendors and reported to Jamison and Jerome until 2013, when Jerome had a stroke, and to Jamison and Donald afterward.

[4] AMM's tenure as the Mall's landlord saw three law enforcement raids there, during which officers executed search warrants, arrested subtenants, and seized alleged counterfeits of Luxottica eyewear and other brands' products. After the first raid, law enforcement left a copy of the search warrant and a list of items seized, including eyewear bearing Luxottica's marks, at the raided booth. The second raid lasted more than 14 hours and involved approximately 30 federal and local law enforcement agents who shut down the Mall to execute search warrants, arrested subtenants for selling counterfeit goods, seized thousands of counterfeit items bearing Luxottica's marks, and loaded the items onto a

514

tractor-trailer parked in front of the Shopping Center. Dickerson witnessed the second raid from the Shopping Center's parking lot and notified Jamison, Donald, and Jerome and Jenny's attorney, Louis Bridges. Dickerson later walked through the Mall to compile a list of the booths where law enforcement had seized goods and informed Jamison, Jerome, and Bridges about his inquiries of subtenants regarding the raid and whether they were selling counterfeit items. Each subtenant denied selling counterfeit merchandise, but Jamison admitted that she would expect the subtenants to lie if they were selling counterfeit goods. On Bridges' advice, the defendants decided to take no action against the subtenants unless the subtenants were convicted of a crime. More than a year after Luxottica filed this lawsuit, police executed several more search warrants at the Mall and seized additional counterfeit items bearing Luxottica's marks.

[5] Luxottica twice sent letters notifying the defendants that their subtenants were not authorized to sell Luxottica's eyewear and that any mark resembling Ray-Ban or Oakley marks would indicate that the glasses were counterfeit. The second letter also identified specific booths Luxottica suspected of selling counterfeit eyewear. Jamison and Donald were aware of both letters. Dickerson visited the booths named in the second letter but made no attempt to determine whether those vendors' eyewear products were counterfeit or to terminate their leases. After Luxottica filed this lawsuit, Jamison and Bridges attended a meeting at the College Park Police Department to discuss the unlawful selling of counterfeit products at the Mall.

[6] Despite the raids, letters, and meeting with law enforcement, the defendants took no steps to evict the infringing subtenants; they even renewed leases with several of the subtenants who had been arrested during the 14-plus-hour raid. In the month leading up to the filing of this lawsuit, Isabel Rozo, an employee of Luxottica's private investigator Geanie Johansen, purchased and photographed $15 and $20 counterfeit Ray-Ban glasses at several booths. Ray-Ban glasses normally retail for $140 to $220 a pair.

[7]... After an 11-day trial, the jury returned a special verdict holding all defendants except Jenny liable for contributory trademark infringement and assessing $100,000 in damages for each infringed trademark, totaling $1.9 million in damages. Having moved for judgment as a matter of law after the close of all the evidence, the defendants renewed their motion, which the district court denied.

. . . .

III. DISCUSSION

. . . .

A. Luxottica Presented Sufficient Evidence to Sustain the Jury's Verdict on Contributory Trademark Infringement.

. . . .

1. Contributory Liability Under the Lanham Act

. . . .

[8] In support of its theory that the defendants had at least constructive knowledge of their subtenants' infringement, Luxottica presented evidence tending to show that the defendants exhibited willful blindness to the subtenants' unlawful conduct. Across the circuits, a consensus has developed that willful blindness is one way to show that a defendant had constructive knowledge in cases of contributory trademark infringement.... *{S}ee also United States v. Baxter Int'l, Inc.*, 345 F.3d 866, 902 (11th Cir. 2003) (holding, in the context of the Medicare Secondary Payer statute, that "[a] party that willfully blinds itself to a fact... can be charged with constructive knowledge of that fact"). Willful blindness occurs when a person "suspect[s] wrongdoing and deliberately fail[s] to investigate." *Hard Rock Cafe*, 955 F.2d at 1149. We agree with the other circuits that willful blindness is a form of constructive knowledge for contributory trademark infringement. We evaluate the strength of Luxottica's evidence regarding willful blindness and constructive knowledge in Part III.A.3.

. . . .

3. The Evidence Was Sufficient to Prove That the Defendants Had at Least Constructive Knowledge of Specific Acts of Infringement.

[9] Pursuing a knowledge theory of contributory trademark infringement, Luxottica sought to prove that the defendants knew or had reason to know that their subtenants were selling counterfeit items yet continued to supply services (space, utilities, maintenance, and parking) that enabled the subtenants to sell their goods. The question that arises—[ ] one of first impression for this Court—is whether the knowledge theory of contributory liability requires the plaintiff to prove that the defendant had actual or constructive knowledge of *specific* infringing acts. We need not answer this question, however, because even if liability for contributory trademark infringement requires the defendant to have knowledge of specific acts of direct infringement, the evidence in this case was sufficient for a reasonable jury to find that the defendants had at least constructive knowledge of (or were willfully blind to) specific acts of direct infringement by their subtenants.

[10] The defendants argue that the district court should have applied what they deem a stricter standard from *Tiffany (NJ) v. eBay Inc.*, 600 F.3d 93 (2d Cir. 2010), in ruling on their renewed motion for judgment as a matter of law. In *Tiffany*, the jewelry titan sued the online listing service eBay for contributory trademark infringement because vendors listed counterfeit Tiffany products for sale on eBay's website. Whenever Tiffany notified eBay of a direct infringer's identity, eBay delisted the vendor within 24 hours. But, by itself, eBay was unable to identify and block each direct infringer, even with 200 employees focused on that task, because its website contained 100 million listings, and eBay lacked the ability to inspect goods in person and the expertise to distinguish Tiffany products from non-Tiffany products. "For contributory trademark infringement liability to lie," the Second Circuit held, "a service provider must have more than a general knowledge or reason to know that its service is being used to sell counterfeit goods. Some contemporary knowledge of which particular listings are infringing or will infringe in the future is necessary." *Id.* at 107. Because Tiffany's demand letters identified no additional sellers of counterfeit goods other than the sellers eBay had already delisted, eBay lacked actual or constructive knowledge of the remaining direct infringers. The court thus upheld the bench trial verdict in favor of eBay.

[11] The defendants articulate *Tiffany*'s legal standard for contributory trademark infringement as whether "Plaintiffs provide[d] notice to Defendants that a particular seller was then selling counterfeit versions of Plaintiffs' product." Appellants' Initial Br. at 22 (internal quotation marks omitted). The defendants err, though, in asserting that *Tiffany* narrowed the sources of a defendant's actual or constructive knowledge to just one: notice by the trademark holders. *Tiffany* did not categorically shift the burden onto trademark holders to provide notice to defendants; it simply clarified that certain facts of the case—a marketplace of 100 million listings and eBay's inability to inspect goods in person and lack of expertise to distinguish Tiffany from non-Tiffany jewelry—made it unlikely that eBay could identify the infringing vendors on its own, without help from Tiffany. *Tiffany*, 600 F.3d at 97-98, 109. In arguing that it was Luxottica's burden to notify the defendants of the infringing subtenants' identities, the defendants fail to acknowledge that actual or constructive knowledge of the direct infringers' identities could arise from many sources, including steps the defendants could have taken to investigate alleged direct infringement at the Mall after being put on notice by Luxottica that unnamed subtenants' may have been selling counterfeit Luxottica products.

[12] In any event, we need not decide today whether a defendant must be found to have had knowledge of specific acts of direct infringement for contributory liability to attach. Even if specific knowledge is necessary, the trial evidence was sufficient to prove that the defendants had at least constructive knowledge of specific instances where their subtenants infringed Luxottica's marks. Unlike in *Tiffany*, the defendants here did not need Luxottica's help to identify the infringing subtenants. Although *Inwood* created "no affirmative duty to take precautions against the sale of counterfeits," *Hard Rock Cafe*, 955 F.2d at 1149, the jury reasonably could have found that Luxottica's notice letters would have prompted a reasonable landlord to do at least a cursory visual inspection of the Mall's 130 booths to determine which vendors displayed eyewear with Luxottica's marks and sold it at prices low enough—$15 or $20 a pair for glasses that typically retail at $140 to $220 a pair—to alert a reasonable

516

person that it was counterfeit. Similarly, the jury reasonably could have found that a cursory visual inspection of 130 booths to see if they displayed what appeared to be counterfeit Luxottica eyewear was not so burdensome as to relieve the defendants of the responsibility to investigate after being informed by Luxottica that unnamed subtenants may have been engaging in illegal activity.

[13] What's more, previously we have held that evidence of "serious and widespread" infringement makes it more likely that a defendant knew about the infringement. *Mini Maid Servs. Co. v. Maid Brigade Sys., Inc.*, 967 F.2d 1516, 1522 (11th Cir. 1992). The three law enforcement raids—one of which lasted over 14 hours and required a tractor-trailer to haul away the seized merchandise—evidenced "serious and widespread" violations that gave the defendants at least constructive knowledge that their subtenants were selling counterfeit goods. *Id.* After the 14-plus-hour raid, Dickerson, the defendants' property manager, walked through the Mall; compiled a list of booths where law enforcement had seized goods; and informed Jerome, Jamison, and Bridges about his conversations with subtenants regarding the raid and whether they were selling counterfeit products. The record evidence of (1) the raids, arrests, and seizures, (2) the meeting at the College Park Police Department Jamison and Bridges attended where they discussed the sale of counterfeit goods at the Mall, and (3) the defendants' ability to visually inspect the approximately 130 booths was, taken together, sufficient to support a jury finding that the defendants had at least constructive knowledge of, or were willfully blind to learning, which subtenants were directly infringing Luxottica's trademarks.

[14] In sum, evidence of the defendants' knowledge of specific infringing acts by subtenants who relied on the services the defendants provided (including space, utilities, and maintenance) amply supported the jury verdict.

Questions and Comments

1. *Tiffany v. eBay and Canal Street.* A Canal Street landlord sought to use the specific knowledge standard in *Tiffany v. eBay* to escape secondary liability for the continuing sale of counterfeit OMEGA watches by unnamed individuals operating out of its building as either tenants or subtenants. (Canal Street is a major street in New York City at the northern edge of Manhattan's Chinatown.) As the defendants would in *Luxxotica*, the landlord 375 Canal argued that while it had been made aware of previous unnamed individuals selling counterfeits from its building, it did not have specific knowledge of the counterfeit sales that were the subject of the current suit, which were made by different unnamed individuals (whom the landlord basically claimed not to be able to tell apart). Omega argued before the jury that 375 Canal was willfully blind to the identities of its tenants and the jury agreed, finding that 375 Canal was contributorily liable (and awarding $1.1 million in statutory damages). Finding no error in the jury instructions, the Second Circuit distinguished eBay's conduct in *Tiffany*:

> Omega introduced evidence from which a jury could find that Canal had a history of turning a blind eye toward counterfeiting at 375 Canal Street and that Canal had taken insufficient steps to root out the counterfeiting it knew or should have known was occurring . . . .

> Canal insists that the verdict below portends widespread liability even for innocent actors. But *Tiffany* made clear that contributory trademark infringement based on willful blindness does not create liability simply because of a defendant's "general knowledge as to counterfeiting on its" property, *id.* at 107, or because a defendant "fail[ed] to anticipate that others would use its service to infringe a protected mark," *id.* at 110 n.15. *Tiffany* provided a test for identifying which scenarios could result in liability: "[C]ontributory liability may arise where a defendant is . . . made aware that there was infringement on its site but . . . ignored that fact." *Id.* There is no inherent duty to look for infringement by others on one's property. Indeed, the district court's jury instructions correctly stated that Canal had no affirmative duty to police trademarks: "Even if 375 Canal has control over the premises, 375 Canal has no affirmative duty to take precautions against the sale of counterfeit goods or to seek out and prevent alleged trademark violations, and cannot be found liable if it simply fails to take reasonable preemptive precautions against sales of counterfeit items." J. App'x 2629. But where a defendant knows or should know of

infringement, whether that defendant may be liable for contributory infringement turns on what the defendant does next. If it undertakes bona fide efforts to root out infringement, such as eBay did in *Tiffany*, that will support a verdict finding no liability, even if the defendant was not fully successful in stopping infringement. But if the defendant decides to take no or little action, it will support a verdict finding liability. *See Coach, Inc. v. Goodfellow*, 717 F.3d 498, 505 (6th Cir. 2013) (upholding liability because the defendant knew or had reason to know of infringement yet continued to lease vending space "without undertaking a reasonable investigation or taking other appropriate remedial measures").

Omega SA v. 375 Canal, LLC, 984 F.3d 244, 254–55 (2d Cir. 2021). Earlier in the opinion, the court referenced such reasonable precautions as "posting anti-counterfeiting signs, conducting walk-throughs, or inspecting the property for hidden compartments that could contain counterfeit goods." *Id.* at 249.

Made in the USA
Middletown, DE
30 November 2023

44037960R00294